MW01040255

MATT WAGNER'S

GRENDEL™

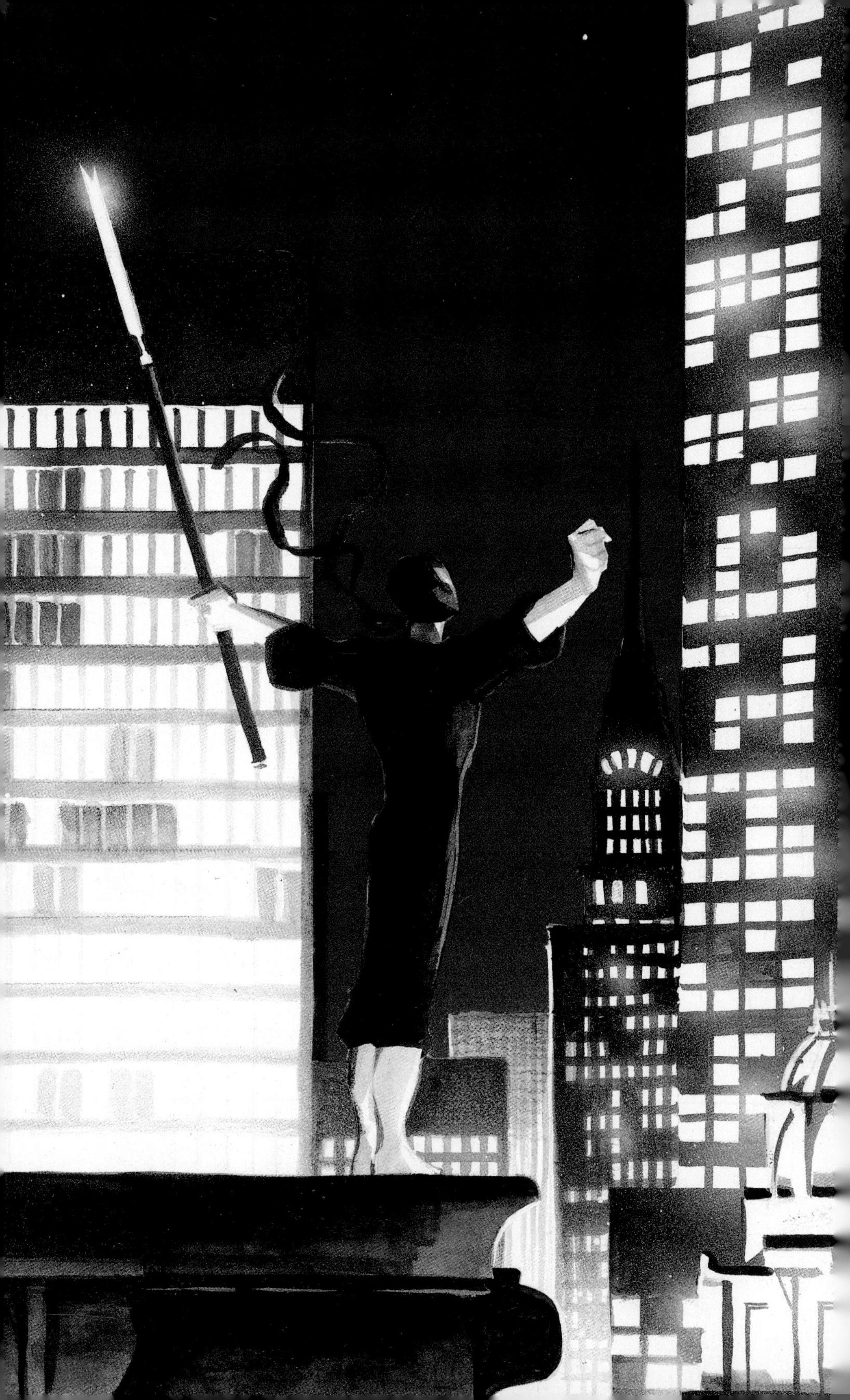

MATT WAGNER'S
GRENDEL™
OMNIBUS
VOLUME 1: HUNTER ROSE

DARK HORSE BOOKS

Publisher MIKE RICHARDSON
Editor DIANA SCHUTZ
Assistant editor BRENDAN WRIGHT
Designer JUSTIN COUCH
Digital production CARY GRAZZINI and CHRIS HORN

GRENDEL™ OMNIBUS VOLUME 1: HUNTER ROSE

This volume collects *Grendel: Devil by the Deed 25th Anniversary Edition;* issues one through four of the Dark Horse comic book series *Grendel: Black, White, & Red;* issues one through four of the Dark Horse comic book series *Grendel: Red, White, & Black;* issues zero through eight of the Dark Horse comic book series *Grendel: Behold the Devil,* along with material that originally appeared on MySpace; stories from the *Comico Collection, Decade: A Dark Horse Short Story Collection,* issues 49 and 50 of *Dark Horse Extra, Dark Horse Maverick 2001,* and *Liberty Annual 2011.*

Published by Dark Horse Books
A division of Dark Horse Comics, Inc.
10956 SE Main Street
Milwaukie, Oregon 97222
United States of America

DarkHorse.com

First edition: August 2012
ISBN 978-1-59582-893-4

10 9 8 7 6 5 4 3 2
Printed by Midas Printing International, Ltd., Huizhou, China.

CONTENTS

DEVIL BY THE DEED

Created, written, & illustrated by MATT WAGNER

Inks by RICH RANKIN
Color by CHRIS PITZER

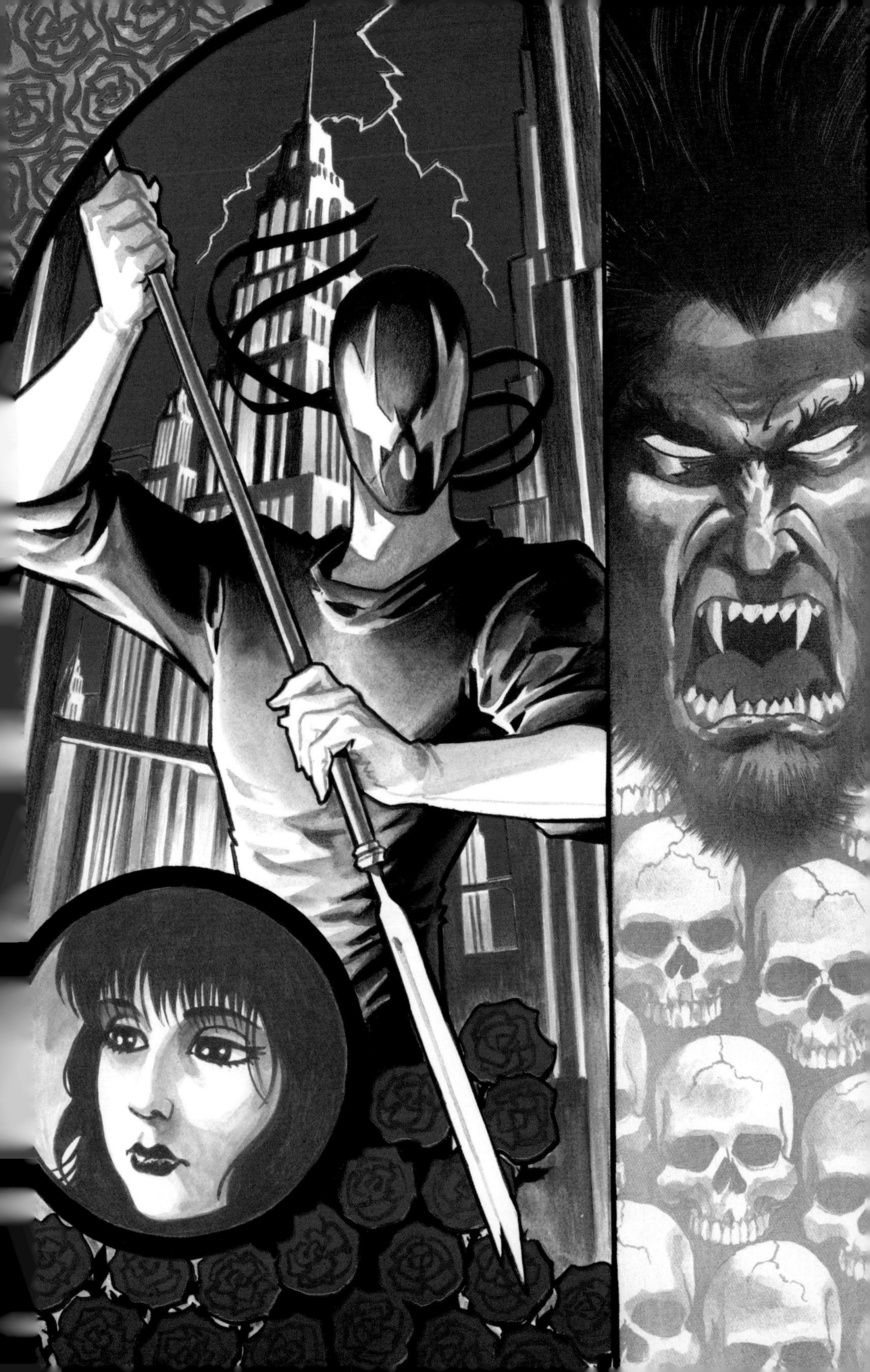

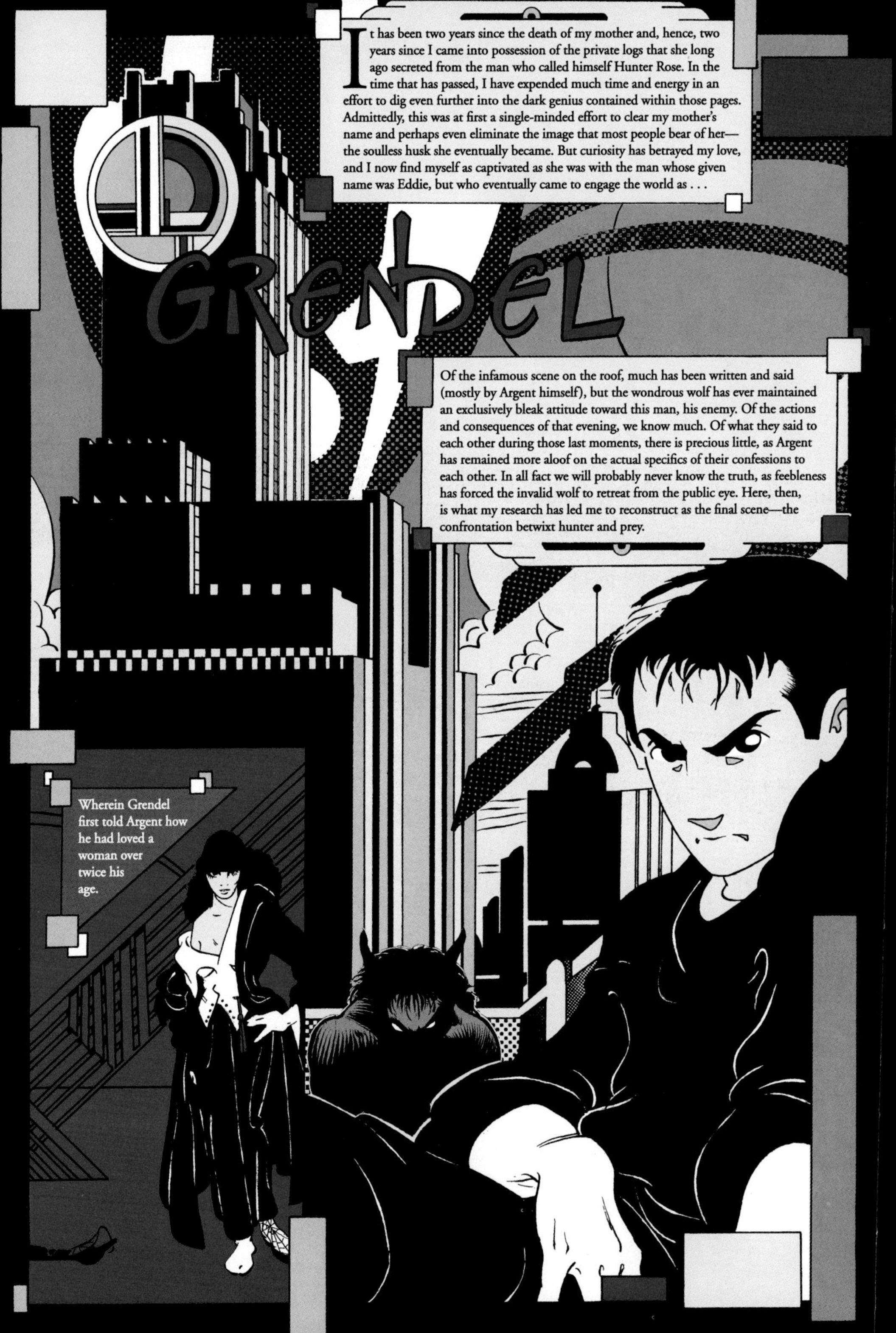
It has been two years since the death of my mother and, hence, two years since I came into possession of the private logs that she long ago secreted from the man who called himself Hunter Rose. In the time that has passed, I have expended much time and energy in an effort to dig even further into the dark genius contained within those pages. Admittedly, this was at first a single-minded effort to clear my mother's name and perhaps even eliminate the image that most people bear of her—the soulless husk she eventually became. But curiosity has betrayed my love, and I now find myself as captivated as she was with the man whose given name was Eddie, but who eventually came to engage the world as . . .
GRENDEL
Of the infamous scene on the roof, much has been written and said (mostly by Argent himself), but the wondrous wolf has ever maintained an exclusively bleak attitude toward this man, his enemy. Of the actions and consequences of that evening, we know much. Of what they said to each other during those last moments, there is precious little, as Argent has remained more aloof on the actual specifics of their confessions to each other. In all fact we will probably never know the truth, as feebleness has forced the invalid wolf to retreat from the public eye. Here, then, is what my research has led me to reconstruct as the final scene—the confrontation betwixt hunter and prey.
Wherein Grendel first told Argent how he had loved a woman over twice his age.

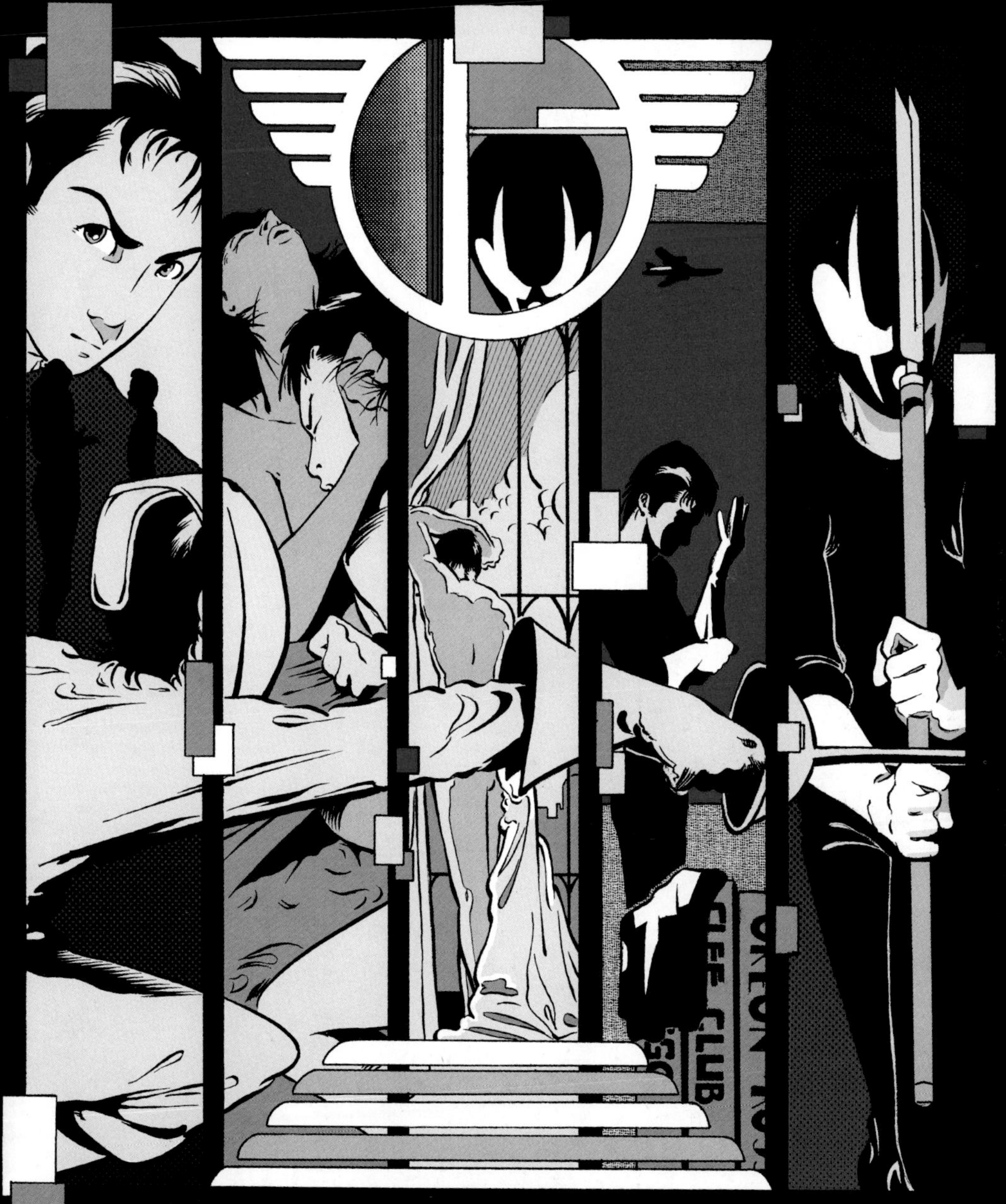
CLEF CLUB

He apparently had no trouble at anything he tried. It all came easy. He makes certain vague references to these quantum leaps in his developmental years but seems not to take much interest in his astounding abilities. It must be remembered, though, that these ledgers were all written long after he had already fallen under the influence of his older love, and so emphatically pursued what he took to be her directions. Police autopsy reports suggest his capabilities were based on some type of advanced genetic mutation, resulting in a much higher usage of our almost limitless mental capacities. And so he achieved and achieved and achieved. And was soon bored off his ass. How often have other restless spirits found solace in the blade? He found his greatest joy in fencing, winning time and time again, and all the while unaware of the classic tragedy he was becoming. Of the competition in London, he raves. Or I guess I should say the time following the tourney, the first time he met *her*. He was primed for the experience, his growing cynicism inflamed by how easily he had just defeated some of the most experienced fencers in the world. He was fourteen. Jocasta Rose was one of the trainers on the British team, and she sought him out. We can't really be sure of her intentions, as his accounts are often visibly naïve. She seduced him, though; that, he admits. She pulled him away from his world, and he went without a glance back. She was thirty-six. He writes of this time often and goes on for pages concerning her fiercely competitive spirit. How she died is unknown (the search for a Jocasta Rose of London has proved, as yet, fruitless—is the name fictional?), for Grendel himself never says more than this: "Then, she died. So I returned to America. My parents had died, too." He apparently didn't care. For he had become someone else by this point. He had taken the name of Hunter Rose (evidencing the true influence on his life) and proceeded to take the literary world by storm. His poignant, and now infamous, best sellers were instant classics, and the mysterious and dashing Hunter Rose quickly became the toast of the literary chic. Inspiringly clear are the descriptions of how he used writing as a Zen-like preparation for what he viewed as his only possible challenge: the complete domination of those around him. First, it was in the mere fashion of life and death. A flamboyant hitman, he captured the public's fascination with the macabre and unknown. The competitiveness that had possessed him drove him on, and soon he found himself in a position of power over one of New York's many underworld "families." At this point he was seventeen—and he was Grendel.

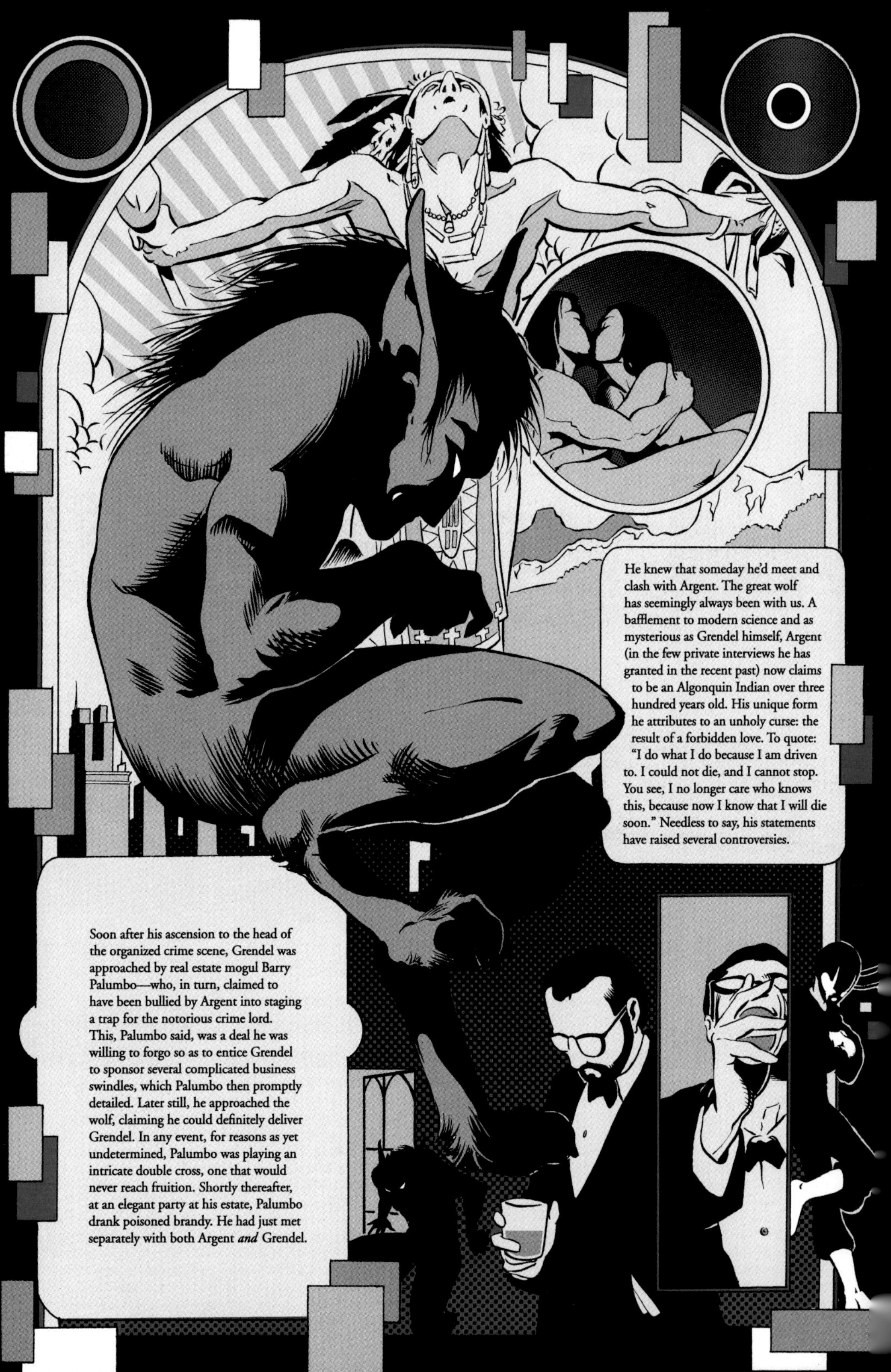
He knew that someday he'd meet and clash with Argent. The great wolf has seemingly always been with us. A bafflement to modern science and as mysterious as Grendel himself, Argent (in the few private interviews he has granted in the recent past) now claims to be an Algonquin Indian over three hundred years old. His unique form he attributes to an unholy curse: the result of a forbidden love. To quote: "I do what I do because I am driven to. I could not die, and I cannot stop. You see, I no longer care who knows this, because now I know that I will die soon." Needless to say, his statements have raised several controversies.
Soon after his ascension to the head of the organized crime scene, Grendel was approached by real estate mogul Barry Palumbo—who, in turn, claimed to have been bullied by Argent into staging a trap for the notorious crime lord. This, Palumbo said, was a deal he was willing to forgo so as to entice Grendel to sponsor several complicated business swindles, which Palumbo then promptly detailed. Later still, he approached the wolf, claiming he could definitely deliver Grendel. In any event, for reasons as yet undetermined, Palumbo was playing an intricate double cross, one that would never reach fruition. Shortly thereafter, at an elegant party at his estate, Palumbo drank poisoned brandy. He had just met separately with both Argent *and* Grendel.

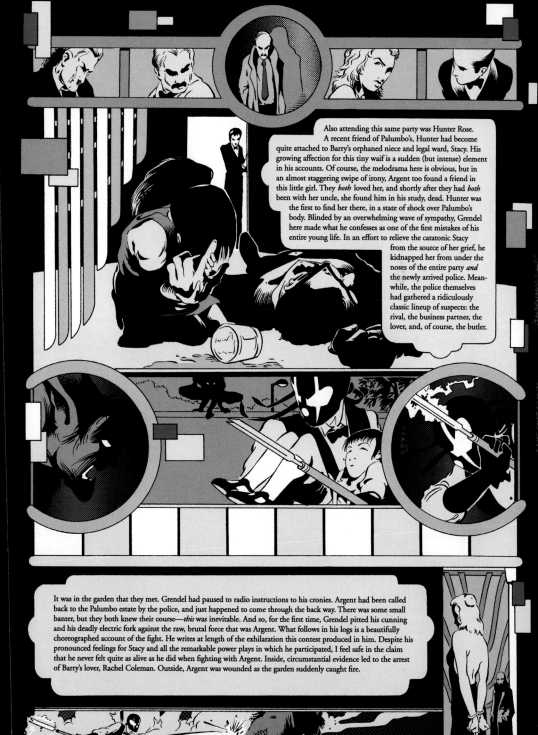

Also attending this same party was Hunter Rose. A recent friend of Palumbo's, Hunter had become quite attached to Barry's orphaned niece and legal ward, Stacy. His growing affection for this tiny waif is a sudden (but intense) element in his accounts. Of course, the melodrama here is obvious, but in an almost staggering swipe of irony, Argent too found a friend in this little girl. They *both* loved her, and shortly after they had *both* been with her uncle, she found him in his study, dead. Hunter was the first to find her there, in a state of shock over Palumbo's body. Blinded by an overwhelming wave of sympathy, Grendel here made what he confesses as one of the first mistakes of his entire young life. In an effort to relieve the catatonic Stacy from the source of her grief, he kidnapped her from under the noses of the entire party *and* the newly arrived police. Meanwhile, the police themselves had gathered a ridiculously classic lineup of suspects: the rival, the business partner, the lover, and, of course, the butler.

It was in the garden that they met. Grendel had paused to radio instructions to his cronies. Argent had been called back to the Palumbo estate by the police, and just happened to come through the back way. There was some small banter, but they both knew their course—*this* was inevitable. And so, for the first time, Grendel pitted his cunning and his deadly electric fork against the raw, brutal force that was Argent. What follows in his logs is a beautifully choreographed account of the fight. He writes at length of the exhilaration this contest produced in him. Despite his pronounced feelings for Stacy and all the remarkable power plays in which he participated, I feel safe in the claim that he never felt quite as alive as he did when fighting with Argent. Inside, circumstantial evidence led to the arrest of Barry's lover, Rachel Coleman. Outside, Argent was wounded as the garden suddenly caught fire.

11

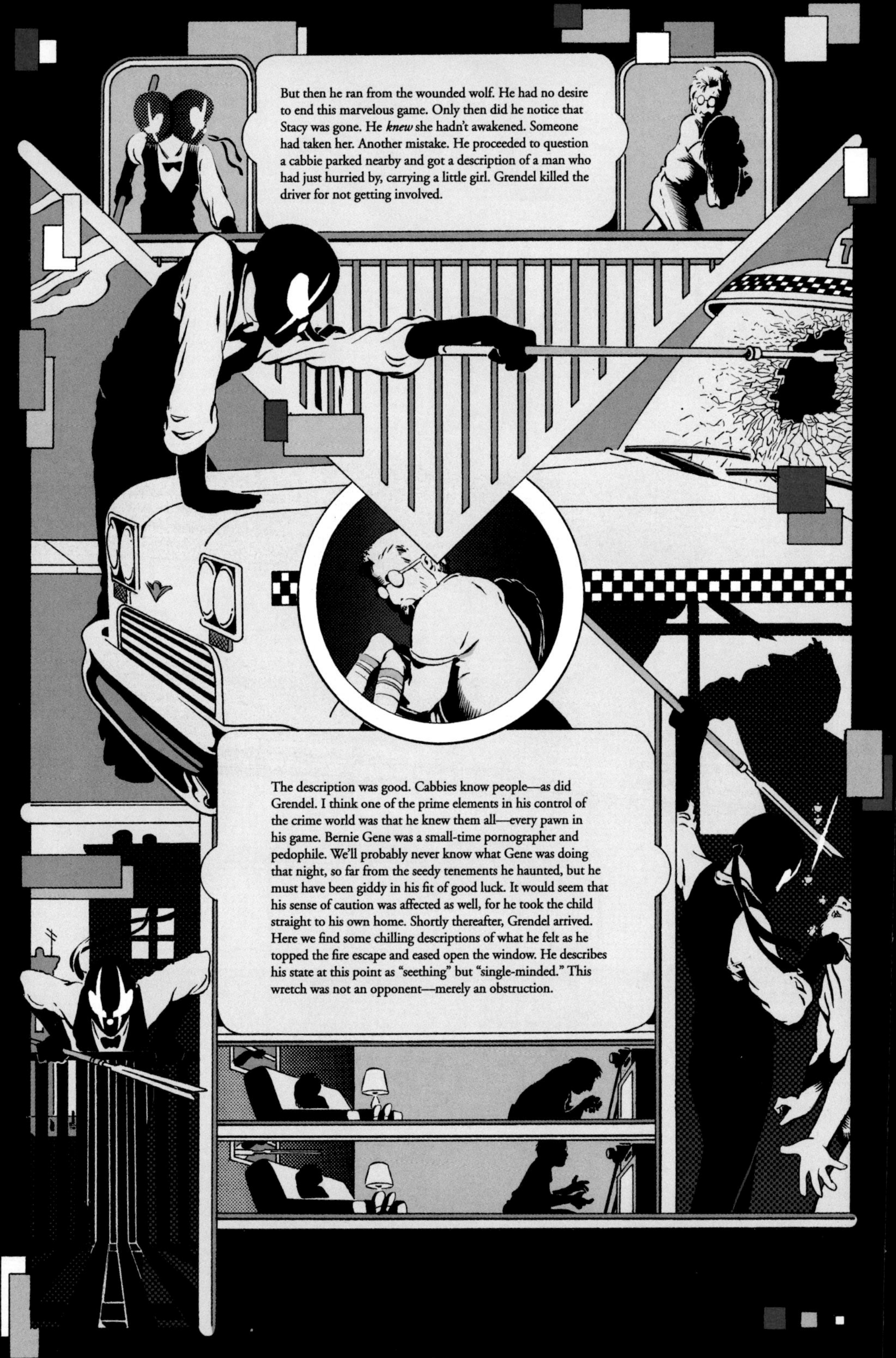
But then he ran from the wounded wolf. He had no desire to end this marvelous game. Only then did he notice that Stacy was gone. He *knew* she hadn't awakened. Someone had taken her. Another mistake. He proceeded to question a cabbie parked nearby and got a description of a man who had just hurried by, carrying a little girl. Grendel killed the driver for not getting involved.
The description was good. Cabbies know people—as did Grendel. I think one of the prime elements in his control of the crime world was that he knew them all—every pawn in his game. Bernie Gene was a small-time pornographer and pedophile. We'll probably never know what Gene was doing that night, so far from the seedy tenements he haunted, but he must have been giddy in his fit of good luck. It would seem that his sense of caution was affected as well, for he took the child straight to his own home. Shortly thereafter, Grendel arrived. Here we find some chilling descriptions of what he felt as he topped the fire escape and eased open the window. He describes his state at this point as "seething" but "single-minded." This wretch was not an opponent—merely an obstruction.

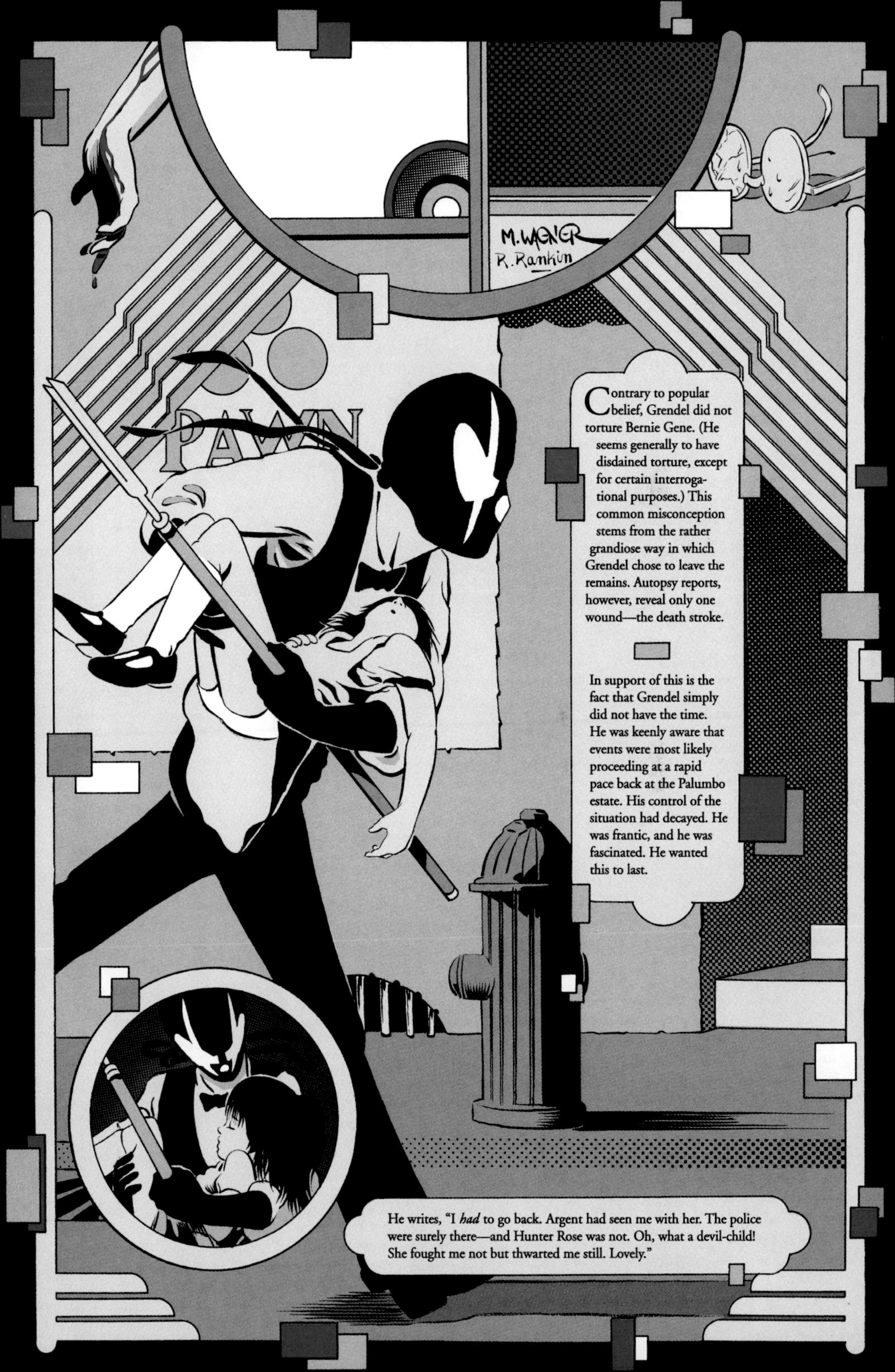
M. WAGNER
R. Rankin
PAWN
Contrary to popular belief, Grendel did not torture Bernie Gene. (He seems generally to have disdained torture, except for certain interrogational purposes.) This common misconception stems from the rather grandiose way in which Grendel chose to leave the remains. Autopsy reports, however, reveal only one wound—the death stroke.
In support of this is the fact that Grendel simply did not have the time. He was keenly aware that events were most likely proceeding at a rapid pace back at the Palumbo estate. His control of the situation had decayed. He was frantic, and he was fascinated. He wanted this to last.
He writes, "I *had* to go back. Argent had seen me with her. The police were surely there—and Hunter Rose was not. Oh, what a devil-child! She fought me not but thwarted me still. Lovely."

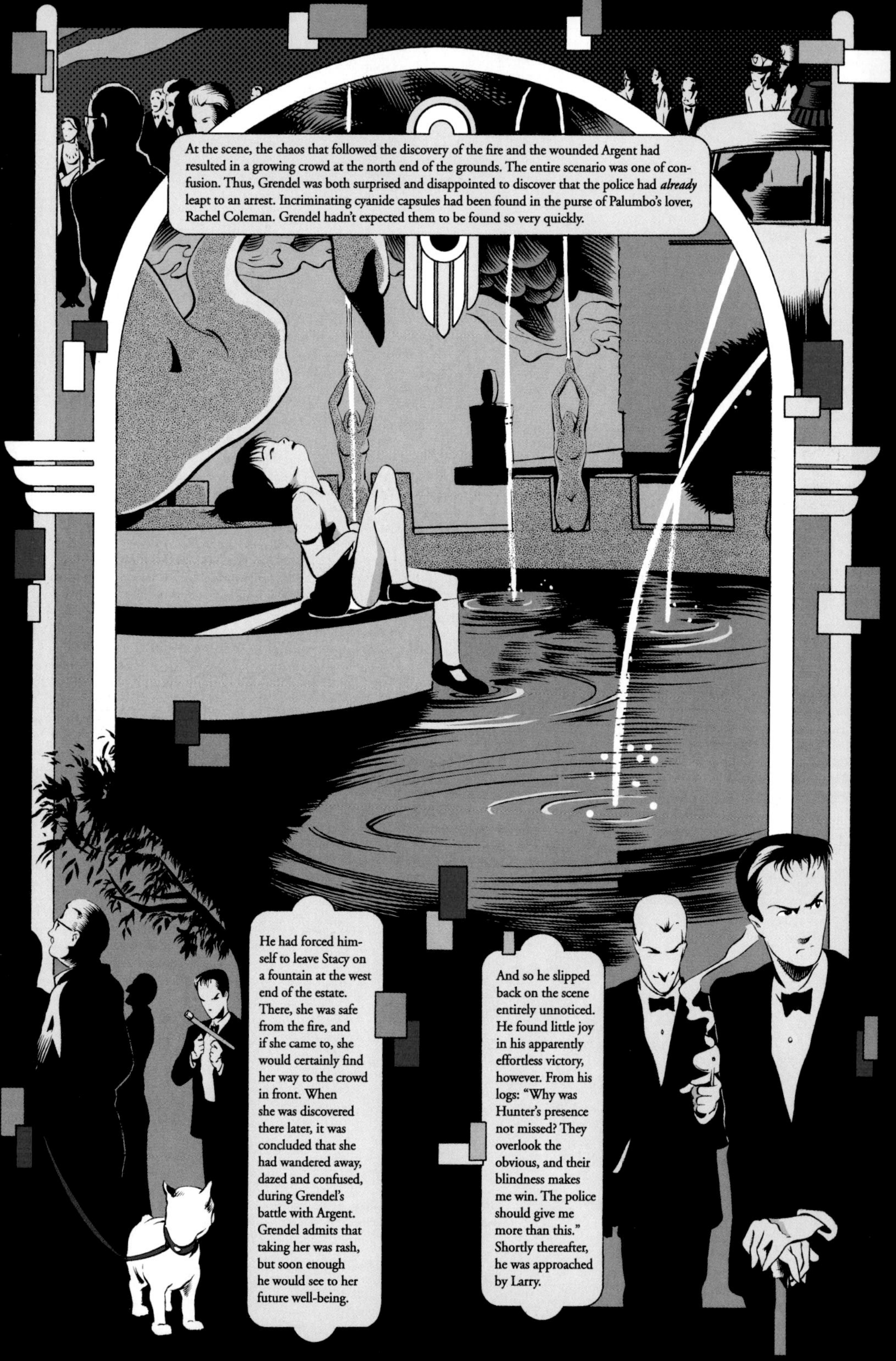
At the scene, the chaos that followed the discovery of the fire and the wounded Argent had resulted in a growing crowd at the north end of the grounds. The entire scenario was one of confusion. Thus, Grendel was both surprised and disappointed to discover that the police had *already* leapt to an arrest. Incriminating cyanide capsules had been found in the purse of Palumbo's lover, Rachel Coleman. Grendel hadn't expected them to be found so very quickly.
He had forced himself to leave Stacy on a fountain at the west end of the estate. There, she was safe from the fire, and if she came to, she would certainly find her way to the crowd in front. When she was discovered there later, it was concluded that she had wandered away, dazed and confused, during Grendel's battle with Argent. Grendel admits that taking her was rash, but soon enough he would see to her future well-being.
And so he slipped back on the scene entirely unnoticed. He found little joy in his apparently effortless victory, however. From his logs: "Why was Hunter's presence not missed? They overlook the obvious, and their blindness makes me win. The police should give me more than this." Shortly thereafter, he was approached by Larry.

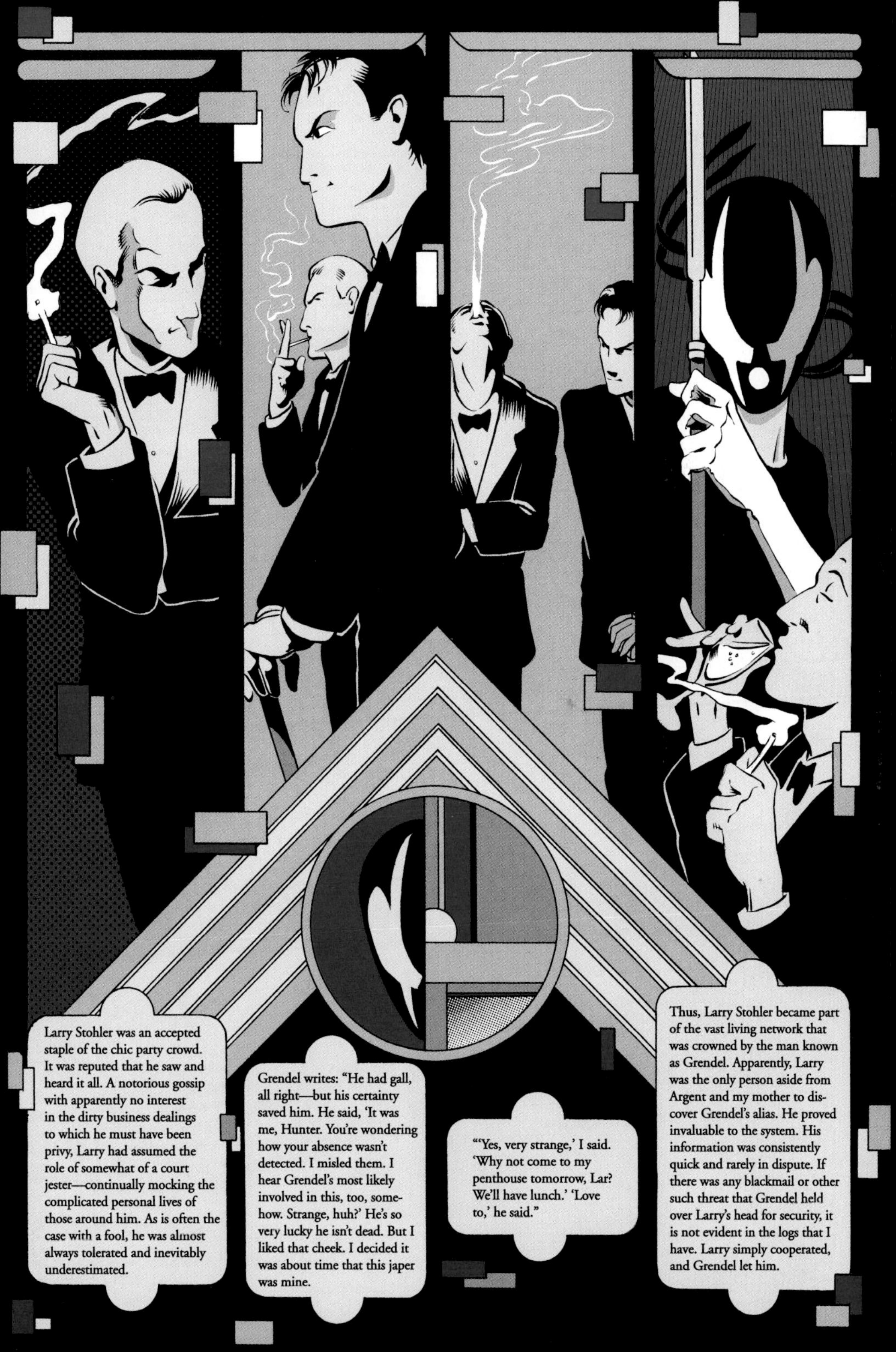

Larry Stohler was an accepted staple of the chic party crowd. It was reputed that he saw and heard it all. A notorious gossip with apparently no interest in the dirty business dealings to which he must have been privy, Larry had assumed the role of somewhat of a court jester—continually mocking the complicated personal lives of those around him. As is often the case with a fool, he was almost always tolerated and inevitably underestimated.
Grendel writes: "He had gall, all right—but his certainty saved him. He said, 'It was me, Hunter. You're wondering how your absence wasn't detected. I misled them. I hear Grendel's most likely involved in this, too, somehow. Strange, huh?' He's so very lucky he isn't dead. But I liked that cheek. I decided it was about time that this japer was mine.
"'Yes, very strange,' I said. 'Why not come to my penthouse tomorrow, Lar? We'll have lunch.' 'Love to,' he said."
Thus, Larry Stohler became part of the vast living network that was crowned by the man known as Grendel. Apparently, Larry was the only person aside from Argent and my mother to discover Grendel's alias. He proved invaluable to the system. His information was consistently quick and rarely in dispute. If there was any blackmail or other such threat that Grendel held over Larry's head for security, it is not evident in the logs that I have. Larry simply cooperated, and Grendel let him.

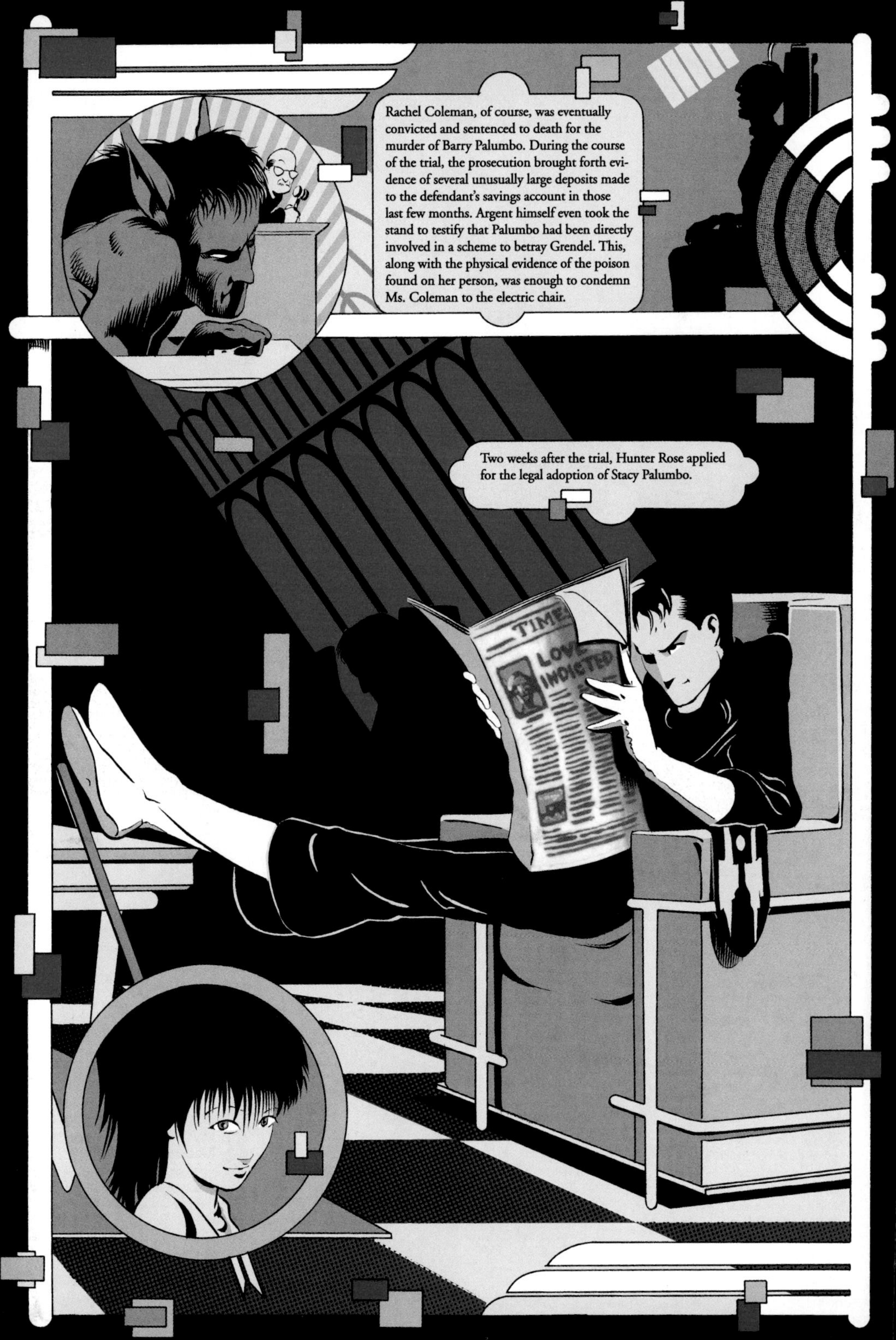
Rachel Coleman, of course, was eventually convicted and sentenced to death for the murder of Barry Palumbo. During the course of the trial, the prosecution brought forth evidence of several unusually large deposits made to the defendant's savings account in those last few months. Argent himself even took the stand to testify that Palumbo had been directly involved in a scheme to betray Grendel. This, along with the physical evidence of the poison found on her person, was enough to condemn Ms. Coleman to the electric chair.
Two weeks after the trial, Hunter Rose applied for the legal adoption of Stacy Palumbo.
TIMES
LOVE INDICTED

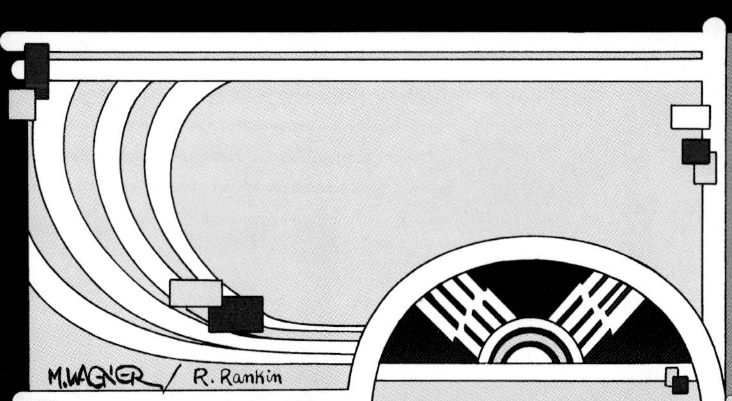
M. WAGNER / R. Rankin

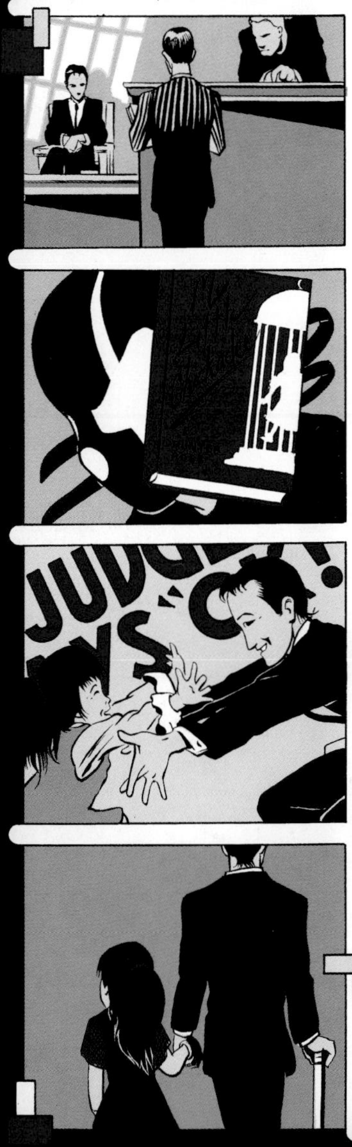

In the wake of the abundant media hype that followed the spectacular murder of Barry Palumbo, the adoption of his only surviving heir was sure to spark the public's vivid imagination. The trial had been intricately covered, and soon Hunter Rose and Stacy Palumbo were household names. Hunter Rose was, of course, also covered intricately—eighteen being a rather controversial age to apply for adoption. Alas, no loophole could be found in either his character or intentions. He had created a persona in complete. Records existed. Character witnesses were brought in by the droves. The fact that not one person (or is there merely no record?) came forth to spoil his story makes the full extent of his reach seem all the more remarkable.

And, of course, sales of all Hunter Rose novels skyrocketed. It was during this time that he published the infamous *My Little Chickadee*. Although actually a subtly constructed (and admittedly manipulative) book, the mere fact of its authorship has assured its place on many lists of "undesirable" literature. In any case, the genius of this work cannot be ignored. The parallels between it and the actual trial exist on an amazing number of levels. Such is the construction that the reader leaves its pages feeling swayed—regardless of preconception. It has been argued that *My Little Chickadee* was the major deciding factor in the custody battle.

In light of the new evidence available from Grendel's private notes, this assumption can no longer be denied. He began work on the book less than a week into the course of the trial and finished it in under three days. In his logs he makes little or no reference to it during the actual production, but afterward refers to it constantly—often quoting passages. He was fully aware of the book's capacity and of its possible repercussions. And in typical fashion, it worked. Inside of three months, the book had swayed both public and judicial opinion in the author's favor. And so, Hunter Rose became Stacy's legal guardian.

Inevitably, Hunter and Stacy became a media "couple" of renown. Their presence about town was in high demand—and could either condone or condemn practically any social event. Thus, Stacy Palumbo was doomed to a childhood enmeshed in the fast life—all from possibly the only good intentions of the man who was Grendel.

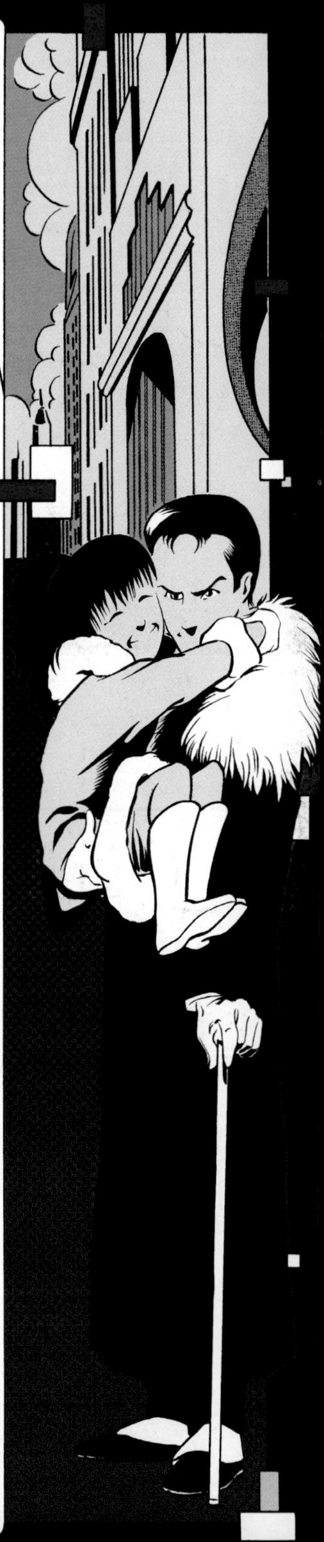

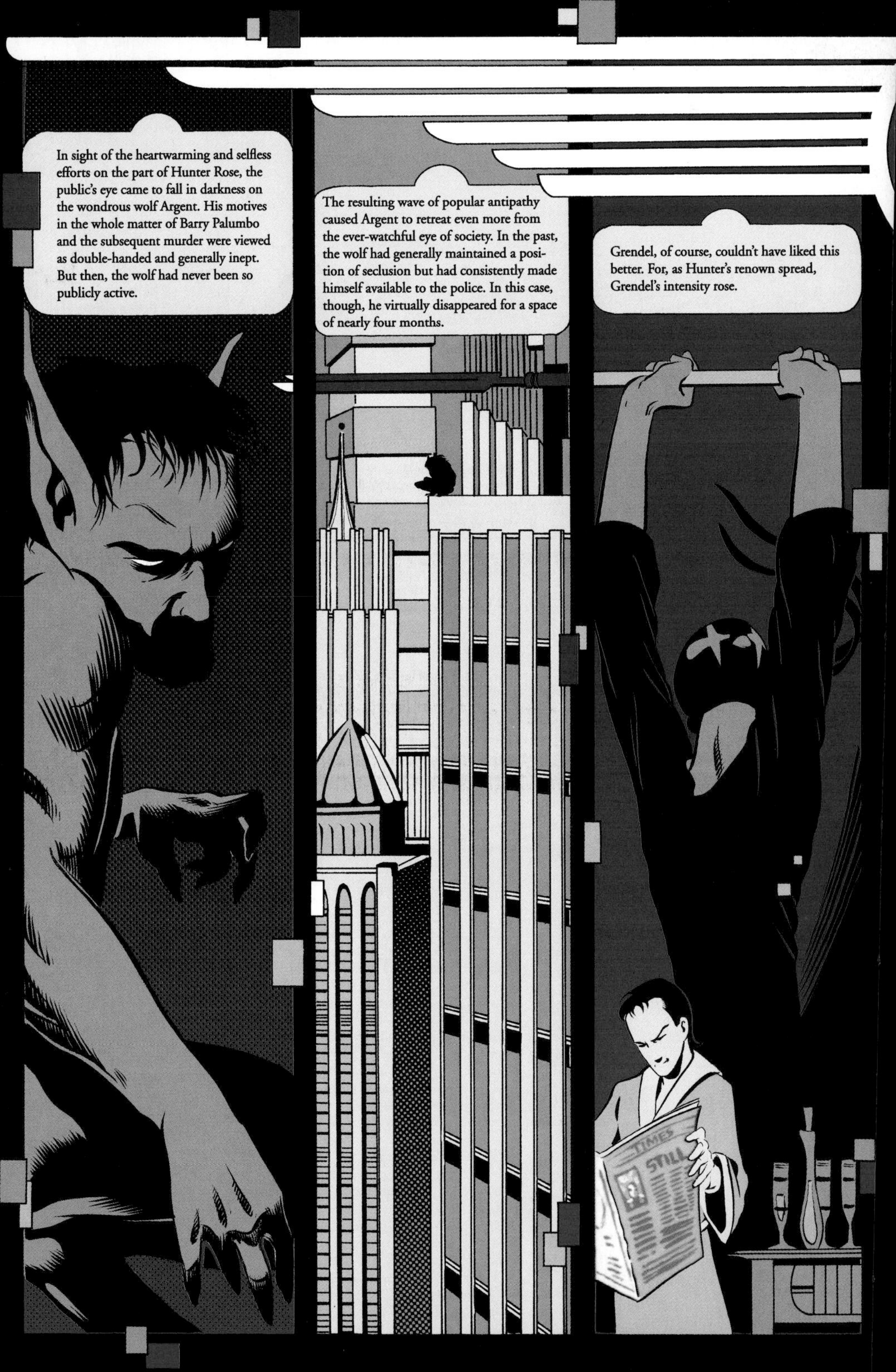
In sight of the heartwarming and selfless efforts on the part of Hunter Rose, the public's eye came to fall in darkness on the wondrous wolf Argent. His motives in the whole matter of Barry Palumbo and the subsequent murder were viewed as double-handed and generally inept. But then, the wolf had never been so publicly active.
The resulting wave of popular antipathy caused Argent to retreat even more from the ever-watchful eye of society. In the past, the wolf had generally maintained a position of seclusion but had consistently made himself available to the police. In this case, though, he virtually disappeared for a space of nearly four months.
Grendel, of course, couldn't have liked this better. For, as Hunter's renown spread, Grendel's intensity rose.

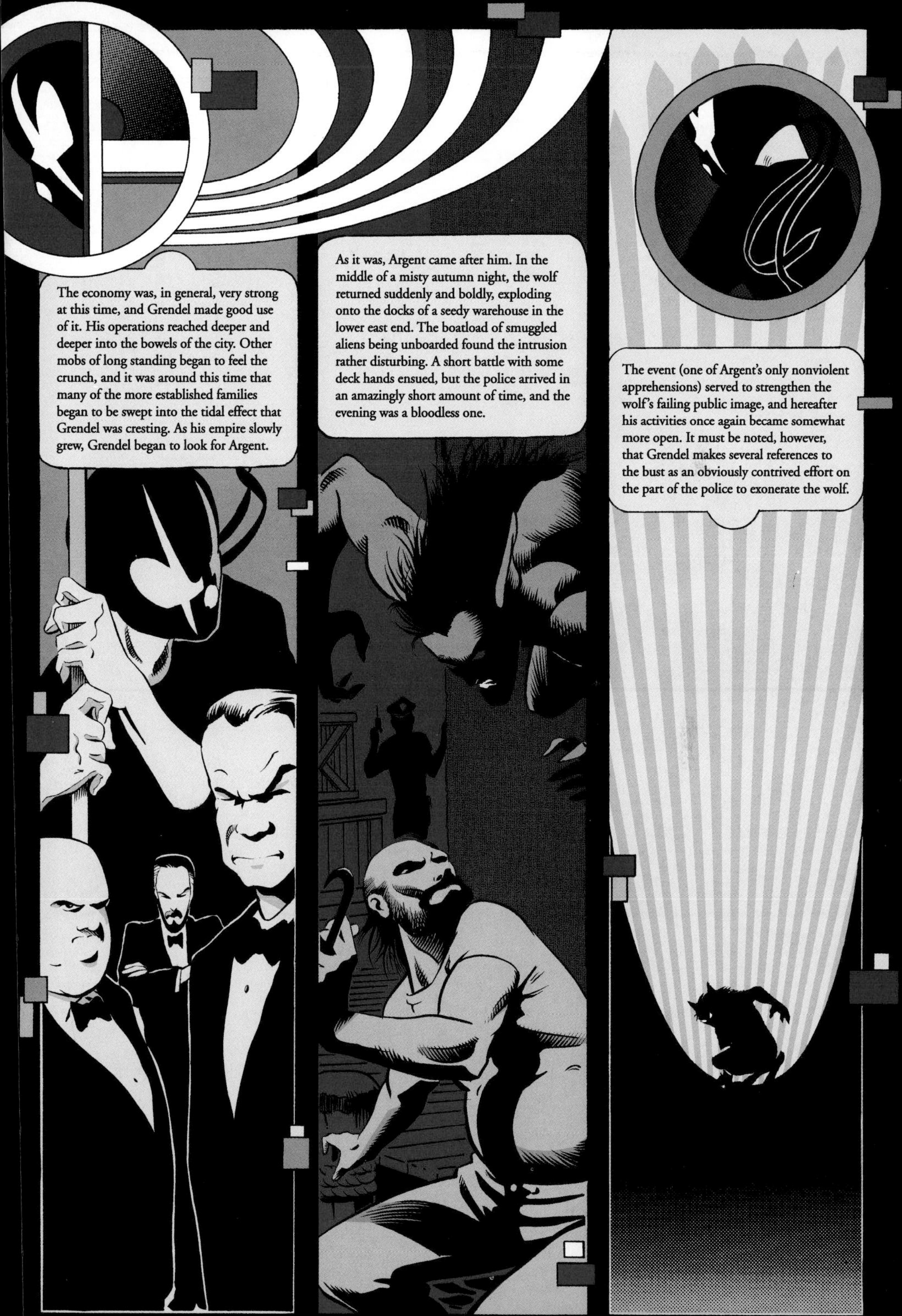
The economy was, in general, very strong at this time, and Grendel made good use of it. His operations reached deeper and deeper into the bowels of the city. Other mobs of long standing began to feel the crunch, and it was around this time that many of the more established families began to be swept into the tidal effect that Grendel was cresting. As his empire slowly grew, Grendel began to look for Argent.
As it was, Argent came after him. In the middle of a misty autumn night, the wolf returned suddenly and boldly, exploding onto the docks of a seedy warehouse in the lower east end. The boatload of smuggled aliens being unboarded found the intrusion rather disturbing. A short battle with some deck hands ensued, but the police arrived in an amazingly short amount of time, and the evening was a bloodless one.
The event (one of Argent's only nonviolent apprehensions) served to strengthen the wolf's failing public image, and hereafter his activities once again became somewhat more open. It must be noted, however, that Grendel makes several references to the bust as an obviously contrived effort on the part of the police to exonerate the wolf.

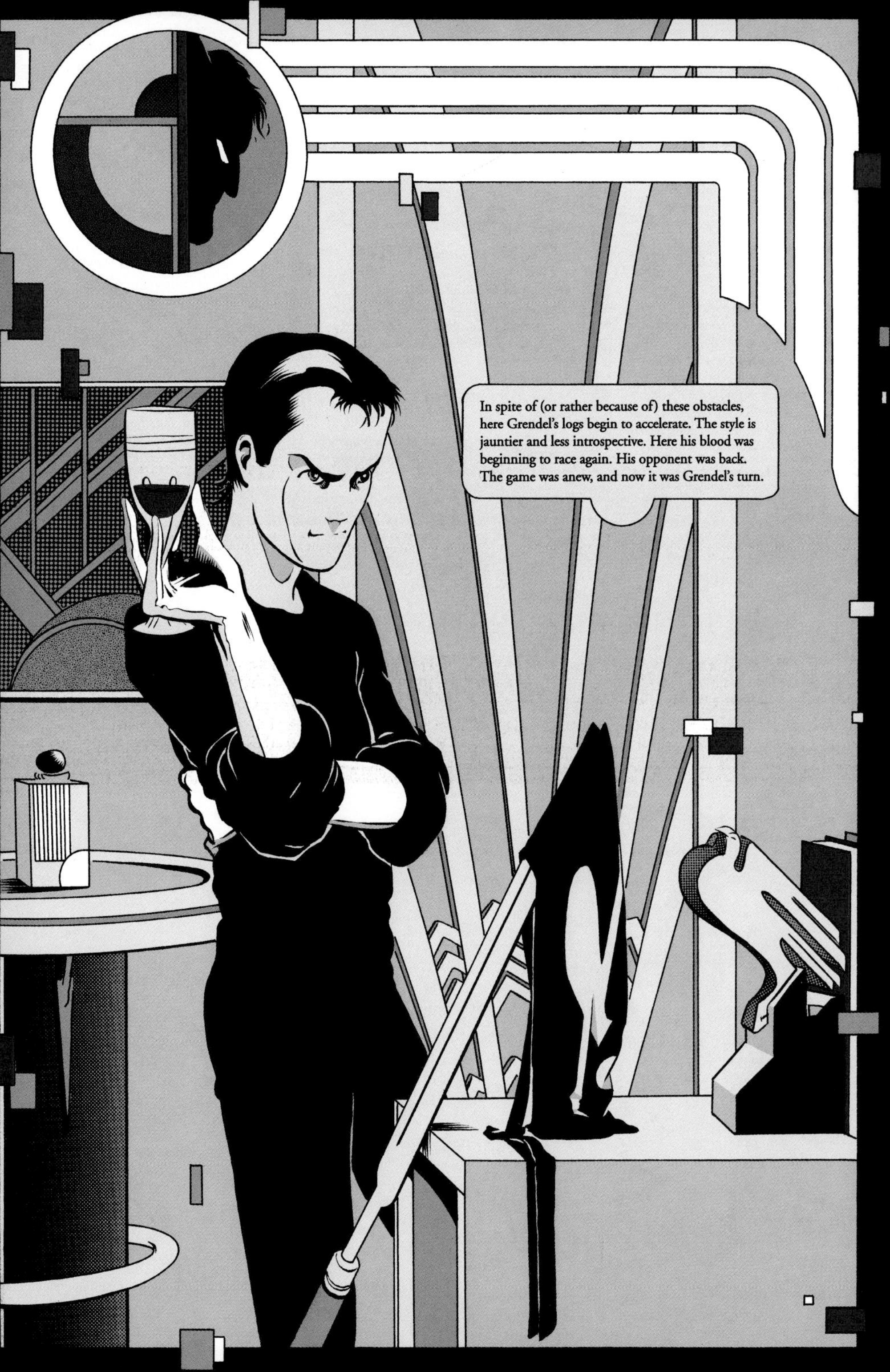
In spite of (or rather because of) these obstacles, here Grendel's logs begin to accelerate. The style is jauntier and less introspective. Here his blood was beginning to race again. His opponent was back. The game was anew, and now it was Grendel's turn.

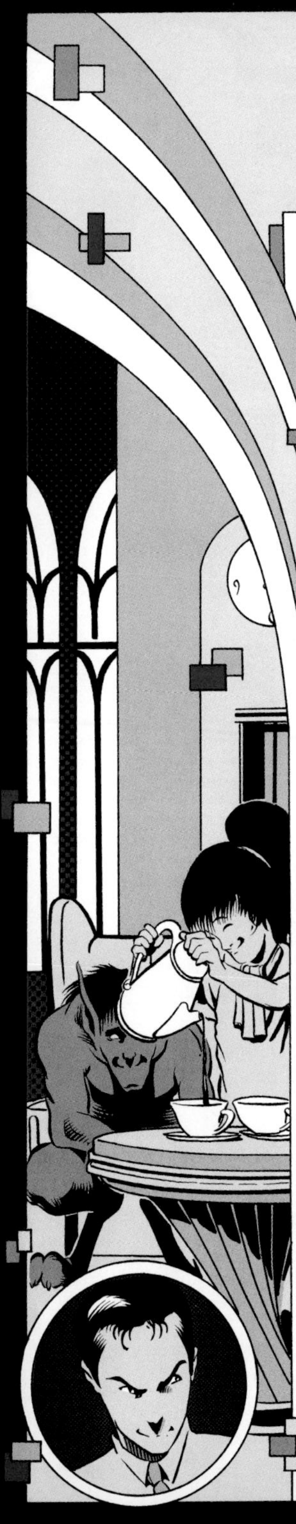

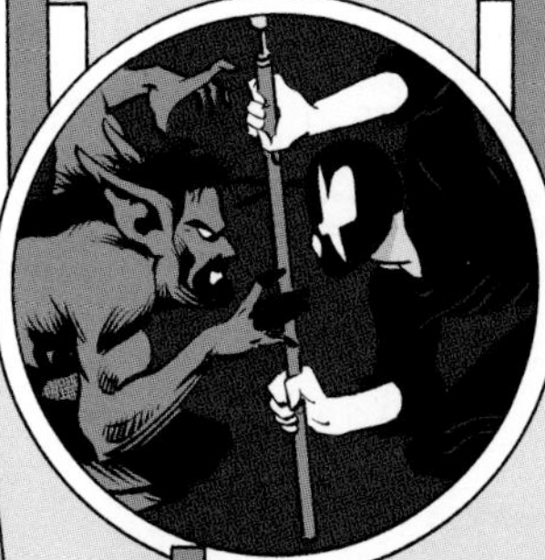

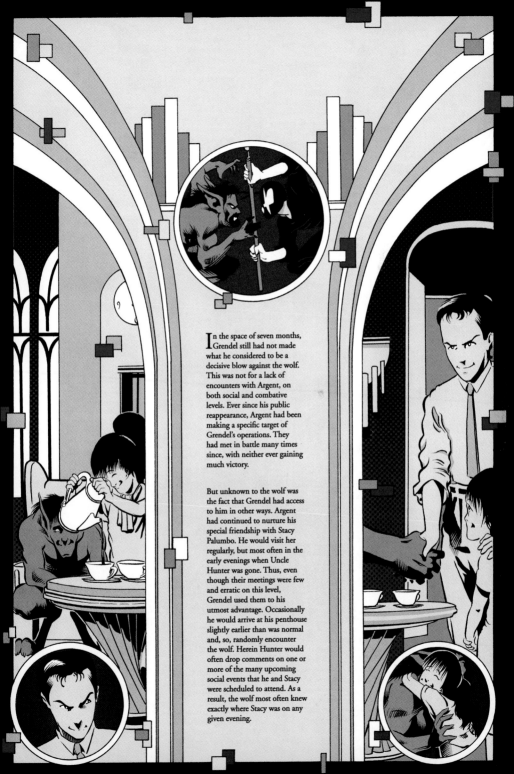

In the space of seven months, Grendel still had not made what he considered to be a decisive blow against the wolf. This was not for a lack of encounters with Argent, on both social and combative levels. Ever since his public reappearance, Argent had been making a specific target of Grendel's operations. They had met in battle many times since, with neither ever gaining much victory.

But unknown to the wolf was the fact that Grendel had access to him in other ways. Argent had continued to nurture his special friendship with Stacy Palumbo. He would visit her regularly, but most often in the early evenings when Uncle Hunter was gone. Thus, even though their meetings were few and erratic on this level, Grendel used them to his utmost advantage. Occasionally he would arrive at his penthouse slightly earlier than was normal and, so, randomly encounter the wolf. Herein Hunter would often drop comments on one or more of the many upcoming social events that he and Stacy were scheduled to attend. As a result, the wolf most often knew exactly where Stacy was on any given evening.

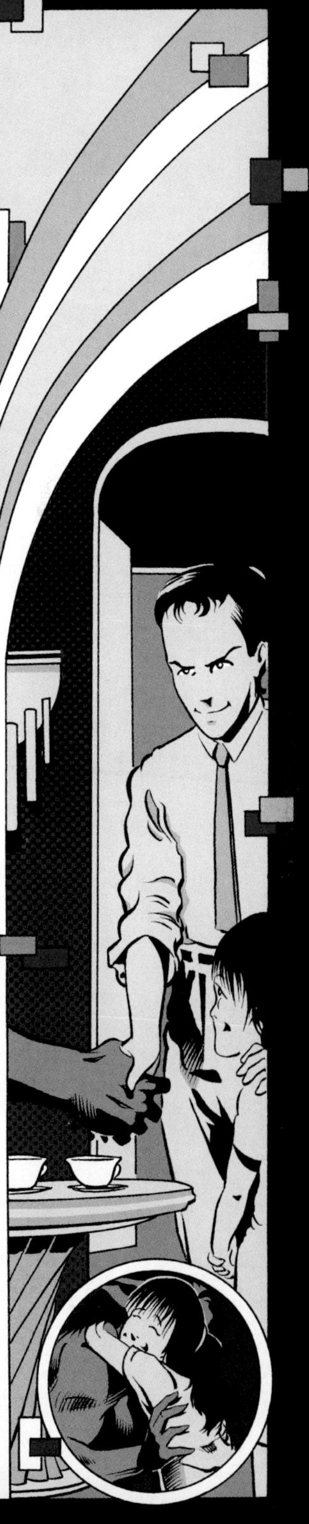

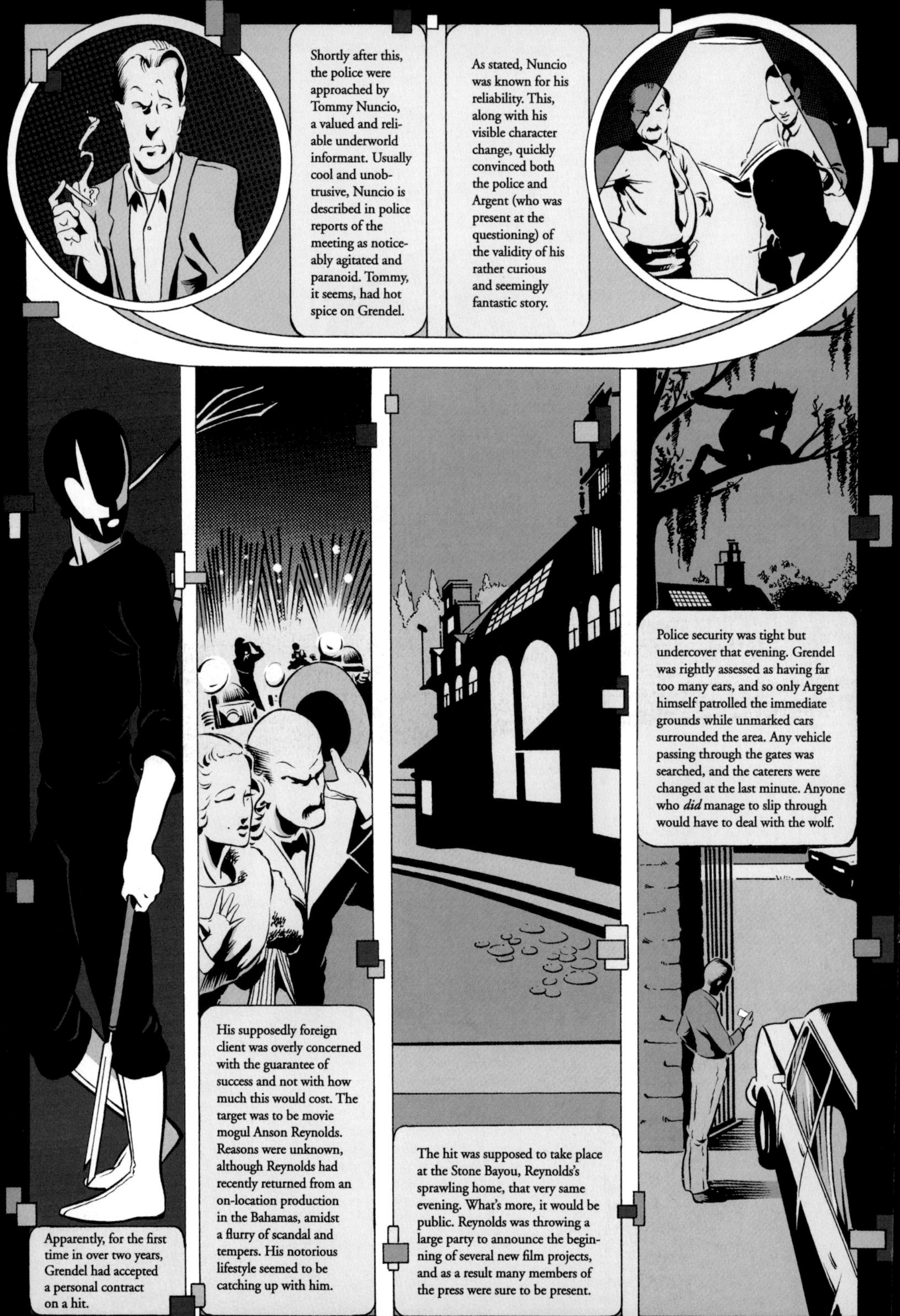
Shortly after this, the police were approached by Tommy Nuncio, a valued and reliable underworld informant. Usually cool and unobtrusive, Nuncio is described in police reports of the meeting as noticeably agitated and paranoid. Tommy, it seems, had hot spice on Grendel.
As stated, Nuncio was known for his reliability. This, along with his visible character change, quickly convinced both the police and Argent (who was present at the questioning) of the validity of his rather curious and seemingly fantastic story.
Apparently, for the first time in over two years, Grendel had accepted a personal contract on a hit.
His supposedly foreign client was overly concerned with the guarantee of success and not with how much this would cost. The target was to be movie mogul Anson Reynolds. Reasons were unknown, although Reynolds had recently returned from an on-location production in the Bahamas, amidst a flurry of scandal and tempers. His notorious lifestyle seemed to be catching up with him.
The hit was supposed to take place at the Stone Bayou, Reynolds's sprawling home, that very same evening. What's more, it would be public. Reynolds was throwing a large party to announce the beginning of several new film projects, and as a result many members of the press were sure to be present.
Police security was tight but undercover that evening. Grendel was rightly assessed as having far too many ears, and so only Argent himself patrolled the immediate grounds while unmarked cars surrounded the area. Any vehicle passing through the gates was searched, and the caterers were changed at the last minute. Anyone who *did* manage to slip through would have to deal with the wolf.

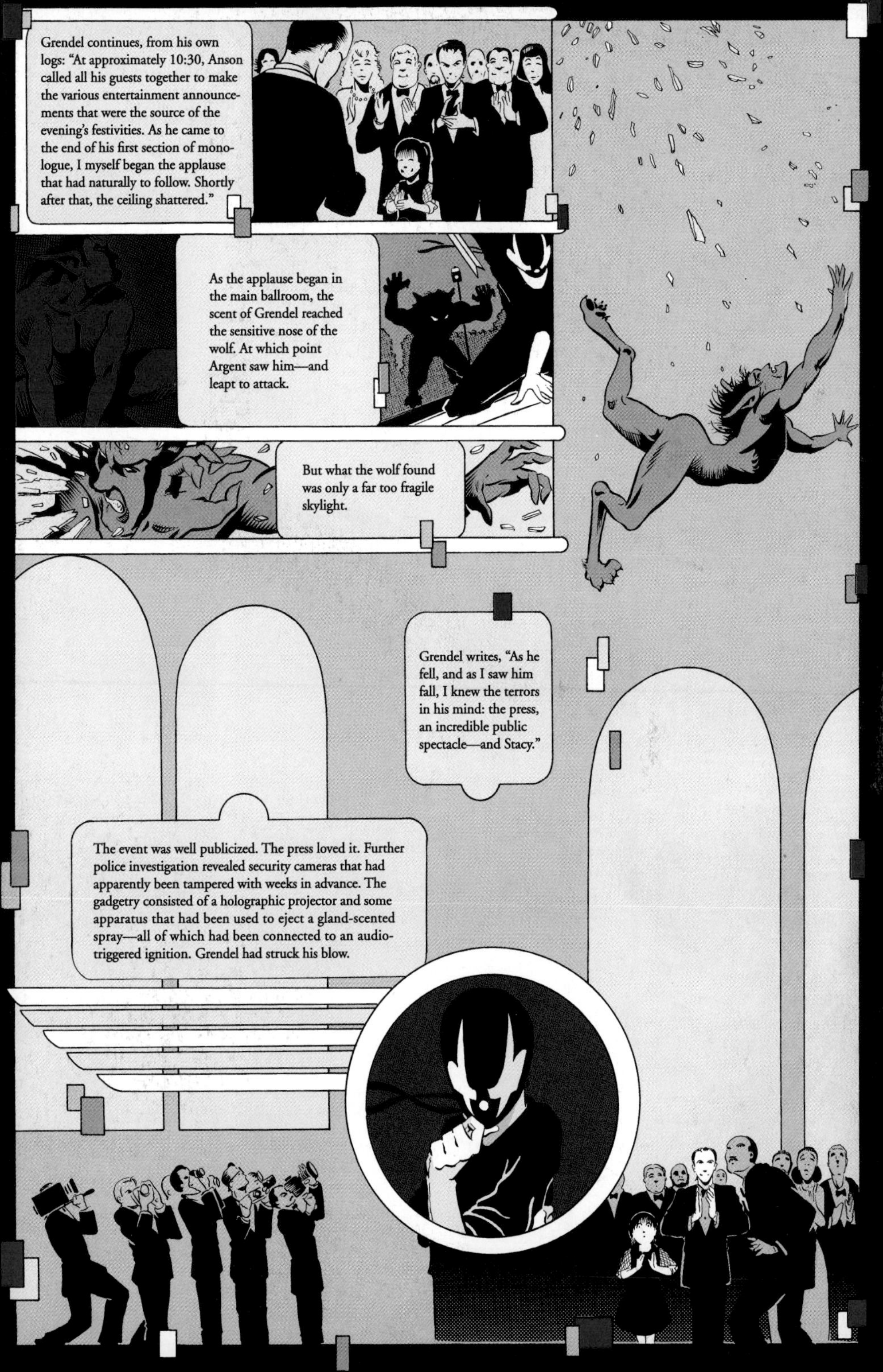
Grendel continues, from his own logs: "At approximately 10:30, Anson called all his guests together to make the various entertainment announcements that were the source of the evening's festivities. As he came to the end of his first section of monologue, I myself began the applause that had naturally to follow. Shortly after that, the ceiling shattered."
As the applause began in the main ballroom, the scent of Grendel reached the sensitive nose of the wolf. At which point Argent saw him—and leapt to attack.
But what the wolf found was only a far too fragile skylight.
Grendel writes, "As he fell, and as I saw him fall, I knew the terrors in his mind: the press, an incredible public spectacle—and Stacy."
The event was well publicized. The press loved it. Further police investigation revealed security cameras that had apparently been tampered with weeks in advance. The gadgetry consisted of a holographic projector and some apparatus that had been used to eject a gland-scented spray—all of which had been connected to an audio-triggered ignition. Grendel had struck his blow.

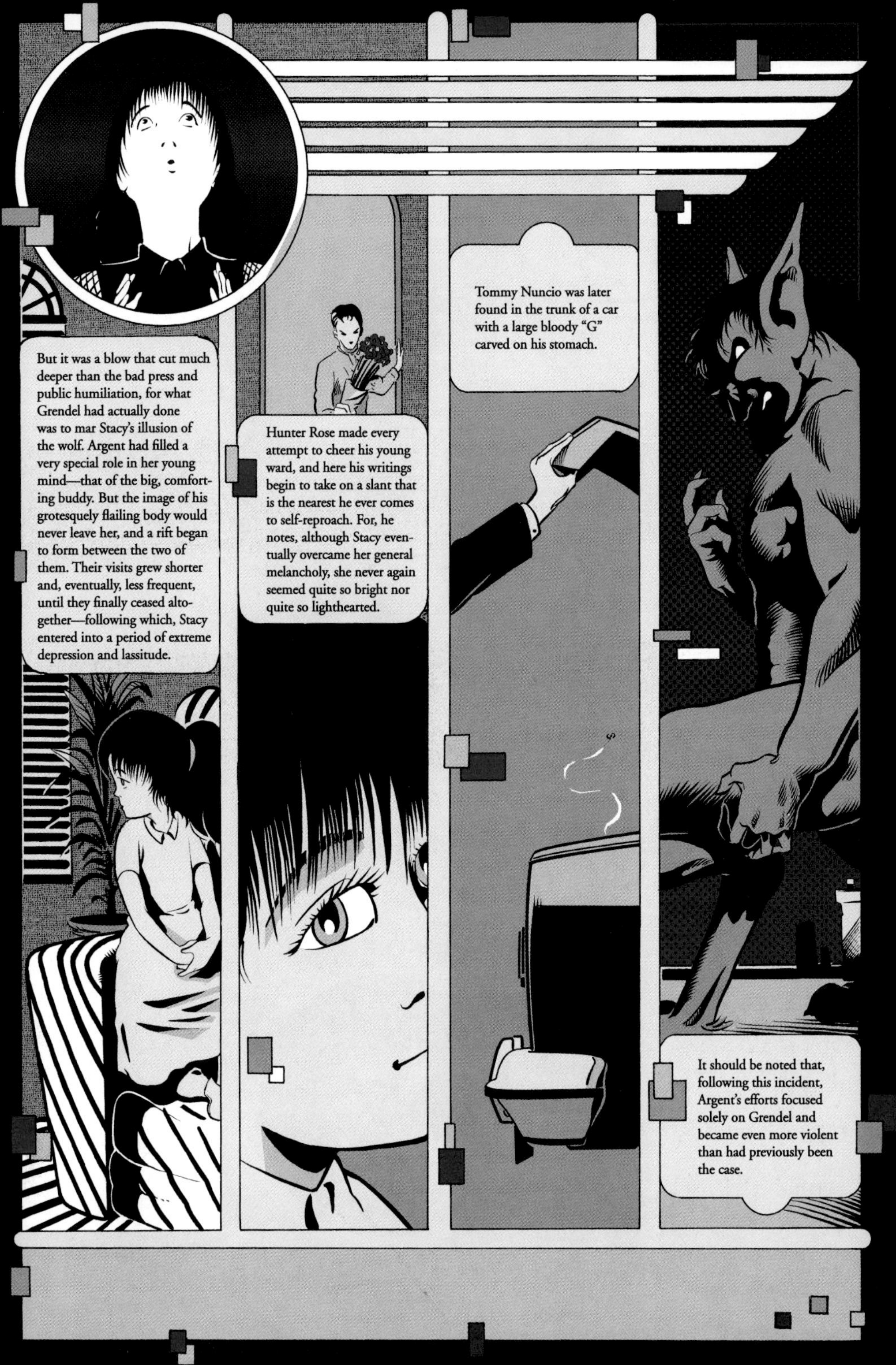
But it was a blow that cut much deeper than the bad press and public humiliation, for what Grendel had actually done was to mar Stacy's illusion of the wolf. Argent had filled a very special role in her young mind—that of the big, comforting buddy. But the image of his grotesquely flailing body would never leave her, and a rift began to form between the two of them. Their visits grew shorter and, eventually, less frequent, until they finally ceased altogether—following which, Stacy entered into a period of extreme depression and lassitude.
Hunter Rose made every attempt to cheer his young ward, and here his writings begin to take on a slant that is the nearest he ever comes to self-reproach. For, he notes, although Stacy eventually overcame her general melancholy, she never again seemed quite so bright nor quite so lighthearted.
Tommy Nuncio was later found in the trunk of a car with a large bloody "G" carved on his stomach.
It should be noted that, following this incident, Argent's efforts focused solely on Grendel and became even more violent than had previously been the case.

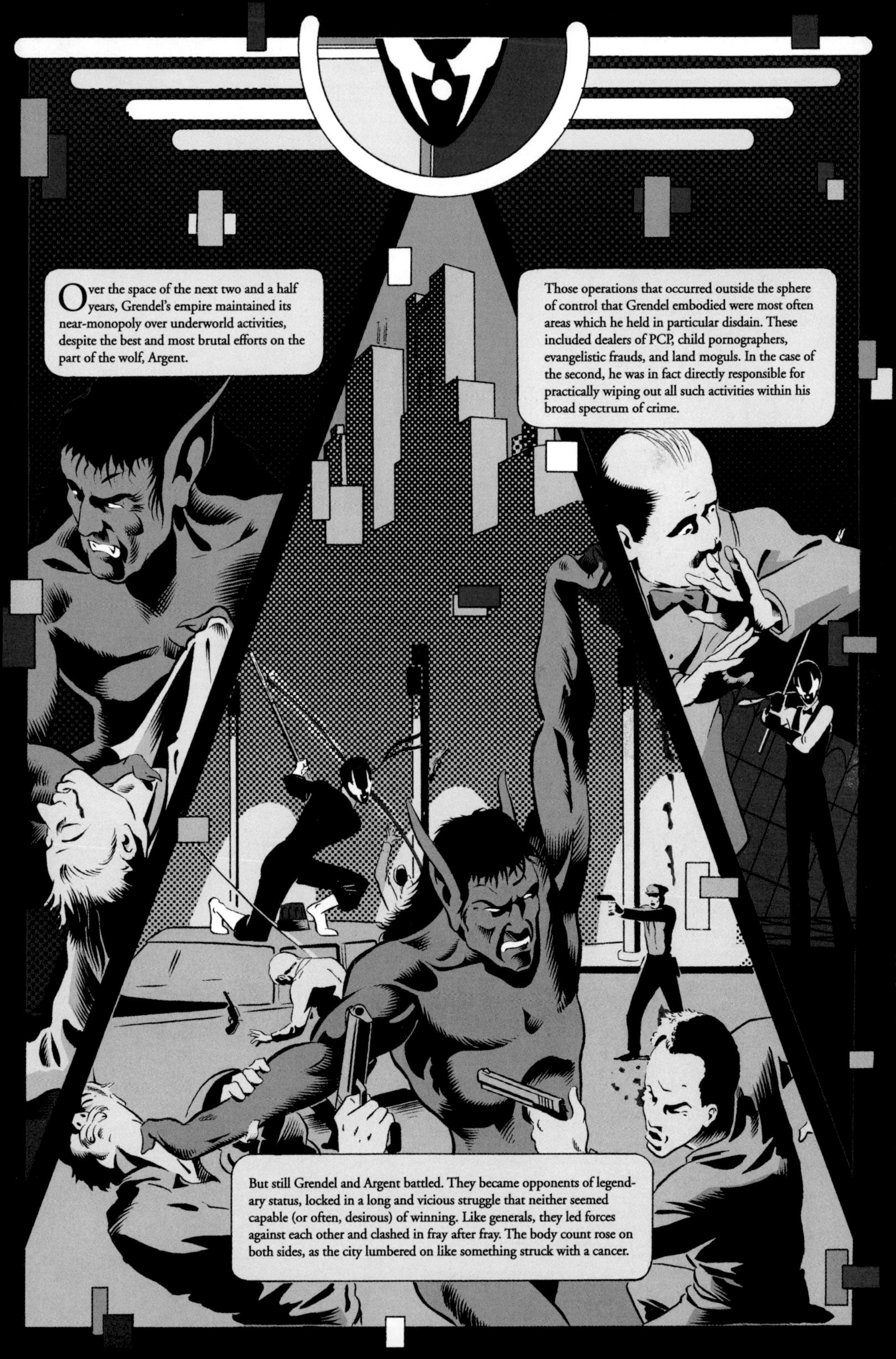
Over the space of the next two and a half years, Grendel's empire maintained its near-monopoly over underworld activities, despite the best and most brutal efforts on the part of the wolf, Argent.
Those operations that occurred outside the sphere of control that Grendel embodied were most often areas which he held in particular disdain. These included dealers of PCP, child pornographers, evangelistic frauds, and land moguls. In the case of the second, he was in fact directly responsible for practically wiping out all such activities within his broad spectrum of crime.
But still Grendel and Argent battled. They became opponents of legendary status, locked in a long and vicious struggle that neither seemed capable (or often, desirous) of winning. Like generals, they led forces against each other and clashed in fray after fray. The body count rose on both sides, as the city lumbered on like something struck with a cancer.

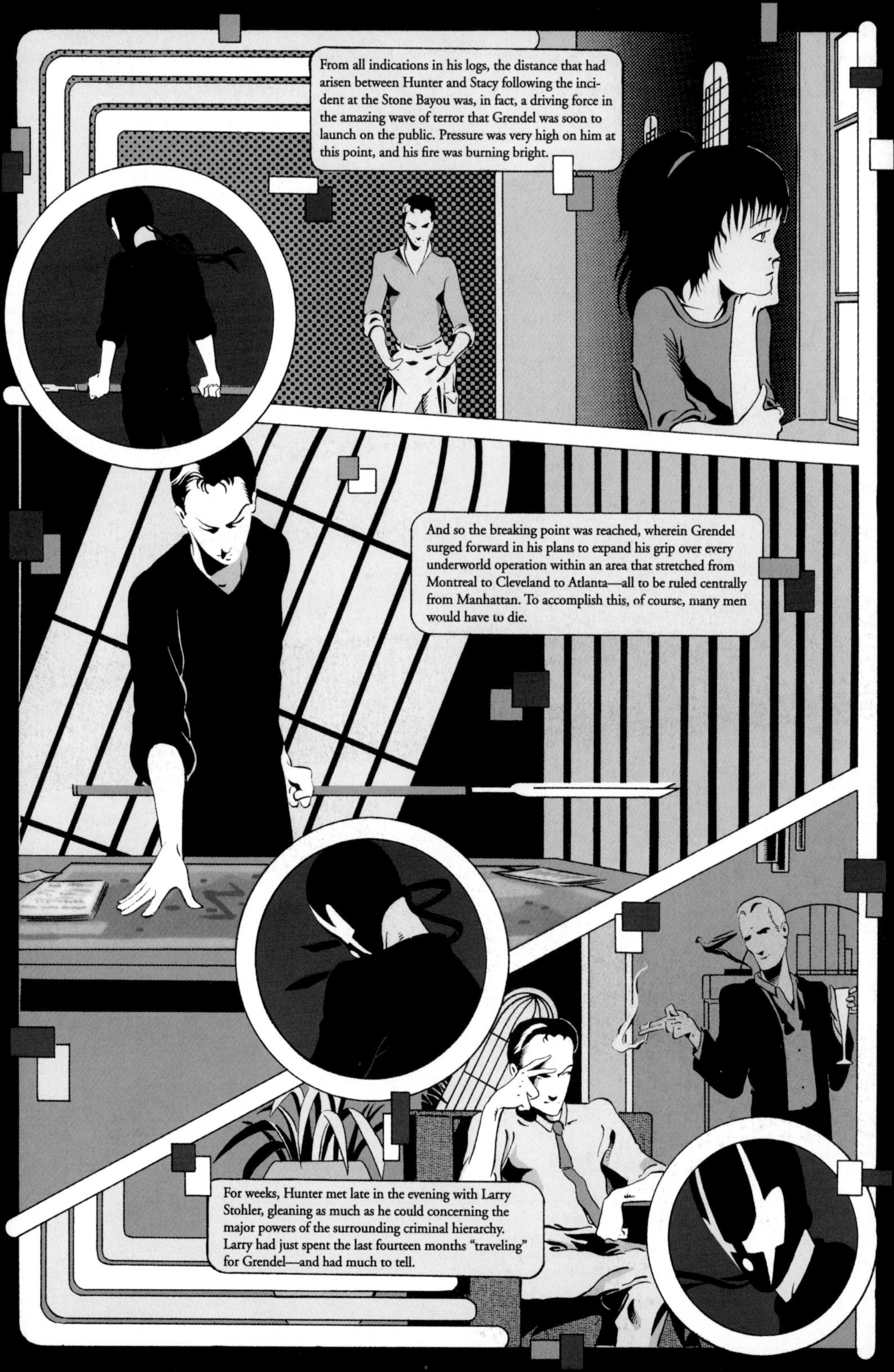
From all indications in his logs, the distance that had arisen between Hunter and Stacy following the incident at the Stone Bayou was, in fact, a driving force in the amazing wave of terror that Grendel was soon to launch on the public. Pressure was very high on him at this point, and his fire was burning bright.
And so the breaking point was reached, wherein Grendel surged forward in his plans to expand his grip over every underworld operation within an area that stretched from Montreal to Cleveland to Atlanta—all to be ruled centrally from Manhattan. To accomplish this, of course, many men would have to die.
For weeks, Hunter met late in the evening with Larry Stohler, gleaning as much as he could concerning the major powers of the surrounding criminal hierarchy. Larry had just spent the last fourteen months "traveling" for Grendel—and had much to tell.

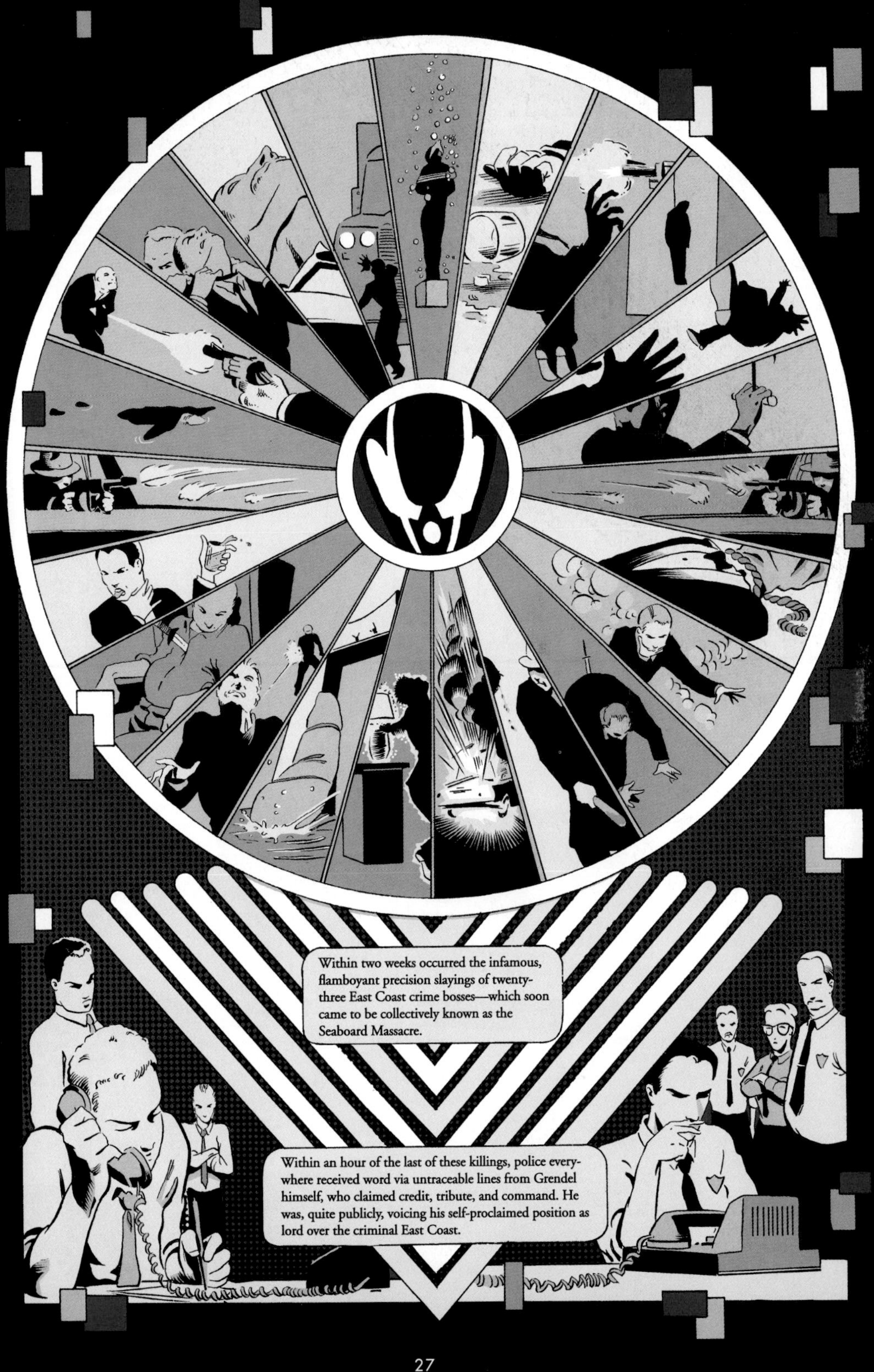
Within two weeks occurred the infamous, flamboyant precision slayings of twenty-three East Coast crime bosses—which soon came to be collectively known as the Seaboard Massacre.
Within an hour of the last of these killings, police everywhere received word via untraceable lines from Grendel himself, who claimed credit, tribute, and command. He was, quite publicly, voicing his self-proclaimed position as lord over the criminal East Coast.

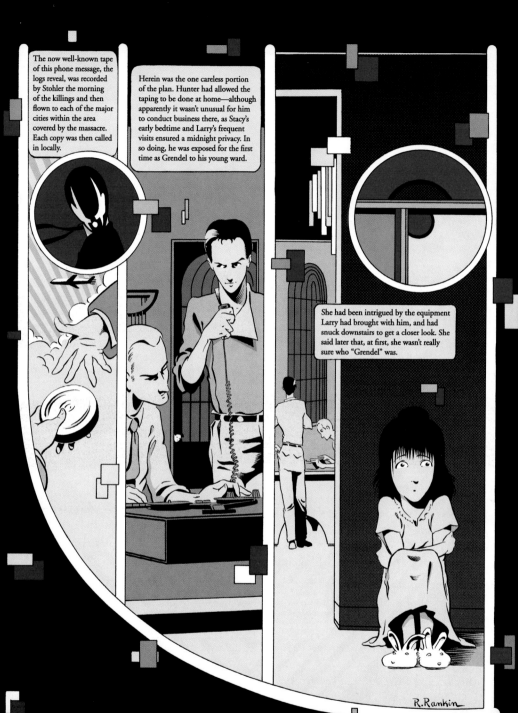

The now well-known tape of this phone message, the logs reveal, was recorded by Stohler the morning of the killings and then flown to each of the major cities within the area covered by the massacre. Each copy was then called in locally.

Herein was the one careless portion of the plan. Hunter had allowed the taping to be done at home—although apparently it wasn't unusual for him to conduct business there, as Stacy's early bedtime and Larry's frequent visits ensured a midnight privacy. In so doing, he was exposed for the first time as Grendel to his young ward.

She had been intrigued by the equipment Larry had brought with him, and had snuck downstairs to get a closer look. She said later that, at first, she wasn't really sure who "Grendel" was.

R. Rankin

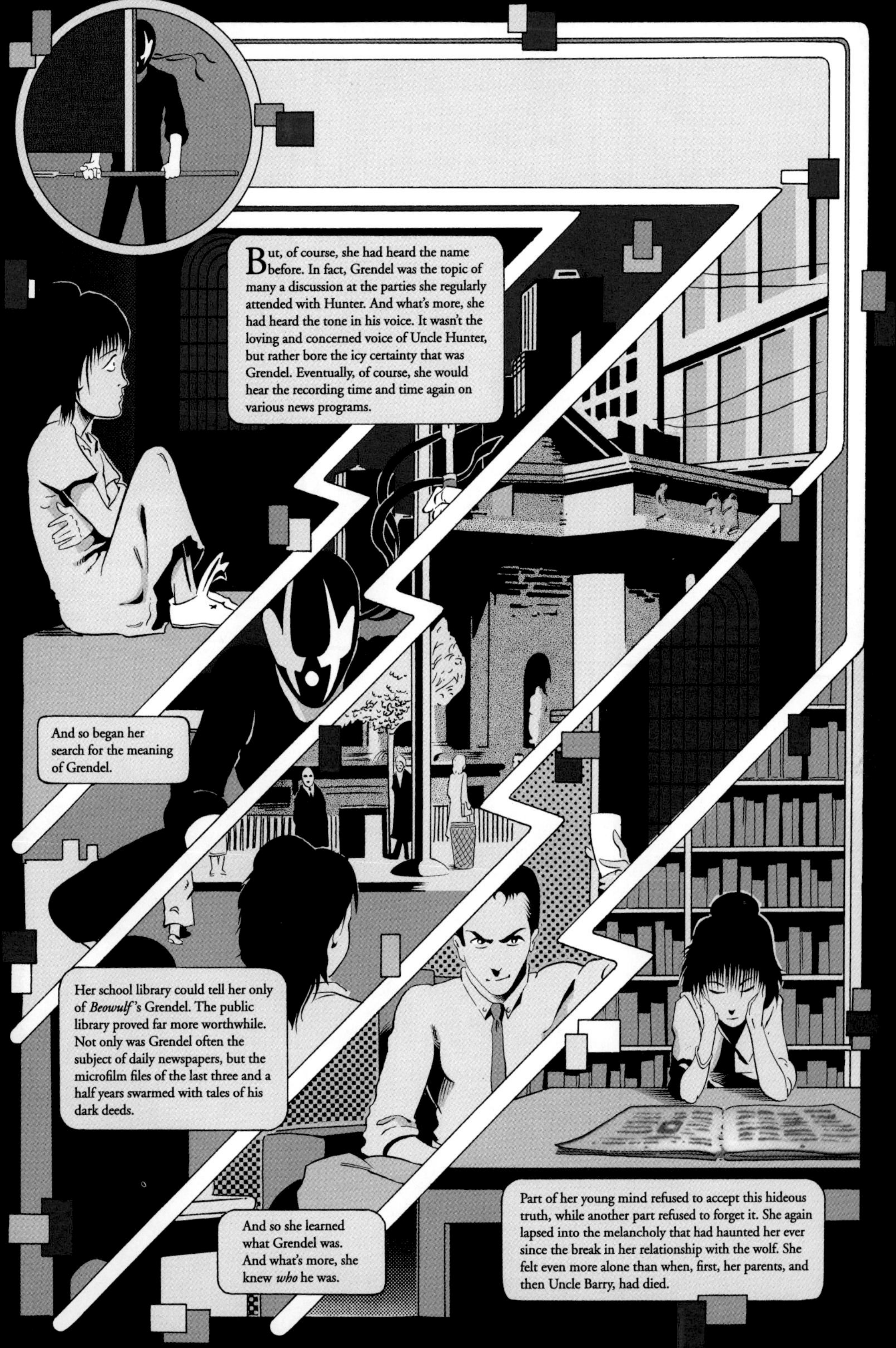

But, of course, she had heard the name before. In fact, Grendel was the topic of many a discussion at the parties she regularly attended with Hunter. And what's more, she had heard the tone in his voice. It wasn't the loving and concerned voice of Uncle Hunter, but rather bore the icy certainty that was Grendel. Eventually, of course, she would hear the recording time and time again on various news programs.
And so began her search for the meaning of Grendel.
Her school library could tell her only of *Beowulf*'s Grendel. The public library proved far more worthwhile. Not only was Grendel often the subject of daily newspapers, but the microfilm files of the last three and a half years swarmed with tales of his dark deeds.
And so she learned what Grendel was. And what's more, she knew *who* he was.
Part of her young mind refused to accept this hideous truth, while another part refused to forget it. She again lapsed into the melancholy that had haunted her ever since the break in her relationship with the wolf. She felt even more alone than when, first, her parents, and then Uncle Barry, had died.

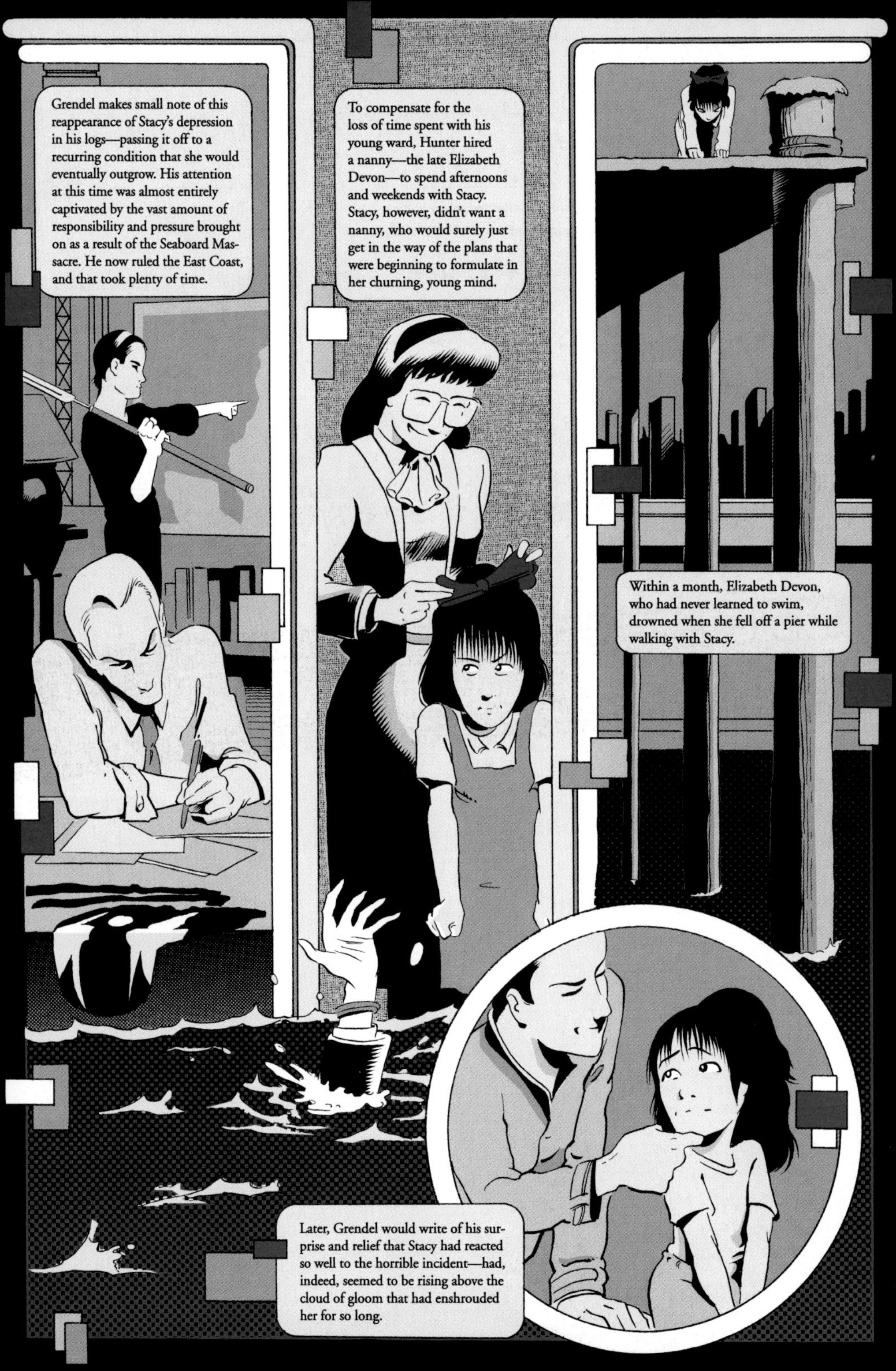
Grendel makes small note of this reappearance of Stacy's depression in his logs—passing it off to a recurring condition that she would eventually outgrow. His attention at this time was almost entirely captivated by the vast amount of responsibility and pressure brought on as a result of the Seaboard Massacre. He now ruled the East Coast, and that took plenty of time.
To compensate for the loss of time spent with his young ward, Hunter hired a nanny—the late Elizabeth Devon—to spend afternoons and weekends with Stacy. Stacy, however, didn't want a nanny, who would surely just get in the way of the plans that were beginning to formulate in her churning, young mind.
Within a month, Elizabeth Devon, who had never learned to swim, drowned when she fell off a pier while walking with Stacy.
Later, Grendel would write of his surprise and relief that Stacy had reacted so well to the horrible incident—had, indeed, seemed to be rising above the cloud of gloom that had enshrouded her for so long.

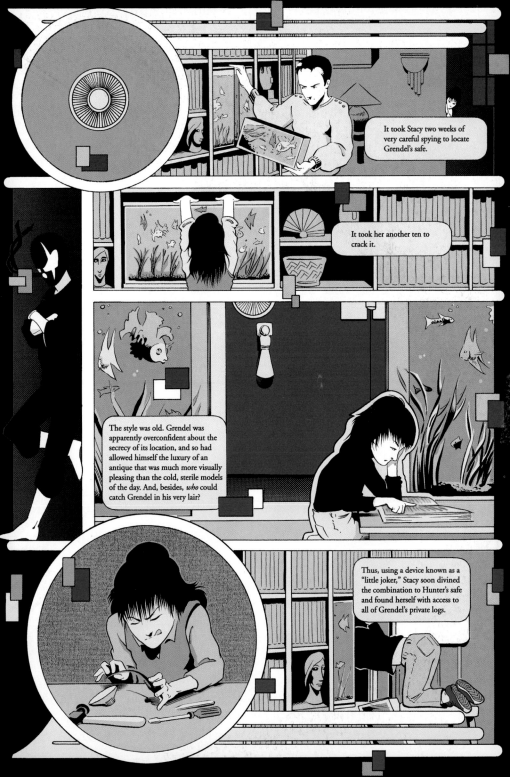

It took Stacy two weeks of very careful spying to locate Grendel's safe.

It took her another ten to crack it.

The style was old. Grendel was apparently overconfident about the secrecy of its location, and so had allowed himself the luxury of an antique that was much more visually pleasing than the cold, sterile models of the day. And, besides, *who* could catch Grendel in his very lair?

Thus, using a device known as a "little joker," Stacy soon divined the combination to Hunter's safe and found herself with access to all of Grendel's private logs.

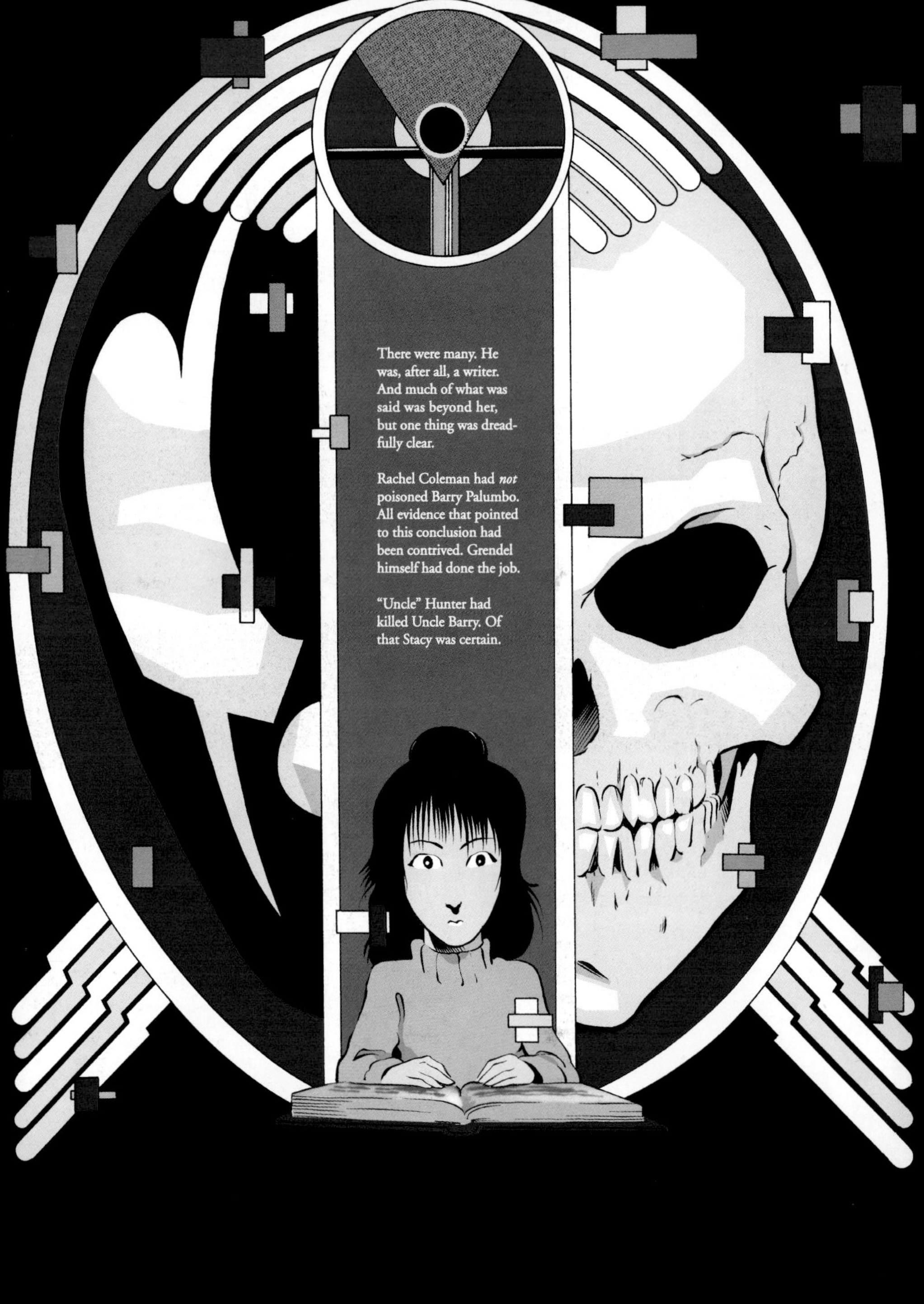
There were many. He was, after all, a writer. And much of what was said was beyond her, but one thing was dread-fully clear.
Rachel Coleman had *not* poisoned Barry Palumbo. All evidence that pointed to this conclusion had been contrived. Grendel himself had done the job.
"Uncle" Hunter had killed Uncle Barry. Of that Stacy was certain.

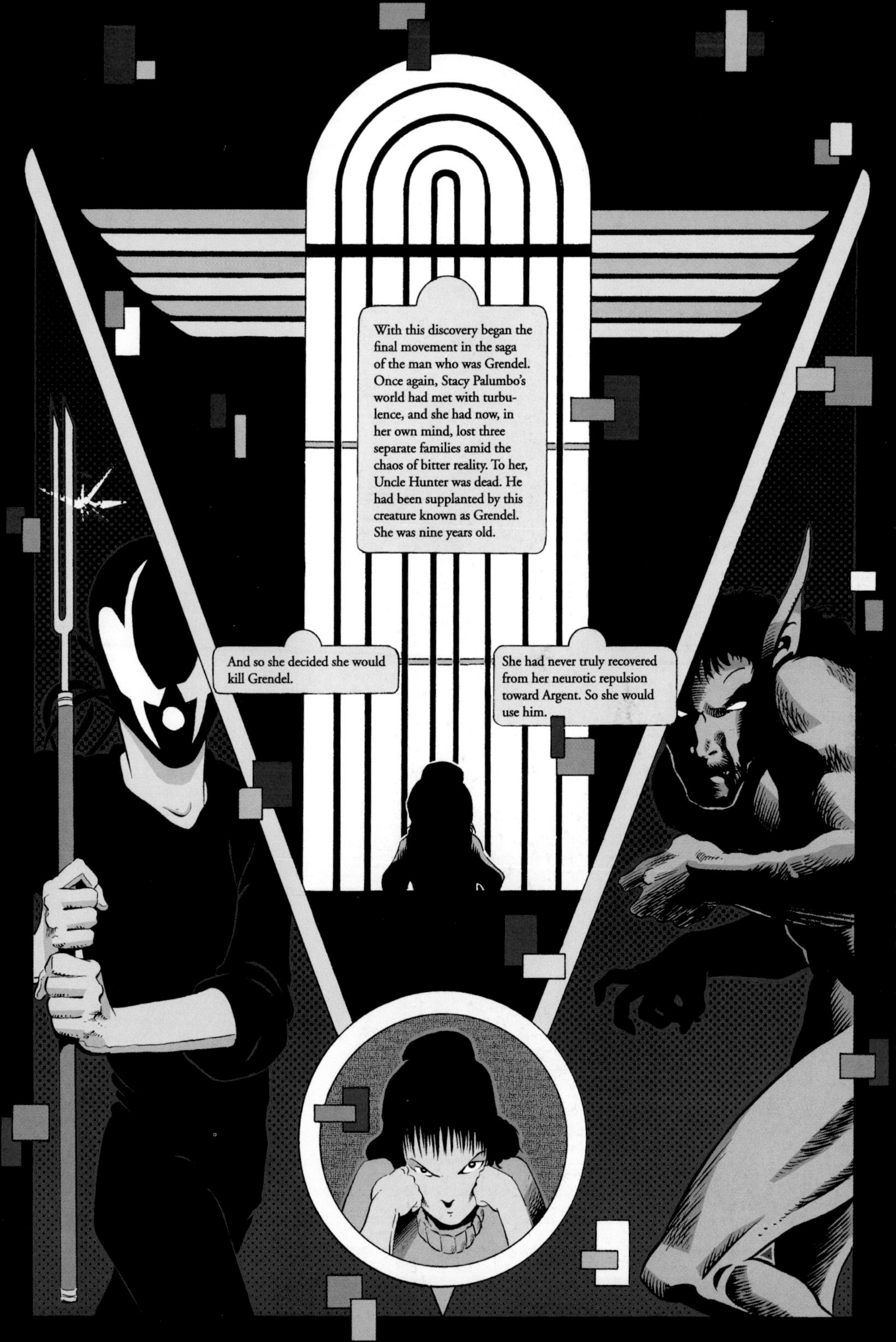
With this discovery began the final movement in the saga of the man who was Grendel. Once again, Stacy Palumbo's world had met with turbulence, and she had now, in her own mind, lost three separate families amid the chaos of bitter reality. To her, Uncle Hunter was dead. He had been supplanted by this creature known as Grendel. She was nine years old.
And so she decided she would kill Grendel.
She had never truly recovered from her neurotic repulsion toward Argent. So she would use him.

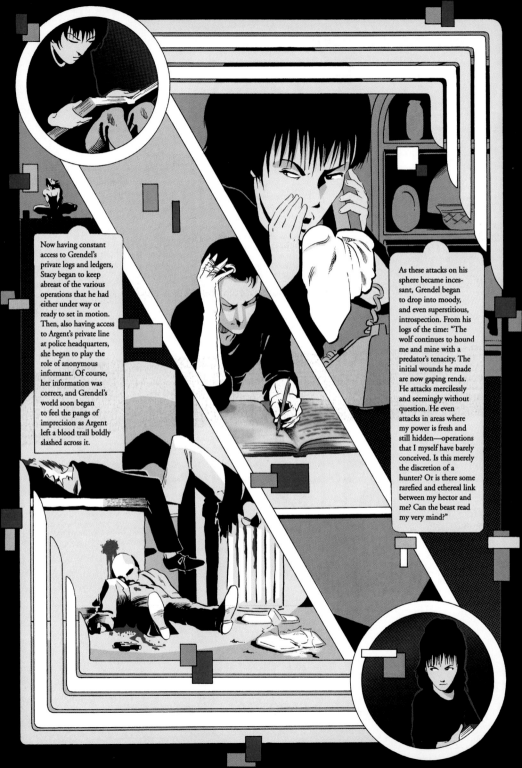

Now having constant access to Grendel's private logs and ledgers, Stacy began to keep abreast of the various operations that he had either under way or ready to set in motion. Then, also having access to Argent's private line at police headquarters, she began to play the role of anonymous informant. Of course, her information was correct, and Grendel's world soon began to feel the pangs of imprecision as Argent left a blood trail boldly slashed across it.

As these attacks on his sphere became incessant, Grendel began to drop into moody, and even superstitious, introspection. From his logs of the time: "The wolf continues to hound me and mine with a predator's tenacity. The initial wounds he made are now gaping rends. He attacks mercilessly and seemingly without question. He even attacks in areas where my power is fresh and still hidden—operations that I myself have barely conceived. Is this merely the discretion of a hunter? Or is there some rarefied and ethereal link between my hector and me? Can the beast read my very mind?"

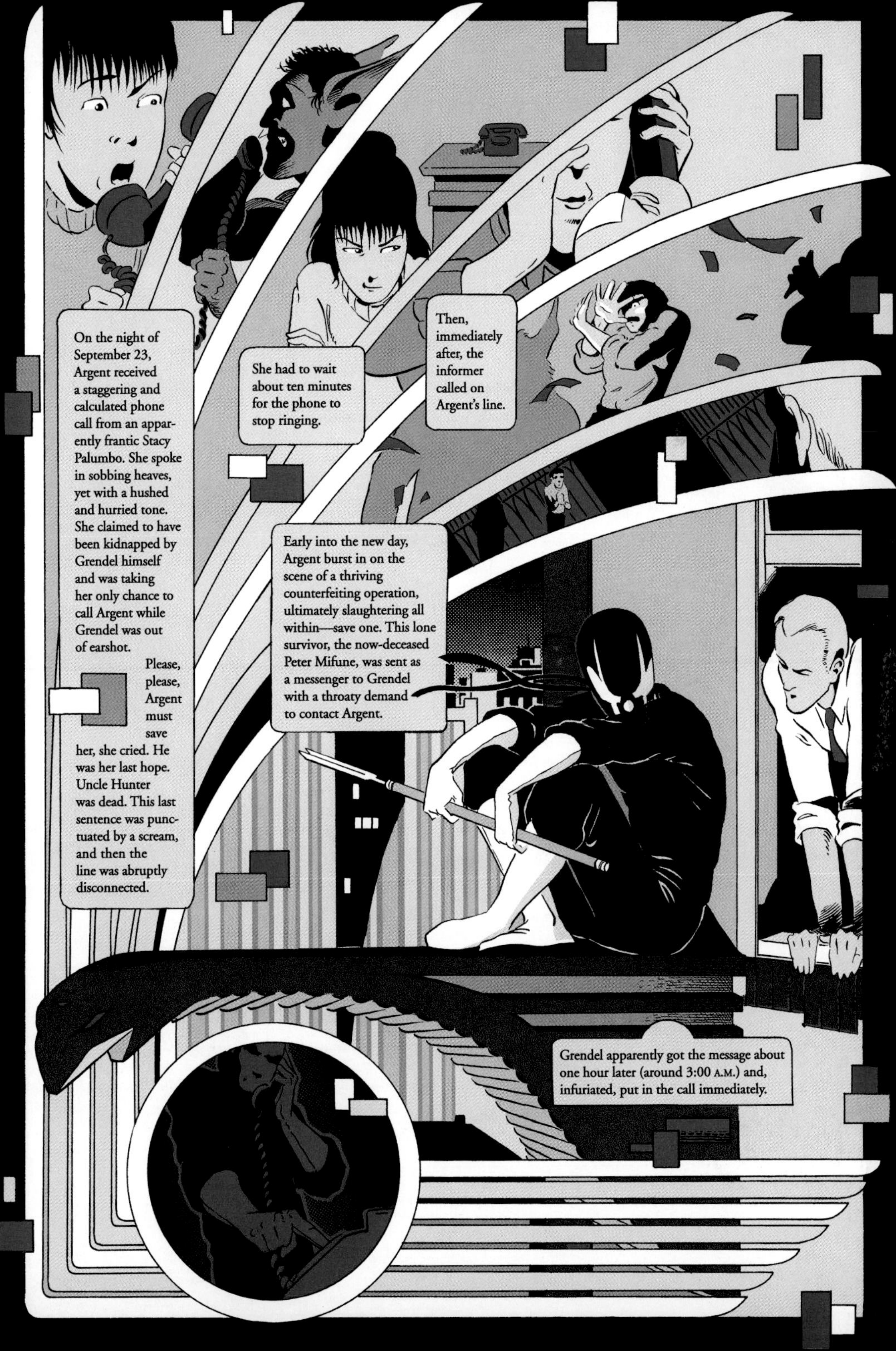
On the night of September 23, Argent received a staggering and calculated phone call from an apparently frantic Stacy Palumbo. She spoke in sobbing heaves, yet with a hushed and hurried tone. She claimed to have been kidnapped by Grendel himself and was taking her only chance to call Argent while Grendel was out of earshot. Please, please, Argent must save her, she cried. He was her last hope. Uncle Hunter was dead. This last sentence was punctuated by a scream, and then the line was abruptly disconnected.
She had to wait about ten minutes for the phone to stop ringing.
Then, immediately after, the informer called on Argent's line.
Early into the new day, Argent burst in on the scene of a thriving counterfeiting operation, ultimately slaughtering all within—save one. This lone survivor, the now-deceased Peter Mifune, was sent as a messenger to Grendel with a throaty demand to contact Argent.
Grendel apparently got the message about one hour later (around 3:00 A.M.) and, infuriated, put in the call immediately.

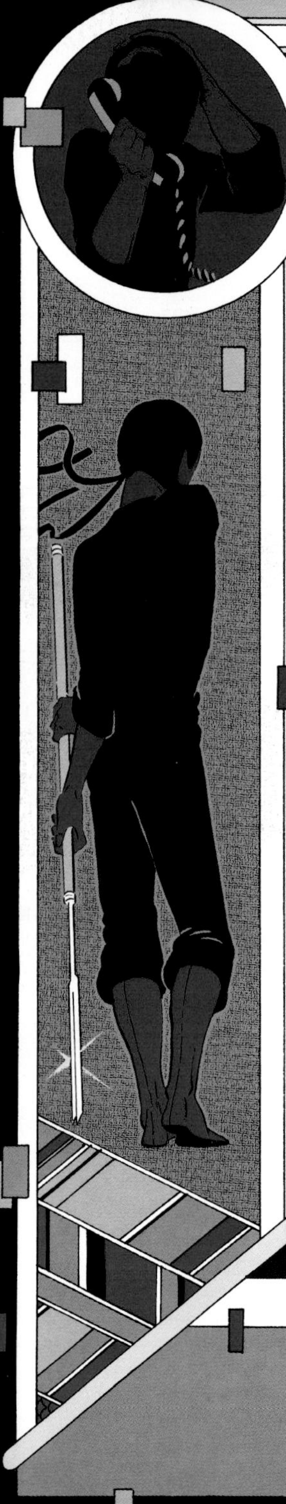

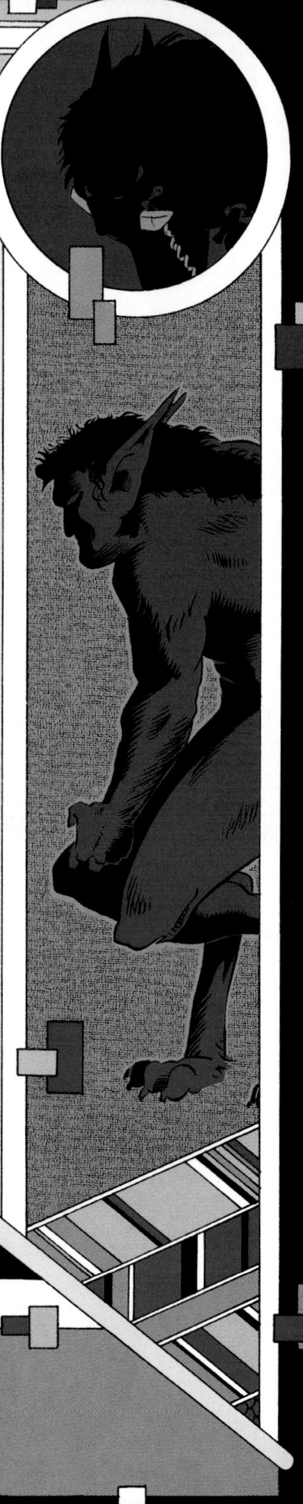

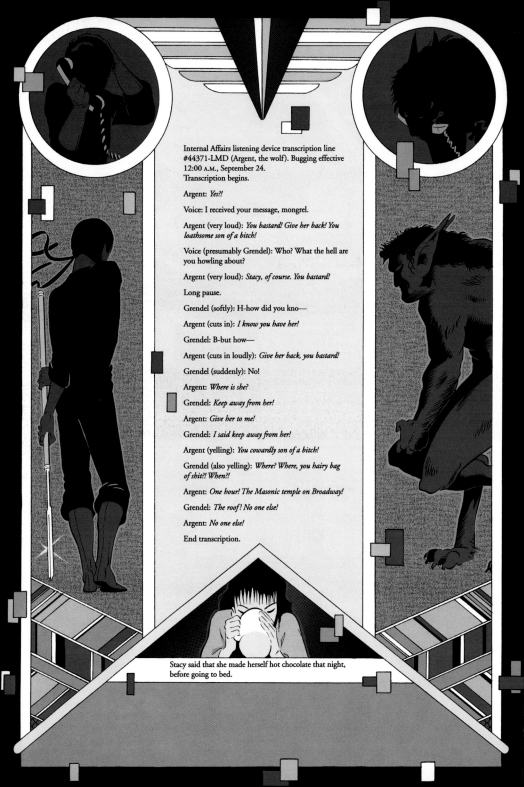

Internal Affairs listening device transcription line #44371-LMD (Argent, the wolf). Bugging effective 12:00 A.M., September 24.
Transcription begins.

Argent: *Yes?!*

Voice: I received your message, mongrel.

Argent (very loud): *You bastard! Give her back! You loathsome son of a bitch!*

Voice (presumably Grendel): Who? What the hell are you howling about?

Argent (very loud): *Stacy, of course. You bastard!*

Long pause.

Grendel (softly): H-how did you kno—

Argent (cuts in): *I know you have her!*

Grendel: B-but how—

Argent (cuts in loudly): *Give her back, you bastard!*

Grendel (suddenly): No!

Argent: *Where is she?*

Grendel: *Keep away from her!*

Argent: *Give her to me!*

Grendel: *I said keep away from her!*

Argent (yelling): *You cowardly son of a bitch!*

Grendel (also yelling): *Where? Where, you hairy bag of shit?! When?!*

Argent: *One hour! The Masonic temple on Broadway!*

Grendel: *The roof! No one else!*

Argent: *No one else!*

End transcription.

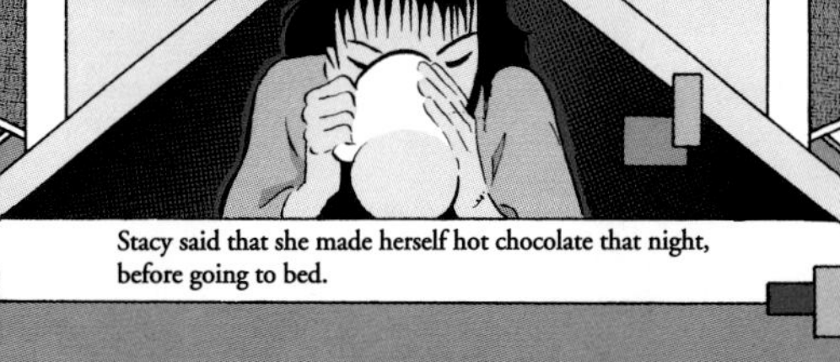

Stacy said that she made herself hot chocolate that night, before going to bed.

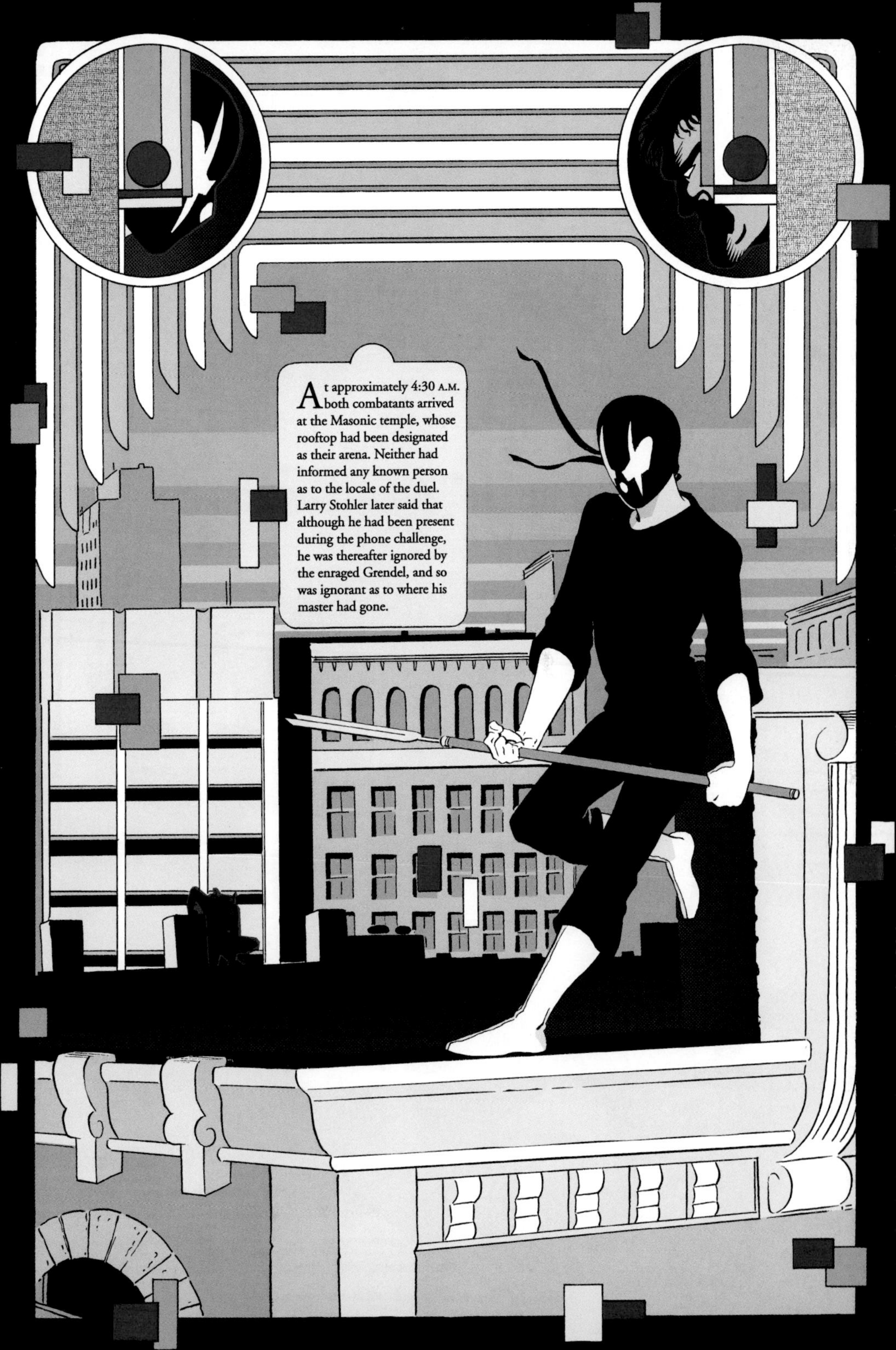
At approximately 4:30 A.M. both combatants arrived at the Masonic temple, whose rooftop had been designated as their arena. Neither had informed any known person as to the locale of the duel. Larry Stohler later said that although he had been present during the phone challenge, he was thereafter ignored by the enraged Grendel, and so was ignorant as to where his master had gone.

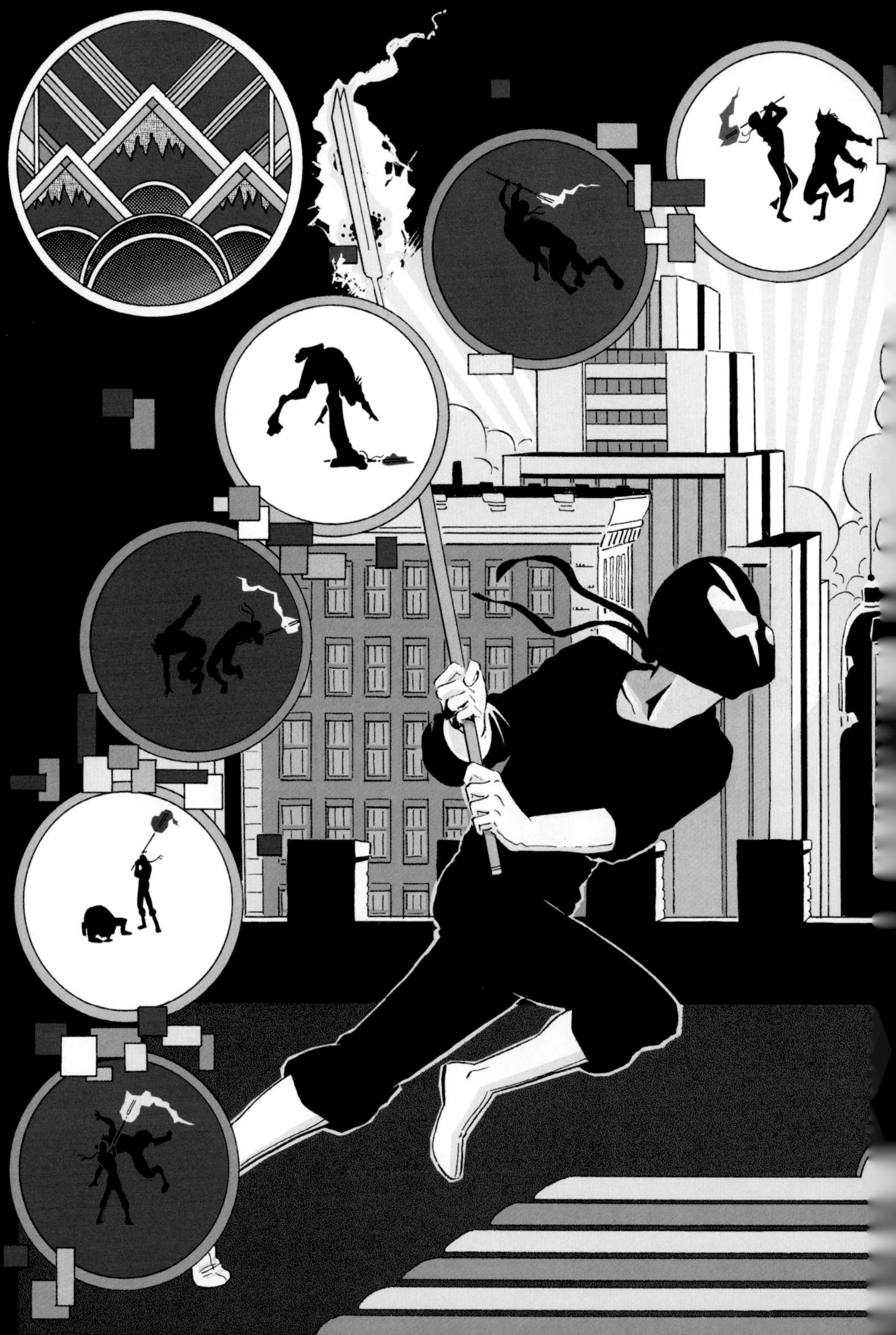

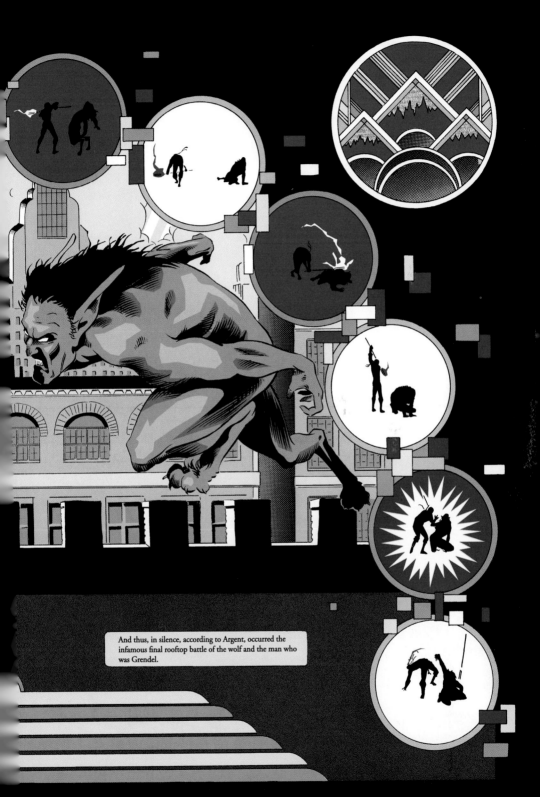

And thus, in silence, according to Argent, occurred the infamous final rooftop battle of the wolf and the man who was Grendel.

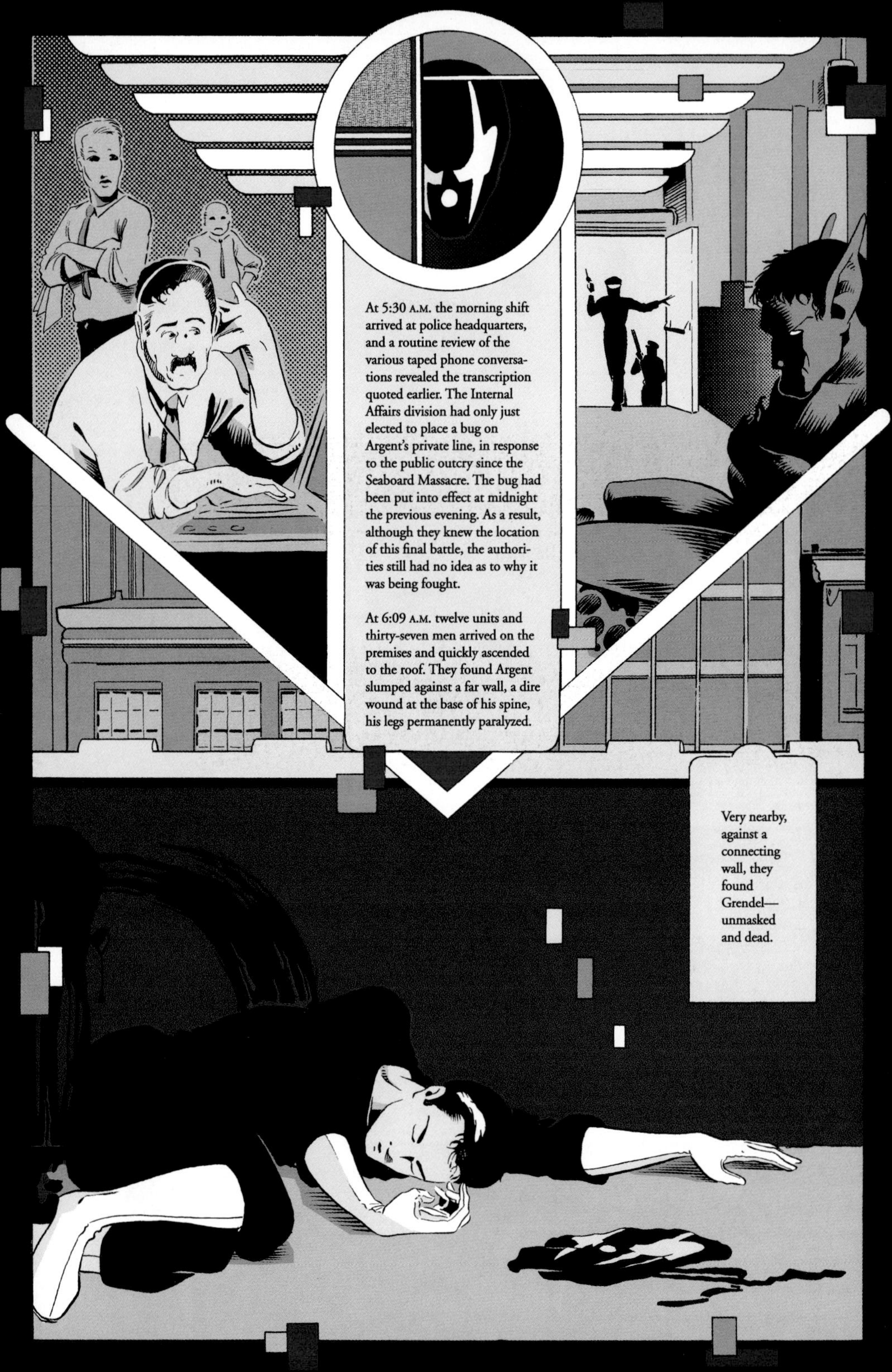
At 5:30 A.M. the morning shift arrived at police headquarters, and a routine review of the various taped phone conversations revealed the transcription quoted earlier. The Internal Affairs division had only just elected to place a bug on Argent's private line, in response to the public outcry since the Seaboard Massacre. The bug had been put into effect at midnight the previous evening. As a result, although they knew the location of this final battle, the authorities still had no idea as to why it was being fought.
At 6:09 A.M. twelve units and thirty-seven men arrived on the premises and quickly ascended to the roof. They found Argent slumped against a far wall, a dire wound at the base of his spine, his legs permanently paralyzed.
Very nearby, against a connecting wall, they found Grendel—unmasked and dead.

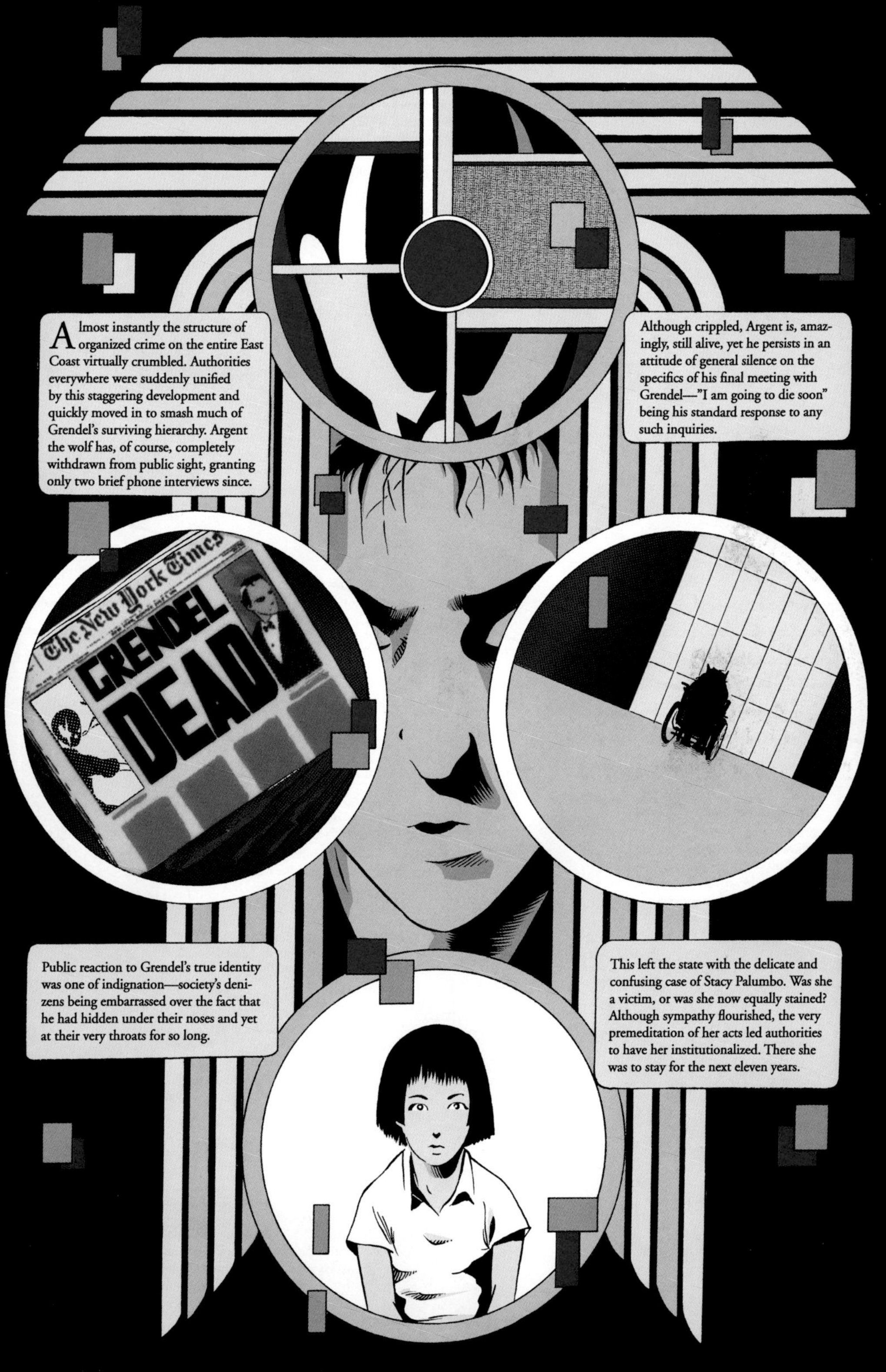
Almost instantly the structure of organized crime on the entire East Coast virtually crumbled. Authorities everywhere were suddenly unified by this staggering development and quickly moved in to smash much of Grendel's surviving hierarchy. Argent the wolf has, of course, completely withdrawn from public sight, granting only two brief phone interviews since.
Although crippled, Argent is, amazingly, still alive, yet he persists in an attitude of general silence on the specifics of his final meeting with Grendel—"I am going to die soon" being his standard response to any such inquiries.
The New York Times
GRENDEL DEAD
Public reaction to Grendel's true identity was one of indignation—society's denizens being embarrassed over the fact that he had hidden under their noses and yet at their very throats for so long.
This left the state with the delicate and confusing case of Stacy Palumbo. Was she a victim, or was she now equally stained? Although sympathy flourished, the very premeditation of her acts led authorities to have her institutionalized. There she was to stay for the next eleven years.

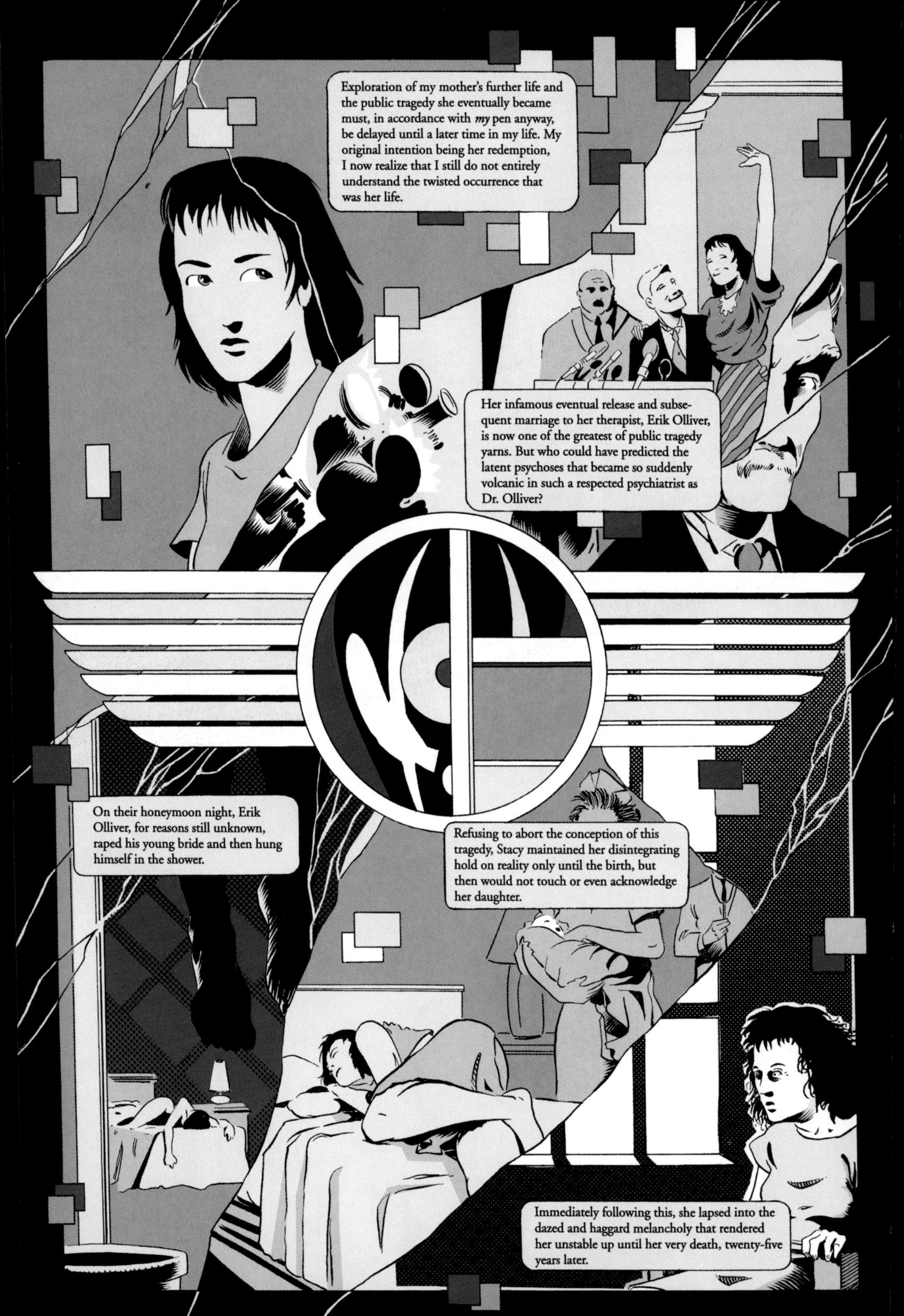
Exploration of my mother's further life and the public tragedy she eventually became must, in accordance with *my* pen anyway, be delayed until a later time in my life. My original intention being her redemption, I now realize that I still do not entirely understand the twisted occurrence that was her life.
Her infamous eventual release and subsequent marriage to her therapist, Erik Olliver, is now one of the greatest of public tragedy yarns. But who could have predicted the latent psychoses that became so suddenly volcanic in such a respected psychiatrist as Dr. Olliver?
On their honeymoon night, Erik Olliver, for reasons still unknown, raped his young bride and then hung himself in the shower.
Refusing to abort the conception of this tragedy, Stacy maintained her disintegrating hold on reality only until the birth, but then would not touch or even acknowledge her daughter.
Immediately following this, she lapsed into the dazed and haggard melancholy that rendered her unstable up until her very death, twenty-five years later.

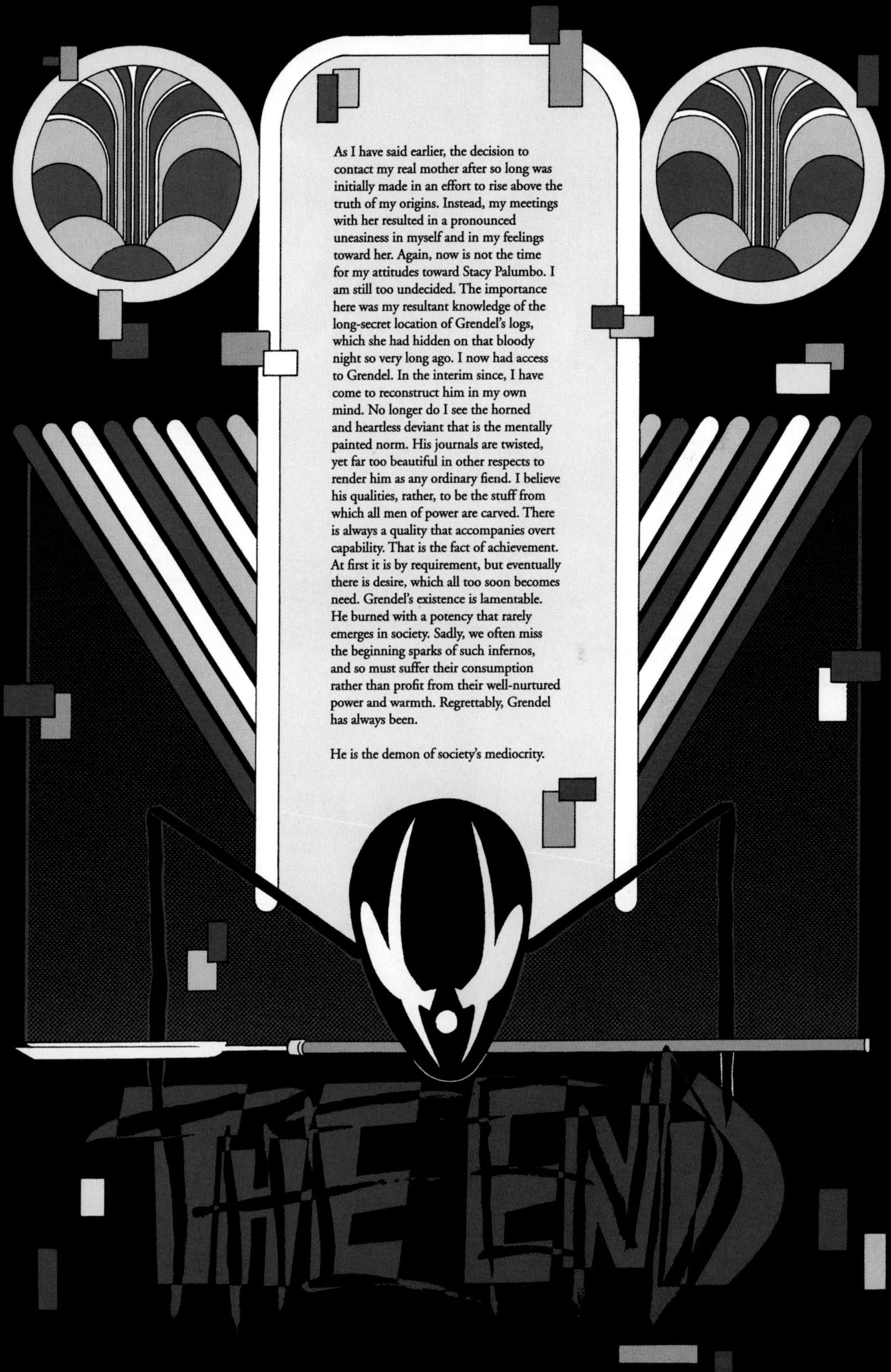
As I have said earlier, the decision to contact my real mother after so long was initially made in an effort to rise above the truth of my origins. Instead, my meetings with her resulted in a pronounced uneasiness in myself and in my feelings toward her. Again, now is not the time for my attitudes toward Stacy Palumbo. I am still too undecided. The importance here was my resultant knowledge of the long-secret location of Grendel's logs, which she had hidden on that bloody night so very long ago. I now had access to Grendel. In the interim since, I have come to reconstruct him in my own mind. No longer do I see the horned and heartless deviant that is the mentally painted norm. His journals are twisted, yet far too beautiful in other respects to render him as any ordinary fiend. I believe his qualities, rather, to be the stuff from which all men of power are carved. There is always a quality that accompanies overt capability. That is the fact of achievement. At first it is by requirement, but eventually there is desire, which all too soon becomes need. Grendel's existence is lamentable. He burned with a potency that rarely emerges in society. Sadly, we often miss the beginning sparks of such infernos, and so must suffer their consumption rather than profit from their well-nurtured power and warmth. Regrettably, Grendel has always been.
He is the demon of society's mediocrity.
THE END

ABOUT THE AUTHOR

Christine Powell Spar lives in Manhattan with her son Anson. She is currently a staff reporter for *The New York Times* and is considered one of the world's foremost experts on Grendel and his history. Ms. Spar is the widow of war correspondent Peter Spar.

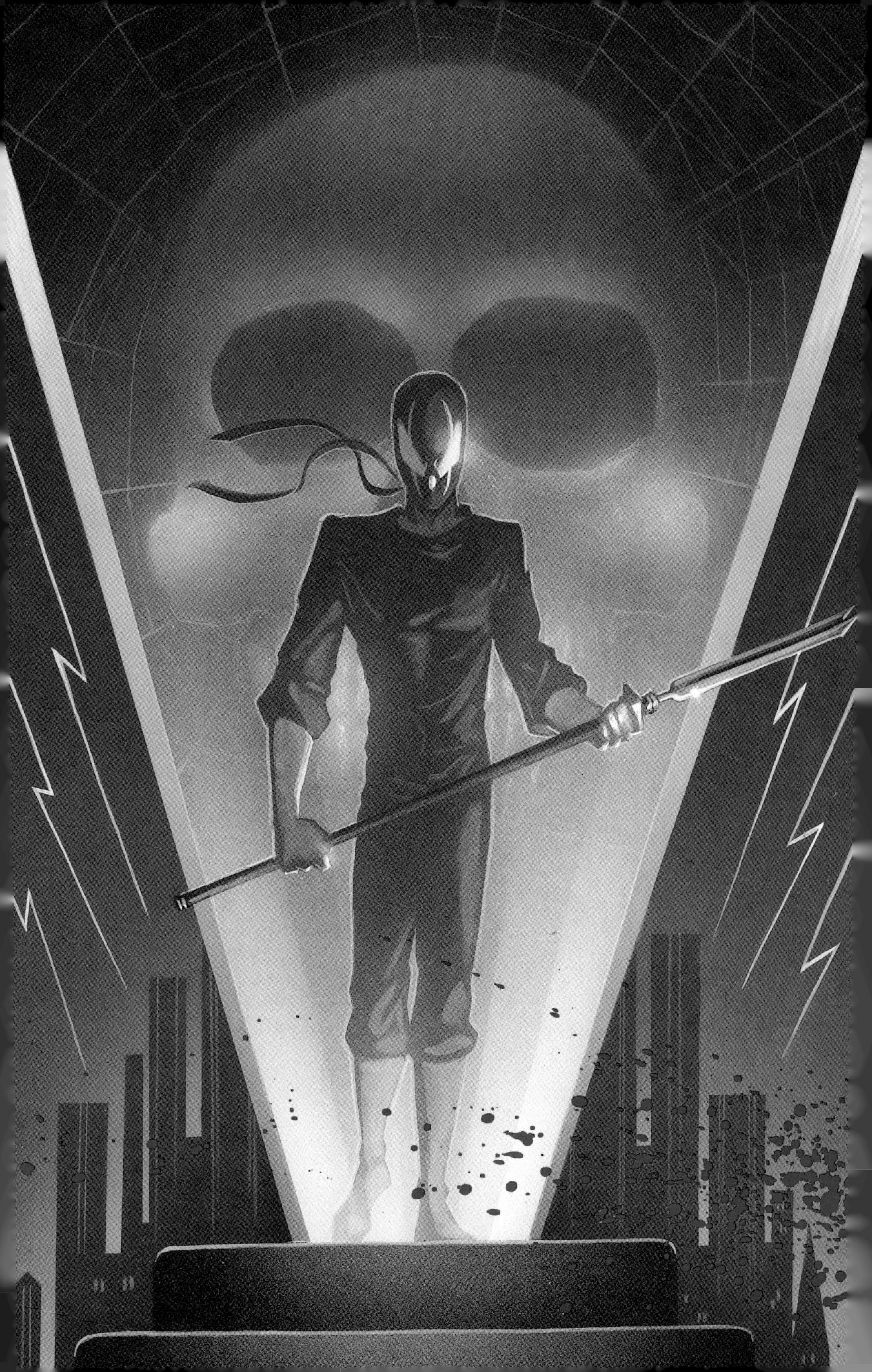

BLACK, WHITE, & RED
All stories written by MATT WAGNER

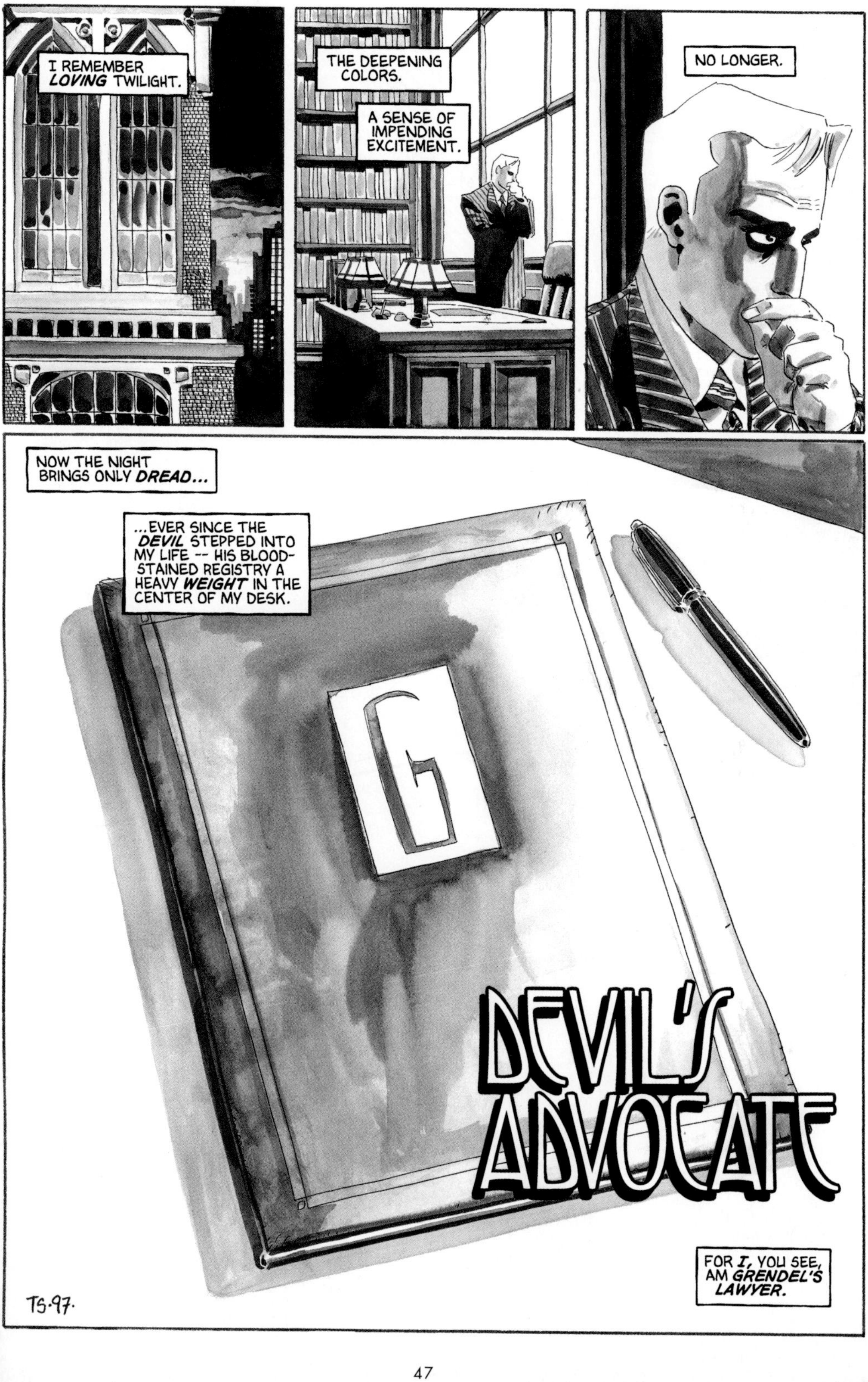
I REMEMBER LOVING TWILIGHT.
THE DEEPENING COLORS.
A SENSE OF IMPENDING EXCITEMENT.
NO LONGER.
NOW THE NIGHT BRINGS ONLY DREAD...
...EVER SINCE THE DEVIL STEPPED INTO MY LIFE -- HIS BLOOD-STAINED REGISTRY A HEAVY WEIGHT IN THE CENTER OF MY DESK.
G
DEVIL'S ADVOCATE
FOR I, YOU SEE, AM GRENDEL'S LAWYER.
TS·97·

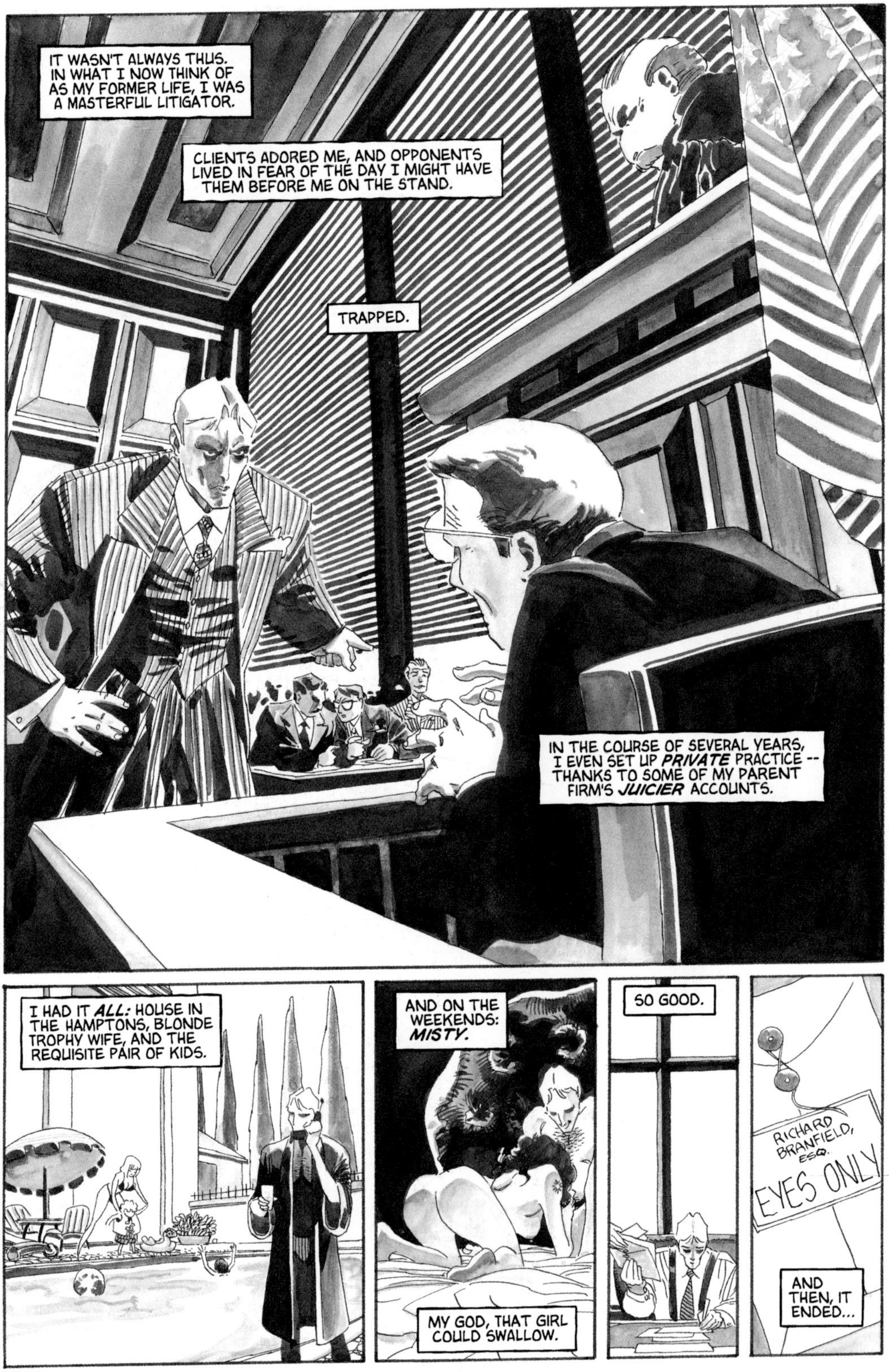
IT WASN'T ALWAYS THUS. IN WHAT I NOW THINK OF AS MY FORMER LIFE, I WAS A MASTERFUL LITIGATOR.
CLIENTS ADORED ME, AND OPPONENTS LIVED IN FEAR OF THE DAY I MIGHT HAVE THEM BEFORE ME ON THE STAND.
TRAPPED.
IN THE COURSE OF SEVERAL YEARS, I EVEN SET UP PRIVATE PRACTICE -- THANKS TO SOME OF MY PARENT FIRM'S JUICIER ACCOUNTS.
I HAD IT ALL: HOUSE IN THE HAMPTONS, BLONDE TROPHY WIFE, AND THE REQUISITE PAIR OF KIDS.
AND ON THE WEEKENDS: MISTY.
MY GOD, THAT GIRL COULD SWALLOW.
SO GOOD.
RICHARD BRANFIELD, ESQ.
EYES ONLY
AND THEN, IT ENDED...

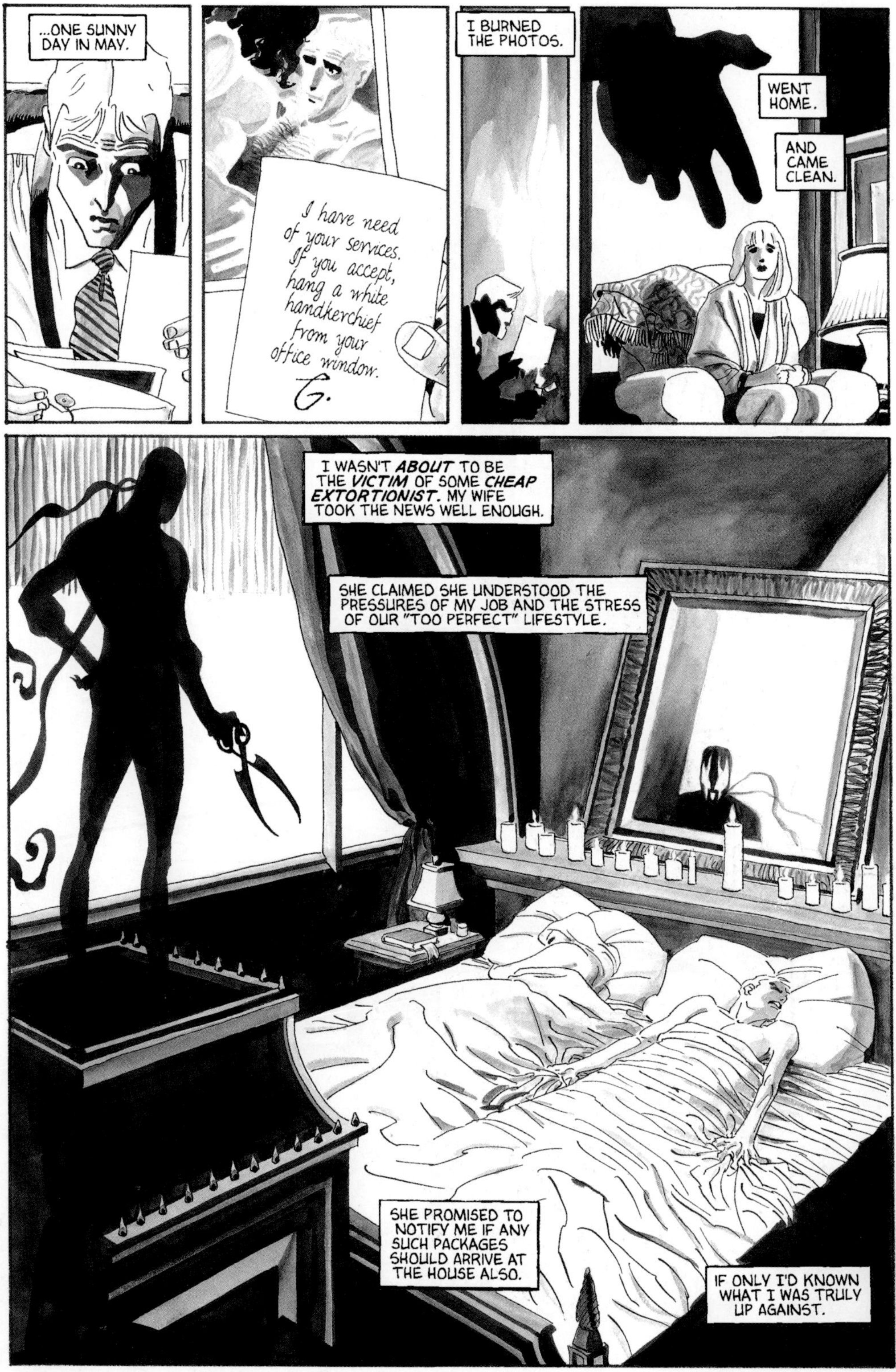
...ONE SUNNY DAY IN MAY.
I have need of your services. If you accept, hang a white handkerchief from your office window. G.
I BURNED THE PHOTOS.
WENT HOME.
AND CAME CLEAN.
I WASN'T ABOUT TO BE THE VICTIM OF SOME CHEAP EXTORTIONIST. MY WIFE TOOK THE NEWS WELL ENOUGH.
SHE CLAIMED SHE UNDERSTOOD THE PRESSURES OF MY JOB AND THE STRESS OF OUR "TOO PERFECT" LIFESTYLE.
SHE PROMISED TO NOTIFY ME IF ANY SUCH PACKAGES SHOULD ARRIVE AT THE HOUSE ALSO.
IF ONLY I'D KNOWN WHAT I WAS TRULY UP AGAINST.

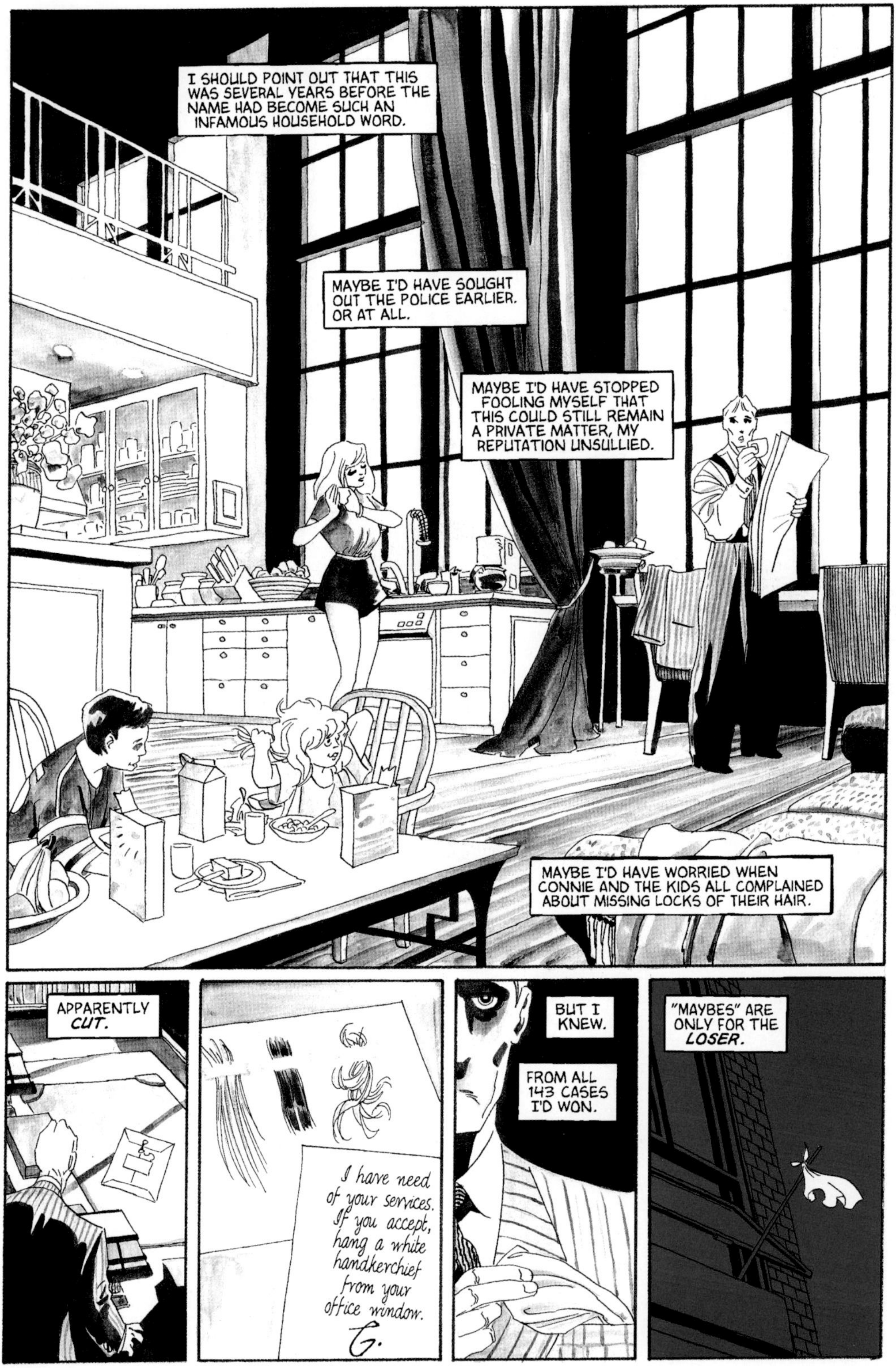
I SHOULD POINT OUT THAT THIS WAS SEVERAL YEARS BEFORE THE NAME HAD BECOME SUCH AN INFAMOUS HOUSEHOLD WORD.
MAYBE I'D HAVE SOUGHT OUT THE POLICE EARLIER. OR AT ALL.
MAYBE I'D HAVE STOPPED FOOLING MYSELF THAT THIS COULD STILL REMAIN A PRIVATE MATTER, MY REPUTATION UNSULLIED.
MAYBE I'D HAVE WORRIED WHEN CONNIE AND THE KIDS ALL COMPLAINED ABOUT MISSING LOCKS OF THEIR HAIR.
APPARENTLY *CUT.*
I have need of your services. If you accept, hang a white handkerchief from your office window. G.
BUT I KNEW.
FROM ALL 143 CASES I'D WON.
"MAYBES" ARE ONLY FOR THE *LOSER.*

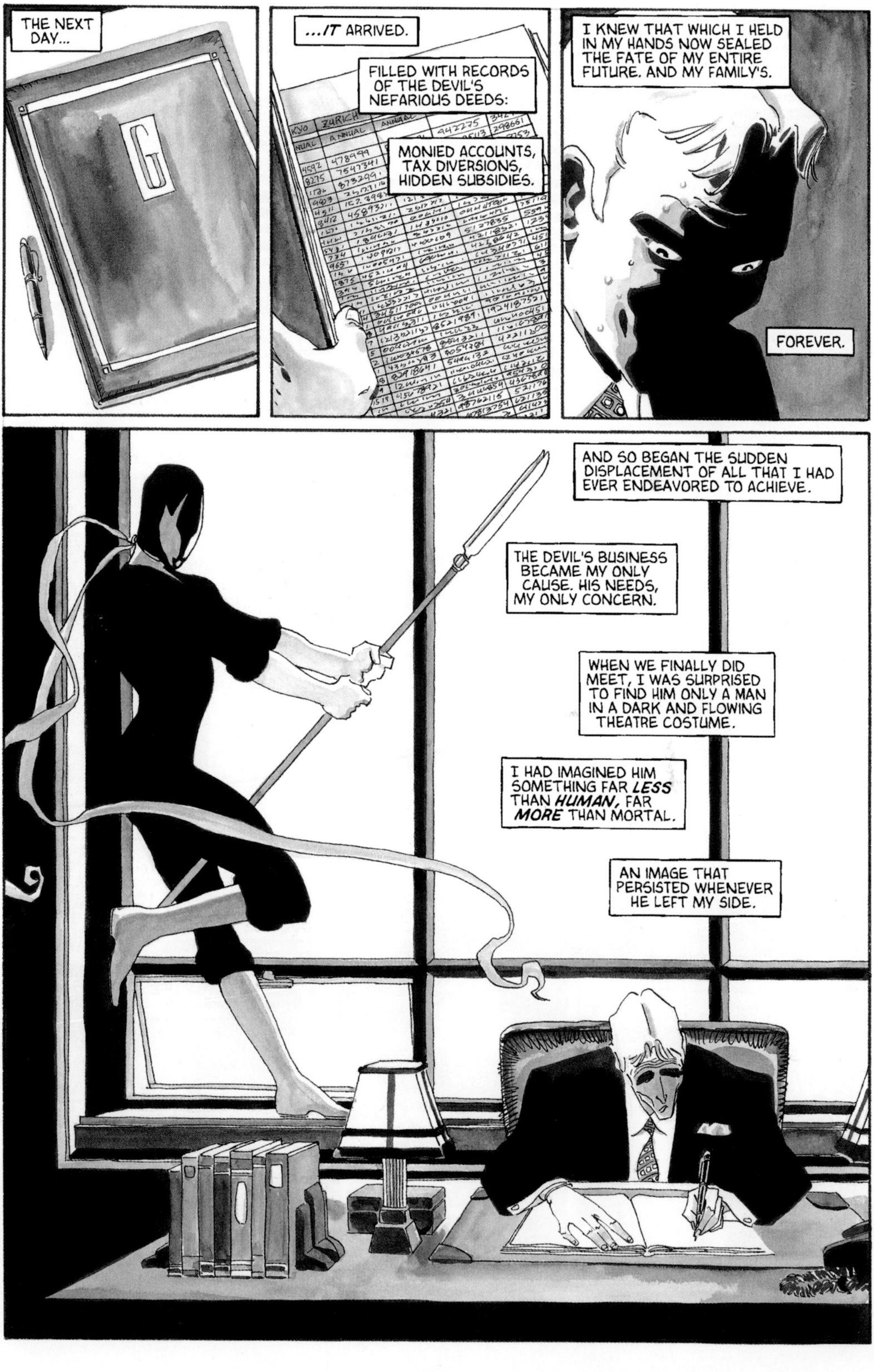
THE NEXT DAY...
...IT ARRIVED.
FILLED WITH RECORDS OF THE DEVIL'S NEFARIOUS DEEDS:
MONIED ACCOUNTS, TAX DIVERSIONS, HIDDEN SUBSIDIES.
I KNEW THAT WHICH I HELD IN MY HANDS NOW SEALED THE FATE OF MY ENTIRE FUTURE. AND MY FAMILY'S.
FOREVER.
AND SO BEGAN THE SUDDEN DISPLACEMENT OF ALL THAT I HAD EVER ENDEAVORED TO ACHIEVE.
THE DEVIL'S BUSINESS BECAME MY ONLY CAUSE. HIS NEEDS, MY ONLY CONCERN.
WHEN WE FINALLY DID MEET, I WAS SURPRISED TO FIND HIM ONLY A MAN IN A DARK AND FLOWING THEATRE COSTUME.
I HAD IMAGINED HIM SOMETHING FAR LESS THAN HUMAN, FAR MORE THAN MORTAL.
AN IMAGE THAT PERSISTED WHENEVER HE LEFT MY SIDE.

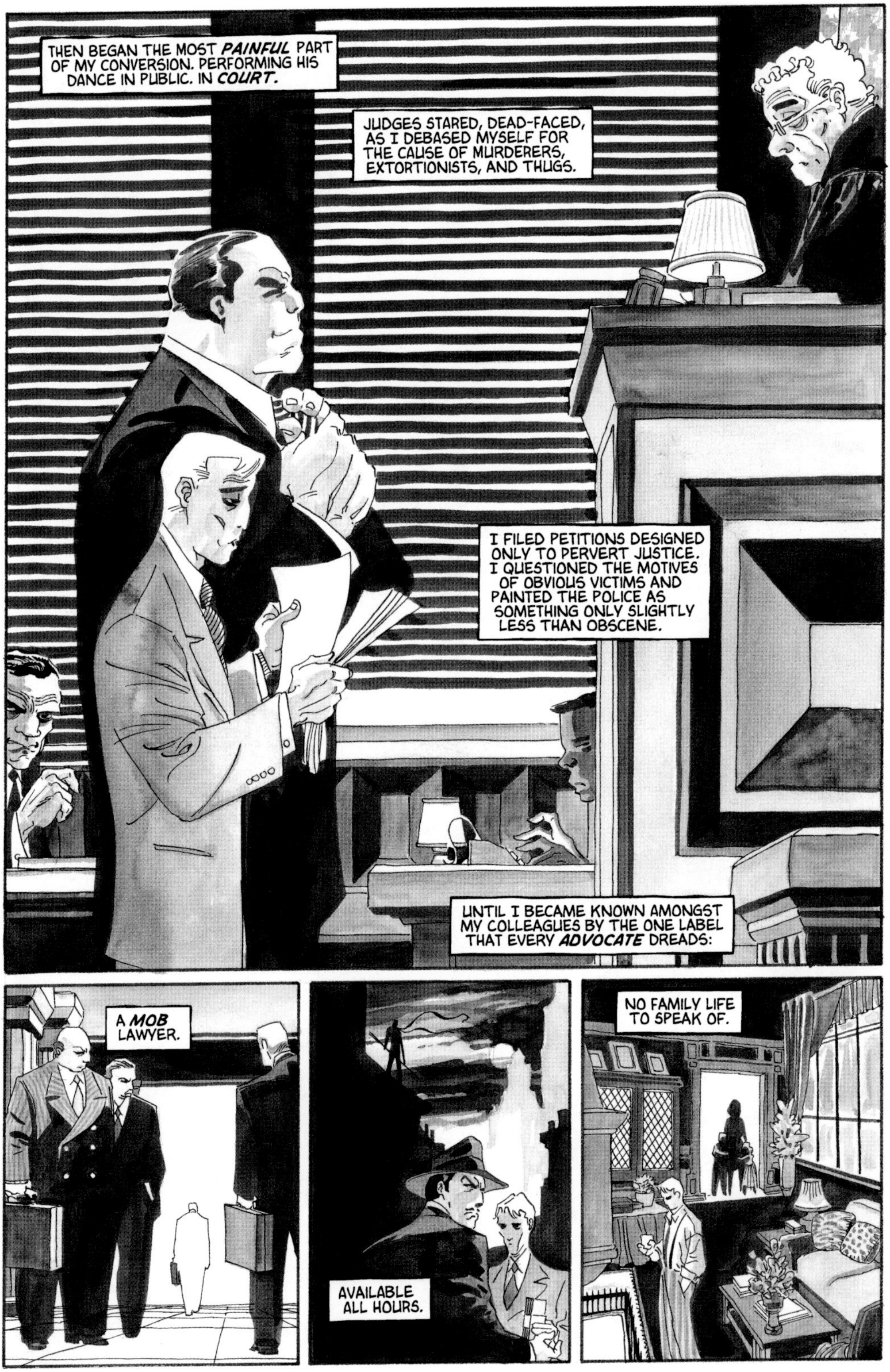
THEN BEGAN THE MOST PAINFUL PART OF MY CONVERSION. PERFORMING HIS DANCE IN PUBLIC. IN COURT.
JUDGES STARED, DEAD-FACED, AS I DEBASED MYSELF FOR THE CAUSE OF MURDERERS, EXTORTIONISTS, AND THUGS.
I FILED PETITIONS DESIGNED ONLY TO PERVERT JUSTICE. I QUESTIONED THE MOTIVES OF OBVIOUS VICTIMS AND PAINTED THE POLICE AS SOMETHING ONLY SLIGHTLY LESS THAN OBSCENE.
UNTIL I BECAME KNOWN AMONGST MY COLLEAGUES BY THE ONE LABEL THAT EVERY ADVOCATE DREADS:
A MOB LAWYER.
AVAILABLE ALL HOURS.
NO FAMILY LIFE TO SPEAK OF.

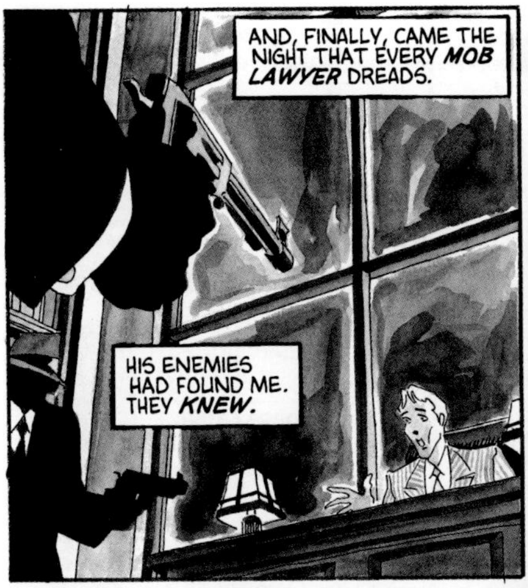
AND, FINALLY, CAME THE NIGHT THAT EVERY *MOB LAWYER* DREADS.
HIS ENEMIES HAD FOUND ME. THEY *KNEW.*

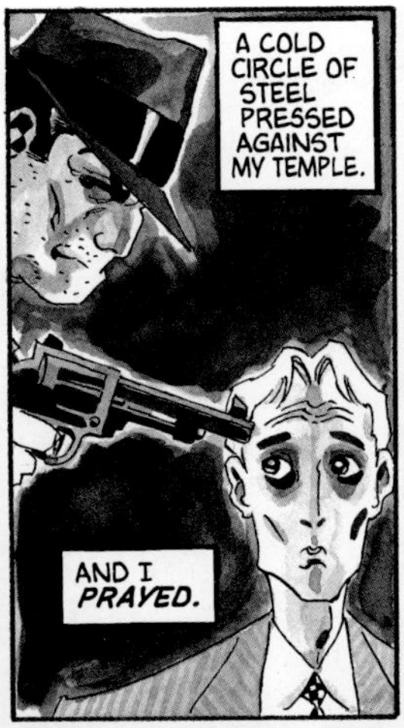
A COLD CIRCLE OF STEEL PRESSED AGAINST MY TEMPLE.
AND I *PRAYED.*

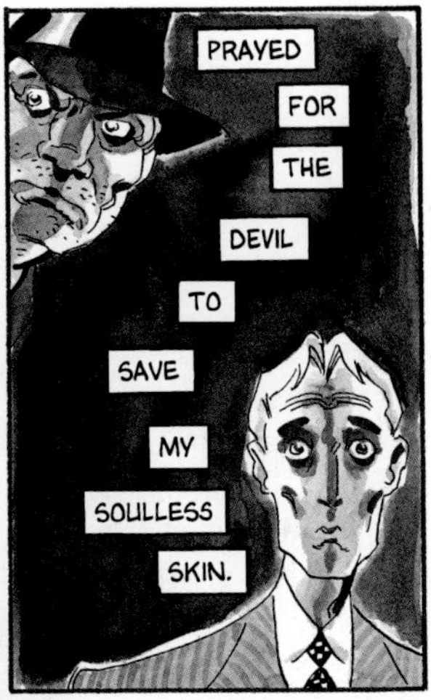
PRAYED FOR THE DEVIL TO SAVE MY SOULLESS SKIN.

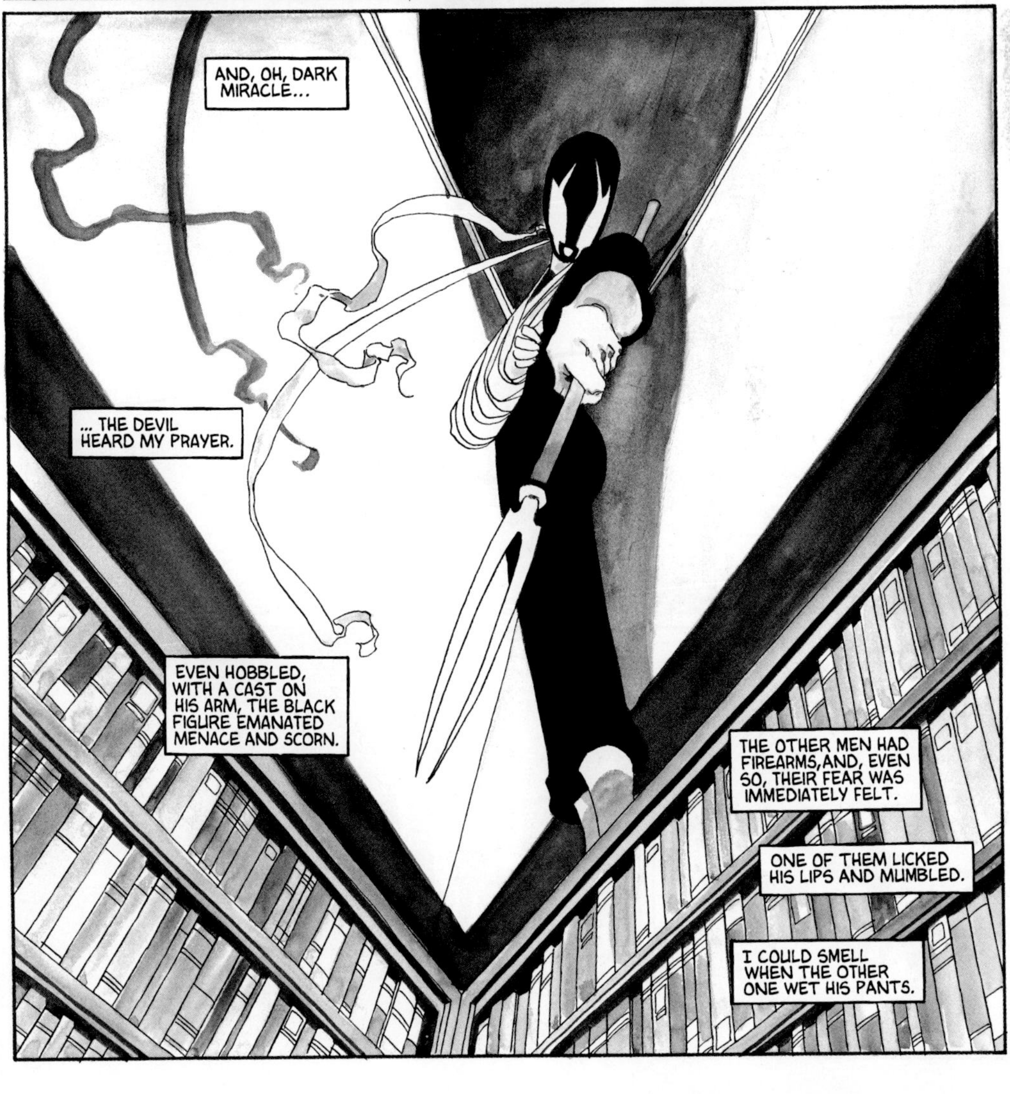
AND, OH, DARK MIRACLE...
... THE DEVIL HEARD MY PRAYER.
EVEN HOBBLED, WITH A CAST ON HIS ARM, THE BLACK FIGURE EMANATED MENACE AND SCORN.
THE OTHER MEN HAD FIREARMS,AND, EVEN SO, THEIR FEAR WAS IMMEDIATELY FELT.
ONE OF THEM LICKED HIS LIPS AND MUMBLED.
I COULD SMELL WHEN THE OTHER ONE WET HIS PANTS.

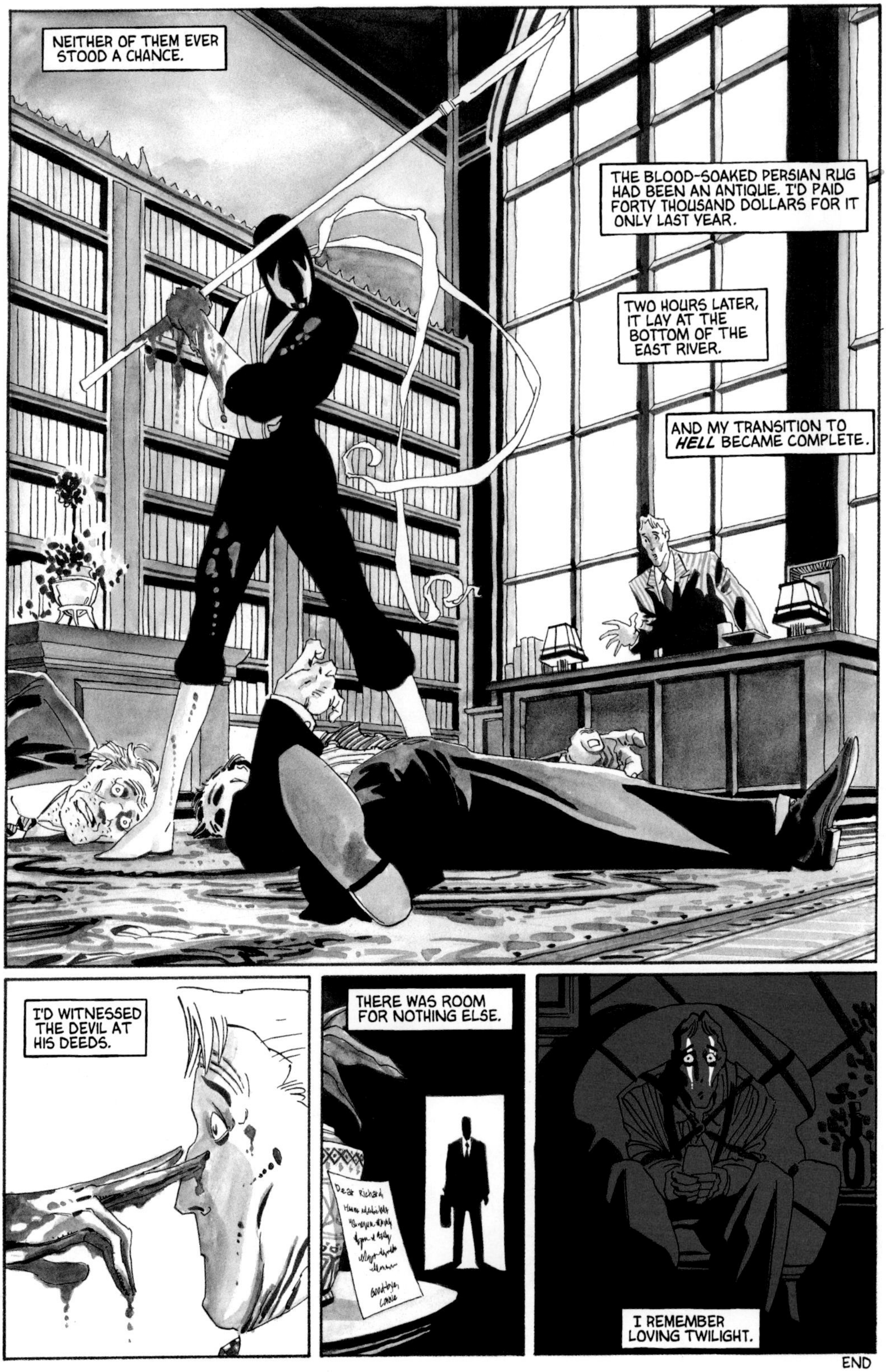
NEITHER OF THEM EVER STOOD A CHANCE.
THE BLOOD-SOAKED PERSIAN RUG HAD BEEN AN ANTIQUE. I'D PAID FORTY THOUSAND DOLLARS FOR IT ONLY LAST YEAR.
TWO HOURS LATER, IT LAY AT THE BOTTOM OF THE EAST RIVER.
AND MY TRANSITION TO ***HELL*** BECAME COMPLETE.
I'D WITNESSED THE DEVIL AT HIS DEEDS.
THERE WAS ROOM FOR NOTHING ELSE.
Dear Richard
Goodbye, Connie
I REMEMBER LOVING TWILIGHT.

END

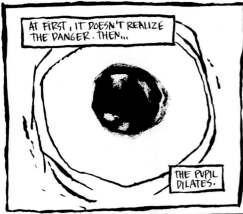

AT FIRST, IT DOESN'T REALIZE THE DANGER. THEN...

THE PUPIL DILATES.

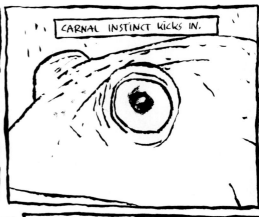

CARNAL INSTINCT KICKS IN.

REGARDLESS, IT'S TRAPPED. THE SCREENING HOLDS AS THE FLAMES BEGIN TO BUILD.

IT'S LIFE--

--EXPLODES IN A SIZZLING ROAR.

ELEVEN MINUTES LATER.

THERE'S LITTLE LEFT BUT A THICK, GOOEY PASTE.

NOW, WHATEVER GAVE ME THE IDEA TO DO THAT?

DEVIL ON MY BACK

55

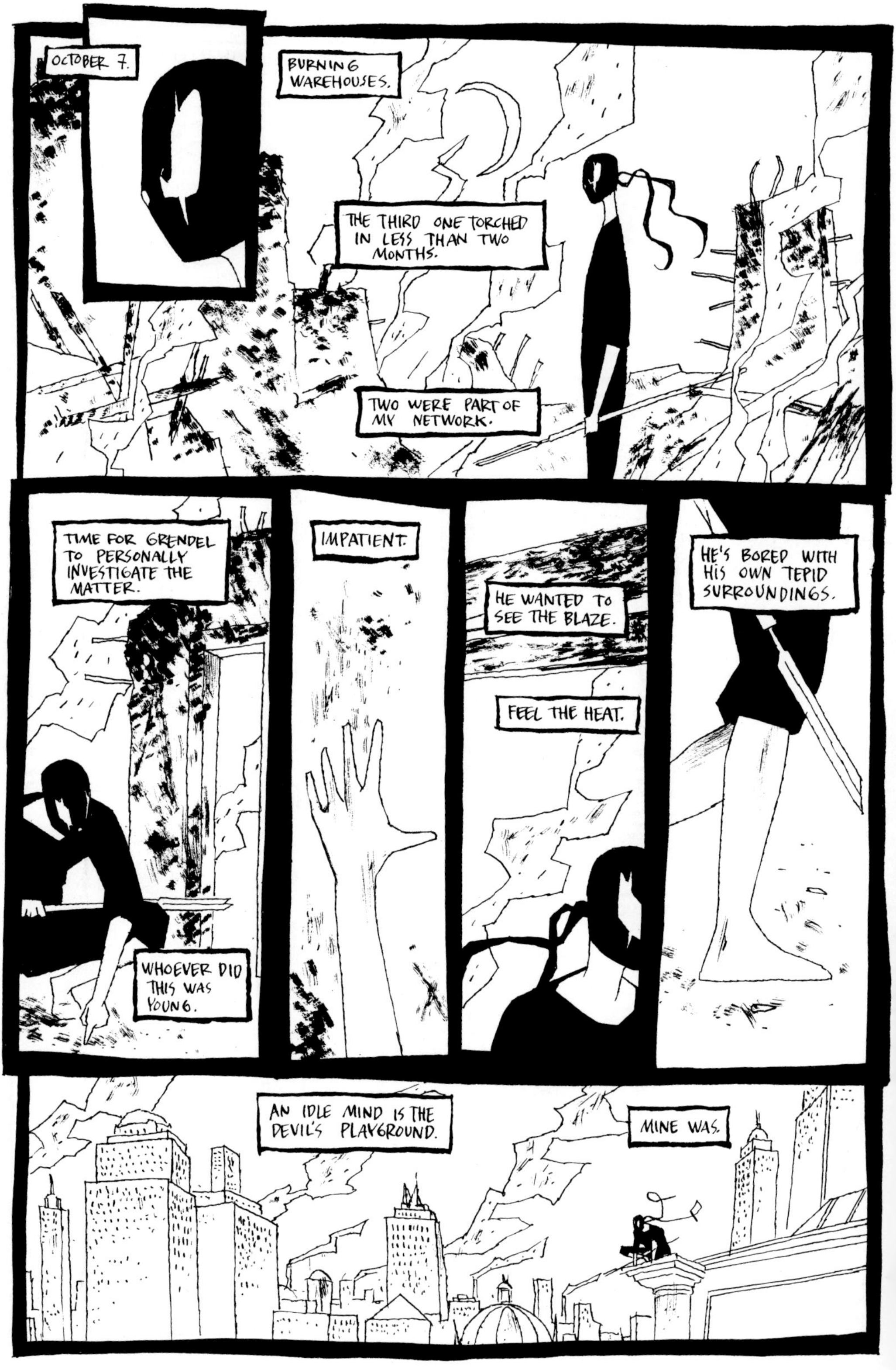
OCTOBER 7.
BURNING WAREHOUSES.
THE THIRD ONE TORCHED IN LESS THAN TWO MONTHS.
TWO WERE PART OF MY NETWORK.
TIME FOR GRENDEL TO PERSONALLY INVESTIGATE THE MATTER.
WHOEVER DID THIS WAS YOUNG.
IMPATIENT.
HE WANTED TO SEE THE BLAZE.
FEEL THE HEAT.
HE'S BORED WITH HIS OWN TEPID SURROUNDINGS.
AN IDLE MIND IS THE DEVIL'S PLAYGROUND.
MINE WAS.

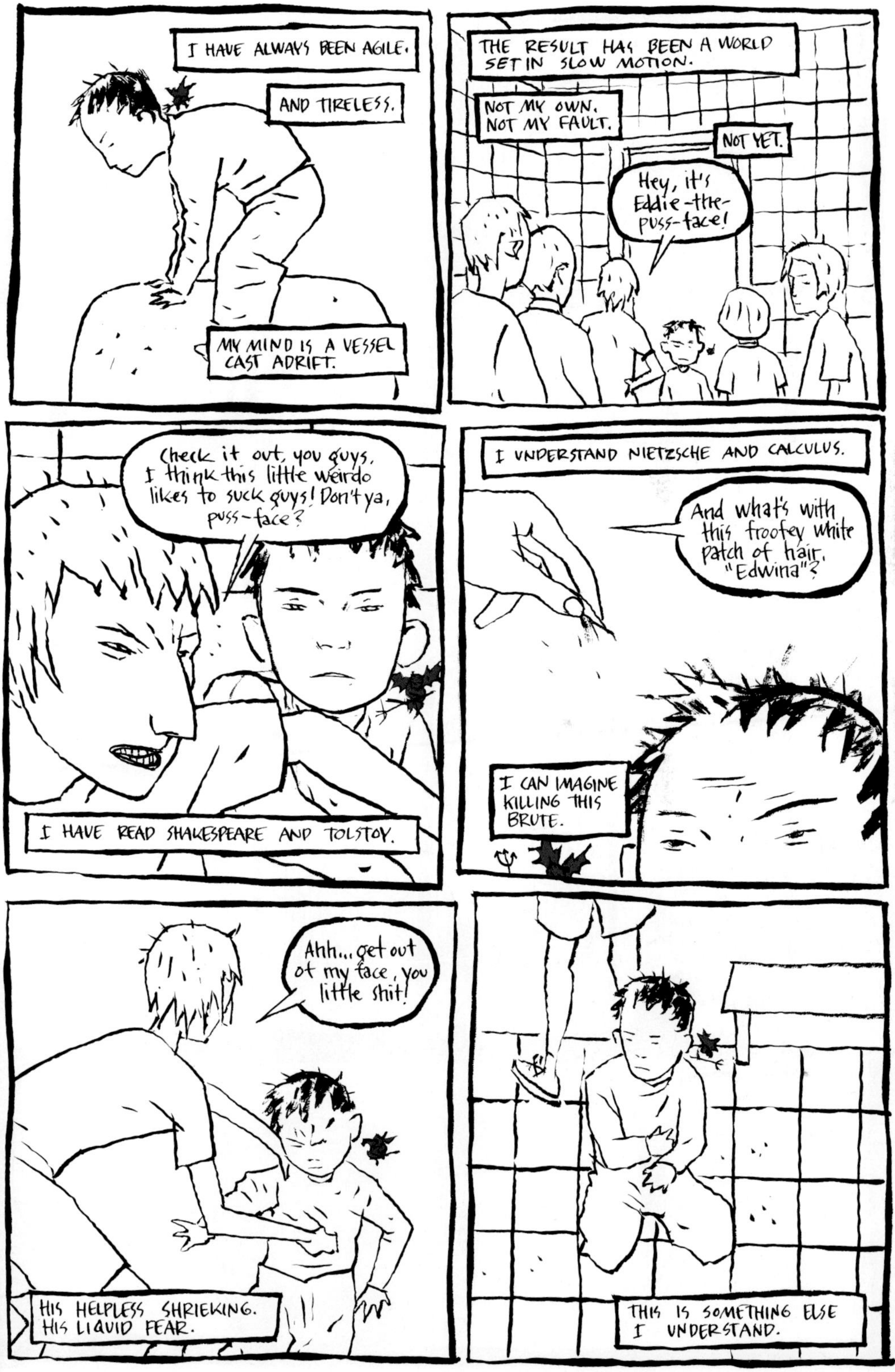
I HAVE ALWAYS BEEN AGILE.
AND TIRELESS.
MY MIND IS A VESSEL CAST ADRIFT.
THE RESULT HAS BEEN A WORLD SET IN SLOW MOTION.
NOT MY OWN. NOT MY FAULT.
NOT YET.
Hey, it's Eddie-the-puss-face!
Check it out, you guys. I think this little weirdo likes to suck guys! Don't ya, puss-face?
I HAVE READ SHAKESPEARE AND TOLSTOY.
I UNDERSTAND NIETZSCHE AND CALCULUS.
And what's with this froofey white patch of hair, "Edwina"?
I CAN IMAGINE KILLING THIS BRUTE.
Ahh... get out of my face, you little shit!
HIS HELPLESS SHRIEKING. HIS LIQUID FEAR.
THIS IS SOMETHING ELSE I UNDERSTAND.

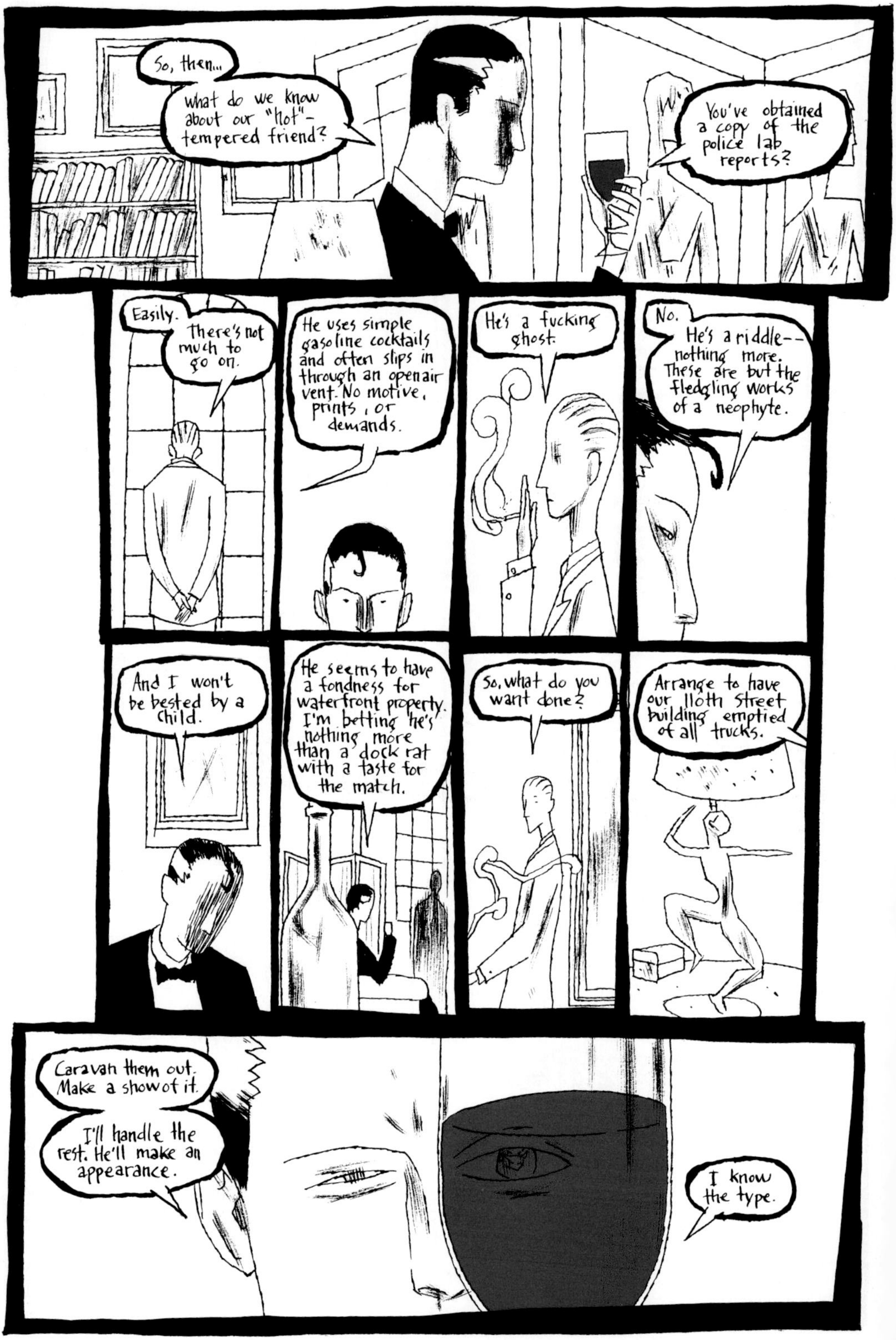
So, then...
what do we know about our "hot"-tempered friend?
You've obtained a copy of the police lab reports?
Easily.
There's not much to go on.
He uses simple gasoline cocktails and often slips in through an open air vent. No motive, prints, or demands.
He's a fucking ghost.
No.
He's a riddle--nothing more. These are but the fledgling works of a neophyte.
And I won't be bested by a child.
He seems to have a fondness for waterfront property. I'm betting he's nothing more than a dock rat with a taste for the match.
So, what do you want done?
Arrange to have our 110th Street building emptied of all trucks.
Caravan them out. Make a show of it.
I'll handle the rest. He'll make an appearance.
I know the type.

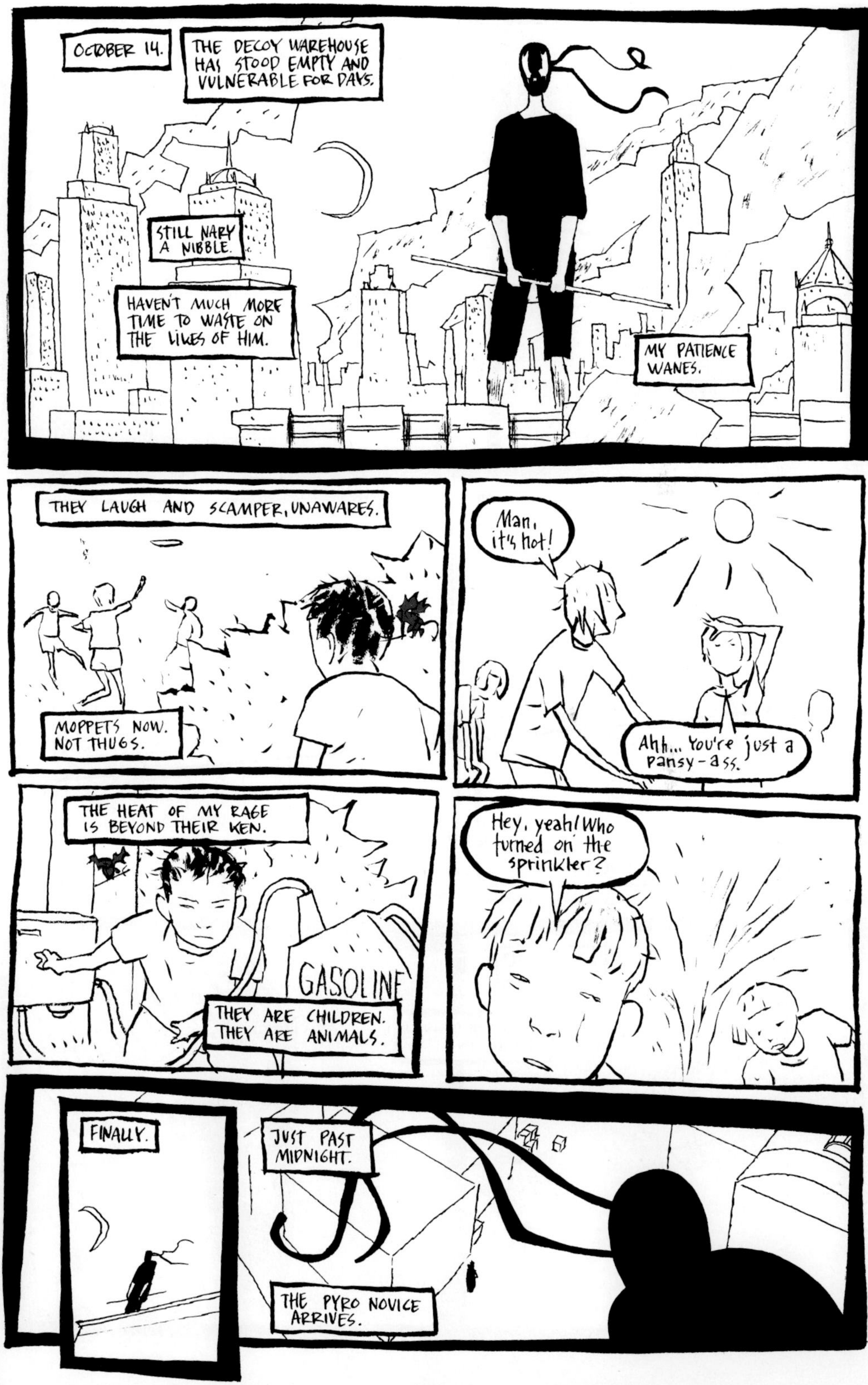
OCTOBER 14.
THE DECOY WAREHOUSE HAS STOOD EMPTY AND VULNERABLE FOR DAYS.
STILL NARY A NIBBLE.
HAVEN'T MUCH MORE TIME TO WASTE ON THE LIKES OF HIM.
MY PATIENCE WANES.
THEY LAUGH AND SCAMPER, UNAWARES.
MOPPETS NOW. NOT THUGS.
Man, it's hot!
Ahh... You're just a pansy-ass.
THE HEAT OF MY RAGE IS BEYOND THEIR KEN.
GASOLINE
THEY ARE CHILDREN. THEY ARE ANIMALS.
Hey, yeah! Who turned on the sprinkler?
FINALLY.
JUST PAST MIDNIGHT.
THE PYRO NOVICE ARRIVES.

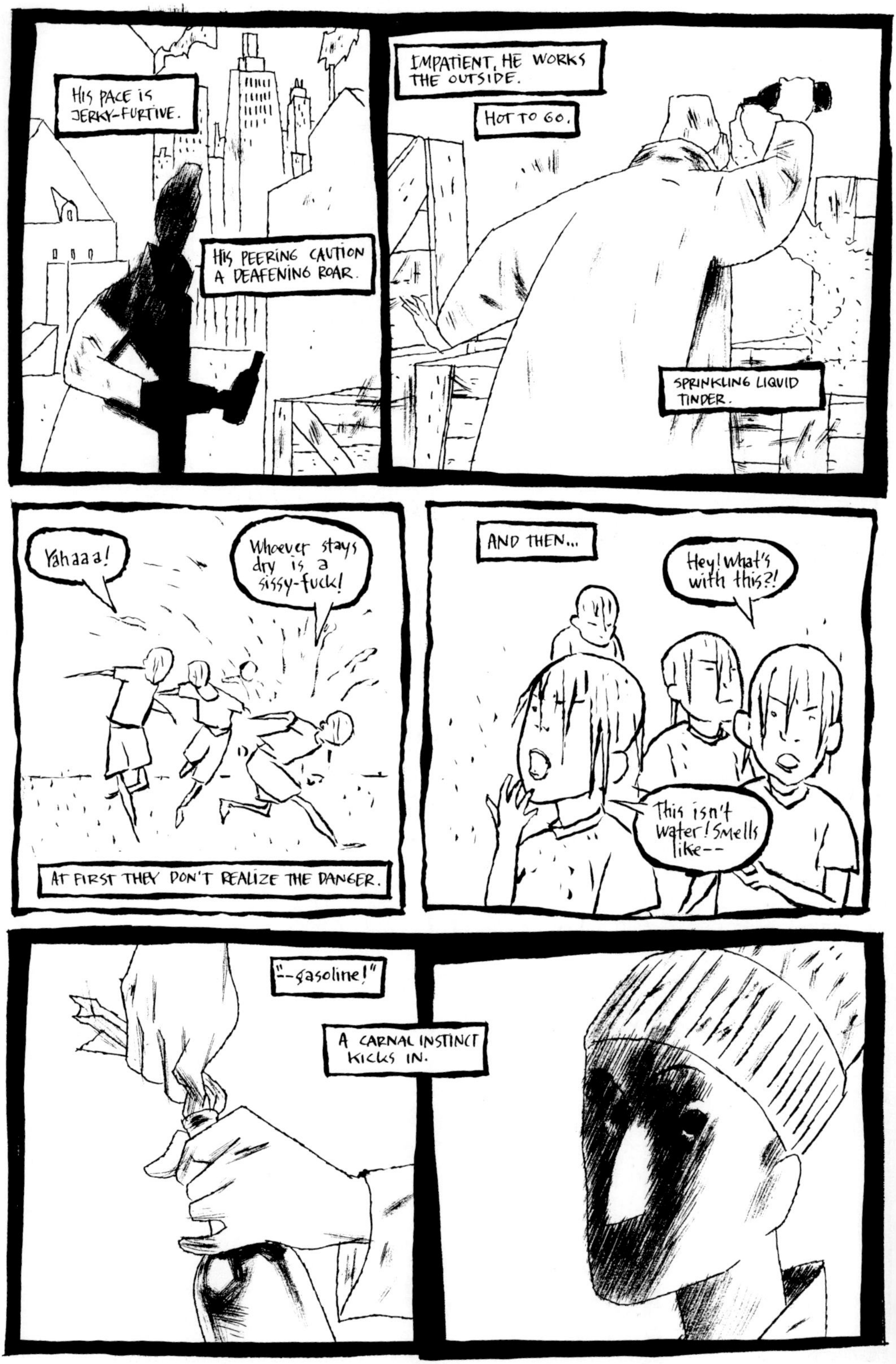
HIS PACE IS JERKY-FURTIVE.
HIS PEERING CAUTION A DEAFENING ROAR.
IMPATIENT, HE WORKS THE OUTSIDE.
HOT TO GO.
SPRINKLING LIQUID TINDER.
Yahaaa!
Whoever stays dry is a sissy-fuck!
AT FIRST THEY DON'T REALIZE THE DANGER.
AND THEN...
Hey! What's with this?!
This isn't water! Smells like--
"--gasoline!"
A CARNAL INSTINCT KICKS IN.

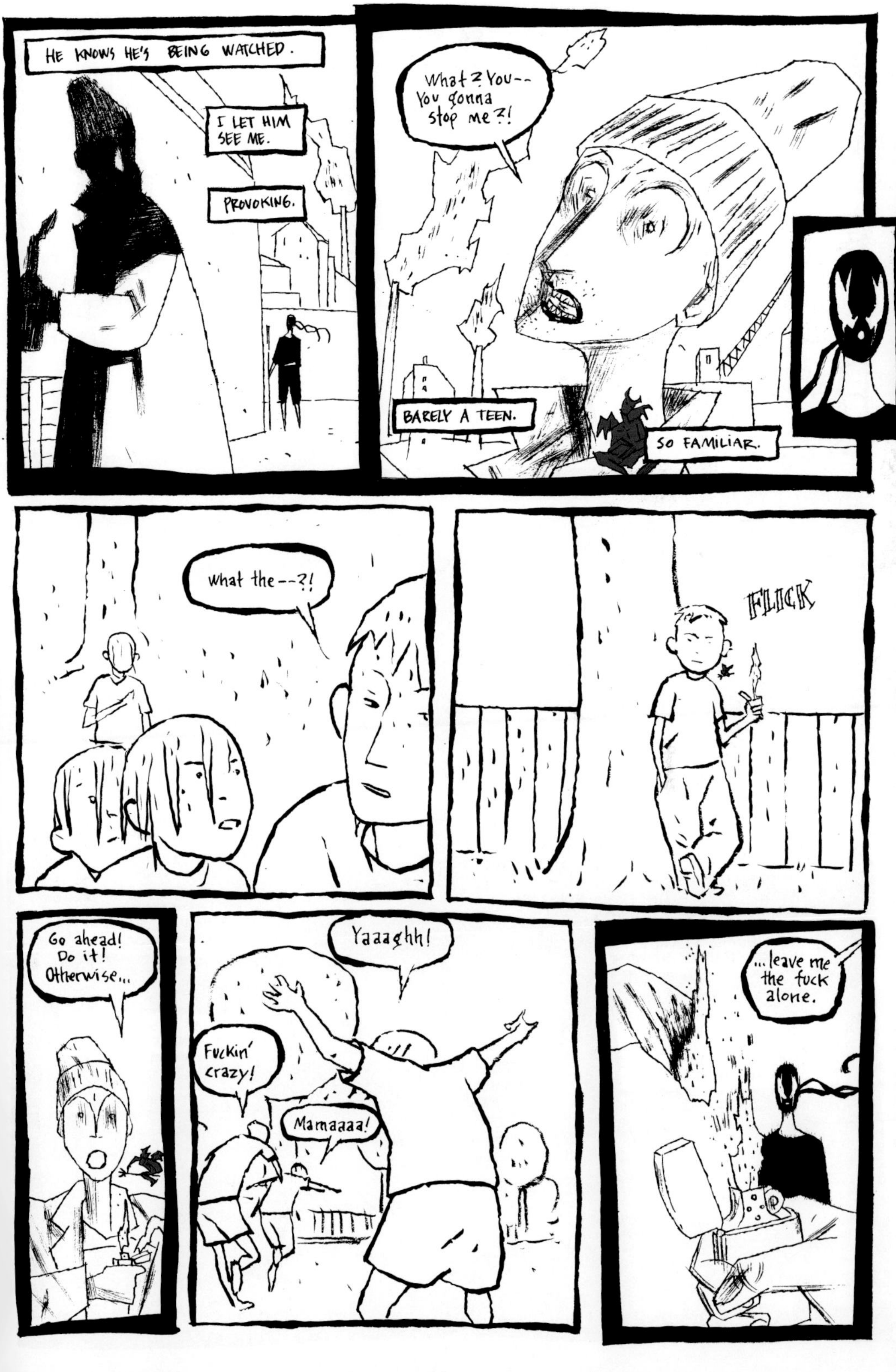
HE KNOWS HE'S BEING WATCHED.
I LET HIM SEE ME.
PROVOKING.
What? You-- You gonna stop me?!
BARELY A TEEN.
SO FAMILIAR.
what the--?!
FLICK
Go ahead! Do it! Otherwise...
Yaaaghh!
Fuckin' crazy!
Mamaaaa!
...leave me the fuck alone.

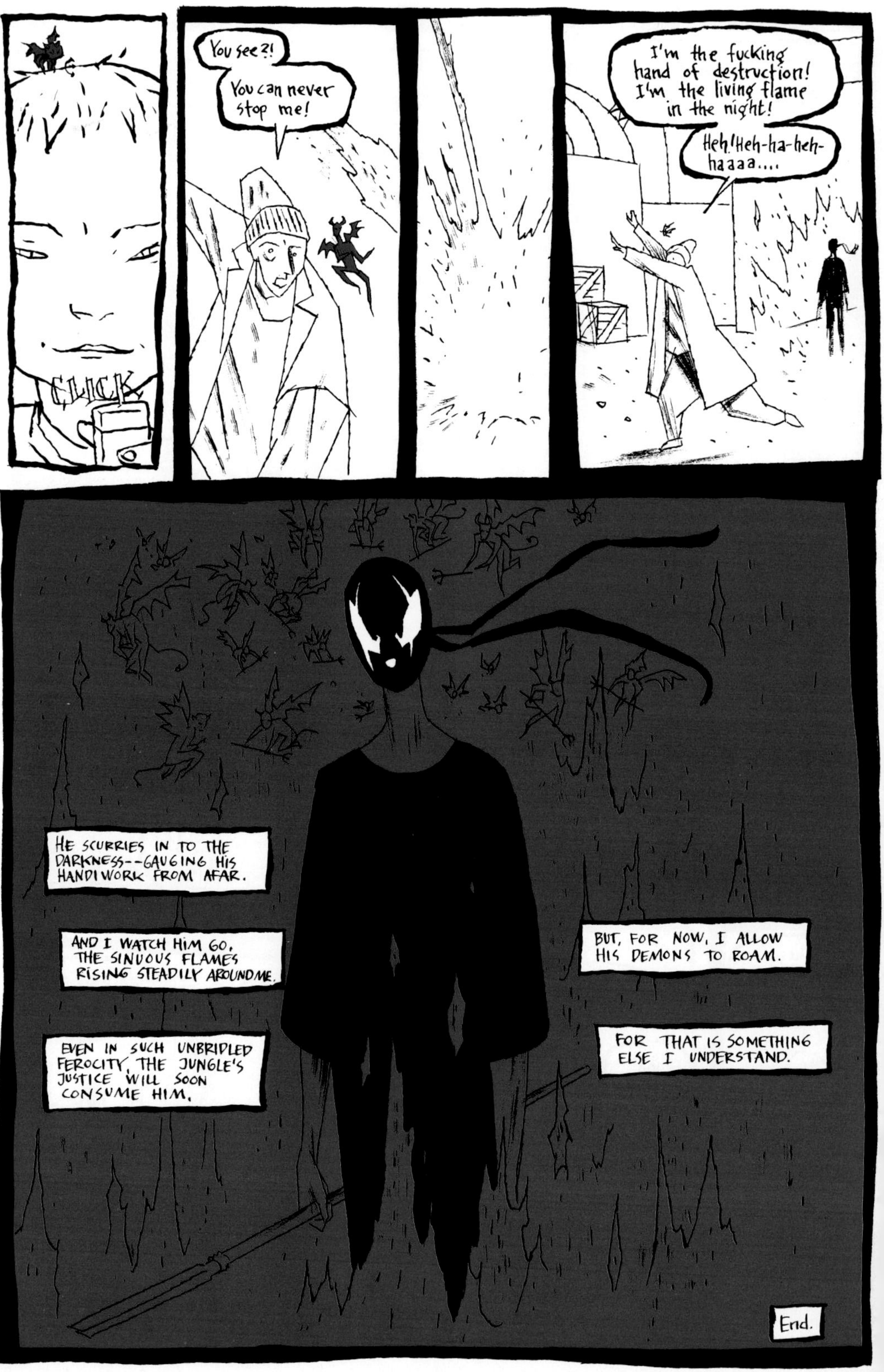
CLICK
You see?!
You can never stop me!
I'm the fucking hand of destruction! I'm the living flame in the night!
Heh! Heh-ha-heh-haaaa....
HE SCURRIES IN TO THE DARKNESS--GAUGING HIS HANDIWORK FROM AFAR.
AND I WATCH HIM GO, THE SINUOUS FLAMES RISING STEADILY AROUND ME.
EVEN IN SUCH UNBRIDLED FEROCITY, THE JUNGLE'S JUSTICE WILL SOON CONSUME HIM.
BUT, FOR NOW, I ALLOW HIS DEMONS TO ROAM.
FOR THAT IS SOMETHING ELSE I UNDERSTAND.
End.

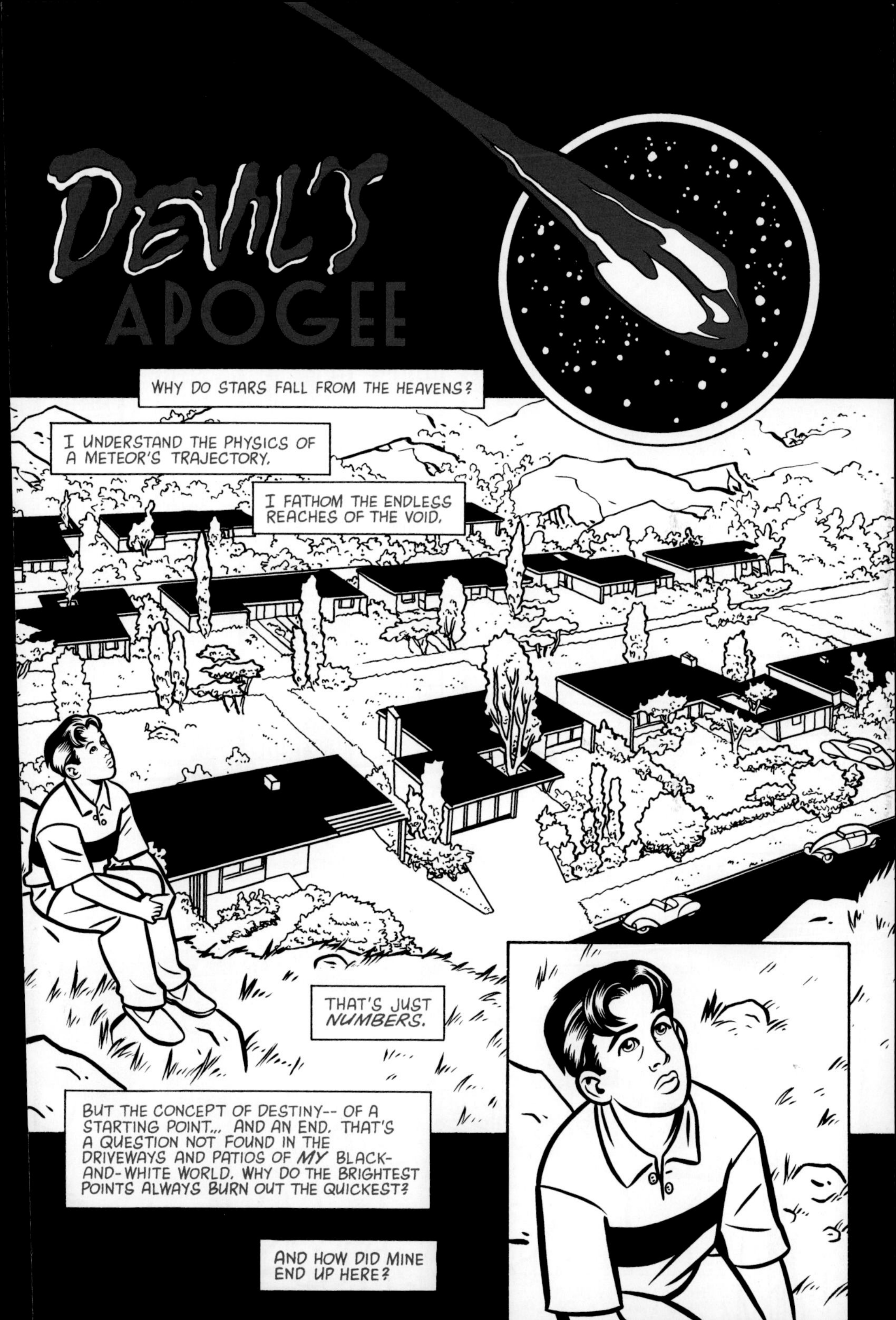
DEVIL'S APOGEE
WHY DO STARS FALL FROM THE HEAVENS?
I UNDERSTAND THE PHYSICS OF A METEOR'S TRAJECTORY.
I FATHOM THE ENDLESS REACHES OF THE VOID.
THAT'S JUST *NUMBERS.*
BUT THE CONCEPT OF DESTINY-- OF A STARTING POINT... AND AN END. THAT'S A QUESTION NOT FOUND IN THE DRIVEWAYS AND PATIOS OF *MY* BLACK-AND-WHITE WORLD. WHY DO THE BRIGHTEST POINTS ALWAYS BURN OUT THE QUICKEST?
AND HOW DID MINE END UP HERE?

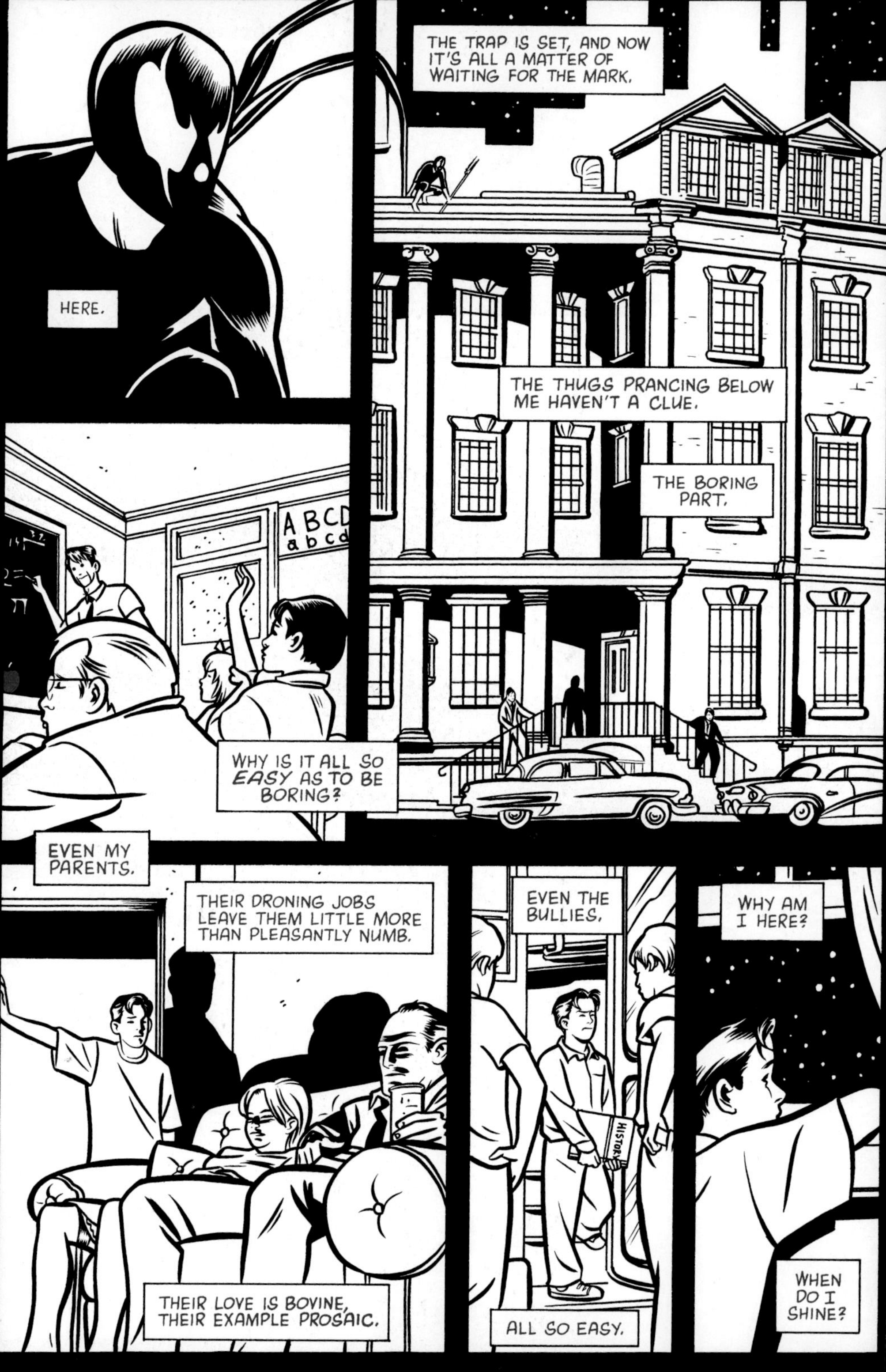
HERE.
THE TRAP IS SET, AND NOW IT'S ALL A MATTER OF WAITING FOR THE MARK.
THE THUGS PRANCING BELOW ME HAVEN'T A CLUE.
THE BORING PART.
A B C D
a b c d
WHY IS IT ALL SO EASY AS TO BE BORING?
EVEN MY PARENTS.
THEIR DRONING JOBS LEAVE THEM LITTLE MORE THAN PLEASANTLY NUMB.
THEIR LOVE IS BOVINE, THEIR EXAMPLE PROSAIC.
EVEN THE BULLIES.
HISTORY
ALL SO EASY.
WHY AM I HERE?
WHEN DO I SHINE?

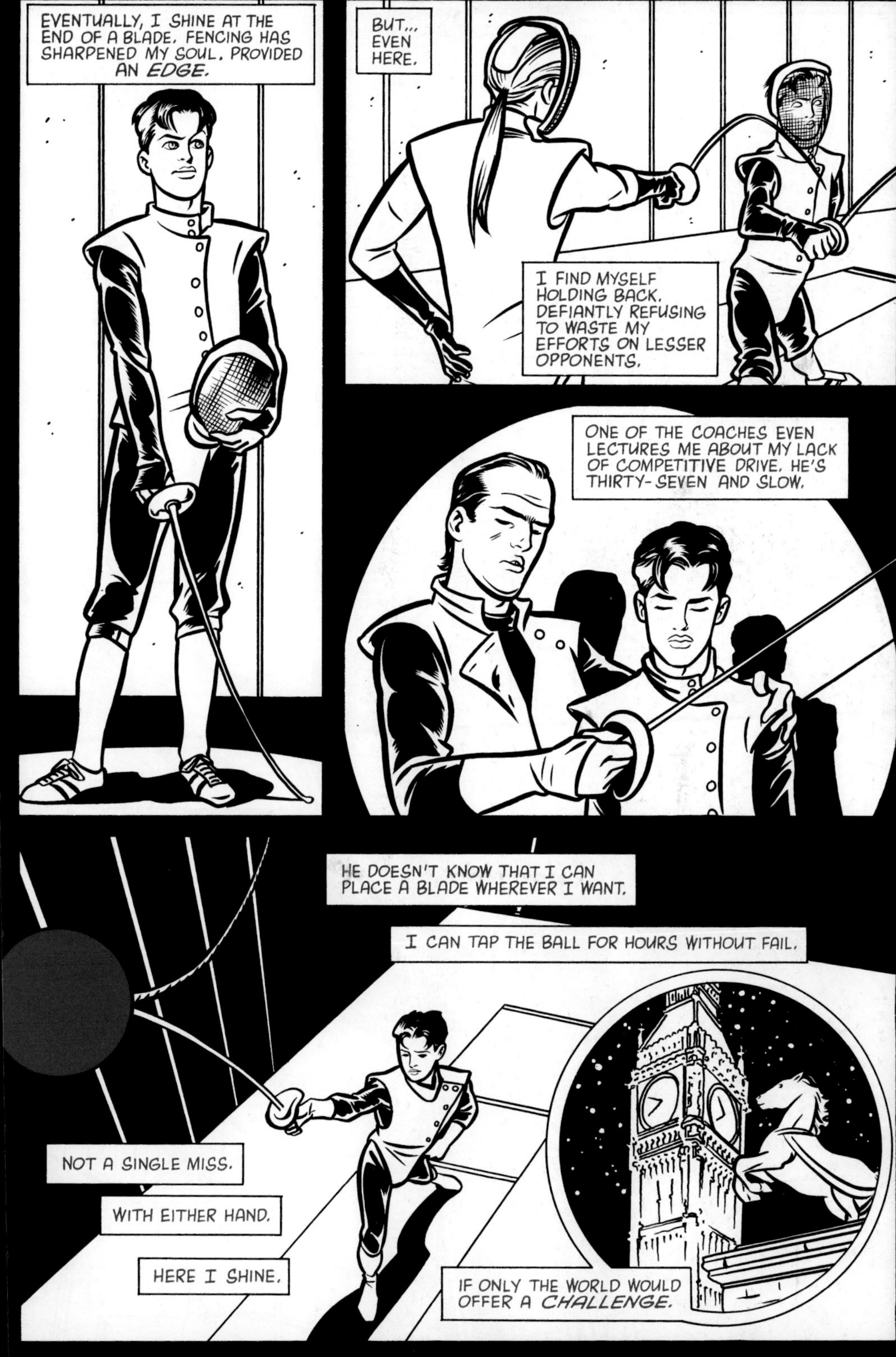
EVENTUALLY, I SHINE AT THE END OF A BLADE. FENCING HAS SHARPENED MY SOUL. PROVIDED AN *EDGE.*
BUT... EVEN HERE.
I FIND MYSELF HOLDING BACK. DEFIANTLY REFUSING TO WASTE MY EFFORTS ON LESSER OPPONENTS.
ONE OF THE COACHES EVEN LECTURES ME ABOUT MY LACK OF COMPETITIVE DRIVE. HE'S THIRTY-SEVEN AND SLOW.
HE DOESN'T KNOW THAT I CAN PLACE A BLADE WHEREVER I WANT.
I CAN TAP THE BALL FOR HOURS WITHOUT FAIL.
NOT A SINGLE MISS.
WITH EITHER HAND.
HERE I SHINE.
IF ONLY THE WORLD WOULD OFFER A *CHALLENGE.*

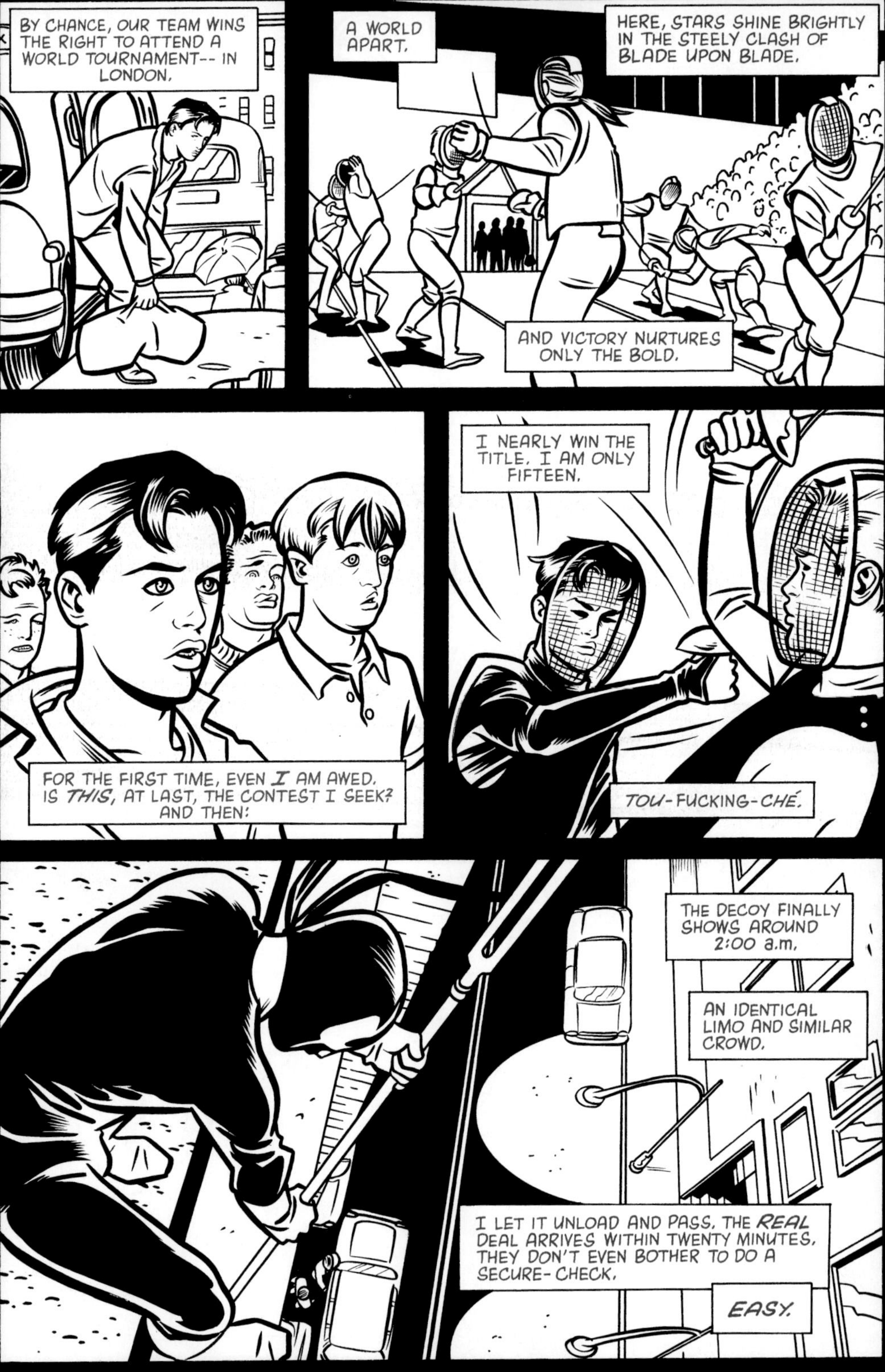
BY CHANCE, OUR TEAM WINS THE RIGHT TO ATTEND A WORLD TOURNAMENT-- IN LONDON.
A WORLD APART.
HERE, STARS SHINE BRIGHTLY IN THE STEELY CLASH OF BLADE UPON BLADE.
AND VICTORY NURTURES ONLY THE BOLD.
FOR THE FIRST TIME, EVEN *I* AM AWED. IS *THIS*, AT LAST, THE CONTEST I SEEK? AND THEN:
I NEARLY WIN THE TITLE. I AM ONLY FIFTEEN.
TOU-FUCKING-*CHÉ*.
THE DECOY FINALLY SHOWS AROUND 2:00 a.m.
AN IDENTICAL LIMO AND SIMILAR CROWD.
I LET IT UNLOAD AND PASS. THE *REAL* DEAL ARRIVES WITHIN TWENTY MINUTES. THEY DON'T EVEN BOTHER TO DO A SECURE-CHECK.
EASY.

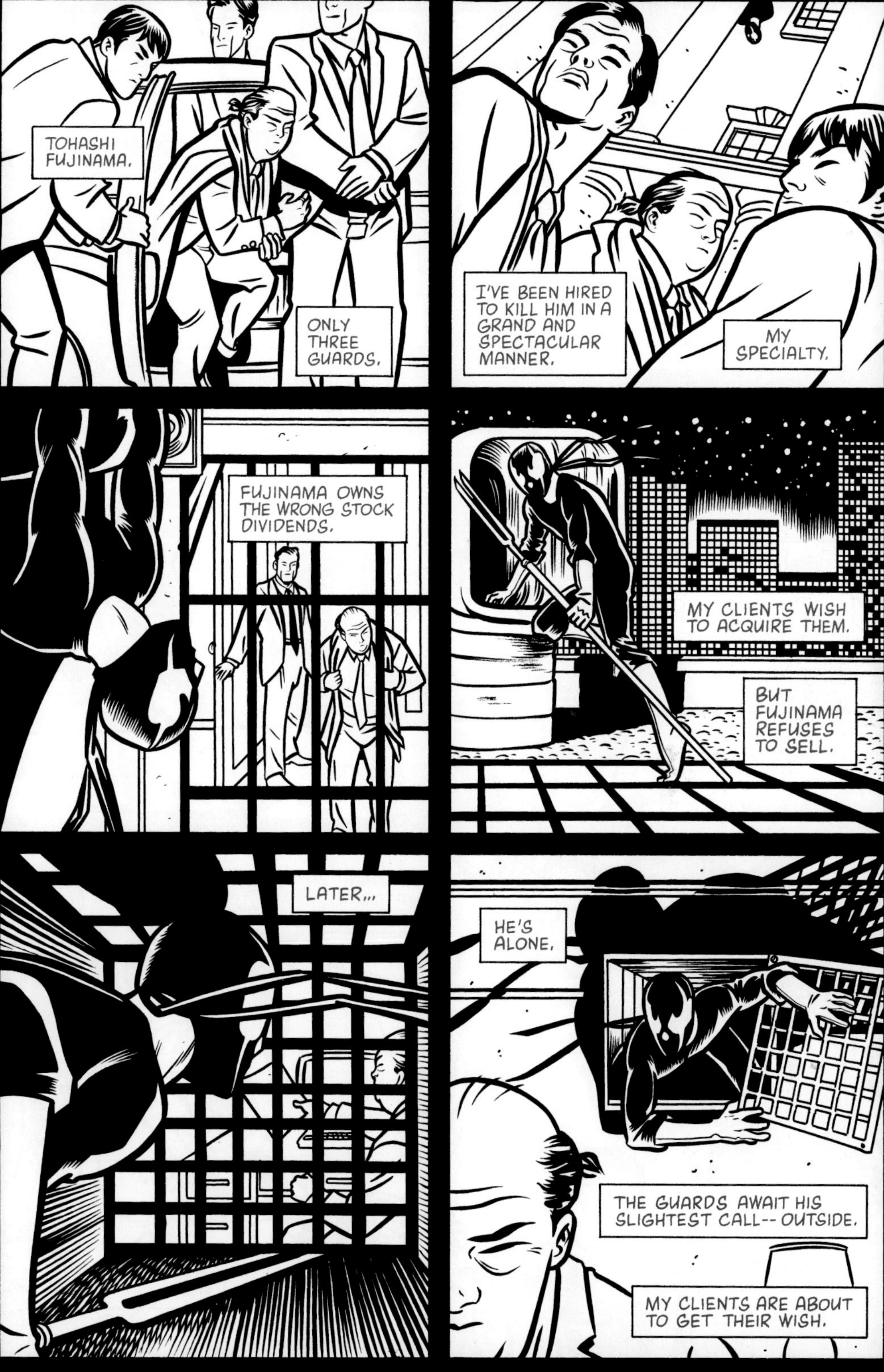
TOHASHI FUJINAMA.
ONLY THREE GUARDS.
I'VE BEEN HIRED TO KILL HIM IN A GRAND AND SPECTACULAR MANNER.
MY SPECIALTY.
FUJINAMA OWNS THE WRONG STOCK DIVIDENDS.
MY CLIENTS WISH TO ACQUIRE THEM.
BUT FUJINAMA REFUSES TO SELL.
LATER...
HE'S ALONE.
THE GUARDS AWAIT HIS SLIGHTEST CALL-- OUTSIDE.
MY CLIENTS ARE ABOUT TO GET THEIR WISH.

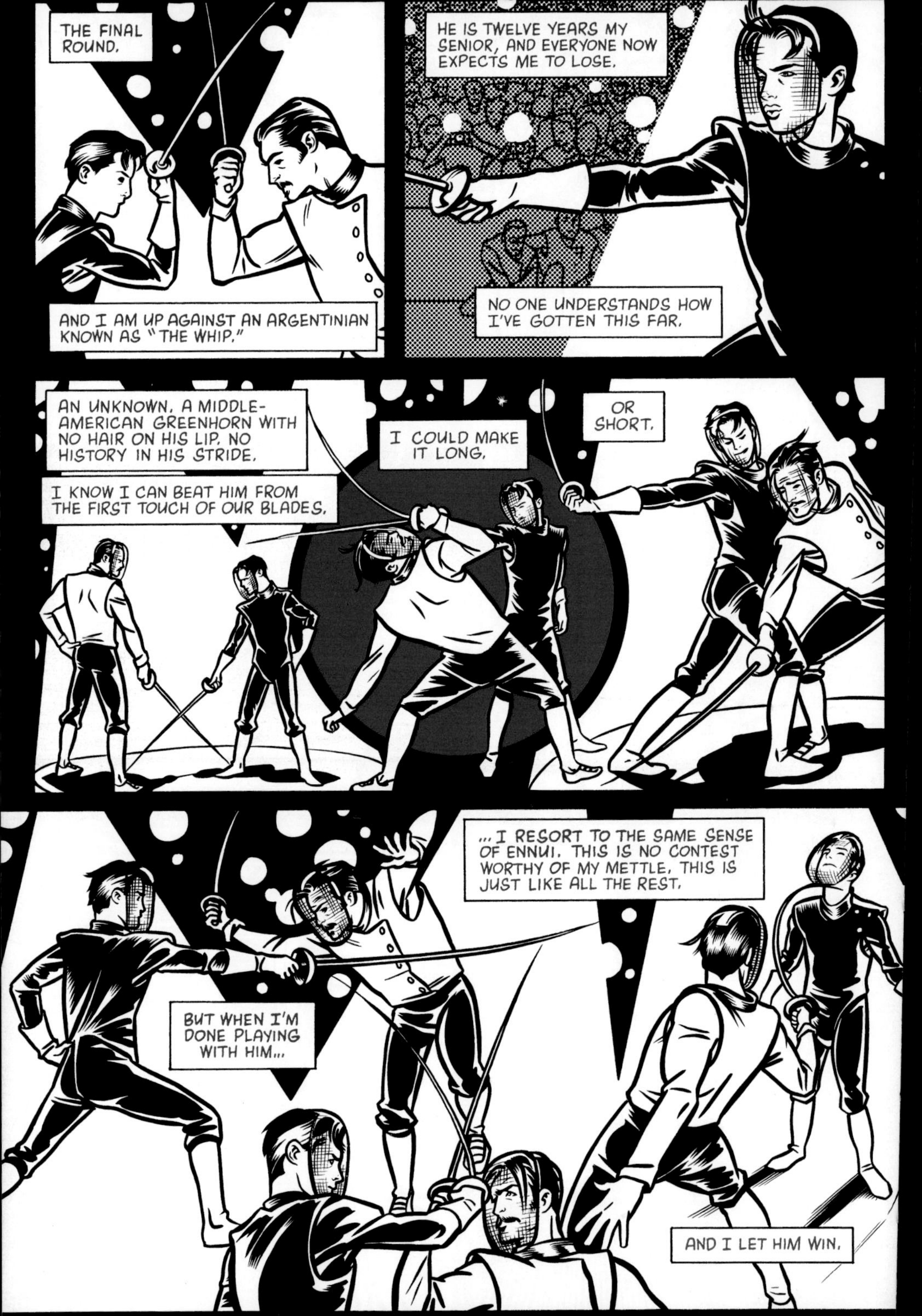

THE FINAL ROUND.
AND I AM UP AGAINST AN ARGENTINIAN KNOWN AS "THE WHIP."
HE IS TWELVE YEARS MY SENIOR, AND EVERYONE NOW EXPECTS ME TO LOSE.
NO ONE UNDERSTANDS HOW I'VE GOTTEN THIS FAR.
AN UNKNOWN. A MIDDLE-AMERICAN GREENHORN WITH NO HAIR ON HIS LIP. NO HISTORY IN HIS STRIDE.
I KNOW I CAN BEAT HIM FROM THE FIRST TOUCH OF OUR BLADES.
I COULD MAKE IT LONG.
OR SHORT.
BUT WHEN I'M DONE PLAYING WITH HIM...
...I RESORT TO THE SAME SENSE OF ENNUI. THIS IS NO CONTEST WORTHY OF MY METTLE. THIS IS JUST LIKE ALL THE REST.
AND I LET HIM WIN.

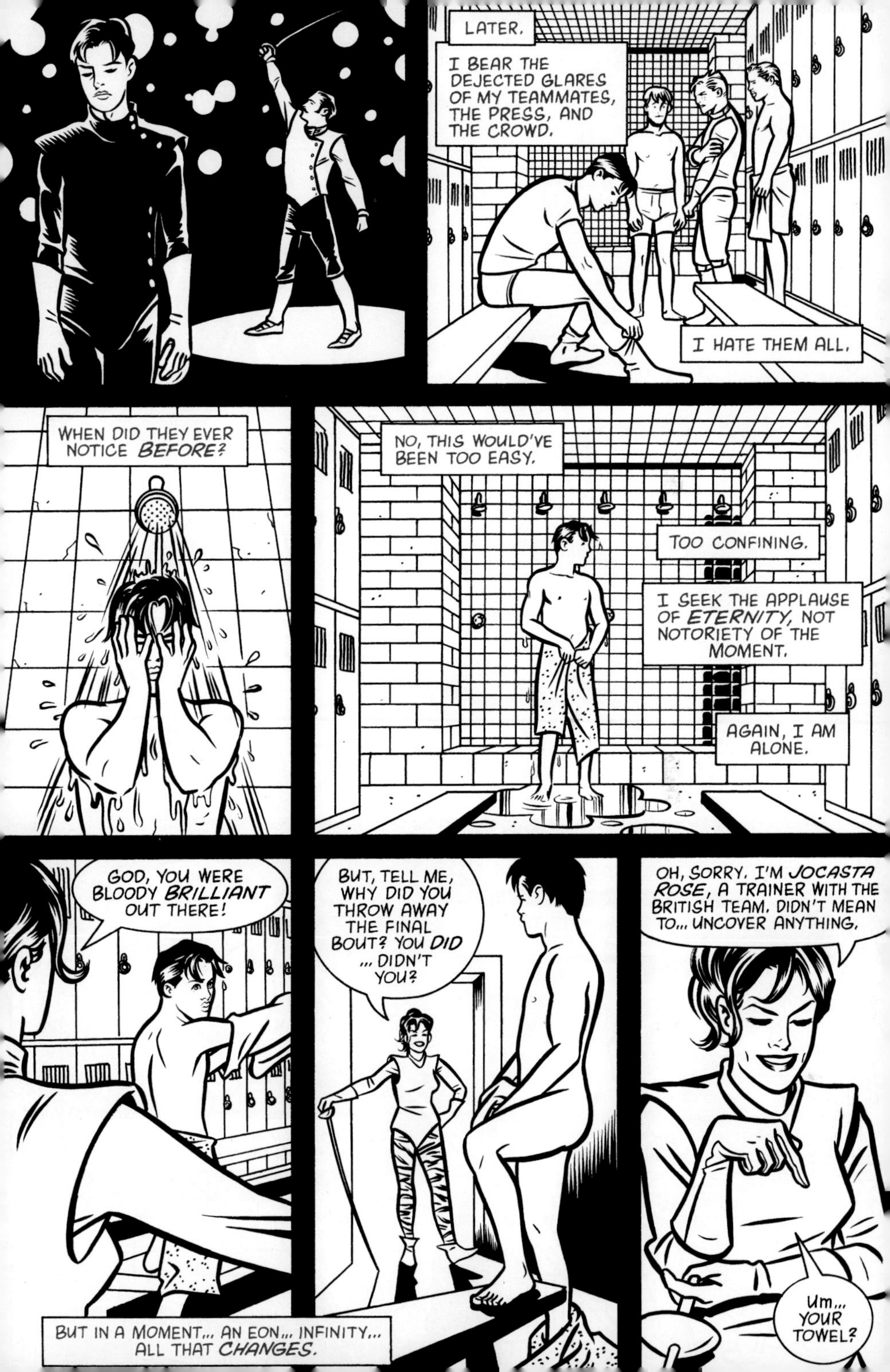
LATER.
I BEAR THE DEJECTED GLARES OF MY TEAMMATES, THE PRESS, AND THE CROWD.
I HATE THEM ALL.
WHEN DID THEY EVER NOTICE BEFORE?
NO, THIS WOULD'VE BEEN TOO EASY.
TOO CONFINING.
I SEEK THE APPLAUSE OF ETERNITY, NOT NOTORIETY OF THE MOMENT.
AGAIN, I AM ALONE.
GOD, YOU WERE BLOODY BRILLIANT OUT THERE!
BUT, TELL ME, WHY DID YOU THROW AWAY THE FINAL BOUT? YOU DID ... DIDN'T YOU?
OH, SORRY. I'M JOCASTA ROSE, A TRAINER WITH THE BRITISH TEAM. DIDN'T MEAN TO... UNCOVER ANYTHING.
Um... YOUR TOWEL?
BUT IN A MOMENT... AN EON... INFINITY... ALL THAT CHANGES.

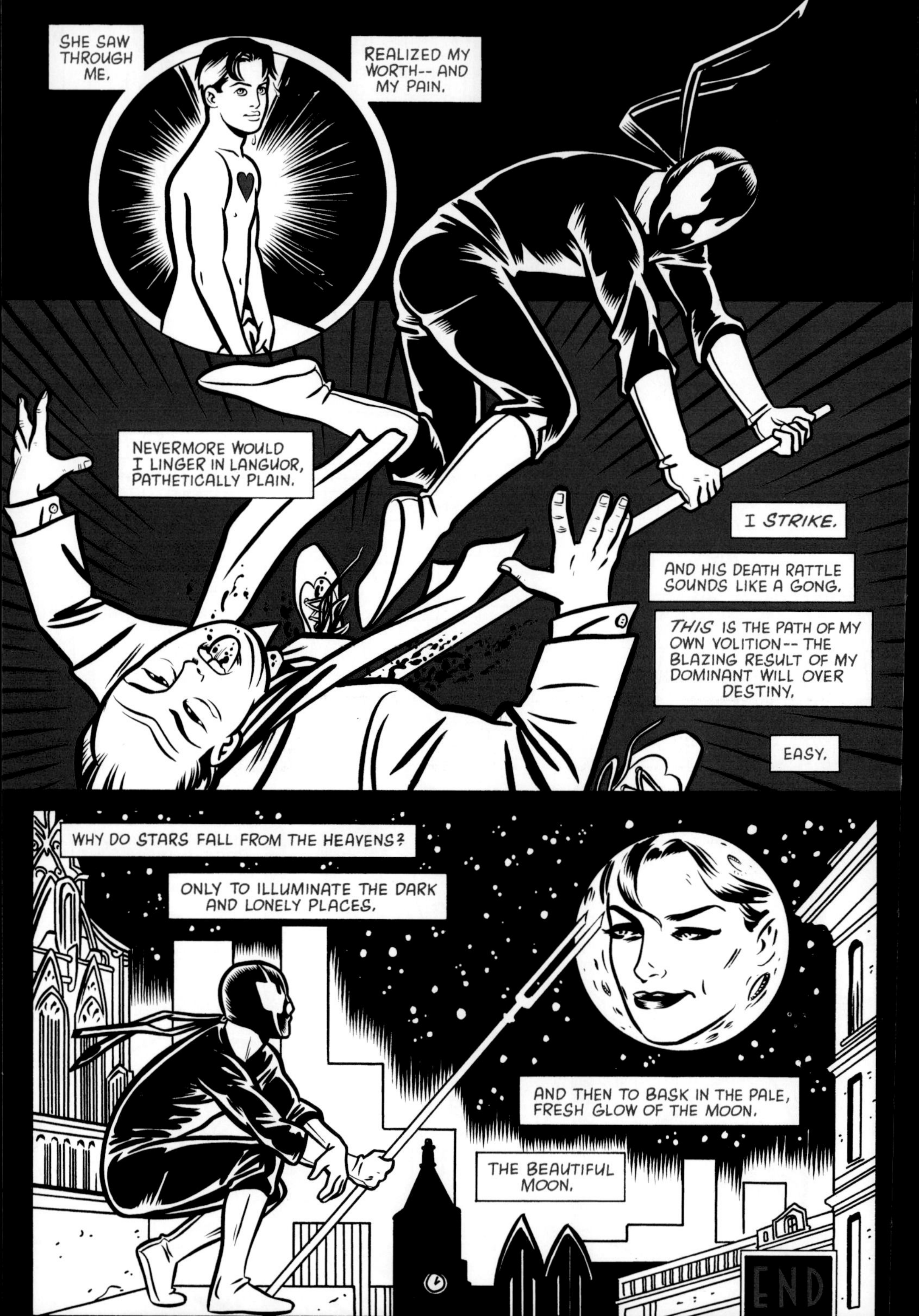
SHE SAW THROUGH ME.
REALIZED MY WORTH-- AND MY PAIN.
NEVERMORE WOULD I LINGER IN LANGUOR, PATHETICALLY PLAIN.
I *STRIKE.*
AND HIS DEATH RATTLE SOUNDS LIKE A GONG.
THIS IS THE PATH OF MY OWN VOLITION-- THE BLAZING RESULT OF MY DOMINANT WILL OVER DESTINY.
EASY.
WHY DO STARS FALL FROM THE HEAVENS?
ONLY TO ILLUMINATE THE DARK AND LONELY PLACES.
AND THEN TO BASK IN THE PALE, FRESH GLOW OF THE MOON.
THE BEAUTIFUL MOON.
END

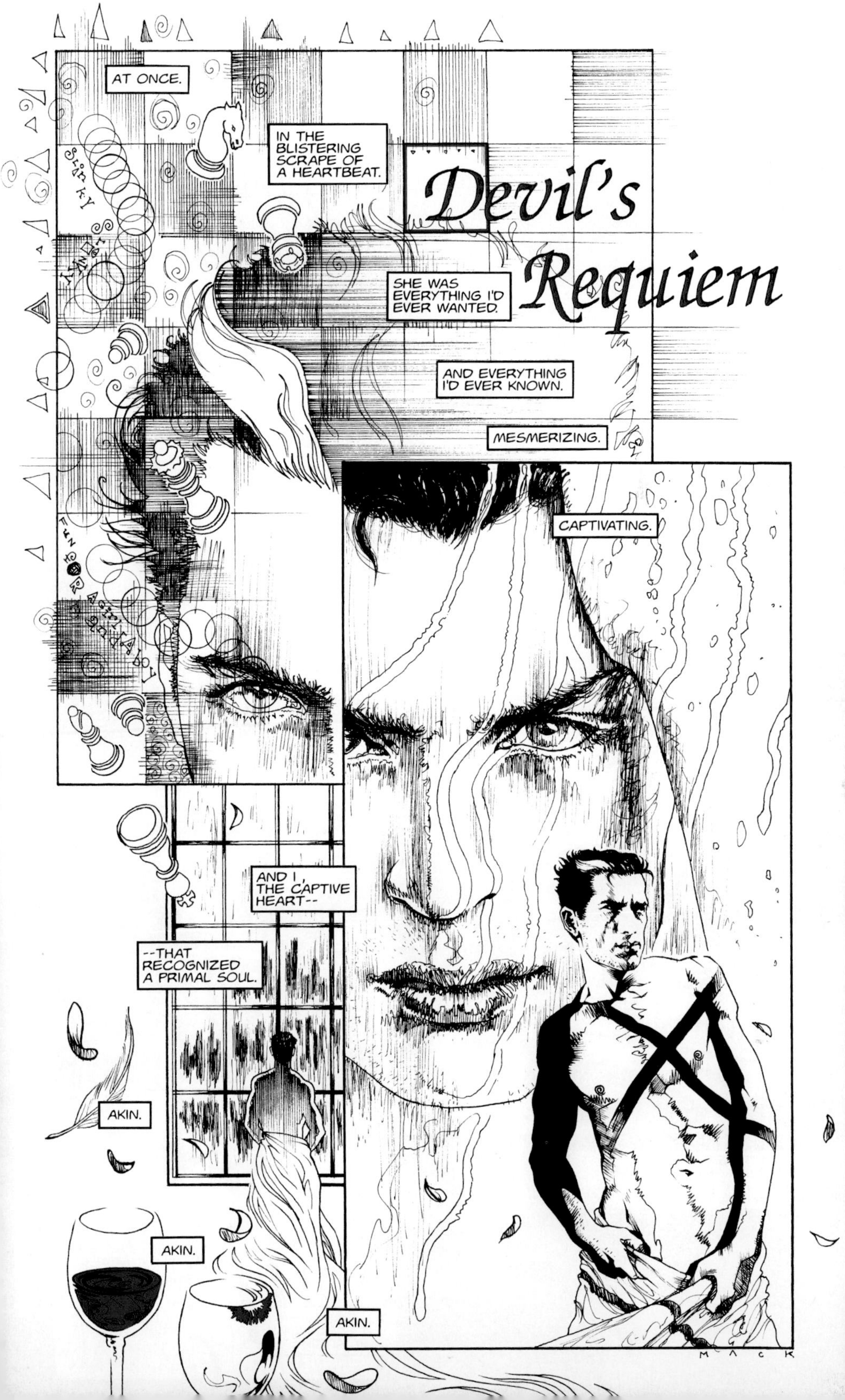
AT ONCE.
IN THE BLISTERING SCRAPE OF A HEARTBEAT.
Devil's Requiem
SHE WAS EVERYTHING I'D EVER WANTED.
AND EVERYTHING I'D EVER KNOWN.
MESMERIZING.
CAPTIVATING.
AND I, THE CAPTIVE HEART--
--THAT RECOGNIZED A PRIMAL SOUL.
AKIN.
AKIN.
AKIN.
M A C K

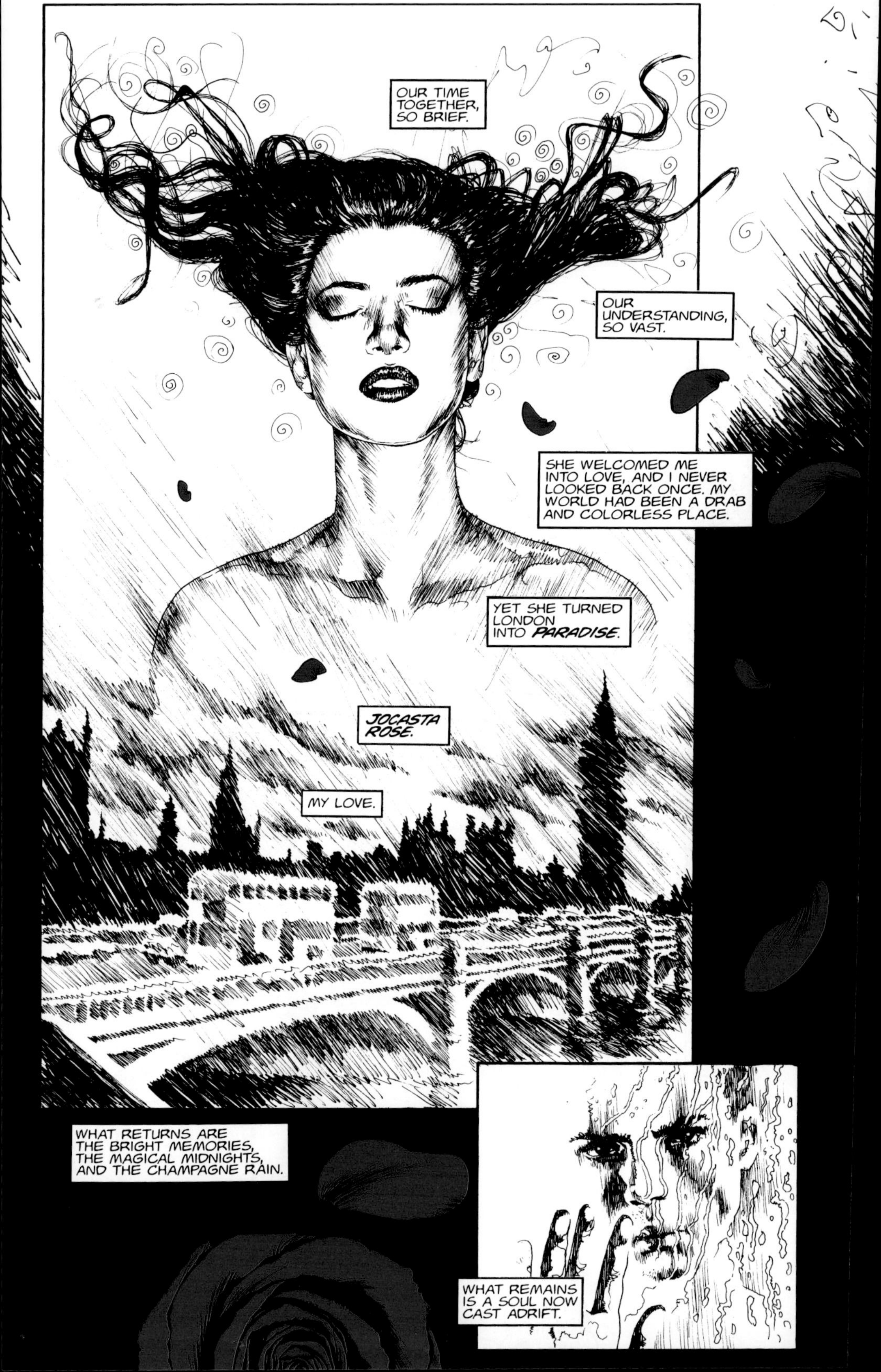
OUR TIME TOGETHER, SO BRIEF.
OUR UNDERSTANDING, SO VAST.
SHE WELCOMED ME INTO LOVE, AND I NEVER LOOKED BACK ONCE. MY WORLD HAD BEEN A DRAB AND COLORLESS PLACE.
YET SHE TURNED LONDON INTO PARADISE.
JOCASTA ROSE.
MY LOVE.
WHAT RETURNS ARE THE BRIGHT MEMORIES, THE MAGICAL MIDNIGHTS, AND THE CHAMPAGNE RAIN.
WHAT REMAINS IS A SOUL NOW CAST ADRIFT.

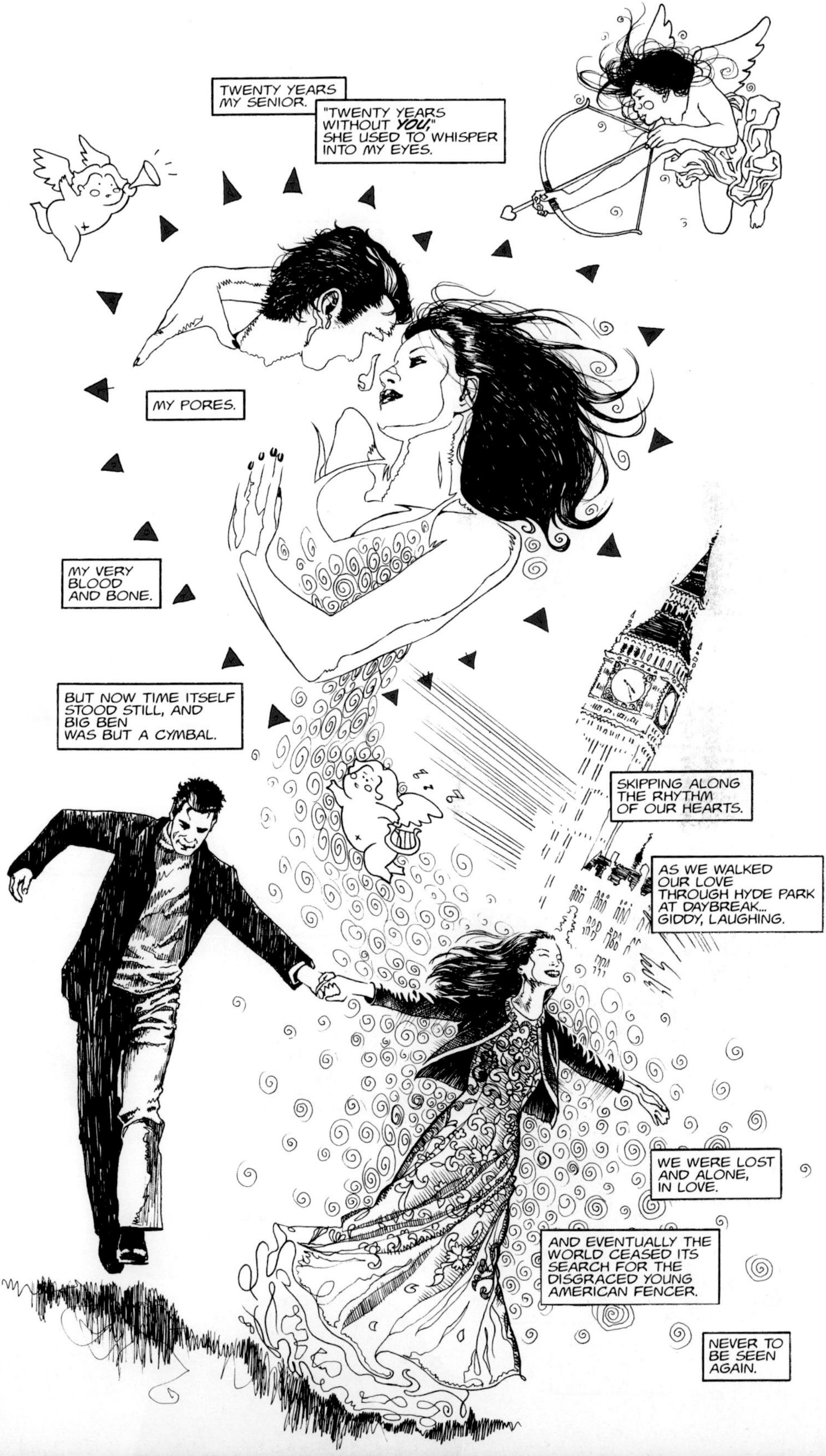

TWENTY YEARS MY SENIOR.
"TWENTY YEARS WITHOUT *YOU*," SHE USED TO WHISPER INTO MY EYES.
MY PORES.
MY VERY BLOOD AND BONE.
BUT NOW TIME ITSELF STOOD STILL, AND BIG BEN WAS BUT A CYMBAL.
SKIPPING ALONG THE RHYTHM OF OUR HEARTS.
AS WE WALKED OUR LOVE THROUGH HYDE PARK AT DAYBREAK... GIDDY, LAUGHING.
WE WERE LOST AND ALONE, IN LOVE.
AND EVENTUALLY THE WORLD CEASED ITS SEARCH FOR THE DISGRACED YOUNG AMERICAN FENCER.
NEVER TO BE SEEN AGAIN.

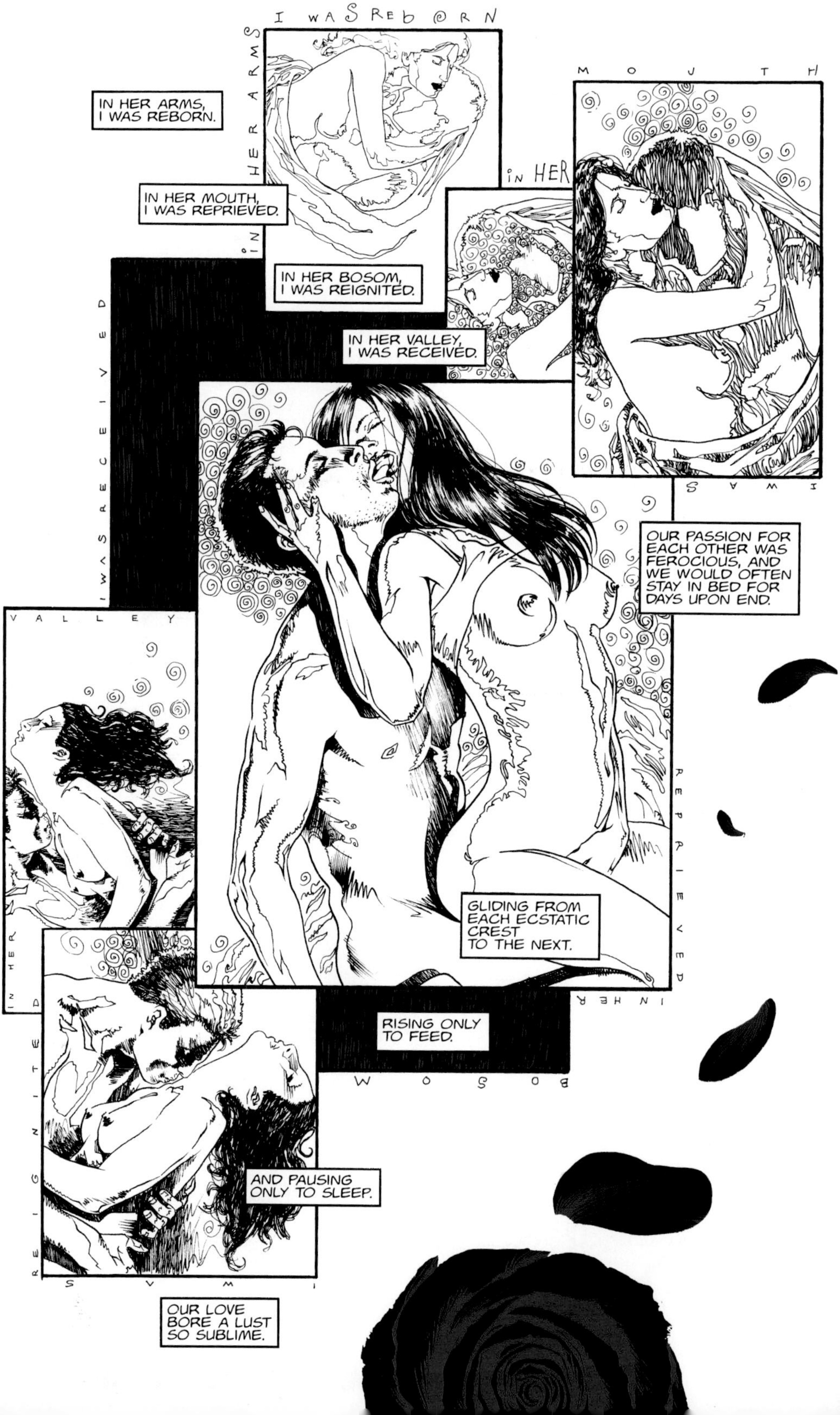
IN HER ARMS, I WAS REBORN.
IN HER MOUTH, I WAS REPRIEVED.
IN HER BOSOM, I WAS REIGNITED.
IN HER VALLEY, I WAS RECEIVED.
OUR PASSION FOR EACH OTHER WAS FEROCIOUS, AND WE WOULD OFTEN STAY IN BED FOR DAYS UPON END.
GLIDING FROM EACH ECSTATIC CREST TO THE NEXT.
RISING ONLY TO FEED.
AND PAUSING ONLY TO SLEEP.
OUR LOVE BORE A LUST SO SUBLIME.

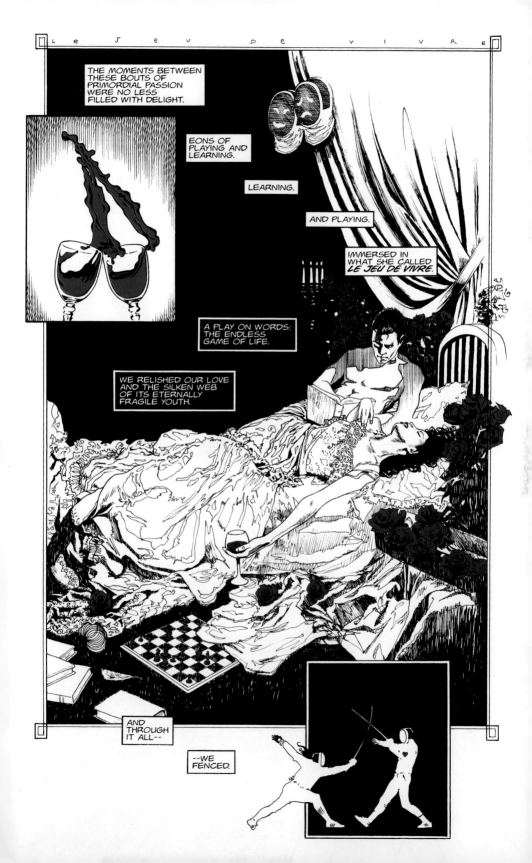

THE MOMENTS BETWEEN THESE BOUTS OF PRIMORDIAL PASSION WERE NO LESS FILLED WITH DELIGHT.

EONS OF PLAYING AND LEARNING.

LEARNING.

AND PLAYING.

IMMERSED IN WHAT SHE CALLED *LE JEU DE VIVRE*.

A PLAY ON WORDS: THE ENDLESS GAME OF LIFE.

WE RELISHED OUR LOVE AND THE SILKEN WEB OF ITS ETERNALLY FRAGILE YOUTH.

AND THROUGH IT ALL--

--WE FENCED.

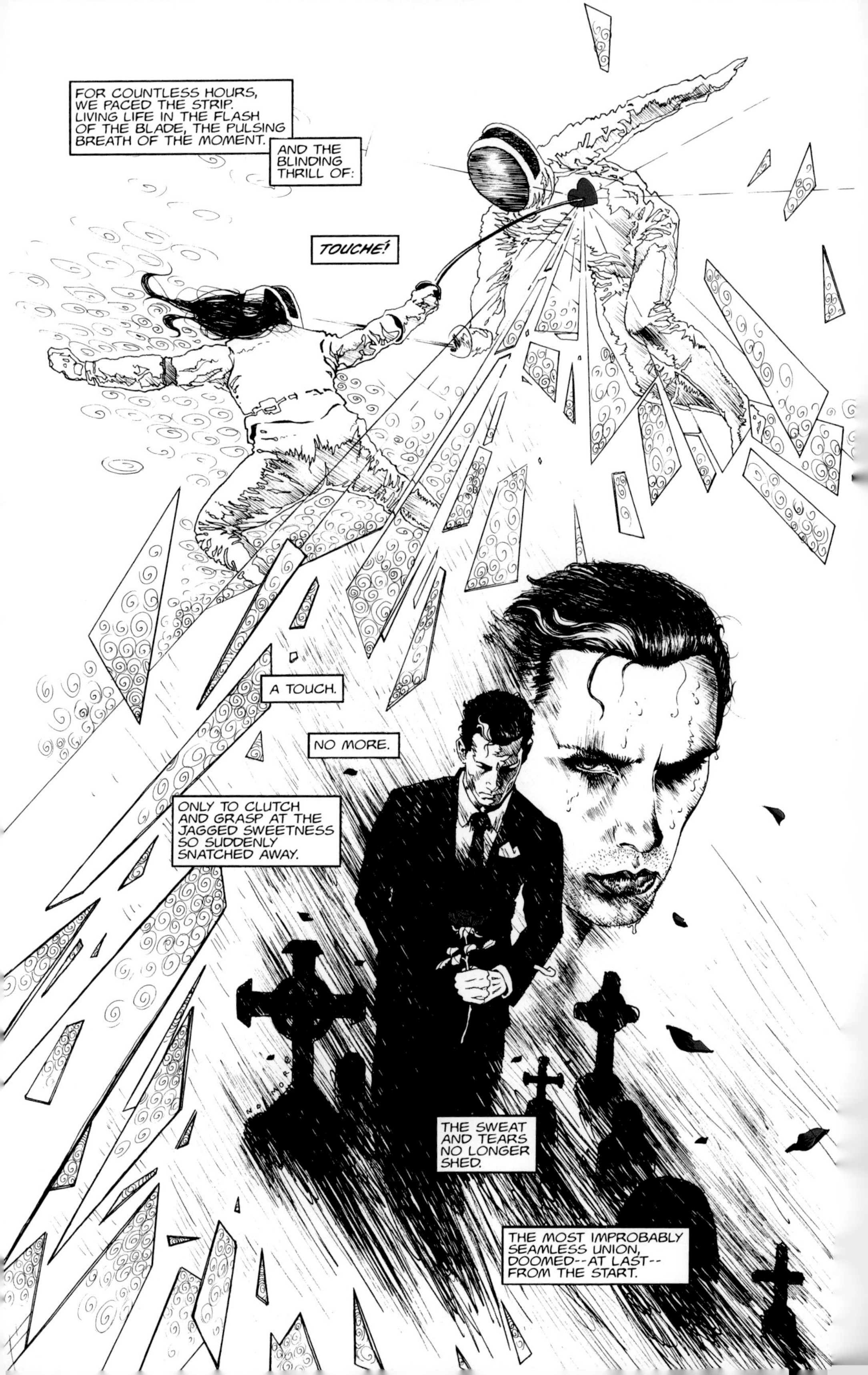
FOR COUNTLESS HOURS, WE PACED THE STRIP. LIVING LIFE IN THE FLASH OF THE BLADE, THE PULSING BREATH OF THE MOMENT.
AND THE BLINDING THRILL OF:
TOUCHE!
A TOUCH.
NO MORE.
ONLY TO CLUTCH AND GRASP AT THE JAGGED SWEETNESS SO SUDDENLY SNATCHED AWAY.
THE SWEAT AND TEARS NO LONGER SHED.
THE MOST IMPROBABLY SEAMLESS UNION, DOOMED--AT LAST--FROM THE START.

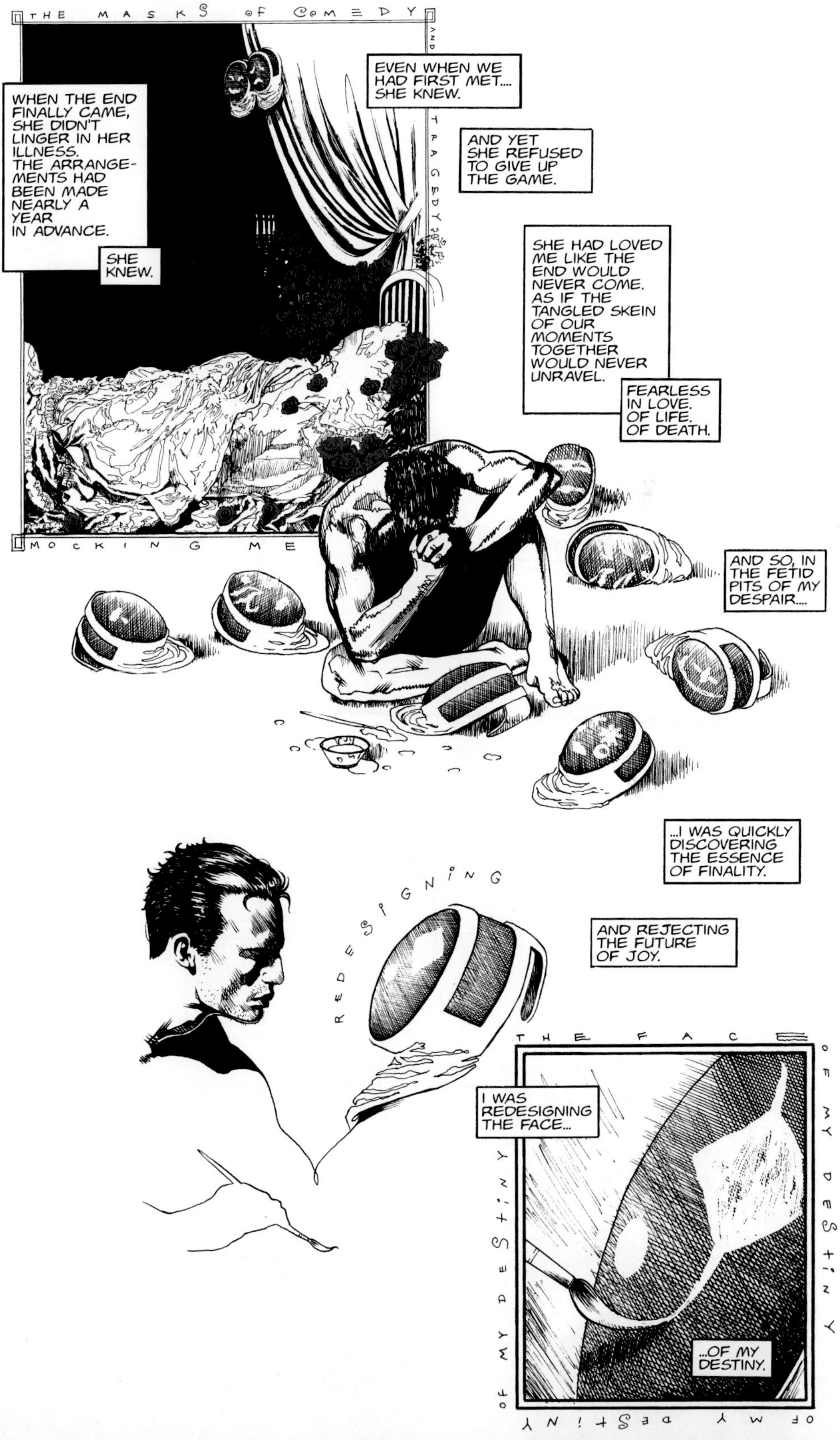
THE MASKS OF COMEDY AND TRAGEDY
MOCKING ME
WHEN THE END FINALLY CAME, SHE DIDN'T LINGER IN HER ILLNESS. THE ARRANGEMENTS HAD BEEN MADE NEARLY A YEAR IN ADVANCE.
SHE KNEW.
EVEN WHEN WE HAD FIRST MET.... SHE KNEW.
AND YET SHE REFUSED TO GIVE UP THE GAME.
SHE HAD LOVED ME LIKE THE END WOULD NEVER COME. AS IF THE TANGLED SKEIN OF OUR MOMENTS TOGETHER WOULD NEVER UNRAVEL.
FEARLESS IN LOVE. OF LIFE. OF DEATH.
AND SO, IN THE FETID PITS OF MY DESPAIR....
...I WAS QUICKLY DISCOVERING THE ESSENCE OF FINALITY.
AND REJECTING THE FUTURE OF JOY.
REDESIGNING
THE FACE OF MY DESTINY
OF MY DESTINY
OF MY DESTINY
I WAS REDESIGNING THE FACE...
...OF MY DESTINY.

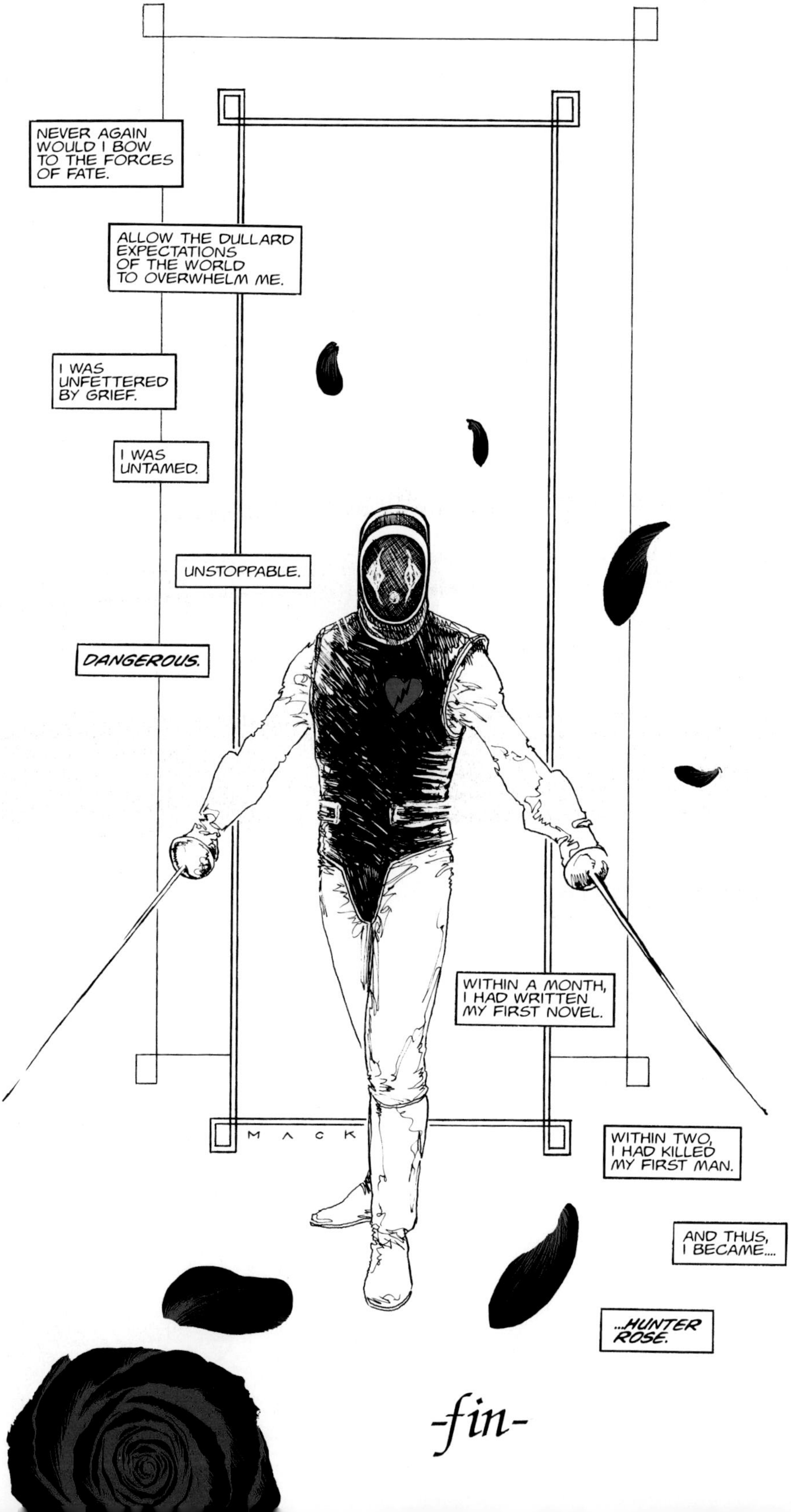
NEVER AGAIN WOULD I BOW TO THE FORCES OF FATE.
ALLOW THE DULLARD EXPECTATIONS OF THE WORLD TO OVERWHELM ME.
I WAS UNFETTERED BY GRIEF.
I WAS UNTAMED.
UNSTOPPABLE.
DANGEROUS.
WITHIN A MONTH, I HAD WRITTEN MY FIRST NOVEL.
MACK
WITHIN TWO, I HAD KILLED MY FIRST MAN.
AND THUS, I BECAME....
...HUNTER ROSE.
-fin-

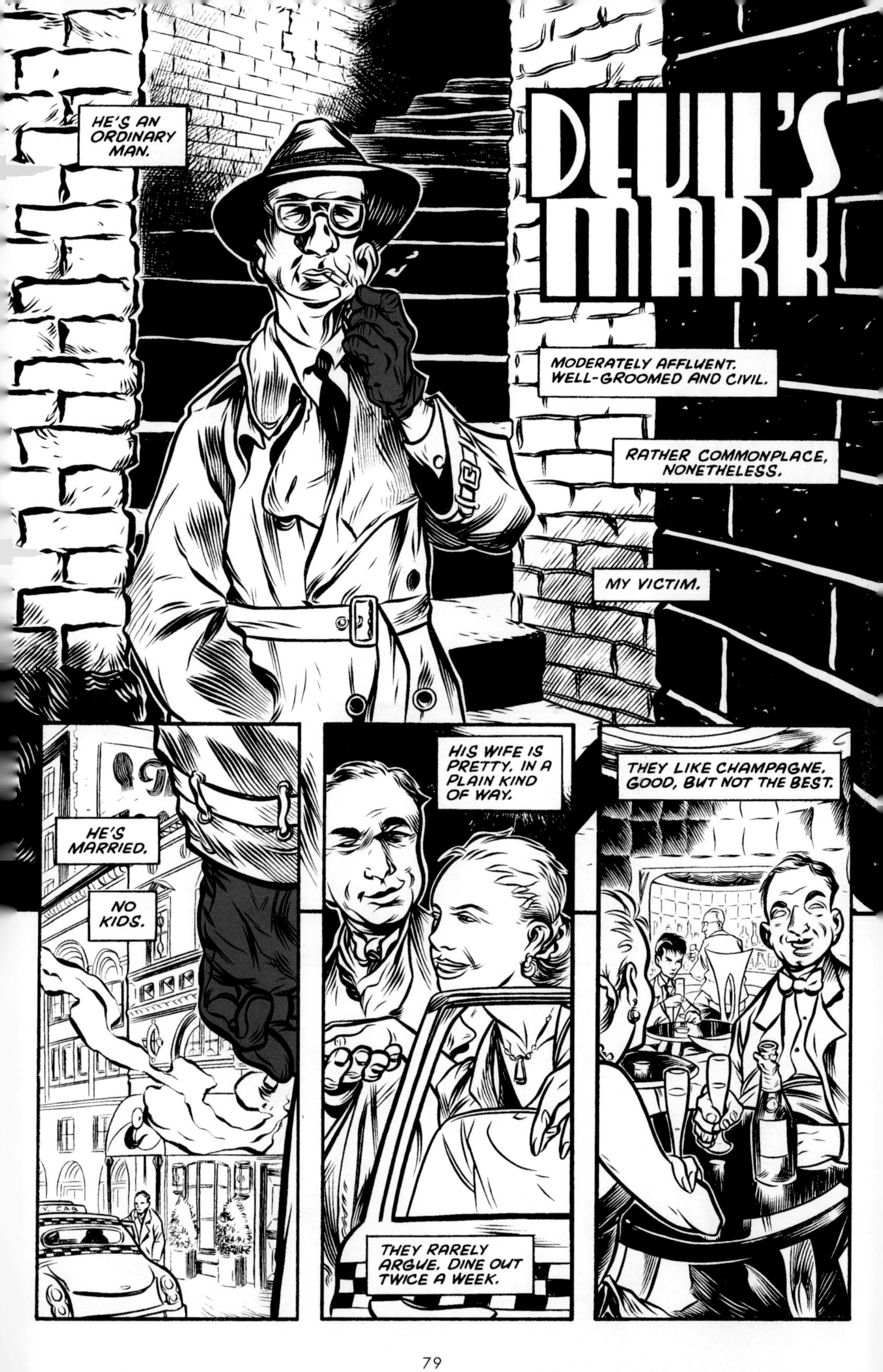
DEVIL'S MARK
HE'S AN ORDINARY MAN.
MODERATELY AFFLUENT. WELL-GROOMED AND CIVIL.
RATHER COMMONPLACE, NONETHELESS.
MY VICTIM.
HE'S MARRIED.
NO KIDS.
HIS WIFE IS PRETTY, IN A PLAIN KIND OF WAY.
THEY RARELY ARGUE. DINE OUT TWICE A WEEK.
THEY LIKE CHAMPAGNE. GOOD, BUT NOT THE BEST.

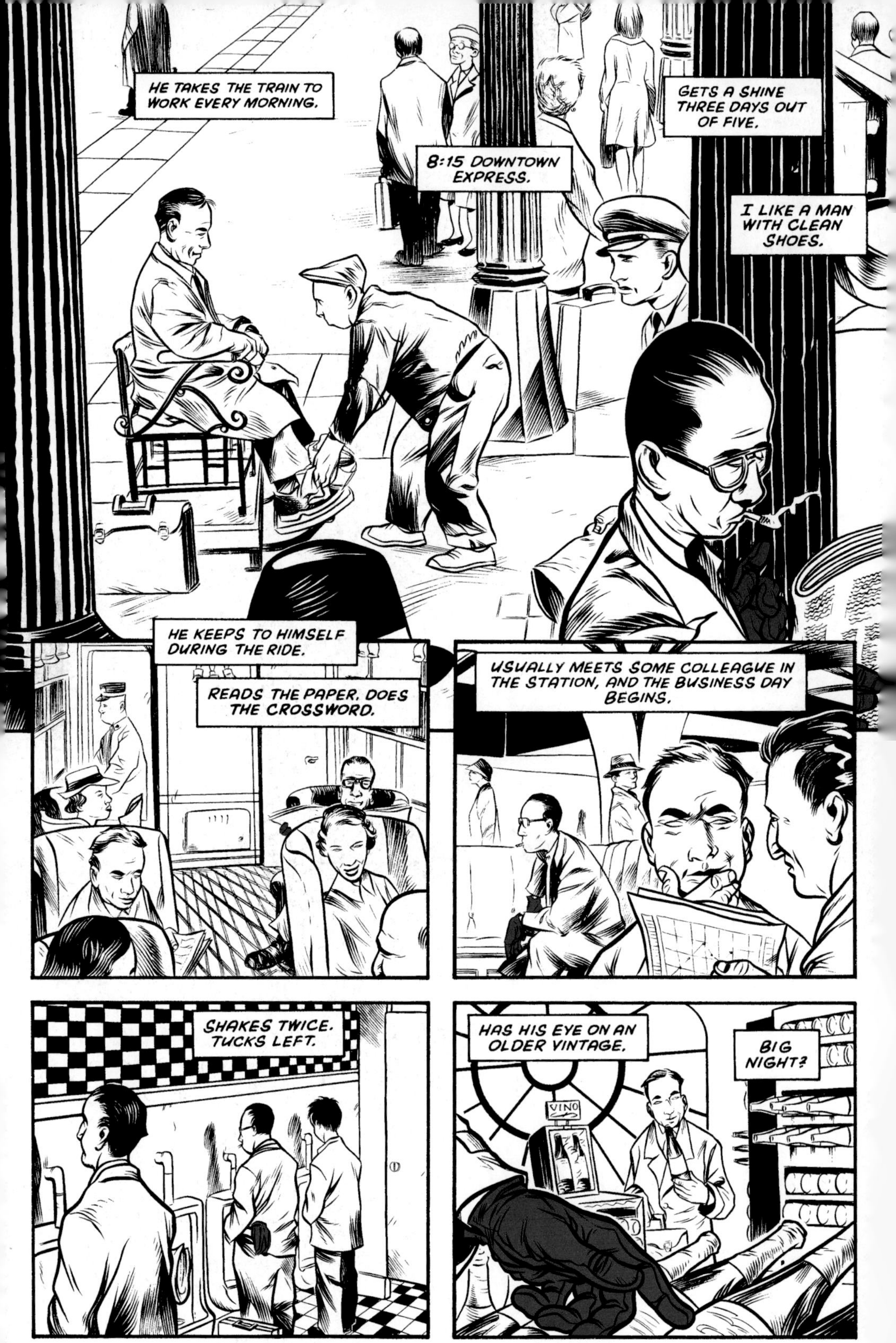
HE TAKES THE TRAIN TO WORK EVERY MORNING.
8:15 DOWNTOWN EXPRESS.
GETS A SHINE THREE DAYS OUT OF FIVE.
I LIKE A MAN WITH CLEAN SHOES.
HE KEEPS TO HIMSELF DURING THE RIDE.
READS THE PAPER. DOES THE CROSSWORD.
USUALLY MEETS SOME COLLEAGUE IN THE STATION, AND THE BUSINESS DAY BEGINS.
SHAKES TWICE. TUCKS LEFT.
HAS HIS EYE ON AN OLDER VINTAGE.
VINO
BIG NIGHT?

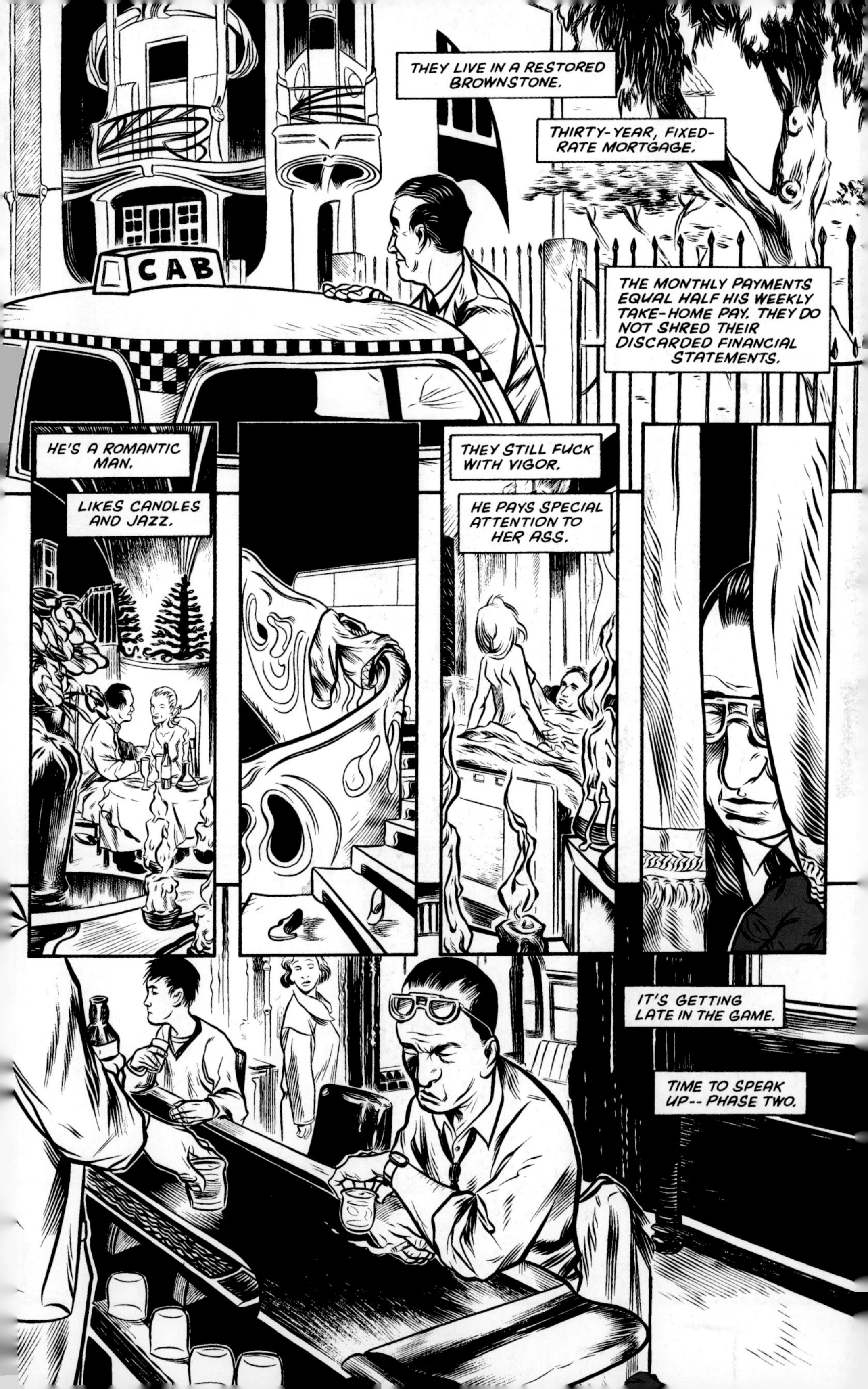
THEY LIVE IN A RESTORED BROWNSTONE.
THIRTY-YEAR, FIXED-RATE MORTGAGE.
CAB
THE MONTHLY PAYMENTS EQUAL HALF HIS WEEKLY TAKE-HOME PAY. THEY DO NOT SHRED THEIR DISCARDED FINANCIAL STATEMENTS.
HE'S A ROMANTIC MAN.
LIKES CANDLES AND JAZZ.
THEY STILL FUCK WITH VIGOR.
HE PAYS SPECIAL ATTENTION TO HER ASS.
IT'S GETTING LATE IN THE GAME.
TIME TO SPEAK UP-- PHASE TWO.

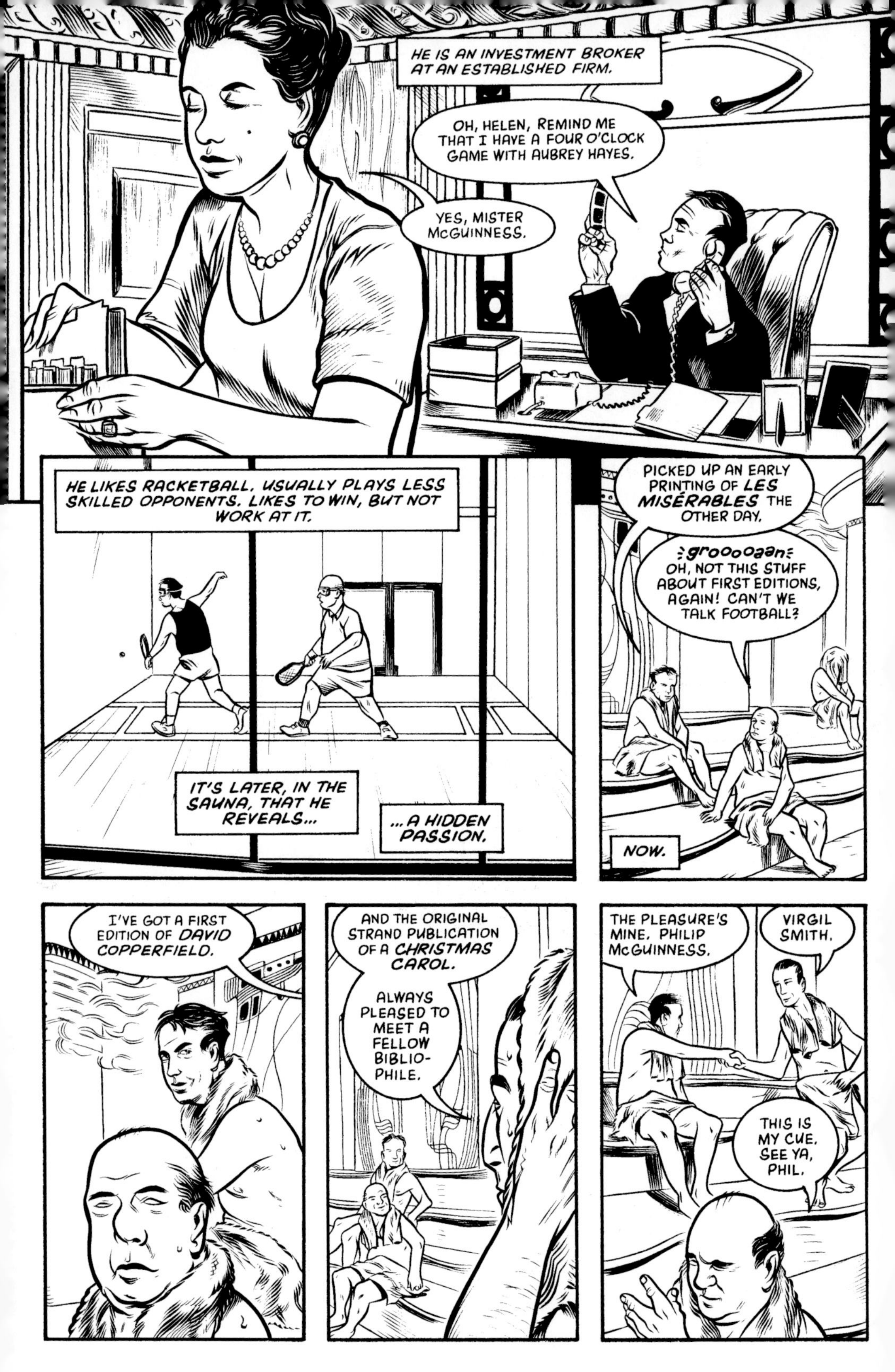

HE IS AN INVESTMENT BROKER AT AN ESTABLISHED FIRM.
OH, HELEN, REMIND ME THAT I HAVE A FOUR O'CLOCK GAME WITH AUBREY HAYES.
YES, MISTER McGUINNESS.
HE LIKES RACKETBALL, USUALLY PLAYS LESS SKILLED OPPONENTS. LIKES TO WIN, BUT NOT WORK AT IT.
IT'S LATER, IN THE SAUNA, THAT HE REVEALS...
...A HIDDEN PASSION.
PICKED UP AN EARLY PRINTING OF LES MISÉRABLES THE OTHER DAY.
groooooaan
OH, NOT THIS STUFF ABOUT FIRST EDITIONS, AGAIN! CAN'T WE TALK FOOTBALL?
NOW.
I'VE GOT A FIRST EDITION OF DAVID COPPERFIELD.
AND THE ORIGINAL STRAND PUBLICATION OF A CHRISTMAS CAROL.
ALWAYS PLEASED TO MEET A FELLOW BIBLIO-PHILE.
THE PLEASURE'S MINE. PHILIP McGUINNESS.
VIRGIL SMITH.
THIS IS MY CUE. SEE YA, PHIL.

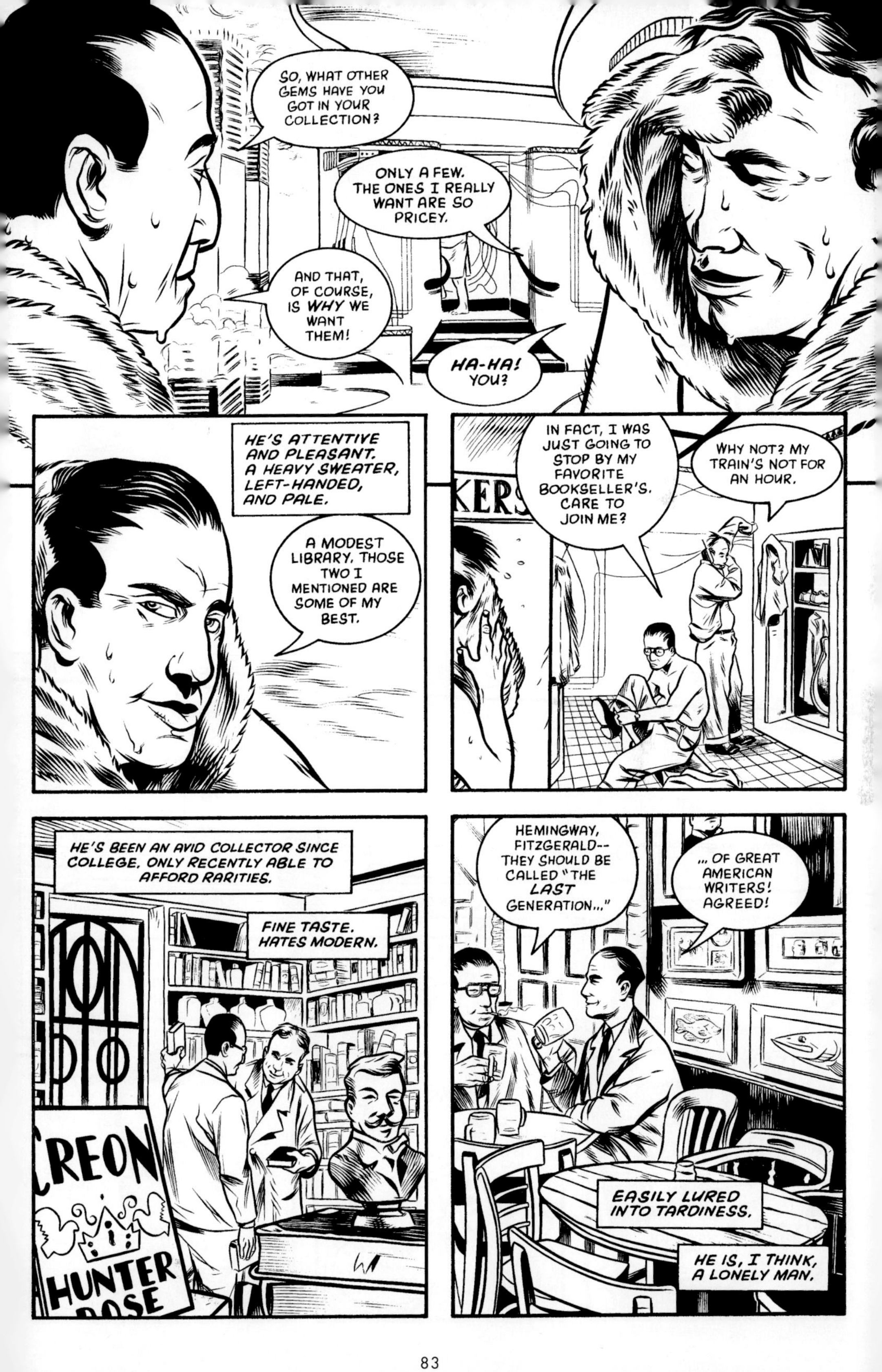
SO, WHAT OTHER GEMS HAVE YOU GOT IN YOUR COLLECTION?
ONLY A FEW. THE ONES I REALLY WANT ARE SO PRICEY.
AND THAT, OF COURSE, IS WHY WE WANT THEM!
HA-HA! YOU?
HE'S ATTENTIVE AND PLEASANT. A HEAVY SWEATER, LEFT-HANDED, AND PALE.
A MODEST LIBRARY. THOSE TWO I MENTIONED ARE SOME OF MY BEST.
KERS
IN FACT, I WAS JUST GOING TO STOP BY MY FAVORITE BOOKSELLER'S. CARE TO JOIN ME?
WHY NOT? MY TRAIN'S NOT FOR AN HOUR.
HE'S BEEN AN AVID COLLECTOR SINCE COLLEGE, ONLY RECENTLY ABLE TO AFFORD RARITIES.
FINE TASTE. HATES MODERN.
CREON
HUNTER ROSE
HEMINGWAY, FITZGERALD-- THEY SHOULD BE CALLED "THE LAST GENERATION..."
... OF GREAT AMERICAN WRITERS! AGREED!
EASILY LURED INTO TARDINESS.
HE IS, I THINK, A LONELY MAN.

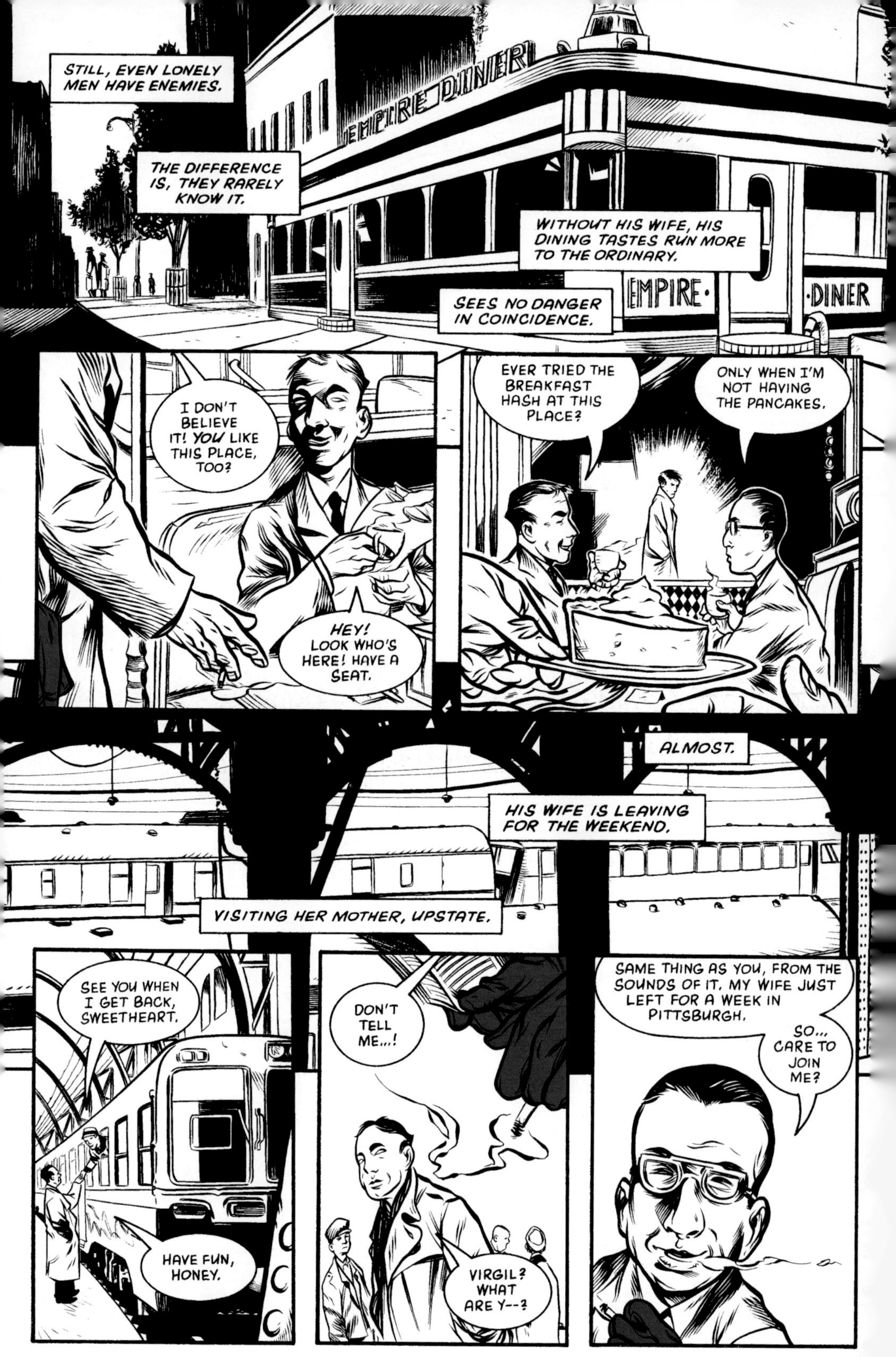
STILL, EVEN LONELY MEN HAVE ENEMIES.
THE DIFFERENCE IS, THEY RARELY KNOW IT.
EMPIRE DINER
WITHOUT HIS WIFE, HIS DINING TASTES RUN MORE TO THE ORDINARY.
SEES NO DANGER IN COINCIDENCE.
EMPIRE · DINER
I DON'T BELIEVE IT! YOU LIKE THIS PLACE, TOO?
HEY! LOOK WHO'S HERE! HAVE A SEAT.
EVER TRIED THE BREAKFAST HASH AT THIS PLACE?
ONLY WHEN I'M NOT HAVING THE PANCAKES.
ALMOST.
HIS WIFE IS LEAVING FOR THE WEEKEND,
VISITING HER MOTHER, UPSTATE.
SEE YOU WHEN I GET BACK, SWEETHEART.
HAVE FUN, HONEY.
DON'T TELL ME...!
VIRGIL? WHAT ARE Y--?
SAME THING AS YOU, FROM THE SOUNDS OF IT. MY WIFE JUST LEFT FOR A WEEK IN PITTSBURGH.
SO... CARE TO JOIN ME?

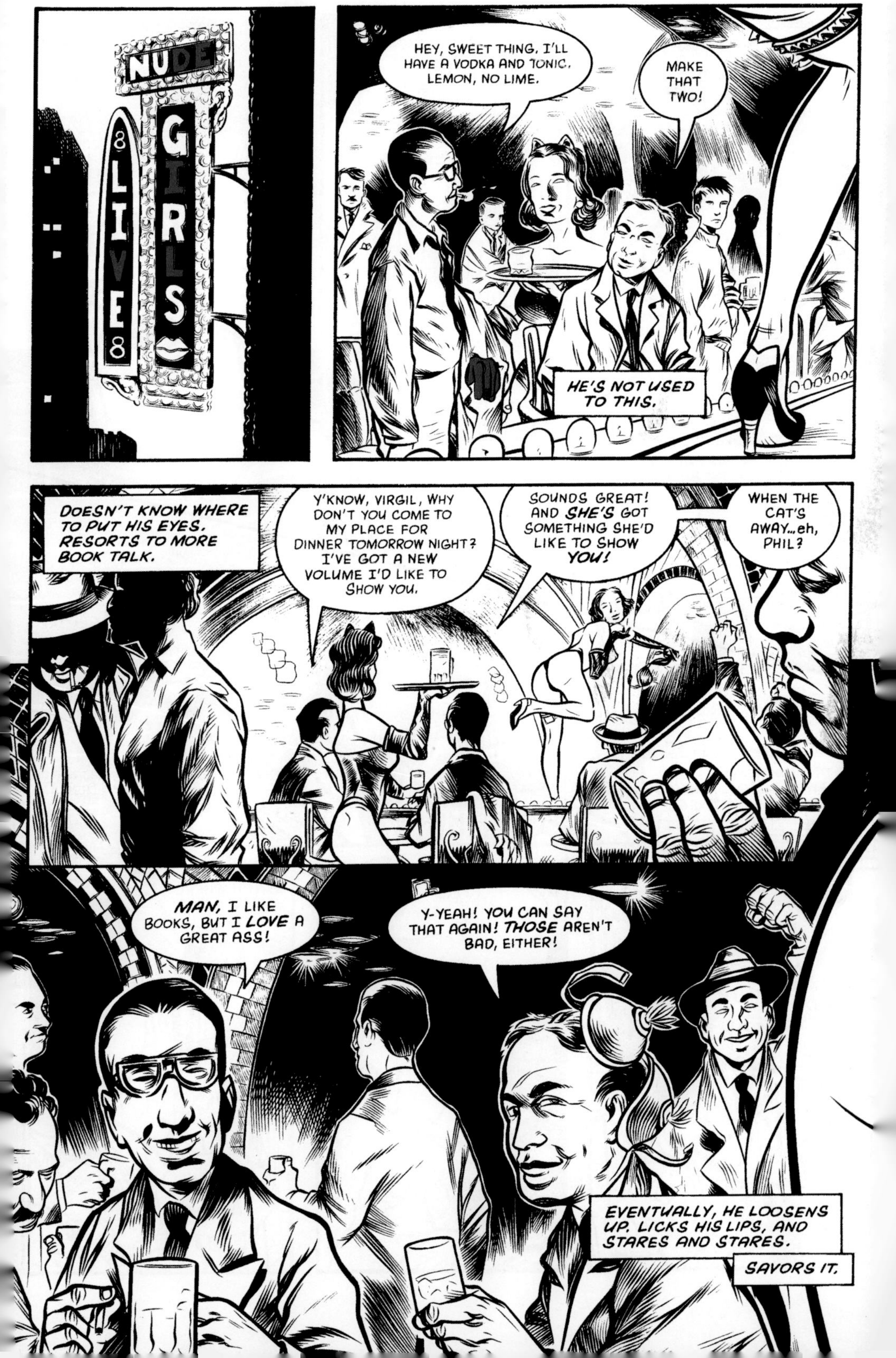
NUDE
LIVE
GIRLS
HEY, SWEET THING, I'LL HAVE A VODKA AND TONIC. LEMON, NO LIME.
MAKE THAT TWO!
HE'S NOT USED TO THIS.
DOESN'T KNOW WHERE TO PUT HIS EYES. RESORTS TO MORE BOOK TALK.
Y'KNOW, VIRGIL, WHY DON'T YOU COME TO MY PLACE FOR DINNER TOMORROW NIGHT? I'VE GOT A NEW VOLUME I'D LIKE TO SHOW YOU.
SOUNDS GREAT! AND SHE'S GOT SOMETHING SHE'D LIKE TO SHOW YOU!
WHEN THE CAT'S AWAY...eh, PHIL?
MAN, I LIKE BOOKS, BUT I LOVE A GREAT ASS!
Y-YEAH! YOU CAN SAY THAT AGAIN! THOSE AREN'T BAD, EITHER!
EVENTUALLY, HE LOOSENS UP. LICKS HIS LIPS, AND STARES AND STARES.
SAVORS IT.

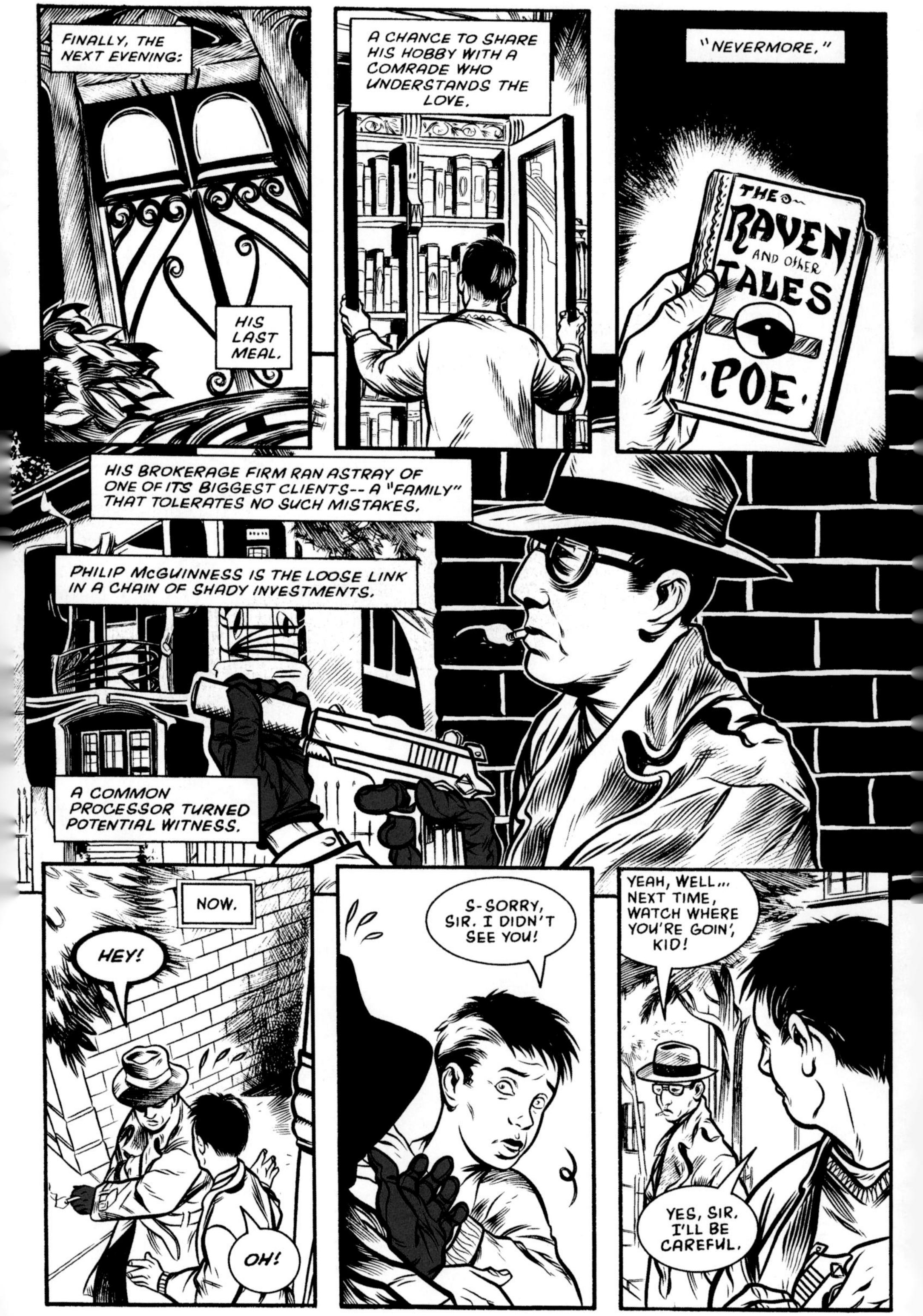
FINALLY, THE NEXT EVENING:
HIS LAST MEAL.
A CHANCE TO SHARE HIS HOBBY WITH A COMRADE WHO UNDERSTANDS THE LOVE.
"NEVERMORE."
THE RAVEN AND OTHER TALES POE
HIS BROKERAGE FIRM RAN ASTRAY OF ONE OF ITS BIGGEST CLIENTS-- A "FAMILY" THAT TOLERATES NO SUCH MISTAKES.
PHILIP McGUINNESS IS THE LOOSE LINK IN A CHAIN OF SHADY INVESTMENTS.
A COMMON PROCESSOR TURNED POTENTIAL WITNESS.
NOW.
HEY!
OH!
S-SORRY, SIR. I DIDN'T SEE YOU!
YEAH, WELL... NEXT TIME, WATCH WHERE YOU'RE GOIN', KID!
YES, SIR. I'LL BE CAREFUL.

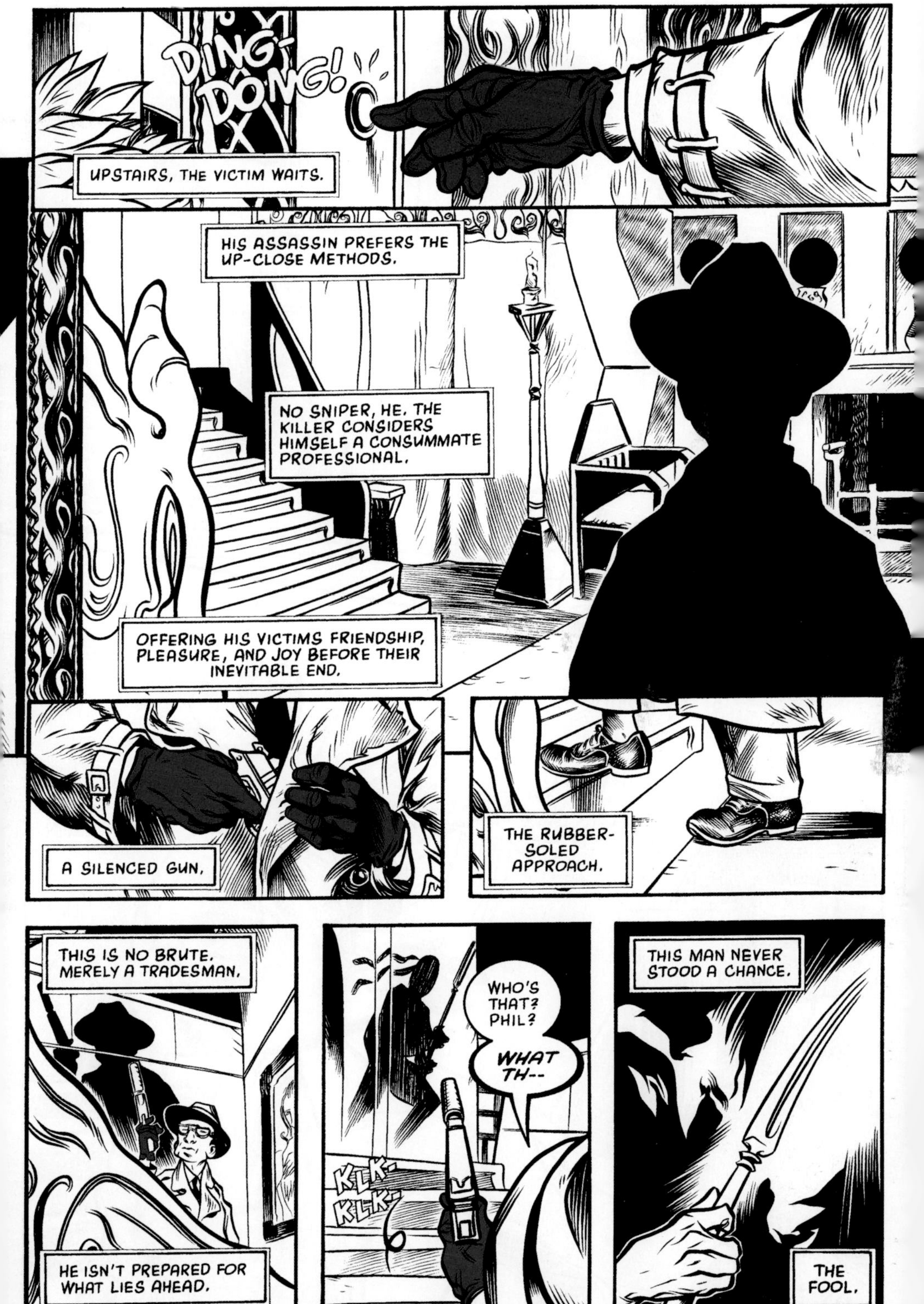
DING-DONG!
UPSTAIRS, THE VICTIM WAITS.
HIS ASSASSIN PREFERS THE UP-CLOSE METHODS.
NO SNIPER, HE. THE KILLER CONSIDERS HIMSELF A CONSUMMATE PROFESSIONAL.
OFFERING HIS VICTIMS FRIENDSHIP, PLEASURE, AND JOY BEFORE THEIR INEVITABLE END.
A SILENCED GUN.
THE RUBBER-SOLED APPROACH.
THIS IS NO BRUTE. MERELY A TRADESMAN.
HE ISN'T PREPARED FOR WHAT LIES AHEAD.
WHO'S THAT? PHIL?
WHAT TH--
KLK-KLK-
THIS MAN NEVER STOOD A CHANCE.
THE FOOL.

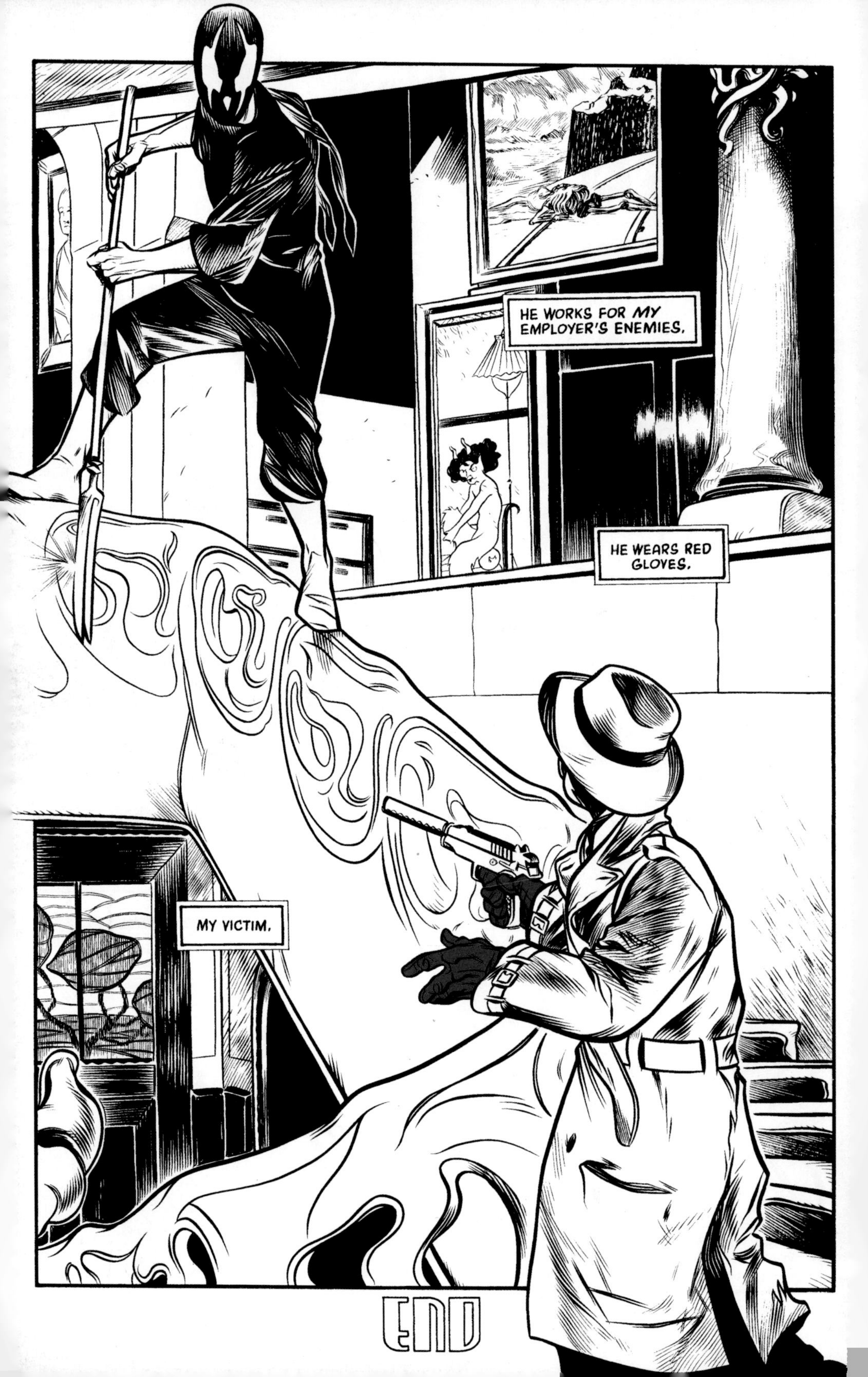
HE WORKS FOR MY EMPLOYER'S ENEMIES.
HE WEARS RED GLOVES.
MY VICTIM.
END

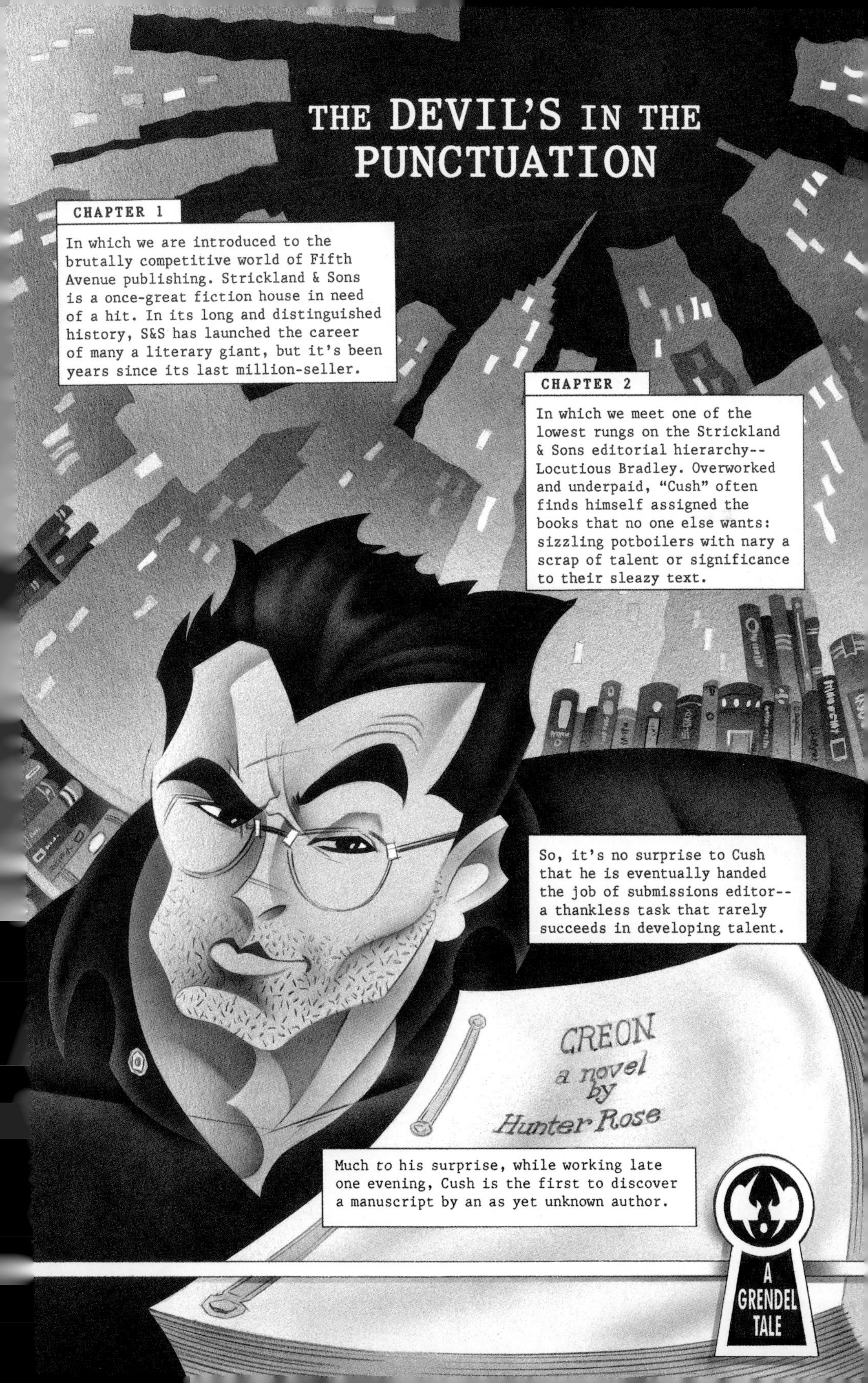
THE DEVIL'S IN THE PUNCTUATION
CHAPTER 1
In which we are introduced to the brutally competitive world of Fifth Avenue publishing. Strickland & Sons is a once-great fiction house in need of a hit. In its long and distinguished history, S&S has launched the career of many a literary giant, but it's been years since its last million-seller.
CHAPTER 2
In which we meet one of the lowest rungs on the Strickland & Sons editorial hierarchy--Locutious Bradley. Overworked and underpaid, "Cush" often finds himself assigned the books that no one else wants: sizzling potboilers with nary a scrap of talent or significance to their sleazy text.
So, it's no surprise to Cush that he is eventually handed the job of submissions editor--a thankless task that rarely succeeds in developing talent.
CREON
a novel
by
Hunter Rose
Much *to* his surprise, while working late one evening, Cush is the first to discover a manuscript by an as yet unknown author.
A GRENDEL TALE

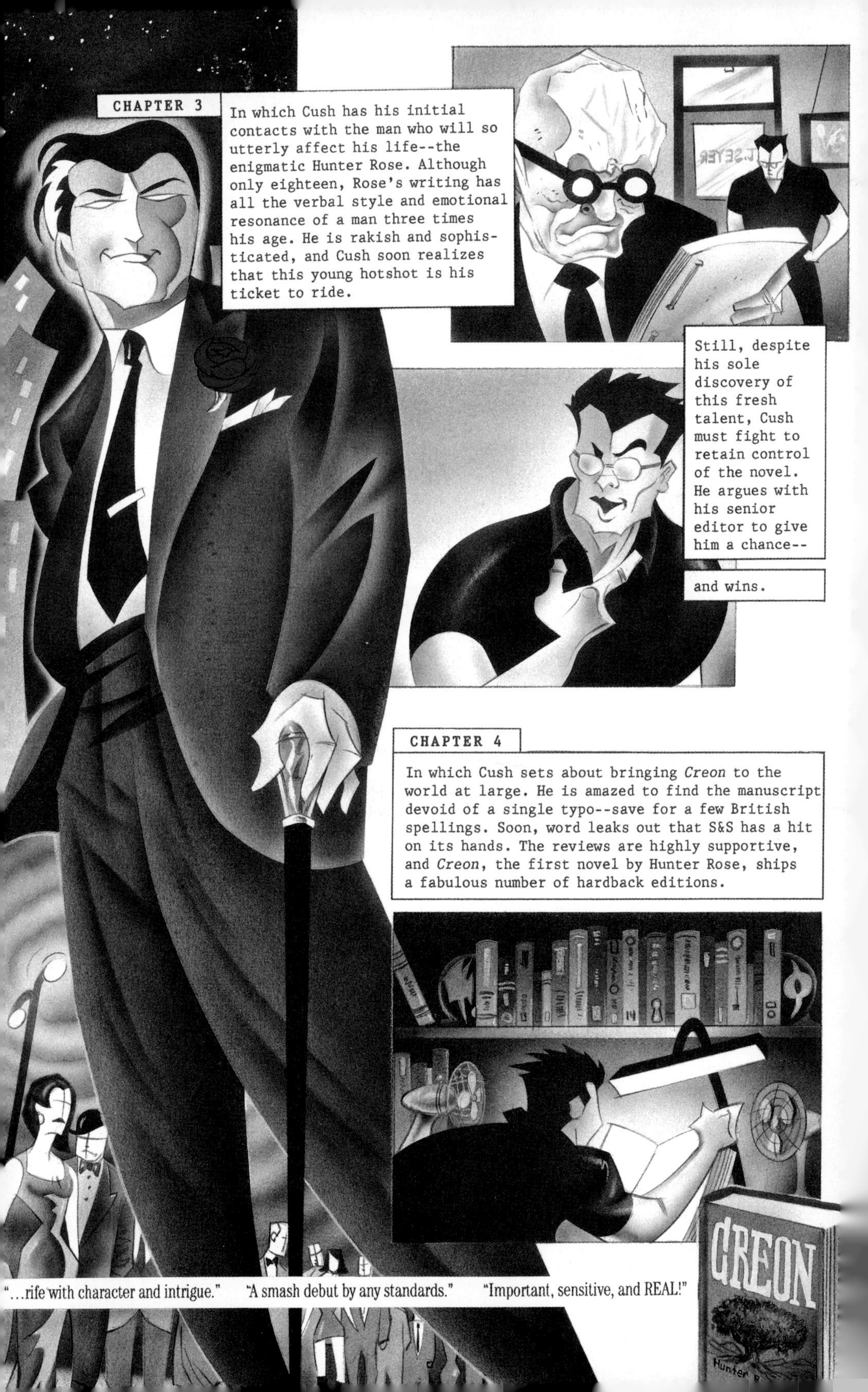
CHAPTER 3
In which Cush has his initial contacts with the man who will so utterly affect his life--the enigmatic Hunter Rose. Although only eighteen, Rose's writing has all the verbal style and emotional resonance of a man three times his age. He is rakish and sophisticated, and Cush soon realizes that this young hotshot is his ticket to ride.
Still, despite his sole discovery of this fresh talent, Cush must fight to retain control of the novel. He argues with his senior editor to give him a chance--
and wins.
CHAPTER 4
In which Cush sets about bringing *Creon* to the world at large. He is amazed to find the manuscript devoid of a single typo--save for a few British spellings. Soon, word leaks out that S&S has a hit on its hands. The reviews are highly supportive, and *Creon*, the first novel by Hunter Rose, ships a fabulous number of hardback editions.
"...rife with character and intrigue."
"A smash debut by any standards."
"Important, sensitive, and REAL!"
CREON

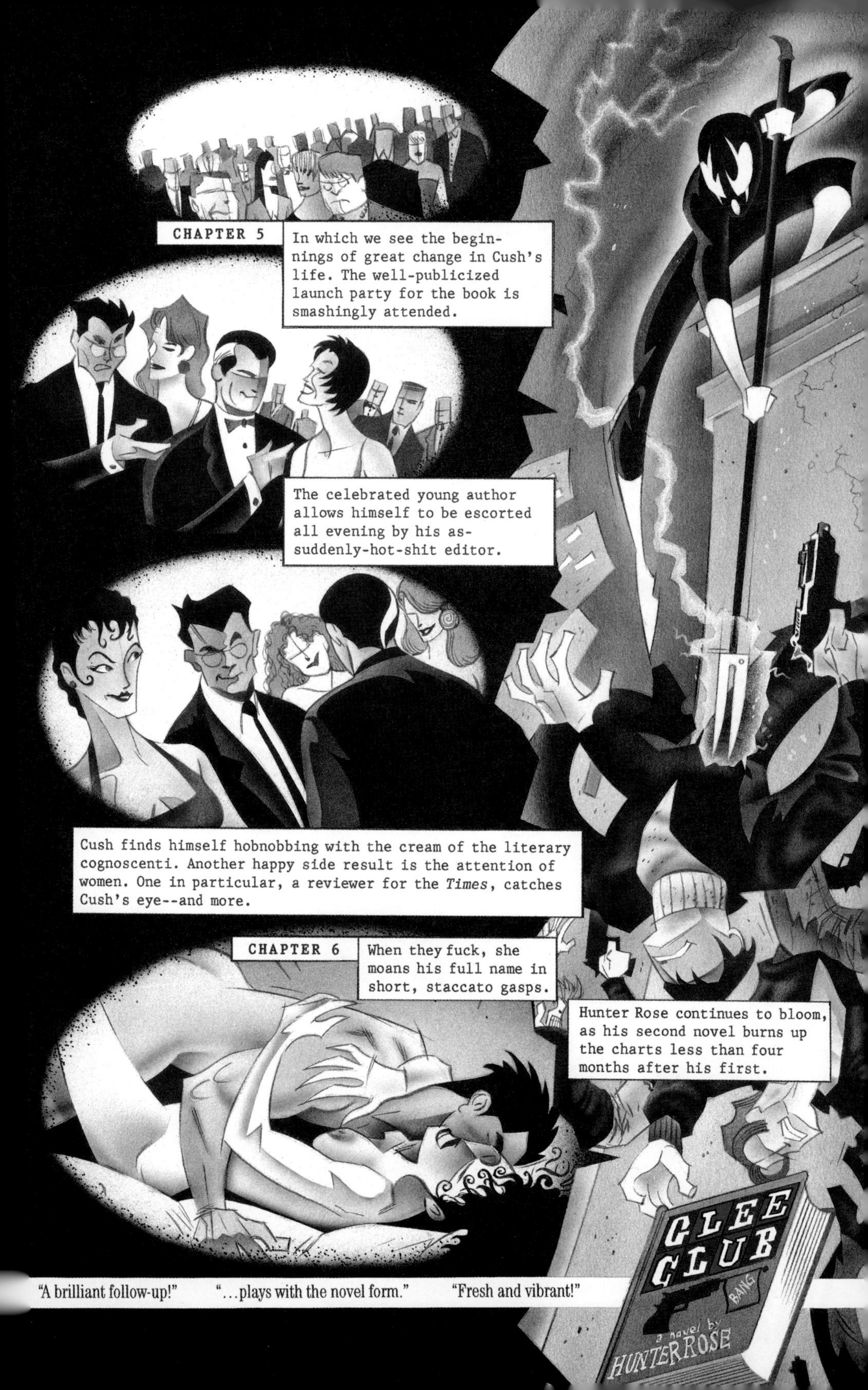
CHAPTER 5
In which we see the beginnings of great change in Cush's life. The well-publicized launch party for the book is smashingly attended.
The celebrated young author allows himself to be escorted all evening by his as-suddenly-hot-shit editor.
Cush finds himself hobnobbing with the cream of the literary cognoscenti. Another happy side result is the attention of women. One in particular, a reviewer for the *Times*, catches Cush's eye--and more.
CHAPTER 6
When they fuck, she moans his full name in short, staccato gasps.
Hunter Rose continues to bloom, as his second novel burns up the charts less than four months after his first.
"A brilliant follow-up!"
"...plays with the novel form."
"Fresh and vibrant!"
GLEE CLUB
BANG
a novel by
HUNTER ROSE

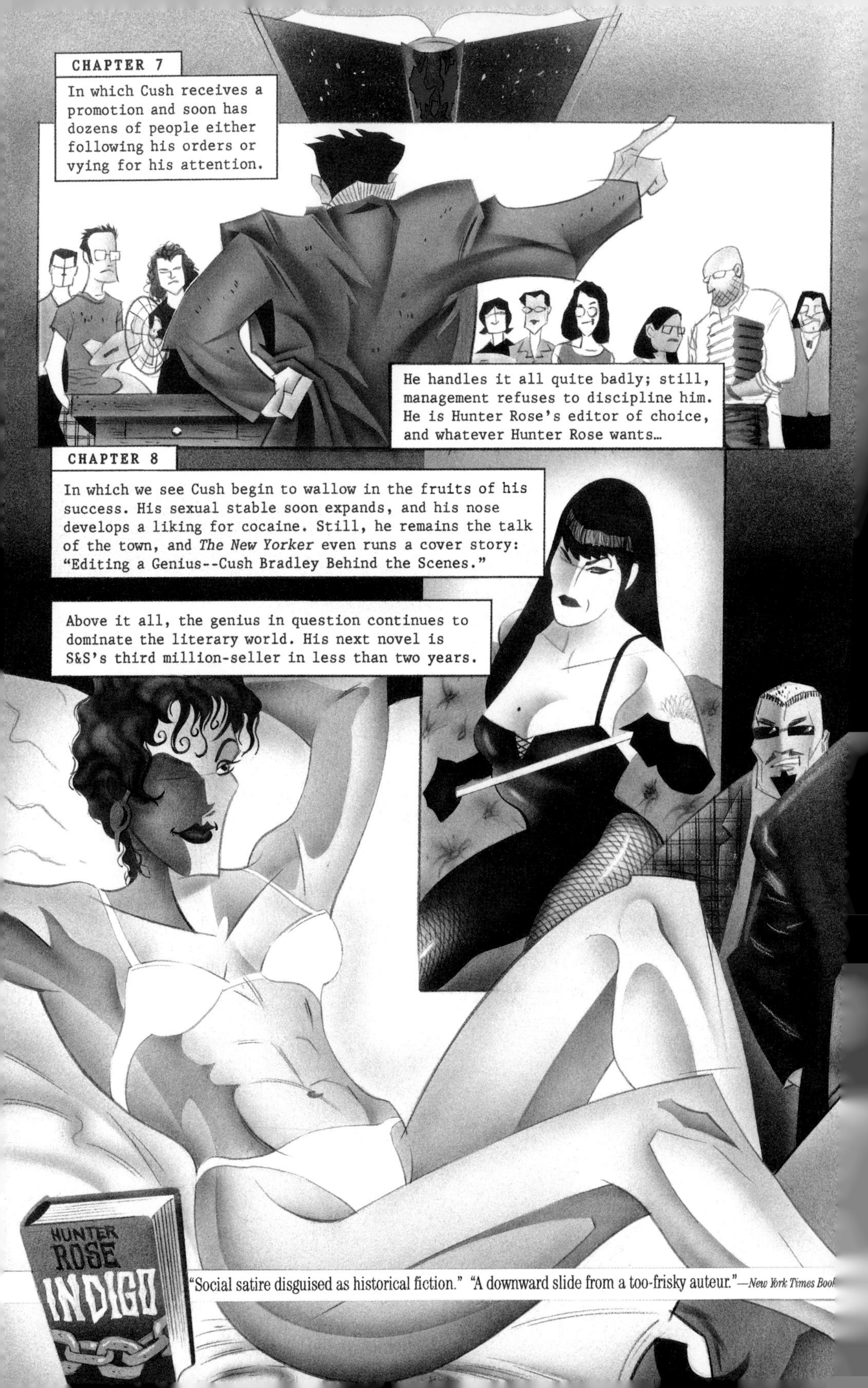
CHAPTER 7
In which Cush receives a promotion and soon has dozens of people either following his orders or vying for his attention.
He handles it all quite badly; still, management refuses to discipline him. He is Hunter Rose's editor of choice, and whatever Hunter Rose wants...
CHAPTER 8
In which we see Cush begin to wallow in the fruits of his success. His sexual stable soon expands, and his nose develops a liking for cocaine. Still, he remains the talk of the town, and *The New Yorker* even runs a cover story: "Editing a Genius--Cush Bradley Behind the Scenes."
Above it all, the genius in question continues to dominate the literary world. His next novel is S&S's third million-seller in less than two years.
HUNTER ROSE
INDIGO
"Social satire disguised as historical fiction." "A downward slide from a too-frisky auteur."—New York Times Book

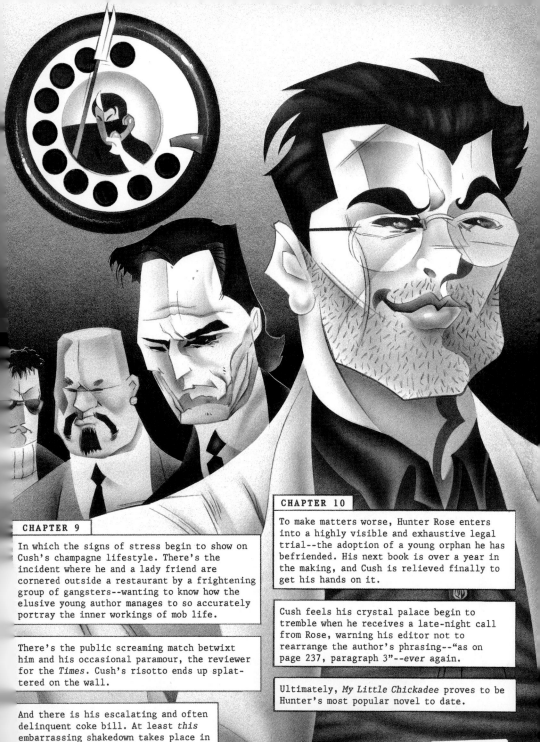

CHAPTER 9

In which the signs of stress begin to show on Cush's champagne lifestyle. There's the incident where he and a lady friend are cornered outside a restaurant by a frightening group of gangsters--wanting to know how the elusive young author manages to so accurately portray the inner workings of mob life.

There's the public screaming match betwixt him and his occasional paramour, the reviewer for the *Times*. Cush's risotto ends up splattered on the wall.

And there is his escalating and often delinquent coke bill. At least *this* embarrassing shakedown takes place in private--but *far* scarier.

CHAPTER 10

To make matters worse, Hunter Rose enters into a highly visible and exhaustive legal trial--the adoption of a young orphan he has befriended. His next book is over a year in the making, and Cush is relieved finally to get his hands on it.

Cush feels his crystal palace begin to tremble when he receives a late-night call from Rose, warning his editor not to rearrange the author's phrasing--"as on page 237, paragraph 3"--*ever* again.

Ultimately, *My Little Chickadee* proves to be Hunter's most popular novel to date.

eting, exhilarating, and fresh!"   "Grabs hold with a vengeance…"   "Overwrought and self-serving."

ROSE
My Little
CHICK
A
DEE

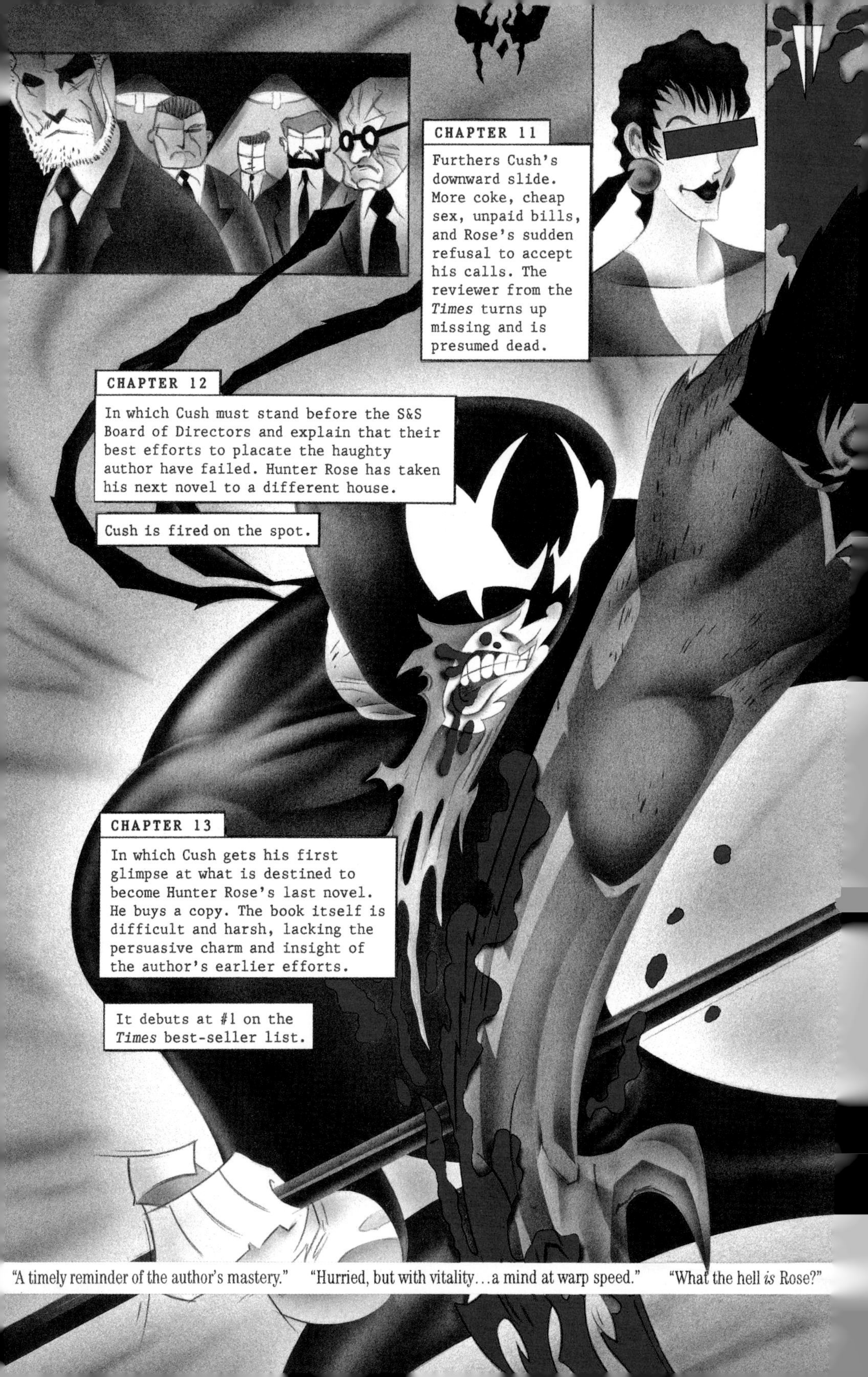
CHAPTER 11
Furthers Cush's downward slide. More coke, cheap sex, unpaid bills, and Rose's sudden refusal to accept his calls. The reviewer from the *Times* turns up missing and is presumed dead.
CHAPTER 12
In which Cush must stand before the S&S Board of Directors and explain that their best efforts to placate the haughty author have failed. Hunter Rose has taken his next novel to a different house.
Cush is fired on the spot.
CHAPTER 13
In which Cush gets his first glimpse at what is destined to become Hunter Rose's last novel. He buys a copy. The book itself is difficult and harsh, lacking the persuasive charm and insight of the author's earlier efforts.
It debuts at #1 on the *Times* best-seller list.
"A timely reminder of the author's mastery."
"Hurried, but with vitality...a mind at warp speed."
"What the hell *is* Rose?"

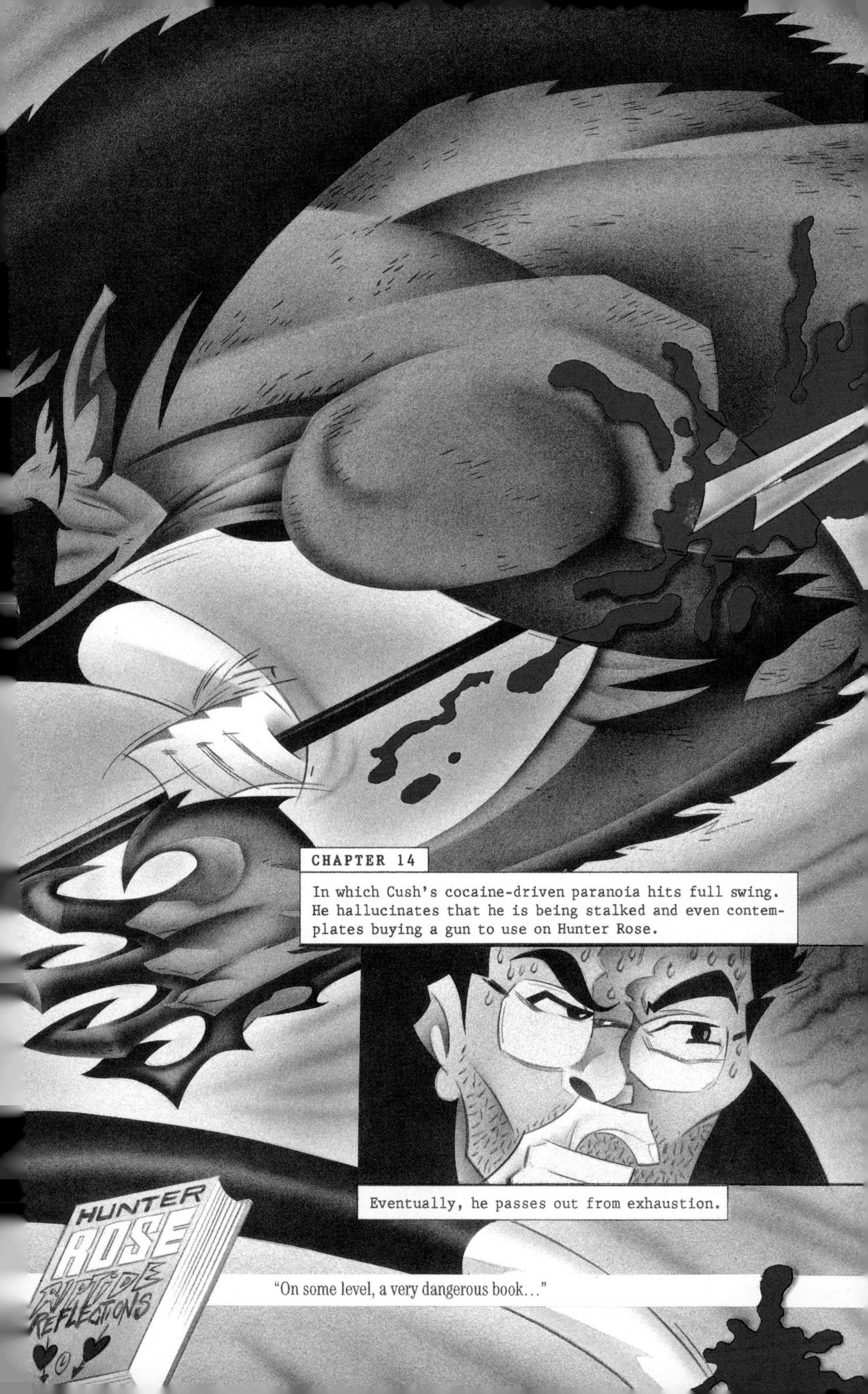
CHAPTER 14
In which Cush's cocaine-driven paranoia hits full swing. He hallucinates that he is being stalked and even contemplates buying a gun to use on Hunter Rose.
Eventually, he passes out from exhaustion.
HUNTER ROSE RIPTIDE REFLECTIONS
"On some level, a very dangerous book..."

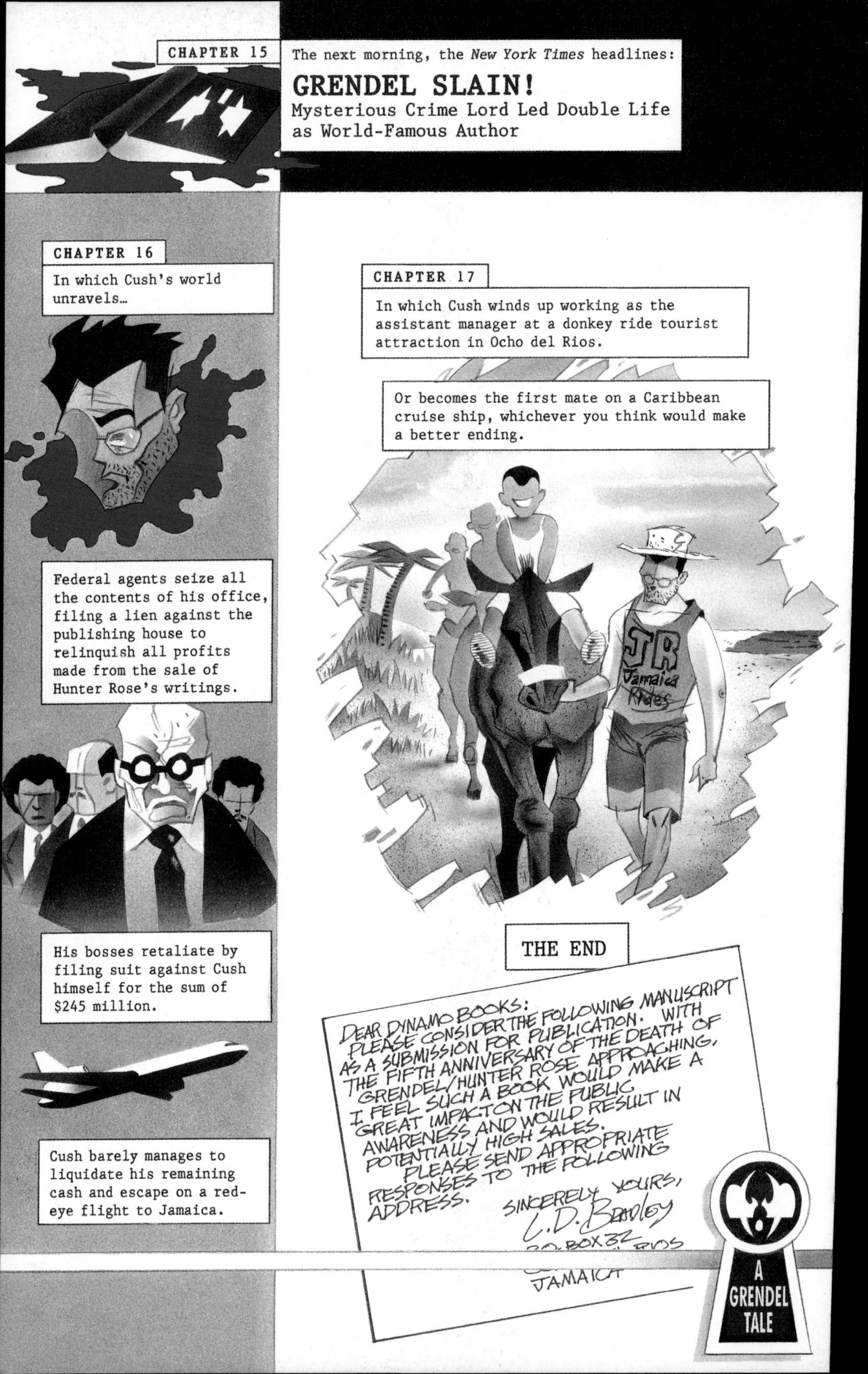
CHAPTER 15
The next morning, the *New York Times* headlines:
GRENDEL SLAIN!
Mysterious Crime Lord Led Double Life as World-Famous Author
CHAPTER 16
In which Cush's world unravels…
Federal agents seize all the contents of his office, filing a lien against the publishing house to relinquish all profits made from the sale of Hunter Rose's writings.
His bosses retaliate by filing suit against Cush himself for the sum of $245 million.
Cush barely manages to liquidate his remaining cash and escape on a red-eye flight to Jamaica.
CHAPTER 17
In which Cush winds up working as the assistant manager at a donkey ride tourist attraction in Ocho del Rios.
Or becomes the first mate on a Caribbean cruise ship, whichever you think would make a better ending.
JR
Jamaica Rides
THE END
DEAR DYNAMO BOOKS:
PLEASE CONSIDER THE FOLLOWING MANUSCRIPT AS A SUBMISSION FOR PUBLICATION. WITH THE FIFTH ANNIVERSARY OF THE DEATH OF GRENDEL/HUNTER ROSE APPROACHING, I FEEL SUCH A BOOK WOULD MAKE A GREAT IMPACT ON THE PUBLIC AWARENESS AND WOULD RESULT IN POTENTIALLY HIGH SALES.
PLEASE SEND APPROPRIATE RESPONSES TO THE FOLLOWING ADDRESS.
SINCERELY YOURS,
L.D. Bradley
P.O. BOX 32
JAMAICA
A GRENDEL TALE

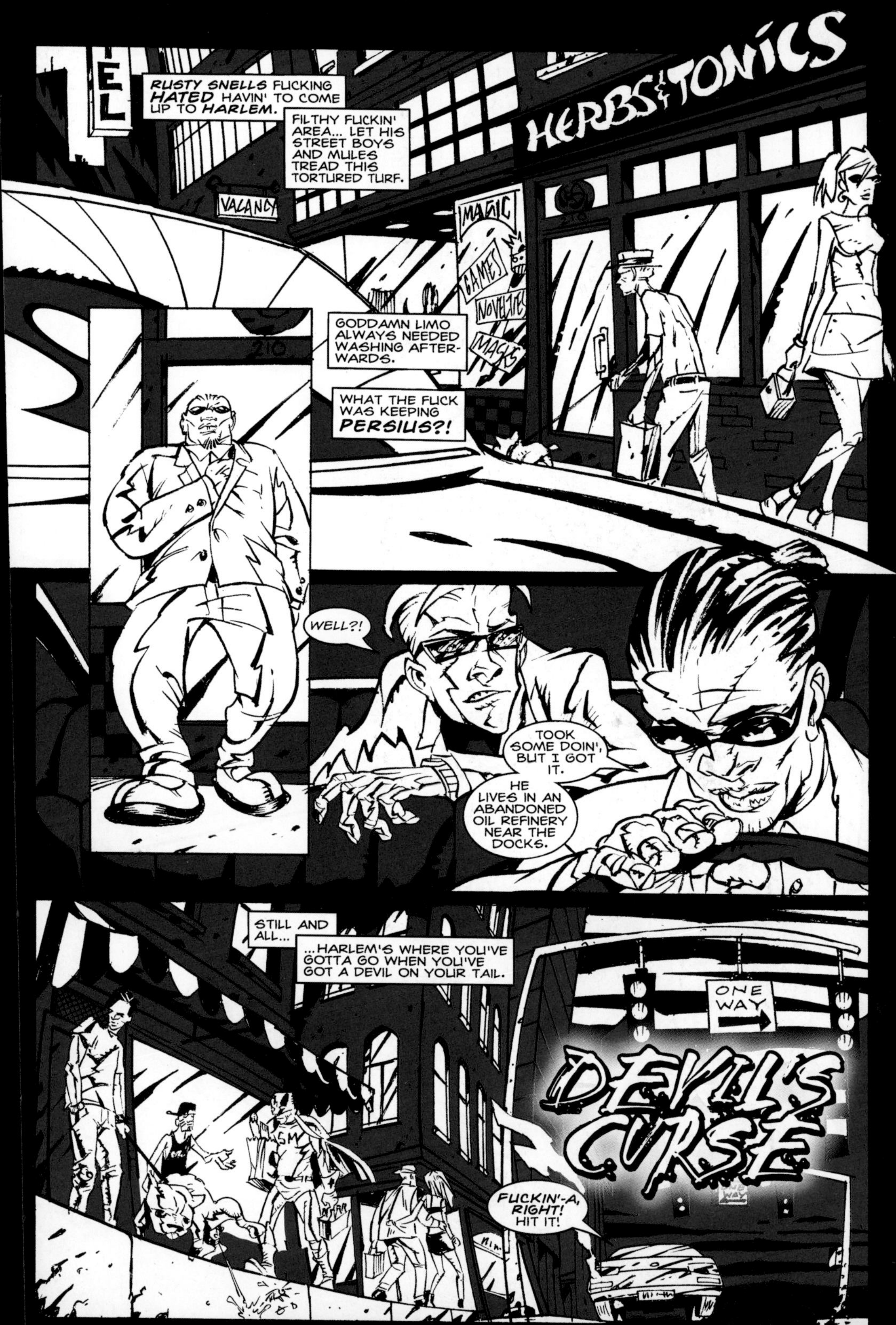
HERBS & TONICS
RUSTY SNELLS FUCKING HATED HAVIN' TO COME UP TO HARLEM.
FILTHY FUCKIN' AREA... LET HIS STREET BOYS AND MULES TREAD THIS TORTURED TURF.
VACANCY
MAGIC
GAMES
NOVELTIES
MASKS
GODDAMN LIMO ALWAYS NEEDED WASHING AFTER-WARDS.
WHAT THE FUCK WAS KEEPING PERSIUS?!
WELL?!
TOOK SOME DOIN', BUT I GOT IT.
HE LIVES IN AN ABANDONED OIL REFINERY NEAR THE DOCKS.
STILL AND ALL...
...HARLEM'S WHERE YOU'VE GOTTA GO WHEN YOU'VE GOT A DEVIL ON YOUR TAIL.
ONE WAY
DEVIL'S CURSE
FUCKIN'-A, RIGHT! HIT IT!

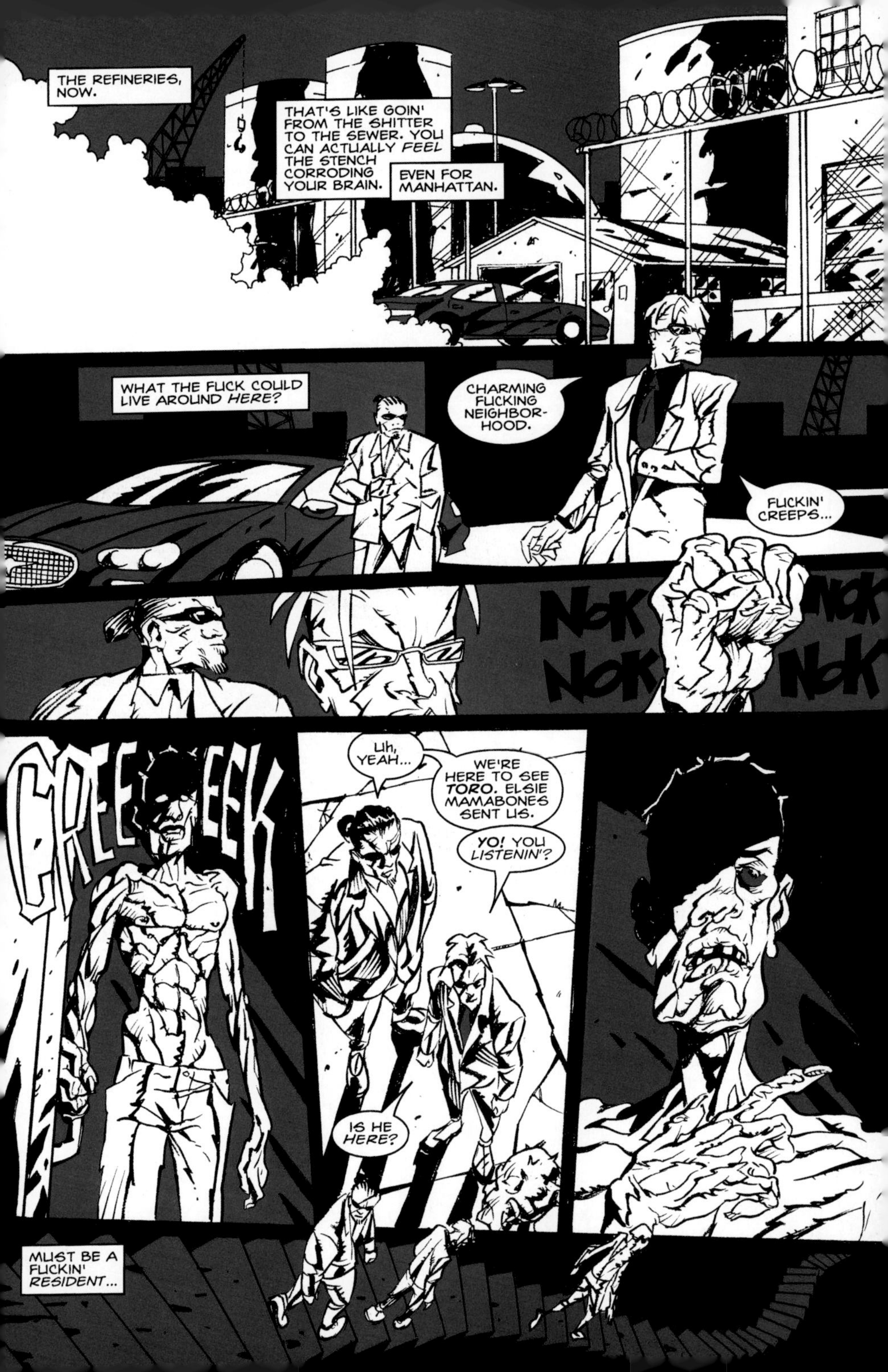
THE REFINERIES, NOW.
THAT'S LIKE GOIN' FROM THE SHITTER TO THE SEWER. YOU CAN ACTUALLY FEEL THE STENCH CORRODING YOUR BRAIN.
EVEN FOR MANHATTAN.
WHAT THE FUCK COULD LIVE AROUND HERE?
CHARMING FUCKING NEIGHBOR-HOOD.
FUCKIN' CREEPS...
NOK NOK NOK NOK
CREEEEK
UH, YEAH...
WE'RE HERE TO SEE TORO. ELSIE MAMABONES SENT US.
YO! YOU LISTENIN'?
IS HE HERE?
MUST BE A FUCKIN' RESIDENT...

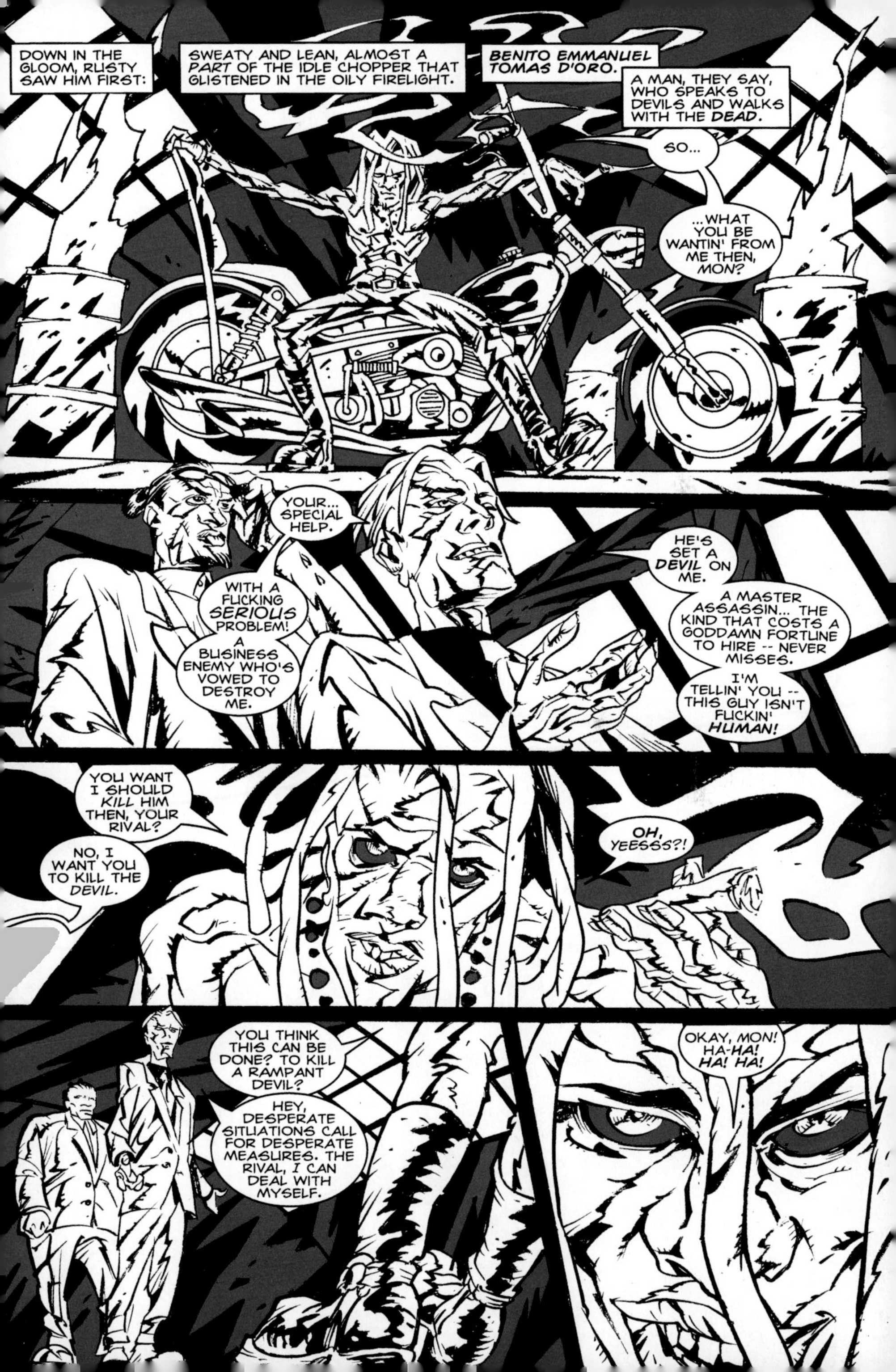

DOWN IN THE GLOOM, RUSTY SAW HIM FIRST:
SWEATY AND LEAN, ALMOST A *PART* OF THE IDLE CHOPPER THAT GLISTENED IN THE OILY FIRELIGHT.
BENITO EMMANUEL TOMAS D'ORO.
A MAN, THEY SAY, WHO SPEAKS TO DEVILS AND WALKS WITH THE *DEAD*.
SO...
...WHAT YOU BE WANTIN' FROM ME THEN, *MON?*
YOUR... SPECIAL HELP.
WITH A FUCKING ***SERIOUS*** PROBLEM!
A BUSINESS ENEMY WHO'S VOWED TO DESTROY ME.
HE'S SET A ***DEVIL*** ON ME.
A MASTER ASSASSIN... THE KIND THAT COSTS A GODDAMN FORTUNE TO HIRE -- NEVER MISSES.
I'M TELLIN' YOU -- THIS GUY ISN'T FUCKIN' ***HUMAN!***
YOU WANT I SHOULD *KILL* HIM THEN, YOUR RIVAL?
NO, I WANT YOU TO KILL THE *DEVIL*.
OH, *YEESSS?!*
YOU THINK THIS CAN BE DONE? TO KILL A RAMPANT DEVIL?
HEY, DESPERATE SITUATIONS CALL FOR DESPERATE MEASURES. THE RIVAL, *I* CAN DEAL WITH MYSELF.
OKAY, MON! HA-***HA!*** ***HA! HA!***

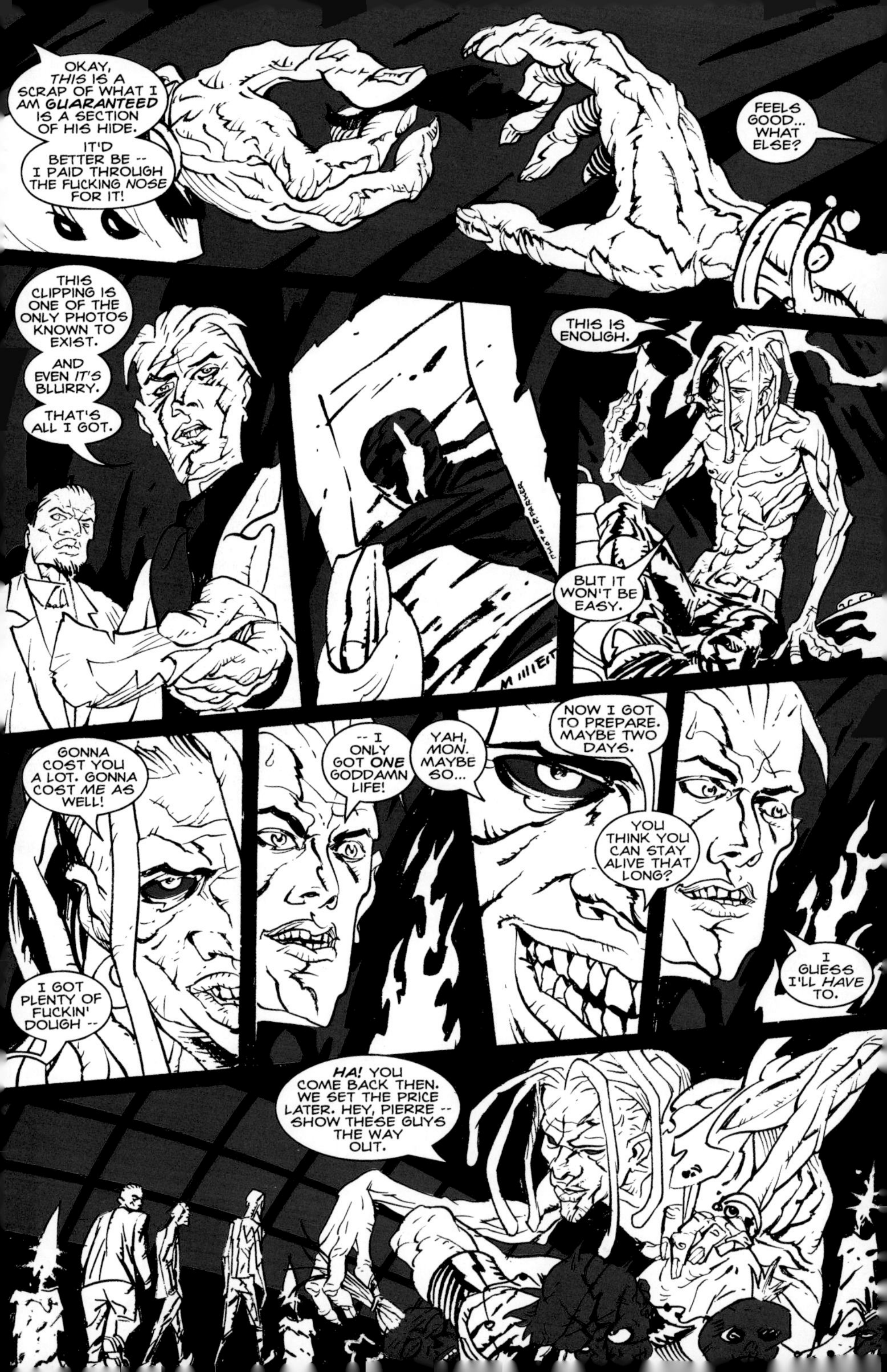

OKAY, THIS IS A SCRAP OF WHAT I AM GUARANTEED IS A SECTION OF HIS HIDE.
IT'D BETTER BE -- I PAID THROUGH THE FUCKING NOSE FOR IT!
FEELS GOOD... WHAT ELSE?
THIS CLIPPING IS ONE OF THE ONLY PHOTOS KNOWN TO EXIST.
AND EVEN IT'S BLURRY.
THAT'S ALL I GOT.
THIS IS ENOUGH.
BUT IT WON'T BE EASY.
GONNA COST YOU A LOT. GONNA COST ME AS WELL!
I GOT PLENTY OF FUCKIN' DOUGH --
-- I ONLY GOT ONE GODDAMN LIFE!
YAH, MON. MAYBE SO...
NOW I GOT TO PREPARE. MAYBE TWO DAYS.
YOU THINK YOU CAN STAY ALIVE THAT LONG?
I GUESS I'LL HAVE TO.
HA! YOU COME BACK THEN. WE SET THE PRICE LATER. HEY, PIERRE -- SHOW THESE GUYS THE WAY OUT.

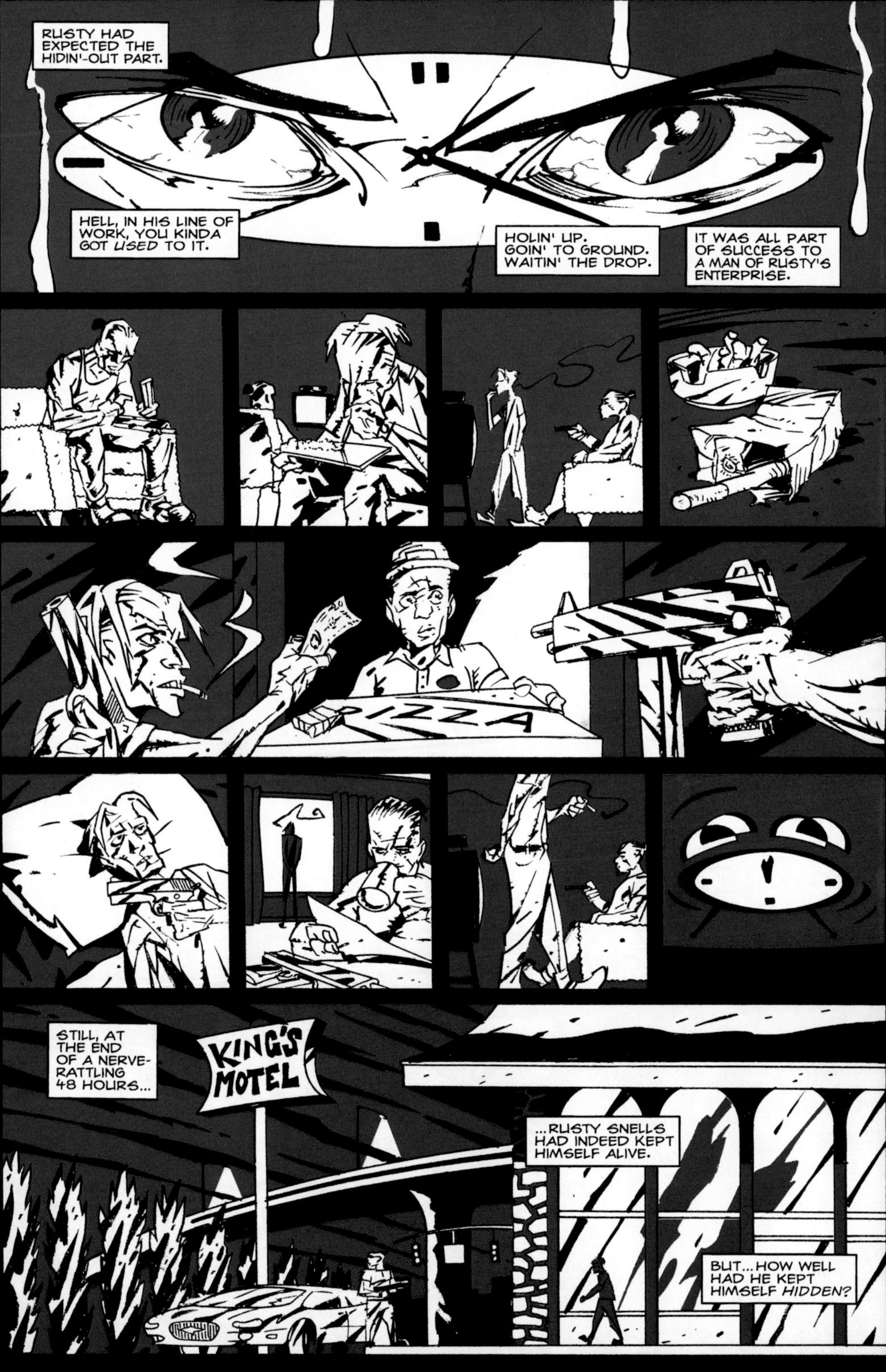
RUSTY HAD EXPECTED THE HIDIN'-OUT PART.
HELL, IN HIS LINE OF WORK, YOU KINDA GOT *USED* TO IT.
HOLIN' UP. GOIN' TO GROUND. WAITIN' THE DROP.
IT WAS ALL PART OF SUCCESS TO A MAN OF RUSTY'S ENTERPRISE.
PIZZA
STILL, AT THE END OF A NERVE-RATTLING 48 HOURS...
KING'S MOTEL
...RUSTY SNELLS HAD INDEED KEPT HIMSELF ALIVE.
BUT...HOW WELL HAD HE KEPT HIMSELF *HIDDEN*?

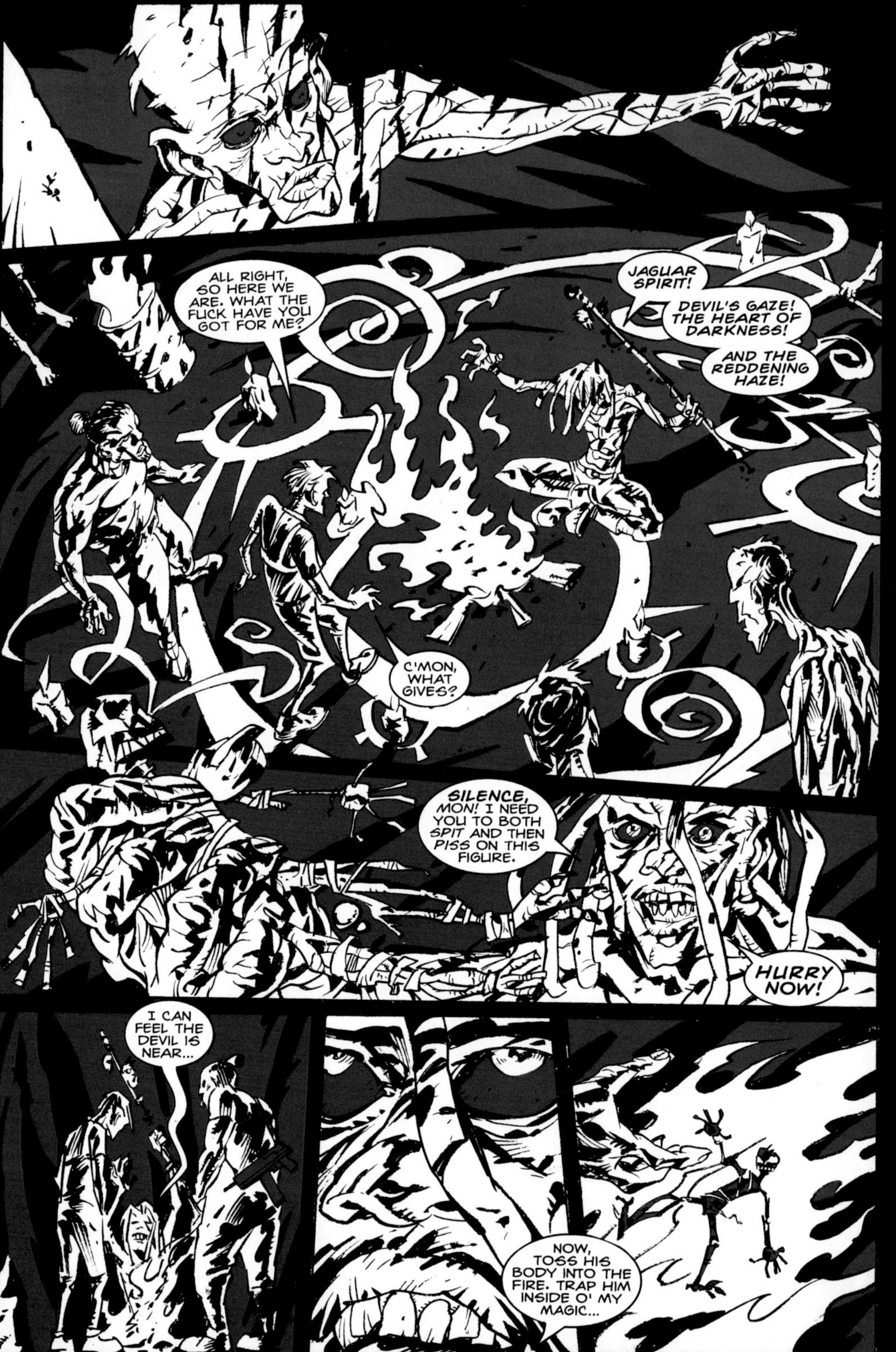
ALL RIGHT, SO HERE WE ARE. WHAT THE FUCK HAVE YOU GOT FOR ME?
JAGUAR SPIRIT!
DEVIL'S GAZE! THE HEART OF DARKNESS!
AND THE REDDENING HAZE!
C'MON, WHAT GIVES?
SILENCE, MON! I NEED YOU TO BOTH SPIT AND THEN PISS ON THIS FIGURE.
HURRY NOW!
I CAN FEEL THE DEVIL IS NEAR...
NOW, TOSS HIS BODY INTO THE FIRE. TRAP HIM INSIDE O' MY MAGIC...

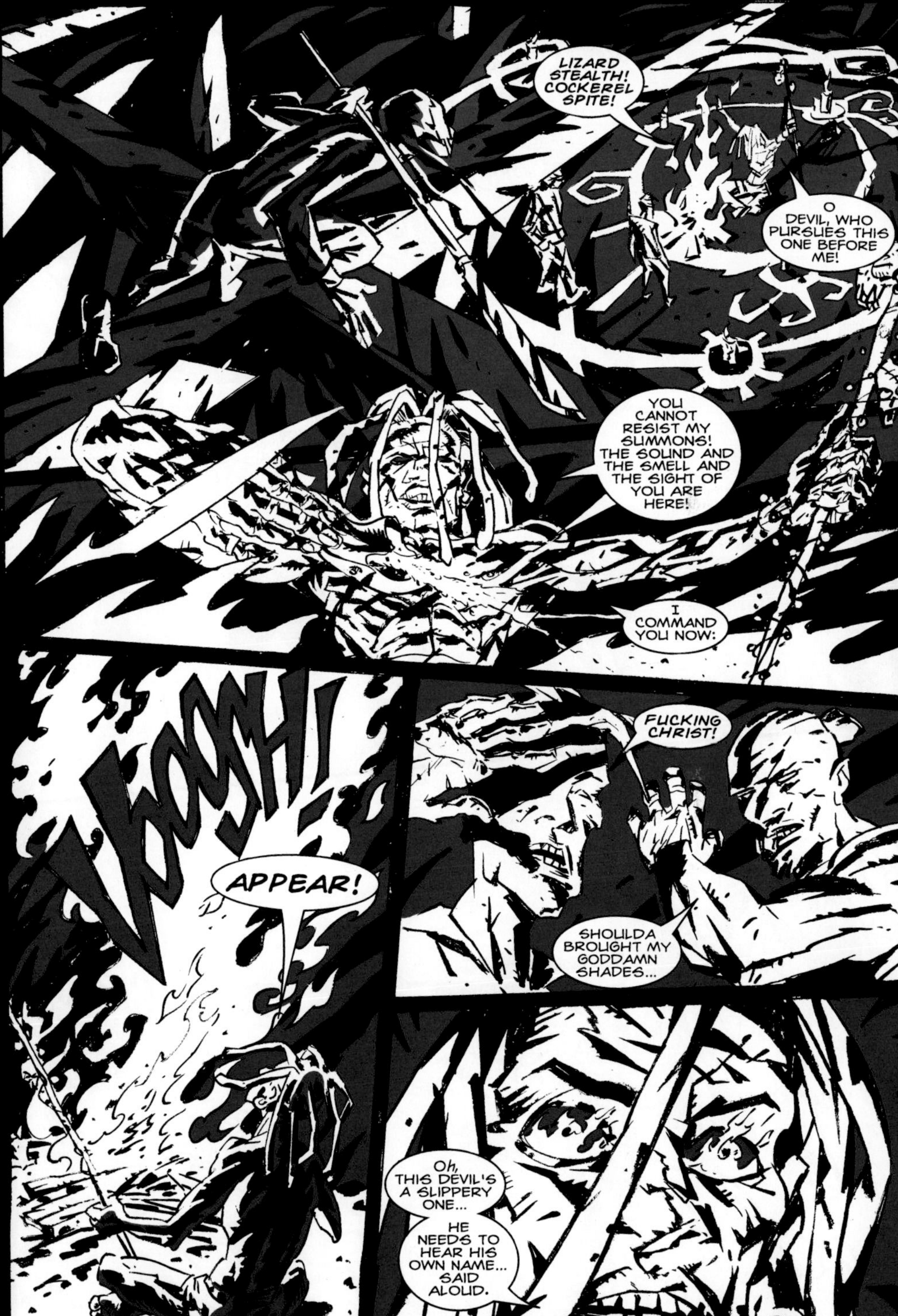
LIZARD STEALTH! COCKEREL SPITE!
O DEVIL, WHO PURSUES THIS ONE BEFORE ME!
YOU CANNOT RESIST MY SUMMONS! THE SOUND AND THE SMELL AND THE SIGHT OF YOU ARE HERE!
I COMMAND YOU NOW:
VOOSH!!
APPEAR!
FUCKING CHRIST!
SHOULDA BROUGHT MY GODDAMN SHADES...
Oh, THIS DEVIL'S A SLIPPERY ONE...
HE NEEDS TO HEAR HIS OWN NAME... SAID ALOUD.

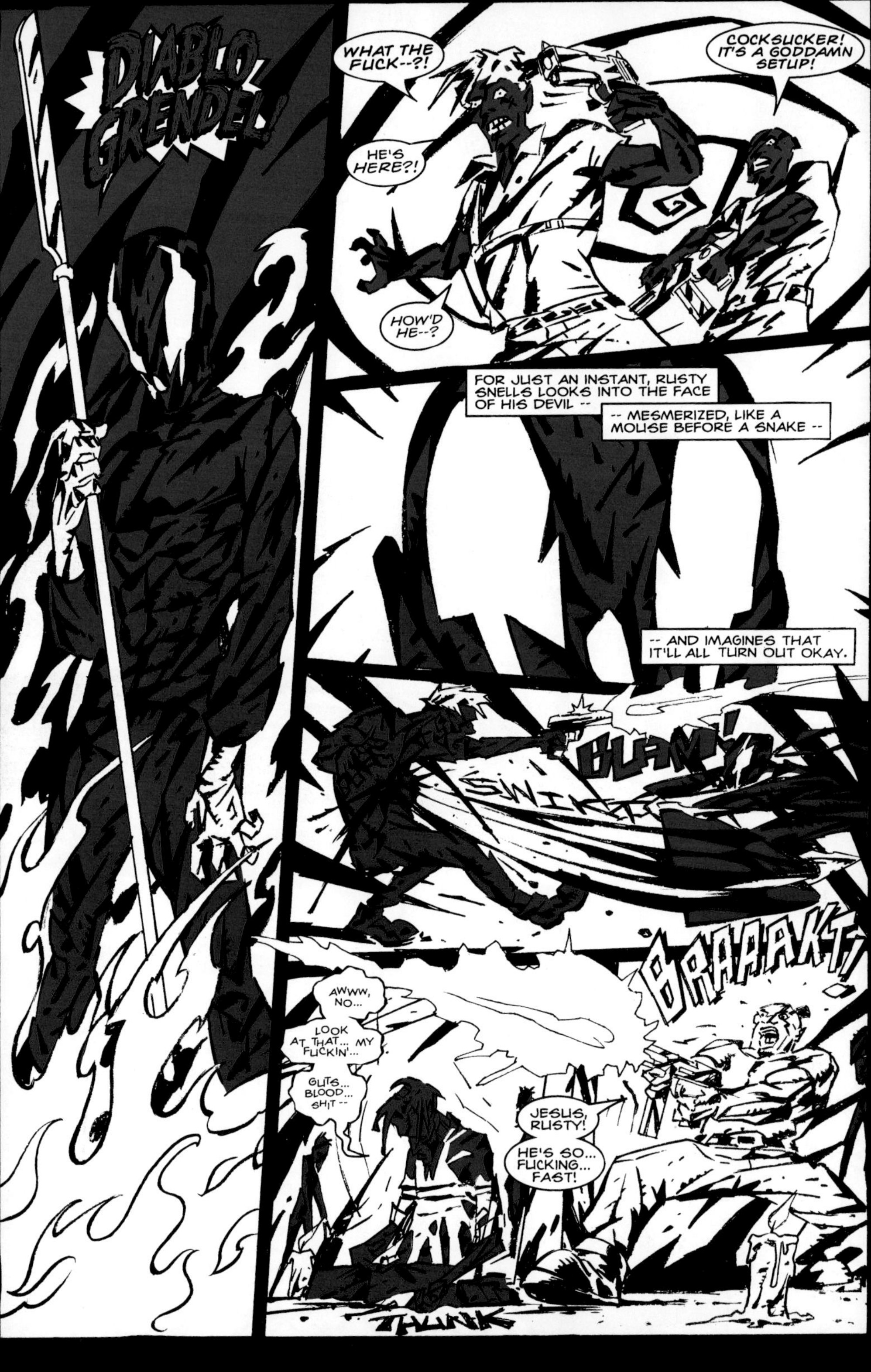
DIABLO GRENDEL!
WHAT THE FUCK--?!
COCKSUCKER! IT'S A GODDAMN SETUP!
HE'S HERE?!
HOW'D HE--?
FOR JUST AN INSTANT, RUSTY SNELLS LOOKS INTO THE FACE OF HIS DEVIL --
-- MESMERIZED, LIKE A MOUSE BEFORE A SNAKE --
-- AND IMAGINES THAT IT'LL ALL TURN OUT OKAY.
BLAM!
SWIFF
BRAAAKT!
AWWW, NO...
LOOK AT THAT... MY FUCKIN'...
GUTS... BLOOD... SHIT --
JESUS, RUSTY!
HE'S SO... FUCKING... FAST!
THUNK

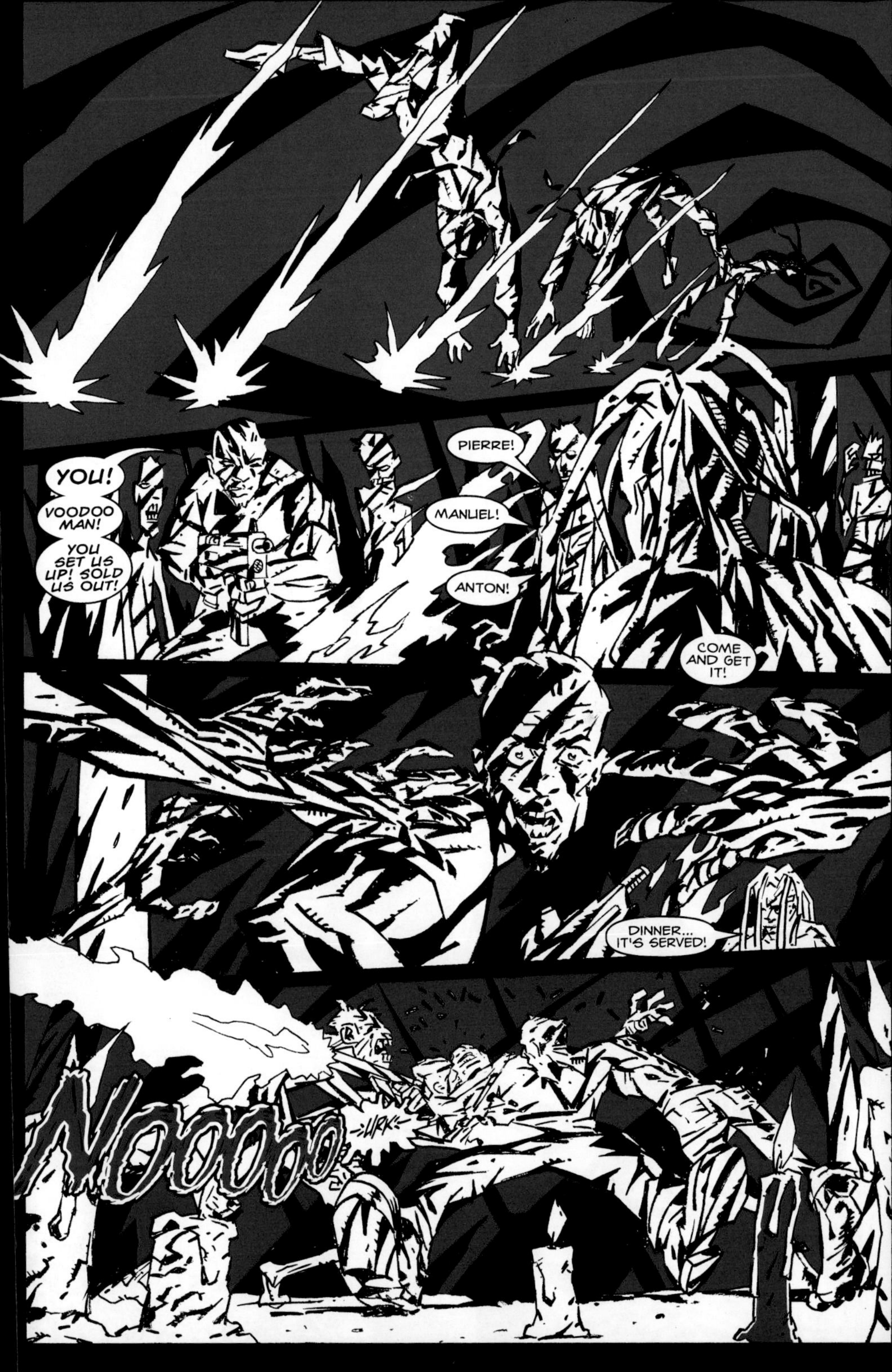
YOU!
VOODOO MAN!
YOU SET US UP! SOLD US OUT!
PIERRE!
MANUEL!
ANTON!
COME AND GET IT!
DINNER... IT'S SERVED!
NOOOOO
URK

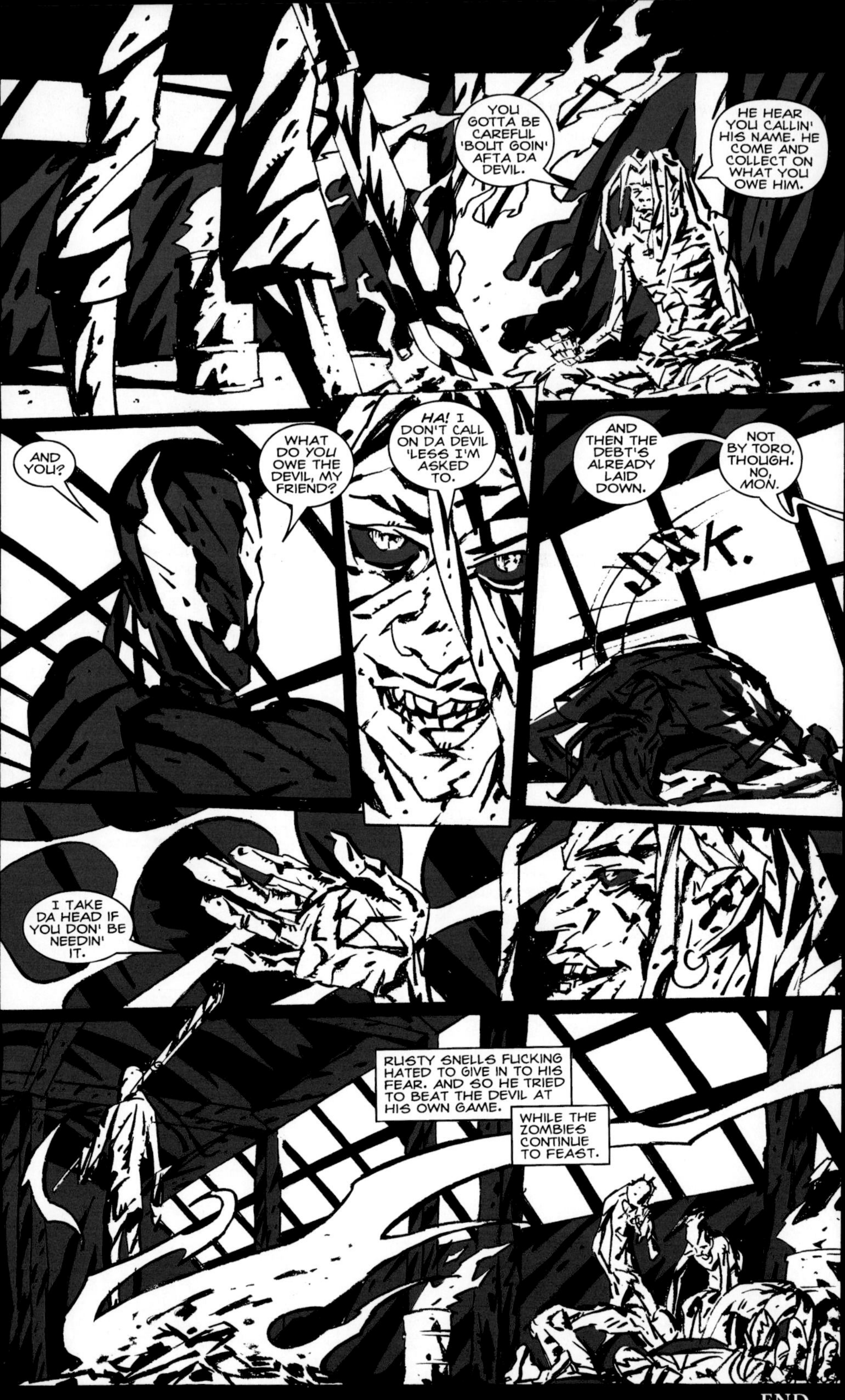
YOU GOTTA BE CAREFUL 'BOUT GOIN' AFTA DA DEVIL.
HE HEAR YOU CALLIN' HIS NAME. HE COME AND COLLECT ON WHAT YOU OWE HIM.
AND YOU?
WHAT DO YOU OWE THE DEVIL, MY FRIEND?
HA! I DON'T CALL ON DA DEVIL 'LESS I'M ASKED TO.
AND THEN THE DEBT'S ALREADY LAID DOWN.
NOT BY TORO, THOUGH. NO, MON.
DSK.
I TAKE DA HEAD IF YOU DON' BE NEEDIN' IT.
RUSTY SNELLS FUCKING HATED TO GIVE IN TO HIS FEAR. AND SO HE TRIED TO BEAT THE DEVIL AT HIS OWN GAME.
WHILE THE ZOMBIES CONTINUE TO FEAST.

END

Devil's Coup

BY
MATT WAGNER
AND
TIMOTHY BRADSTREET

CICCONE FAMILY UNDER INVESTIGATION

U.S. District Attorneys today announced their official investigation of the Ciccone crime family, whose underworld activities allegedly include racketeering, drug trafficking, prostitution, and weapons brokering. Although the Ciccones are commonly thought to be one of the major forces in the New York and Tri-State crime scene, police have thus far been unable to actually connect them to any evidence of wrongdoing. Attorneys for the family claim that their clients are a legitimate business dynasty whose interests include importing, commercial trucking, and coin-operated vending machines. "This investigation is a sham! Nothing more than an attempt to bully and coerce tax-paying citizens.

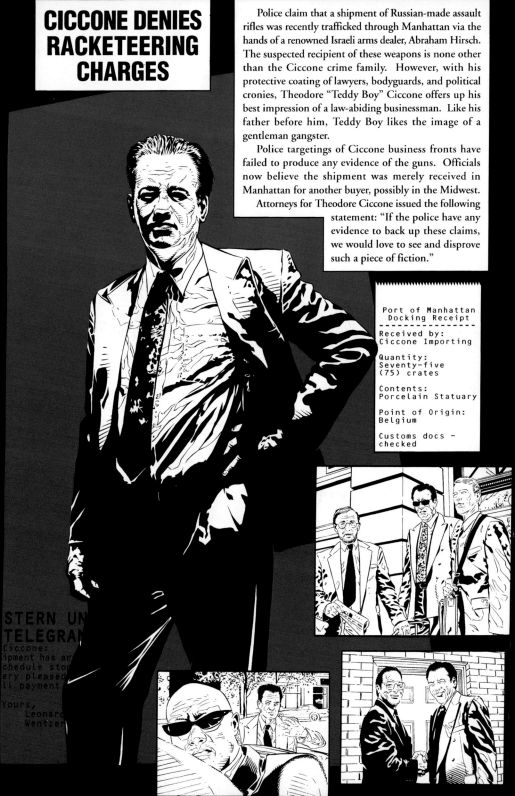

CICCONE DENIES RACKETEERING CHARGES

Police claim that a shipment of Russian-made assault rifles was recently trafficked through Manhattan via the hands of a renowned Israeli arms dealer, Abraham Hirsch. The suspected recipient of these weapons is none other than the Ciccone crime family. However, with his protective coating of lawyers, bodyguards, and political cronies, Theodore "Teddy Boy" Ciccone offers up his best impression of a law-abiding businessman. Like his father before him, Teddy Boy likes the image of a gentleman gangster.

Police targetings of Ciccone business fronts have failed to produce any evidence of the guns. Officials now believe the shipment was merely received in Manhattan for another buyer, possibly in the Midwest.

Attorneys for Theodore Ciccone issued the following statement: "If the police have any evidence to back up these claims, we would love to see and disprove such a piece of fiction."

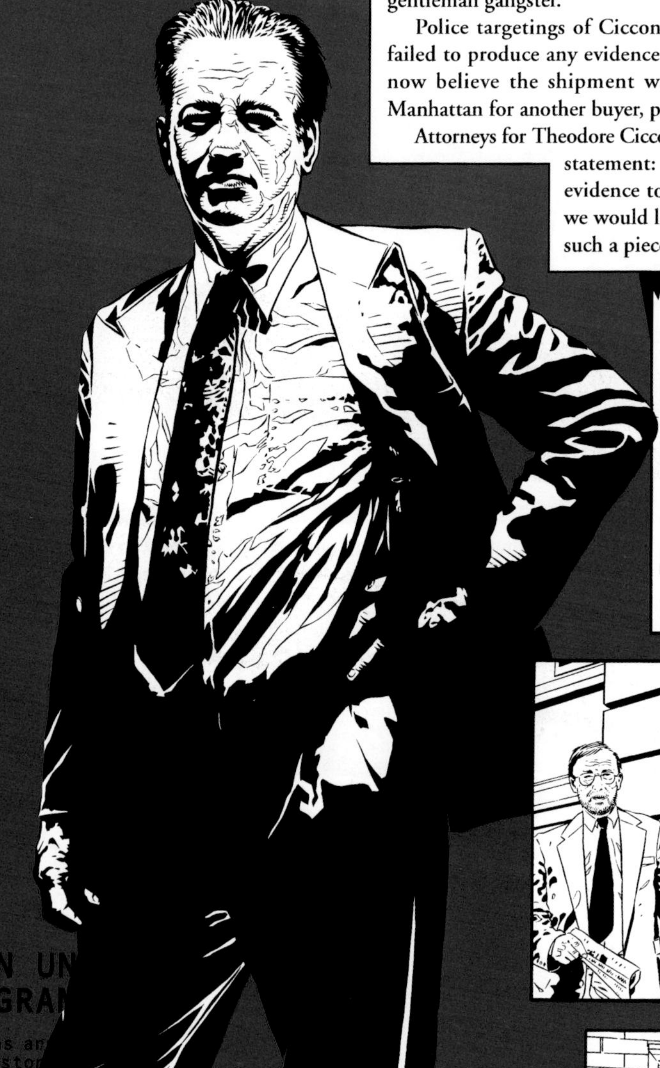

Port of Manhattan
Docking Receipt

Received by:
Ciccone Importing

Quantity:
Seventy-five
(75) crates

Contents:
Porcelain Statuary

Point of Origin:
Belgium

Customs docs -
checked

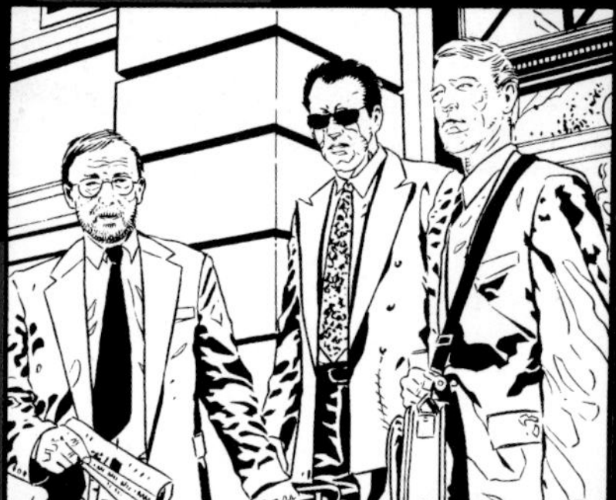

STERN UN
TELEGRAM
Ciccone:
ipment has ar
chedule stor
ery pleased
ll payment

Yours,
Leonard
Wentzer

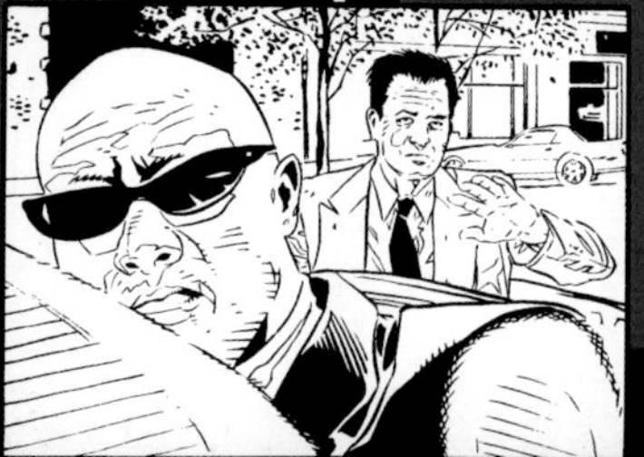

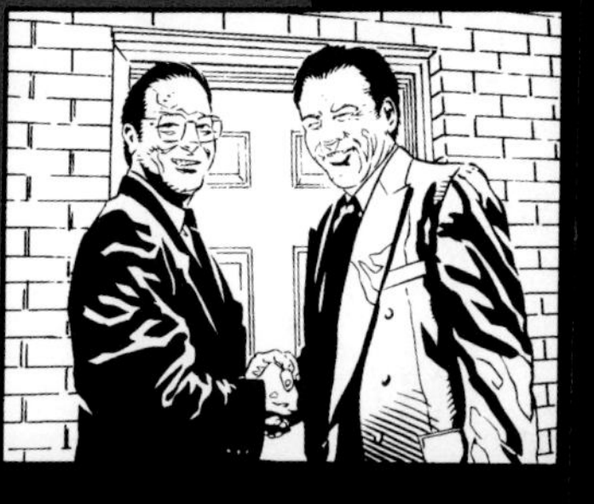

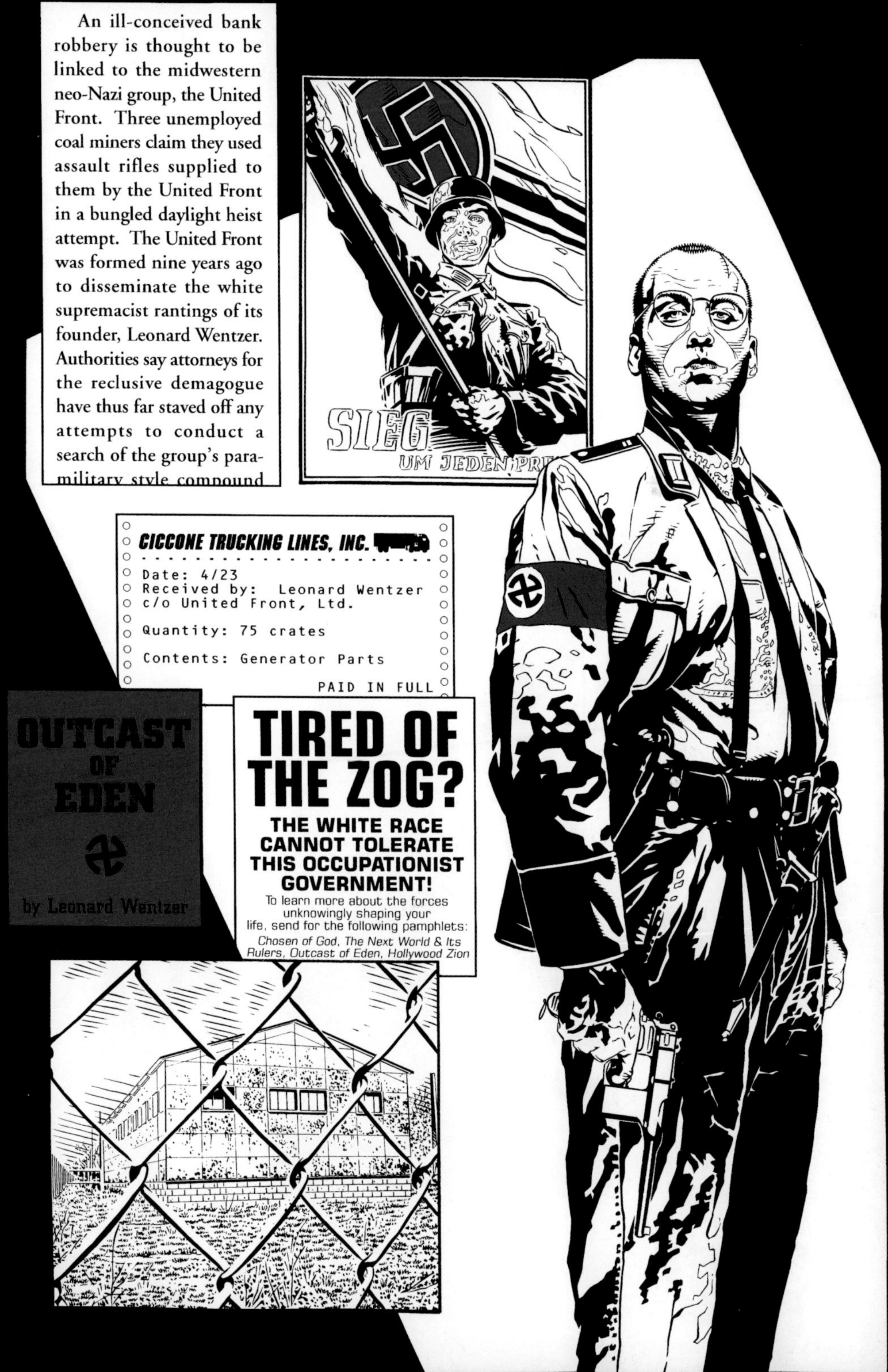

An ill-conceived bank robbery is thought to be linked to the midwestern neo-Nazi group, the United Front. Three unemployed coal miners claim they used assault rifles supplied to them by the United Front in a bungled daylight heist attempt. The United Front was formed nine years ago to disseminate the white supremacist rantings of its founder, Leonard Wentzer. Authorities say attorneys for the reclusive demagogue have thus far staved off any attempts to conduct a search of the group's paramilitary style compound
SIEG
UM JEDEN
CICCONE TRUCKING LINES, INC.
Date: 4/23
Received by: Leonard Wentzer
c/o United Front, Ltd.
Quantity: 75 crates
Contents: Generator Parts
PAID IN FULL
OUTCAST OF EDEN
by Leonard Wentzer
TIRED OF THE ZOG?
THE WHITE RACE CANNOT TOLERATE THIS OCCUPATIONIST GOVERNMENT!
To learn more about the forces unknowingly shaping your life, send for the following pamphlets:
Chosen of God, The Next World & Its Rulers, Outcast of Eden, Hollywood Zion

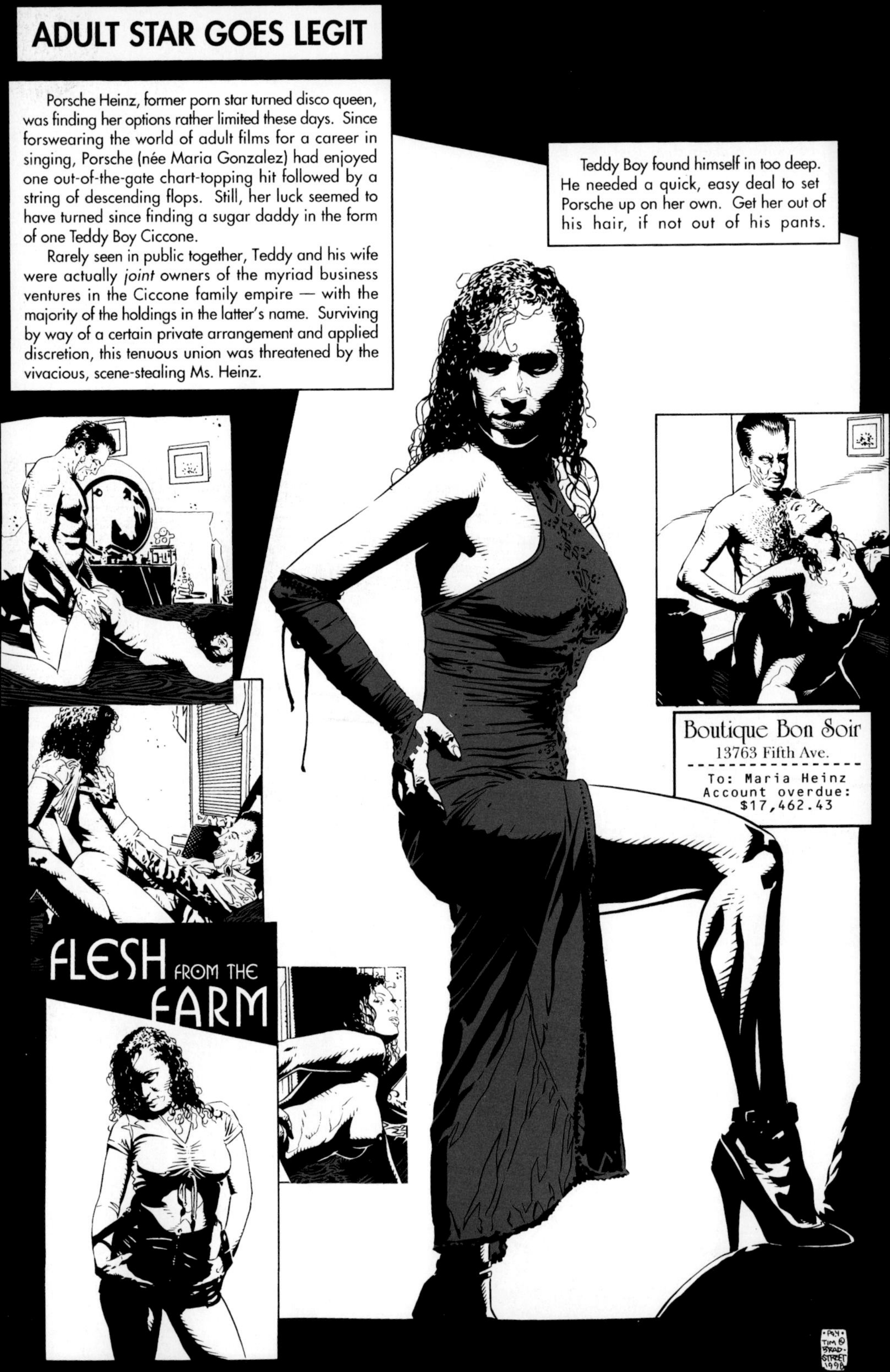

ADULT STAR GOES LEGIT
Porsche Heinz, former porn star turned disco queen, was finding her options rather limited these days. Since forswearing the world of adult films for a career in singing, Porsche (née Maria Gonzalez) had enjoyed one out-of-the-gate chart-topping hit followed by a string of descending flops. Still, her luck seemed to have turned since finding a sugar daddy in the form of one Teddy Boy Ciccone.
Rarely seen in public together, Teddy and his wife were actually *joint* owners of the myriad business ventures in the Ciccone family empire — with the majority of the holdings in the latter's name. Surviving by way of a certain private arrangement and applied discretion, this tenuous union was threatened by the vivacious, scene-stealing Ms. Heinz.
Teddy Boy found himself in too deep. He needed a quick, easy deal to set Porsche up on her own. Get her out of his hair, if not out of his pants.
Boutique Bon Soir
13763 Fifth Ave.
To: Maria Heinz
Account overdue:
$17,462.43
FLESH FROM THE FARM

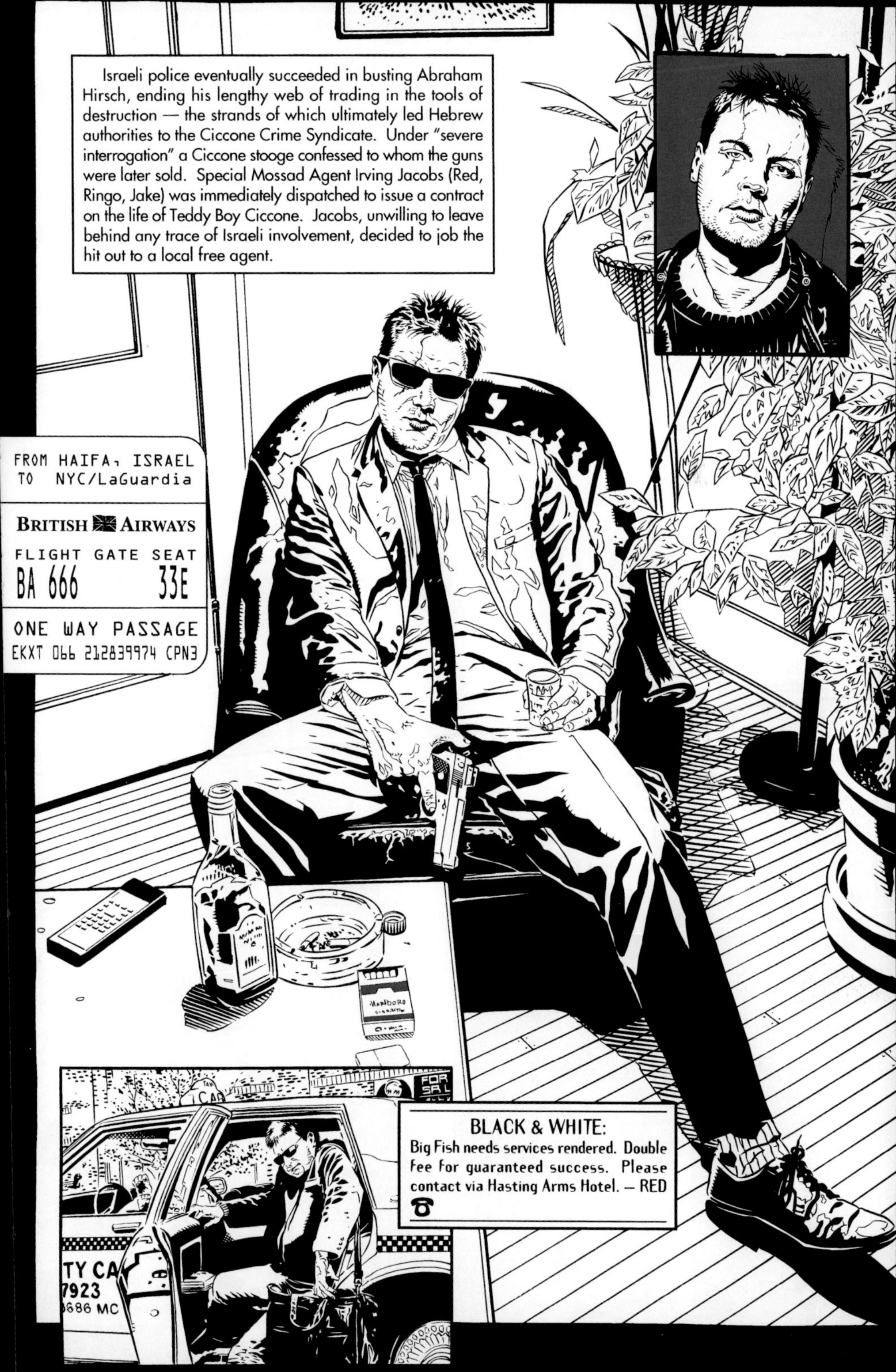

Israeli police eventually succeeded in busting Abraham Hirsch, ending his lengthy web of trading in the tools of destruction — the strands of which ultimately led Hebrew authorities to the Ciccone Crime Syndicate. Under "severe interrogation" a Ciccone stooge confessed to whom the guns were later sold. Special Mossad Agent Irving Jacobs (Red, Ringo, Jake) was immediately dispatched to issue a contract on the life of Teddy Boy Ciccone. Jacobs, unwilling to leave behind any trace of Israeli involvement, decided to job the hit out to a local free agent.
FROM HAIFA, ISRAEL
TO NYC/LaGuardia
BRITISH AIRWAYS
FLIGHT GATE SEAT
BA 666 33E
ONE WAY PASSAGE
EKXT 066 212839974 CPN3
BLACK & WHITE:
Big Fish needs services rendered. Double Fee for guaranteed success. Please contact via Hasting Arms Hotel. — RED
TY CA
7923
3686 MC

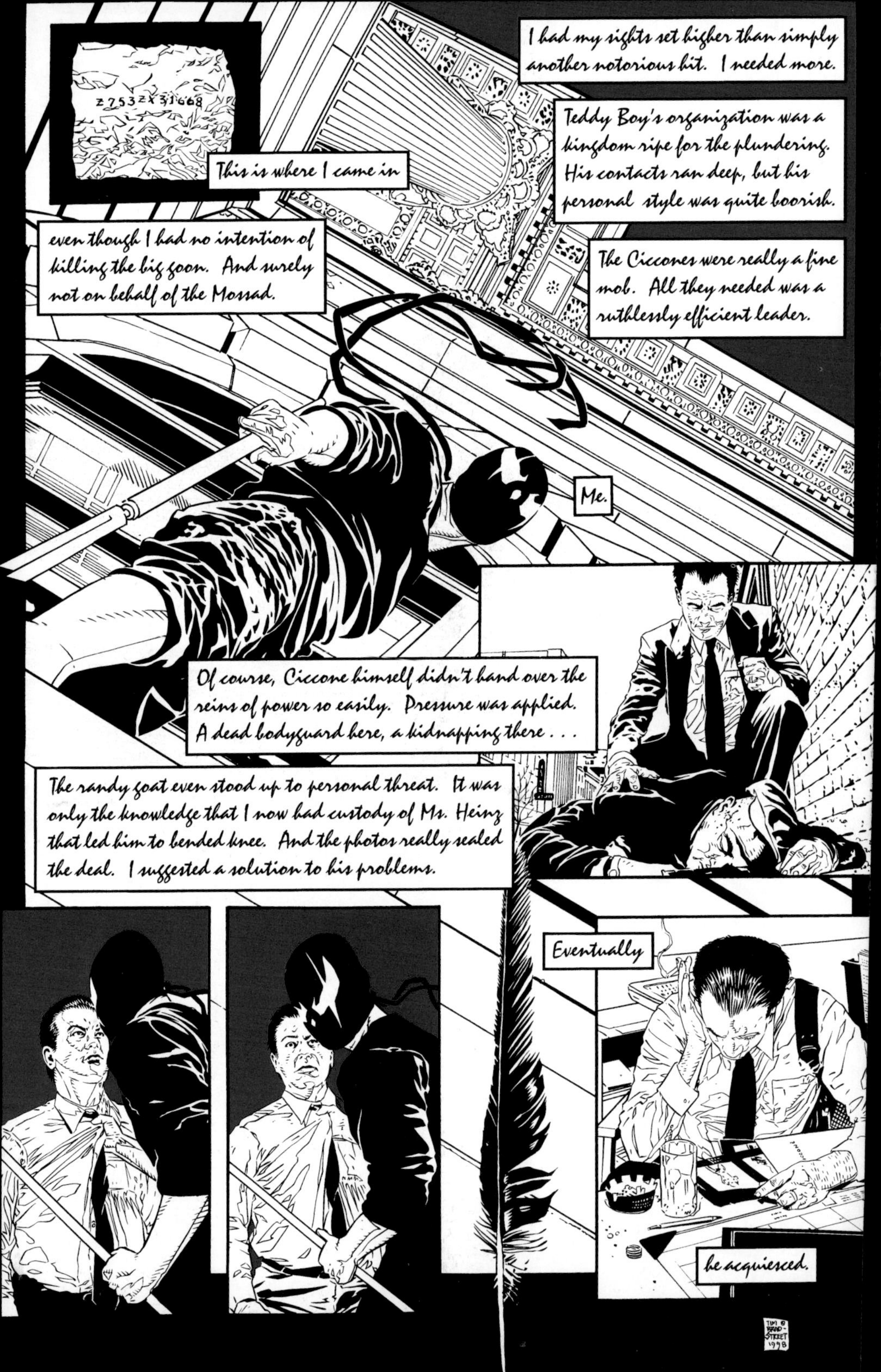
ZZ53ZX31668
This is where I came in
even though I had no intention of killing the big goon. And surely not on behalf of the Mossad.
I had my sights set higher than simply another notorious hit. I needed more.
Teddy Boy's organization was a kingdom ripe for the plundering. His contacts ran deep, but his personal style was quite boorish.
The Ciccones were really a fine mob. All they needed was a ruthlessly efficient leader.
Me.
Of course, Ciccone himself didn't hand over the reins of power so easily. Pressure was applied. A dead bodyguard here, a kidnapping there . . .
The randy goat even stood up to personal threat. It was only the knowledge that I now had custody of Ms. Heinz that led him to bended knee. And the photos really sealed the deal. I suggested a solution to his problems.
Eventually
he acquiesced.
TIM © BROADSTREET 1998

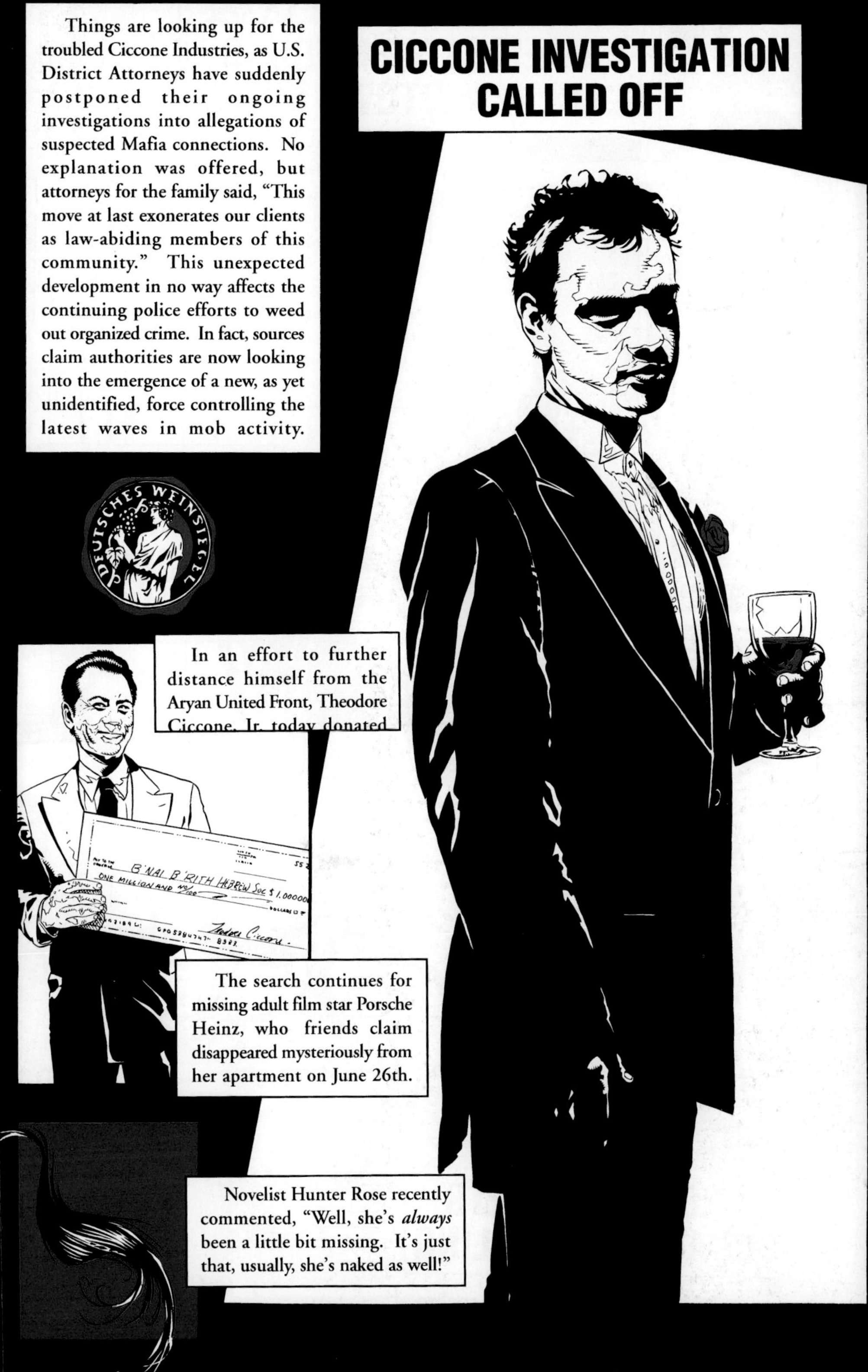

CICCONE INVESTIGATION CALLED OFF
Things are looking up for the troubled Ciccone Industries, as U.S. District Attorneys have suddenly postponed their ongoing investigations into allegations of suspected Mafia connections. No explanation was offered, but attorneys for the family said, "This move at last exonerates our clients as law-abiding members of this community." This unexpected development in no way affects the continuing police efforts to weed out organized crime. In fact, sources claim authorities are now looking into the emergence of a new, as yet unidentified, force controlling the latest waves in mob activity.
DEUTSCHES WEINSIEGEL
In an effort to further distance himself from the Aryan United Front, Theodore Ciccone, Jr. today donated
B'NAI B'RITH HEBREW SOC
ONE MILLION AND 00/100
The search continues for missing adult film star Porsche Heinz, who friends claim disappeared mysteriously from her apartment on June 26th.
Novelist Hunter Rose recently commented, "Well, she's *always* been a little bit missing. It's just that, usually, she's naked as well!"

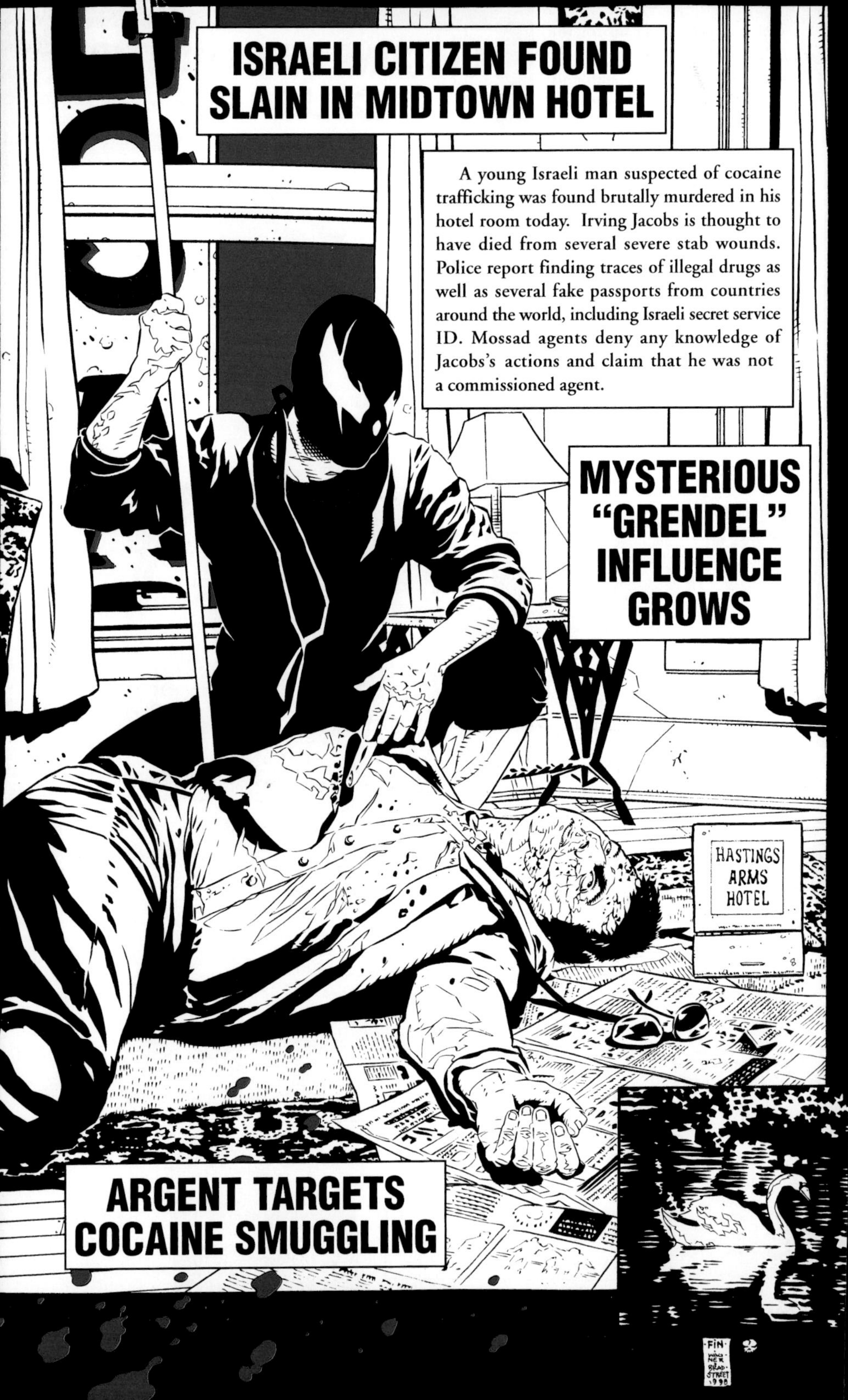

ISRAELI CITIZEN FOUND SLAIN IN MIDTOWN HOTEL
A young Israeli man suspected of cocaine trafficking was found brutally murdered in his hotel room today. Irving Jacobs is thought to have died from several severe stab wounds. Police report finding traces of illegal drugs as well as several fake passports from countries around the world, including Israeli secret service ID. Mossad agents deny any knowledge of Jacobs's actions and claim that he was not a commissioned agent.
MYSTERIOUS "GRENDEL" INFLUENCE GROWS
HASTINGS ARMS HOTEL
ARGENT TARGETS COCAINE SMUGGLING
FIN

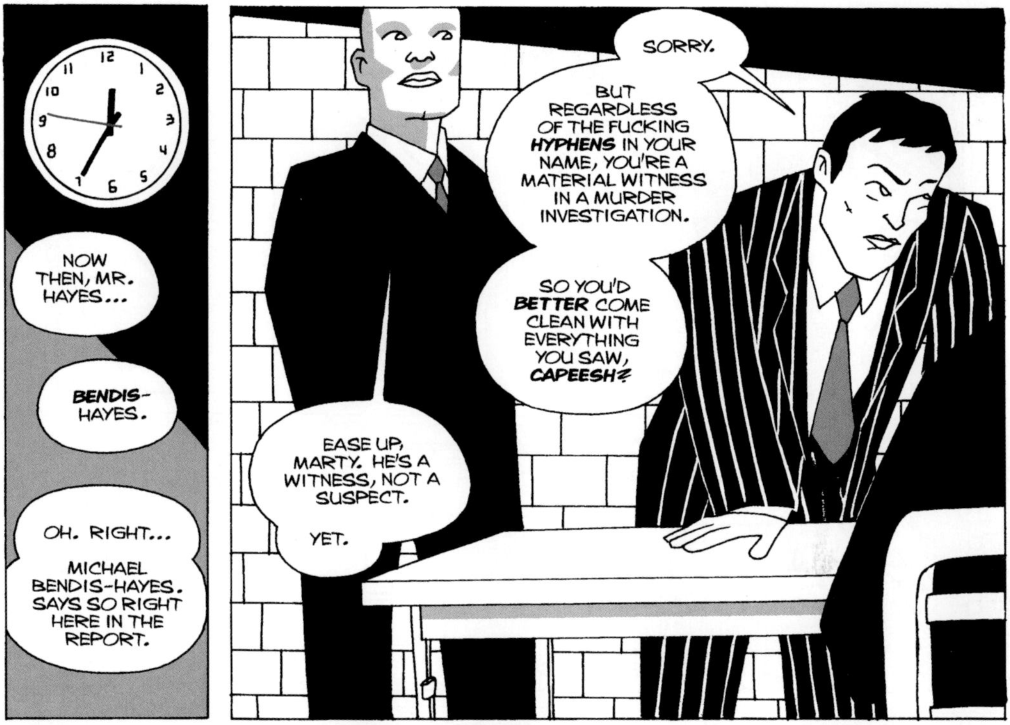
NOW THEN, MR. HAYES...
BENDIS-HAYES.
SORRY.
BUT REGARDLESS OF THE FUCKING HYPHENS IN YOUR NAME, YOU'RE A MATERIAL WITNESS IN A MURDER INVESTIGATION.
SO YOU'D BETTER COME CLEAN WITH EVERYTHING YOU SAW, CAPEESH?
EASE UP, MARTY. HE'S A WITNESS, NOT A SUSPECT.
YET.
OH. RIGHT...
MICHAEL BENDIS-HAYES. SAYS SO RIGHT HERE IN THE REPORT.

devil's witness

wagner — phoenix

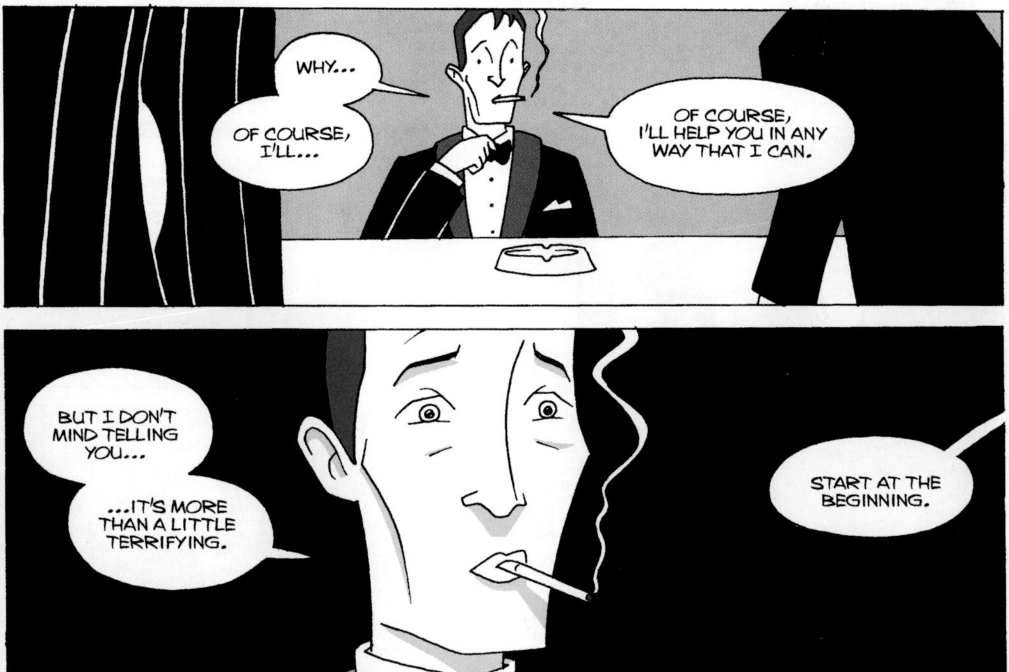
WHY...
OF COURSE, I'LL...
OF COURSE, I'LL HELP YOU IN ANY WAY THAT I CAN.
BUT I DON'T MIND TELLING YOU...
...IT'S MORE THAN A LITTLE TERRIFYING.
START AT THE BEGINNING.

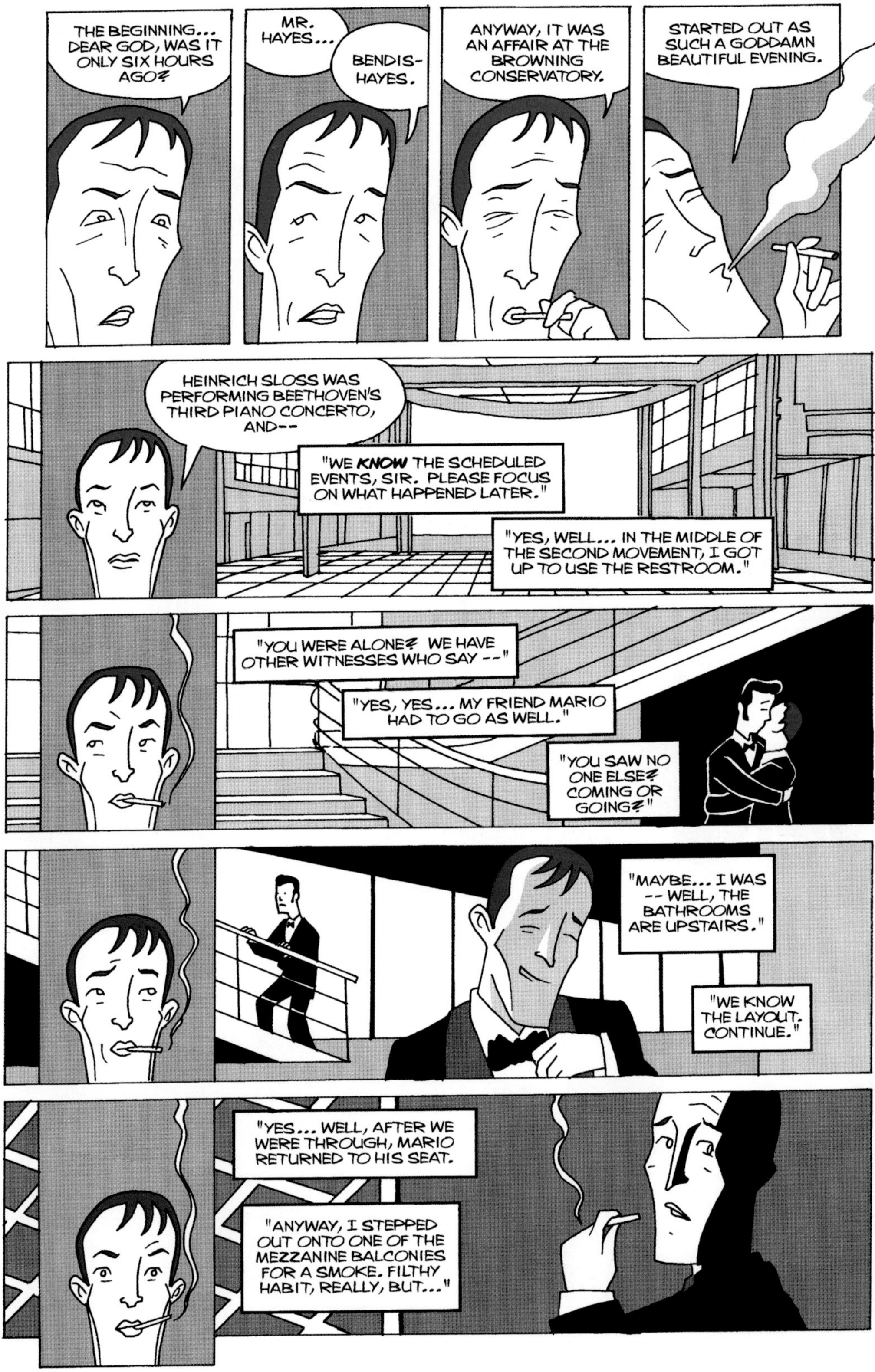
THE BEGINNING... DEAR GOD, WAS IT ONLY SIX HOURS AGO?
MR. HAYES...
BENDIS-HAYES.
ANYWAY, IT WAS AN AFFAIR AT THE BROWNING CONSERVATORY.
STARTED OUT AS SUCH A GODDAMN BEAUTIFUL EVENING.
HEINRICH SLOSS WAS PERFORMING BEETHOVEN'S THIRD PIANO CONCERTO, AND--
"WE KNOW THE SCHEDULED EVENTS, SIR. PLEASE FOCUS ON WHAT HAPPENED LATER."
"YES, WELL... IN THE MIDDLE OF THE SECOND MOVEMENT, I GOT UP TO USE THE RESTROOM."
"YOU WERE ALONE? WE HAVE OTHER WITNESSES WHO SAY --"
"YES, YES... MY FRIEND MARIO HAD TO GO AS WELL."
"YOU SAW NO ONE ELSE? COMING OR GOING?"
"MAYBE... I WAS -- WELL, THE BATHROOMS ARE UPSTAIRS."
"WE KNOW THE LAYOUT. CONTINUE."
"YES... WELL, AFTER WE WERE THROUGH, MARIO RETURNED TO HIS SEAT.
"ANYWAY, I STEPPED OUT ONTO ONE OF THE MEZZANINE BALCONIES FOR A SMOKE. FILTHY HABIT, REALLY, BUT..."

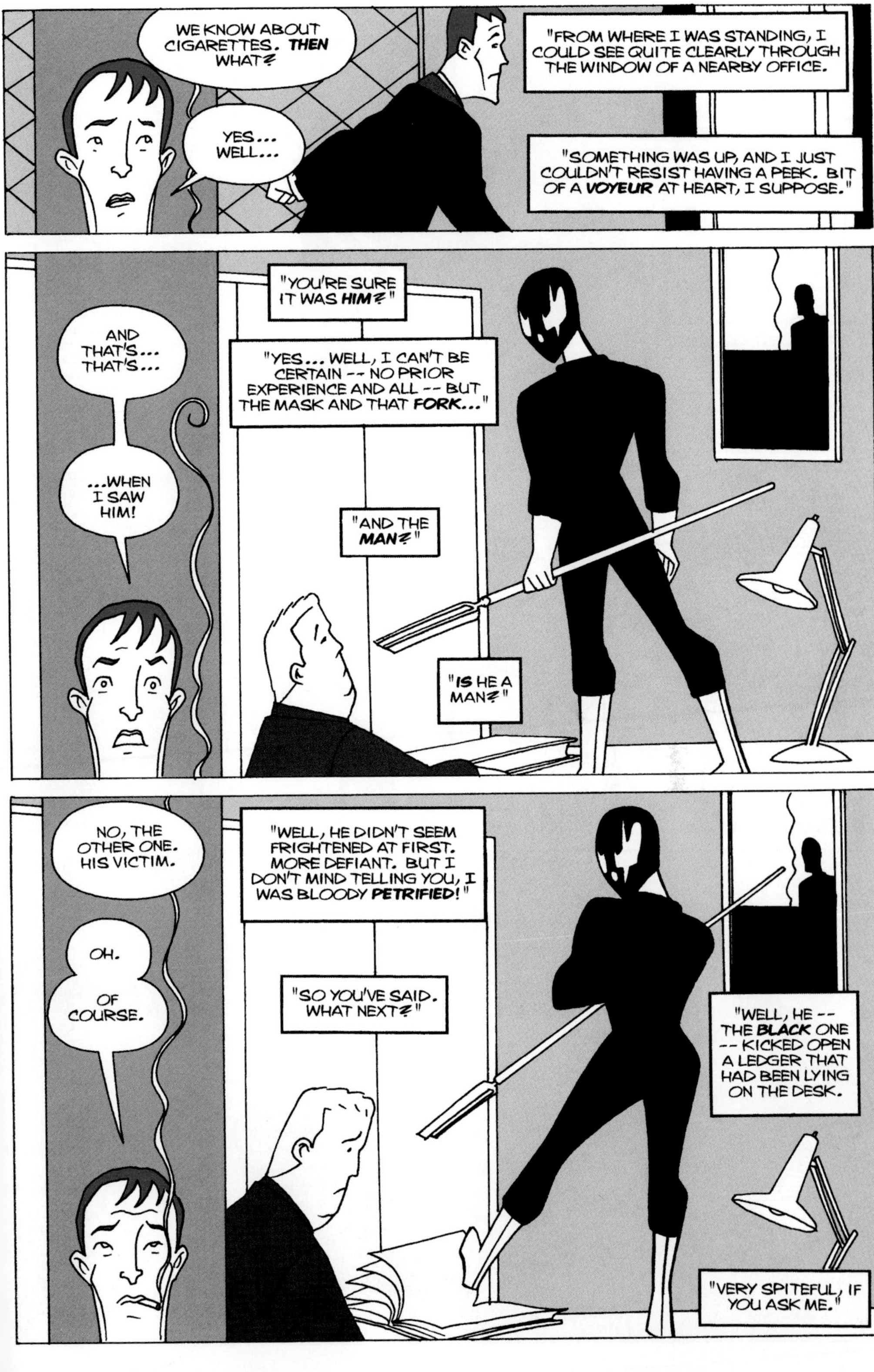
WE KNOW ABOUT CIGARETTES. THEN WHAT?
YES... WELL...
"FROM WHERE I WAS STANDING, I COULD SEE QUITE CLEARLY THROUGH THE WINDOW OF A NEARBY OFFICE.
"SOMETHING WAS UP, AND I JUST COULDN'T RESIST HAVING A PEEK. BIT OF A VOYEUR AT HEART, I SUPPOSE."
"YOU'RE SURE IT WAS HIM?"
AND THAT'S... THAT'S...
"YES... WELL, I CAN'T BE CERTAIN -- NO PRIOR EXPERIENCE AND ALL -- BUT THE MASK AND THAT FORK..."
...WHEN I SAW HIM!
"AND THE MAN?"
"IS HE A MAN?"
NO, THE OTHER ONE. HIS VICTIM.
"WELL, HE DIDN'T SEEM FRIGHTENED AT FIRST. MORE DEFIANT. BUT I DON'T MIND TELLING YOU, I WAS BLOODY PETRIFIED!"
OH.
OF COURSE.
"SO YOU'VE SAID. WHAT NEXT?"
"WELL, HE -- THE BLACK ONE -- KICKED OPEN A LEDGER THAT HAD BEEN LYING ON THE DESK.
"VERY SPITEFUL, IF YOU ASK ME."

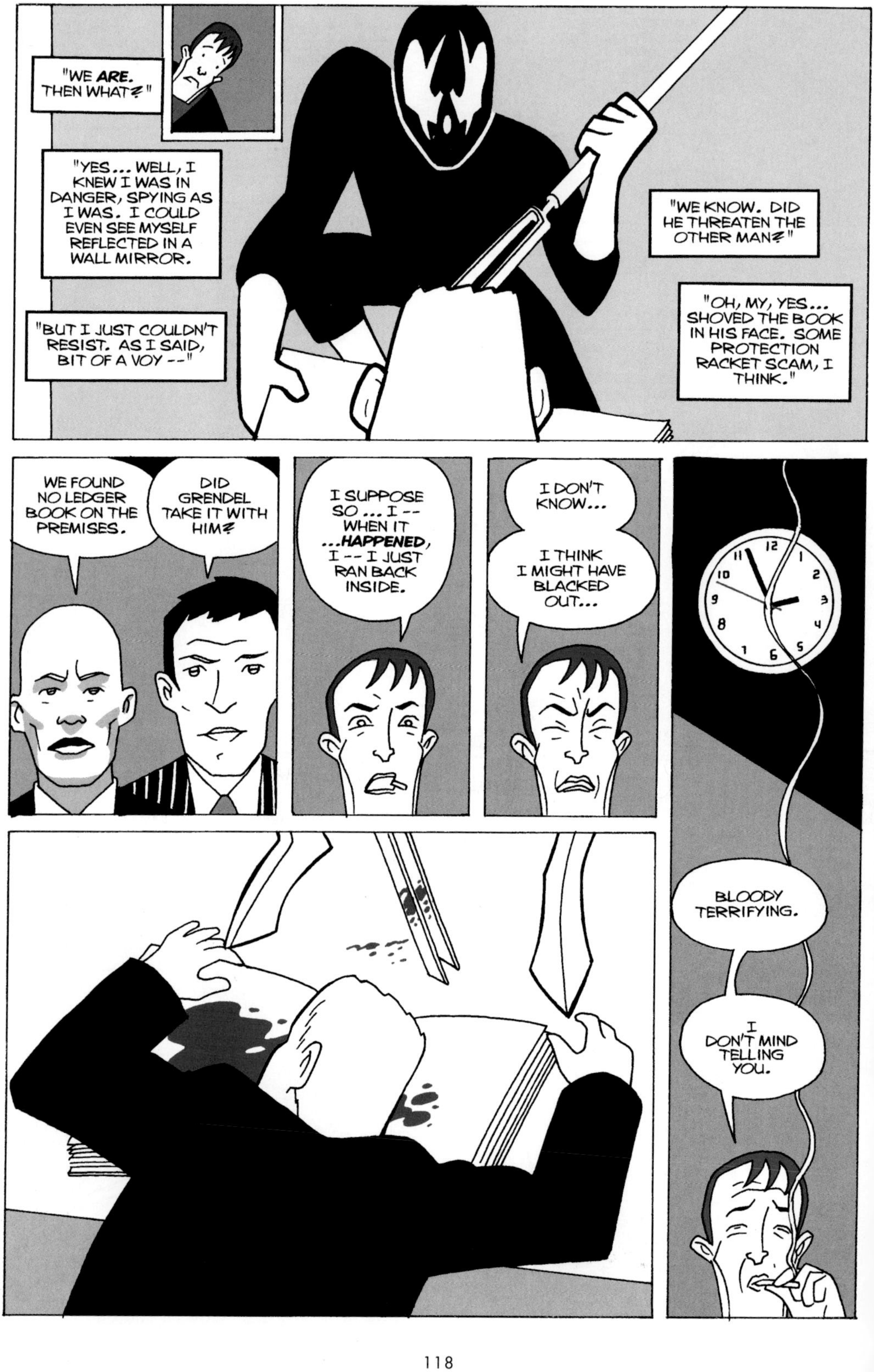
"WE ARE. THEN WHAT?"
"YES... WELL, I KNEW I WAS IN DANGER, SPYING AS I WAS. I COULD EVEN SEE MYSELF REFLECTED IN A WALL MIRROR.
"BUT I JUST COULDN'T RESIST. AS I SAID, BIT OF A VOY --"
"WE KNOW. DID HE THREATEN THE OTHER MAN?"
"OH, MY, YES... SHOVED THE BOOK IN HIS FACE. SOME PROTECTION RACKET SCAM, I THINK."
WE FOUND NO LEDGER BOOK ON THE PREMISES.
DID GRENDEL TAKE IT WITH HIM?
I SUPPOSE SO... I -- WHEN IT ...HAPPENED, I -- I JUST RAN BACK INSIDE.
I DON'T KNOW...
I THINK I MIGHT HAVE BLACKED OUT...
BLOODY TERRIFYING.
I DON'T MIND TELLING YOU.

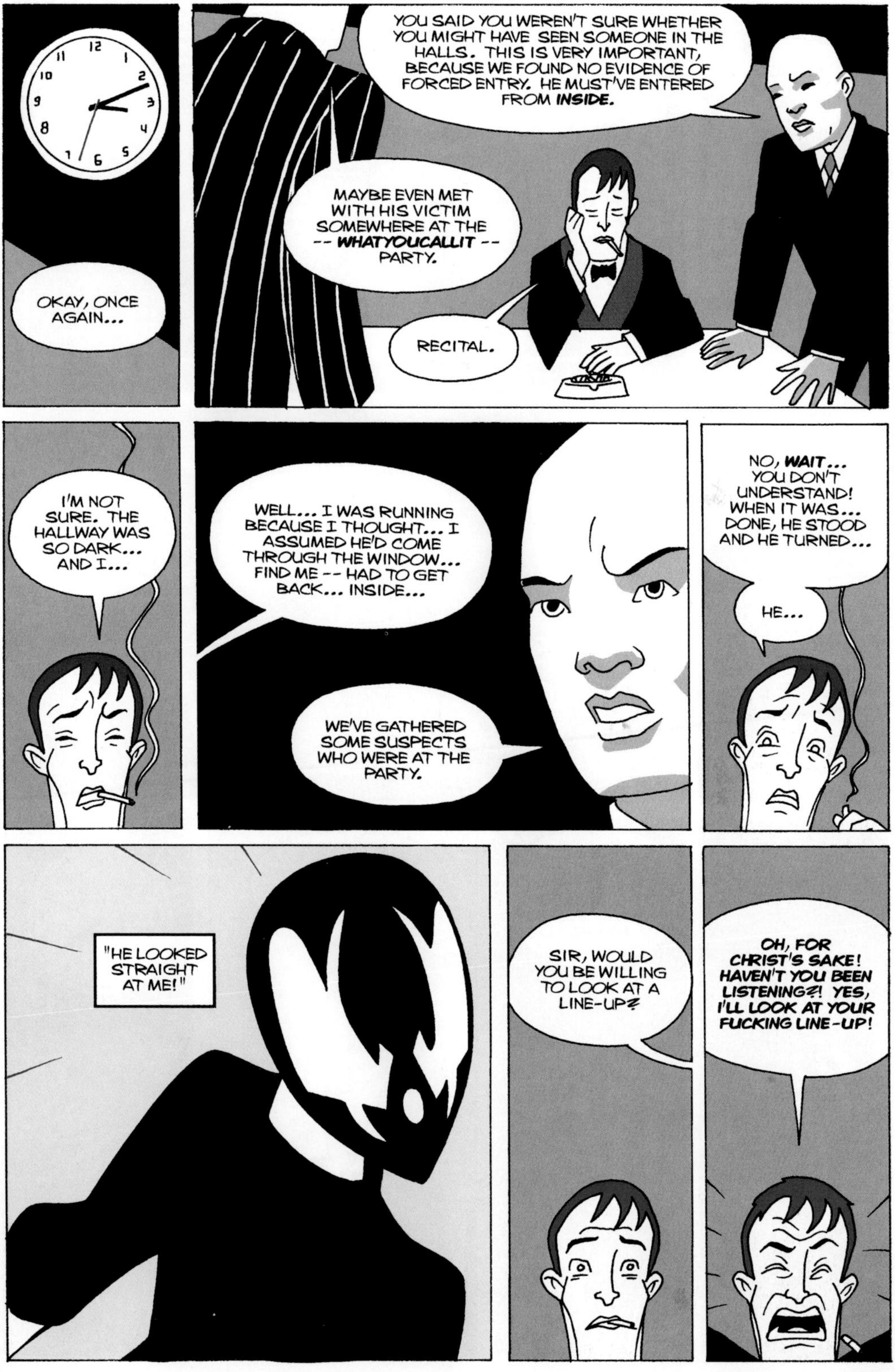
OKAY, ONCE AGAIN...
YOU SAID YOU WEREN'T SURE WHETHER YOU MIGHT HAVE SEEN SOMEONE IN THE HALLS. THIS IS VERY IMPORTANT, BECAUSE WE FOUND NO EVIDENCE OF FORCED ENTRY. HE MUST'VE ENTERED FROM **INSIDE.**
MAYBE EVEN MET WITH HIS VICTIM SOMEWHERE AT THE -- **WHATYOUCALLIT** -- PARTY.
RECITAL.
I'M NOT SURE. THE HALLWAY WAS SO DARK... AND I...
WELL... I WAS RUNNING BECAUSE I THOUGHT... I ASSUMED HE'D COME THROUGH THE WINDOW... FIND ME -- HAD TO GET BACK... INSIDE...
WE'VE GATHERED SOME SUSPECTS WHO WERE AT THE PARTY.
NO, **WAIT...** YOU DON'T UNDERSTAND! WHEN IT WAS... DONE, HE STOOD AND HE TURNED...
HE...
"HE LOOKED STRAIGHT AT ME!"
SIR, WOULD YOU BE WILLING TO LOOK AT A LINE-UP?
OH, FOR CHRIST'S SAKE! HAVEN'T YOU BEEN LISTENING?! YES, I'LL LOOK AT YOUR FUCKING LINE-UP!

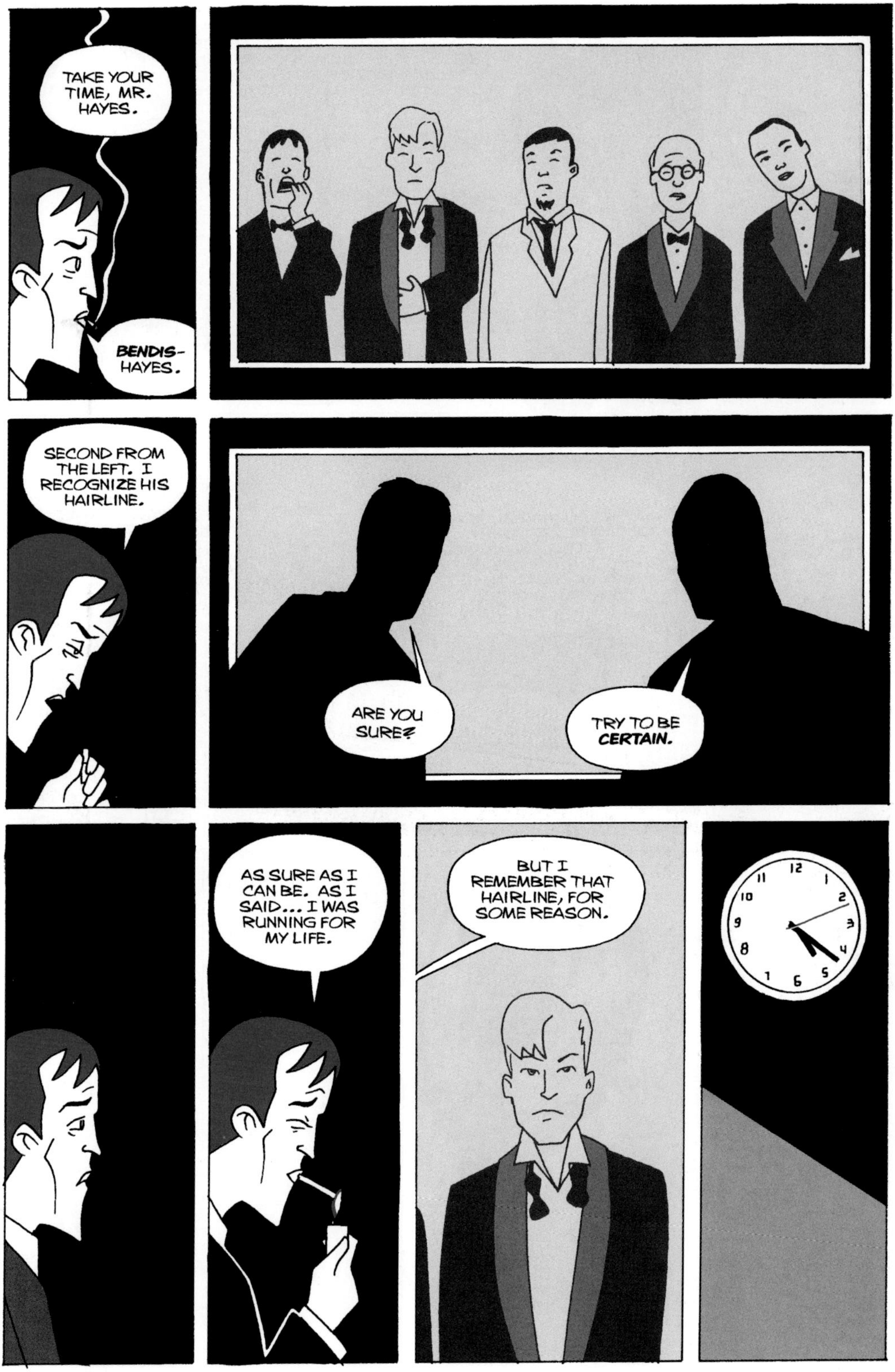
TAKE YOUR TIME, MR. HAYES.
BENDIS-HAYES.
SECOND FROM THE LEFT. I RECOGNIZE HIS HAIRLINE.
ARE YOU SURE?
TRY TO BE CERTAIN.
AS SURE AS I CAN BE. AS I SAID... I WAS RUNNING FOR MY LIFE.
BUT I REMEMBER THAT HAIRLINE, FOR SOME REASON.

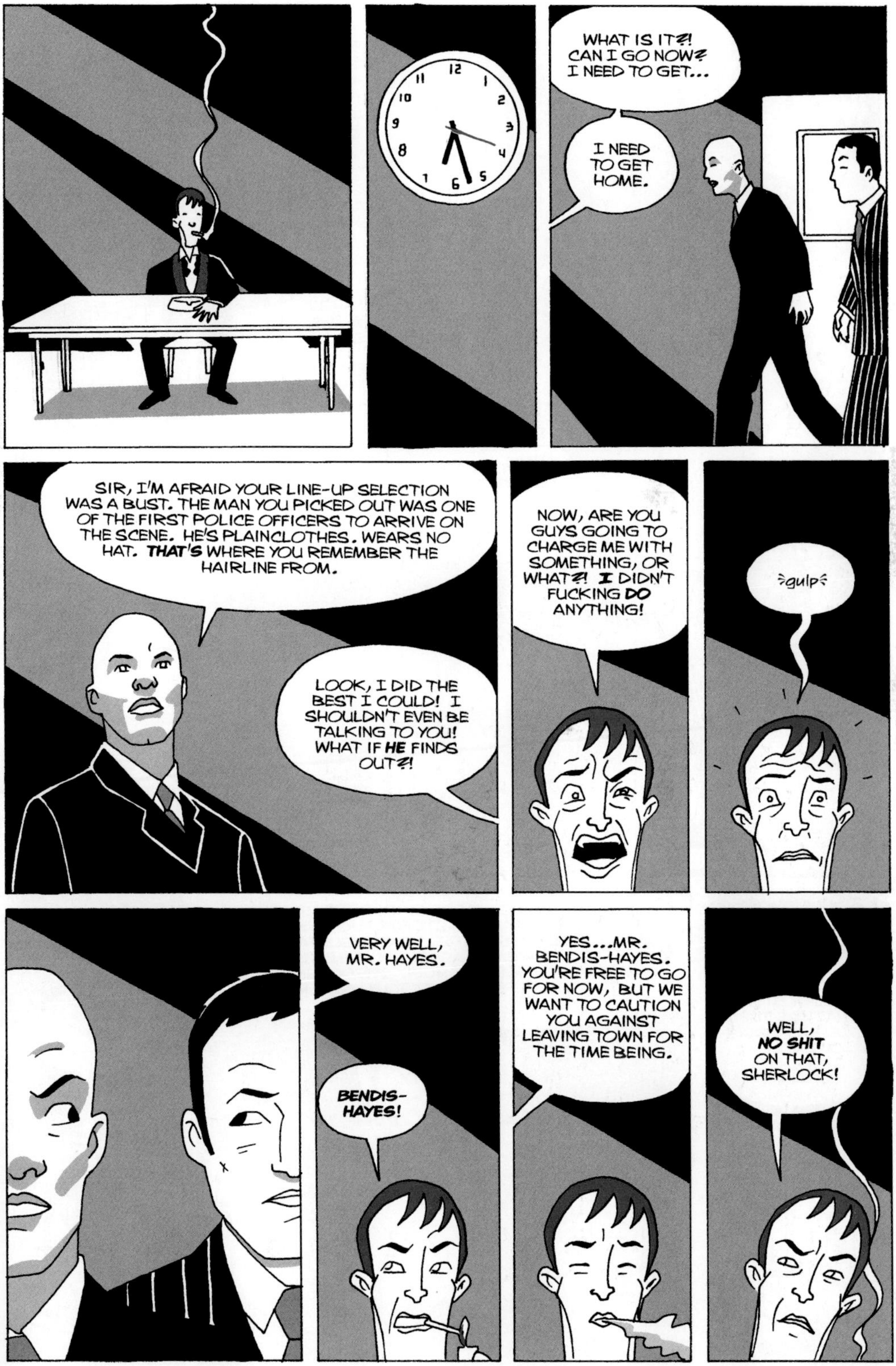
WHAT IS IT?! CAN I GO NOW? I NEED TO GET...
I NEED TO GET HOME.
SIR, I'M AFRAID YOUR LINE-UP SELECTION WAS A BUST. THE MAN YOU PICKED OUT WAS ONE OF THE FIRST POLICE OFFICERS TO ARRIVE ON THE SCENE. HE'S PLAINCLOTHES. WEARS NO HAT. THAT'S WHERE YOU REMEMBER THE HAIRLINE FROM.
LOOK, I DID THE BEST I COULD! I SHOULDN'T EVEN BE TALKING TO YOU! WHAT IF HE FINDS OUT?!
NOW, ARE YOU GUYS GOING TO CHARGE ME WITH SOMETHING, OR WHAT?! I DIDN'T FUCKING DO ANYTHING!
gulp
VERY WELL, MR. HAYES.
BENDIS-HAYES!
YES...MR. BENDIS-HAYES. YOU'RE FREE TO GO FOR NOW, BUT WE WANT TO CAUTION YOU AGAINST LEAVING TOWN FOR THE TIME BEING.
WELL, NO SHIT ON THAT, SHERLOCK!

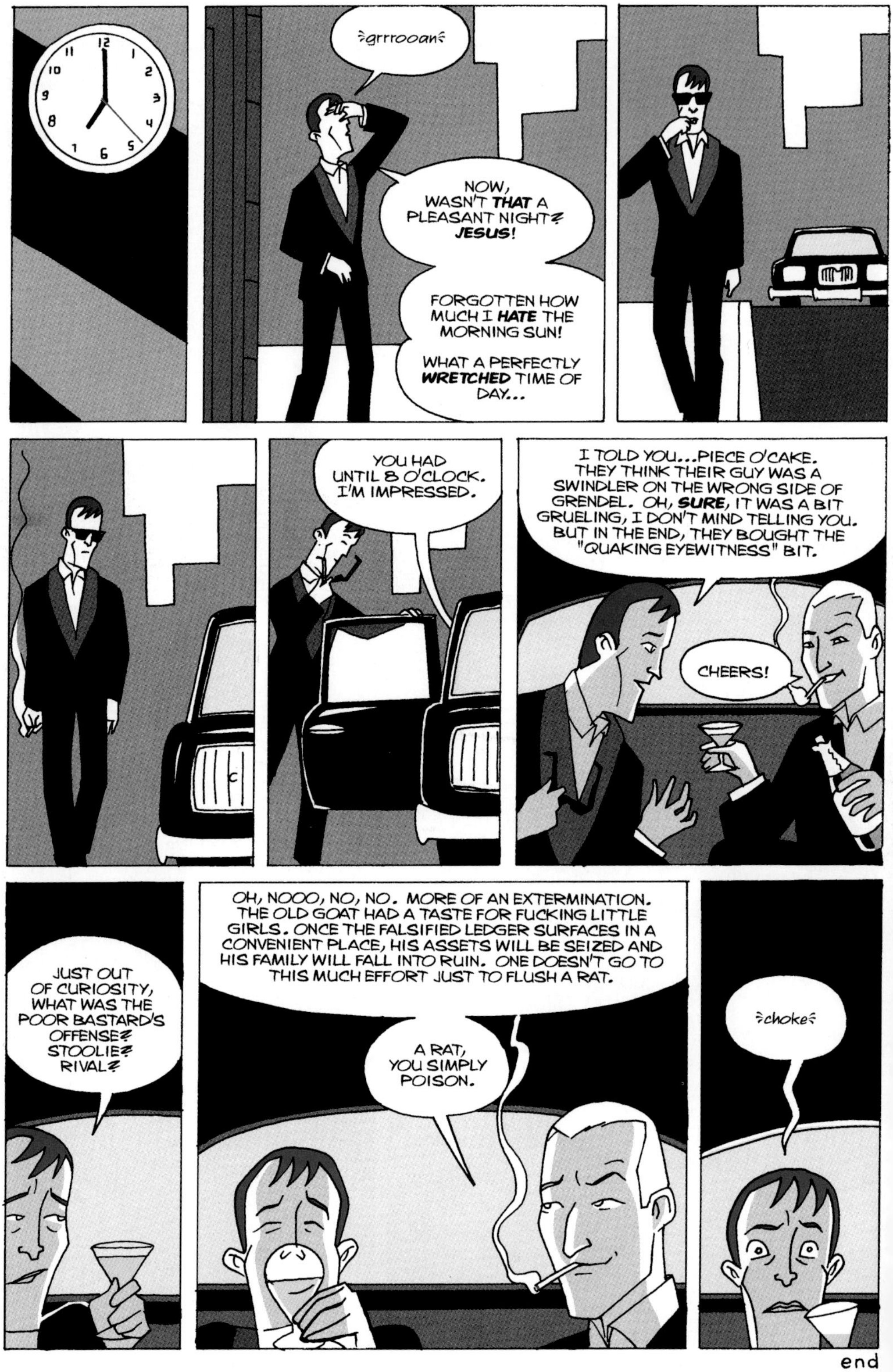

≈grrrooan≈
NOW, WASN'T **THAT** A PLEASANT NIGHT? **JESUS**!
FORGOTTEN HOW MUCH I **HATE** THE MORNING SUN!
WHAT A PERFECTLY **WRETCHED** TIME OF DAY...
YOU HAD UNTIL 8 O'CLOCK. I'M IMPRESSED.
I TOLD YOU...PIECE O'CAKE. THEY THINK THEIR GUY WAS A SWINDLER ON THE WRONG SIDE OF GRENDEL. OH, **SURE**, IT WAS A BIT GRUELING, I DON'T MIND TELLING YOU. BUT IN THE END, THEY BOUGHT THE "QUAKING EYEWITNESS" BIT.
CHEERS!
JUST OUT OF CURIOSITY, WHAT WAS THE POOR BASTARD'S OFFENSE? STOOLIE? RIVAL?
OH, NOOO, NO, NO. MORE OF AN EXTERMINATION. THE OLD GOAT HAD A TASTE FOR FUCKING LITTLE GIRLS. ONCE THE FALSIFIED LEDGER SURFACES IN A CONVENIENT PLACE, HIS ASSETS WILL BE SEIZED AND HIS FAMILY WILL FALL INTO RUIN. ONE DOESN'T GO TO THIS MUCH EFFORT JUST TO FLUSH A RAT.
A RAT, YOU SIMPLY POISON.
≈choke≈
end

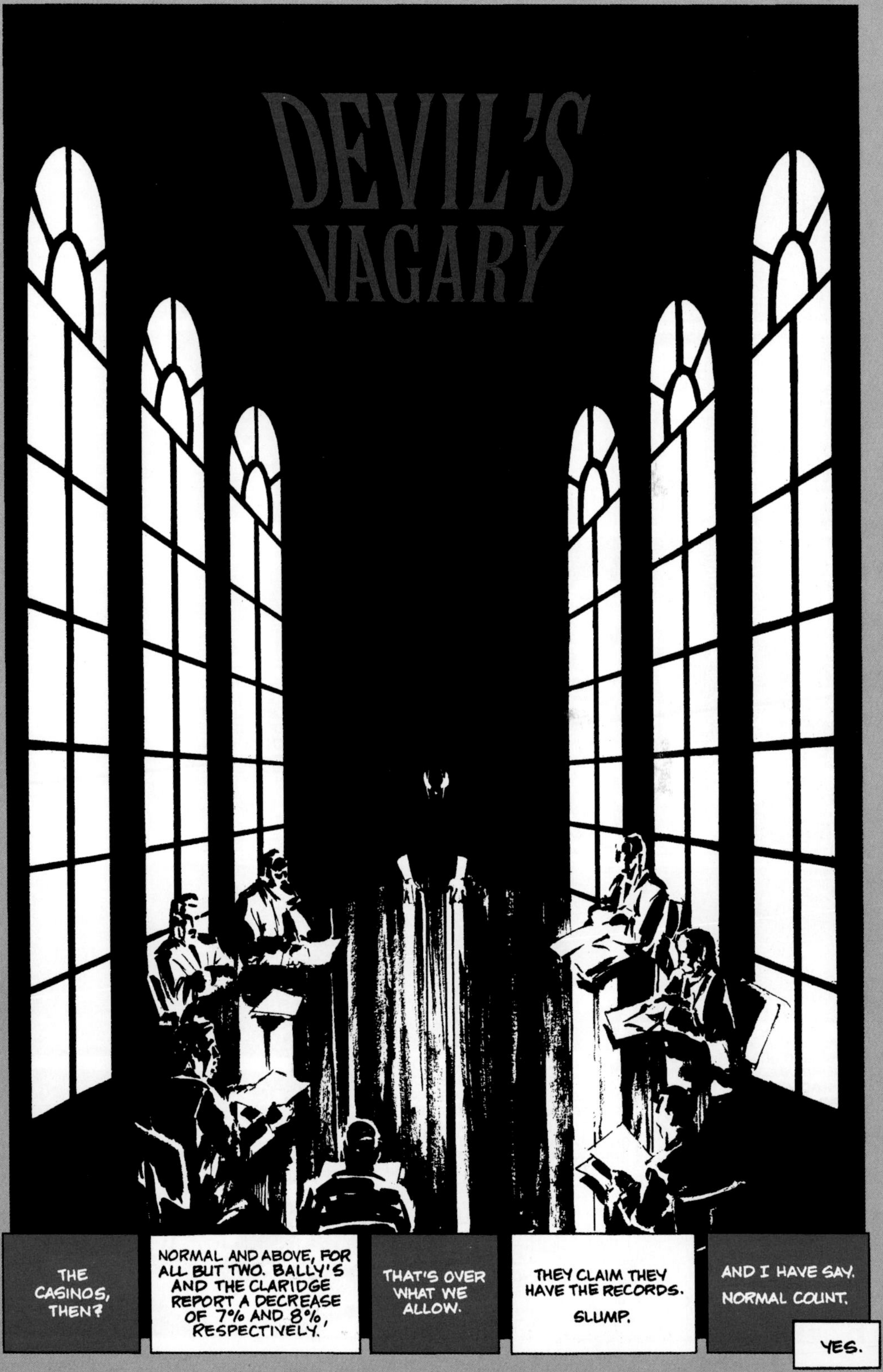
DEVIL'S VAGARY
THE CASINOS, THEN?
NORMAL AND ABOVE, FOR ALL BUT TWO. BALLY'S AND THE CLARIDGE REPORT A DECREASE OF 7% AND 8%, RESPECTIVELY.
THAT'S OVER WHAT WE ALLOW.
THEY CLAIM THEY HAVE THE RECORDS.
SLUMP.
AND I HAVE SAY.
NORMAL COUNT.
YES.

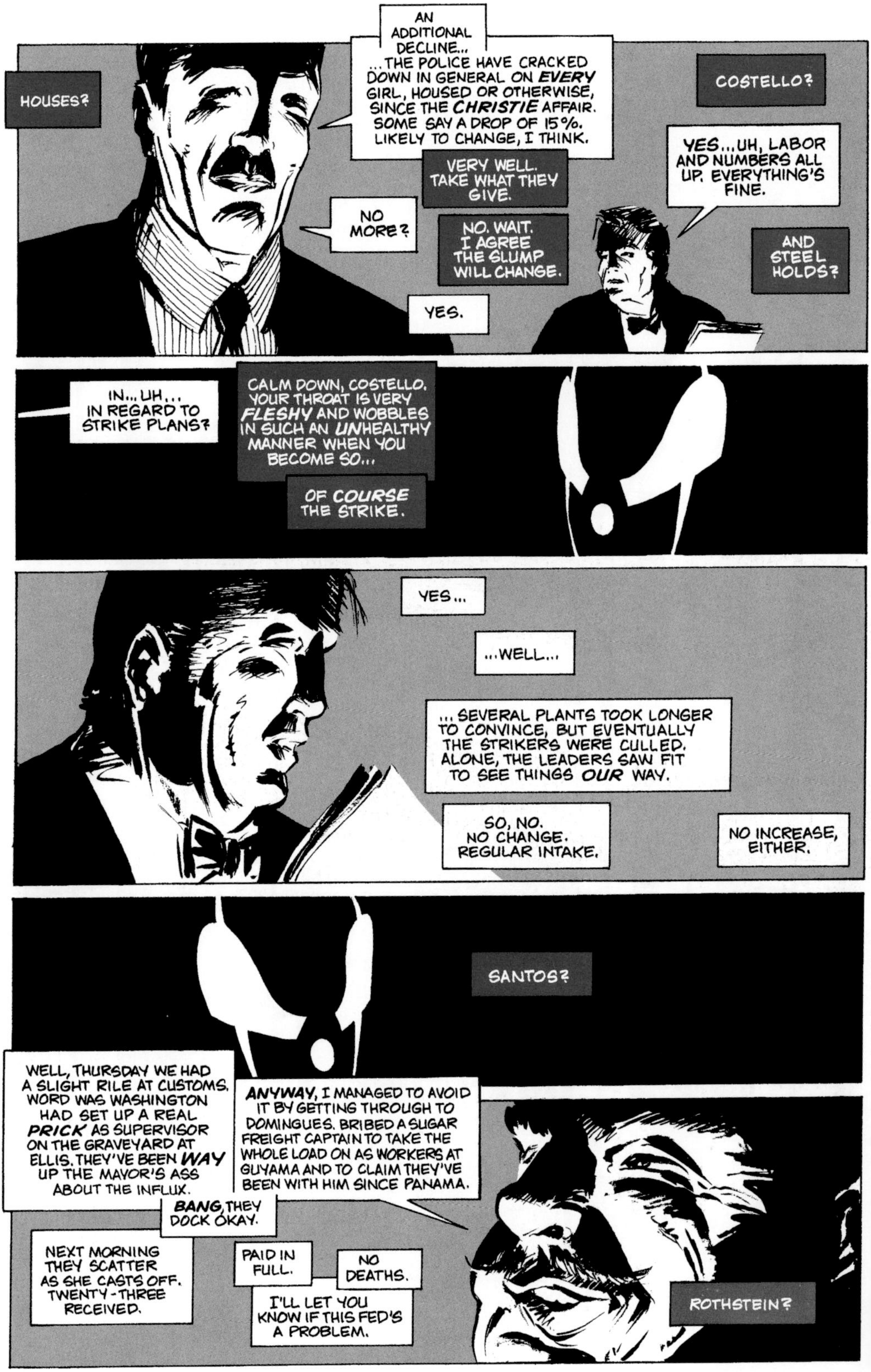

HOUSES?
AN ADDITIONAL DECLINE... ...THE POLICE HAVE CRACKED DOWN IN GENERAL ON EVERY GIRL, HOUSED OR OTHERWISE, SINCE THE CHRISTIE AFFAIR. SOME SAY A DROP OF 15%. LIKELY TO CHANGE, I THINK.
VERY WELL. TAKE WHAT THEY GIVE.
NO MORE?
NO. WAIT. I AGREE THE SLUMP WILL CHANGE.
YES.
COSTELLO?
YES...UH, LABOR AND NUMBERS ALL UP. EVERYTHING'S FINE.
AND STEEL HOLDS?
IN... UH... IN REGARD TO STRIKE PLANS?
CALM DOWN, COSTELLO. YOUR THROAT IS VERY FLESHY AND WOBBLES IN SUCH AN UNHEALTHY MANNER WHEN YOU BECOME SO...
OF COURSE THE STRIKE.
YES...
...WELL...
... SEVERAL PLANTS TOOK LONGER TO CONVINCE, BUT EVENTUALLY THE STRIKERS WERE CULLED. ALONE, THE LEADERS SAW FIT TO SEE THINGS OUR WAY.
SO, NO. NO CHANGE. REGULAR INTAKE.
NO INCREASE, EITHER.
SANTOS?
WELL, THURSDAY WE HAD A SLIGHT RILE AT CUSTOMS. WORD WAS WASHINGTON HAD SET UP A REAL PRICK AS SUPERVISOR ON THE GRAVEYARD AT ELLIS. THEY'VE BEEN WAY UP THE MAYOR'S ASS ABOUT THE INFLUX.
ANYWAY, I MANAGED TO AVOID IT BY GETTING THROUGH TO DOMINGUES. BRIBED A SUGAR FREIGHT CAPTAIN TO TAKE THE WHOLE LOAD ON AS WORKERS AT GUYAMA AND TO CLAIM THEY'VE BEEN WITH HIM SINCE PANAMA.
BANG, THEY DOCK OKAY.
NEXT MORNING THEY SCATTER AS SHE CASTS OFF. TWENTY-THREE RECEIVED.
PAID IN FULL.
NO DEATHS.
I'LL LET YOU KNOW IF THIS FED'S A PROBLEM.
ROTHSTEIN?

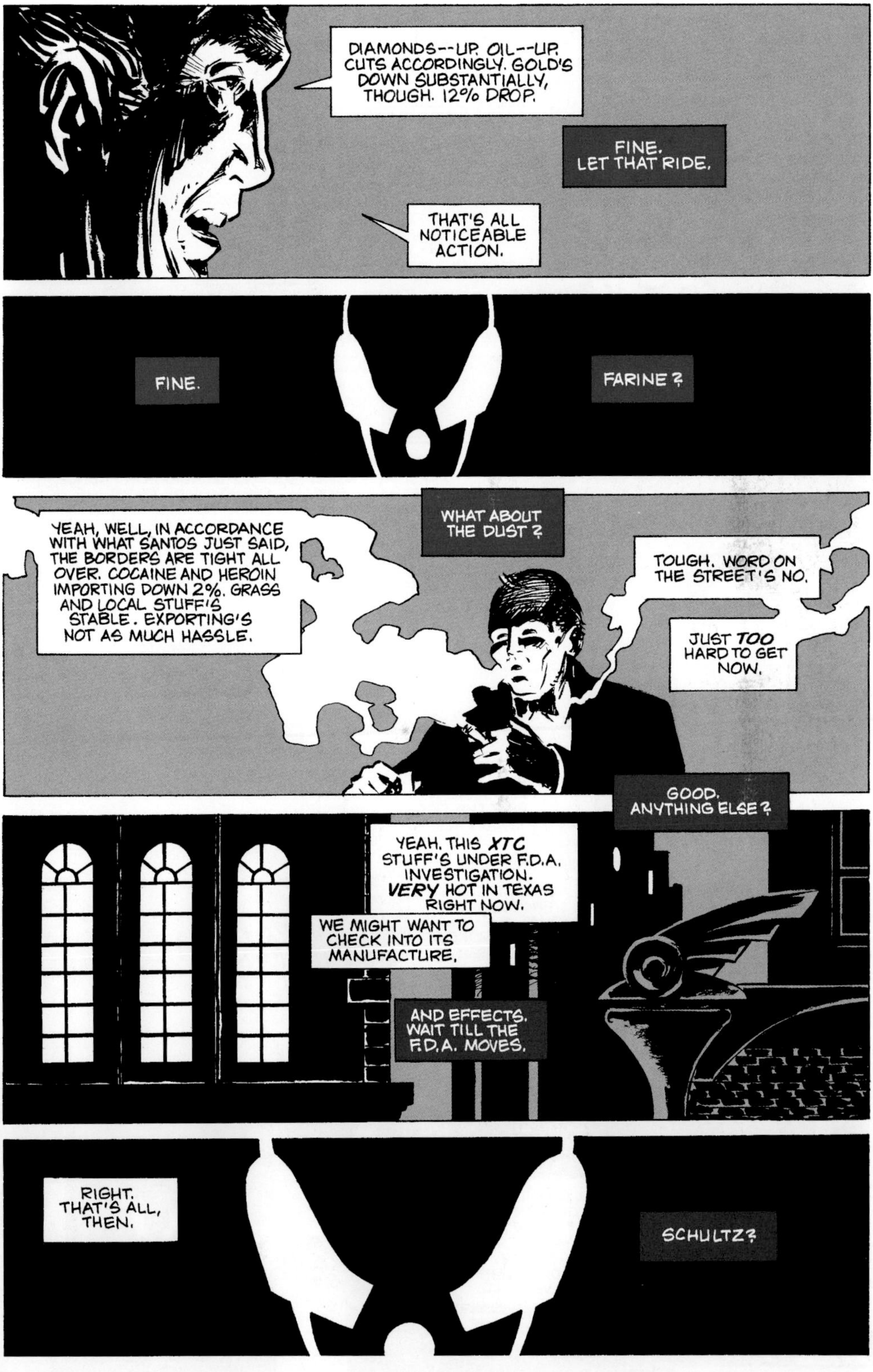

DIAMONDS--UP. OIL--UP. CUTS ACCORDINGLY. GOLD'S DOWN SUBSTANTIALLY, THOUGH. 12% DROP.
FINE. LET THAT RIDE.
THAT'S ALL NOTICEABLE ACTION.
FINE.
FARINE?
WHAT ABOUT THE DUST?
YEAH, WELL, IN ACCORDANCE WITH WHAT SANTOS JUST SAID, THE BORDERS ARE TIGHT ALL OVER. COCAINE AND HEROIN IMPORTING DOWN 2%. GRASS AND LOCAL STUFF'S STABLE. EXPORTING'S NOT AS MUCH HASSLE.
TOUGH. WORD ON THE STREET'S NO.
JUST TOO HARD TO GET NOW.
GOOD. ANYTHING ELSE?
YEAH. THIS XTC STUFF'S UNDER F.D.A. INVESTIGATION. VERY HOT IN TEXAS RIGHT NOW.
WE MIGHT WANT TO CHECK INTO ITS MANUFACTURE.
AND EFFECTS. WAIT TILL THE F.D.A. MOVES.
RIGHT. THAT'S ALL, THEN.
SCHULTZ?

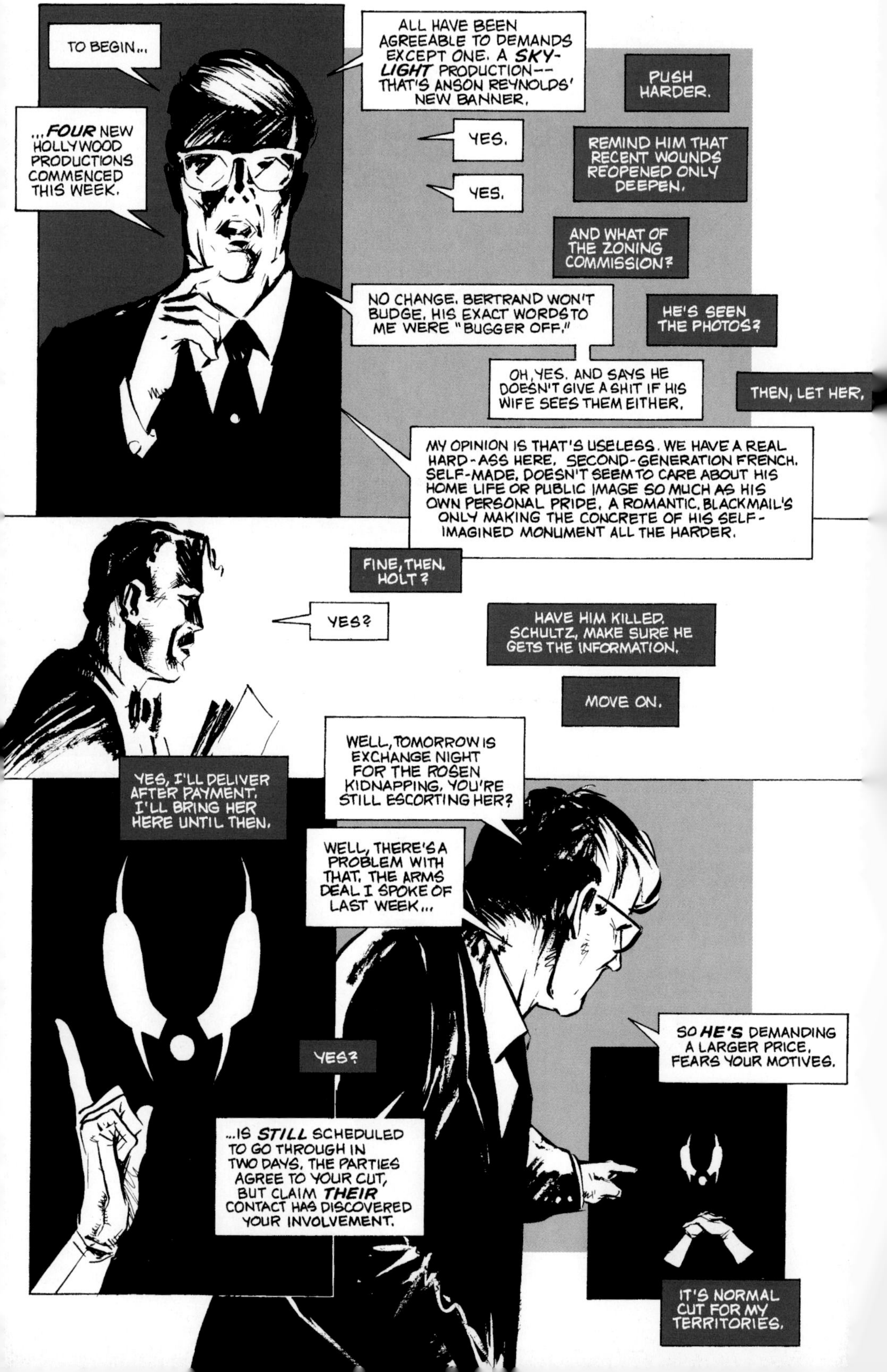

TO BEGIN...
...FOUR NEW HOLLYWOOD PRODUCTIONS COMMENCED THIS WEEK.
ALL HAVE BEEN AGREEABLE TO DEMANDS EXCEPT ONE. A SKY-LIGHT PRODUCTION-- THAT'S ANSON REYNOLDS' NEW BANNER.
PUSH HARDER.
YES.
REMIND HIM THAT RECENT WOUNDS REOPENED ONLY DEEPEN.
YES.
AND WHAT OF THE ZONING COMMISSION?
NO CHANGE. BERTRAND WON'T BUDGE. HIS EXACT WORDS TO ME WERE "BUGGER OFF."
HE'S SEEN THE PHOTOS?
OH, YES. AND SAYS HE DOESN'T GIVE A SHIT IF HIS WIFE SEES THEM EITHER.
THEN, LET HER.
MY OPINION IS THAT'S USELESS. WE HAVE A REAL HARD-ASS HERE. SECOND-GENERATION FRENCH. SELF-MADE. DOESN'T SEEM TO CARE ABOUT HIS HOME LIFE OR PUBLIC IMAGE SO MUCH AS HIS OWN PERSONAL PRIDE. A ROMANTIC. BLACKMAIL'S ONLY MAKING THE CONCRETE OF HIS SELF-IMAGINED MONUMENT ALL THE HARDER.
FINE, THEN. HOLT?
YES?
HAVE HIM KILLED. SCHULTZ, MAKE SURE HE GETS THE INFORMATION.
MOVE ON.
WELL, TOMORROW IS EXCHANGE NIGHT FOR THE ROSEN KIDNAPPING. YOU'RE STILL ESCORTING HER?
YES, I'LL DELIVER AFTER PAYMENT. I'LL BRING HER HERE UNTIL THEN.
WELL, THERE'S A PROBLEM WITH THAT. THE ARMS DEAL I SPOKE OF LAST WEEK...
YES?
...IS STILL SCHEDULED TO GO THROUGH IN TWO DAYS. THE PARTIES AGREE TO YOUR CUT, BUT CLAIM THEIR CONTACT HAS DISCOVERED YOUR INVOLVEMENT.
SO HE'S DEMANDING A LARGER PRICE. FEARS YOUR MOTIVES.
IT'S NORMAL CUT FOR MY TERRITORIES.

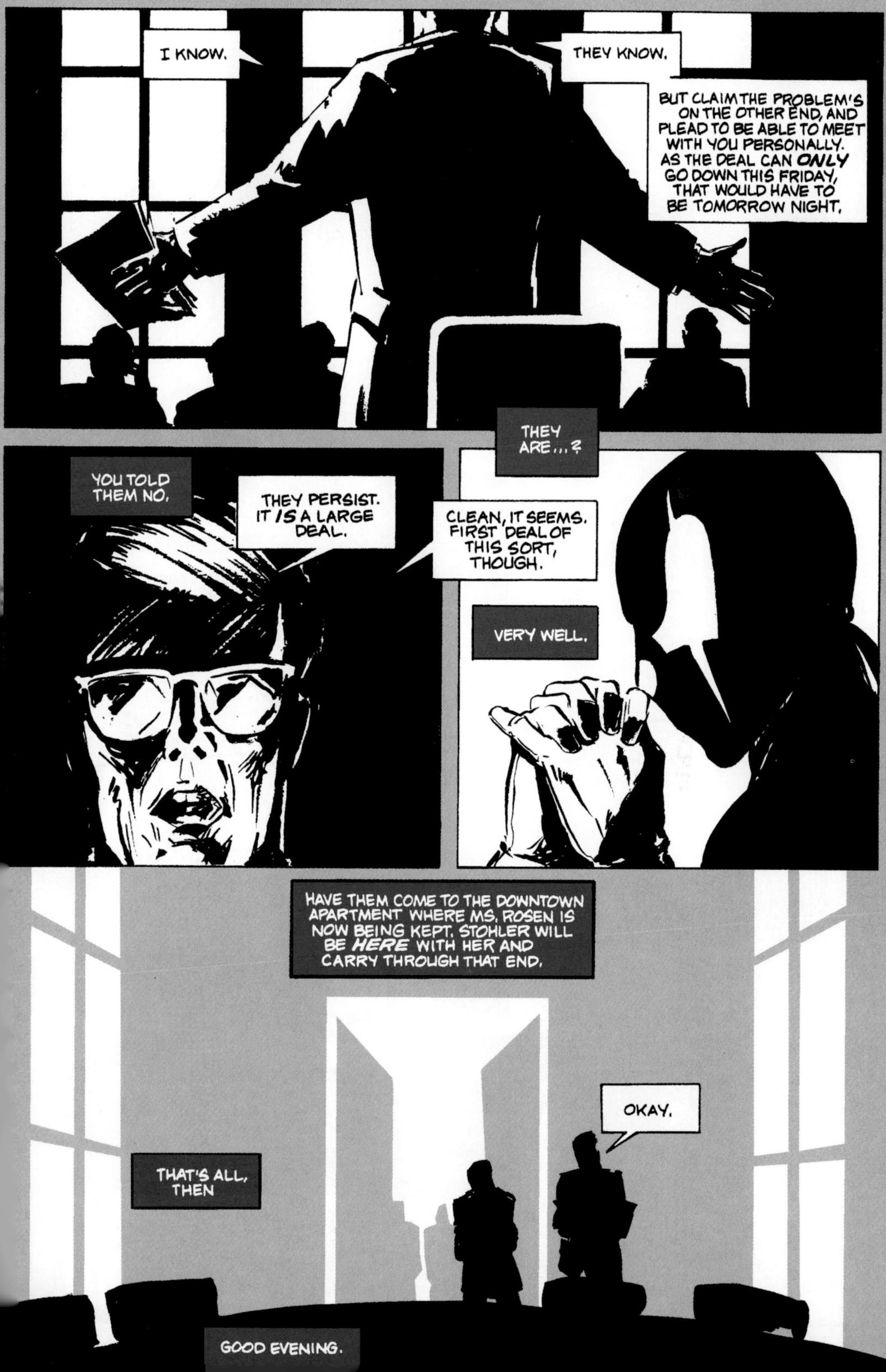
I KNOW.
THEY KNOW.
BUT CLAIM THE PROBLEM'S ON THE OTHER END, AND PLEAD TO BE ABLE TO MEET WITH YOU PERSONALLY. AS THE DEAL CAN ONLY GO DOWN THIS FRIDAY, THAT WOULD HAVE TO BE TOMORROW NIGHT.
YOU TOLD THEM NO.
THEY PERSIST. IT IS A LARGE DEAL.
THEY ARE...?
CLEAN, IT SEEMS. FIRST DEAL OF THIS SORT, THOUGH.
VERY WELL.
HAVE THEM COME TO THE DOWNTOWN APARTMENT WHERE MS. ROSEN IS NOW BEING KEPT. STOHLER WILL BE HERE WITH HER AND CARRY THROUGH THAT END.
OKAY.
THAT'S ALL, THEN
GOOD EVENING.

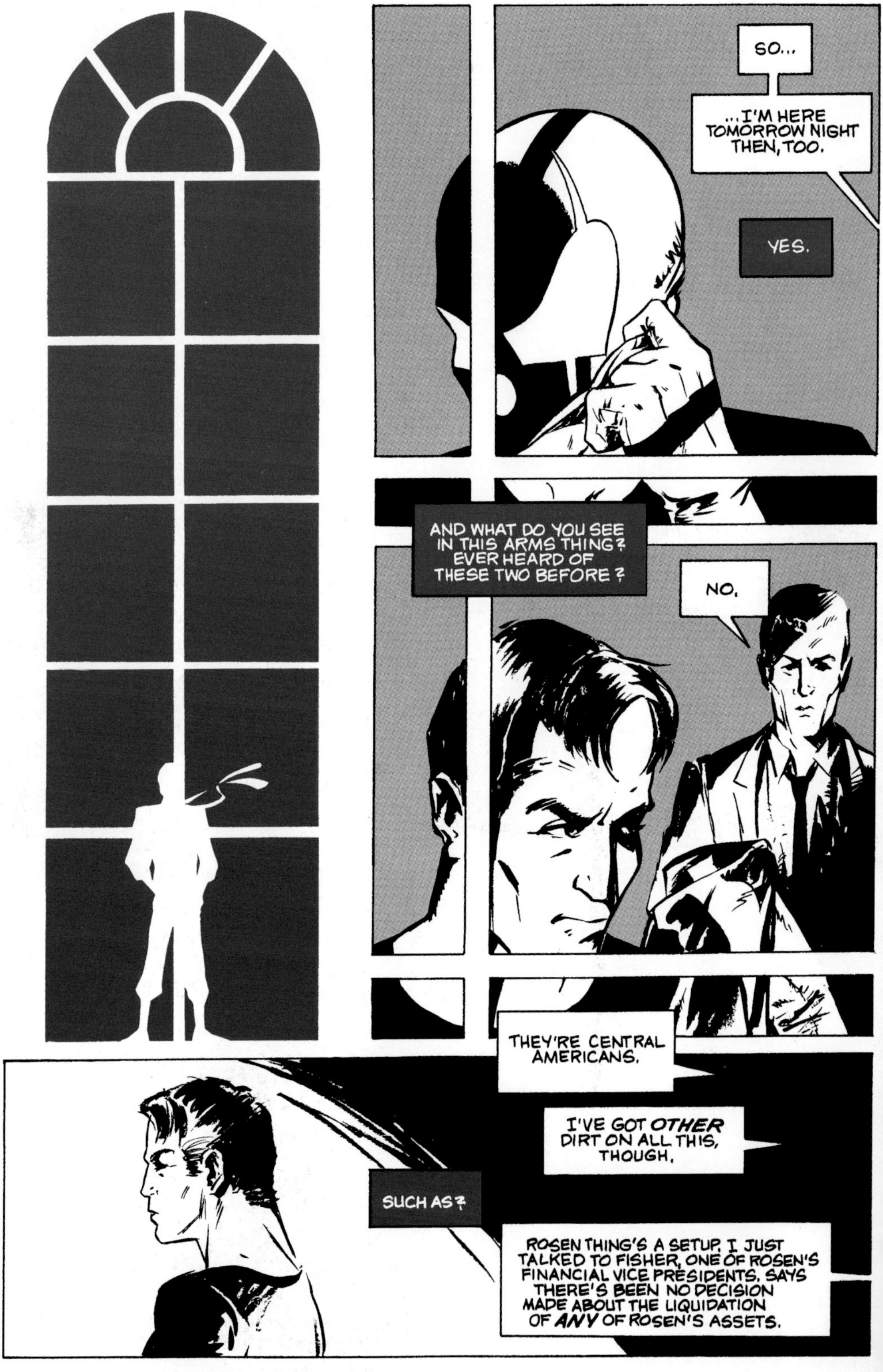
SO...
...I'M HERE TOMORROW NIGHT THEN, TOO.
YES.
AND WHAT DO YOU SEE IN THIS ARMS THING? EVER HEARD OF THESE TWO BEFORE?
NO.
THEY'RE CENTRAL AMERICANS.
I'VE GOT *OTHER* DIRT ON ALL THIS, THOUGH.
SUCH AS?
ROSEN THING'S A SETUP. I JUST TALKED TO FISHER, ONE OF ROSEN'S FINANCIAL VICE PRESIDENTS. SAYS THERE'S BEEN NO DECISION MADE ABOUT THE LIQUIDATION OF *ANY* OF ROSEN'S ASSETS.

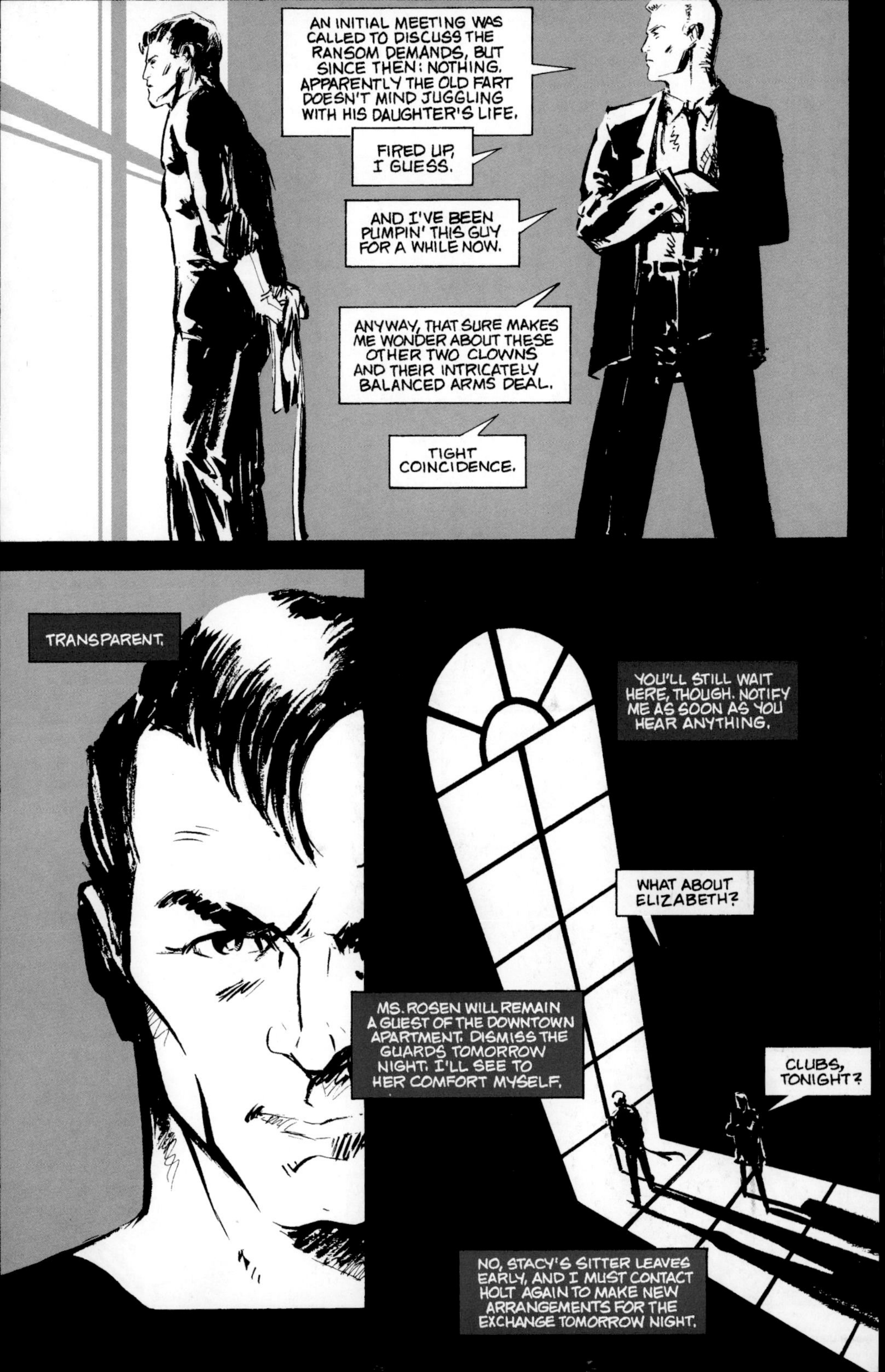
AN INITIAL MEETING WAS CALLED TO DISCUSS THE RANSOM DEMANDS, BUT SINCE THEN: NOTHING. APPARENTLY THE OLD FART DOESN'T MIND JUGGLING WITH HIS DAUGHTER'S LIFE.
FIRED UP, I GUESS.
AND I'VE BEEN PUMPIN' THIS GUY FOR A WHILE NOW.
ANYWAY, THAT SURE MAKES ME WONDER ABOUT THESE OTHER TWO CLOWNS AND THEIR INTRICATELY BALANCED ARMS DEAL.
TIGHT COINCIDENCE.
TRANSPARENT.
YOU'LL STILL WAIT HERE, THOUGH. NOTIFY ME AS SOON AS YOU HEAR ANYTHING.
WHAT ABOUT ELIZABETH?
MS. ROSEN WILL REMAIN A GUEST OF THE DOWNTOWN APARTMENT. DISMISS THE GUARDS TOMORROW NIGHT. I'LL SEE TO HER COMFORT MYSELF.
CLUBS, TONIGHT?
NO, STACY'S SITTER LEAVES EARLY, AND I MUST CONTACT HOLT AGAIN TO MAKE NEW ARRANGEMENTS FOR THE EXCHANGE TOMORROW NIGHT.

I WONDERED IF I'D EVER SET EYES ON YOU AGAIN. AM I *STILL* TO BE RELEASED TONIGHT?

THE VERDICT ON THAT'S STILL FORTHCOMING. DO RELAX. FOR NOW, WE WAIT.

WAIT ON WHAT?

ON A NUMBER OF MEN...

...AND A NUMBER OF SITUATIONS.

I *DON'T LIKE* WAITING ON SITUATIONS, AND I'M *NOT USED* TO WAITING ON MEN.

AND *YOU'VE* KEPT ME WAITING FOR THREE WEEKS ALREADY...

MIGHT'VE BEEN FOUR. YOUR FATHER'S A GOAT.

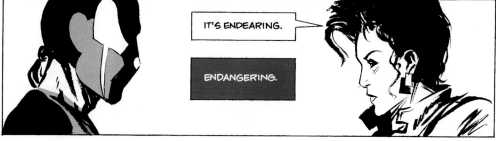

IT'S ENDEARING.

ENDANGERING.

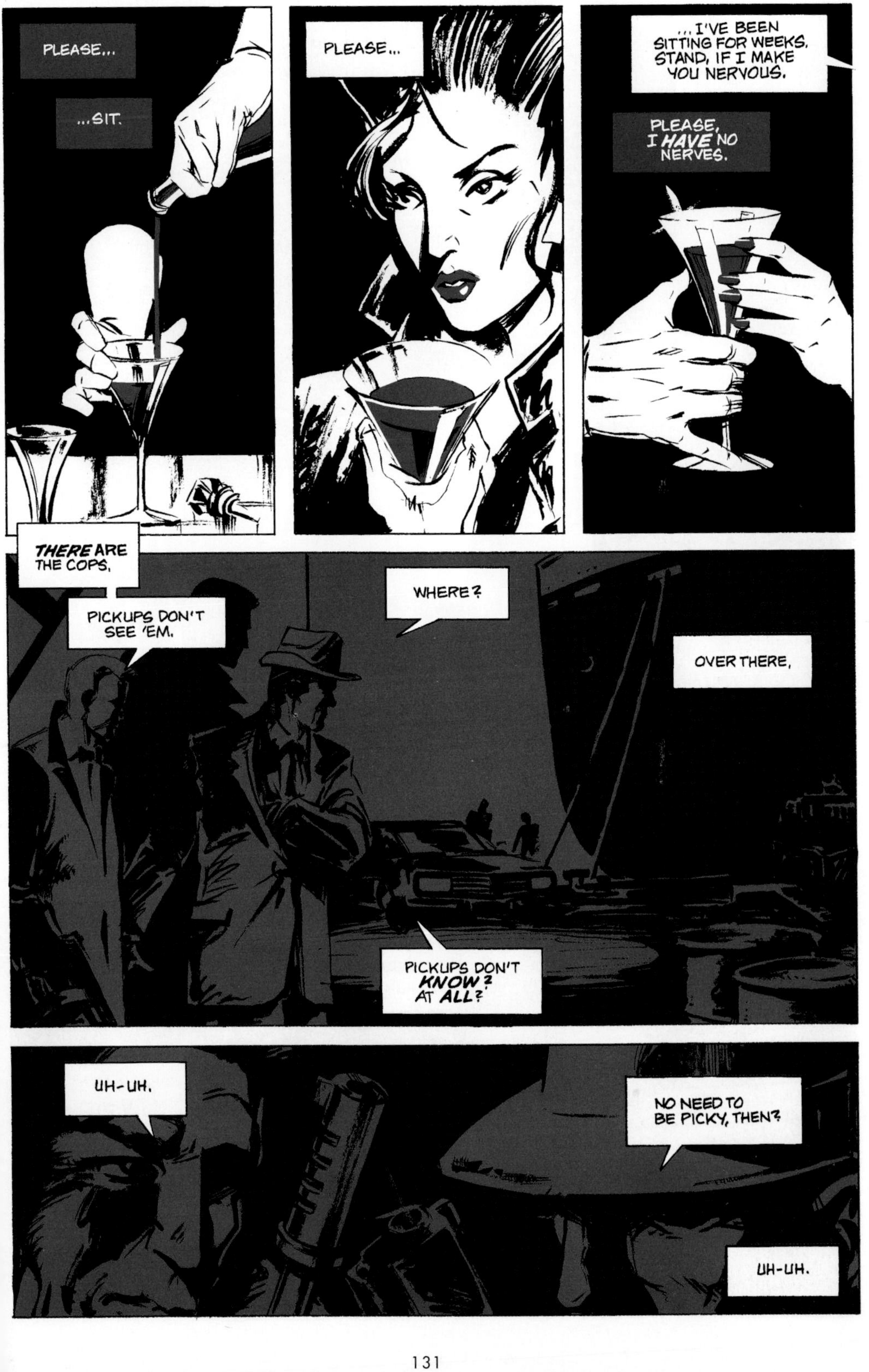
PLEASE...
...SIT.
PLEASE...
...I'VE BEEN SITTING FOR WEEKS. STAND, IF I MAKE YOU NERVOUS.
PLEASE, I HAVE NO NERVES.
THERE ARE THE COPS.
PICKUPS DON'T SEE 'EM.
WHERE?
OVER THERE.
PICKUPS DON'T KNOW? AT ALL?
UH-UH.
NO NEED TO BE PICKY, THEN?
UH-UH.

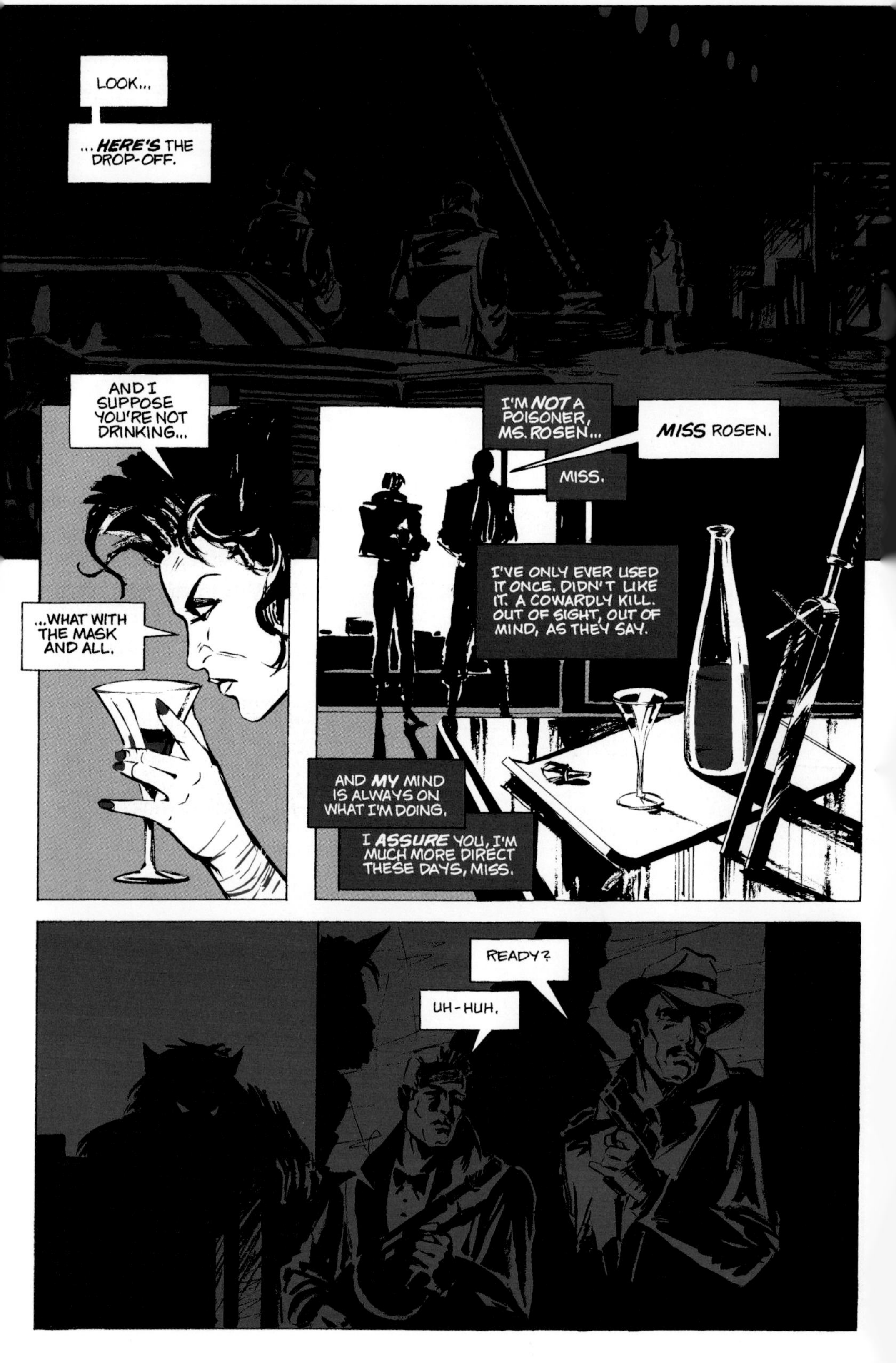
LOOK...
...HERE'S THE DROP-OFF.
AND I SUPPOSE YOU'RE NOT DRINKING...
...WHAT WITH THE MASK AND ALL.
I'M NOT A POISONER, MS. ROSEN...
MISS ROSEN.
MISS.
I'VE ONLY EVER USED IT ONCE. DIDN'T LIKE IT. A COWARDLY KILL. OUT OF SIGHT, OUT OF MIND, AS THEY SAY.
AND MY MIND IS ALWAYS ON WHAT I'M DOING.
I ASSURE YOU, I'M MUCH MORE DIRECT THESE DAYS, MISS.
READY?
UH-HUH.

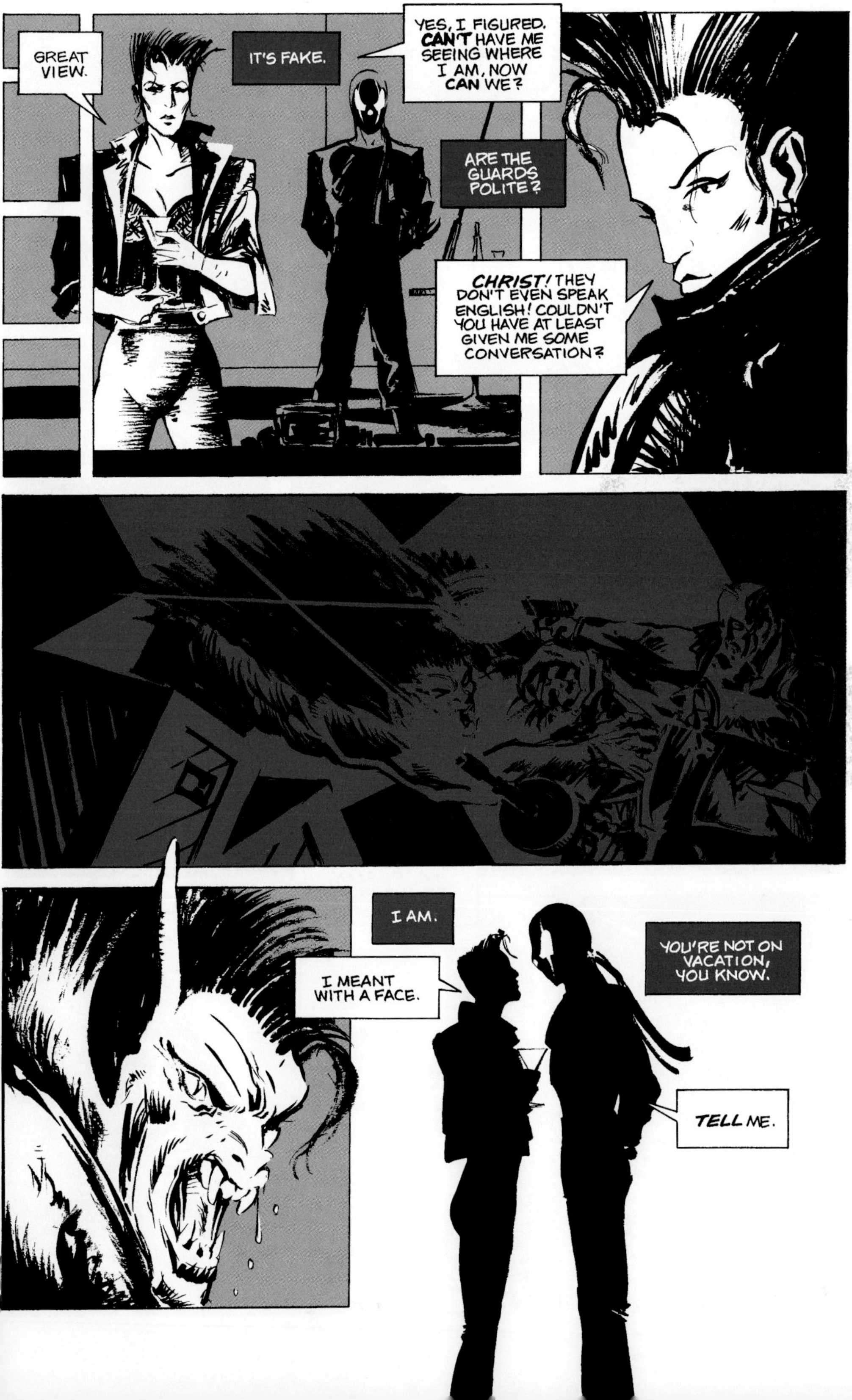
GREAT VIEW.
IT'S FAKE.
YES, I FIGURED. CAN'T HAVE ME SEEING WHERE I AM, NOW CAN WE?
ARE THE GUARDS POLITE?
CHRIST! THEY DON'T EVEN SPEAK ENGLISH! COULDN'T YOU HAVE AT LEAST GIVEN ME SOME CONVERSATION?
I AM.
I MEANT WITH A FACE.
YOU'RE NOT ON VACATION, YOU KNOW.
TELL ME.

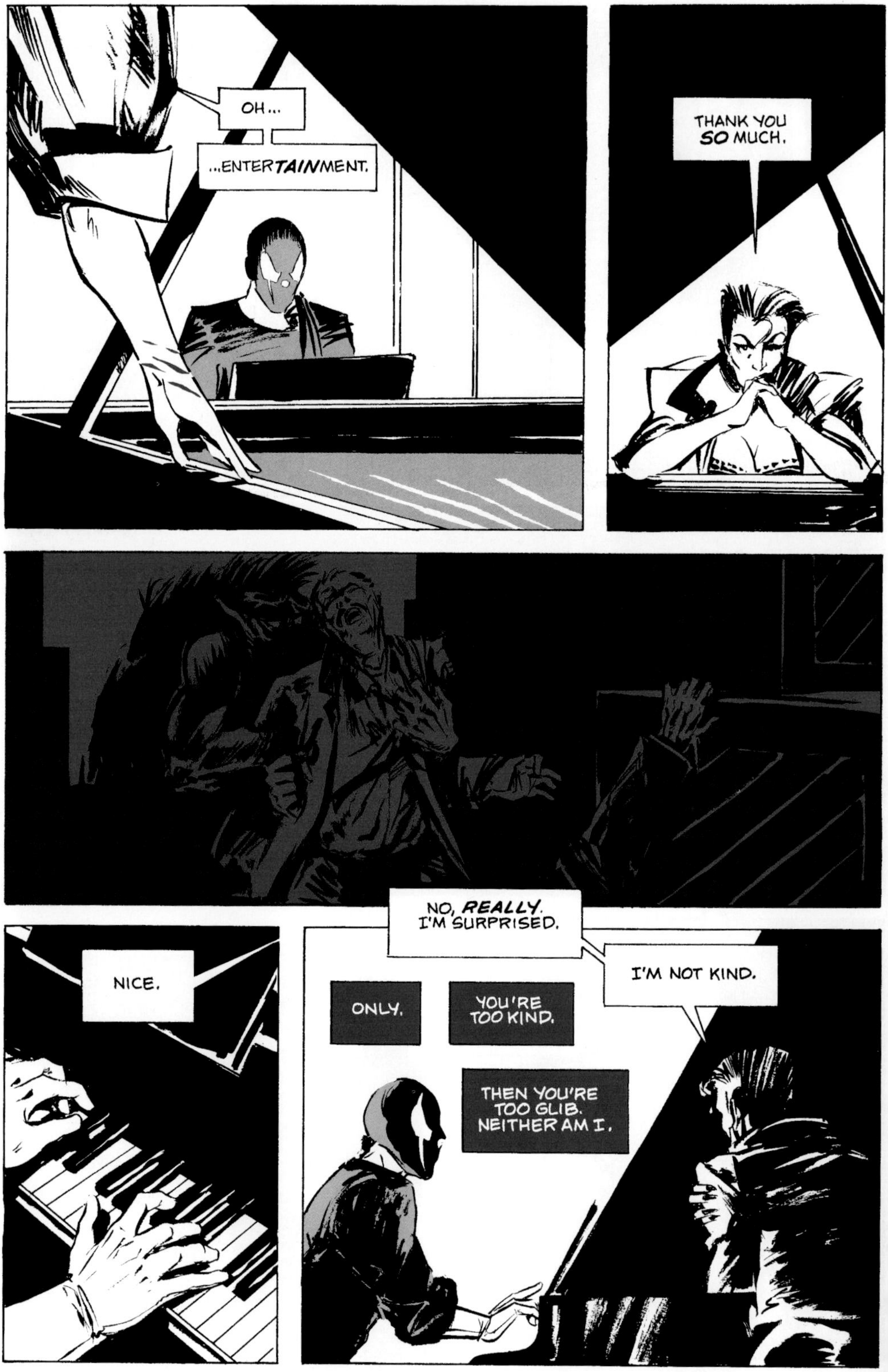
OH...
...ENTERTAINMENT.
THANK YOU SO MUCH.
NICE.
ONLY.
NO, REALLY. I'M SURPRISED.
YOU'RE TOO KIND.
I'M NOT KIND.
THEN YOU'RE TOO GLIB. NEITHER AM I.

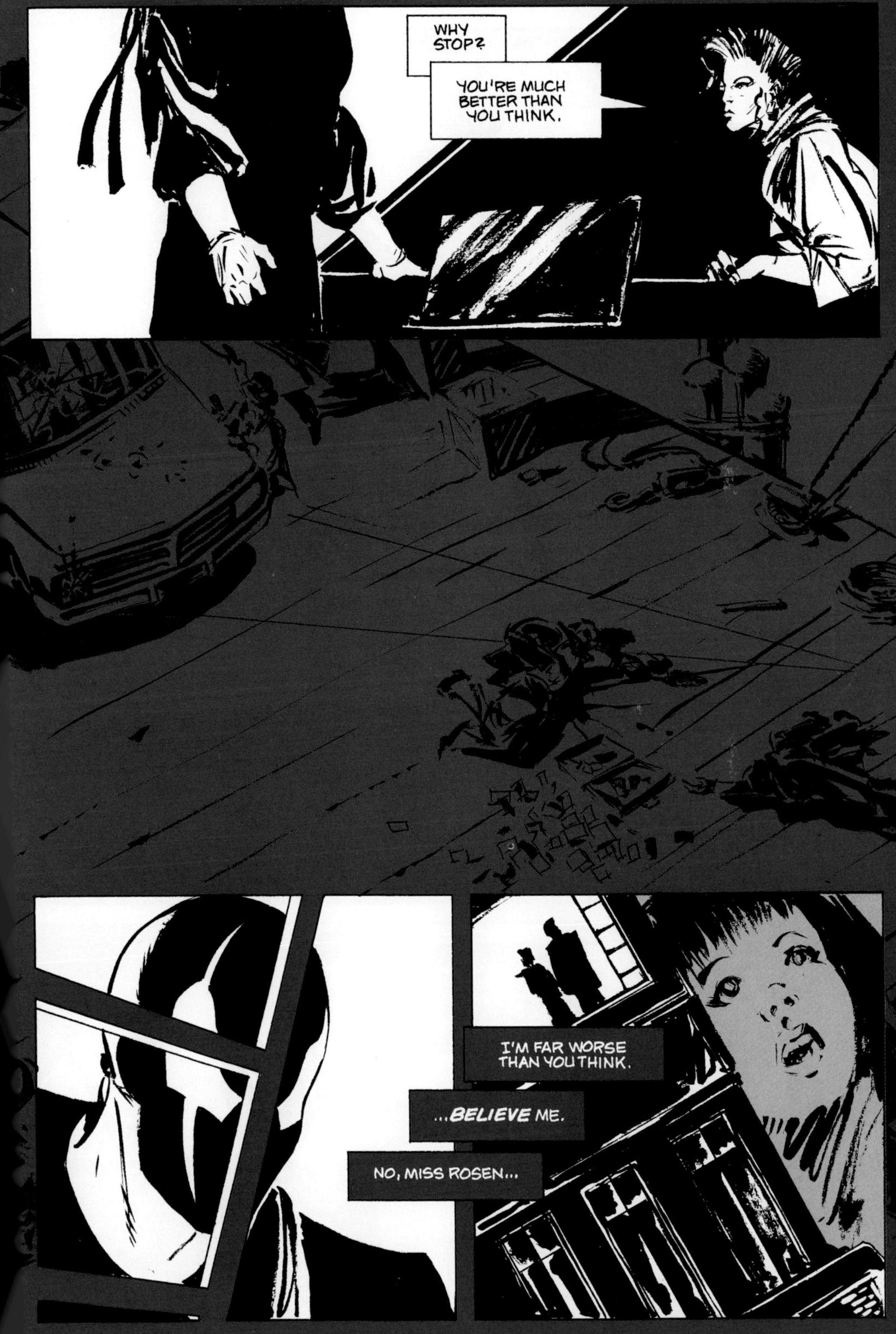
WHY STOP?
YOU'RE MUCH BETTER THAN YOU THINK.
I'M FAR WORSE THAN YOU THINK.
...BELIEVE ME.
NO, MISS ROSEN...

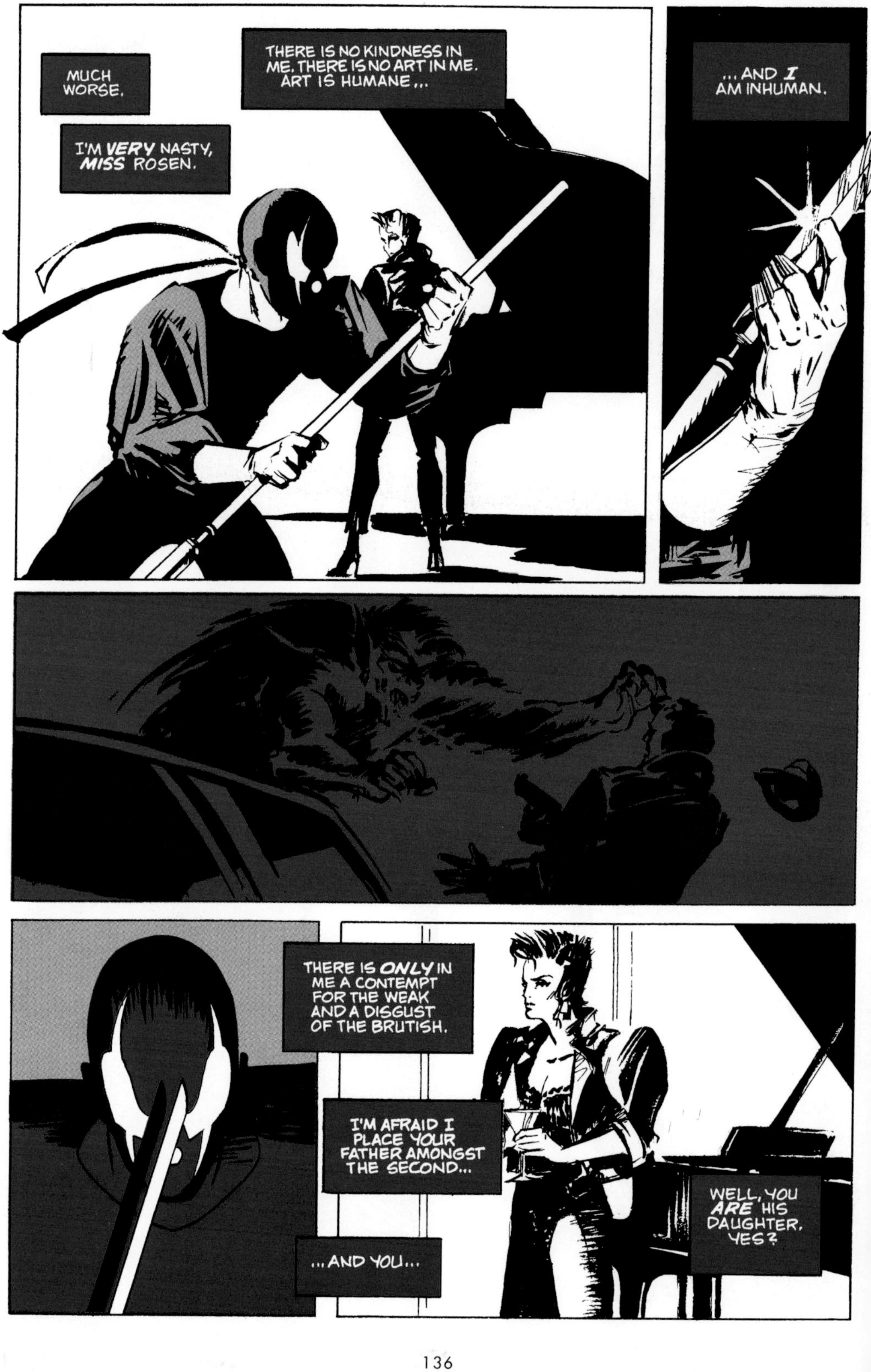
MUCH WORSE.
I'M VERY NASTY, MISS ROSEN.
THERE IS NO KINDNESS IN ME. THERE IS NO ART IN ME. ART IS HUMANE...
...AND I AM INHUMAN.
THERE IS ONLY IN ME A CONTEMPT FOR THE WEAK AND A DISGUST OF THE BRUTISH.
I'M AFRAID I PLACE YOUR FATHER AMONGST THE SECOND...
...AND YOU...
WELL, YOU ARE HIS DAUGHTER, YES?

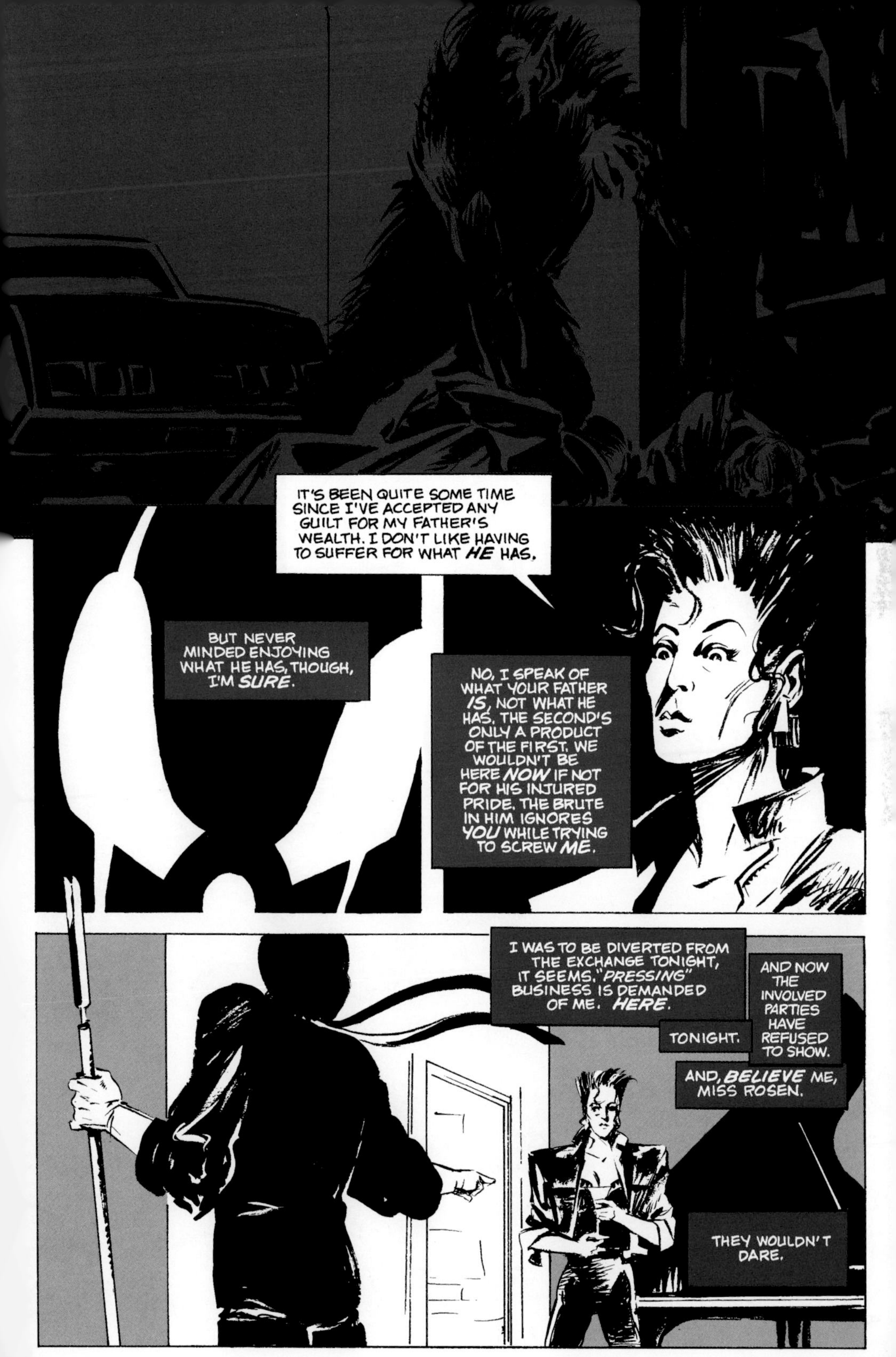

IT'S BEEN QUITE SOME TIME SINCE I'VE ACCEPTED ANY GUILT FOR MY FATHER'S WEALTH. I DON'T LIKE HAVING TO SUFFER FOR WHAT *HE* HAS.
BUT NEVER MINDED ENJOYING WHAT HE HAS, THOUGH, I'M *SURE*.
NO, I SPEAK OF WHAT YOUR FATHER *IS*, NOT WHAT HE HAS. THE SECOND'S ONLY A PRODUCT OF THE FIRST. WE WOULDN'T BE HERE *NOW* IF NOT FOR HIS INJURED PRIDE. THE BRUTE IN HIM IGNORES *YOU* WHILE TRYING TO SCREW *ME*.
I WAS TO BE DIVERTED FROM THE EXCHANGE TONIGHT, IT SEEMS. "*PRESSING*" BUSINESS IS DEMANDED OF ME. *HERE*.
TONIGHT.
AND NOW THE INVOLVED PARTIES HAVE REFUSED TO SHOW.
AND, *BELIEVE* ME, MISS ROSEN.
THEY WOULDN'T DARE.

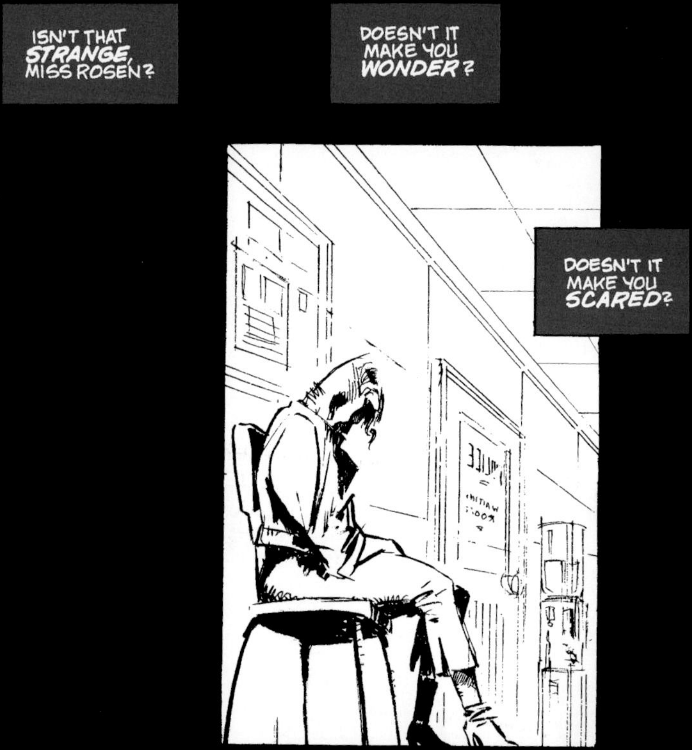
ISN'T THAT STRANGE, MISS ROSEN?
DOESN'T IT MAKE YOU WONDER?
DOESN'T IT MAKE YOU SCARED?

Samuel Rosen had, in fact, worked with the police to arrange an arms scam so as to draw Grendel off from the kidnapping scene. As the Wolf was to be involved, Elizabeth's safety was feared for, should the two clash. The swindle was detected and tragedy resulted, as the arrests were bloody and the hostage not retrieved. Two days later, Elizabeth Rosen was found sitting in the waiting room of Police Headquarters, quite dead.

Excerpt from Devil by the Deed

by Christine Spar

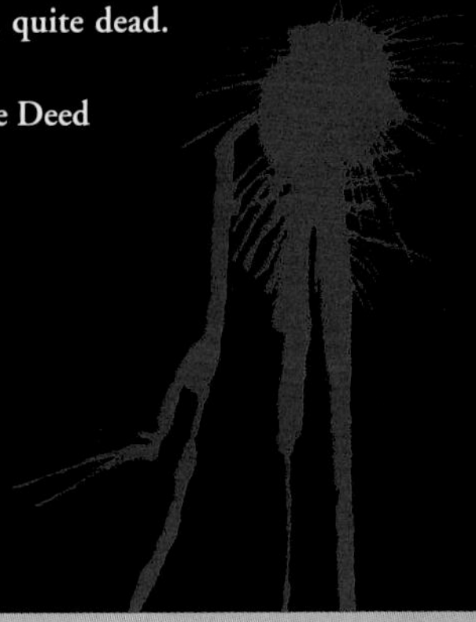

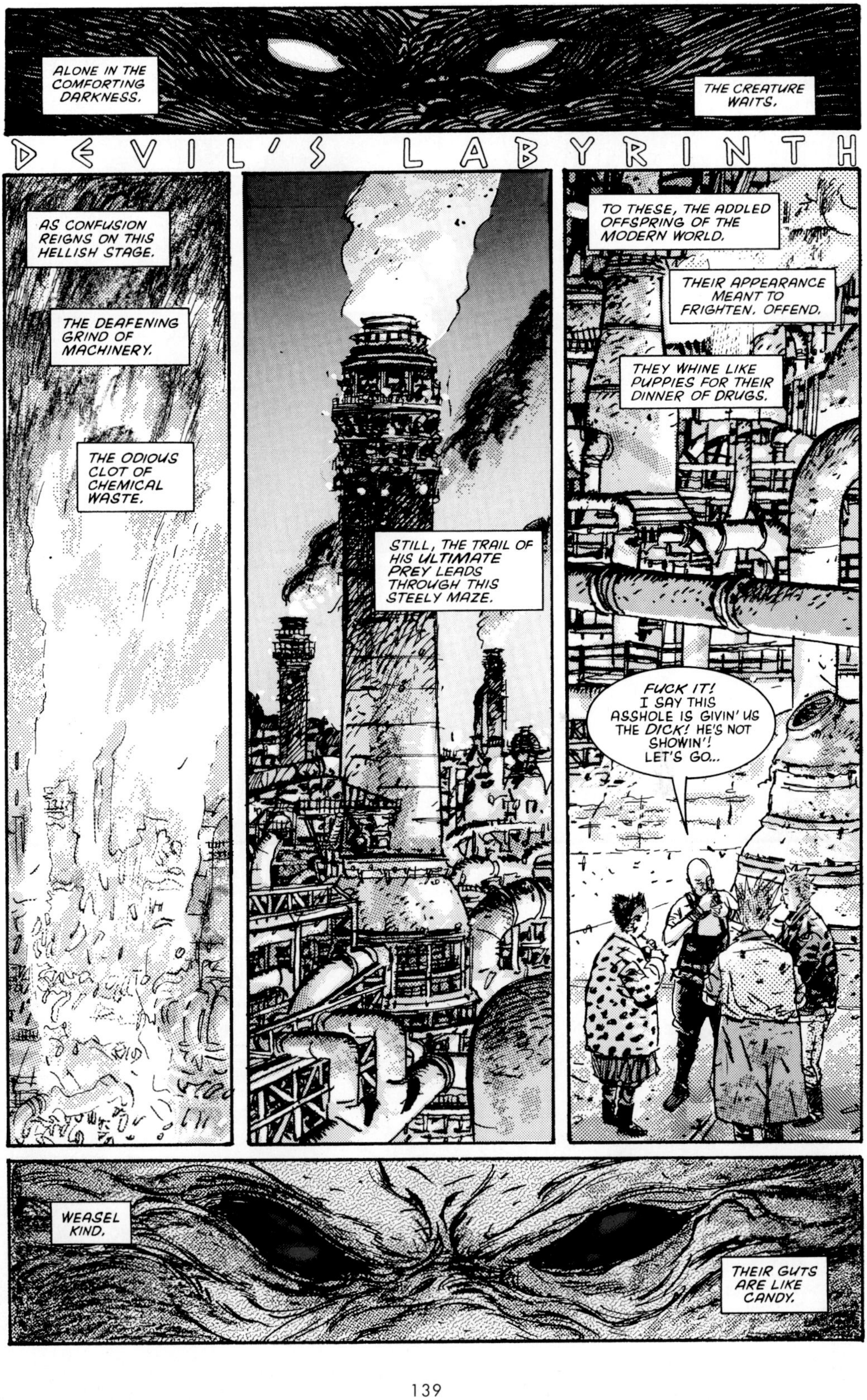

ALONE IN THE COMFORTING DARKNESS.
THE CREATURE WAITS.
DEVIL'S LABYRINTH
AS CONFUSION REIGNS ON THIS HELLISH STAGE.
THE DEAFENING GRIND OF MACHINERY.
THE ODIOUS CLOT OF CHEMICAL WASTE.
STILL, THE TRAIL OF HIS ULTIMATE PREY LEADS THROUGH THIS STEELY MAZE.
TO THESE, THE ADDLED OFFSPRING OF THE MODERN WORLD.
THEIR APPEARANCE MEANT TO FRIGHTEN. OFFEND.
THEY WHINE LIKE PUPPIES FOR THEIR DINNER OF DRUGS.
FUCK IT! I SAY THIS ASSHOLE IS GIVIN' US THE DICK! HE'S NOT SHOWIN'! LET'S GO...
WEASEL KIND.
THEIR GUTS ARE LIKE CANDY.

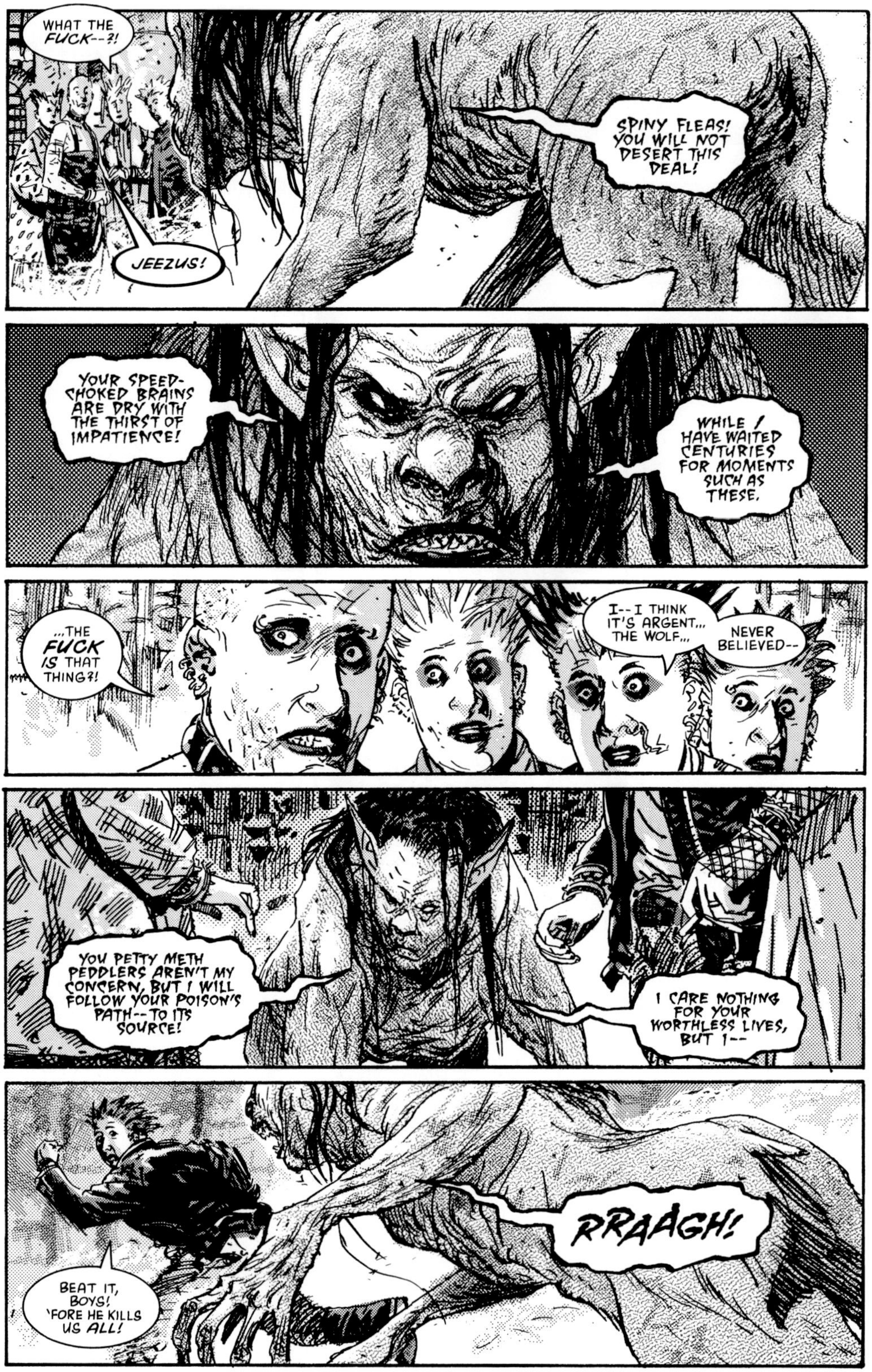
WHAT THE FUCK--?!
JEEZUS!
SPINY FLEAS! YOU WILL NOT DESERT THIS DEAL!
YOUR SPEED-CHOKED BRAINS ARE DRY WITH THE THIRST OF IMPATIENCE!
WHILE I HAVE WAITED CENTURIES FOR MOMENTS SUCH AS THESE.
...THE FUCK IS THAT THING?!
I-- I THINK IT'S ARGENT... THE WOLF...
NEVER BELIEVED--
YOU PETTY METH PEDDLERS AREN'T MY CONCERN, BUT I WILL FOLLOW YOUR POISON'S PATH--TO ITS SOURCE!
I CARE NOTHING FOR YOUR WORTHLESS LIVES, BUT I--
RRAAGH!
BEAT IT, BOYS! 'FORE HE KILLS US ALL!

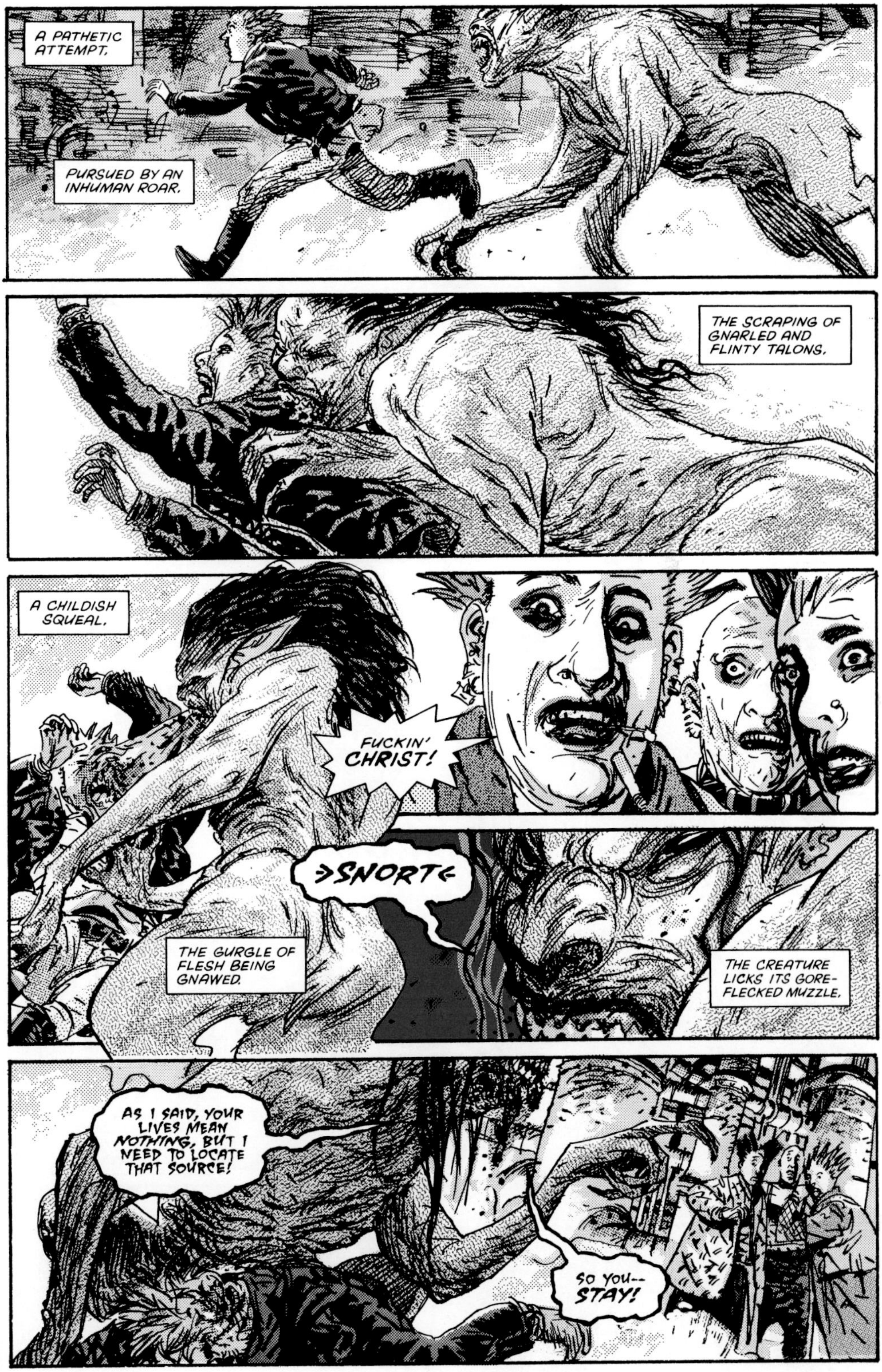
A PATHETIC ATTEMPT,
PURSUED BY AN INHUMAN ROAR.
THE SCRAPING OF GNARLED AND FLINTY TALONS.
A CHILDISH SQUEAL.
FUCKIN' CHRIST!
>SNORT<
THE GURGLE OF FLESH BEING GNAWED.
THE CREATURE LICKS ITS GORE-FLECKED MUZZLE.
AS I SAID, YOUR LIVES MEAN NOTHING, BUT I NEED TO LOCATE THAT SOURCE!
SO YOU-- STAY!

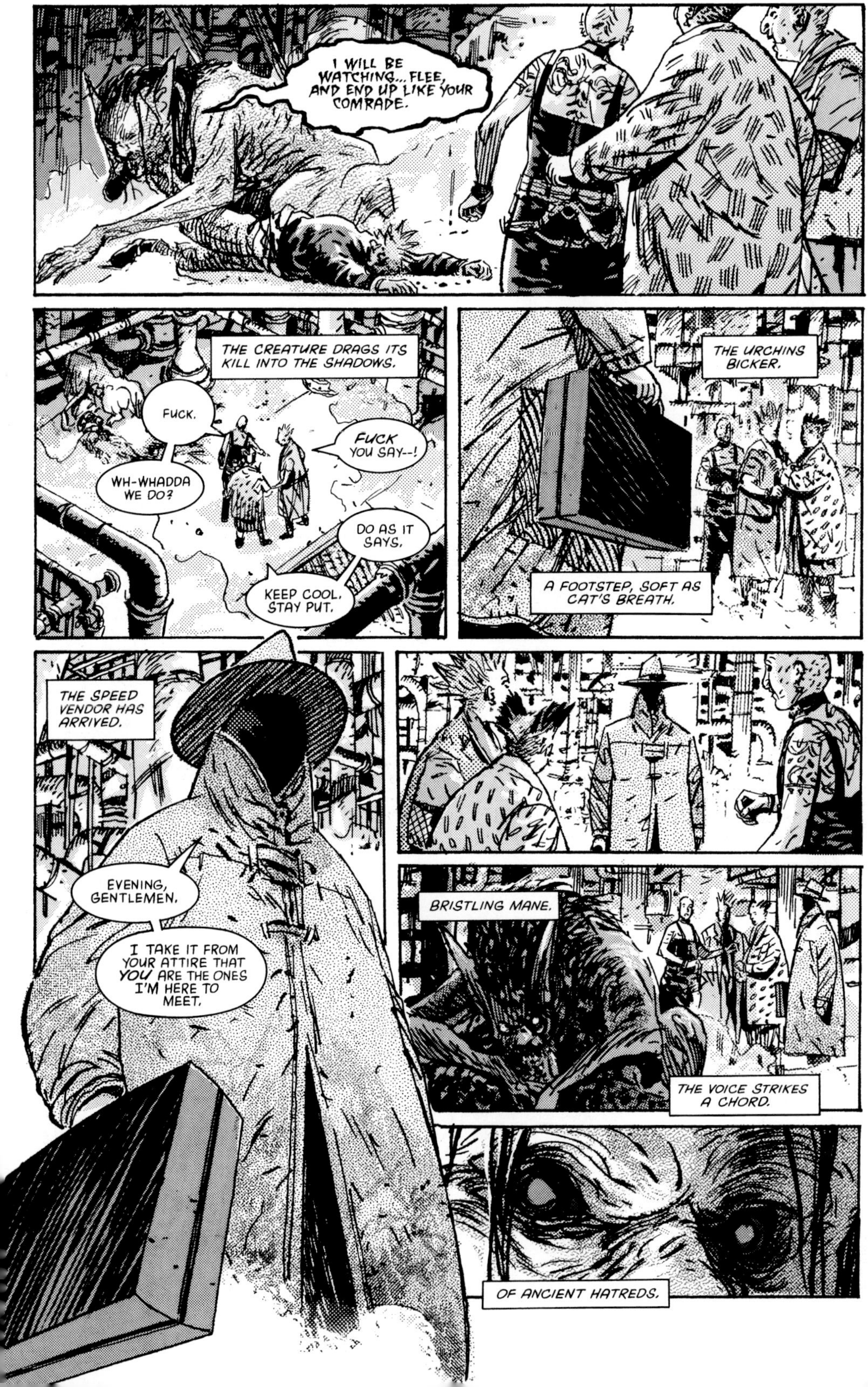
I WILL BE WATCHING... FLEE, AND END UP LIKE YOUR COMRADE.
THE CREATURE DRAGS ITS KILL INTO THE SHADOWS.
FUCK.
FUCK YOU SAY--!
WH-WHADDA WE DO?
DO AS IT SAYS.
KEEP COOL, STAY PUT.
THE URCHINS BICKER.
A FOOTSTEP, SOFT AS CAT'S BREATH.
THE SPEED VENDOR HAS ARRIVED.
EVENING, GENTLEMEN.
I TAKE IT FROM YOUR ATTIRE THAT YOU ARE THE ONES I'M HERE TO MEET.
BRISTLING MANE.
THE VOICE STRIKES A CHORD.
OF ANCIENT HATREDS.

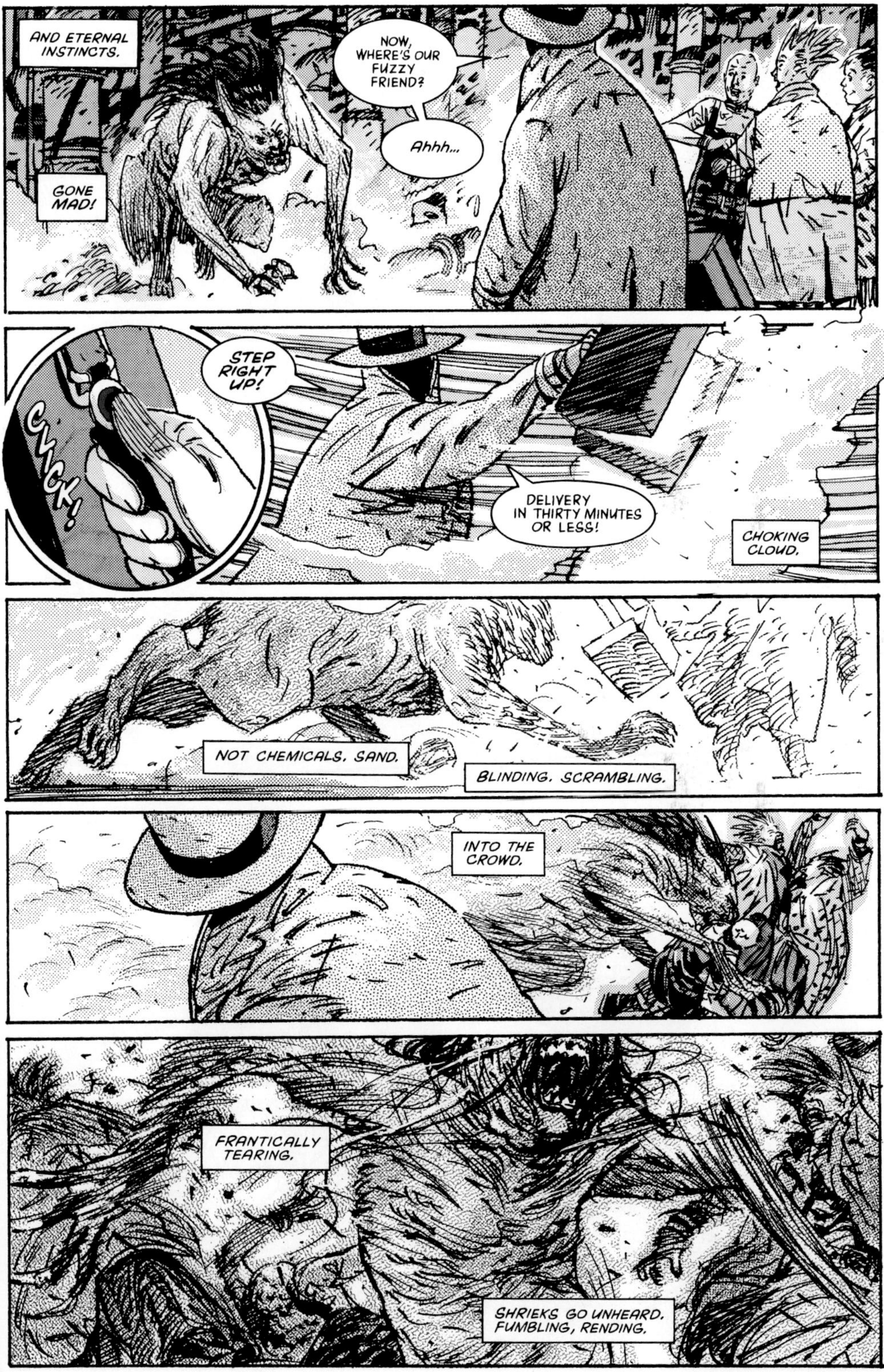
AND ETERNAL INSTINCTS.
GONE MAD!
NOW, WHERE'S OUR FUZZY FRIEND?
Ahhh...
STEP RIGHT UP!
CLICK!
DELIVERY IN THIRTY MINUTES OR LESS!
CHOKING CLOUD.
NOT CHEMICALS. SAND.
BLINDING. SCRAMBLING.
INTO THE CROWD.
FRANTICALLY TEARING.
SHRIEKS GO UNHEARD. FUMBLING, RENDING.

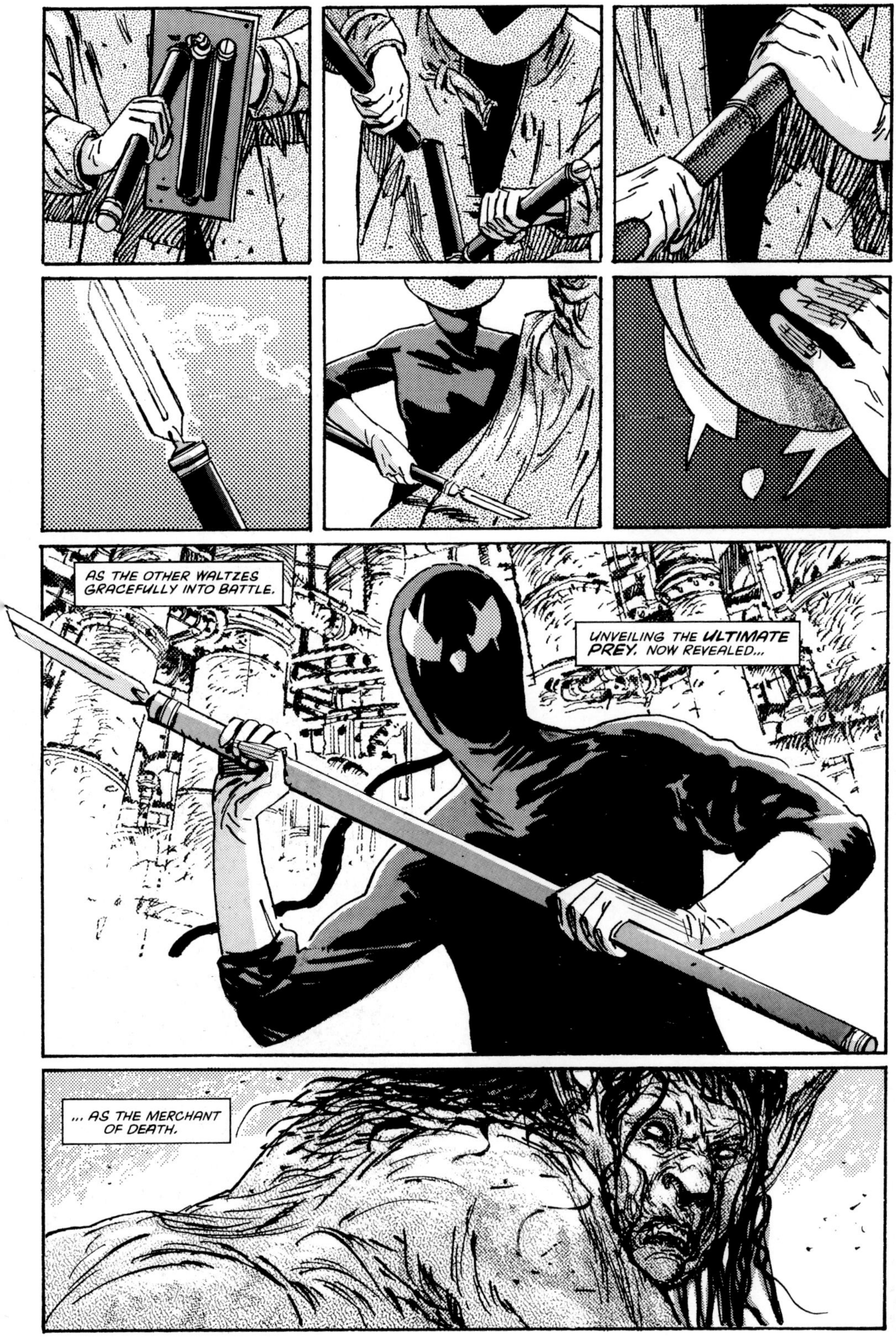

AS THE OTHER WALTZES GRACEFULLY INTO BATTLE.
UNVEILING THE ULTIMATE PREY. NOW REVEALED...
... AS THE MERCHANT OF DEATH.

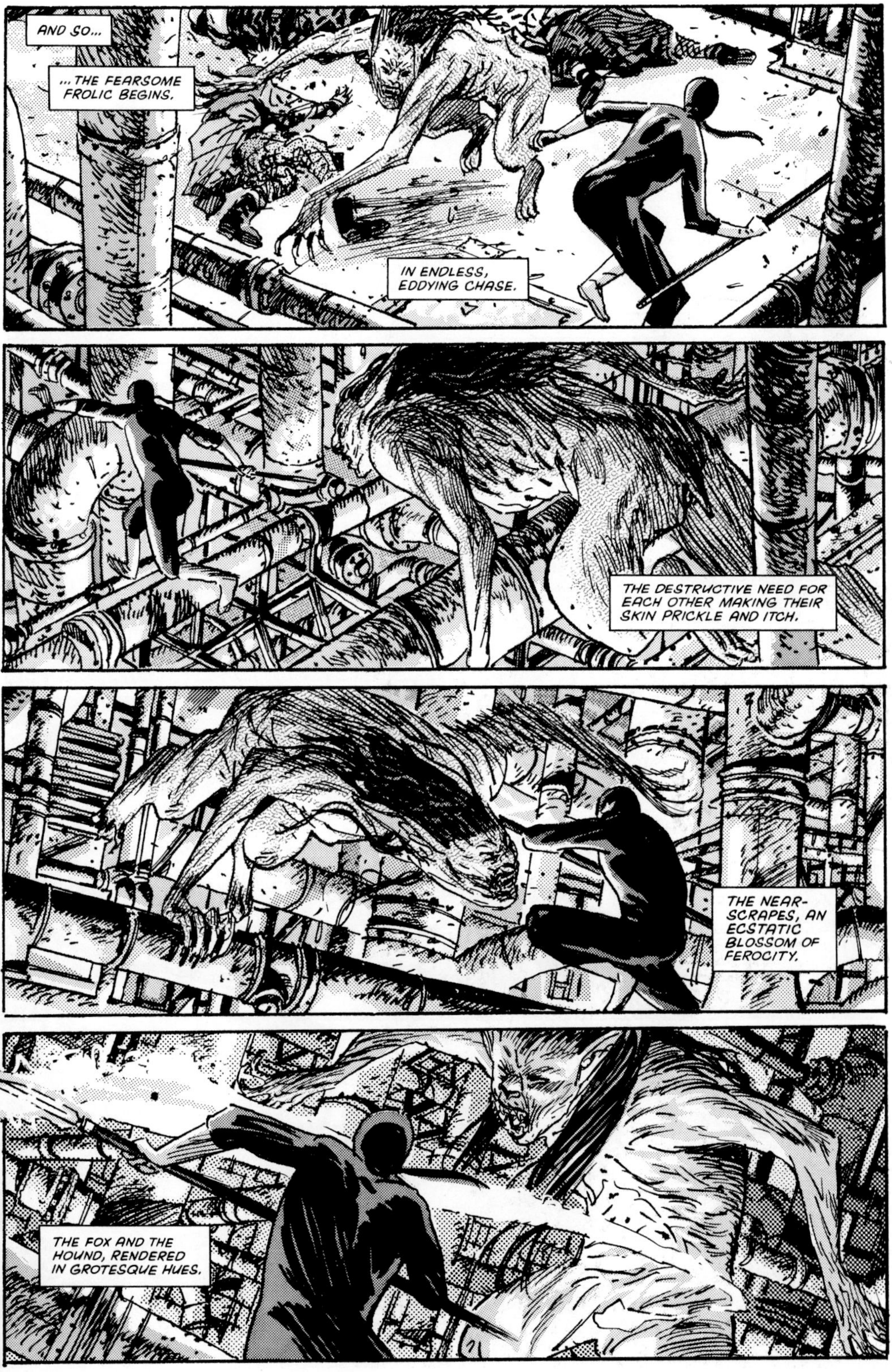
AND SO...
...THE FEARSOME FROLIC BEGINS.
IN ENDLESS, EDDYING CHASE.
THE DESTRUCTIVE NEED FOR EACH OTHER MAKING THEIR SKIN PRICKLE AND ITCH.
THE NEAR-SCRAPES, AN ECSTATIC BLOSSOM OF FEROCITY.
THE FOX AND THE HOUND, RENDERED IN GROTESQUE HUES.

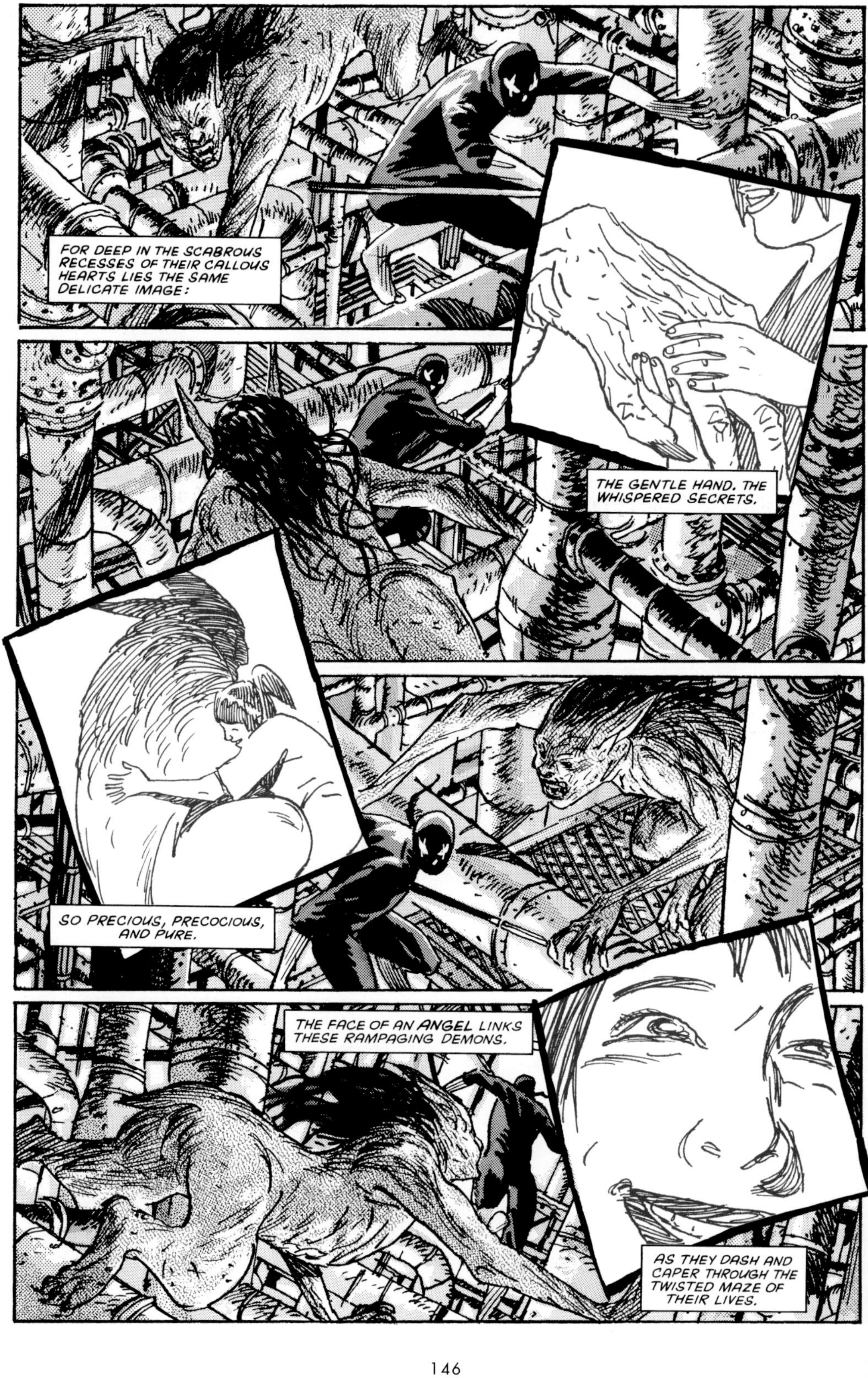
FOR DEEP IN THE SCABROUS RECESSES OF THEIR CALLOUS HEARTS LIES THE SAME DELICATE IMAGE:
THE GENTLE HAND. THE WHISPERED SECRETS.
SO PRECIOUS, PRECOCIOUS, AND PURE.
THE FACE OF AN ANGEL LINKS THESE RAMPAGING DEMONS.
AS THEY DASH AND CAPER THROUGH THE TWISTED MAZE OF THEIR LIVES.

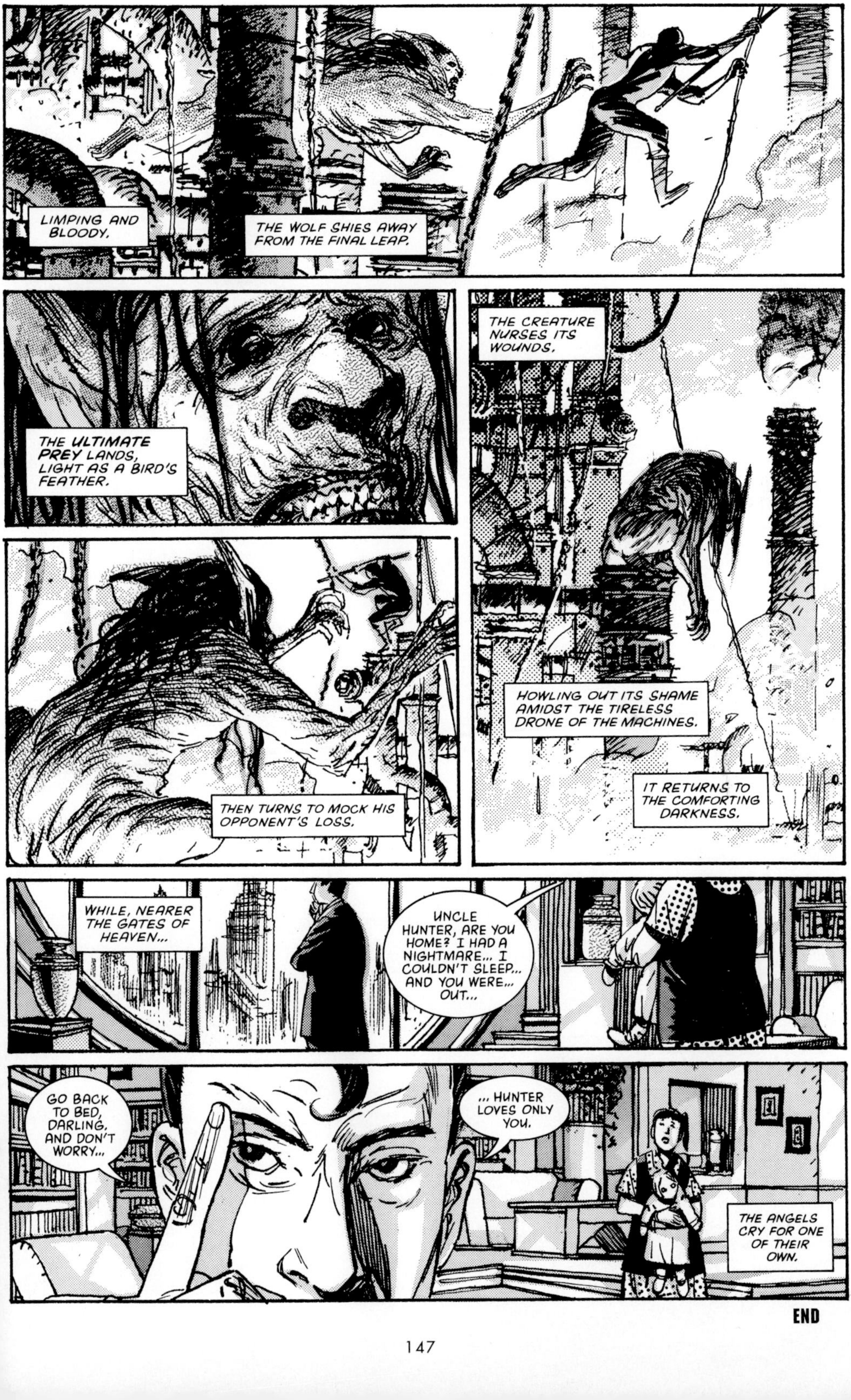
LIMPING AND BLOODY.
THE WOLF SHIES AWAY FROM THE FINAL LEAP.
THE ULTIMATE PREY LANDS, LIGHT AS A BIRD'S FEATHER.
THEN TURNS TO MOCK HIS OPPONENT'S LOSS.
THE CREATURE NURSES ITS WOUNDS.
HOWLING OUT ITS SHAME AMIDST THE TIRELESS DRONE OF THE MACHINES.
IT RETURNS TO THE COMFORTING DARKNESS.
WHILE, NEARER THE GATES OF HEAVEN...
UNCLE HUNTER, ARE YOU HOME? I HAD A NIGHTMARE... I COULDN'T SLEEP... AND YOU WERE... OUT...
GO BACK TO BED, DARLING, AND DON'T WORRY...
... HUNTER LOVES ONLY YOU.
THE ANGELS CRY FOR ONE OF THEIR OWN.
END

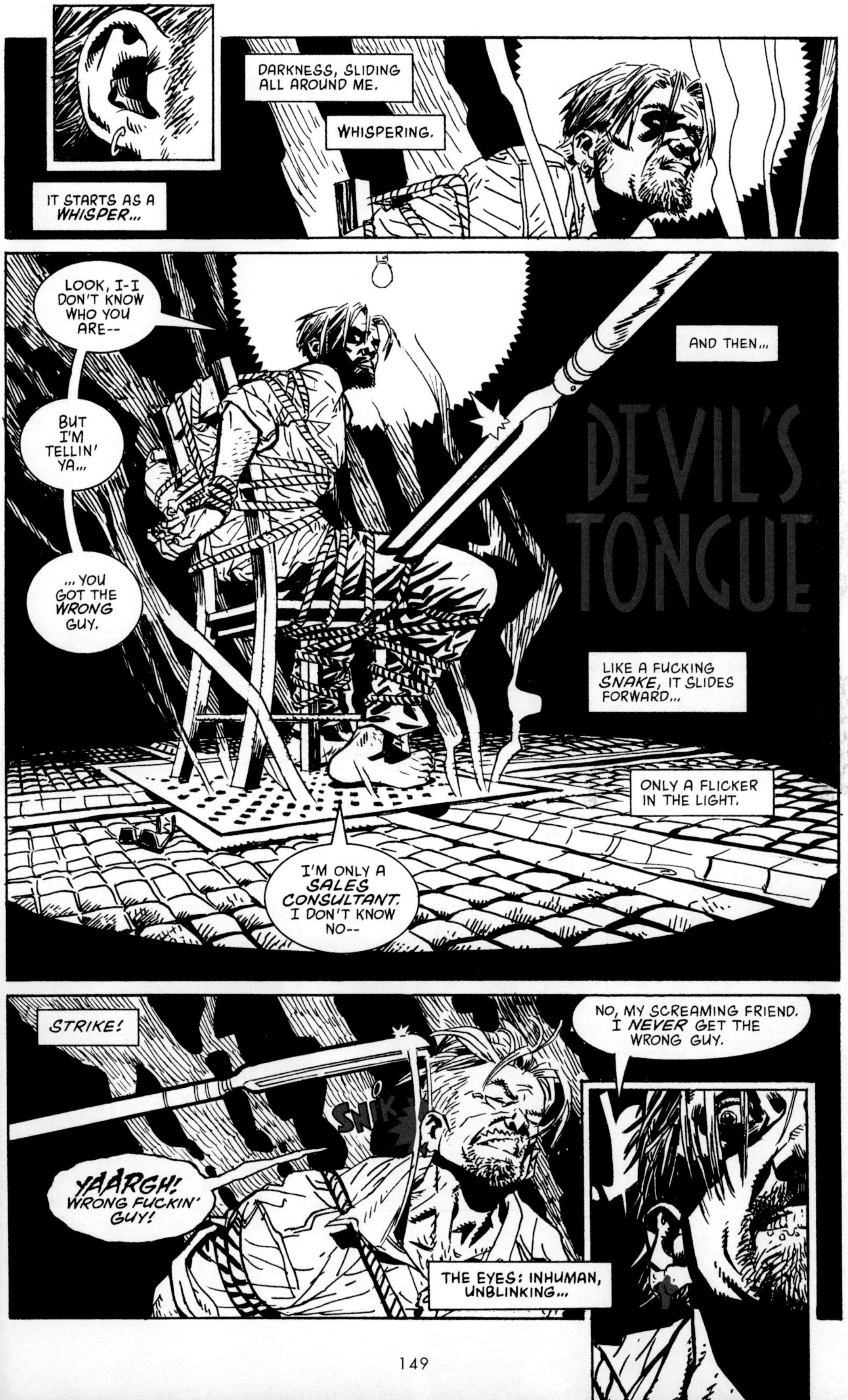
IT STARTS AS A WHISPER...
DARKNESS, SLIDING ALL AROUND ME.
WHISPERING.
LOOK, I-I DON'T KNOW WHO YOU ARE--
BUT I'M TELLIN' YA...
...YOU GOT THE WRONG GUY.
AND THEN...
DEVIL'S TONGUE
LIKE A FUCKING SNAKE, IT SLIDES FORWARD...
ONLY A FLICKER IN THE LIGHT.
I'M ONLY A SALES CONSULTANT. I DON'T KNOW NO--
STRIKE!
SNIK
YAARGH! WRONG FUCKIN' GUY!
NO, MY SCREAMING FRIEND. I NEVER GET THE WRONG GUY.
THE EYES: INHUMAN, UNBLINKING...

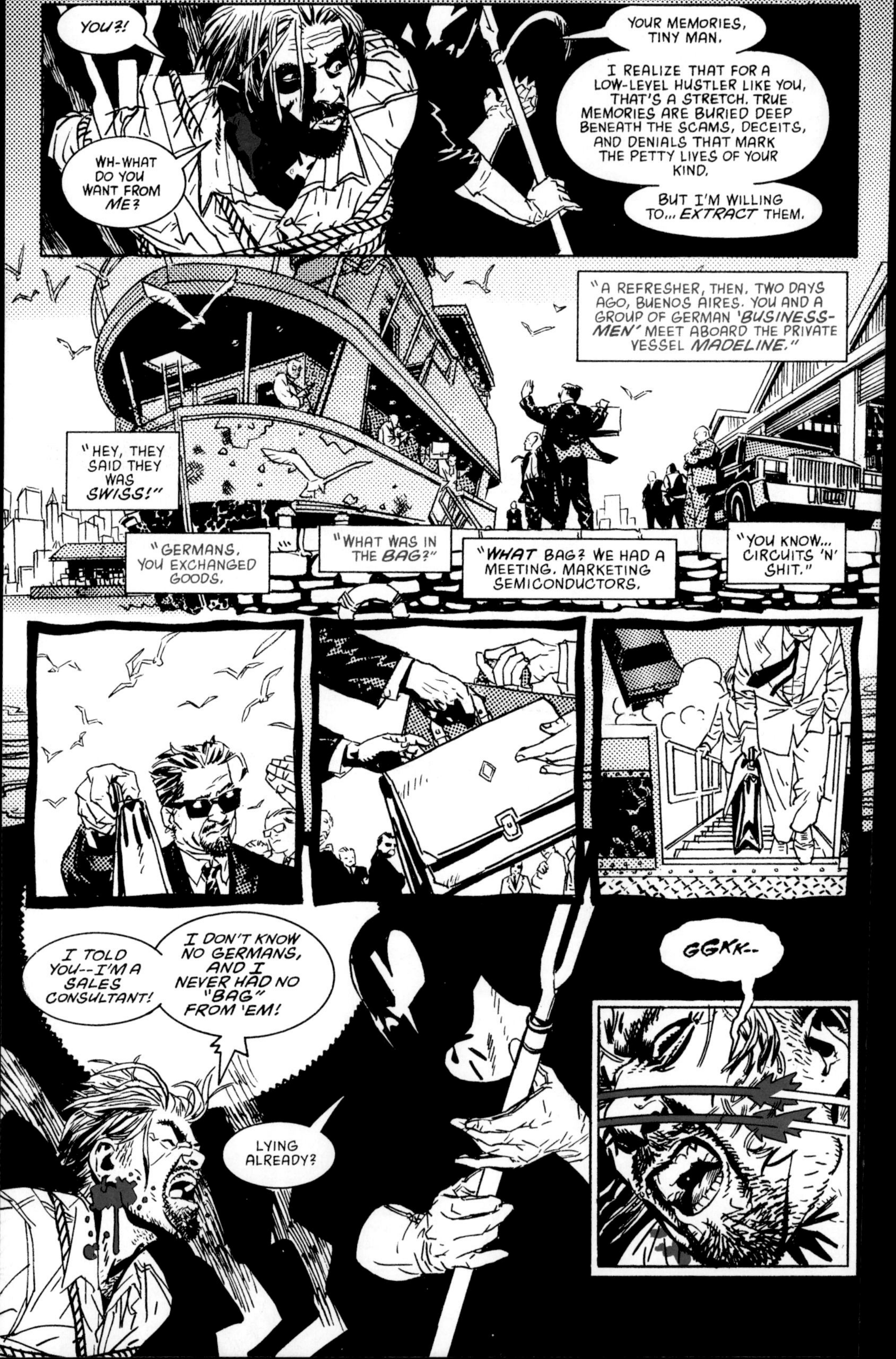
YOU?!
WH-WHAT DO YOU WANT FROM ME?
YOUR MEMORIES, TINY MAN.
I REALIZE THAT FOR A LOW-LEVEL HUSTLER LIKE YOU, THAT'S A STRETCH. TRUE MEMORIES ARE BURIED DEEP BENEATH THE SCAMS, DECEITS, AND DENIALS THAT MARK THE PETTY LIVES OF YOUR KIND.
BUT I'M WILLING TO... EXTRACT THEM.
"A REFRESHER, THEN. TWO DAYS AGO, BUENOS AIRES. YOU AND A GROUP OF GERMAN 'BUSINESS-MEN' MEET ABOARD THE PRIVATE VESSEL MADELINE."
"HEY, THEY SAID THEY WAS SWISS!"
"GERMANS. YOU EXCHANGED GOODS.
"WHAT WAS IN THE BAG?"
"WHAT BAG? WE HAD A MEETING. MARKETING SEMICONDUCTORS.
"YOU KNOW... CIRCUITS 'N' SHIT."
I TOLD YOU--I'M A SALES CONSULTANT!
I DON'T KNOW NO GERMANS, AND I NEVER HAD NO "BAG" FROM 'EM!
LYING ALREADY?
GGKK--

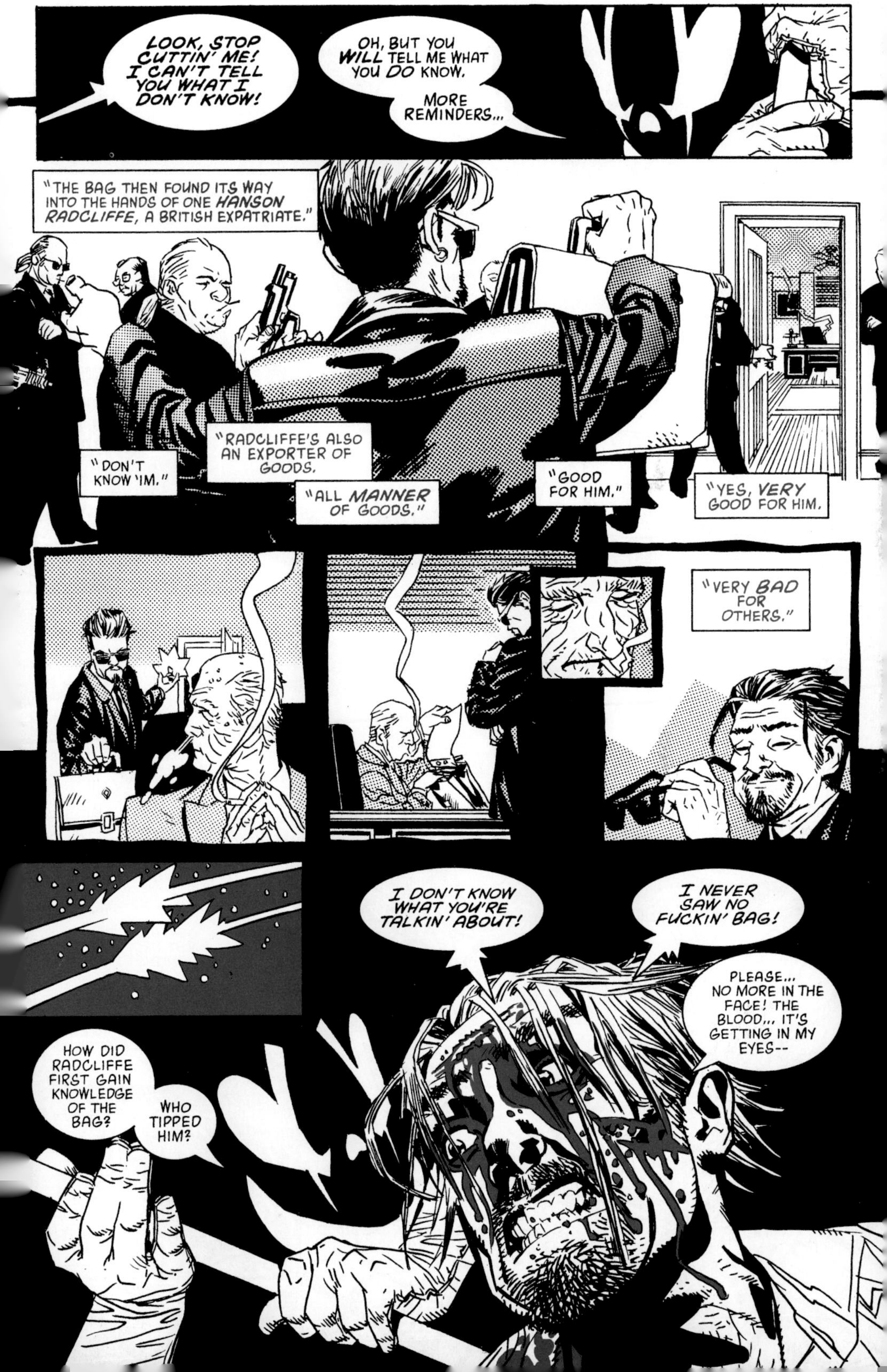
LOOK, STOP CUTTIN' ME! I CAN'T TELL YOU WHAT I DON'T KNOW!
OH, BUT YOU WILL TELL ME WHAT YOU DO KNOW.
MORE REMINDERS...
"THE BAG THEN FOUND ITS WAY INTO THE HANDS OF ONE HANSON RADCLIFFE, A BRITISH EXPATRIATE."
"DON'T KNOW 'IM."
"RADCLIFFE'S ALSO AN EXPORTER OF GOODS.
"ALL MANNER OF GOODS."
"GOOD FOR HIM."
"YES, VERY GOOD FOR HIM.
"VERY BAD FOR OTHERS."
I DON'T KNOW WHAT YOU'RE TALKIN' ABOUT!
I NEVER SAW NO FUCKIN' BAG!
PLEASE... NO MORE IN THE FACE! THE BLOOD... IT'S GETTING IN MY EYES--
HOW DID RADCLIFFE FIRST GAIN KNOWLEDGE OF THE BAG?
WHO TIPPED HIM?

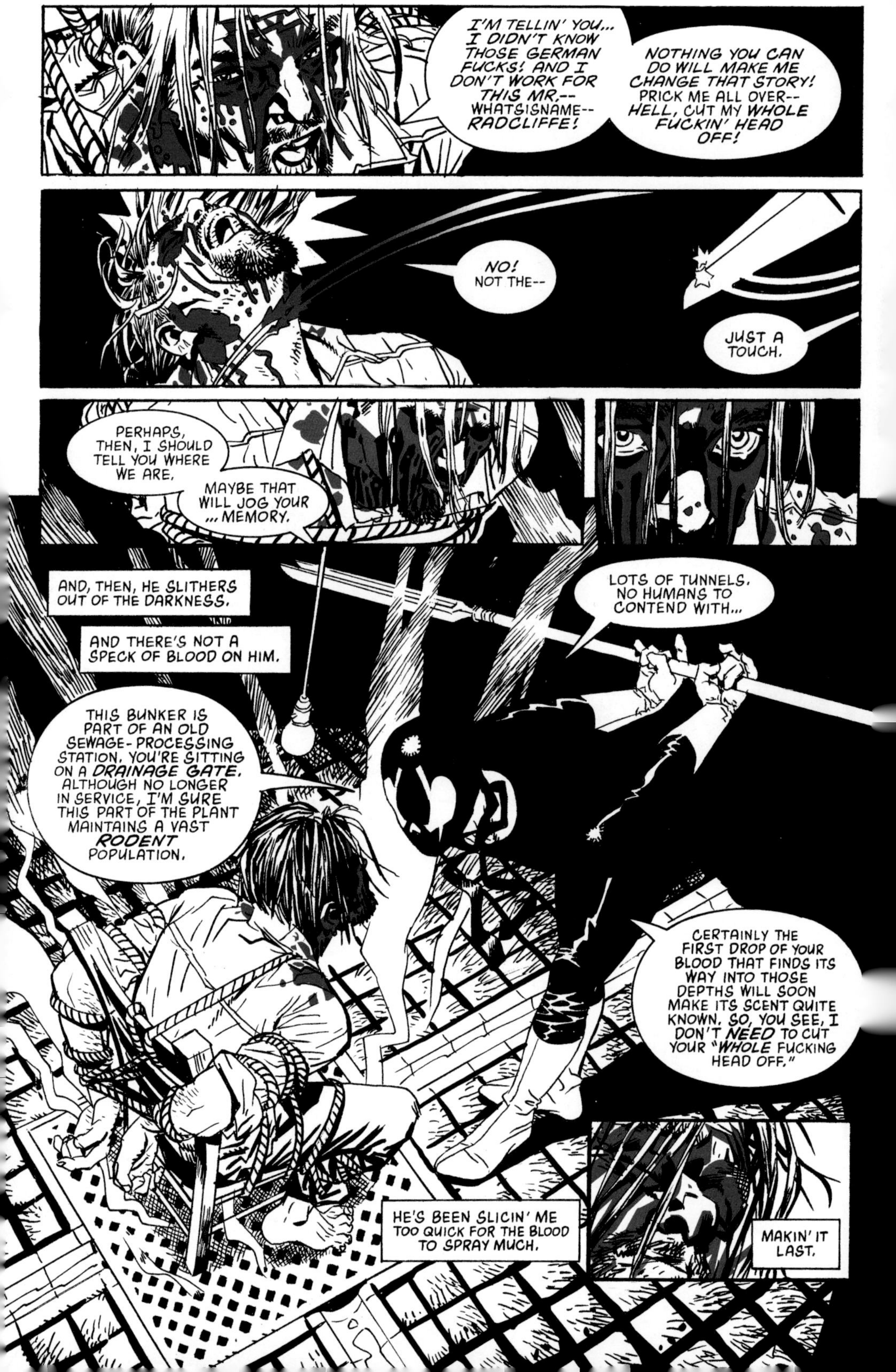
I'M TELLIN' YOU... I DIDN'T KNOW THOSE GERMAN FUCKS! AND I DON'T WORK FOR THIS MR.-- WHATSISNAME-- RADCLIFFE!
NOTHING YOU CAN DO WILL MAKE ME CHANGE THAT STORY! PRICK ME ALL OVER-- HELL, CUT MY WHOLE FUCKIN' HEAD OFF!
NO! NOT THE--
JUST A TOUCH.
PERHAPS, THEN, I SHOULD TELL YOU WHERE WE ARE.
MAYBE THAT WILL JOG YOUR ... MEMORY.
AND, THEN, HE SLITHERS OUT OF THE DARKNESS.
AND THERE'S NOT A SPECK OF BLOOD ON HIM.
LOTS OF TUNNELS. NO HUMANS TO CONTEND WITH...
THIS BUNKER IS PART OF AN OLD SEWAGE-PROCESSING STATION. YOU'RE SITTING ON A DRAINAGE GATE. ALTHOUGH NO LONGER IN SERVICE, I'M SURE THIS PART OF THE PLANT MAINTAINS A VAST RODENT POPULATION.
CERTAINLY THE FIRST DROP OF YOUR BLOOD THAT FINDS ITS WAY INTO THOSE DEPTHS WILL SOON MAKE ITS SCENT QUITE KNOWN. SO, YOU SEE, I DON'T NEED TO CUT YOUR "WHOLE FUCKING HEAD OFF."
HE'S BEEN SLICIN' ME TOO QUICK FOR THE BLOOD TO SPRAY MUCH.
MAKIN' IT LAST.

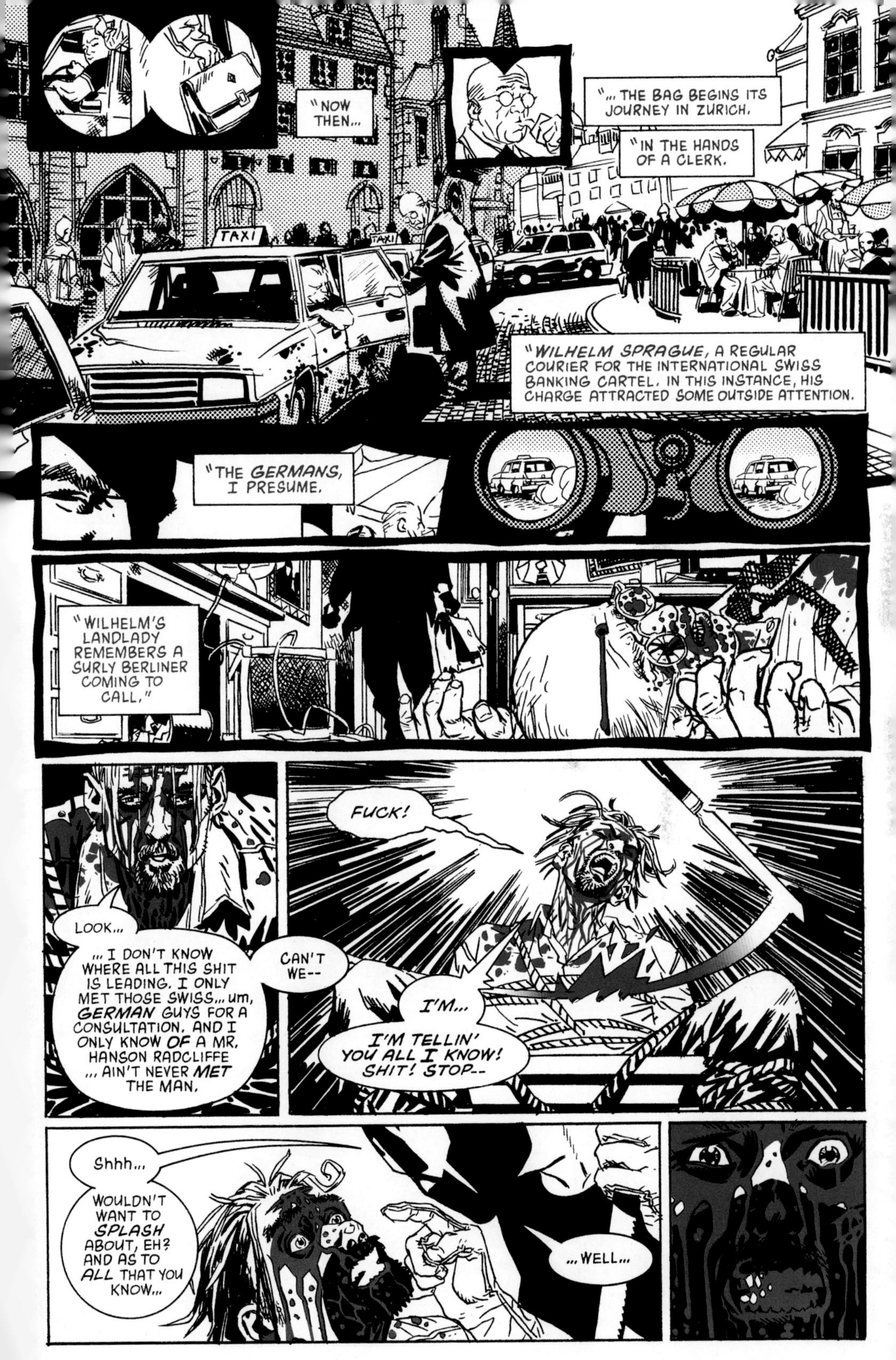
"NOW THEN...
"... THE BAG BEGINS ITS JOURNEY IN ZURICH.
"IN THE HANDS OF A CLERK.
TAXI
TAXI
"WILHELM SPRAGUE, A REGULAR COURIER FOR THE INTERNATIONAL SWISS BANKING CARTEL. IN THIS INSTANCE, HIS CHARGE ATTRACTED SOME OUTSIDE ATTENTION.
"THE GERMANS, I PRESUME.
"WILHELM'S LANDLADY REMEMBERS A SURLY BERLINER COMING TO CALL."
LOOK...
... I DON'T KNOW WHERE ALL THIS SHIT IS LEADING. I ONLY MET THOSE SWISS... um, GERMAN GUYS FOR A CONSULTATION. AND I ONLY KNOW OF A MR. HANSON RADCLIFFE ... AIN'T NEVER MET THE MAN.
FUCK!
CAN'T WE--
I'M...
I'M TELLIN' YOU ALL I KNOW! SHIT! STOP--
Shhh...
WOULDN'T WANT TO SPLASH ABOUT, EH? AND AS TO ALL THAT YOU KNOW...
... WELL...

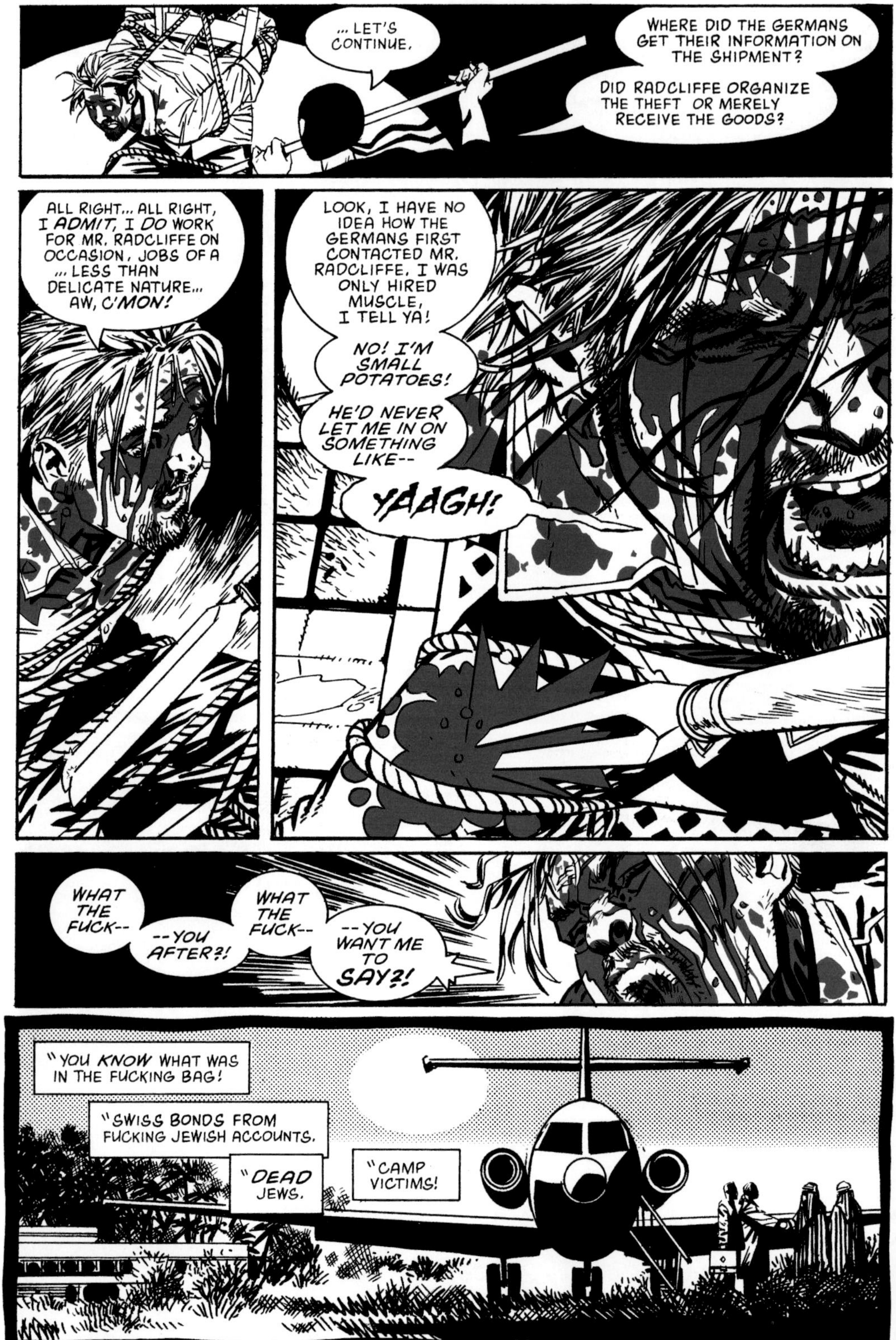
...LET'S CONTINUE.
WHERE DID THE GERMANS GET THEIR INFORMATION ON THE SHIPMENT?
DID RADCLIFFE ORGANIZE THE THEFT OR MERELY RECEIVE THE GOODS?
ALL RIGHT... ALL RIGHT, I *ADMIT*, I *DO* WORK FOR MR. RADCLIFFE ON OCCASION, JOBS OF A ...LESS THAN DELICATE NATURE... AW, *C'MON!*
LOOK, I HAVE NO IDEA HOW THE GERMANS FIRST CONTACTED MR. RADCLIFFE. I WAS ONLY HIRED MUSCLE, I TELL YA!
NO! I'M SMALL POTATOES!
HE'D NEVER LET ME IN ON SOMETHING LIKE--
YAAGH!
WHAT THE FUCK--
--YOU AFTER?!
WHAT THE FUCK--
--YOU WANT ME TO SAY?!
"YOU *KNOW* WHAT WAS IN THE FUCKING BAG!
"SWISS BONDS FROM FUCKING JEWISH ACCOUNTS.
"*DEAD* JEWS.
"CAMP VICTIMS!

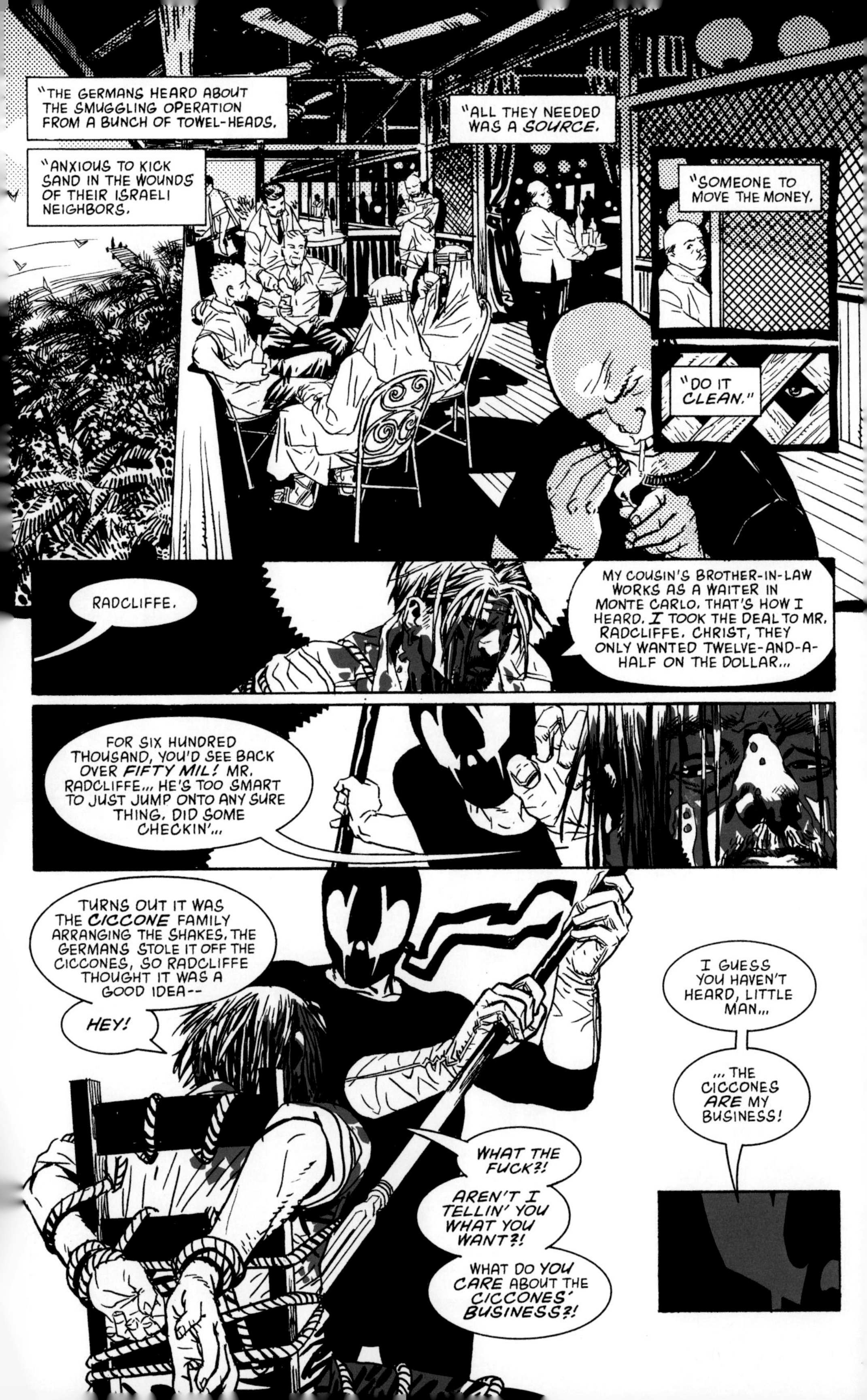
"THE GERMANS HEARD ABOUT THE SMUGGLING OPERATION FROM A BUNCH OF TOWEL-HEADS.
"ANXIOUS TO KICK SAND IN THE WOUNDS OF THEIR ISRAELI NEIGHBORS.
"ALL THEY NEEDED WAS A *SOURCE.*
"SOMEONE TO MOVE THE MONEY.
"DO IT *CLEAN.*"
RADCLIFFE.
MY COUSIN'S BROTHER-IN-LAW WORKS AS A WAITER IN MONTE CARLO. THAT'S HOW I HEARD. *I* TOOK THE DEAL TO MR. RADCLIFFE. CHRIST, THEY ONLY WANTED TWELVE-AND-A-HALF ON THE DOLLAR...
FOR SIX HUNDRED THOUSAND, YOU'D SEE BACK OVER *FIFTY MIL!* MR. RADCLIFFE... HE'S TOO SMART TO JUST JUMP ONTO ANY SURE THING. DID SOME CHECKIN'...
TURNS OUT IT WAS THE *CICCONE* FAMILY ARRANGING THE SHAKES. THE GERMANS STOLE IT OFF THE CICCONES, SO RADCLIFFE THOUGHT IT WAS A GOOD IDEA--
HEY!
WHAT THE FUCK?!
AREN'T I TELLIN' YOU WHAT YOU WANT?!
WHAT DO *YOU CARE* ABOUT THE *CICCONES' BUSINESS?!*
I GUESS YOU HAVEN'T HEARD, LITTLE MAN...
... THE CICCONES *ARE* MY BUSINESS!

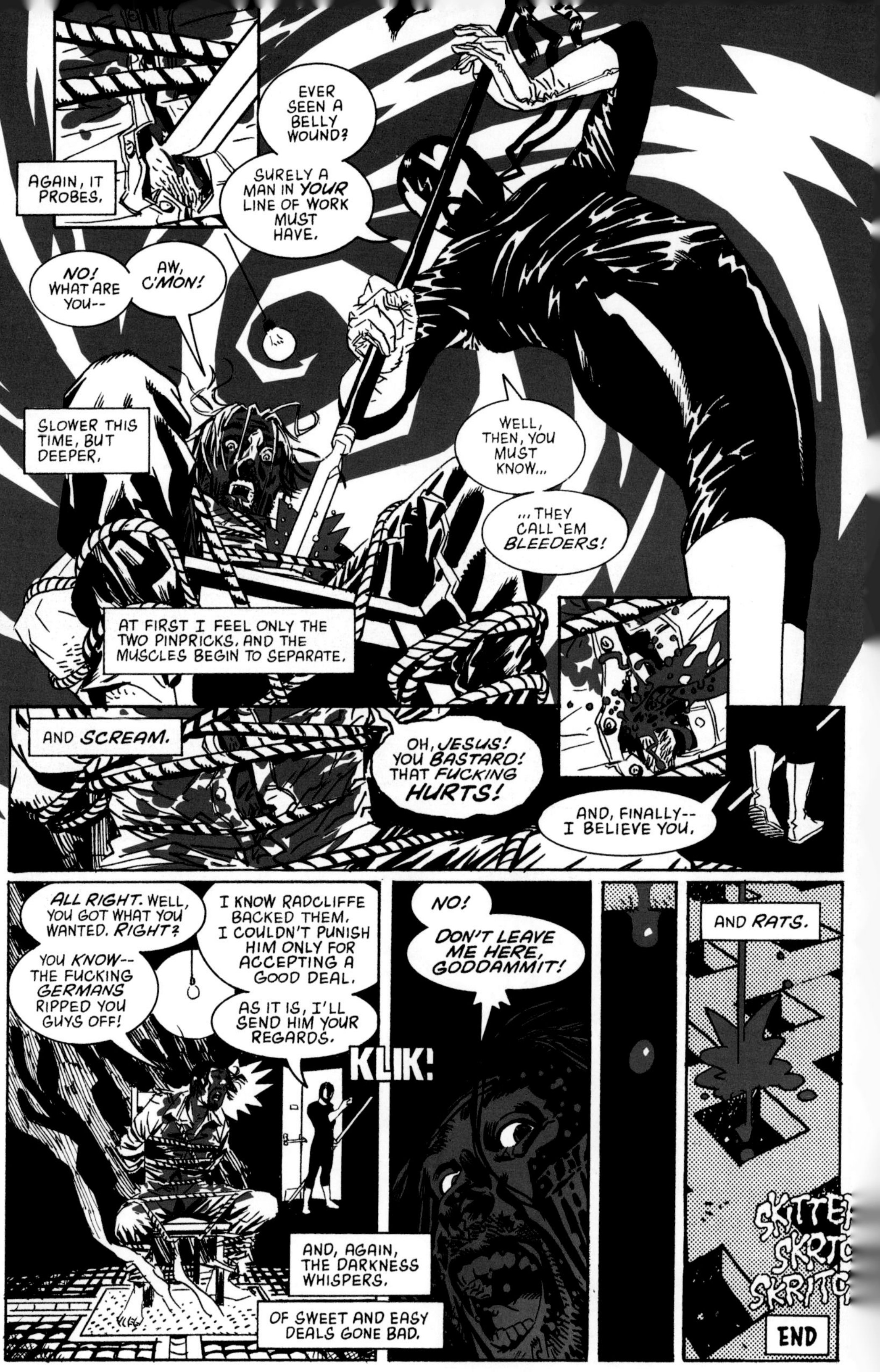

AGAIN, IT PROBES.
EVER SEEN A BELLY WOUND?
SURELY A MAN IN YOUR LINE OF WORK MUST HAVE.
NO! WHAT ARE YOU--
AW, C'MON!
SLOWER THIS TIME, BUT DEEPER.
WELL, THEN, YOU MUST KNOW...
...THEY CALL 'EM BLEEDERS!
AT FIRST I FEEL ONLY THE TWO PINPRICKS, AND THE MUSCLES BEGIN TO SEPARATE.
AND SCREAM.
OH, JESUS! YOU BASTARD! THAT FUCKING HURTS!
AND, FINALLY-- I BELIEVE YOU.
ALL RIGHT. WELL, YOU GOT WHAT YOU WANTED. RIGHT?
YOU KNOW-- THE FUCKING GERMANS RIPPED YOU GUYS OFF!
I KNOW RADCLIFFE BACKED THEM. I COULDN'T PUNISH HIM ONLY FOR ACCEPTING A GOOD DEAL.
AS IT IS, I'LL SEND HIM YOUR REGARDS.
KLIK!
AND, AGAIN, THE DARKNESS WHISPERS.
OF SWEET AND EASY DEALS GONE BAD.
NO!
DON'T LEAVE ME HERE, GODDAMMIT!
AND RATS.
END

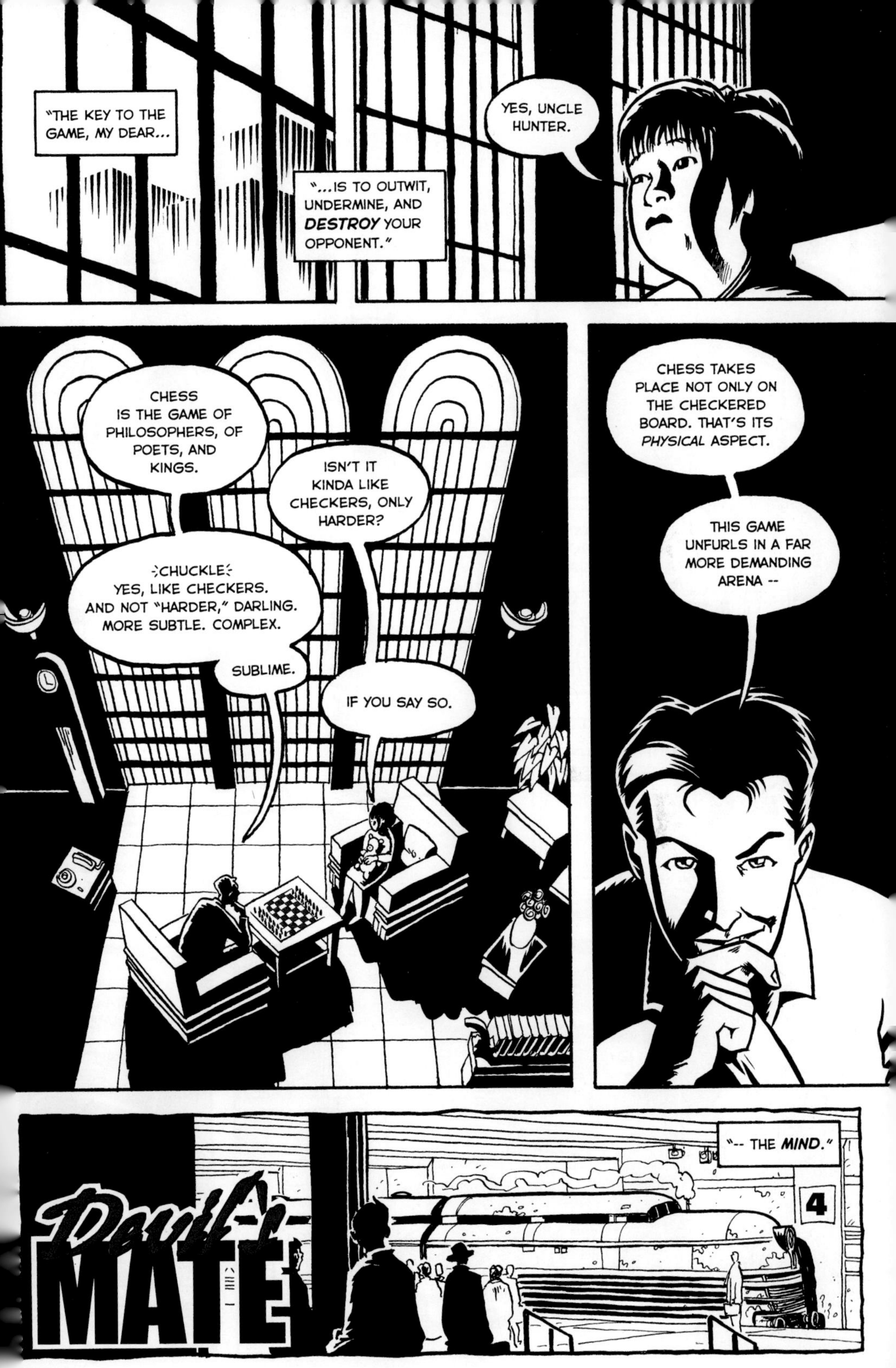

"THE KEY TO THE GAME, MY DEAR...
"...IS TO OUTWIT, UNDERMINE, AND DESTROY YOUR OPPONENT."
YES, UNCLE HUNTER.
CHESS IS THE GAME OF PHILOSOPHERS, OF POETS, AND KINGS.
ISN'T IT KINDA LIKE CHECKERS, ONLY HARDER?
CHUCKLE YES, LIKE CHECKERS. AND NOT "HARDER," DARLING. MORE SUBTLE. COMPLEX.
SUBLIME.
IF YOU SAY SO.
CHESS TAKES PLACE NOT ONLY ON THE CHECKERED BOARD. THAT'S ITS PHYSICAL ASPECT.
THIS GAME UNFURLS IN A FAR MORE DEMANDING ARENA --
"-- THE MIND."
Devil's MATE
4

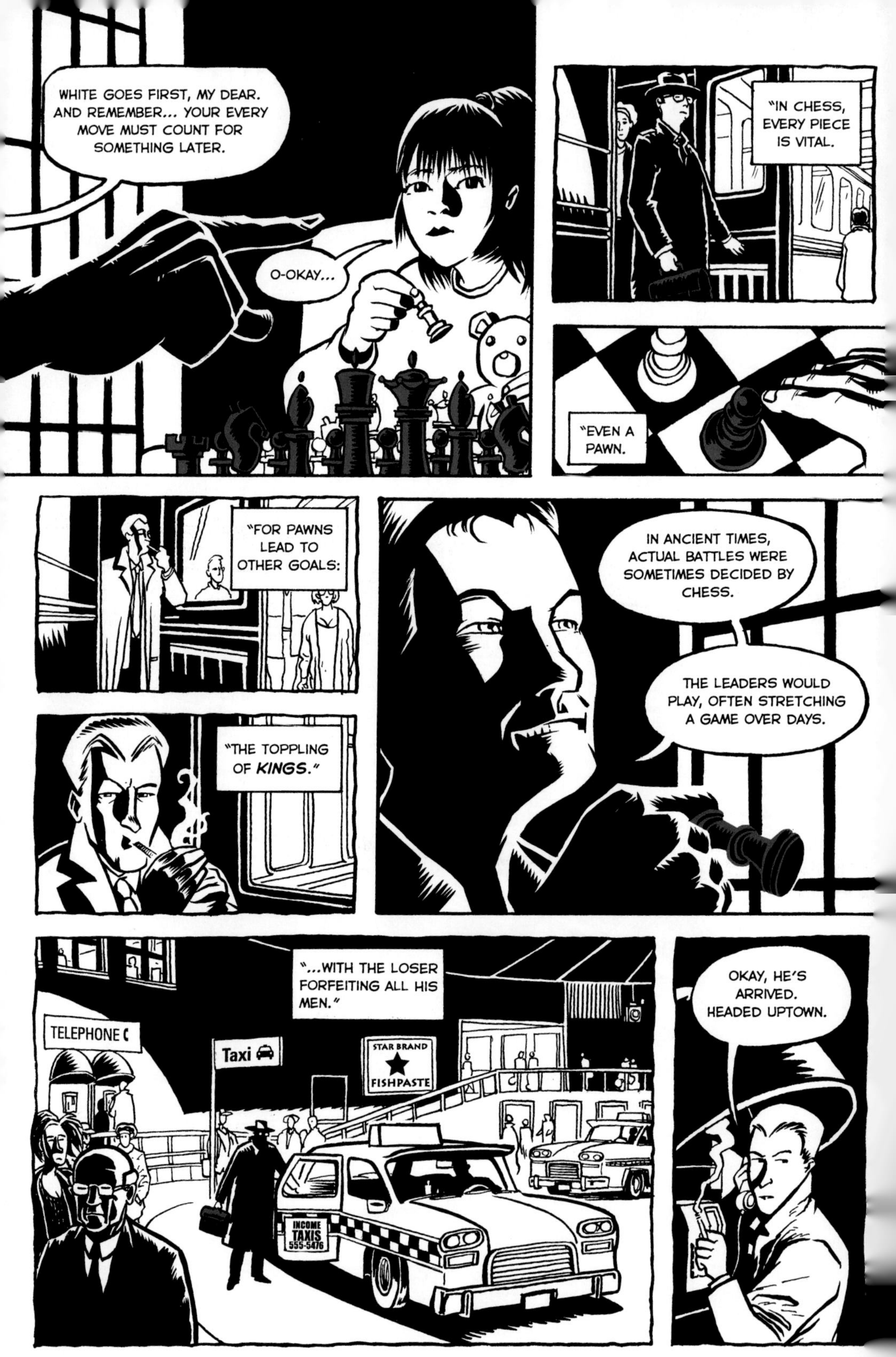
WHITE GOES FIRST, MY DEAR. AND REMEMBER... YOUR EVERY MOVE MUST COUNT FOR SOMETHING LATER.
O-OKAY...
"IN CHESS, EVERY PIECE IS VITAL.
"EVEN A PAWN.
"FOR PAWNS LEAD TO OTHER GOALS:
"THE TOPPLING OF *KINGS*."
IN ANCIENT TIMES, ACTUAL BATTLES WERE SOMETIMES DECIDED BY CHESS.
THE LEADERS WOULD PLAY, OFTEN STRETCHING A GAME OVER DAYS.
"...WITH THE LOSER FORFEITING ALL HIS MEN."
TELEPHONE
Taxi
STAR BRAND FISHPASTE
INCOME TAXIS 555-5476
OKAY, HE'S ARRIVED. HEADED UPTOWN.

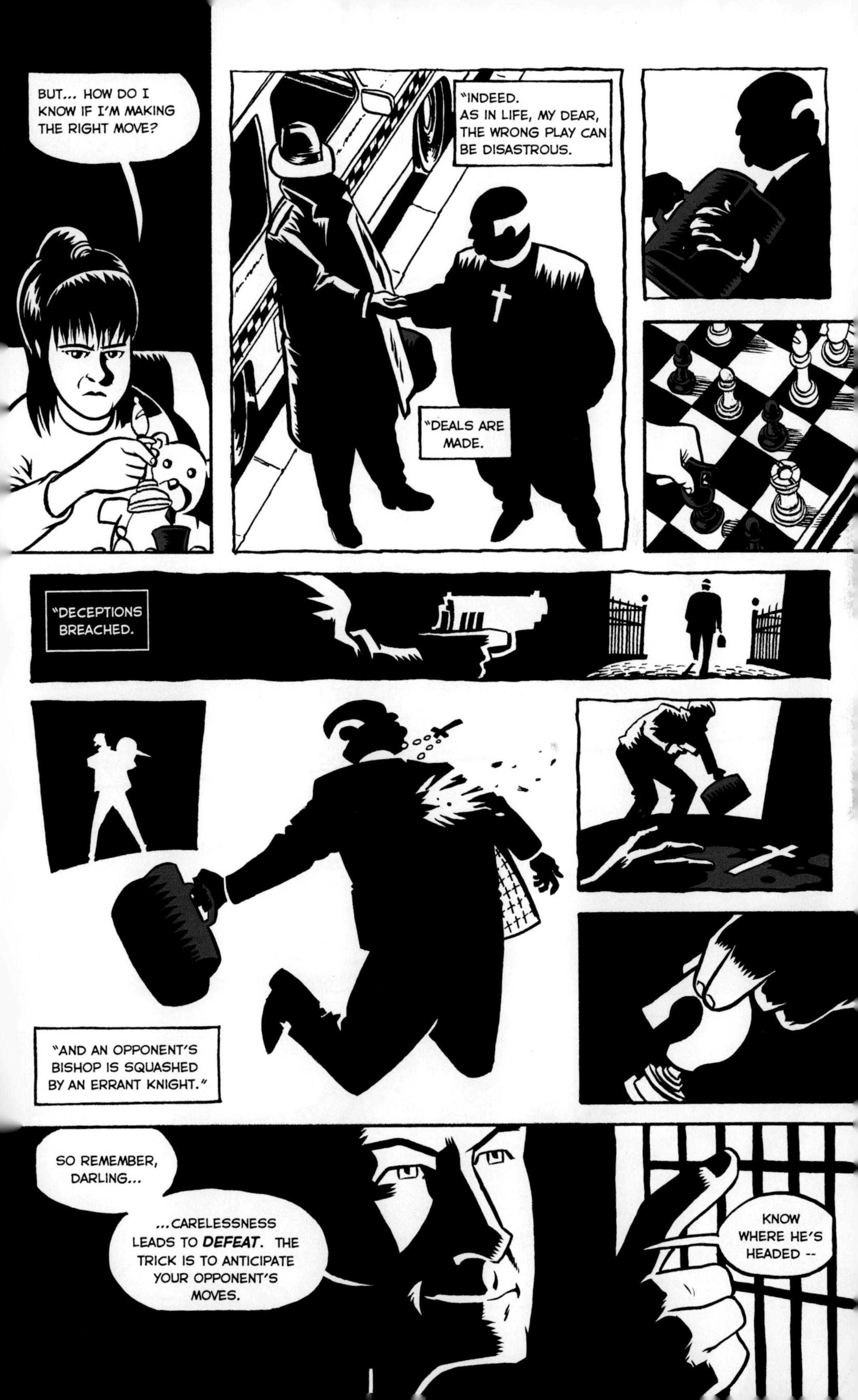
BUT... HOW DO I KNOW IF I'M MAKING THE RIGHT MOVE?
"INDEED. AS IN LIFE, MY DEAR, THE WRONG PLAY CAN BE DISASTROUS.
"DEALS ARE MADE.
"DECEPTIONS BREACHED.
"AND AN OPPONENT'S BISHOP IS SQUASHED BY AN ERRANT KNIGHT."
SO REMEMBER, DARLING...
...CARELESSNESS LEADS TO ***DEFEAT***. THE TRICK IS TO ANTICIPATE YOUR OPPONENT'S MOVES.
KNOW WHERE HE'S HEADED --

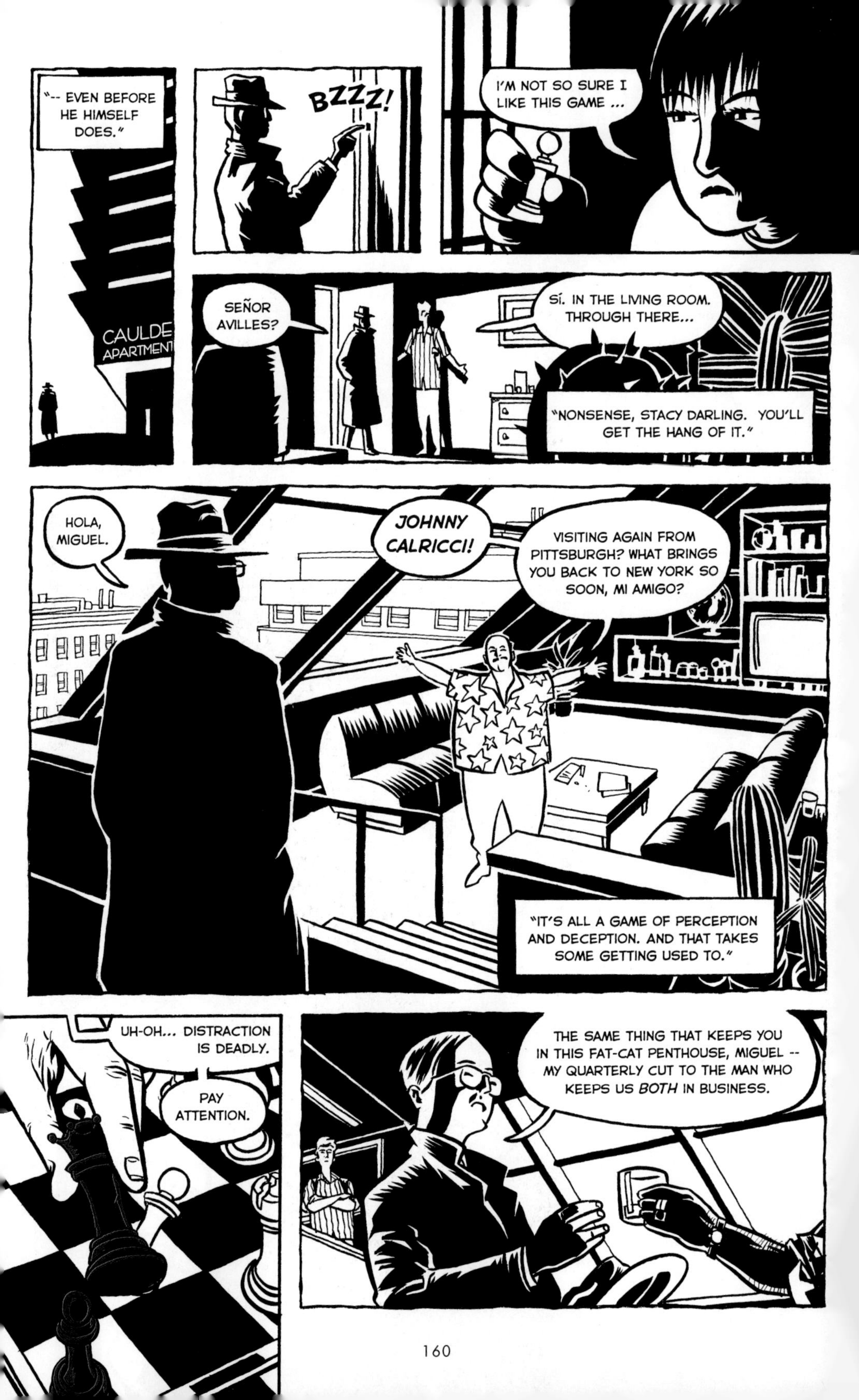
"-- EVEN BEFORE HE HIMSELF DOES."
CAULDE
APARTMENT
BZZZ!
I'M NOT SO SURE I LIKE THIS GAME ...
SEÑOR AVILLES?
SÍ. IN THE LIVING ROOM. THROUGH THERE...
"NONSENSE, STACY DARLING. YOU'LL GET THE HANG OF IT."
HOLA, MIGUEL.
JOHNNY CALRICCI!
VISITING AGAIN FROM PITTSBURGH? WHAT BRINGS YOU BACK TO NEW YORK SO SOON, MI AMIGO?
"IT'S ALL A GAME OF PERCEPTION AND DECEPTION. AND THAT TAKES SOME GETTING USED TO."
UH-OH... DISTRACTION IS DEADLY.
PAY ATTENTION.
THE SAME THING THAT KEEPS YOU IN THIS FAT-CAT PENTHOUSE, MIGUEL -- MY QUARTERLY CUT TO THE MAN WHO KEEPS US *BOTH* IN BUSINESS.

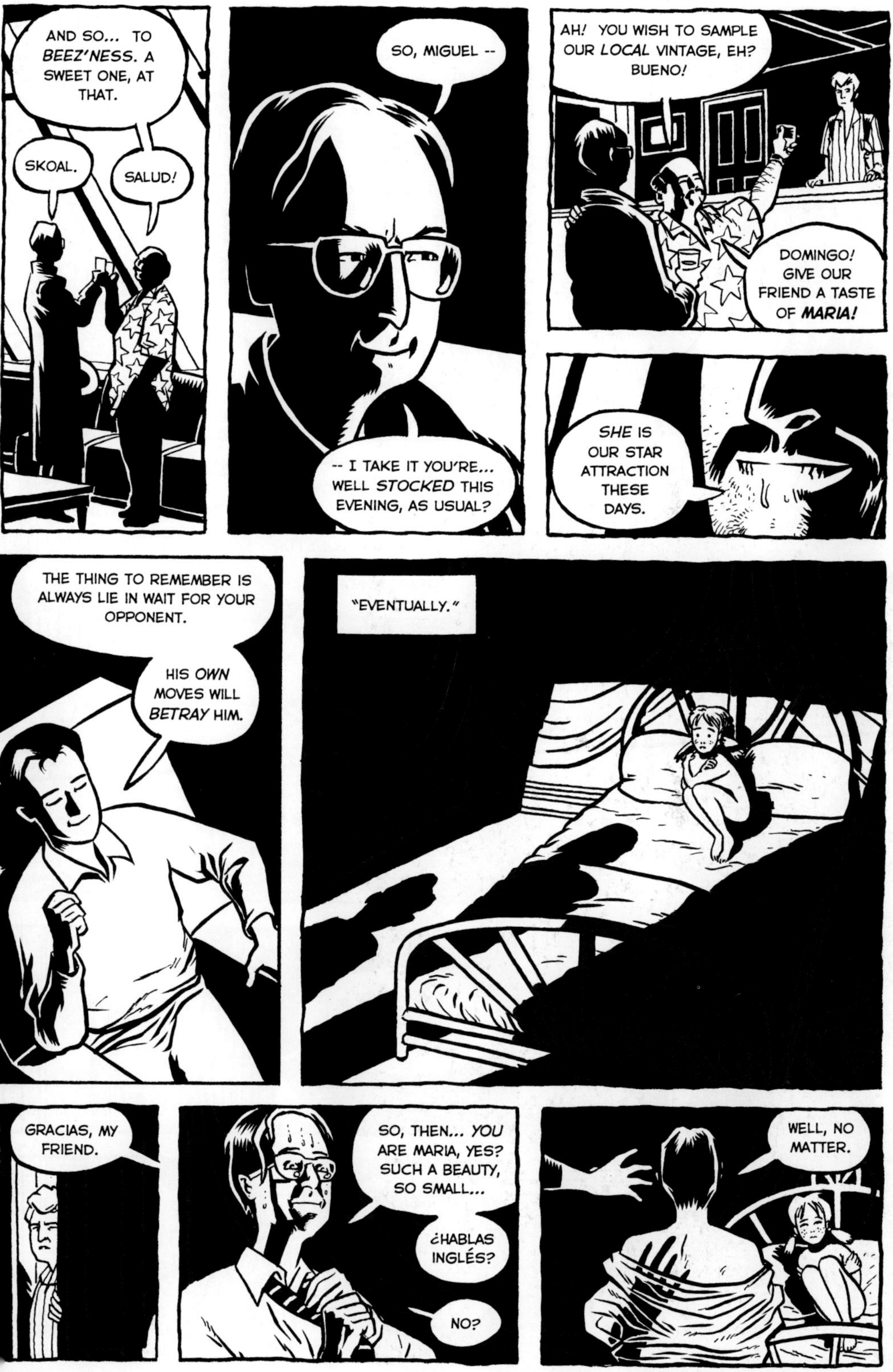
AND SO... TO BEEZ'NESS. A SWEET ONE, AT THAT.
SKOAL.
SALUD!
SO, MIGUEL --
-- I TAKE IT YOU'RE... WELL STOCKED THIS EVENING, AS USUAL?
AH! YOU WISH TO SAMPLE OUR LOCAL VINTAGE, EH? BUENO!
DOMINGO! GIVE OUR FRIEND A TASTE OF MARIA!
SHE IS OUR STAR ATTRACTION THESE DAYS.
THE THING TO REMEMBER IS ALWAYS LIE IN WAIT FOR YOUR OPPONENT.
HIS OWN MOVES WILL BETRAY HIM.
"EVENTUALLY."
GRACIAS, MY FRIEND.
SO, THEN... YOU ARE MARIA, YES? SUCH A BEAUTY, SO SMALL...
¿HABLAS INGLÉS?
NO?
WELL, NO MATTER.

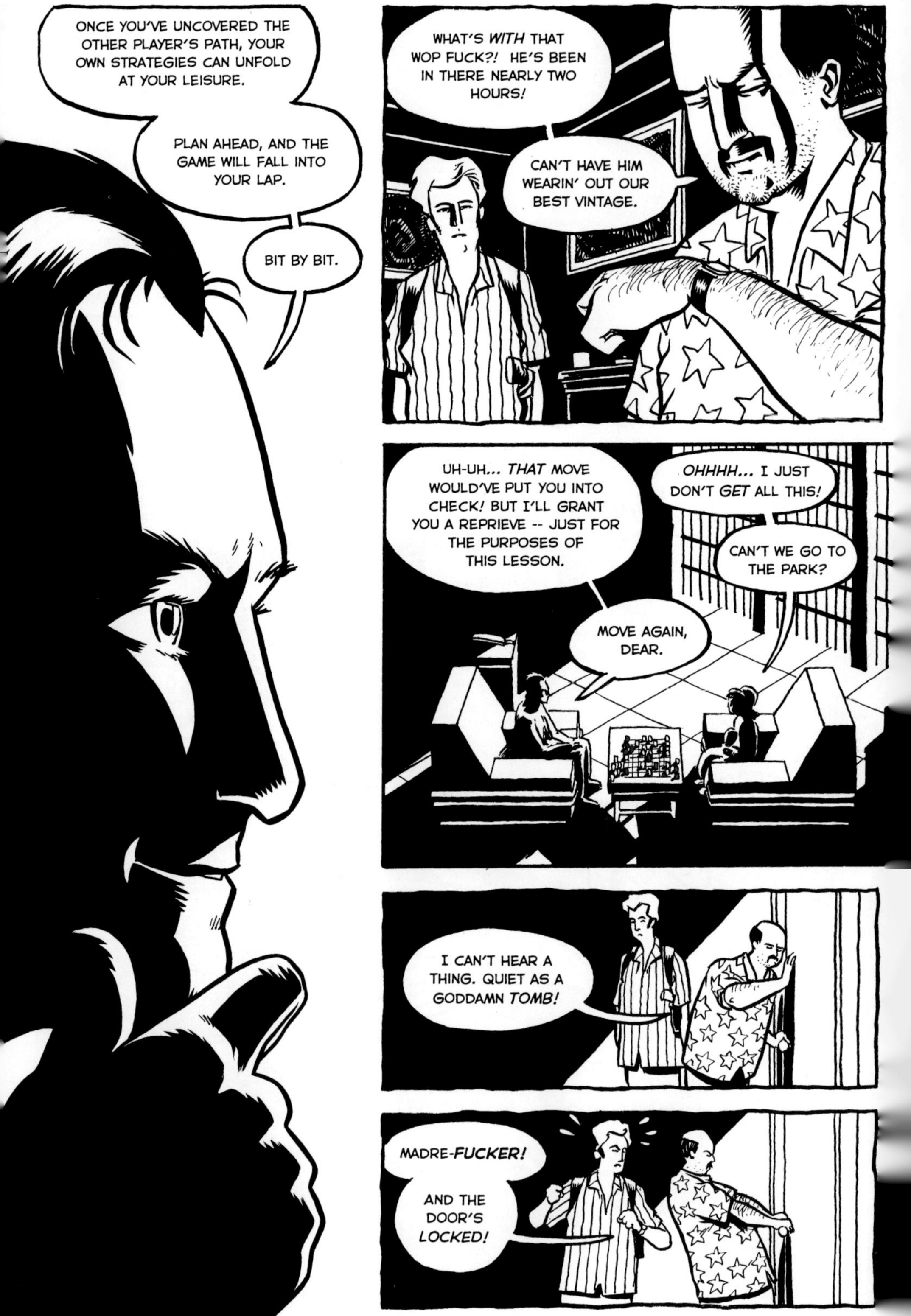
ONCE YOU'VE UNCOVERED THE OTHER PLAYER'S PATH, YOUR OWN STRATEGIES CAN UNFOLD AT YOUR LEISURE.
PLAN AHEAD, AND THE GAME WILL FALL INTO YOUR LAP.
BIT BY BIT.
WHAT'S *WITH* THAT WOP FUCK?! HE'S BEEN IN THERE NEARLY TWO HOURS!
CAN'T HAVE HIM WEARIN' OUT OUR BEST VINTAGE.
UH-UH... *THAT* MOVE WOULD'VE PUT YOU INTO CHECK! BUT I'LL GRANT YOU A REPRIEVE -- JUST FOR THE PURPOSES OF THIS LESSON.
MOVE AGAIN, DEAR.
OHHHH... I JUST DON'T *GET* ALL THIS!
CAN'T WE GO TO THE PARK?
I CAN'T HEAR A THING. QUIET AS A GODDAMN *TOMB!*
MADRE-*FUCKER!*
AND THE DOOR'S *LOCKED!*

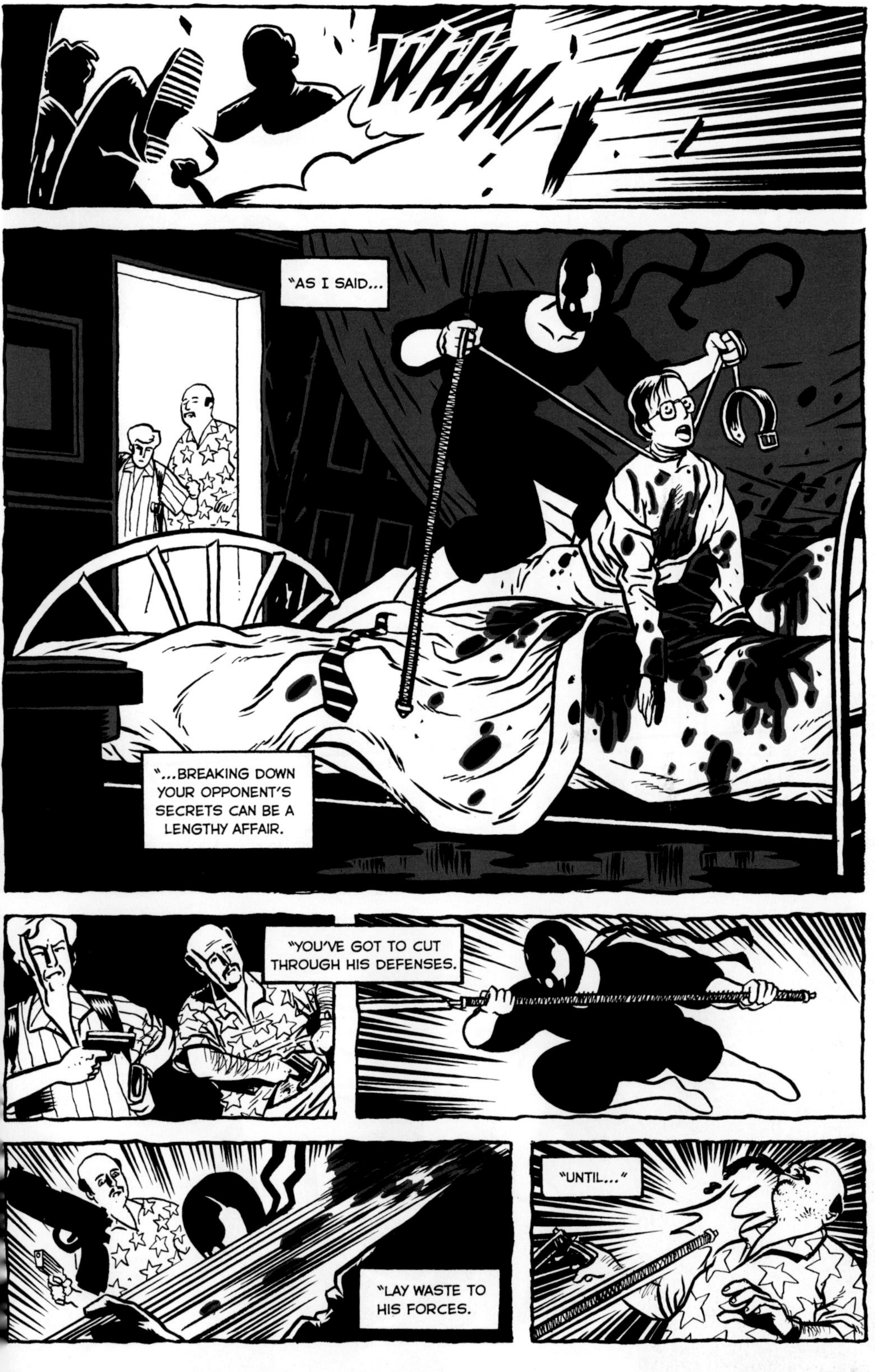
WHAM!
"AS I SAID...
"...BREAKING DOWN YOUR OPPONENT'S SECRETS CAN BE A LENGTHY AFFAIR.
"YOU'VE GOT TO CUT THROUGH HIS DEFENSES.
"LAY WASTE TO HIS FORCES.
"UNTIL..."

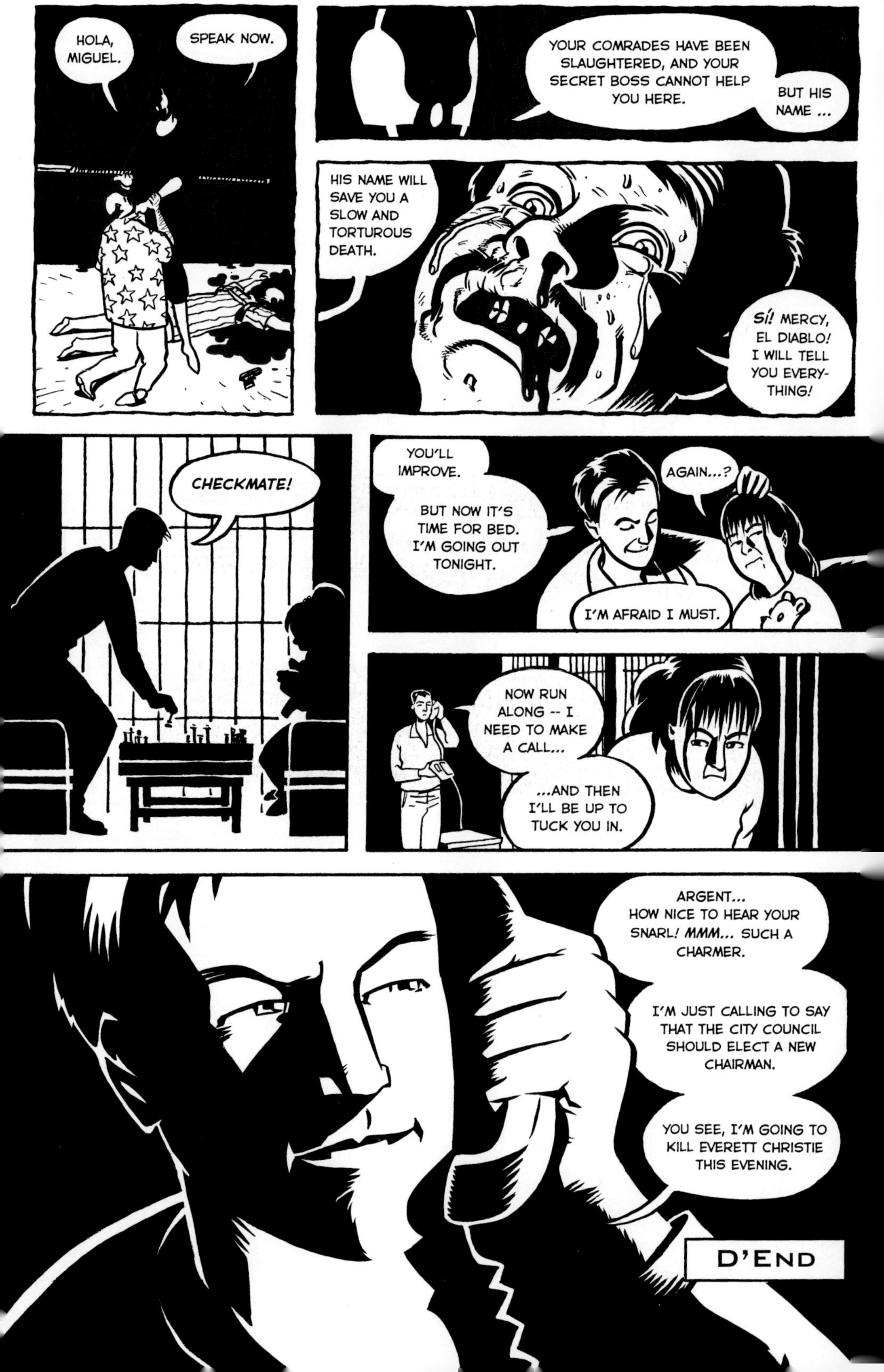
HOLA, MIGUEL.
SPEAK NOW.
YOUR COMRADES HAVE BEEN SLAUGHTERED, AND YOUR SECRET BOSS CANNOT HELP YOU HERE.
BUT HIS NAME ...
HIS NAME WILL SAVE YOU A SLOW AND TORTUROUS DEATH.
SÍ! MERCY, EL DIABLO! I WILL TELL YOU EVERY-THING!
CHECKMATE!
YOU'LL IMPROVE.
AGAIN...?
BUT NOW IT'S TIME FOR BED. I'M GOING OUT TONIGHT.
I'M AFRAID I MUST.
NOW RUN ALONG -- I NEED TO MAKE A CALL...
...AND THEN I'LL BE UP TO TUCK YOU IN.
ARGENT... HOW NICE TO HEAR YOUR SNARL! MMM... SUCH A CHARMER.
I'M JUST CALLING TO SAY THAT THE CITY COUNCIL SHOULD ELECT A NEW CHAIRMAN.
YOU SEE, I'M GOING TO KILL EVERETT CHRISTIE THIS EVENING.
D'END

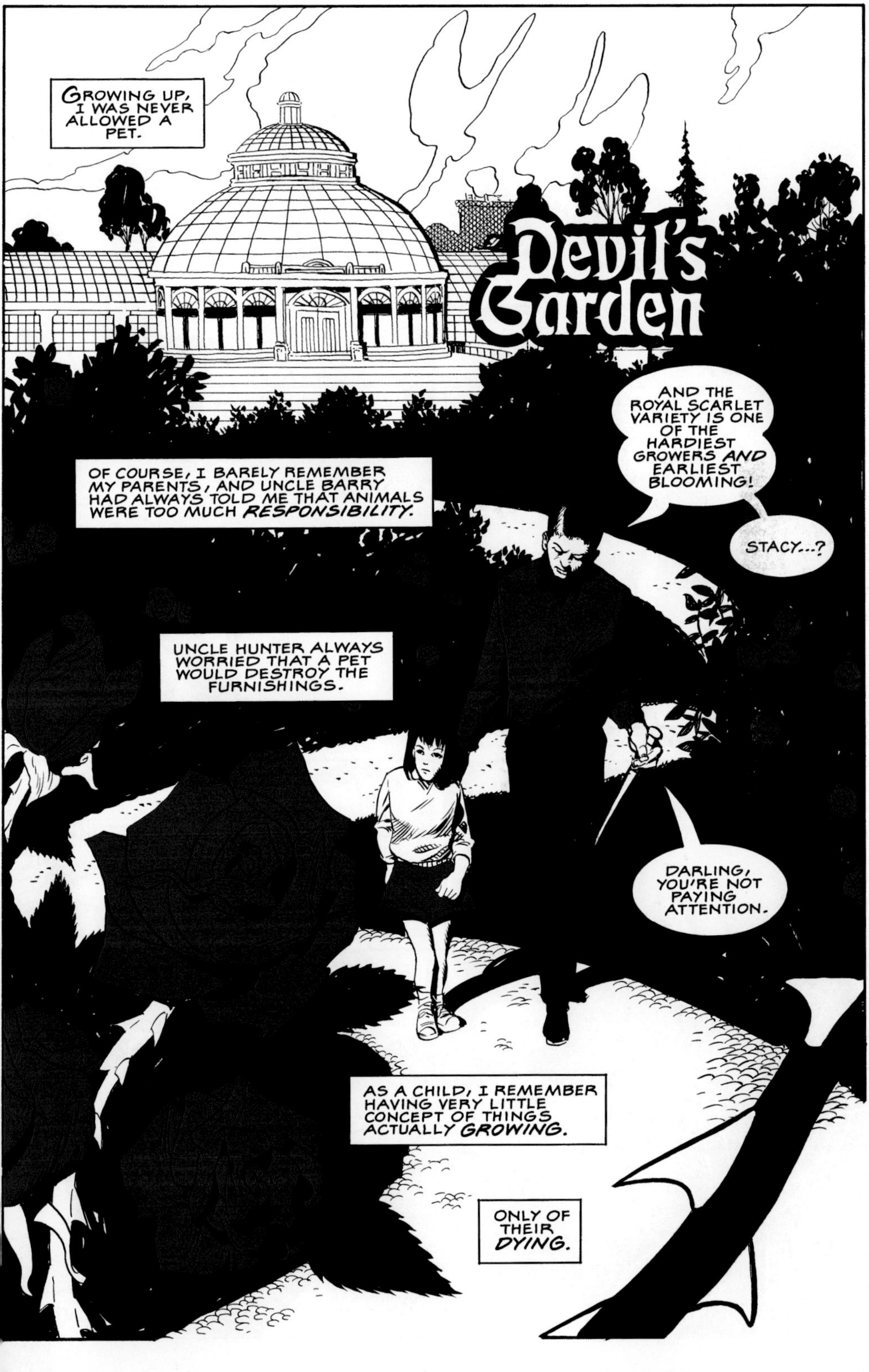
GROWING UP, I WAS NEVER ALLOWED A PET.
Devil's Garden
AND THE ROYAL SCARLET VARIETY IS ONE OF THE HARDIEST GROWERS AND EARLIEST BLOOMING!
OF COURSE, I BARELY REMEMBER MY PARENTS, AND UNCLE BARRY HAD ALWAYS TOLD ME THAT ANIMALS WERE TOO MUCH RESPONSIBILITY.
STACY...?
UNCLE HUNTER ALWAYS WORRIED THAT A PET WOULD DESTROY THE FURNISHINGS.
DARLING, YOU'RE NOT PAYING ATTENTION.
AS A CHILD, I REMEMBER HAVING VERY LITTLE CONCEPT OF THINGS ACTUALLY GROWING.
ONLY OF THEIR DYING.

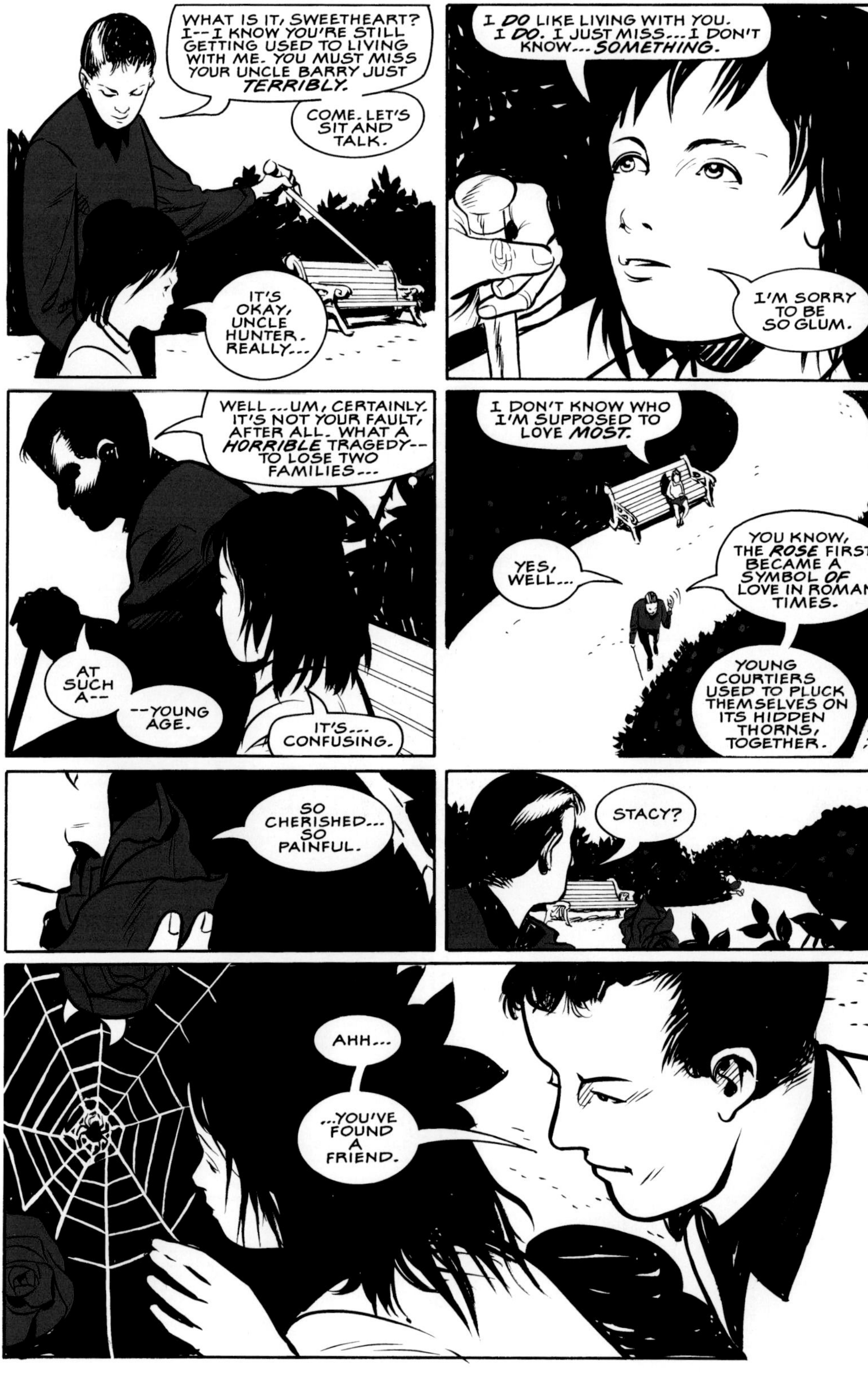

WHAT IS IT, SWEETHEART? I-- I KNOW YOU'RE STILL GETTING USED TO LIVING WITH ME. YOU MUST MISS YOUR UNCLE BARRY JUST TERRIBLY.
COME. LET'S SIT AND TALK.
IT'S OKAY, UNCLE HUNTER. REALLY...
I DO LIKE LIVING WITH YOU. I DO. I JUST MISS... I DON'T KNOW... SOMETHING.
I'M SORRY TO BE SO GLUM.
WELL... UM, CERTAINLY. IT'S NOT YOUR FAULT, AFTER ALL. WHAT A HORRIBLE TRAGEDY-- TO LOSE TWO FAMILIES...
AT SUCH A--
--YOUNG AGE.
IT'S... CONFUSING.
I DON'T KNOW WHO I'M SUPPOSED TO LOVE MOST.
YES, WELL...
YOU KNOW, THE ROSE FIRST BECAME A SYMBOL OF LOVE IN ROMAN TIMES.
YOUNG COURTIERS USED TO PLUCK THEMSELVES ON ITS HIDDEN THORNS, TOGETHER.
SO CHERISHED... SO PAINFUL.
STACY?
AHH...
...YOU'VE FOUND A FRIEND.

SPIDERS ARE CREATURES OF PURE EXISTENCE, DEAR.

THEY LIVE ONLY TO KILL AND CREATE.

SOLITARY. AND SERENE.

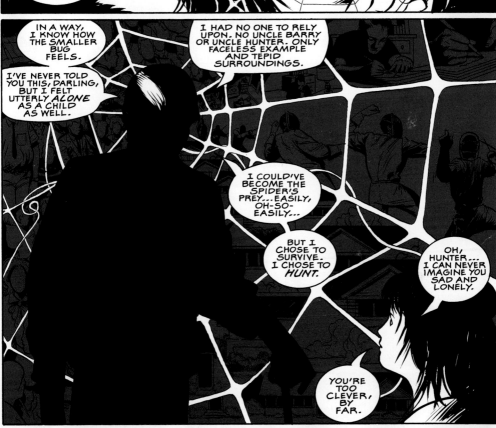

IN A WAY, I KNOW HOW THE SMALLER BUG FEELS.

I'VE NEVER TOLD YOU THIS, DARLING, BUT I FELT UTTERLY *ALONE* AS A CHILD AS WELL.

I HAD NO ONE TO RELY UPON. NO UNCLE BARRY OR UNCLE HUNTER. ONLY FACELESS EXAMPLE AND TEPID SURROUNDINGS.

I COULD'VE BECOME THE SPIDER'S PREY...EASILY, OH-SO-EASILY...

BUT I CHOSE TO SURVIVE. I CHOSE TO *HUNT.*

OH, HUNTER... I CAN NEVER IMAGINE YOU SAD AND LONELY.

YOU'RE TOO CLEVER, BY FAR.

AND YOU'RE TOO KIND-HEARTED, BY FAR.

OH-ME-OH-MY... LOOK AT THE TIME. I'VE GOT A PUBLICITY MEETING IN HALF AN HOUR...

COME ALONG, SWEET-HEART.

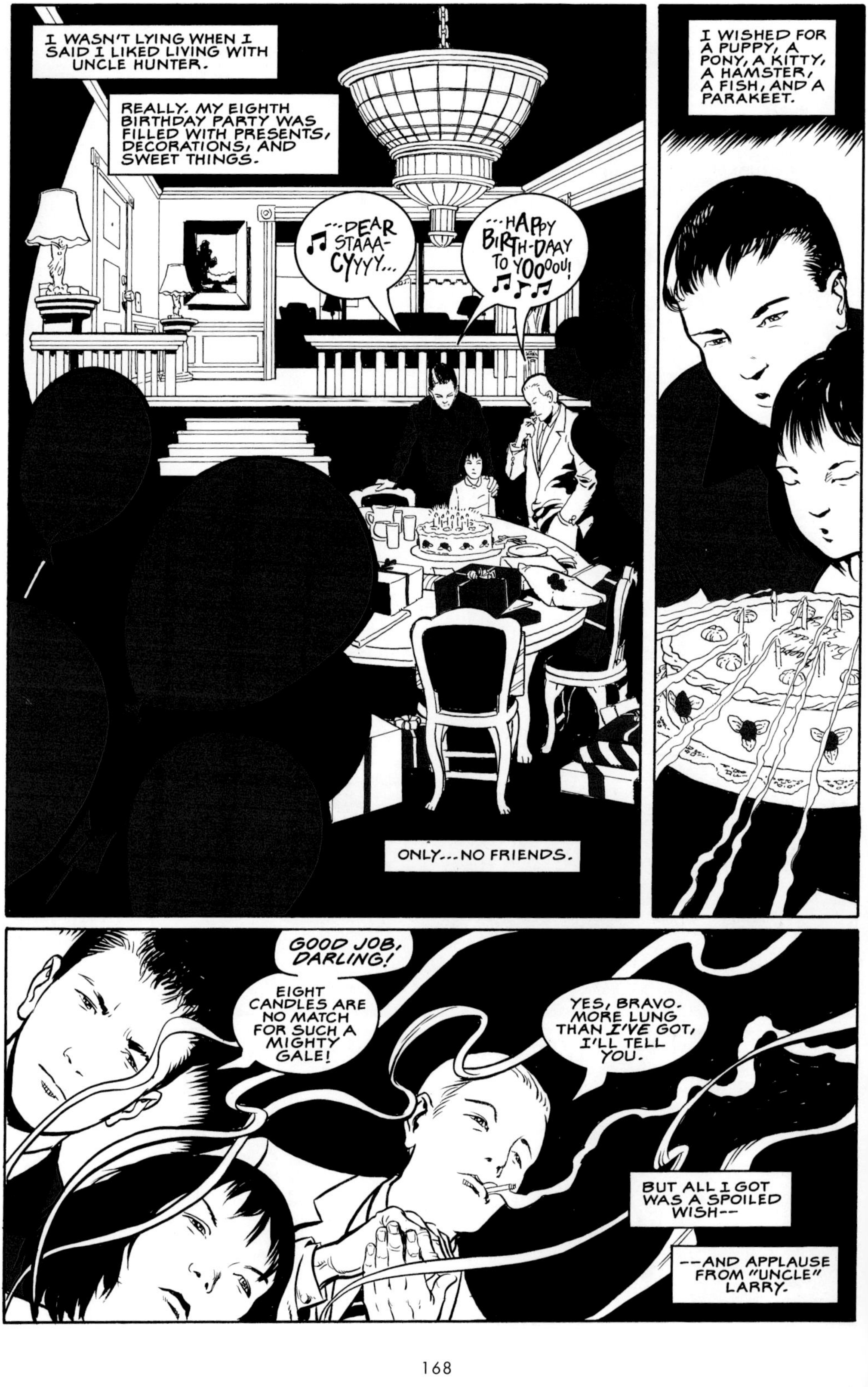
I WASN'T LYING WHEN I SAID I LIKED LIVING WITH UNCLE HUNTER.
REALLY. MY EIGHTH BIRTHDAY PARTY WAS FILLED WITH PRESENTS, DECORATIONS, AND SWEET THINGS.
...DEAR STAAA-CYYYY...
...HAPPY BIRTH-DAAY TO YOOOOU!
ONLY...NO FRIENDS.
I WISHED FOR A PUPPY, A PONY, A KITTY, A HAMSTER, A FISH, AND A PARAKEET.
GOOD JOB, DARLING!
EIGHT CANDLES ARE NO MATCH FOR SUCH A MIGHTY GALE!
YES, BRAVO. MORE LUNG THAN I'VE GOT, I'LL TELL YOU.
BUT ALL I GOT WAS A SPOILED WISH--
--AND APPLAUSE FROM "UNCLE" LARRY.

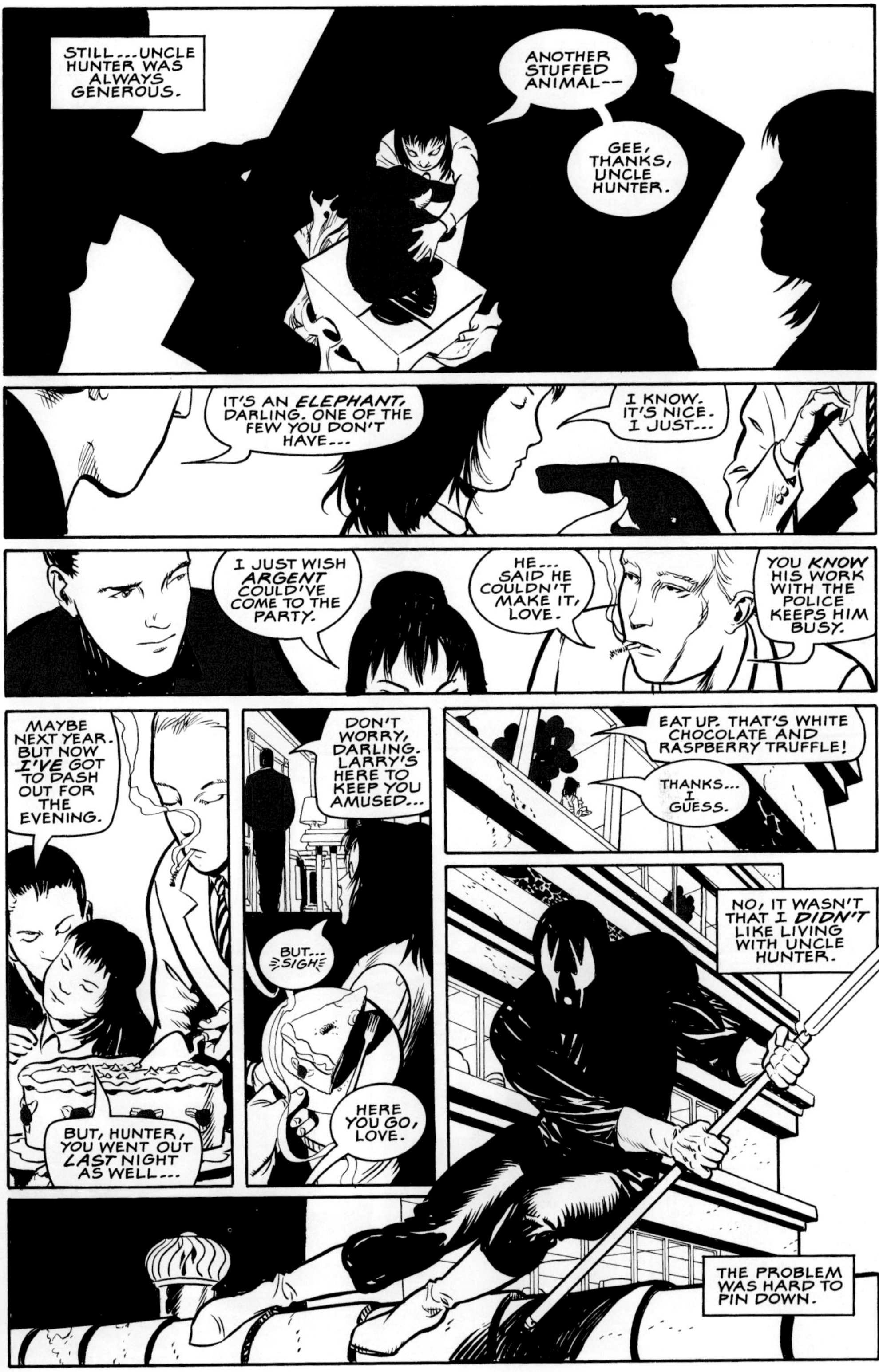
STILL... UNCLE HUNTER WAS ALWAYS GENEROUS.
ANOTHER STUFFED ANIMAL--
GEE, THANKS, UNCLE HUNTER.
IT'S AN *ELEPHANT,* DARLING. ONE OF THE FEW YOU DON'T HAVE...
I KNOW. IT'S NICE. I JUST...
I JUST WISH *ARGENT* COULD'VE COME TO THE PARTY.
HE... SAID HE COULDN'T MAKE IT, LOVE.
YOU *KNOW* HIS WORK WITH THE POLICE KEEPS HIM BUSY.
MAYBE NEXT YEAR. BUT NOW *I'VE* GOT TO DASH OUT FOR THE EVENING.
BUT, HUNTER, YOU WENT OUT *LAST* NIGHT AS WELL...
DON'T WORRY, DARLING. LARRY'S HERE TO KEEP YOU AMUSED...
BUT... *SIGH*
HERE YOU GO, LOVE.
EAT UP. THAT'S WHITE CHOCOLATE AND RASPBERRY TRUFFLE!
THANKS... I GUESS.
NO, IT WASN'T THAT I *DIDN'T* LIKE LIVING WITH UNCLE HUNTER.
THE PROBLEM WAS HARD TO PIN DOWN.

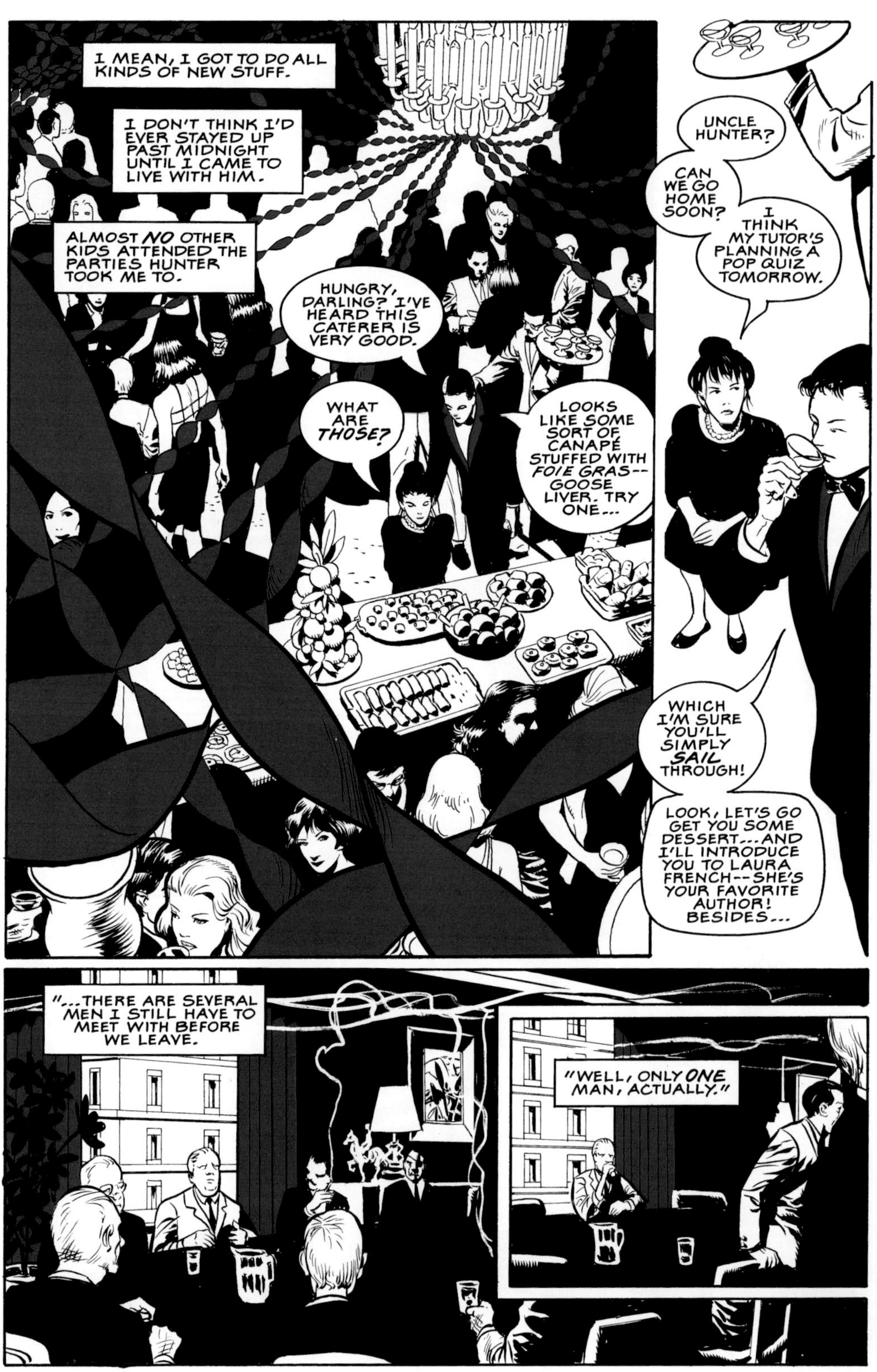
I MEAN, I GOT TO DO ALL KINDS OF NEW STUFF.
I DON'T THINK I'D EVER STAYED UP PAST MIDNIGHT UNTIL I CAME TO LIVE WITH HIM.
ALMOST NO OTHER KIDS ATTENDED THE PARTIES HUNTER TOOK ME TO.
HUNGRY, DARLING? I'VE HEARD THIS CATERER IS VERY GOOD.
WHAT ARE THOSE?
LOOKS LIKE SOME SORT OF CANAPÉ STUFFED WITH FOIE GRAS-- GOOSE LIVER. TRY ONE...
UNCLE HUNTER?
CAN WE GO HOME SOON?
I THINK MY TUTOR'S PLANNING A POP QUIZ TOMORROW.
WHICH I'M SURE YOU'LL SIMPLY SAIL THROUGH!
LOOK, LET'S GO GET YOU SOME DESSERT... AND I'LL INTRODUCE YOU TO LAURA FRENCH--SHE'S YOUR FAVORITE AUTHOR! BESIDES...
"...THERE ARE SEVERAL MEN I STILL HAVE TO MEET WITH BEFORE WE LEAVE.
"WELL, ONLY ONE MAN, ACTUALLY."

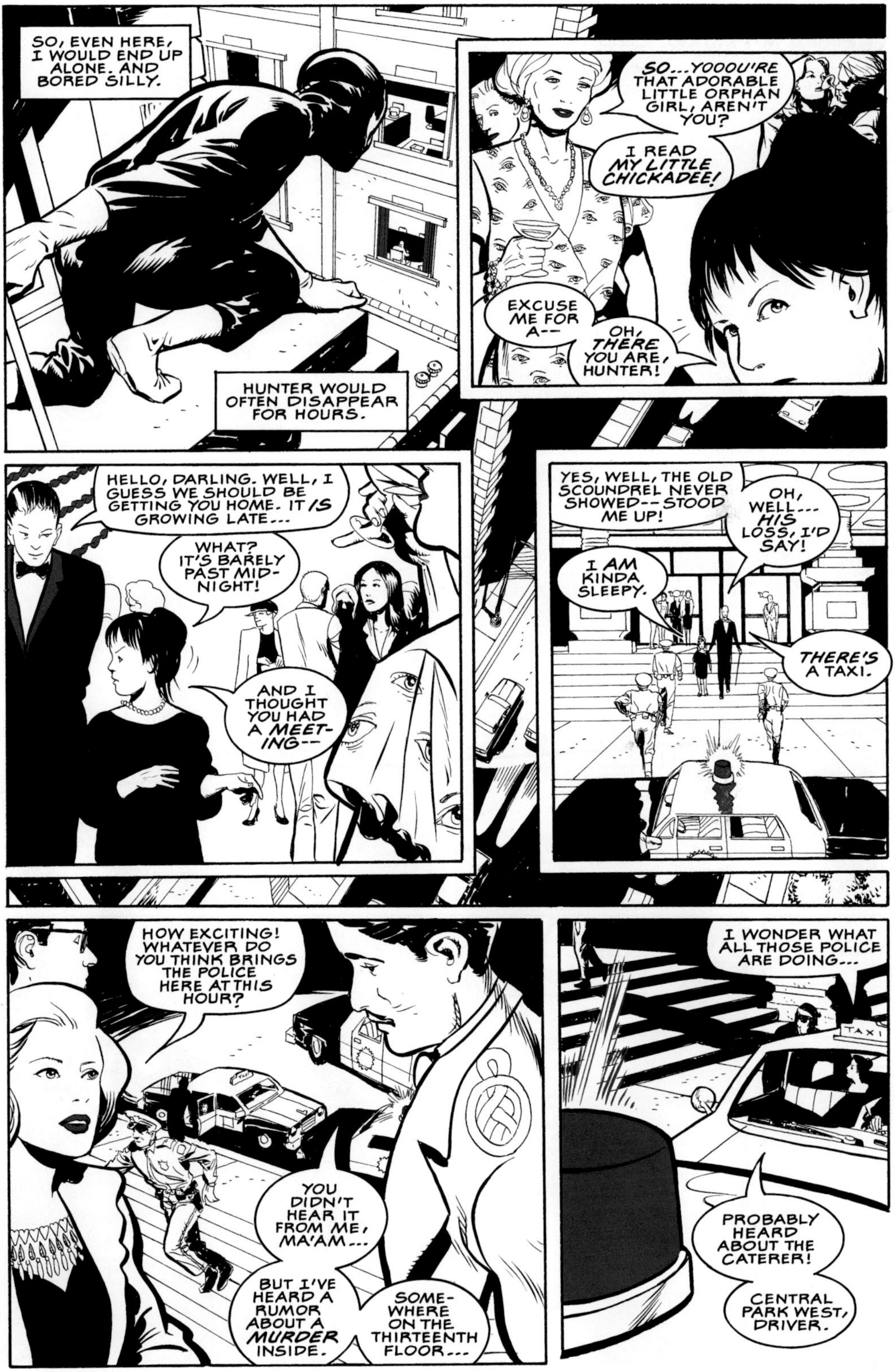
SO, EVEN HERE, I WOULD END UP ALONE. AND BORED SILLY.
HUNTER WOULD OFTEN DISAPPEAR FOR HOURS.
SO...YOOOU'RE THAT ADORABLE LITTLE ORPHAN GIRL, AREN'T YOU?
I READ MY LITTLE CHICKADEE!
EXCUSE ME FOR A--
OH, THERE YOU ARE, HUNTER!
HELLO, DARLING. WELL, I GUESS WE SHOULD BE GETTING YOU HOME. IT IS GROWING LATE...
WHAT? IT'S BARELY PAST MID-NIGHT!
AND I THOUGHT YOU HAD A MEET-ING--
YES, WELL, THE OLD SCOUNDREL NEVER SHOWED--STOOD ME UP!
OH, WELL... HIS LOSS, I'D SAY!
I AM KINDA SLEEPY.
THERE'S A TAXI.
HOW EXCITING! WHATEVER DO YOU THINK BRINGS THE POLICE HERE AT THIS HOUR?
YOU DIDN'T HEAR IT FROM ME, MA'AM...
BUT I'VE HEARD A RUMOR ABOUT A MURDER INSIDE.
SOME-WHERE ON THE THIRTEENTH FLOOR...
I WONDER WHAT ALL THOSE POLICE ARE DOING...
TAXI
PROBABLY HEARD ABOUT THE CATERER!
CENTRAL PARK WEST, DRIVER.

I THINK I ACTUALLY BELIEVED I WOULD REMAIN A LITTLE GIRL FOREVER.

SIMPLY MOVING FROM FAMILY TO FAMILY AFTER THEY HAD ALL DIED.

I EXPECTED IT.

STACY, DARLING-- EH?

UP AND OUT ALREADY?

HMMM... MUST'VE GONE TO THE PARK.

EVEN HUNTER WOULD LEAVE ME SOMEDAY.

I NEVER IMAGINED GROWING UP.

OR OLD.

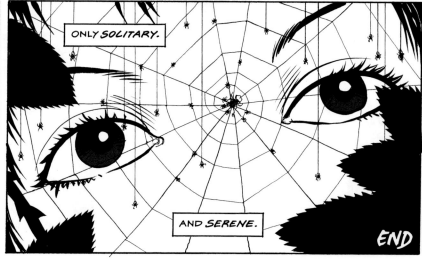

ONLY SOLITARY.

AND SERENE.

END

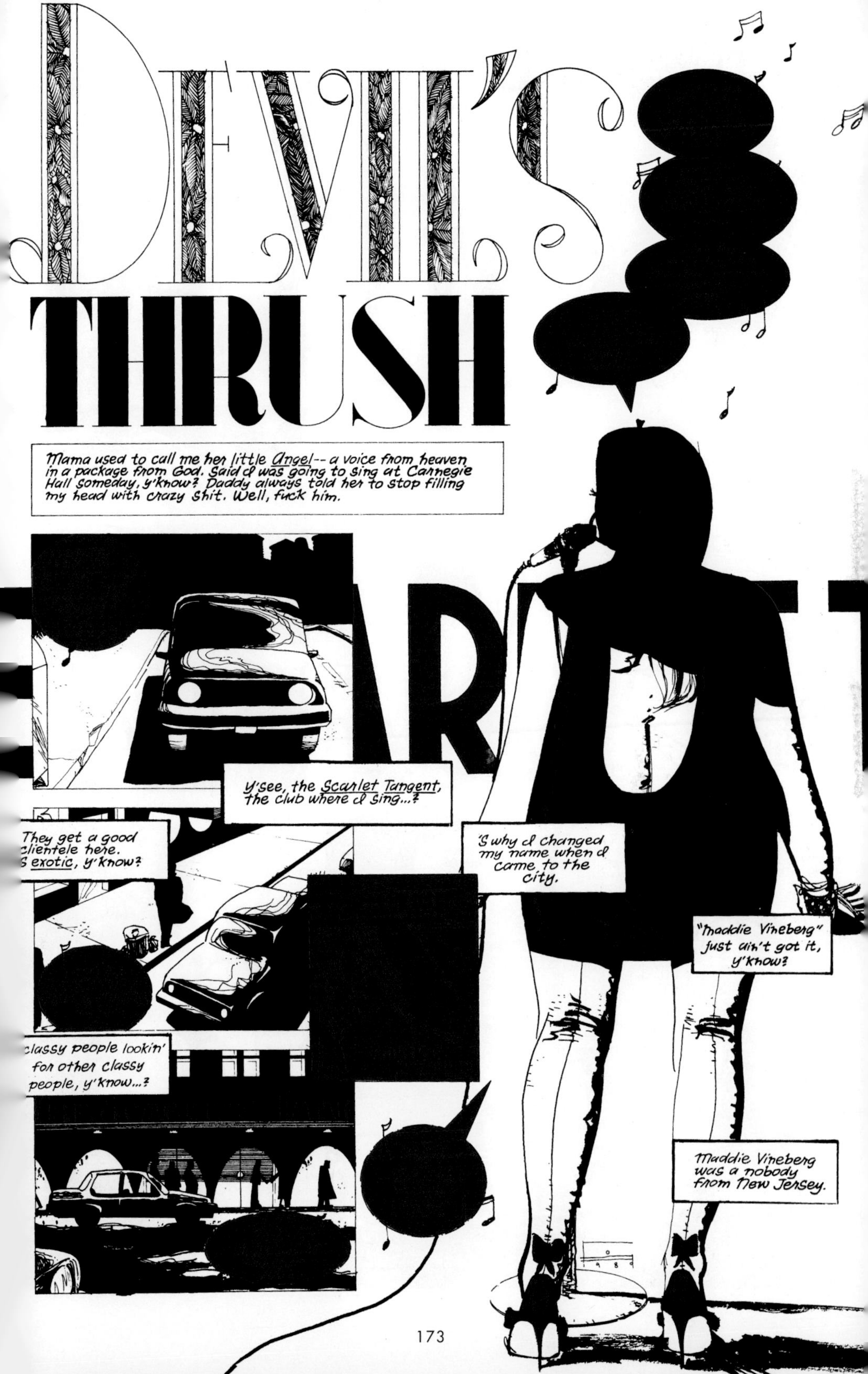

DEVIL'S THRUSH
Mama used to call me her little Angel-- a voice from heaven in a package from God. Said I was going to sing at Carnegie Hall someday, y'know? Daddy always told her to stop filling my head with crazy shit. Well, fuck him.
Y'see, the Scarlet Tangent, the club where I sing...?
They get a good clientele here. S exotic, y'know?
classy people lookin' for other classy people, y'know...?
'S why I changed my name when I came to the city.
"Maddie Vineberg" just ain't got it, y'know?
Maddie Vineberg was a nobody from New Jersey.

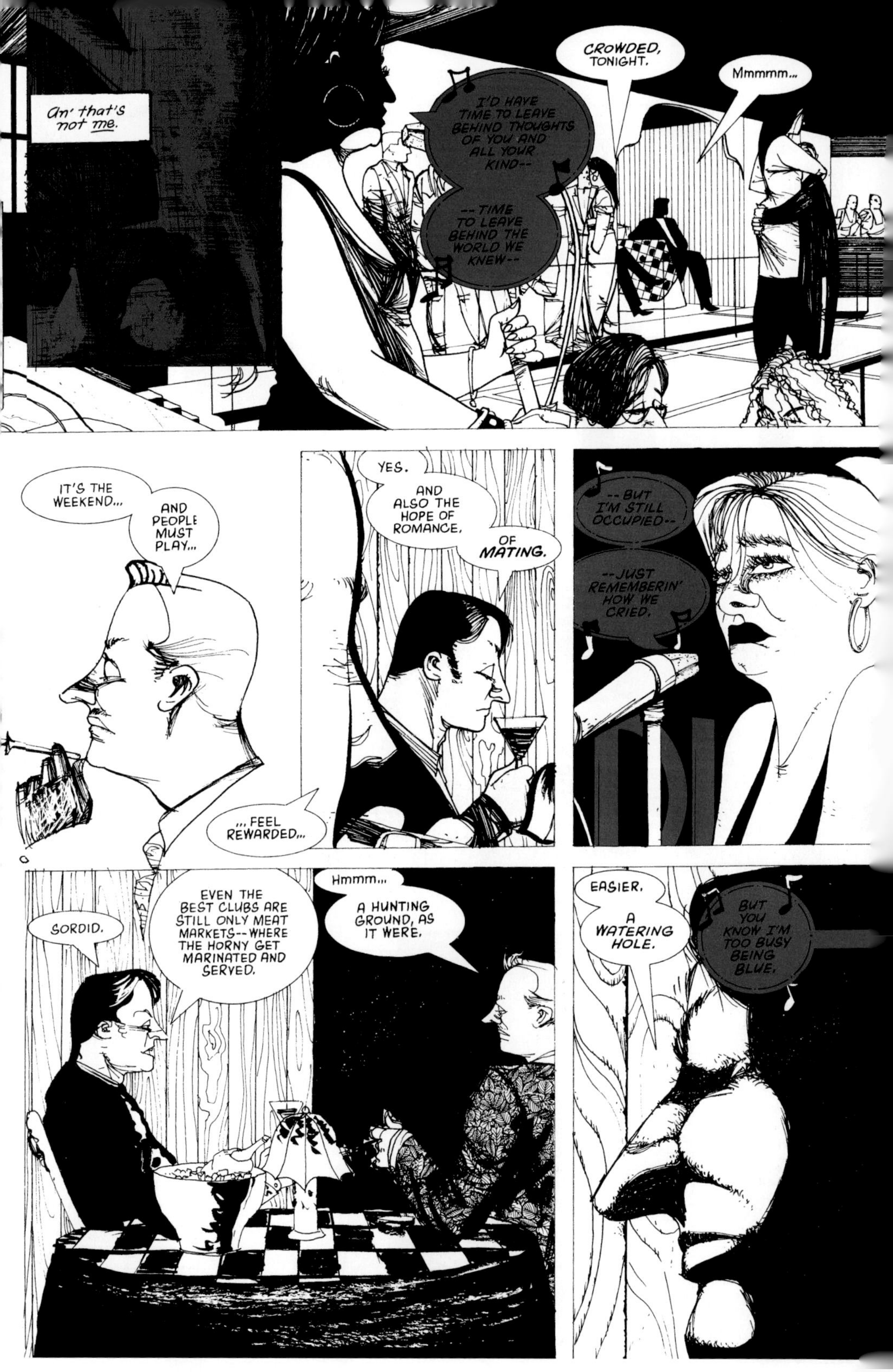
An' that's not me.
I'D HAVE TIME TO LEAVE BEHIND THOUGHTS OF YOU AND ALL YOUR KIND--
--TIME TO LEAVE BEHIND THE WORLD WE KNEW--
CROWDED, TONIGHT.
Mmmmm...
IT'S THE WEEKEND...
AND PEOPLE MUST PLAY...
...FEEL REWARDED...
YES.
AND ALSO THE HOPE OF ROMANCE.
OF MATING.
--BUT I'M STILL OCCUPIED--
--JUST REMEMBERIN' HOW WE CRIED.
SORDID.
EVEN THE BEST CLUBS ARE STILL ONLY MEAT MARKETS--WHERE THE HORNY GET MARINATED AND SERVED.
Hmmm...
A HUNTING GROUND, AS IT WERE.
EASIER.
A WATERING HOLE.
BUT YOU KNOW I'M TOO BUSY BEING BLUE.

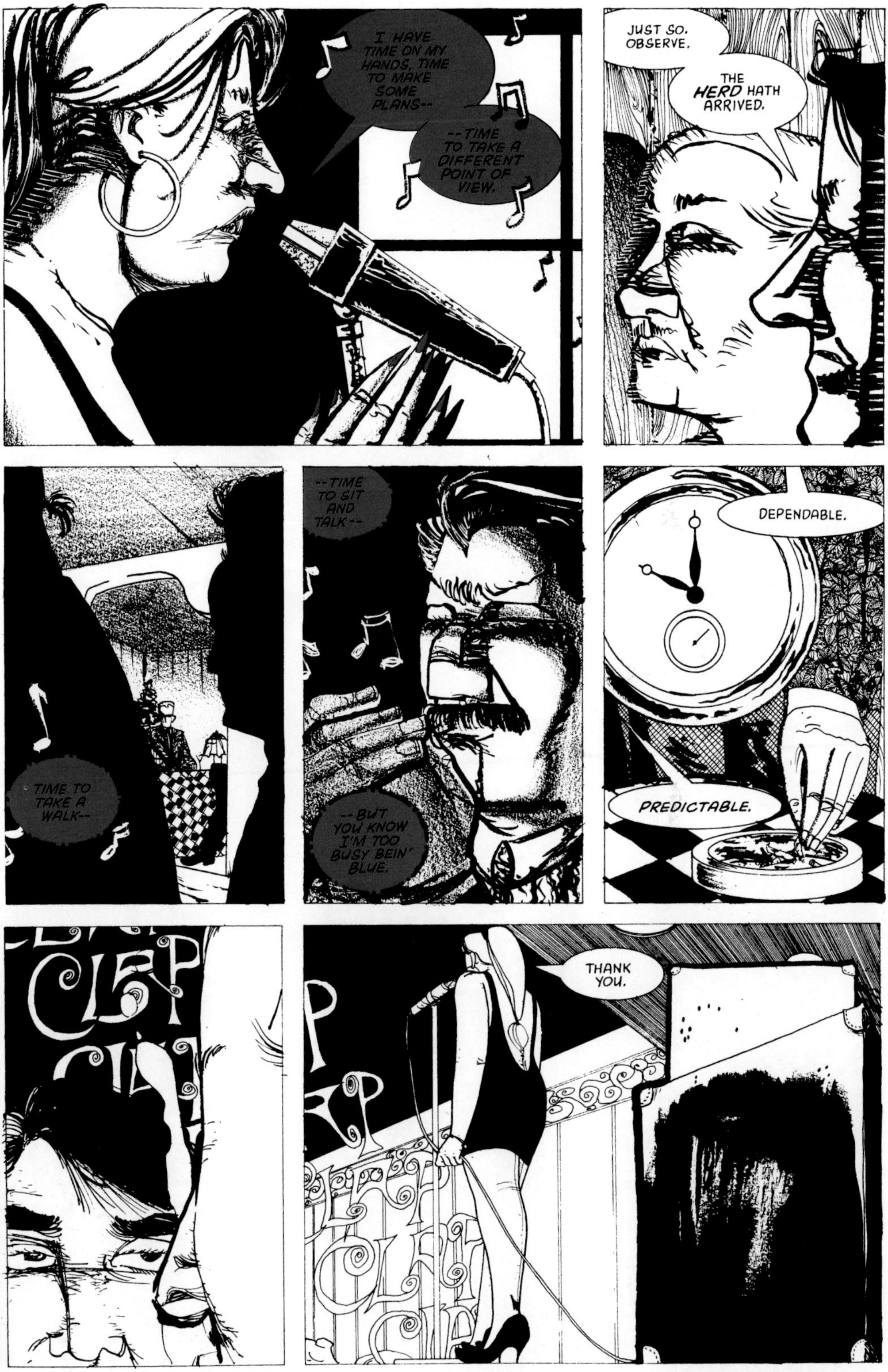
I HAVE TIME ON MY HANDS, TIME TO MAKE SOME PLANS--
--TIME TO TAKE A DIFFERENT POINT OF VIEW.
JUST SO. OBSERVE.
THE HERD HATH ARRIVED.
TIME TO TAKE A WALK--
--TIME TO SIT AND TALK--
--BUT YOU KNOW I'M TOO BUSY BEIN' BLUE.
DEPENDABLE.
PREDICTABLE.
THANK YOU.

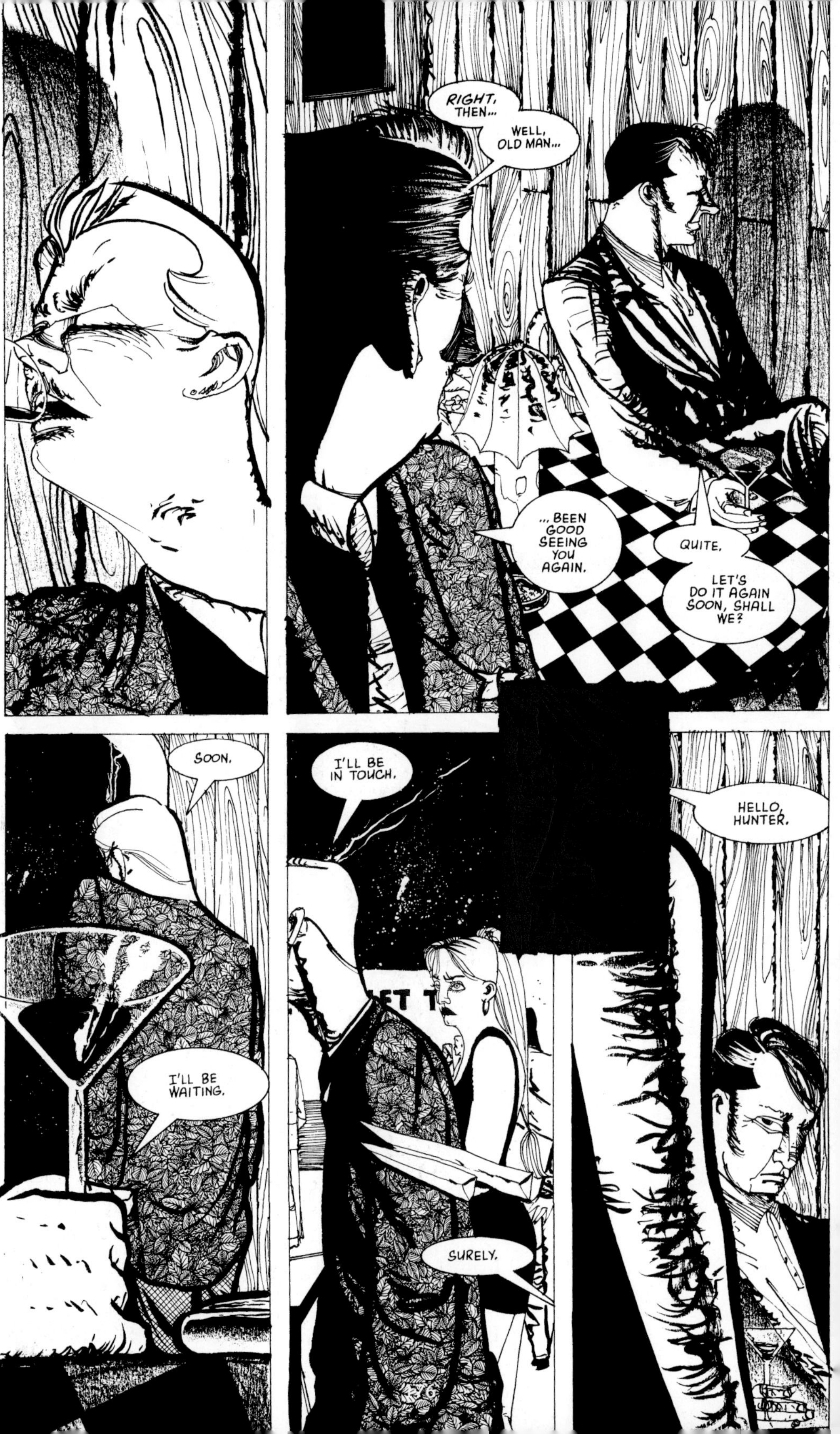

RIGHT, THEN...
WELL, OLD MAN...
...BEEN GOOD SEEING YOU AGAIN.
QUITE.
LET'S DO IT AGAIN SOON, SHALL WE?
SOON.
I'LL BE WAITING.
I'LL BE IN TOUCH.
SURELY.
HELLO, HUNTER.

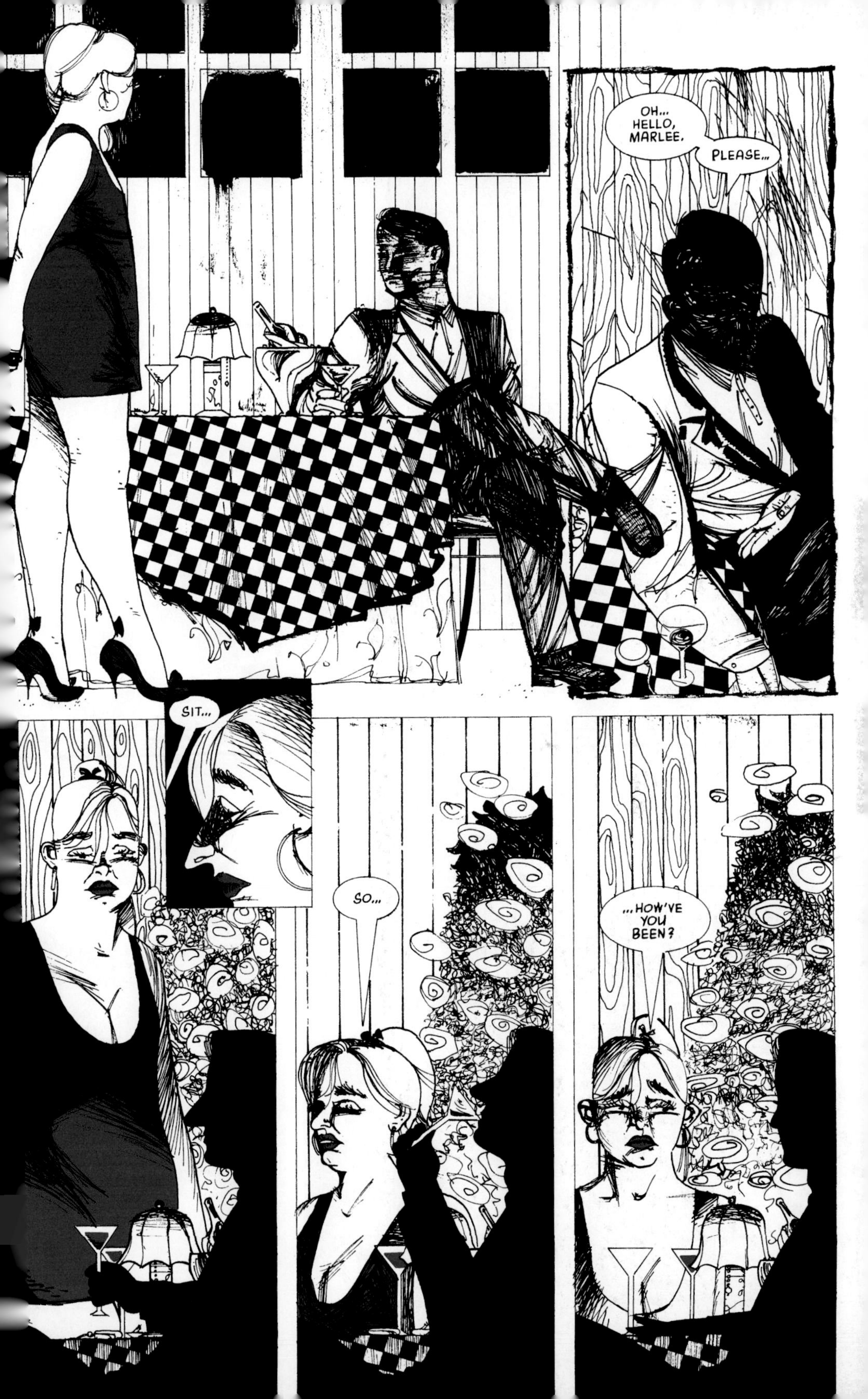
OH... HELLO, MARLEE.
PLEASE...
SIT...
SO...
...HOW'VE YOU BEEN?

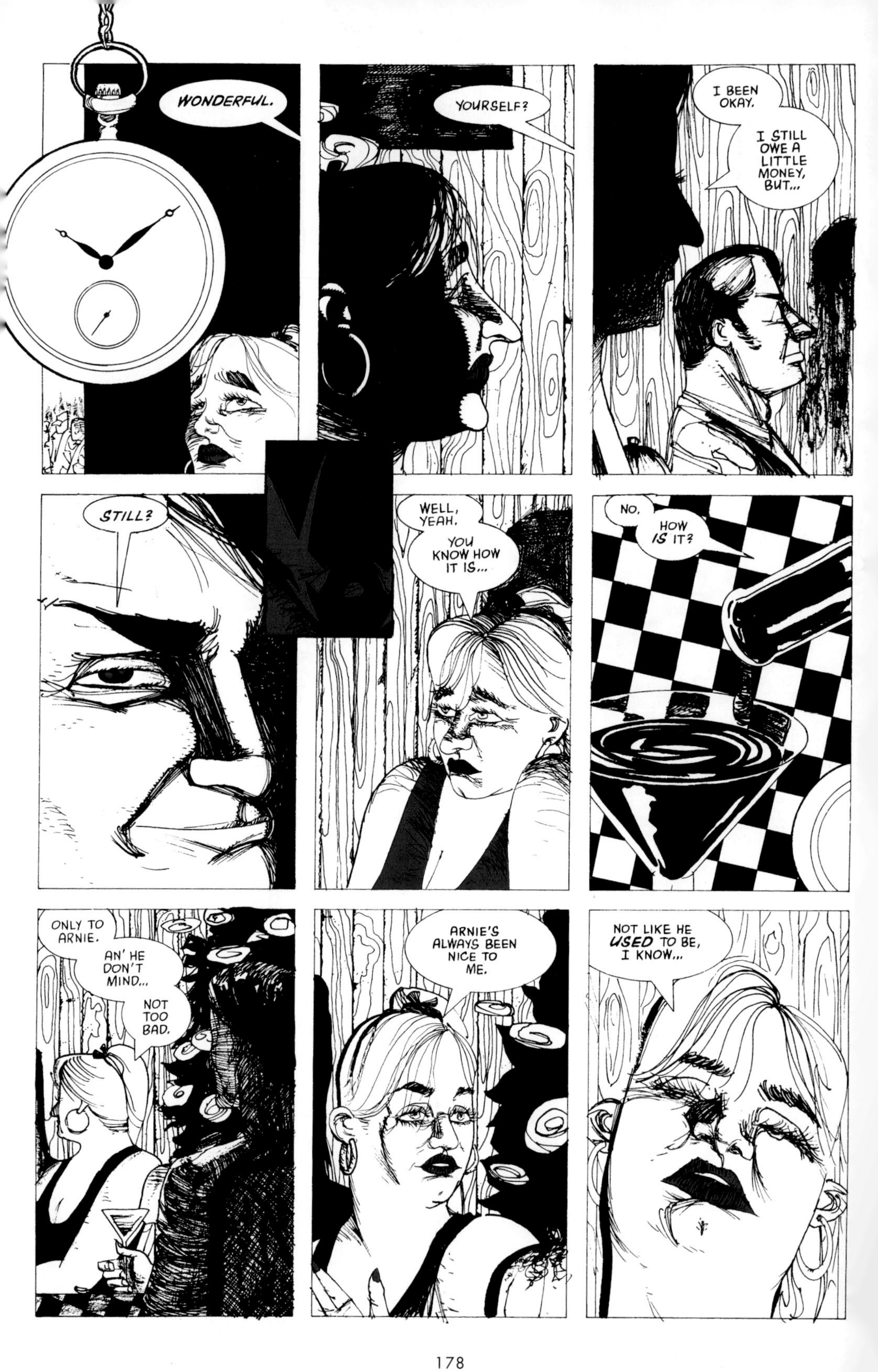
WONDERFUL.
YOURSELF?
I BEEN OKAY.
I STILL OWE A LITTLE MONEY, BUT...
STILL?
WELL, YEAH.
YOU KNOW HOW IT IS...
NO,
HOW IS IT?
ONLY TO ARNIE.
AN' HE DON'T MIND...
NOT TOO BAD.
ARNIE'S ALWAYS BEEN NICE TO ME.
NOT LIKE HE USED TO BE, I KNOW...

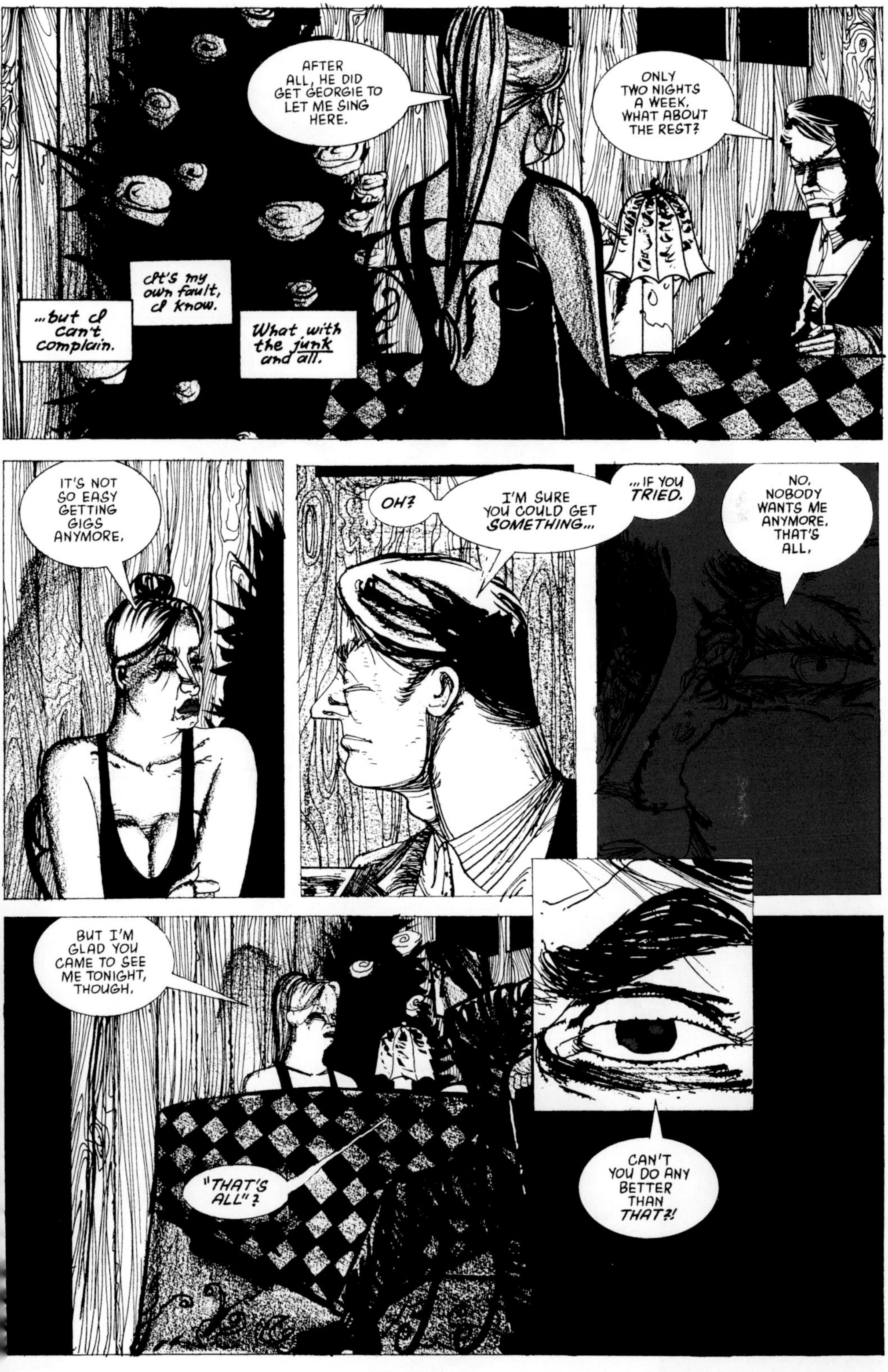
...but I can't complain.
It's my own fault, I know.
What with the junk and all.
AFTER ALL, HE DID GET GEORGIE TO LET ME SING HERE.
ONLY TWO NIGHTS A WEEK. WHAT ABOUT THE REST?
IT'S NOT SO EASY GETTING GIGS ANYMORE.
OH?
I'M SURE YOU COULD GET SOMETHING...
...IF YOU TRIED.
NO. NOBODY WANTS ME ANYMORE. THAT'S ALL.
BUT I'M GLAD YOU CAME TO SEE ME TONIGHT, THOUGH.
"THAT'S ALL"?
CAN'T YOU DO ANY BETTER THAN THAT?!

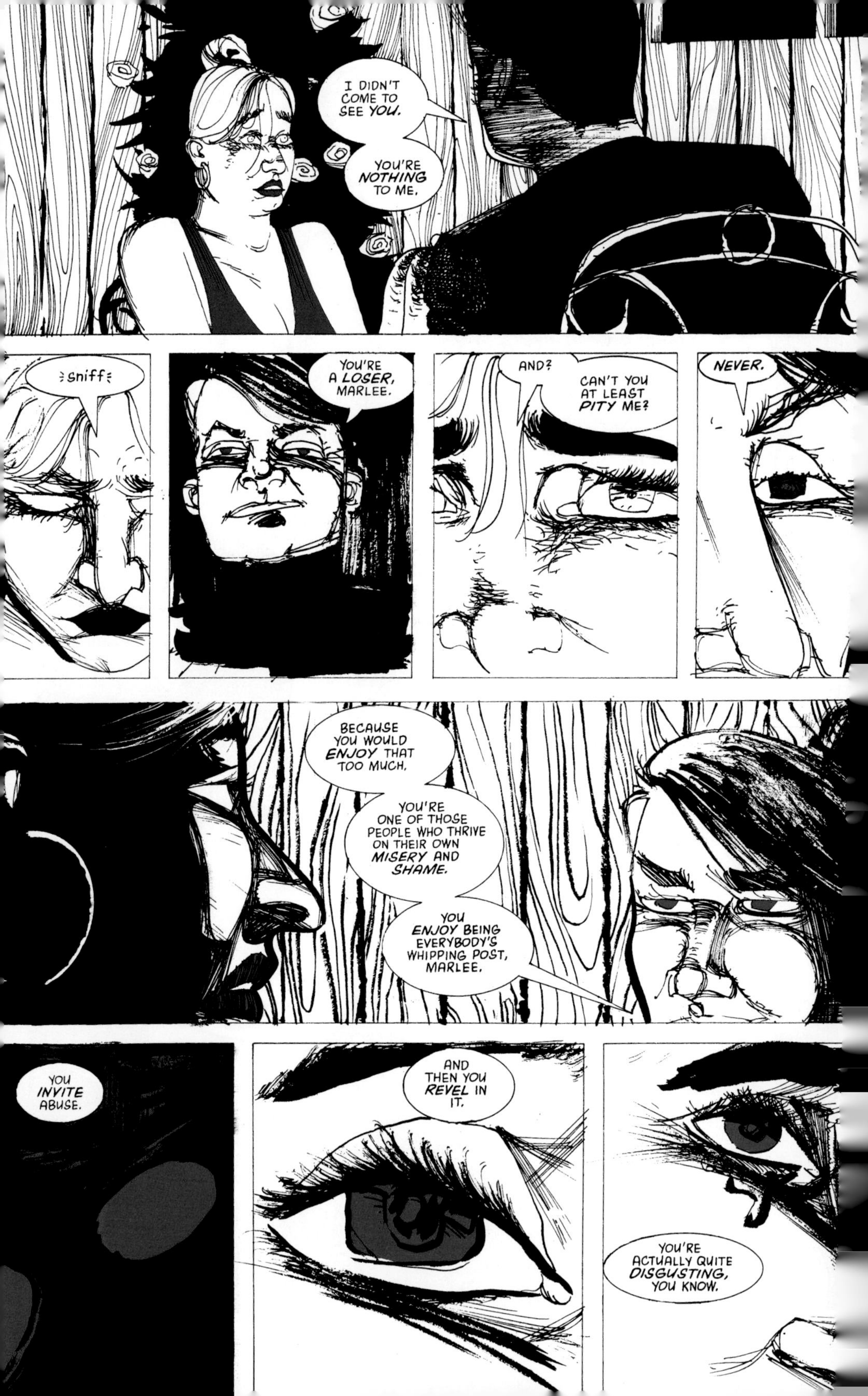
I DIDN'T COME TO SEE YOU.
YOU'RE NOTHING TO ME.
sniff
YOU'RE A LOSER, MARLEE.
AND?
CAN'T YOU AT LEAST PITY ME?
NEVER.
BECAUSE YOU WOULD ENJOY THAT TOO MUCH.
YOU'RE ONE OF THOSE PEOPLE WHO THRIVE ON THEIR OWN MISERY AND SHAME.
YOU ENJOY BEING EVERYBODY'S WHIPPING POST, MARLEE.
YOU INVITE ABUSE.
AND THEN YOU REVEL IN IT.
YOU'RE ACTUALLY QUITE DISGUSTING, YOU KNOW.

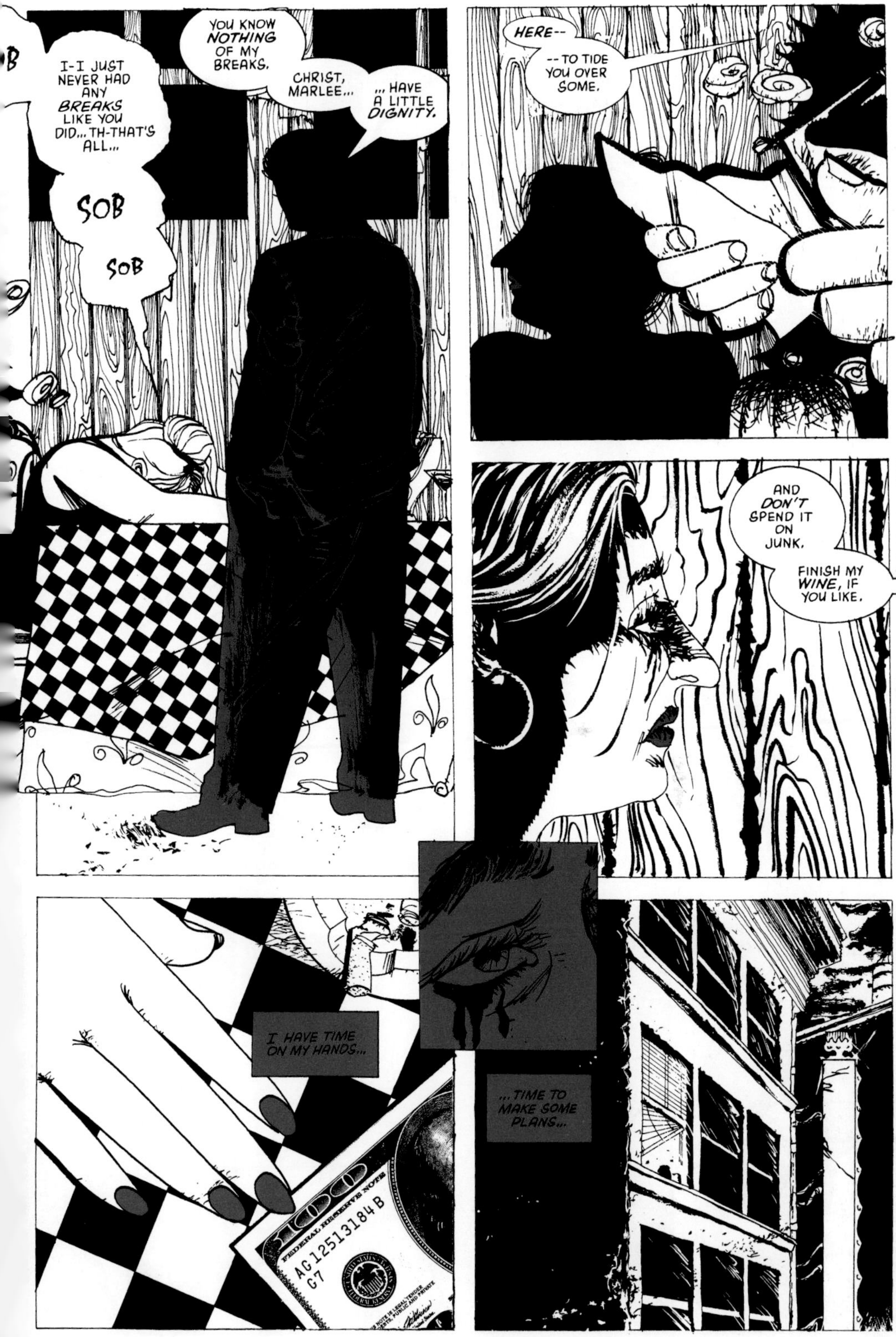

I-I JUST NEVER HAD ANY BREAKS LIKE YOU DID... TH-THAT'S ALL...
SOB
SOB
YOU KNOW NOTHING OF MY BREAKS.
CHRIST, MARLEE...
...HAVE A LITTLE DIGNITY.
HERE--
--TO TIDE YOU OVER SOME.
AND DON'T SPEND IT ON JUNK.
FINISH MY WINE, IF YOU LIKE.
I HAVE TIME ON MY HANDS...
...TIME TO MAKE SOME PLANS...
FEDERAL RESERVE NOTE
AG12513184B
G7

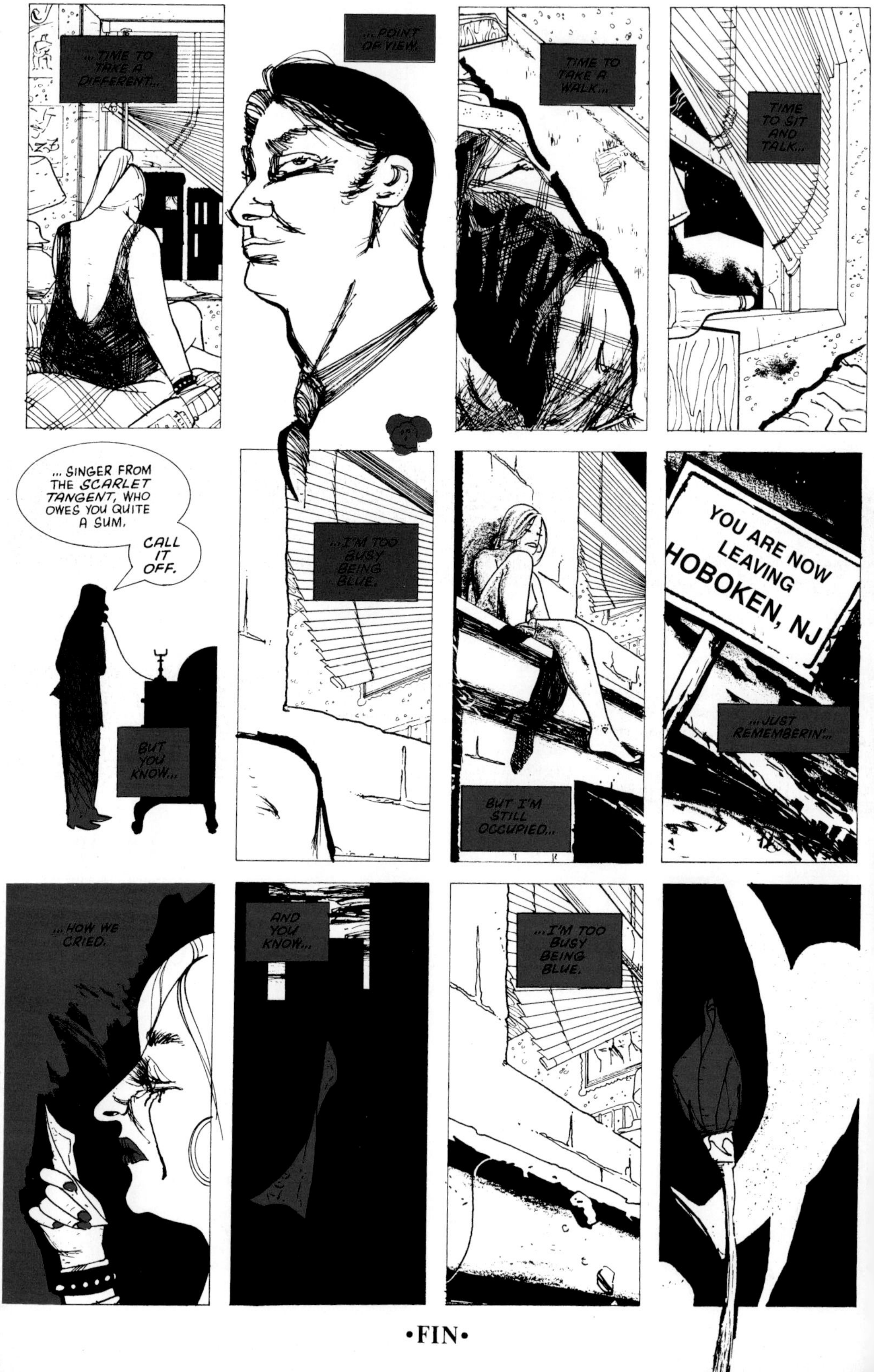
...TIME TO TAKE A DIFFERENT...
...POINT OF VIEW.
TIME TO TAKE A WALK...
TIME TO SIT AND TALK...
... SINGER FROM THE SCARLET TANGENT, WHO OWES YOU QUITE A SUM.
CALL IT OFF.
BUT YOU KNOW...
...I'M TOO BUSY BEING BLUE.
BUT I'M STILL OCCUPIED...
YOU ARE NOW LEAVING HOBOKEN, NJ
...JUST REMEMBERIN'...
...HOW WE CRIED.
AND YOU KNOW...
...I'M TOO BUSY BEING BLUE.

•FIN•

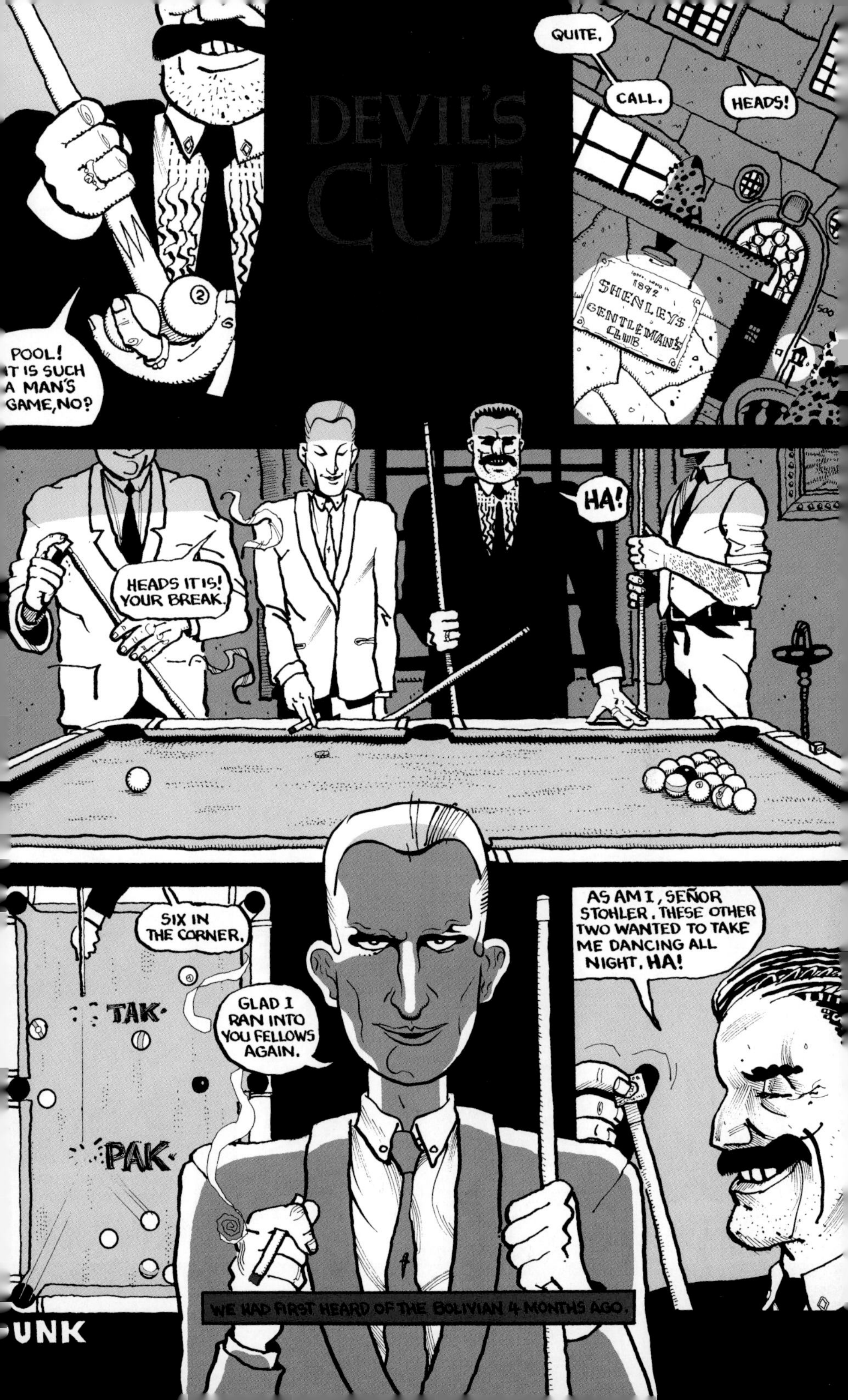
DEVIL'S
CUE
POOL!
IT IS SUCH
A MAN'S
GAME, NO?
QUITE.
CALL.
HEADS!
1892
SHENLEYS
GENTLEMAN'S
CLUB
HEADS IT IS!
YOUR BREAK.
HA!
SIX IN
THE CORNER.
TAK
PAK
UNK
GLAD I
RAN INTO
YOU FELLOWS
AGAIN.
AS AM I, SEÑOR
STOHLER. THESE OTHER
TWO WANTED TO TAKE
ME DANCING ALL
NIGHT. HA!
WE HAD FIRST HEARD OF THE BOLIVIAN 4 MONTHS AGO.

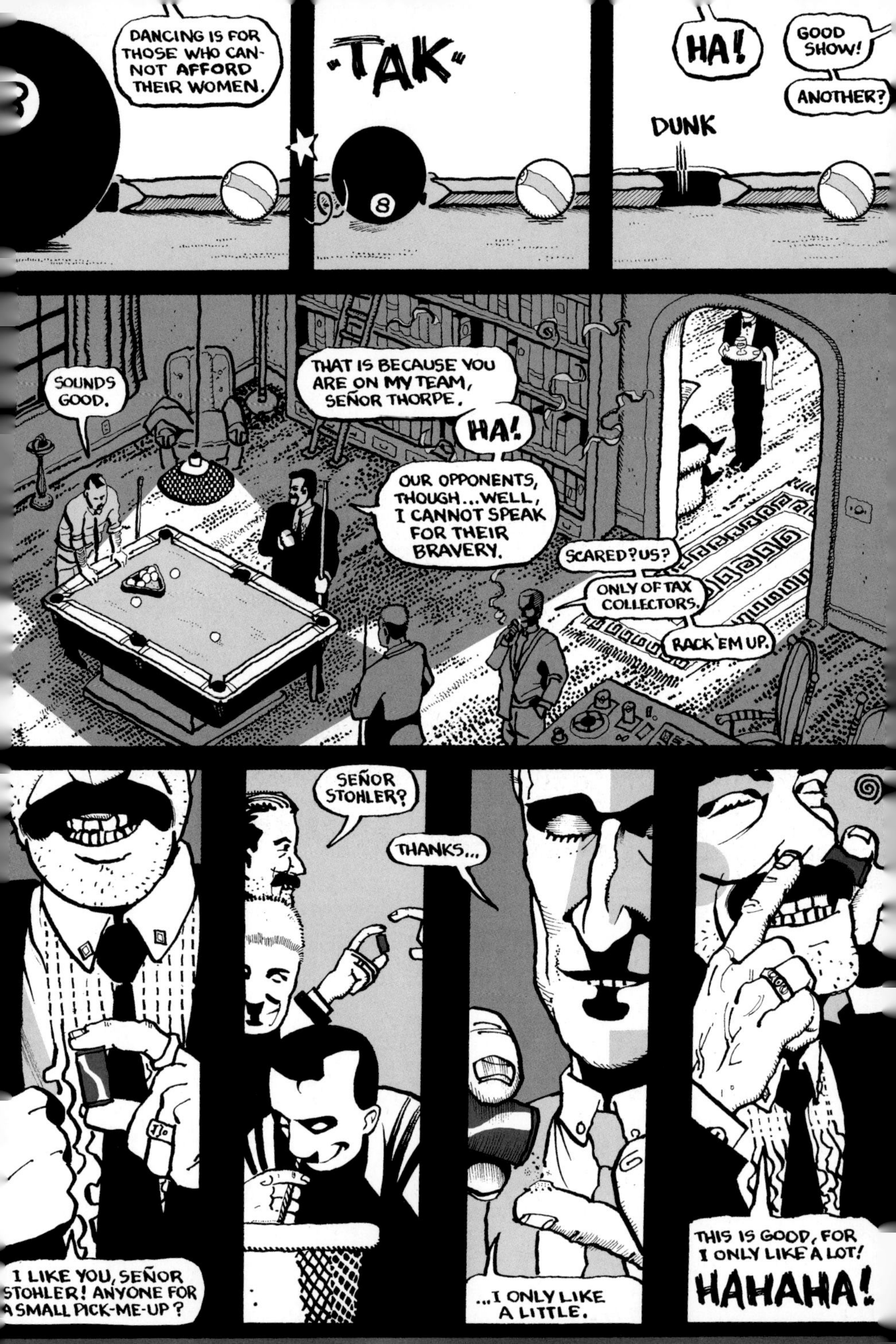
DANCING IS FOR THOSE WHO CANNOT AFFORD THEIR WOMEN.
"TAK"
HA!
GOOD SHOW!
ANOTHER?
DUNK
SOUNDS GOOD.
THAT IS BECAUSE YOU ARE ON MY TEAM, SEÑOR THORPE.
HA!
OUR OPPONENTS, THOUGH... WELL, I CANNOT SPEAK FOR THEIR BRAVERY.
SCARED? US?
ONLY OF TAX COLLECTORS.
RACK 'EM UP.
I LIKE YOU, SEÑOR STOHLER! ANYONE FOR A SMALL PICK-ME-UP?
SEÑOR STOHLER?
THANKS...
...I ONLY LIKE A LITTLE.
THIS IS GOOD, FOR I ONLY LIKE A LOT!
HAHAHA!

HE WAS LOUD ABOUT HIMSELF, THIS BOLIVIAN, AND HE ALWAYS HAD THE FINEST BLOW AROUND.

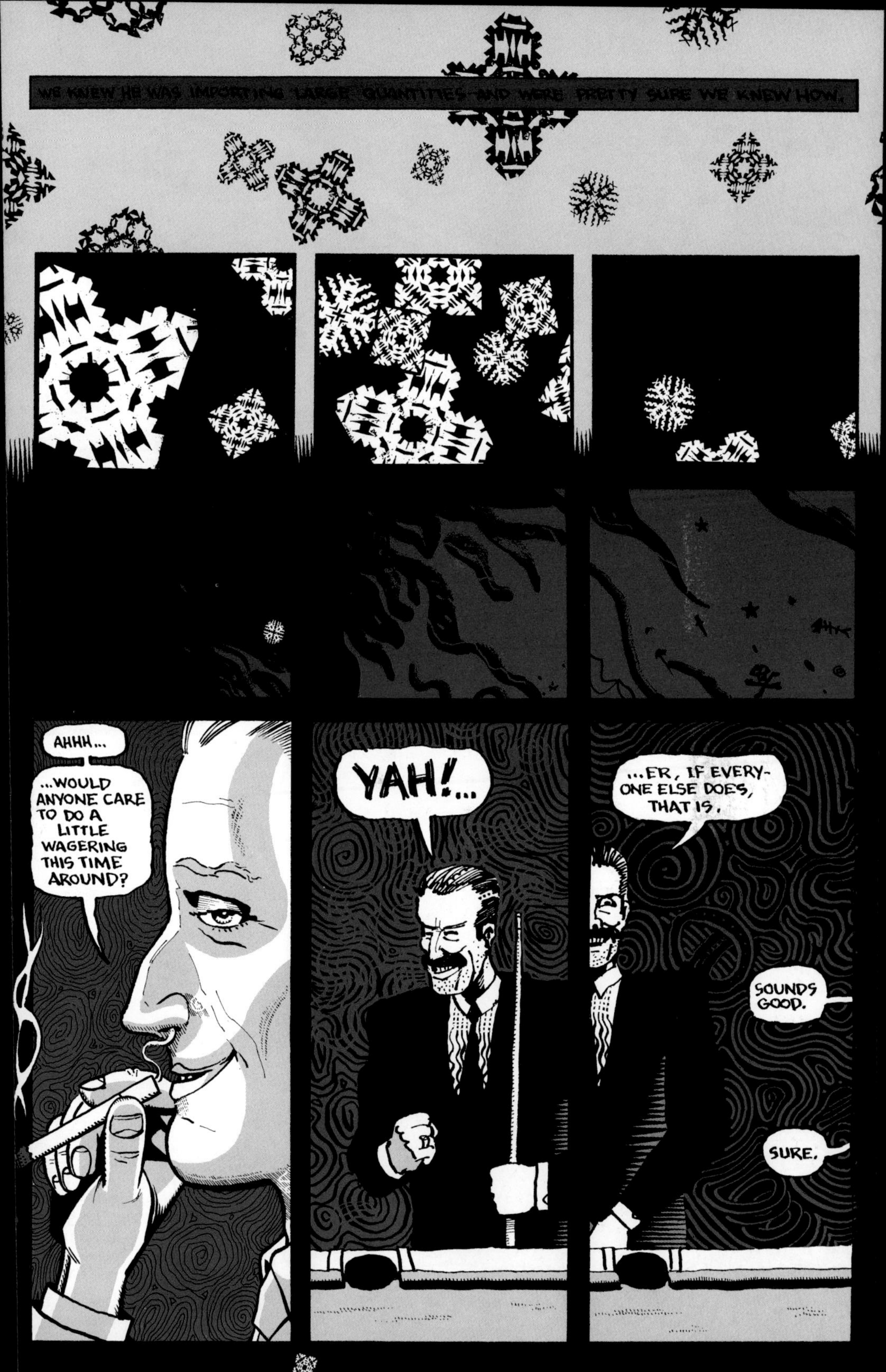
WE KNEW HE WAS IMPORTING LARGE QUANTITIES--AND WERE PRETTY SURE WE KNEW HOW.
AHHH...
...WOULD ANYONE CARE TO DO A LITTLE WAGERING THIS TIME AROUND?
YAH!...
...ER, IF EVERY-ONE ELSE DOES, THAT IS.
SOUNDS GOOD.
SURE.

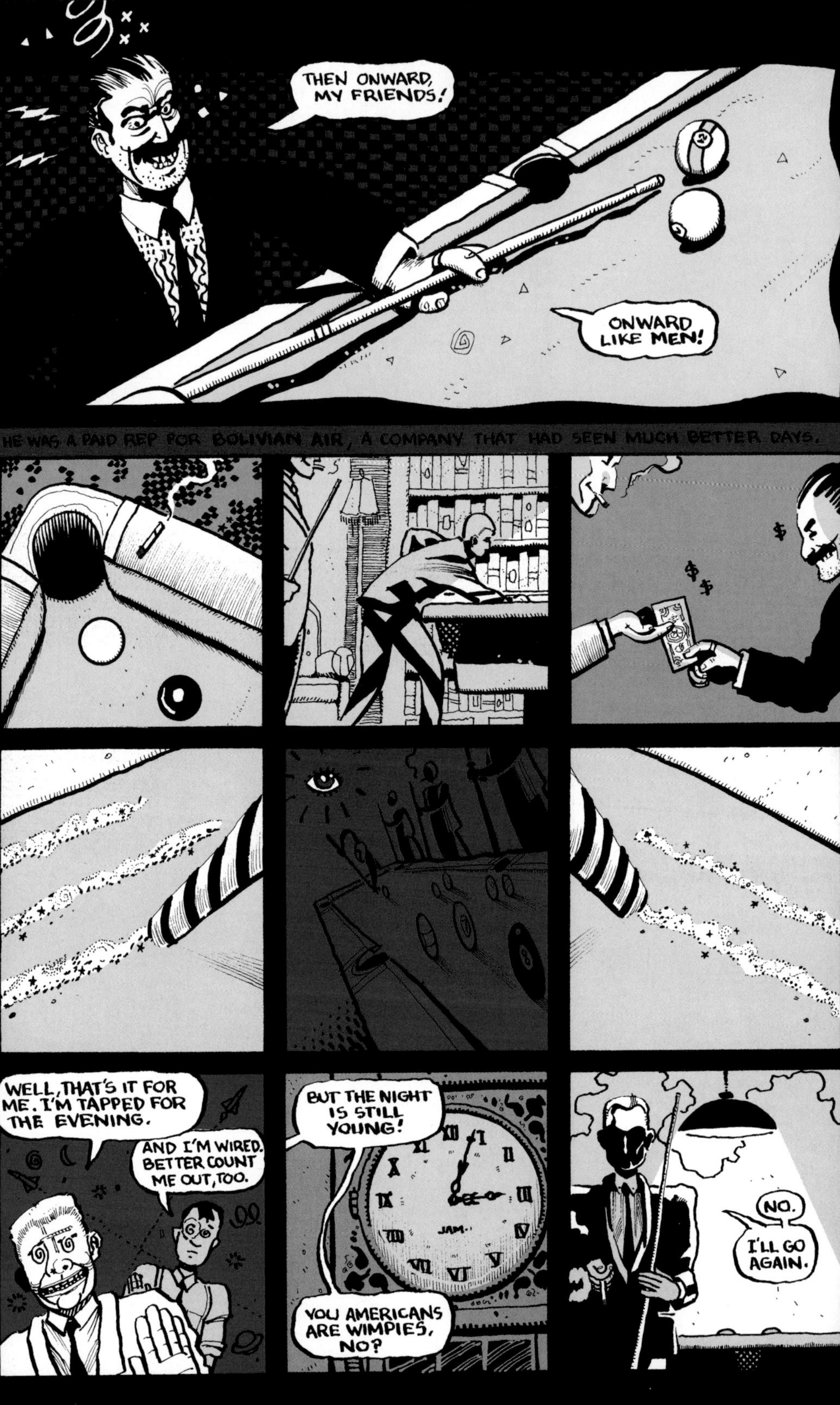
THEN ONWARD, MY FRIENDS!
ONWARD LIKE MEN!
HE WAS A PAID REP FOR BOLIVIAN AIR, A COMPANY THAT HAD SEEN MUCH BETTER DAYS.
WELL, THAT'S IT FOR ME. I'M TAPPED FOR THE EVENING.
AND I'M WIRED. BETTER COUNT ME OUT, TOO.
BUT THE NIGHT IS STILL YOUNG!
YOU AMERICANS ARE WIMPIES, NO?
NO.
I'LL GO AGAIN.

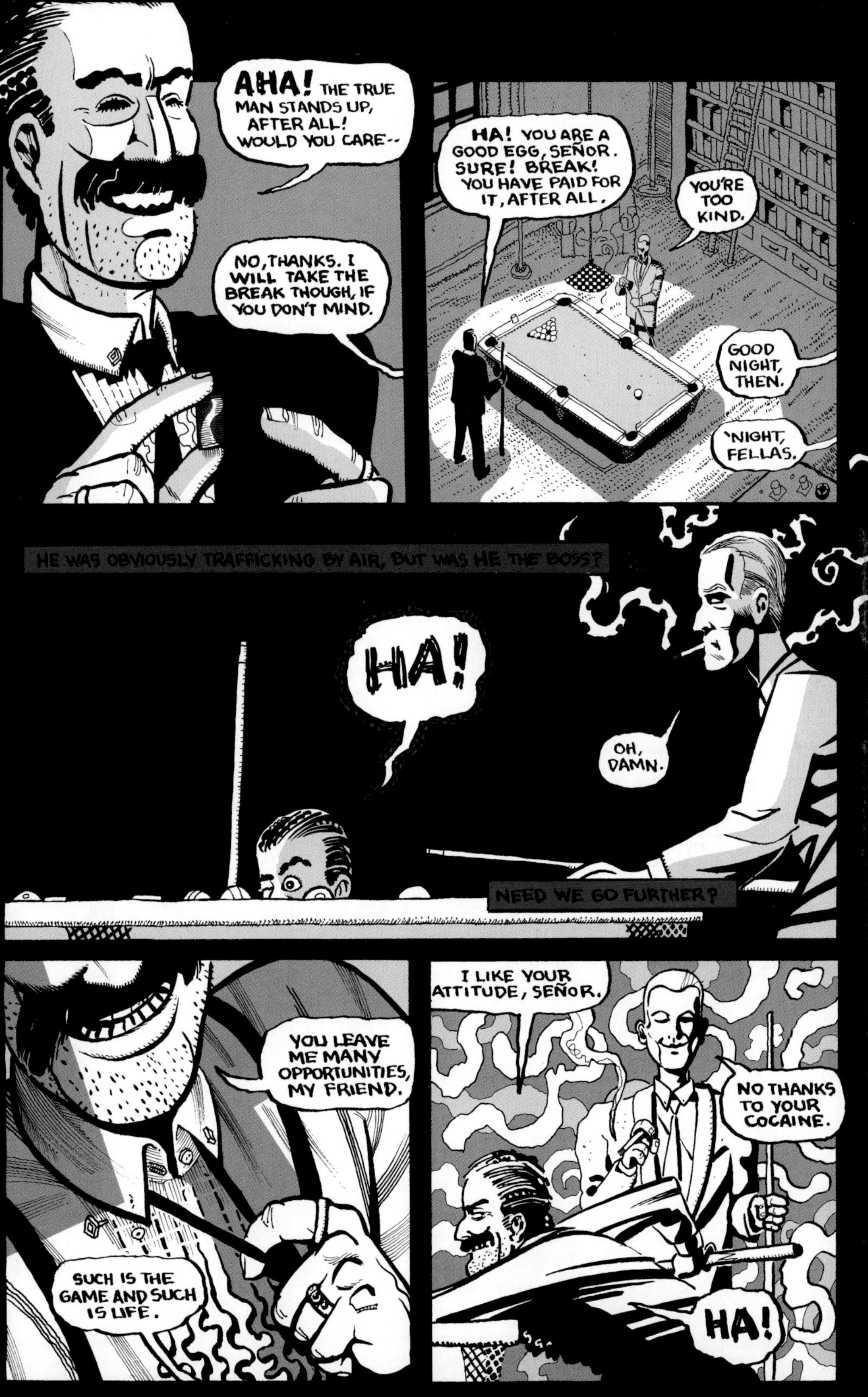
AHA! THE TRUE MAN STANDS UP, AFTER ALL! WOULD YOU CARE--
NO, THANKS. I WILL TAKE THE BREAK THOUGH, IF YOU DON'T MIND.
HA! YOU ARE A GOOD EGG, SEÑOR. SURE! BREAK! YOU HAVE PAID FOR IT, AFTER ALL.
YOU'RE TOO KIND.
GOOD NIGHT, THEN.
'NIGHT, FELLAS.
HE WAS OBVIOUSLY TRAFFICKING BY AIR, BUT WAS HE THE BOSS?
HA!
OH, DAMN.
NEED WE GO FURTHER?
YOU LEAVE ME MANY OPPORTUNITIES, MY FRIEND.
SUCH IS THE GAME AND SUCH IS LIFE.
I LIKE YOUR ATTITUDE, SEÑOR.
NO THANKS TO YOUR COCAINE.
HA!

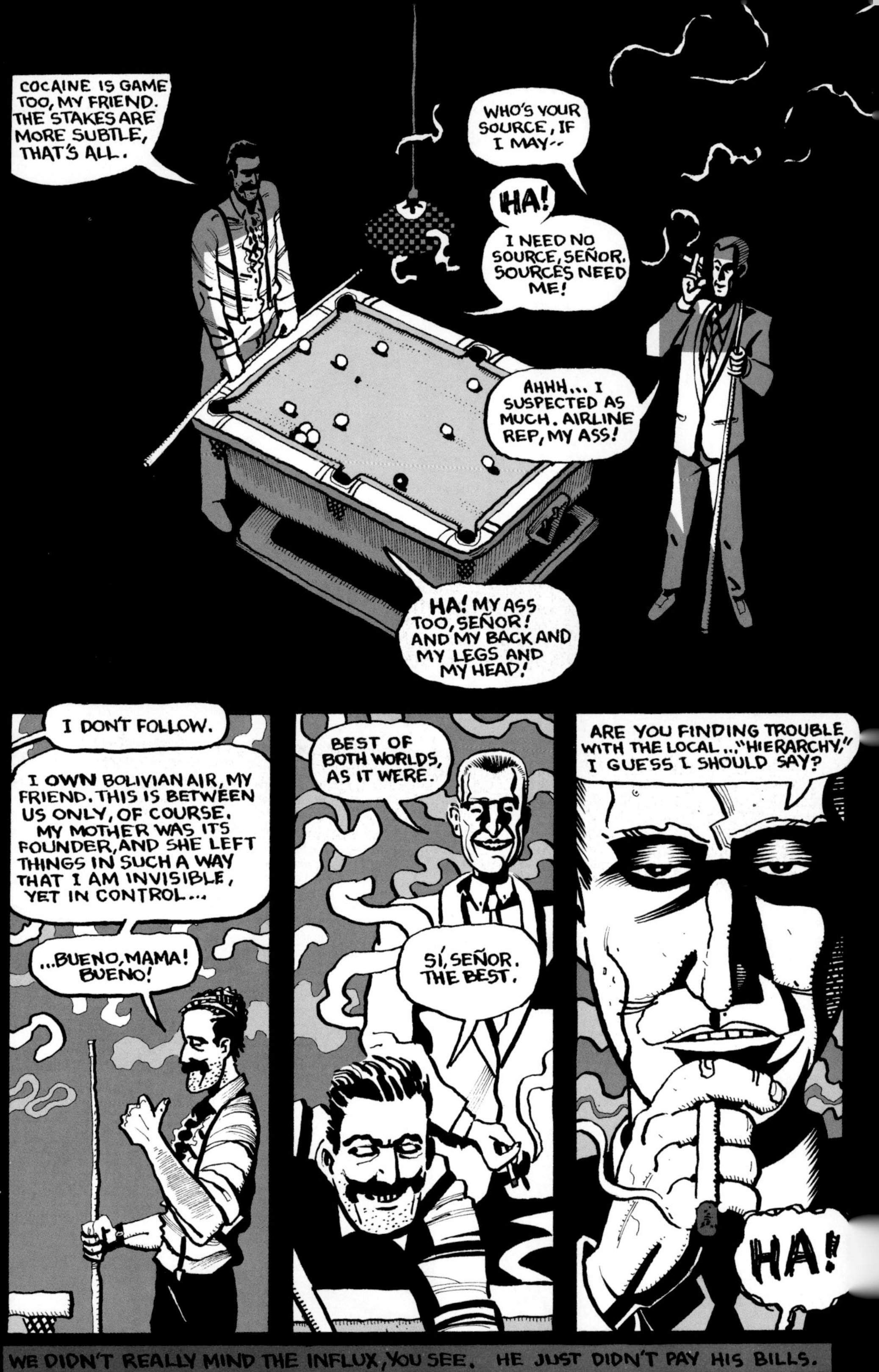
COCAINE IS GAME TOO, MY FRIEND. THE STAKES ARE MORE SUBTLE, THAT'S ALL.
WHO'S YOUR SOURCE, IF I MAY--
HA!
I NEED NO SOURCE, SEÑOR. SOURCES NEED ME!
AHHH... I SUSPECTED AS MUCH. AIRLINE REP, MY ASS!
HA! MY ASS TOO, SEÑOR! AND MY BACK AND MY LEGS AND MY HEAD!
I DON'T FOLLOW.
I OWN BOLIVIAN AIR, MY FRIEND. THIS IS BETWEEN US ONLY, OF COURSE. MY MOTHER WAS ITS FOUNDER, AND SHE LEFT THINGS IN SUCH A WAY THAT I AM INVISIBLE, YET IN CONTROL...
...BUENO, MAMA! BUENO!
BEST OF BOTH WORLDS, AS IT WERE.
SÍ, SEÑOR. THE BEST.
ARE YOU FINDING TROUBLE WITH THE LOCAL... "HIERARCHY," I GUESS I SHOULD SAY?
HA!
WE DIDN'T REALLY MIND THE INFLUX, YOU SEE. HE JUST DIDN'T PAY HIS BILLS.

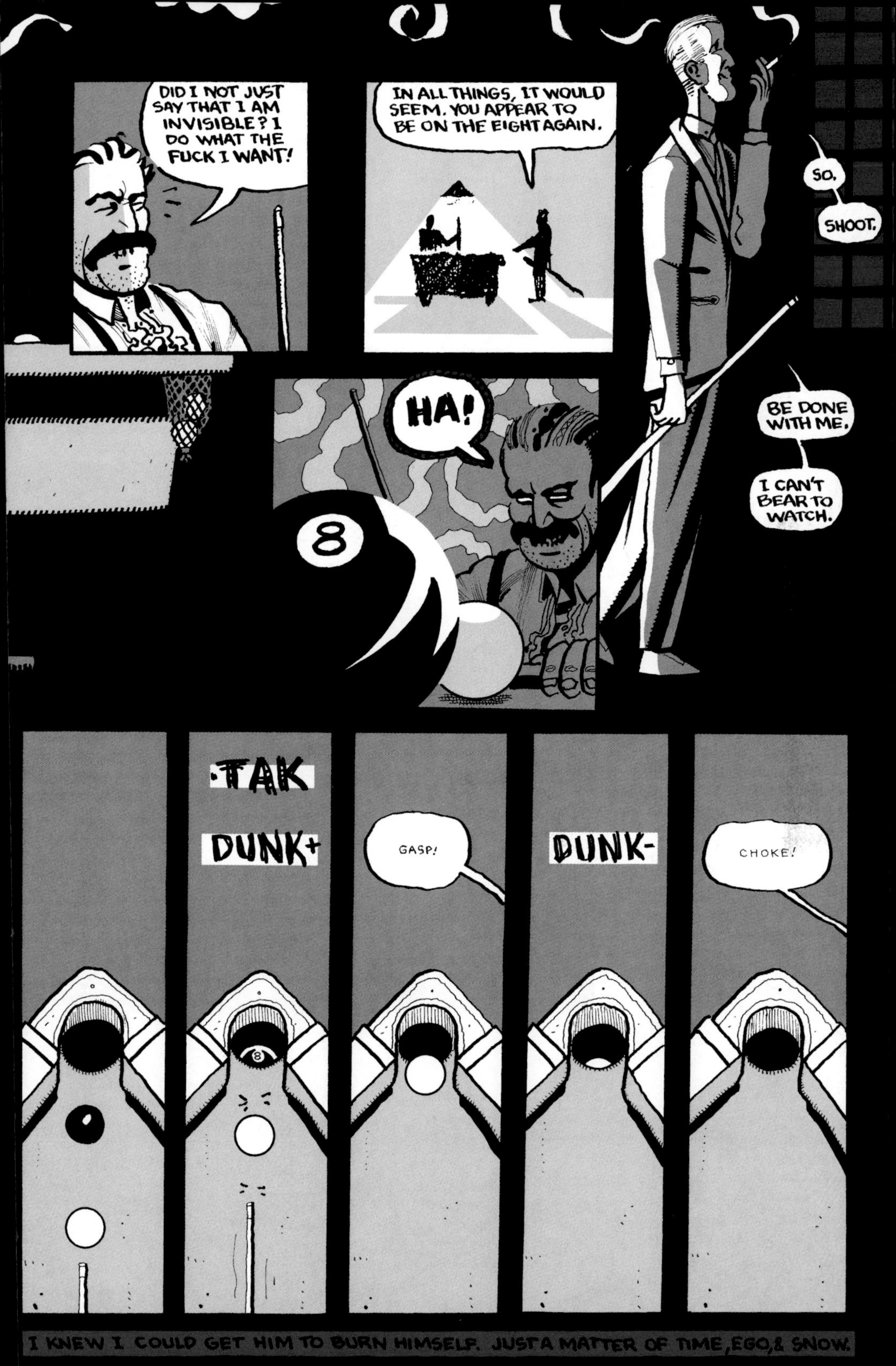
DID I NOT JUST SAY THAT I AM INVISIBLE? I DO WHAT THE FUCK I WANT!
IN ALL THINGS, IT WOULD SEEM. YOU APPEAR TO BE ON THE EIGHT AGAIN.
SO.
SHOOT.
HA!
BE DONE WITH ME.
I CAN'T BEAR TO WATCH.
TAK
DUNK+
GASP!
DUNK-
CHOKE!
I KNEW I COULD GET HIM TO BURN HIMSELF. JUST A MATTER OF TIME, EGO, & SNOW.

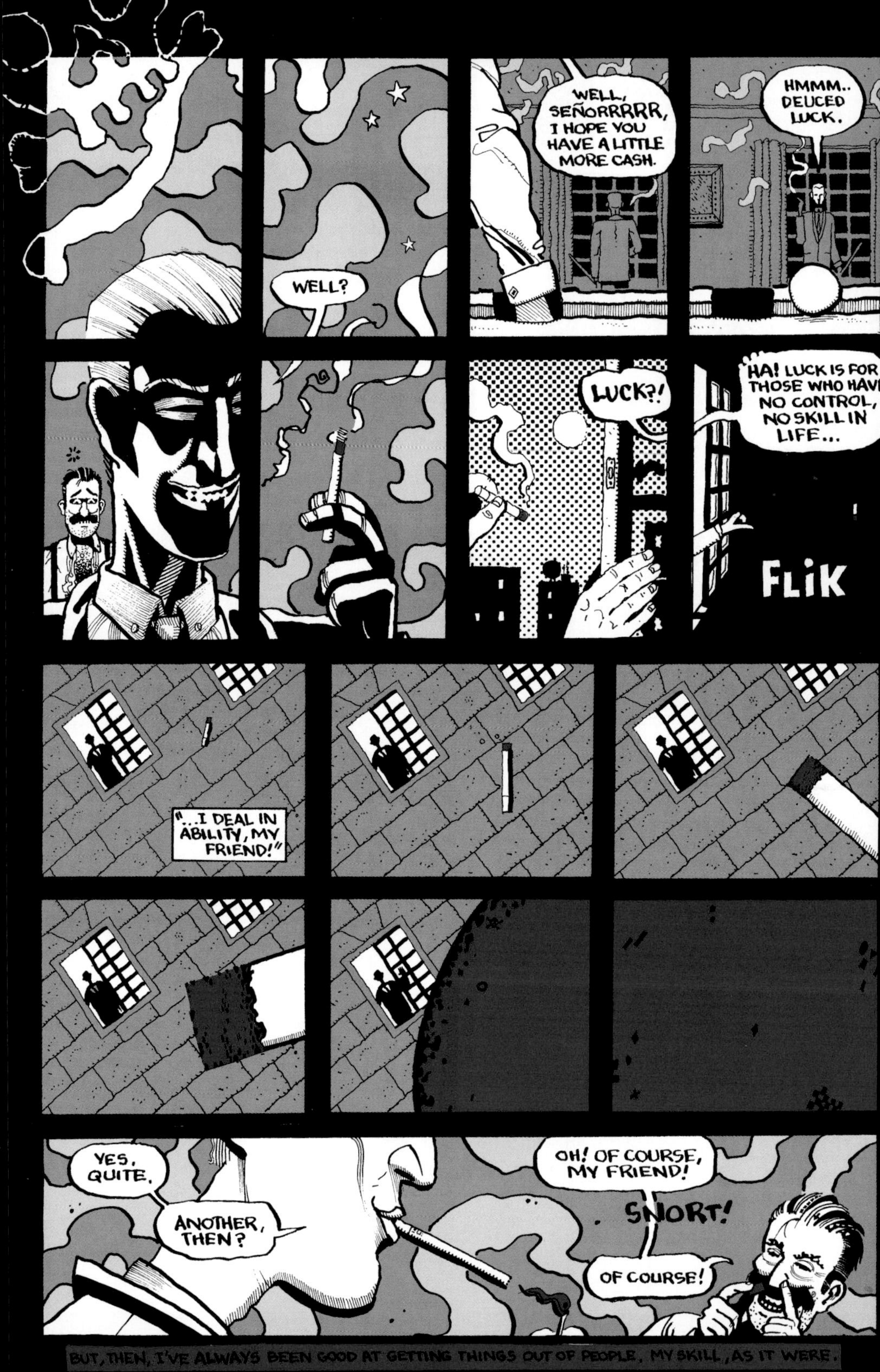
WELL?
WELL, SEÑORRRRR, I HOPE YOU HAVE A LITTLE MORE CASH.
HMMM.. DEUCED LUCK.
LUCK?!
HA! LUCK IS FOR THOSE WHO HAVE NO CONTROL, NO SKILL IN LIFE...
FLIK
"...I DEAL IN ABILITY, MY FRIEND!"
YES, QUITE.
ANOTHER, THEN?
OH! OF COURSE, MY FRIEND!
SNORT!
OF COURSE!
BUT, THEN, I'VE ALWAYS BEEN GOOD AT GETTING THINGS OUT OF PEOPLE. MY SKILL, AS IT WERE.

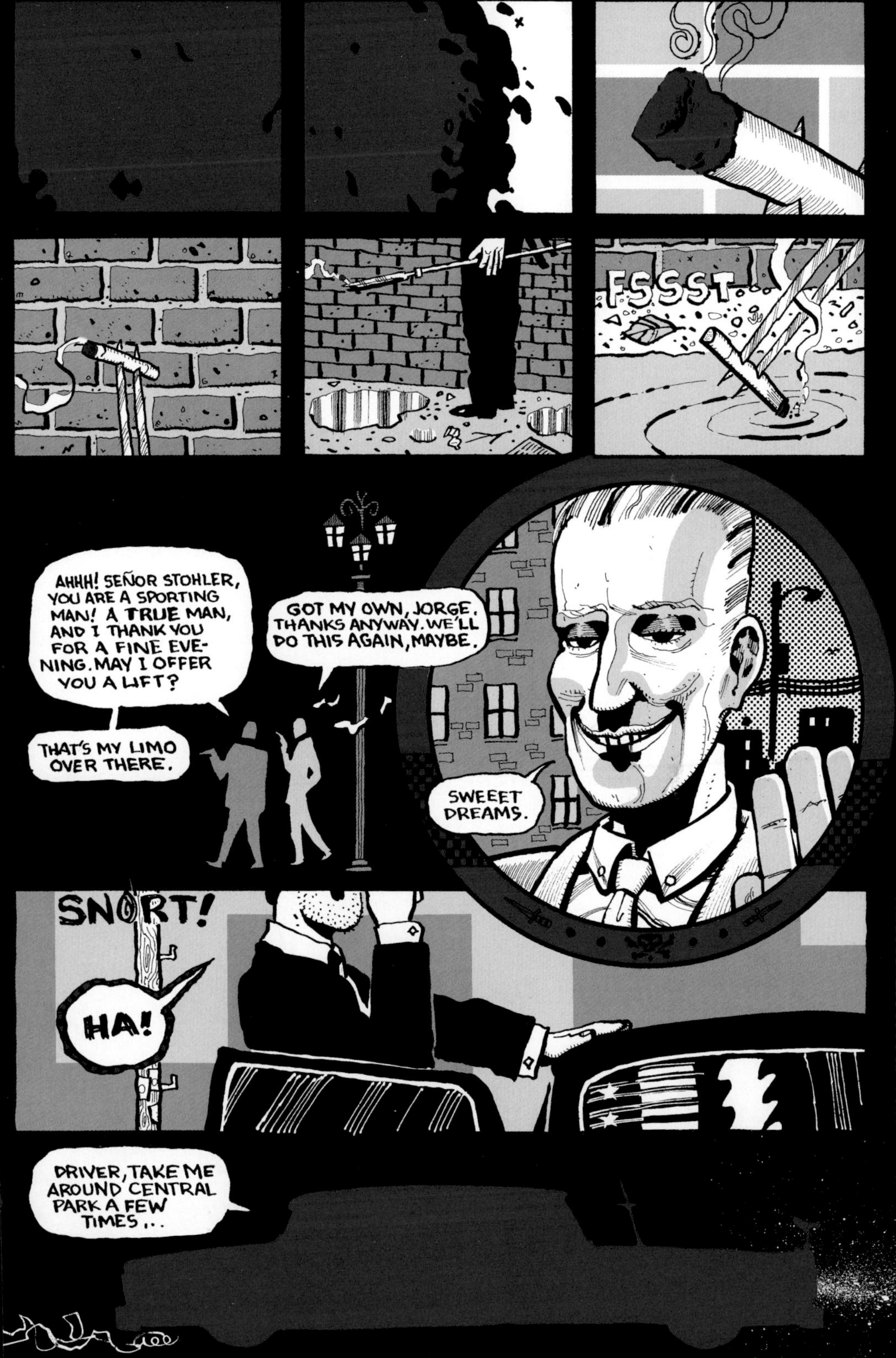
FSSST
AHHH! SEÑOR STOHLER, YOU ARE A SPORTING MAN! A TRUE MAN, AND I THANK YOU FOR A FINE EVENING. MAY I OFFER YOU A LIFT?
THAT'S MY LIMO OVER THERE.
GOT MY OWN, JORGE. THANKS ANYWAY. WE'LL DO THIS AGAIN, MAYBE.
SWEEET DREAMS.
SNORT!
HA!
DRIVER, TAKE ME AROUND CENTRAL PARK A FEW TIMES...

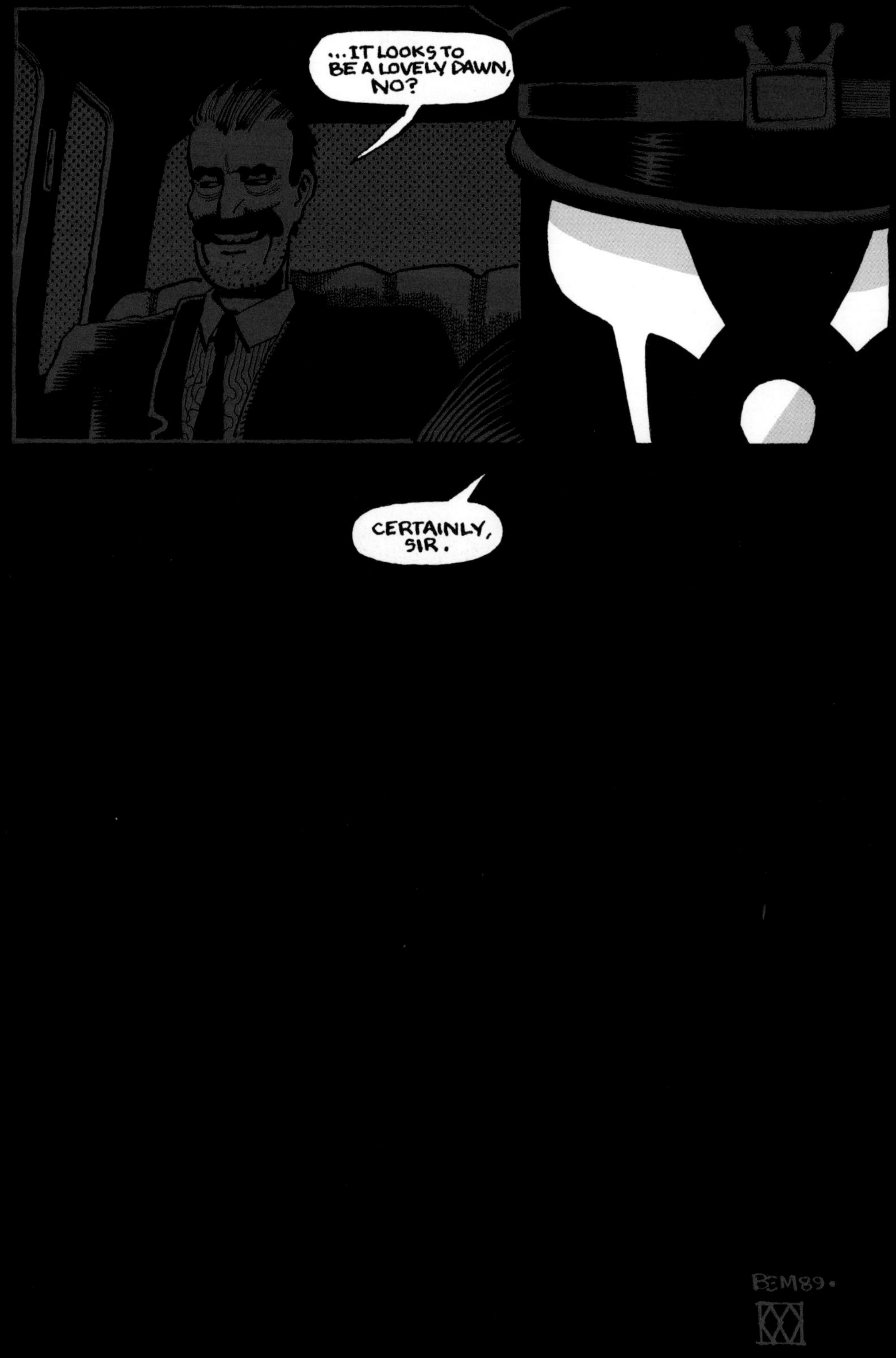
...IT LOOKS TO BE A LOVELY DAWN, NO?
CERTAINLY, SIR.
BEM89.

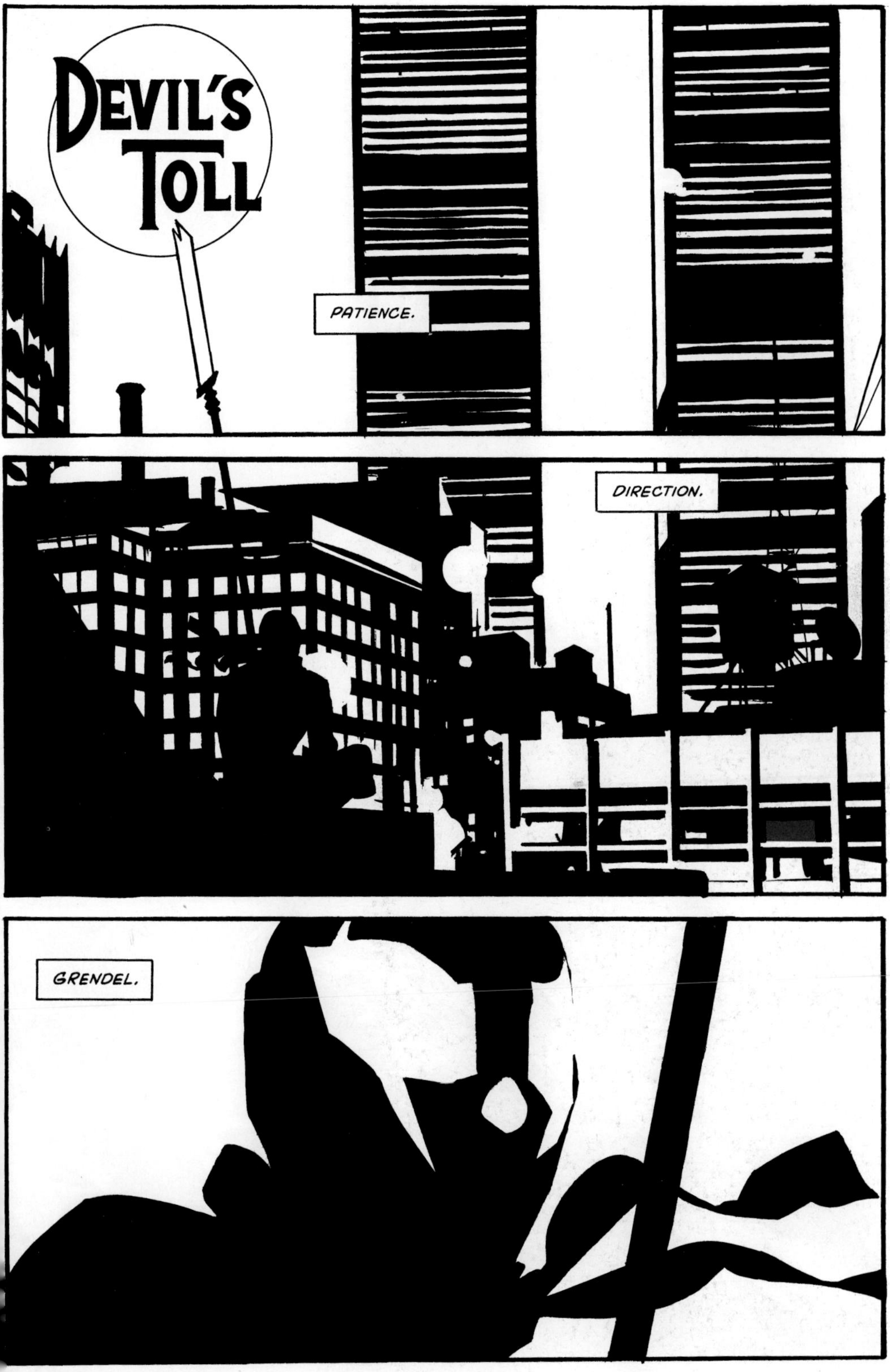
DEVIL'S TOLL
PATIENCE.
DIRECTION.
GRENDEL.

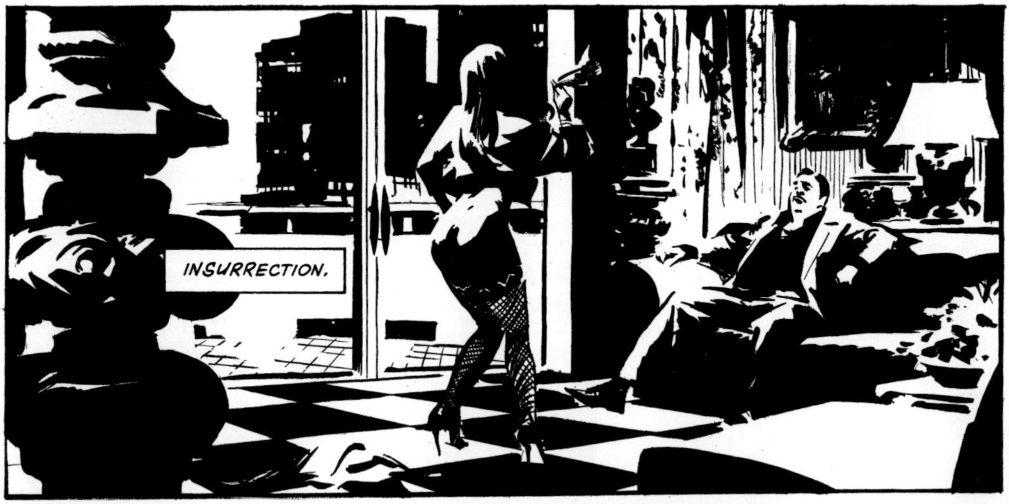
INSURRECTION.

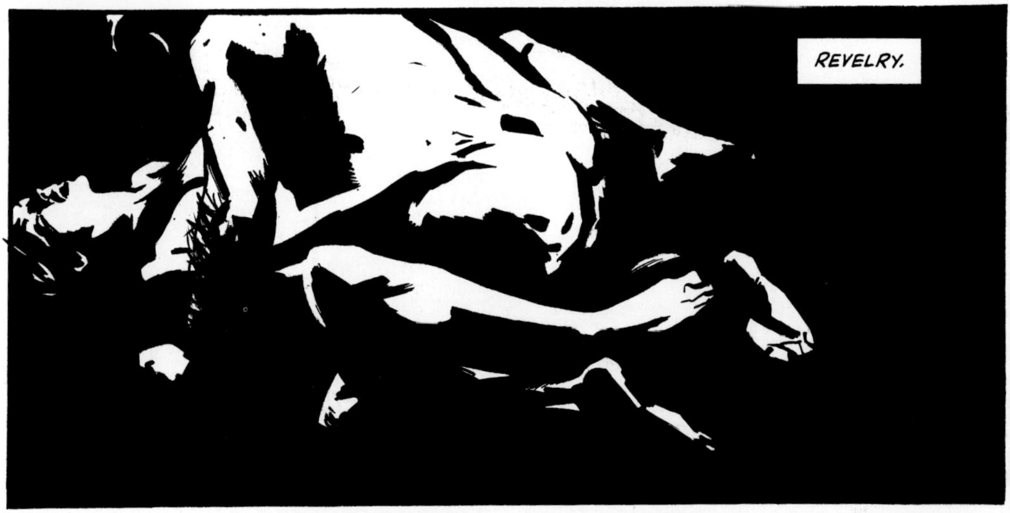
REVELRY.

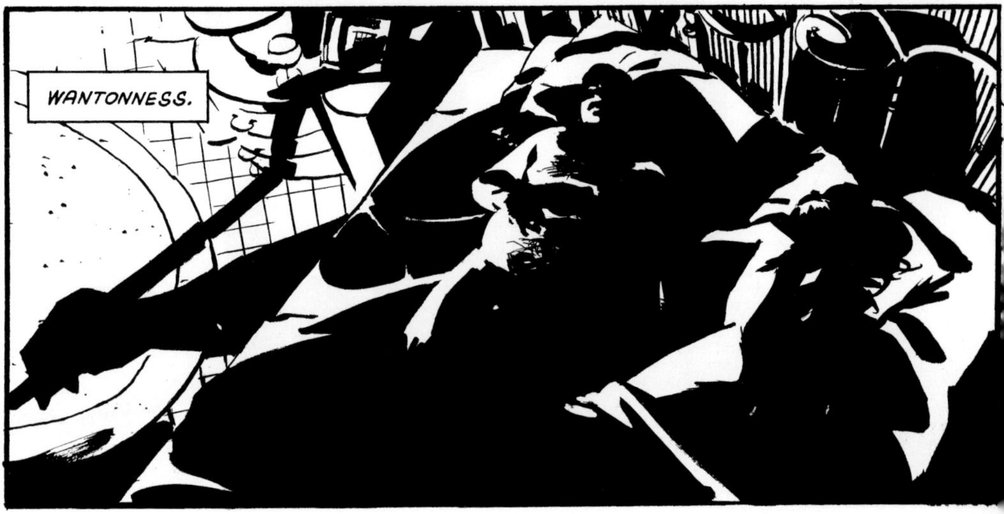
WANTONNESS.

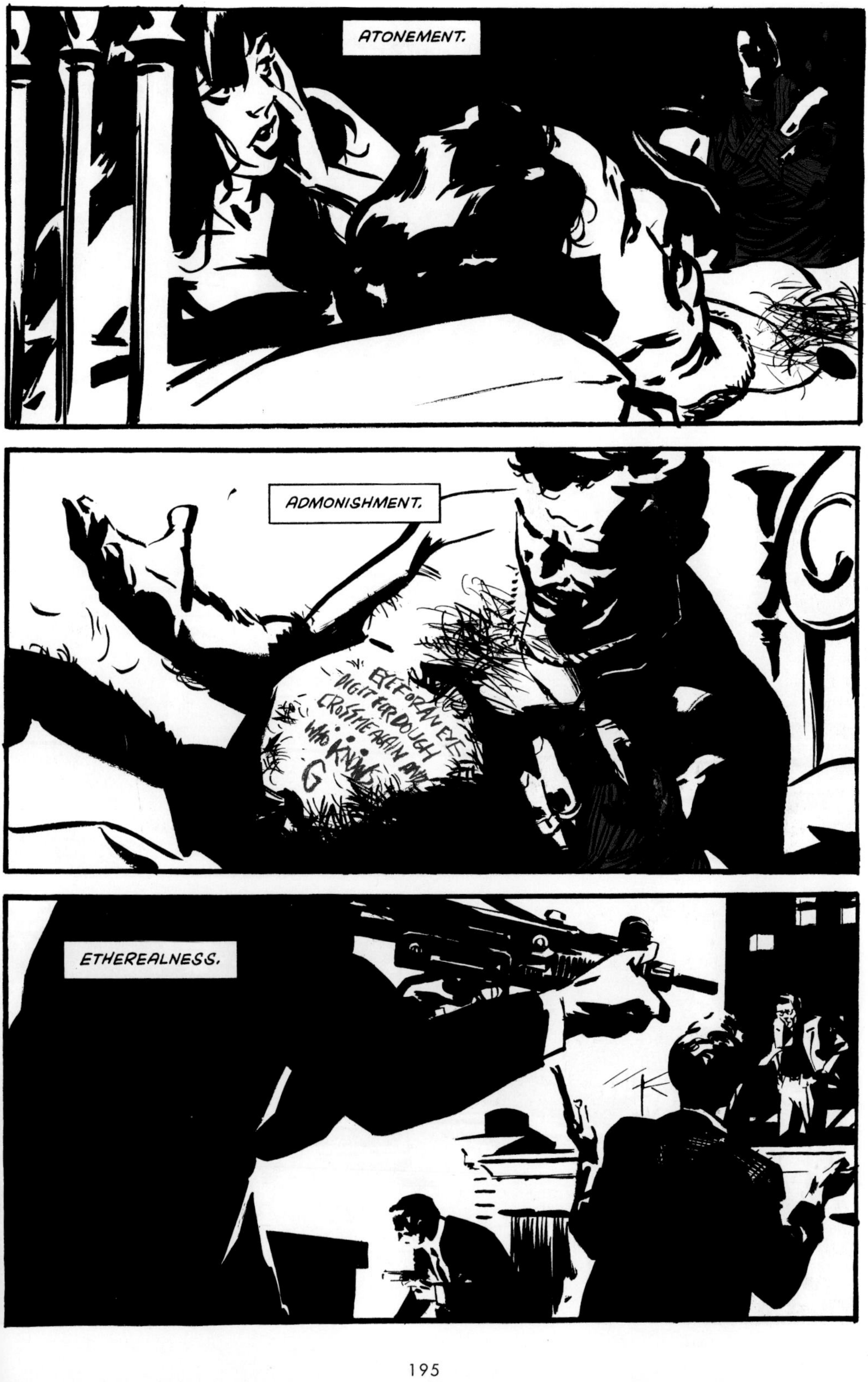
ATONEMENT.
ADMONISHMENT.
EYE FOR AN EYE
DIGIT FOR DOUGH
CROSS ME AGAIN
WHO
G
ETHEREALNESS.

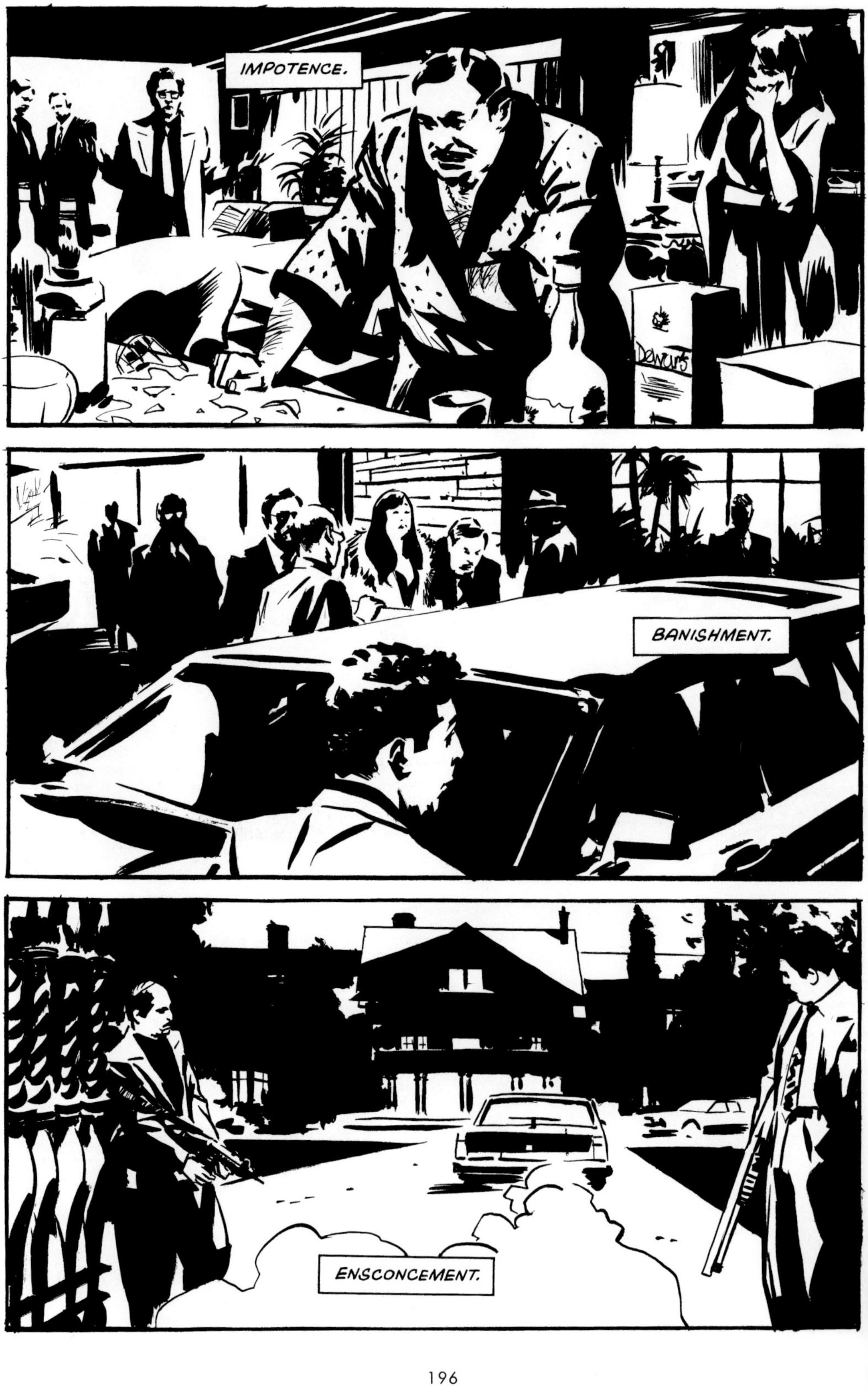
IMPOTENCE.
Dewar's
BANISHMENT.
ENSCONCEMENT.

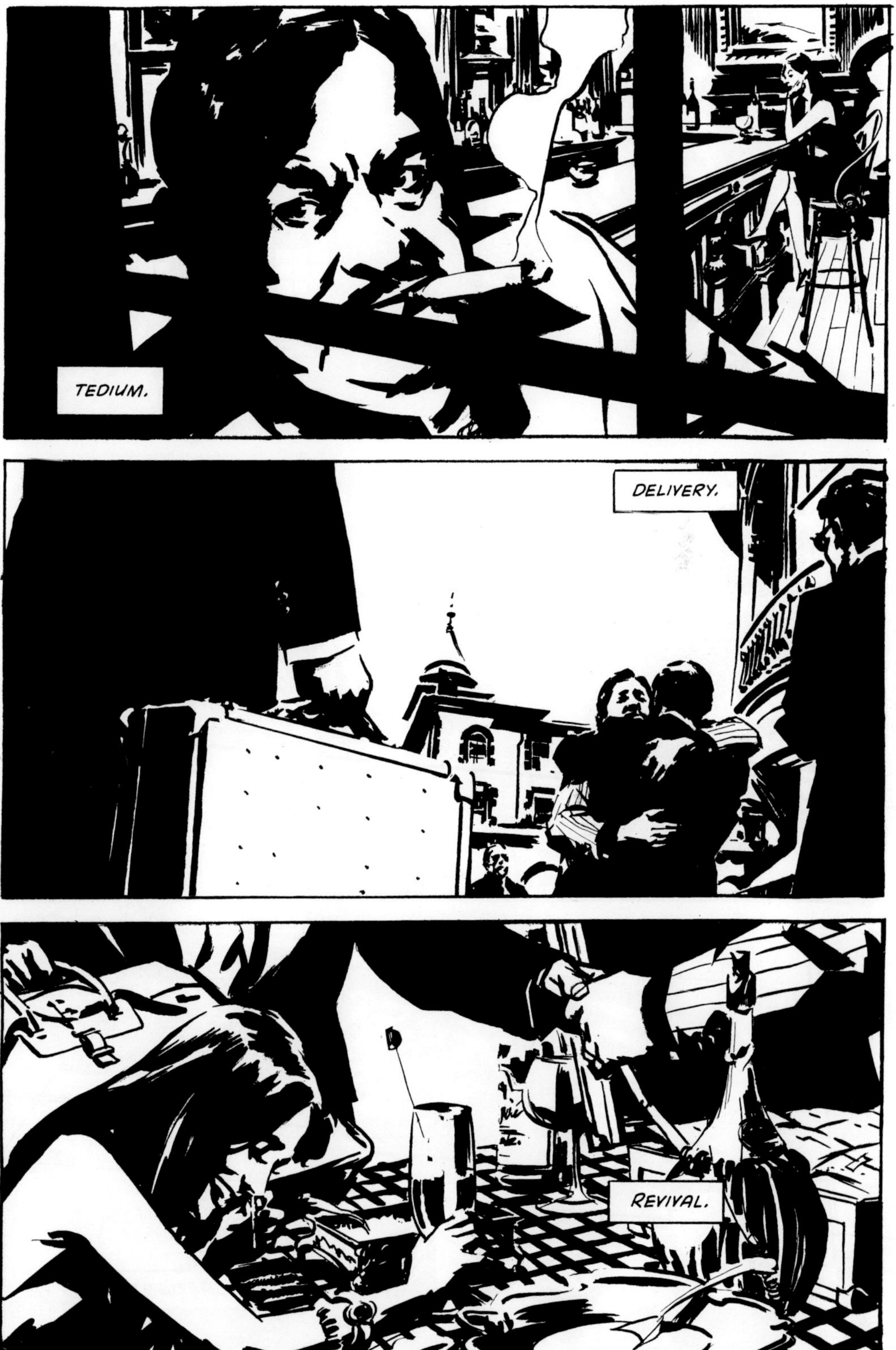
TEDIUM.
DELIVERY.
REVIVAL.

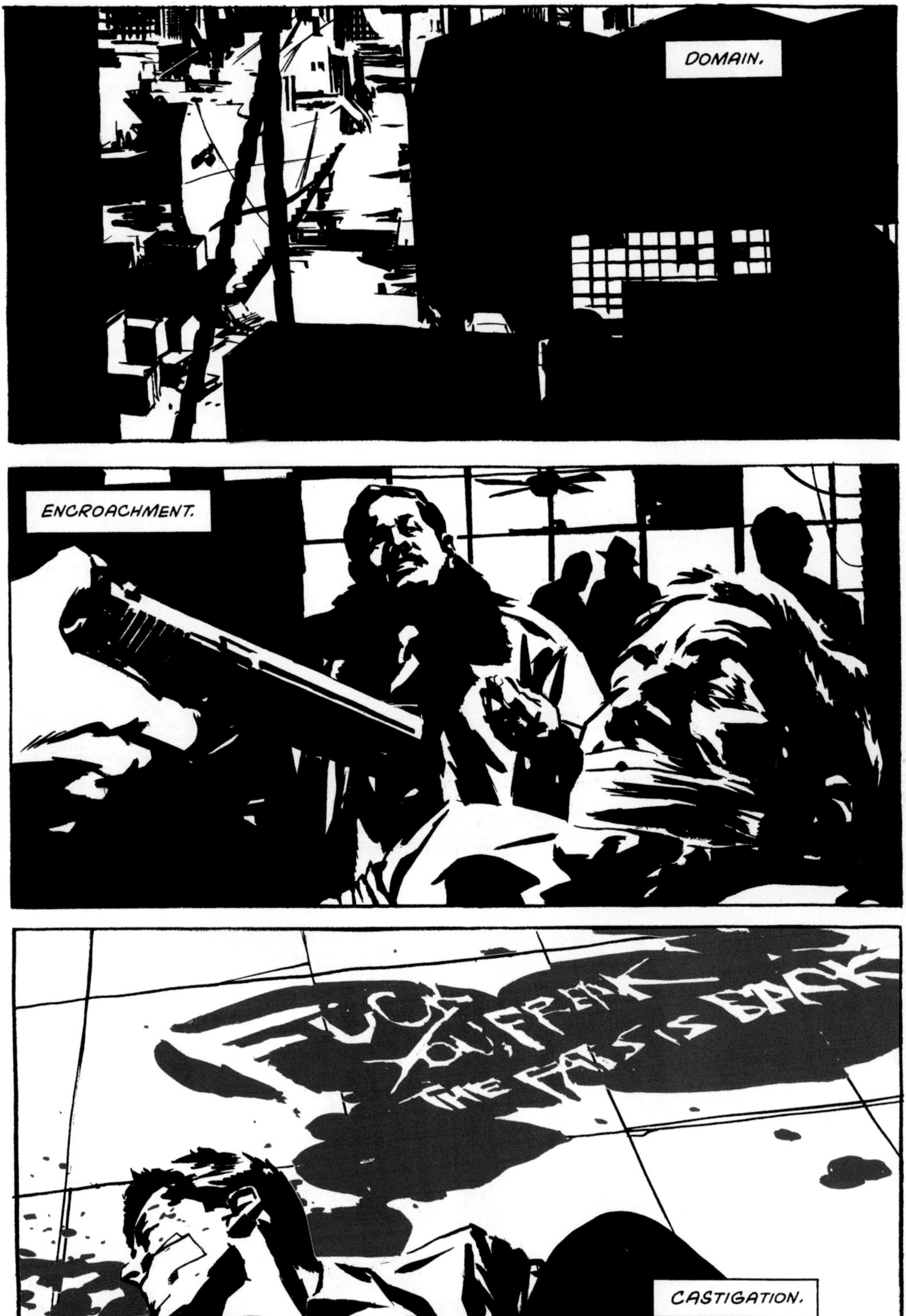
DOMAIN.
ENCROACHMENT.
CASTIGATION.

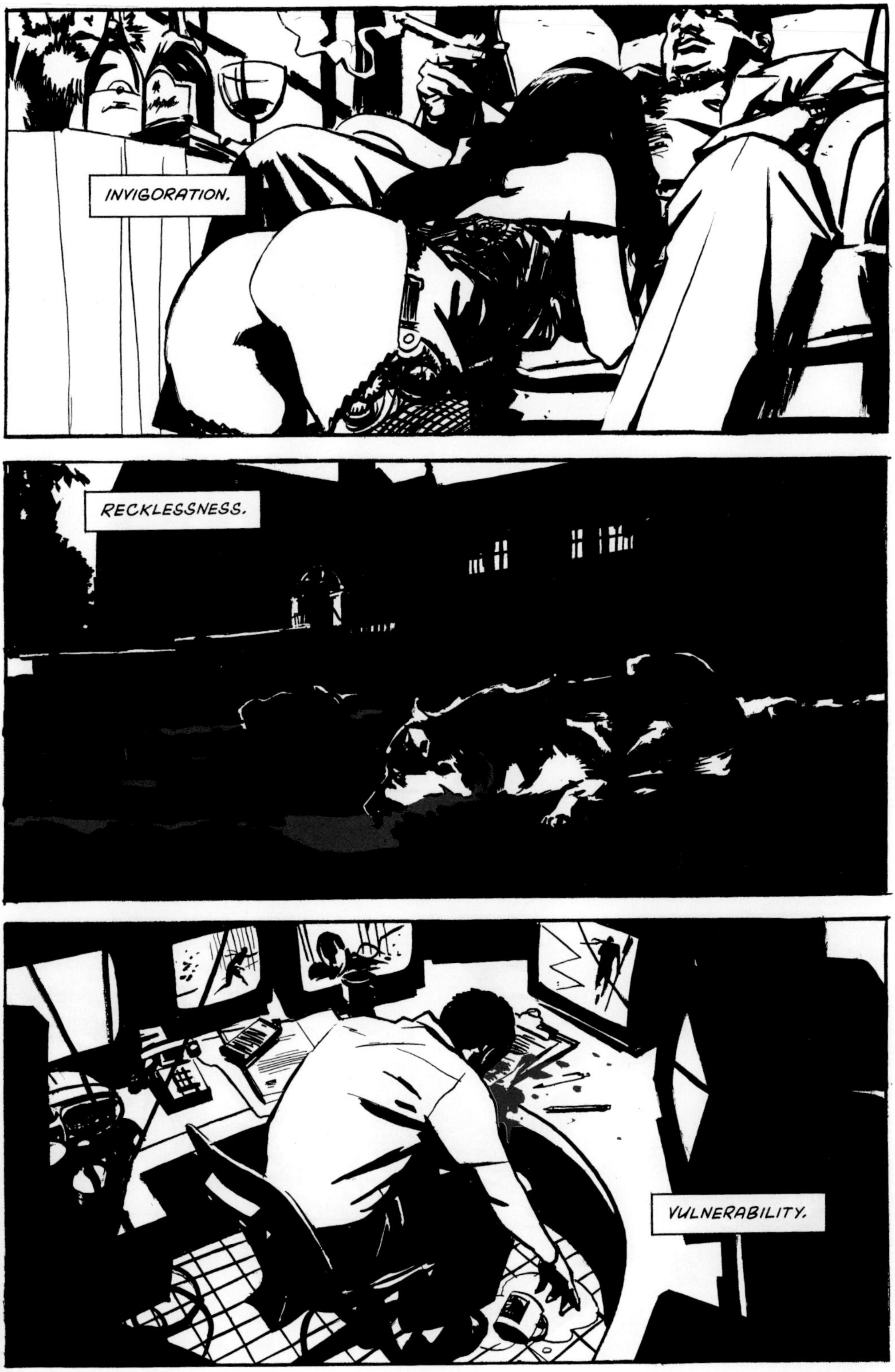
INVIGORATION.
RECKLESSNESS.
VULNERABILITY.

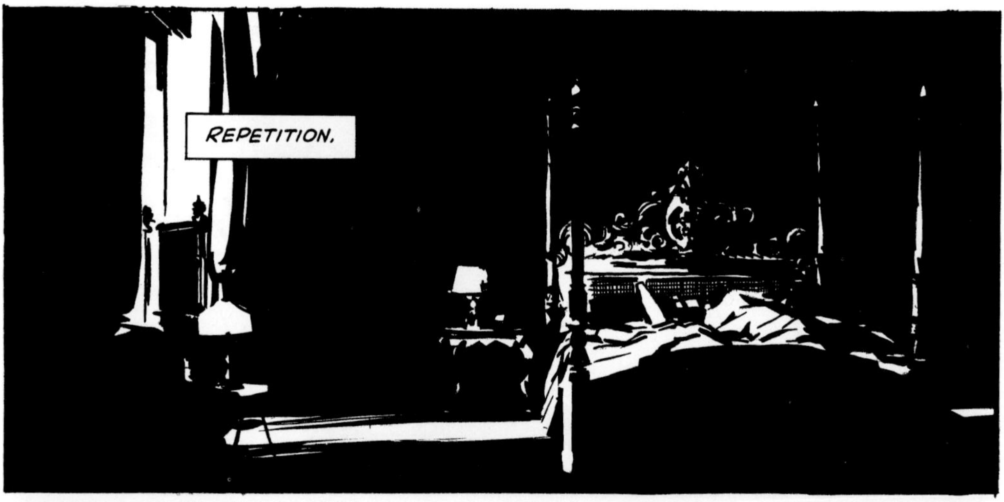
REPETITION.

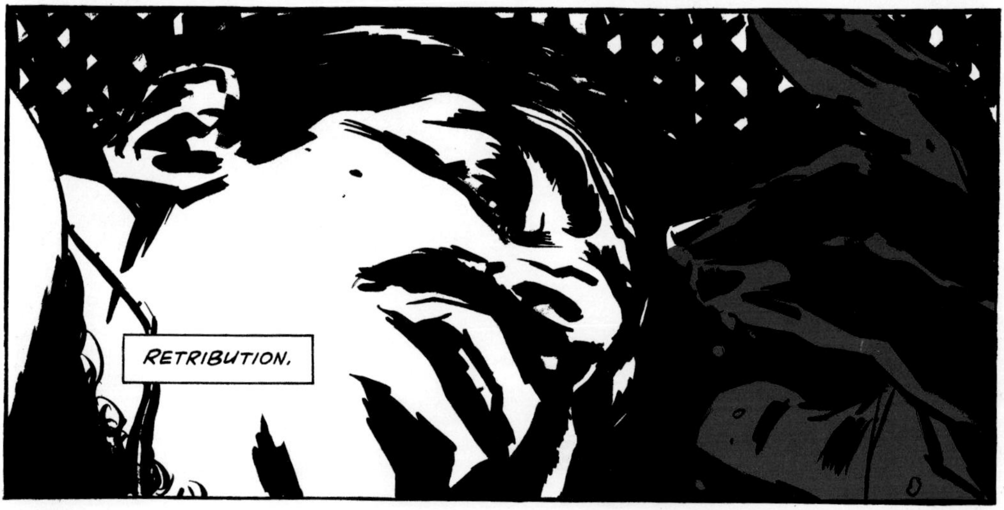
RETRIBUTION.

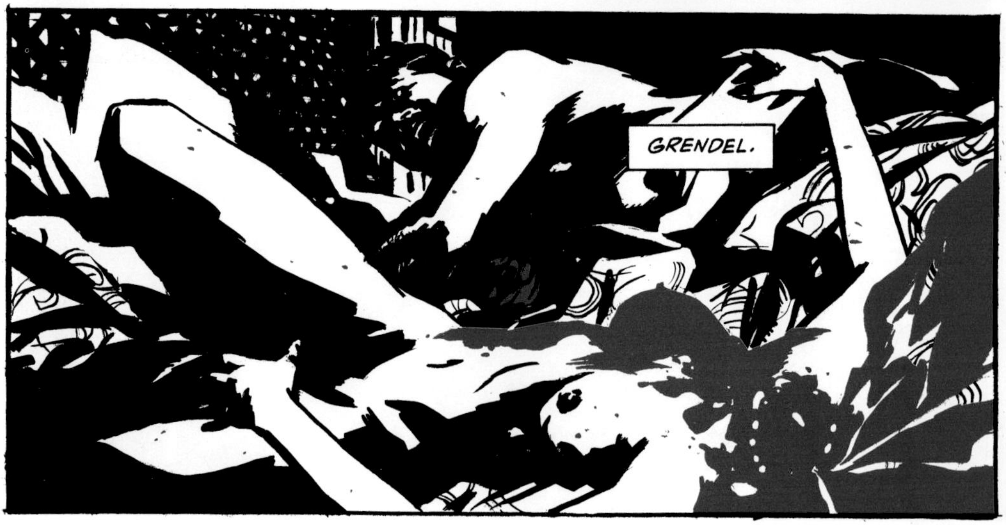
GRENDEL.

-END-

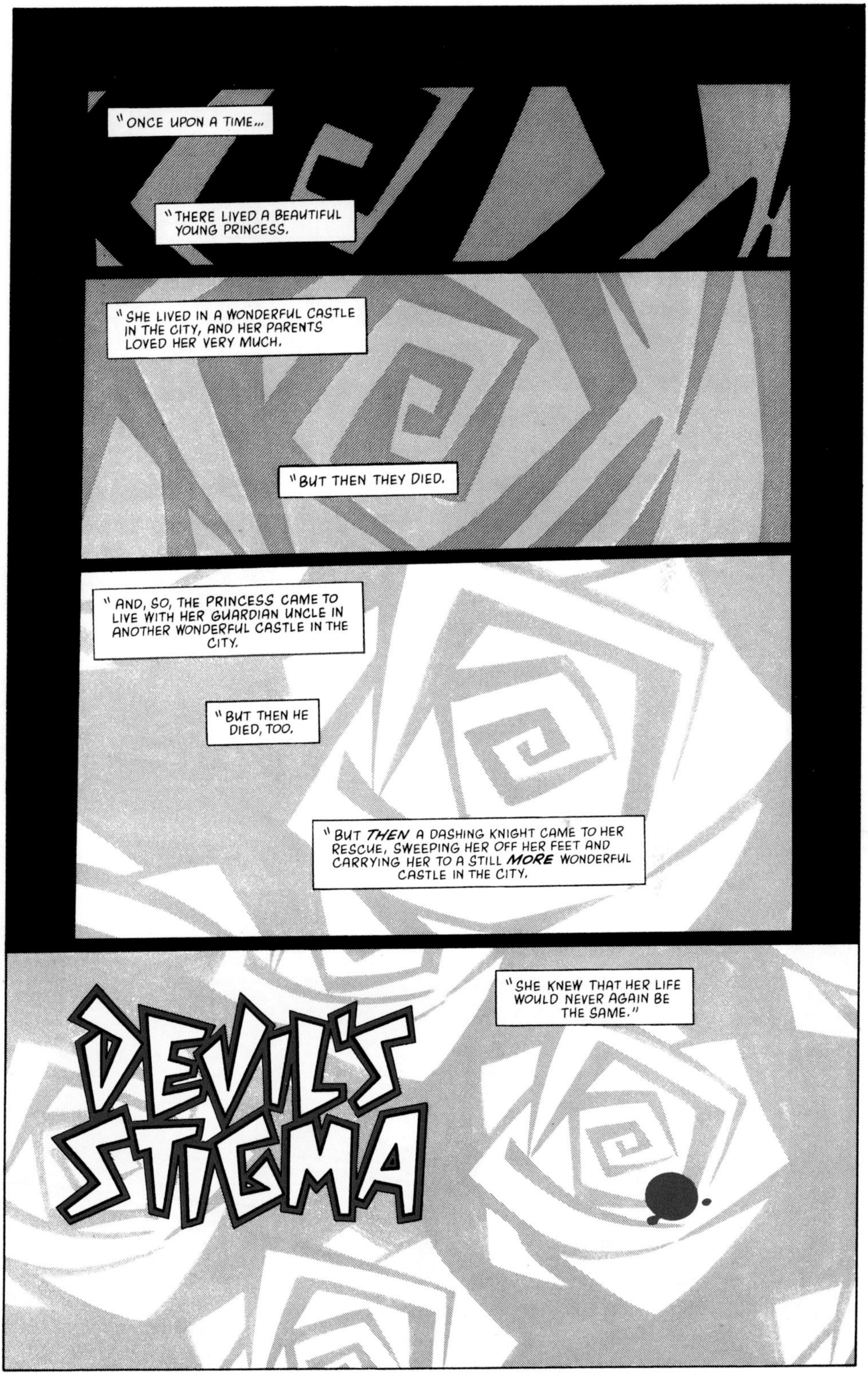
"ONCE UPON A TIME...
"THERE LIVED A BEAUTIFUL YOUNG PRINCESS.
"SHE LIVED IN A WONDERFUL CASTLE IN THE CITY, AND HER PARENTS LOVED HER VERY MUCH.
"BUT THEN THEY DIED.
"AND, SO, THE PRINCESS CAME TO LIVE WITH HER GUARDIAN UNCLE IN ANOTHER WONDERFUL CASTLE IN THE CITY.
"BUT THEN HE DIED, TOO.
"BUT THEN A DASHING KNIGHT CAME TO HER RESCUE, SWEEPING HER OFF HER FEET AND CARRYING HER TO A STILL MORE WONDERFUL CASTLE IN THE CITY.
"SHE KNEW THAT HER LIFE WOULD NEVER AGAIN BE THE SAME."
DEVIL'S STIGMA

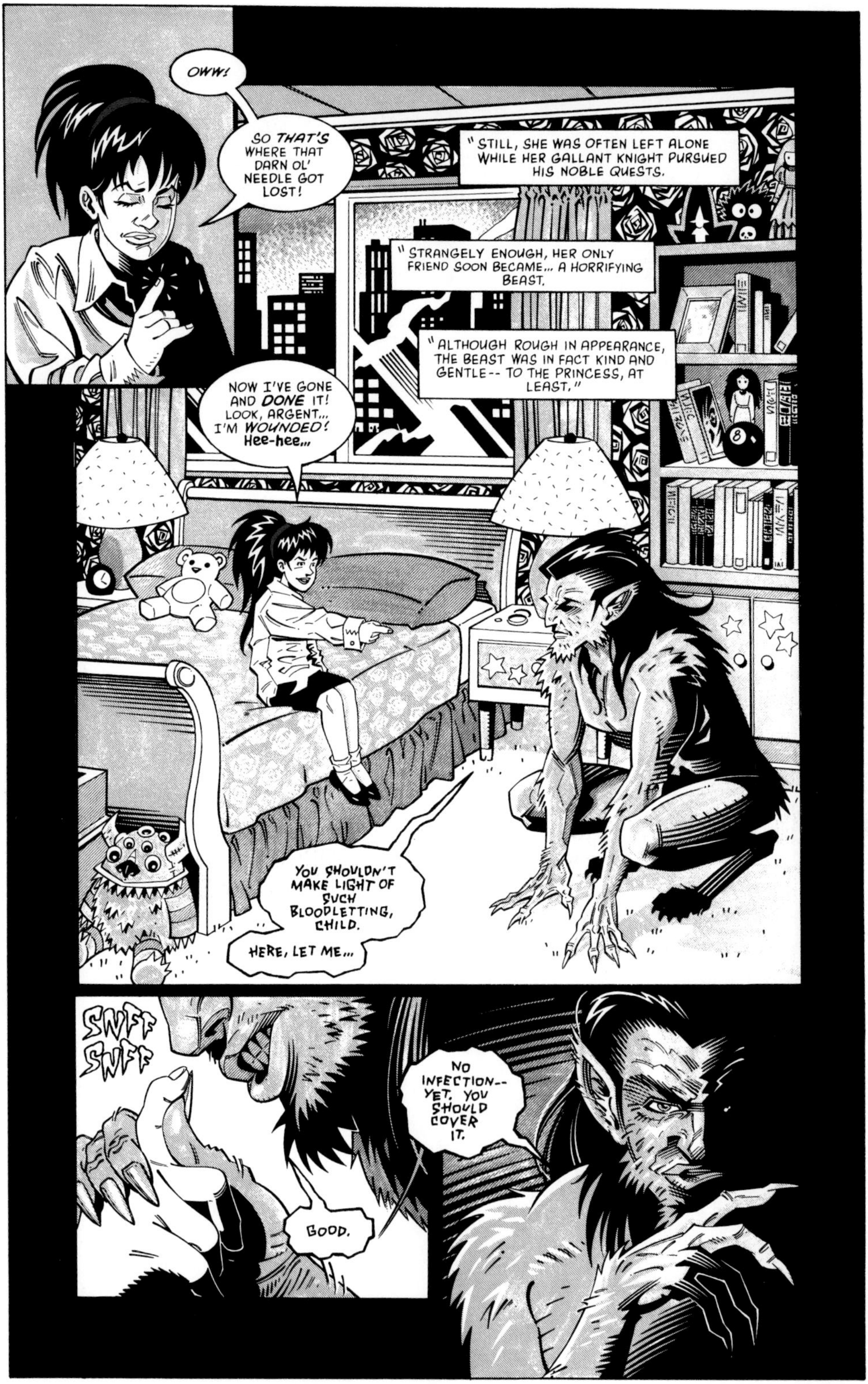
OWW!
SO THAT'S WHERE THAT DARN OL' NEEDLE GOT LOST!
"STILL, SHE WAS OFTEN LEFT ALONE WHILE HER GALLANT KNIGHT PURSUED HIS NOBLE QUESTS.
"STRANGELY ENOUGH, HER ONLY FRIEND SOON BECAME... A HORRIFYING BEAST.
"ALTHOUGH ROUGH IN APPEARANCE, THE BEAST WAS IN FACT KIND AND GENTLE-- TO THE PRINCESS, AT LEAST."
NOW I'VE GONE AND DONE IT! LOOK, ARGENT... I'M WOUNDED! Hee-hee...
YOU SHOULDN'T MAKE LIGHT OF SUCH BLOODLETTING, CHILD.
HERE, LET ME...
SNFF SNFF
NO INFECTION-- YET. YOU SHOULD COVER IT.
GOOD.

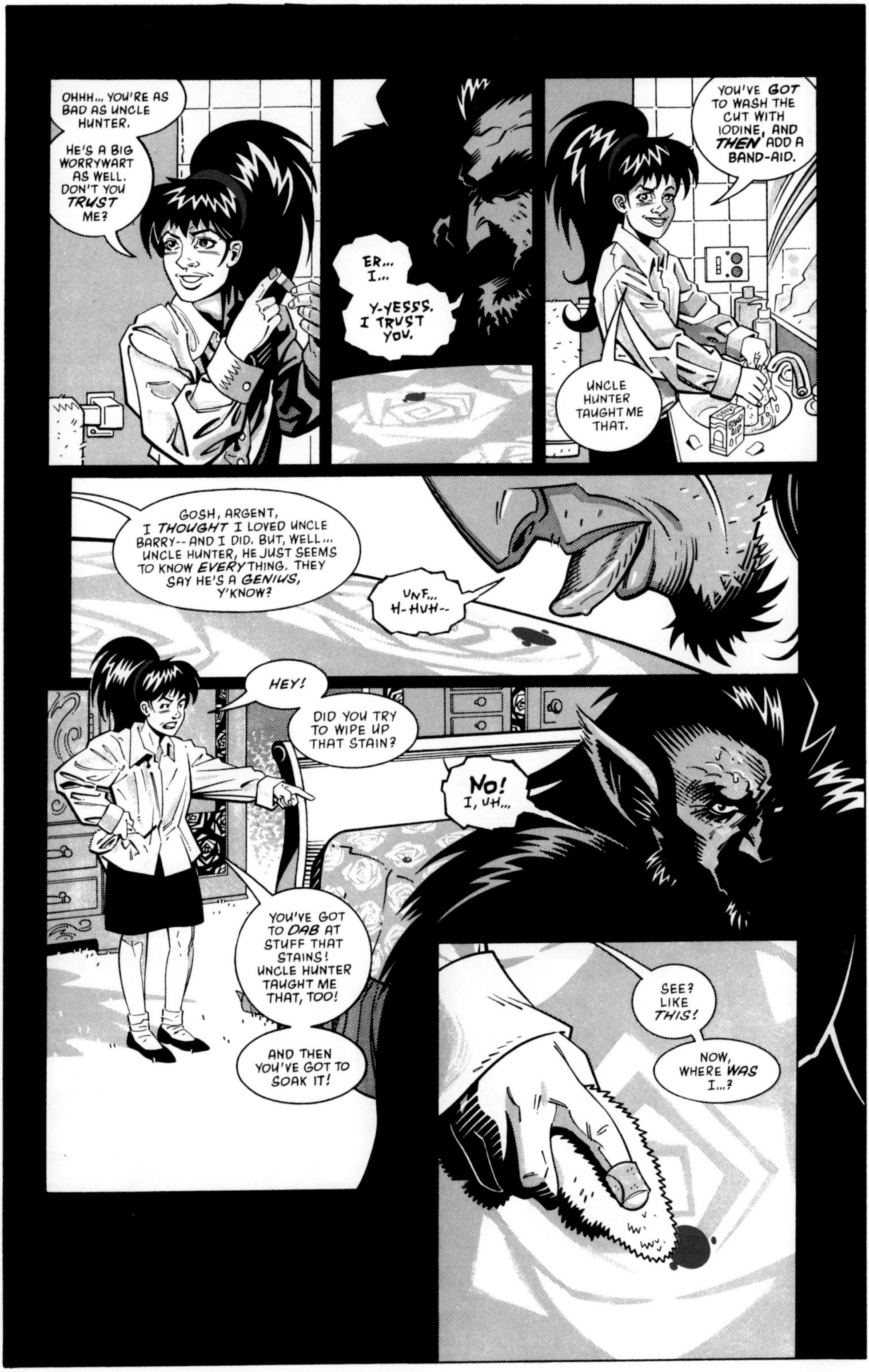
OHHH... YOU'RE AS BAD AS UNCLE HUNTER.
HE'S A BIG WORRYWART AS WELL. DON'T YOU TRUST ME?
ER... I...
Y-YESSS. I TRUST YOU.
YOU'VE GOT TO WASH THE CUT WITH IODINE, AND THEN ADD A BAND-AID.
UNCLE HUNTER TAUGHT ME THAT.
BAND AID
GOSH, ARGENT, I THOUGHT I LOVED UNCLE BARRY-- AND I DID. BUT, WELL... UNCLE HUNTER, HE JUST SEEMS TO KNOW EVERYTHING. THEY SAY HE'S A GENIUS, Y'KNOW?
UNF... H-HUH--
HEY!
DID YOU TRY TO WIPE UP THAT STAIN?
NO! I, UH...
YOU'VE GOT TO DAB AT STUFF THAT STAINS! UNCLE HUNTER TAUGHT ME THAT, TOO!
AND THEN YOU'VE GOT TO SOAK IT!
SEE? LIKE THIS!
NOW, WHERE WAS I...?

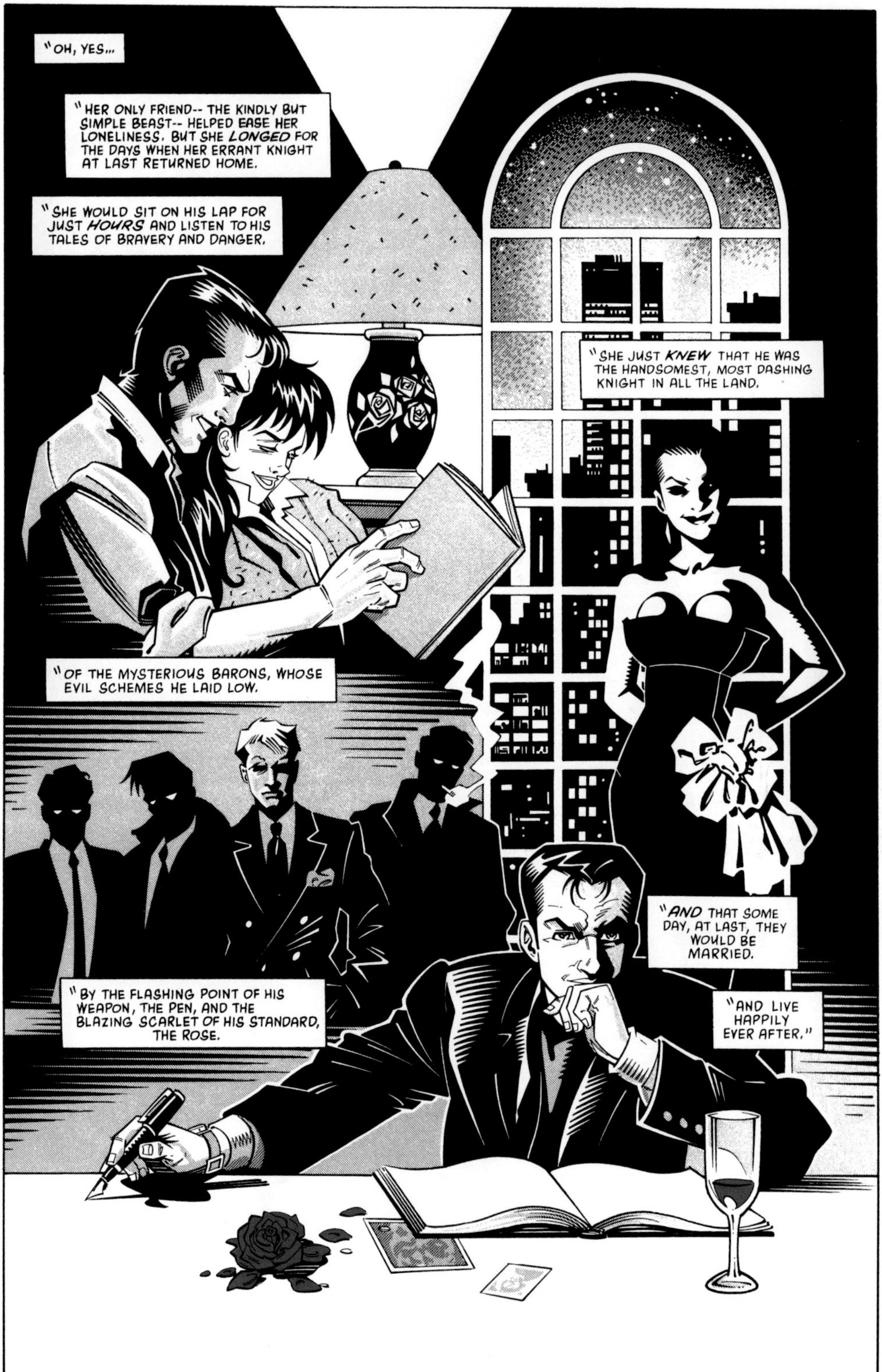
"OH, YES...
"HER ONLY FRIEND-- THE KINDLY BUT SIMPLE BEAST-- HELPED EASE HER LONELINESS. BUT SHE LONGED FOR THE DAYS WHEN HER ERRANT KNIGHT AT LAST RETURNED HOME.
"SHE WOULD SIT ON HIS LAP FOR JUST HOURS AND LISTEN TO HIS TALES OF BRAVERY AND DANGER.
"SHE JUST KNEW THAT HE WAS THE HANDSOMEST, MOST DASHING KNIGHT IN ALL THE LAND.
"OF THE MYSTERIOUS BARONS, WHOSE EVIL SCHEMES HE LAID LOW.
"BY THE FLASHING POINT OF HIS WEAPON, THE PEN, AND THE BLAZING SCARLET OF HIS STANDARD, THE ROSE.
"AND THAT SOME DAY, AT LAST, THEY WOULD BE MARRIED.
"AND LIVE HAPPILY EVER AFTER."

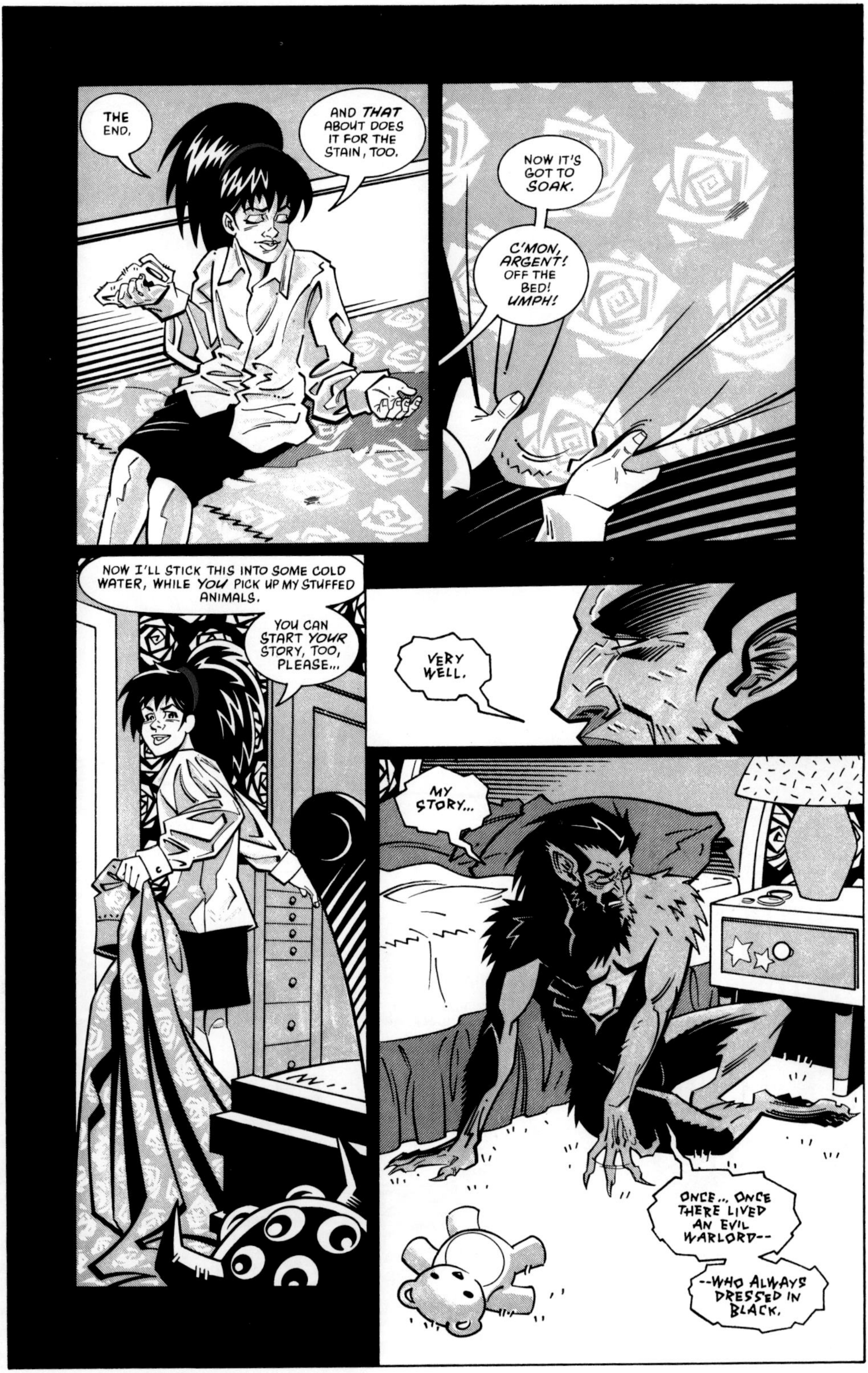
THE END.
AND THAT ABOUT DOES IT FOR THE STAIN, TOO.
NOW IT'S GOT TO SOAK.
C'MON, ARGENT! OFF THE BED! UMPH!
NOW I'LL STICK THIS INTO SOME COLD WATER, WHILE YOU PICK UP MY STUFFED ANIMALS.
YOU CAN START YOUR STORY, TOO, PLEASE...
VERY WELL.
MY STORY...
ONCE... ONCE THERE LIVED AN EVIL WARLORD--
--WHO ALWAYS DRESSED IN BLACK.

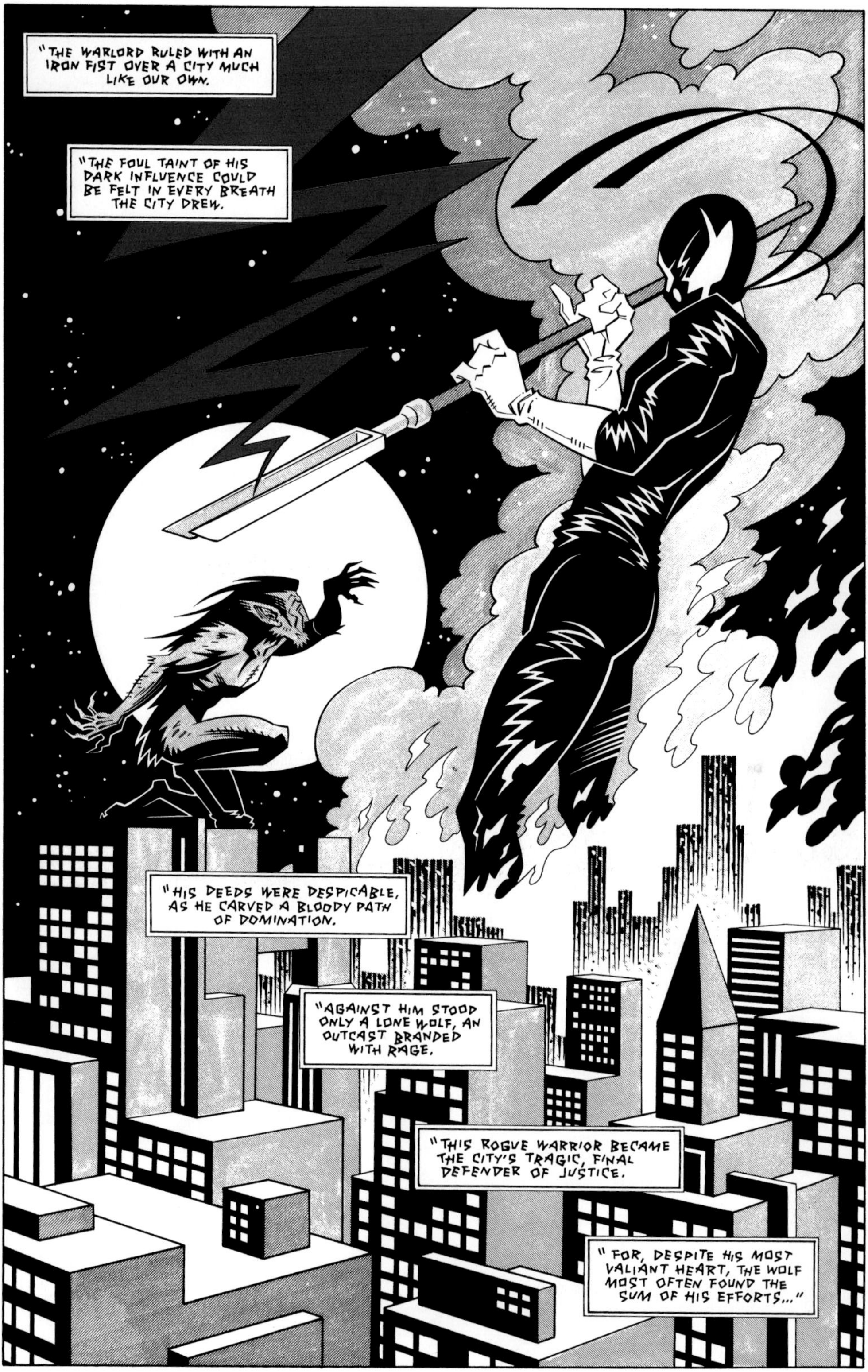
"THE WARLORD RULED WITH AN IRON FIST OVER A CITY MUCH LIKE OUR OWN.
"THE FOUL TAINT OF HIS DARK INFLUENCE COULD BE FELT IN EVERY BREATH THE CITY DREW.
"HIS DEEDS WERE DESPICABLE, AS HE CARVED A BLOODY PATH OF DOMINATION.
"AGAINST HIM STOOD ONLY A LONE WOLF, AN OUTCAST BRANDED WITH RAGE.
"THIS ROGUE WARRIOR BECAME THE CITY'S TRAGIC, FINAL DEFENDER OF JUSTICE.
"FOR, DESPITE HIS MOST VALIANT HEART, THE WOLF MOST OFTEN FOUND THE SUM OF HIS EFFORTS..."

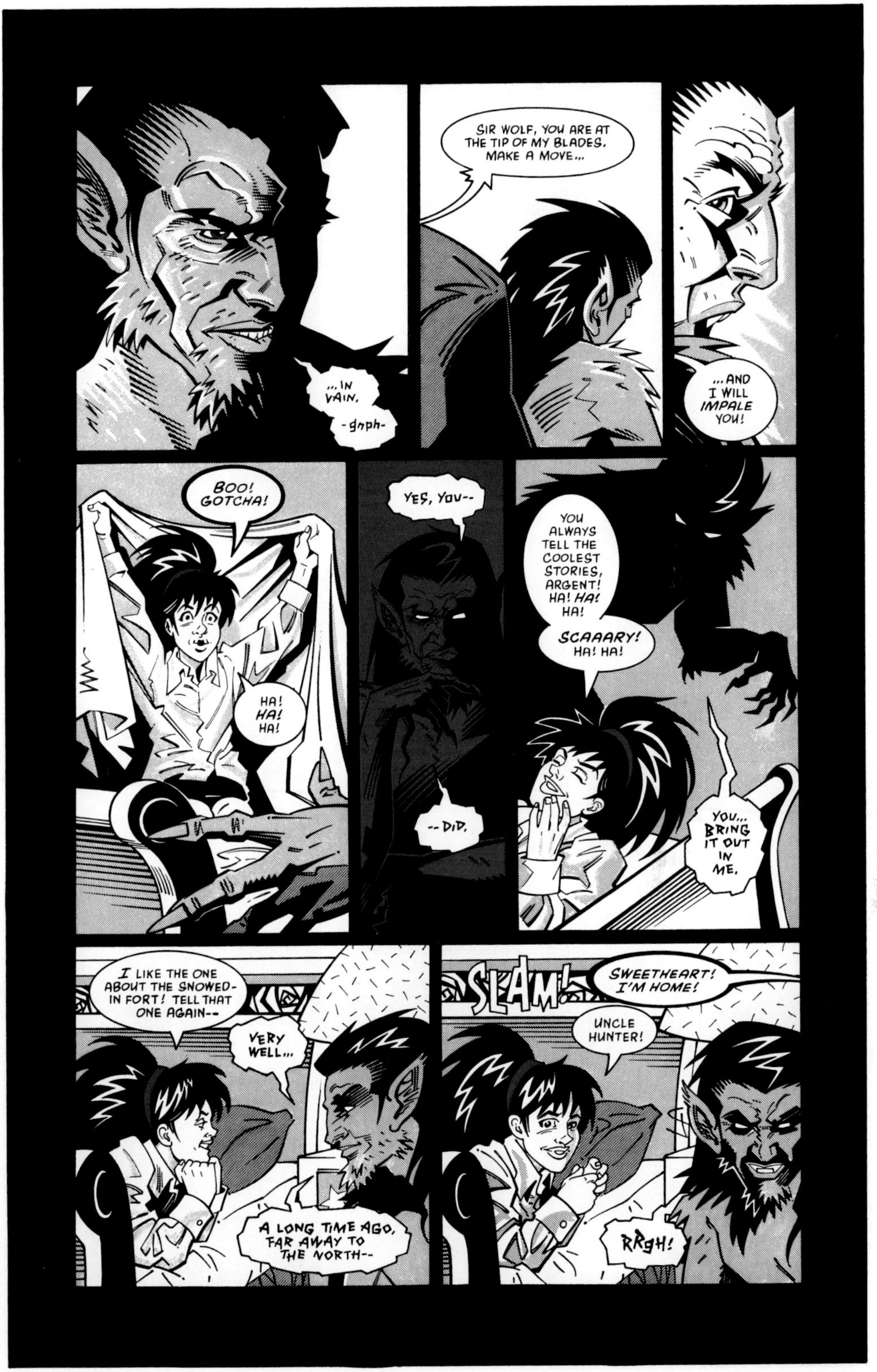
...IN VAIN.
-gnph-
SIR WOLF, YOU ARE AT THE TIP OF MY BLADES. MAKE A MOVE...
...AND I WILL IMPALE YOU!
BOO! GOTCHA!
HA! HA! HA!
YES, YOU--
--DID.
YOU ALWAYS TELL THE COOLEST STORIES, ARGENT! HA! HA! HA!
SCAAARY! HA! HA!
YOU... BRING IT OUT IN ME.
I LIKE THE ONE ABOUT THE SNOWED-IN FORT! TELL THAT ONE AGAIN--
VERY WELL...
A LONG TIME AGO, FAR AWAY TO THE NORTH--
SLAM!
SWEETHEART! I'M HOME!
UNCLE HUNTER!
RRGH!

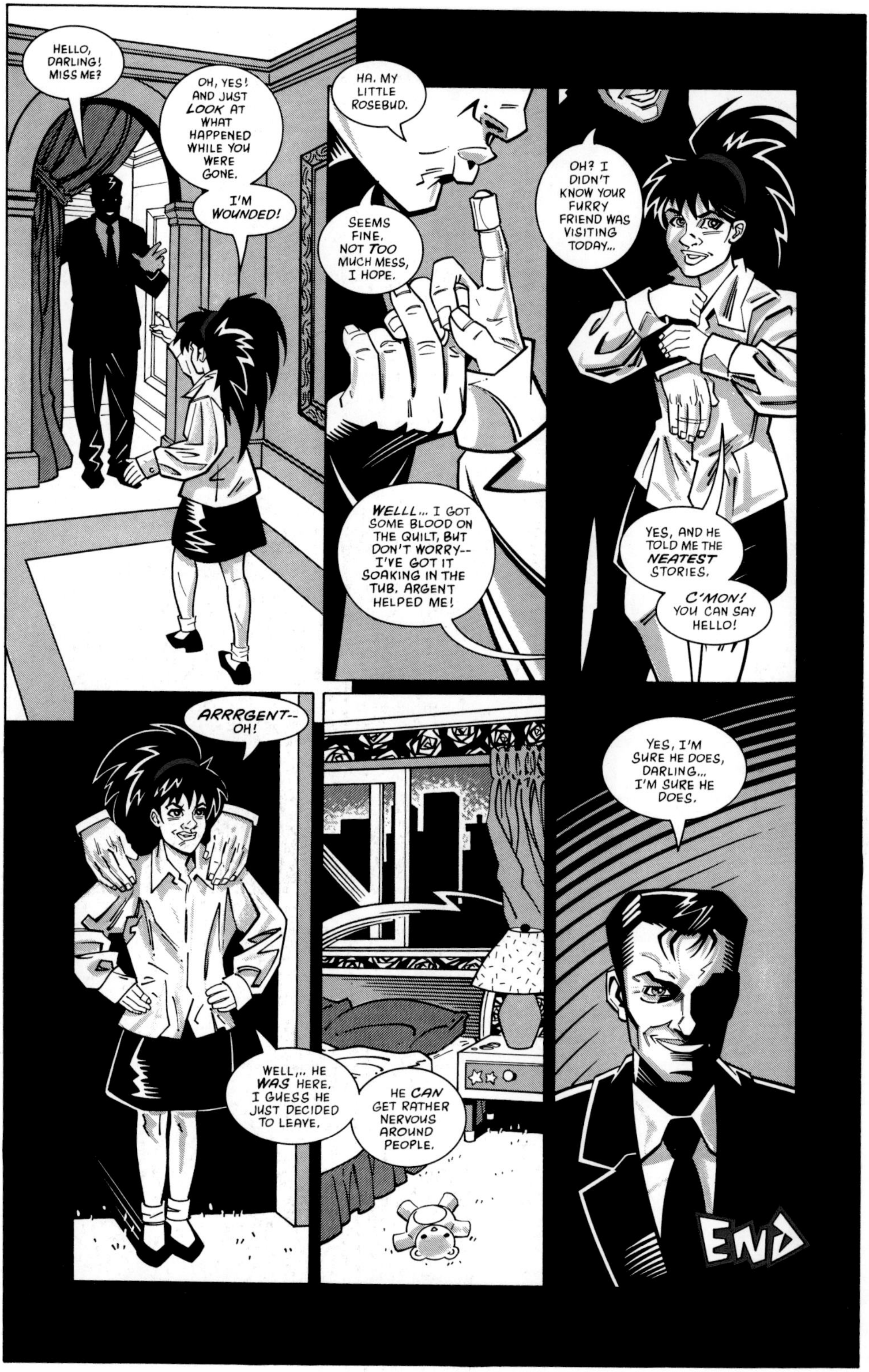
HELLO, DARLING! MISS ME?
OH, YES! AND JUST LOOK AT WHAT HAPPENED WHILE YOU WERE GONE.
I'M WOUNDED!
HA. MY LITTLE ROSEBUD.
SEEMS FINE. NOT TOO MUCH MESS, I HOPE.
WELLL... I GOT SOME BLOOD ON THE QUILT, BUT DON'T WORRY-- I'VE GOT IT SOAKING IN THE TUB. ARGENT HELPED ME!
OH? I DIDN'T KNOW YOUR FURRY FRIEND WAS VISITING TODAY...
YES, AND HE TOLD ME THE NEATEST STORIES.
C'MON! YOU CAN SAY HELLO!
ARRRGENT-- OH!
WELL,.. HE WAS HERE. I GUESS HE JUST DECIDED TO LEAVE.
HE CAN GET RATHER NERVOUS AROUND PEOPLE.
YES, I'M SURE HE DOES, DARLING... I'M SURE HE DOES.
END

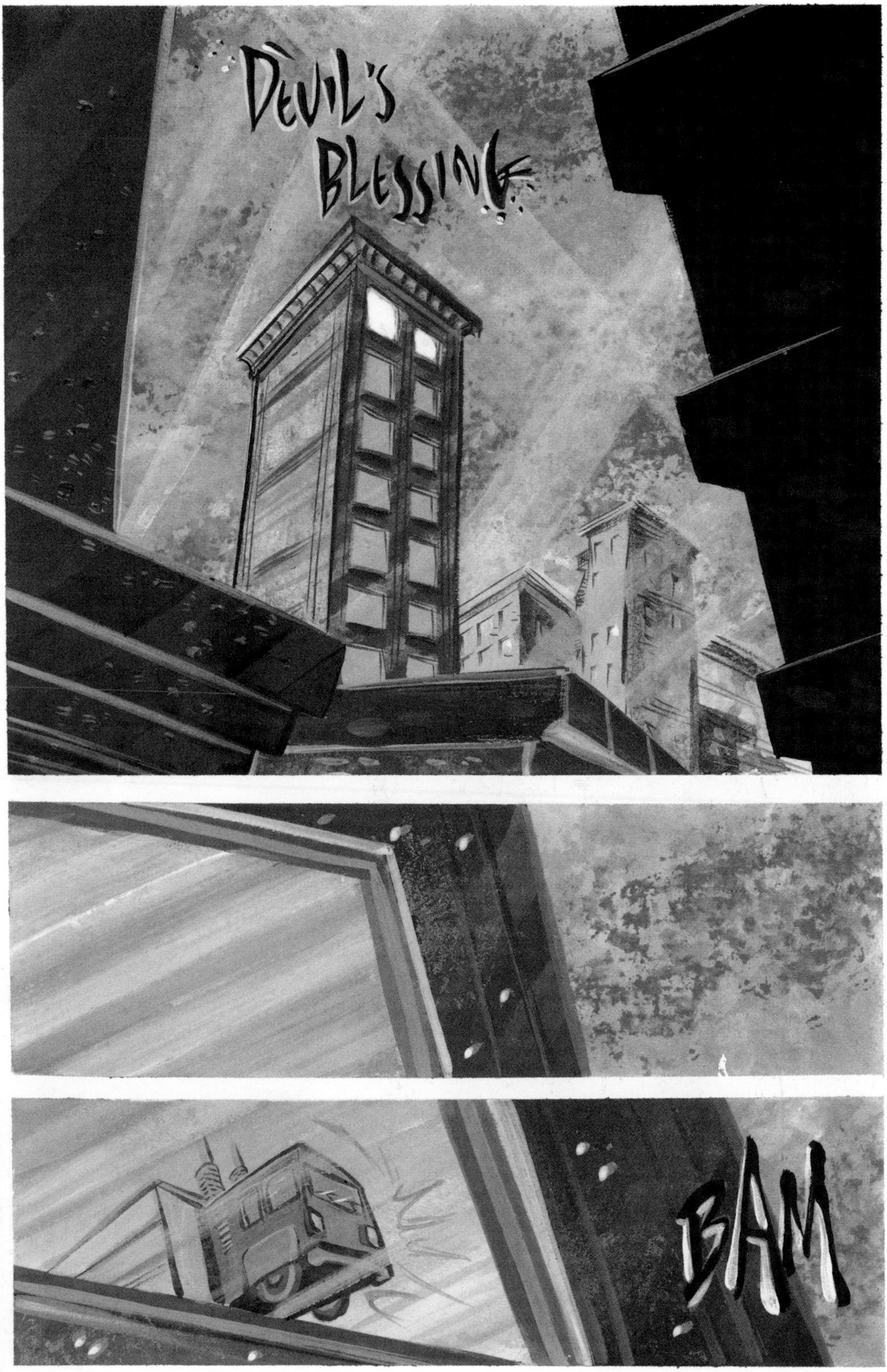
DEVIL'S BLESSING
BAM

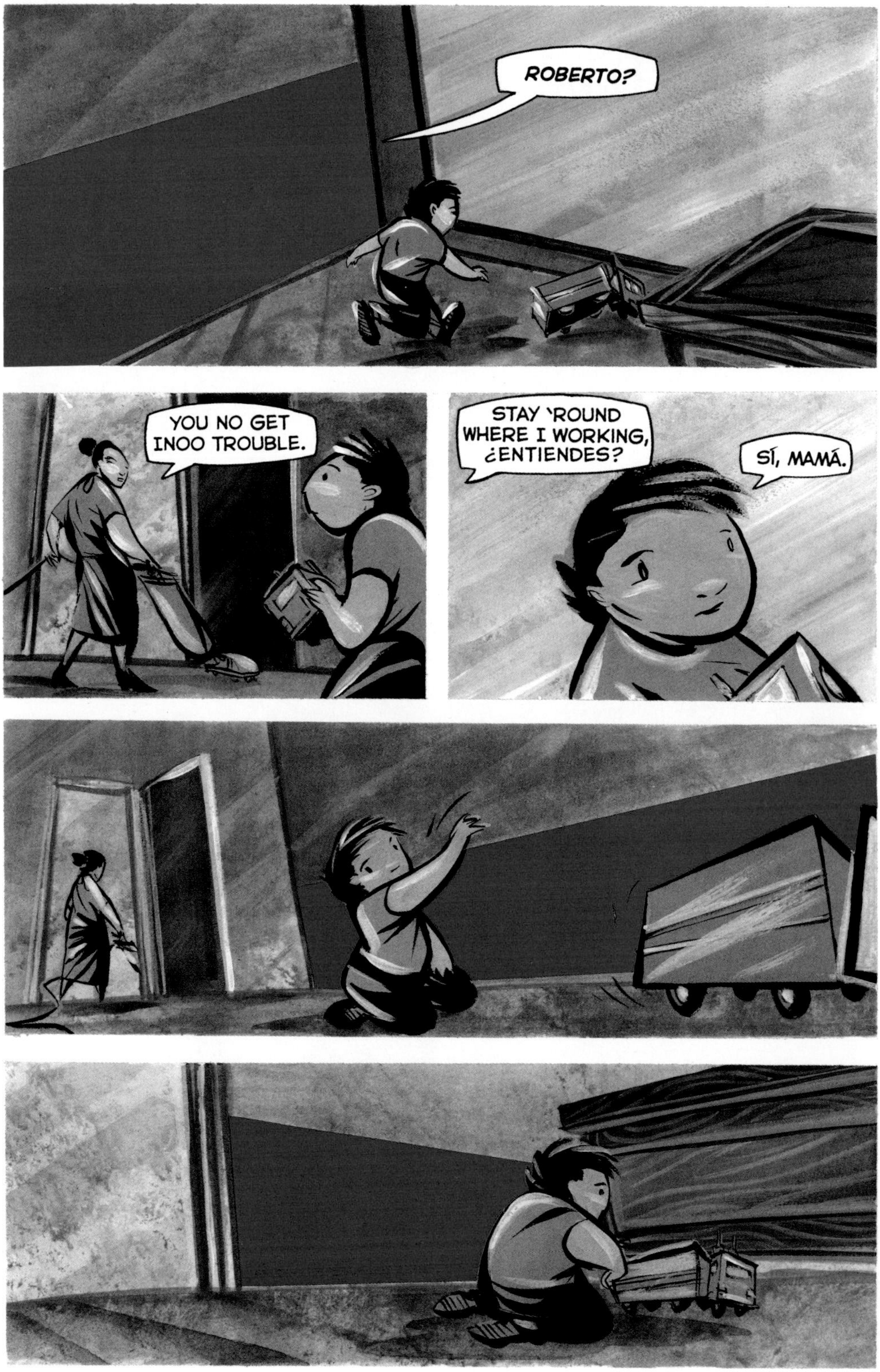
ROBERTO?
YOU NO GET INOO TROUBLE.
STAY 'ROUND WHERE I WORKING, ¿ENTIENDES?
SÍ, MAMÁ.

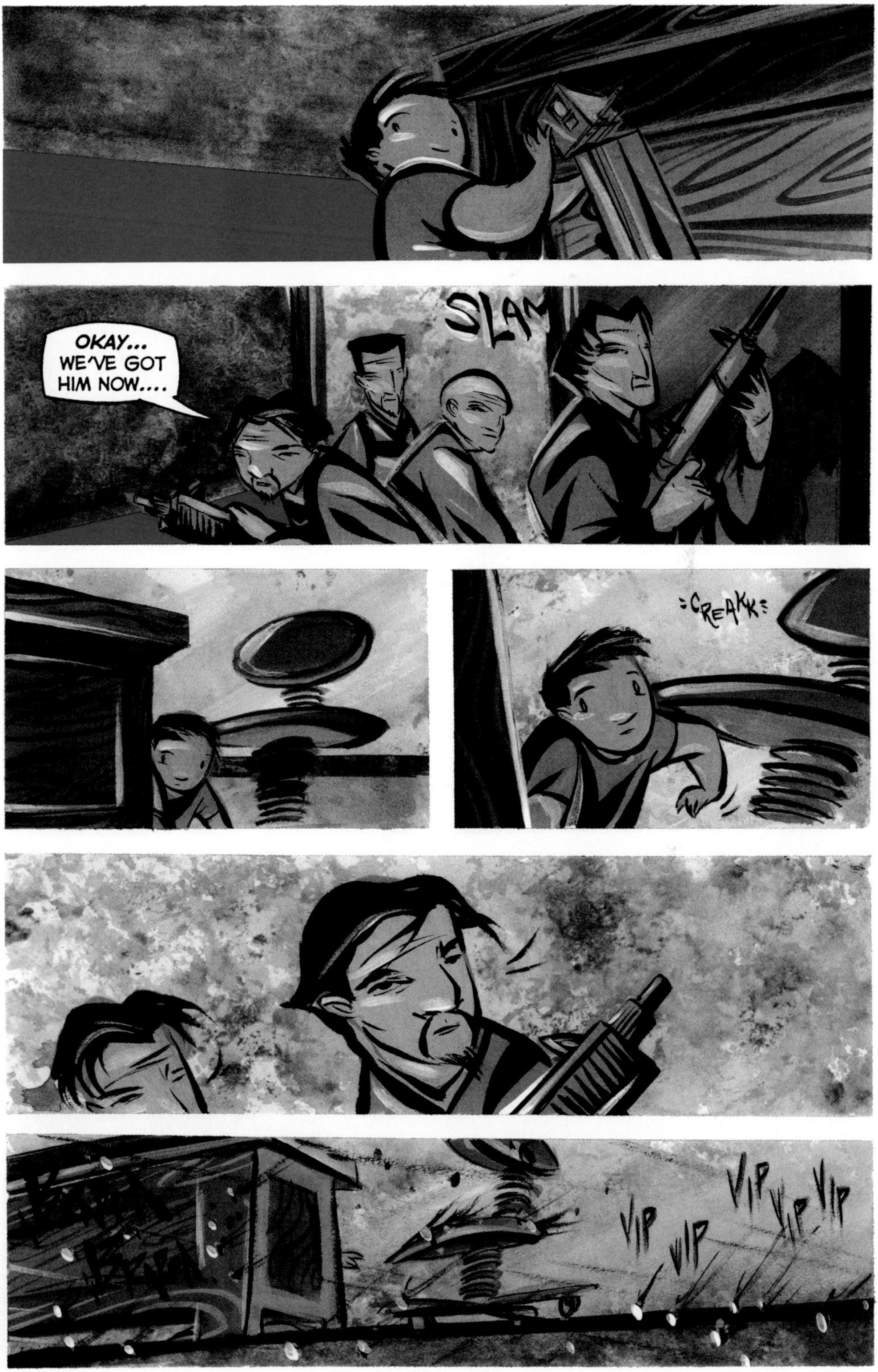
SLAM
OKAY... WE'VE GOT HIM NOW....
CREAKK
VIP
VIP
VIP VIP VIP

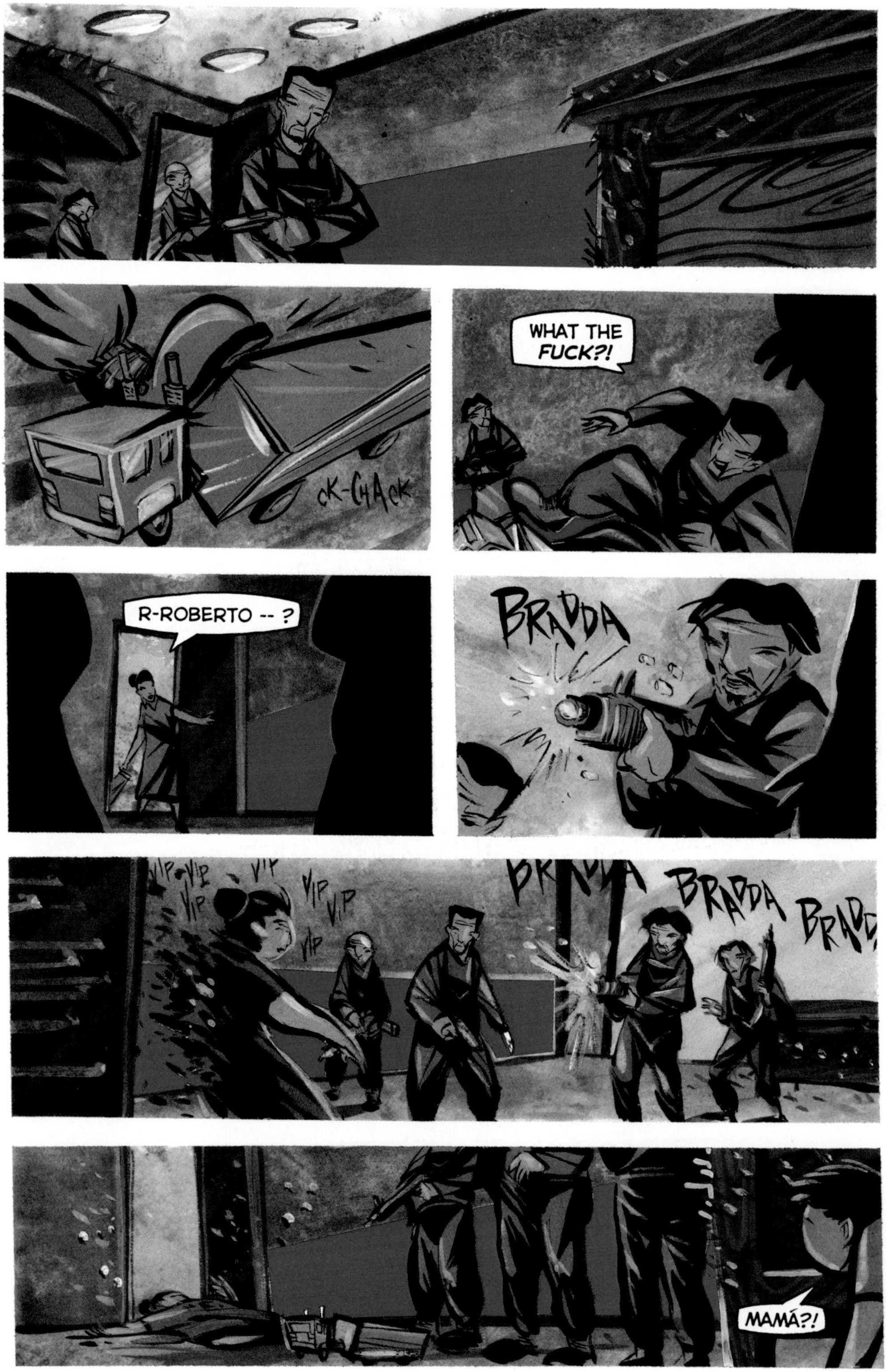
CK-CHACK
WHAT THE FUCK?!
R-ROBERTO -- ?
BRADDA
BRADDA
MAMÁ?!

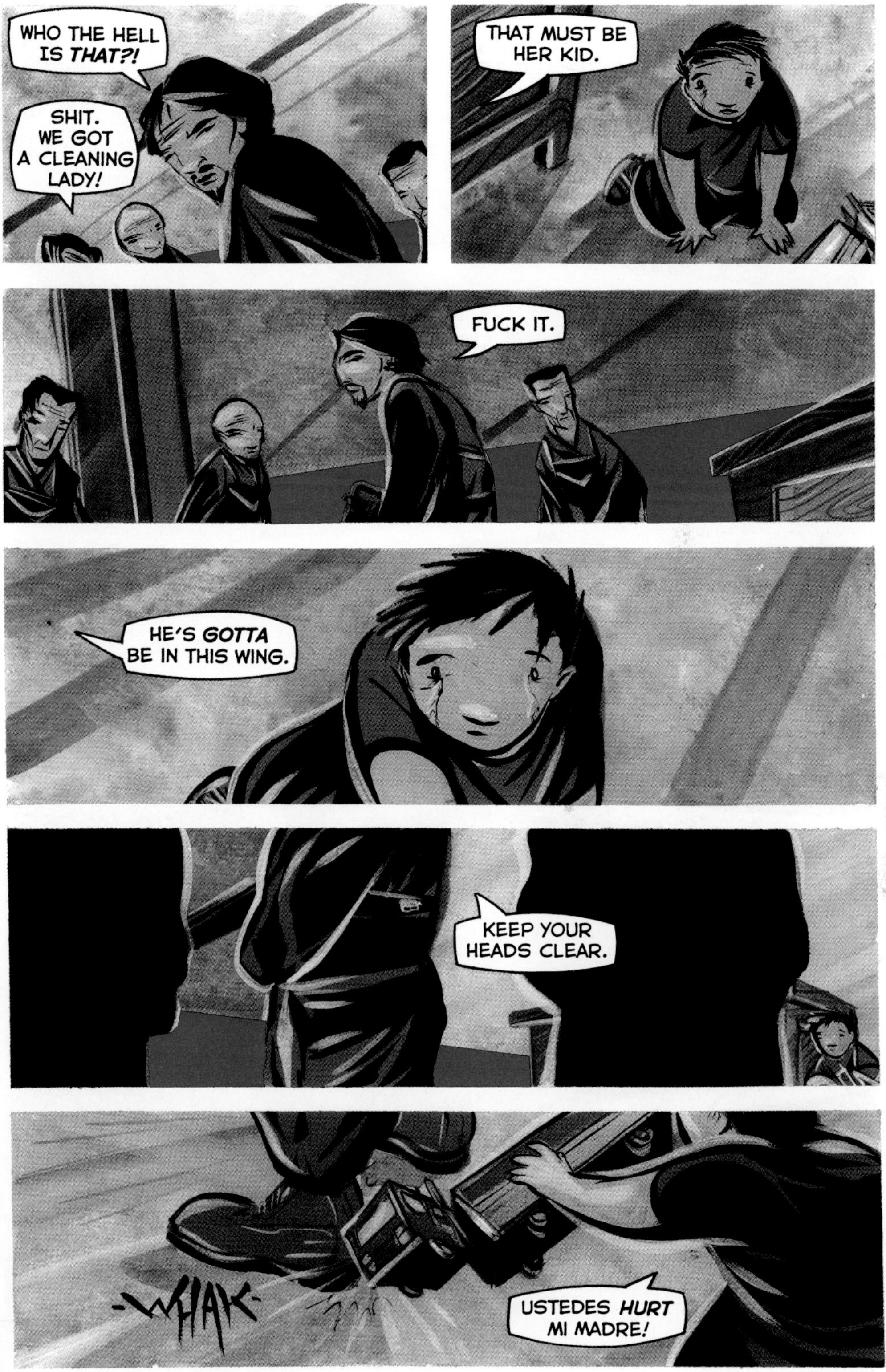
WHO THE HELL IS *THAT?!*
SHIT. WE GOT A CLEANING LADY!
THAT MUST BE HER KID.
FUCK IT.
HE'S *GOTTA* BE IN THIS WING.
KEEP YOUR HEADS CLEAR.
-WHAK-
USTEDES *HURT* MI MADRE!

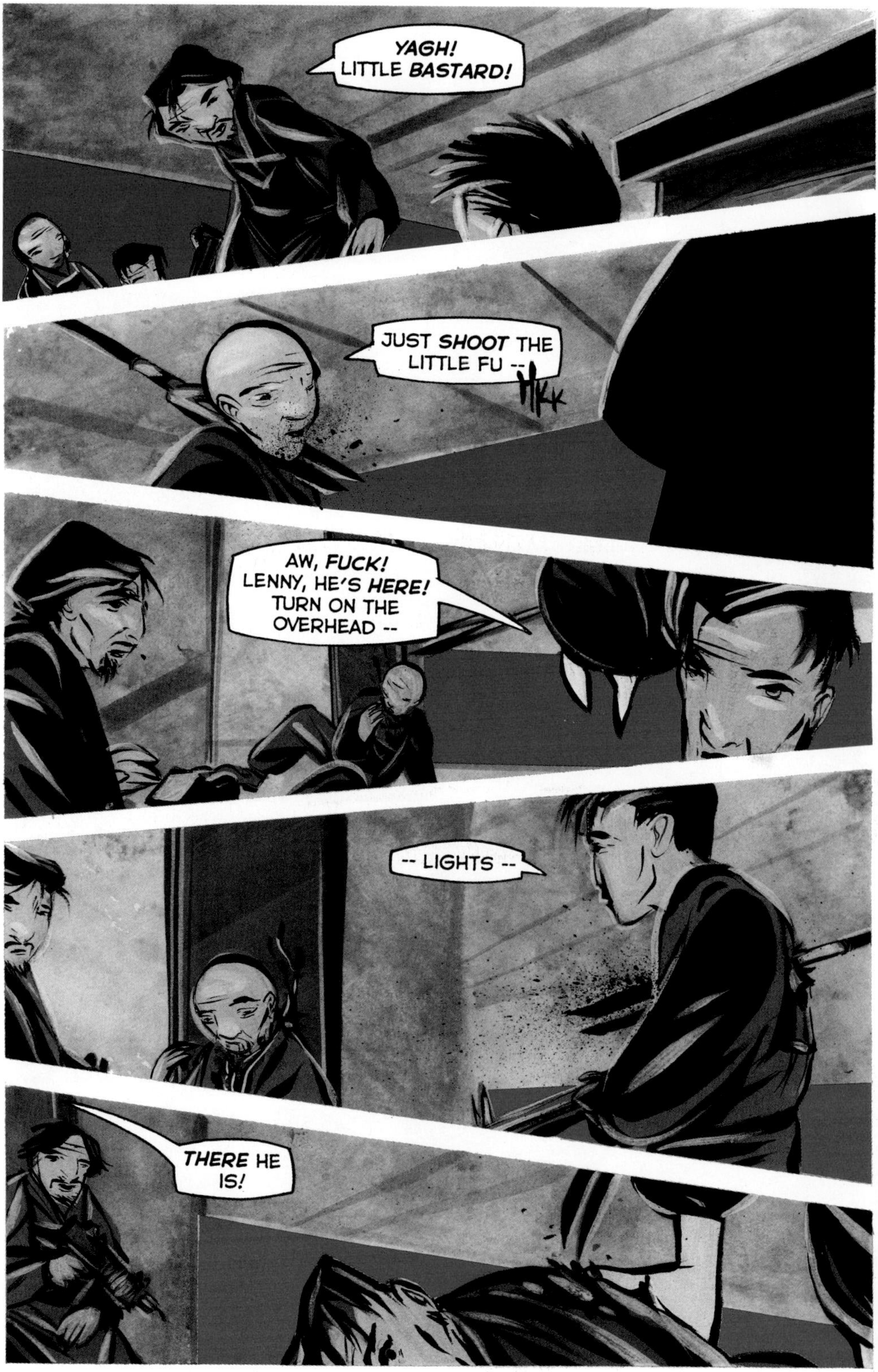
YAGH! LITTLE BASTARD!
JUST SHOOT THE LITTLE FU --
HKK
AW, FUCK! LENNY, HE'S HERE! TURN ON THE OVERHEAD --
-- LIGHTS --
THERE HE IS!

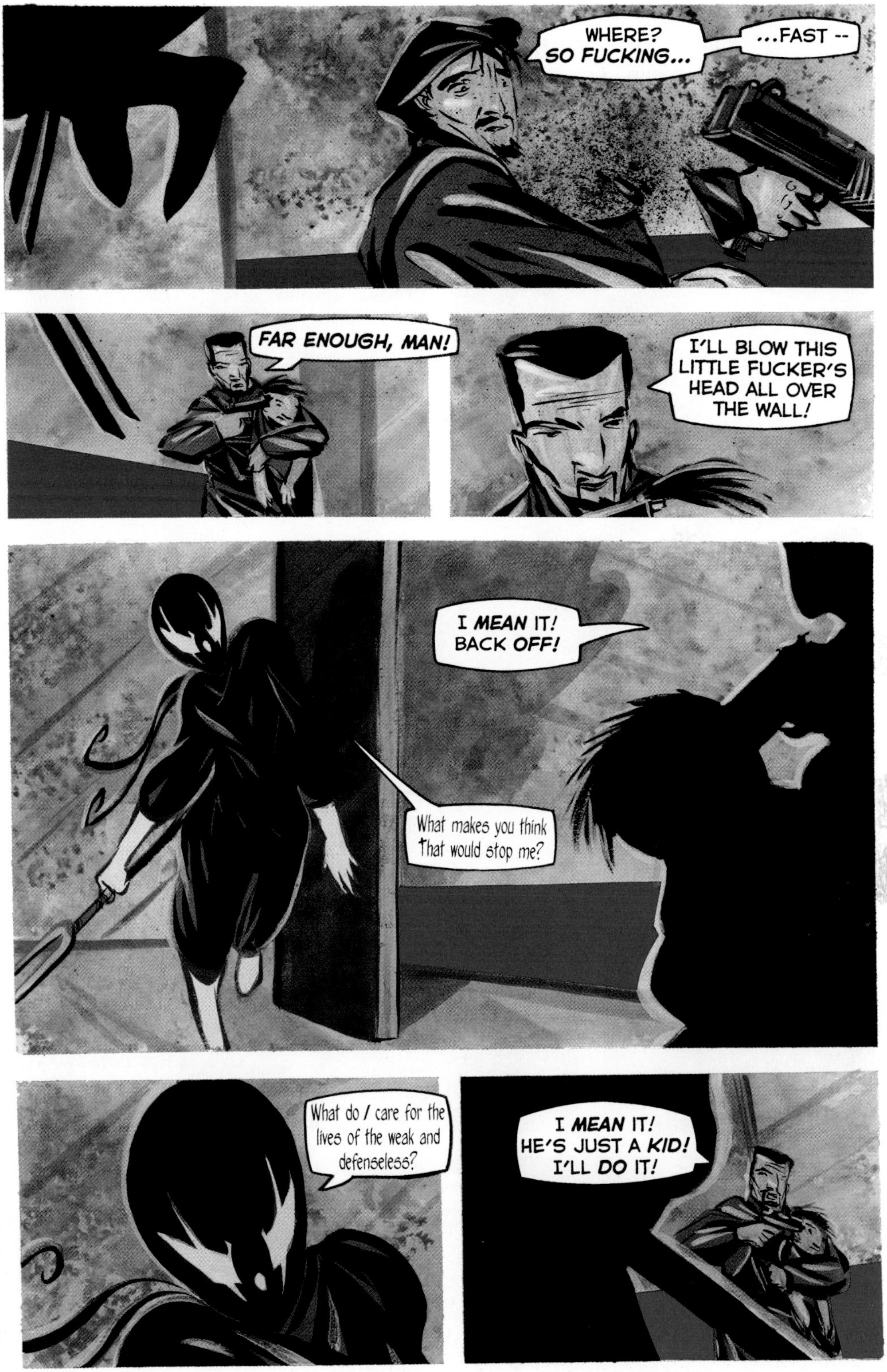
WHERE? SO FUCKING...
...FAST --
FAR ENOUGH, MAN!
I'LL BLOW THIS LITTLE FUCKER'S HEAD ALL OVER THE WALL!
I MEAN IT! BACK OFF!
What makes you think that would stop me?
What do I care for the lives of the weak and defenseless?
I MEAN IT! HE'S JUST A KID! I'LL DO IT!

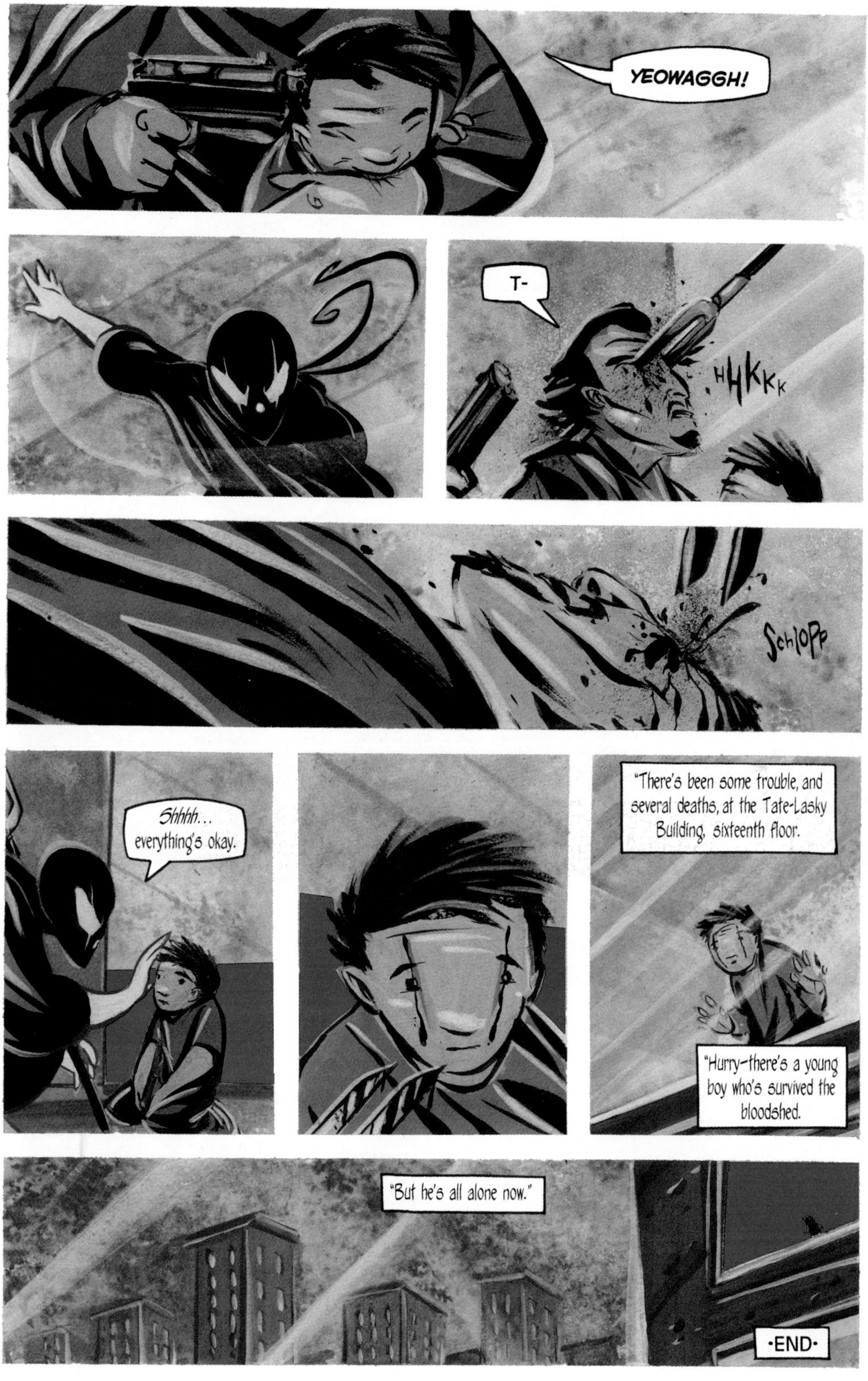
YEOWAGGH!
T-
HHKKK
SCHLOPP
Shhhh... everything's okay.
"There's been some trouble, and several deaths, at the Tate-Lasky Building, sixteenth floor.
"Hurry—there's a young boy who's survived the bloodshed.
"But he's all alone now."
•END•

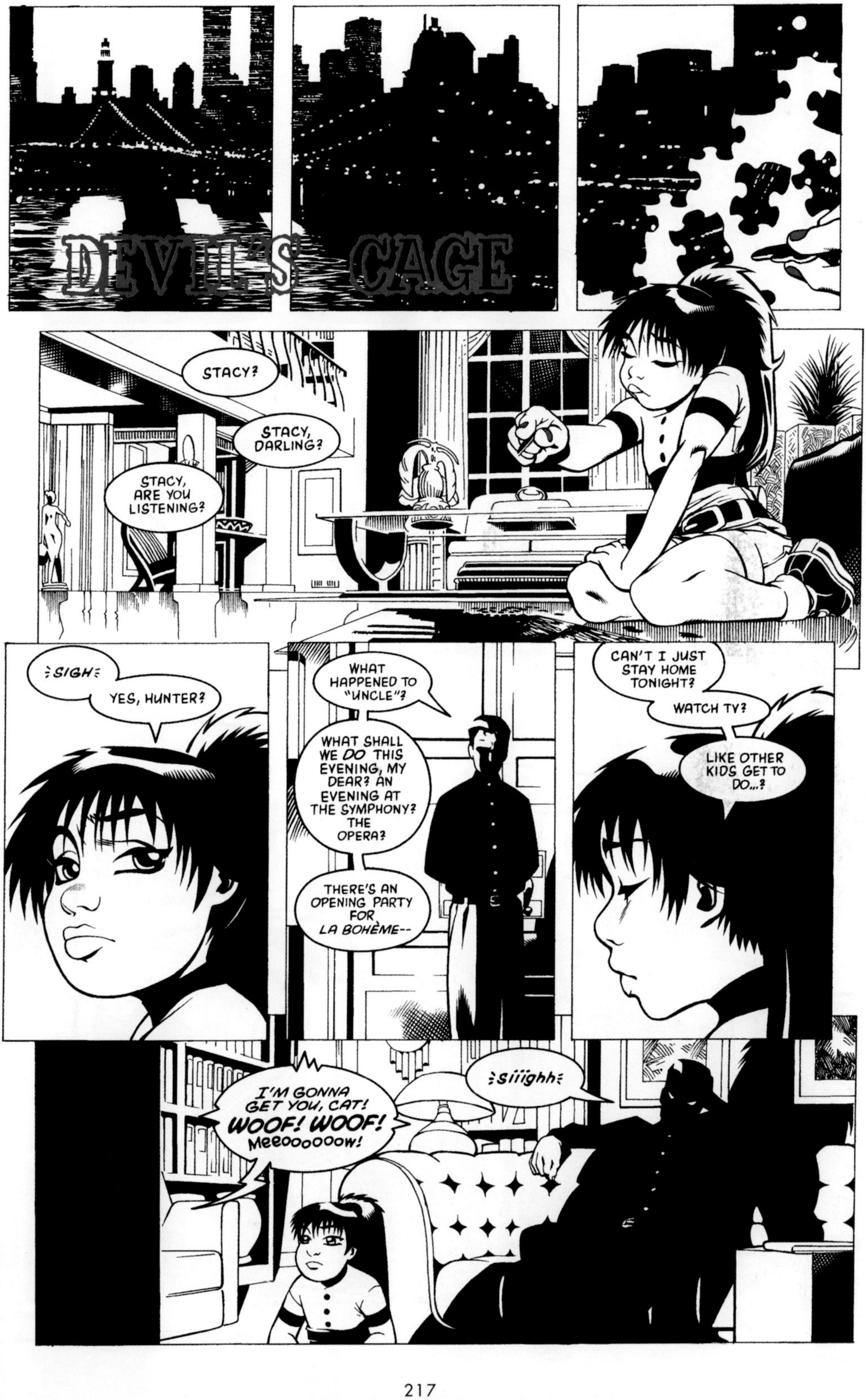
DEVIL'S CAGE
STACY?
STACY, DARLING?
STACY, ARE YOU LISTENING?
SIGH
YES, HUNTER?
WHAT HAPPENED TO "UNCLE"?
WHAT SHALL WE DO THIS EVENING, MY DEAR? AN EVENING AT THE SYMPHONY? THE OPERA?
THERE'S AN OPENING PARTY FOR LA BOHÈME--
CAN'T I JUST STAY HOME TONIGHT?
WATCH TV?
LIKE OTHER KIDS GET TO DO...?
I'M GONNA GET YOU, CAT! WOOF! WOOF! MEEOOOOOOOW!
SIIIGHH

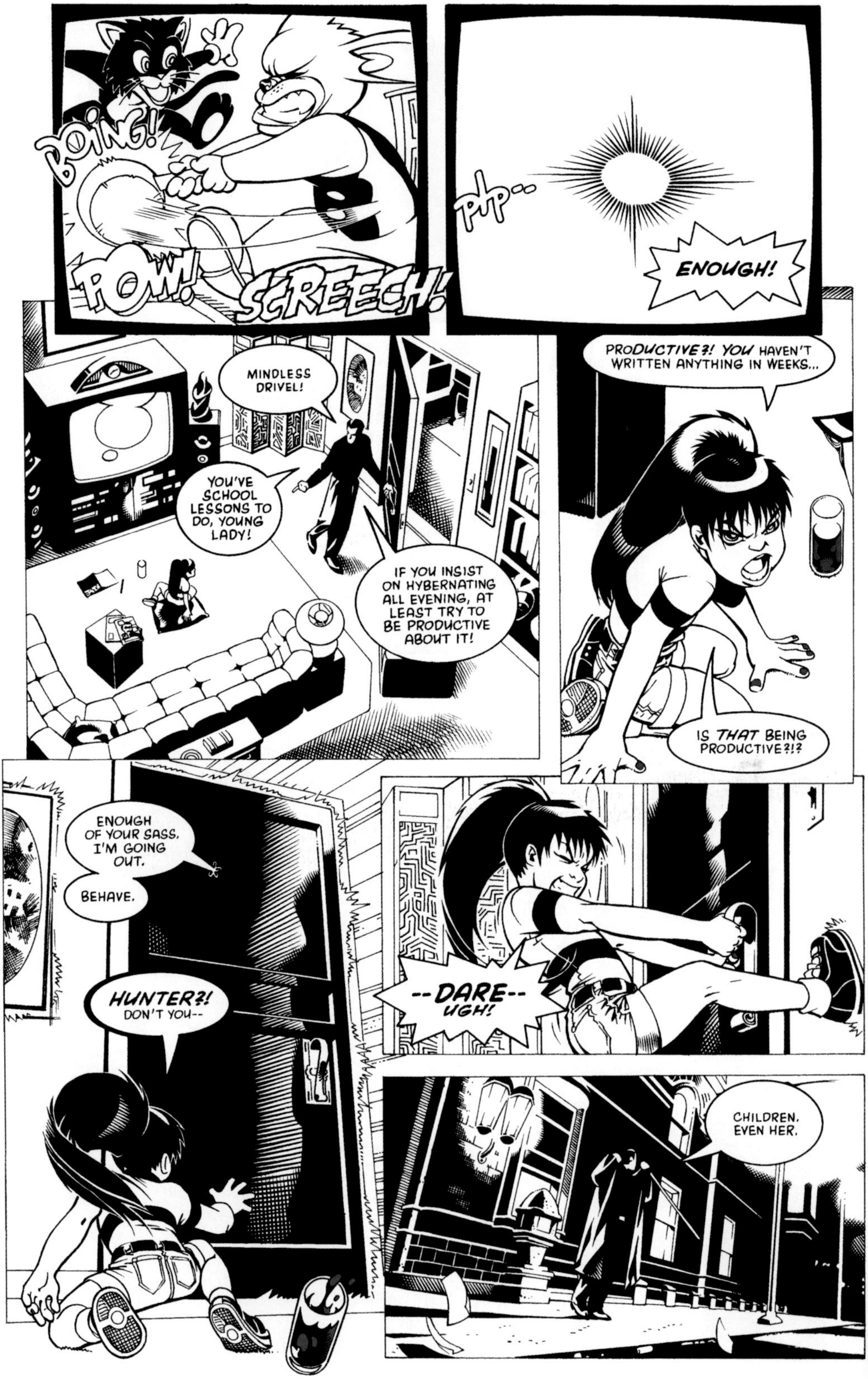
BOING!
POW!
SCREECH!
php--
ENOUGH!
MINDLESS DRIVEL!
YOU'VE SCHOOL LESSONS TO DO, YOUNG LADY!
IF YOU INSIST ON HYBERNATING ALL EVENING, AT LEAST TRY TO BE PRODUCTIVE ABOUT IT!
PRODUCTIVE?! YOU HAVEN'T WRITTEN ANYTHING IN WEEKS...
IS THAT BEING PRODUCTIVE?!?
ENOUGH OF YOUR SASS. I'M GOING OUT.
BEHAVE.
HUNTER?! DON'T YOU--
--DARE-- UGH!
CHILDREN. EVEN HER.

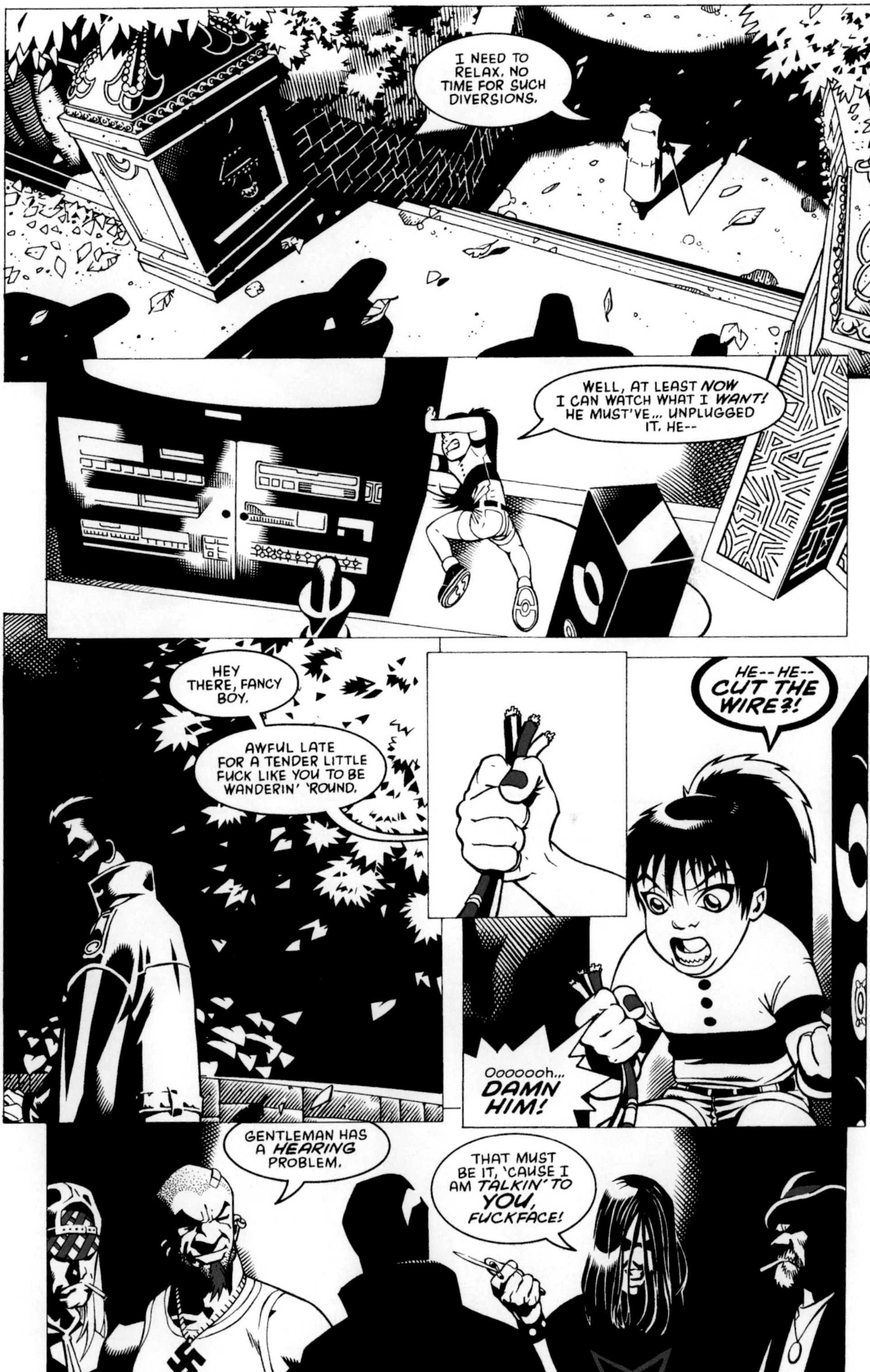
I NEED TO RELAX. NO TIME FOR SUCH DIVERSIONS.
WELL, AT LEAST NOW I CAN WATCH WHAT I WANT! HE MUST'VE... UNPLUGGED IT. HE--
HEY THERE, FANCY BOY.
AWFUL LATE FOR A TENDER LITTLE FUCK LIKE YOU TO BE WANDERIN' 'ROUND.
HE-- HE-- CUT THE WIRE?!
Ooooooh... DAMN HIM!
GENTLEMAN HAS A HEARING PROBLEM.
THAT MUST BE IT, 'CAUSE I AM TALKIN' TO YOU, FUCKFACE!

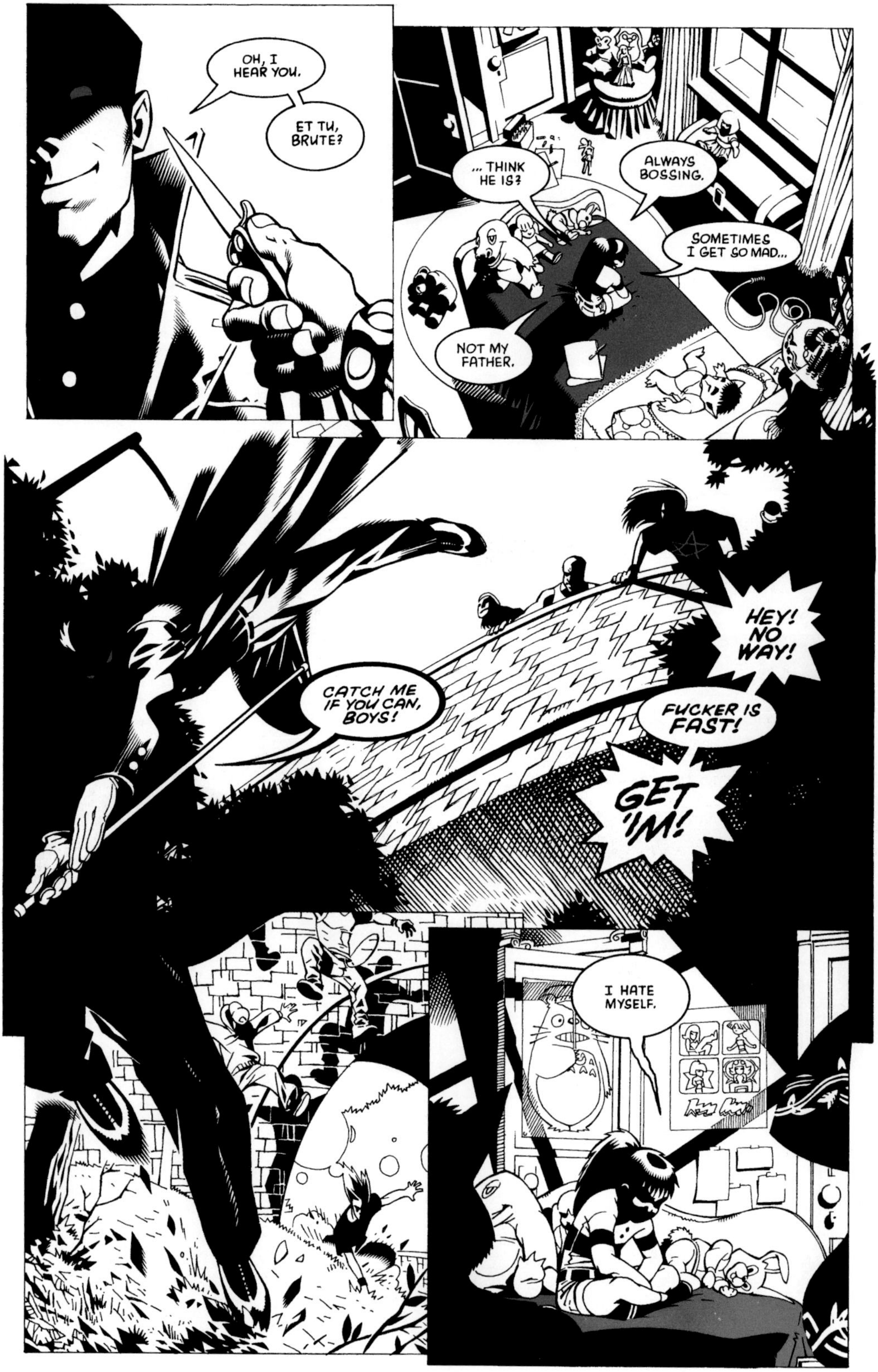
OH, I HEAR YOU.
ET TU, BRUTE?
... THINK HE IS?
ALWAYS BOSSING.
SOMETIMES I GET SO MAD...
NOT MY FATHER.
CATCH ME IF YOU CAN, BOYS!
HEY! NO WAY!
FUCKER IS FAST!
GET 'IM!
I HATE MYSELF.

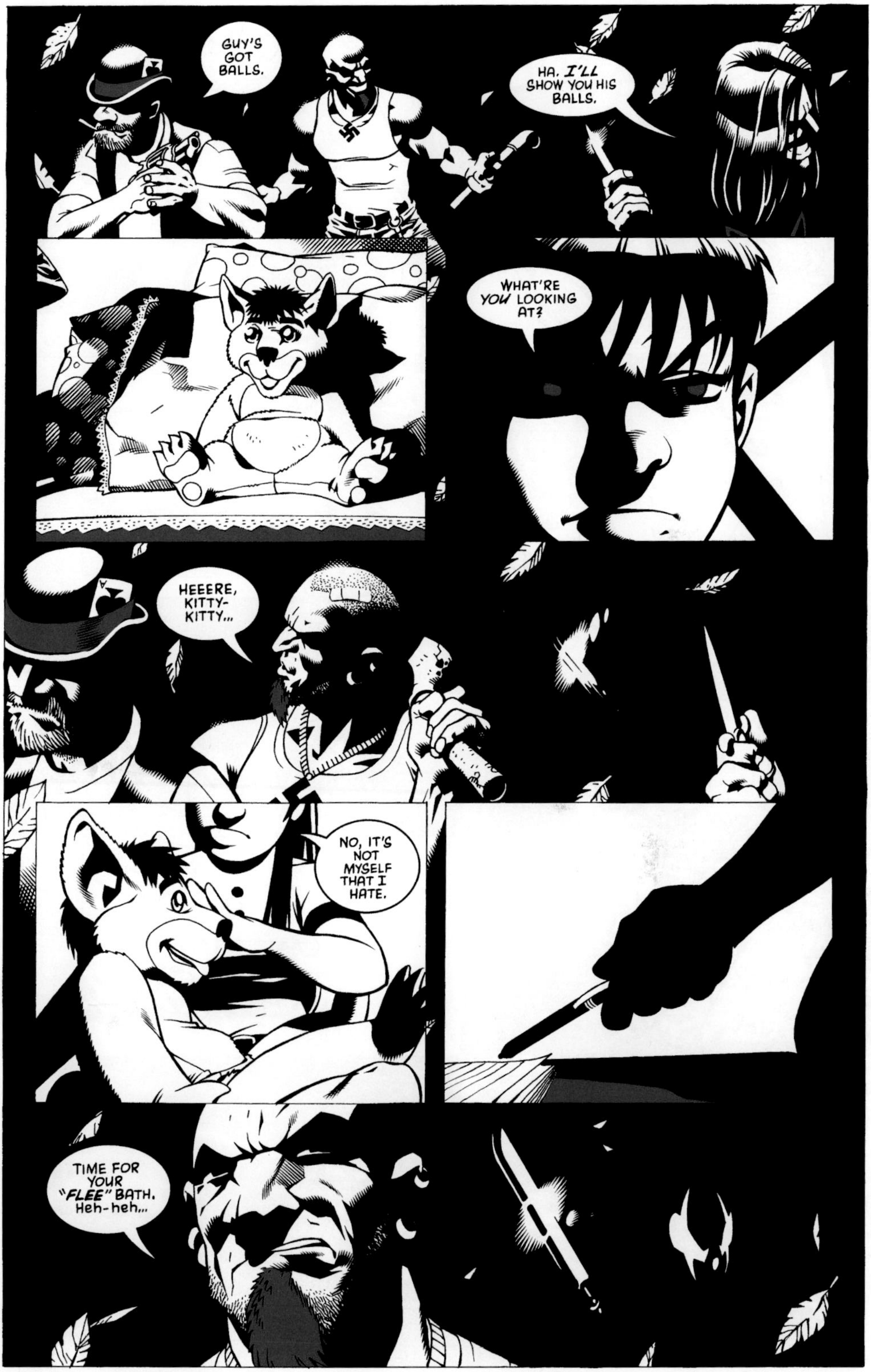
GUY'S GOT BALLS.
HA. I'LL SHOW YOU HIS BALLS.
WHAT'RE YOU LOOKING AT?
HEEERE, KITTY-KITTY...
NO, IT'S NOT MYSELF THAT I HATE.
TIME FOR YOUR "FLEE" BATH. Heh-heh...

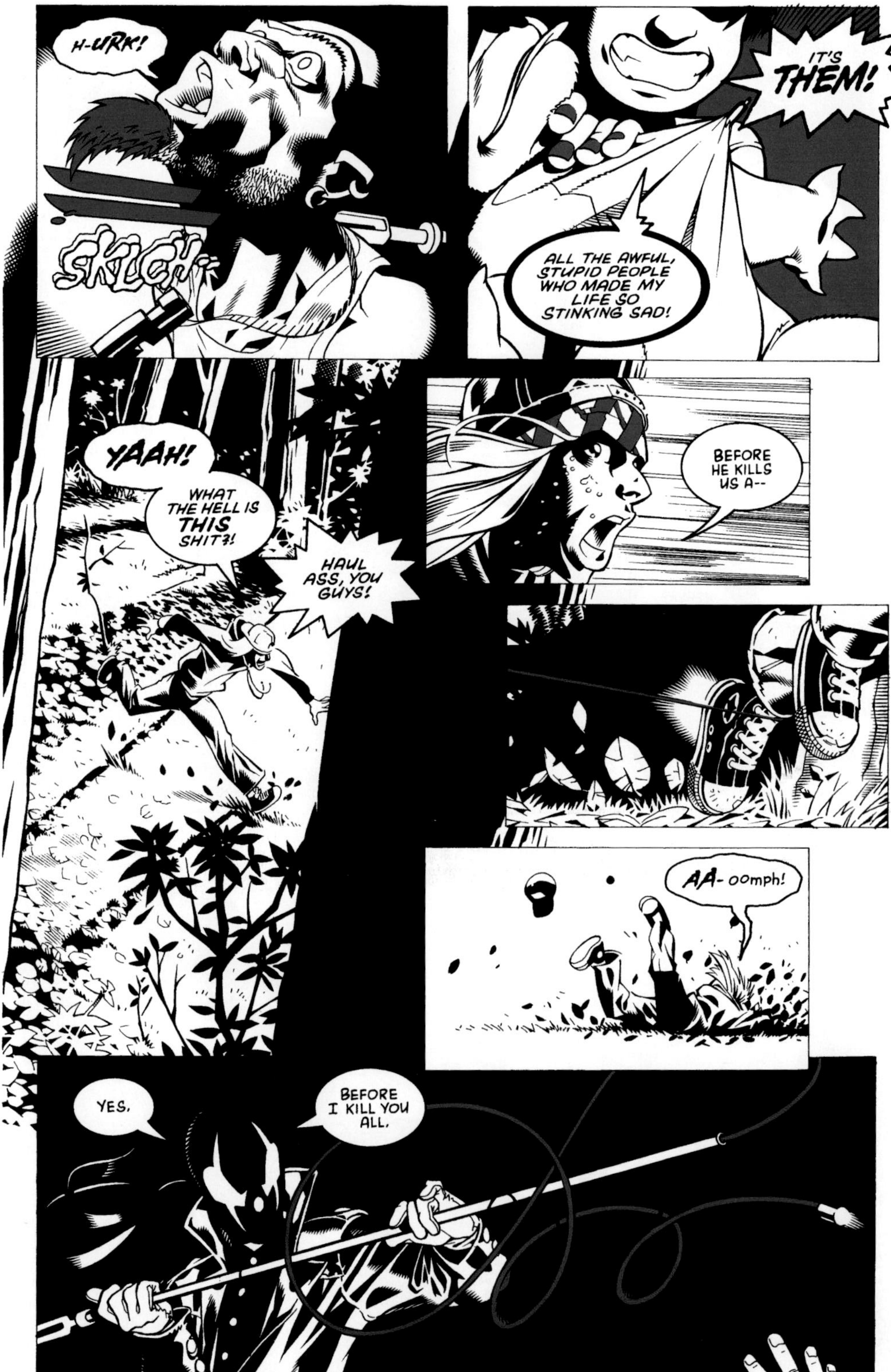
H-URK!
SKLCH
IT'S THEM!
ALL THE AWFUL, STUPID PEOPLE WHO MADE MY LIFE SO STINKING SAD!
YAAH!
WHAT THE HELL IS THIS SHIT?!
HAUL ASS, YOU GUYS!
BEFORE HE KILLS US A--
AA- oomph!
YES.
BEFORE I KILL YOU ALL.

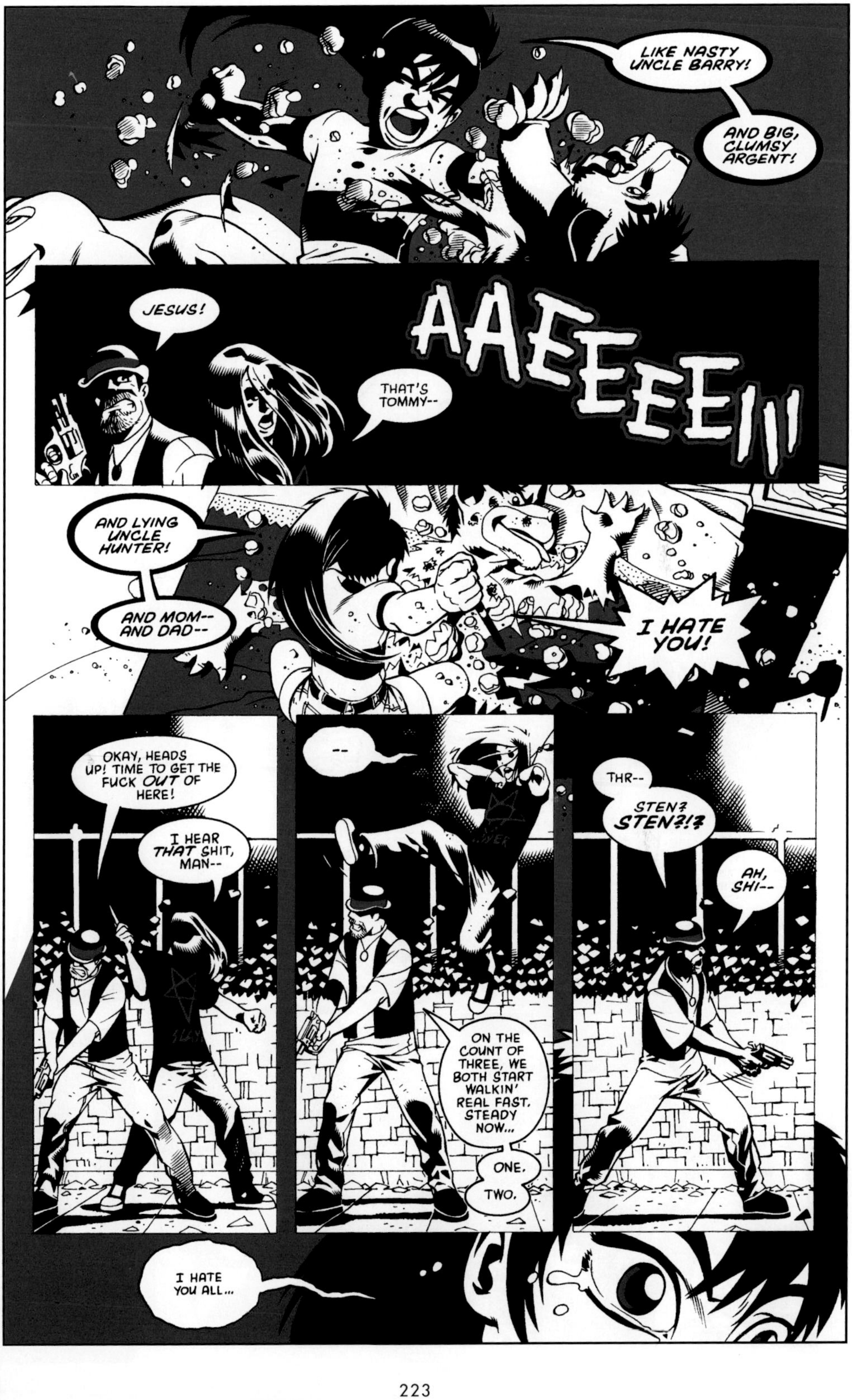
LIKE NASTY UNCLE BARRY!
AND BIG, CLUMSY ARGENT!
JESUS!
THAT'S TOMMY--
AAEEEE!!!
AND LYING UNCLE HUNTER!
AND MOM-- AND DAD--
I HATE YOU!
OKAY, HEADS UP! TIME TO GET THE FUCK OUT OF HERE!
I HEAR THAT SHIT, MAN--
--
ON THE COUNT OF THREE, WE BOTH START WALKIN' REAL FAST. STEADY NOW...
ONE.
TWO.
THR--
STEN? STEN?!?
AH, SHI--
I HATE YOU ALL...

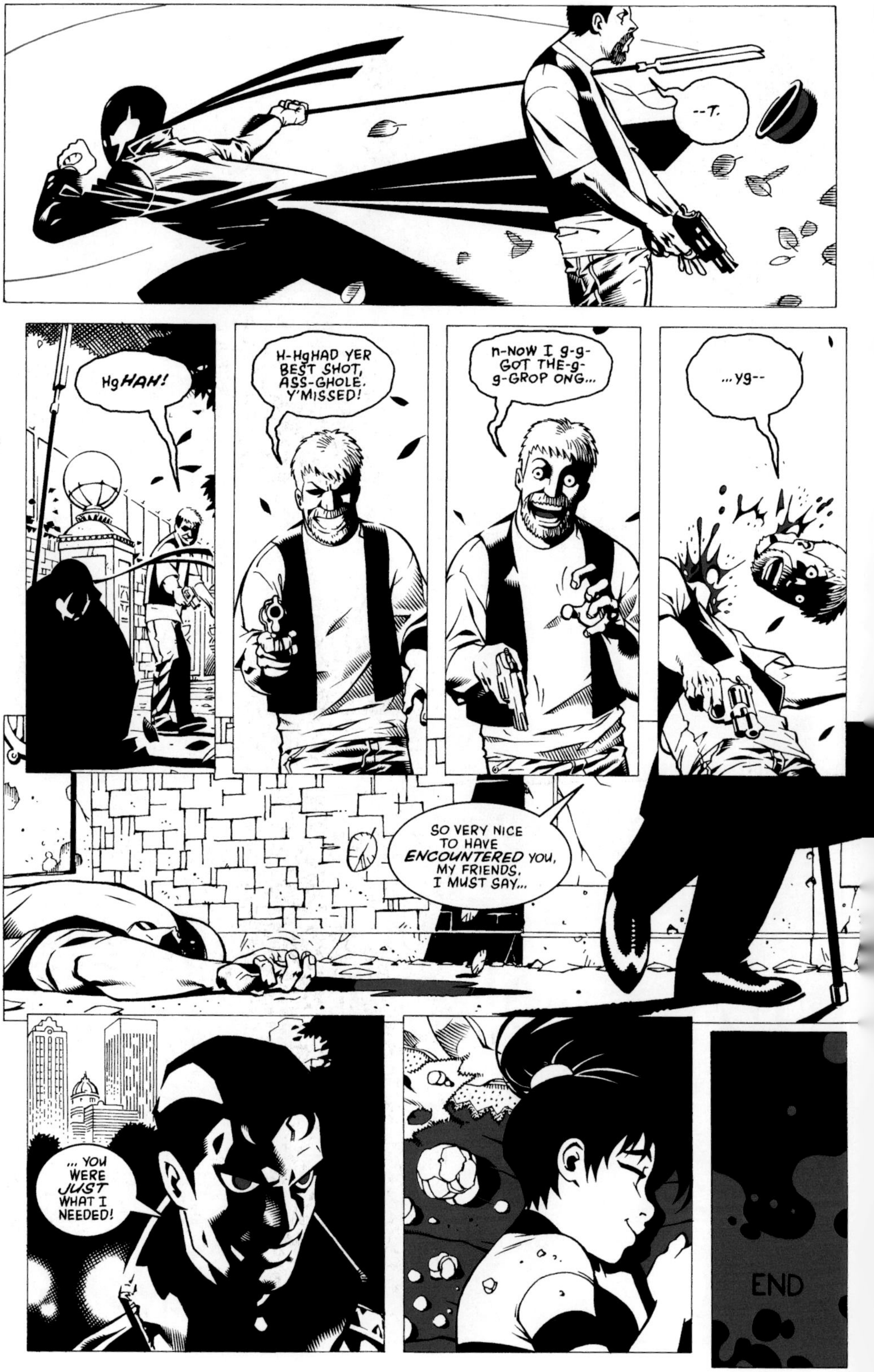

--T.
HgHAH!
H-HgHAD YER BEST SHOT, ASS-GHOLE. Y'MISSED!
n-NOW I g-g-GOT THE-g-g-GROP ONG...
...yg--
SO VERY NICE TO HAVE ENCOUNTERED YOU, MY FRIENDS, I MUST SAY...
... YOU WERE JUST WHAT I NEEDED!
END

Devil's Domain

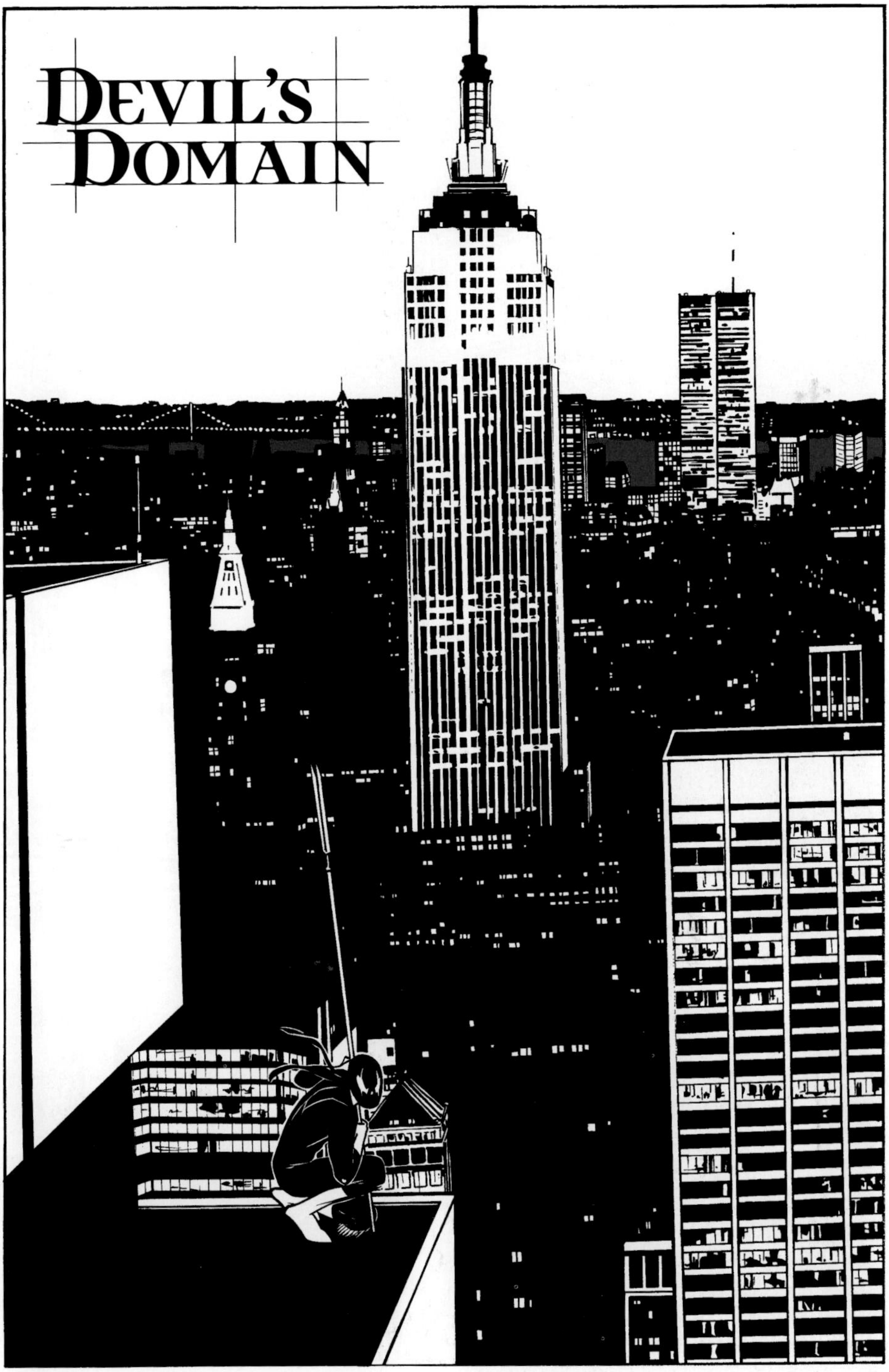

Steely plane, as dark as pitch. The rearing spines of mankind's modern totems. The crossroads piled beneath in termite patterns, hive upon hive upon hive. Above it all, the one who hunts. His will, the flinty stuff of legend.

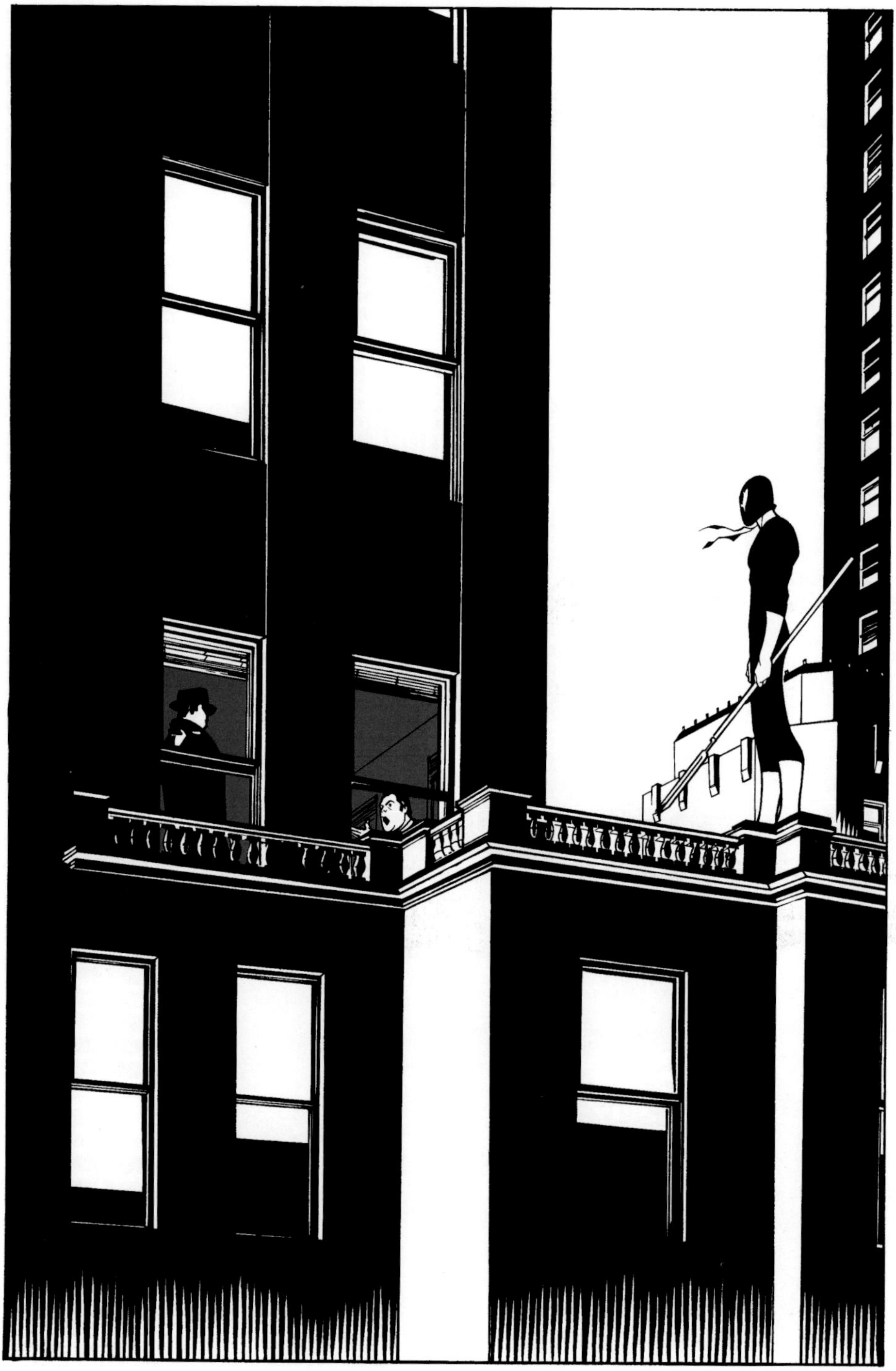

In urban castles are hot deals struck, larcenies juggled, betrayals unveiled. The hunter transcends them, his awful blades gashing dominion and dread. His ghost-walk knows no boundaries, fears no heights, has no ebb.

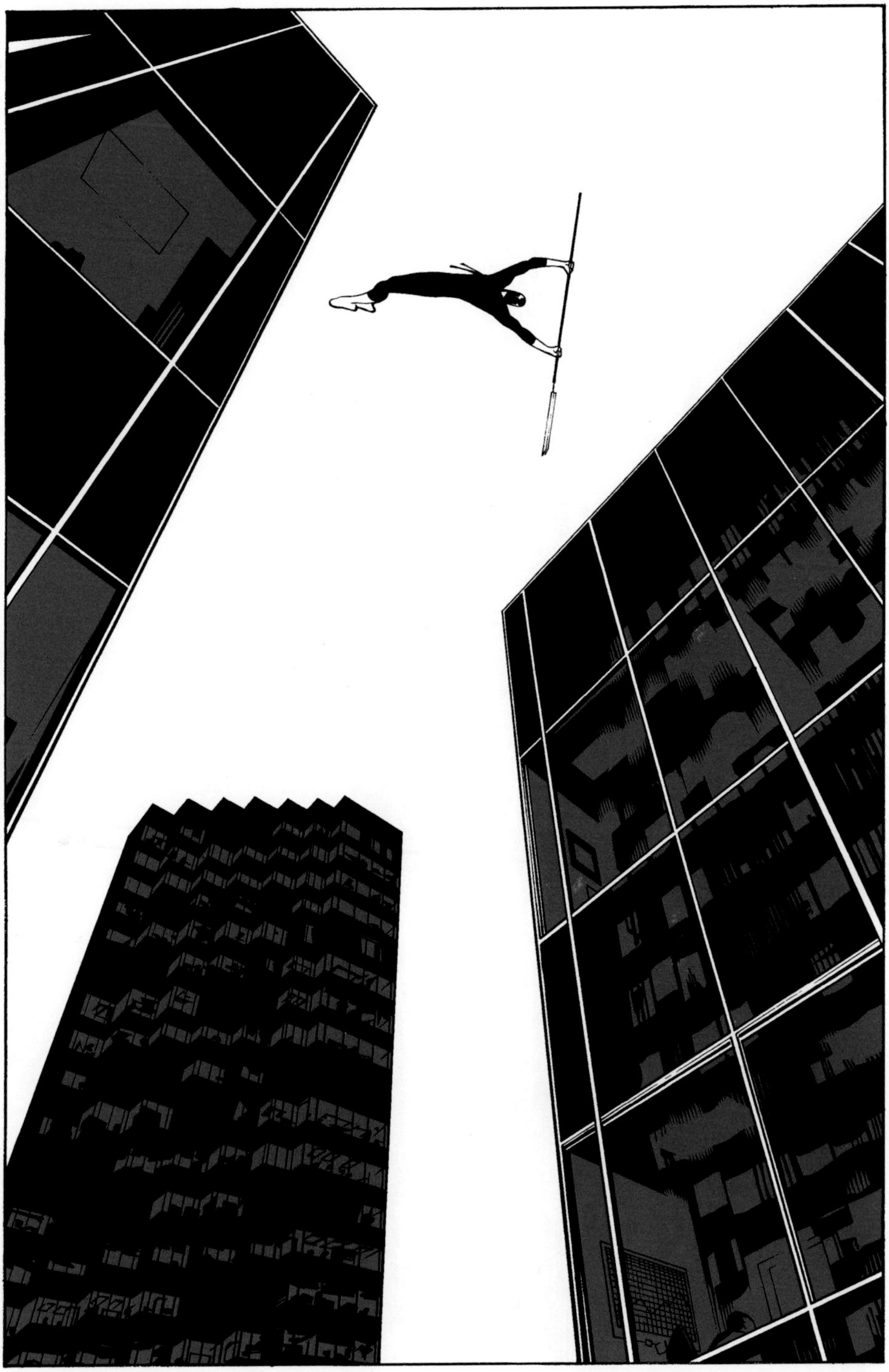

The hunter's dance, absolute license. His soaring prance, a contemptuous yowl that echoes 'midst the daunting canyons of stone, steel, and glass. In endless rebuke: I fear nothing of this dark and lonely world. I am fear.

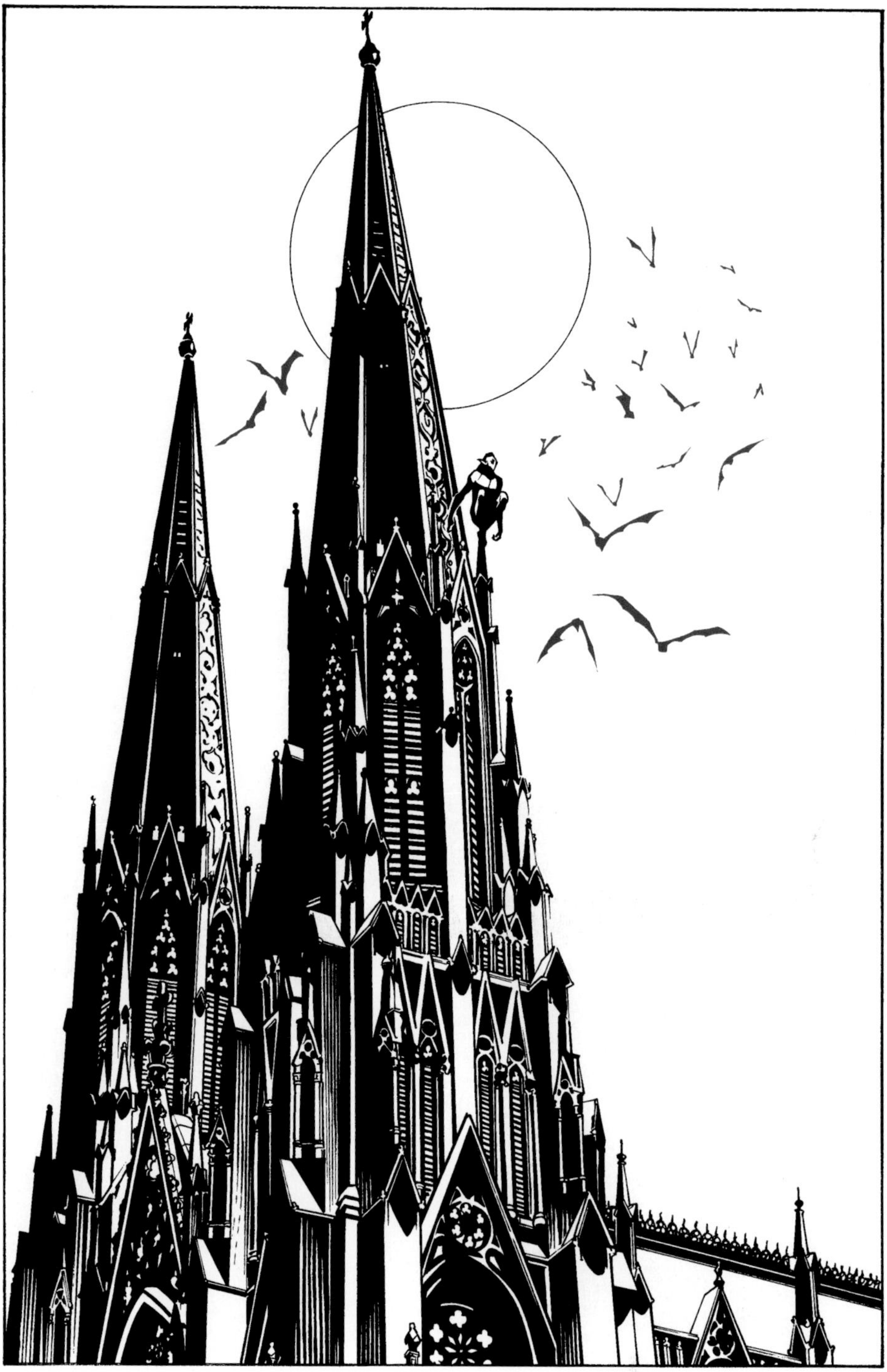

The hunter's insolent scent summons up gorgons, coughed out of hell to pursue, pounce, and purge. The were-thing decries its own freedom, suffers its curse in howling objection. Its aching body, the terrible tool of justice and rage.

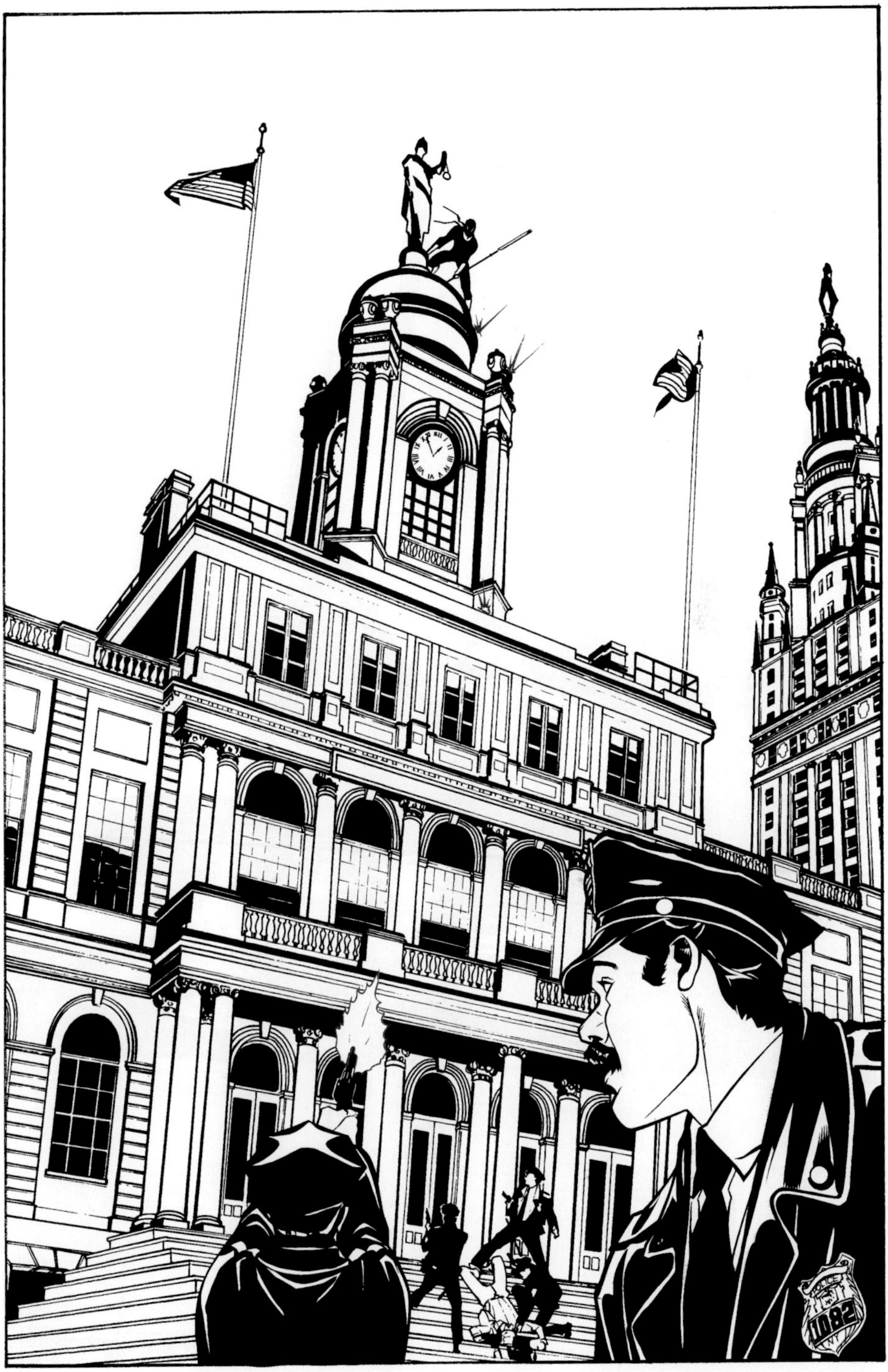
POLICE
1082

Relentless, the hunter endures. Justice, her indolent forces lapping at his heels — ever shambling, arid, and blind. He tramples and flies, no escaping the mark. His fork flashes ardent through the crackle of firearms and haste.

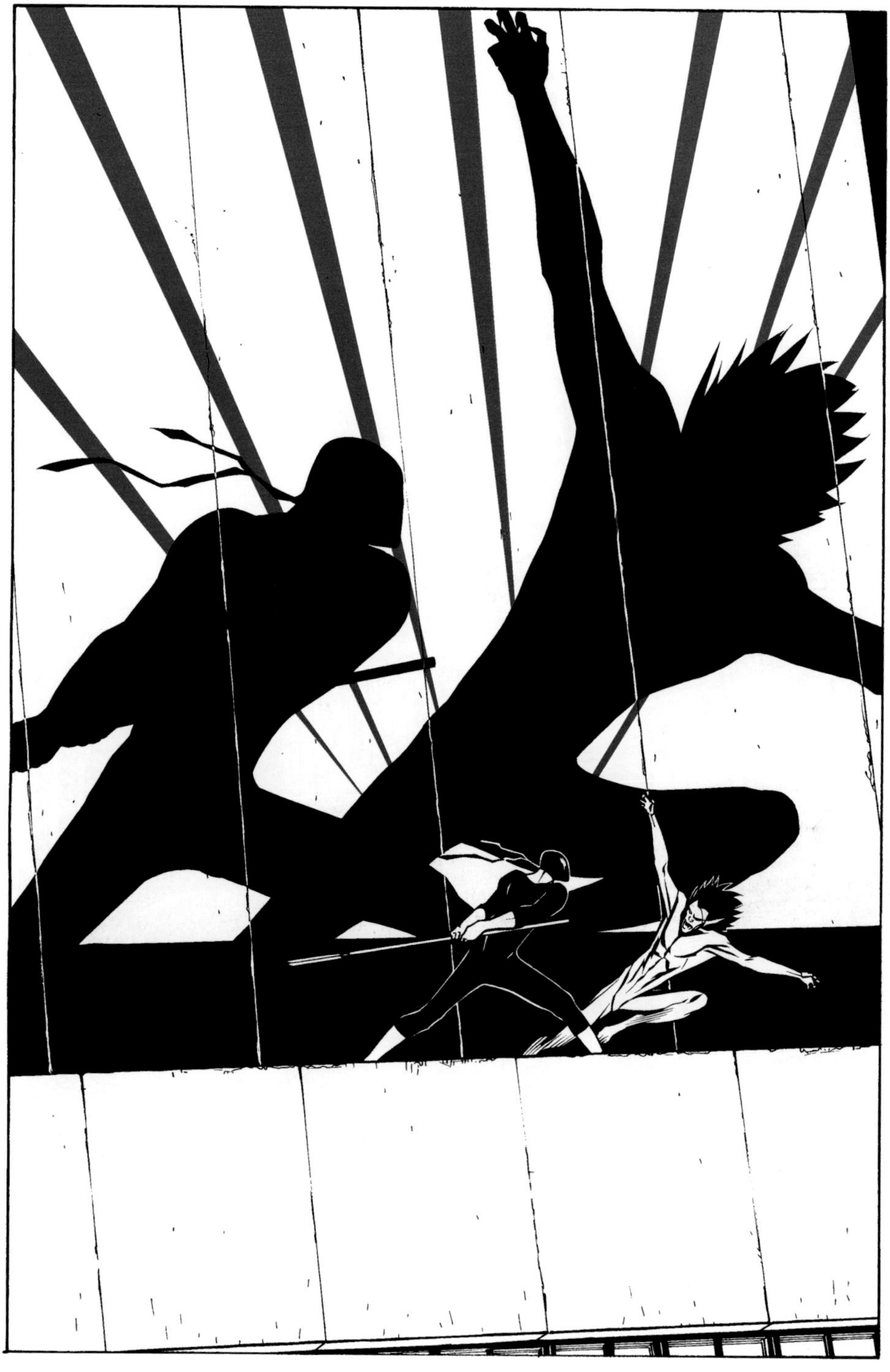

Shadows writhe, the brutal ballet unwinds. Olympian gyrations free the forces of thunder and lightning. Devil eyes and burning snarl, their deafening clash. Raining tragedy, vast bloody ripples staining the ages to come.

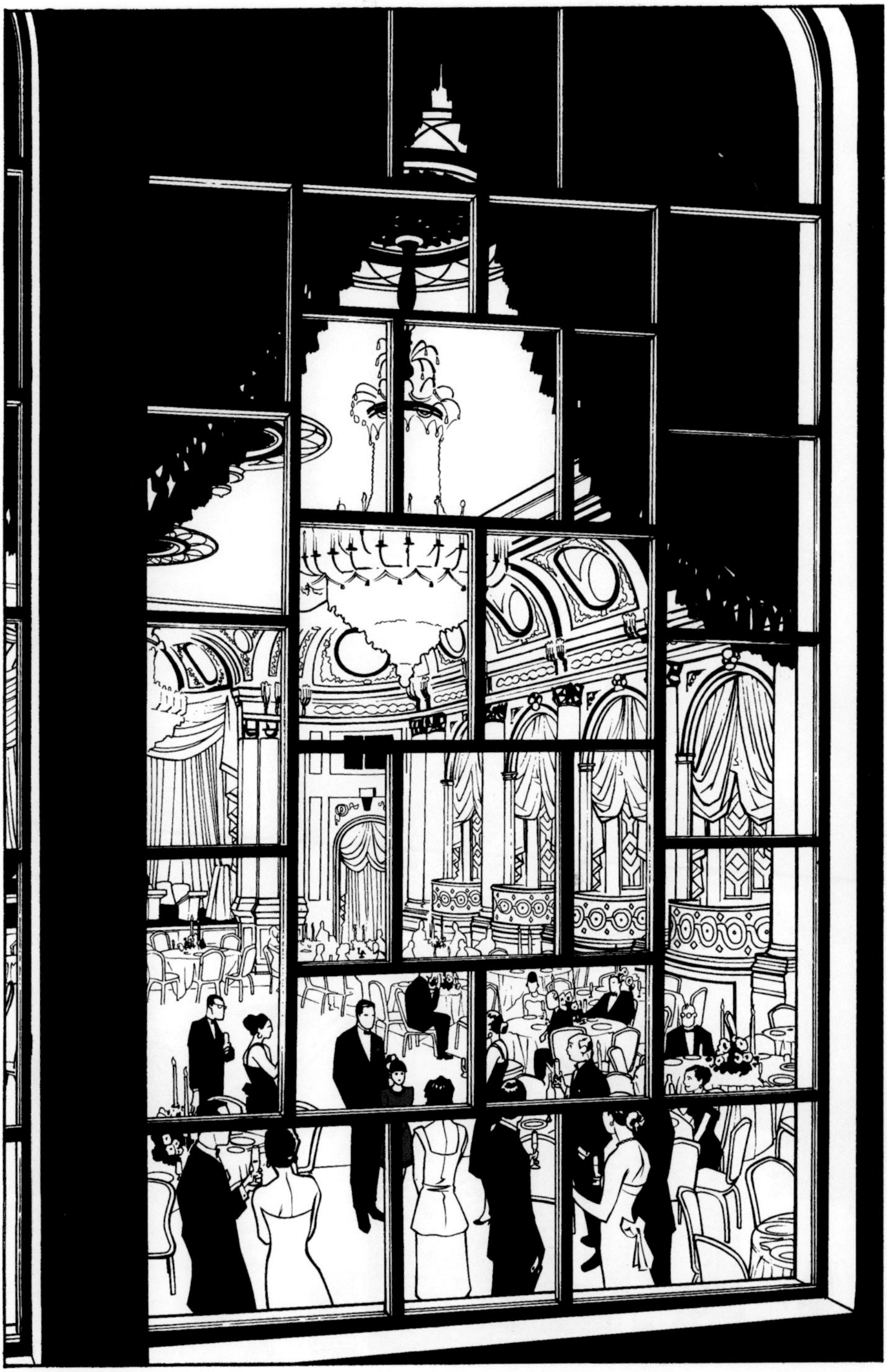

For, in a gilded cage, the hunter tends his precious prize. Parading fashion, preened in peacock pride. She, the fragile chink in his veil of mastery and scorn. Clipped of wing, the forlorn songbird sings beware — oh, beware.

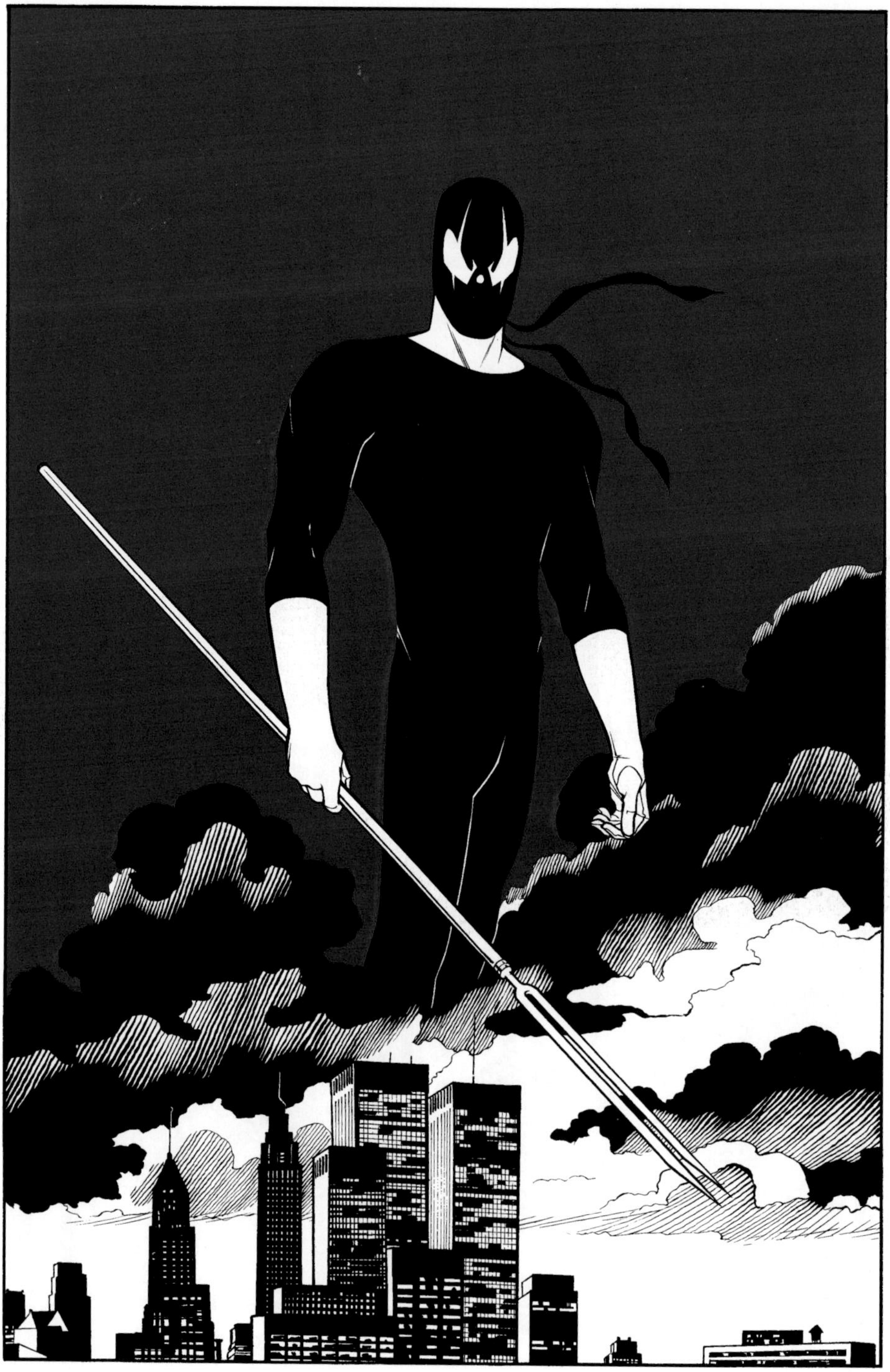

Bestrides this dark colossus, the snapping bonfire of mankind's petty dreams. His, the brightest spark cast high in the firmament of doom. His, the defiant slash 'cross the reeking storm clouds of destiny. His, hell on earth.

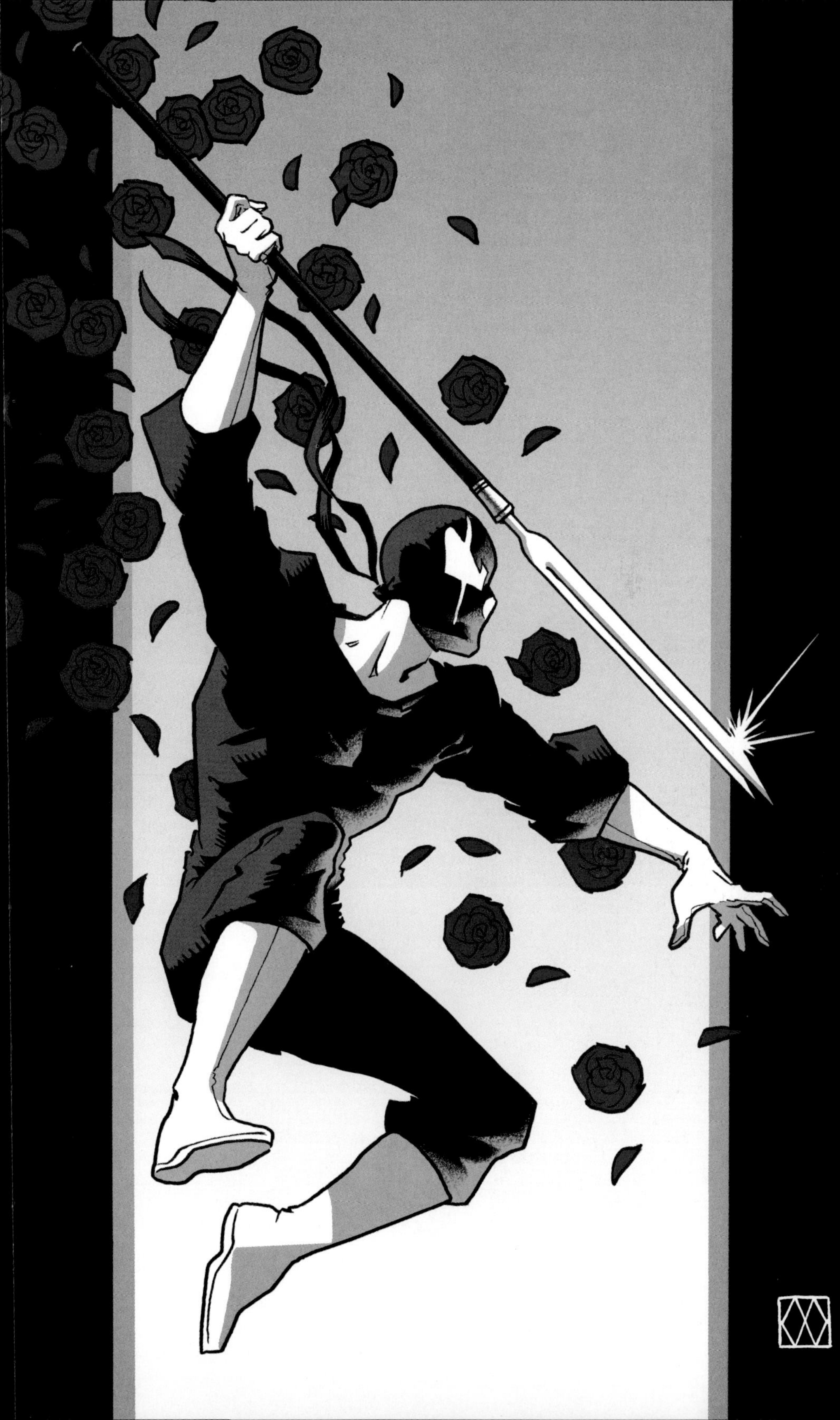

SYMPATHY FROM THE DEVIL
Created, written, & illustrated by MATT WAGNER

Lettering by SEAN KONOT
Color by DAVE STEWART

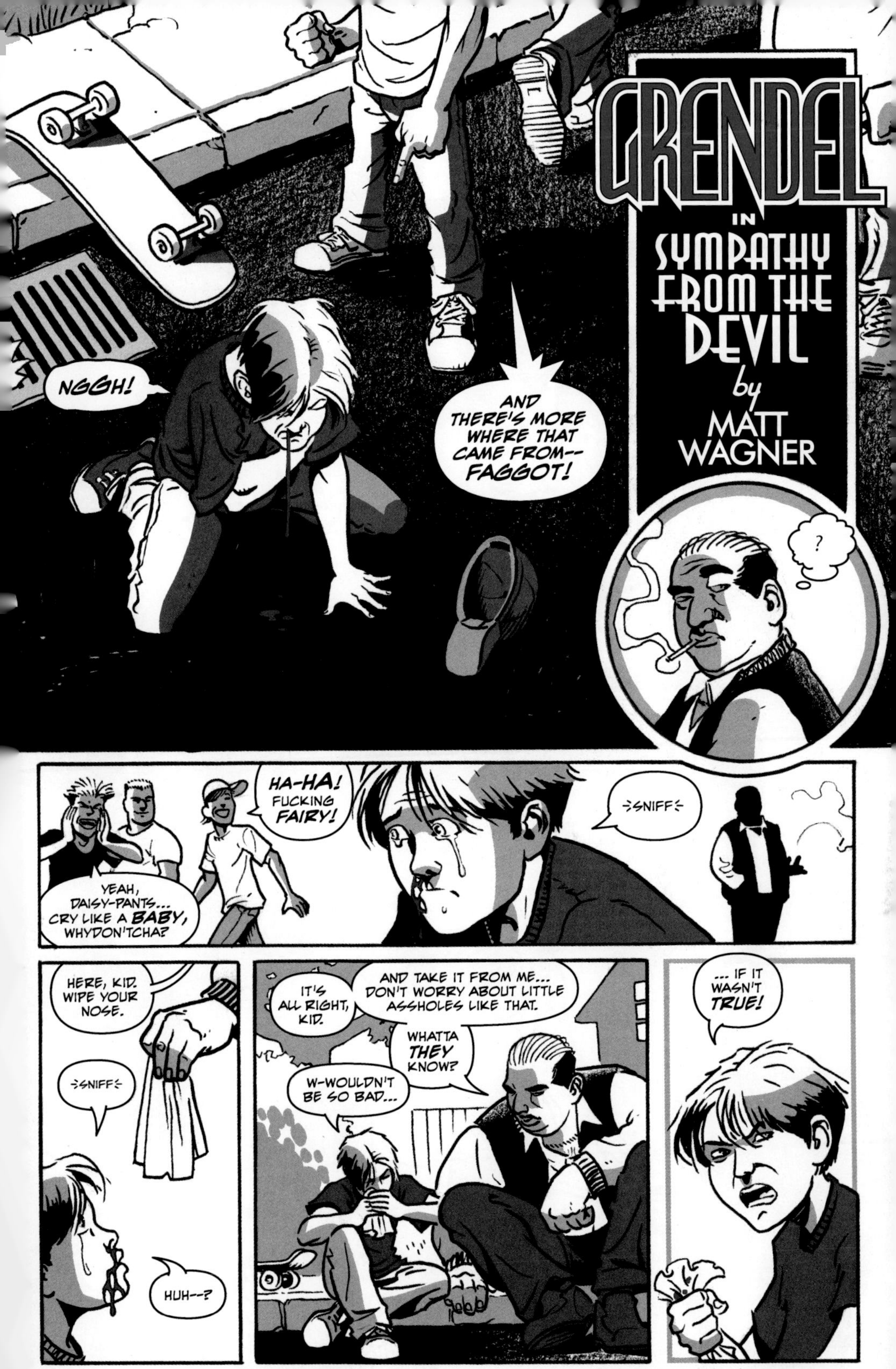
GRENDEL
IN
SYMPATHY FROM THE DEVIL
by
MATT WAGNER
NGGH!
AND THERE'S MORE WHERE THAT CAME FROM-- FAGGOT!
?
HA-HA! FUCKING FAIRY!
YEAH, DAISY-PANTS... CRY LIKE A BABY, WHYDON'TCHA?
SNIFF
HERE, KID. WIPE YOUR NOSE.
SNIFF
HUH--?
IT'S ALL RIGHT, KID.
AND TAKE IT FROM ME... DON'T WORRY ABOUT LITTLE ASSHOLES LIKE THAT.
WHATTA THEY KNOW?
W-WOULDN'T BE SO BAD...
... IF IT WASN'T TRUE!

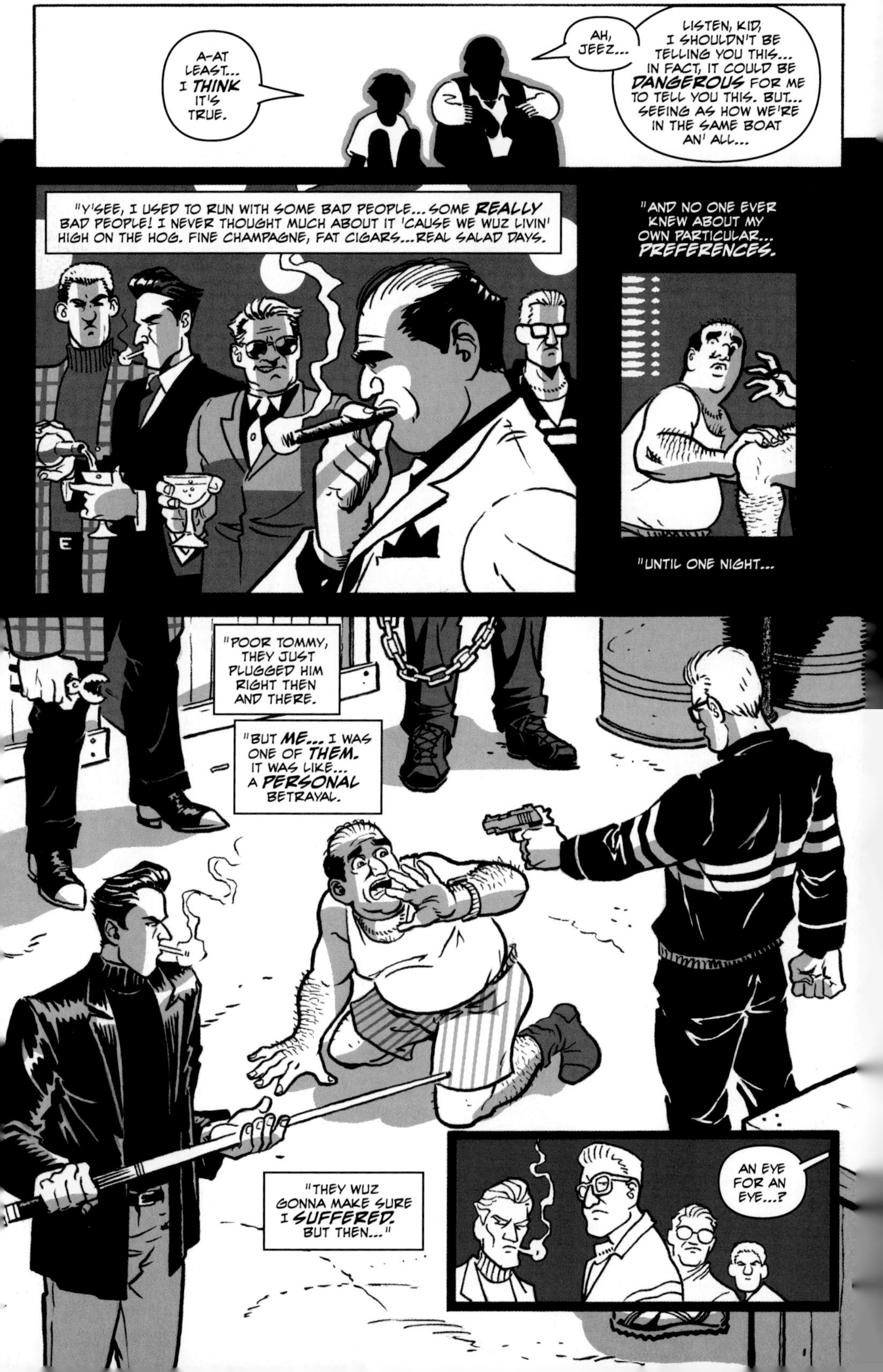
A-AT LEAST... I THINK IT'S TRUE.
AH, JEEZ...
LISTEN, KID, I SHOULDN'T BE TELLING YOU THIS... IN FACT, IT COULD BE DANGEROUS FOR ME TO TELL YOU THIS. BUT... SEEING AS HOW WE'RE IN THE SAME BOAT AN' ALL...
"Y'SEE, I USED TO RUN WITH SOME BAD PEOPLE... SOME REALLY BAD PEOPLE! I NEVER THOUGHT MUCH ABOUT IT 'CAUSE WE WUZ LIVIN' HIGH ON THE HOG. FINE CHAMPAGNE, FAT CIGARS... REAL SALAD DAYS.
"AND NO ONE EVER KNEW ABOUT MY OWN PARTICULAR... PREFERENCES.
"UNTIL ONE NIGHT...
"POOR TOMMY, THEY JUST PLUGGED HIM RIGHT THEN AND THERE.
"BUT ME... I WAS ONE OF THEM. IT WAS LIKE... A PERSONAL BETRAYAL.
"THEY WUZ GONNA MAKE SURE I SUFFERED. BUT THEN..."
AN EYE FOR AN EYE...?

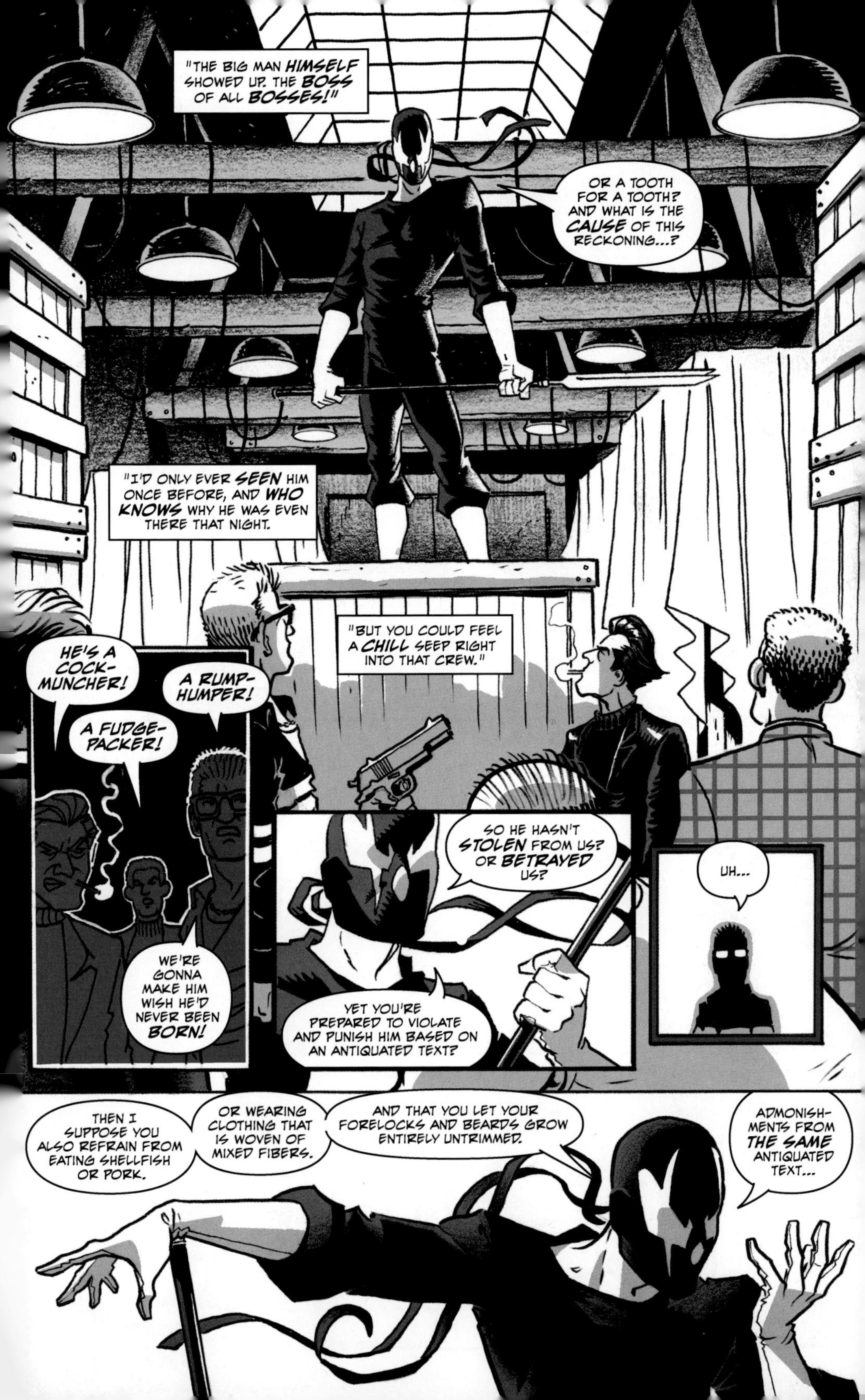
"THE BIG MAN HIMSELF SHOWED UP. THE BOSS OF ALL BOSSES!"
OR A TOOTH FOR A TOOTH? AND WHAT IS THE CAUSE OF THIS RECKONING...?
"I'D ONLY EVER SEEN HIM ONCE BEFORE, AND WHO KNOWS WHY HE WAS EVEN THERE THAT NIGHT.
"BUT YOU COULD FEEL A CHILL SEEP RIGHT INTO THAT CREW."
HE'S A COCK-MUNCHER!
A RUMP-HUMPER!
A FUDGE-PACKER!
WE'RE GONNA MAKE HIM WISH HE'D NEVER BEEN BORN!
SO HE HASN'T STOLEN FROM US? OR BETRAYED US?
UH...
YET YOU'RE PREPARED TO VIOLATE AND PUNISH HIM BASED ON AN ANTIQUATED TEXT?
THEN I SUPPOSE YOU ALSO REFRAIN FROM EATING SHELLFISH OR PORK.
OR WEARING CLOTHING THAT IS WOVEN OF MIXED FIBERS.
AND THAT YOU LET YOUR FORELOCKS AND BEARDS GROW ENTIRELY UNTRIMMED.
ADMONISHMENTS FROM THE SAME ANTIQUATED TEXT...

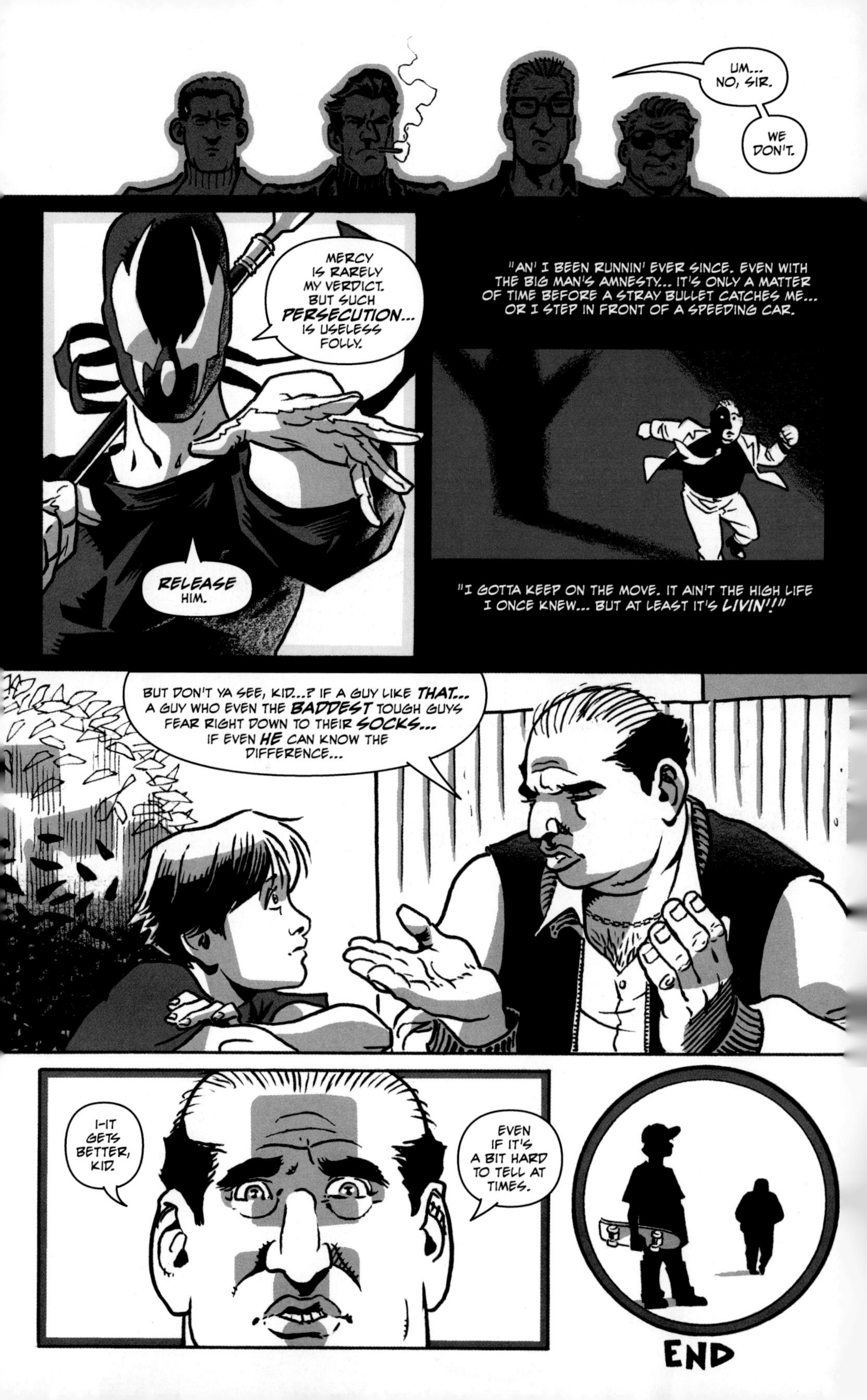
UM... NO, SIR.
WE DON'T.
MERCY IS RARELY MY VERDICT. BUT SUCH PERSECUTION... IS USELESS FOLLY.
RELEASE HIM.
"AN' I BEEN RUNNIN' EVER SINCE. EVEN WITH THE BIG MAN'S AMNESTY... IT'S ONLY A MATTER OF TIME BEFORE A STRAY BULLET CATCHES ME... OR I STEP IN FRONT OF A SPEEDING CAR.
"I GOTTA KEEP ON THE MOVE. IT AIN'T THE HIGH LIFE I ONCE KNEW... BUT AT LEAST IT'S LIVIN'!"
BUT DON'T YA SEE, KID...? IF A GUY LIKE THAT... A GUY WHO EVEN THE BADDEST TOUGH GUYS FEAR RIGHT DOWN TO THEIR SOCKS... IF EVEN HE CAN KNOW THE DIFFERENCE...
I-IT GETS BETTER, KID.
EVEN IF IT'S A BIT HARD TO TELL AT TIMES.
END

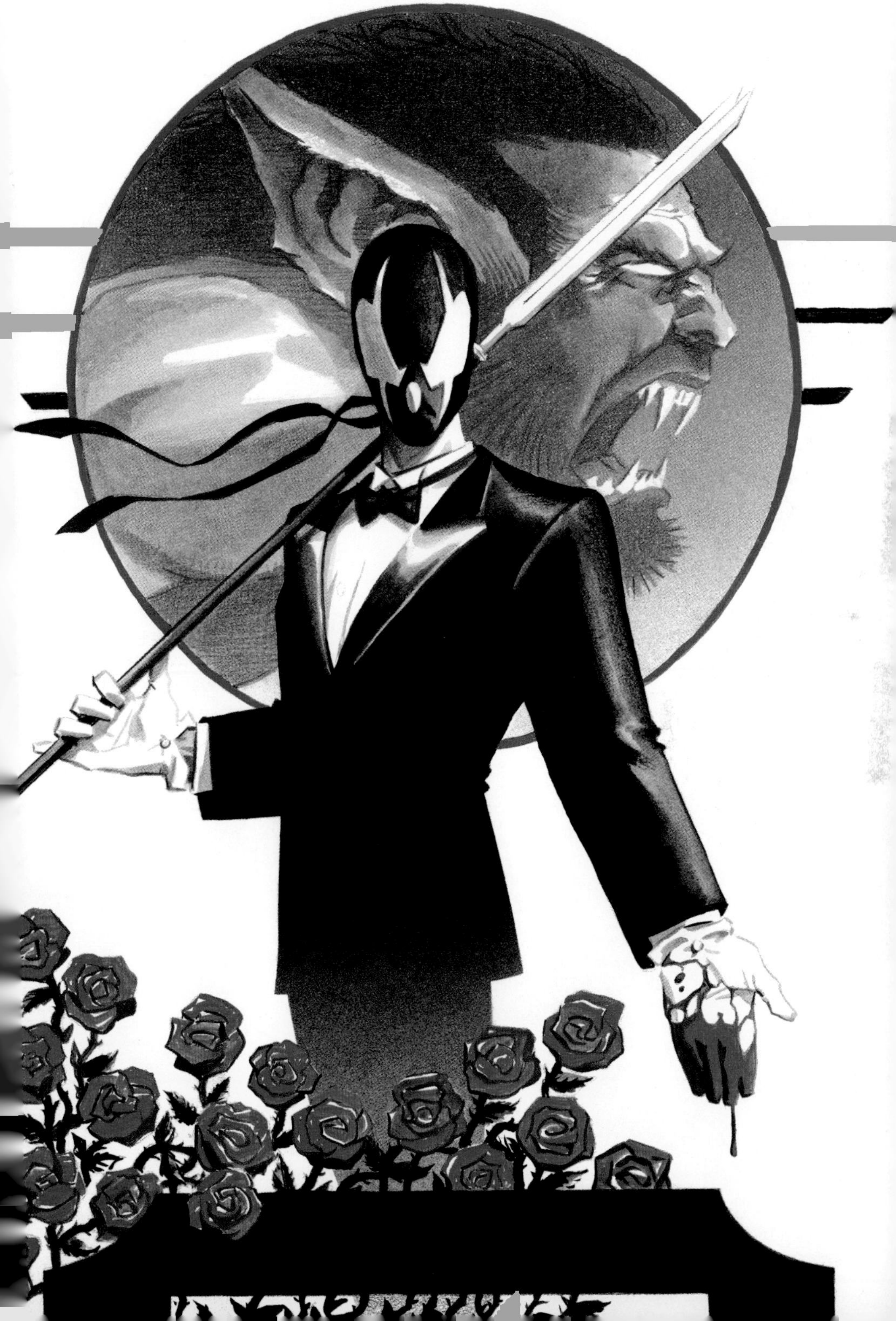

RED, WHITE, & BLACK

All stories written by MATT WAGNER

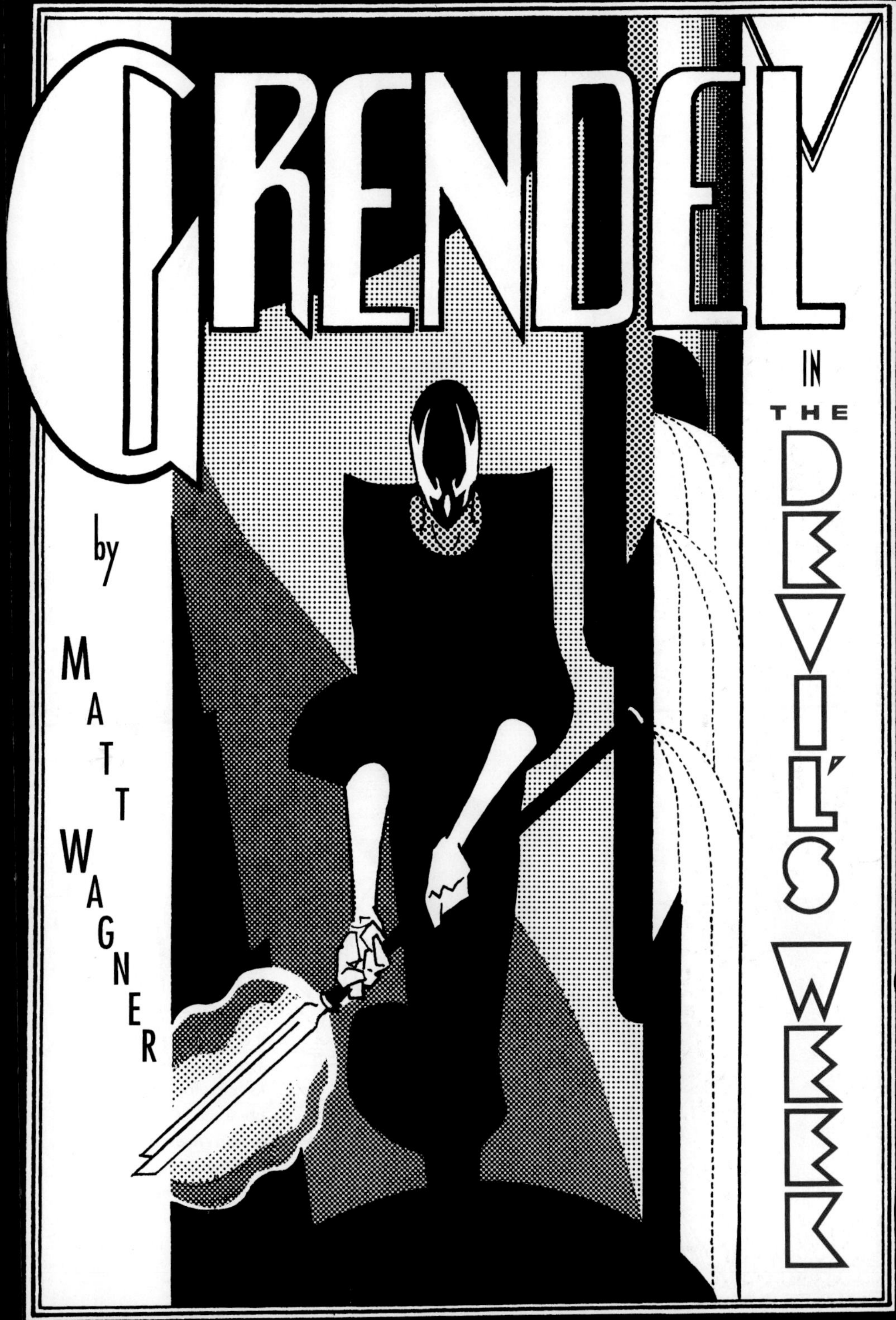
GRENDEL
by MATT WAGNER
IN THE DEVIL'S WEEK

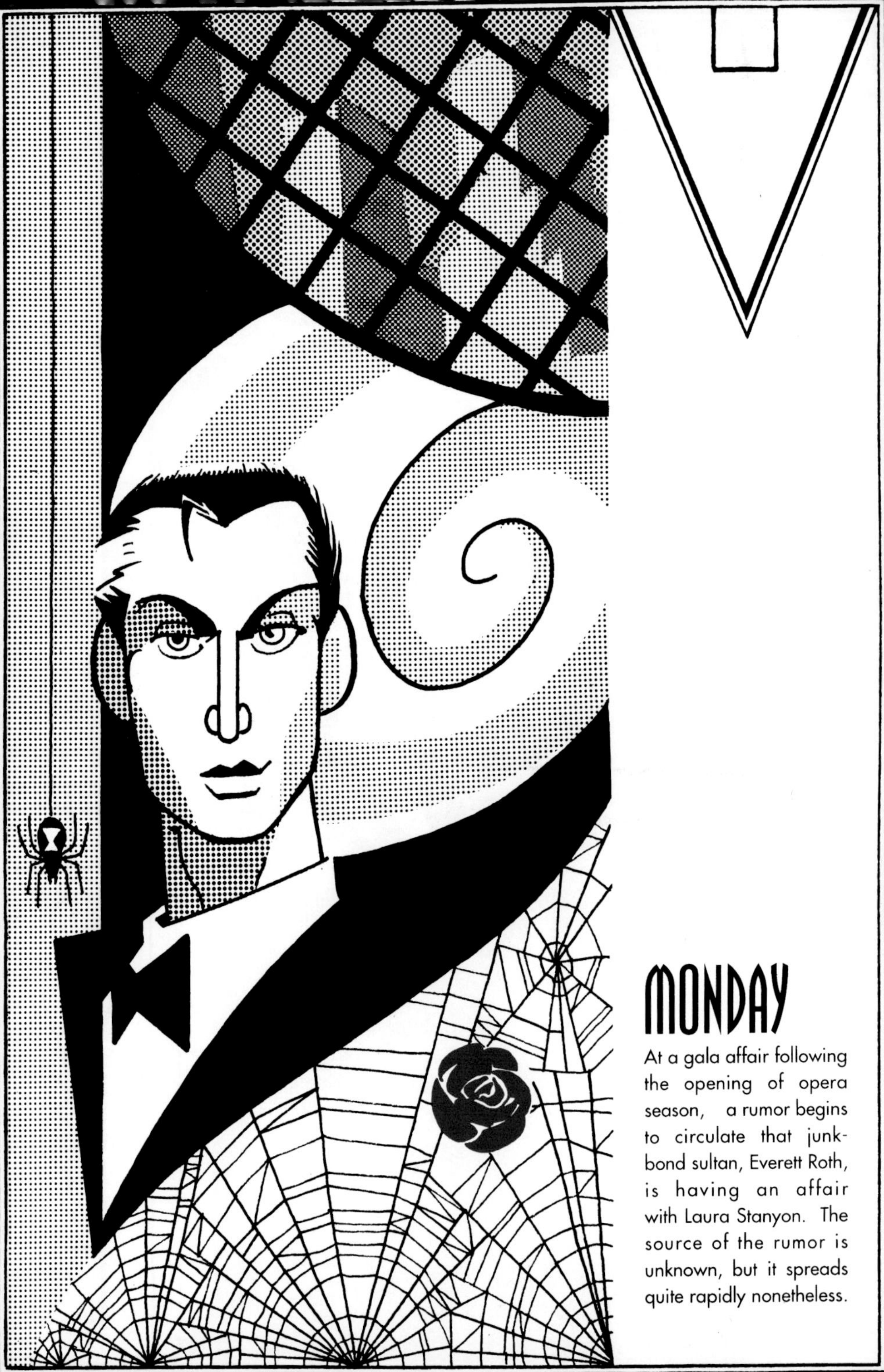

MONDAY

At a gala affair following the opening of opera season, a rumor begins to circulate that junk-bond sultan, Everett Roth, is having an affair with Laura Stanyon. The source of the rumor is unknown, but it spreads quite rapidly nonetheless.

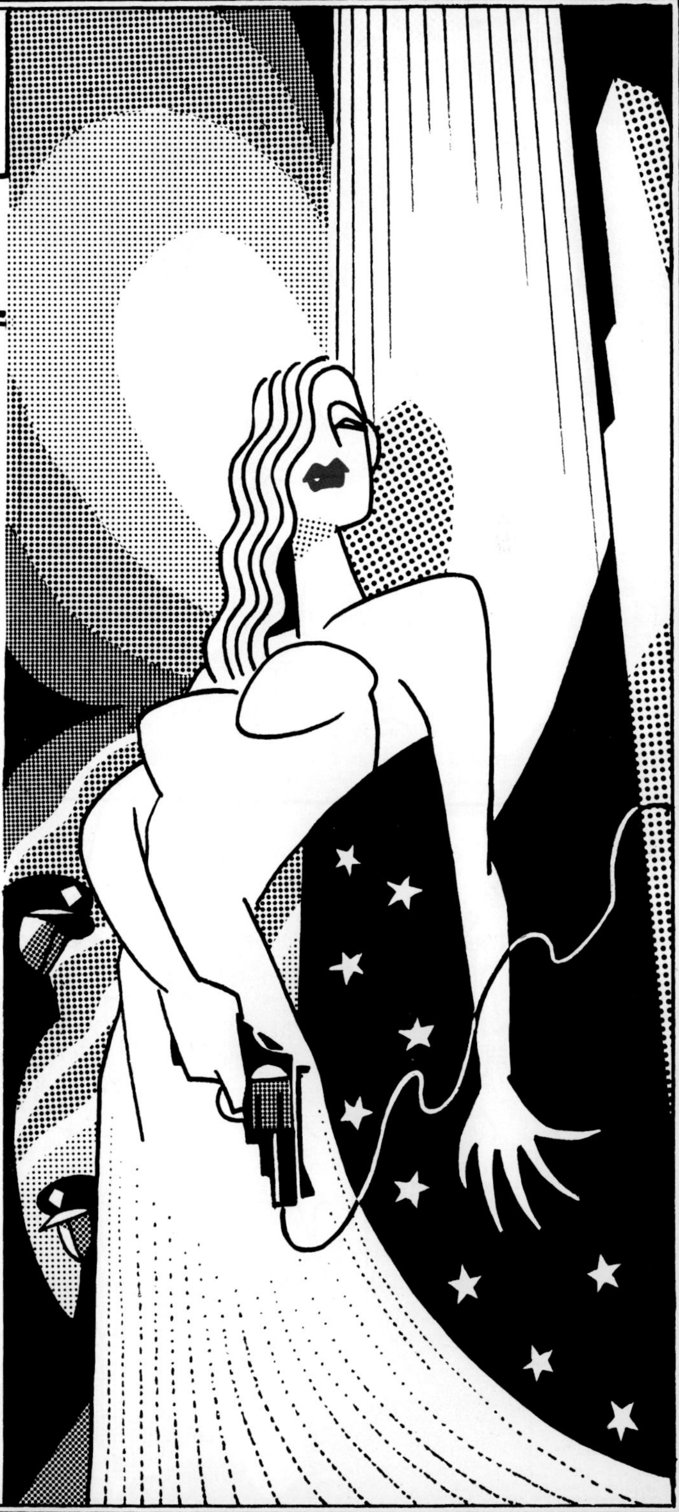

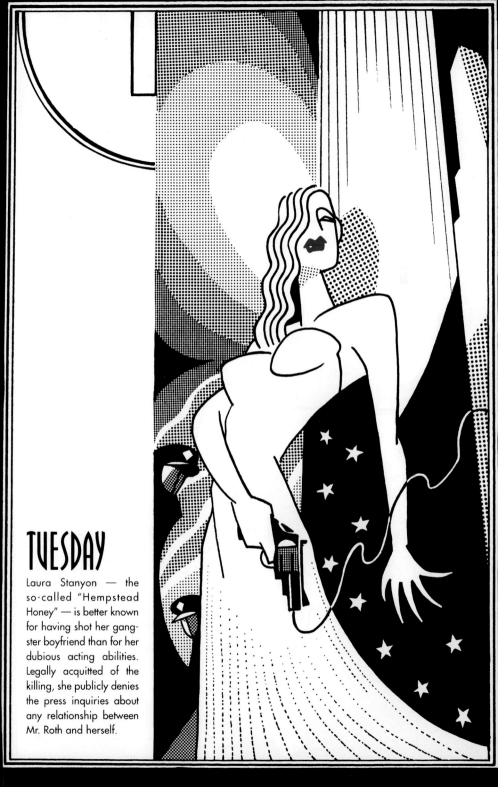

TUESDAY

Laura Stanyon — the so-called "Hempstead Honey" — is better known for having shot her gangster boyfriend than for her dubious acting abilities. Legally acquitted of the killing, she publicly denies the press inquiries about any relationship between Mr. Roth and herself.

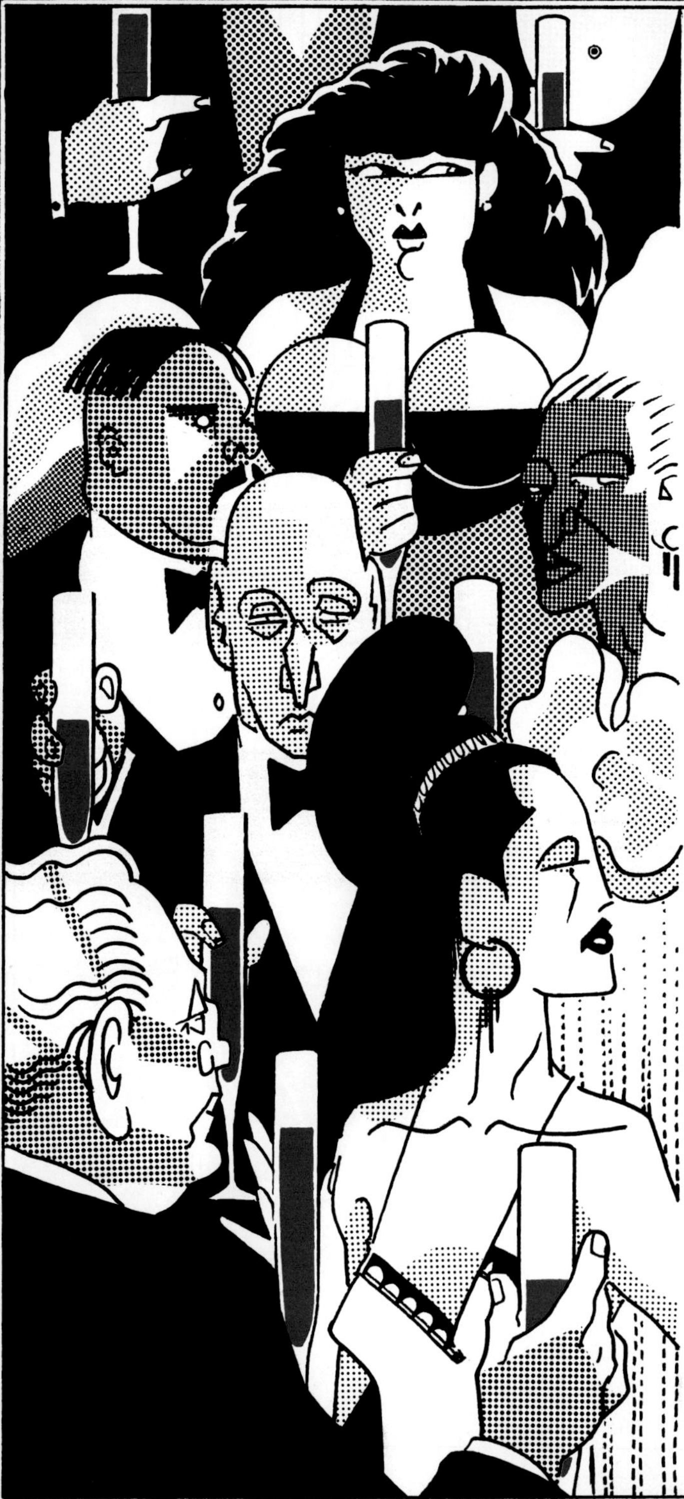

WEDNESDAY

At a prestigious stockholders' party, Everett Roth and his wife engage in a furiously heated disagreement. An anonymous source has mailed her photos of Roth and Stanyon in a tryst. His claims that the photos are faked become lost amidst Lucinda Roth's shrieking.

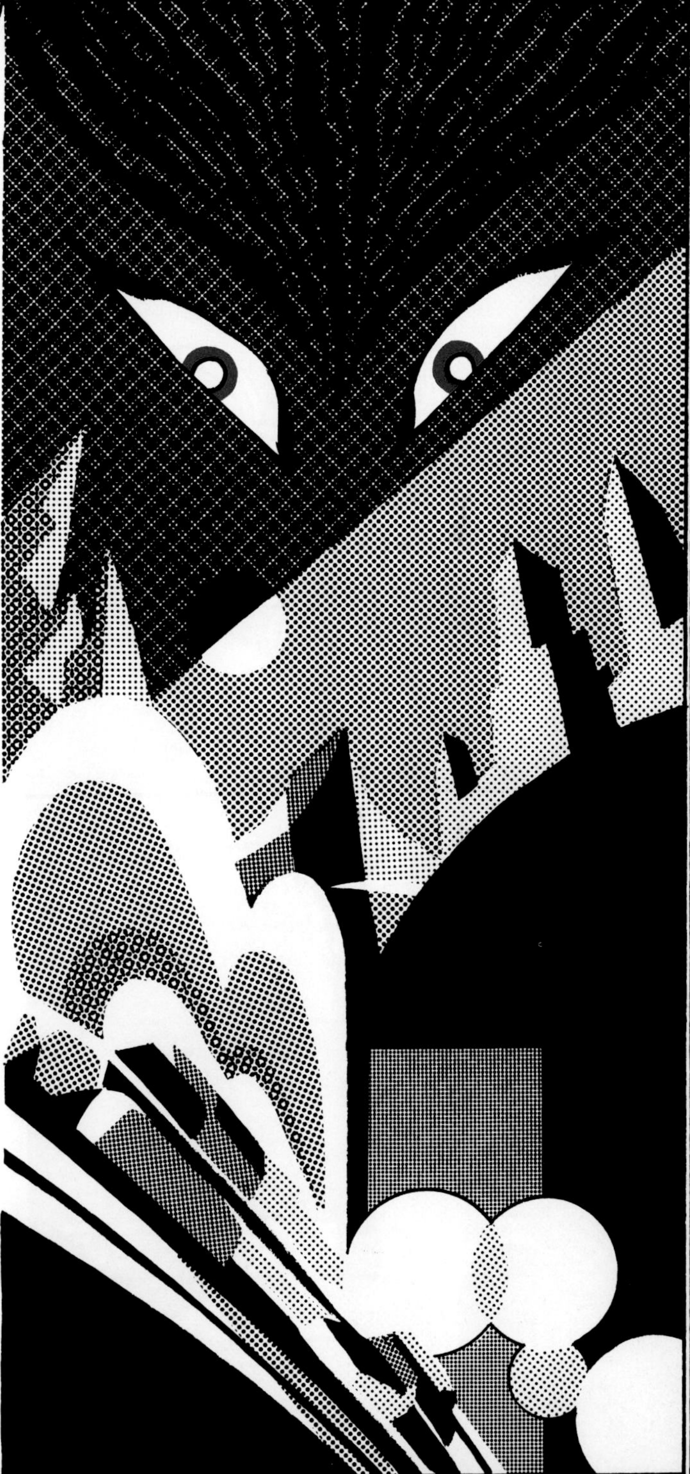

THURSDAY

Argent the Wolf receives an anonymous tip that sets police on the trail of a major cocaine delivery. The resultant high-speed chase leads officers some forty miles out of town. A shoot-out leaves two of the suspects dead. The wounded survivor claims to work for Roth.

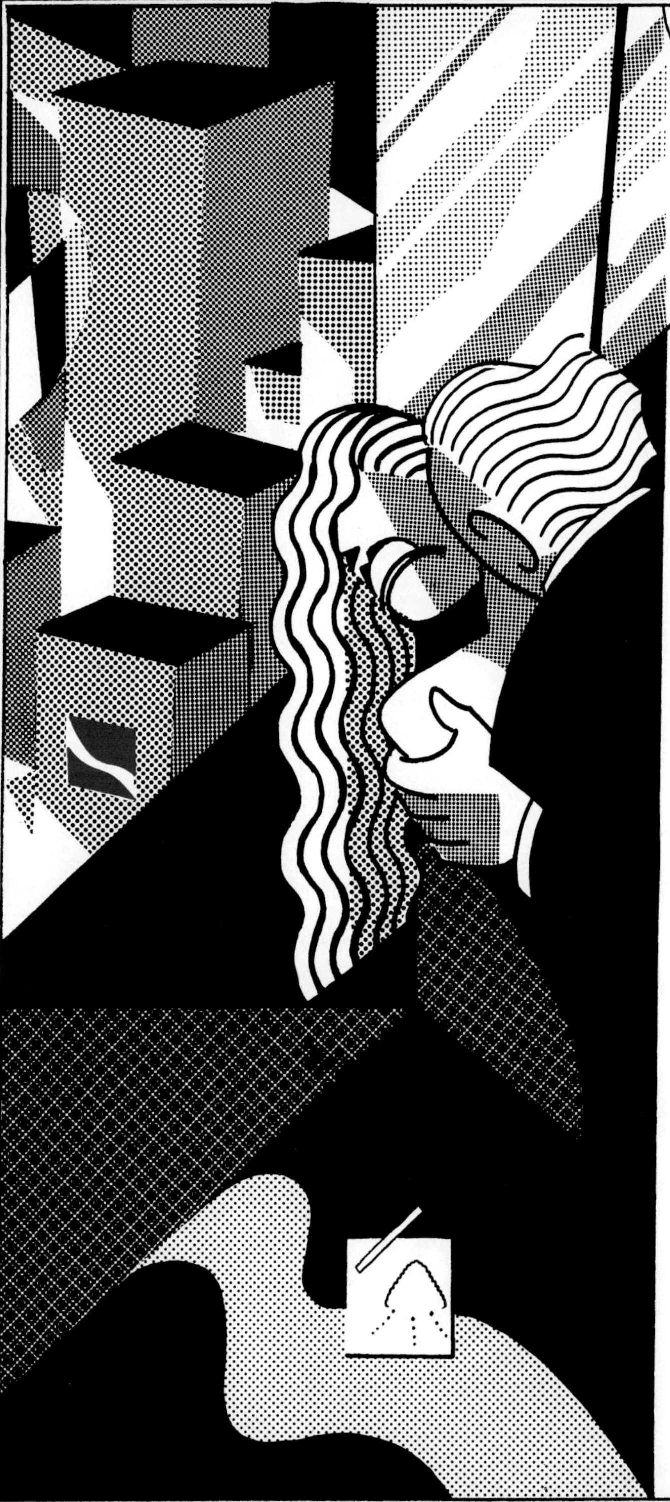

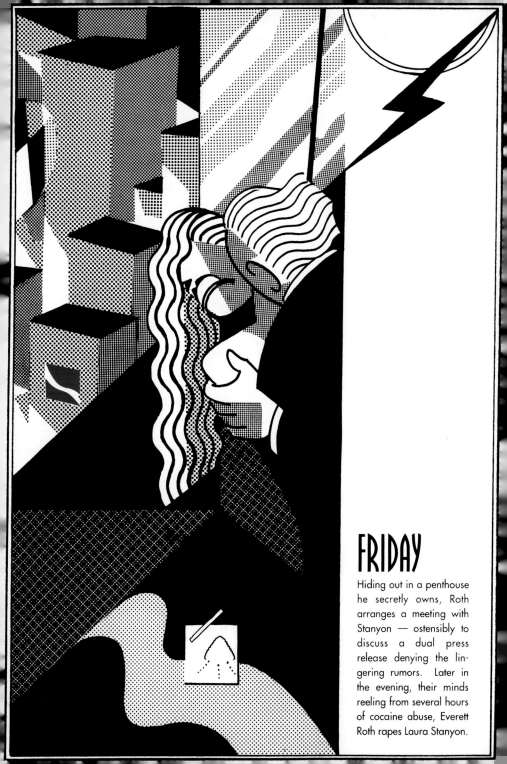

FRIDAY

Hiding out in a penthouse he secretly owns, Roth arranges a meeting with Stanyon — ostensibly to discuss a dual press release denying the lingering rumors. Later in the evening, their minds reeling from several hours of cocaine abuse, Everett Roth rapes Laura Stanyon.

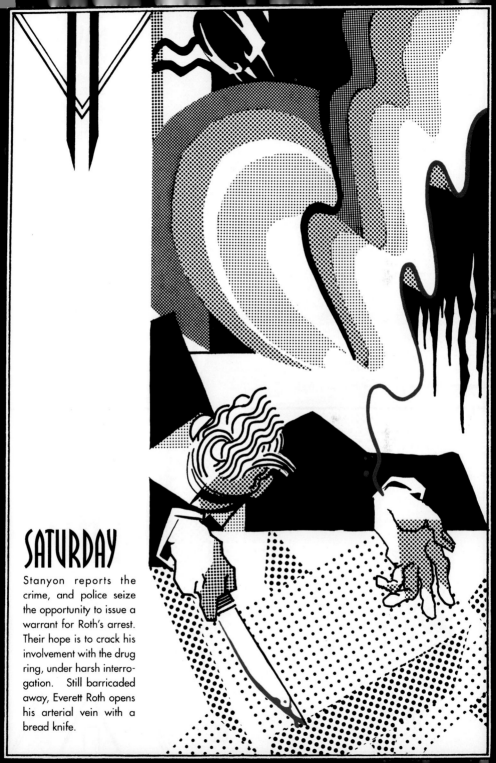

SATURDAY

Stanyon reports the crime, and police seize the opportunity to issue a warrant for Roth's arrest. Their hope is to crack his involvement with the drug ring, under harsh interrogation. Still barricaded away, Everett Roth opens his arterial vein with a bread knife.

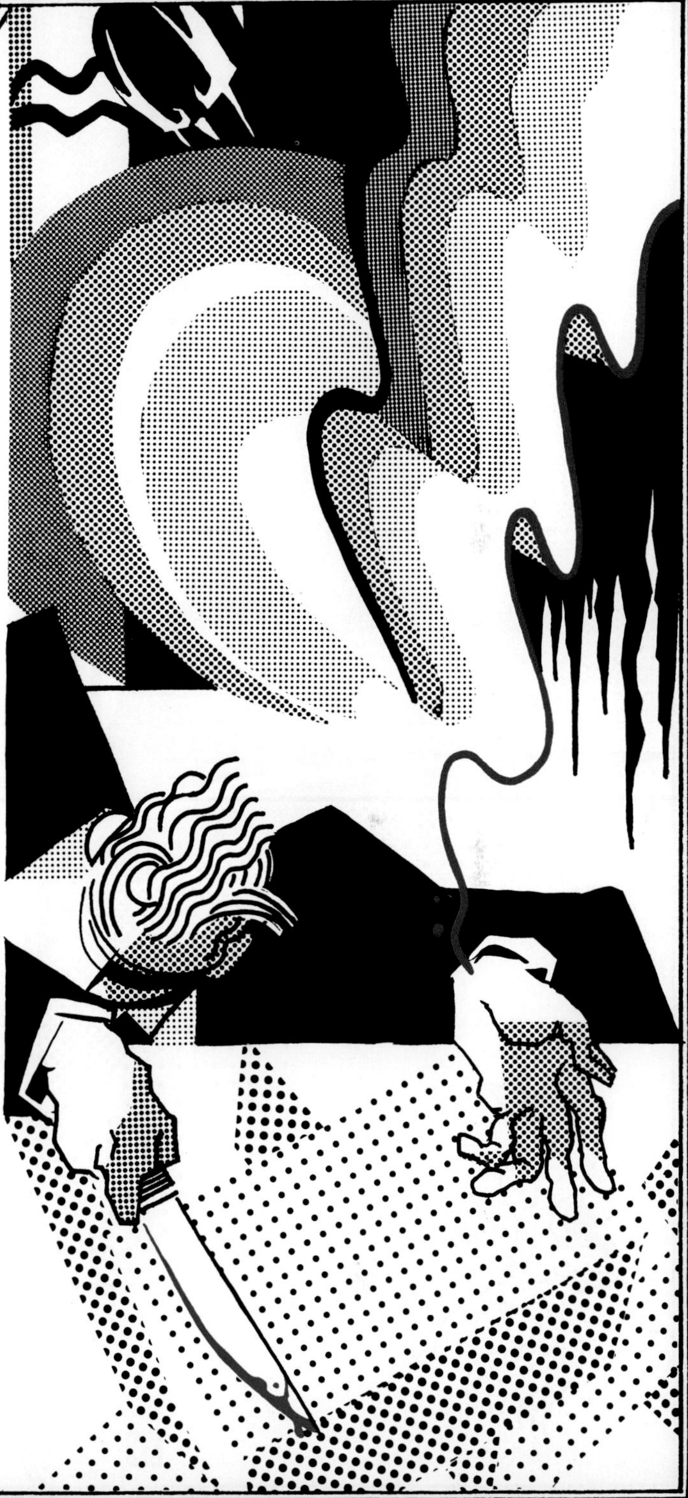

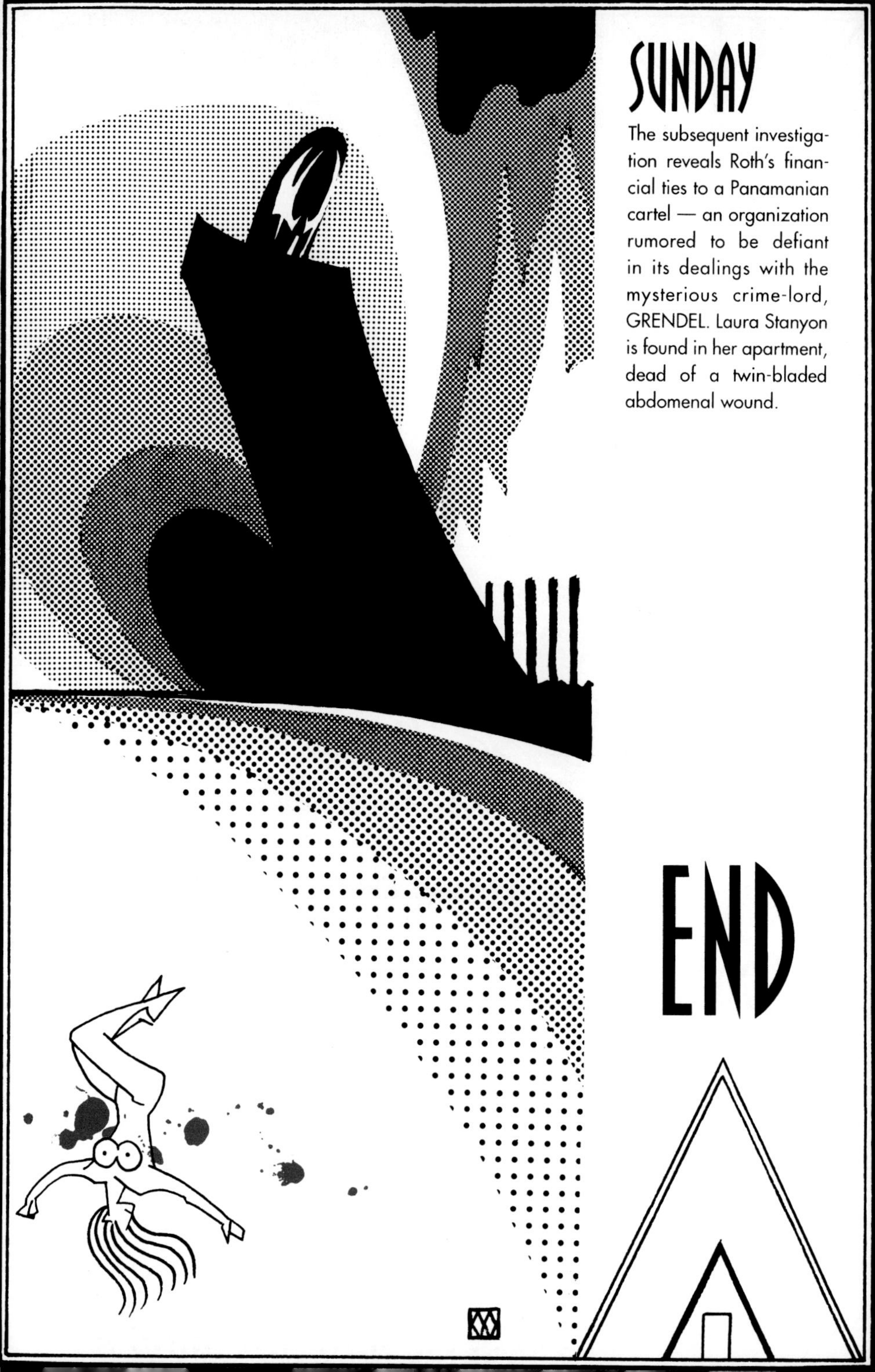
SUNDAY
The subsequent investigation reveals Roth's financial ties to a Panamanian cartel — an organization rumored to be defiant in its dealings with the mysterious crime-lord, GRENDEL. Laura Stanyon is found in her apartment, dead of a twin-bladed abdomenal wound.
END

THE NASTY LI'L DEVIL

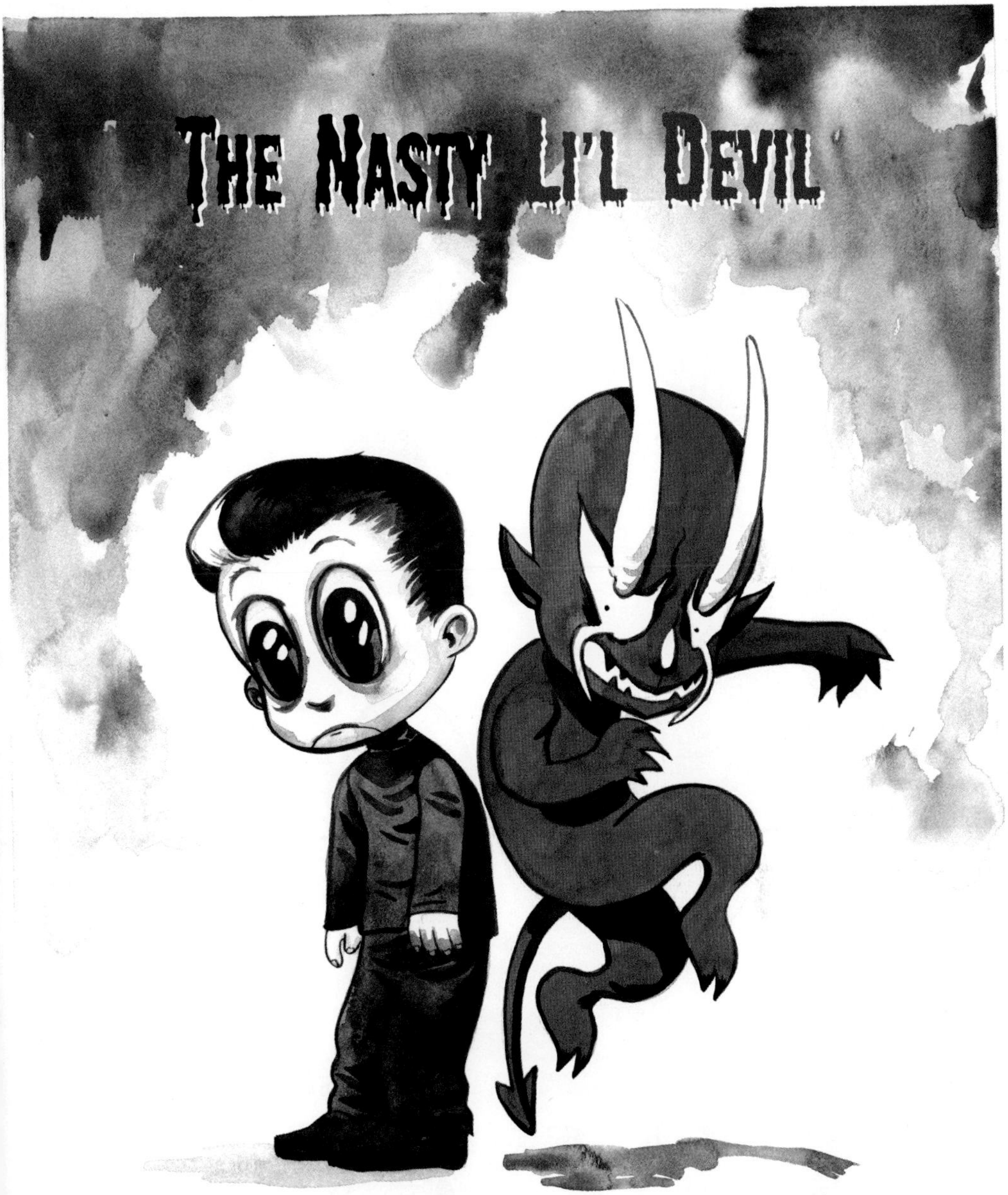

There was once a Li'l Devil who came up out of HELL,

Whereupon he found a suitable host:

One who had a bright and beautiful capacity

but a soul that was quite empty and vast.

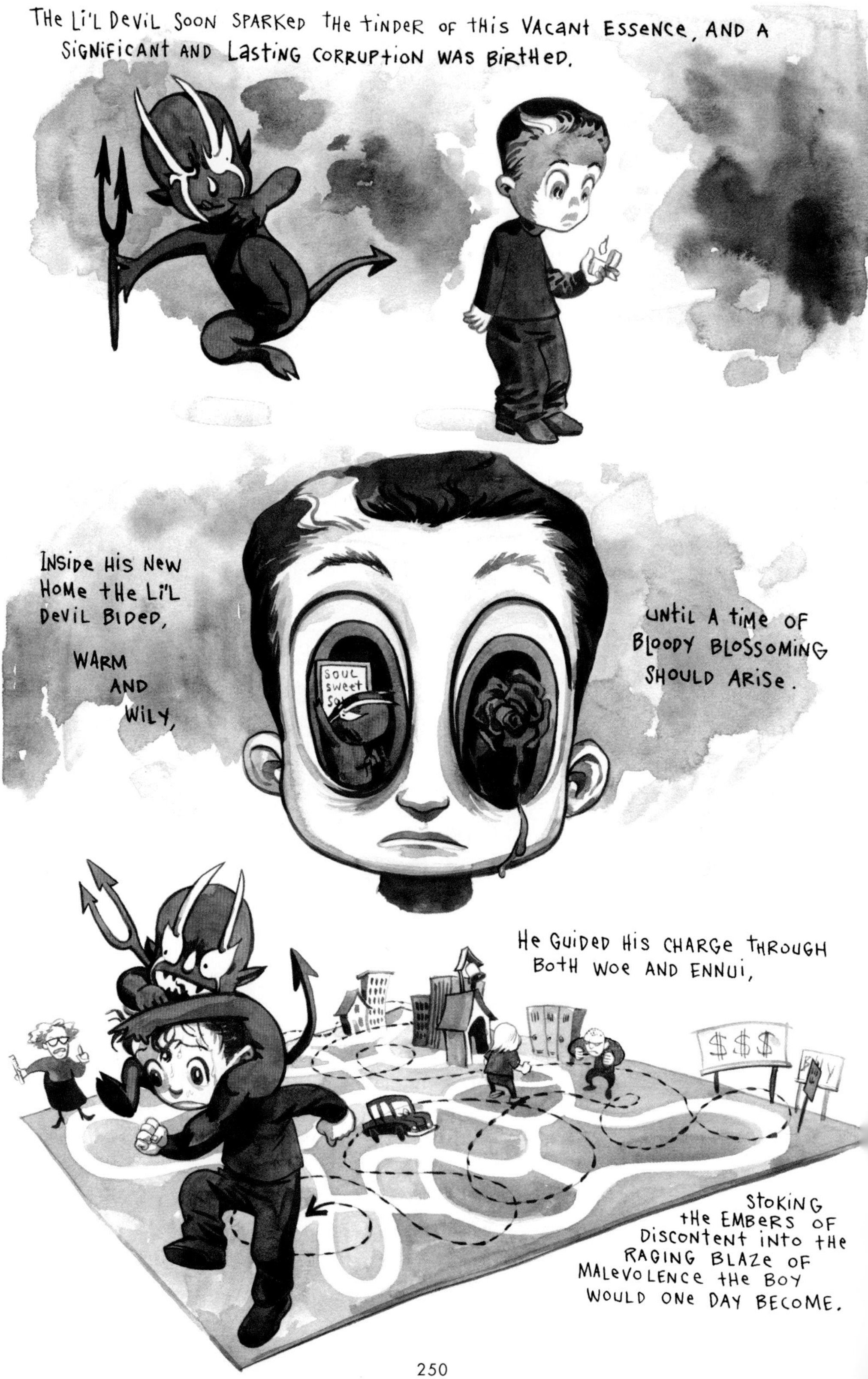
THE LI'L DEVIL SOON SPARKED THE TINDER OF THIS VACANT ESSENCE, AND A SIGNIFICANT AND LASTING CORRUPTION WAS BIRTHED.
INSIDE HIS NEW HOME THE LI'L DEVIL BIDED,
WARM AND WILY,
UNTIL A TIME OF BLOODY BLOSSOMING SHOULD ARISE.
HE GUIDED HIS CHARGE THROUGH BOTH WOE AND ENNUI,
$$$
STOKING THE EMBERS OF DISCONTENT INTO THE RAGING BLAZE OF MALEVOLENCE THE BOY WOULD ONE DAY BECOME.

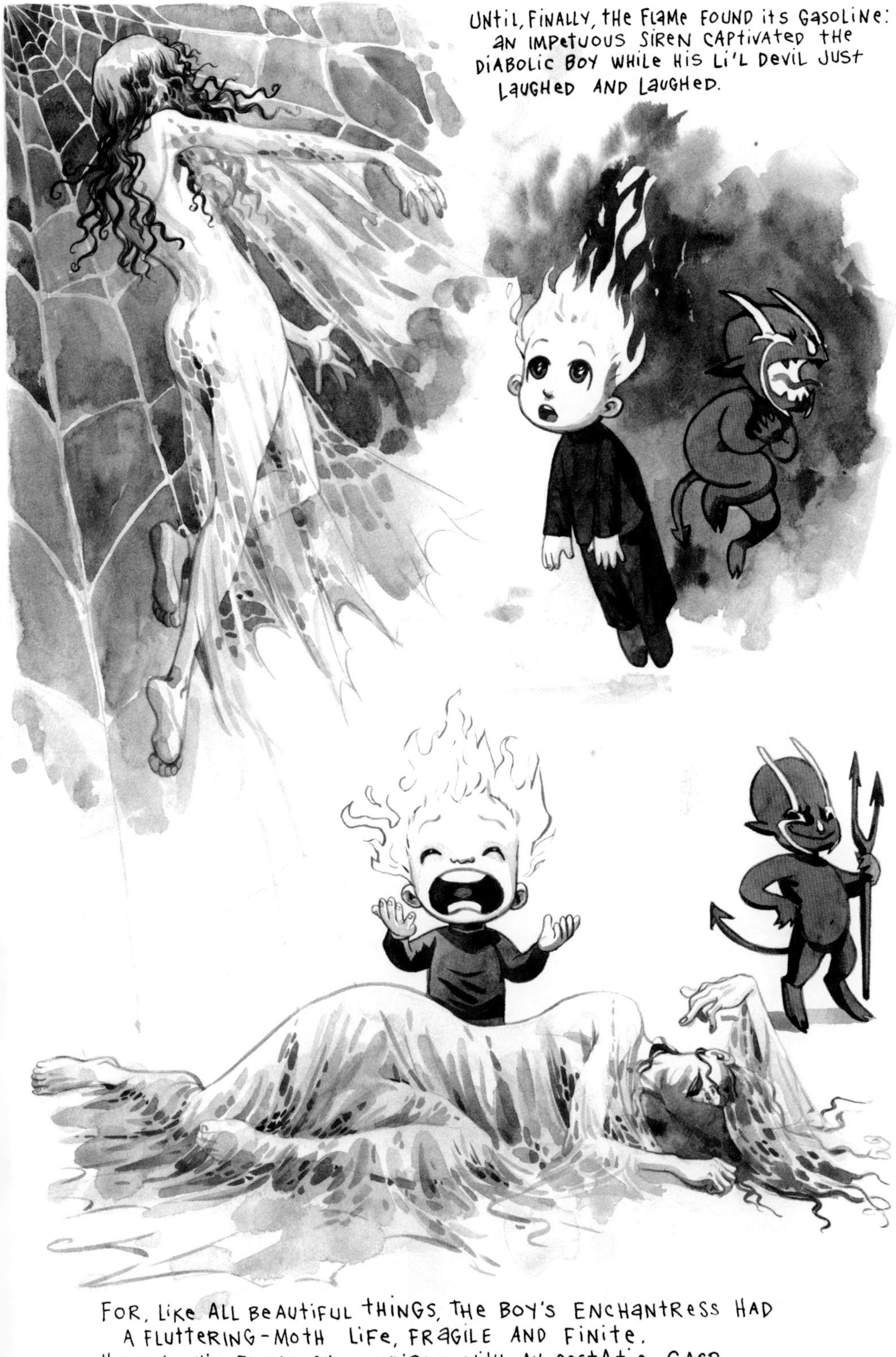
UNTIL, FINALLY, THE FLAME FOUND ITS GASOLINE: AN IMPETUOUS SIREN CAPTIVATED THE DIABOLIC BOY WHILE HIS LI'L DEVIL JUST LAUGHED AND LAUGHED.
FOR, LIKE ALL BEAUTIFUL THINGS, THE BOY'S ENCHANTRESS HAD A FLUTTERING-MOTH LIFE, FRAGILE AND FINITE. HELD TO HIS FLAME, SHE EXPIRED WITH AN ECSTATIC GASP.

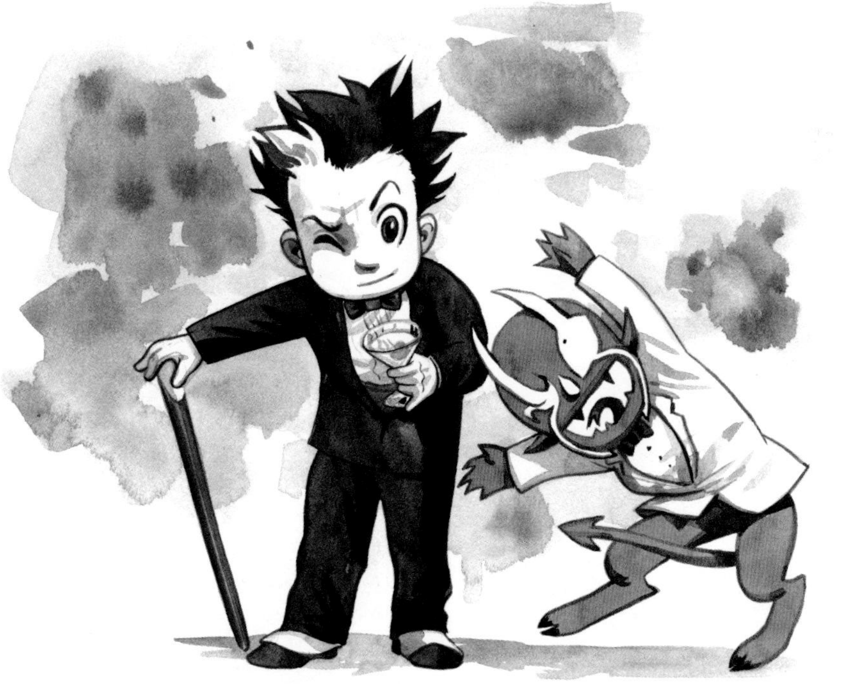

Yet the Hellish Surge of His Mettle, once loosed, was unquenchable.
The boy became a man, deadly and undaunted.
The Grief of His Loss had freed Him of all care and concern.

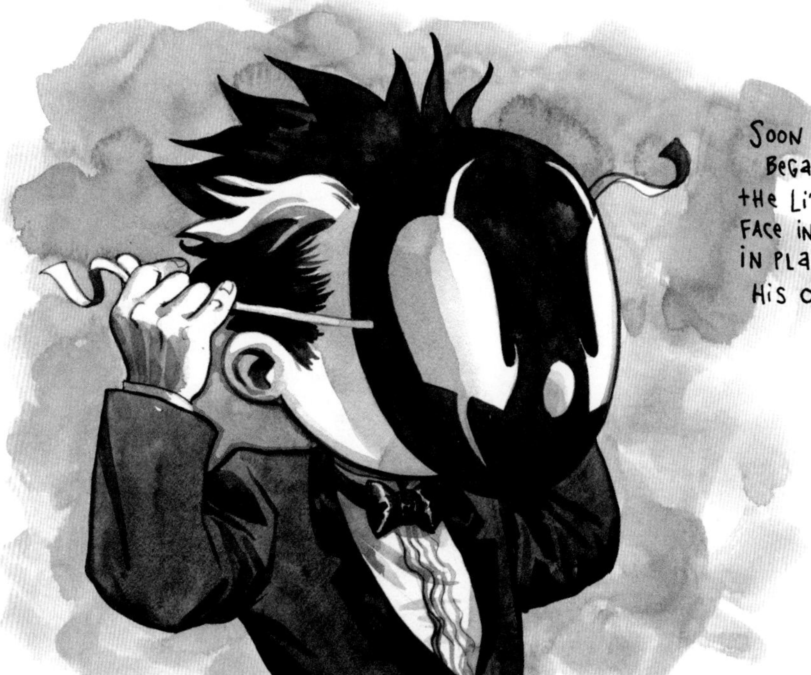

Soon He began to See the Li'l Devil's Face in the Mirror, in Place of His own.

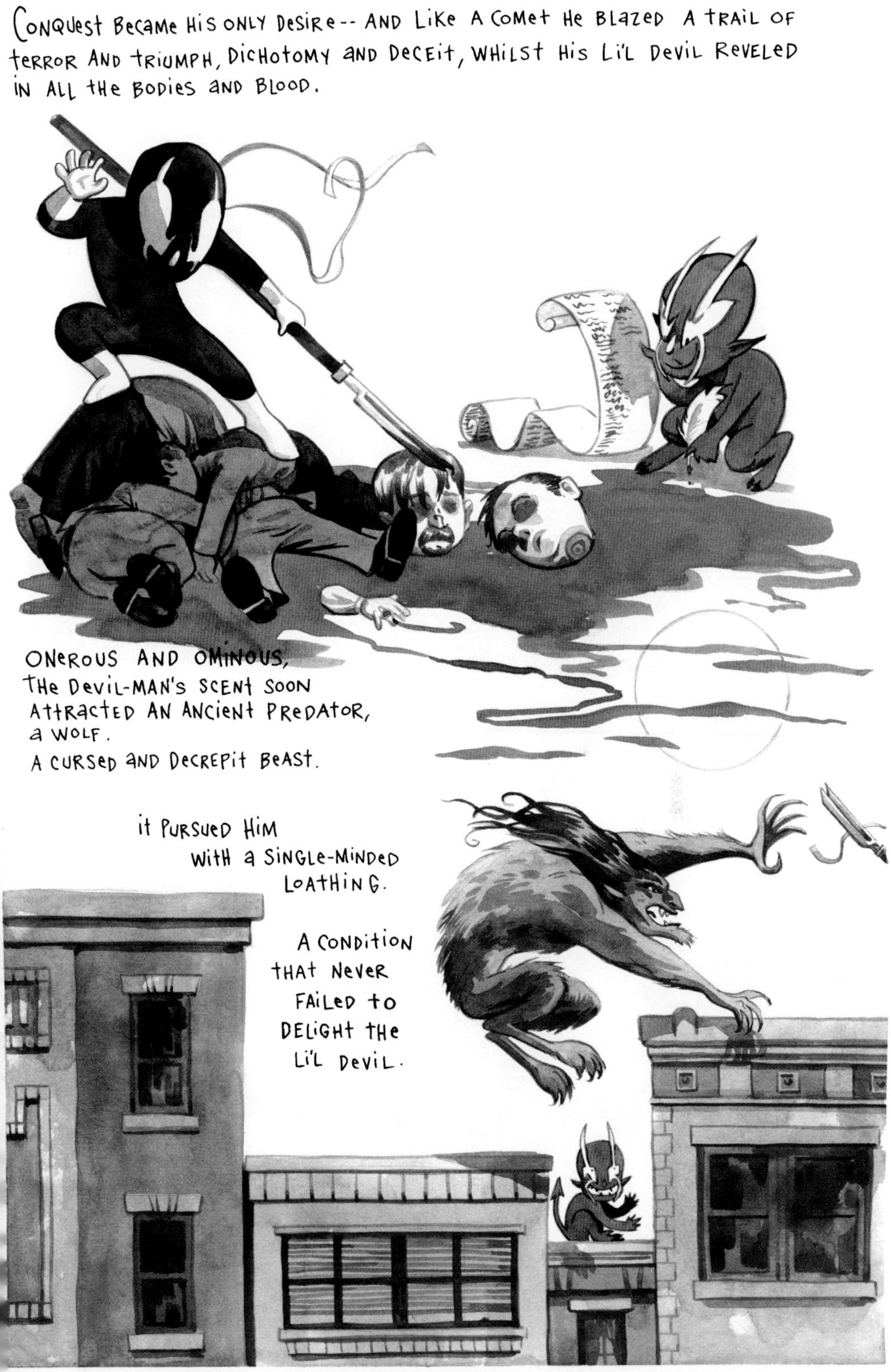
CONQUEST BECAME HIS ONLY DESIRE-- AND LIKE A COMET HE BLAZED A TRAIL OF TERROR AND TRIUMPH, DICHOTOMY AND DECEIT, WHILST HIS LI'L DEVIL REVELED IN ALL THE BODIES AND BLOOD.
ONEROUS AND OMINOUS, THE DEVIL-MAN'S SCENT SOON ATTRACTED AN ANCIENT PREDATOR, A WOLF.
A CURSED AND DECREPIT BEAST.
IT PURSUED HIM WITH A SINGLE-MINDED LOATHING.
A CONDITION THAT NEVER FAILED TO DELIGHT THE LI'L DEVIL.

AND SO THEY THRASHED AND FLAILED, THRASHED AND FLAILED.
NEITHER SEEMING EVER TO GAIN GROUND. NEITHER SEEMING EVER TO WEAKEN.

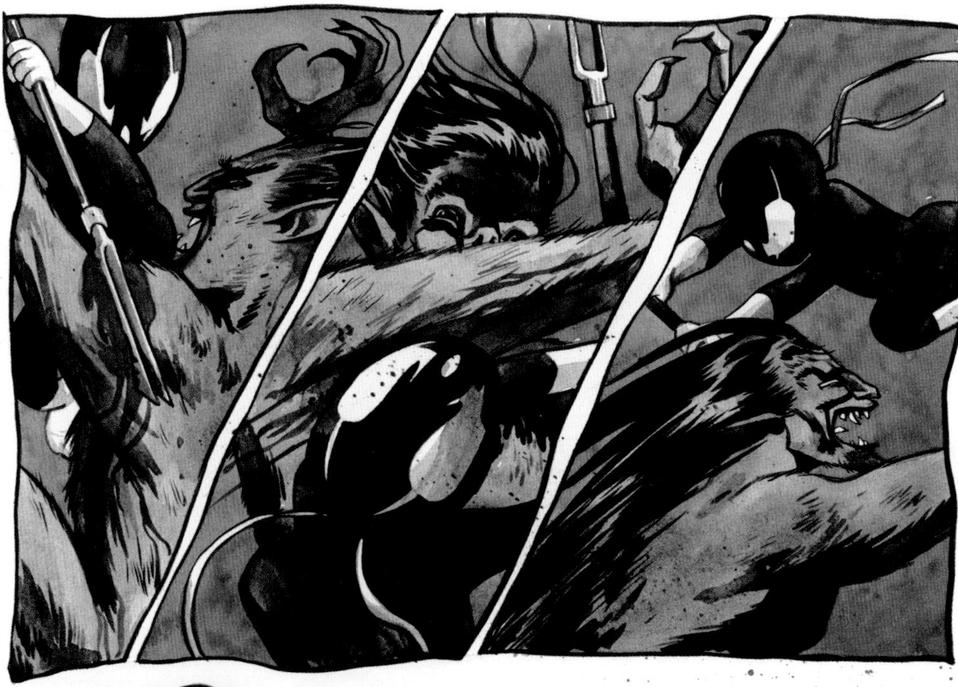

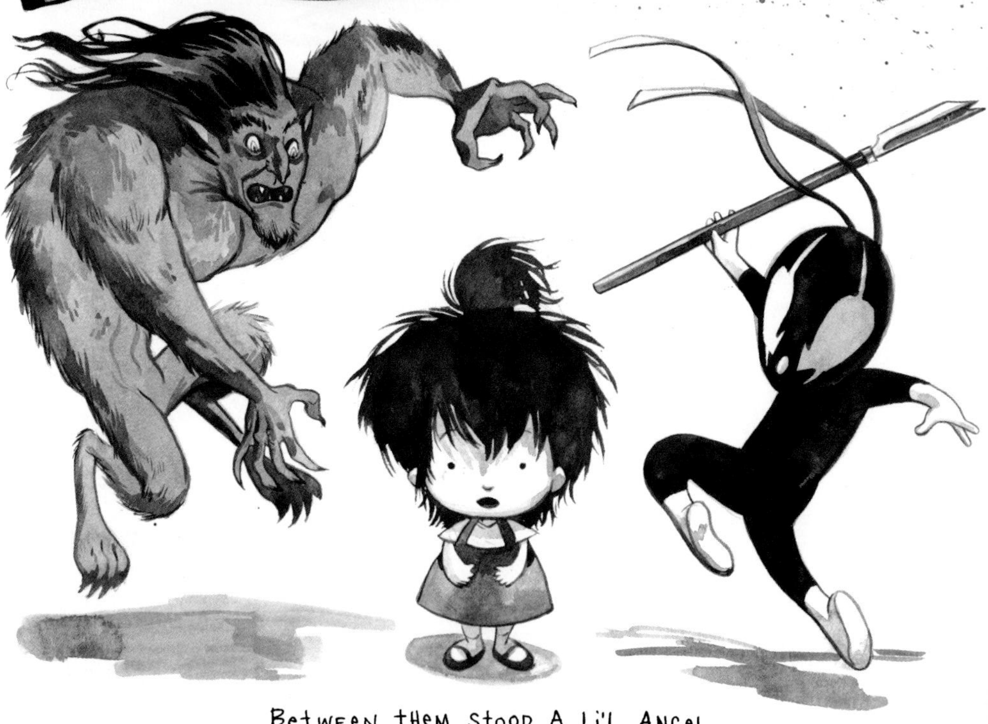

BETWEEN THEM STOOD A LI'L ANGEL,
NAIVE AND PURE.

DESTINY'S LAMB, THE LI'L ANGEL, WAS BELOVED OF BOTH DEVIL-MAN AND WOLF. UNFORTUNATELY, THE AFFECTIONS OF EVIL ARE OF THE MOST INFECTIOUS, INSIDIOUS KIND.

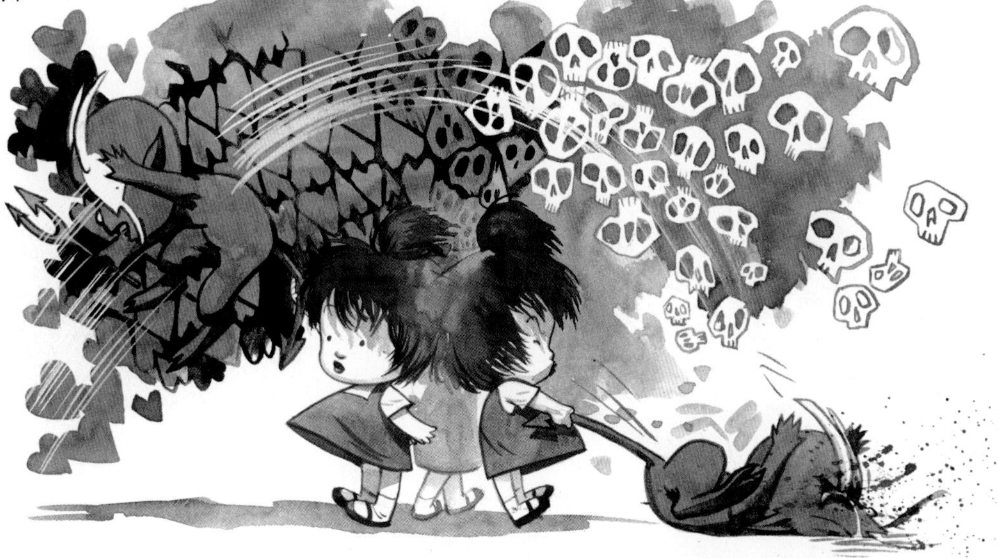

EXPOSED TO SUCH ESCAPADES, THE LI'L ANGEL FOUND HERSELF ABSORBING SOME OF THESE WICKED SPIRITS. IN TIME, SHE FOUND THAT SHE COULD SEE ONLY A LI'L DEVIL'S FACE IN THE MIRROR.

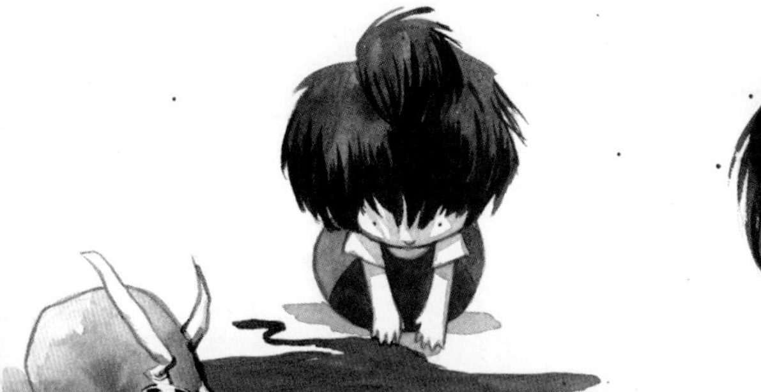

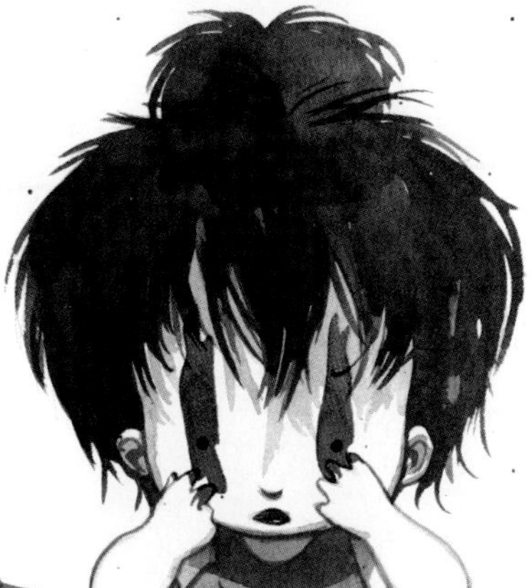

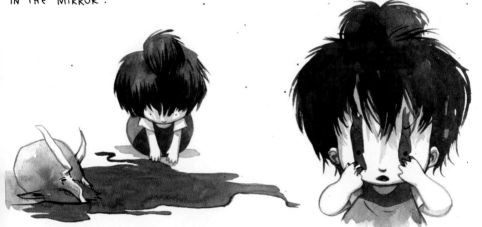

IN THE END, HER INNOCENCE FELL IN SHATTERED SACRIFICE, TO THE DEFEAT BY EVIL AND RAGE....

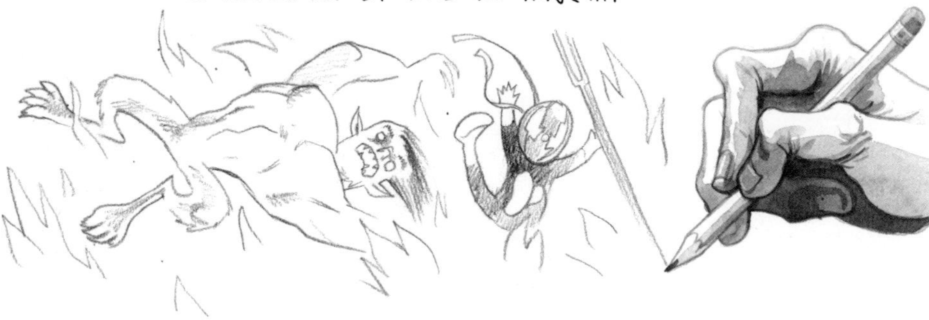

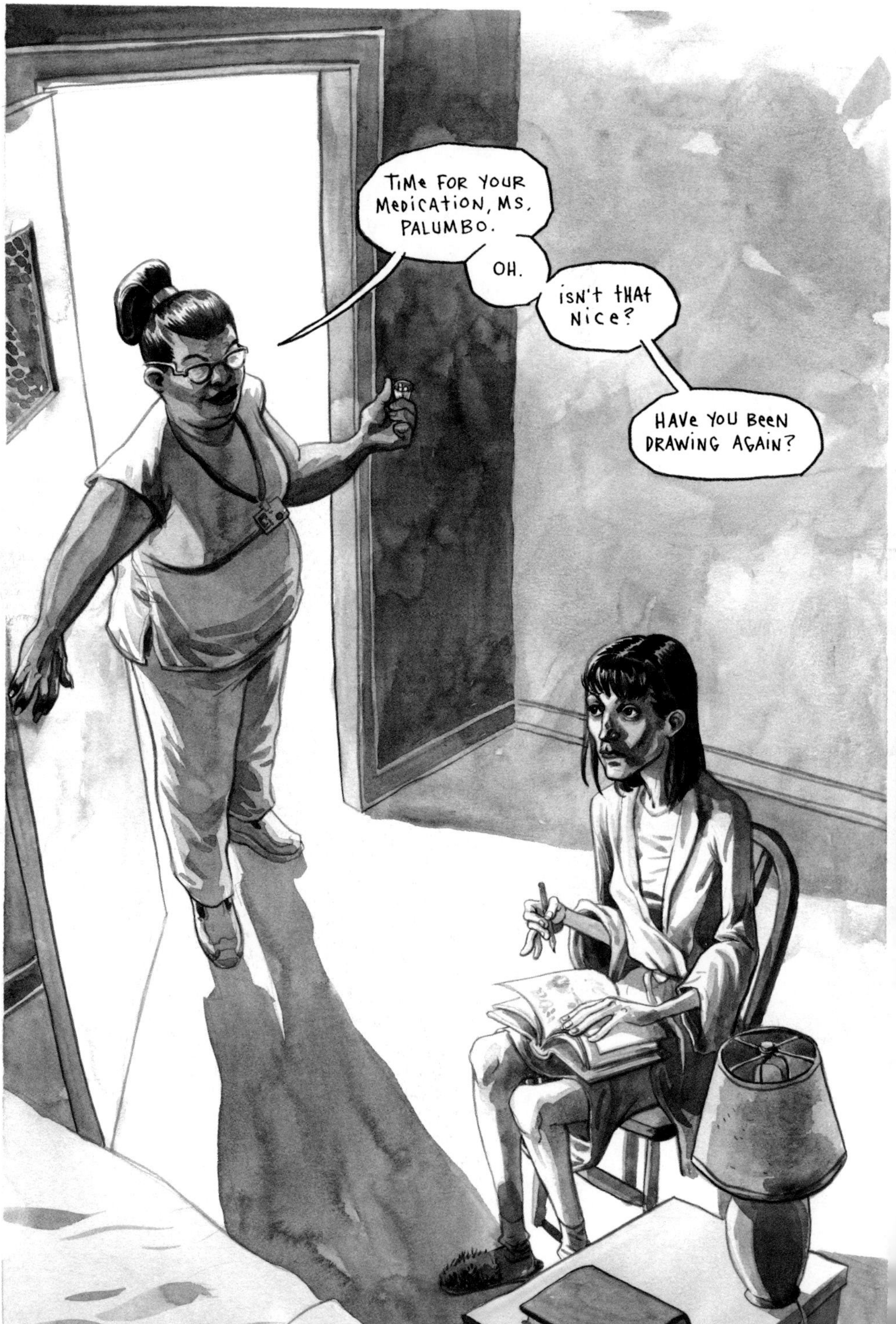
TIME FOR YOUR MEDICATION, MS. PALUMBO.
OH.
ISN'T THAT NICE?
HAVE YOU BEEN DRAWING AGAIN?

BY MATT WAGNER AND JILL THOMPSON
APRIL 2002

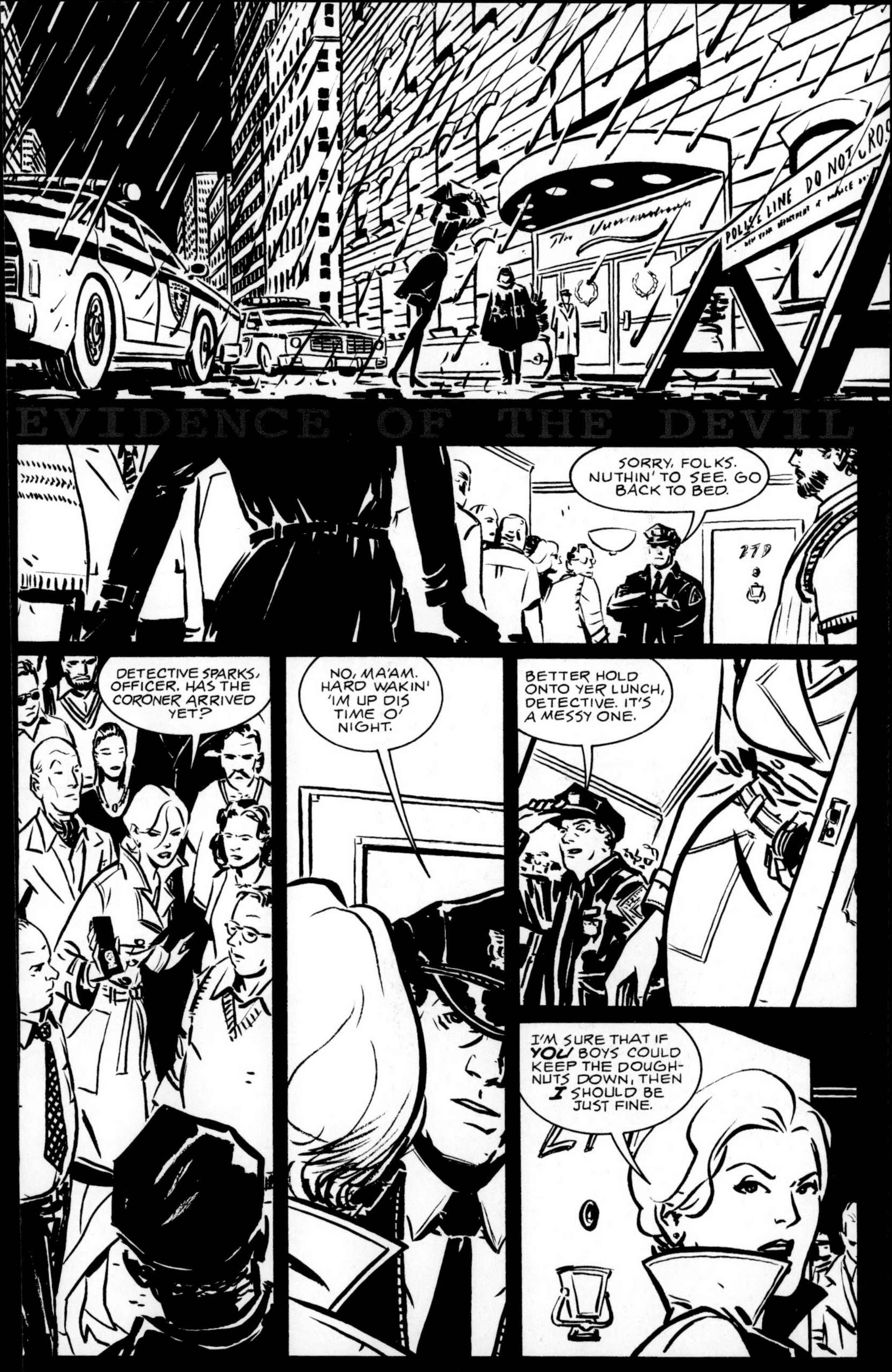
POLICE LINE DO NOT CROS
EVIDENCE OF THE DEVIL
SORRY, FOLKS. NUTHIN' TO SEE. GO BACK TO BED.
DETECTIVE SPARKS, OFFICER. HAS THE CORONER ARRIVED YET?
NO, MA'AM. HARD WAKIN' 'IM UP DIS TIME O' NIGHT.
BETTER HOLD ONTO YER LUNCH, DETECTIVE. IT'S A MESSY ONE.
I'M SURE THAT IF *YOU* BOYS COULD KEEP THE DOUGHNUTS DOWN, THEN *I* SHOULD BE JUST FINE.

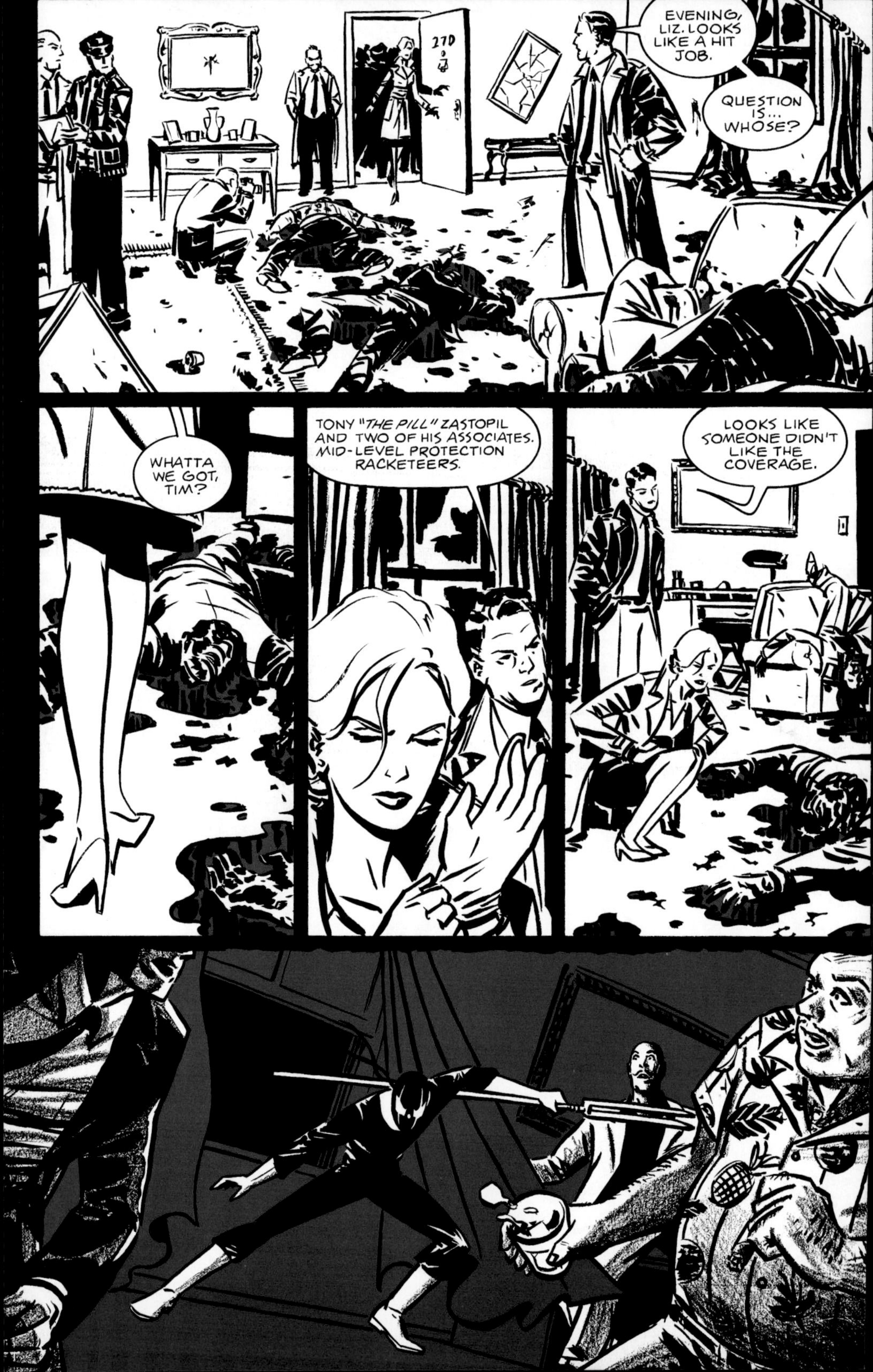

27D
EVENING, LIZ. LOOKS LIKE A HIT JOB.
QUESTION IS... WHOSE?
WHATTA WE GOT, TIM?
TONY "*THE PILL*" ZASTOPIL AND TWO OF HIS ASSOCIATES. MID-LEVEL PROTECTION RACKETEERS.
LOOKS LIKE SOMEONE DIDN'T LIKE THE COVERAGE.

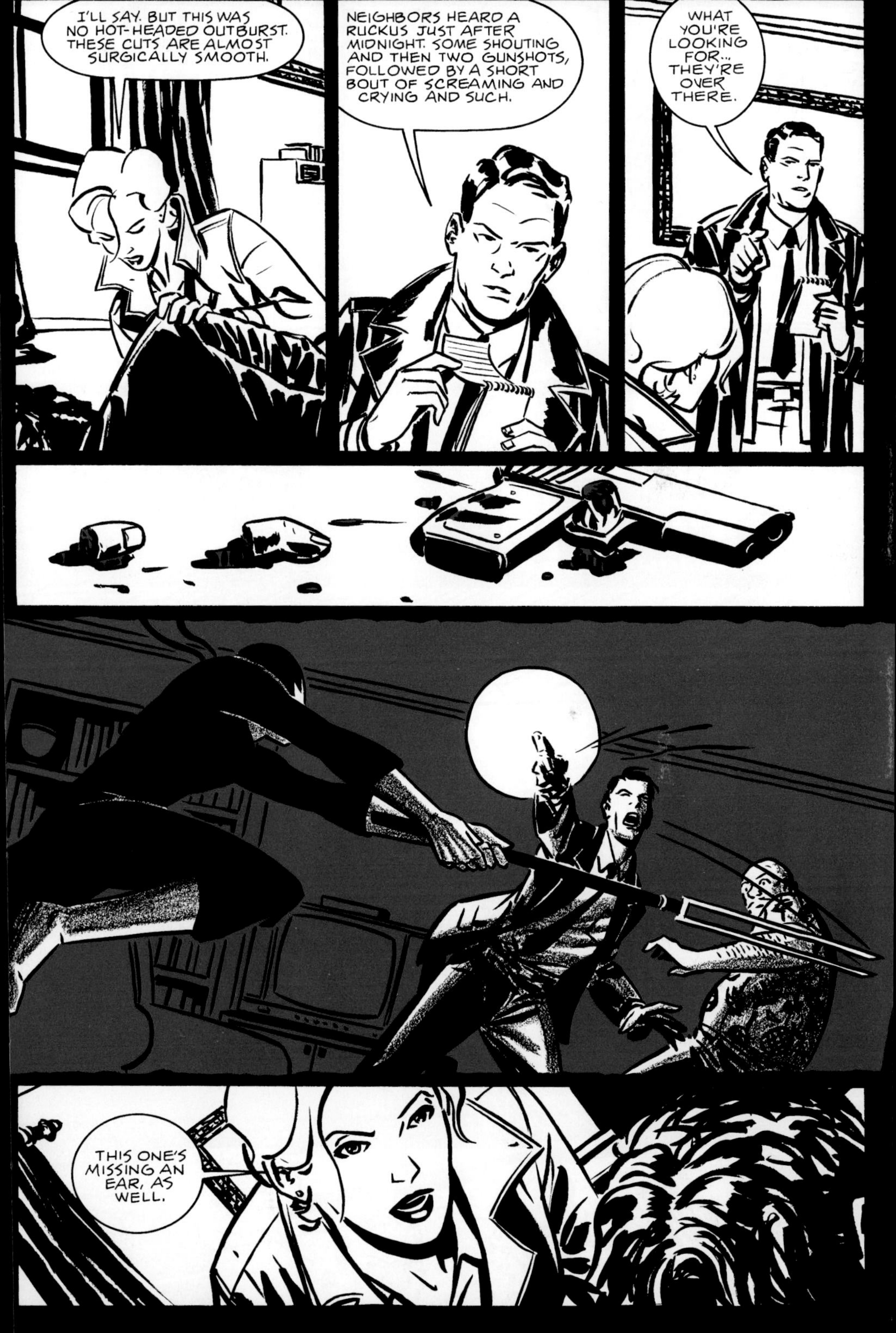
I'LL SAY. BUT THIS WAS NO HOT-HEADED OUTBURST. THESE CUTS ARE ALMOST SURGICALLY SMOOTH.
NEIGHBORS HEARD A RUCKUS JUST AFTER MIDNIGHT. SOME SHOUTING AND THEN TWO GUNSHOTS, FOLLOWED BY A SHORT BOUT OF SCREAMING AND CRYING AND SUCH.
WHAT YOU'RE LOOKING FOR... THEY'RE OVER THERE.
THIS ONE'S MISSING AN EAR, AS WELL.

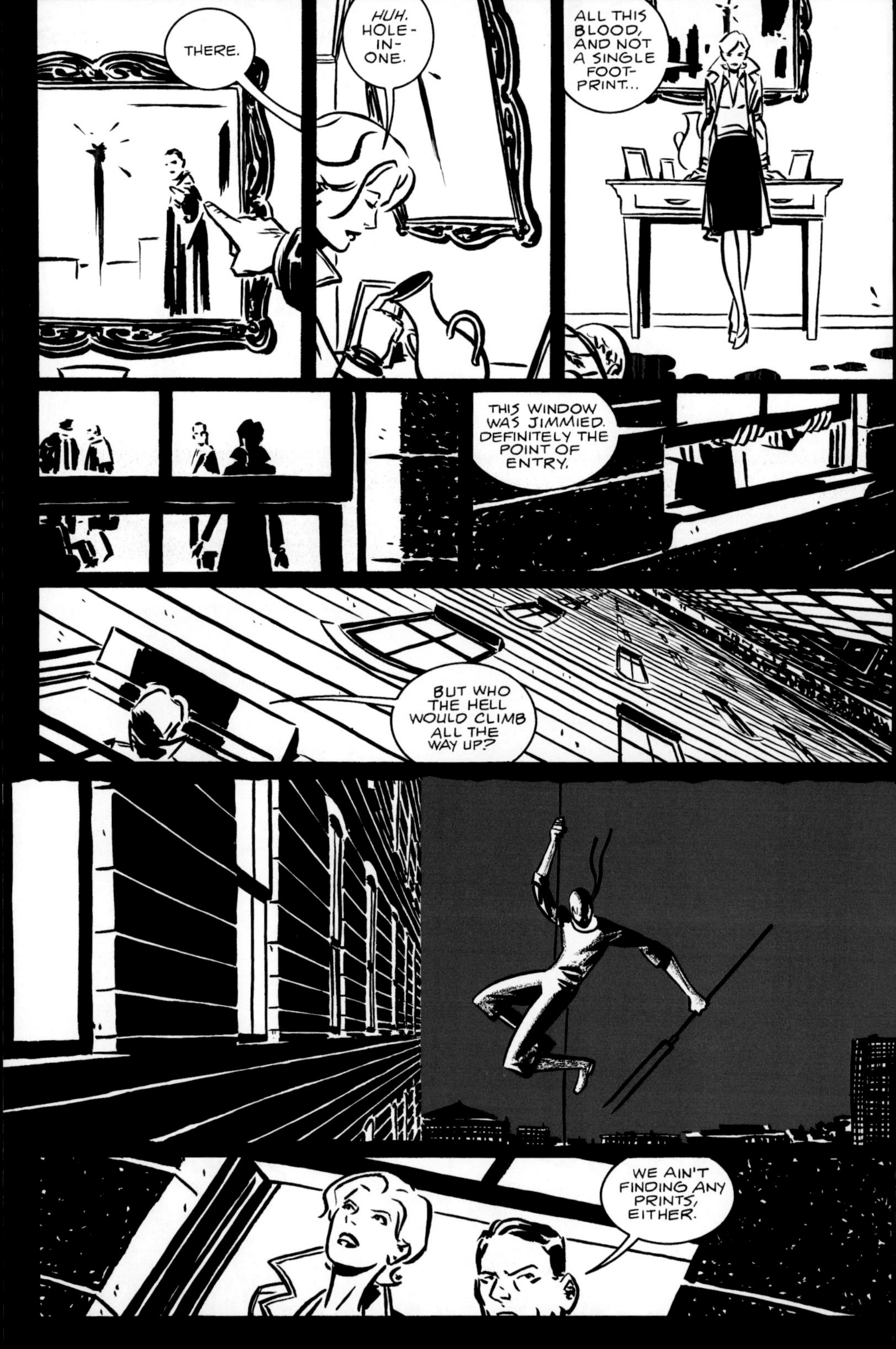

THERE.
HUH. HOLE-IN-ONE.
ALL THIS BLOOD, AND NOT A SINGLE FOOTPRINT...
THIS WINDOW WAS JIMMIED. DEFINITELY THE POINT OF ENTRY.
BUT WHO THE HELL WOULD CLIMB ALL THE WAY UP?
WE AIN'T FINDING ANY PRINTS, EITHER.

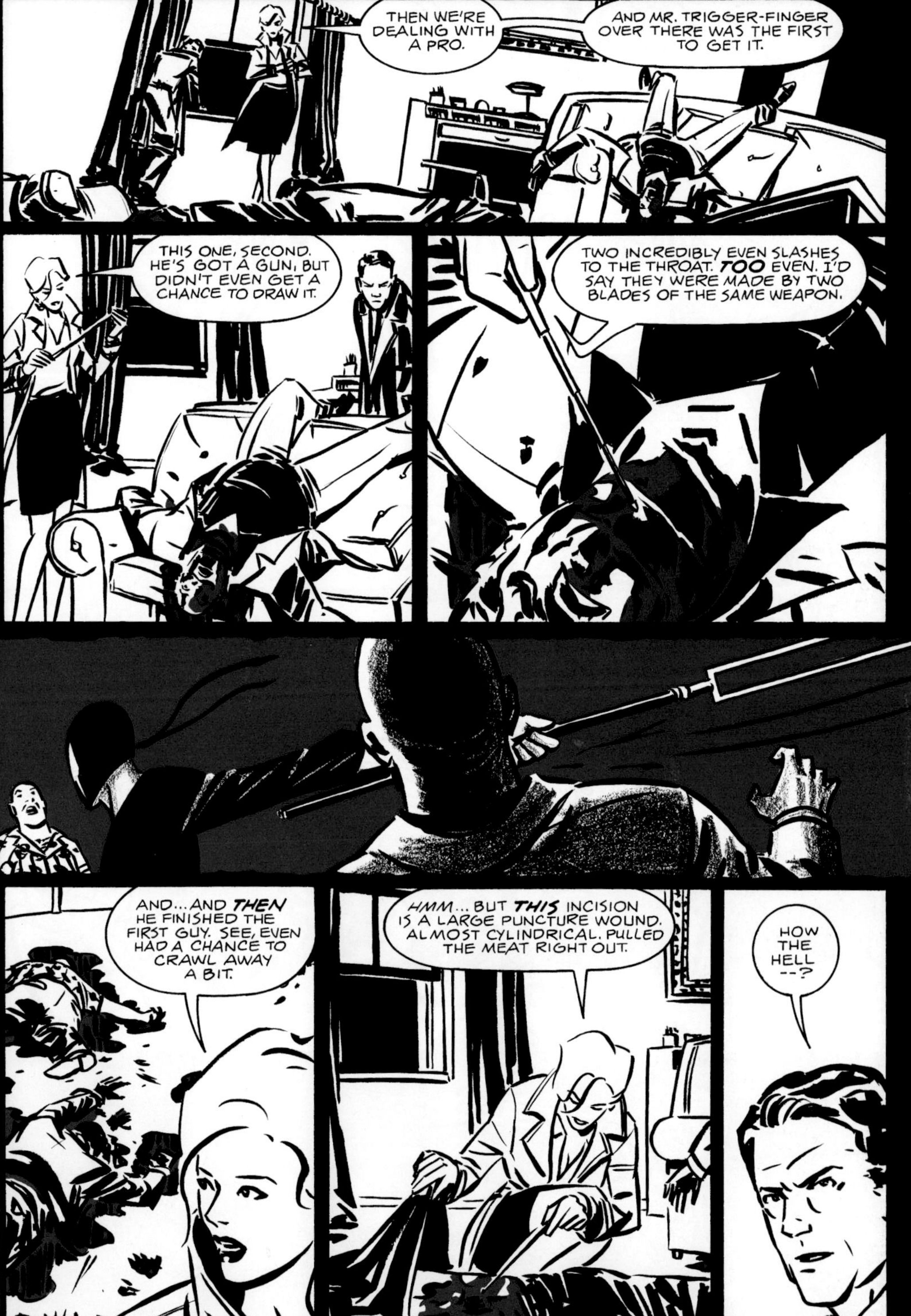
THEN WE'RE DEALING WITH A PRO.
AND MR. TRIGGER-FINGER OVER THERE WAS THE FIRST TO GET IT.
THIS ONE, SECOND. HE'S GOT A GUN, BUT DIDN'T EVEN GET A CHANCE TO DRAW IT.
TWO INCREDIBLY EVEN SLASHES TO THE THROAT. TOO EVEN. I'D SAY THEY WERE MADE BY TWO BLADES OF THE SAME WEAPON.
AND... AND THEN HE FINISHED THE FIRST GUY. SEE, EVEN HAD A CHANCE TO CRAWL AWAY A BIT.
HMM... BUT THIS INCISION IS A LARGE PUNCTURE WOUND. ALMOST CYLINDRICAL. PULLED THE MEAT RIGHT OUT.
HOW THE HELL --?

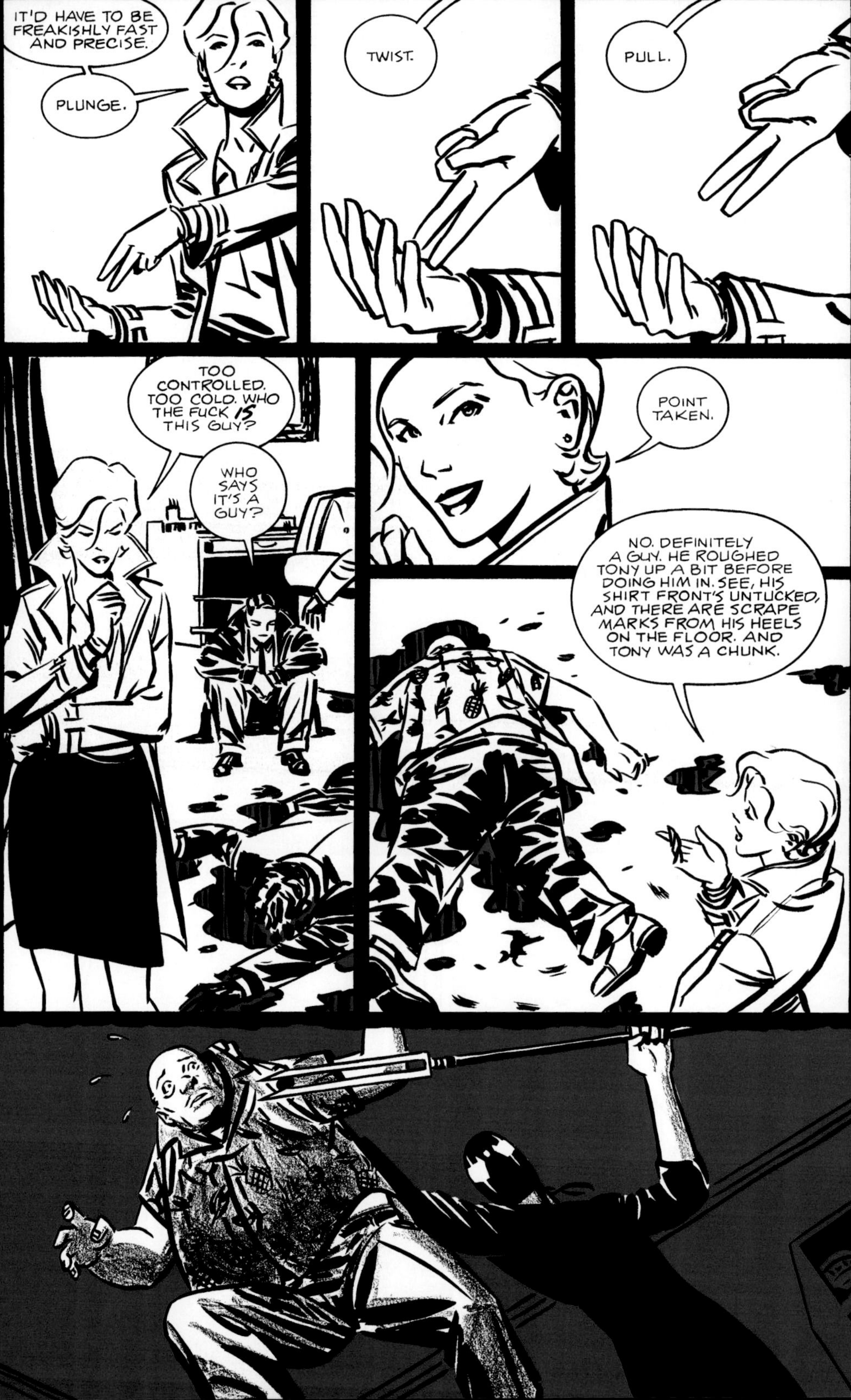
IT'D HAVE TO BE FREAKISHLY FAST AND PRECISE.
PLUNGE.
TWIST.
PULL.
TOO CONTROLLED. TOO COLD. WHO THE FUCK IS THIS GUY?
WHO SAYS IT'S A GUY?
POINT TAKEN.
NO. DEFINITELY A GUY. HE ROUGHED TONY UP A BIT BEFORE DOING HIM IN. SEE, HIS SHIRT FRONT'S UNTUCKED, AND THERE ARE SCRAPE MARKS FROM HIS HEELS ON THE FLOOR. AND TONY WAS A CHUNK.

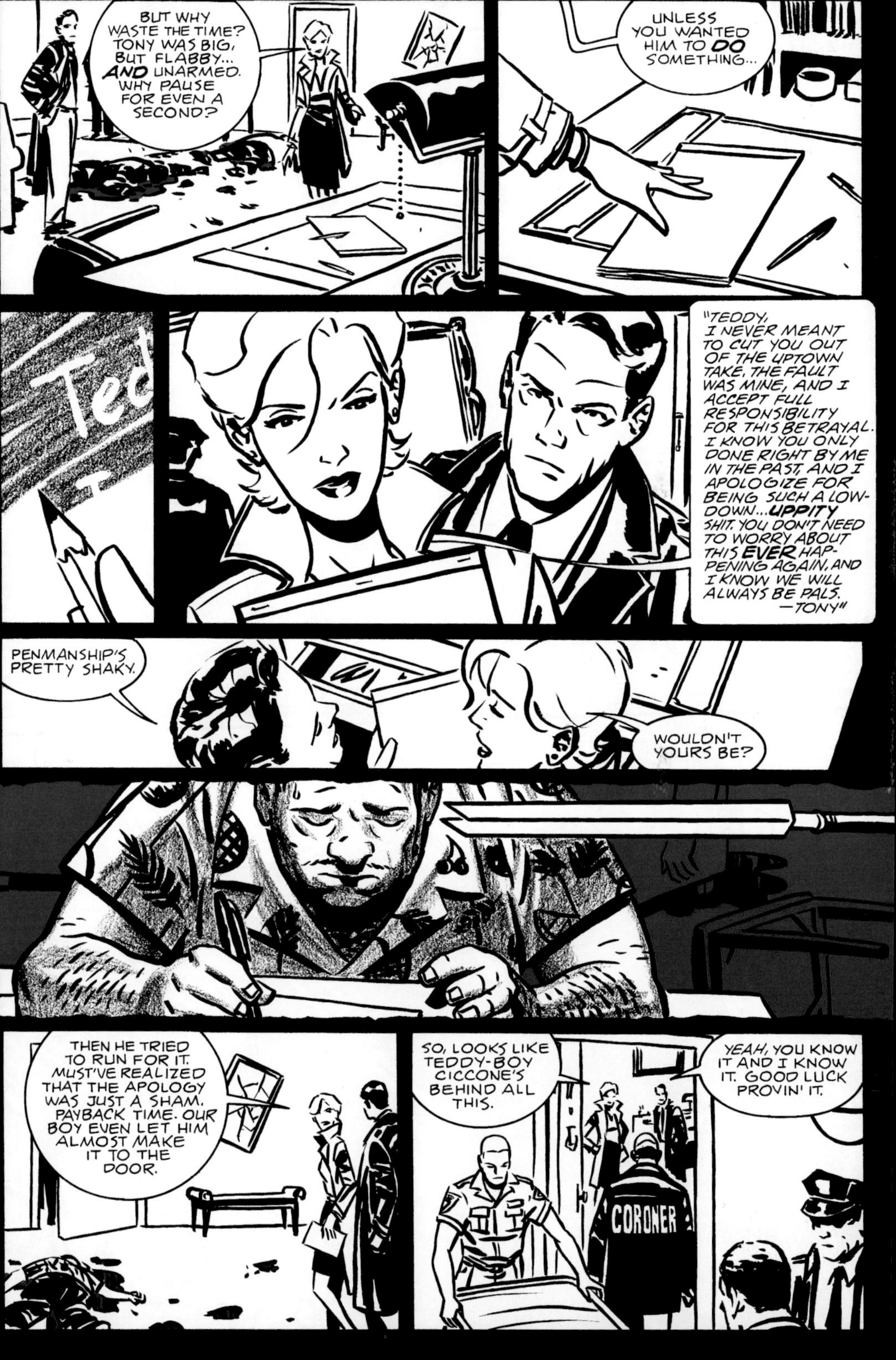

BUT WHY WASTE THE TIME? TONY WAS BIG, BUT FLABBY... AND UNARMED. WHY PAUSE FOR EVEN A SECOND?
UNLESS YOU WANTED HIM TO DO SOMETHING...
Ted
"TEDDY, I NEVER MEANT TO CUT YOU OUT OF THE UPTOWN TAKE. THE FAULT WAS MINE, AND I ACCEPT FULL RESPONSIBILITY FOR THIS BETRAYAL. I KNOW YOU ONLY DONE RIGHT BY ME IN THE PAST, AND I APOLOGIZE FOR BEING SUCH A LOW-DOWN...UPPITY SHIT. YOU DON'T NEED TO WORRY ABOUT THIS EVER HAPPENING AGAIN. AND I KNOW WE WILL ALWAYS BE PALS. —TONY"
PENMANSHIP'S PRETTY SHAKY.
WOULDN'T YOURS BE?
THEN HE TRIED TO RUN FOR IT. MUST'VE REALIZED THAT THE APOLOGY WAS JUST A SHAM. PAYBACK TIME. OUR BOY EVEN LET HIM ALMOST MAKE IT TO THE DOOR.
SO, LOOKS LIKE TEDDY-BOY CICCONE'S BEHIND ALL THIS.
YEAH, YOU KNOW IT AND I KNOW IT. GOOD LUCK PROVIN' IT.
CORONER

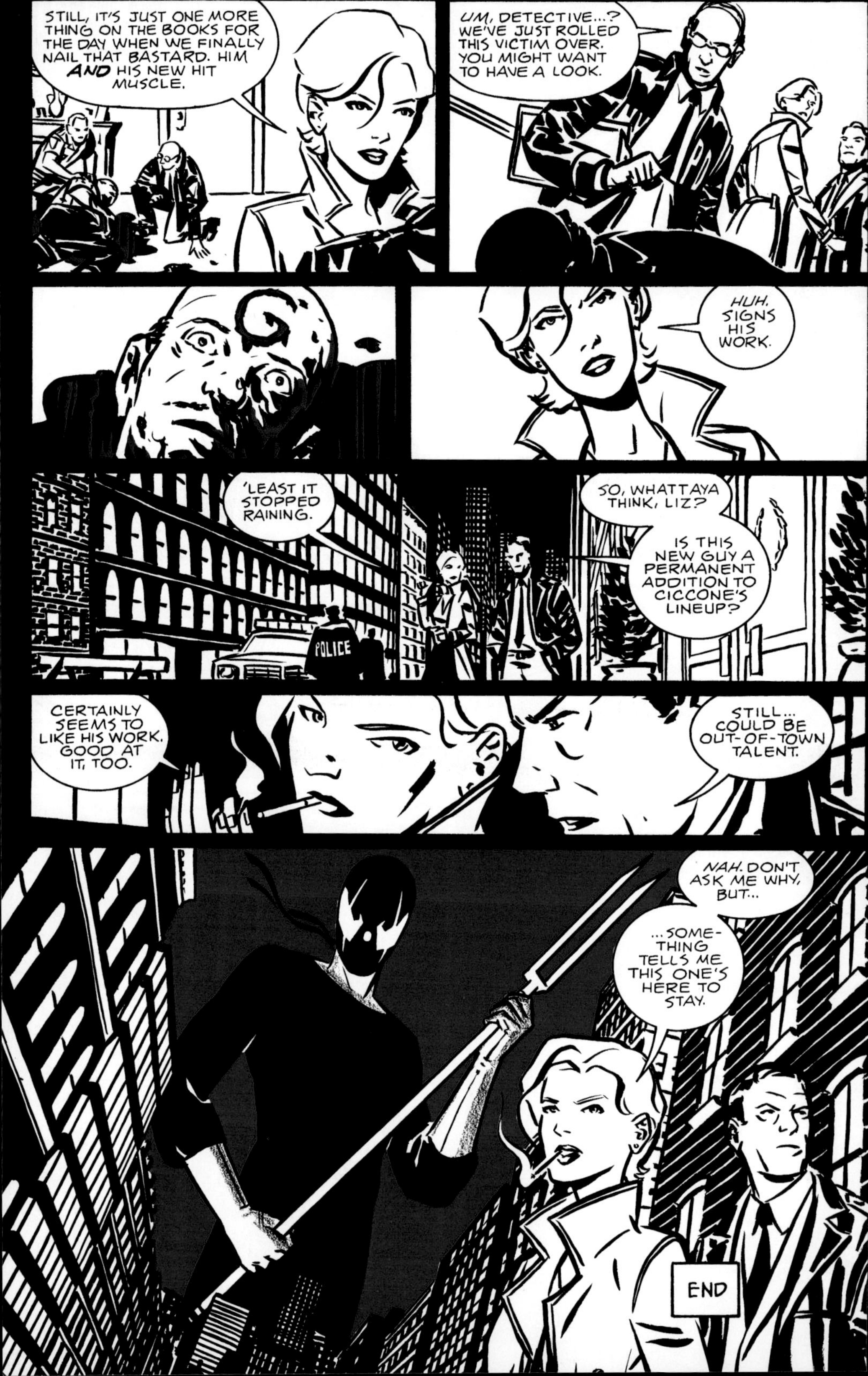
STILL, IT'S JUST ONE MORE THING ON THE BOOKS FOR THE DAY WHEN WE FINALLY NAIL THAT BASTARD. HIM AND HIS NEW HIT MUSCLE.
UM, DETECTIVE...? WE'VE JUST ROLLED THIS VICTIM OVER. YOU MIGHT WANT TO HAVE A LOOK.
HUH. SIGNS HIS WORK.
'LEAST IT STOPPED RAINING.
POLICE
SO, WHATTAYA THINK, LIZ?
IS THIS NEW GUY A PERMANENT ADDITION TO CICCONE'S LINEUP?
CERTAINLY SEEMS TO LIKE HIS WORK. GOOD AT IT, TOO.
STILL... COULD BE OUT-OF-TOWN TALENT.
NAH. DON'T ASK ME WHY, BUT...
...SOME-THING TELLS ME THIS ONE'S HERE TO STAY.
END

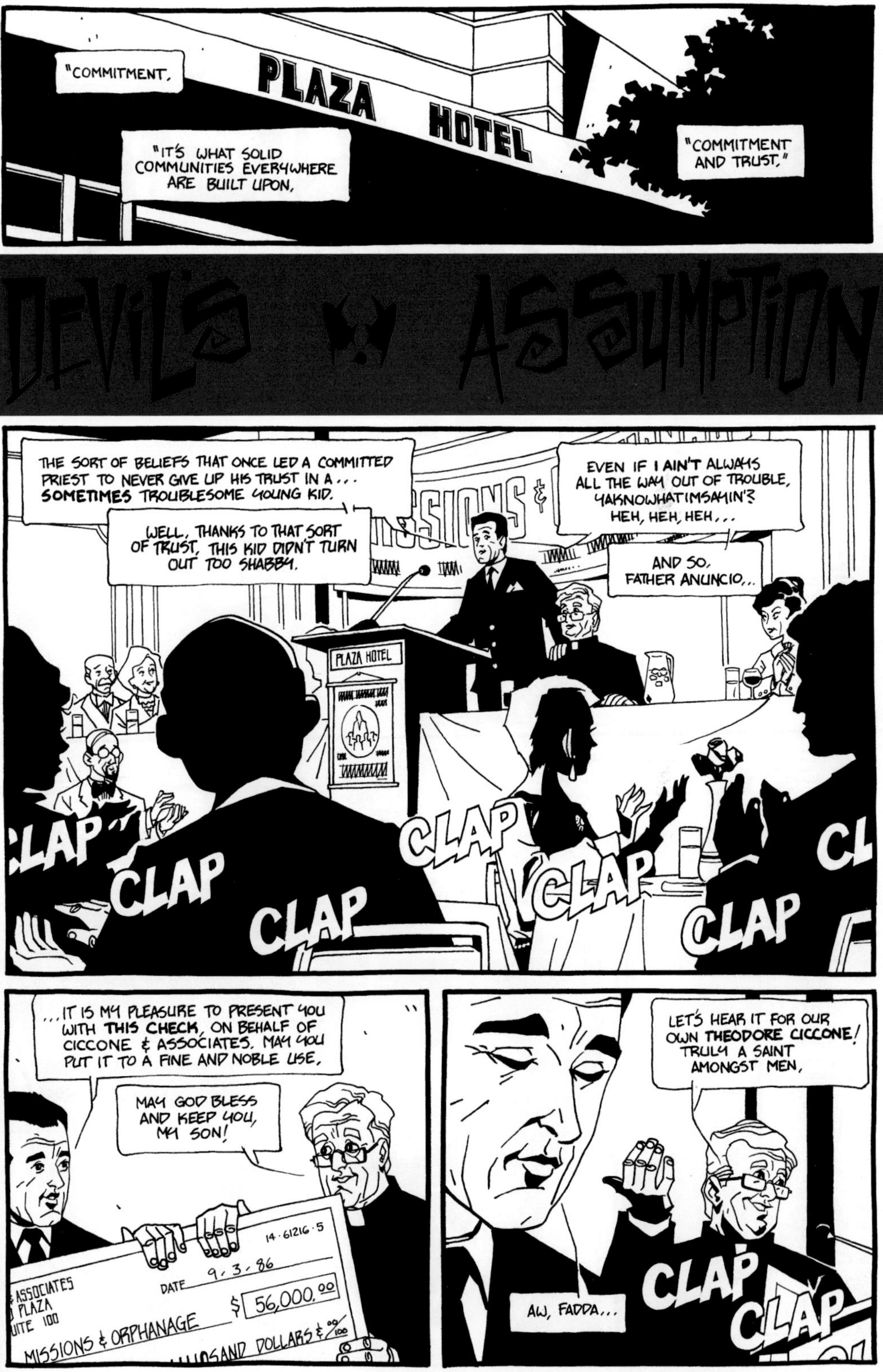
"COMMITMENT.
PLAZA HOTEL
"IT'S WHAT SOLID COMMUNITIES EVERYWHERE ARE BUILT UPON.
"COMMITMENT AND TRUST."
DEVIL'S ASSUMPTION
THE SORT OF BELIEFS THAT ONCE LED A COMMITTED PRIEST TO NEVER GIVE UP HIS TRUST IN A... SOMETIMES TROUBLESOME YOUNG KID.
WELL, THANKS TO THAT SORT OF TRUST, THIS KID DIDN'T TURN OUT TOO SHABBY.
EVEN IF I AIN'T ALWAYS ALL THE WAY OUT OF TROUBLE, YAKNOWHATIMSAYIN'? HEH, HEH, HEH...
AND SO, FATHER ANUNCIO...
PLAZA HOTEL
CLAP
CLAP
CLAP
CLAP
CLAP
CLAP
CL
...IT IS MY PLEASURE TO PRESENT YOU WITH THIS CHECK, ON BEHALF OF CICCONE & ASSOCIATES. MAY YOU PUT IT TO A FINE AND NOBLE USE.
MAY GOD BLESS AND KEEP YOU, MY SON!
14·61216·5
DATE 9-3-86
$ 56,000.00
MISSIONS & ORPHANAGE
LET'S HEAR IT FOR OUR OWN THEODORE CICCONE! TRULY A SAINT AMONGST MEN.
AW, FADDA...
CLAP
CLAP

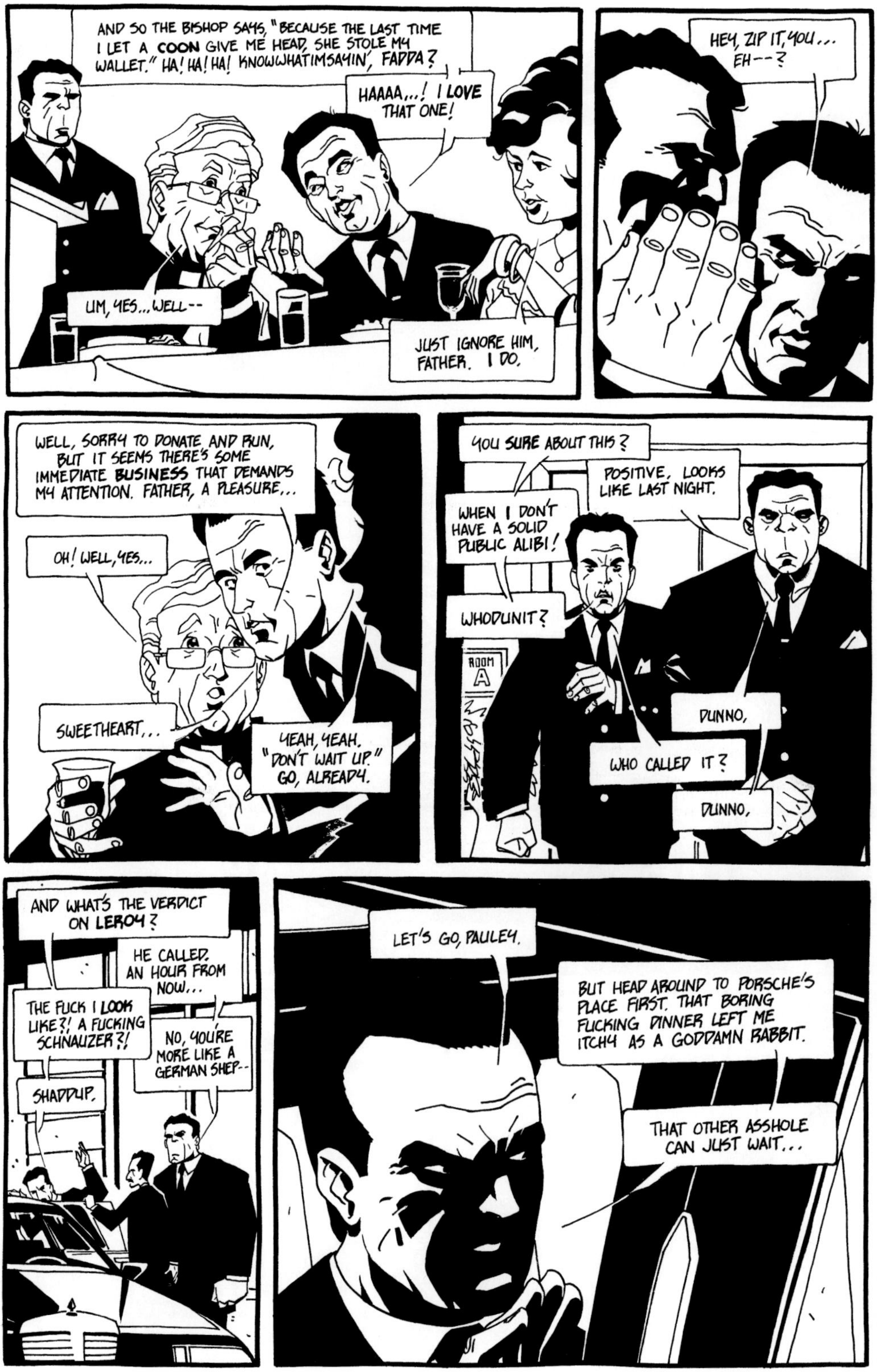
AND SO THE BISHOP SAYS, "BECAUSE THE LAST TIME I LET A COON GIVE ME HEAD, SHE STOLE MY WALLET." HA! HA! HA! KNOWWHATIMSAYIN', FADDA?
HAAAA...! I LOVE THAT ONE!
UM, YES... WELL--
JUST IGNORE HIM, FATHER. I DO.
HEY, ZIP IT, YOU... EH--?
WELL, SORRY TO DONATE AND RUN, BUT IT SEEMS THERE'S SOME IMMEDIATE BUSINESS THAT DEMANDS MY ATTENTION. FATHER, A PLEASURE...
OH! WELL, YES...
SWEETHEART...
YEAH, YEAH. "DON'T WAIT UP." GO, ALREADY.
YOU SURE ABOUT THIS?
POSITIVE. LOOKS LIKE LAST NIGHT.
WHEN I DON'T HAVE A SOLID PUBLIC ALIBI!
WHODUNIT?
ROOM A
DUNNO.
WHO CALLED IT?
DUNNO.
AND WHAT'S THE VERDICT ON LEROY?
HE CALLED. AN HOUR FROM NOW...
THE FUCK I LOOK LIKE?! A FUCKING SCHNAUZER?!
NO, YOU'RE MORE LIKE A GERMAN SHEP--
SHADDUP.
LET'S GO, PAULEY.
BUT HEAD AROUND TO PORSCHE'S PLACE FIRST. THAT BORING FUCKING DINNER LEFT ME ITCHY AS A GODDAMN RABBIT.
THAT OTHER ASSHOLE CAN JUST WAIT...

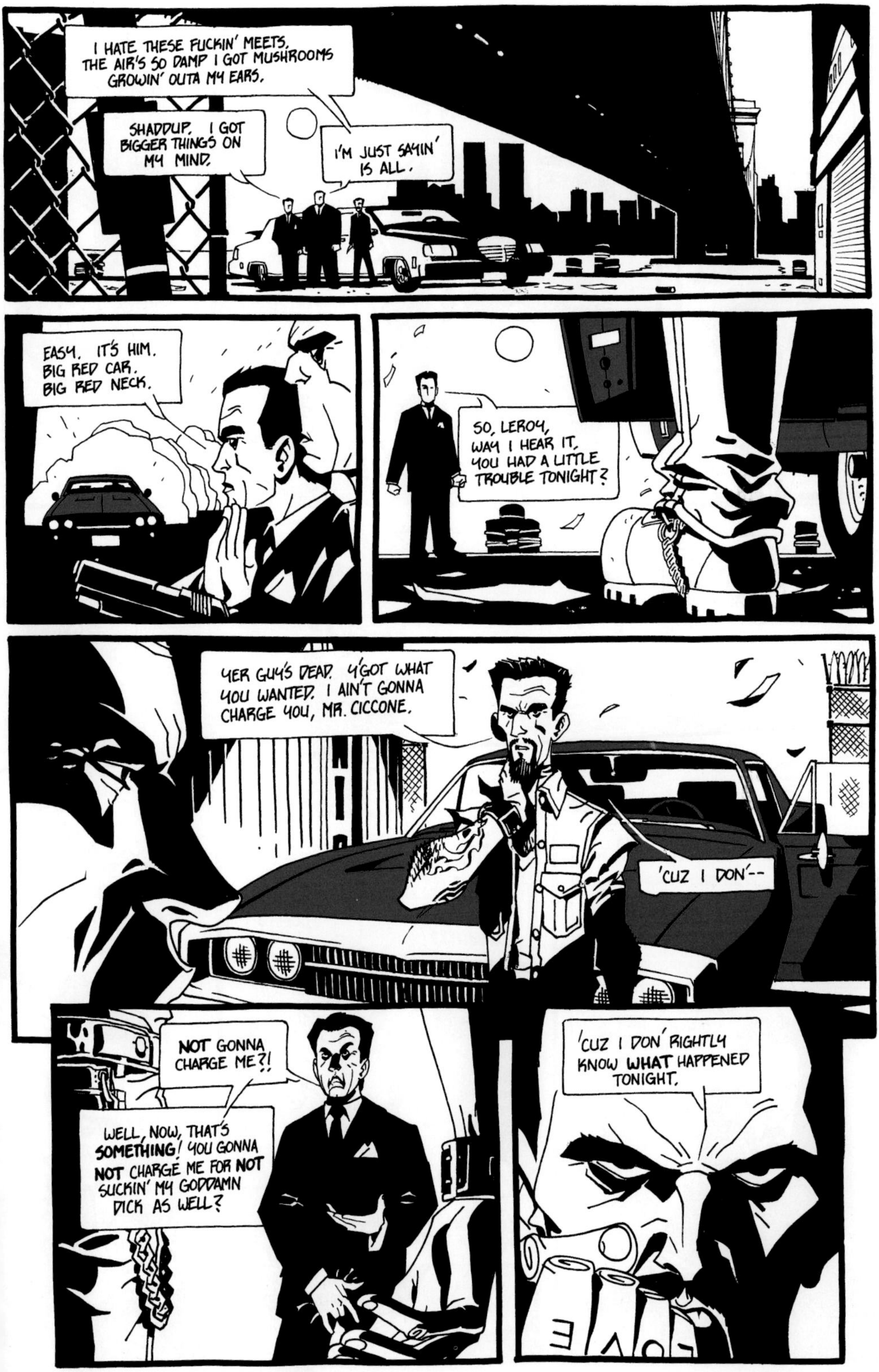
I HATE THESE FUCKIN' MEETS. THE AIR'S SO DAMP I GOT MUSHROOMS GROWIN' OUTA MY EARS.
SHADDUP. I GOT BIGGER THINGS ON MY MIND.
I'M JUST SAYIN' IS ALL.
EASY. IT'S HIM. BIG RED CAR. BIG RED NECK.
SO, LEROY, WAY I HEAR IT, YOU HAD A LITTLE TROUBLE TONIGHT?
YER GUY'S DEAD. Y'GOT WHAT YOU WANTED. I AIN'T GONNA CHARGE YOU, MR. CICCONE.
'CUZ I DON'--
NOT GONNA CHARGE ME?!
WELL, NOW, THAT'S SOMETHING! YOU GONNA NOT CHARGE ME FOR NOT SUCKIN' MY GODDAMN DICK AS WELL?
'CUZ I DON' RIGHTLY KNOW WHAT HAPPENED TONIGHT.

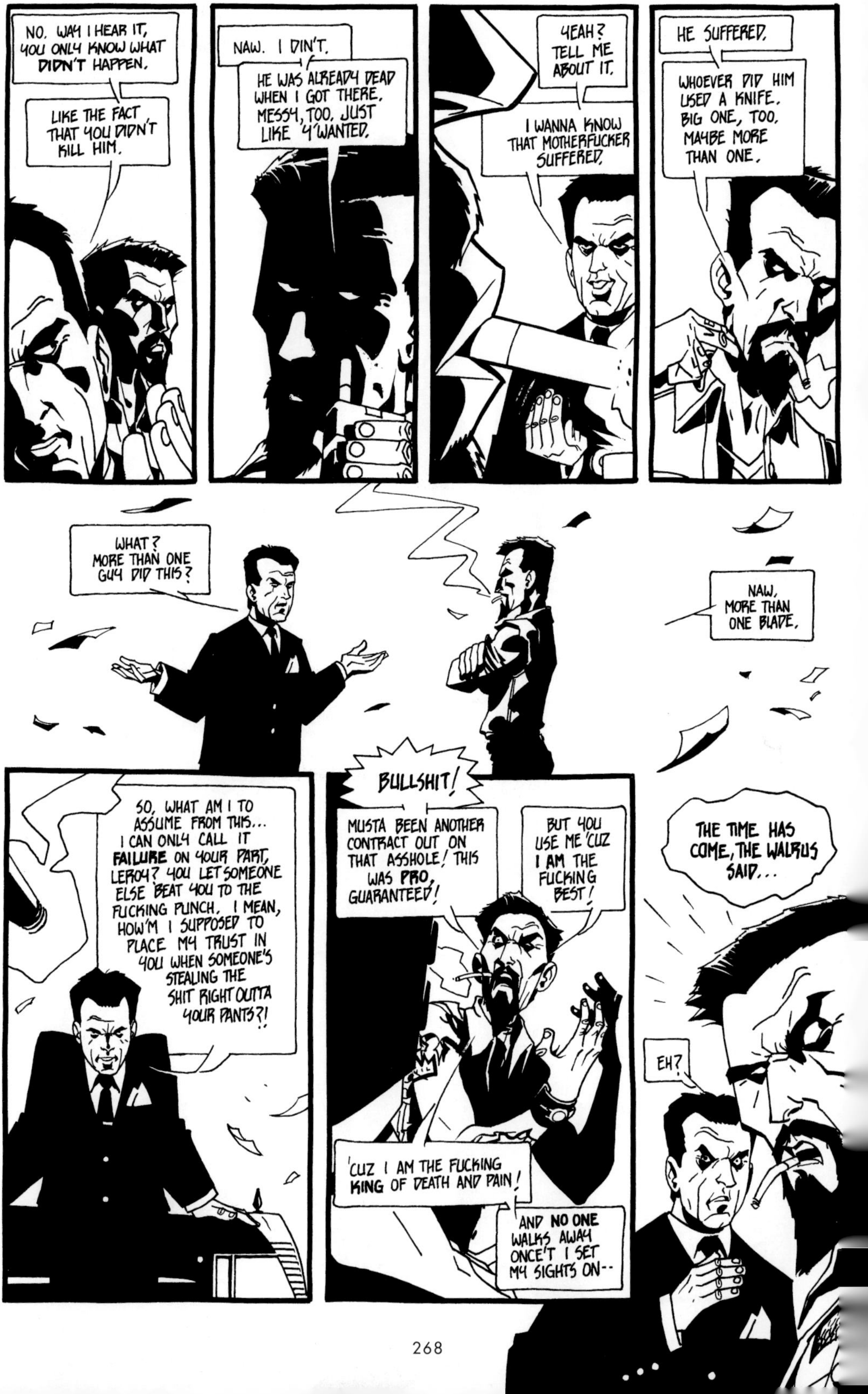
NO, WAY I HEAR IT, YOU ONLY KNOW WHAT **DIDN'T** HAPPEN.
LIKE THE FACT THAT YOU DIDN'T KILL HIM.
NAW. I DIN'T.
HE WAS ALREADY DEAD WHEN I GOT THERE. MESSY, TOO, JUST LIKE 'Y'WANTED.
YEAH? TELL ME ABOUT IT.
I WANNA KNOW THAT MOTHERFUCKER SUFFERED.
HE SUFFERED.
WHOEVER DID HIM USED A KNIFE. BIG ONE, TOO. MAYBE MORE THAN ONE.
WHAT? MORE THAN ONE GUY DID THIS?
NAW, MORE THAN ONE BLADE.
SO, WHAT AM I TO ASSUME FROM THIS... I CAN ONLY CALL IT **FAILURE** ON YOUR PART, LEROY? YOU LET SOMEONE ELSE BEAT YOU TO THE FUCKING PUNCH. I MEAN, HOW'M I SUPPOSED TO PLACE MY TRUST IN YOU WHEN SOMEONE'S STEALING THE SHIT RIGHT OUTTA YOUR PANTS?!
BULLSHIT!
MUSTA BEEN ANOTHER CONTRACT OUT ON THAT ASSHOLE! THIS WAS **PRO**, GUARANTEED!
BUT YOU USE ME 'CUZ **I AM** THE FUCKING BEST!
'CUZ I AM THE FUCKING **KING** OF DEATH AND PAIN!
AND **NO ONE** WALKS AWAY ONCE'T I SET MY SIGHTS ON--
THE TIME HAS COME, THE WALRUS SAID...
EH?

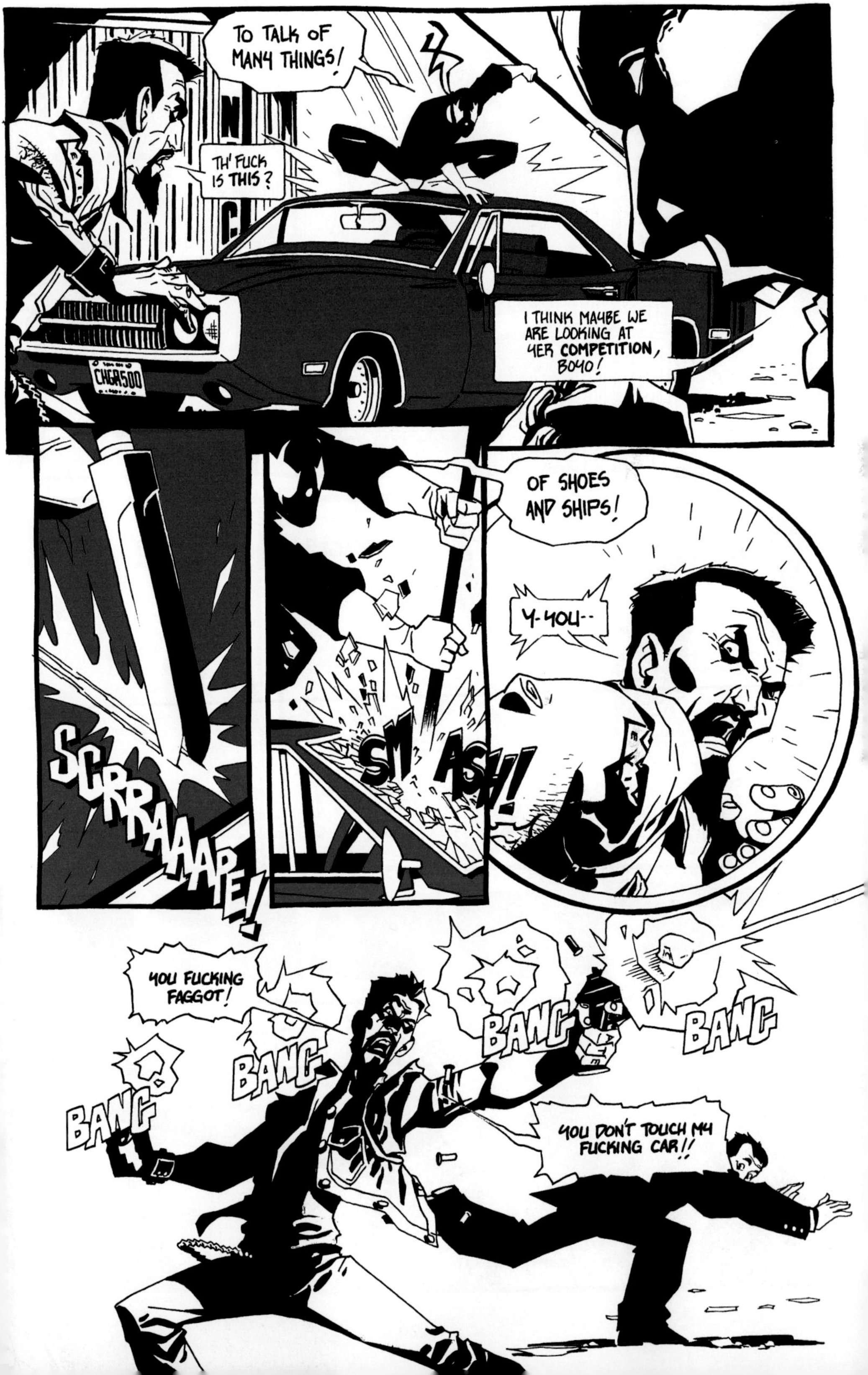
TO TALK OF MANY THINGS!
TH' FUCK IS THIS?
CHGR500
I THINK MAYBE WE ARE LOOKING AT YER COMPETITION, BOYO!
SCRRAAAAPE!
SMASH!
OF SHOES AND SHIPS!
Y-YOU--
YOU FUCKING FAGGOT!
BANG
BANG
BANG
BANG
YOU DON'T TOUCH MY FUCKING CAR!!

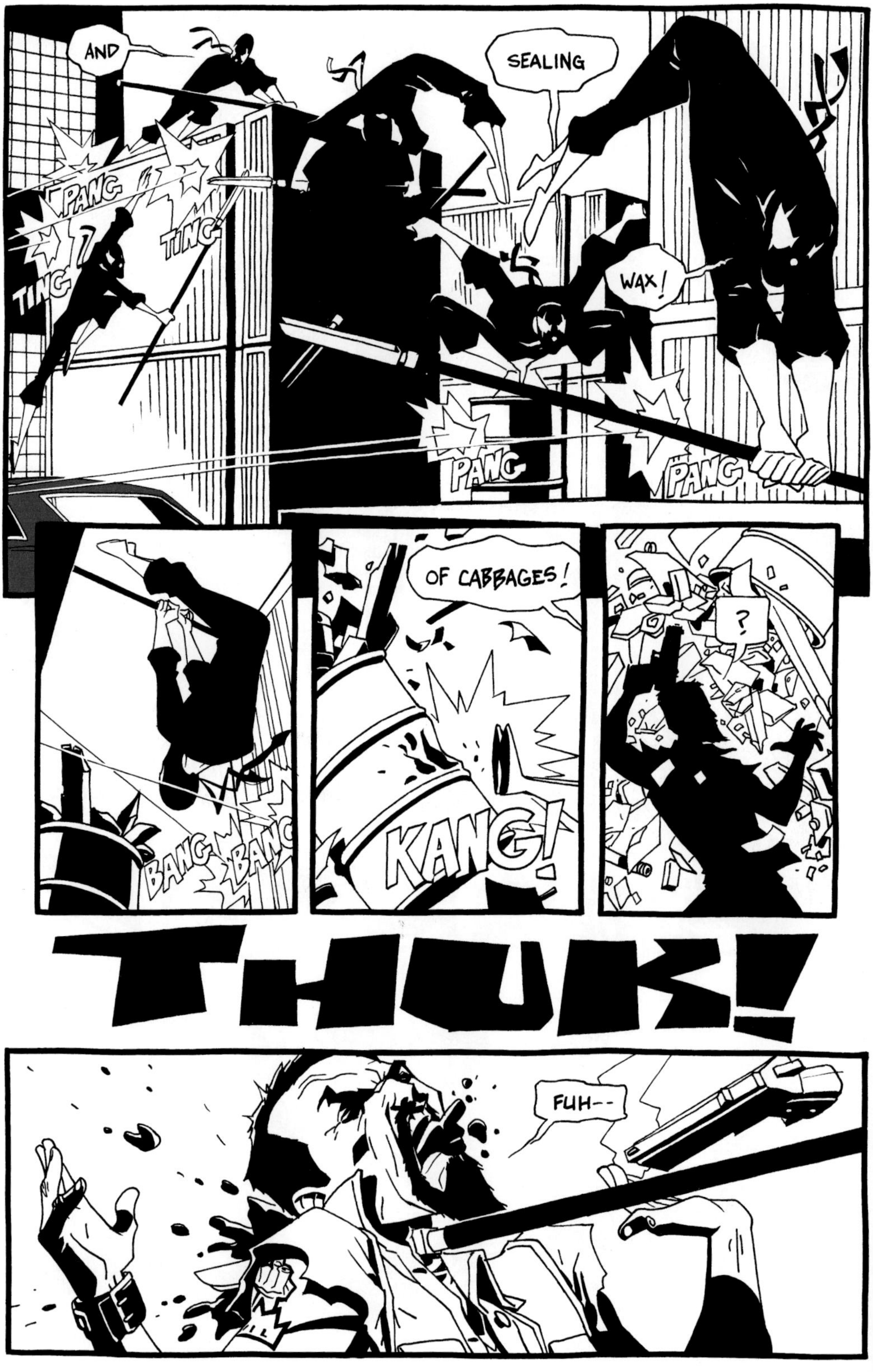
AND
SEALING
PANG
TING
TING
WAX!
PANG
PANG
BANG
BANG
OF CABBAGES!
KANG!
?
THUK!
FUH--

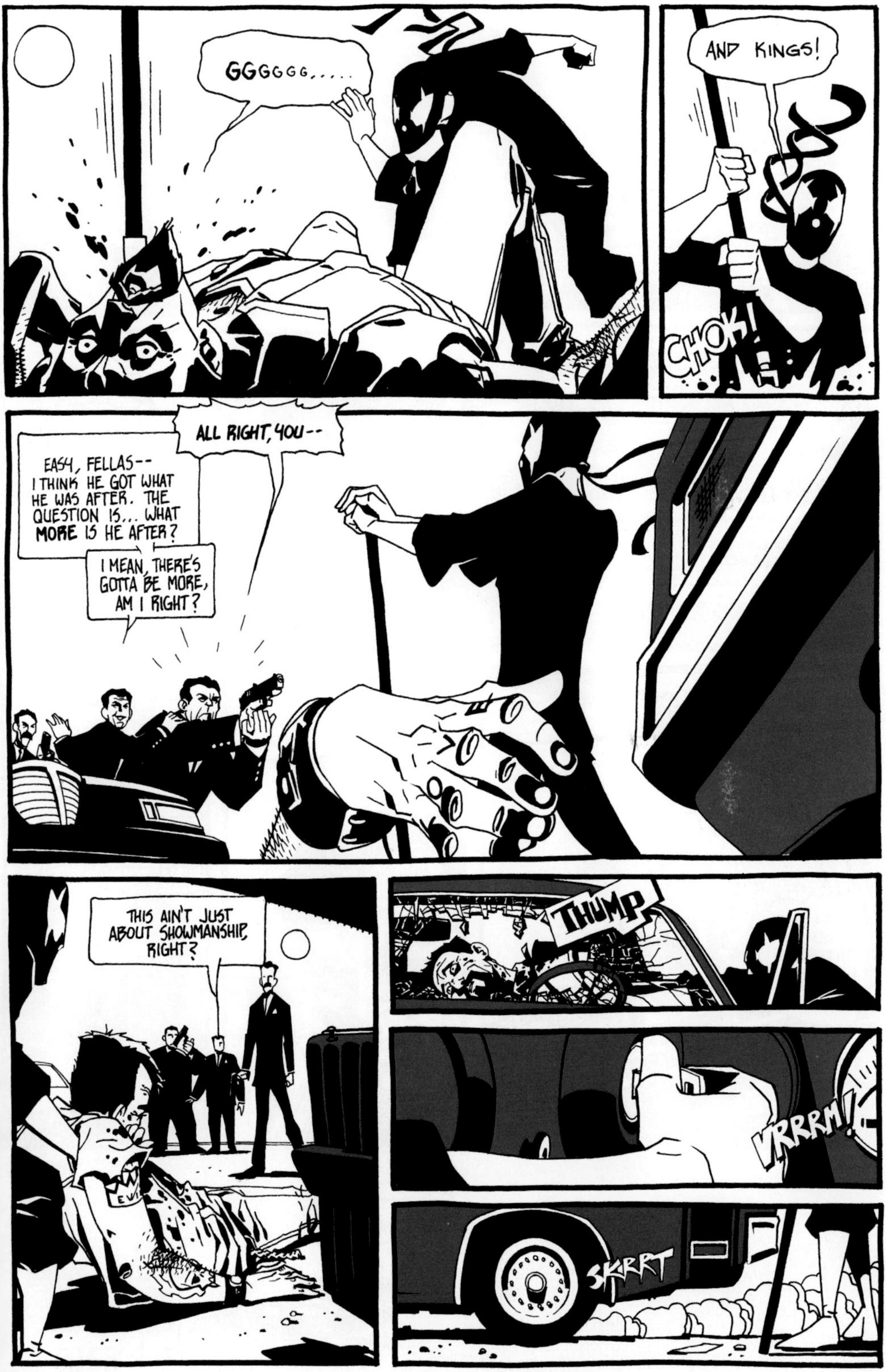

GGGGGG,.....
AND KINGS!
CHOK!
ALL RIGHT, YOU--
EASY, FELLAS-- I THINK HE GOT WHAT HE WAS AFTER. THE QUESTION IS... WHAT MORE IS HE AFTER?
I MEAN, THERE'S GOTTA BE MORE, AM I RIGHT?
THIS AIN'T JUST ABOUT SHOWMANSHIP, RIGHT?
THUMP
VRRRM!
SKRRT

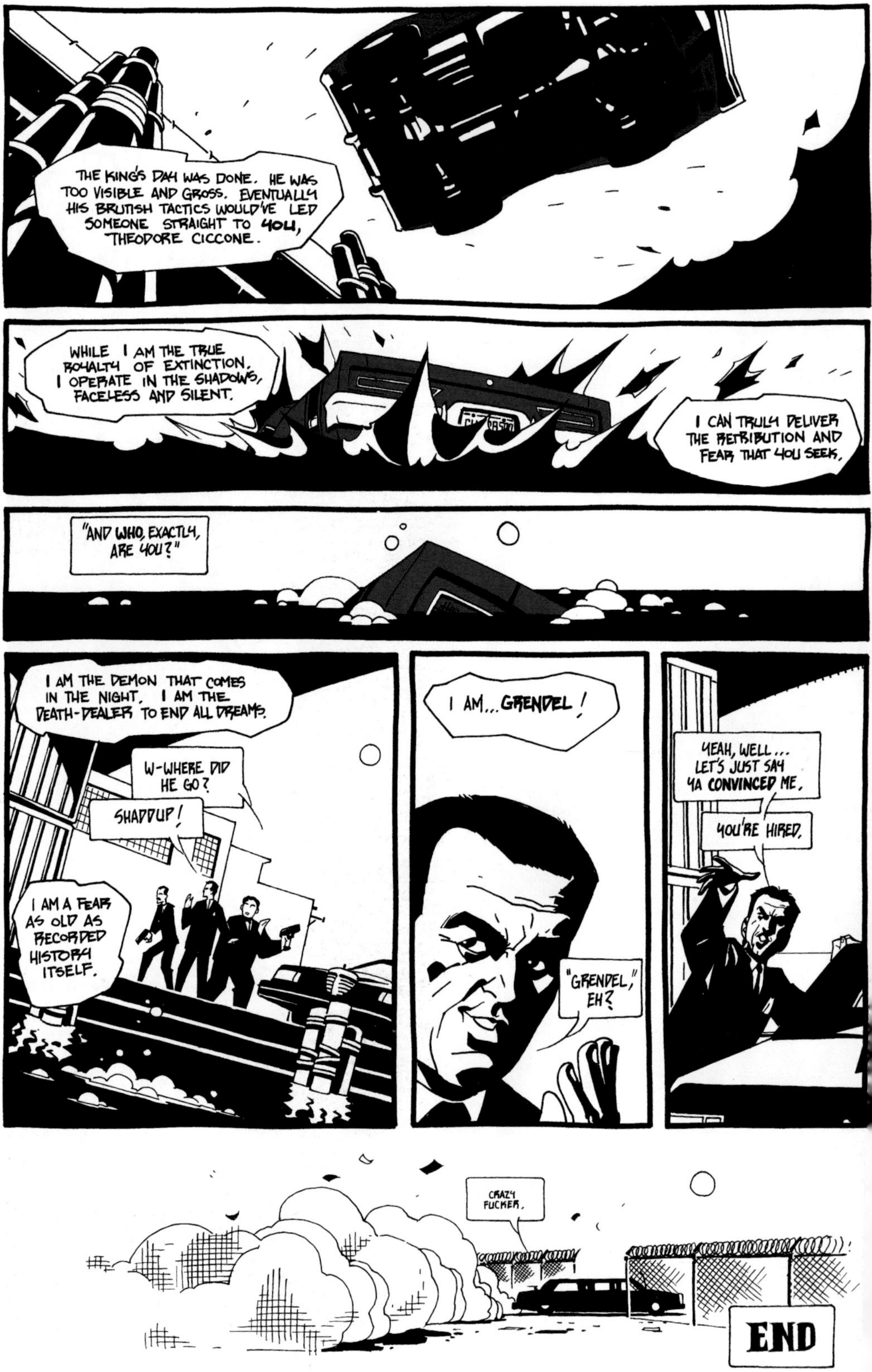
THE KING'S DAY WAS DONE. HE WAS TOO VISIBLE AND GROSS. EVENTUALLY HIS BRUTISH TACTICS WOULD'VE LED SOMEONE STRAIGHT TO YOU, THEODORE CICCONE.
WHILE I AM THE TRUE ROYALTY OF EXTINCTION, I OPERATE IN THE SHADOWS, FACELESS AND SILENT.
I CAN TRULY DELIVER THE RETRIBUTION AND FEAR THAT YOU SEEK.
"AND WHO, EXACTLY, ARE YOU?"
I AM THE DEMON THAT COMES IN THE NIGHT. I AM THE DEATH-DEALER TO END ALL DREAMS.
W-WHERE DID HE GO?
SHADDUP!
I AM A FEAR AS OLD AS RECORDED HISTORY ITSELF.
I AM... GRENDEL!
"GRENDEL," EH?
YEAH, WELL... LET'S JUST SAY YA CONVINCED ME.
YOU'RE HIRED.
CRAZY FUCKER.
END

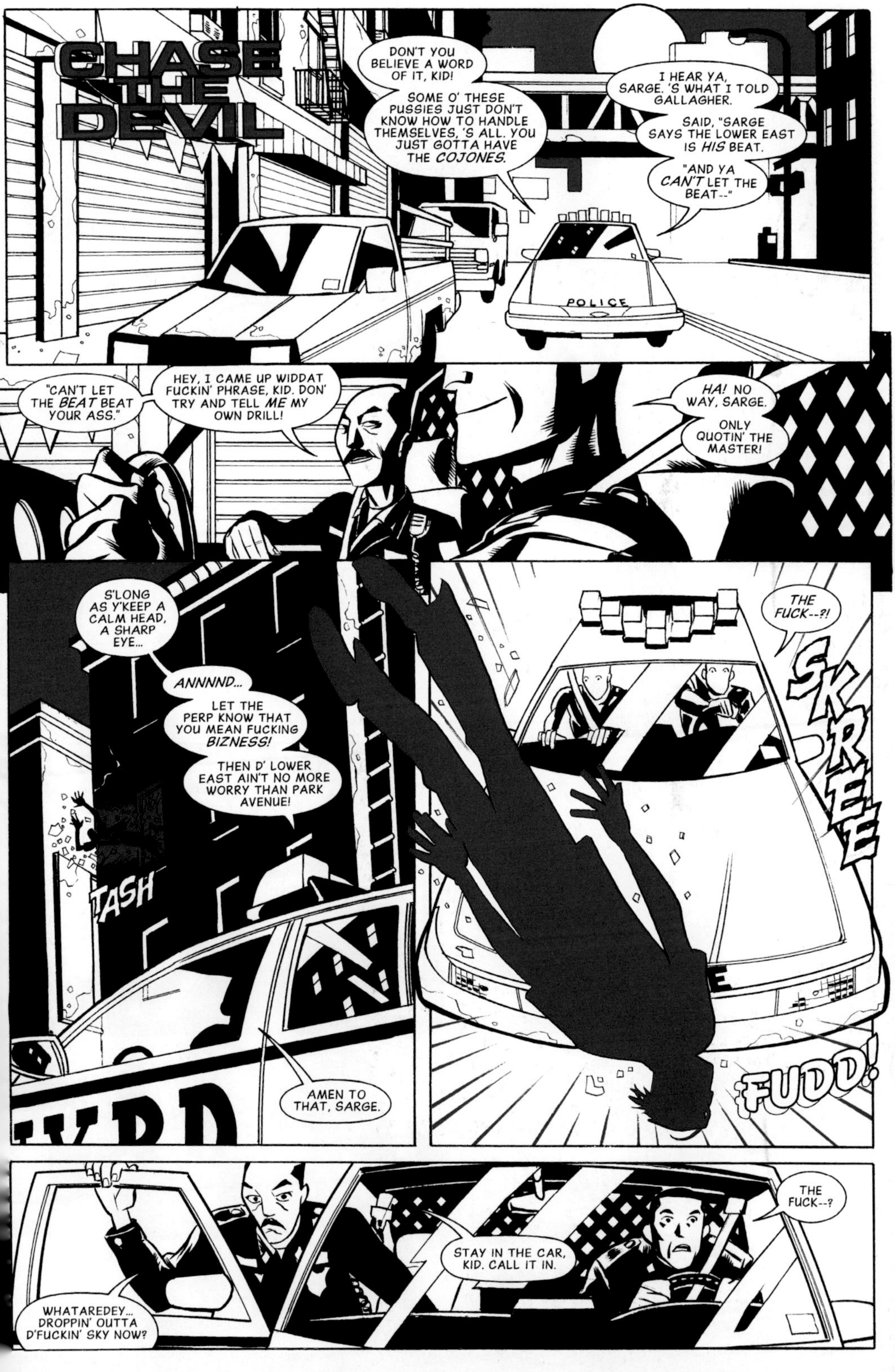
CHASE THE DEVIL
DON'T YOU BELIEVE A WORD OF IT, KID!
SOME O' THESE PUSSIES JUST DON'T KNOW HOW TO HANDLE THEMSELVES, 'S ALL. YOU JUST GOTTA HAVE THE COJONES.
I HEAR YA, SARGE. 'S WHAT I TOLD GALLAGHER.
SAID, "SARGE SAYS THE LOWER EAST IS HIS BEAT.
"AND YA CAN'T LET THE BEAT--"
POLICE
"CAN'T LET THE BEAT BEAT YOUR ASS."
HEY, I CAME UP WIDDAT FUCKIN' PHRASE, KID. DON' TRY AND TELL ME MY OWN DRILL!
HA! NO WAY, SARGE.
ONLY QUOTIN' THE MASTER!
S'LONG AS Y'KEEP A CALM HEAD, A SHARP EYE...
ANNNND...
LET THE PERP KNOW THAT YOU MEAN FUCKING BIZNESS!
THEN D' LOWER EAST AIN'T NO MORE WORRY THAN PARK AVENUE!
TASH
AMEN TO THAT, SARGE.
THE FUCK--?!
SKREE
FUDD!
THE FUCK--?
STAY IN THE CAR, KID. CALL IT IN.
WHATAREDEY... DROPPIN' OUTTA D'FUCKIN' SKY NOW?

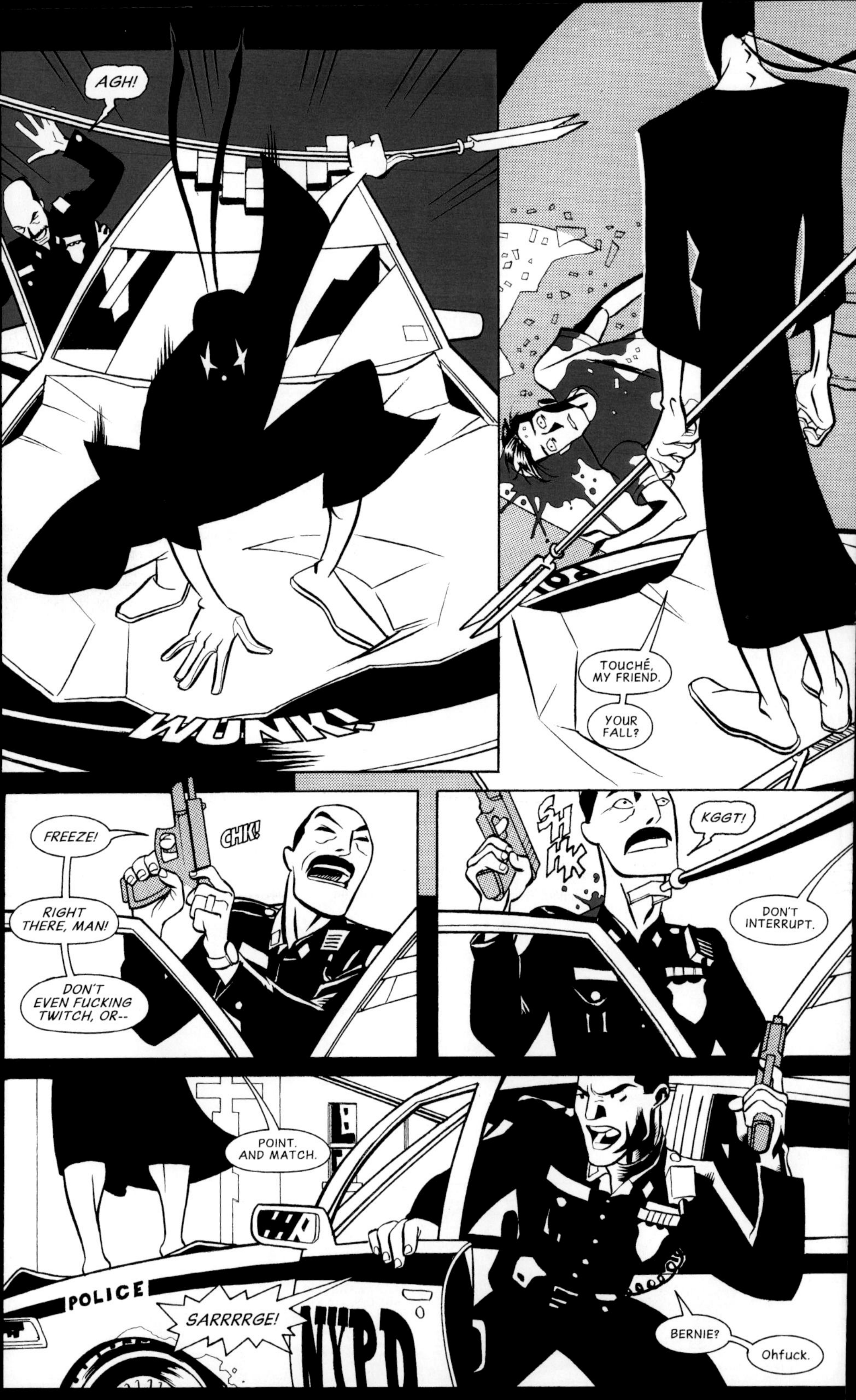
AGH!
WUNK!
TOUCHÉ, MY FRIEND.
YOUR FALL?
FREEZE!
CHK!
RIGHT THERE, MAN!
DON'T EVEN FUCKING TWITCH, OR--
SHHK
KGGT!
DON'T INTERRUPT.
POINT. AND MATCH.
POLICE
SARRRRGE!
NYPD
BERNIE?
Ohfuck.

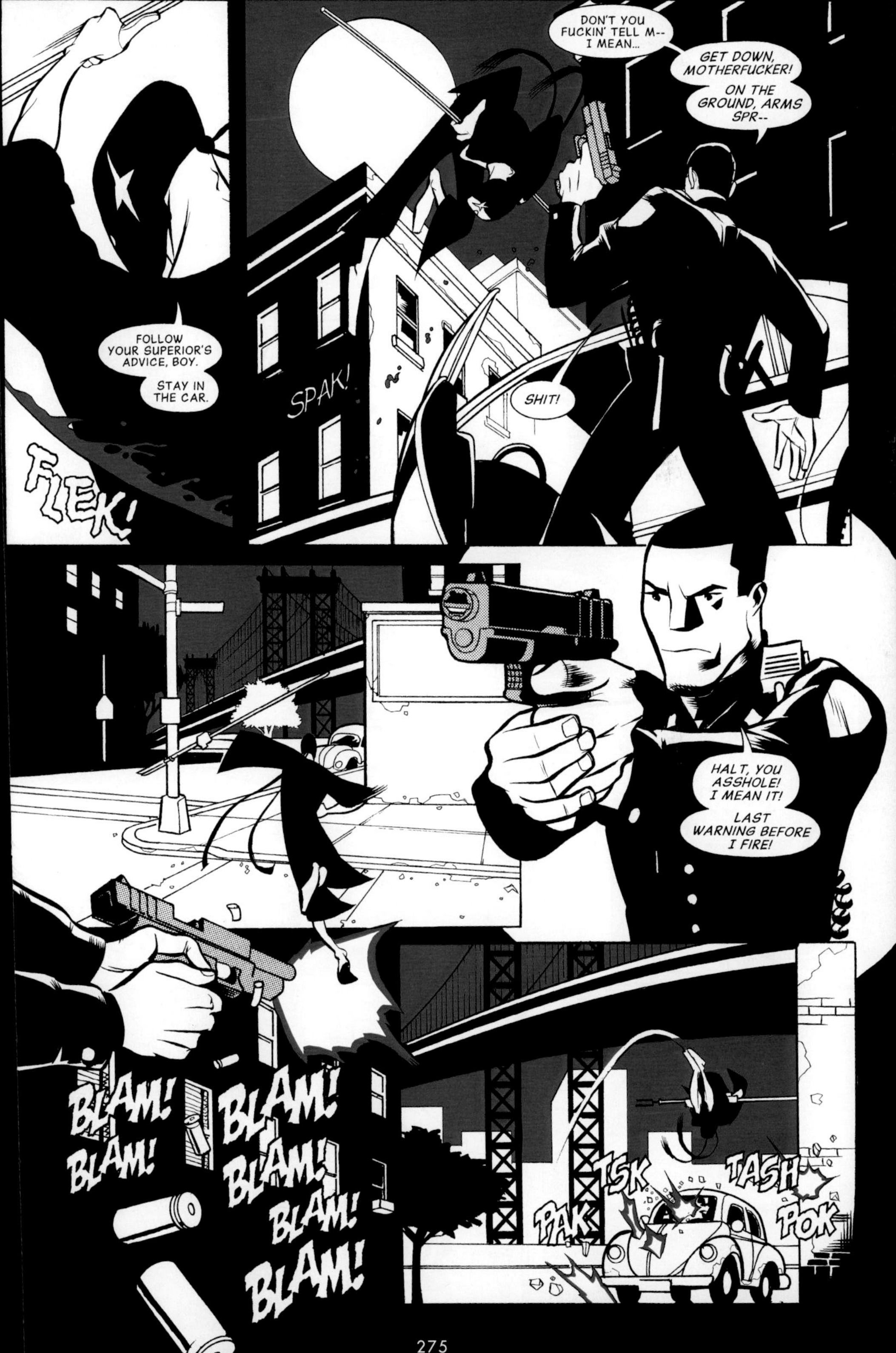
FOLLOW YOUR SUPERIOR'S ADVICE, BOY.
STAY IN THE CAR.
FLEK!
DON'T YOU FUCKIN' TELL M-- I MEAN...
GET DOWN, MOTHERFUCKER!
ON THE GROUND, ARMS SPR--
SPAK!
SHIT!
HALT, YOU ASSHOLE! I MEAN IT!
LAST WARNING BEFORE I FIRE!
BLAM! BLAM!
BLAM! BLAM! BLAM! BLAM!
PAK
TSK
TASH
POK

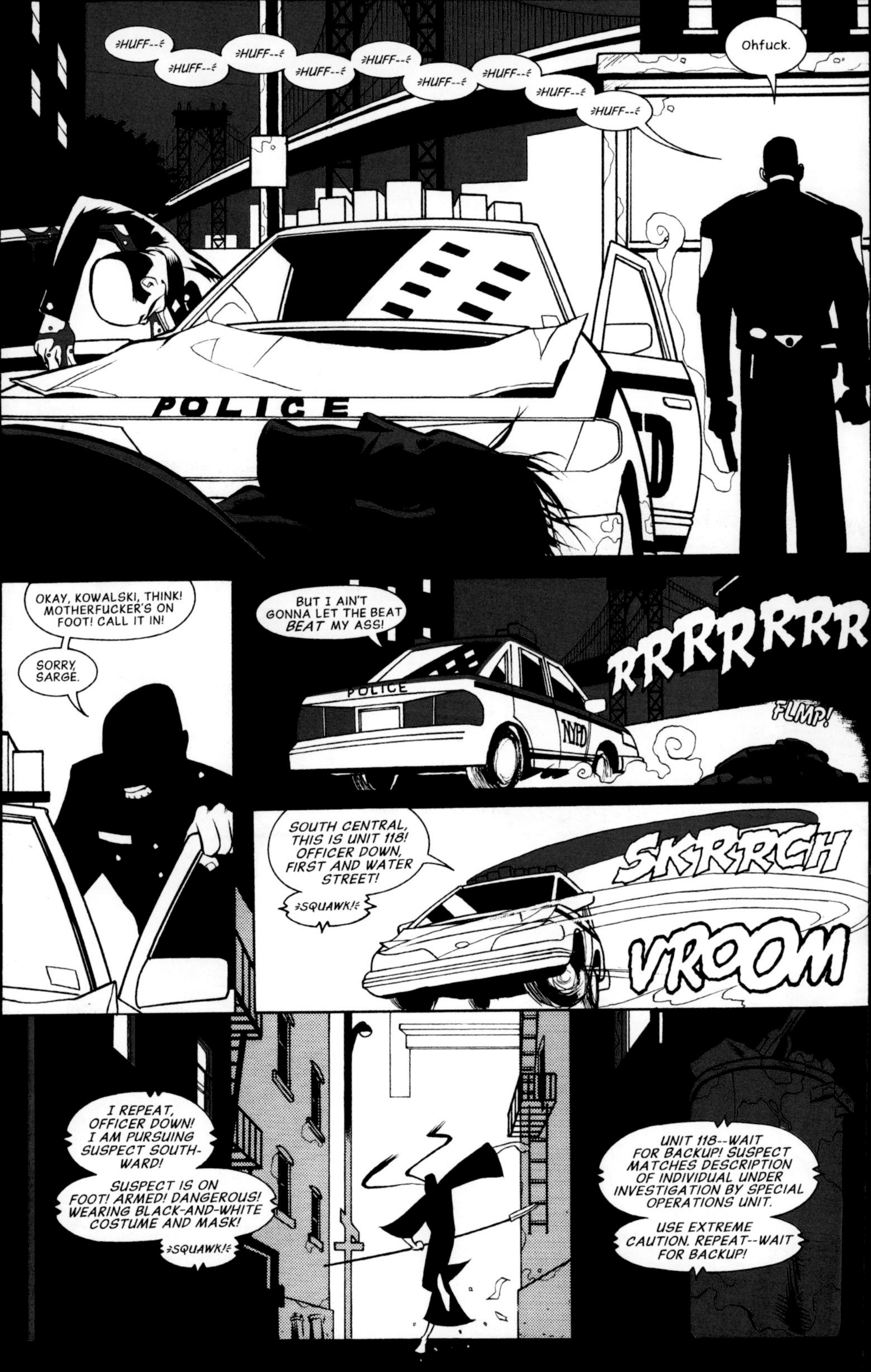

HUFF--
HUFF--
HUFF--
HUFF--
HUFF--
HUFF--
HUFF--
HUFF--
Ohfuck.
POLICE
OKAY, KOWALSKI, THINK! MOTHERFUCKER'S ON FOOT! CALL IT IN!
SORRY, SARGE.
BUT I AIN'T GONNA LET THE BEAT BEAT MY ASS!
POLICE
NYPD
RRRRRRR
FLMP!
SOUTH CENTRAL, THIS IS UNIT 118! OFFICER DOWN, FIRST AND WATER STREET!
SQUAWK!
SKRRCH
VROOM
I REPEAT, OFFICER DOWN! I AM PURSUING SUSPECT SOUTH-WARD!
SUSPECT IS ON FOOT! ARMED! DANGEROUS! WEARING BLACK-AND-WHITE COSTUME AND MASK!
SQUAWK!
UNIT 118--WAIT FOR BACKUP! SUSPECT MATCHES DESCRIPTION OF INDIVIDUAL UNDER INVESTIGATION BY SPECIAL OPERATIONS UNIT.
USE EXTREME CAUTION. REPEAT--WAIT FOR BACKUP!

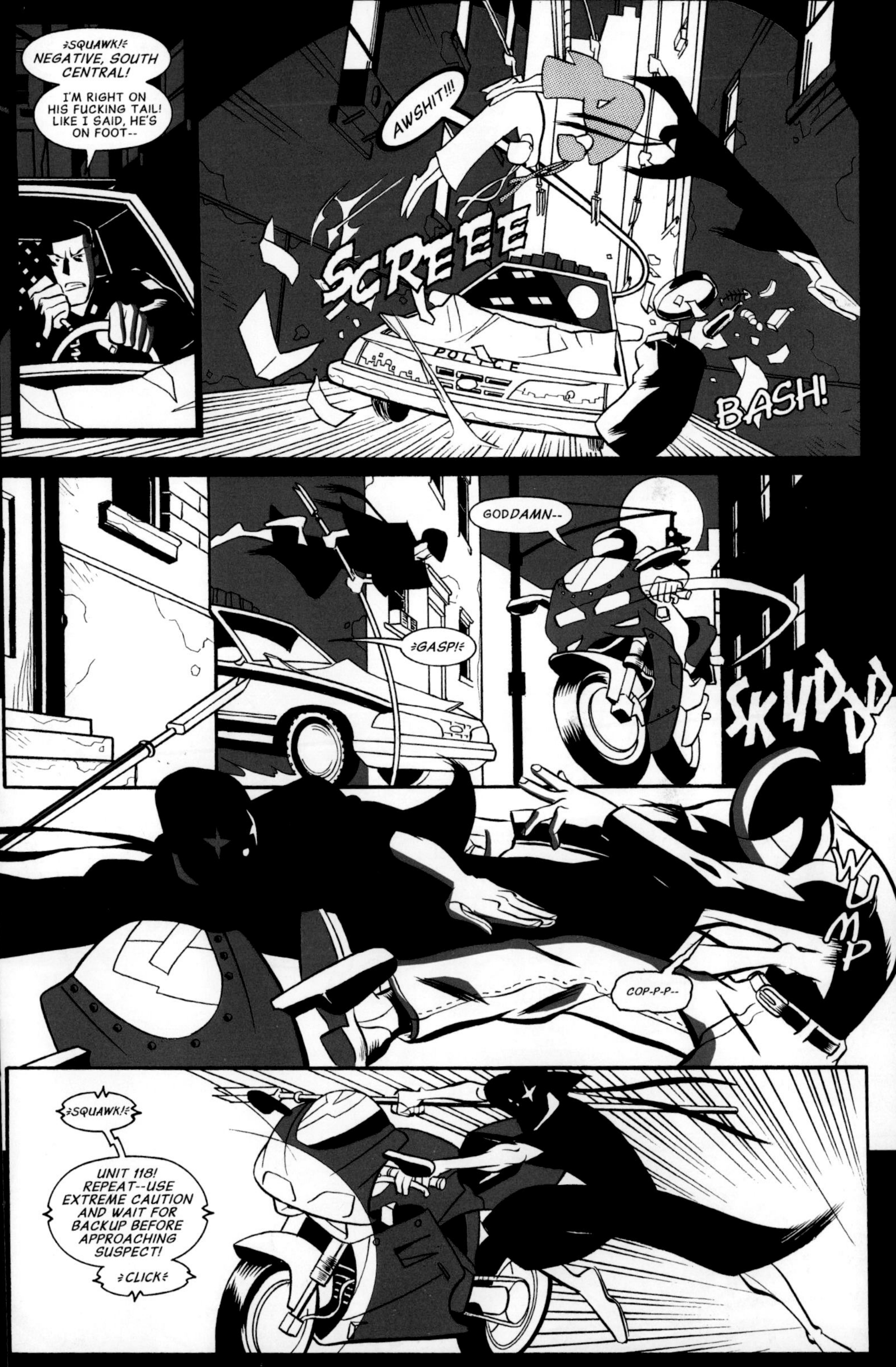

SQUAWK!
NEGATIVE, SOUTH CENTRAL!
I'M RIGHT ON HIS FUCKING TAIL! LIKE I SAID, HE'S ON FOOT--
AWSHIT!!!
SCREEE
POLICE
BASH!
GODDAMN--
GASP!
SKUDDD
WUMP
COP-P-P--
SQUAWK!
UNIT 118! REPEAT--USE EXTREME CAUTION AND WAIT FOR BACKUP BEFORE APPROACHING SUSPECT!
CLICK

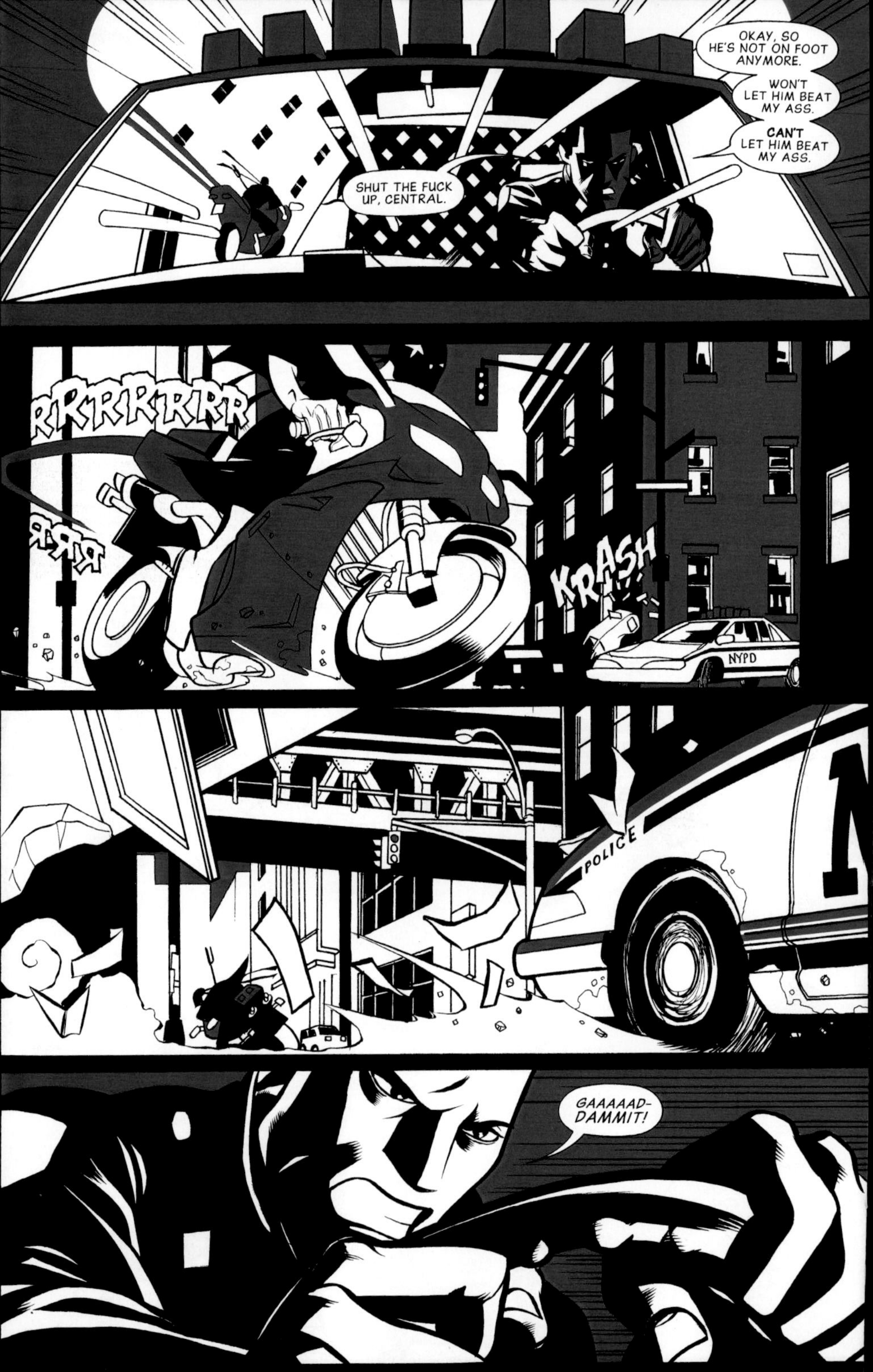
OKAY, SO HE'S NOT ON FOOT ANYMORE.
WON'T LET HIM BEAT MY ASS.
CAN'T LET HIM BEAT MY ASS.
SHUT THE FUCK UP, CENTRAL.
RRRRRRRR
RRR
KRASH
NYPD
POLICE
GAAAAAD-DAMMIT!

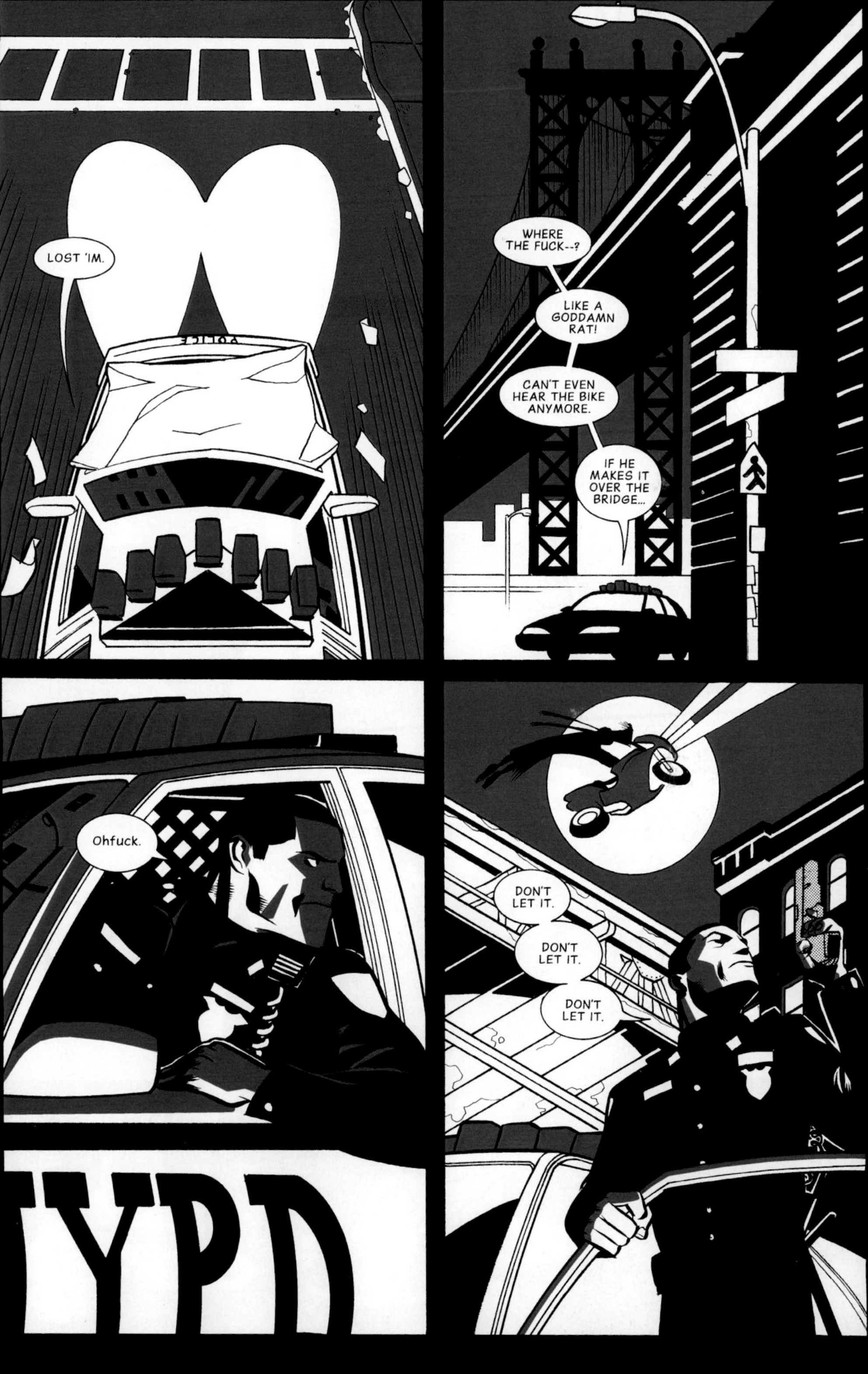
LOST 'IM.
WHERE THE FUCK--?
LIKE A GODDAMN RAT!
CAN'T EVEN HEAR THE BIKE ANYMORE.
IF HE MAKES IT OVER THE BRIDGE...
Ohfuck.
YPD
DON'T LET IT.
DON'T LET IT.
DON'T LET IT.

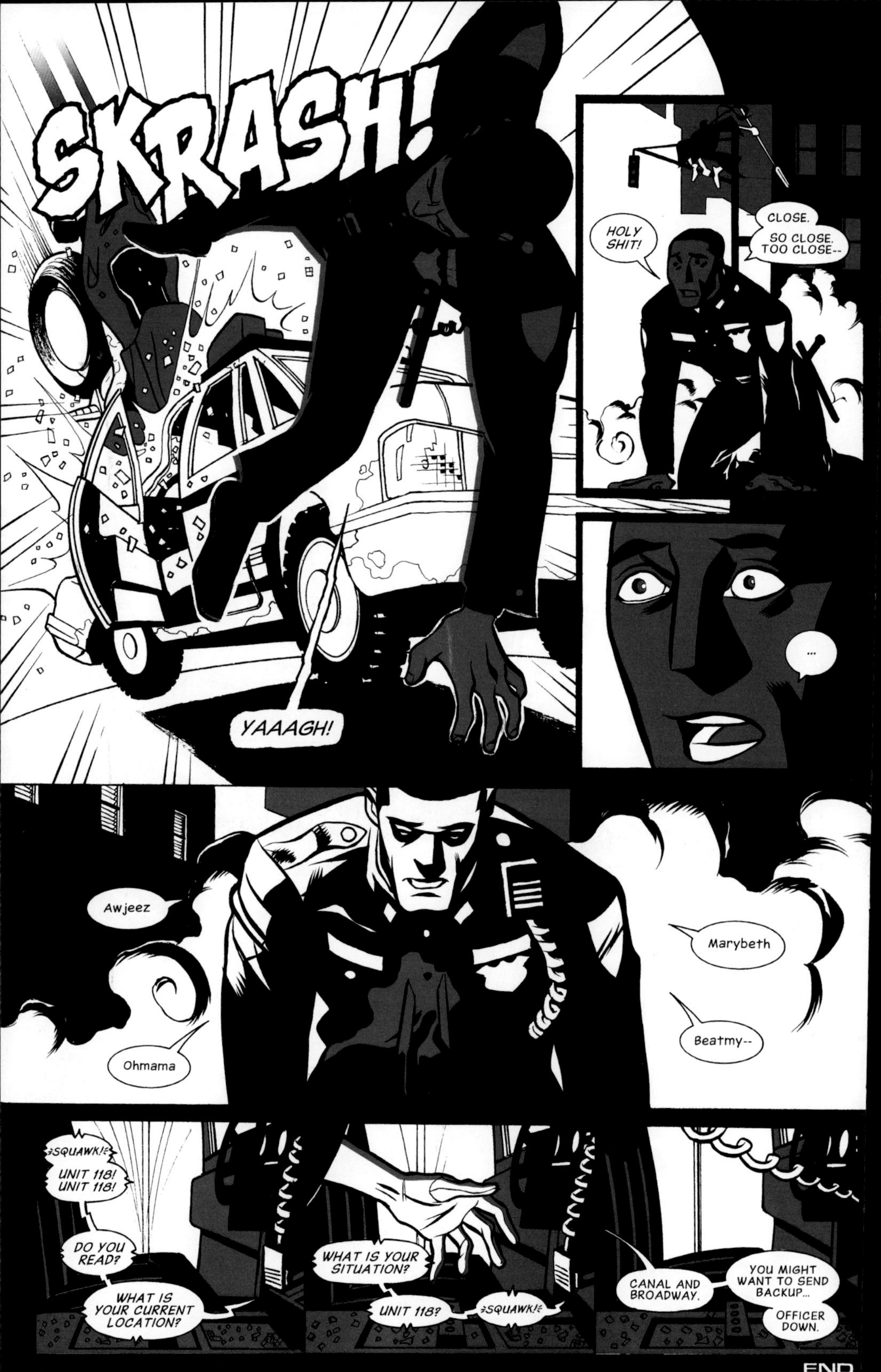

SKRASH!
YAAAGH!
HOLY SHIT!
CLOSE.
SO CLOSE. TOO CLOSE--
...
Awjeez
Ohmama
Marybeth
Beatmy--
SQUAWK!
UNIT 118! UNIT 118!
DO YOU READ?
WHAT IS YOUR CURRENT LOCATION?
WHAT IS YOUR SITUATION?
UNIT 118?
SQUAWK!
CANAL AND BROADWAY.
YOU MIGHT WANT TO SEND BACKUP...
OFFICER DOWN.
END

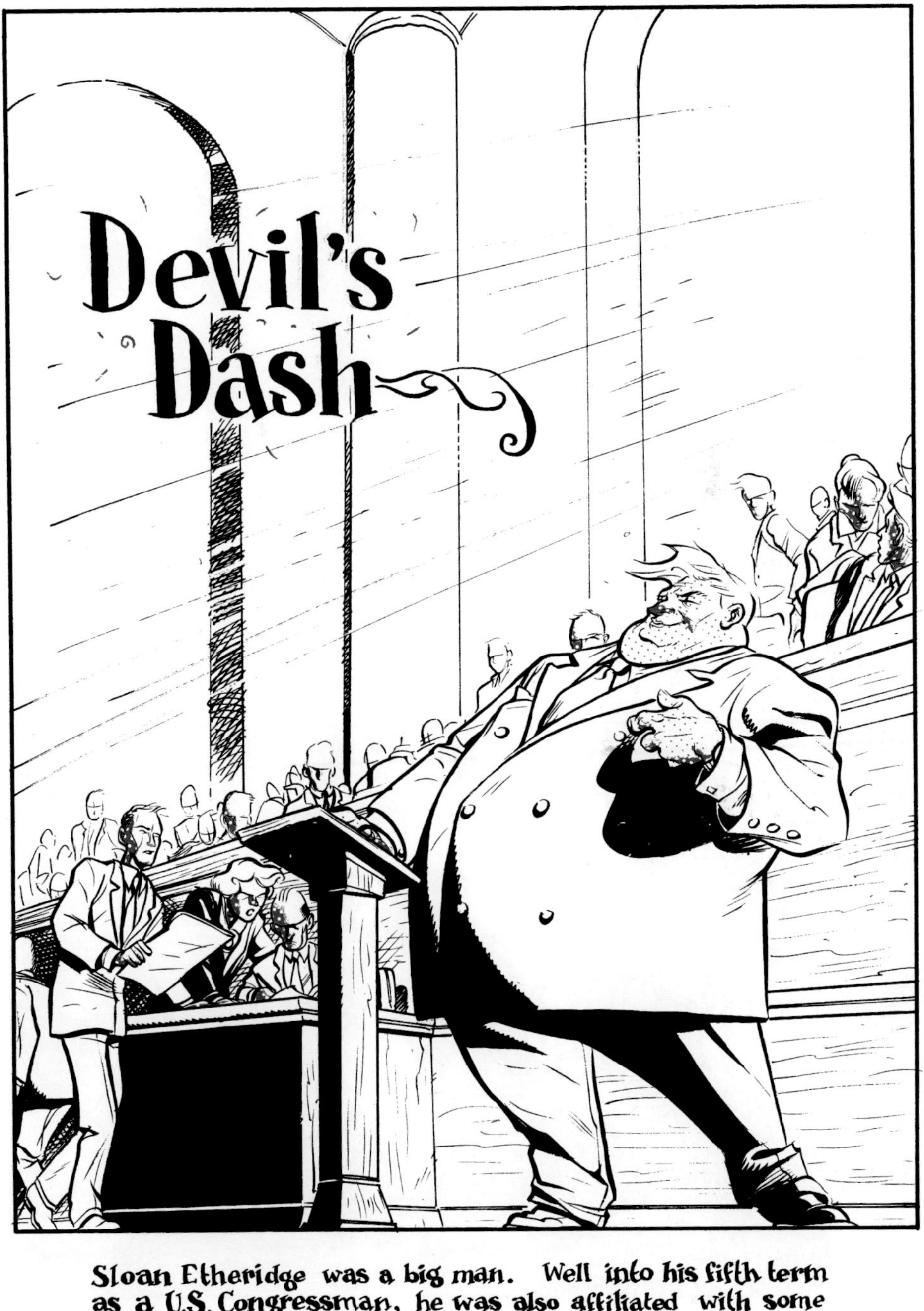
Devil's Dash

Sloan Etheridge was a big man. Well into his fifth term as a U.S. Congressman, he was also affiliated with some of the most ruthlessly successful members of the organized crime syndicates. Additionally, Sloan Etheridge weighed in at a healthy 427 lbs.

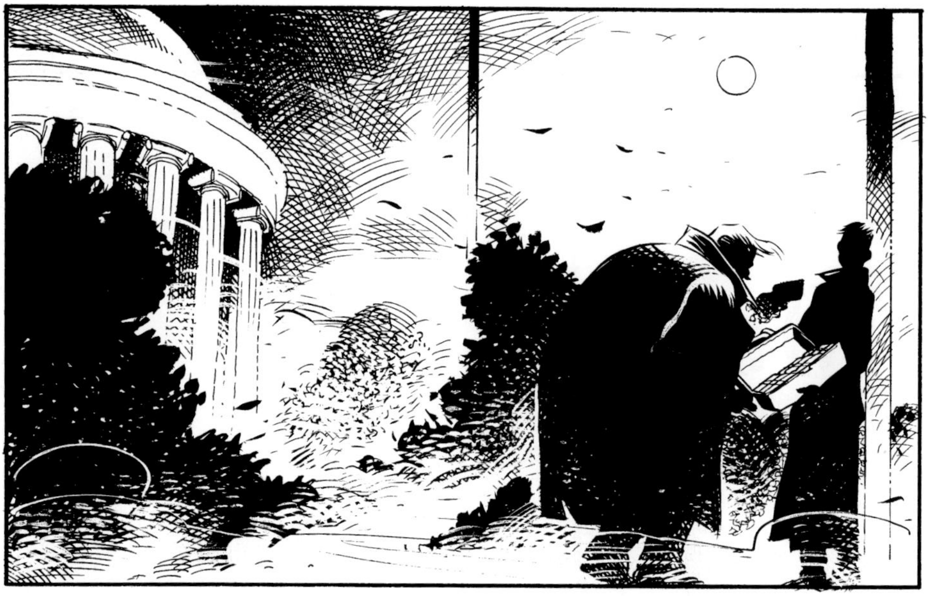

Made fearless by his protected status in the political arena, Sloan took comfort that his underworld connections guaranteed he was never investigated by those very same authorities from the Department of Justice. He was impervious to any attack.

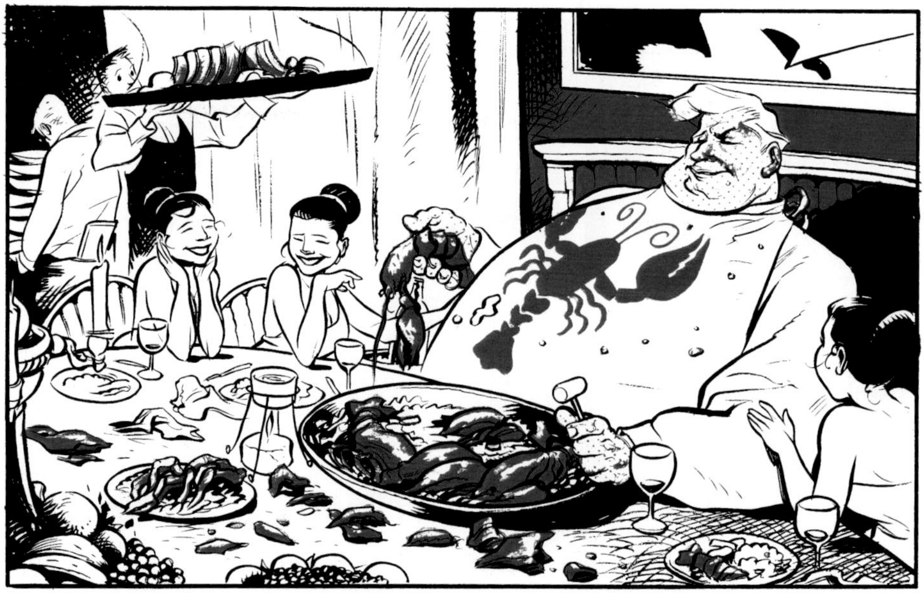

The Respected Gentleman from New York enjoyed a privileged life in every regard and exhibited a voracious appetite for all the finer things of life. His tastes ranged from caviar to lobster, from silken shirts to young Asian prostitutes, Scotch whisky to Bolivian cocaine.

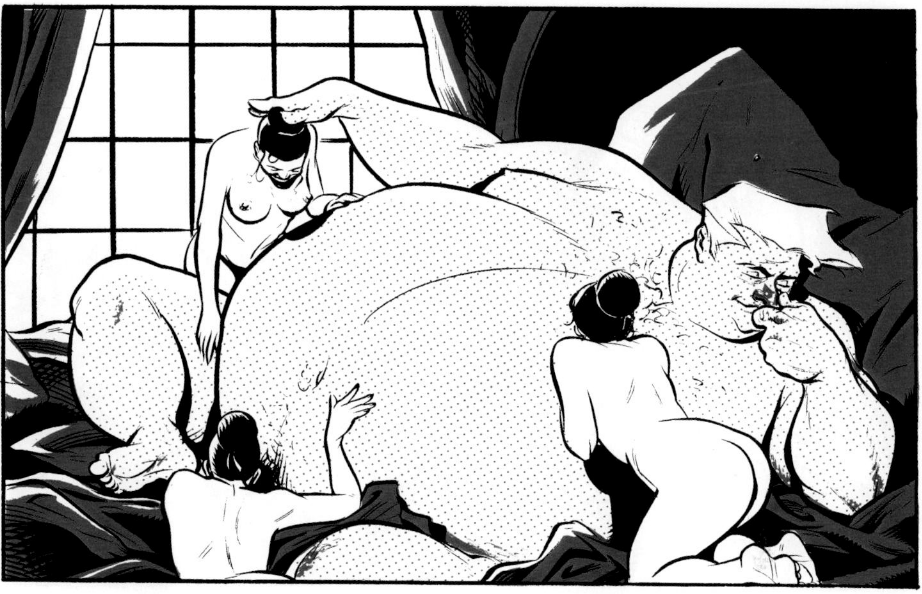

Between sessions of Congress, Sloan always returned to his penthouse apartment in Manhattan, a visit that often found Mrs. Etheridge out of town on vacation. Still, his more entrepreneurial constituents always saw to it that Sloan was far from ever lonely.

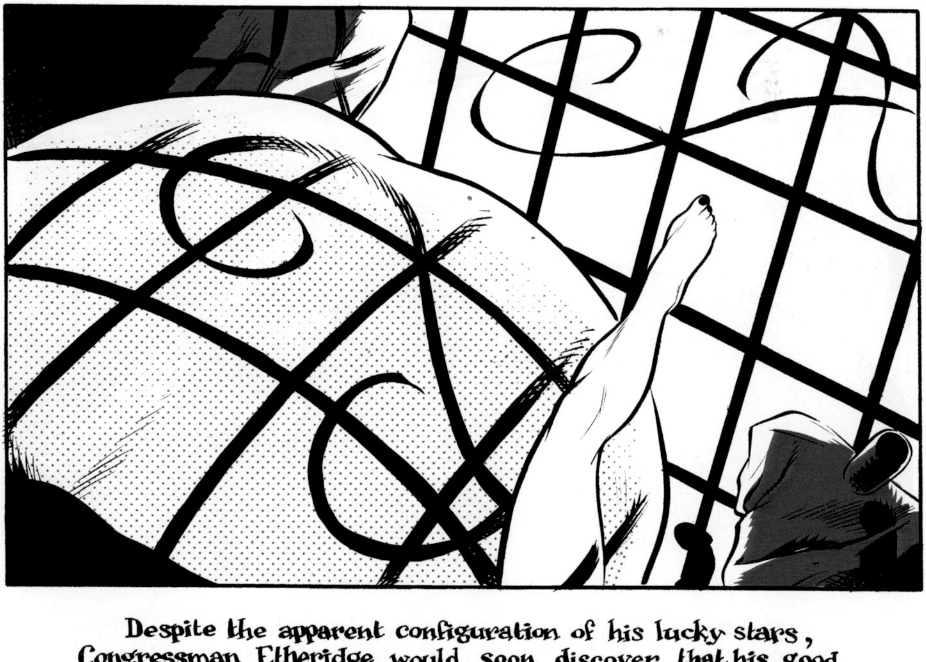

Despite the apparent configuration of his lucky stars, Congressman Etheridge would soon discover that his good fortunes were about to run out. His associations within Mafia circles had unwittingly brought him into opposition with the rival Ciccone Family.

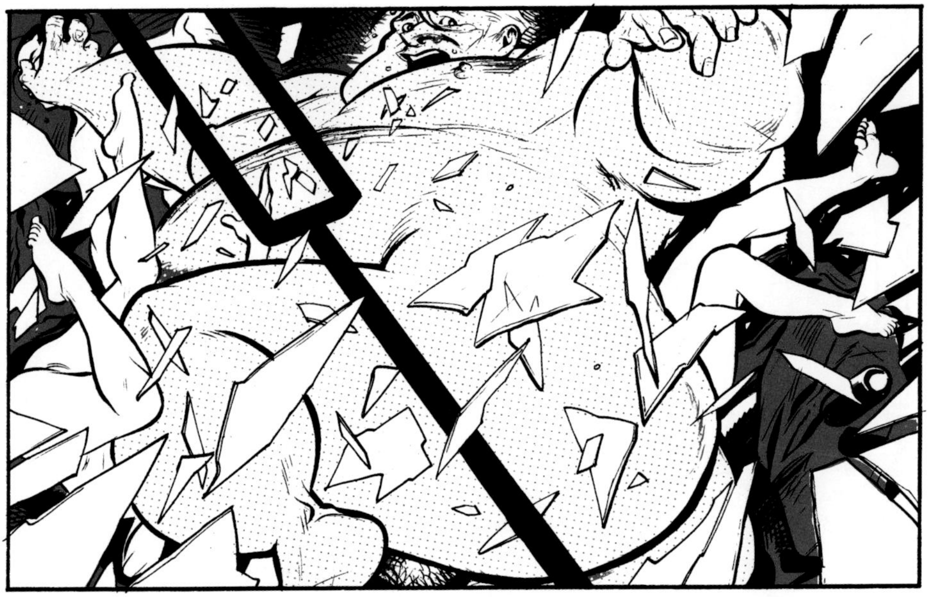

Even the aloof and pampered Sloan had heard the fearful name of the Ciccones' enforcer, whispered in the most hushed and somber tones ever uttered by his mobster buddies. In that moment of recognition, the very big man squealed and fled with all the hysteria of a very small girl.

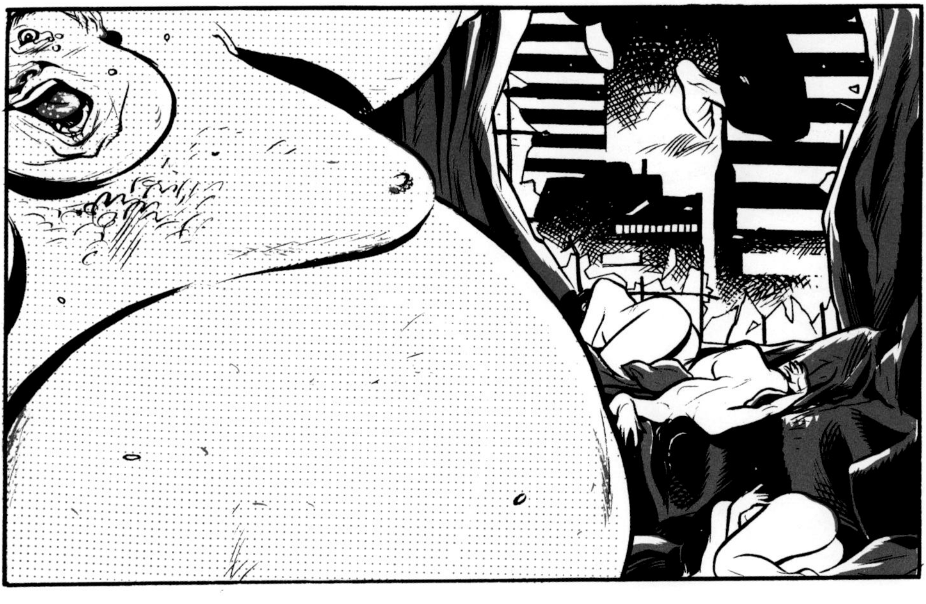

Heedless of his companions' safety, Sloan's rampaging exit left one of the ladies with a broken hand and another with several fractured ribs. The assassin ignored the whores and came on, relentless in his pursuit of the blubbering, terrified manipulator.

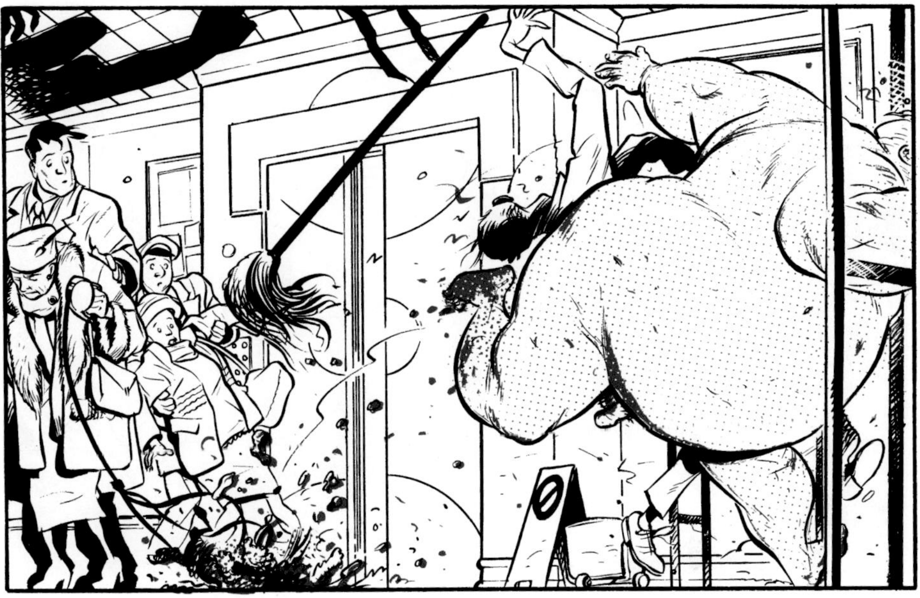

Bounding through the lobby of his building and bellowing for the police, Etheridge accidentally trampled a brace of poodles and snapped the neck of an elderly custodian. His trembling heart leapt sideways as a darkened figure emerged from the emergency staircase.

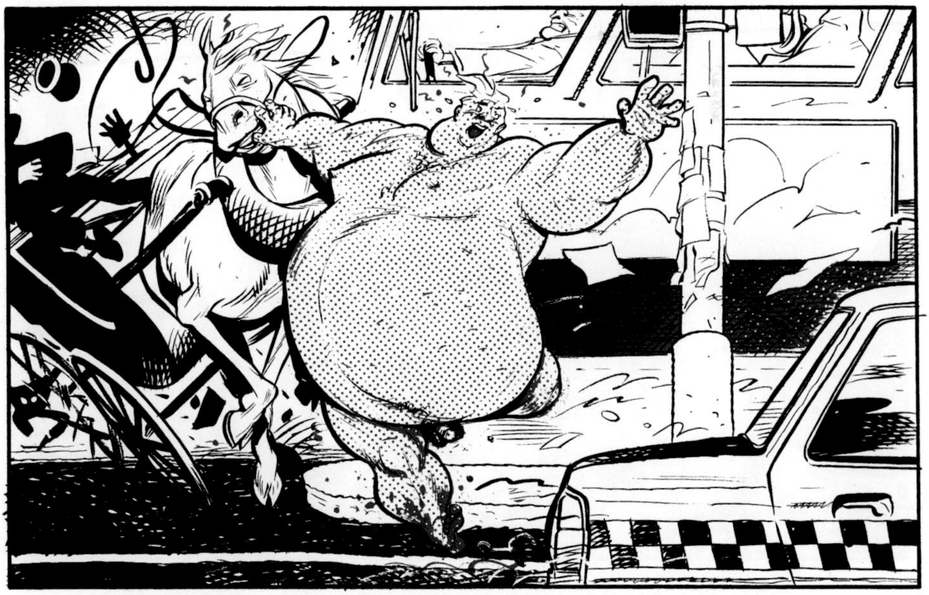

One block away, Sloan waved desperately for a cab, scaring a hansom horse into bolting and dislodging its driver. As it careened out into traffic, the carriage was struck by a bus and the elderly couple inside were both killed instantly. No taxis stopped.

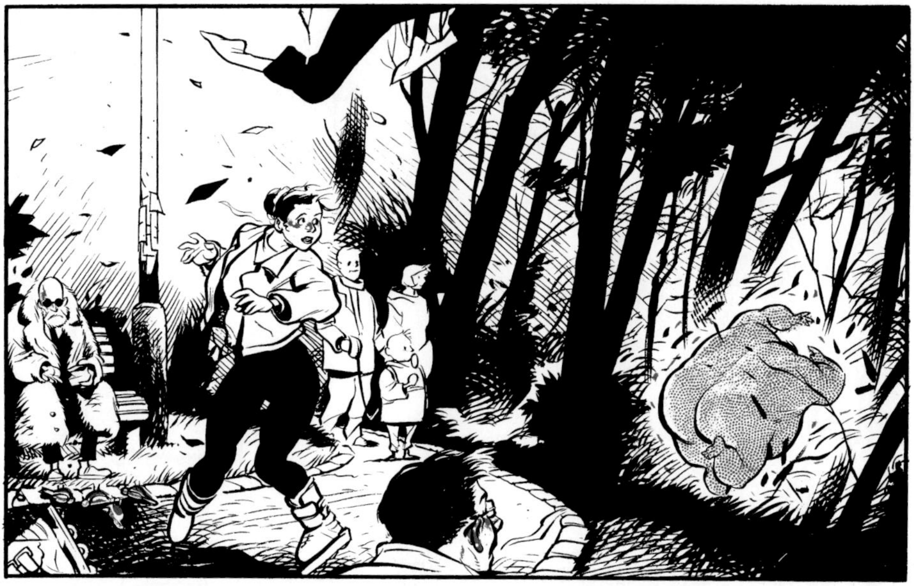

Witless, Etheridge's frantic dash led him into Central Park where his bizarre appearance elicited less alarm than bemused smiles. Through the shadowy brush raced along his pursuer, allowing Sloan occasionally to catch sight of him with the grimmest panache.

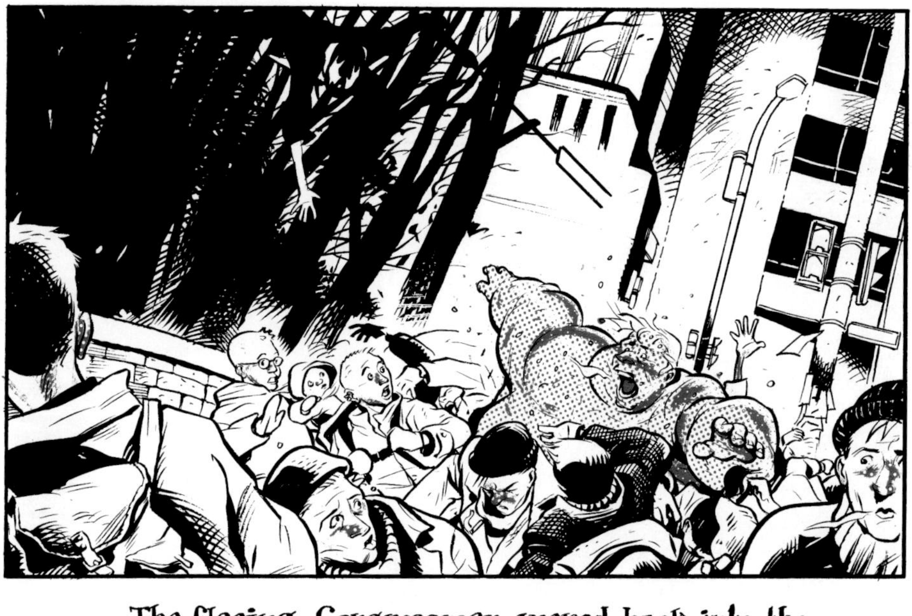

The fleeing Congressman veered back into the streets, seeking the safety of the crowds, his senses numbed by the utter panic that surged every time he looked over his shoulder. His own demise was chasing him, a vision that his gluttonous mind had never considered.

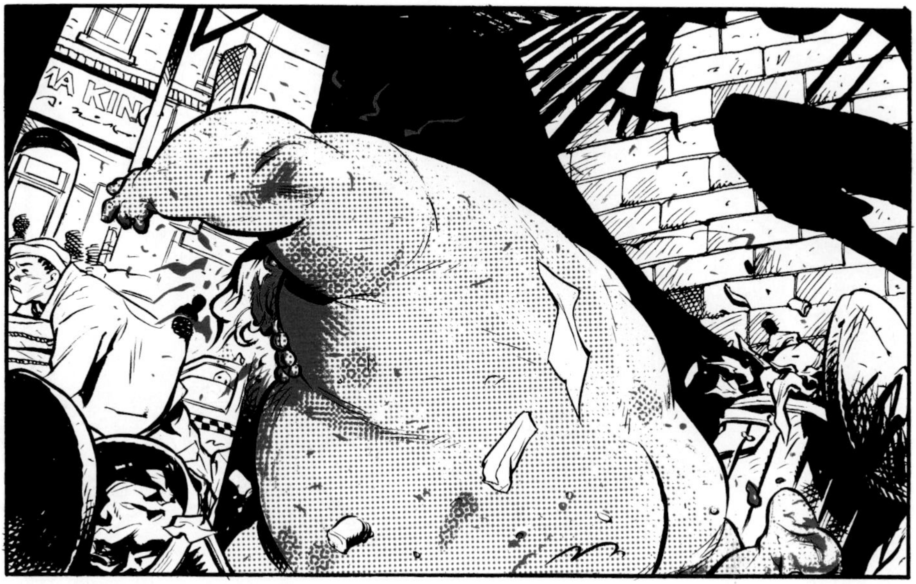

Finally, Sloan's heart began to seize. His dreadful sprint had reached its end. Still, his panic-ridden body refused to accept the only possible conclusion, as the specter of death began its fateful descent. With a terminal effort of dying will, Etheridge once again turned and dashed.

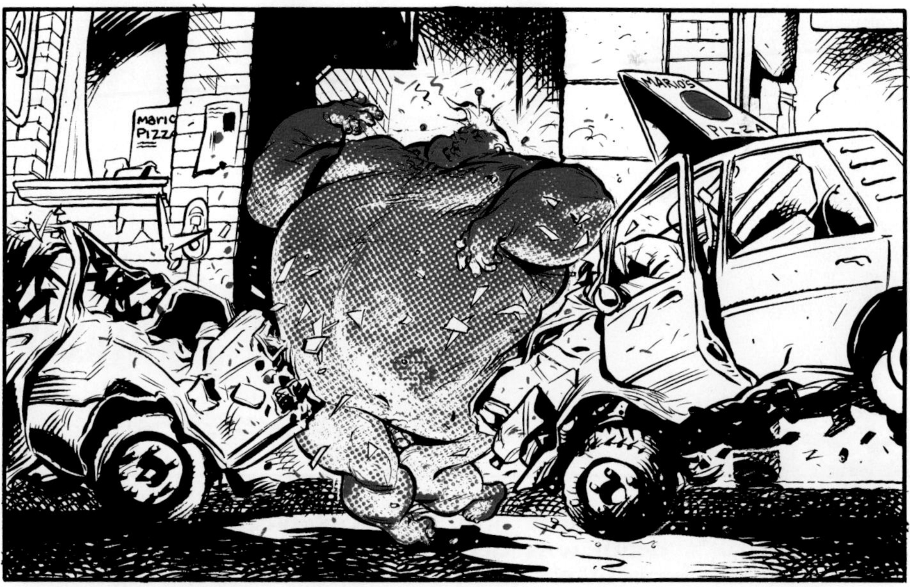
MARIO'S
PIZZA

The skidding collision of a pizza delivery vehicle and an empty limousine sandwiched Congressman Etheridge in a quelling embrace. The accident broke over eighty percent of his bones and ruptured many of his internal organs. One of his eyes was dislodged from its socket, and fourteen teeth were shattered.

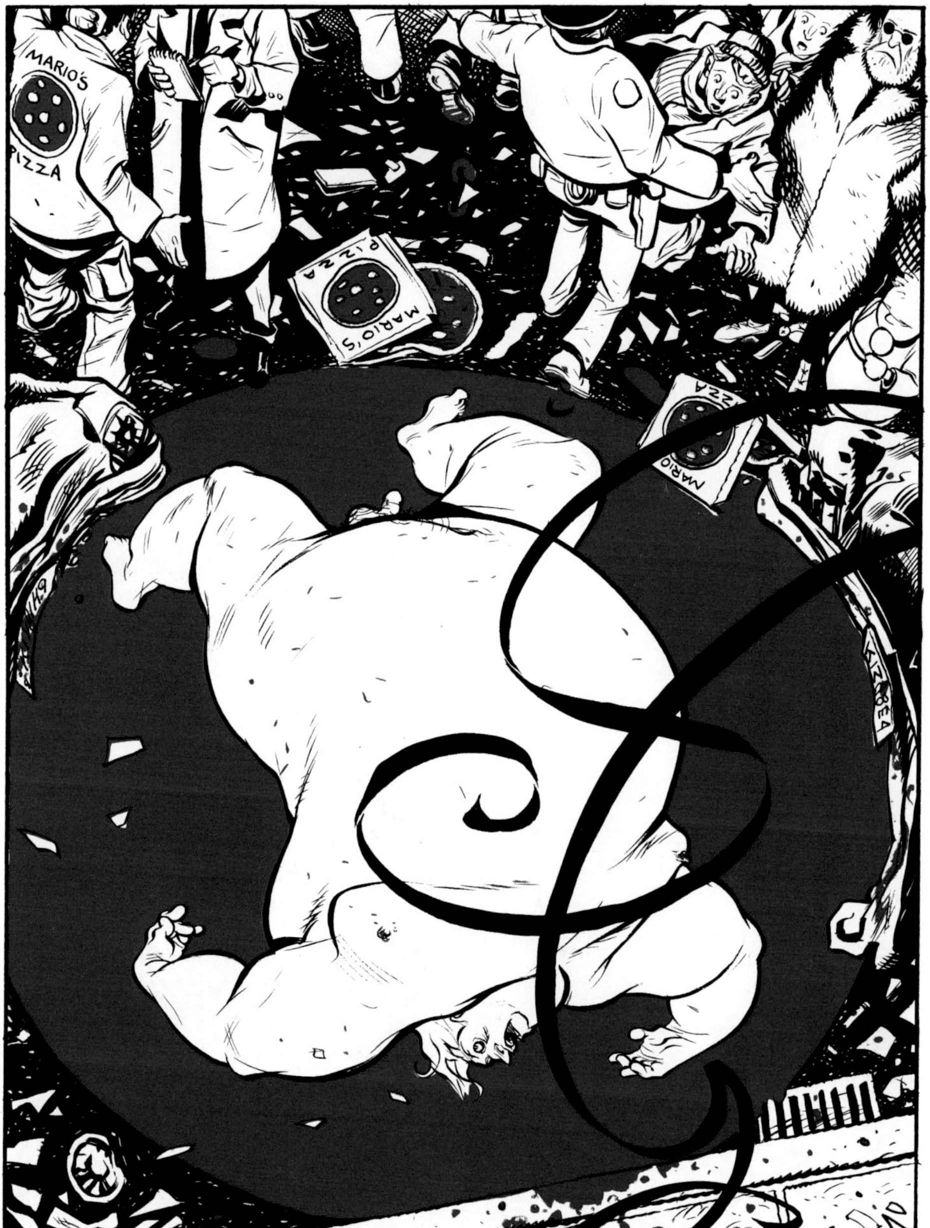
MARIO'S
PIZZA
PIZZA
MARIO'S

In the end, United States Representative Sloan Etheridge's death was deemed a tragically bizarre accident, brought about by his own hysteria during a massive heart attack, which, in turn, was probably triggered by the high amount of cocaine found in his system. Such personal transgressions were brought to the forefront of the death inquiry, but no trace of his connections to organized crime was ever found.

·End·

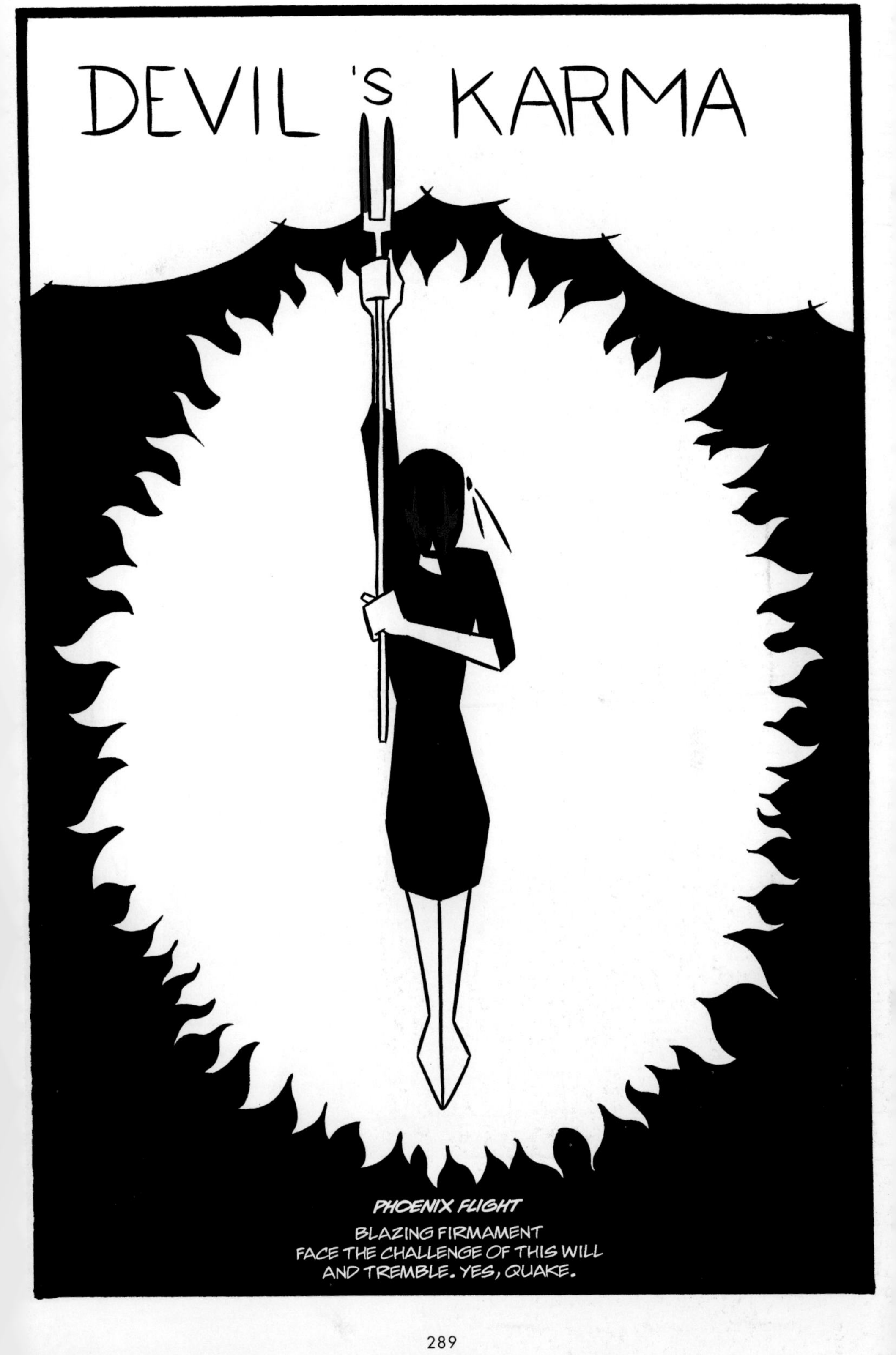
DEVIL'S KARMA
PHOENIX FLIGHT
BLAZING FIRMAMENT
FACE THE CHALLENGE OF THIS WILL
AND TREMBLE. YES, QUAKE.

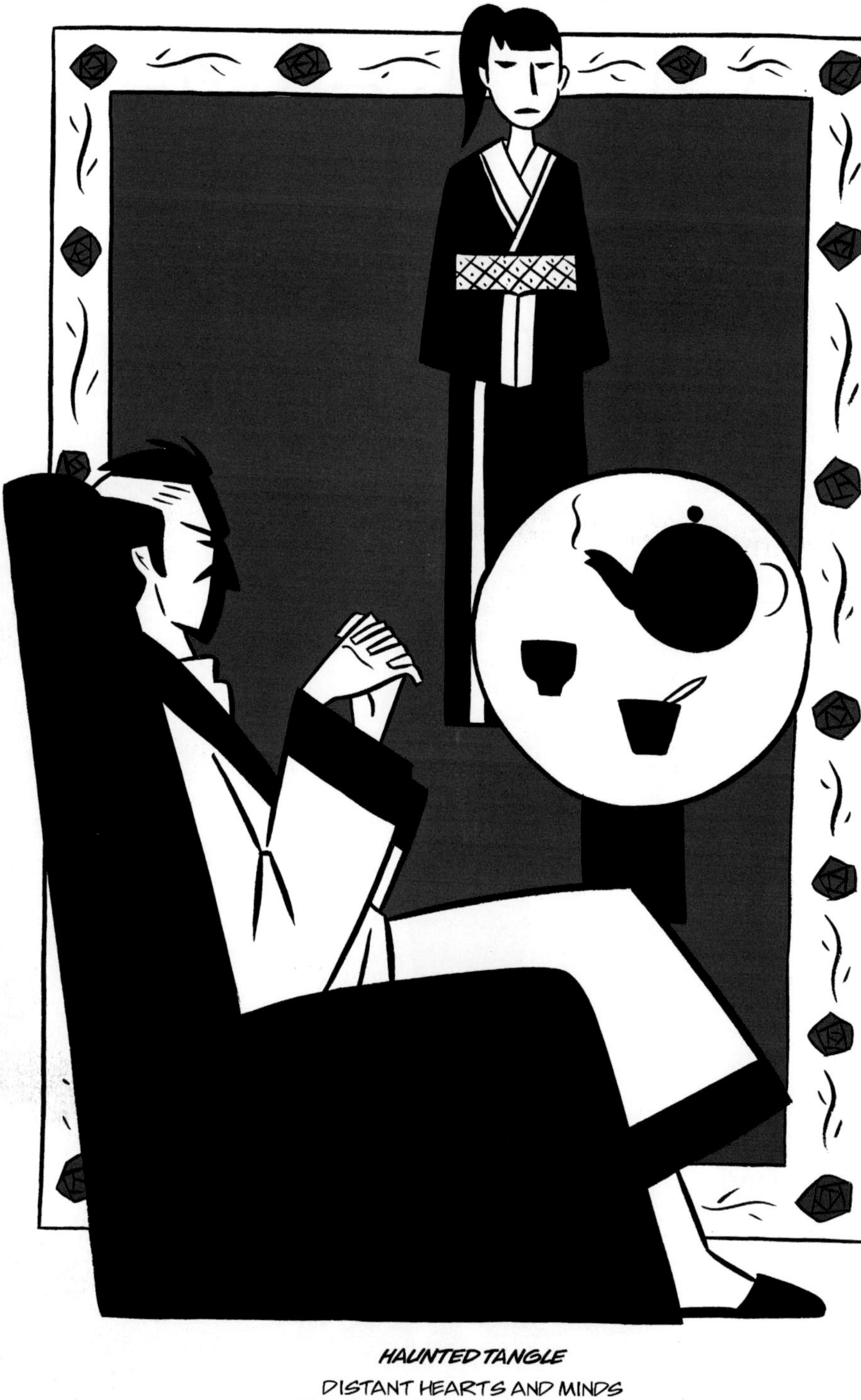

HAUNTED TANGLE

DISTANT HEARTS AND MINDS
CONTEMPLATE BEAUTY AND DEATH.
THEIR FATES BOUND BY BOTH.

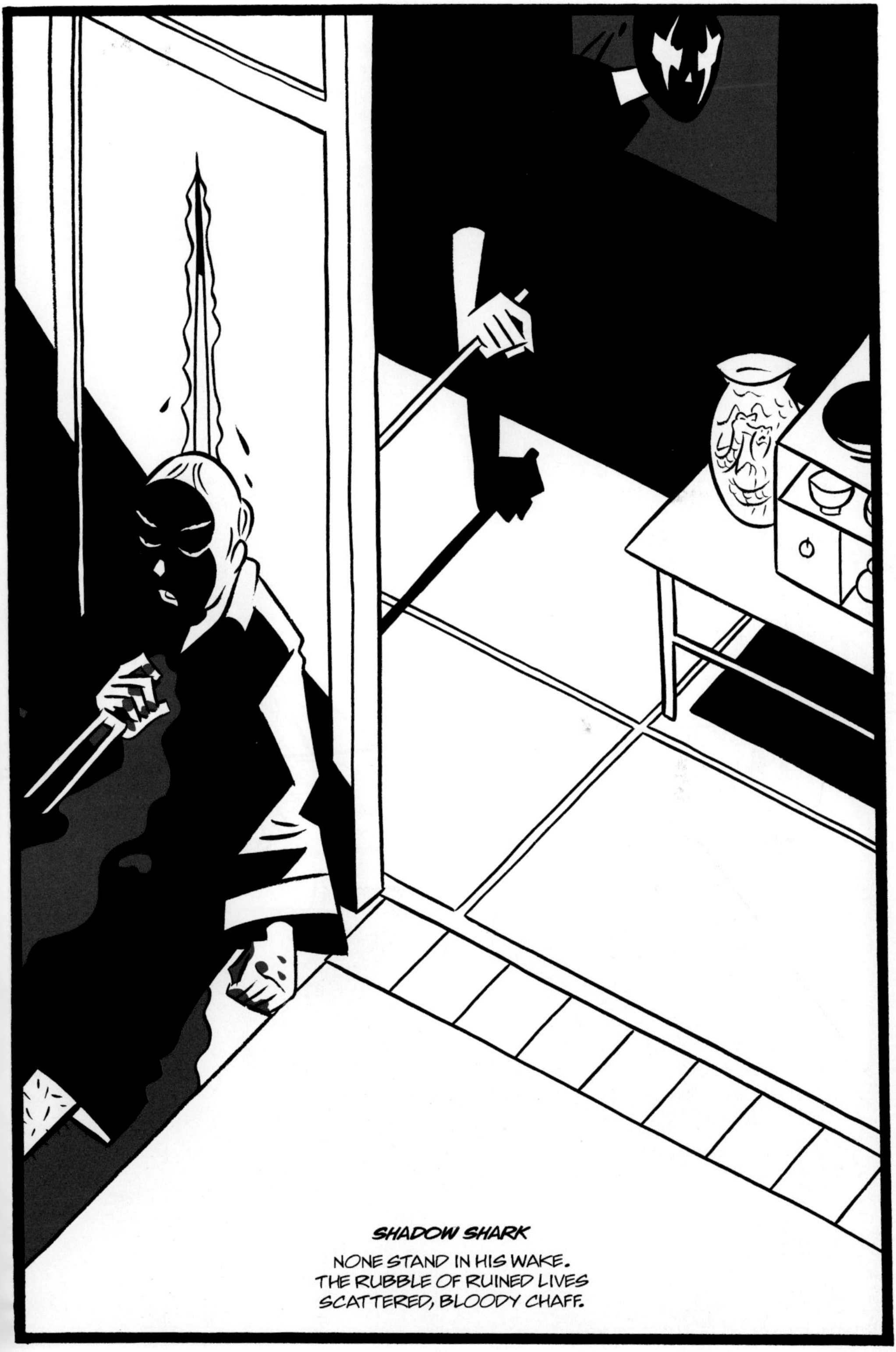
SHADOW SHARK
NONE STAND IN HIS WAKE.
THE RUBBLE OF RUINED LIVES
SCATTERED, BLOODY CHAFF.

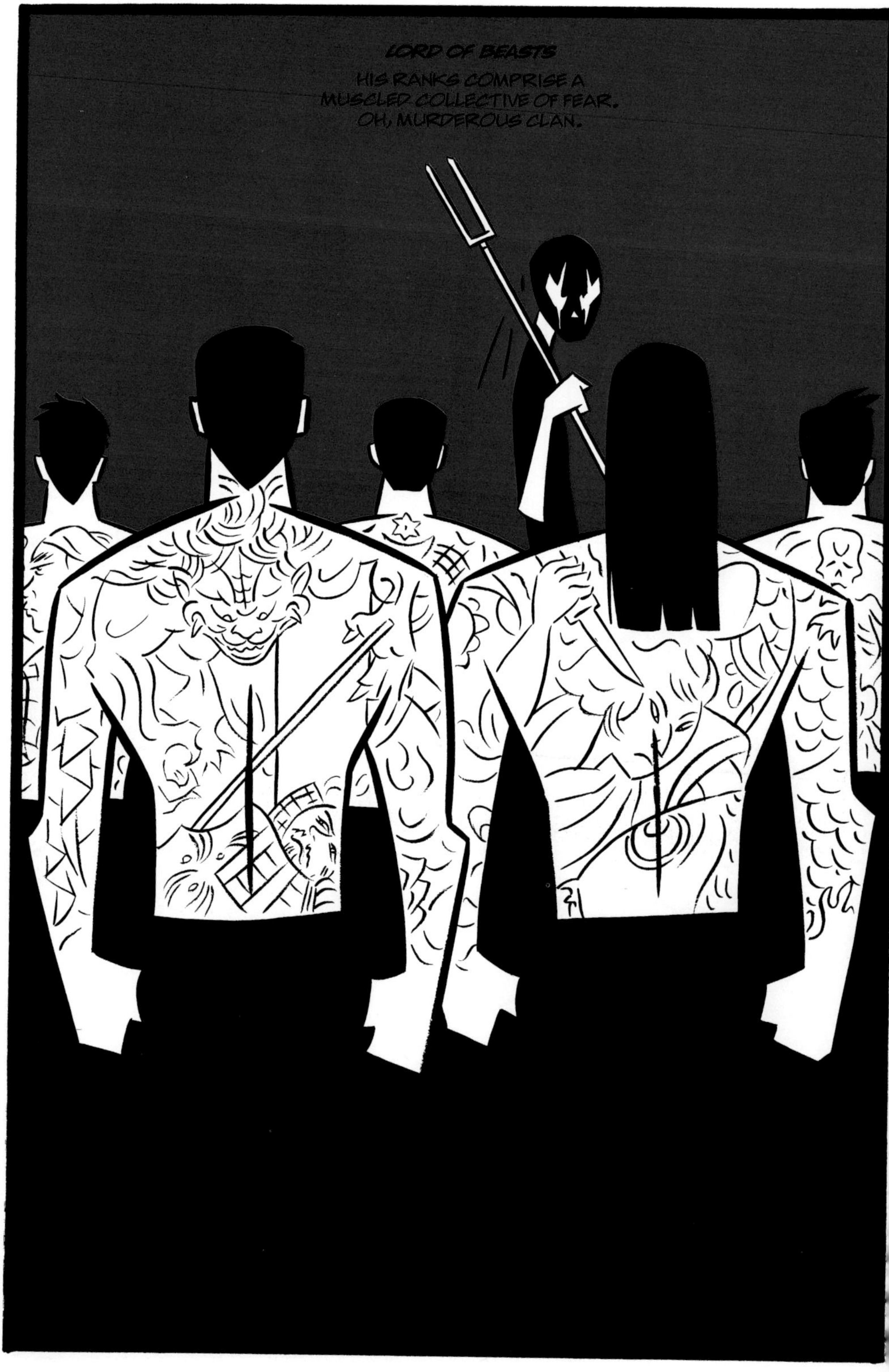
LORD OF BEASTS
HIS RANKS COMPRISE A
MUSCLED COLLECTIVE OF FEAR.
OH, MURDEROUS CLAN.

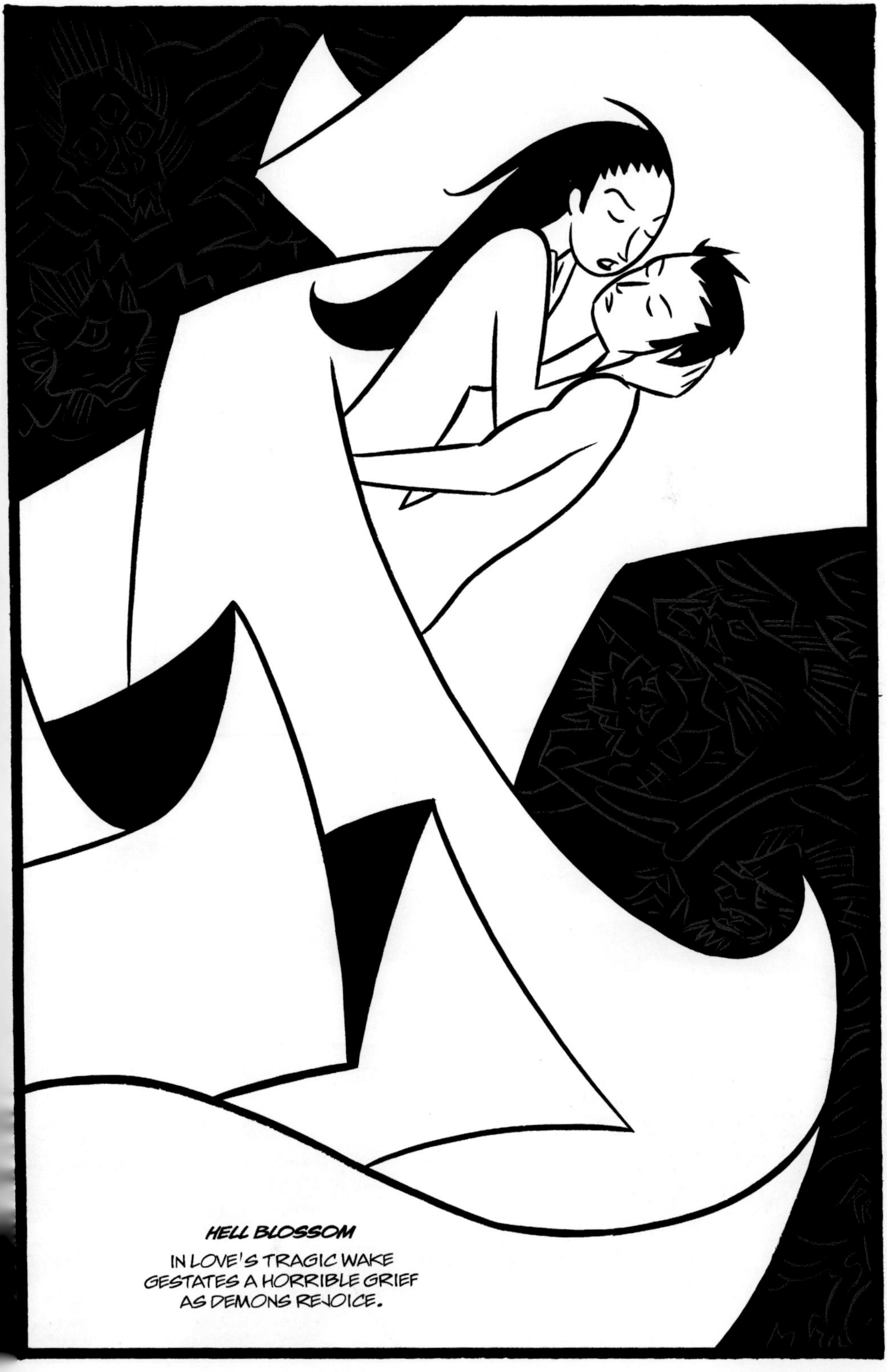
HELL BLOSSOM
IN LOVE'S TRAGIC WAKE
GESTATES A HORRIBLE GRIEF
AS DEMONS REJOICE.

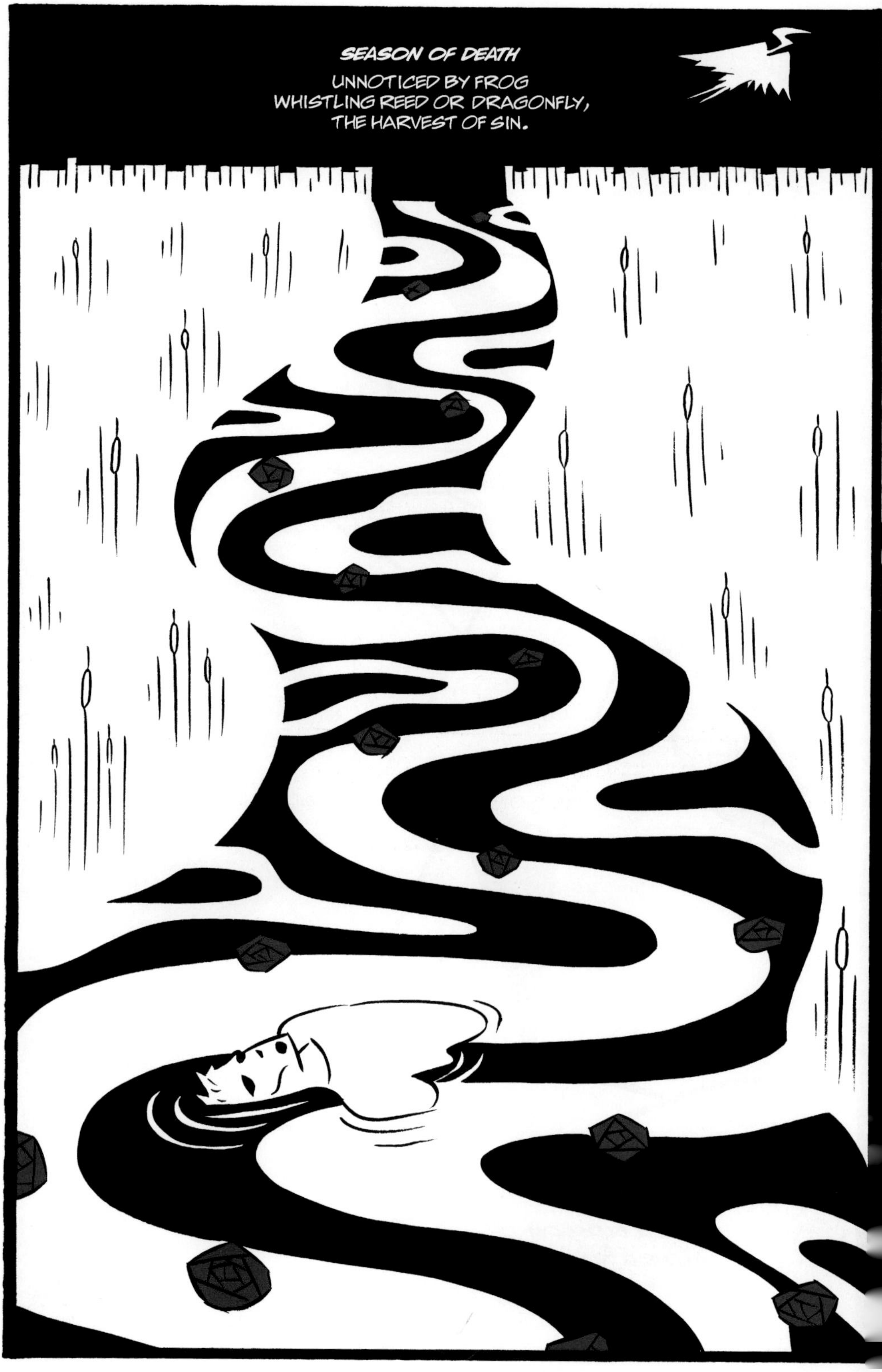
SEASON OF DEATH
UNNOTICED BY FROG
WHISTLING REED OR DRAGONFLY,
THE HARVEST OF SIN.

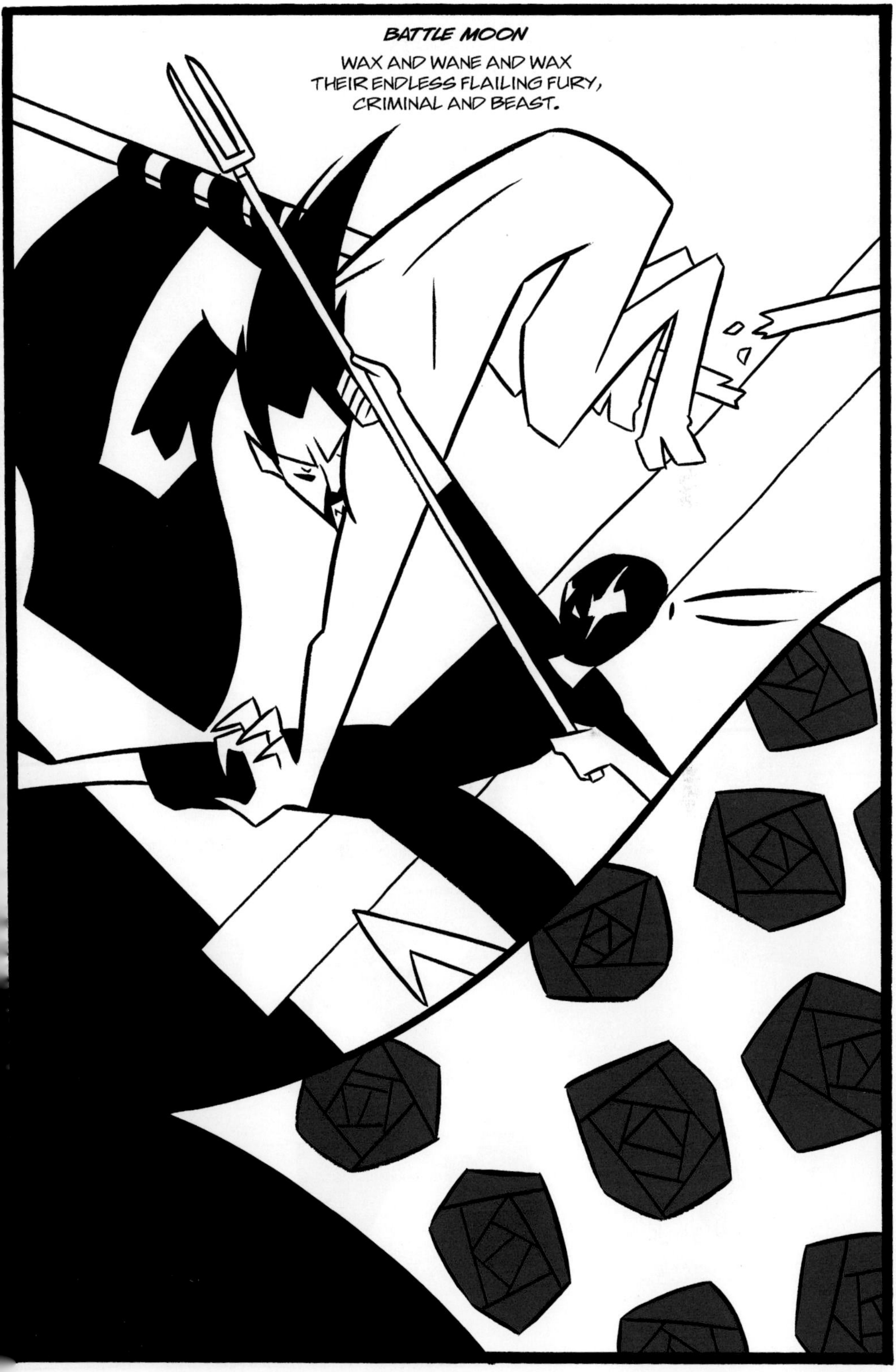
BATTLE MOON
WAX AND WANE AND WAX
THEIR ENDLESS FLAILING FURY,
CRIMINAL AND BEAST.

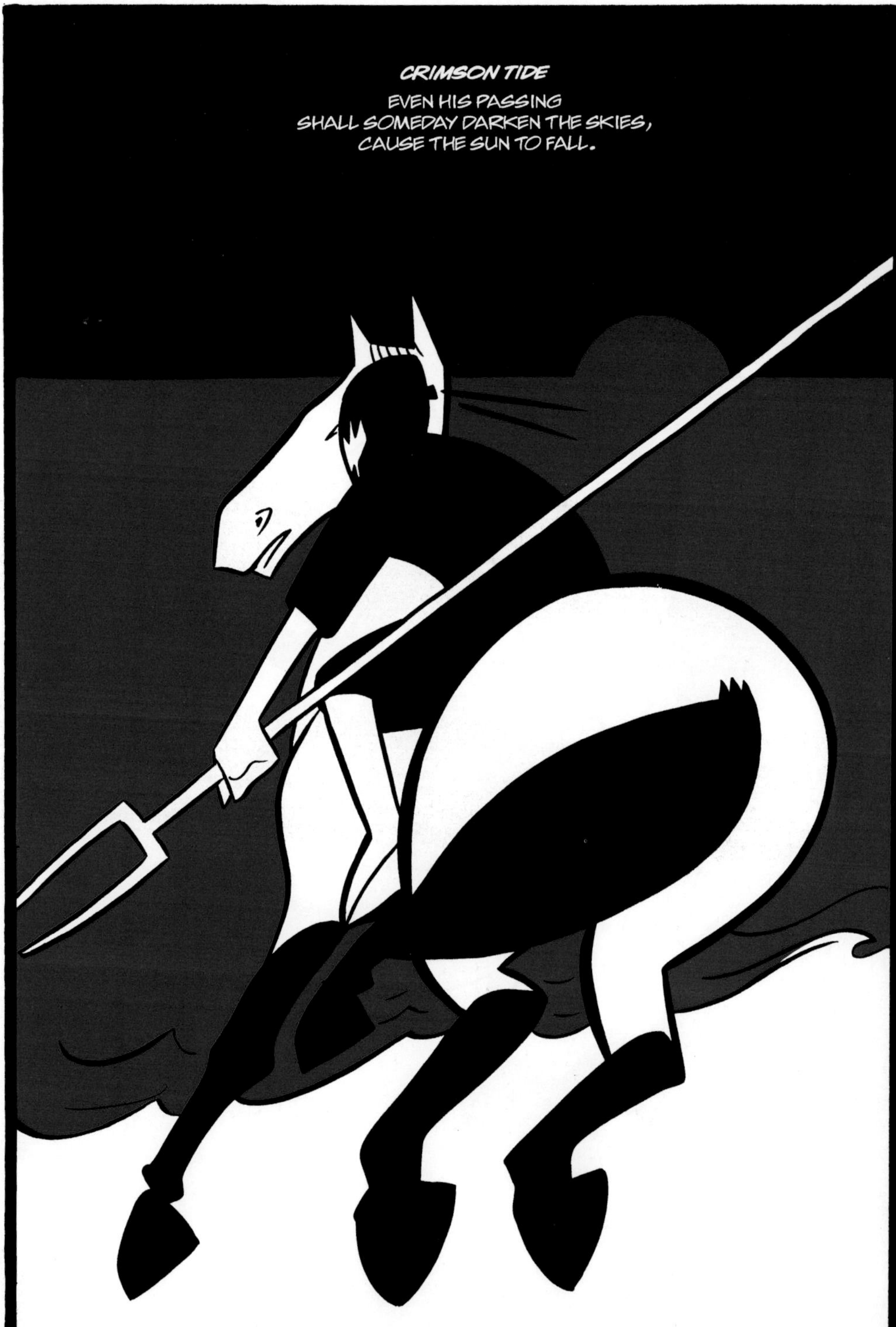
CRIMSON TIDE
EVEN HIS PASSING
SHALL SOMEDAY DARKEN THE SKIES,
CAUSE THE SUN TO FALL.

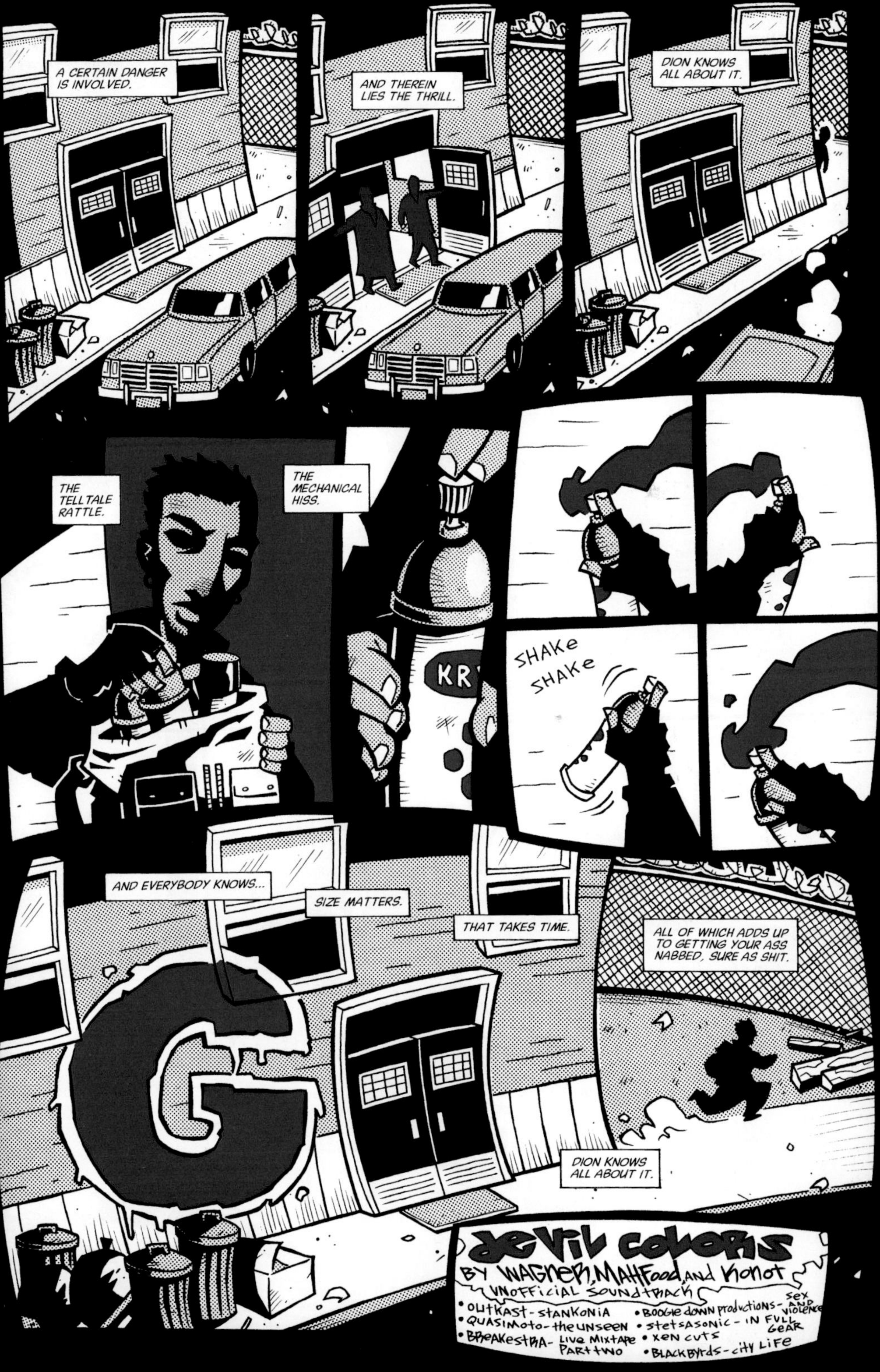

A CERTAIN DANGER IS INVOLVED.
AND THEREIN LIES THE THRILL.
DION KNOWS ALL ABOUT IT.
THE TELLTALE RATTLE.
THE MECHANICAL HISS.
KR
SHAKE
SHAKE
AND EVERYBODY KNOWS...
SIZE MATTERS.
THAT TAKES TIME.
ALL OF WHICH ADDS UP TO GETTING YOUR ASS NABBED, SURE AS SHIT.
DION KNOWS ALL ABOUT IT.
devil colors
BY WAGNER, MAHFOOD, AND KONOT
UNOFFICIAL SOUNDTRACK
• OUTKAST - STANKONIA
• QUASIMOTO - THE UNSEEN
• BREAKESTRA - LIVE MIXTAPE PART TWO
• BOOGIE DOWN PRODUCTIONS - SEX AND VIOLENCE
• STETSASONIC - IN FULL GEAR
• XEN CUTS
• BLACKBYRDS - CITY LIFE

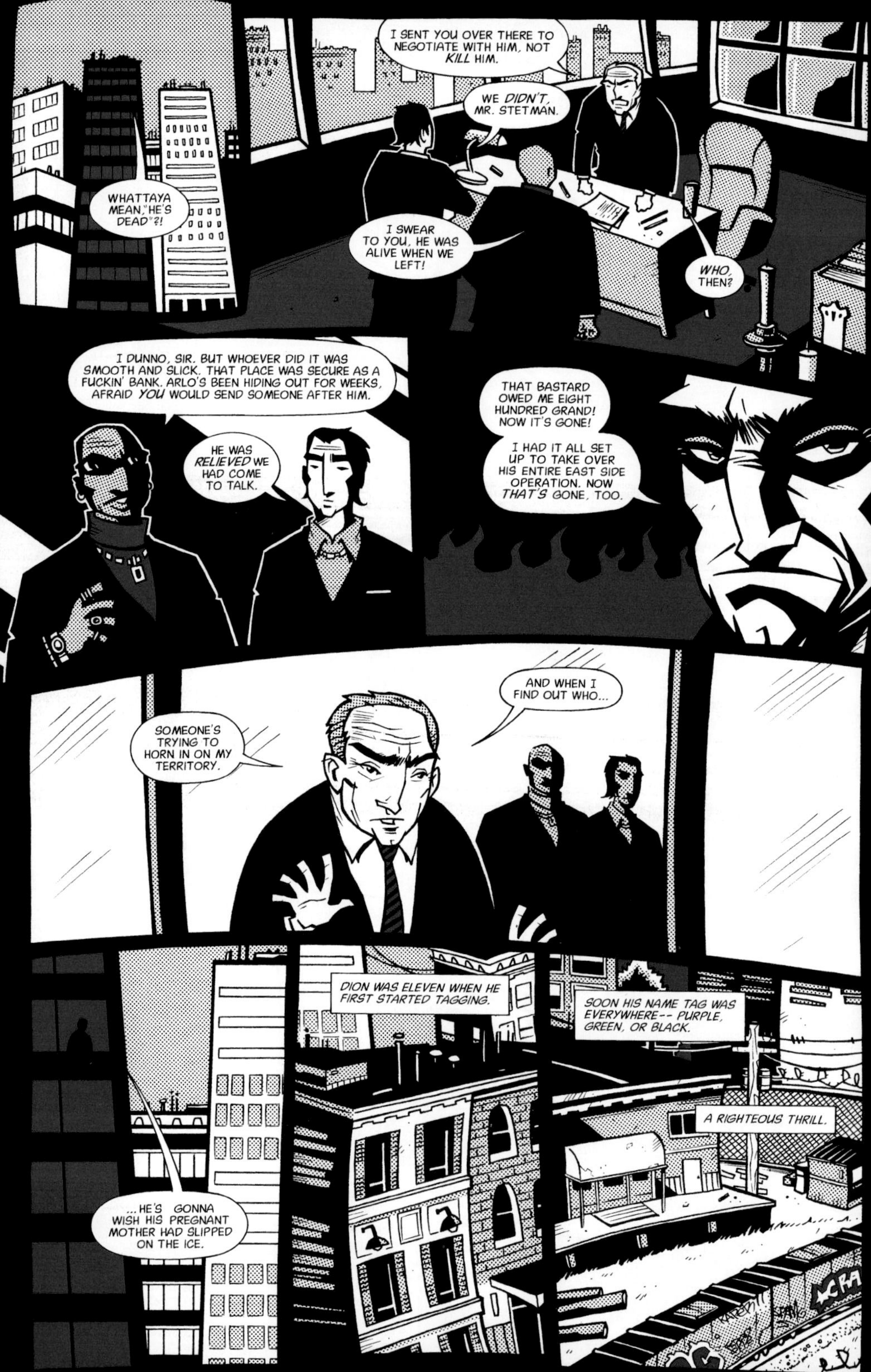
WHATTAYA MEAN, "HE'S DEAD"?!
I SENT YOU OVER THERE TO NEGOTIATE WITH HIM, NOT KILL HIM.
WE DIDN'T, MR. STETMAN.
I SWEAR TO YOU, HE WAS ALIVE WHEN WE LEFT!
WHO, THEN?
I DUNNO, SIR. BUT WHOEVER DID IT WAS SMOOTH AND SLICK. THAT PLACE WAS SECURE AS A FUCKIN' BANK. ARLO'S BEEN HIDING OUT FOR WEEKS, AFRAID YOU WOULD SEND SOMEONE AFTER HIM.
HE WAS RELIEVED WE HAD COME TO TALK.
THAT BASTARD OWED ME EIGHT HUNDRED GRAND! NOW IT'S GONE!
I HAD IT ALL SET UP TO TAKE OVER HIS ENTIRE EAST SIDE OPERATION. NOW THAT'S GONE, TOO.
SOMEONE'S TRYING TO HORN IN ON MY TERRITORY.
AND WHEN I FIND OUT WHO...
...HE'S GONNA WISH HIS PREGNANT MOTHER HAD SLIPPED ON THE ICE.
DION WAS ELEVEN WHEN HE FIRST STARTED TAGGING.
SOON HIS NAME TAG WAS EVERYWHERE-- PURPLE, GREEN, OR BLACK.
A RIGHTEOUS THRILL.

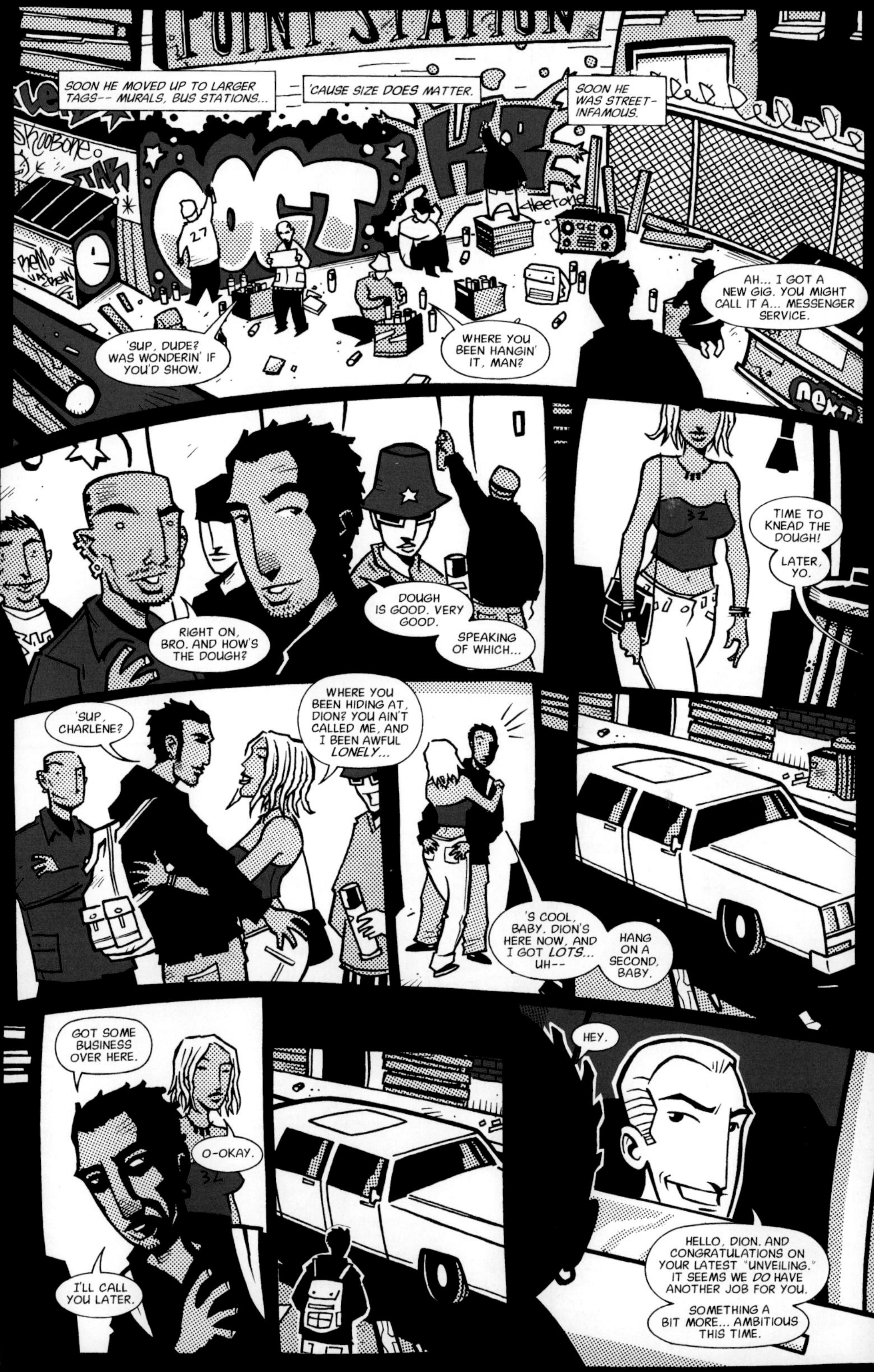

POINT STATION
SOON HE MOVED UP TO LARGER TAGS-- MURALS, BUS STATIONS...
'CAUSE SIZE DOES MATTER.
SOON HE WAS STREET-INFAMOUS.
'SUP, DUDE? WAS WONDERIN' IF YOU'D SHOW.
WHERE YOU BEEN HANGIN' IT, MAN?
AH... I GOT A NEW GIG. YOU MIGHT CALL IT A... MESSENGER SERVICE.
RIGHT ON, BRO. AND HOW'S THE DOUGH?
DOUGH IS GOOD. VERY GOOD.
SPEAKING OF WHICH...
TIME TO KNEAD THE DOUGH!
LATER, YO.
'SUP, CHARLENE?
WHERE YOU BEEN HIDING AT, DION? YOU AIN'T CALLED ME, AND I BEEN AWFUL LONELY...
'S COOL, BABY, DION'S HERE NOW, AND I GOT LOTS... UH--
HANG ON A SECOND, BABY.
GOT SOME BUSINESS OVER HERE.
O-OKAY.
I'LL CALL YOU LATER.
HEY.
HELLO, DION. AND CONGRATULATIONS ON YOUR LATEST "UNVEILING." IT SEEMS WE DO HAVE ANOTHER JOB FOR YOU.
SOMETHING A BIT MORE... AMBITIOUS THIS TIME.

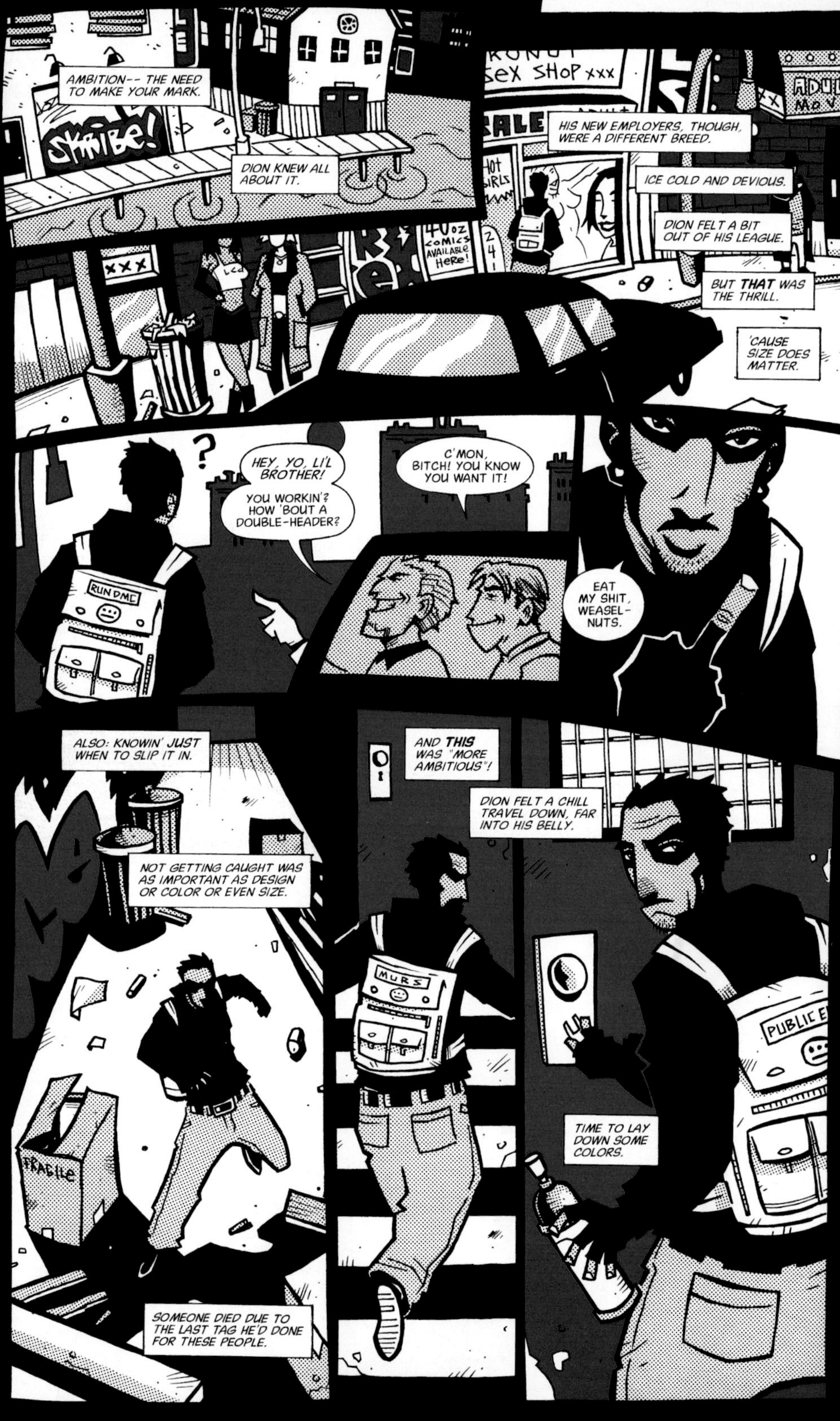
AMBITION-- THE NEED TO MAKE YOUR MARK.
SKRIBE!
DION KNEW ALL ABOUT IT.
SEX SHOP XXX
ADULT MOVIE
HIS NEW EMPLOYERS, THOUGH, WERE A DIFFERENT BREED.
ICE COLD AND DEVIOUS.
DION FELT A BIT OUT OF HIS LEAGUE.
40oz COMICS AVAILABLE HERE!
XXX
BUT THAT WAS THE THRILL.
'CAUSE SIZE DOES MATTER.
?
HEY, YO, LI'L BROTHER!
YOU WORKIN'? HOW 'BOUT A DOUBLE-HEADER?
C'MON, BITCH! YOU KNOW YOU WANT IT!
RUN DMC
EAT MY SHIT, WEASEL-NUTS.
ALSO: KNOWIN' JUST WHEN TO SLIP IT IN.
NOT GETTING CAUGHT WAS AS IMPORTANT AS DESIGN OR COLOR OR EVEN SIZE.
FRAGILE
SOMEONE DIED DUE TO THE LAST TAG HE'D DONE FOR THESE PEOPLE.
AND THIS WAS "MORE AMBITIOUS"!
DION FELT A CHILL TRAVEL DOWN, FAR INTO HIS BELLY.
MURS
PUBLIC E
TIME TO LAY DOWN SOME COLORS.

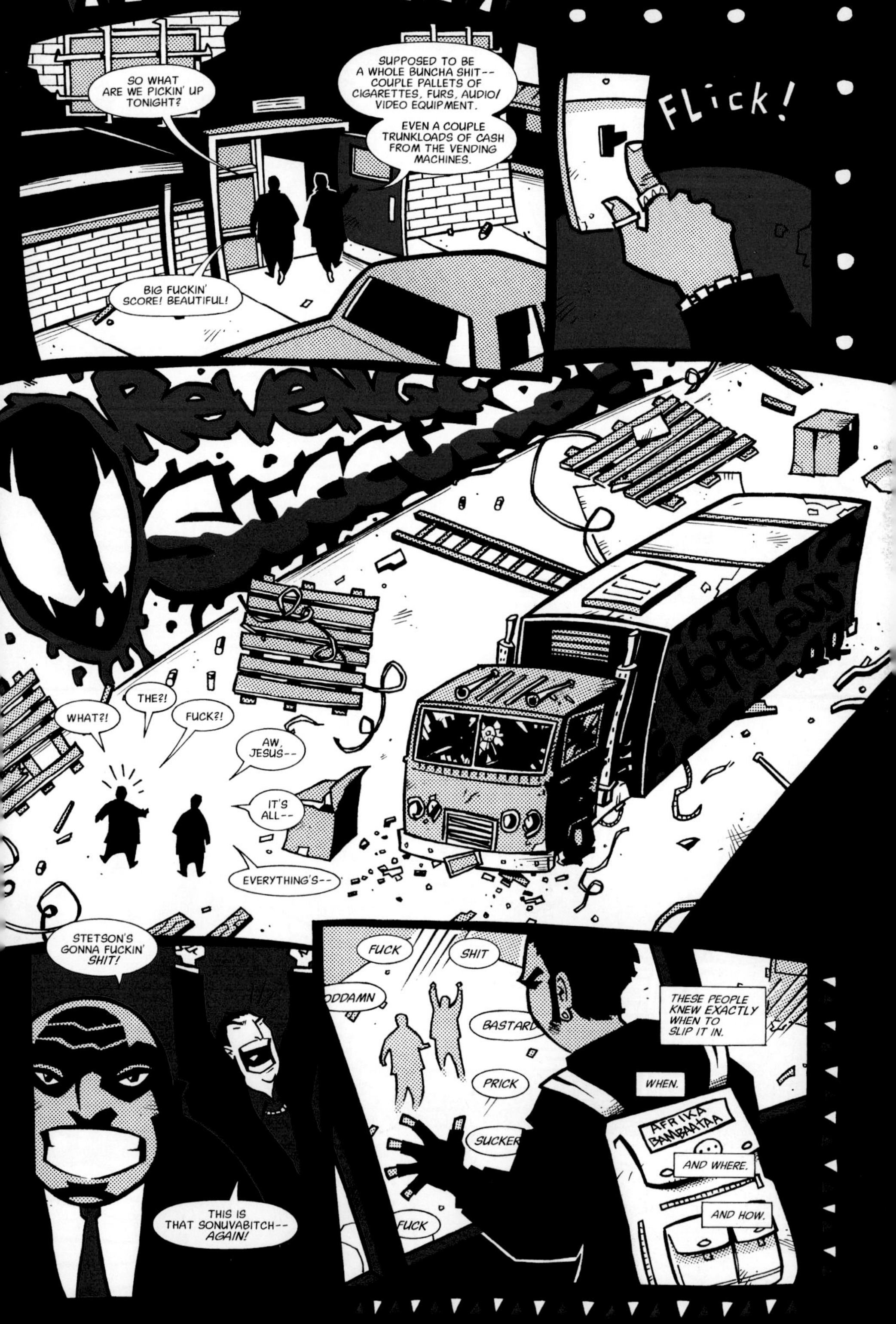

SO WHAT ARE WE PICKIN' UP TONIGHT?
SUPPOSED TO BE A WHOLE BUNCHA SHIT-- COUPLE PALLETS OF CIGARETTES, FURS, AUDIO/ VIDEO EQUIPMENT.
EVEN A COUPLE TRUNKLOADS OF CASH FROM THE VENDING MACHINES.
BIG FUCKIN' SCORE! BEAUTIFUL!
FLICK!
WHAT?!
THE?!
FUCK?!
AW, JESUS--
IT'S ALL--
EVERYTHING'S--
STETSON'S GONNA FUCKIN' SHIT!
THIS IS THAT SONUVABITCH-- AGAIN!
FUCK
SHIT
ODDAMN
BASTARD
PRICK
SUCKER
FUCK
THESE PEOPLE KNEW EXACTLY WHEN TO SLIP IT IN.
WHEN.
AND WHERE.
AND HOW.
AFRIKA BAMBAATAA

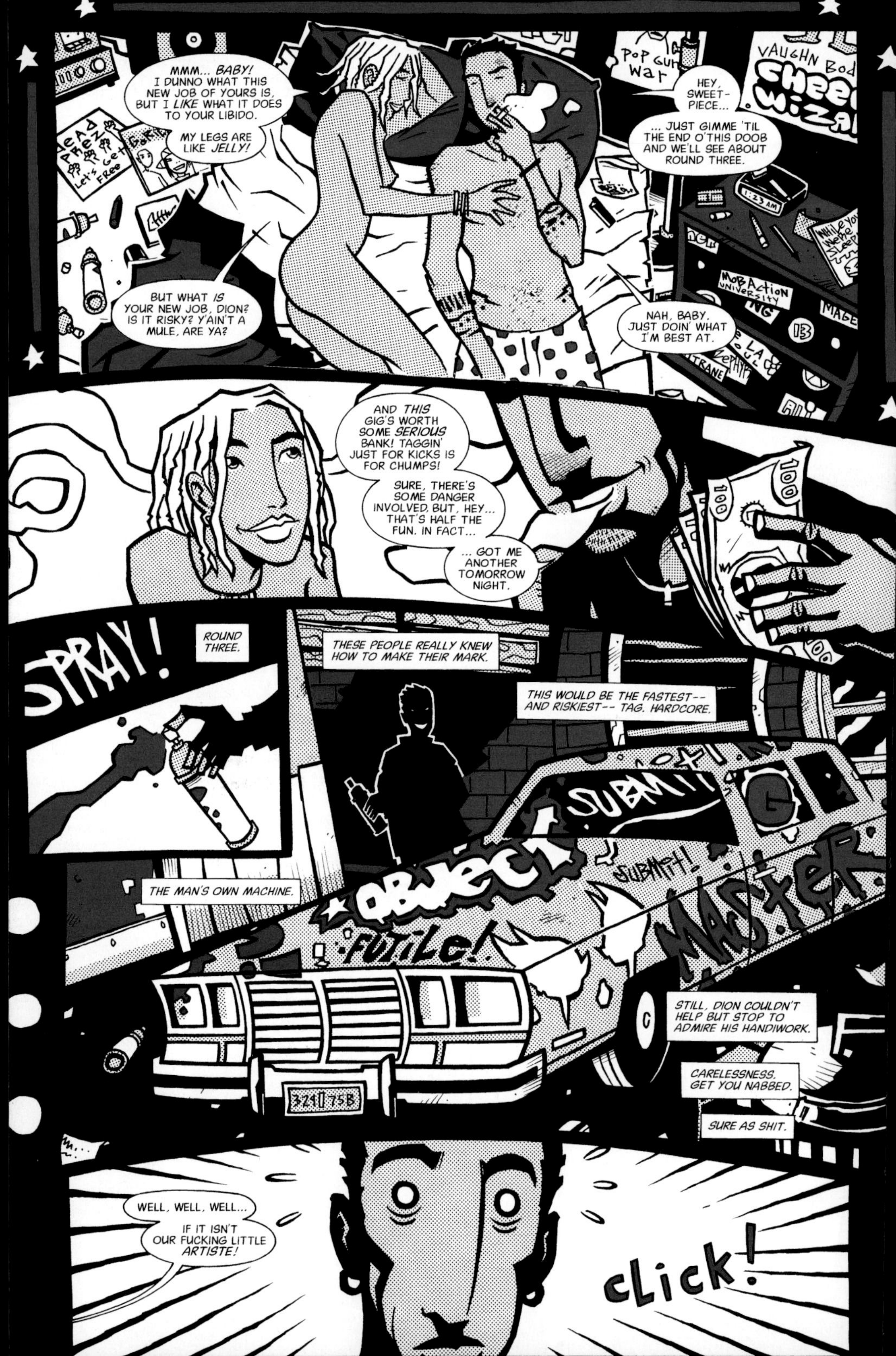
MMM... BABY! I DUNNO WHAT THIS NEW JOB OF YOURS IS, BUT I LIKE WHAT IT DOES TO YOUR LIBIDO.
MY LEGS ARE LIKE JELLY!
HEY, SWEET-PIECE...
... JUST GIMME 'TIL THE END O'THIS DOOB AND WE'LL SEE ABOUT ROUND THREE.
BUT WHAT IS YOUR NEW JOB, DION? IS IT RISKY? Y'AIN'T A MULE, ARE YA?
NAH, BABY. JUST DOIN' WHAT I'M BEST AT.
AND THIS GIG'S WORTH SOME SERIOUS BANK! TAGGIN' JUST FOR KICKS IS FOR CHUMPS!
SURE, THERE'S SOME DANGER INVOLVED, BUT, HEY... THAT'S HALF THE FUN. IN FACT...
... GOT ME ANOTHER TOMORROW NIGHT.
SPRAY!
ROUND THREE.
THESE PEOPLE REALLY KNEW HOW TO MAKE THEIR MARK.
THIS WOULD BE THE FASTEST-- AND RISKIEST-- TAG. HARDCORE.
SUBMIT!
OBJECT
FUTILE!
MASTER
THE MAN'S OWN MACHINE.
STILL, DION COULDN'T HELP BUT STOP TO ADMIRE HIS HANDIWORK.
CARELESSNESS. GET YOU NABBED.
SURE AS SHIT.
WELL, WELL, WELL...
IF IT ISN'T OUR FUCKING LITTLE ARTISTE!
CLICK!

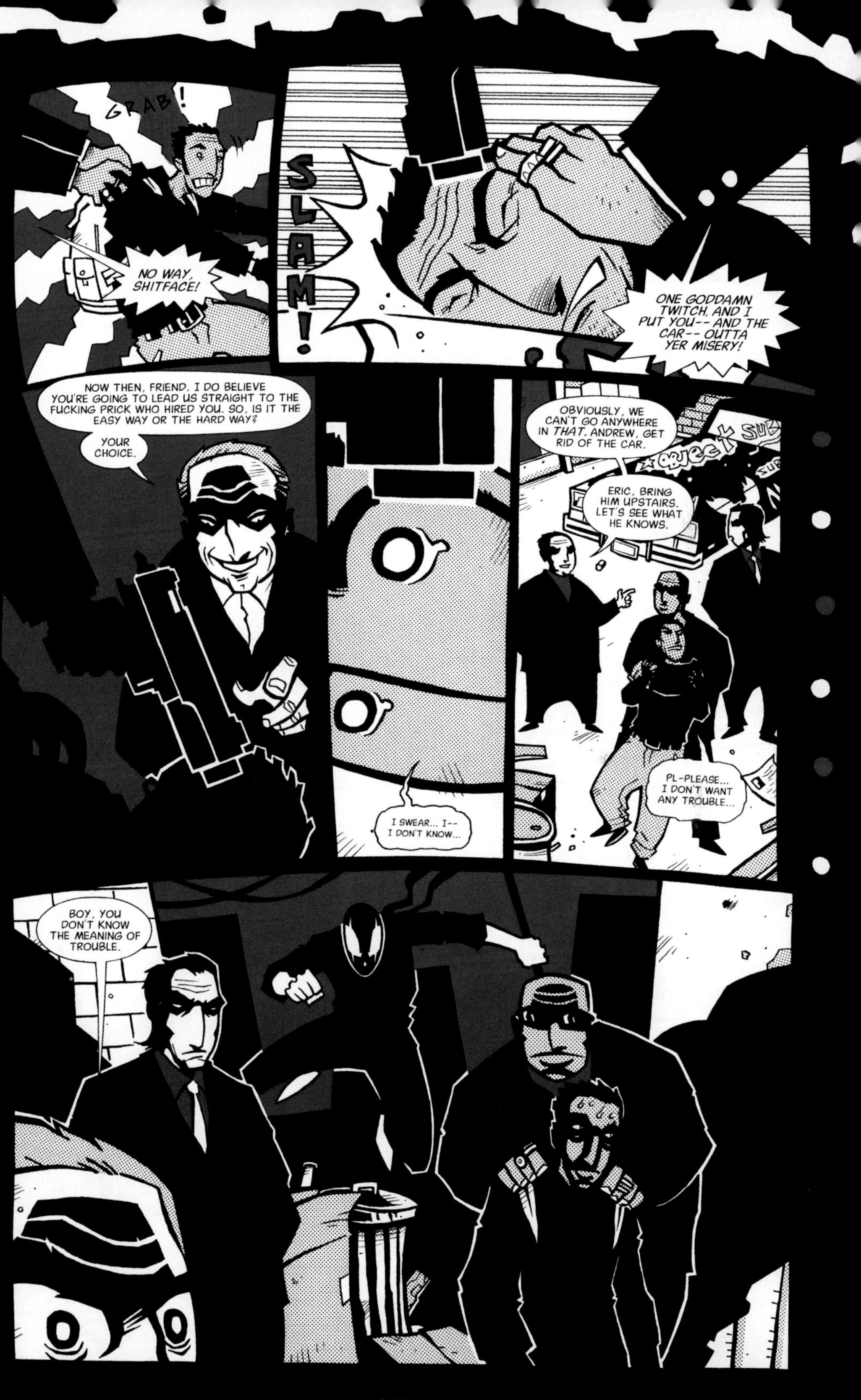
GRAB!
NO WAY, SHITFACE!
SLAM!
ONE GODDAMN TWITCH, AND I PUT YOU-- AND THE CAR-- OUTTA YER MISERY!
NOW THEN, FRIEND. I DO BELIEVE YOU'RE GOING TO LEAD US STRAIGHT TO THE FUCKING PRICK WHO HIRED YOU. SO, IS IT THE EASY WAY OR THE HARD WAY?
YOUR CHOICE.
I SWEAR... I-- I DON'T KNOW...
OBVIOUSLY, WE CAN'T GO ANYWHERE IN THAT. ANDREW, GET RID OF THE CAR.
ERIC, BRING HIM UPSTAIRS. LET'S SEE WHAT HE KNOWS.
PL-PLEASE... I DON'T WANT ANY TROUBLE...
BOY, YOU DON'T KNOW THE MEANING OF TROUBLE.

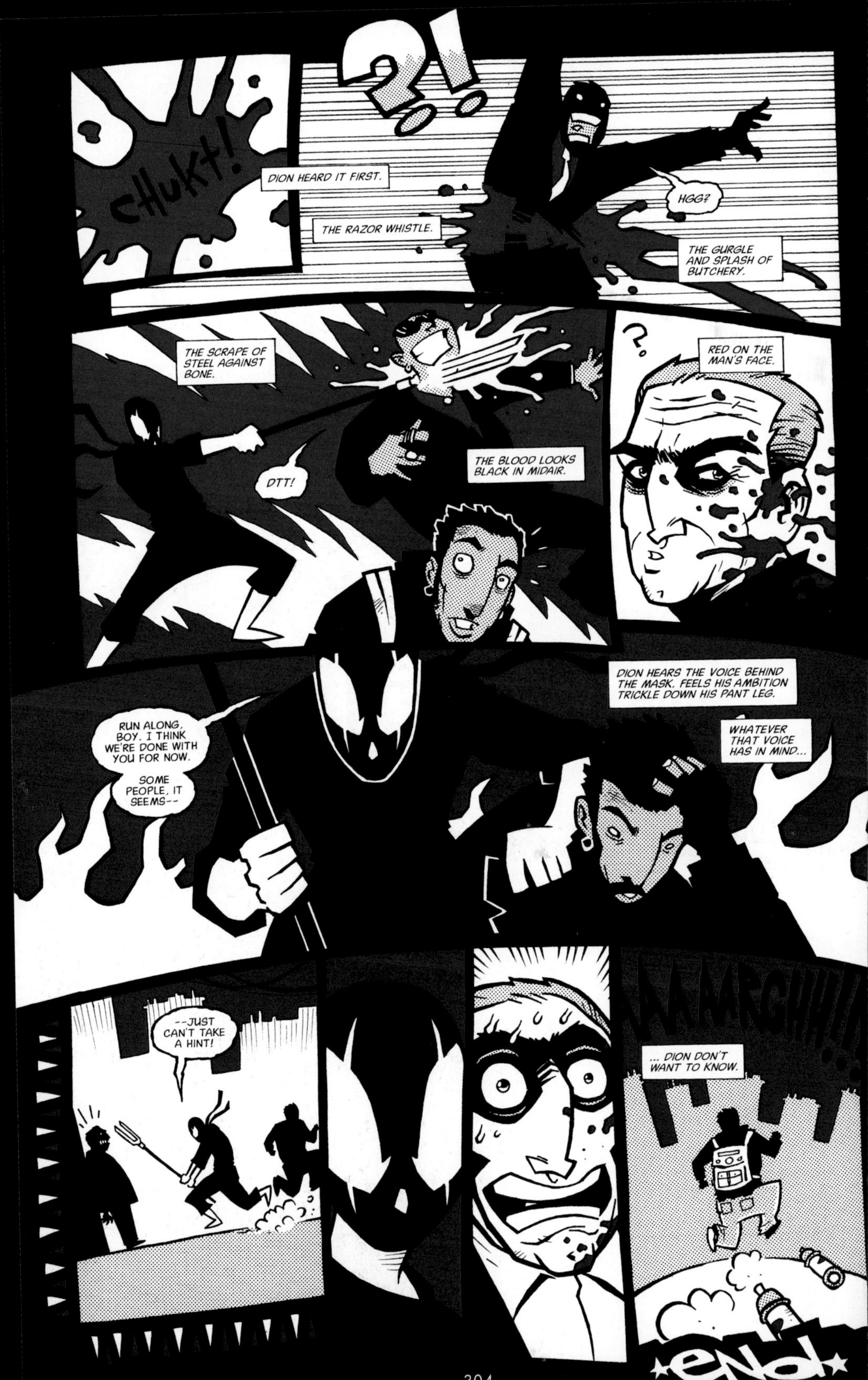
CHUKT!
?!
DION HEARD IT FIRST.
THE RAZOR WHISTLE.
HGG?
THE GURGLE AND SPLASH OF BUTCHERY.
THE SCRAPE OF STEEL AGAINST BONE.
DTT!
THE BLOOD LOOKS BLACK IN MIDAIR.
?
RED ON THE MAN'S FACE.
DION HEARS THE VOICE BEHIND THE MASK. FEELS HIS AMBITION TRICKLE DOWN HIS PANT LEG.
RUN ALONG, BOY. I THINK WE'RE DONE WITH YOU FOR NOW.
SOME PEOPLE, IT SEEMS--
WHATEVER THAT VOICE HAS IN MIND...
--JUST CAN'T TAKE A HINT!
AAAARGHH!!!
... DION DON'T WANT TO KNOW.
END

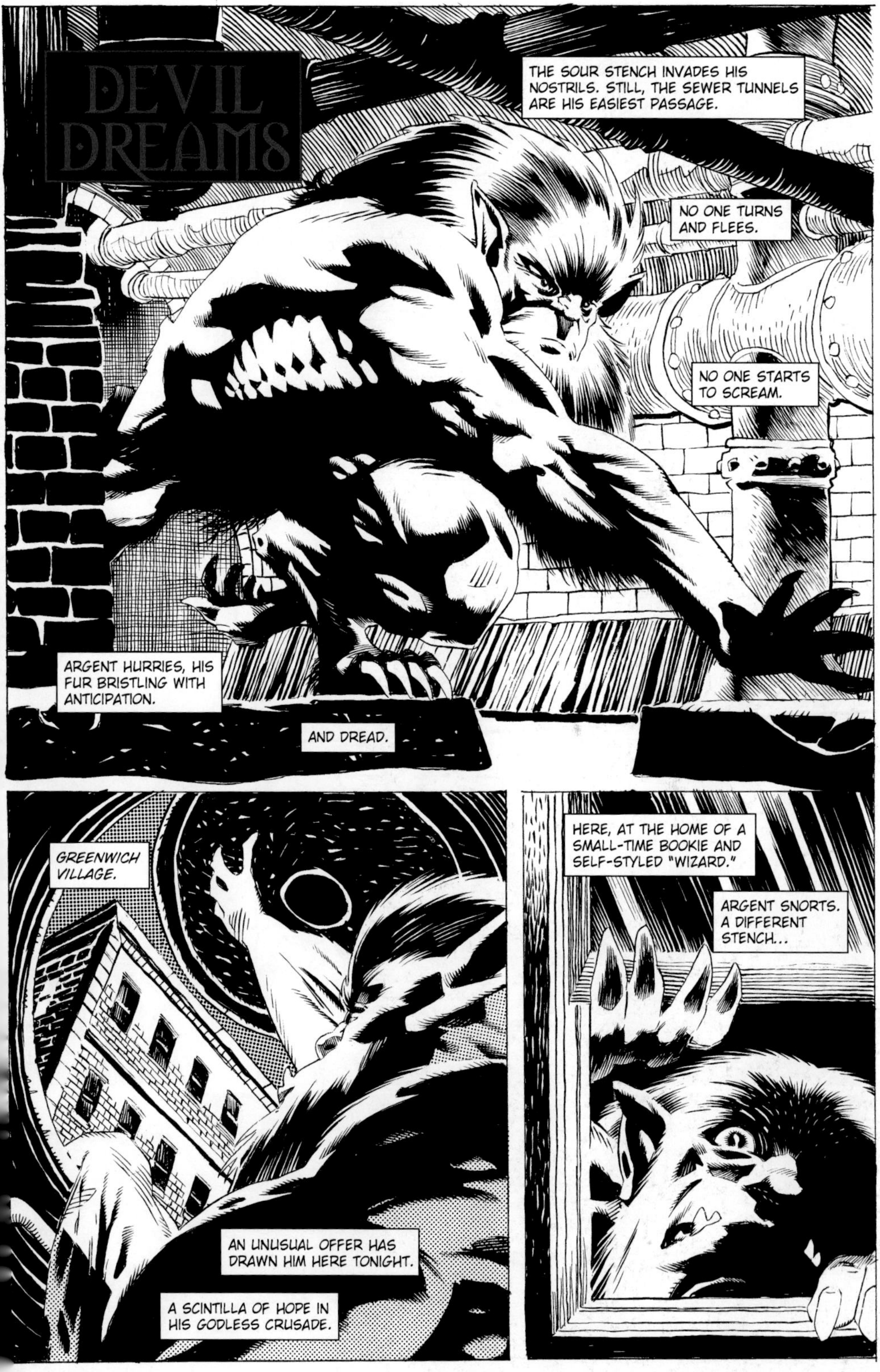
DEVIL DREAMS
THE SOUR STENCH INVADES HIS NOSTRILS. STILL, THE SEWER TUNNELS ARE HIS EASIEST PASSAGE.
NO ONE TURNS AND FLEES.
NO ONE STARTS TO SCREAM.
ARGENT HURRIES, HIS FUR BRISTLING WITH ANTICIPATION.
AND DREAD.
GREENWICH VILLAGE.
AN UNUSUAL OFFER HAS DRAWN HIM HERE TONIGHT.
A SCINTILLA OF HOPE IN HIS GODLESS CRUSADE.
HERE, AT THE HOME OF A SMALL-TIME BOOKIE AND SELF-STYLED "WIZARD."
ARGENT SNORTS. A DIFFERENT STENCH...

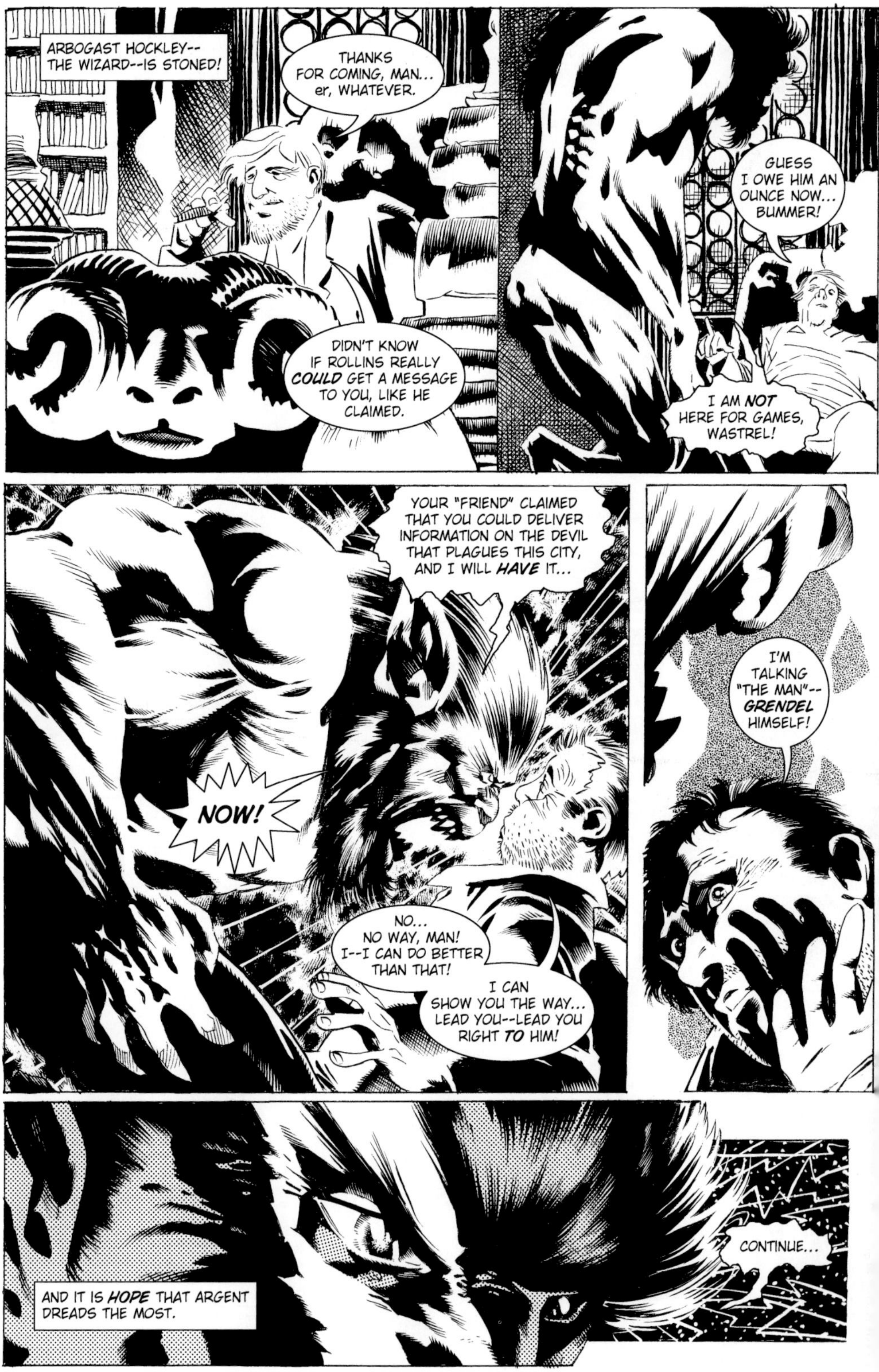
ARBOGAST HOCKLEY--
THE WIZARD--IS STONED!
THANKS FOR COMING, MAN... er, WHATEVER.
DIDN'T KNOW IF ROLLINS REALLY COULD GET A MESSAGE TO YOU, LIKE HE CLAIMED.
GUESS I OWE HIM AN OUNCE NOW... BUMMER!
I AM NOT HERE FOR GAMES, WASTREL!
YOUR "FRIEND" CLAIMED THAT YOU COULD DELIVER INFORMATION ON THE DEVIL THAT PLAGUES THIS CITY, AND I WILL HAVE IT...
NOW!
NO... NO WAY, MAN! I--I CAN DO BETTER THAN THAT!
I CAN SHOW YOU THE WAY... LEAD YOU--LEAD YOU RIGHT TO HIM!
I'M TALKING "THE MAN"--GRENDEL HIMSELF!
AND IT IS HOPE THAT ARGENT DREADS THE MOST.
CONTINUE...

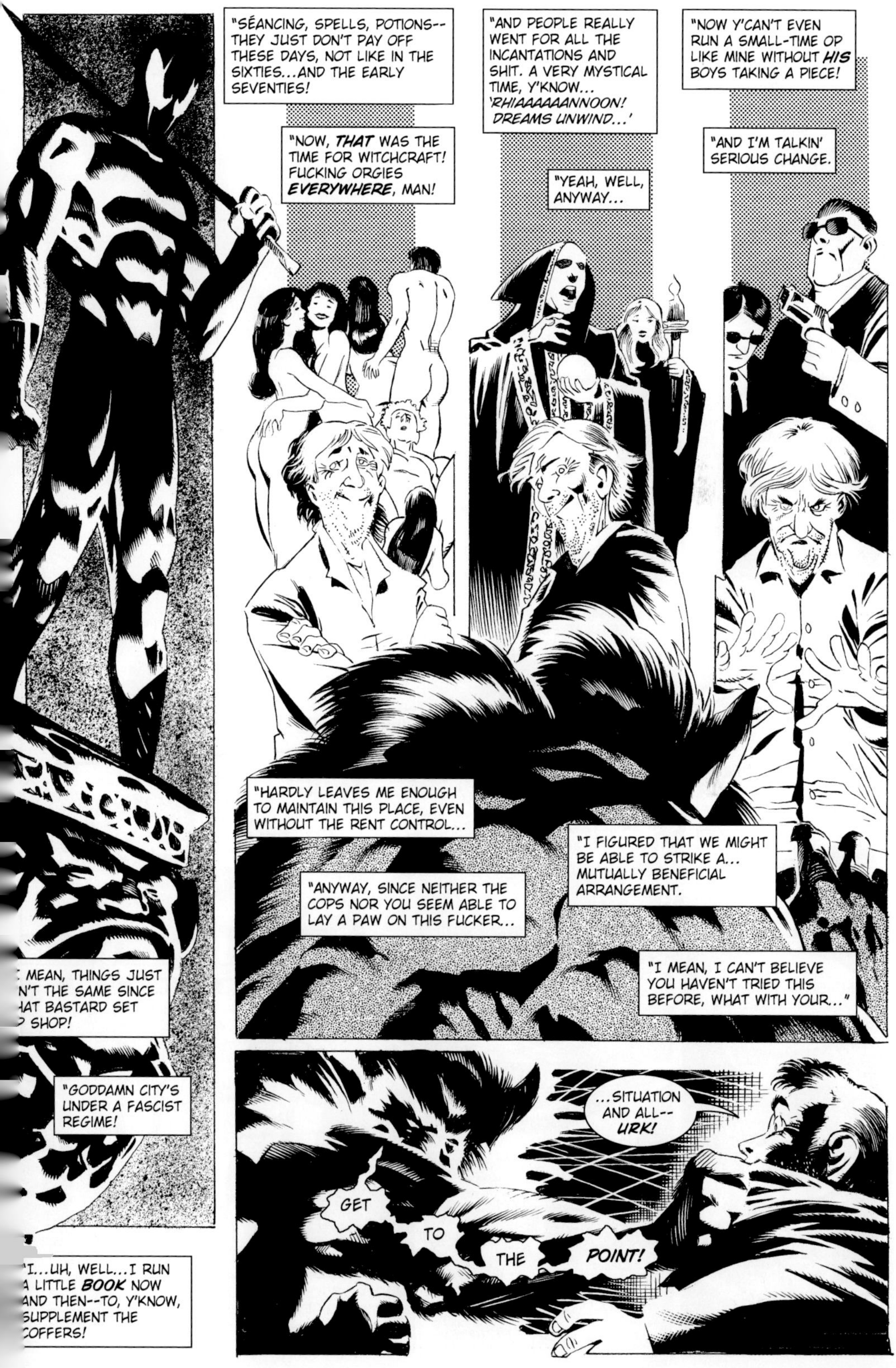

"SÉANCING, SPELLS, POTIONS--THEY JUST DON'T PAY OFF THESE DAYS, NOT LIKE IN THE SIXTIES...AND THE EARLY SEVENTIES!
"NOW, THAT WAS THE TIME FOR WITCHCRAFT! FUCKING ORGIES EVERYWHERE, MAN!
"AND PEOPLE REALLY WENT FOR ALL THE INCANTATIONS AND SHIT. A VERY MYSTICAL TIME, Y'KNOW... 'RHIAAAAAANNOON! DREAMS UNWIND...'
"YEAH, WELL, ANYWAY...
"NOW Y'CAN'T EVEN RUN A SMALL-TIME OP LIKE MINE WITHOUT HIS BOYS TAKING A PIECE!
"AND I'M TALKIN' SERIOUS CHANGE.
MEAN, THINGS JUST N'T THE SAME SINCE HAT BASTARD SET SHOP!
"GODDAMN CITY'S UNDER A FASCIST REGIME!
"I...UH, WELL...I RUN A LITTLE BOOK NOW AND THEN--TO, Y'KNOW, SUPPLEMENT THE COFFERS!
"HARDLY LEAVES ME ENOUGH TO MAINTAIN THIS PLACE, EVEN WITHOUT THE RENT CONTROL...
"ANYWAY, SINCE NEITHER THE COPS NOR YOU SEEM ABLE TO LAY A PAW ON THIS FUCKER...
"I FIGURED THAT WE MIGHT BE ABLE TO STRIKE A... MUTUALLY BENEFICIAL ARRANGEMENT.
"I MEAN, I CAN'T BELIEVE YOU HAVEN'T TRIED THIS BEFORE, WHAT WITH YOUR..."
...SITUATION AND ALL-- URK!
GET TO THE POINT!

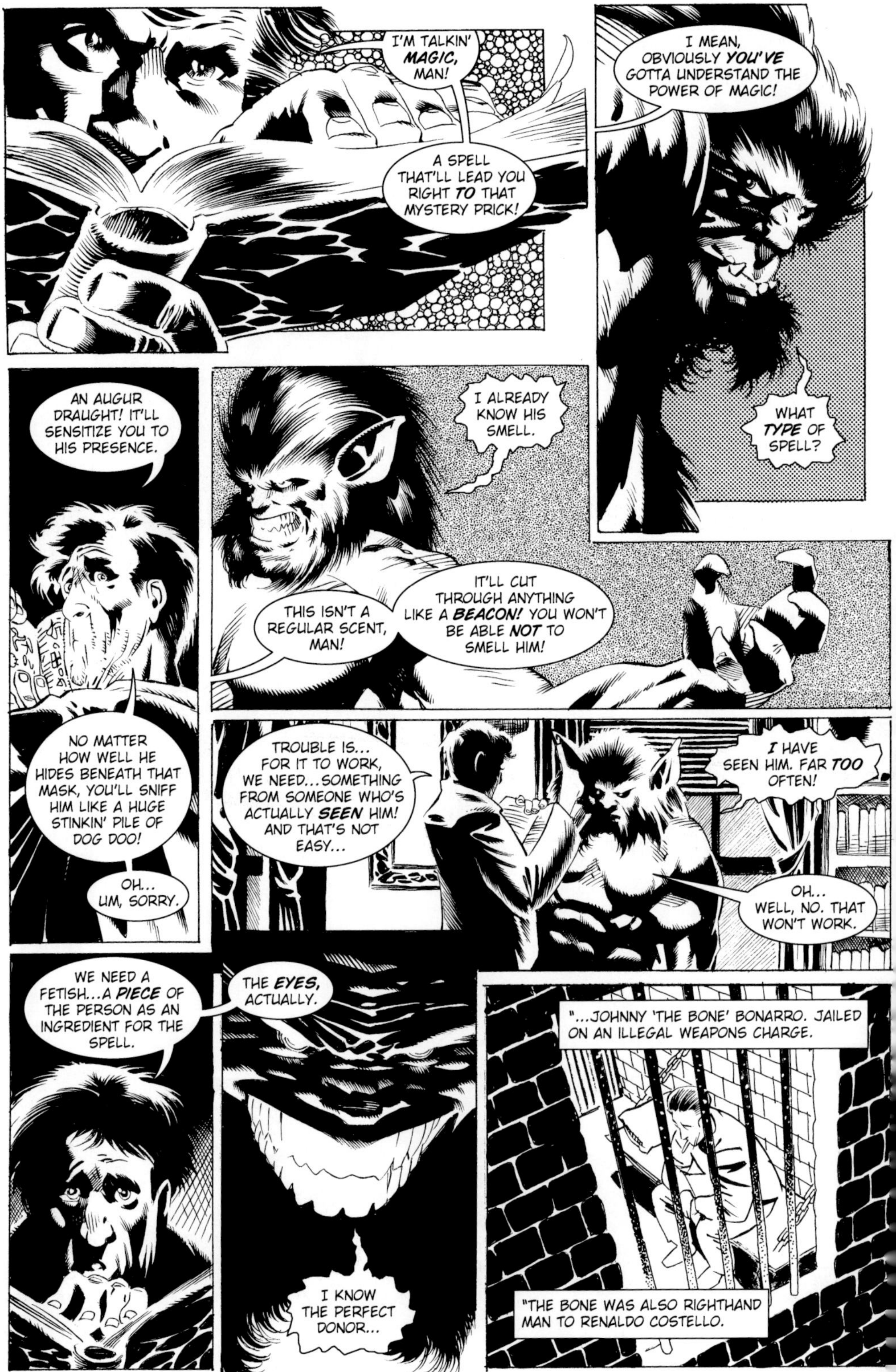

I'M TALKIN' *MAGIC,* MAN!
A SPELL THAT'LL LEAD YOU RIGHT *TO* THAT MYSTERY PRICK!
I MEAN, OBVIOUSLY *YOU'VE* GOTTA UNDERSTAND THE POWER OF MAGIC!
WHAT *TYPE* OF SPELL?
AN AUGUR DRAUGHT! IT'LL SENSITIZE YOU TO HIS PRESENCE.
I ALREADY KNOW HIS SMELL.
THIS ISN'T A REGULAR SCENT, MAN!
IT'LL CUT THROUGH ANYTHING LIKE A *BEACON!* YOU WON'T BE ABLE *NOT* TO SMELL HIM!
NO MATTER HOW WELL HE HIDES BENEATH THAT MASK, YOU'LL SNIFF HIM LIKE A HUGE STINKIN' PILE OF DOG DOO!
OH... UM, SORRY.
TROUBLE IS... FOR IT TO WORK, WE NEED...SOMETHING FROM SOMEONE WHO'S ACTUALLY *SEEN* HIM! AND THAT'S NOT EASY...
I HAVE SEEN HIM. FAR *TOO* OFTEN!
OH... WELL, NO. THAT WON'T WORK.
WE NEED A FETISH...A *PIECE* OF THE PERSON AS AN INGREDIENT FOR THE SPELL.
THE *EYES,* ACTUALLY.
I KNOW THE PERFECT DONOR...
"...JOHNNY 'THE BONE' BONARRO. JAILED ON AN ILLEGAL WEAPONS CHARGE.
"THE BONE WAS ALSO RIGHTHAND MAN TO RENALDO COSTELLO.

"RUMORED TO BE ONE OF GRENDEL'S INNER CIRCLE OF LIEUTENANTS."

Y'KNOW, JOHNNY, THEY'RE WAITIN' TO HEAR YOU SING. COULD MEAN NICER... ACCOMMODATIONS.

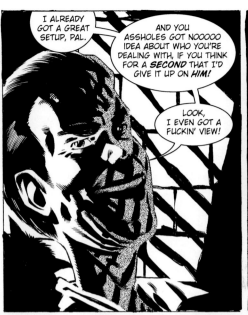

I ALREADY GOT A GREAT SETUP, PAL.

AND YOU ASSHOLES GOT NOOOOO IDEA ABOUT WHO YOU'RE DEALING WITH, IF YOU THINK FOR A SECOND THAT I'D GIVE IT UP ON HIM!

LOOK, I EVEN GOT A FUCKIN' VIEW!

I CAN JUST SEE A GLINT OF THE GODDAMN MOON OVER ALL THE RAZOR WIRE!

SUIT Y'SELF, DIRTBAG...

YEAH, I'M SAFE AS A BABY RIGHT WHERE I AM--

GLLGG!

YAAAAAAAAGH!

WHAT THE FUCK?!

HOLY MOTHER OF GOD!

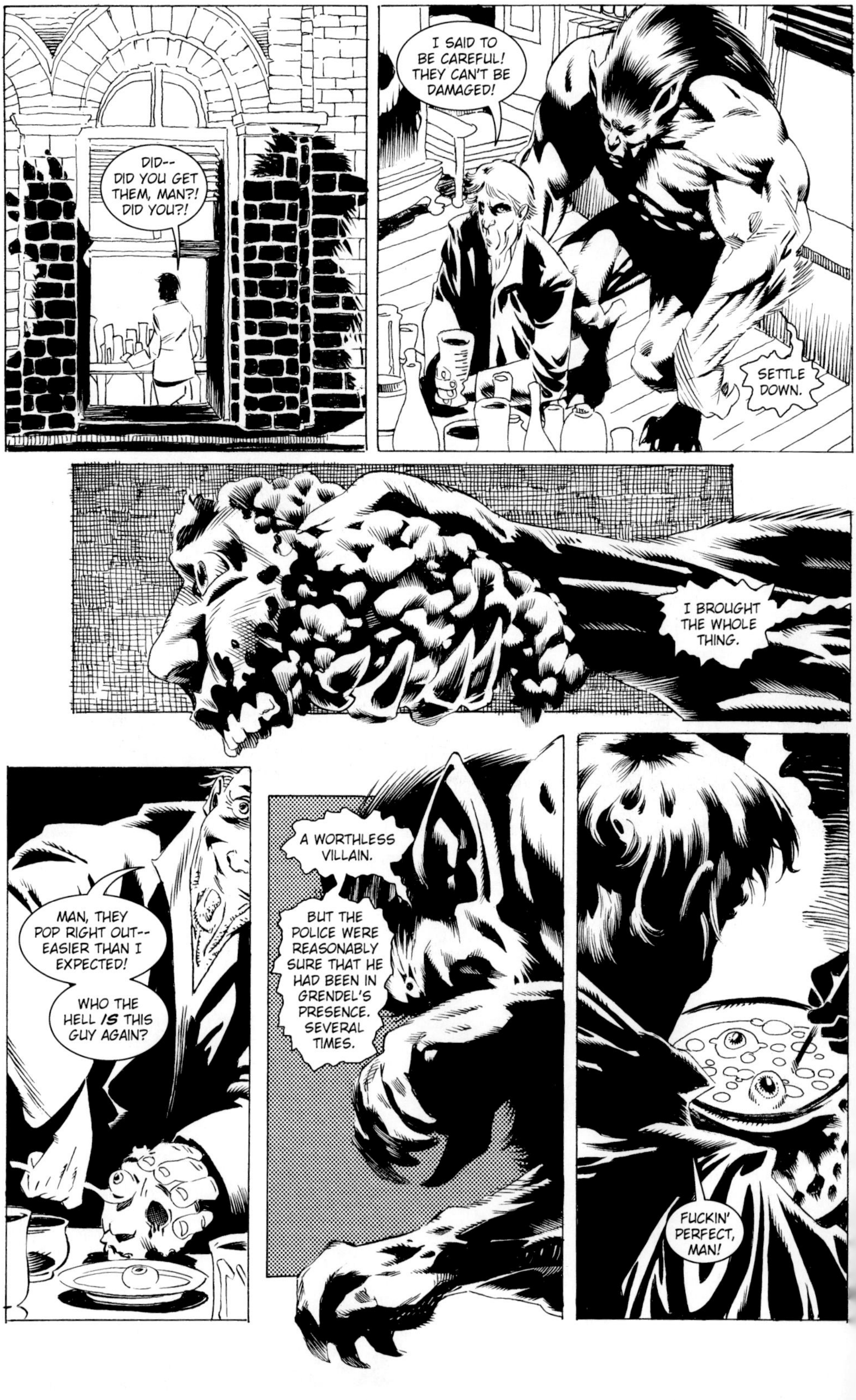
DID-- DID YOU GET THEM, MAN?! DID YOU?!
I SAID TO BE CAREFUL! THEY CAN'T BE DAMAGED!
SETTLE DOWN.
I BROUGHT THE WHOLE THING.
MAN, THEY POP RIGHT OUT-- EASIER THAN I EXPECTED!
WHO THE HELL *IS* THIS GUY AGAIN?
A WORTHLESS VILLAIN.
BUT THE POLICE WERE REASONABLY SURE THAT HE HAD BEEN IN GRENDEL'S PRESENCE. SEVERAL TIMES.
FUCKIN' PERFECT, MAN!

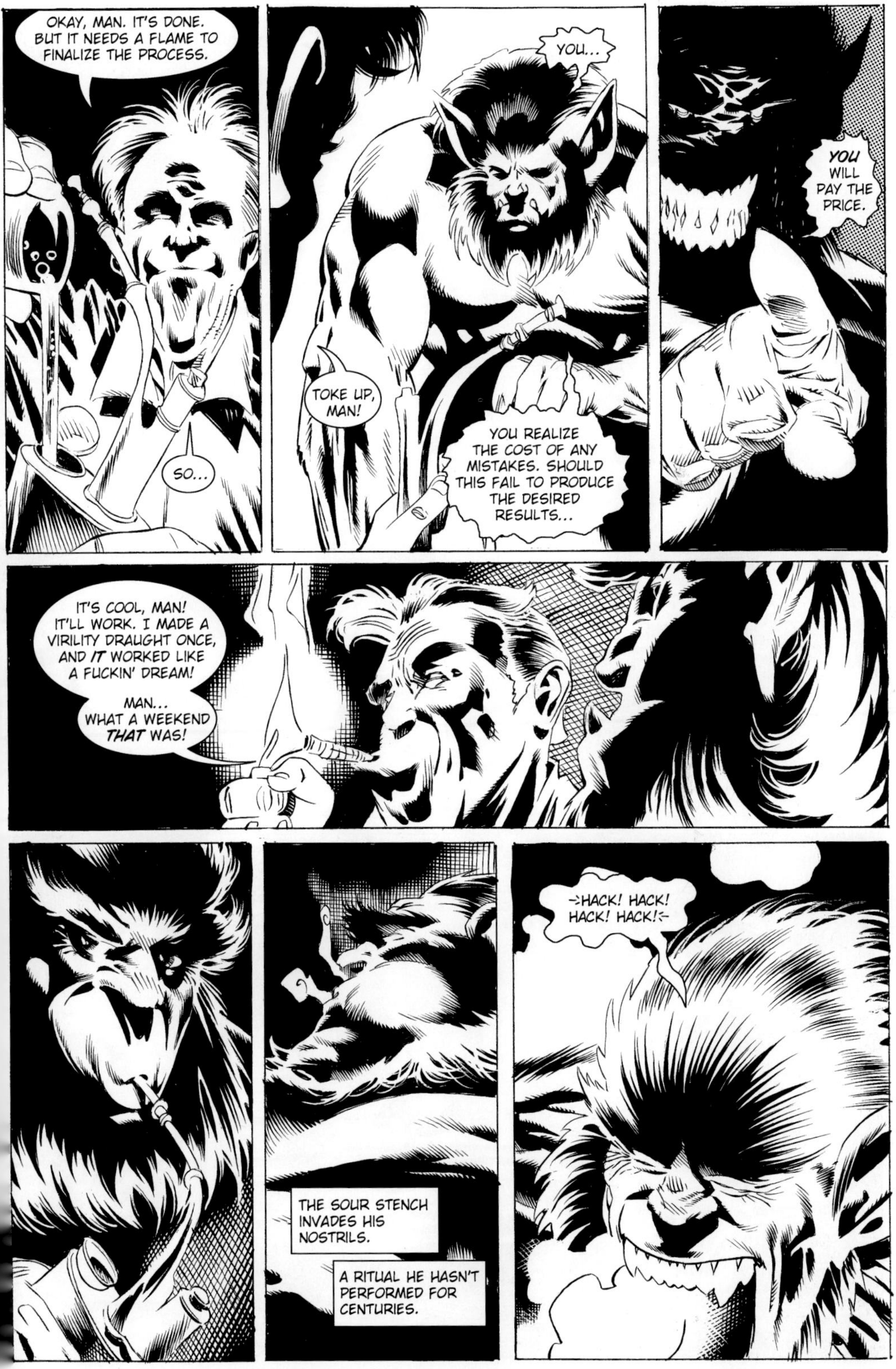
OKAY, MAN. IT'S DONE. BUT IT NEEDS A FLAME TO FINALIZE THE PROCESS.
SO...
YOU...
TOKE UP, MAN!
YOU REALIZE THE COST OF ANY MISTAKES. SHOULD THIS FAIL TO PRODUCE THE DESIRED RESULTS...
YOU WILL PAY THE PRICE.
IT'S COOL, MAN! IT'LL WORK. I MADE A VIRILITY DRAUGHT ONCE, AND IT WORKED LIKE A FUCKIN' DREAM!
MAN... WHAT A WEEKEND THAT WAS!
THE SOUR STENCH INVADES HIS NOSTRILS.
A RITUAL HE HASN'T PERFORMED FOR CENTURIES.
HACK! HACK! HACK! HACK!

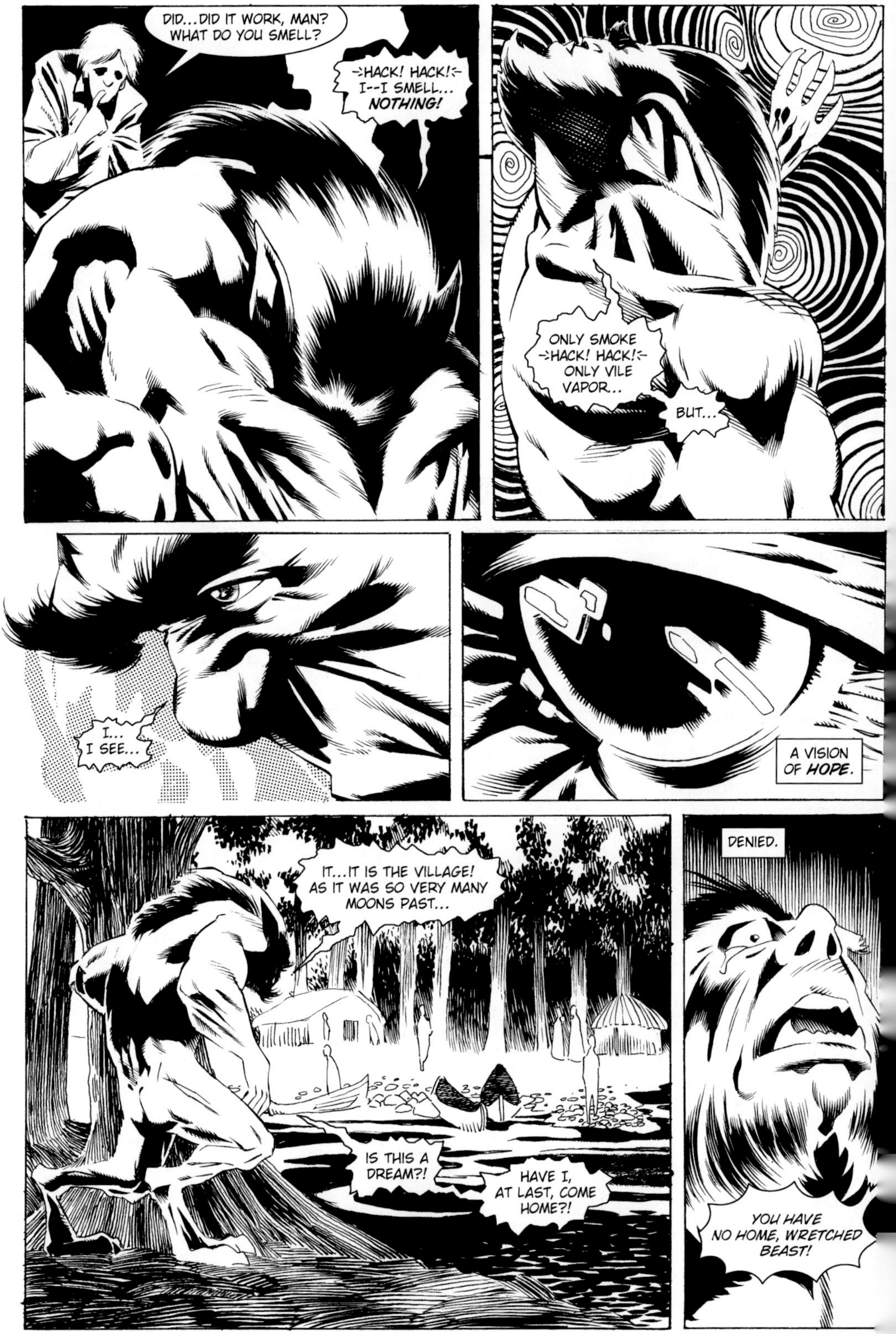

DID...DID IT WORK, MAN? WHAT DO YOU SMELL?
-HACK! HACK!- I--I SMELL... NOTHING!
ONLY SMOKE -HACK! HACK!- ONLY VILE VAPOR...
BUT...
I... I SEE...
A VISION OF HOPE.
IT...IT IS THE VILLAGE! AS IT WAS SO VERY MANY MOONS PAST...
IS THIS A DREAM?!
HAVE I, AT LAST, COME HOME?!
DENIED.
YOU HAVE NO HOME, WRETCHED BEAST!

YOU ARE AN OUTCAST, DREAM-PICKER! A PARIAH, SHUNNED BY ALL!

NOW AND FOREVER-MORE!

MASLUN!

SHADOW-WOLF!

DEATH-SPIRIT!

WHY... WHY MUST YOU TORMENT ME SO?!

I?!

I MERELY GRANTED WHAT YOU DESIRED.

I--I NEVER DESERVED THIS FATE!

WHAT OTHER COURSE DID YOU EXPECT?!

YOU INVITED MY PRESENCE, KNAVE!

YOUR OWN PASSIONS ARE WHAT FUELED THIS CURSE!

NO... NO, I--

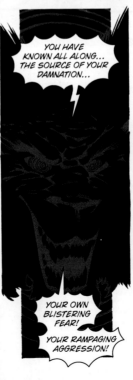

YOU HAVE KNOWN ALL ALONG... THE SOURCE OF YOUR DAMNATION...

YOUR OWN BLISTERING FEAR!

YOUR RAMPAGING AGGRESSION!

YES, YOU HAVE ALWAYS KNOWN ME BY ONE NAME...

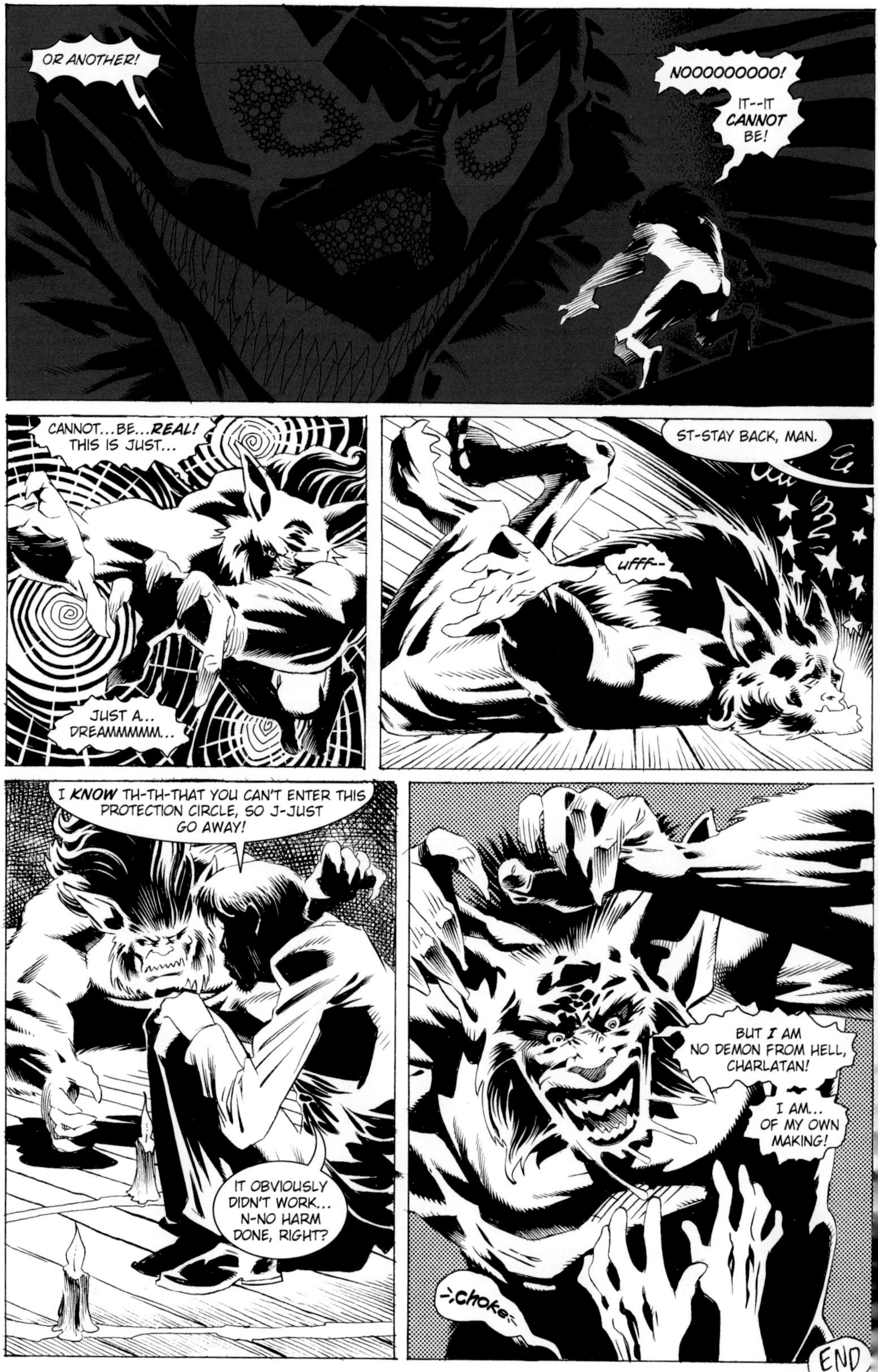
OR ANOTHER!
NOOOOOOOOO!
IT--IT CANNOT BE!
CANNOT...BE...REAL! THIS IS JUST...
JUST A... DREAMMMMMM...
ST-STAY BACK, MAN.
uffff--
I KNOW TH-TH-THAT YOU CAN'T ENTER THIS PROTECTION CIRCLE, SO J-JUST GO AWAY!
IT OBVIOUSLY DIDN'T WORK... N-NO HARM DONE, RIGHT?
BUT I AM NO DEMON FROM HELL, CHARLATAN!
I AM... OF MY OWN MAKING!
choke
END

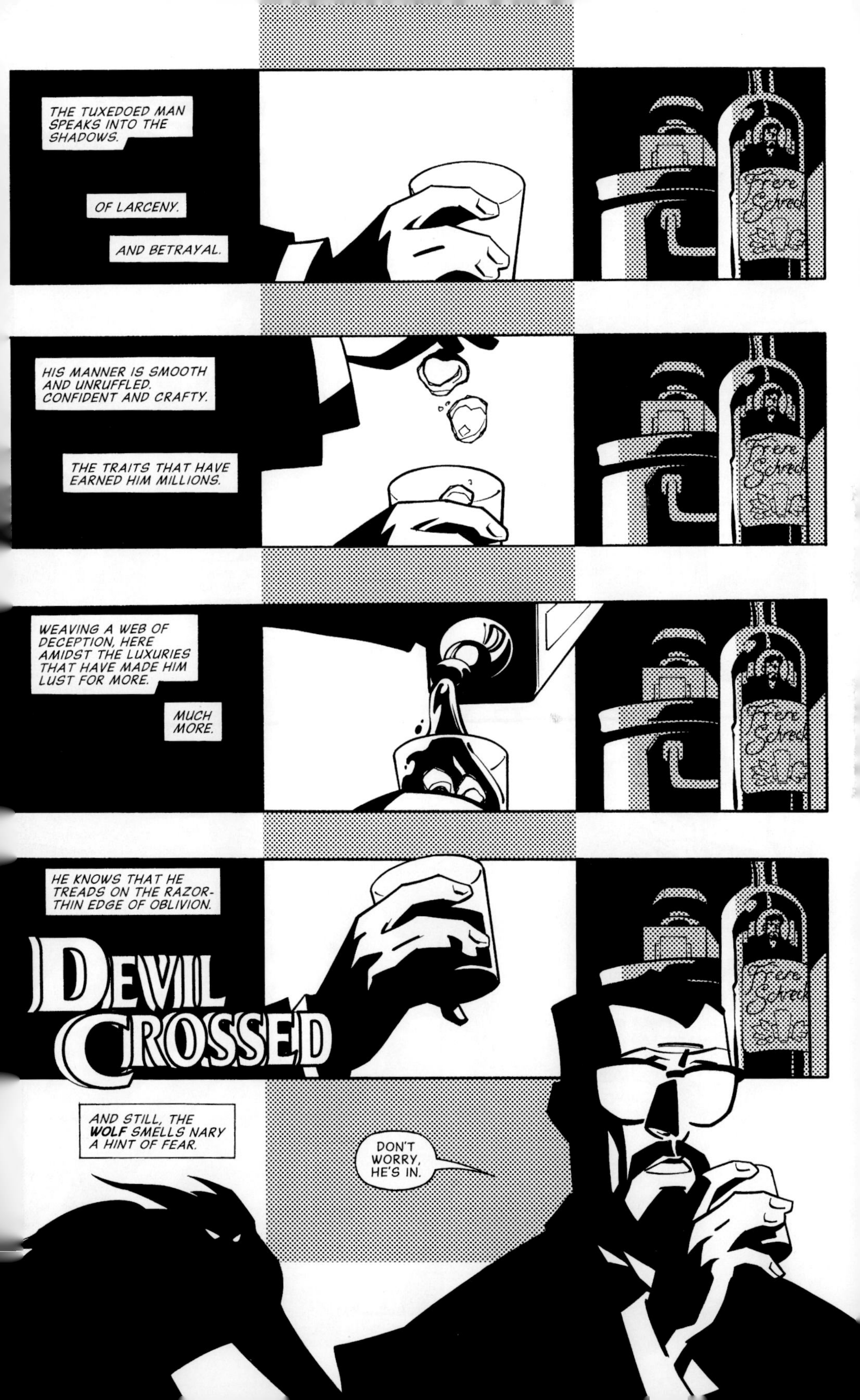
THE TUXEDOED MAN SPEAKS INTO THE SHADOWS.
OF LARCENY.
AND BETRAYAL.
HIS MANNER IS SMOOTH AND UNRUFFLED. CONFIDENT AND CRAFTY.
THE TRAITS THAT HAVE EARNED HIM MILLIONS.
WEAVING A WEB OF DECEPTION, HERE AMIDST THE LUXURIES THAT HAVE MADE HIM LUST FOR MORE.
MUCH MORE.
HE KNOWS THAT HE TREADS ON THE RAZOR-THIN EDGE OF OBLIVION.
DEVIL CROSSED
AND STILL, THE WOLF SMELLS NARY A HINT OF FEAR.
DON'T WORRY, HE'S IN.

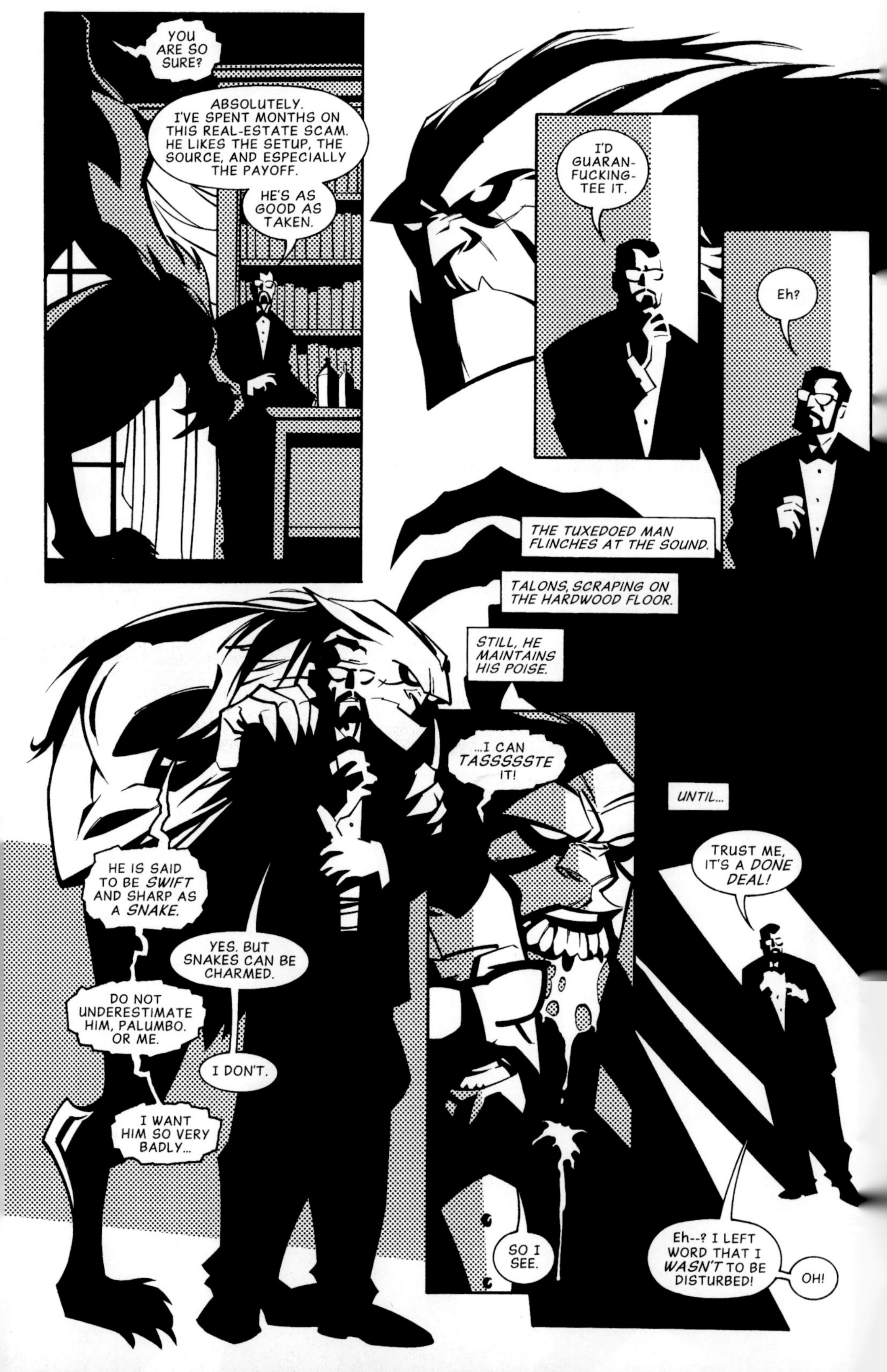
YOU ARE SO SURE?
ABSOLUTELY. I'VE SPENT MONTHS ON THIS REAL-ESTATE SCAM. HE LIKES THE SETUP, THE SOURCE, AND ESPECIALLY THE PAYOFF.
HE'S AS GOOD AS TAKEN.
I'D GUARAN-FUCKING-TEE IT.
Eh?
THE TUXEDOED MAN FLINCHES AT THE SOUND.
TALONS, SCRAPING ON THE HARDWOOD FLOOR.
STILL, HE MAINTAINS HIS POISE.
UNTIL...
TRUST ME, IT'S A DONE DEAL!
Eh--? I LEFT WORD THAT I WASN'T TO BE DISTURBED!
OH!
...I CAN TASSSSSTE IT!
SO I SEE.
HE IS SAID TO BE SWIFT AND SHARP AS A SNAKE.
YES. BUT SNAKES CAN BE CHARMED.
DO NOT UNDERESTIMATE HIM, PALUMBO. OR ME.
I DON'T.
I WANT HIM SO VERY BADLY...

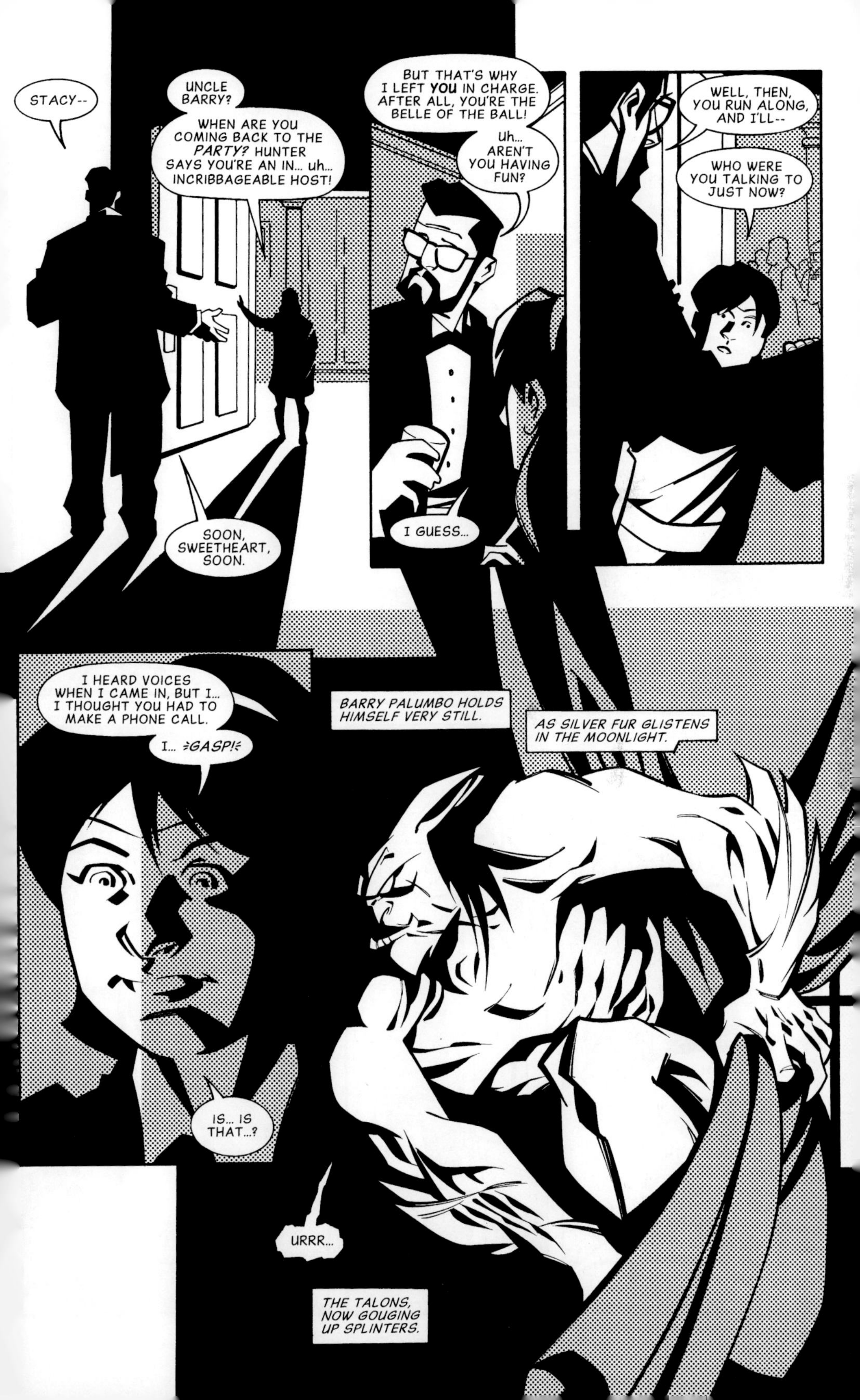
STACY--
UNCLE BARRY?
WHEN ARE YOU COMING BACK TO THE *PARTY?* HUNTER SAYS YOU'RE AN IN... uh... INCRIBBAGEABLE HOST!
SOON, SWEETHEART, SOON.
BUT THAT'S WHY I LEFT **YOU** IN CHARGE. AFTER ALL, YOU'RE THE BELLE OF THE BALL!
uh... AREN'T YOU HAVING FUN?
I GUESS...
WELL, THEN, YOU RUN ALONG, AND I'LL--
WHO WERE YOU TALKING TO JUST NOW?
I HEARD VOICES WHEN I CAME IN, BUT I... I THOUGHT YOU HAD TO MAKE A PHONE CALL.
I... *GASP!*
BARRY PALUMBO HOLDS HIMSELF VERY STILL.
AS SILVER FUR GLISTENS IN THE MOONLIGHT.
IS... IS THAT...?
URRR...
THE TALONS, NOW GOUGING UP SPLINTERS.

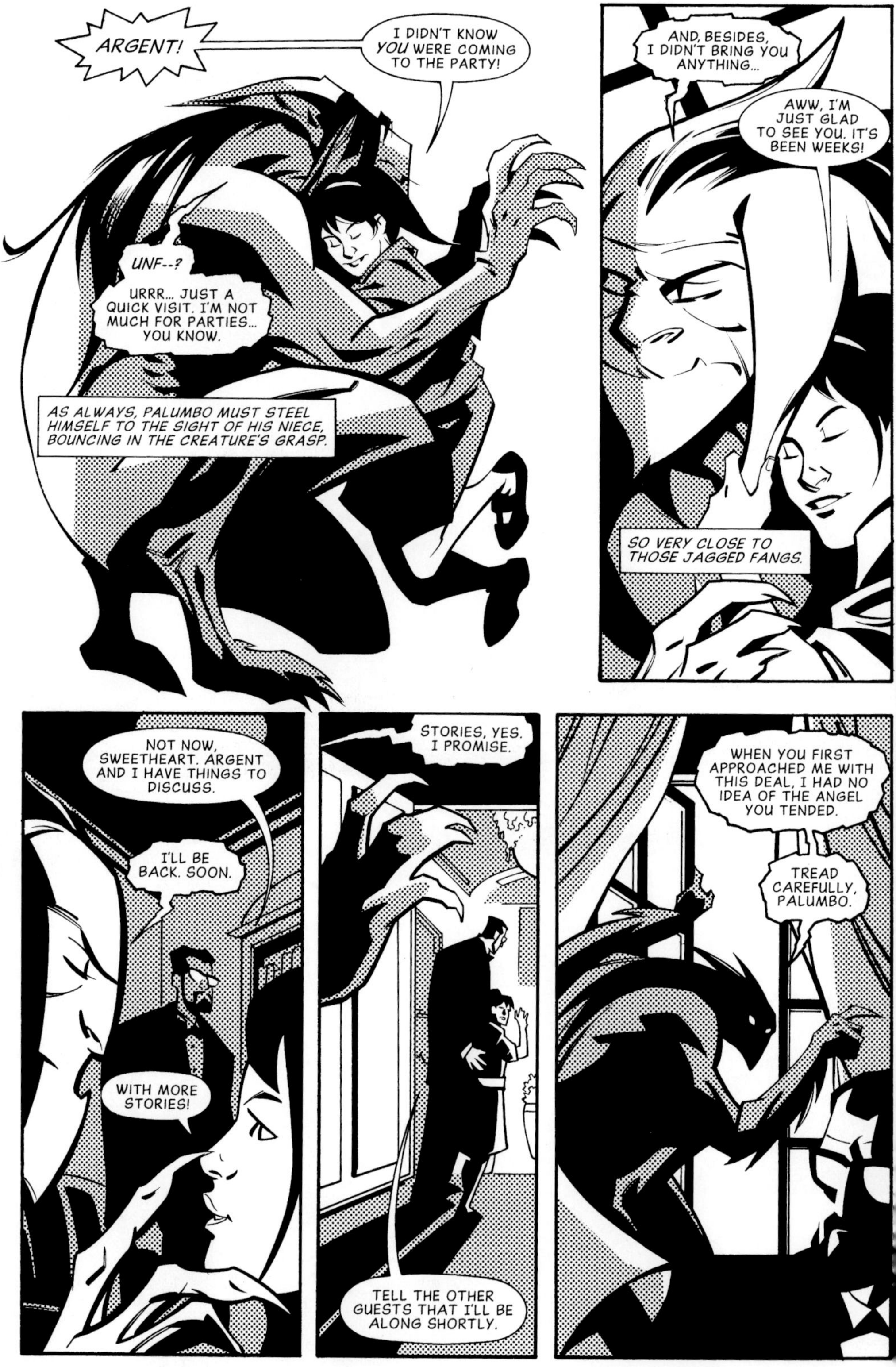
ARGENT!
I DIDN'T KNOW YOU WERE COMING TO THE PARTY!
UNF--?
URRR... JUST A QUICK VISIT. I'M NOT MUCH FOR PARTIES... YOU KNOW.
AS ALWAYS, PALUMBO MUST STEEL HIMSELF TO THE SIGHT OF HIS NIECE, BOUNCING IN THE CREATURE'S GRASP.
AND, BESIDES, I DIDN'T BRING YOU ANYTHING...
AWW, I'M JUST GLAD TO SEE YOU. IT'S BEEN WEEKS!
SO VERY CLOSE TO THOSE JAGGED FANGS.
NOT NOW, SWEETHEART. ARGENT AND I HAVE THINGS TO DISCUSS.
I'LL BE BACK. SOON.
WITH MORE STORIES!
STORIES, YES. I PROMISE.
TELL THE OTHER GUESTS THAT I'LL BE ALONG SHORTLY.
WHEN YOU FIRST APPROACHED ME WITH THIS DEAL, I HAD NO IDEA OF THE ANGEL YOU TENDED.
TREAD CAREFULLY, PALUMBO.

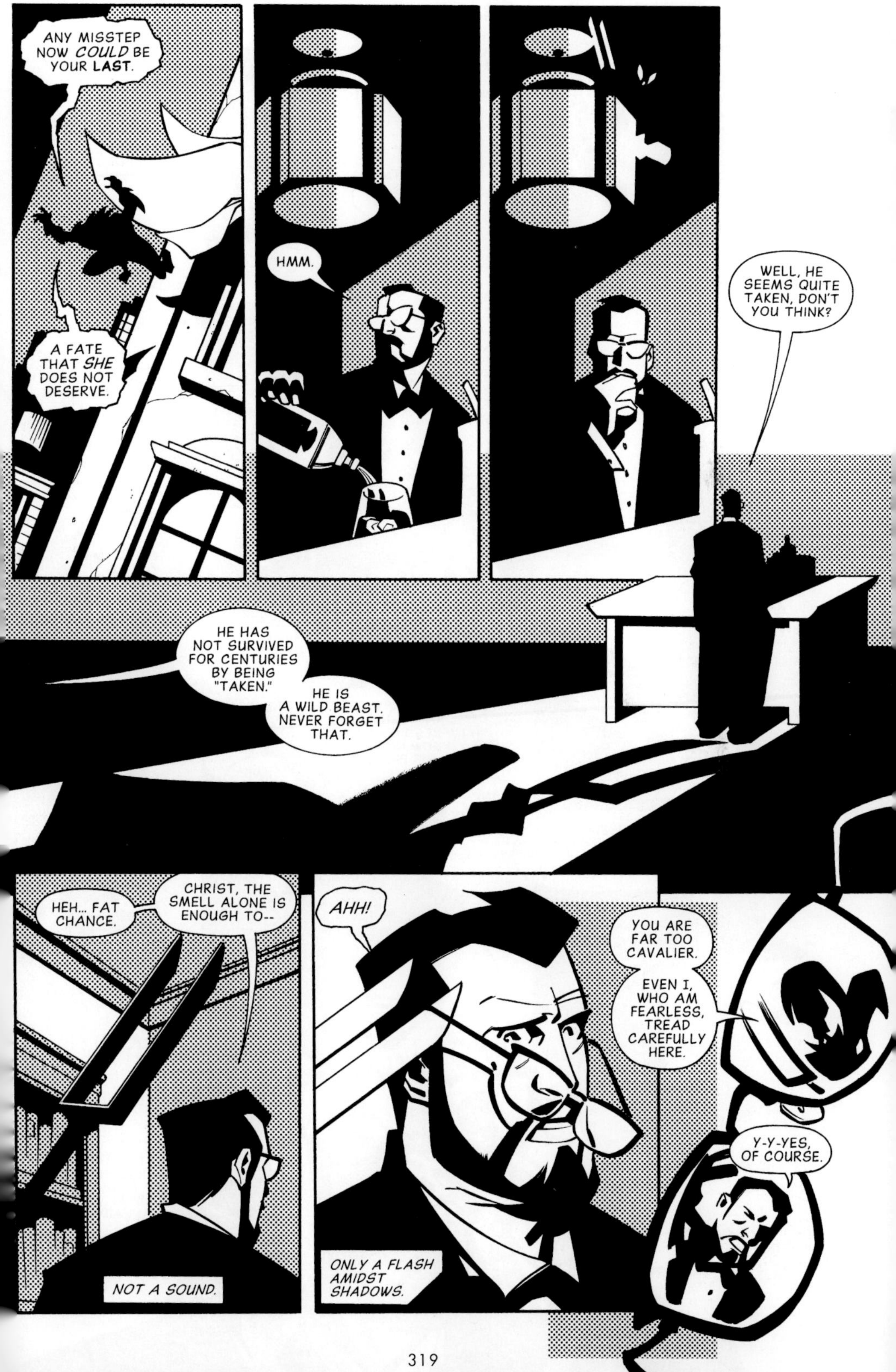
ANY MISSTEP NOW COULD BE YOUR LAST.
A FATE THAT SHE DOES NOT DESERVE.
HMM.
WELL, HE SEEMS QUITE TAKEN, DON'T YOU THINK?
HE HAS NOT SURVIVED FOR CENTURIES BY BEING "TAKEN."
HE IS A WILD BEAST. NEVER FORGET THAT.
HEH... FAT CHANCE.
CHRIST, THE SMELL ALONE IS ENOUGH TO--
NOT A SOUND.
AHH!
ONLY A FLASH AMIDST SHADOWS.
YOU ARE FAR TOO CAVALIER.
EVEN I, WHO AM FEARLESS, TREAD CAREFULLY HERE.
Y-Y-YES, OF COURSE.

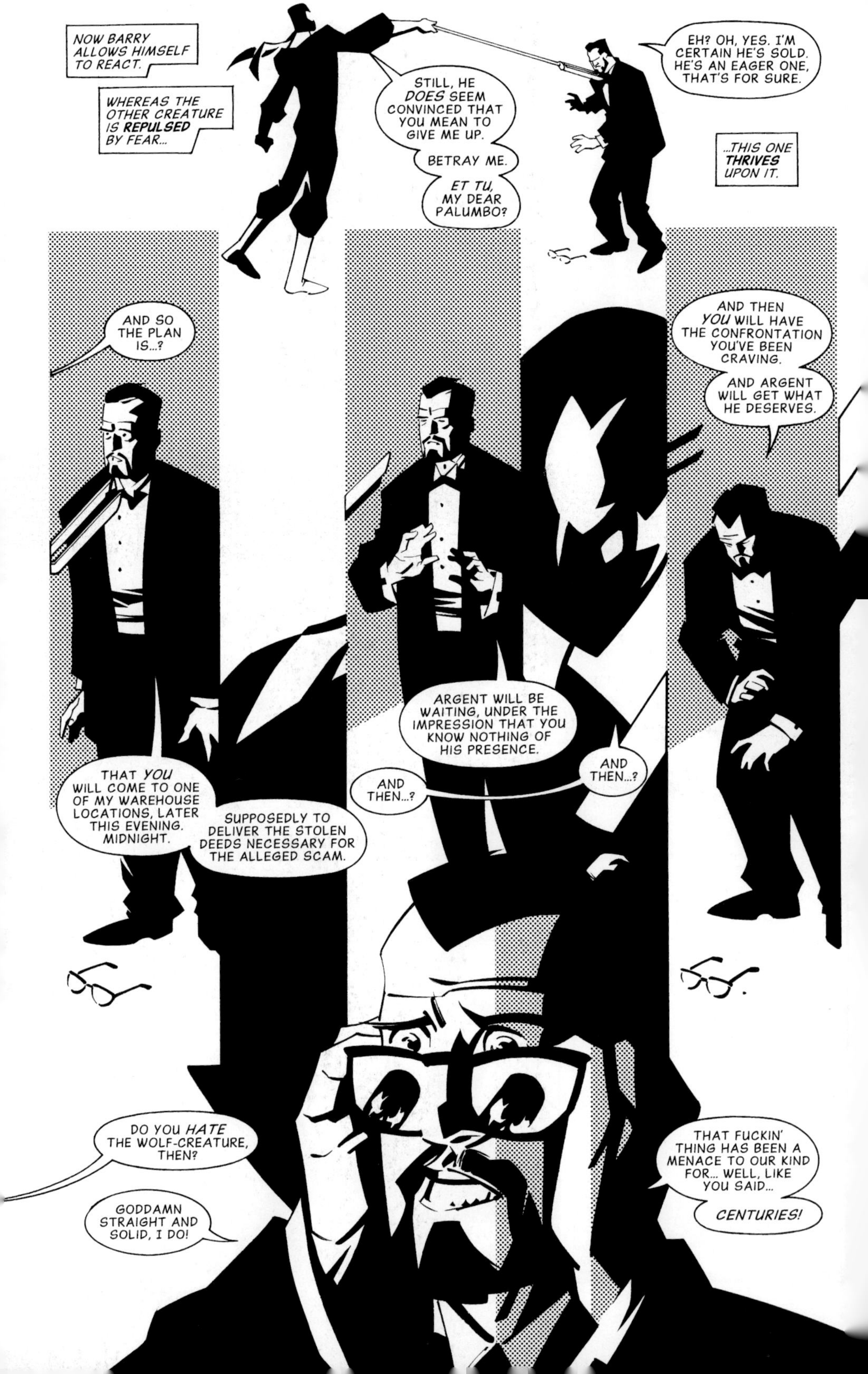
NOW BARRY ALLOWS HIMSELF TO REACT.
WHEREAS THE OTHER CREATURE IS **REPULSED** BY FEAR...
STILL, HE *DOES* SEEM CONVINCED THAT YOU MEAN TO GIVE ME UP.
BETRAY ME.
ET TU, MY DEAR PALUMBO?
EH? OH, YES. I'M CERTAIN HE'S SOLD. HE'S AN EAGER ONE, THAT'S FOR SURE.
...THIS ONE **THRIVES** UPON IT.
AND SO THE PLAN IS...?
THAT *YOU* WILL COME TO ONE OF MY WAREHOUSE LOCATIONS, LATER THIS EVENING. MIDNIGHT.
SUPPOSEDLY TO DELIVER THE STOLEN DEEDS NECESSARY FOR THE ALLEGED SCAM.
ARGENT WILL BE WAITING, UNDER THE IMPRESSION THAT YOU KNOW NOTHING OF HIS PRESENCE.
AND THEN...?
AND THEN...?
AND THEN *YOU* WILL HAVE THE CONFRONTATION YOU'VE BEEN CRAVING.
AND ARGENT WILL GET WHAT HE DESERVES.
DO YOU *HATE* THE WOLF-CREATURE, THEN?
GODDAMN STRAIGHT AND SOLID, I DO!
THAT FUCKIN' THING HAS BEEN A MENACE TO OUR KIND FOR... WELL, LIKE YOU SAID...
CENTURIES!

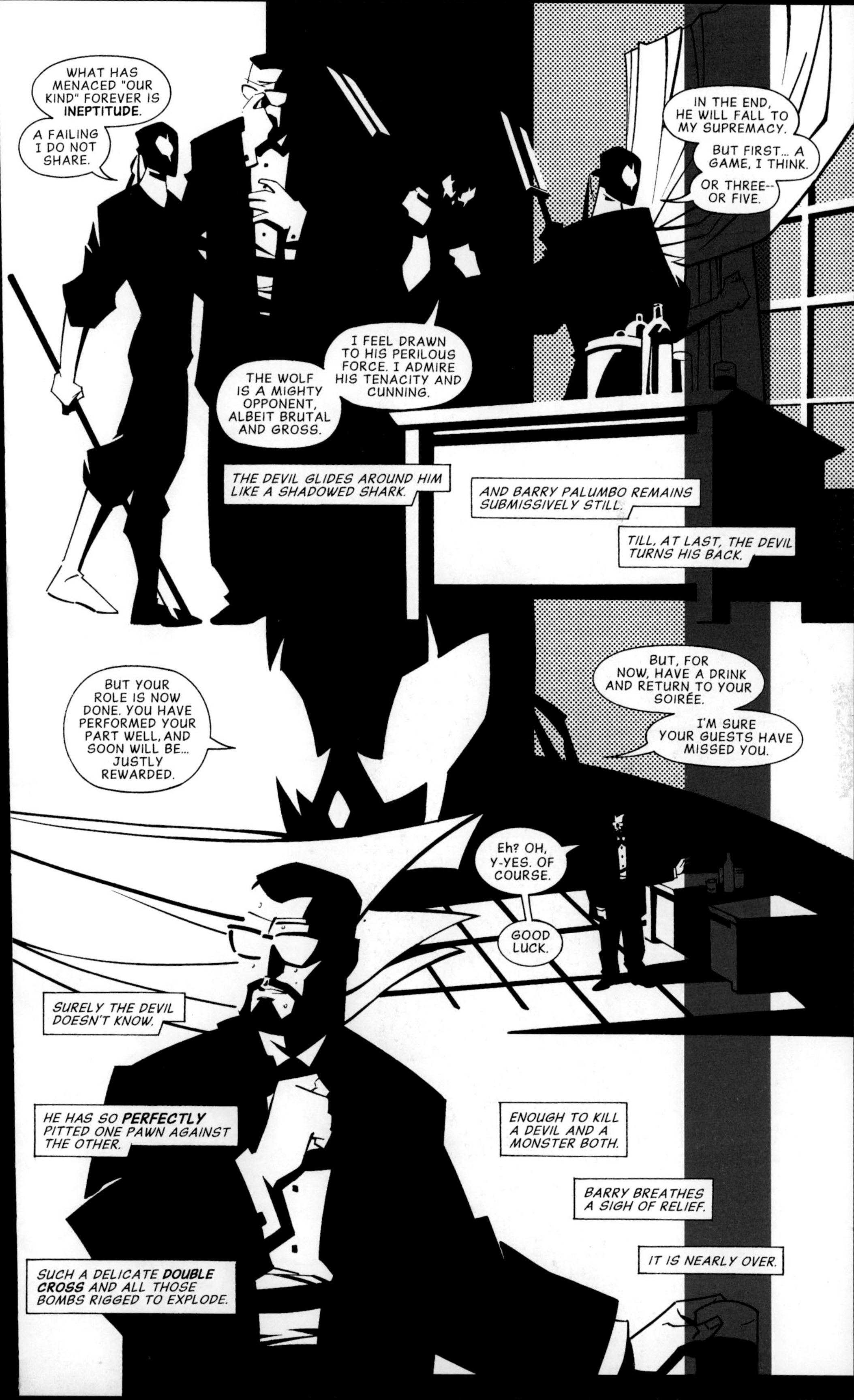
WHAT HAS MENACED "OUR KIND" FOREVER IS **INEPTITUDE**.
A FAILING I DO NOT SHARE.
IN THE END, HE WILL FALL TO MY SUPREMACY.
BUT FIRST... A GAME, I THINK.
OR THREE-- OR FIVE.
THE WOLF IS A MIGHTY OPPONENT, ALBEIT BRUTAL AND GROSS.
I FEEL DRAWN TO HIS PERILOUS FORCE. I ADMIRE HIS TENACITY AND CUNNING.
THE DEVIL GLIDES AROUND HIM LIKE A SHADOWED SHARK.
AND BARRY PALUMBO REMAINS SUBMISSIVELY STILL.
TILL, AT LAST, THE DEVIL TURNS HIS BACK.
BUT YOUR ROLE IS NOW DONE. YOU HAVE PERFORMED YOUR PART WELL, AND SOON WILL BE... JUSTLY REWARDED.
BUT, FOR NOW, HAVE A DRINK AND RETURN TO YOUR SOIRÉE.
I'M SURE YOUR GUESTS HAVE MISSED YOU.
Eh? OH, Y-YES. OF COURSE.
GOOD LUCK.
SURELY THE DEVIL DOESN'T KNOW.
*HE HAS SO **PERFECTLY** PITTED ONE PAWN AGAINST THE OTHER.*
*SUCH A DELICATE **DOUBLE CROSS** AND ALL THOSE BOMBS RIGGED TO EXPLODE.*
ENOUGH TO KILL A DEVIL AND A MONSTER BOTH.
BARRY BREATHES A SIGH OF RELIEF.
IT IS NEARLY OVER.

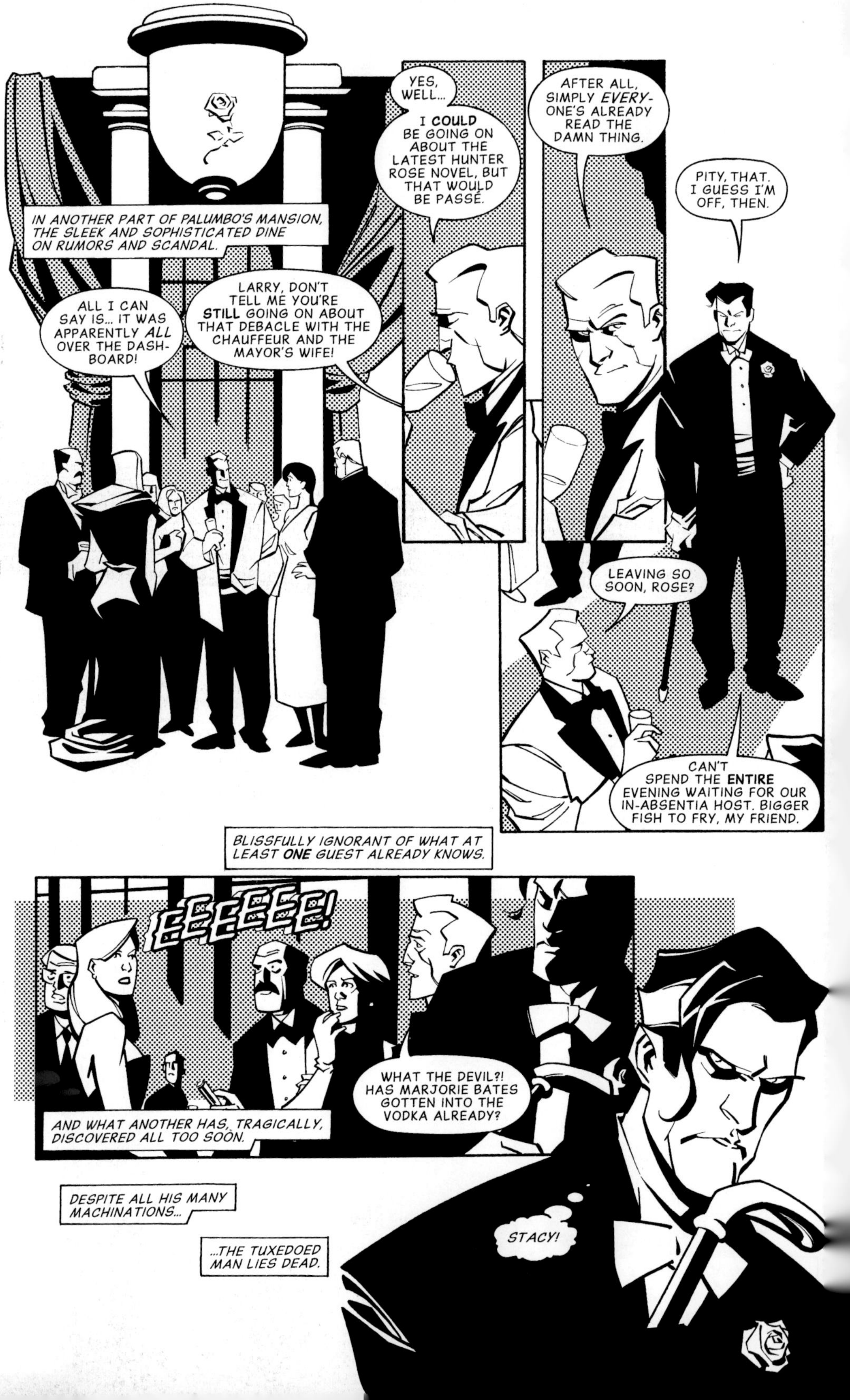
IN ANOTHER PART OF PALUMBO'S MANSION, THE SLEEK AND SOPHISTICATED DINE ON RUMORS AND SCANDAL.
ALL I CAN SAY IS... IT WAS APPARENTLY ALL OVER THE DASH-BOARD!
LARRY, DON'T TELL ME YOU'RE STILL GOING ON ABOUT THAT DEBACLE WITH THE CHAUFFEUR AND THE MAYOR'S WIFE!
YES, WELL...
I COULD BE GOING ON ABOUT THE LATEST HUNTER ROSE NOVEL, BUT THAT WOULD BE PASSÉ.
AFTER ALL, SIMPLY EVERY-ONE'S ALREADY READ THE DAMN THING.
PITY, THAT. I GUESS I'M OFF, THEN.
LEAVING SO SOON, ROSE?
CAN'T SPEND THE ENTIRE EVENING WAITING FOR OUR IN-ABSENTIA HOST. BIGGER FISH TO FRY, MY FRIEND.
BLISSFULLY IGNORANT OF WHAT AT LEAST ONE GUEST ALREADY KNOWS.
EEEEEEE!
WHAT THE DEVIL?! HAS MARJORIE BATES GOTTEN INTO THE VODKA ALREADY?
AND WHAT ANOTHER HAS, TRAGICALLY, DISCOVERED ALL TOO SOON.
DESPITE ALL HIS MANY MACHINATIONS...
...THE TUXEDOED MAN LIES DEAD.
STACY!

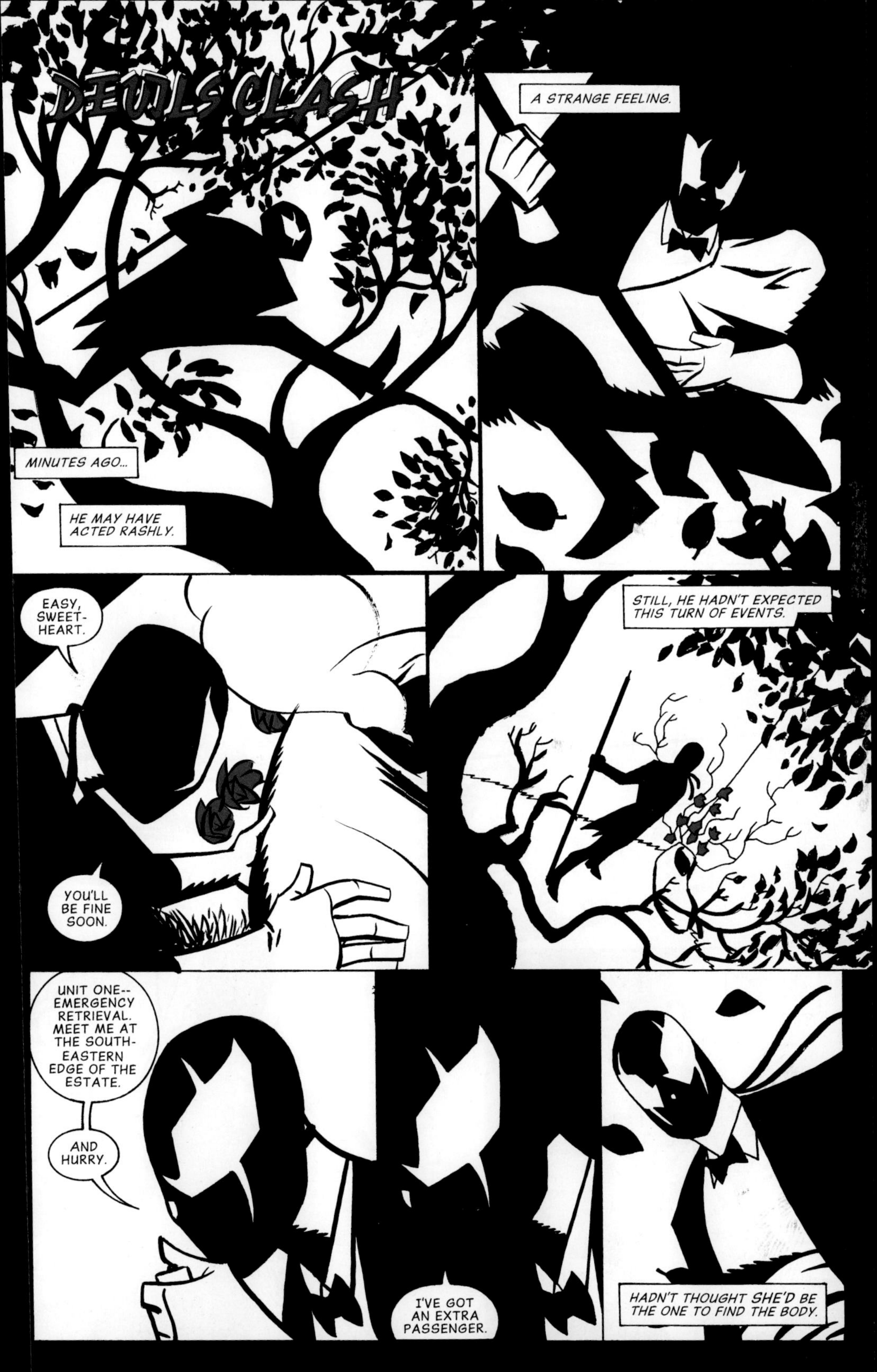
DEVILS CLASH
MINUTES AGO...
HE MAY HAVE ACTED RASHLY.
A STRANGE FEELING.
EASY, SWEET-HEART.
YOU'LL BE FINE SOON.
STILL, HE HADN'T EXPECTED THIS TURN OF EVENTS.
UNIT ONE-- EMERGENCY RETRIEVAL. MEET ME AT THE SOUTH-EASTERN EDGE OF THE ESTATE.
AND HURRY.
I'VE GOT AN EXTRA PASSENGER.
HADN'T THOUGHT SHE'D BE THE ONE TO FIND THE BODY.

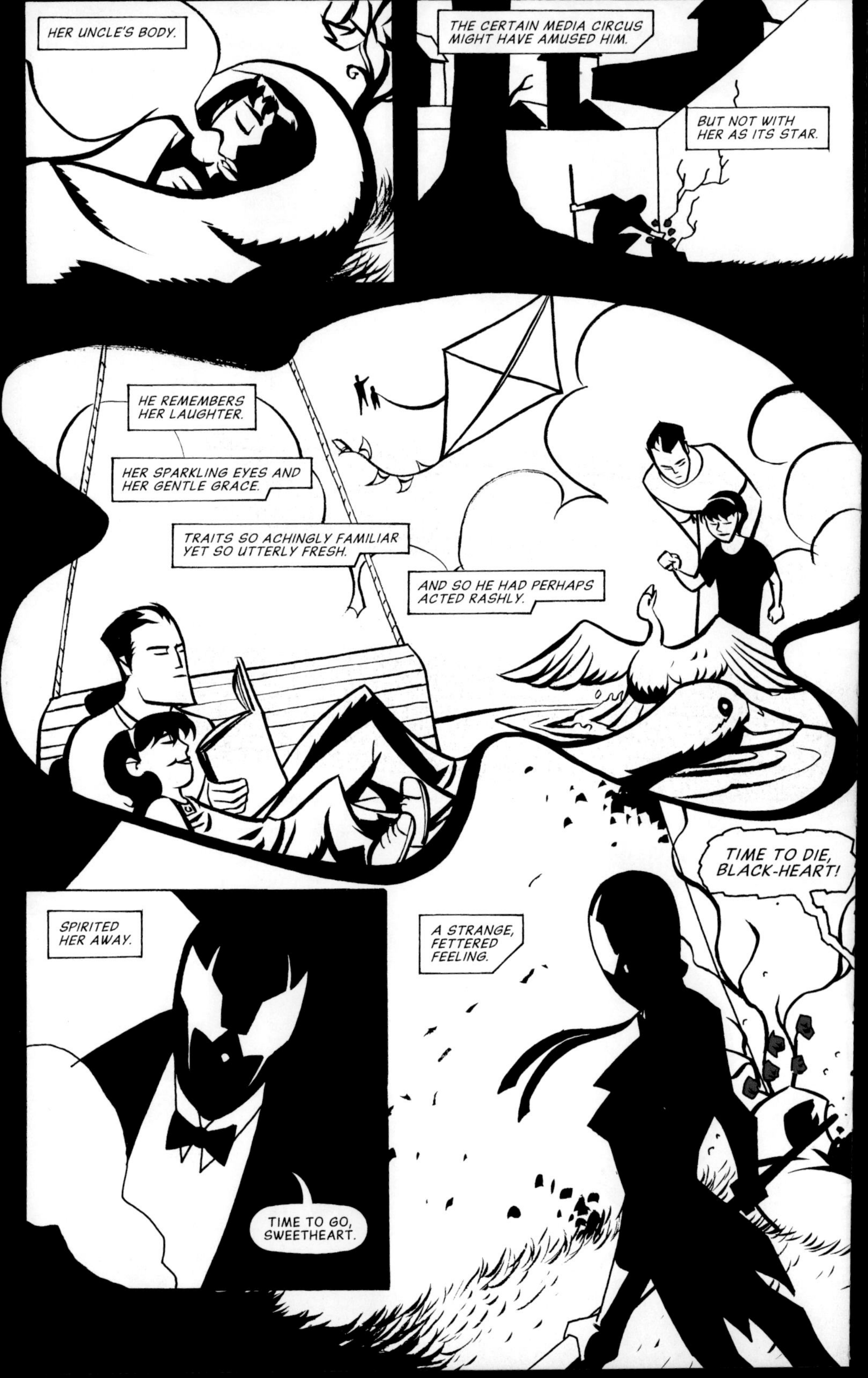
HER UNCLE'S BODY.
THE CERTAIN MEDIA CIRCUS MIGHT HAVE AMUSED HIM.
BUT NOT WITH HER AS ITS STAR.
HE REMEMBERS HER LAUGHTER.
HER SPARKLING EYES AND HER GENTLE GRACE.
TRAITS SO ACHINGLY FAMILIAR YET SO UTTERLY FRESH.
AND SO HE HAD PERHAPS ACTED RASHLY.
SPIRITED HER AWAY.
TIME TO GO, SWEETHEART.
A STRANGE, FETTERED FEELING.
TIME TO DIE, BLACK-HEART!

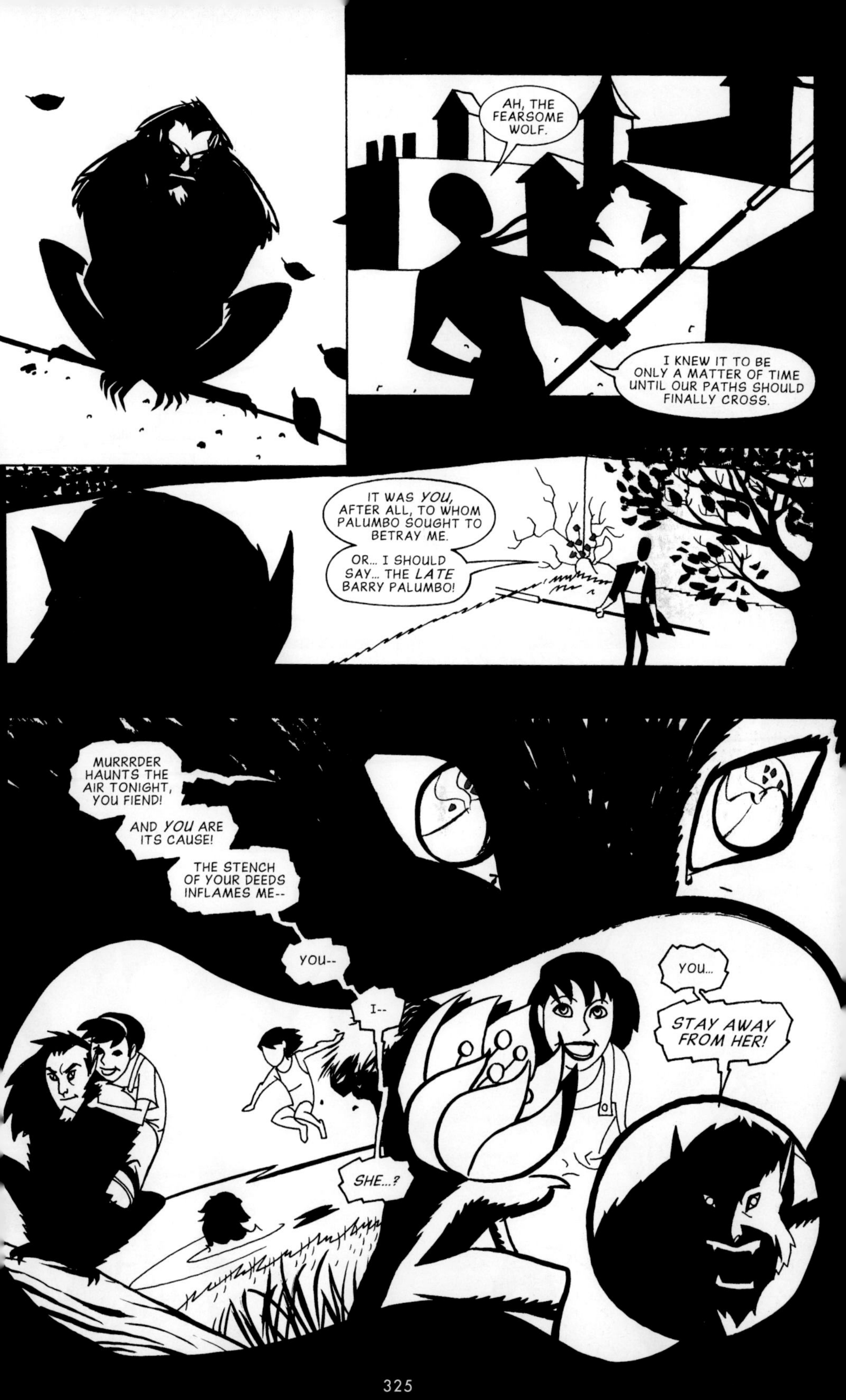
AH, THE FEARSOME WOLF.
I KNEW IT TO BE ONLY A MATTER OF TIME UNTIL OUR PATHS SHOULD FINALLY CROSS.
IT WAS *YOU*, AFTER ALL, TO WHOM PALUMBO SOUGHT TO BETRAY ME.
OR... I SHOULD SAY... THE *LATE* BARRY PALUMBO!
MURRRDER HAUNTS THE AIR TONIGHT, YOU FIEND!
AND *YOU* ARE ITS CAUSE!
THE STENCH OF YOUR DEEDS INFLAMES ME--
YOU--
I--
SHE...?
YOU...
STAY AWAY FROM HER!

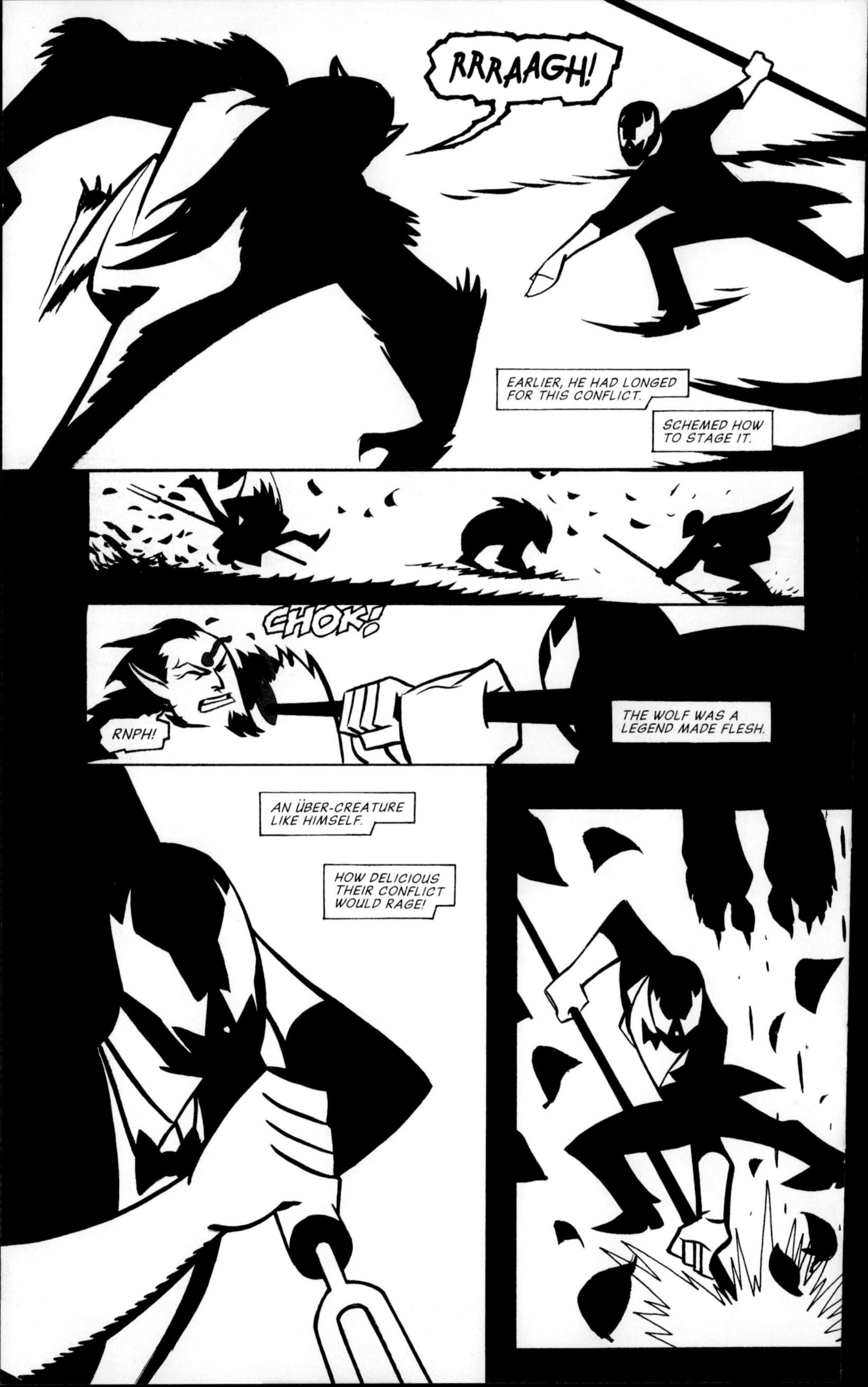
RRRAAGH!
EARLIER, HE HAD LONGED FOR THIS CONFLICT.
SCHEMED HOW TO STAGE IT.
CHOK!
RNPH!
THE WOLF WAS A LEGEND MADE FLESH.
AN ÜBER-CREATURE LIKE HIMSELF.
HOW DELICIOUS THEIR CONFLICT WOULD RAGE!

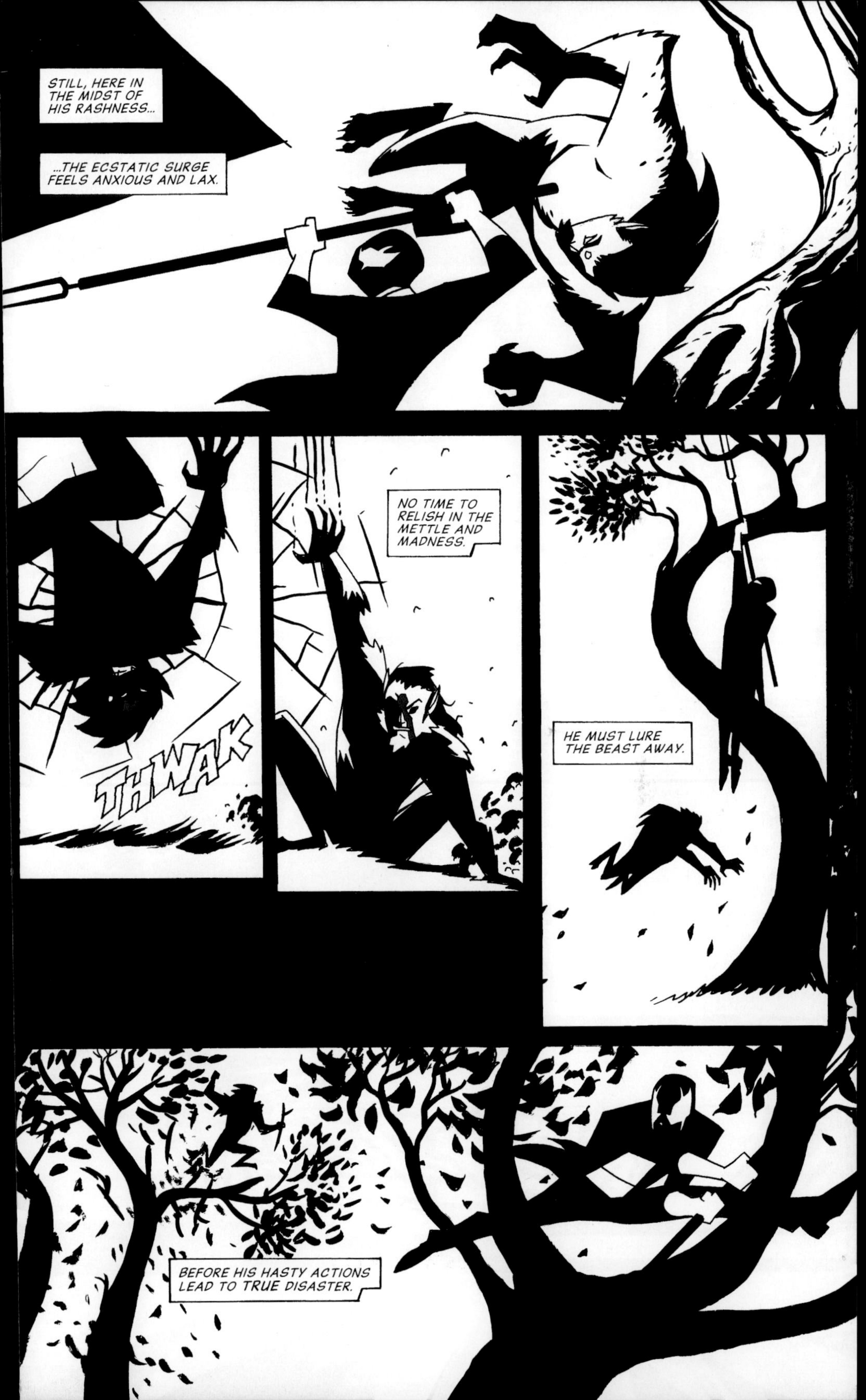
STILL, HERE IN THE MIDST OF HIS RASHNESS...
...THE ECSTATIC SURGE FEELS ANXIOUS AND LAX.
THWAK
NO TIME TO RELISH IN THE METTLE AND MADNESS.
HE MUST LURE THE BEAST AWAY.
BEFORE HIS HASTY ACTIONS LEAD TO TRUE DISASTER.

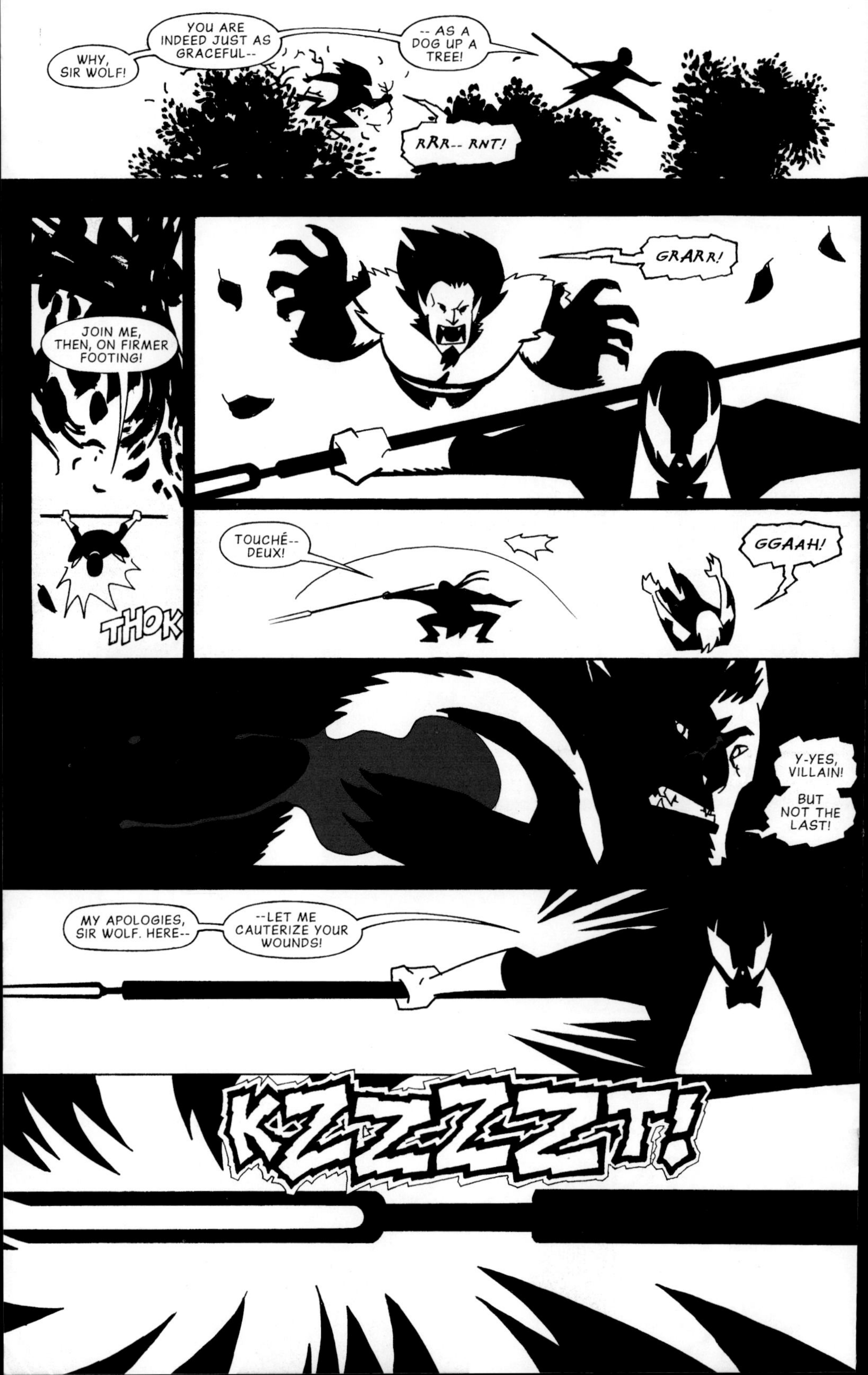
WHY, SIR WOLF!
YOU ARE INDEED JUST AS GRACEFUL--
-- AS A DOG UP A TREE!
RRR-- RNT!
JOIN ME, THEN, ON FIRMER FOOTING!
GRARR!
THOK
TOUCHÉ-- DEUX!
GGAAH!
Y-YES, VILLAIN!
BUT NOT THE LAST!
MY APOLOGIES, SIR WOLF. HERE--
--LET ME CAUTERIZE YOUR WOUNDS!
KZZZZT!

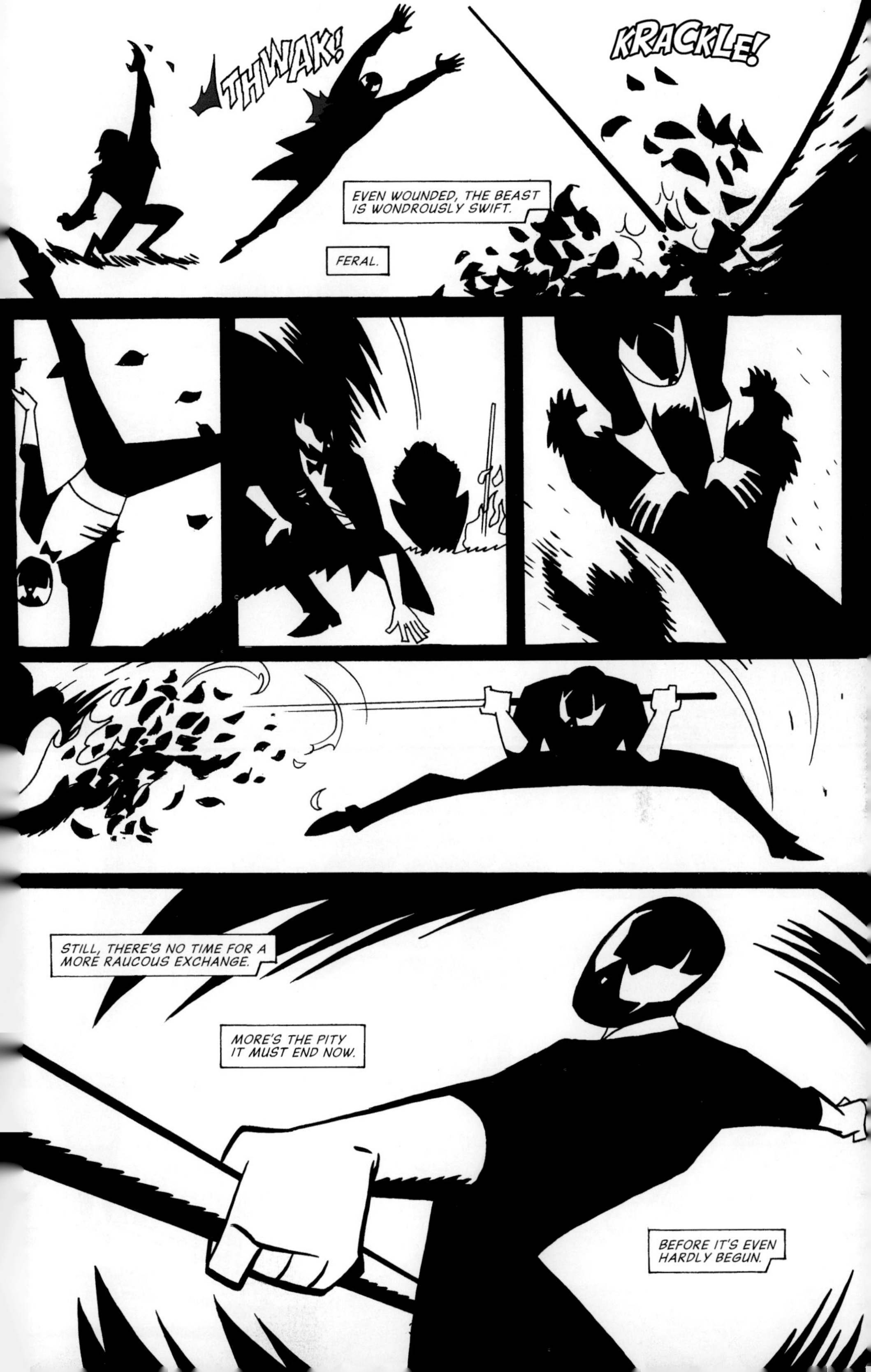
THWAK!
KRACKLE!
EVEN WOUNDED, THE BEAST IS WONDROUSLY SWIFT.
FERAL.
STILL, THERE'S NO TIME FOR A MORE RAUCOUS EXCHANGE.
MORE'S THE PITY IT MUST END NOW.
BEFORE IT'S EVEN HARDLY BEGUN.

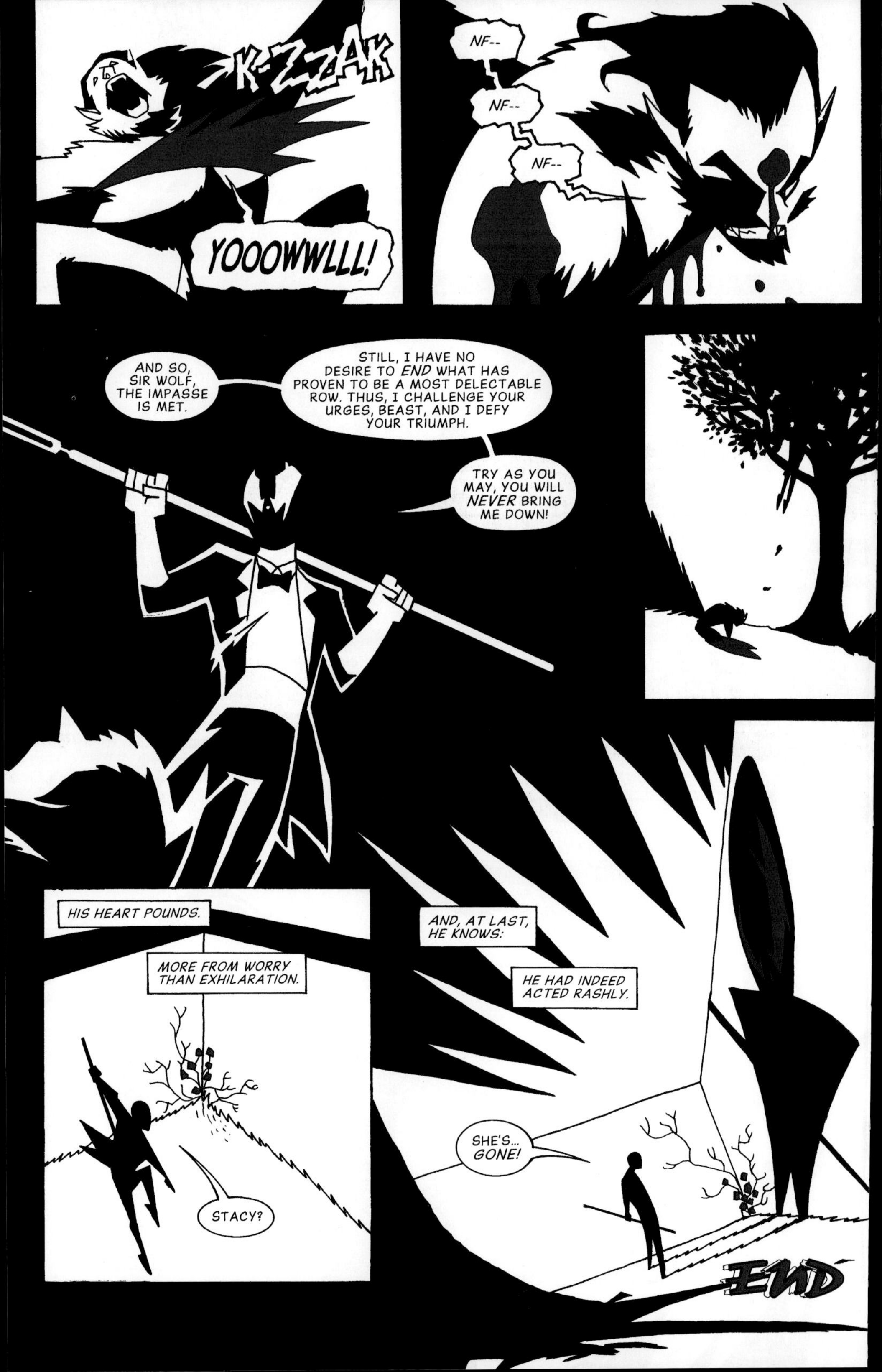
K-ZZAK
YOOOWWLLL!
NF--
NF--
NF--
AND SO, SIR WOLF, THE IMPASSE IS MET.
STILL, I HAVE NO DESIRE TO *END* WHAT HAS PROVEN TO BE A MOST DELECTABLE ROW. THUS, I CHALLENGE YOUR URGES, BEAST, AND I DEFY YOUR TRIUMPH.
TRY AS YOU MAY, YOU WILL *NEVER* BRING ME DOWN!
HIS HEART POUNDS.
MORE FROM WORRY THAN EXHILARATION.
STACY?
AND, AT LAST, HE KNOWS:
HE HAD INDEED ACTED RASHLY.
SHE'S... GONE!
END

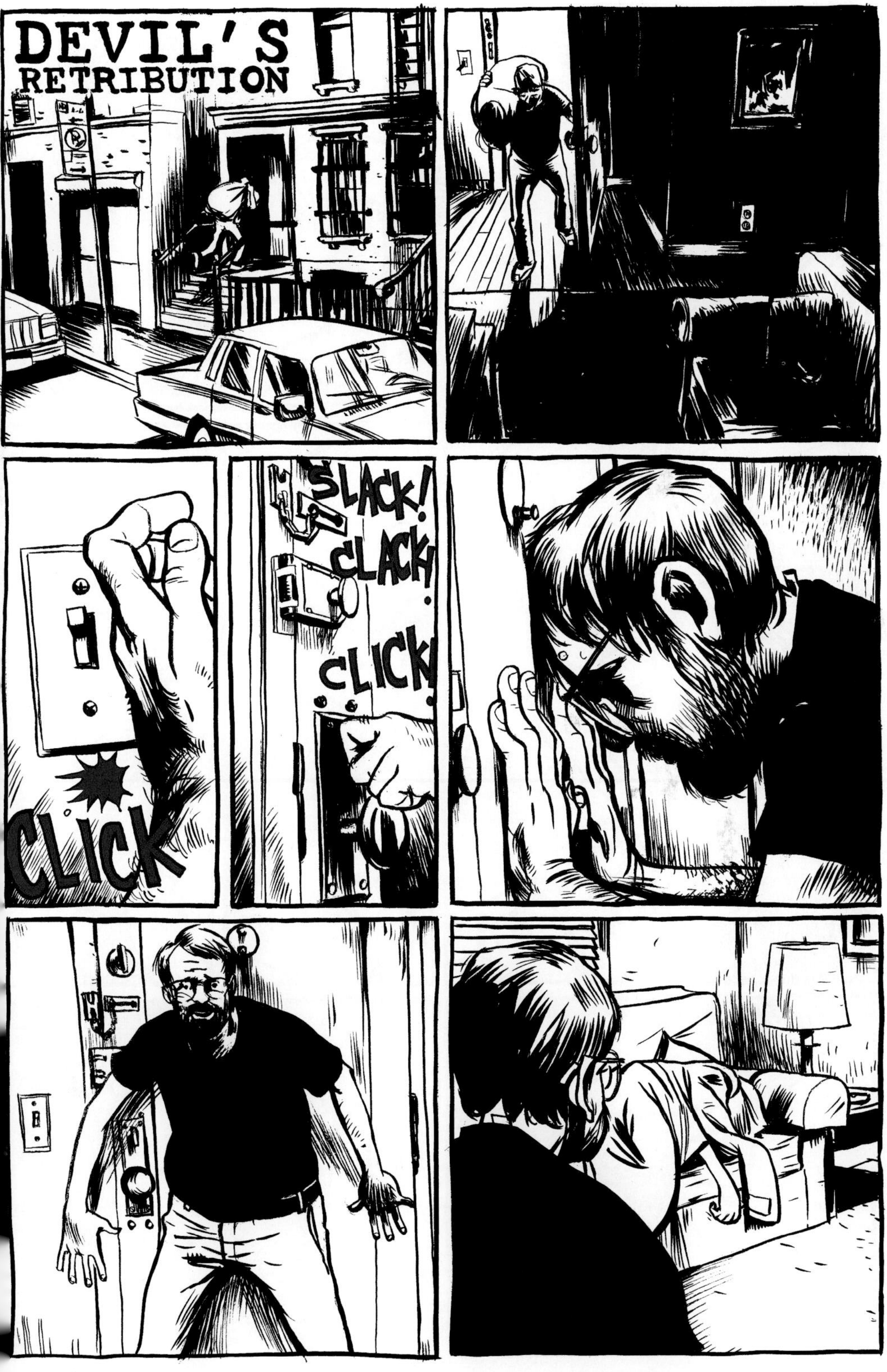
DEVIL'S RETRIBUTION
CLICK
SLACK!
CLACK!
CLICK!

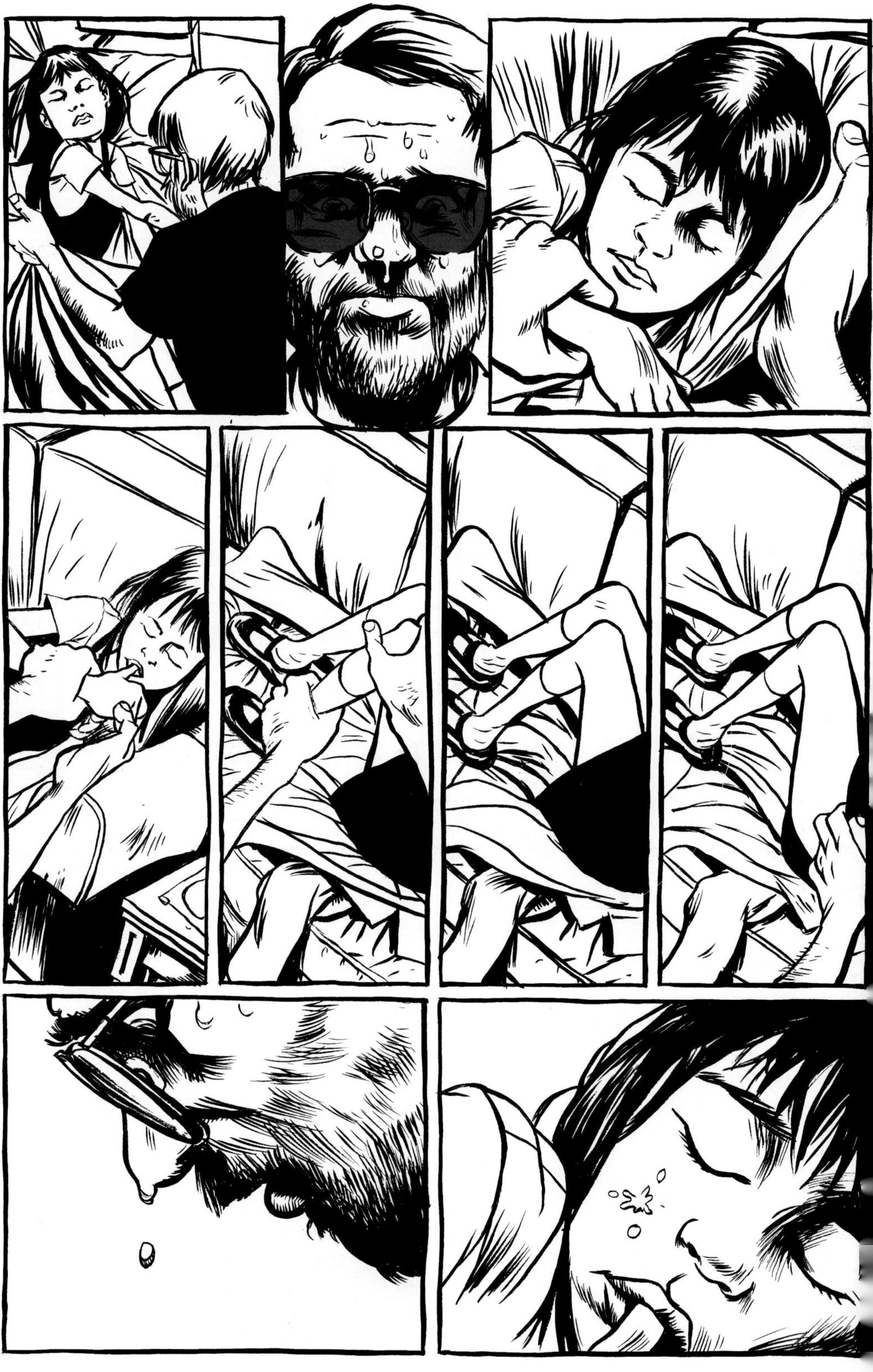

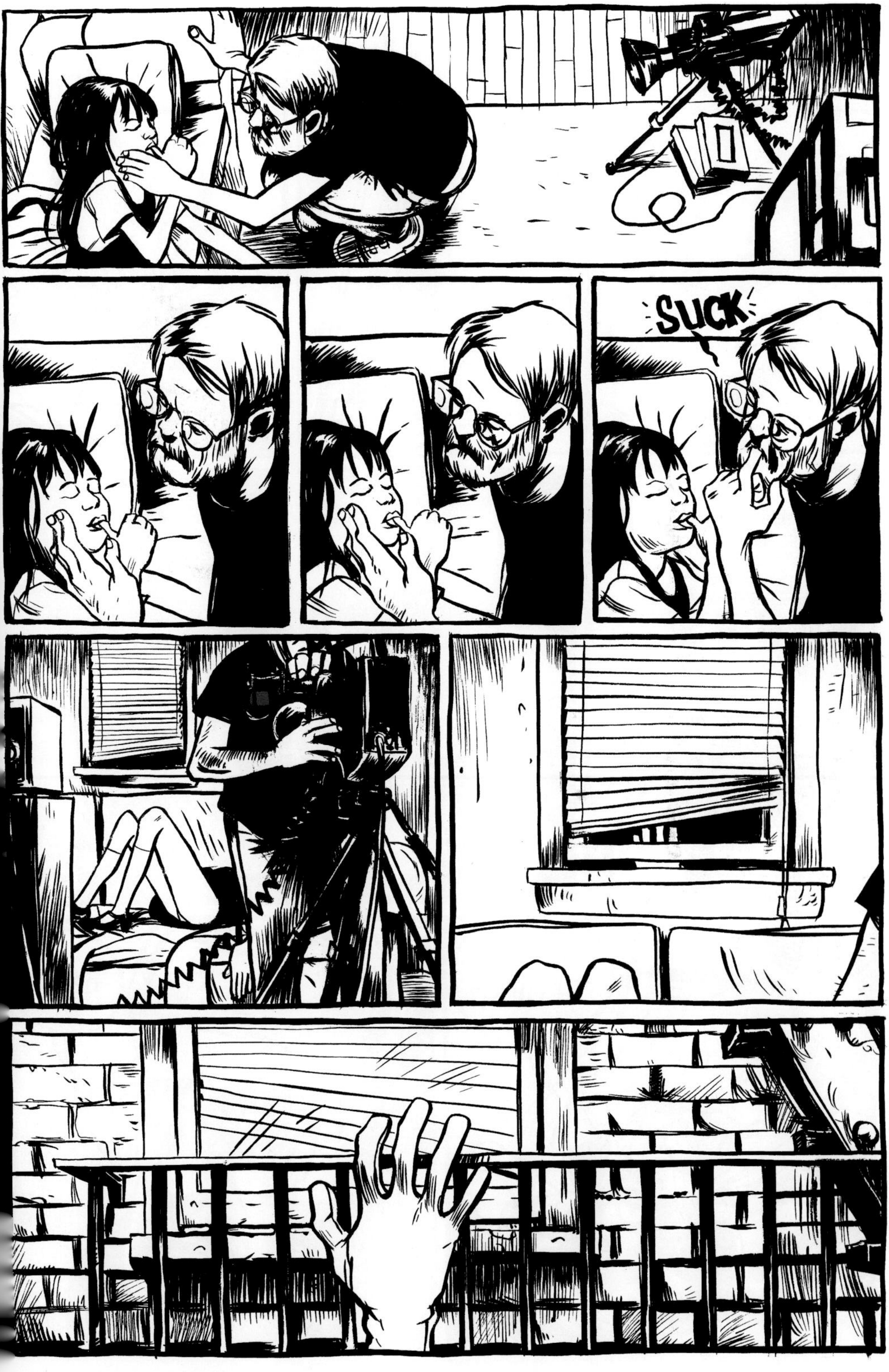
SUCK

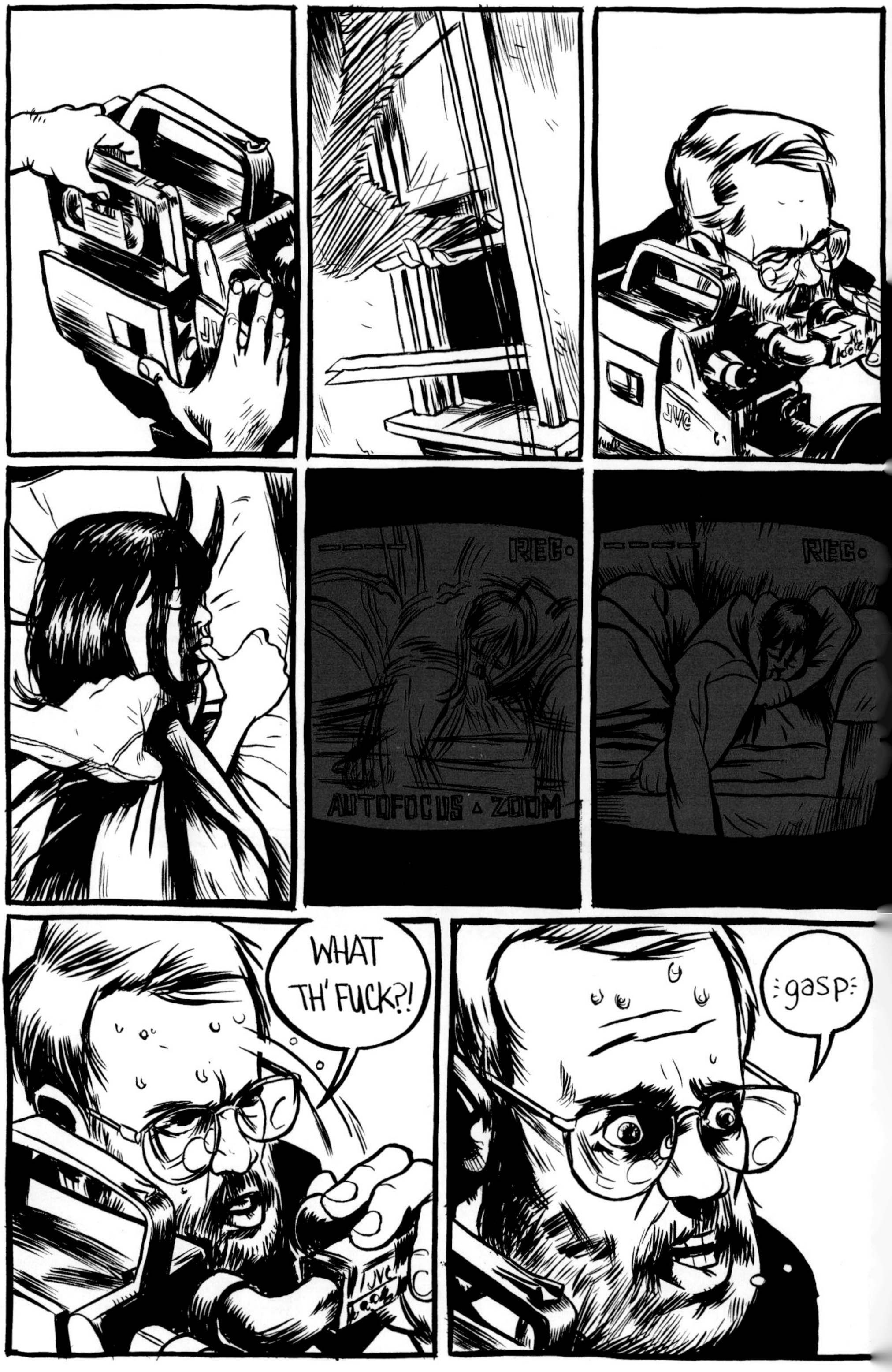
REC
AUTOFOCUS ZOOM
REC
WHAT TH' FUCK?!
gasp

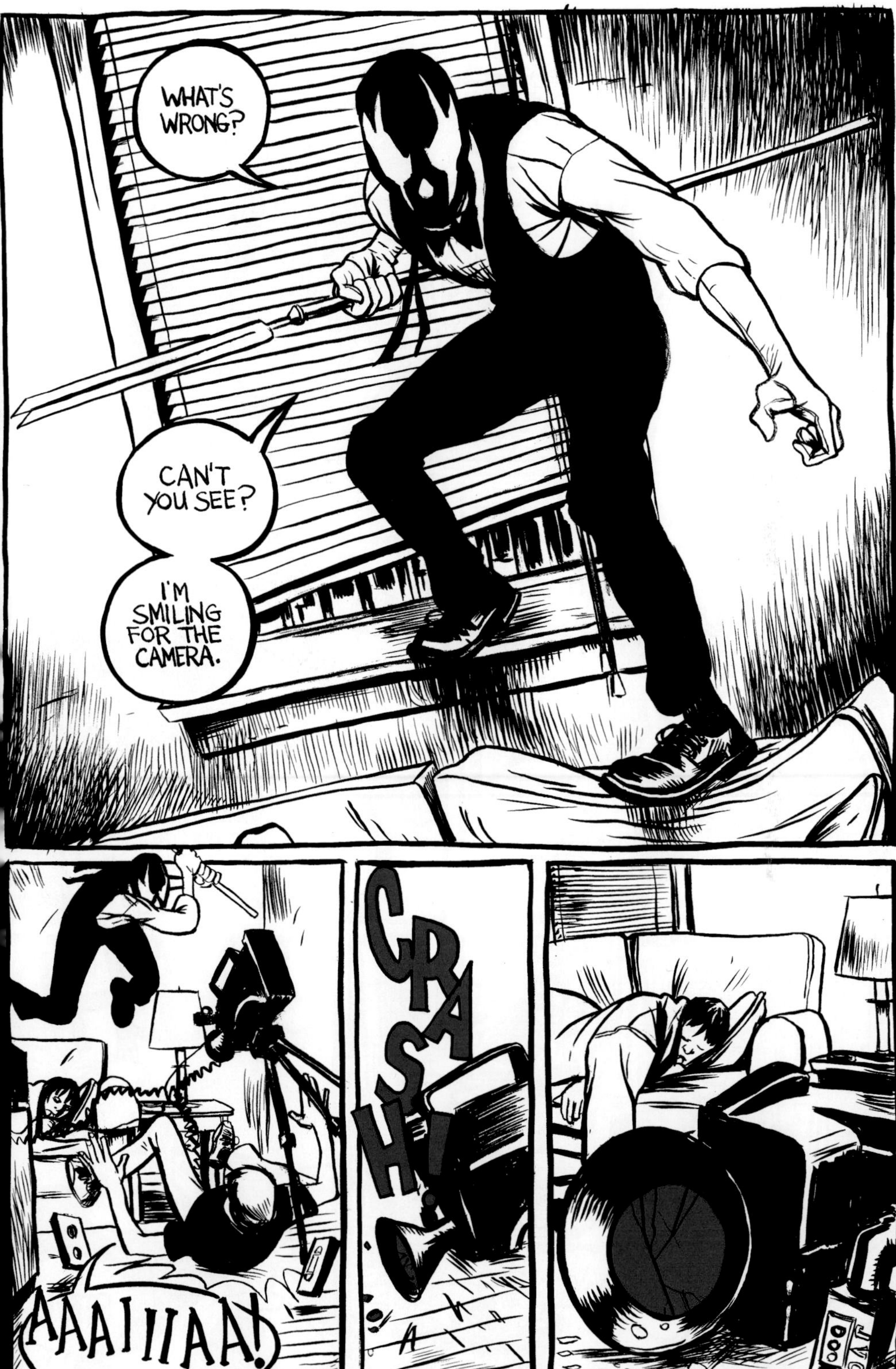
WHAT'S WRONG?
CAN'T YOU SEE?
I'M SMILING FOR THE CAMERA.
AAAIIIAA!
CRASH!

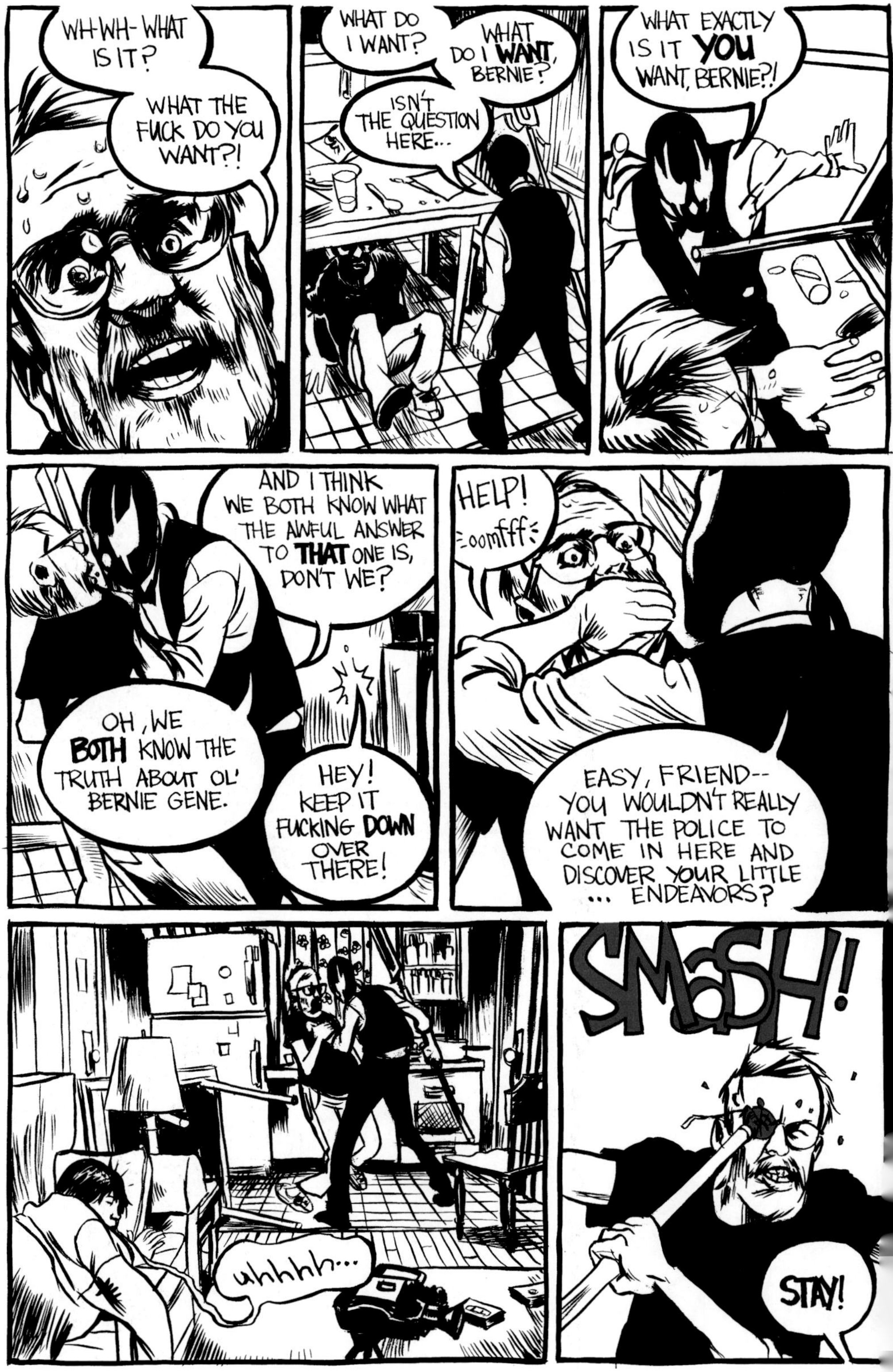
WH-WH- WHAT IS IT?
WHAT THE FUCK DO YOU WANT?!
WHAT DO I WANT?
WHAT DO I WANT, BERNIE?
ISN'T THE QUESTION HERE...
WHAT EXACTLY IS IT YOU WANT, BERNIE?!
AND I THINK WE BOTH KNOW WHAT THE AWFUL ANSWER TO THAT ONE IS, DON'T WE?
OH, WE BOTH KNOW THE TRUTH ABOUT OL' BERNIE GENE.
HEY! KEEP IT FUCKING DOWN OVER THERE!
HELP!
oomfff
EASY, FRIEND-- YOU WOULDN'T REALLY WANT THE POLICE TO COME IN HERE AND DISCOVER YOUR LITTLE ... ENDEAVORS?
uhhhh...
SMASH!
STAY!

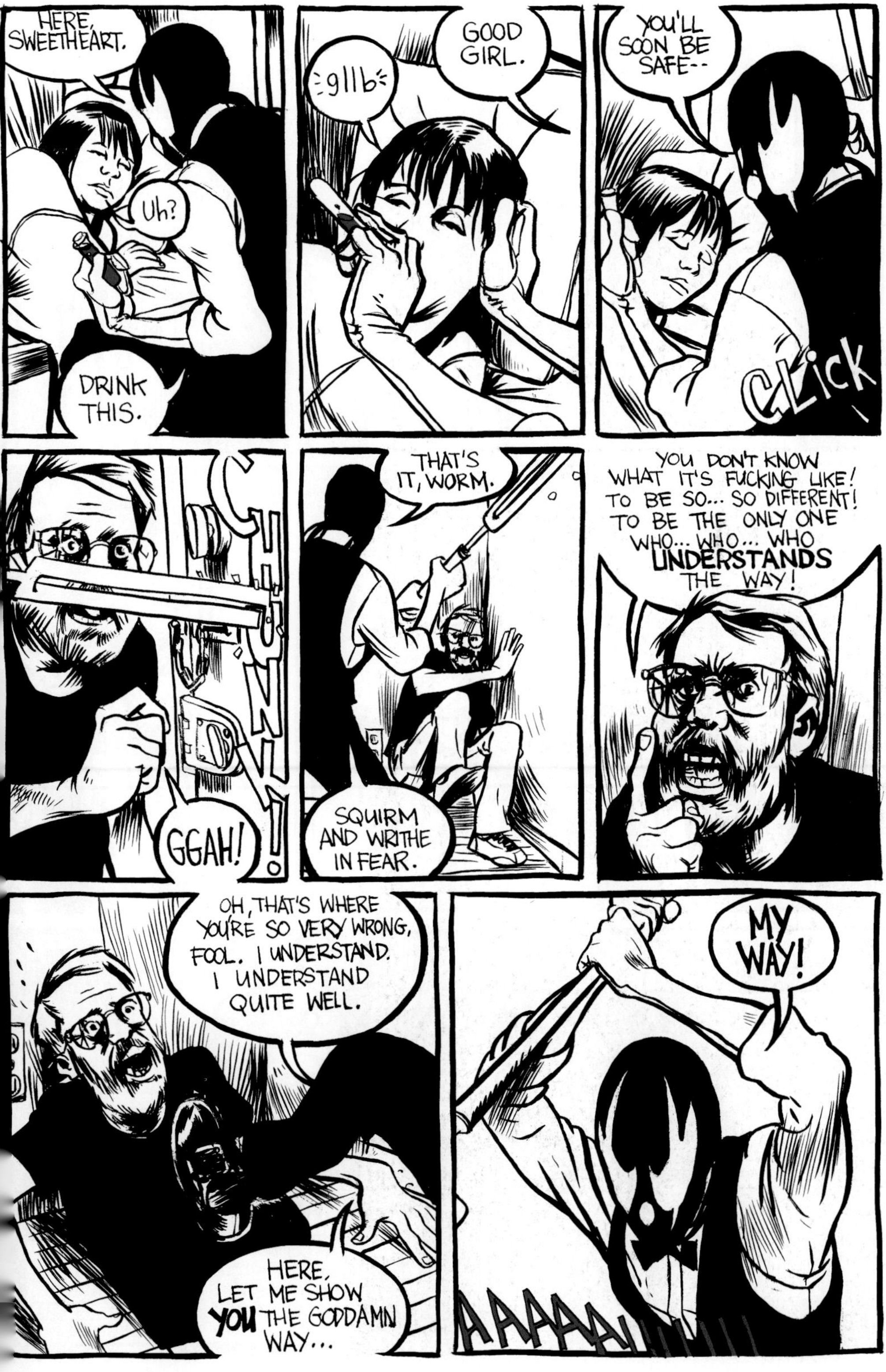
HERE, SWEETHEART.
Uh?
DRINK THIS.
gllb
GOOD GIRL.
YOU'LL SOON BE SAFE--
CLICK
CHUNK!
GGAH!
THAT'S IT, WORM.
SQUIRM AND WRITHE IN FEAR.
YOU DON'T KNOW WHAT IT'S FUCKING LIKE! TO BE SO... SO DIFFERENT! TO BE THE ONLY ONE WHO... WHO... WHO UNDERSTANDS THE WAY!
OH, THAT'S WHERE YOU'RE SO VERY WRONG, FOOL. I UNDERSTAND. I UNDERSTAND QUITE WELL.
HERE, LET ME SHOW YOU THE GODDAMN WAY...
MY WAY!
AAAAAA

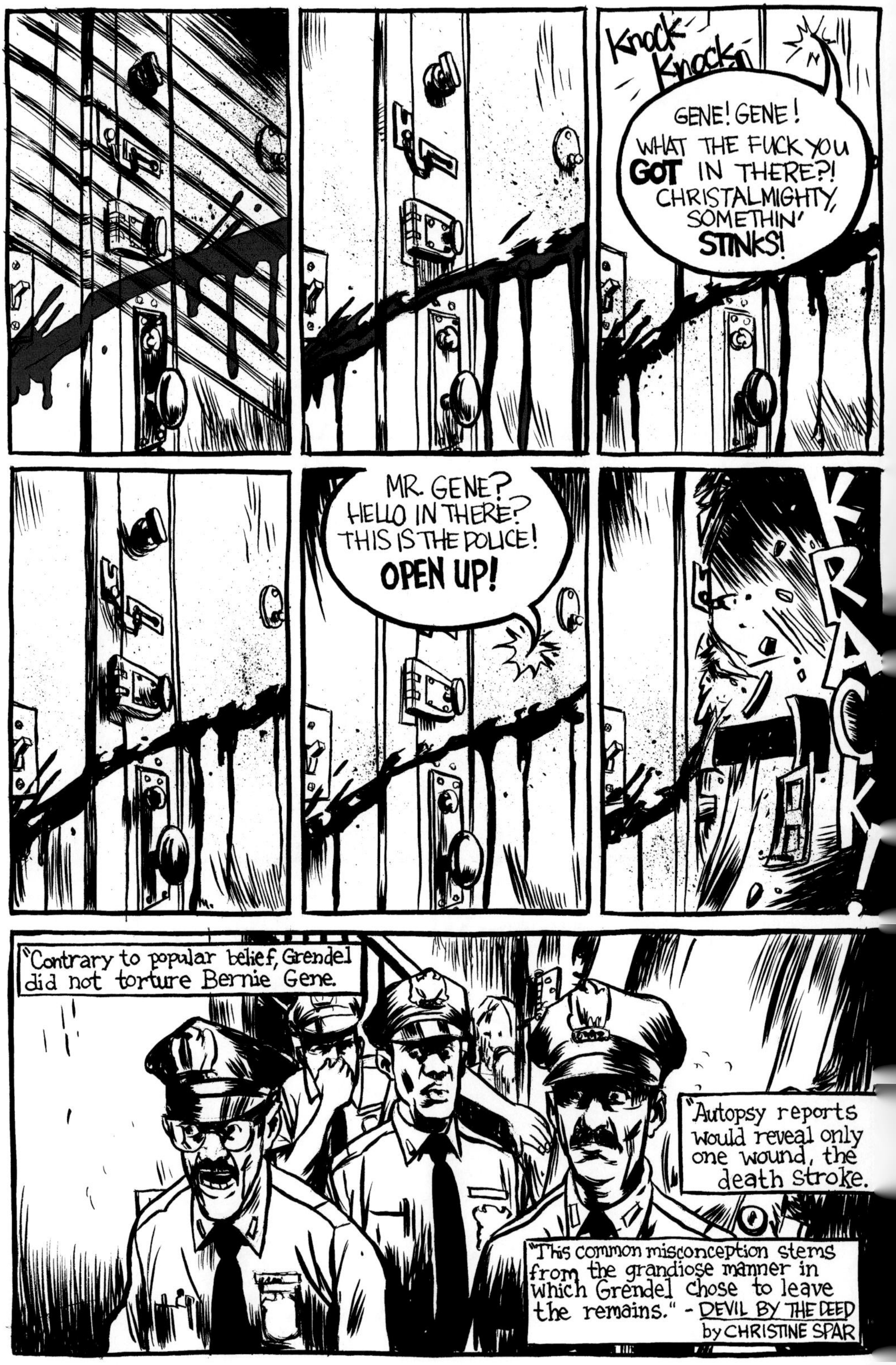

Knock
Knock
GENE! GENE! WHAT THE FUCK YOU GOT IN THERE?! CHRISTALMIGHTY, SOMETHIN' STINKS!
MR. GENE? HELLO IN THERE? THIS IS THE POLICE! OPEN UP!
KRACK!
"Contrary to popular belief, Grendel did not torture Bernie Gene.
"Autopsy reports would reveal only one wound, the death stroke.
"This common misconception stems from the grandiose manner in which Grendel chose to leave the remains." - DEVIL BY THE DEED by CHRISTINE SPAR

POK POK POK POK POK POK POK POK POK POK POK POK POK POK POK POK POK POK POK

POK POK POK POK

POK POK POK POK

PANT PANT PANT PANT PANT

PANT PANT PANT PANT PANT PANT

POK POK POK POK POK POK POK

DEVIL SAY, DEVIL DO

RUN.

POK POK POK POK POK POK POK POK POK POK

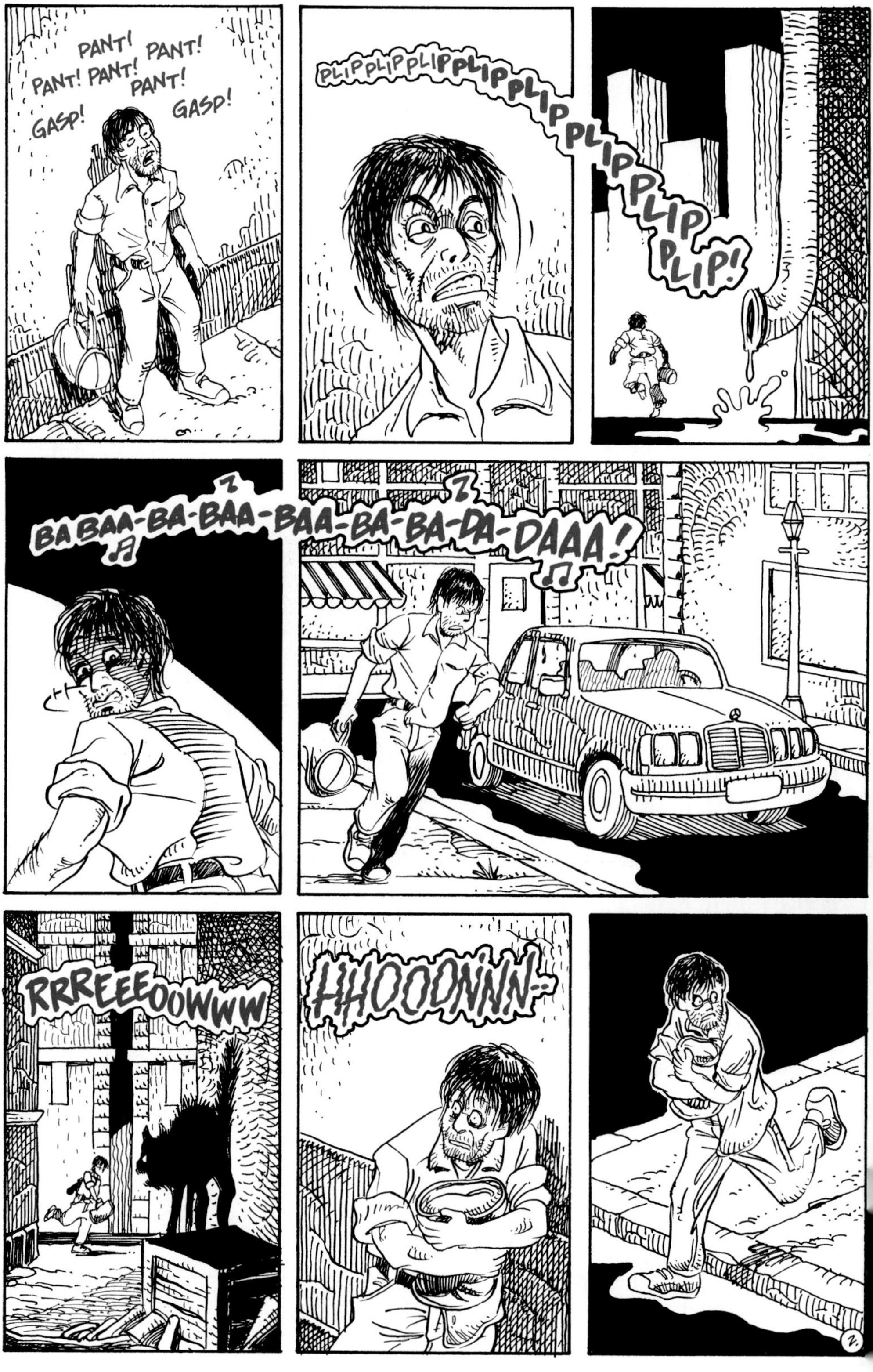
PANT! PANT! PANT! PANT! PANT!
GASP! GASP!
PLIP PLIP PLIP PLIP PLIP PLIP PLIP PLIP PLIP PLIP!
BA BAA-BA-BAA-BAA-BA-BA-DA-DAAA!
RRREEEOOWWW
HHOOONNN-

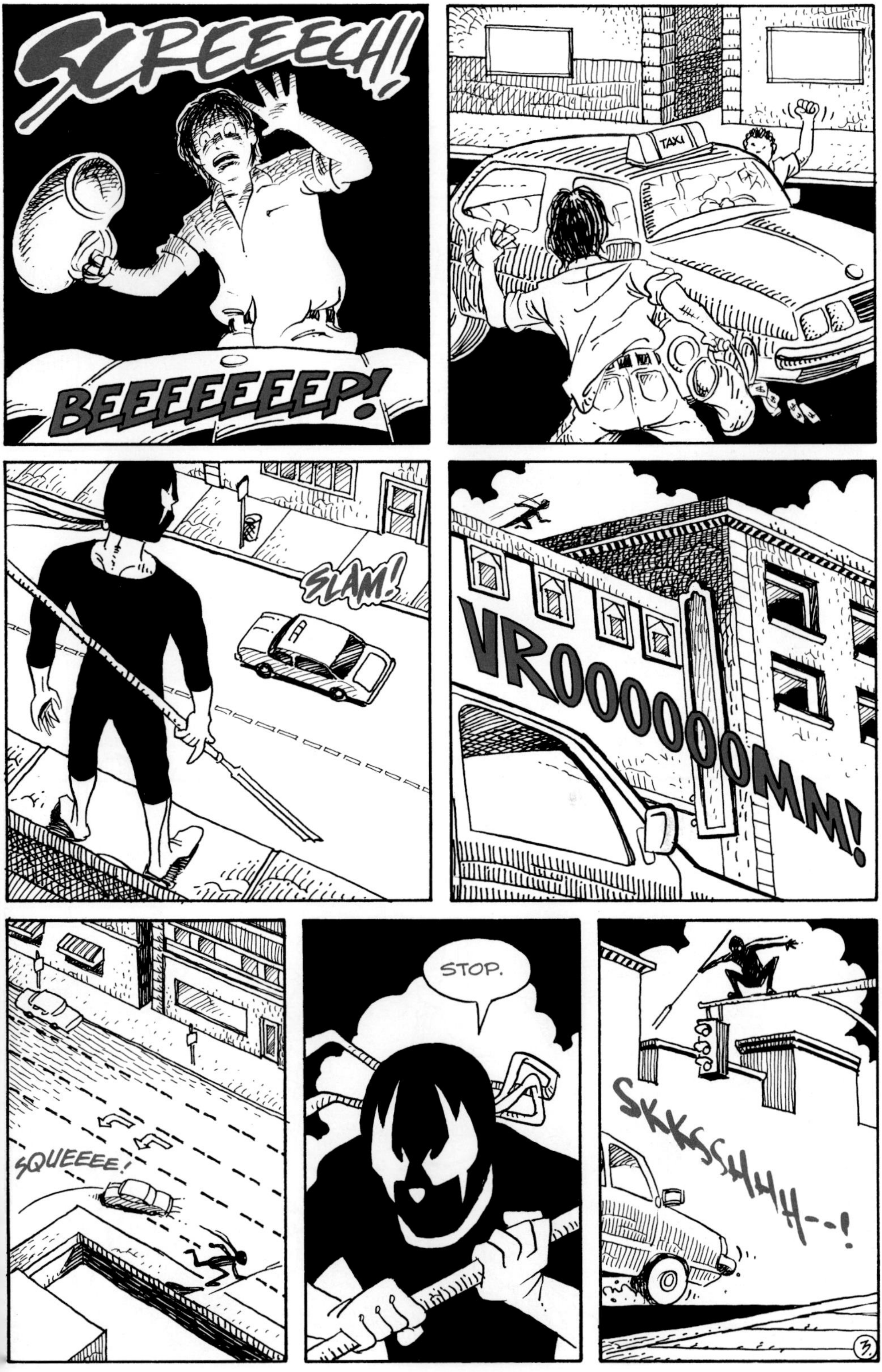
SCREEECH!!
BEEEEEEEP!
SLAM!
VROOOOOOOMM!
SQUEEEE!
STOP.
SKKSSHHH--!
3.

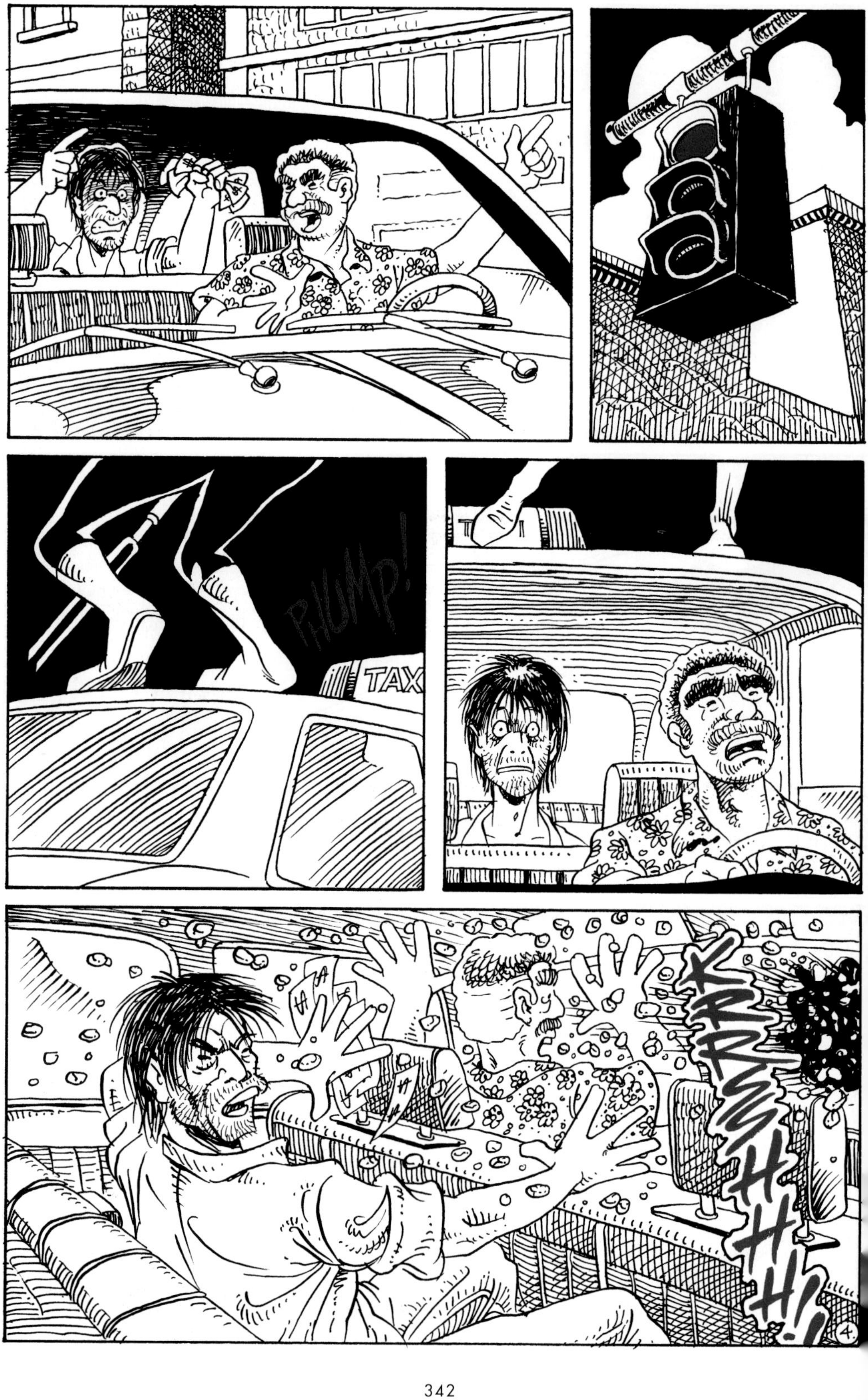
PHUMP!
KRRSSHHHH!

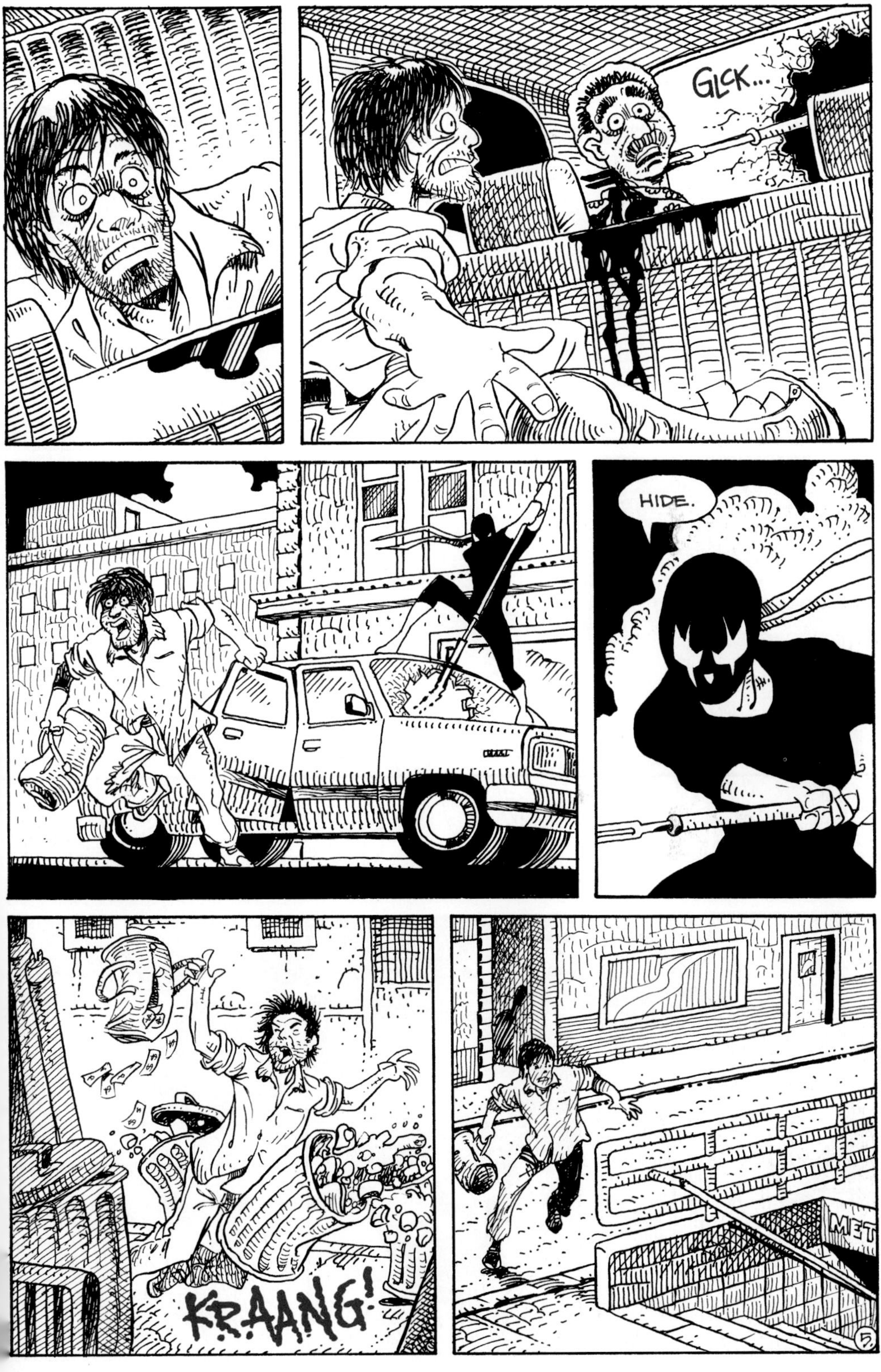
GLCK...
HIDE.
KRAANG!
MET
5

CHUKK-CHUKKA-CHUKKA-SSS

RACKTA-RACKTA-RACKTA-RACKTA-RACKTA-RACKTAIR,

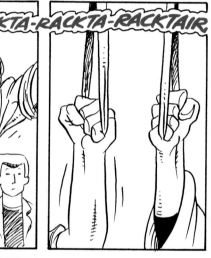

KTA-RACKTA-RACKTA-RACKTA-RACKTA-RACKTA-RACKT,

BOO.

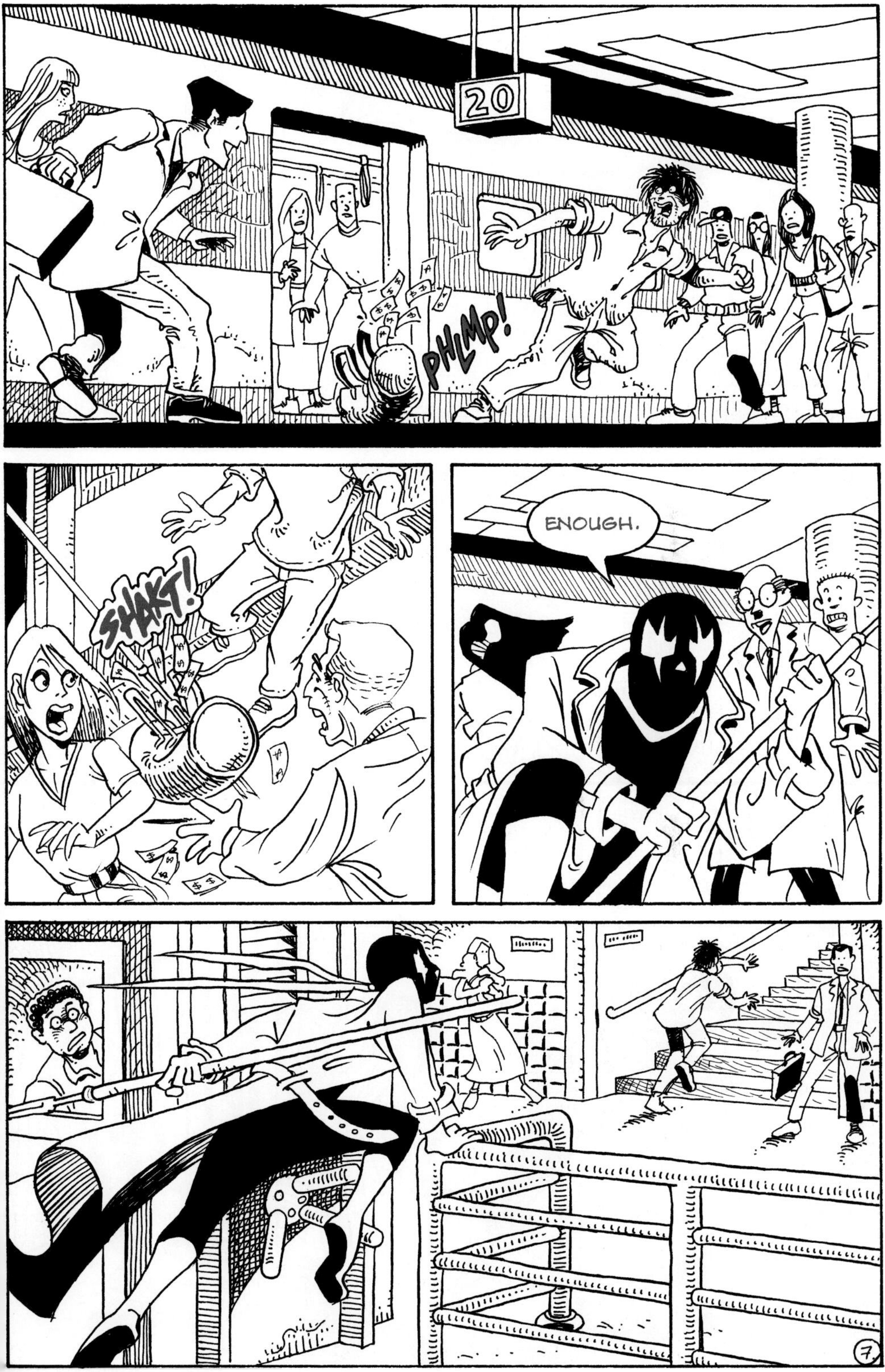
20
PHLMP!
SHAKT!
ENOUGH.
7

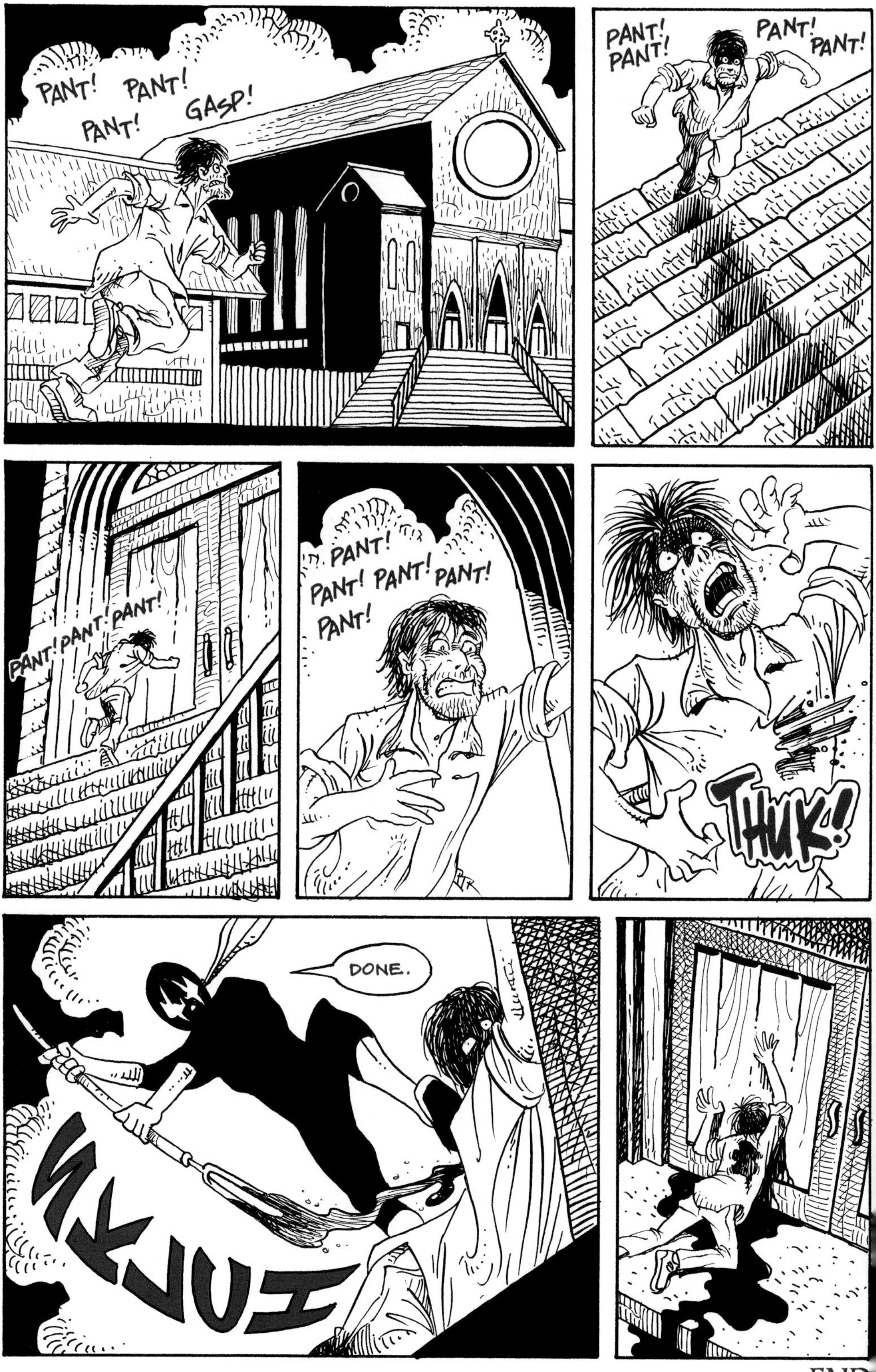

PANT! PANT!
PANT! GASP!
PANT!
PANT!
PANT! PANT!
PANT!
PANT!PANT!PANT!
PANT!
PANT! PANT! PANT!
PANT!
THUK!
DONE.
HUNK

END

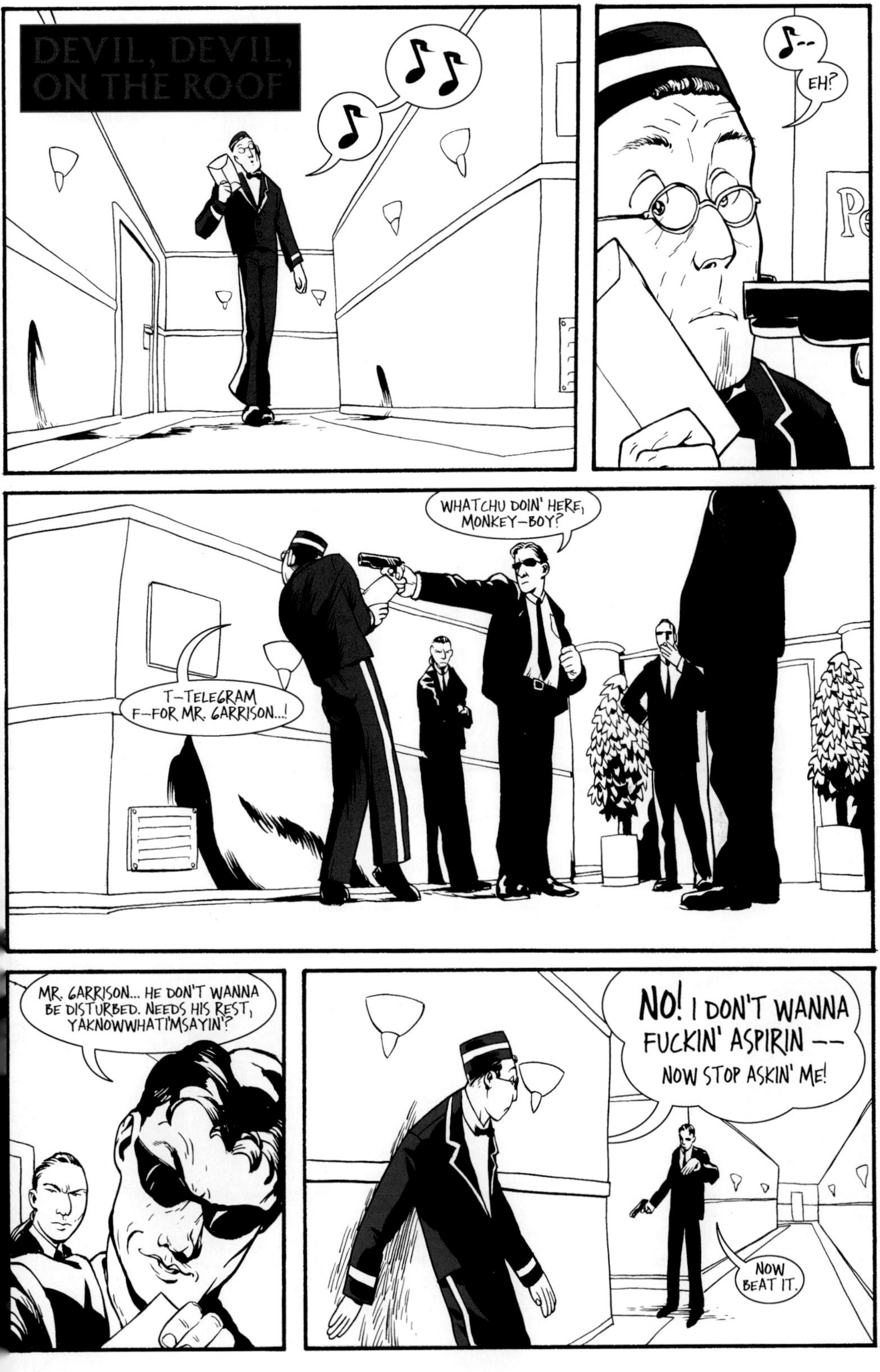
DEVIL, DEVIL, ON THE ROOF
EH?
WHATCHU DOIN' HERE, MONKEY-BOY?
T-TELEGRAM F-FOR MR. GARRISON...!
MR. GARRISON... HE DON'T WANNA BE DISTURBED. NEEDS HIS REST, YAKNOWWHATI'MSAYIN'?
NO! I DON'T WANNA FUCKIN' ASPIRIN -- NOW STOP ASKIN' ME!
NOW BEAT IT.

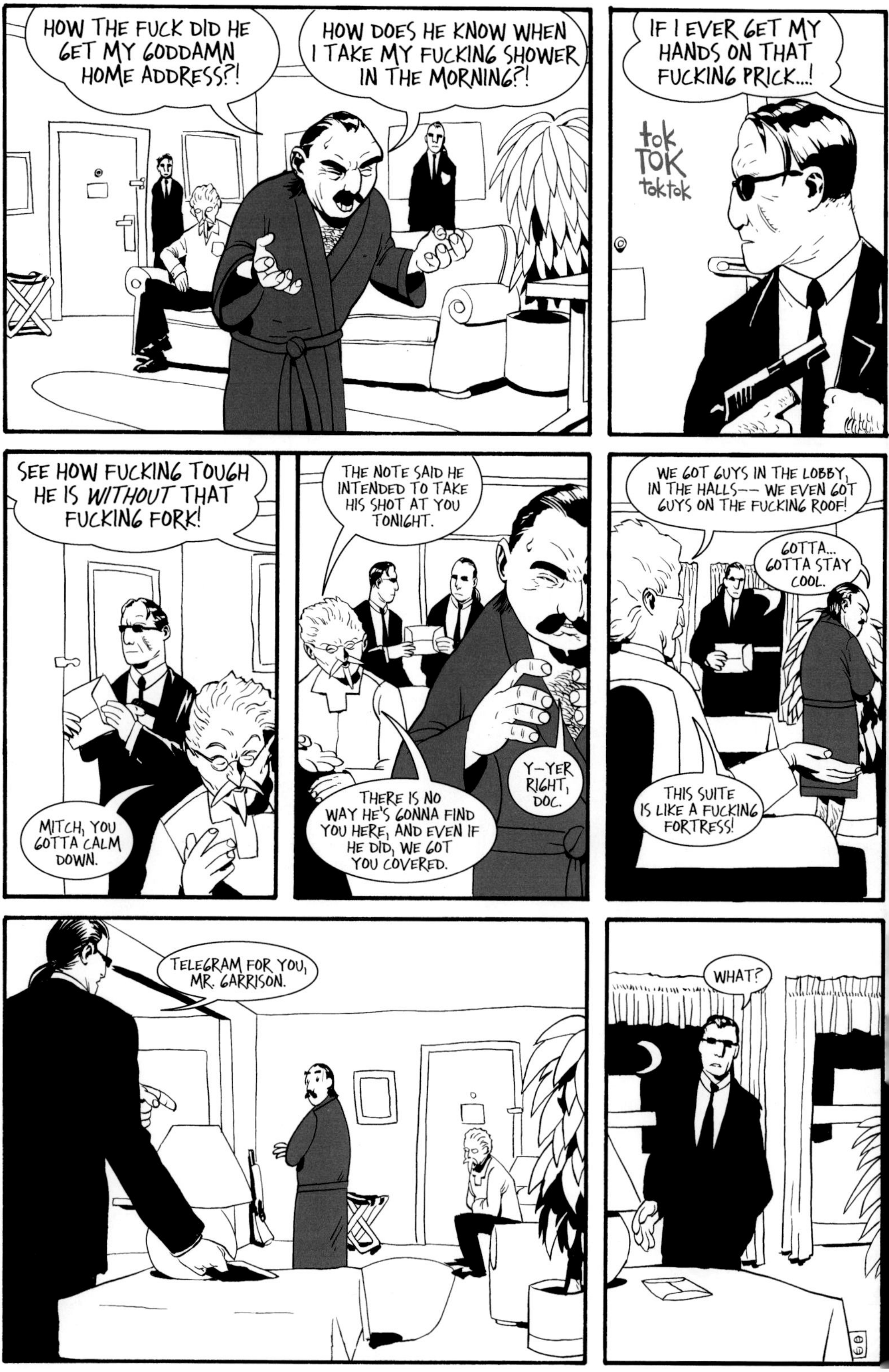
HOW THE FUCK DID HE GET MY GODDAMN HOME ADDRESS?!
HOW DOES HE KNOW WHEN I TAKE MY FUCKING SHOWER IN THE MORNING?!
IF I EVER GET MY HANDS ON THAT FUCKING PRICK...!
tok TOK toktok
SEE HOW FUCKING TOUGH HE IS *WITHOUT* THAT FUCKING FORK!
MITCH, YOU GOTTA CALM DOWN.
THE NOTE SAID HE INTENDED TO TAKE HIS SHOT AT YOU TONIGHT.
THERE IS NO WAY HE'S GONNA FIND YOU HERE, AND EVEN IF HE DID, WE GOT YOU COVERED.
Y-YER RIGHT, DOC.
WE GOT GUYS IN THE LOBBY, IN THE HALLS-- WE EVEN GOT GUYS ON THE FUCKING ROOF!
GOTTA... GOTTA STAY COOL.
THIS SUITE IS LIKE A FUCKING FORTRESS!
TELEGRAM FOR YOU, MR. GARRISON.
WHAT?

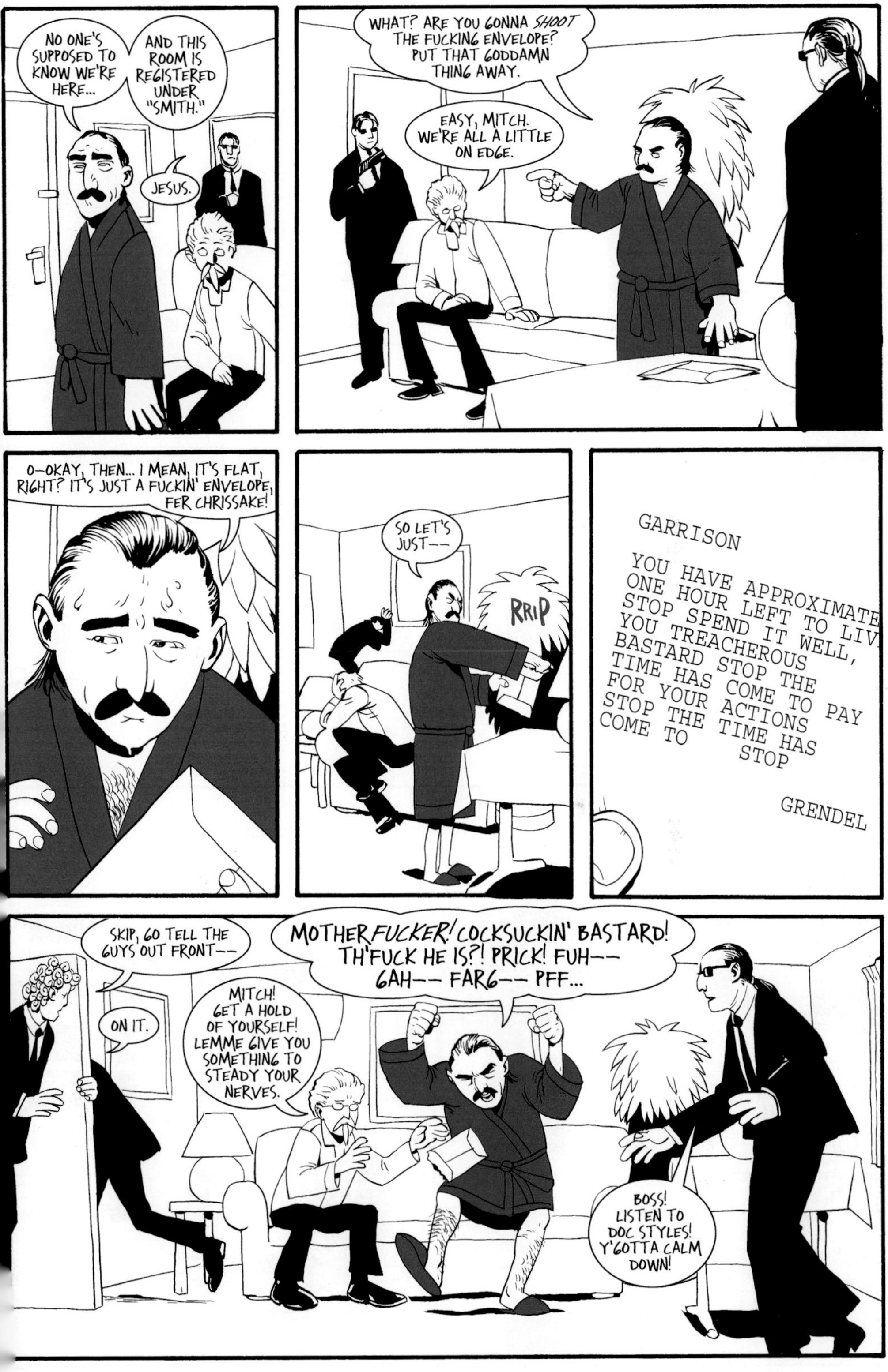
NO ONE'S SUPPOSED TO KNOW WE'RE HERE...
AND THIS ROOM IS REGISTERED UNDER "SMITH."
JESUS.
WHAT? ARE YOU GONNA *SHOOT* THE FUCKING ENVELOPE? PUT THAT GODDAMN THING AWAY.
EASY, MITCH. WE'RE ALL A LITTLE ON EDGE.
O—OKAY, THEN... I MEAN, IT'S FLAT, RIGHT? IT'S JUST A FUCKIN' ENVELOPE, FER CHRISSAKE!
SO LET'S JUST——
RRIP
GARRISON
YOU HAVE APPROXIMATE
ONE HOUR LEFT TO LIV
STOP SPEND IT WELL,
YOU TREACHEROUS
BASTARD STOP THE
TIME HAS COME TO PAY
FOR YOUR ACTIONS
STOP THE TIME HAS
COME TO STOP
GRENDEL
SKIP, GO TELL THE GUYS OUT FRONT——
ON IT.
MOTHER*FUCKER*! COCKSUCKIN' BASTARD! TH'FUCK HE IS?! PRICK! FUH—— GAH—— FARG—— PFF...
MITCH! GET A HOLD OF YOURSELF! LEMME GIVE YOU SOMETHING TO STEADY YOUR NERVES.
BOSS! LISTEN TO DOC STYLES! Y'GOTTA CALM DOWN!

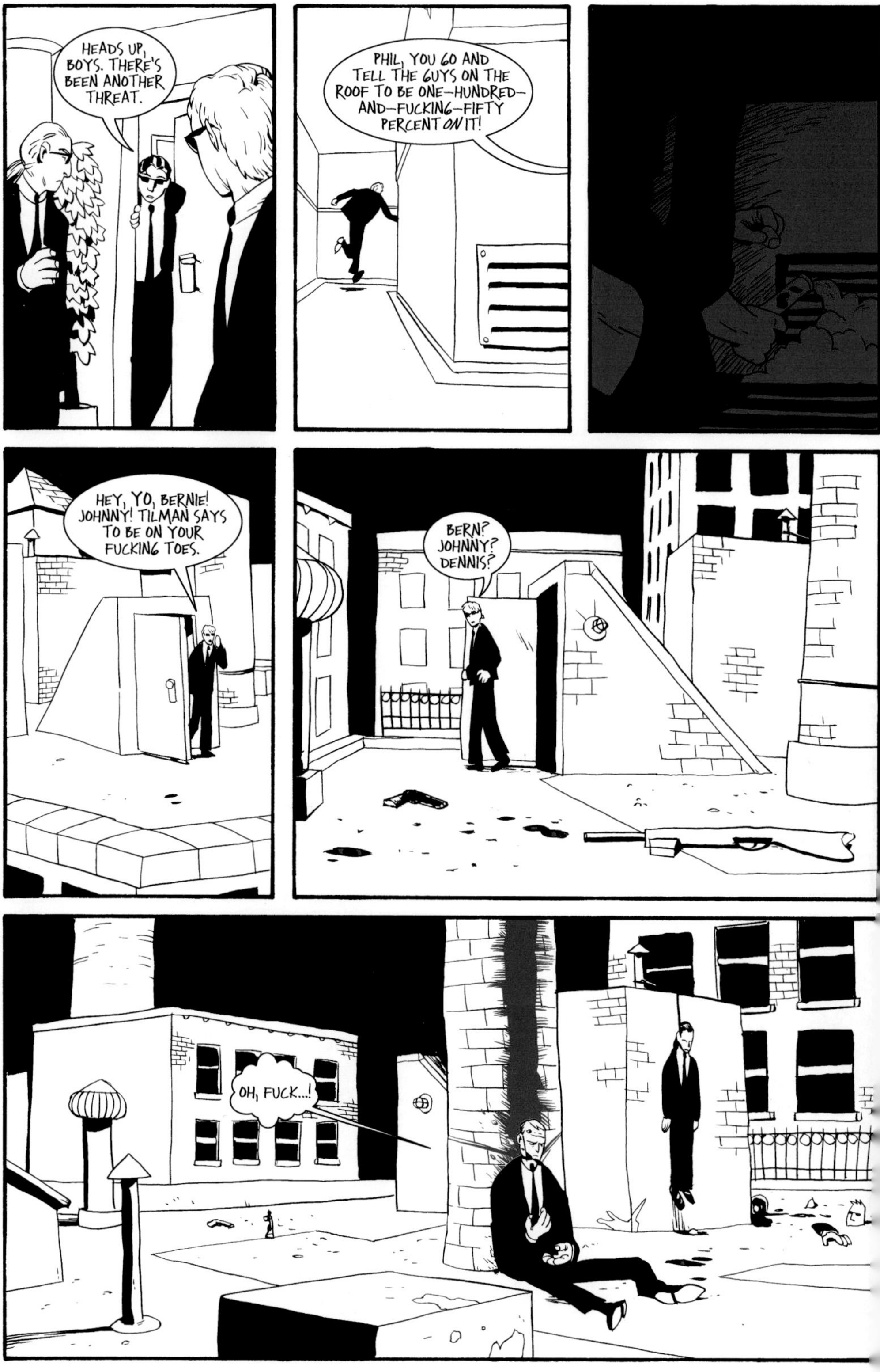
HEADS UP, BOYS. THERE'S BEEN ANOTHER THREAT.
PHIL, YOU GO AND TELL THE GUYS ON THE ROOF TO BE ONE--HUNDRED--AND--FUCKING--FIFTY PERCENT ON IT!
HEY, YO, BERNIE! JOHNNY! TILMAN SAYS TO BE ON YOUR FUCKING TOES.
BERN? JOHNNY? DENNIS?
OH, FUCK...!

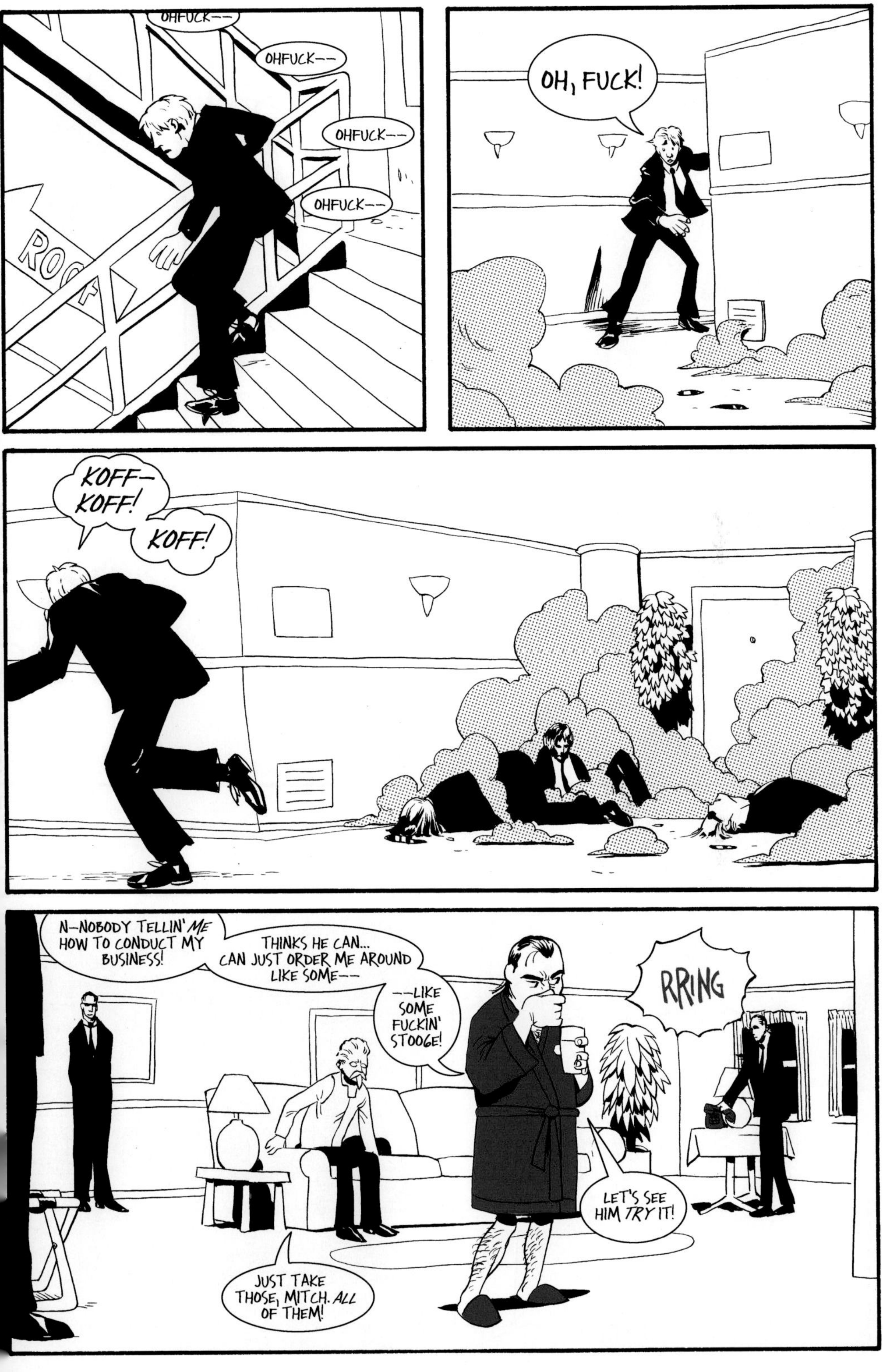
OHFUCK--
OHFUCK--
OHFUCK--
OHFUCK--
ROOF
OH, FUCK!
KOFF-KOFF!
KOFF!
N-NOBODY TELLIN' ME HOW TO CONDUCT MY BUSINESS!
THINKS HE CAN... CAN JUST ORDER ME AROUND LIKE SOME--
--LIKE SOME FUCKIN' STOOGE!
RRING
LET'S SEE HIM TRY IT!
JUST TAKE THOSE, MITCH. ALL OF THEM!

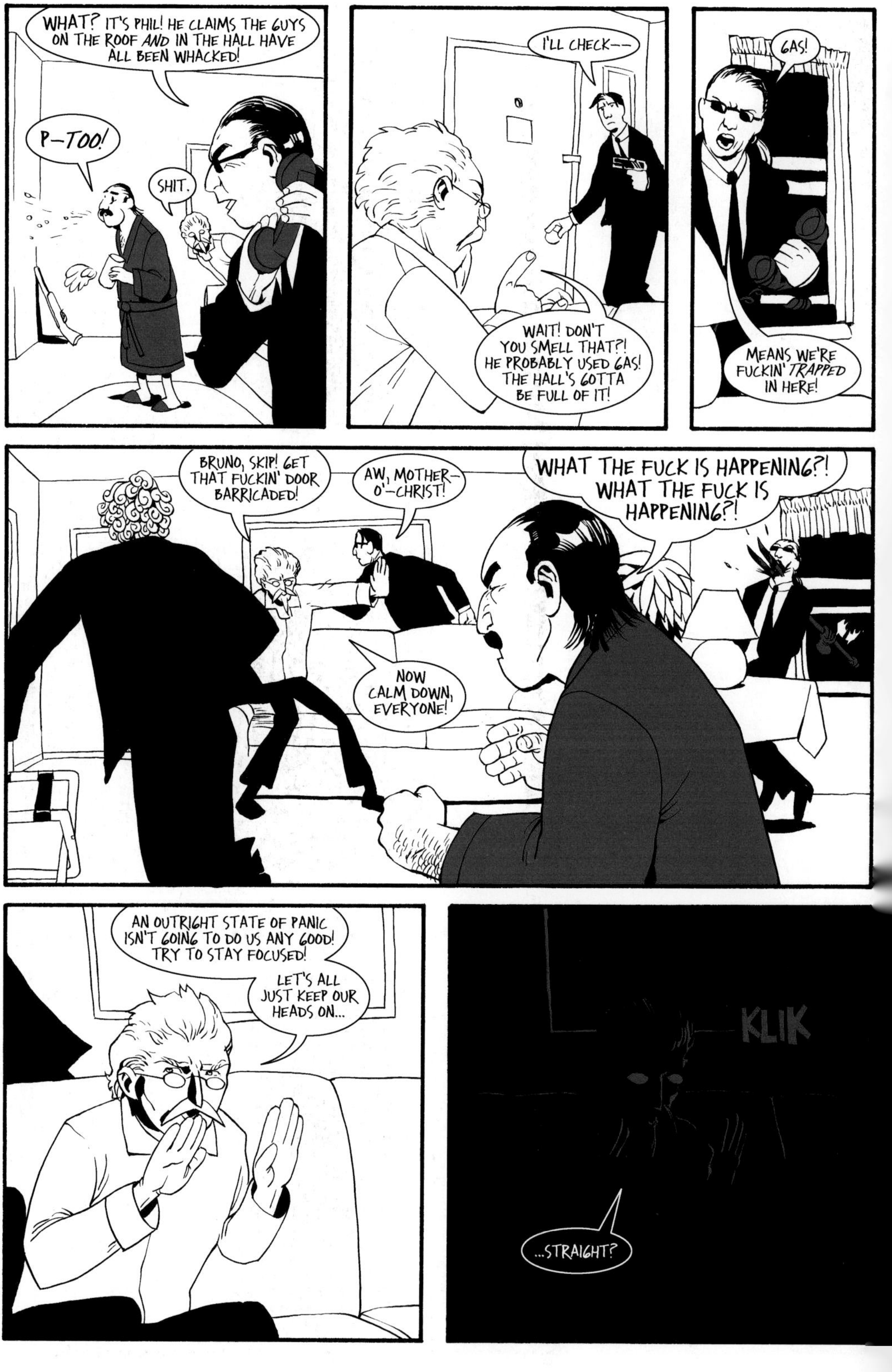

WHAT? IT'S PHIL! HE CLAIMS THE GUYS ON THE ROOF AND IN THE HALL HAVE ALL BEEN WHACKED!
P-TOO!
SHIT.
I'LL CHECK--
WAIT! DON'T YOU SMELL THAT?! HE PROBABLY USED GAS! THE HALL'S GOTTA BE FULL OF IT!
GAS!
MEANS WE'RE FUCKIN' TRAPPED IN HERE!
BRUNO, SKIP! GET THAT FUCKIN' DOOR BARRICADED!
AW, MOTHER-O'-CHRIST!
WHAT THE FUCK IS HAPPENING?! WHAT THE FUCK IS HAPPENING?!
NOW CALM DOWN, EVERYONE!
AN OUTRIGHT STATE OF PANIC ISN'T GOING TO DO US ANY GOOD! TRY TO STAY FOCUSED!
LET'S ALL JUST KEEP OUR HEADS ON...
KLIK
...STRAIGHT?

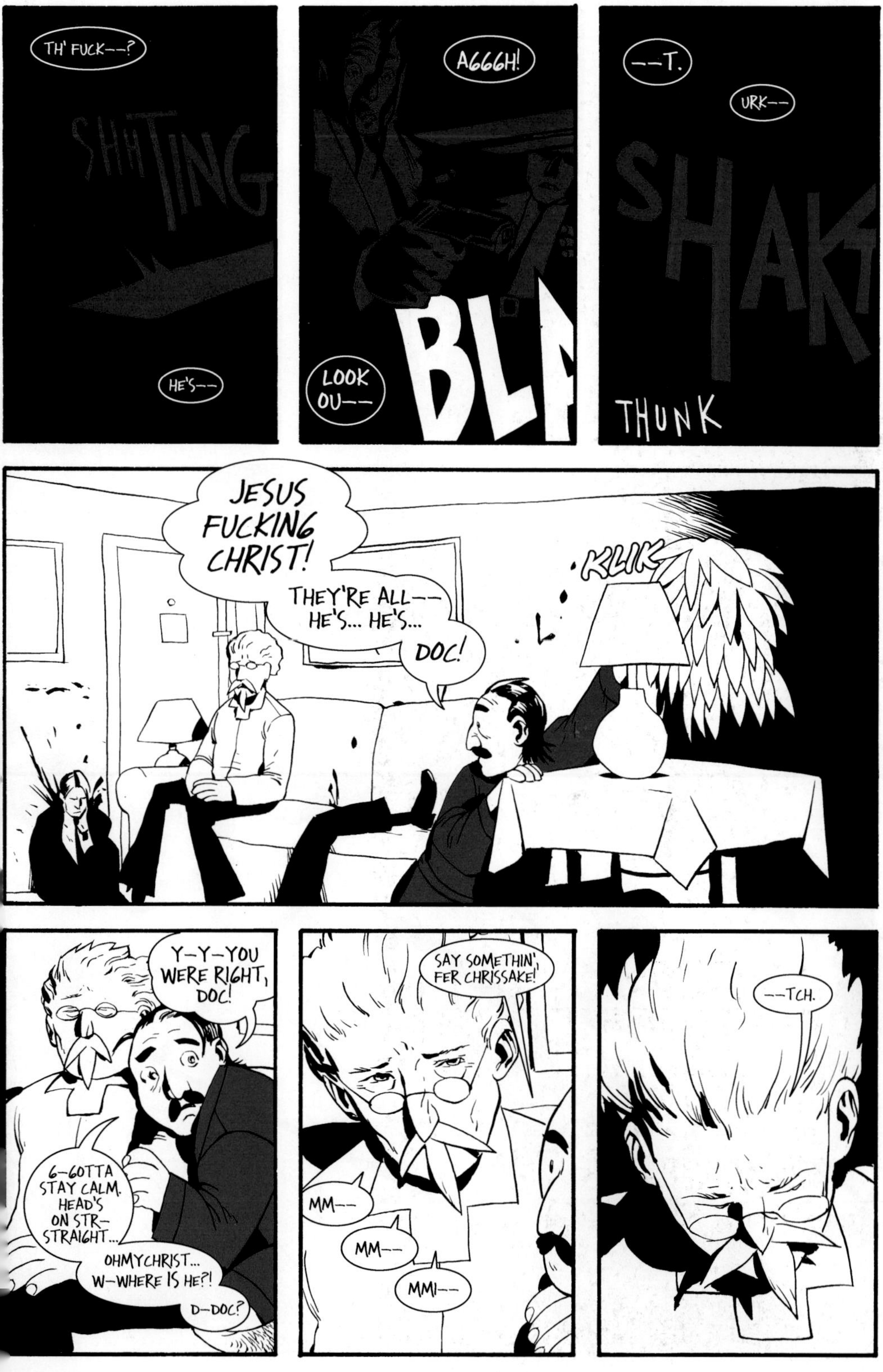
TH' FUCK--?
SHHTING
HE'S--
AGGGH!
LOOK OU--
BLF
--T.
URK--
SHAK
THUNK
JESUS FUCKING CHRIST!
THEY'RE ALL-- HE'S... HE'S...
DOC!
KLIK
Y-Y-YOU WERE RIGHT, DOC!
G-GOTTA STAY CALM. HEAD'S ON STR-STRAIGHT...
OHMYCHRIST... W-WHERE IS HE?!
D-DOC?
SAY SOMETHIN', FER CHRISSAKE!
MM--
MM--
MMI--
--TCH.

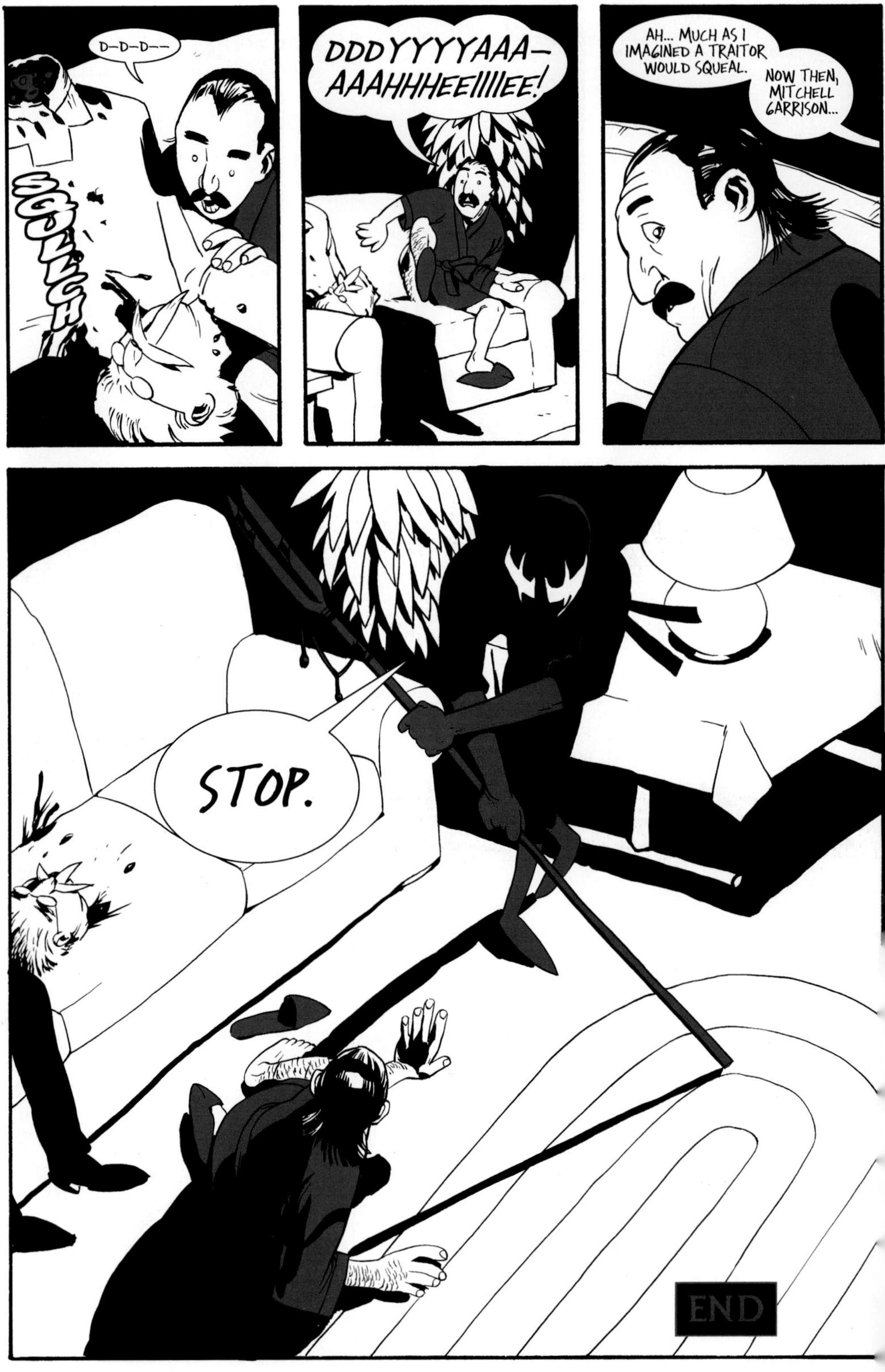
D-D-D--
SQUELCH
DDDYYYYAAA-AAAHHHEEIIIIIEE!
AH... MUCH AS I IMAGINED A TRAITOR WOULD SQUEAL.
NOW THEN, MITCHELL GARRISON...
STOP.
END

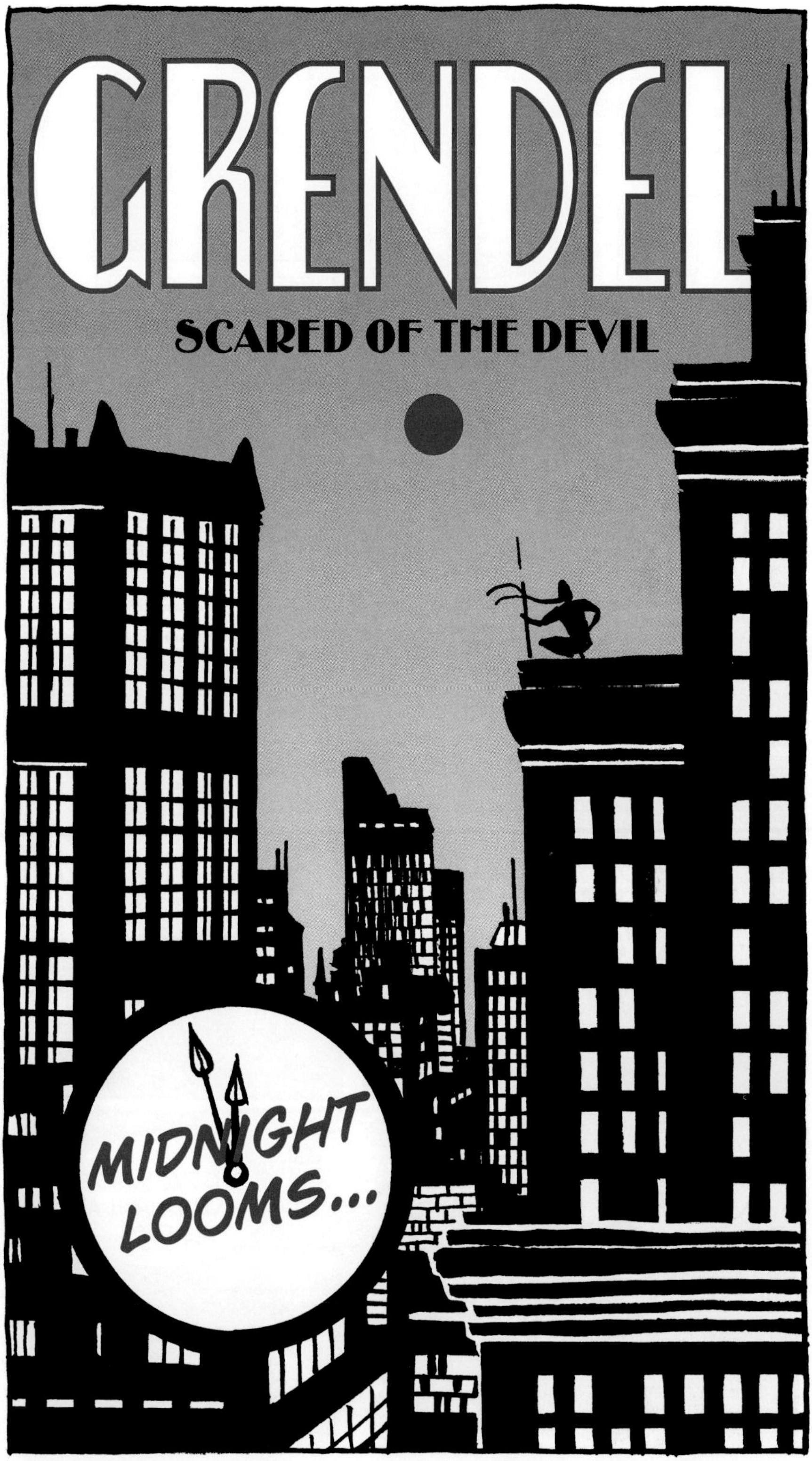
GRENDEL
SCARED OF THE DEVIL
MIDNIGHT LOOMS...

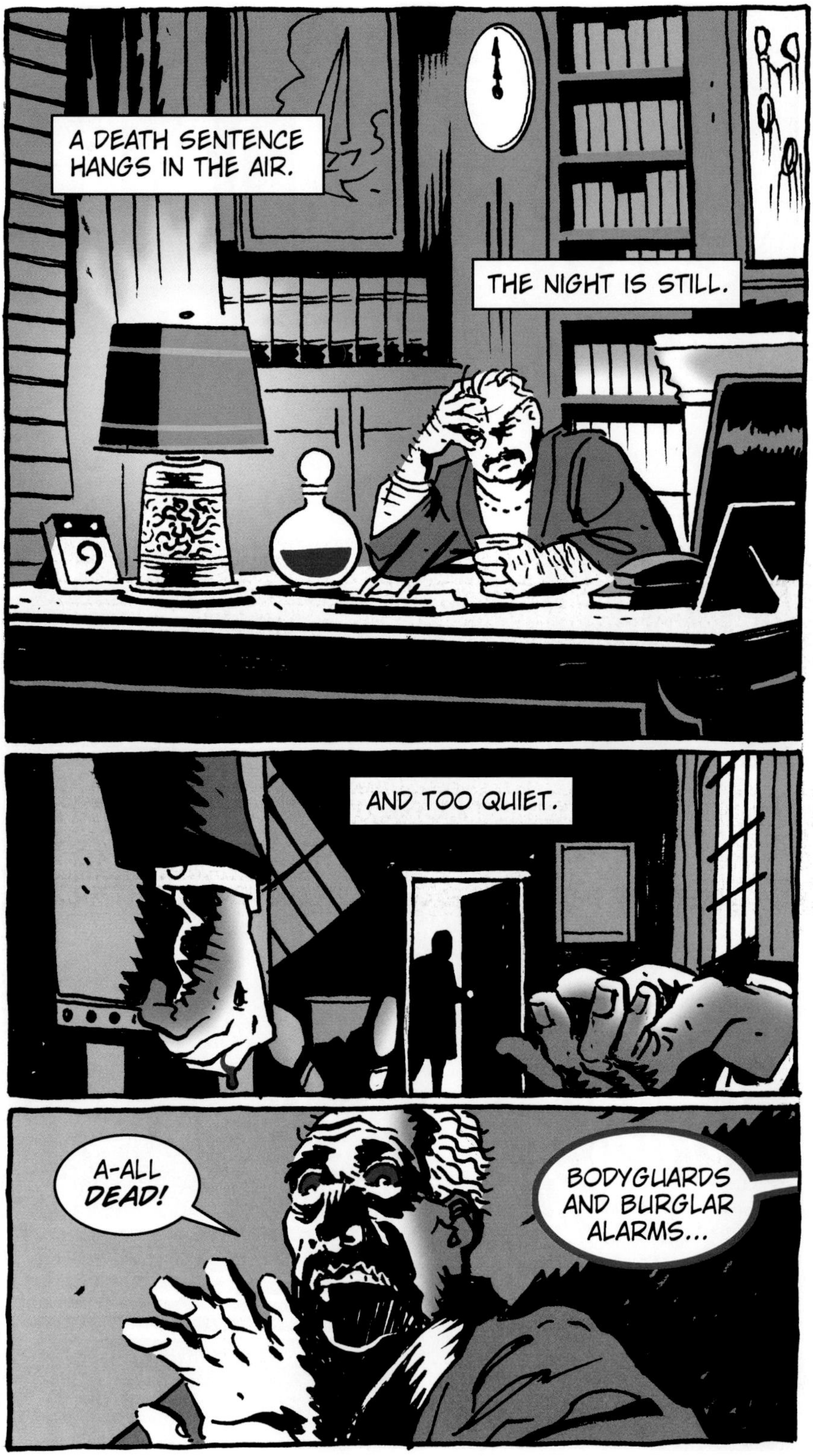
A DEATH SENTENCE HANGS IN THE AIR.
THE NIGHT IS STILL.
AND TOO QUIET.
A-ALL DEAD!
BODYGUARDS AND BURGLAR ALARMS...

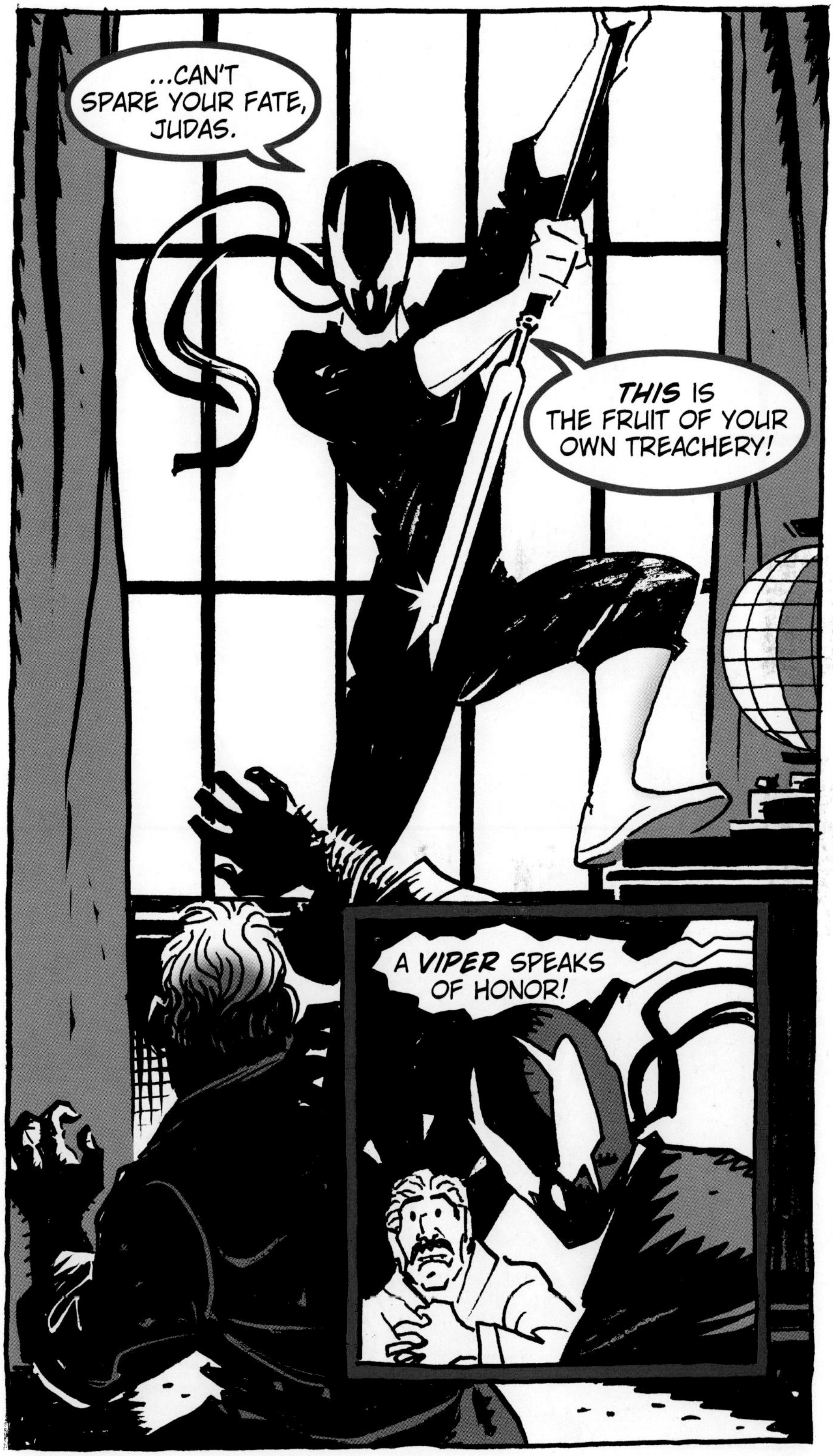
...CAN'T SPARE YOUR FATE, JUDAS.
THIS IS THE FRUIT OF YOUR OWN TREACHERY!
A VIPER SPEAKS OF HONOR!

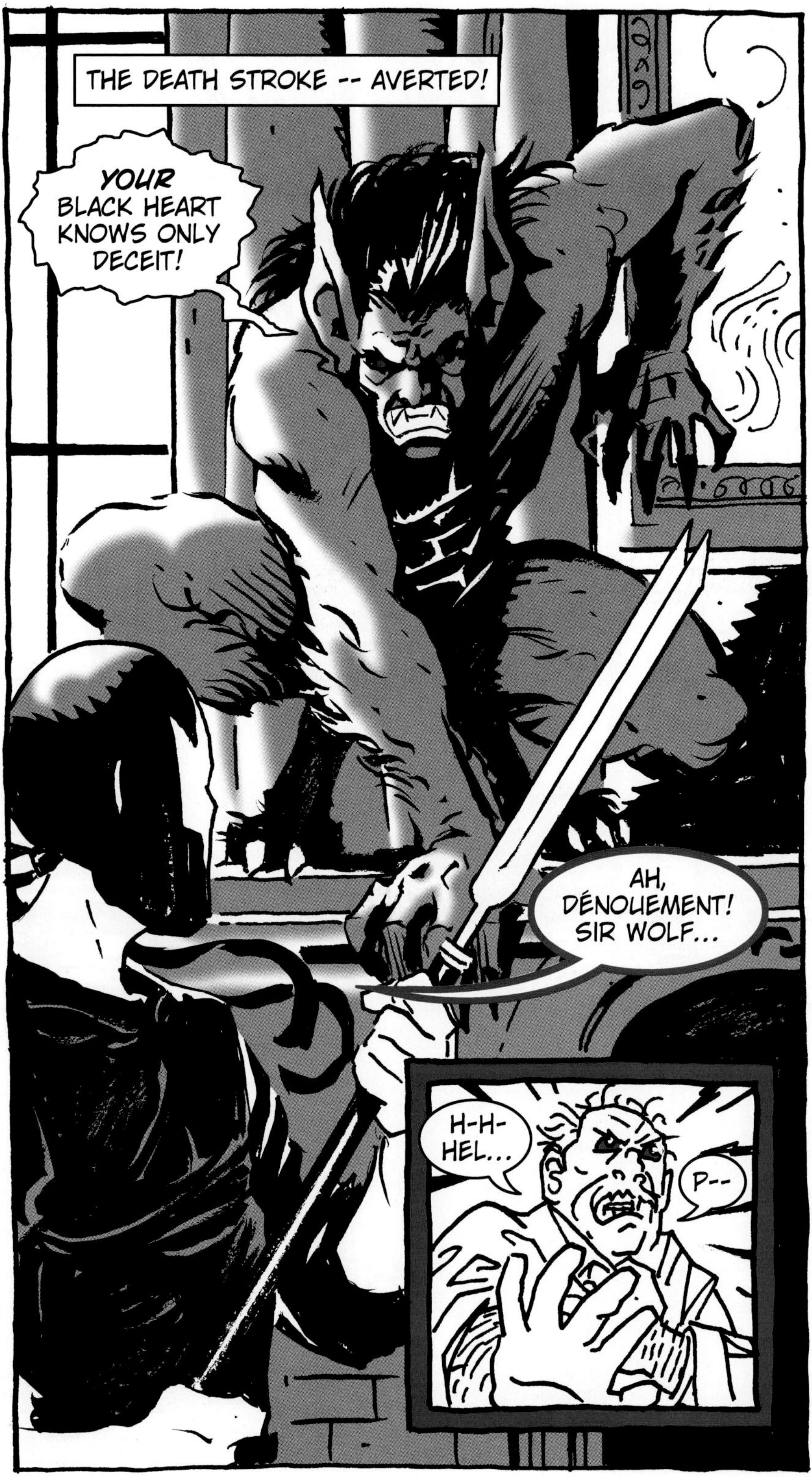
THE DEATH STROKE -- AVERTED!
YOUR BLACK HEART KNOWS ONLY DECEIT!
AH, DÉNOUEMENT! SIR WOLF...
H-H-HEL...
P--

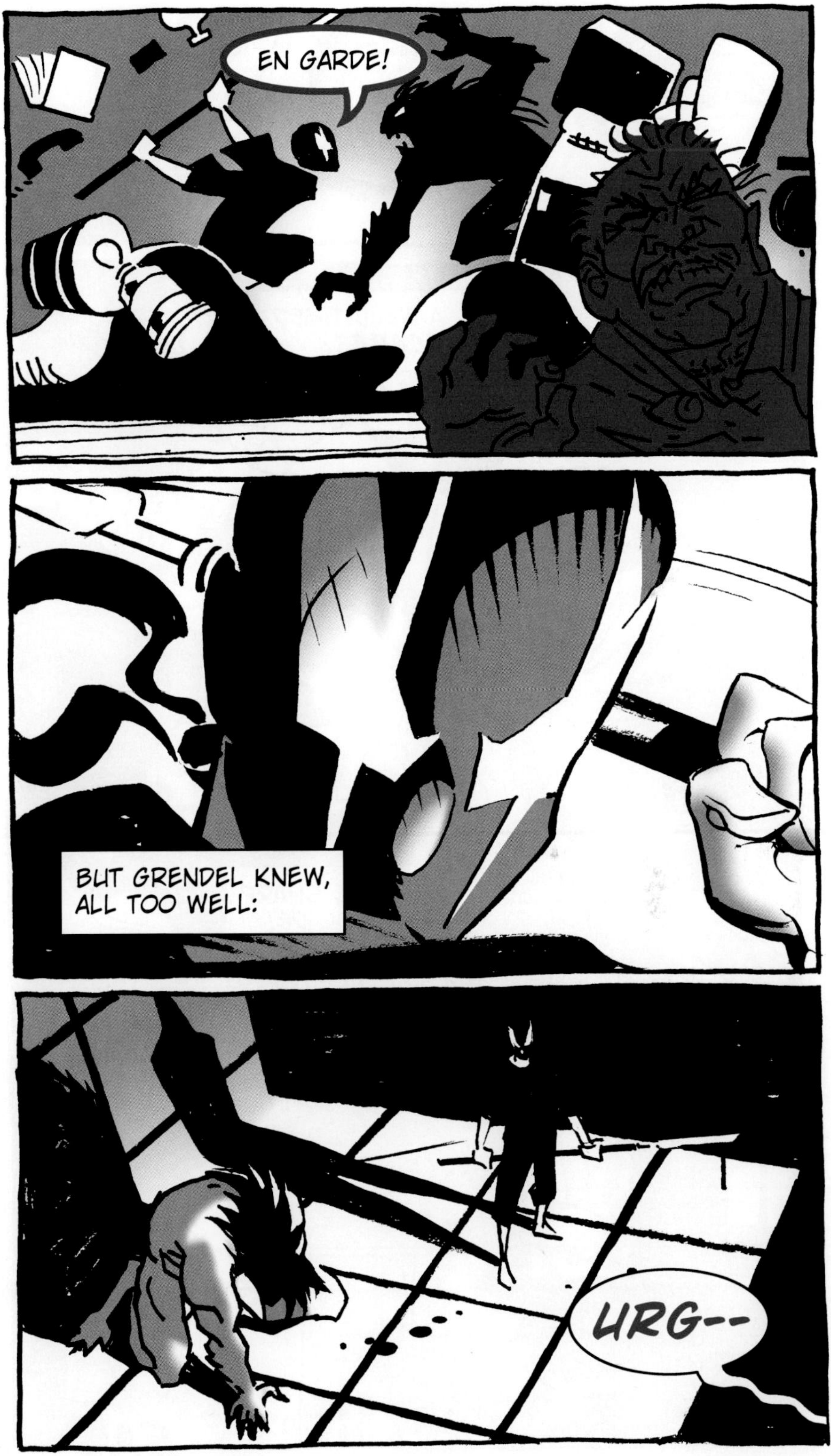
EN GARDE!
BUT GRENDEL KNEW, ALL TOO WELL:
URG--

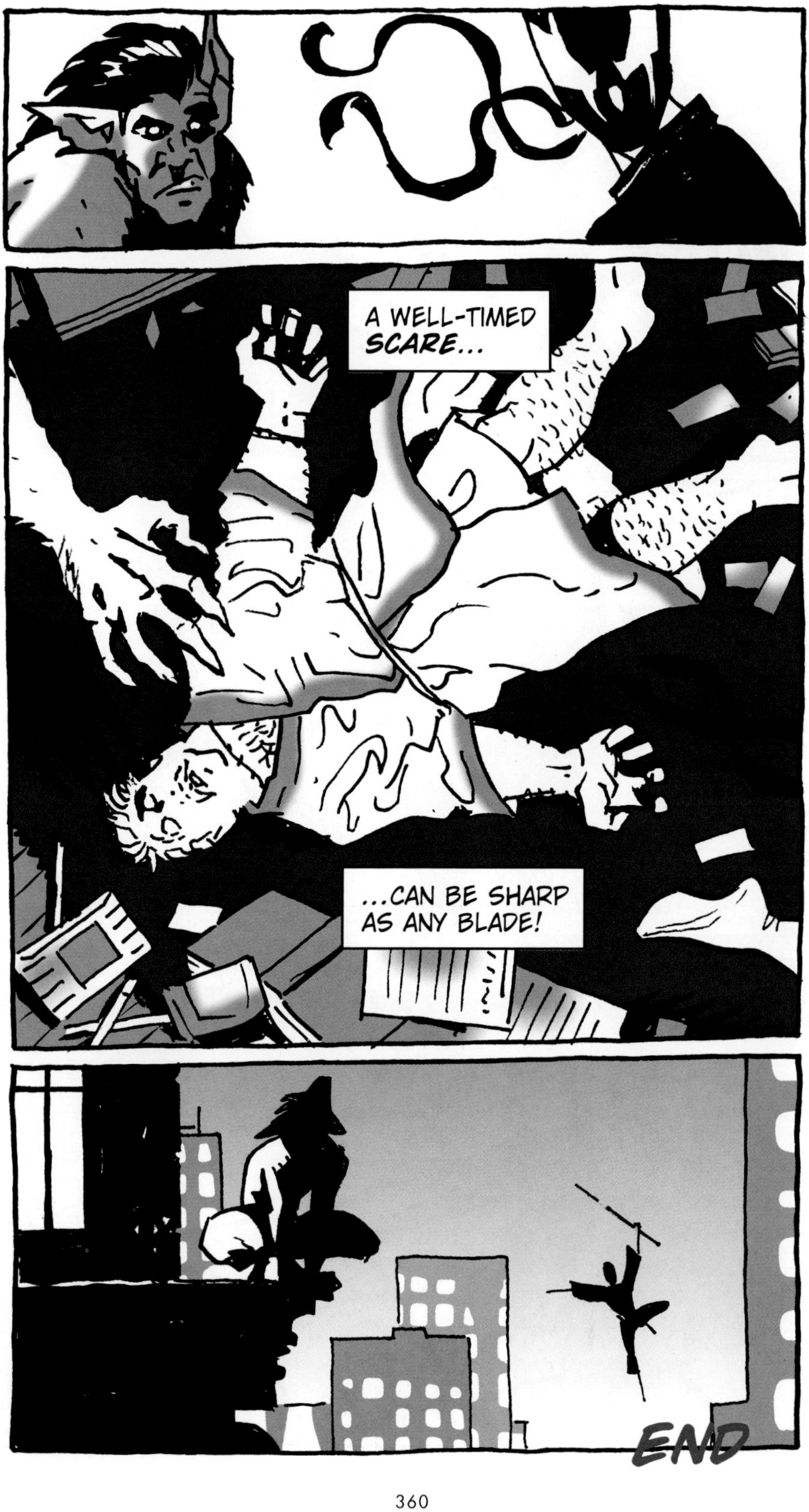
A WELL-TIMED SCARE...
...CAN BE SHARP AS ANY BLADE!
END

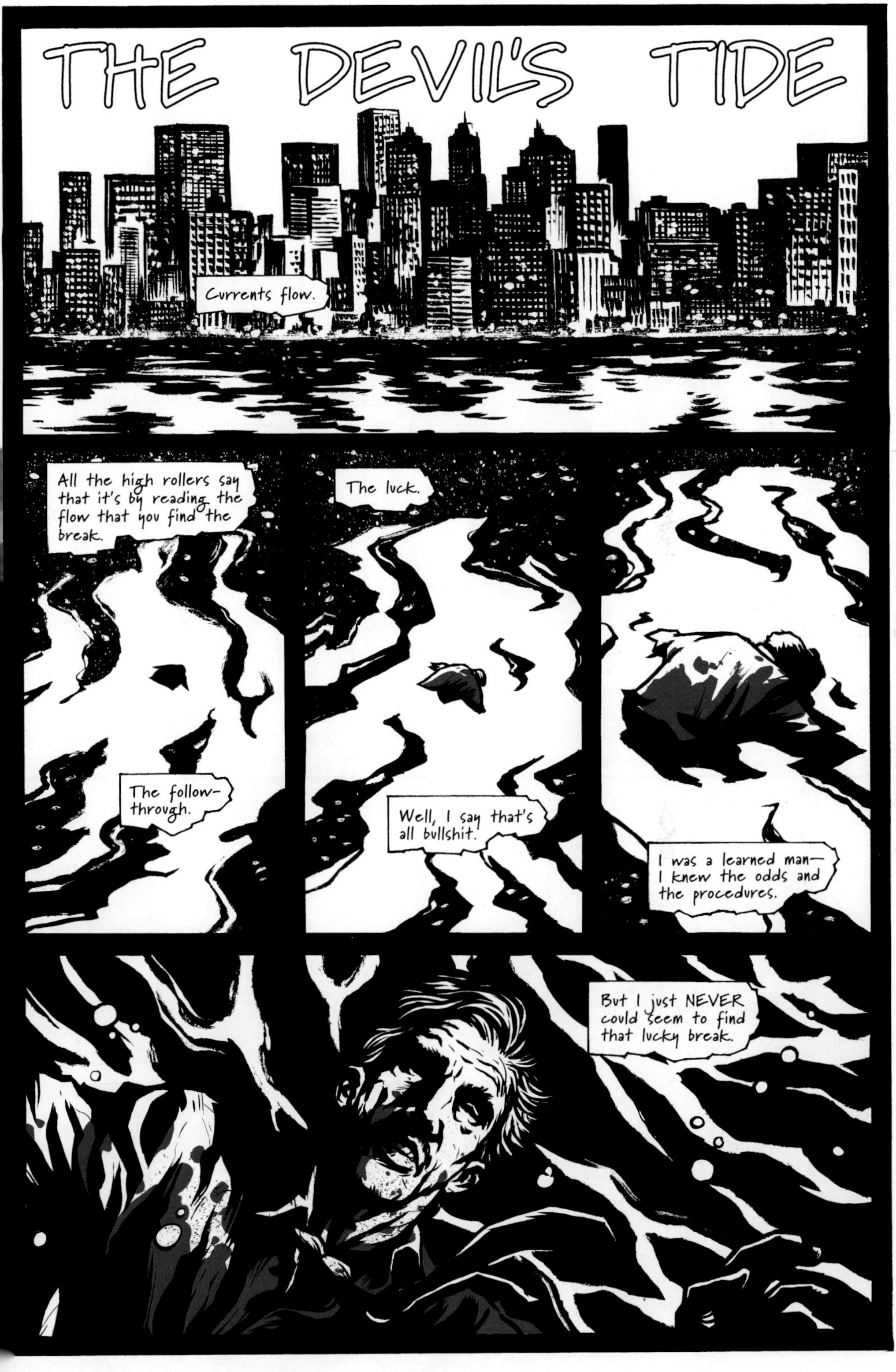
THE DEVIL'S TIDE
Currents flow.
All the high rollers say that it's by reading the flow that you find the break.
The follow-through.
The luck.
Well, I say that's all bullshit.
I was a learned man—I knew the odds and the procedures.
But I just NEVER could seem to find that lucky break.

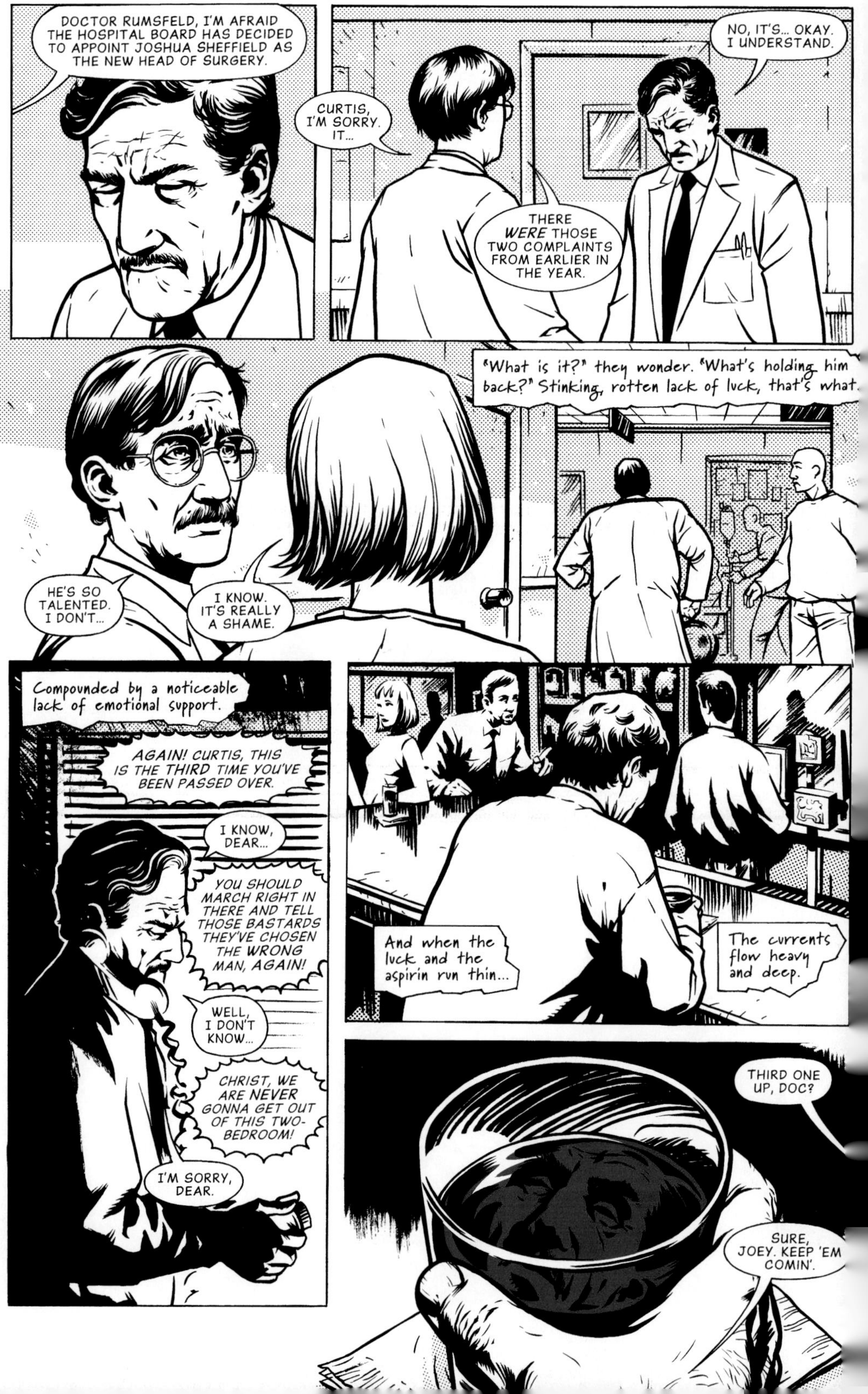
DOCTOR RUMSFELD, I'M AFRAID THE HOSPITAL BOARD HAS DECIDED TO APPOINT JOSHUA SHEFFIELD AS THE NEW HEAD OF SURGERY.
CURTIS, I'M SORRY. IT...
NO, IT'S... OKAY. I UNDERSTAND.
THERE WERE THOSE TWO COMPLAINTS FROM EARLIER IN THE YEAR.
"What is it?" they wonder. "What's holding him back?" Stinking, rotten lack of luck, that's what.
HE'S SO TALENTED. I DON'T...
I KNOW. IT'S REALLY A SHAME.
Compounded by a noticeable lack of emotional support.
AGAIN! CURTIS, THIS IS THE THIRD TIME YOU'VE BEEN PASSED OVER.
I KNOW, DEAR...
YOU SHOULD MARCH RIGHT IN THERE AND TELL THOSE BASTARDS THEY'VE CHOSEN THE WRONG MAN, AGAIN!
WELL, I DON'T KNOW...
CHRIST, WE ARE NEVER GONNA GET OUT OF THIS TWO-BEDROOM!
I'M SORRY, DEAR.
And when the luck and the aspirin run thin...
The currents flow heavy and deep.
THIRD ONE UP, DOC?
SURE, JOEY. KEEP 'EM COMIN'.

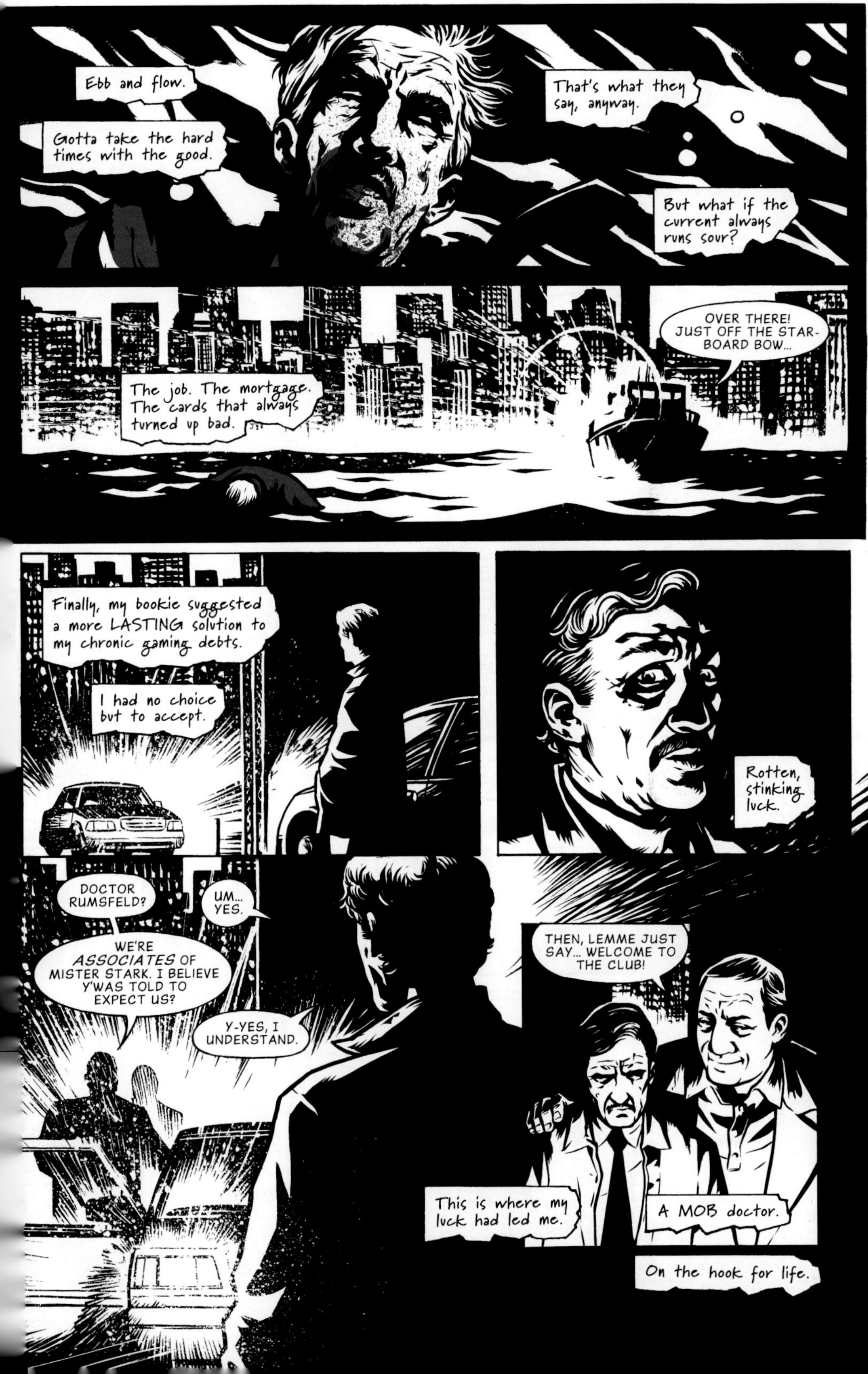

Ebb and flow.
Gotta take the hard times with the good.
That's what they say, anyway.
But what if the current always runs sour?
The job. The mortgage. The cards that always turned up bad.
OVER THERE! JUST OFF THE STARBOARD BOW...
Finally, my bookie suggested a more LASTING solution to my chronic gaming debts.
I had no choice but to accept.
Rotten, stinking luck.
DOCTOR RUMSFELD?
UM... YES.
WE'RE ASSOCIATES OF MISTER STARK. I BELIEVE Y'WAS TOLD TO EXPECT US?
Y-YES, I UNDERSTAND.
THEN, LEMME JUST SAY... WELCOME TO THE CLUB!
This is where my luck had led me.
A MOB doctor.
On the hook for life.

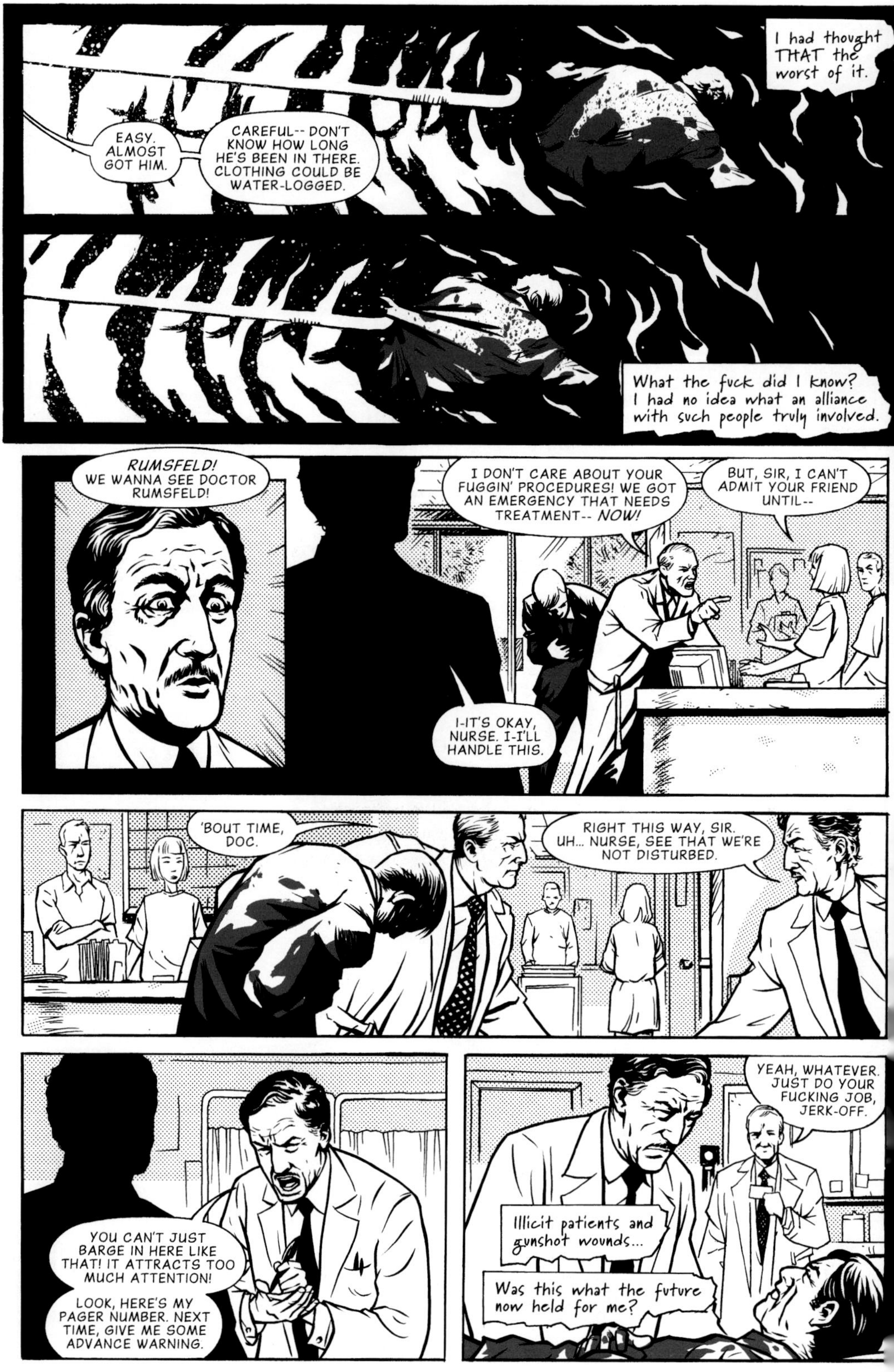
I had thought THAT the worst of it.
EASY. ALMOST GOT HIM.
CAREFUL-- DON'T KNOW HOW LONG HE'S BEEN IN THERE. CLOTHING COULD BE WATER-LOGGED.
What the fuck did I know? I had no idea what an alliance with such people truly involved.
RUMSFELD! WE WANNA SEE DOCTOR RUMSFELD!
I DON'T CARE ABOUT YOUR FUGGIN' PROCEDURES! WE GOT AN EMERGENCY THAT NEEDS TREATMENT-- NOW!
BUT, SIR, I CAN'T ADMIT YOUR FRIEND UNTIL--
I-IT'S OKAY, NURSE. I-I'LL HANDLE THIS.
'BOUT TIME, DOC.
RIGHT THIS WAY, SIR. UH... NURSE, SEE THAT WE'RE NOT DISTURBED.
YOU CAN'T JUST BARGE IN HERE LIKE THAT! IT ATTRACTS TOO MUCH ATTENTION!
LOOK, HERE'S MY PAGER NUMBER. NEXT TIME, GIVE ME SOME ADVANCE WARNING.
YEAH, WHATEVER. JUST DO YOUR FUCKING JOB, JERK-OFF.
Illicit patients and gunshot wounds...
Was this what the future now held for me?

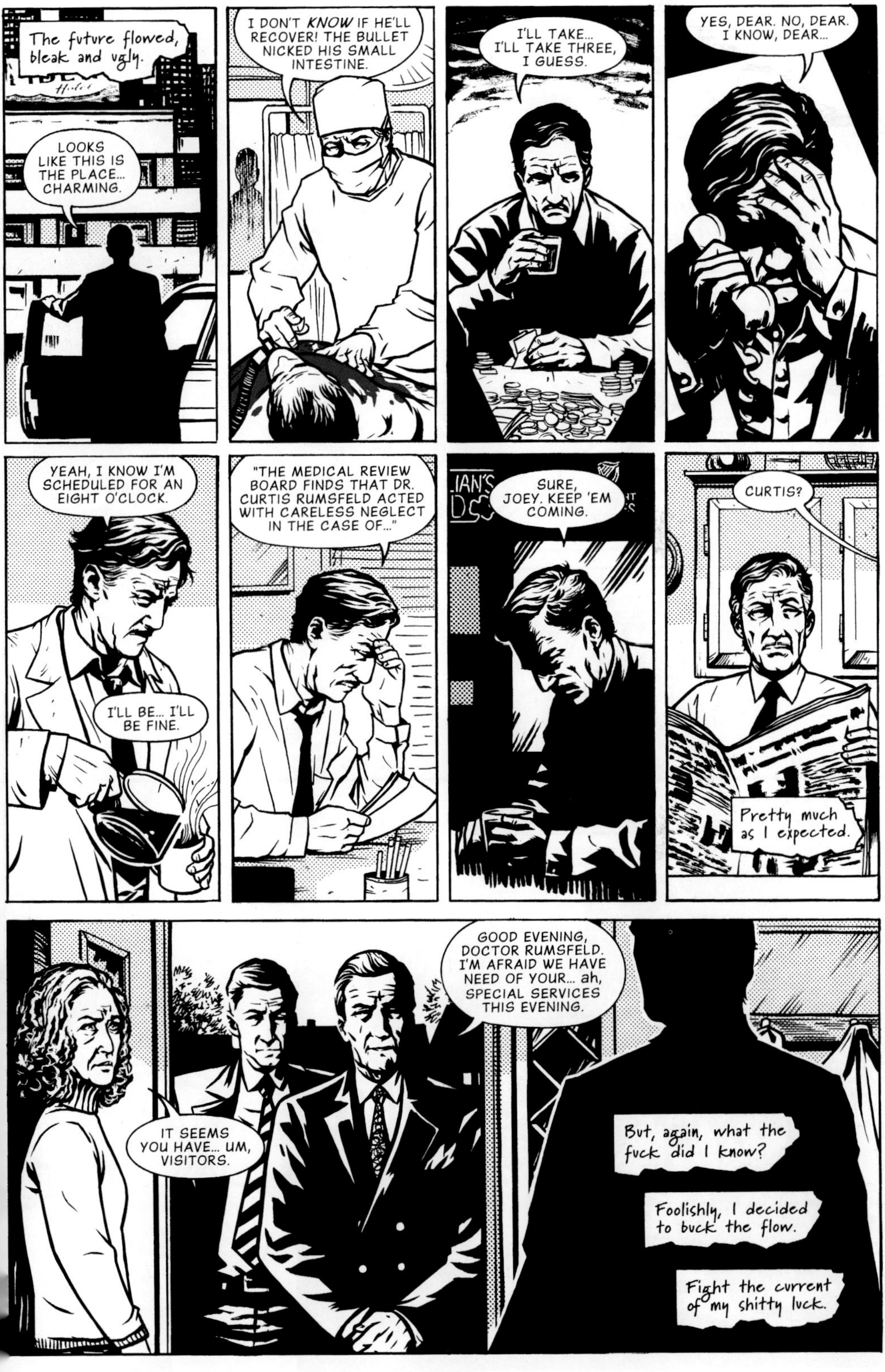
The future flowed, bleak and ugly.
LOOKS LIKE THIS IS THE PLACE... CHARMING.
I DON'T *KNOW* IF HE'LL RECOVER! THE BULLET NICKED HIS SMALL INTESTINE.
I'LL TAKE... I'LL TAKE THREE, I GUESS.
YES, DEAR. NO, DEAR. I KNOW, DEAR...
YEAH, I KNOW I'M SCHEDULED FOR AN EIGHT O'CLOCK.
I'LL BE... I'LL BE FINE.
"THE MEDICAL REVIEW BOARD FINDS THAT DR. CURTIS RUMSFELD ACTED WITH CARELESS NEGLECT IN THE CASE OF..."
SURE, JOEY. KEEP 'EM COMING.
CURTIS?
Pretty much as I expected.
GOOD EVENING, DOCTOR RUMSFELD. I'M AFRAID WE HAVE NEED OF YOUR... ah, SPECIAL SERVICES THIS EVENING.
IT SEEMS YOU HAVE... UM, VISITORS.
But, again, what the fuck did I know?
Foolishly, I decided to buck the flow.
Fight the current of my shitty luck.

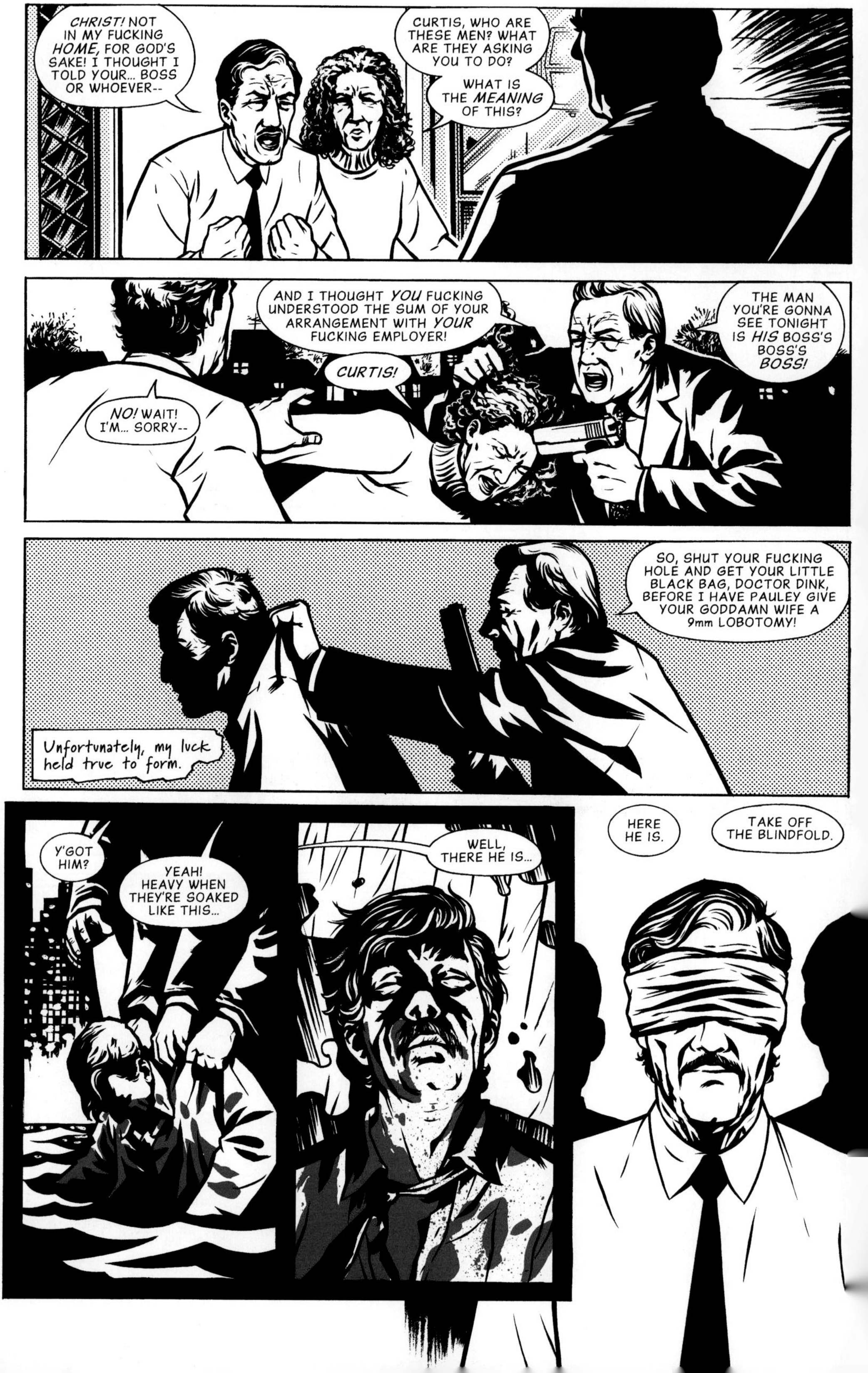
CHRIST! NOT IN MY FUCKING HOME, FOR GOD'S SAKE! I THOUGHT I TOLD YOUR... BOSS OR WHOEVER--
CURTIS, WHO ARE THESE MEN? WHAT ARE THEY ASKING YOU TO DO?
WHAT IS THE MEANING OF THIS?
AND I THOUGHT YOU FUCKING UNDERSTOOD THE SUM OF YOUR ARRANGEMENT WITH YOUR FUCKING EMPLOYER!
CURTIS!
THE MAN YOU'RE GONNA SEE TONIGHT IS HIS BOSS'S BOSS'S BOSS!
NO! WAIT! I'M... SORRY--
SO, SHUT YOUR FUCKING HOLE AND GET YOUR LITTLE BLACK BAG, DOCTOR DINK, BEFORE I HAVE PAULEY GIVE YOUR GODDAMN WIFE A 9mm LOBOTOMY!
Unfortunately, my luck held true to form.
Y'GOT HIM?
YEAH! HEAVY WHEN THEY'RE SOAKED LIKE THIS...
WELL, THERE HE IS...
HERE HE IS.
TAKE OFF THE BLINDFOLD.

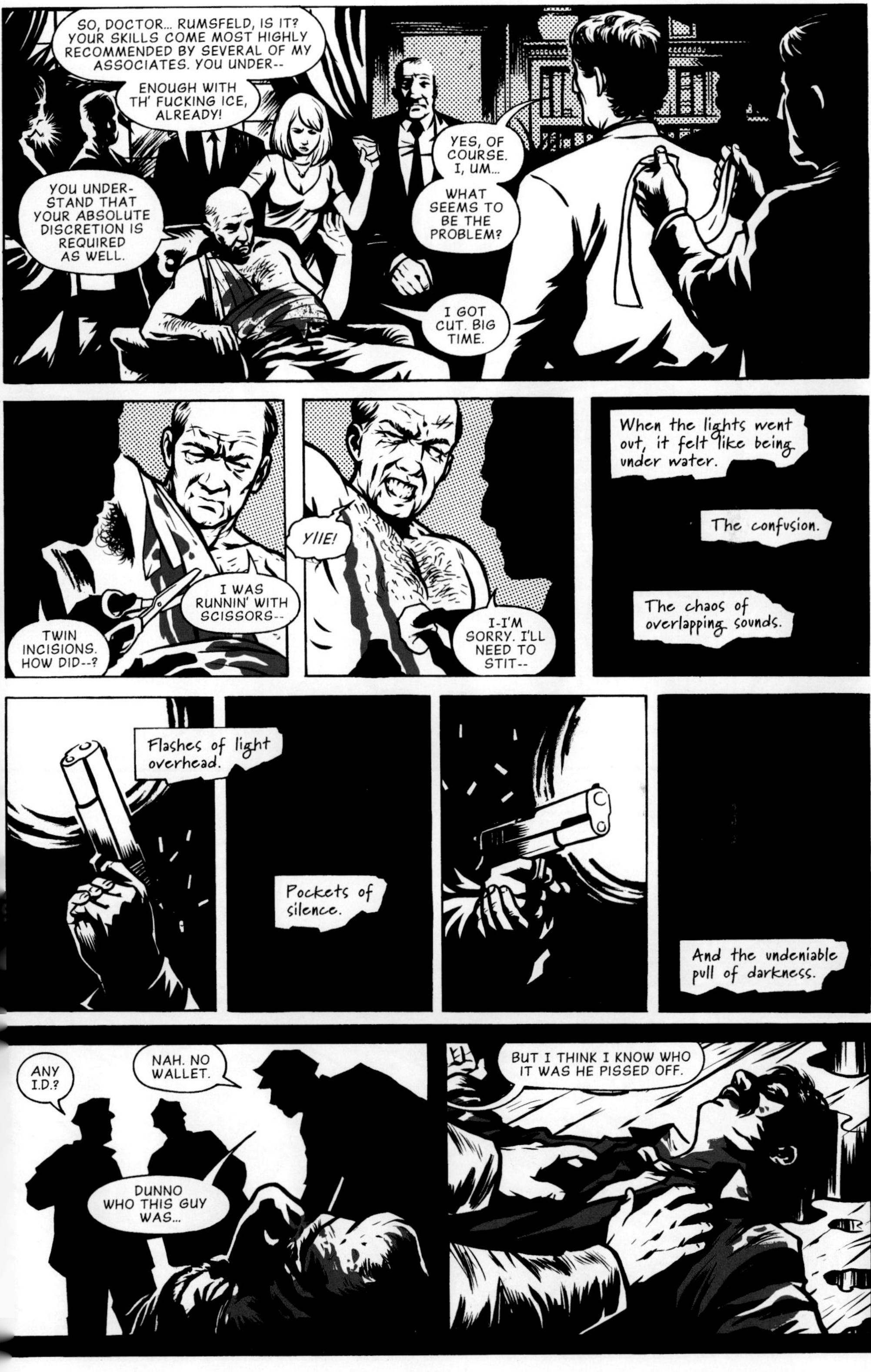
SO, DOCTOR... RUMSFELD, IS IT? YOUR SKILLS COME MOST HIGHLY RECOMMENDED BY SEVERAL OF MY ASSOCIATES. YOU UNDER--
ENOUGH WITH TH' FUCKING ICE, ALREADY!
YOU UNDERSTAND THAT YOUR ABSOLUTE DISCRETION IS REQUIRED AS WELL.
YES, OF COURSE. I, UM...
WHAT SEEMS TO BE THE PROBLEM?
I GOT CUT. BIG TIME.
TWIN INCISIONS. HOW DID--?
I WAS RUNNIN' WITH SCISSORS--
YIIE!
I-I'M SORRY. I'LL NEED TO STIT--
When the lights went out, it felt like being under water.
The confusion.
The chaos of overlapping sounds.
Flashes of light overhead.
Pockets of silence.
And the undeniable pull of darkness.
ANY I.D.?
NAH. NO WALLET.
DUNNO WHO THIS GUY WAS...
BUT I THINK I KNOW WHO IT WAS HE PISSED OFF.

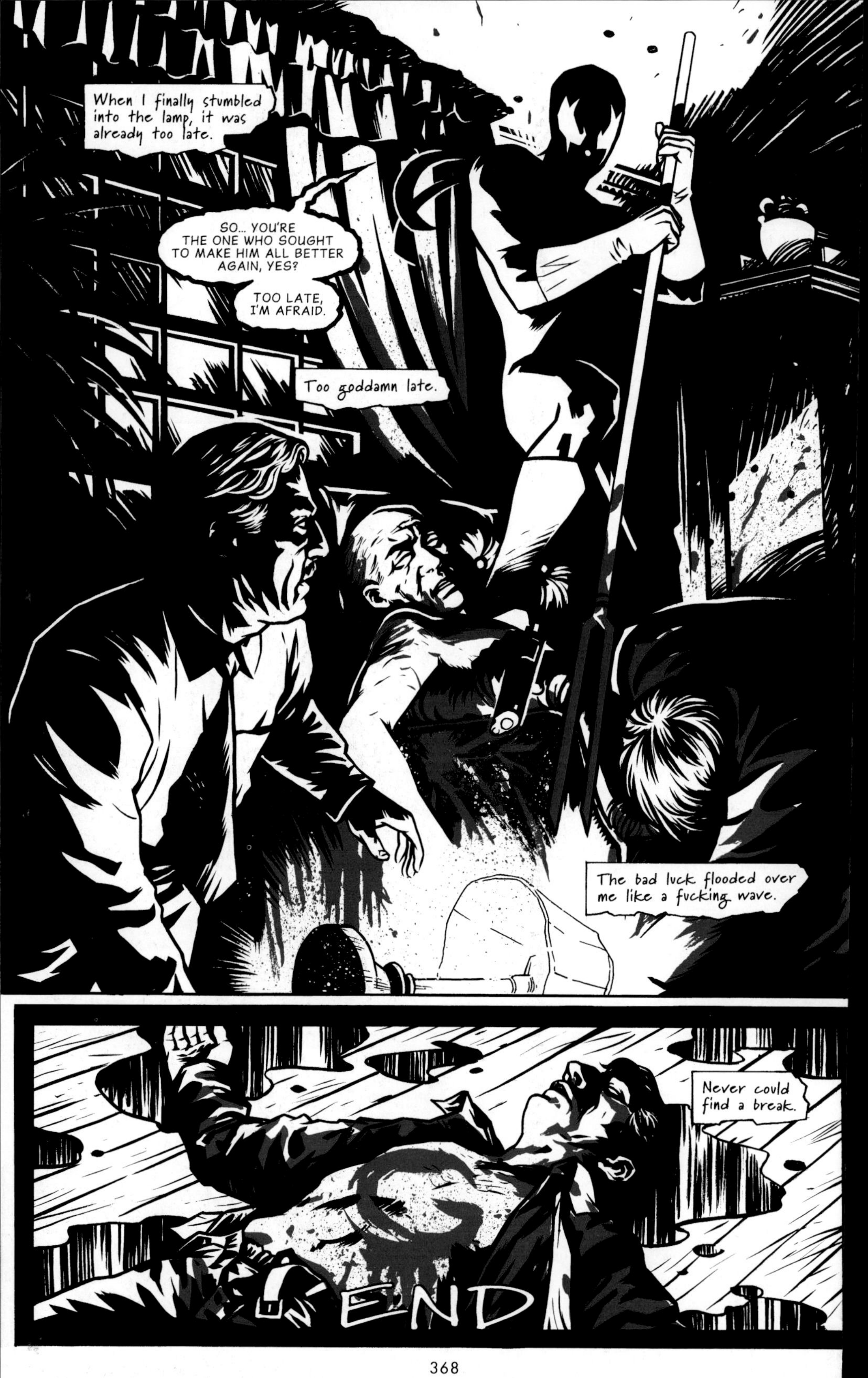
When I finally stumbled into the lamp, it was already too late.
SO... YOU'RE THE ONE WHO SOUGHT TO MAKE HIM ALL BETTER AGAIN, YES?
TOO LATE, I'M AFRAID.
Too goddamn late.
The bad luck flooded over me like a fucking wave.
Never could find a break.
END

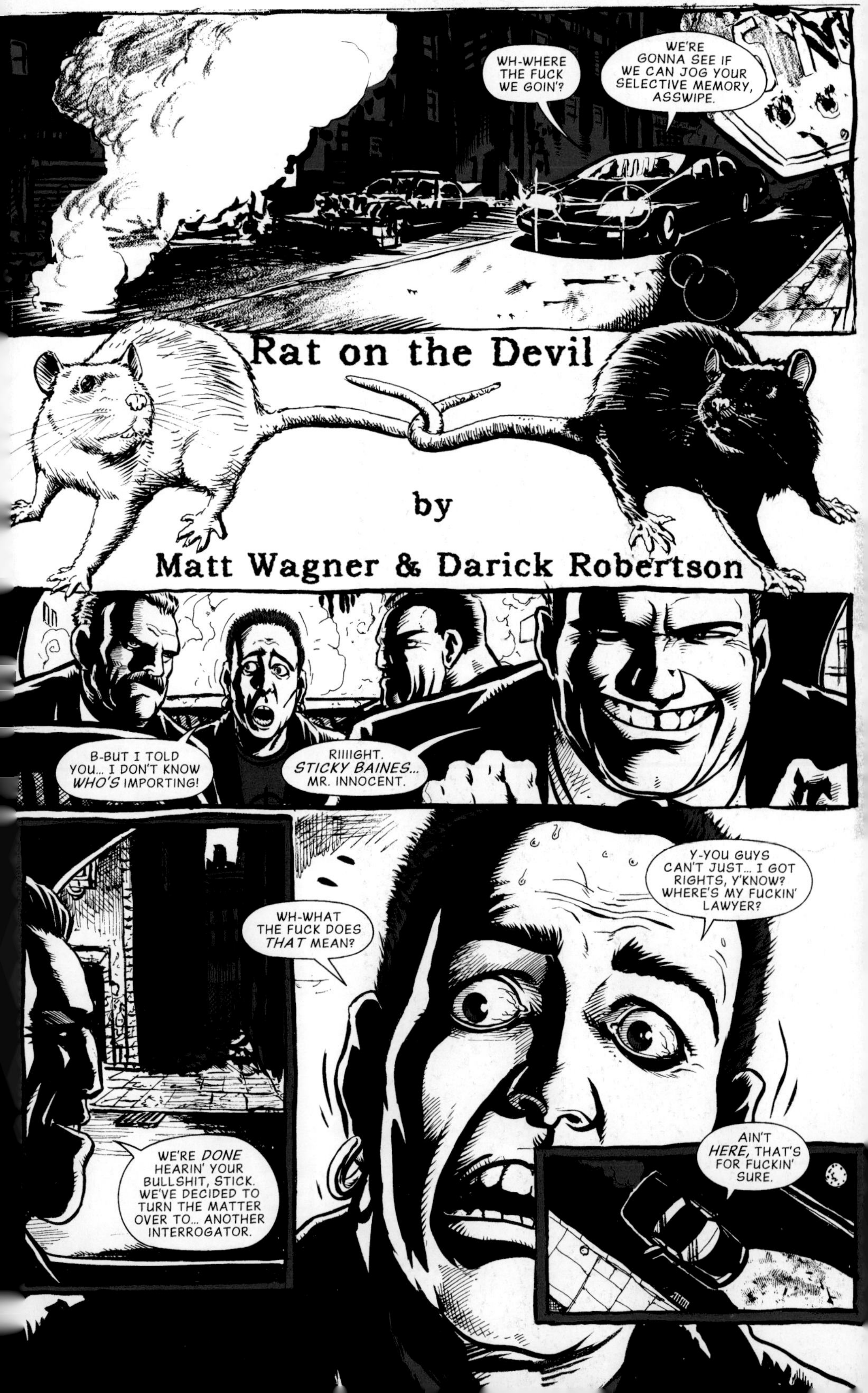

WH-WHERE THE FUCK WE GOIN'?
WE'RE GONNA SEE IF WE CAN JOG YOUR SELECTIVE MEMORY, ASSWIPE.
Rat on the Devil
by
Matt Wagner & Darick Robertson
B-BUT I TOLD YOU... I DON'T KNOW WHO'S IMPORTING!
RIIIGHT. STICKY BAINES... MR. INNOCENT.
WE'RE DONE HEARIN' YOUR BULLSHIT, STICK. WE'VE DECIDED TO TURN THE MATTER OVER TO... ANOTHER INTERROGATOR.
WH-WHAT THE FUCK DOES THAT MEAN?
Y-YOU GUYS CAN'T JUST... I GOT RIGHTS, Y'KNOW? WHERE'S MY FUCKIN' LAWYER?
AIN'T HERE, THAT'S FOR FUCKIN' SURE.

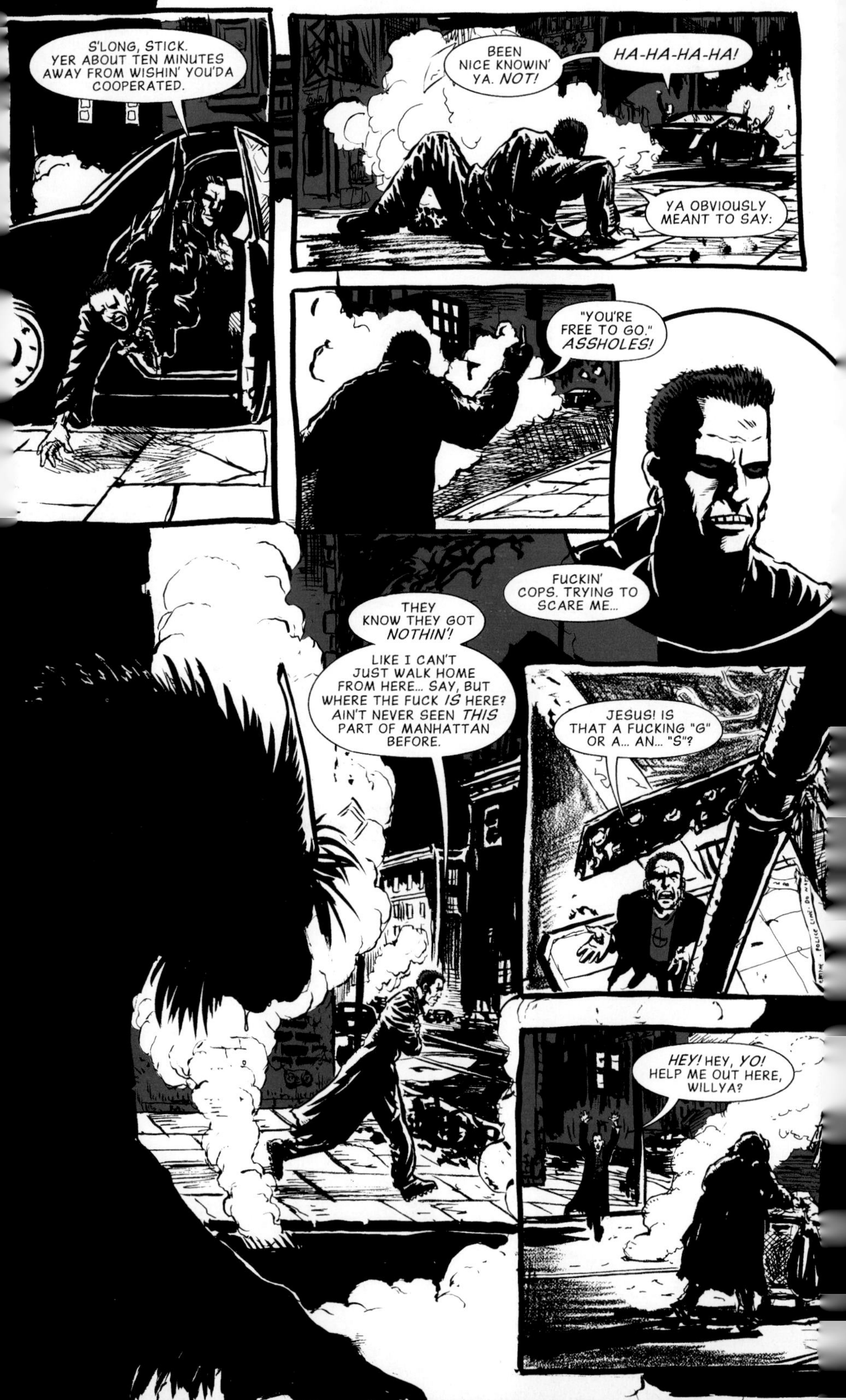

S'LONG, STICK. YER ABOUT TEN MINUTES AWAY FROM WISHIN' YOU'DA COOPERATED.
BEEN NICE KNOWIN' YA. NOT!
HA-HA-HA-HA!
YA OBVIOUSLY MEANT TO SAY:
"YOU'RE FREE TO GO." ASSHOLES!
FUCKIN' COPS. TRYING TO SCARE ME...
THEY KNOW THEY GOT NOTHIN'!
LIKE I CAN'T JUST WALK HOME FROM HERE... SAY, BUT WHERE THE FUCK IS HERE? AIN'T NEVER SEEN THIS PART OF MANHATTAN BEFORE.
JESUS! IS THAT A FUCKING "G" OR A... AN... "S"?
HEY! HEY, YO! HELP ME OUT HERE, WILLYA?

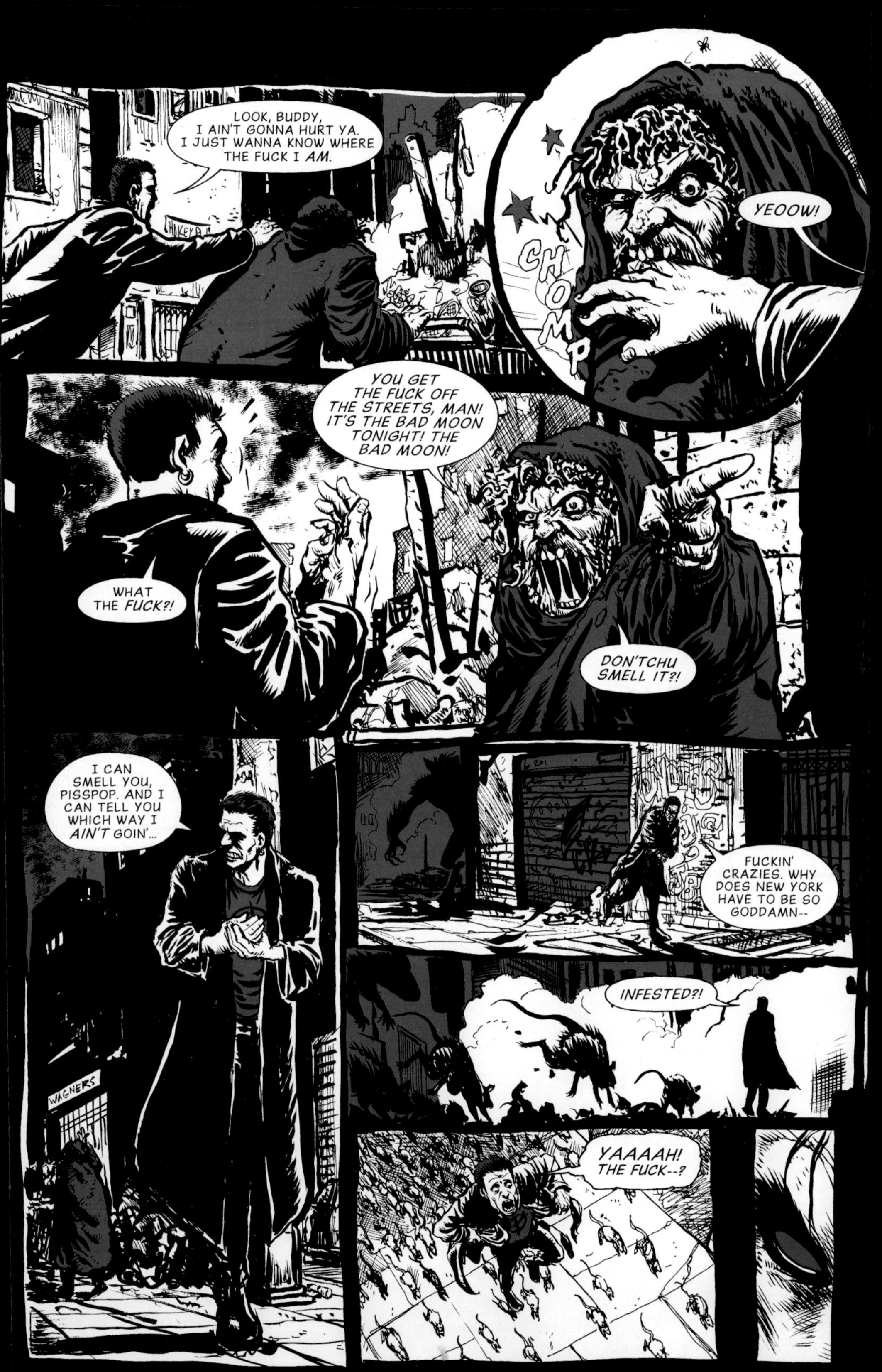
LOOK, BUDDY, I AIN'T GONNA HURT YA. I JUST WANNA KNOW WHERE THE FUCK I AM.
YEOOW!
CHOMP
YOU GET THE FUCK OFF THE STREETS, MAN! IT'S THE BAD MOON TONIGHT! THE BAD MOON!
WHAT THE FUCK?!
DON'TCHU SMELL IT?!
I CAN SMELL YOU, PISSPOP. AND I CAN TELL YOU WHICH WAY I AIN'T GOIN'...
WAGNERS
FUCKIN' CRAZIES. WHY DOES NEW YORK HAVE TO BE SO GODDAMN--
INFESTED?!
YAAAAH! THE FUCK--?

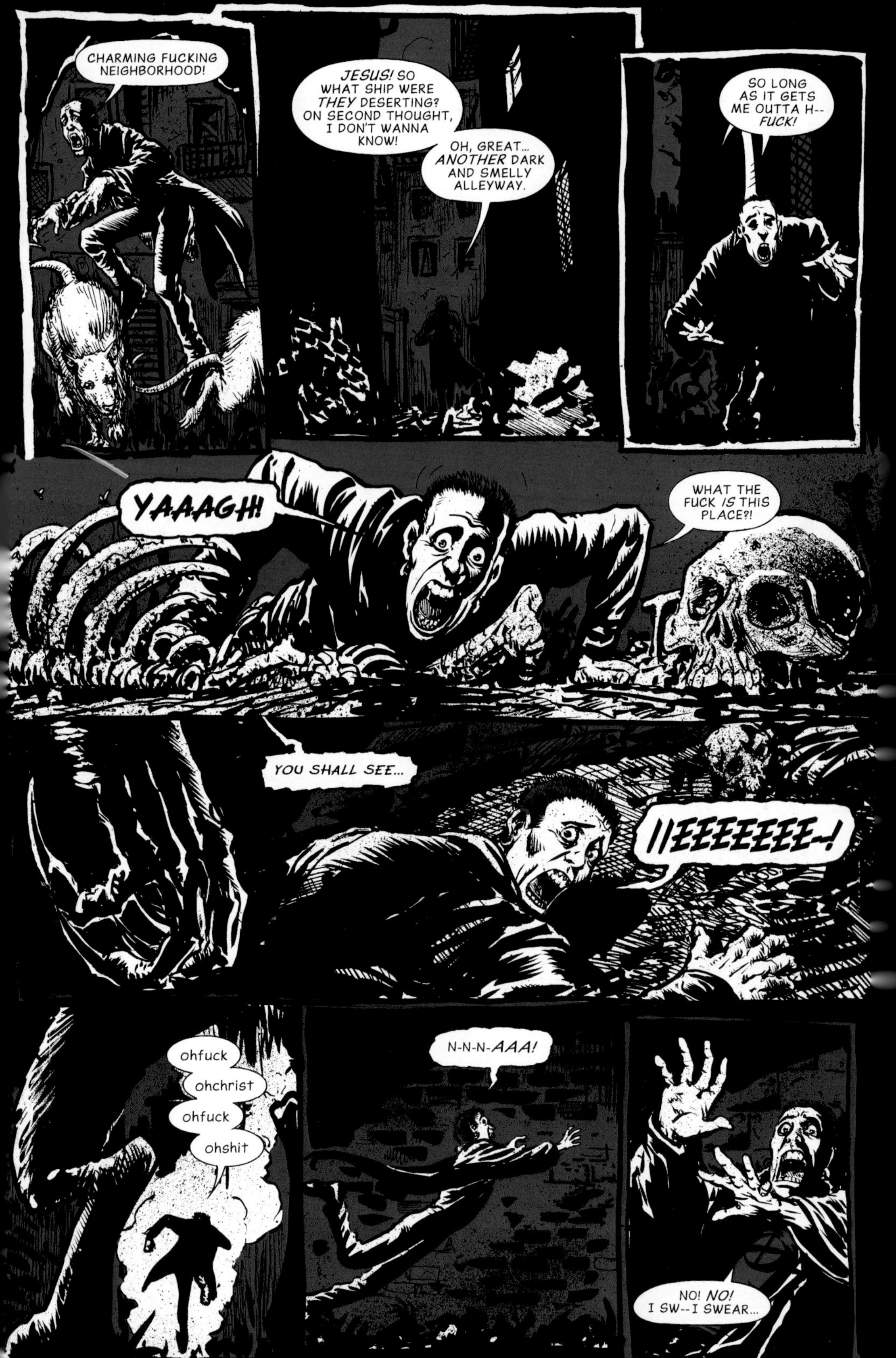
CHARMING FUCKING NEIGHBORHOOD!
JESUS! SO WHAT SHIP WERE THEY DESERTING? ON SECOND THOUGHT, I DON'T WANNA KNOW!
OH, GREAT... ANOTHER DARK AND SMELLY ALLEYWAY.
SO LONG AS IT GETS ME OUTTA H-- FUCK!
YAAAGH!
WHAT THE FUCK IS THIS PLACE?!
YOU SHALL SEE...
IIEEEEEEEE-!
ohfuck
ohchrist
ohfuck
ohshit
N-N-N-AAA!
NO! NO! I SW--I SWEAR...

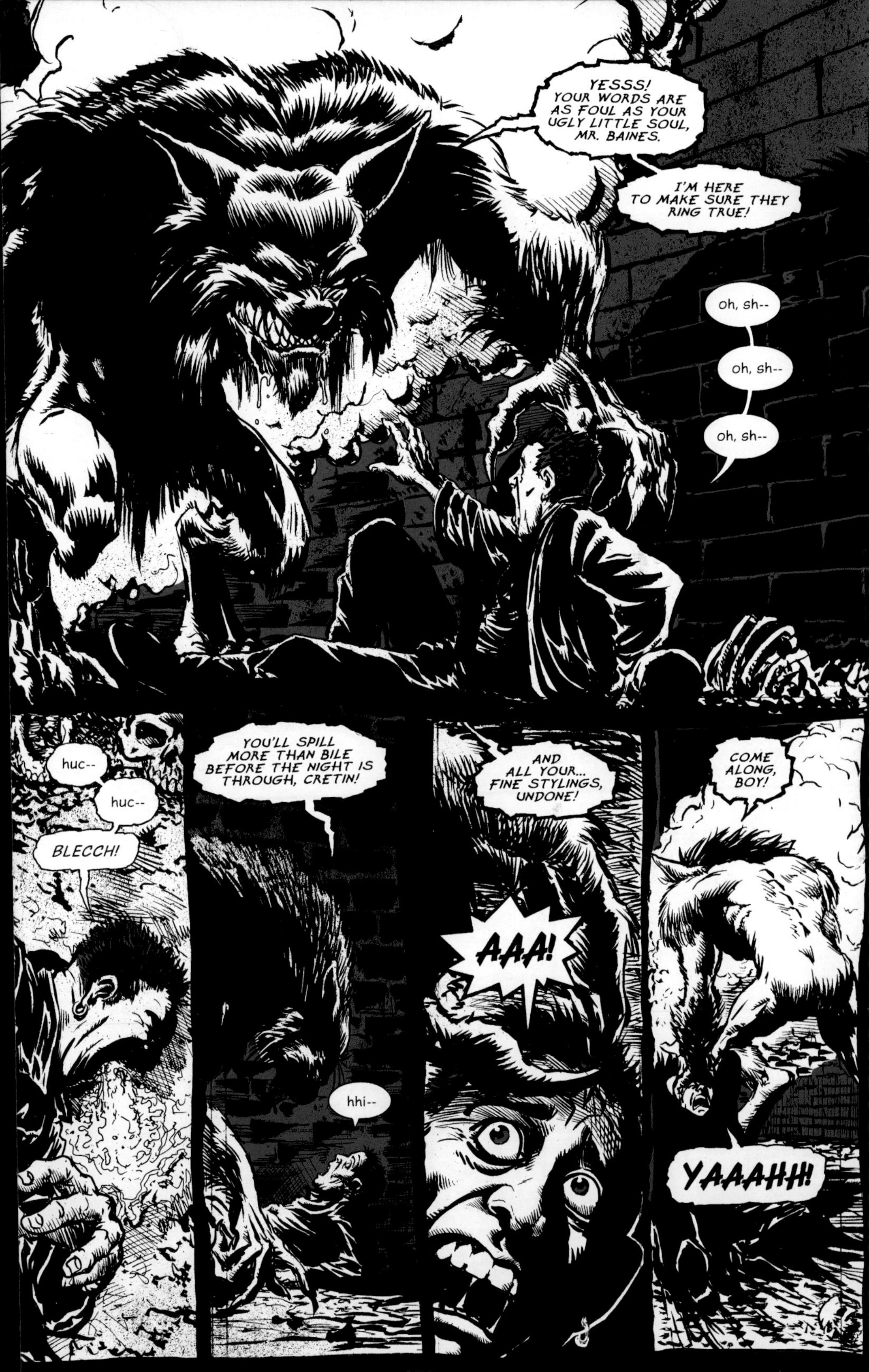
YESSS! YOUR WORDS ARE AS FOUL AS YOUR UGLY LITTLE SOUL, MR. BAINES.
I'M HERE TO MAKE SURE THEY RING TRUE!
oh, sh--
oh, sh--
oh, sh--
huc--
huc--
BLECCH!
YOU'LL SPILL MORE THAN BILE BEFORE THE NIGHT IS THROUGH, CRETIN!
hhi--
AND ALL YOUR... FINE STYLINGS, UNDONE!
AAA!
COME ALONG, BOY!
YAAAHH!

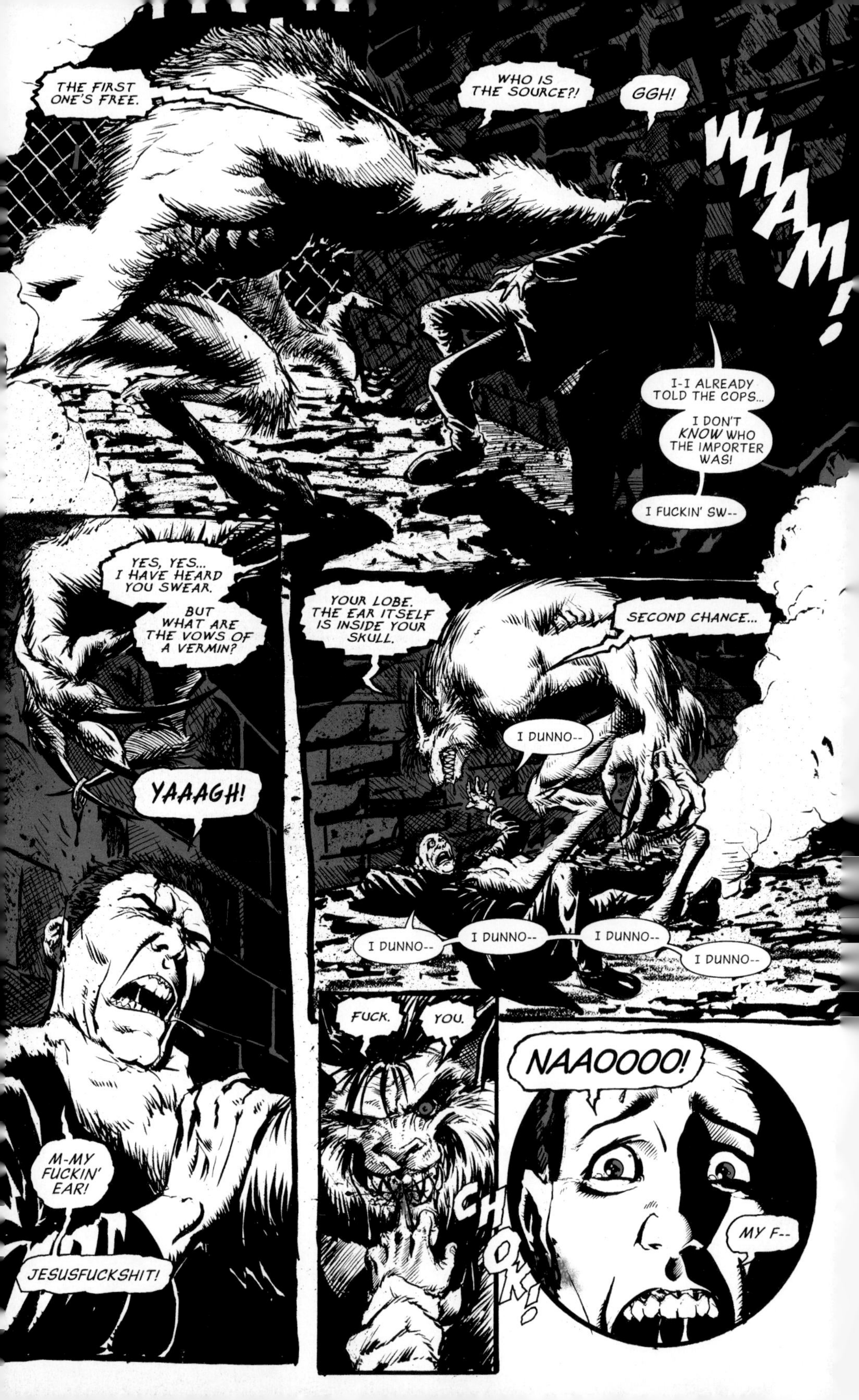
THE FIRST ONE'S FREE.
WHO IS THE SOURCE?!
GGH!
WHAM!
I-I ALREADY TOLD THE COPS...
I DON'T KNOW WHO THE IMPORTER WAS!
I FUCKIN' SW--
YES, YES... I HAVE HEARD YOU SWEAR.
BUT WHAT ARE THE VOWS OF A VERMIN?
YAAAGH!
M-MY FUCKIN' EAR!
JESUSFUCKSHIT!
YOUR LOBE. THE EAR ITSELF IS INSIDE YOUR SKULL.
SECOND CHANCE...
I DUNNO--
I DUNNO--
I DUNNO--
I DUNNO--
I DUNNO--
FUCK.
YOU.
CHOMP!
NAAOOOO!
MY F--

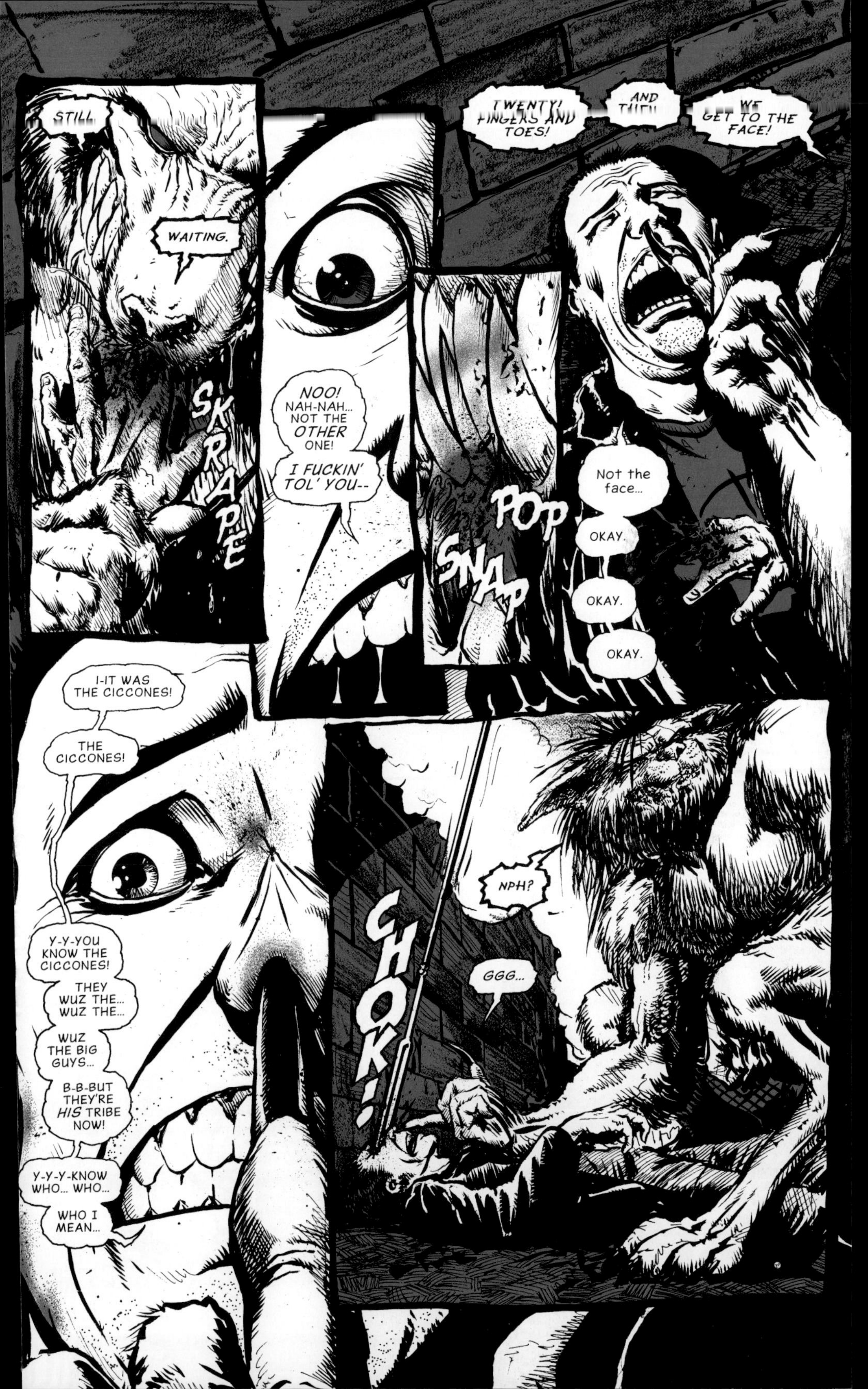
STILL.
WAITING.
SKRAPE
NOO! NAH-NAH... NOT THE OTHER ONE!
I FUCKIN' TOL' YOU--
TWENTY! FINGERS AND TOES!
AND
WE GET TO THE FACE!
POP
SNAP
Not the face...
OKAY.
OKAY.
OKAY.
I-IT WAS THE CICCONES!
THE CICCONES!
Y-Y-YOU KNOW THE CICCONES!
THEY WUZ THE... WUZ THE...
WUZ THE BIG GUYS...
B-B-BUT THEY'RE *HIS* TRIBE NOW!
Y-Y-Y-KNOW WHO... WHO...
WHO I MEAN...
CHOK!!
NPH?
GGG...

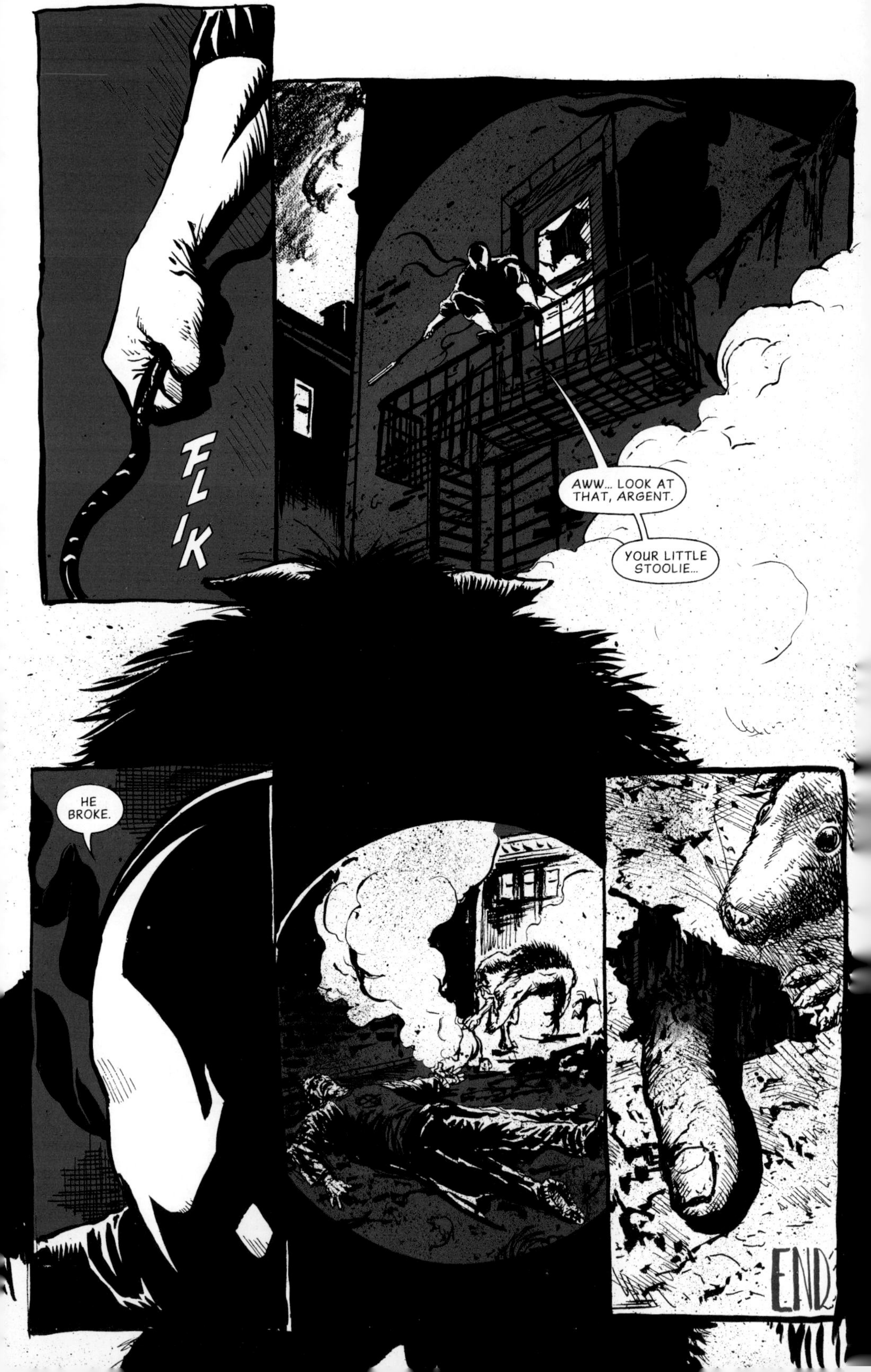
FLIK
AWW... LOOK AT THAT, ARGENT.
YOUR LITTLE STOOLIE...
HE BROKE.
END

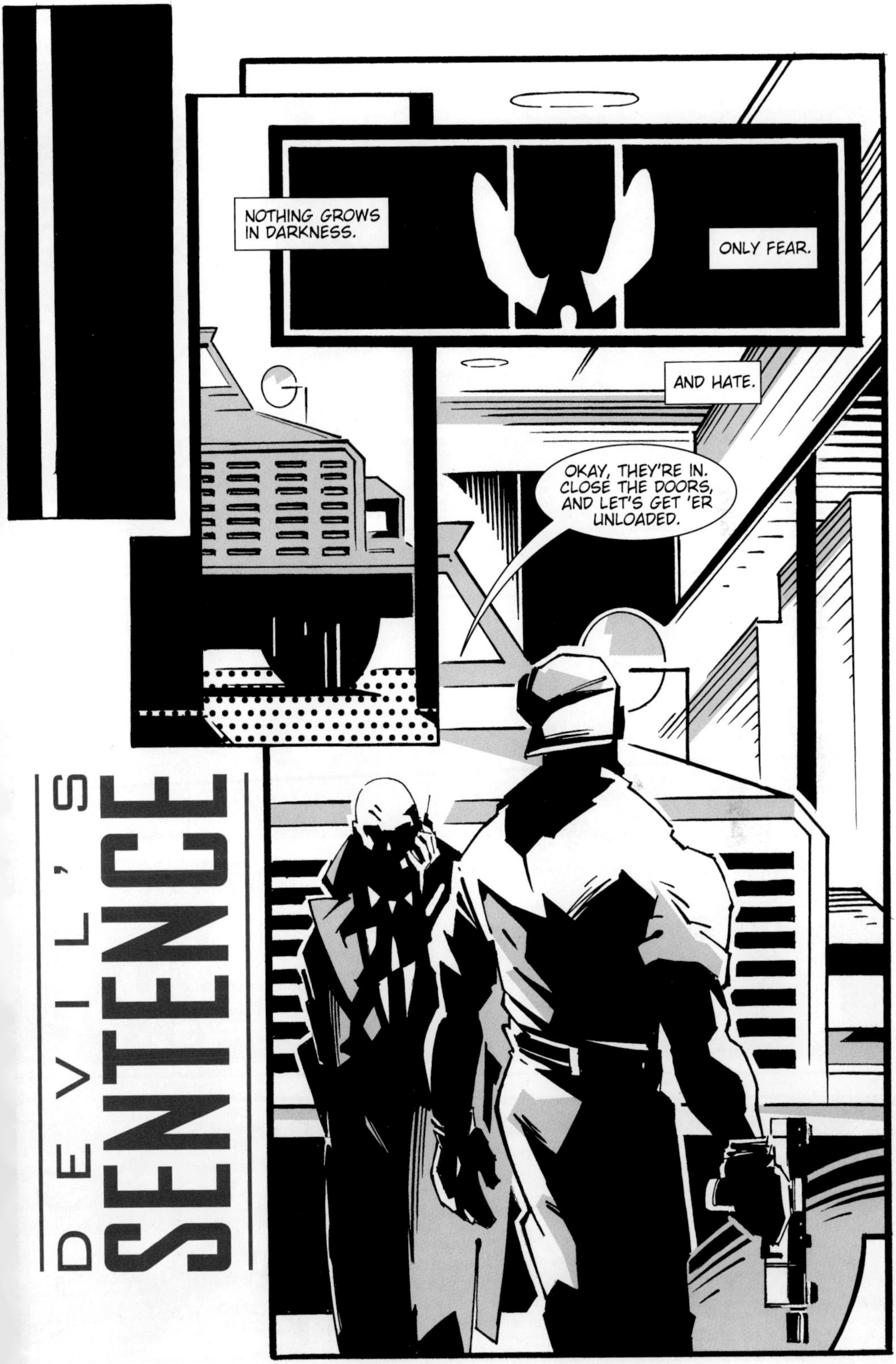
DEVIL'S
SENTENCE
NOTHING GROWS IN DARKNESS.
ONLY FEAR.
AND HATE.
OKAY, THEY'RE IN. CLOSE THE DOORS, AND LET'S GET 'ER UNLOADED.

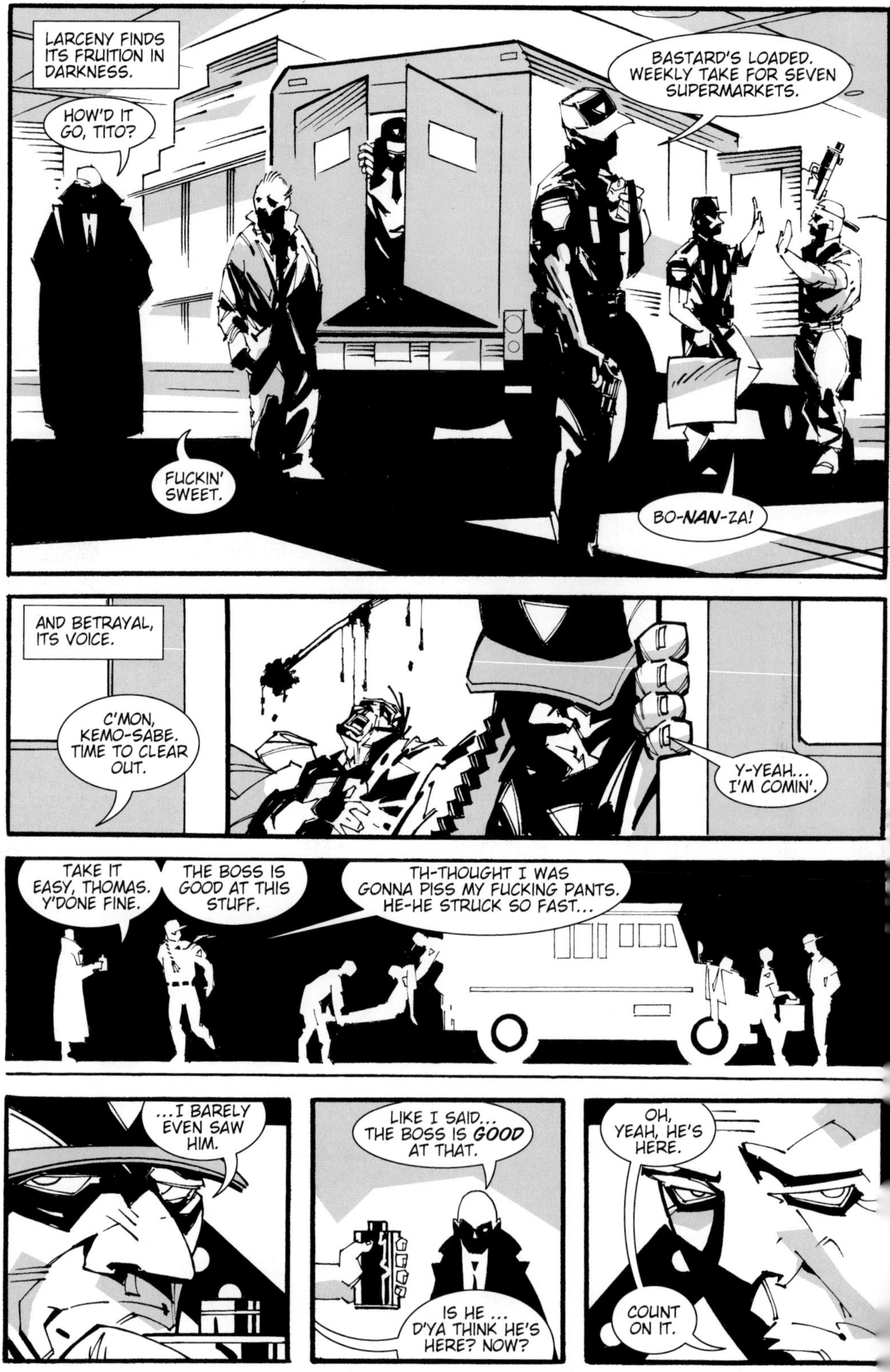

LARCENY FINDS ITS FRUITION IN DARKNESS.
HOW'D IT GO, TITO?
BASTARD'S LOADED. WEEKLY TAKE FOR SEVEN SUPERMARKETS.
FUCKIN' SWEET.
BO-NAN-ZA!
AND BETRAYAL, ITS VOICE.
C'MON, KEMO-SABE. TIME TO CLEAR OUT.
Y-YEAH... I'M COMIN'.
TAKE IT EASY, THOMAS. Y'DONE FINE.
THE BOSS IS GOOD AT THIS STUFF.
TH-THOUGHT I WAS GONNA PISS MY FUCKING PANTS. HE-HE STRUCK SO FAST...
...I BARELY EVEN SAW HIM.
LIKE I SAID... THE BOSS IS *GOOD* AT THAT.
IS HE ... D'YA THINK HE'S HERE? NOW?
OH, YEAH, HE'S HERE.
COUNT ON IT.

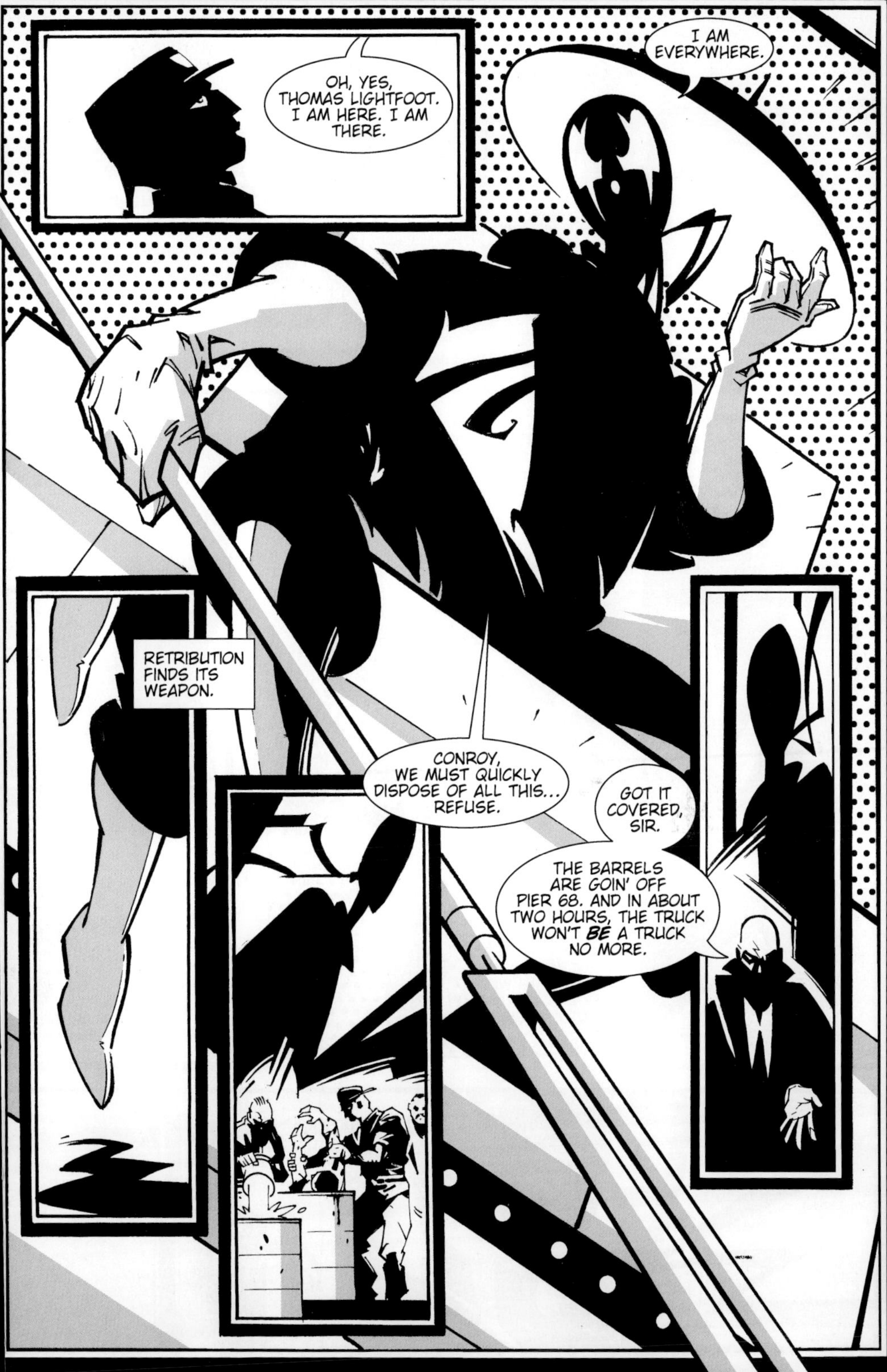
OH, YES, THOMAS LIGHTFOOT. I AM HERE. I AM THERE.
I AM EVERYWHERE.
RETRIBUTION FINDS ITS WEAPON.
CONROY, WE MUST QUICKLY DISPOSE OF ALL THIS... REFUSE.
GOT IT COVERED, SIR.
THE BARRELS ARE GOIN' OFF PIER 68. AND IN ABOUT TWO HOURS, THE TRUCK WON'T *BE* A TRUCK NO MORE.

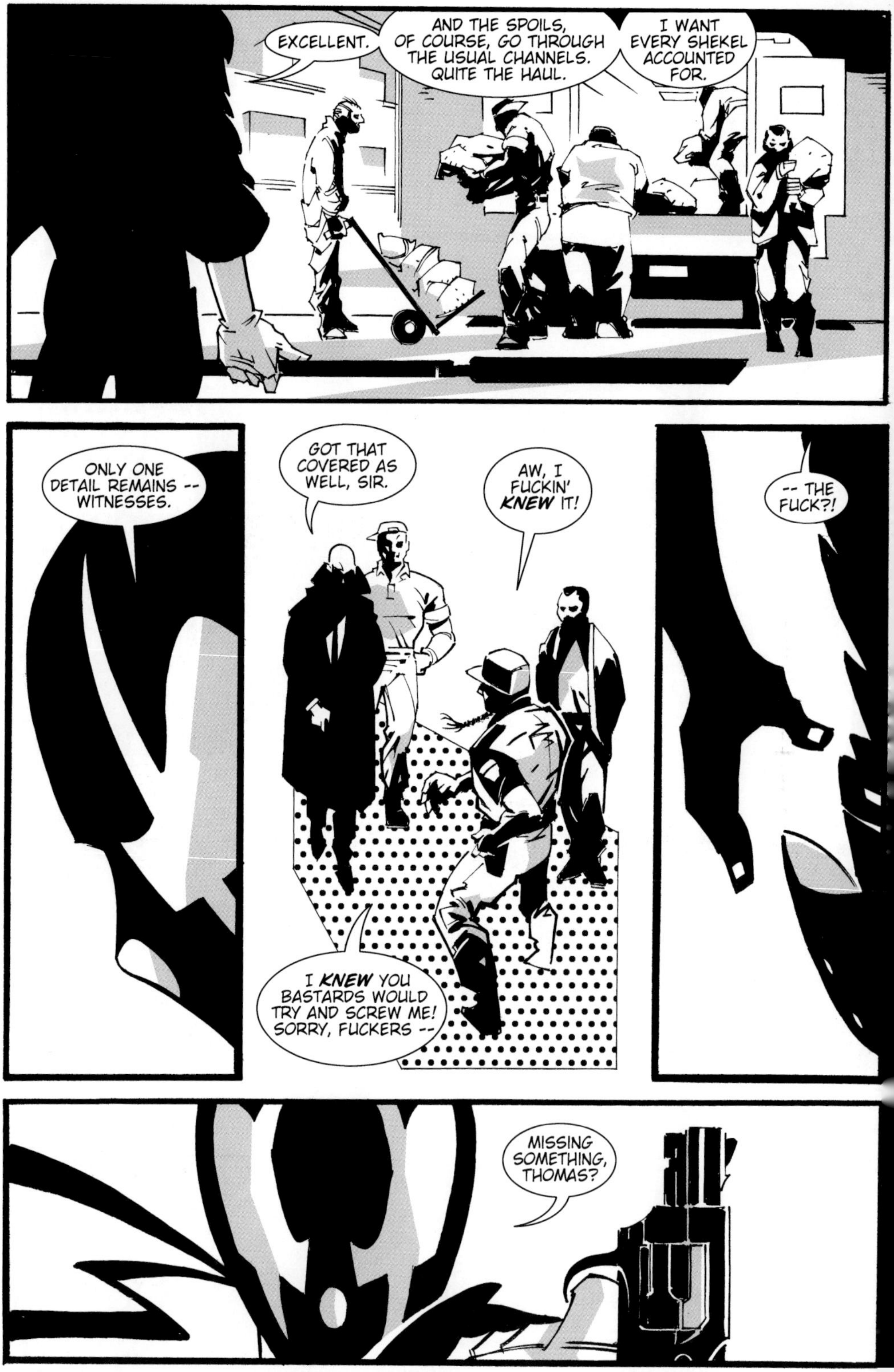
EXCELLENT.
AND THE SPOILS, OF COURSE, GO THROUGH THE USUAL CHANNELS. QUITE THE HAUL.
I WANT EVERY SHEKEL ACCOUNTED FOR.
ONLY ONE DETAIL REMAINS -- WITNESSES.
GOT THAT COVERED AS WELL, SIR.
AW, I FUCKIN' KNEW IT!
I KNEW YOU BASTARDS WOULD TRY AND SCREW ME! SORRY, FUCKERS --
-- THE FUCK?!
MISSING SOMETHING, THOMAS?

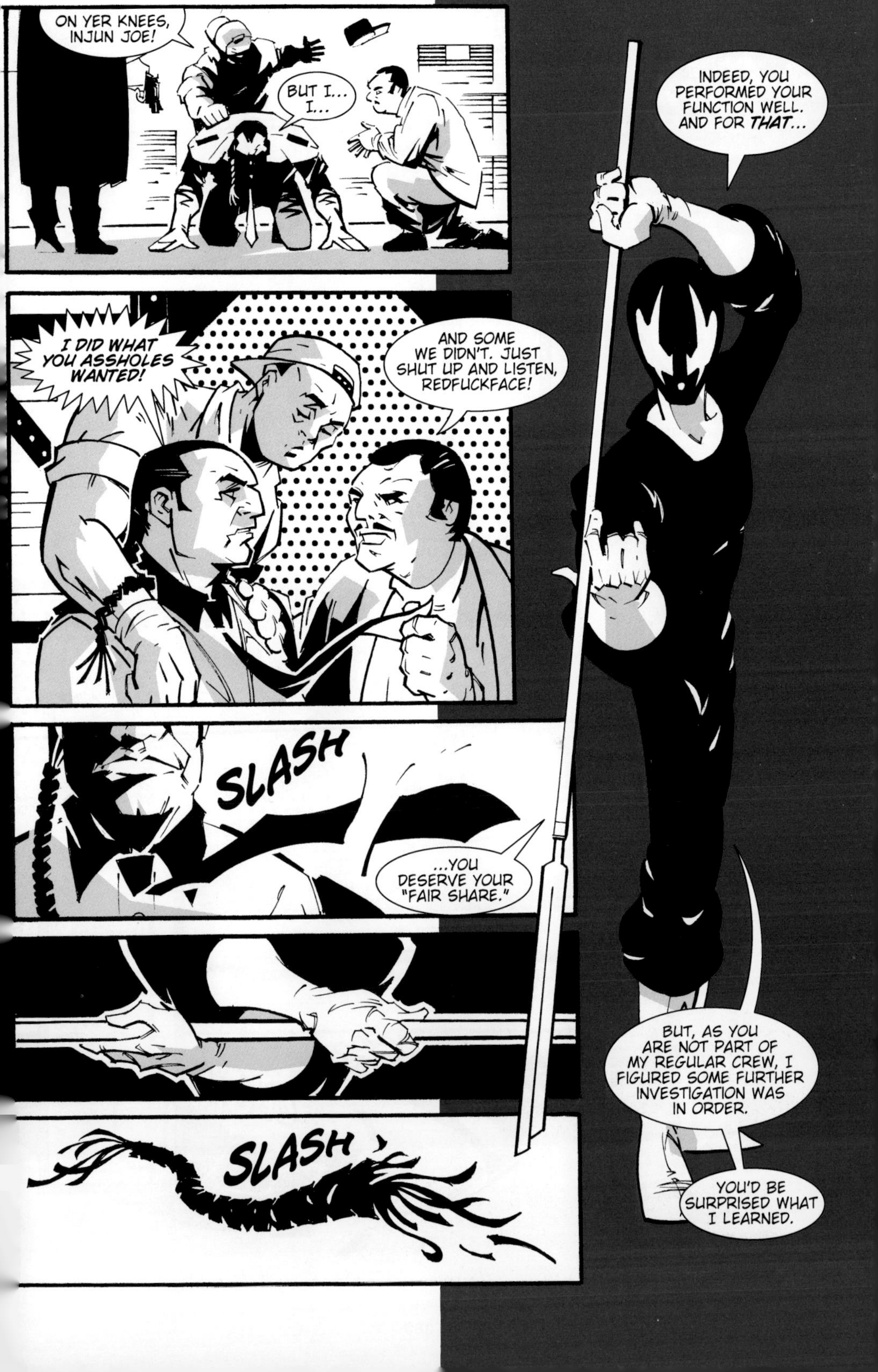
ON YER KNEES, INJUN JOE!
BUT I... I...
INDEED, YOU PERFORMED YOUR FUNCTION WELL. AND FOR *THAT*...
I DID WHAT YOU ASSHOLES WANTED!
AND SOME WE DIDN'T. JUST SHUT UP AND LISTEN, REDFUCKFACE!
SLASH
...YOU DESERVE YOUR "FAIR SHARE."
BUT, AS YOU ARE NOT PART OF MY REGULAR CREW, I FIGURED SOME FURTHER INVESTIGATION WAS IN ORDER.
SLASH
YOU'D BE SURPRISED WHAT I LEARNED.

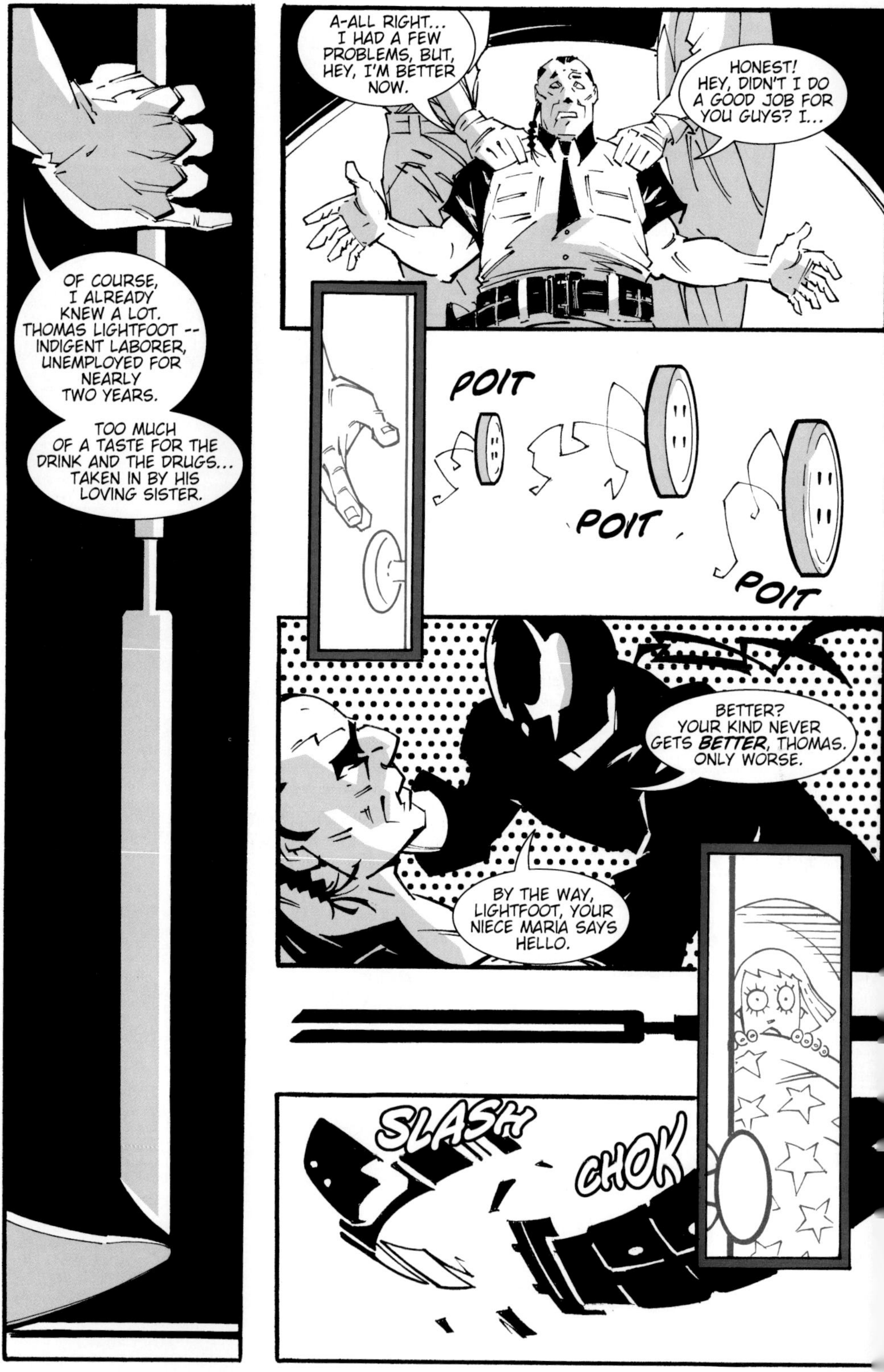
OF COURSE, I ALREADY KNEW A LOT. THOMAS LIGHTFOOT -- INDIGENT LABORER, UNEMPLOYED FOR NEARLY TWO YEARS.
TOO MUCH OF A TASTE FOR THE DRINK AND THE DRUGS... TAKEN IN BY HIS LOVING SISTER.
A-ALL RIGHT... I HAD A FEW PROBLEMS, BUT, HEY, I'M BETTER NOW.
HONEST! HEY, DIDN'T I DO A GOOD JOB FOR YOU GUYS? I...
POIT
POIT
POIT
BETTER? YOUR KIND NEVER GETS *BETTER*, THOMAS. ONLY WORSE.
BY THE WAY, LIGHTFOOT, YOUR NIECE MARIA SAYS HELLO.
SLASH
CHOK

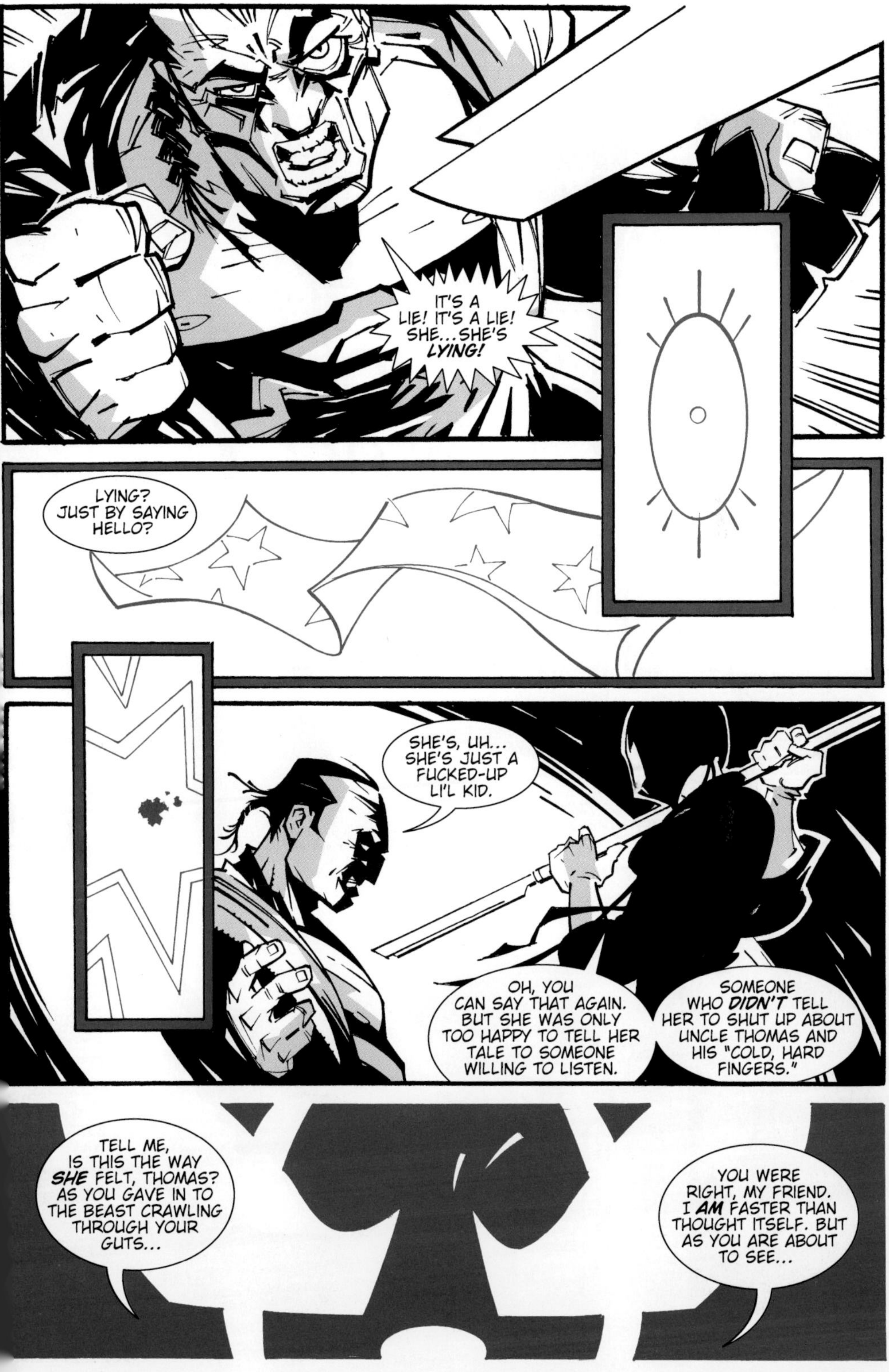

IT'S A LIE! IT'S A LIE! SHE...SHE'S *LYING!*
LYING? JUST BY SAYING HELLO?
SHE'S, UH... SHE'S JUST A FUCKED-UP LI'L KID.
OH, YOU CAN SAY THAT AGAIN. BUT SHE WAS ONLY TOO HAPPY TO TELL HER TALE TO SOMEONE WILLING TO LISTEN.
SOMEONE WHO *DIDN'T* TELL HER TO SHUT UP ABOUT UNCLE THOMAS AND HIS "COLD, HARD FINGERS."
TELL ME, IS THIS THE WAY *SHE* FELT, THOMAS? AS YOU GAVE IN TO THE BEAST CRAWLING THROUGH YOUR GUTS...
YOU WERE RIGHT, MY FRIEND. I *AM* FASTER THAN THOUGHT ITSELF. BUT AS YOU ARE ABOUT TO SEE...

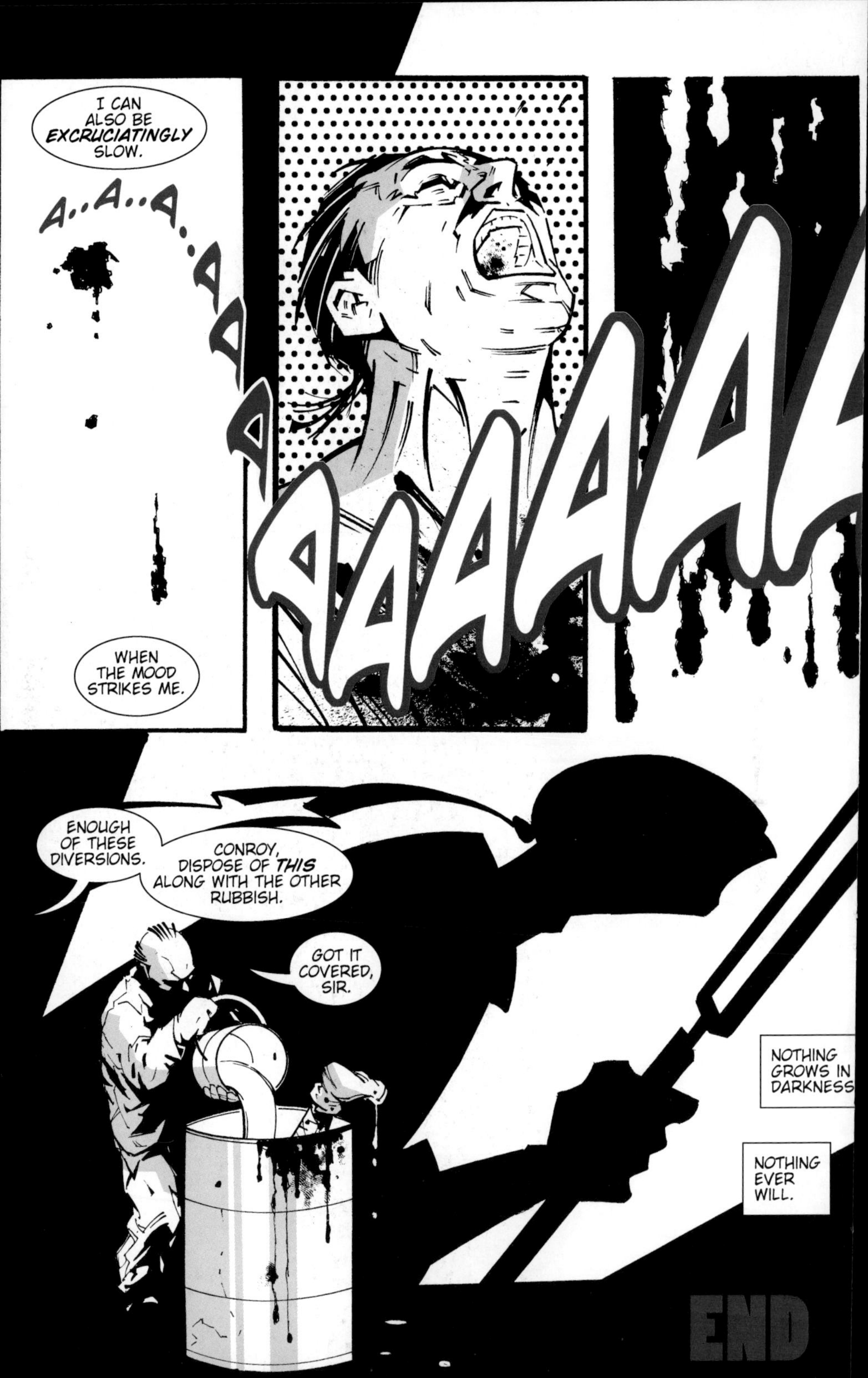
I CAN ALSO BE EXCRUCIATINGLY SLOW.
A..A..A..A
AAAAAAAA
WHEN THE MOOD STRIKES ME.
ENOUGH OF THESE DIVERSIONS.
CONROY, DISPOSE OF THIS ALONG WITH THE OTHER RUBBISH.
GOT IT COVERED, SIR.
NOTHING GROWS IN DARKNESS
NOTHING EVER WILL.
END

DEVILISH
ESCAPADES

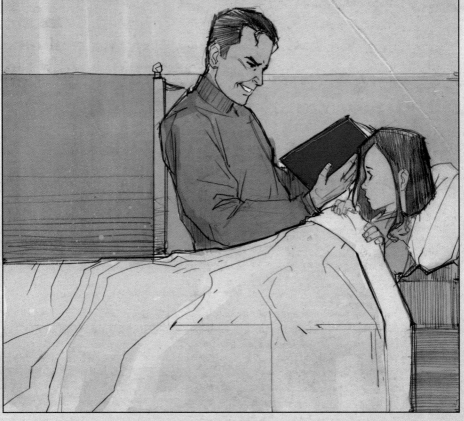

by
MATT WAGNER
and
PHIL NOTO

SEVEN *MINUTE MYSTERIES* ACCOMPANIED BY PICTURES.
ALL NEW TALES OF EVIL AND MAYHEM!

DEATH IN THE BASEMENT

The day on which my husband would later die began ordinarily enough. I saw him off to work and then went downstairs to put on a load of laundry. It was only on the final rinse cycle that I realized someone was living in the basement. I heard a noise, and at first I thought we had rats, but then I saw the slight glint as a gun poked out of the shadows underneath the stairs. The man's speech was ragged and coarse as he demanded a telephone and a bottle of aspirin. I … I guess I was just too frightened to even think of refusing. As I handed him a glass of water, I noticed the blood. There was some sort of deep gash on his left calf, which he had tied off with a strip of cloth. I later discovered a broken transom window, and I suppose that is how he gained entry, crawling in from the rear alley. He muttered into the phone for several minutes, alternately angry and pleading. Eventually, he hung up and seemed to forget for a while that I was still there. At last he waved the gun at me again and told me that he'd kill anyone other than me who came down the stairs. I knew my daughter would be home from school in less than two hours, and so I offered to phone a doctor, which he adamantly refused. "I jus — just need to rest. And, believe me, you don't want *anyone* comin' to find me here. Not with … not with who's after me." He kept the phone so I couldn't call the police, and I … I went upstairs and started making dinner. I was halfway through the roast when I heard the shots. Of course, I'd forgotten it was Thursday and that my husband always came home early to check that the oil delivery man had correctly refilled the furnace. He's never trusted service people.

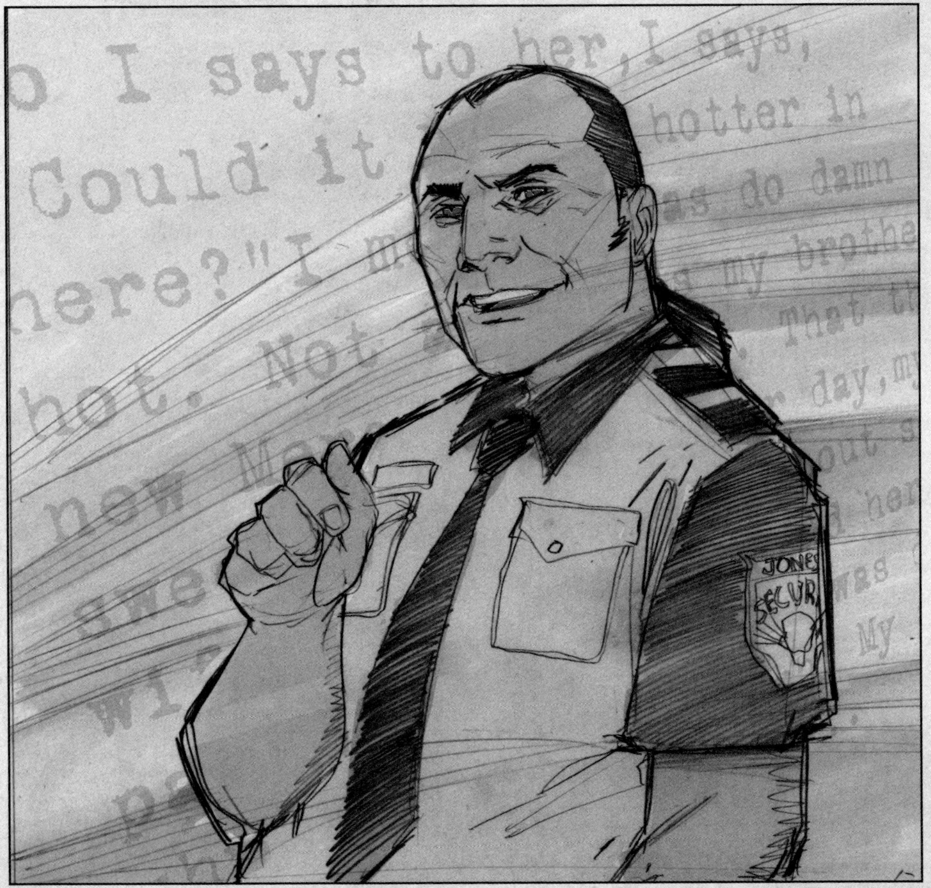
I says to her, I says,
Could it
hotter in
do damn
my
hot. Not
day,
My

THE STEEL COFFIN

Contrary to what you might think, my line of work isn't very exciting at all, although it *is* interesting. Holed away inside an armored vehicle for most of the day, you get a different angle on the way things in the world transpire. From in here, it all seems too random, so disordered and dangerous. Still, the banks do what they do for a reason. There are very few actual robberies carried out against money transport vehicles. I mean, I'm licensed to carry a firearm, but I've never once had to draw it from the holster. All that changed the day the Indian came on board. He was new to the guard business, and none of the other security personnel seemed to know him. He followed procedure to the letter but generally kept to himself. Then, one day, after almost three weeks of being locked up in this steel box for nearly seven hours a day together, the Indian starts talking a mile a minute. I remember thinking, "Bastards can't handle their whiskey *or* their coffee," just as the truck came to a stoplight. We stayed there for a long time. *Too* long. And then the truck bounced a bit, but the Indian just kept yakkin' away. About nothing — the thermostat in his apartment, his brother's Mercedes, his wife's hernia. Just as I was getting ready to check in with the driver, that's when I heard it. The latch on the back door moved — which it isn't supposed to do. The door's supposed to be locked tight from the inside. But listening like I was to the damn Indian go on and on, I hadn't noticed. I remember a flash of black and white ... so fast. And then falling backwards as everything went red. Didn't even get to draw the gun.

CROSSFIRE REPORT

The suspect maintains a steady pace as she travels north on Seventh Avenue. Just south of 98th Street, suspect enters a five-storey building and proceeds to the third floor rear apartment. Surveillance devices record transfer of controlled substances to suspect in standard-issue army backpack. Suspect returns to own apartment and remains there, with backpack, until next evening. Phone taps reveal drop-off point, located in lower Soho. Contact time, 23:00 hours. Suspect carries backpack via subway line to general area. Spends nearly an hour wandering, seemingly to avoid any trail or detection. Suspect enters café and purchases 16-oz. cappuccino. To go. Suspect rendezvous with drop mule at 22:58. Enters alley off Mercer Avenue to complete hand-off. Agents standing ready, as unknown parties arrive at the scene. Altercation ensues, as apparent rival gang attempts to obtain backpack from suspect and mule. Mule refuses and is subdued. Agents in position, as gang members circle suspect. Situation escalates with the sudden arrival of unknown, masked assailant. Assailant somehow slips through agents' surveillance net and enters fray only when contraband threatened. Masked assailant wields some manner of bladed weapon and dispatches rival gang members in short order — before agents can intervene. Signal is given, and agents close on the scene. Assailant ignores orders to halt and quickly exits scene via pre-positioned safety line from fire escape. Shots are fired, and suspect is cut down in the salvo. Further investigation required.

THE VISITOR

Third day of the month meant it was time to wash out the empty stalls. Zoo policy. It was in front of the tiger cages that I saw him: Italian shoes and an eagle's stance. Not a hair out of place. Seemed a little young for the walking stick. I told him that it was past closing and that the gates were already locked. He never apologized, but said that he must've lost track of time. I asked if he was there on zoo business, but he said no — "just visiting." I reached for my key chain, but when I looked up again he was gone. Spotted him about a week later, again in front of the tiger's cage. The Bengal. Visiting again. I'd nearly forgotten him by the end of month, before the mauling. It was late, and a commotion in the monkey house led me to something amiss with the big cat. I heard a muffled keening and realized that the Bengal wasn't pacing — its attention on the human intruder in the corner of its den. Bound and gagged, the man was trying to scream but only suceeded in getting the tiger all worked up. Knowing I'd be too late, I turned to run for help when I saw him again. Perched in a tree, masked and hidden, but still visiting. As before, he didn't pay much attention to my presence, as he watched the slaughter begin. The Bengal went through forty pounds before we could sedate her. The victim was later identified as an illegal arms dealer, and the cause of death listed as unknown. But I know the cause. I know the keys to survival, and I know the name that the police are loath to utter. So I've done nothing. Nothing but try and forget the sight of his face. Forget his stance. Forget I ever saw him.

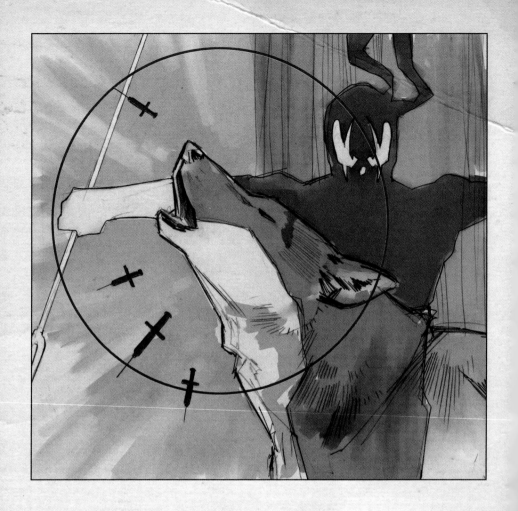

WOLF TRACKS

I seen the Wolf on more than one occasion. Once, when my cousin Stavros was scoring a bag, we was walkin' north on the lower east side. Suddenly, this fucking … *shape* just dashes across the street in front of us. So fast you could hardly see it, but we found the scrape marks it left as it bounded over some cars. I wanted to split, but Stavie really wanted that smack. Luckily we got out okay, but I never went back with him. Then, once, I was sittin' on the roof of Stavie's place, sparkin' a bone, when I could hear this ragged breathing from nearby. And then this *howl* cuts loose, like some *huge* fucking animal caught in a trap. Another time, I was hanging out near the docks, at a bar called the Rusty Nail, and I hadda take a leak. The john was out of order, so I stepped out back in the alley. From up above I could hear the whispered lines of a deal going down. Well, a second later I heard that fire escape rattle and shake like it was coming off the fucking wall! One of the dealers gave a little gurgle, and the other one started crying, real high like a little girl, before both of them were drowned out by the growling. Jesus, I pissed all over my left leg when the blood began to hit the ground — first just in drops and then a steady stream, like a bucket tipped over. And then, when that goddamn howling started again … man, I fucking bolted outta there and didn't stop until I was safe at home. They say the Wolf doesn't give a shit about small-timers. That his only concern is the higher-ups, the mystery bosses who control the way this city actually runs. I say that's all bullshit. They don't know the truth. They ain't seen what I seen.

PRESCRIPTION FOR MURDER

The patient had lost a lot of blood and was in shock by the time I arrived. Or, I should say, *was brought*. Awakened in the middle of the night, once again, I was told to leave my family at home alone. Unaware, they slept peacefully as I was forced to attend yet another wounded gangster in the darkened recesses of some mysterious warehouse. As always, a crude hood prevented me from knowing the exact location. The patient was young, black, and instead of being shot up in the normal manner of such miscreants, was the victim of many long and ugly slashes of varying depth. The result of some testosterone-driven confrontation involving knives, I supposed. My escorts, normally a gruffly effusive bunch, were this time strangely silent as I examined their fading charge. "Well, gentlemen, this time you may have come too late. This man needs several transfusions of whole blood and probably more morphine and adrenaline than I've got in my bag. Still …" A muffled but commanding voice spoke from the surrounding shadows, and my escorts all visibly stiffened. "Still, you will keep him alive, Doctor. He has information that is *vital* to my interests." As I gazed around, trying to locate the source of this directive, I was horrified to see a pair of long, thin blades slide out of the darkness. Scalpel-sharp, they nicked the patient's ear, cleanly slicing off much of the lobe and adding fresh blood to the crusty table on which he lay. "And my interests," the voice continued, "are *not* to be denied." Deep in the surrounding darkness, I could barely discern the distended white shapes that suggested a pair of inhuman eyes — a sight I will not soon forget. Nonetheless, despite my best efforts to the contrary, the patient died some hours later. I was released unharmed and my services were never again requested, but I am left with the residual image of this faceless phantom in the shadows. Despite escalating medications, I have hardly slept since.

EYEWITNESS OF DOOM

Windows are funny. To spend your time gazing out of them is considered a natural thing, even a God-given right. To spend your time gazing *into* them is condemned as downright criminal. That was one of the only requirements for this job — that you keep your nose, and your peepers, outta the client's business. Oh, sure, there're all the safety concerns, etc. … but, mostly, you don't even get into this business if you ain't a careful sort. And not scared o' heights. Me, I've always been a climber, so window-washing skyscrapers ain't no big shakes. And I know how to mind my own business. I've got this special way, see, of looking at the surface of the glass without actually looking through it. Oh, I'm sure there's plenty to observe inside the buildings I work on: business, politics, sex, drugs. This is Manhattan, after all. But I don't see none of it, 'cause that's just part of my job. 'Course, all that changed for good when a bullet shot out of the third western plate on the twenty-eighth floor, less than a foot away from my freakin' nose. Then, I couldn't *help* but look. And, damn it all, don't I wish that I hadn't? There was several guys inside, all flailing about and waving guns. Trying to find what to aim at. Two more rounds went into the ceiling when one of the guys, the big one in the dark blue suit, just seemed to sort of split in half, his blood making a mess of the inside of the glass and partly obstructing my view. And so, what I *should've* seen — the most important thing I'd *ever* see — I missed. But the bullet didn't. The next round caught me right in the chest before the shooting stopped altogether. I dangled from my rig for a bit before *it* passed over me. Guess it must've been the angel of death, all black and billowy. Cut me loose, and then used the rig to climb onto the roof. They say it's the fall that kills you and not the impact. They're right.

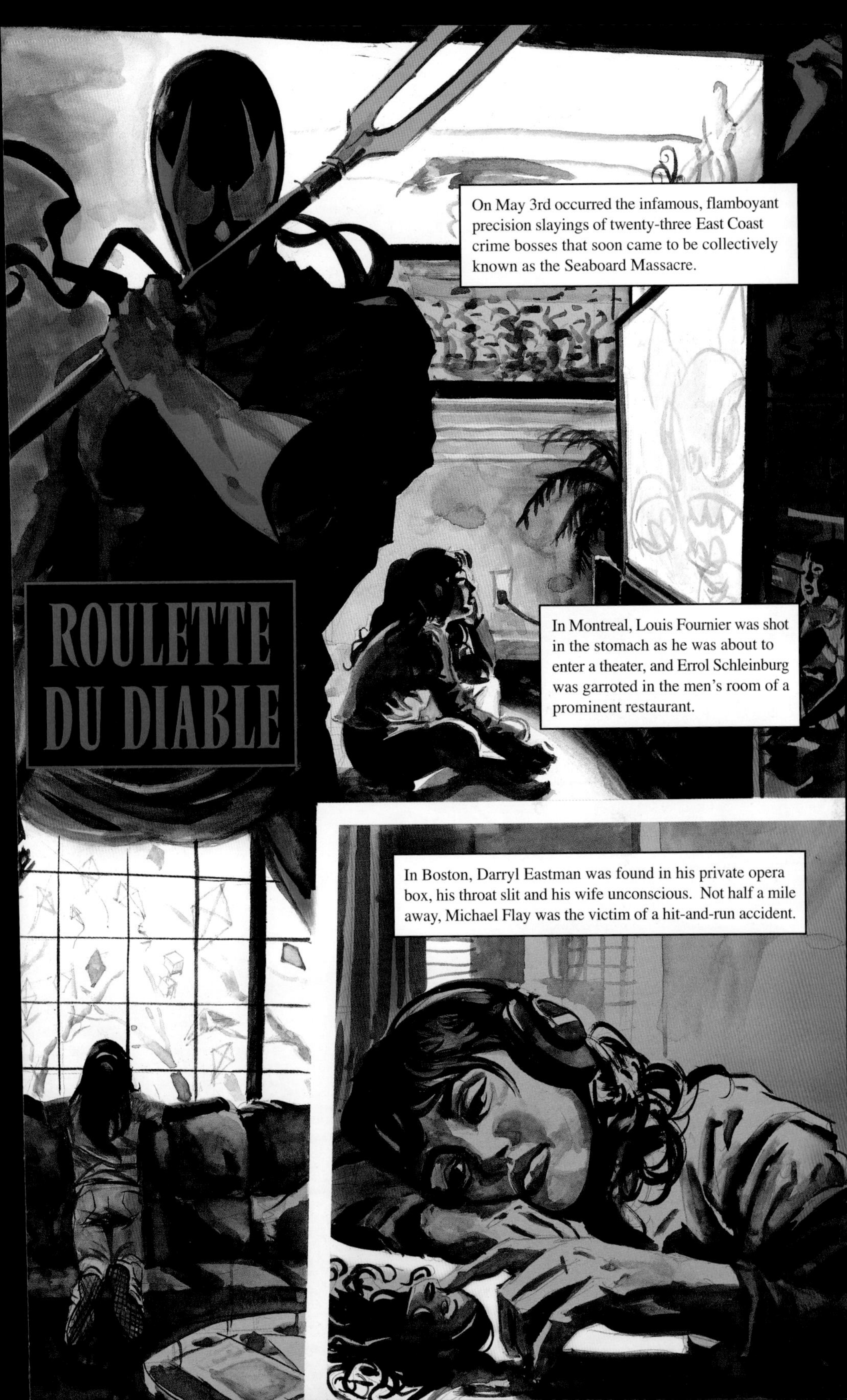
On May 3rd occurred the infamous, flamboyant precision slayings of twenty-three East Coast crime bosses that soon came to be collectively known as the Seaboard Massacre.
ROULETTE DU DIABLE
In Montreal, Louis Fournier was shot in the stomach as he was about to enter a theater, and Errol Schleinburg was garroted in the men's room of a prominent restaurant.
In Boston, Darryl Eastman was found in his private opera box, his throat slit and his wife unconscious. Not half a mile away, Michael Flay was the victim of a hit-and-run accident.

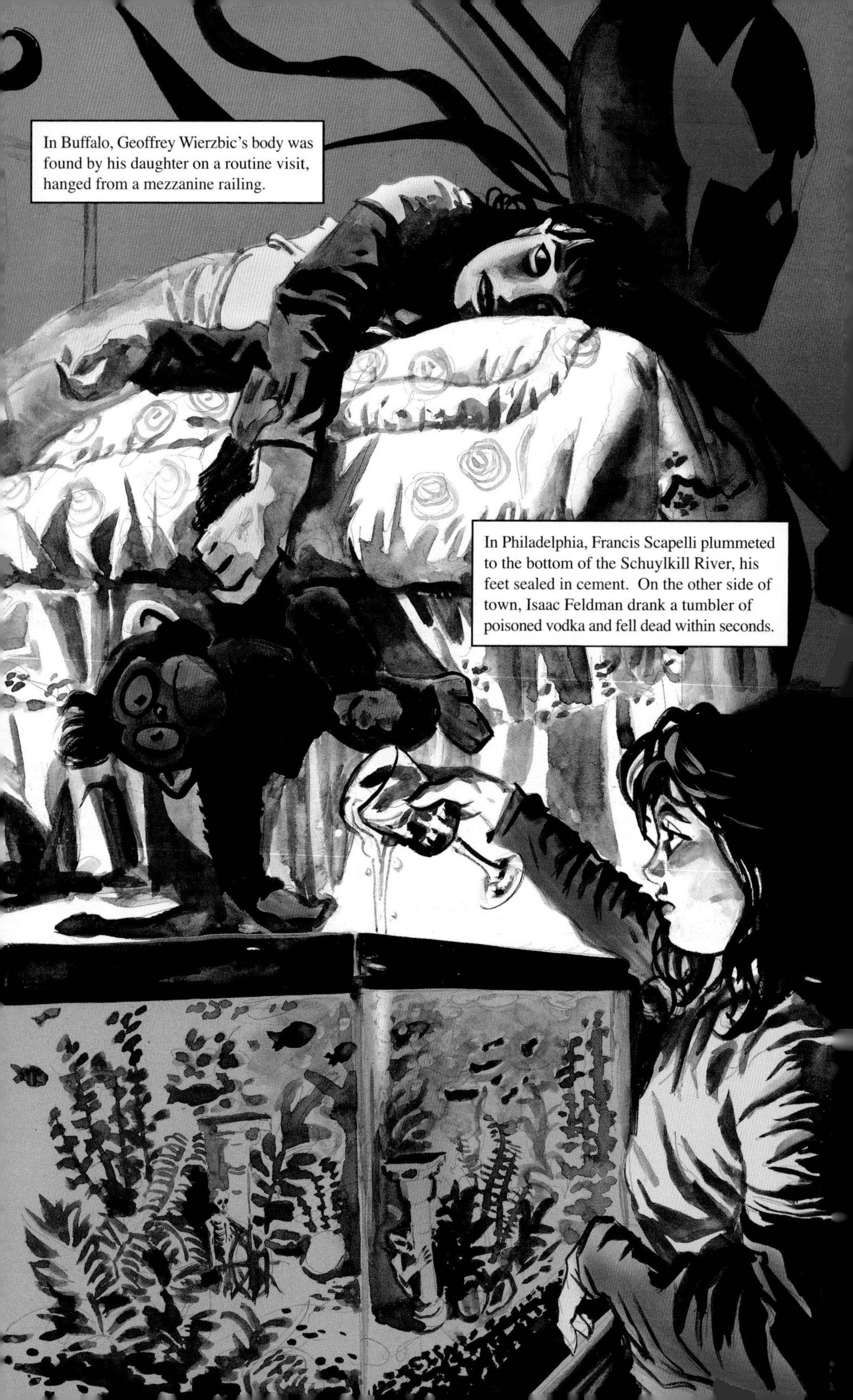
In Buffalo, Geoffrey Wierzbic's body was found by his daughter on a routine visit, hanged from a mezzanine railing.
In Philadelphia, Francis Scapelli plummeted to the bottom of the Schuylkill River, his feet sealed in cement. On the other side of town, Isaac Feldman drank a tumbler of poisoned vodka and fell dead within seconds.

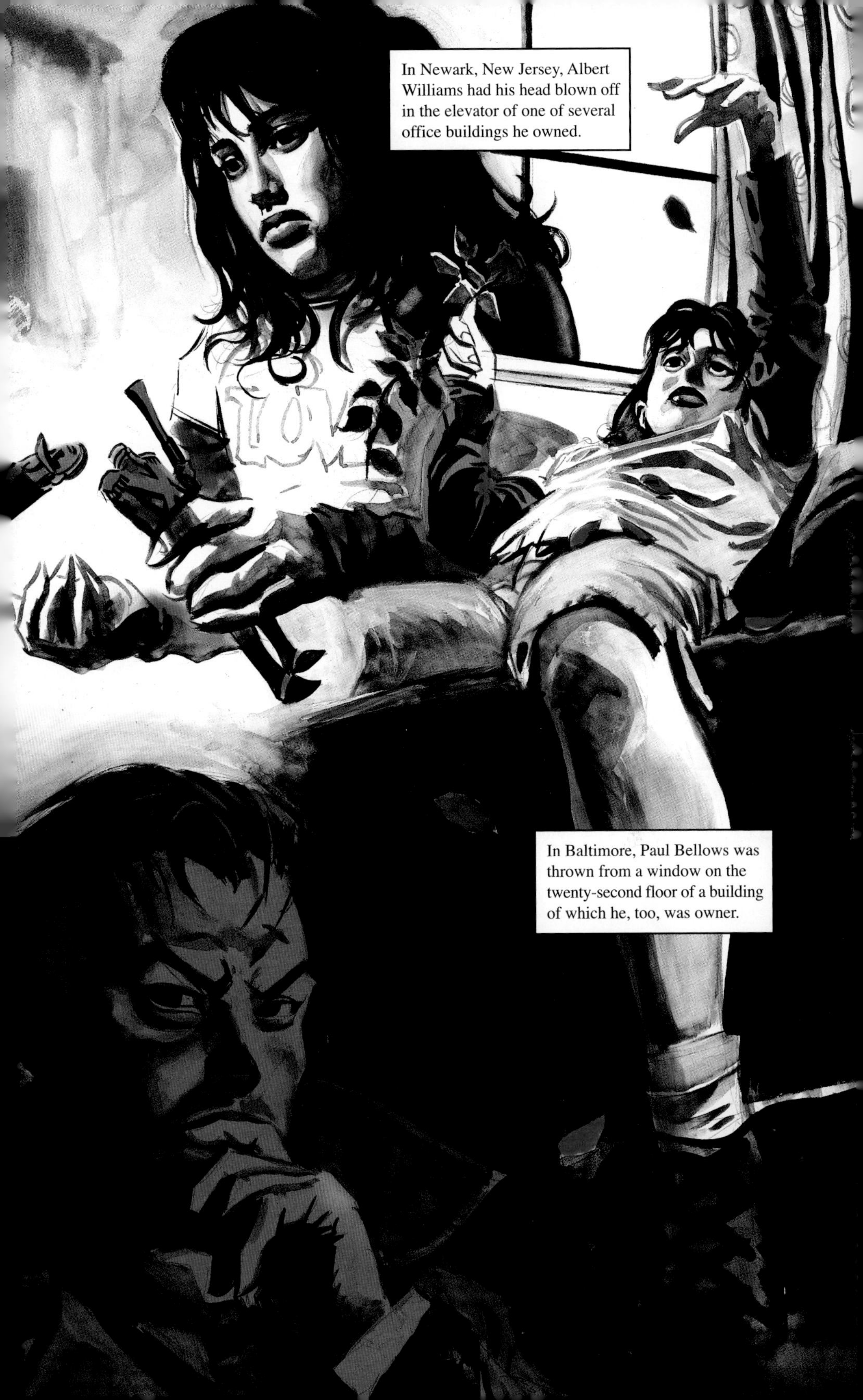
In Newark, New Jersey, Albert Williams had his head blown off in the elevator of one of several office buildings he owned.
LOV
In Baltimore, Paul Bellows was thrown from a window on the twenty-second floor of a building of which he, too, was owner.

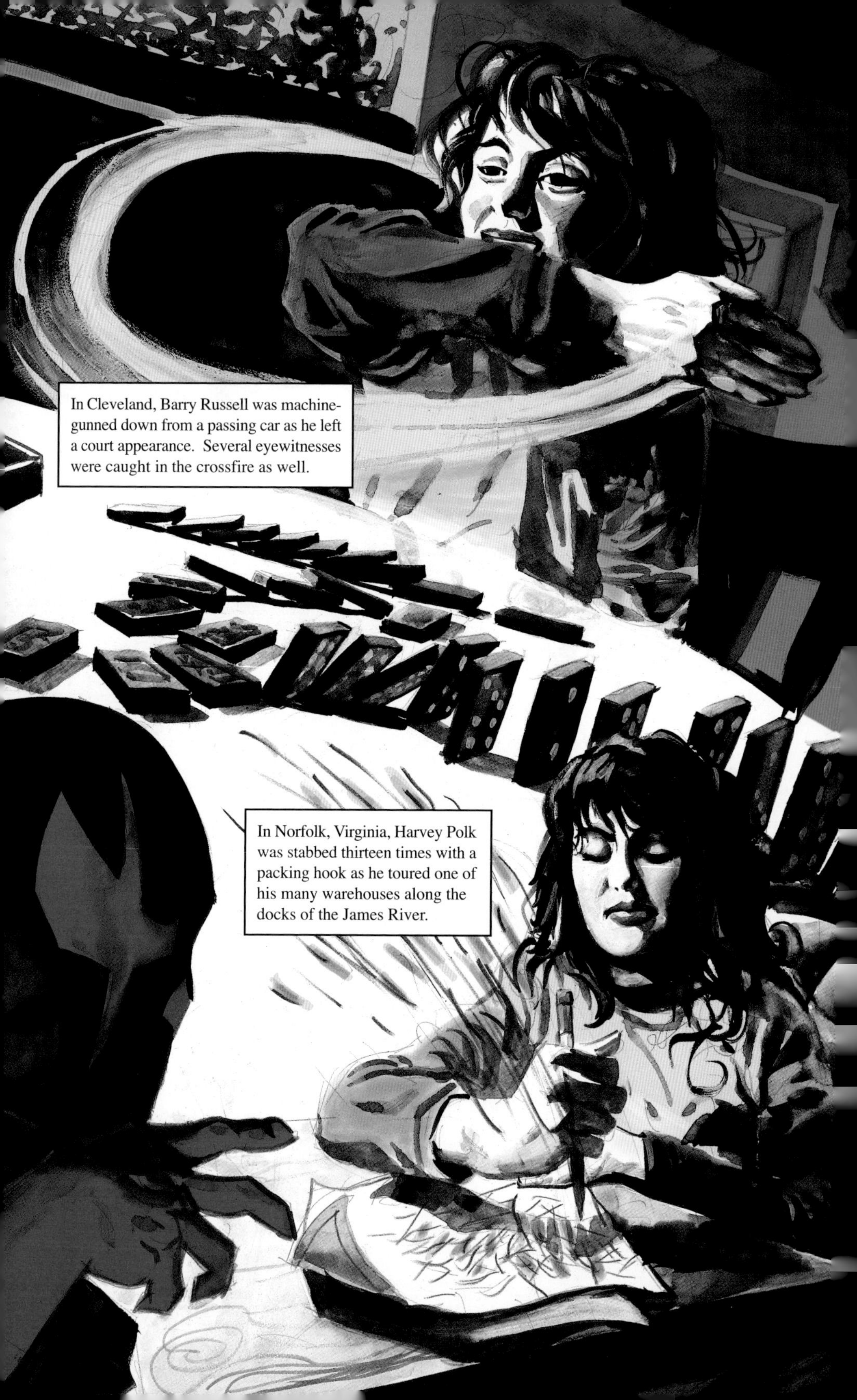
In Cleveland, Barry Russell was machine-gunned down from a passing car as he left a court appearance. Several eyewitnesses were caught in the crossfire as well.
In Norfolk, Virginia, Harvey Polk was stabbed thirteen times with a packing hook as he toured one of his many warehouses along the docks of the James River.

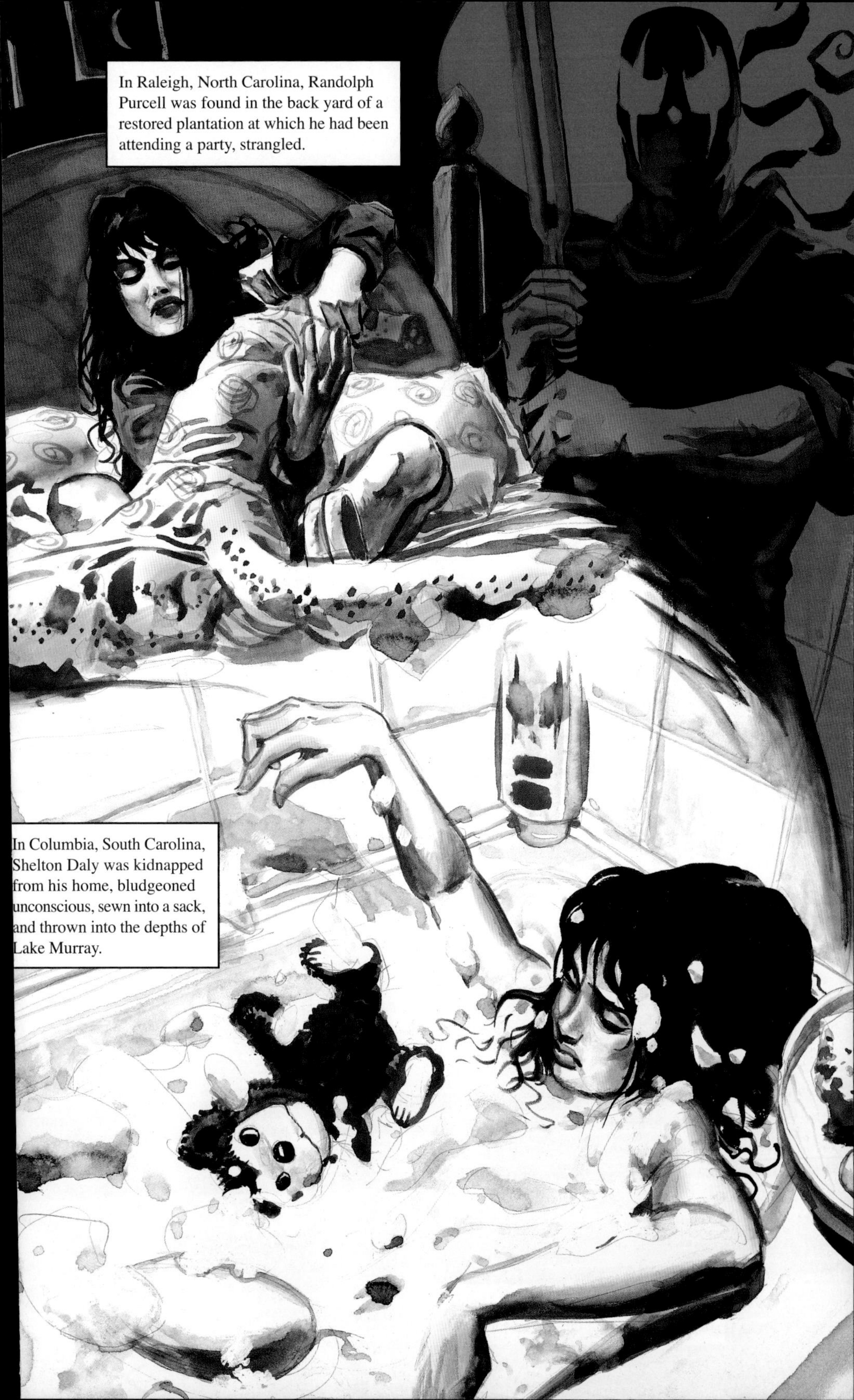
In Raleigh, North Carolina, Randolph Purcell was found in the back yard of a restored plantation at which he had been attending a party, strangled.
In Columbia, South Carolina, Shelton Daly was kidnapped from his home, bludgeoned unconscious, sewn into a sack, and thrown into the depths of Lake Murray.

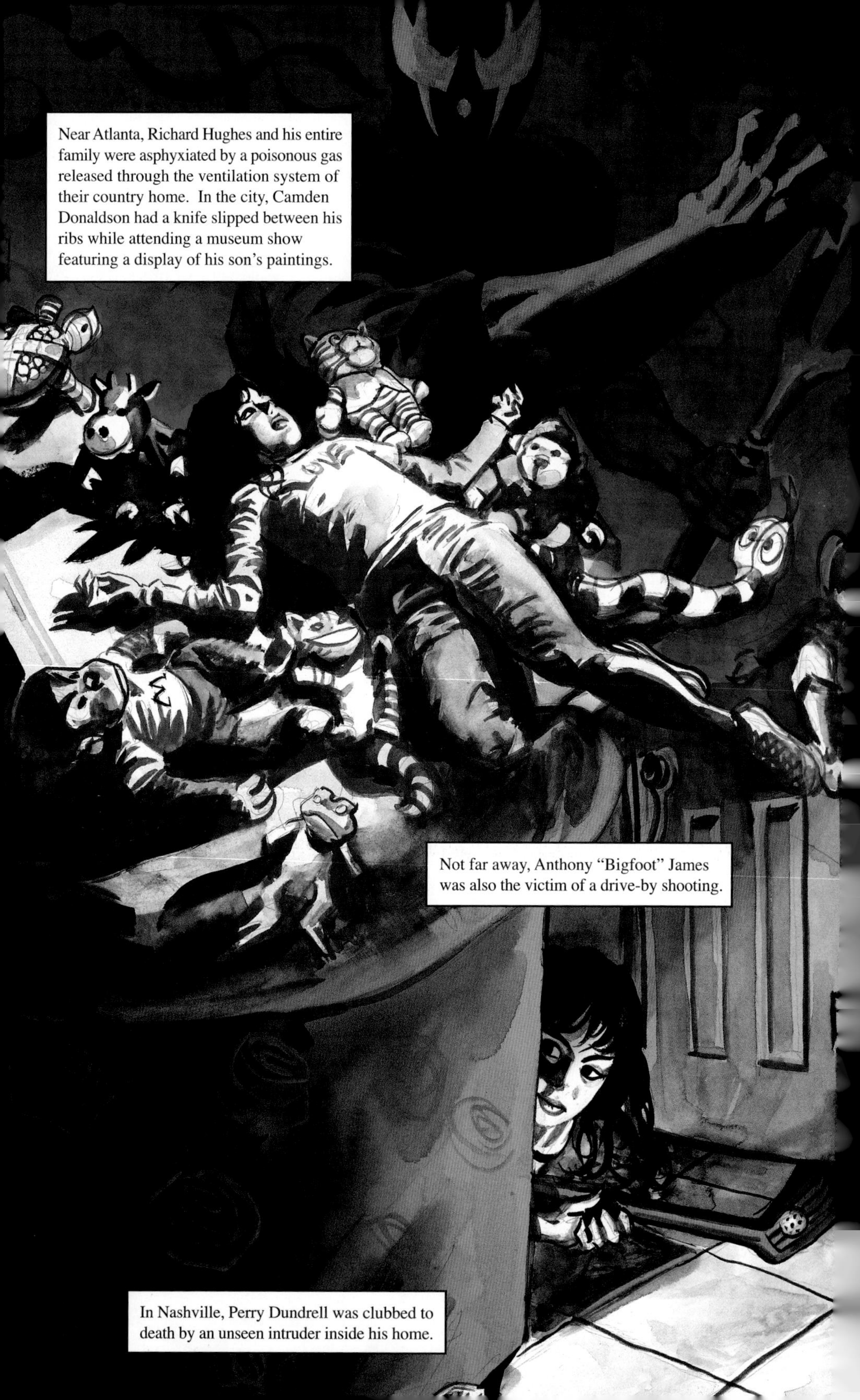

Near Atlanta, Richard Hughes and his entire family were asphyxiated by a poisonous gas released through the ventilation system of their country home. In the city, Camden Donaldson had a knife slipped between his ribs while attending a museum show featuring a display of his son's paintings.
LOVE
Not far away, Anthony "Bigfoot" James was also the victim of a drive-by shooting.
In Nashville, Perry Dundrell was clubbed to death by an unseen intruder inside his home.

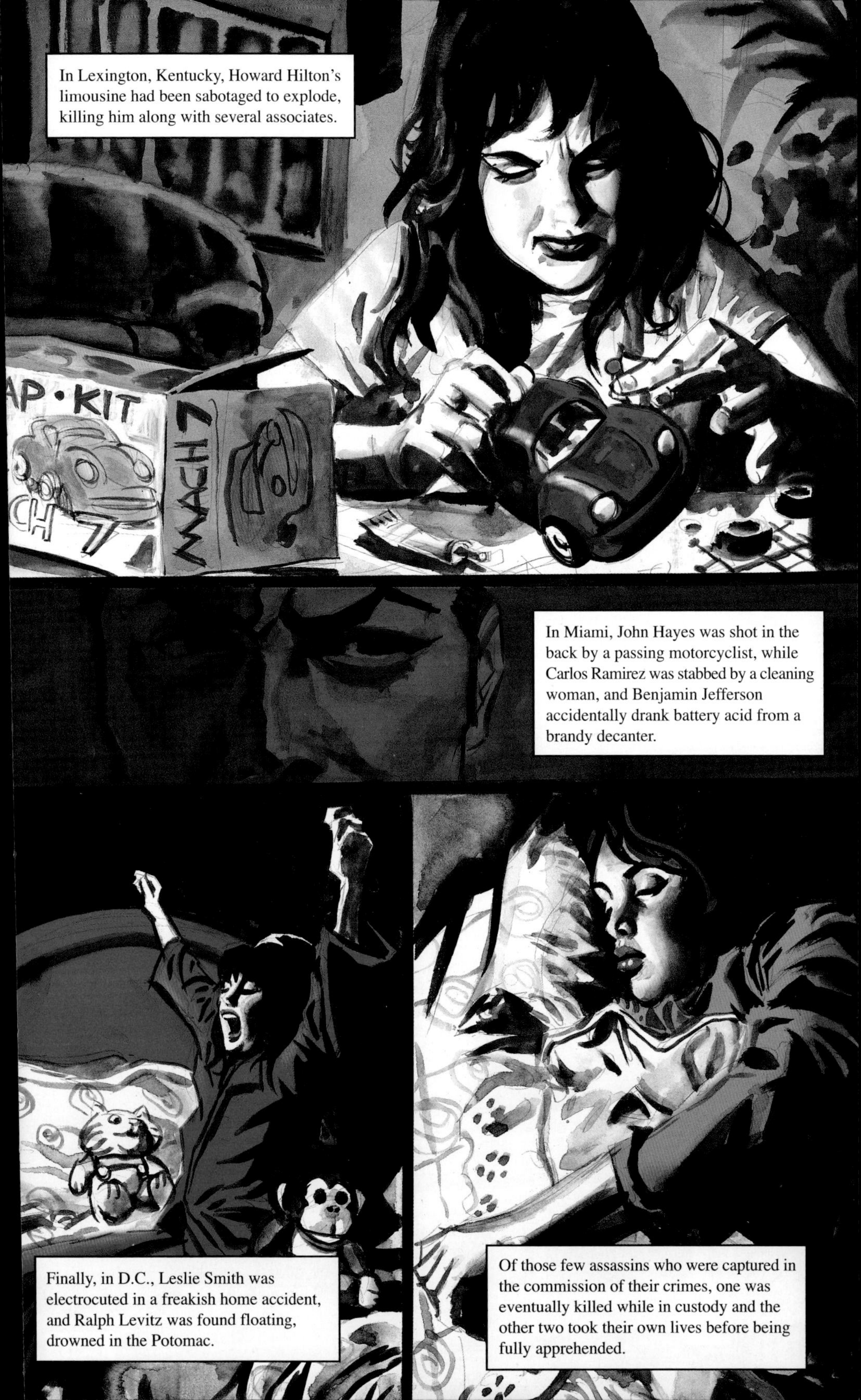
In Lexington, Kentucky, Howard Hilton's limousine had been sabotaged to explode, killing him along with several associates.
In Miami, John Hayes was shot in the back by a passing motorcyclist, while Carlos Ramirez was stabbed by a cleaning woman, and Benjamin Jefferson accidentally drank battery acid from a brandy decanter.
Finally, in D.C., Leslie Smith was electrocuted in a freakish home accident, and Ralph Levitz was found floating, drowned in the Potomac.
Of those few assassins who were captured in the commission of their crimes, one was eventually killed while in custody and the other two took their own lives before being fully apprehended.

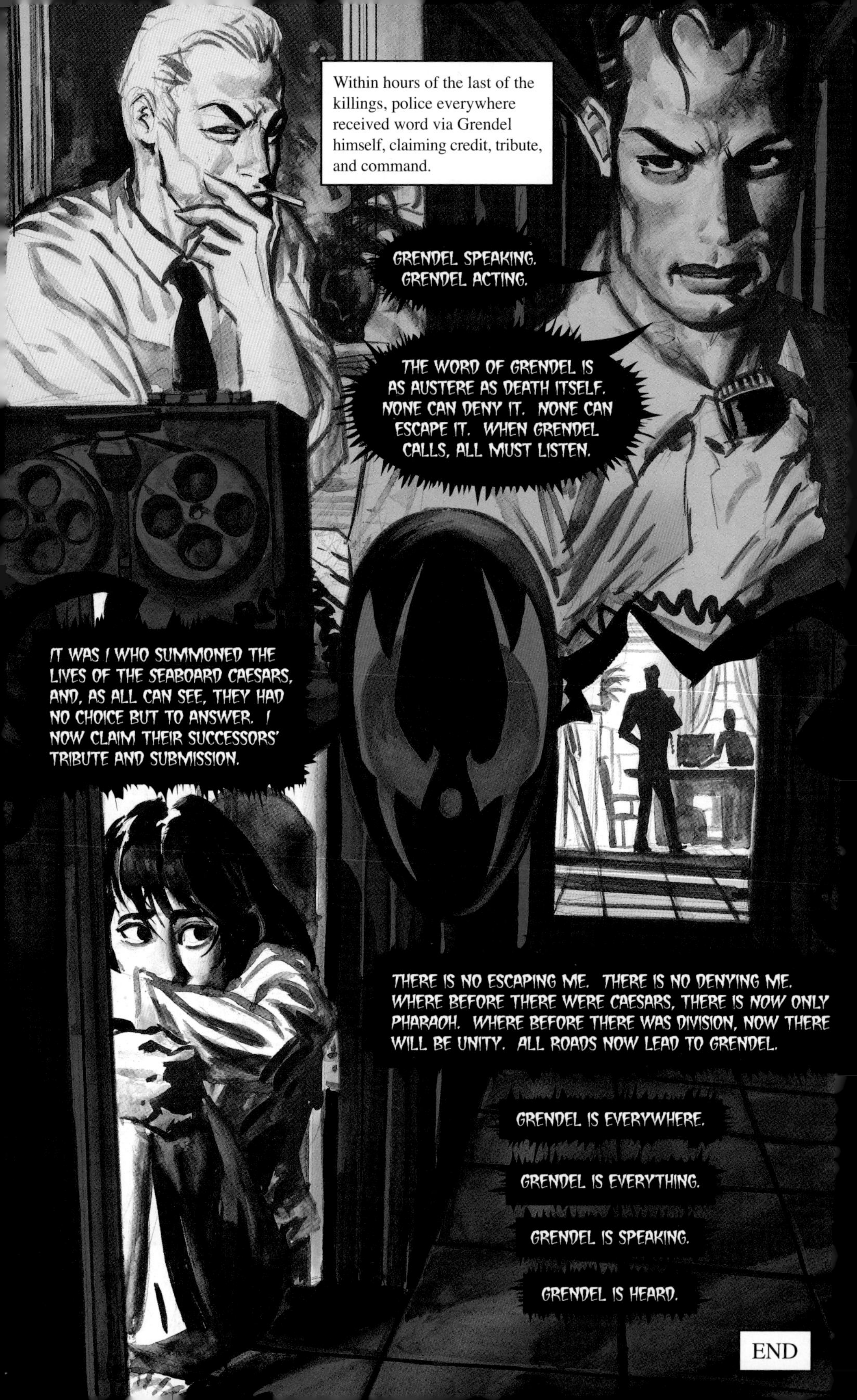

Within hours of the last of the killings, police everywhere received word via Grendel himself, claiming credit, tribute, and command.
GRENDEL SPEAKING. GRENDEL ACTING.
THE WORD OF GRENDEL IS AS AUSTERE AS DEATH ITSELF. NONE CAN DENY IT. NONE CAN ESCAPE IT. WHEN GRENDEL CALLS, ALL MUST LISTEN.
IT WAS I WHO SUMMONED THE LIVES OF THE SEABOARD CAESARS, AND, AS ALL CAN SEE, THEY HAD NO CHOICE BUT TO ANSWER. I NOW CLAIM THEIR SUCCESSORS' TRIBUTE AND SUBMISSION.
THERE IS NO ESCAPING ME. THERE IS NO DENYING ME. WHERE BEFORE THERE WERE CAESARS, THERE IS NOW ONLY PHARAOH. WHERE BEFORE THERE WAS DIVISION, NOW THERE WILL BE UNITY. ALL ROADS NOW LEAD TO GRENDEL.
GRENDEL IS EVERYWHERE.
GRENDEL IS EVERYTHING.
GRENDEL IS SPEAKING.
GRENDEL IS HEARD.
END

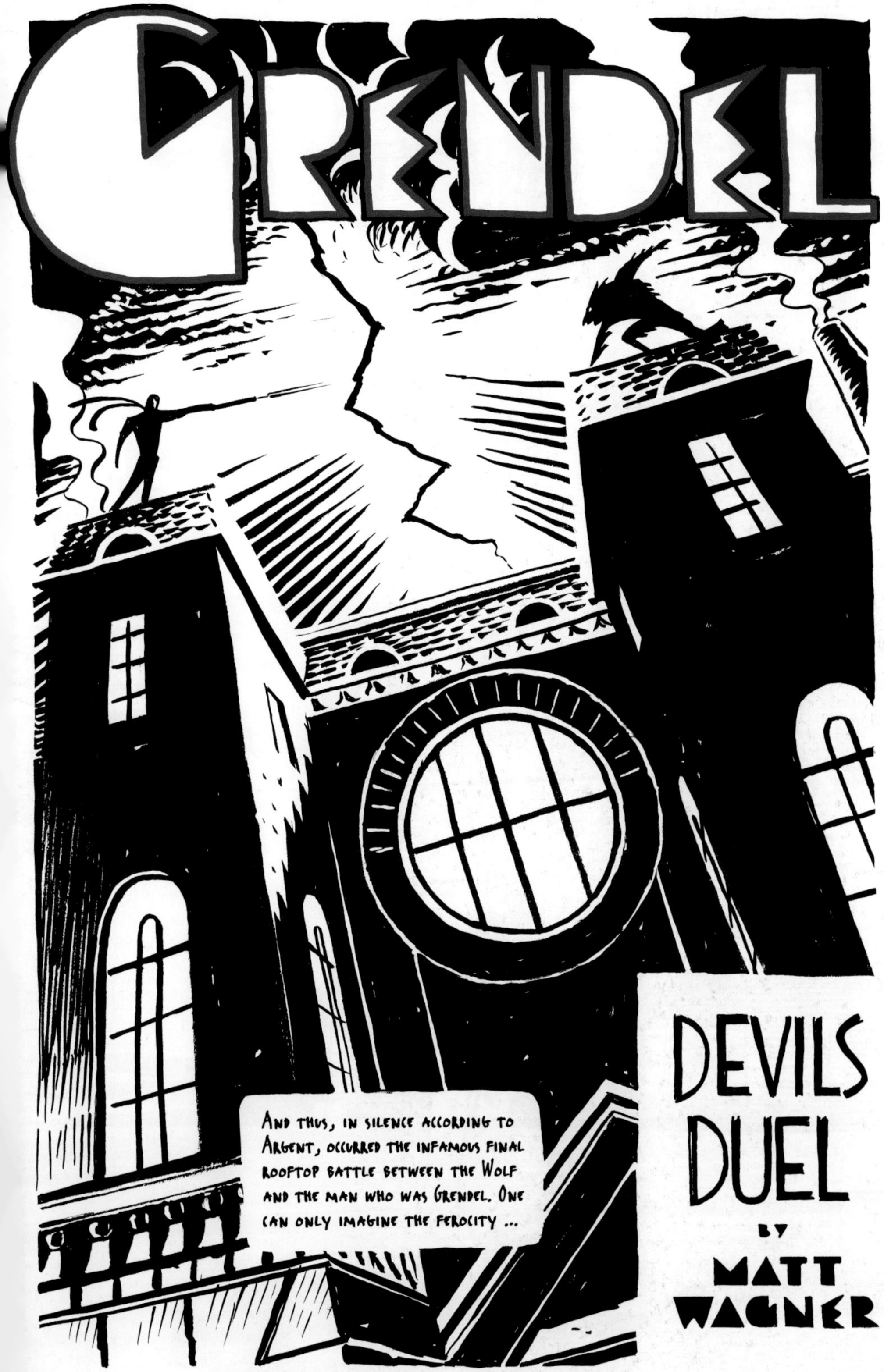
GRENDEL
AND THUS, IN SILENCE ACCORDING TO ARGENT, OCCURRED THE INFAMOUS FINAL ROOFTOP BATTLE BETWEEN THE WOLF AND THE MAN WHO WAS GRENDEL. ONE CAN ONLY IMAGINE THE FEROCITY ...
DEVILS DUEL
BY
MATT WAGNER

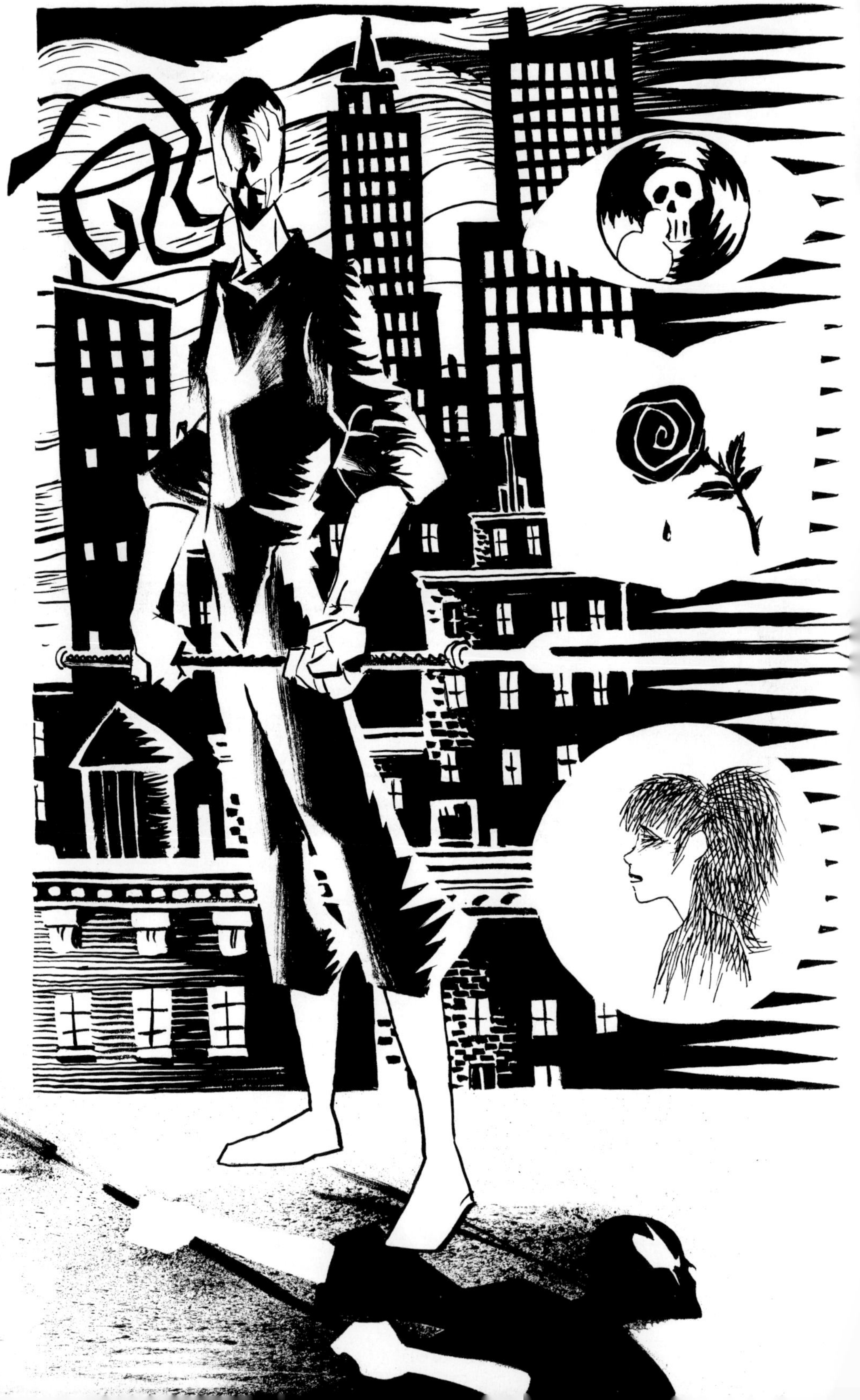

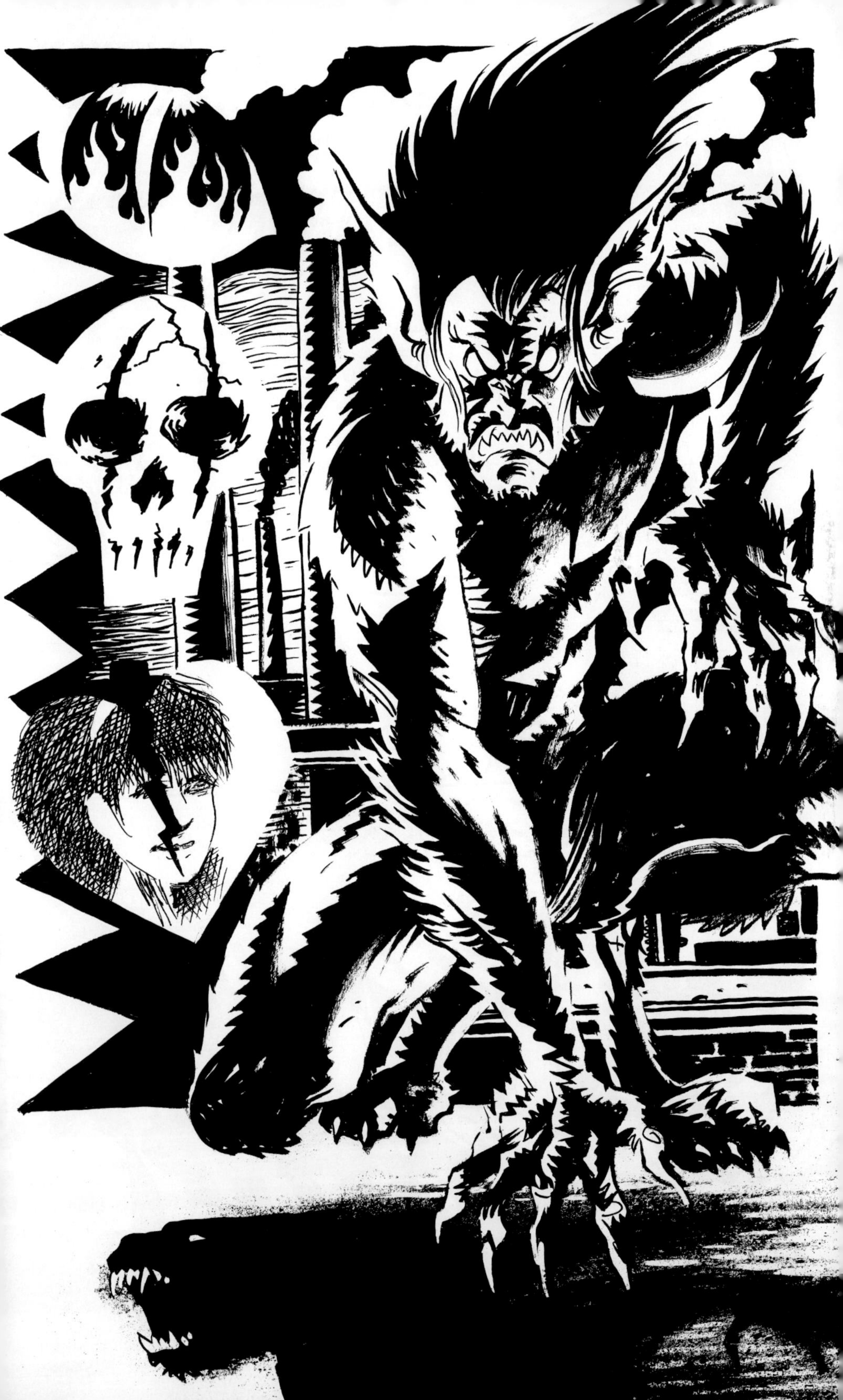

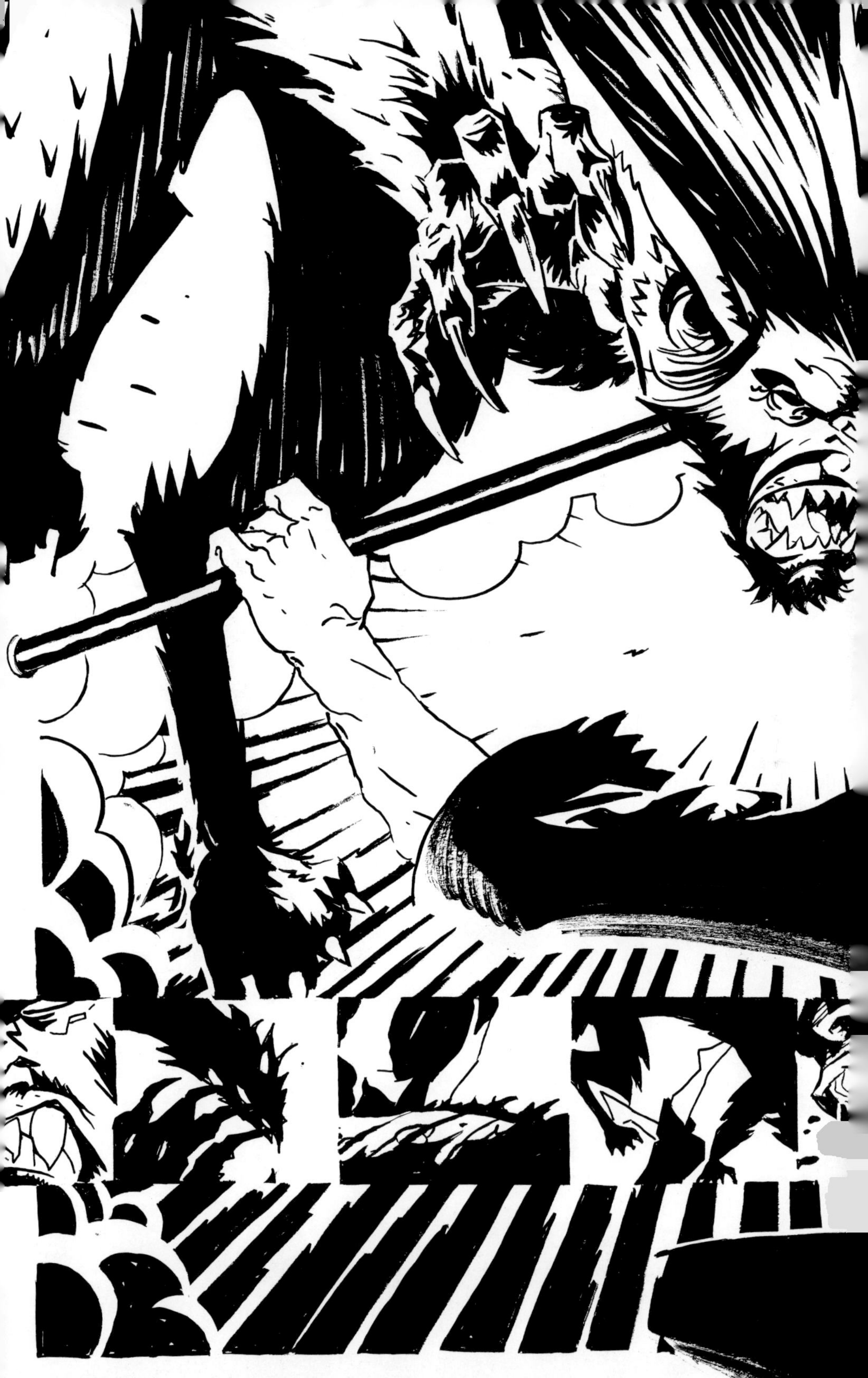

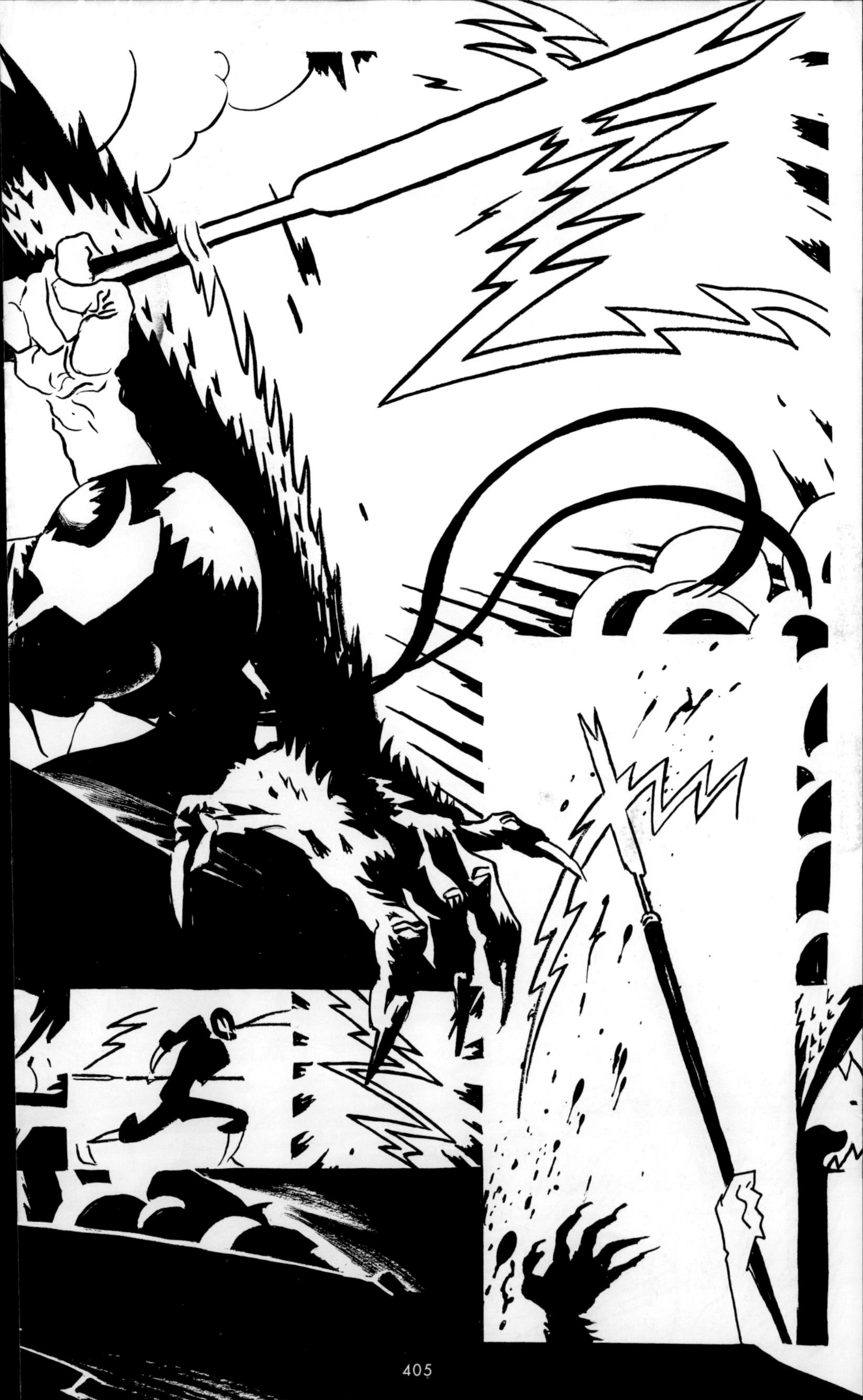

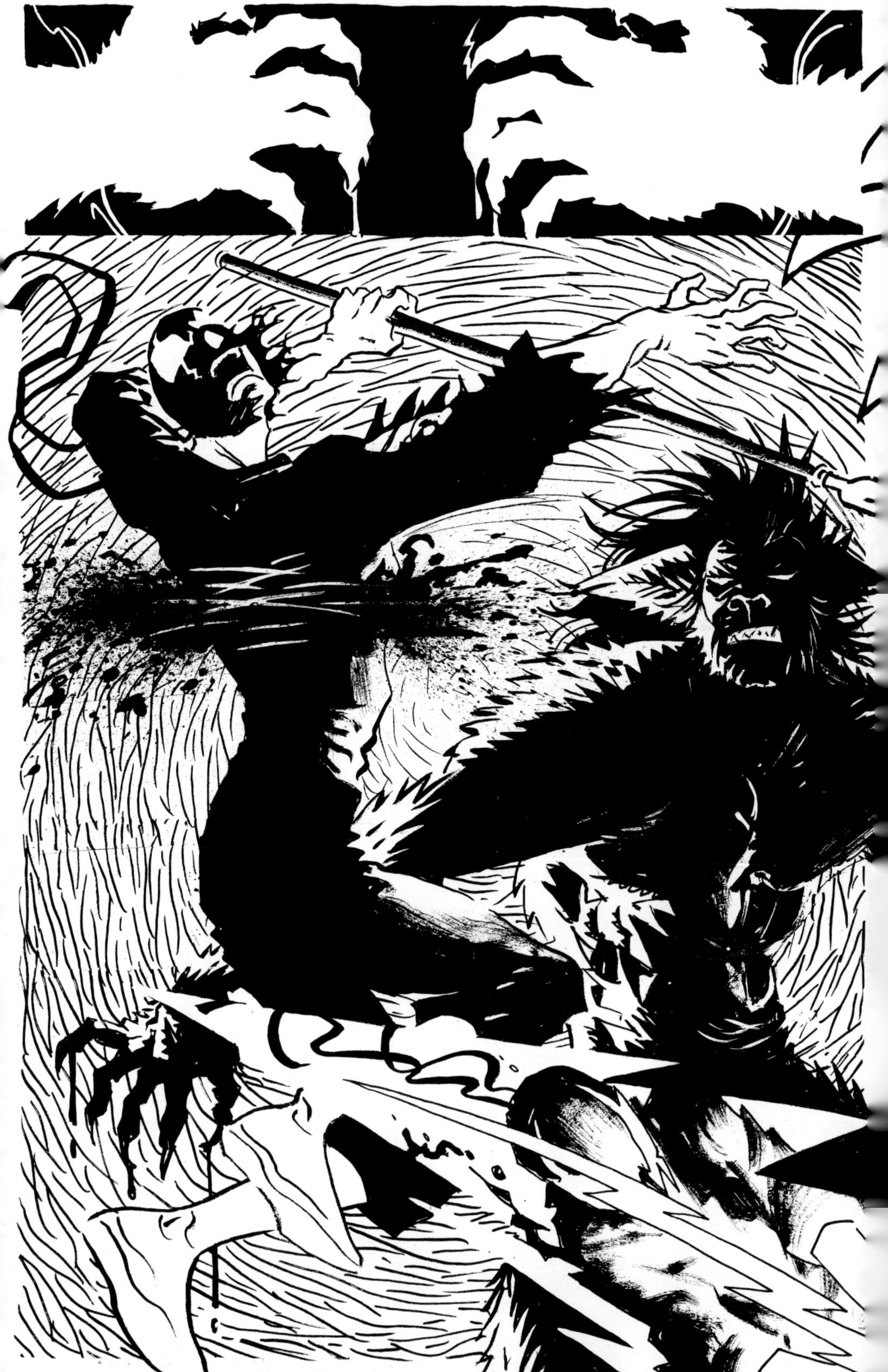

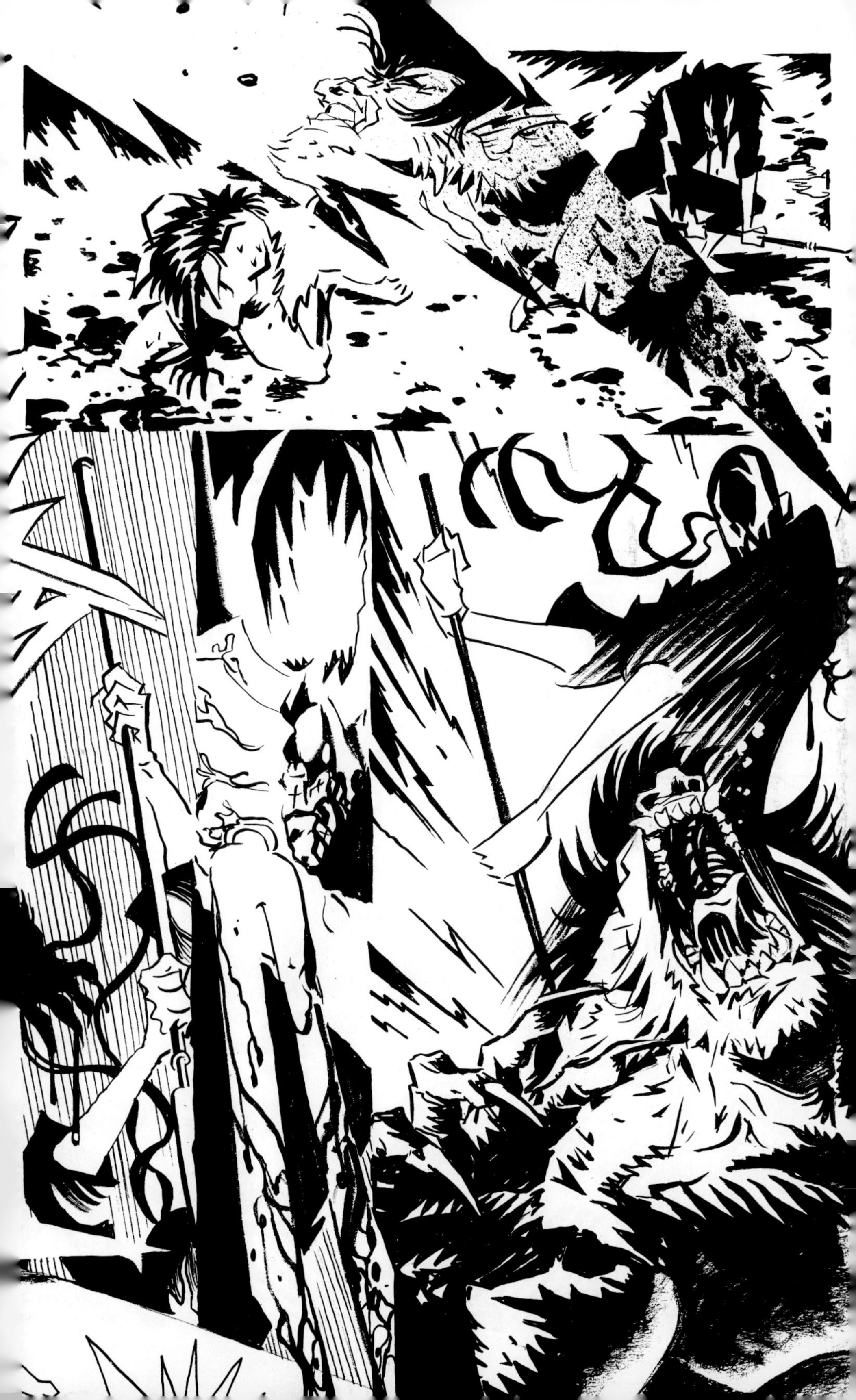

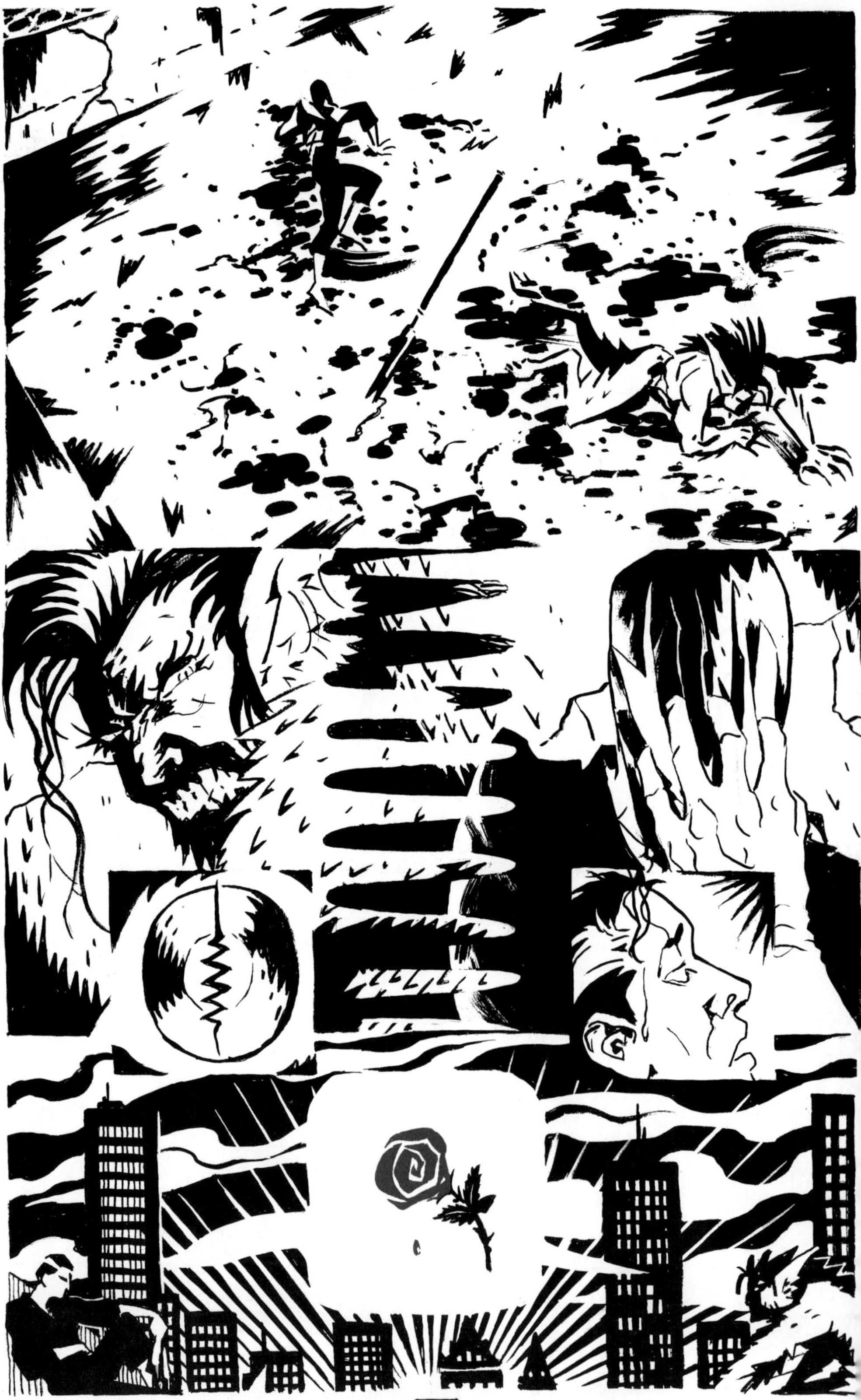

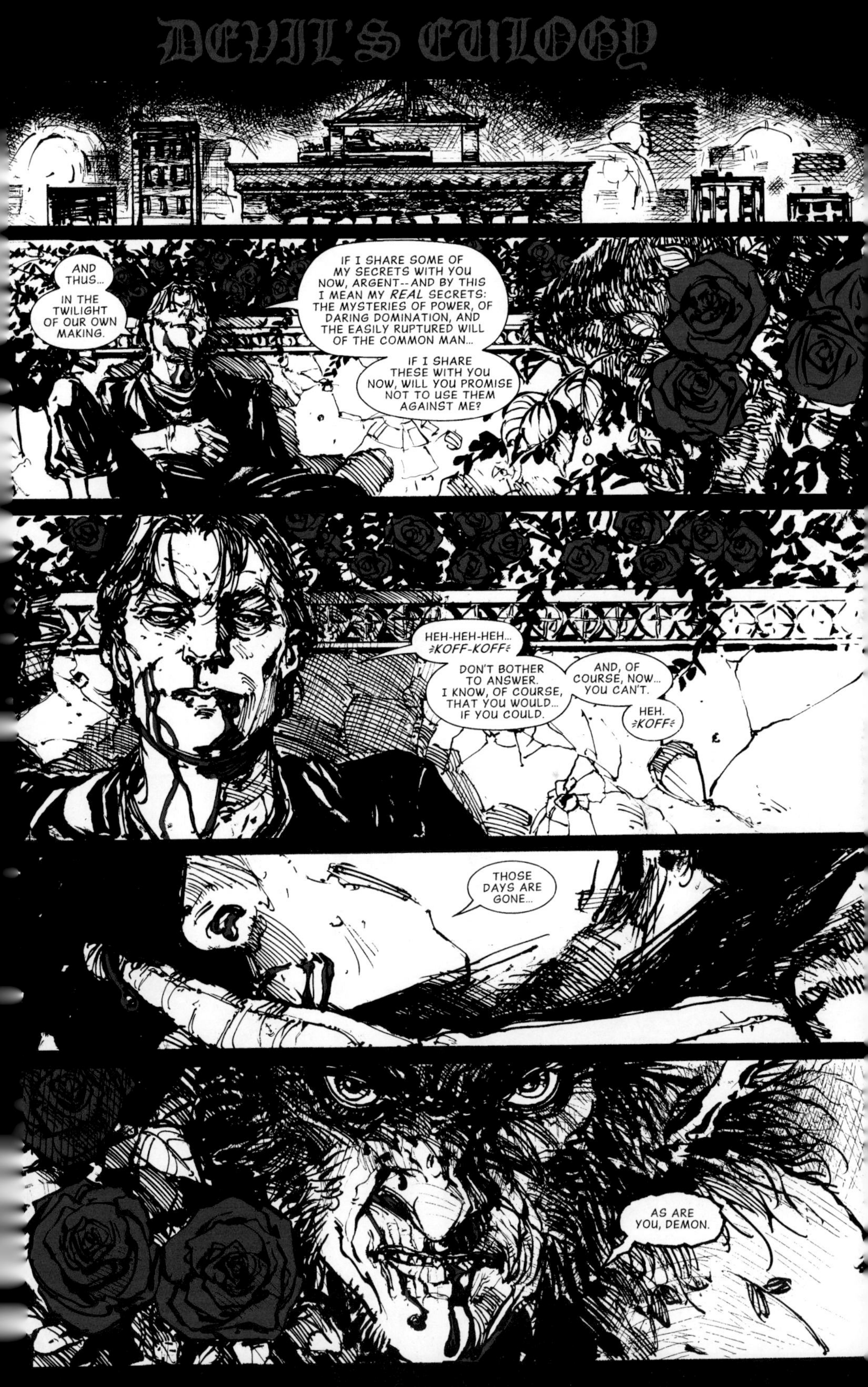
DEVIL'S EULOGY
AND THUS... IN THE TWILIGHT OF OUR OWN MAKING.
IF I SHARE SOME OF MY SECRETS WITH YOU NOW, ARGENT--AND BY THIS I MEAN MY REAL SECRETS: THE MYSTERIES OF POWER, OF DARING DOMINATION, AND THE EASILY RUPTURED WILL OF THE COMMON MAN...
IF I SHARE THESE WITH YOU NOW, WILL YOU PROMISE NOT TO USE THEM AGAINST ME?
HEH-HEH-HEH... KOFF-KOFF
DON'T BOTHER TO ANSWER. I KNOW, OF COURSE, THAT YOU WOULD... IF YOU COULD.
AND, OF COURSE, NOW... YOU CAN'T.
HEH. KOFF
THOSE DAYS ARE GONE...
AS ARE YOU, DEMON.

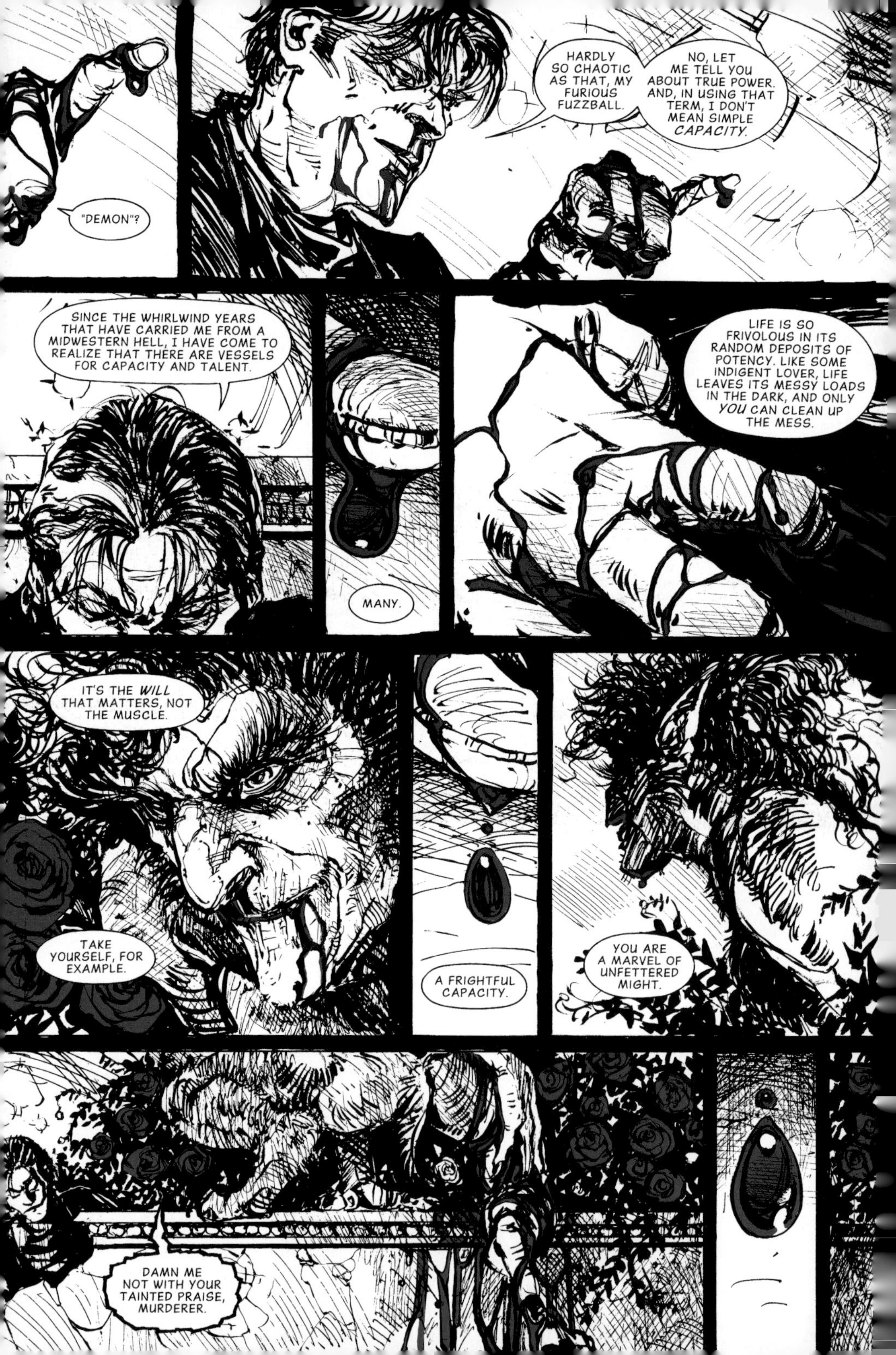
"DEMON"?
HARDLY SO CHAOTIC AS THAT, MY FURIOUS FUZZBALL.
NO, LET ME TELL YOU ABOUT TRUE POWER. AND, IN USING THAT TERM, I DON'T MEAN SIMPLE *CAPACITY.*
SINCE THE WHIRLWIND YEARS THAT HAVE CARRIED ME FROM A MIDWESTERN HELL, I HAVE COME TO REALIZE THAT THERE ARE VESSELS FOR CAPACITY AND TALENT.
MANY.
LIFE IS SO FRIVOLOUS IN ITS RANDOM DEPOSITS OF POTENCY. LIKE SOME INDIGENT LOVER, LIFE LEAVES ITS MESSY LOADS IN THE DARK, AND ONLY *YOU* CAN CLEAN UP THE MESS.
IT'S THE *WILL* THAT MATTERS, NOT THE MUSCLE.
TAKE YOURSELF, FOR EXAMPLE.
A FRIGHTFUL CAPACITY.
YOU ARE A MARVEL OF UNFETTERED MIGHT.
DAMN ME NOT WITH YOUR TAINTED PRAISE, MURDERER.

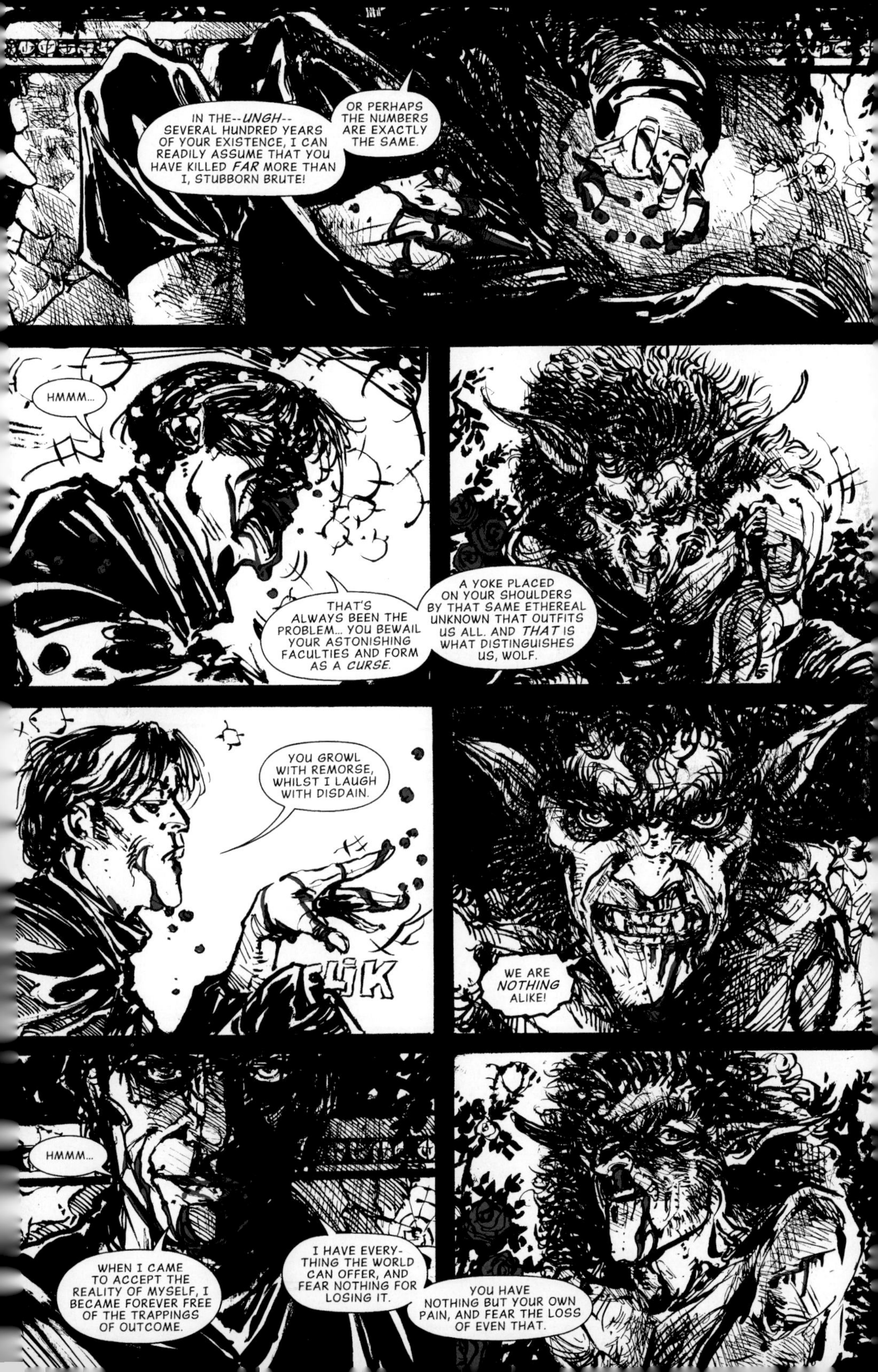
IN THE--UNGH--SEVERAL HUNDRED YEARS OF YOUR EXISTENCE, I CAN READILY ASSUME THAT YOU HAVE KILLED FAR MORE THAN I, STUBBORN BRUTE!
OR PERHAPS THE NUMBERS ARE EXACTLY THE SAME.
HMMM...
THAT'S ALWAYS BEEN THE PROBLEM... YOU BEWAIL YOUR ASTONISHING FACULTIES AND FORM AS A CURSE.
A YOKE PLACED ON YOUR SHOULDERS BY THAT SAME ETHEREAL UNKNOWN THAT OUTFITS US ALL. AND THAT IS WHAT DISTINGUISHES US, WOLF.
YOU GROWL WITH REMORSE, WHILST I LAUGH WITH DISDAIN.
TLIK
WE ARE NOTHING ALIKE!
HMMM...
WHEN I CAME TO ACCEPT THE REALITY OF MYSELF, I BECAME FOREVER FREE OF THE TRAPPINGS OF OUTCOME.
I HAVE EVERY-THING THE WORLD CAN OFFER, AND FEAR NOTHING FOR LOSING IT.
YOU HAVE NOTHING BUT YOUR OWN PAIN, AND FEAR THE LOSS OF EVEN THAT.

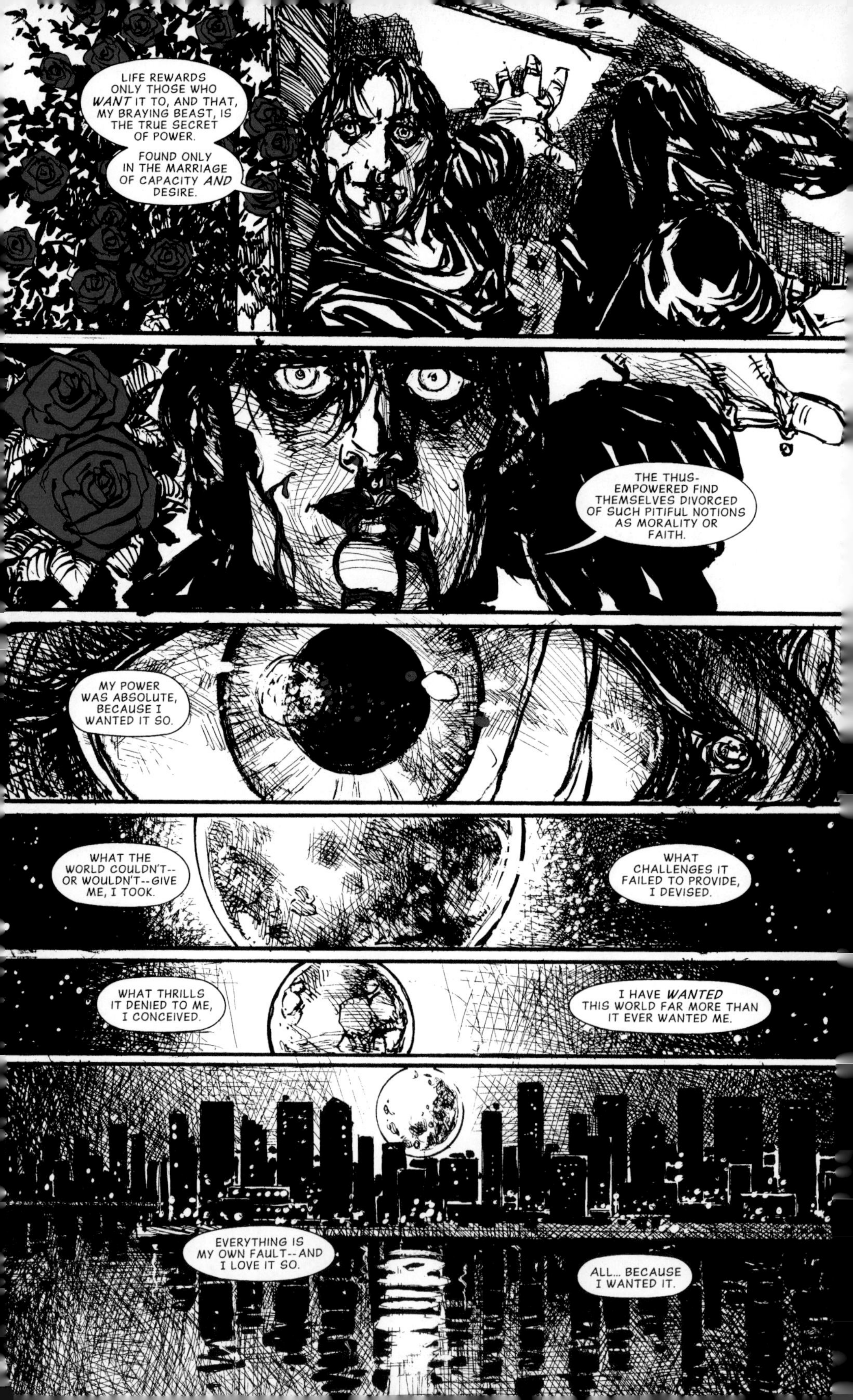
LIFE REWARDS ONLY THOSE WHO WANT IT TO, AND THAT, MY BRAYING BEAST, IS THE TRUE SECRET OF POWER.
FOUND ONLY IN THE MARRIAGE OF CAPACITY AND DESIRE.
THE THUS-EMPOWERED FIND THEMSELVES DIVORCED OF SUCH PITIFUL NOTIONS AS MORALITY OR FAITH.
MY POWER WAS ABSOLUTE, BECAUSE I WANTED IT SO.
WHAT THE WORLD COULDN'T--OR WOULDN'T--GIVE ME, I TOOK.
WHAT CHALLENGES IT FAILED TO PROVIDE, I DEVISED.
WHAT THRILLS IT DENIED TO ME, I CONCEIVED.
I HAVE WANTED THIS WORLD FAR MORE THAN IT EVER WANTED ME.
EVERYTHING IS MY OWN FAULT--AND I LOVE IT SO.
ALL... BECAUSE I WANTED IT.

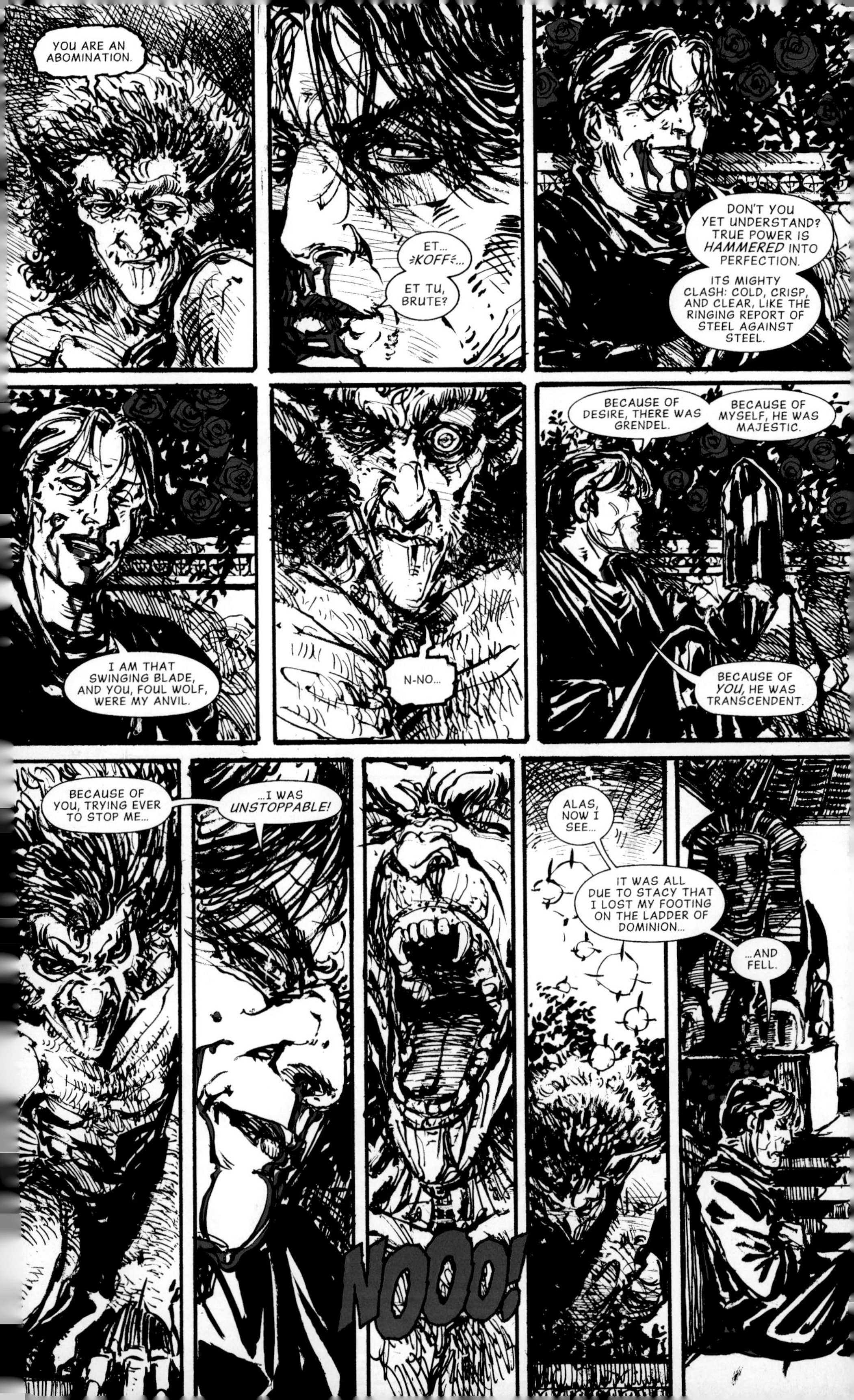
YOU ARE AN ABOMINATION.
ET... *KOFF*...
ET TU, BRUTE?
DON'T YOU YET UNDERSTAND? TRUE POWER IS *HAMMERED* INTO PERFECTION.
ITS MIGHTY CLASH: COLD, CRISP, AND CLEAR, LIKE THE RINGING REPORT OF STEEL AGAINST STEEL.
I AM THAT SWINGING BLADE, AND YOU, FOUL WOLF, WERE MY ANVIL.
N-NO...
BECAUSE OF DESIRE, THERE WAS GRENDEL.
BECAUSE OF MYSELF, HE WAS MAJESTIC.
BECAUSE OF *YOU,* HE WAS TRANSCENDENT.
BECAUSE OF YOU, TRYING EVER TO STOP ME...
...I WAS *UNSTOPPABLE!*
NOOO!
ALAS, NOW I SEE...
IT WAS ALL DUE TO STACY THAT I LOST MY FOOTING ON THE LADDER OF DOMINION...
...AND FELL.

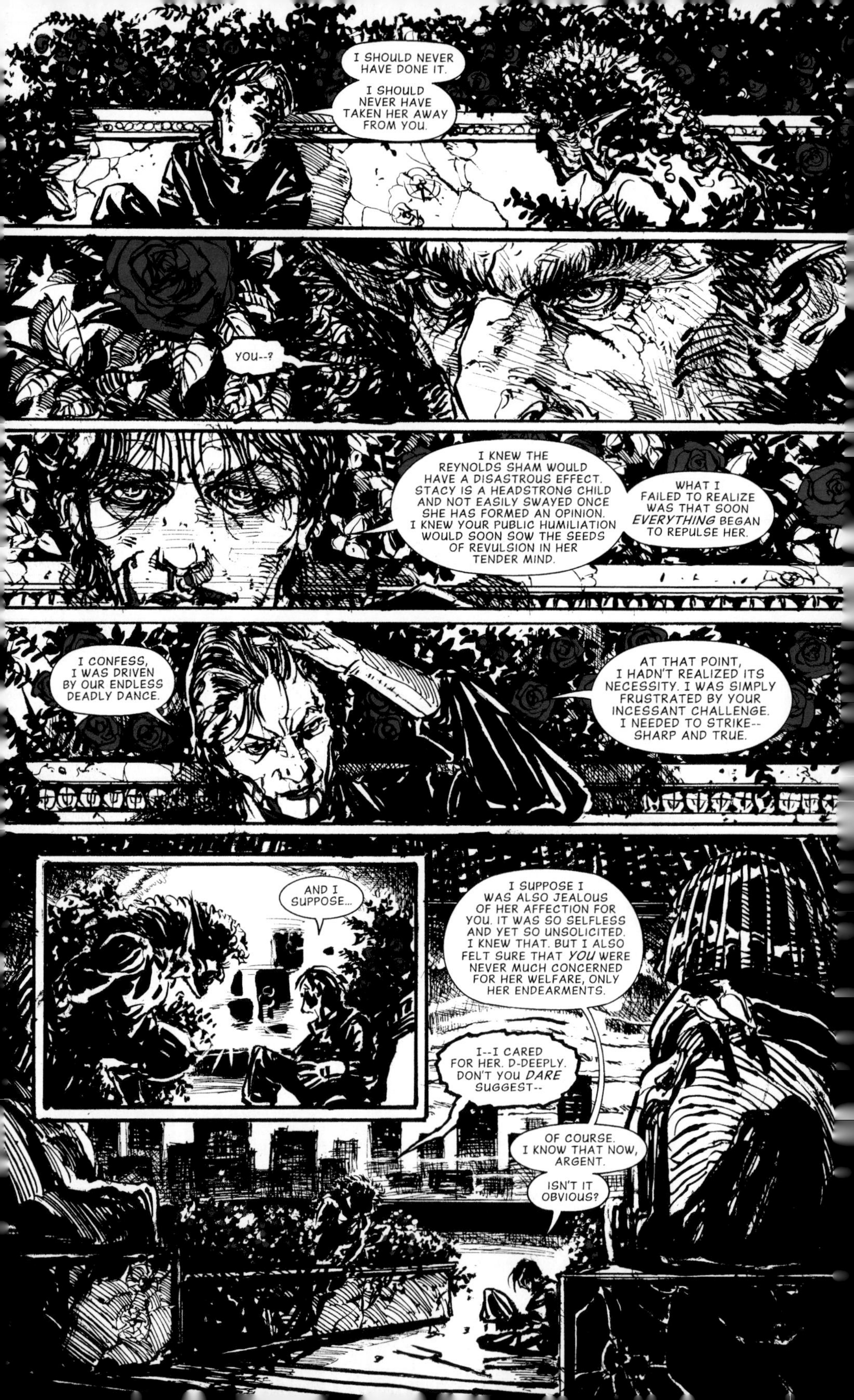
I SHOULD NEVER HAVE DONE IT.
I SHOULD NEVER HAVE TAKEN HER AWAY FROM YOU.
YOU--?
I KNEW THE REYNOLDS SHAM WOULD HAVE A DISASTROUS EFFECT. STACY IS A HEADSTRONG CHILD AND NOT EASILY SWAYED ONCE SHE HAS FORMED AN OPINION. I KNEW YOUR PUBLIC HUMILIATION WOULD SOON SOW THE SEEDS OF REVULSION IN HER TENDER MIND.
WHAT I FAILED TO REALIZE WAS THAT SOON *EVERYTHING* BEGAN TO REPULSE HER.
I CONFESS, I WAS DRIVEN BY OUR ENDLESS DEADLY DANCE.
AT THAT POINT, I HADN'T REALIZED ITS NECESSITY. I WAS SIMPLY FRUSTRATED BY YOUR INCESSANT CHALLENGE. I NEEDED TO STRIKE-- SHARP AND TRUE.
AND I SUPPOSE...
I SUPPOSE I WAS ALSO JEALOUS OF HER AFFECTION FOR YOU. IT WAS SO SELFLESS AND YET SO UNSOLICITED. I KNEW THAT. BUT I ALSO FELT SURE THAT *YOU* WERE NEVER MUCH CONCERNED FOR HER WELFARE, ONLY HER ENDEARMENTS.
I--I CARED FOR HER. D-DEEPLY. DON'T YOU *DARE* SUGGEST--
OF COURSE. I KNOW THAT NOW, ARGENT.
ISN'T IT OBVIOUS?

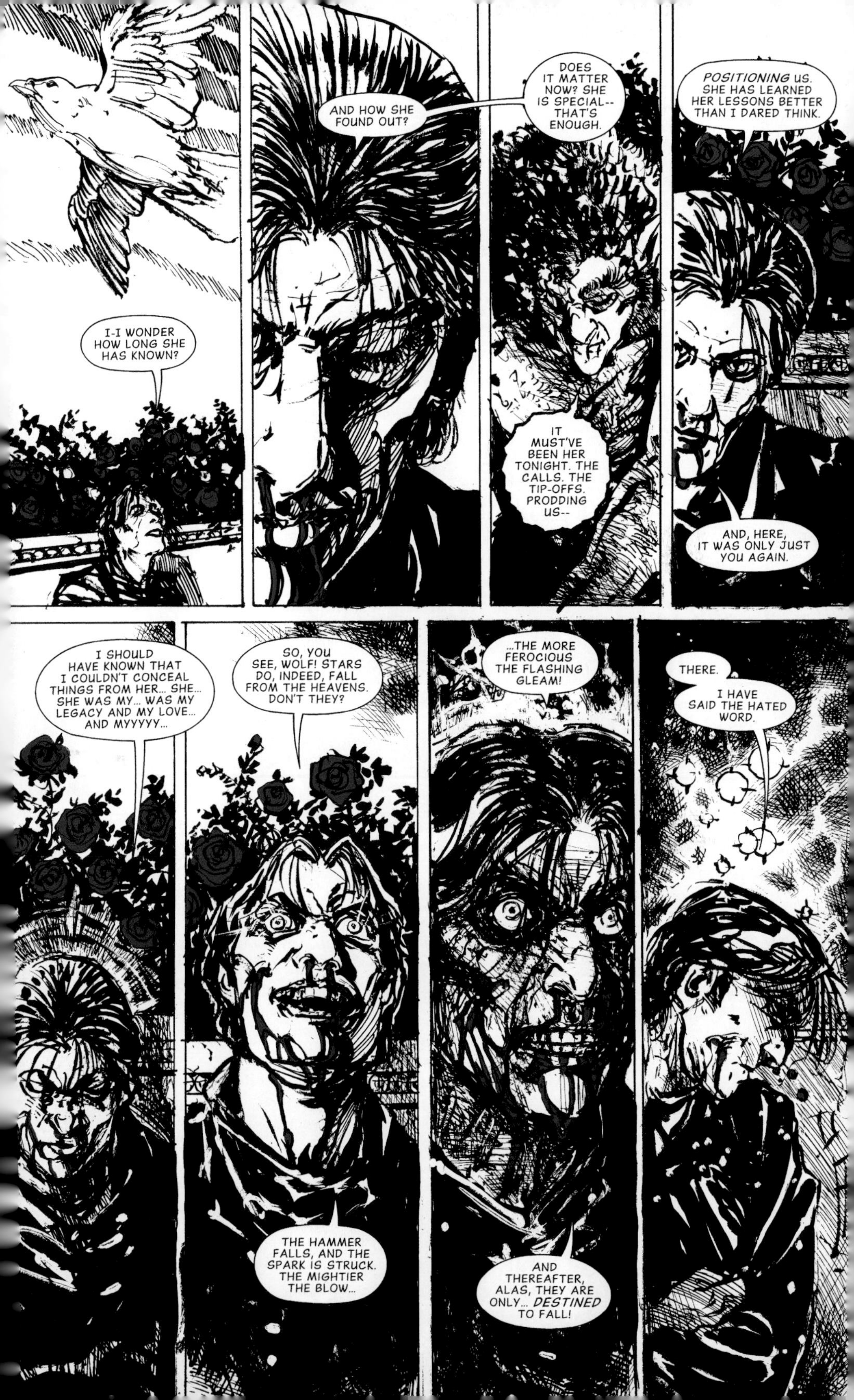
I-I WONDER HOW LONG SHE HAS KNOWN?
AND HOW SHE FOUND OUT?
DOES IT MATTER NOW? SHE IS SPECIAL-- THAT'S ENOUGH.
IT MUST'VE BEEN HER TONIGHT. THE CALLS. THE TIP-OFFS. PRODDING US--
POSITIONING US. SHE HAS LEARNED HER LESSONS BETTER THAN I DARED THINK.
AND, HERE, IT WAS ONLY JUST YOU AGAIN.
I SHOULD HAVE KNOWN THAT I COULDN'T CONCEAL THINGS FROM HER... SHE... SHE WAS MY... WAS MY LEGACY AND MY LOVE... AND MYYYYY...
SO, YOU SEE, WOLF! STARS DO, INDEED, FALL FROM THE HEAVENS. DON'T THEY?
THE HAMMER FALLS, AND THE SPARK IS STRUCK. THE MIGHTIER THE BLOW...
...THE MORE FEROCIOUS THE FLASHING GLEAM!
AND THEREAFTER, ALAS, THEY ARE ONLY... DESTINED TO FALL!
THERE.
I HAVE SAID THE HATED WORD.

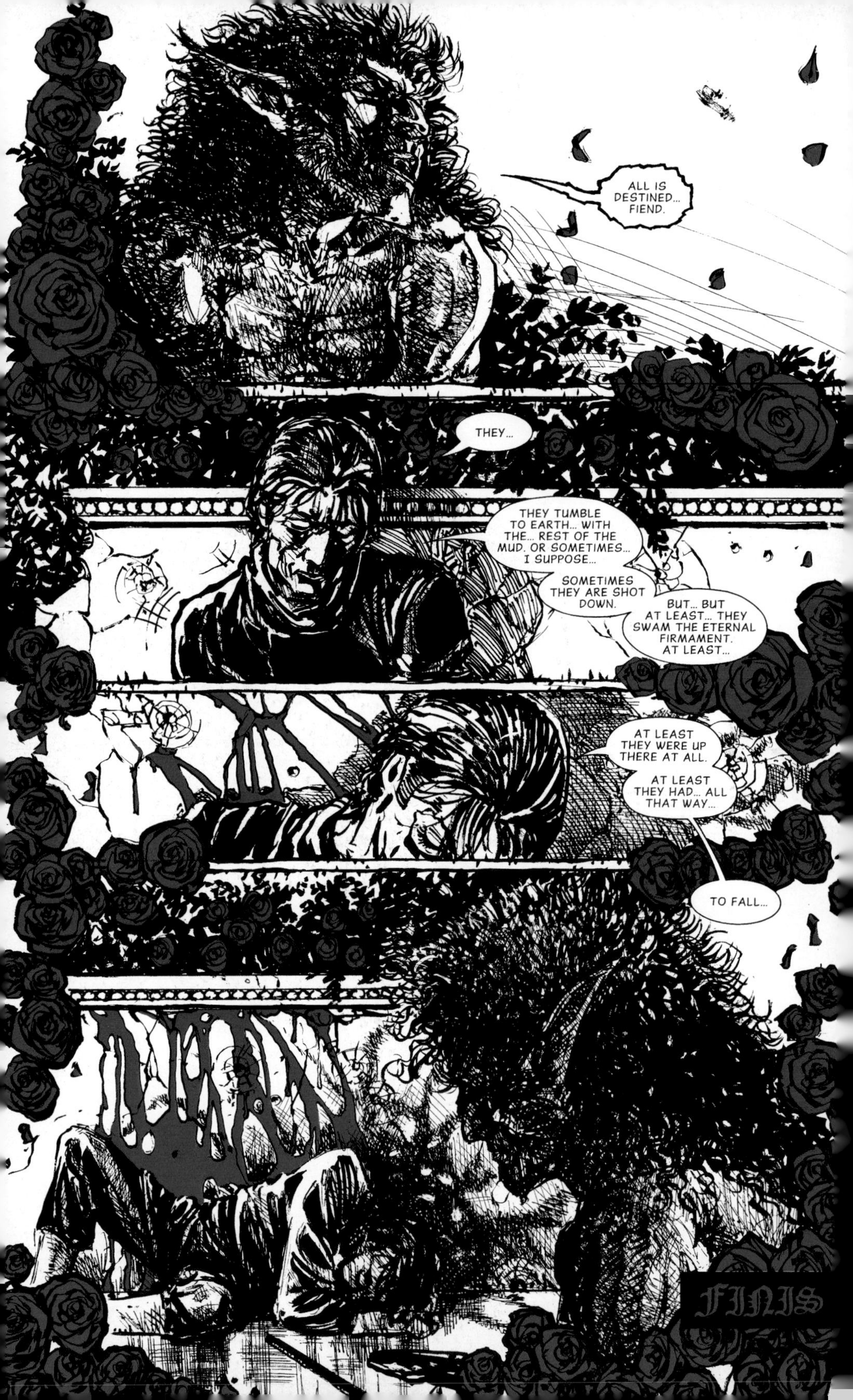
ALL IS DESTINED... FIEND.
THEY...
THEY TUMBLE TO EARTH... WITH THE... REST OF THE MUD. OR SOMETIMES... I SUPPOSE...
SOMETIMES THEY ARE SHOT DOWN.
BUT... BUT AT LEAST... THEY SWAM THE ETERNAL FIRMAMENT. AT LEAST...
AT LEAST THEY WERE UP THERE AT ALL.
AT LEAST THEY HAD... ALL THAT WAY...
TO FALL...
FINIS

DÉVIL, DEED, DÉNOUEMENT

Not so very long ago,
Back when it all began,
There stood a most exceptional
Yet borderline young man.
Alone and undirected,
He longed to strike and shine,
'Til something took hold of his
Fertile, ripe, young mind.

'Cuz the devil don't care
What you need or want.
It's only Devil, Deed,
And Dénouement.

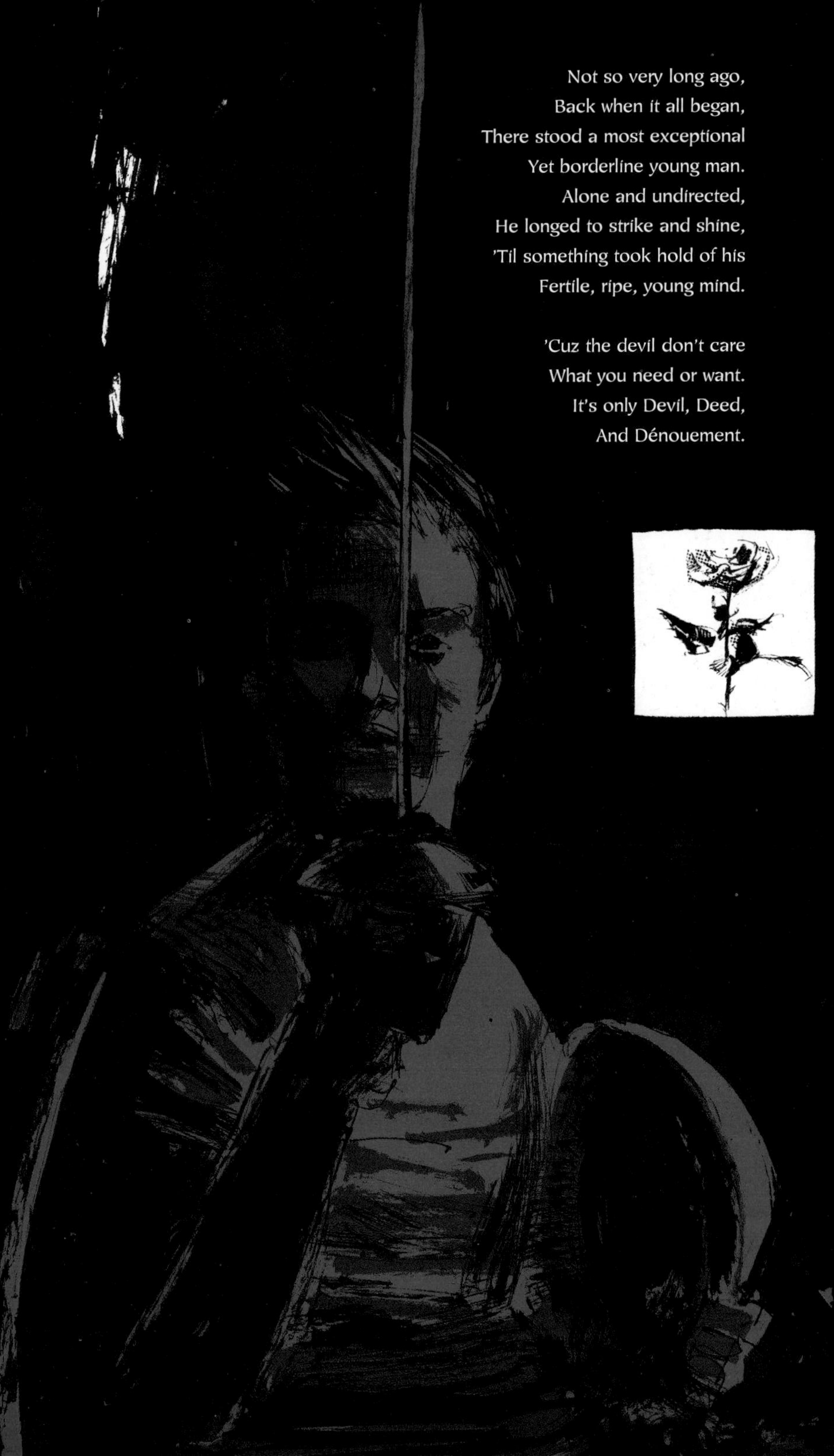

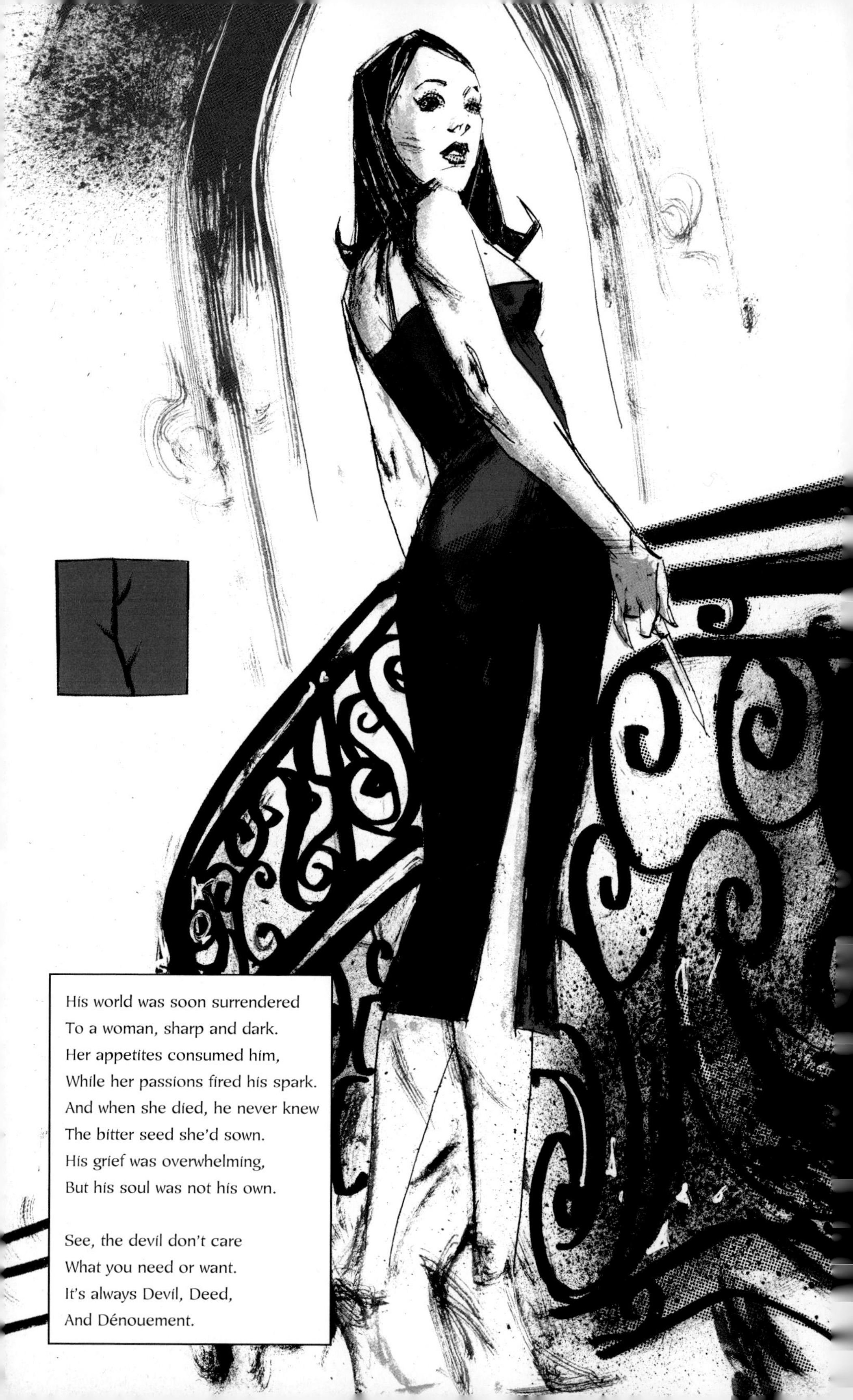
His world was soon surrendered
To a woman, sharp and dark.
Her appetites consumed him,
While her passions fired his spark.
And when she died, he never knew
The bitter seed she'd sown.
His grief was overwhelming,
But his soul was not his own.

See, the devil don't care
What you need or want.
It's always Devil, Deed,
And Dénouement.

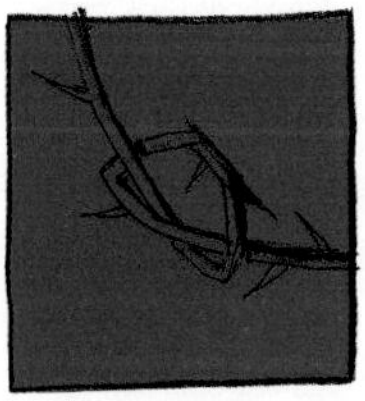

Then soon emerged a different life,
One of wealth and fame.
The hunter rose and set his sights
On vain and vapid game.
They fawned on him and ate his words,
Such sport was much too plain.
None of them quite realized
What lay hidden in his cane.

Now, the devil don't care
What you need or want.
He's into Devil, Deed,
And Dénouement.

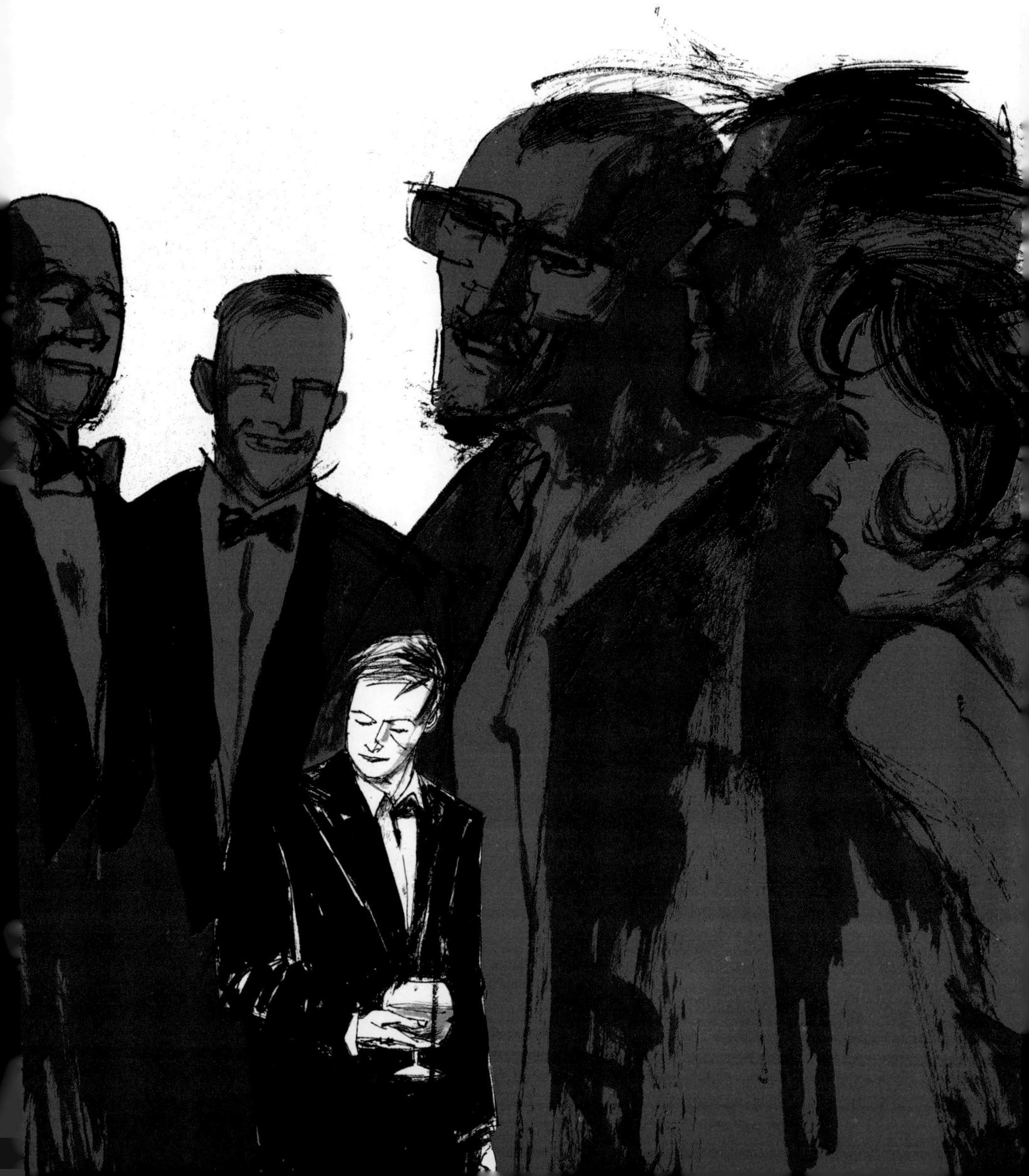

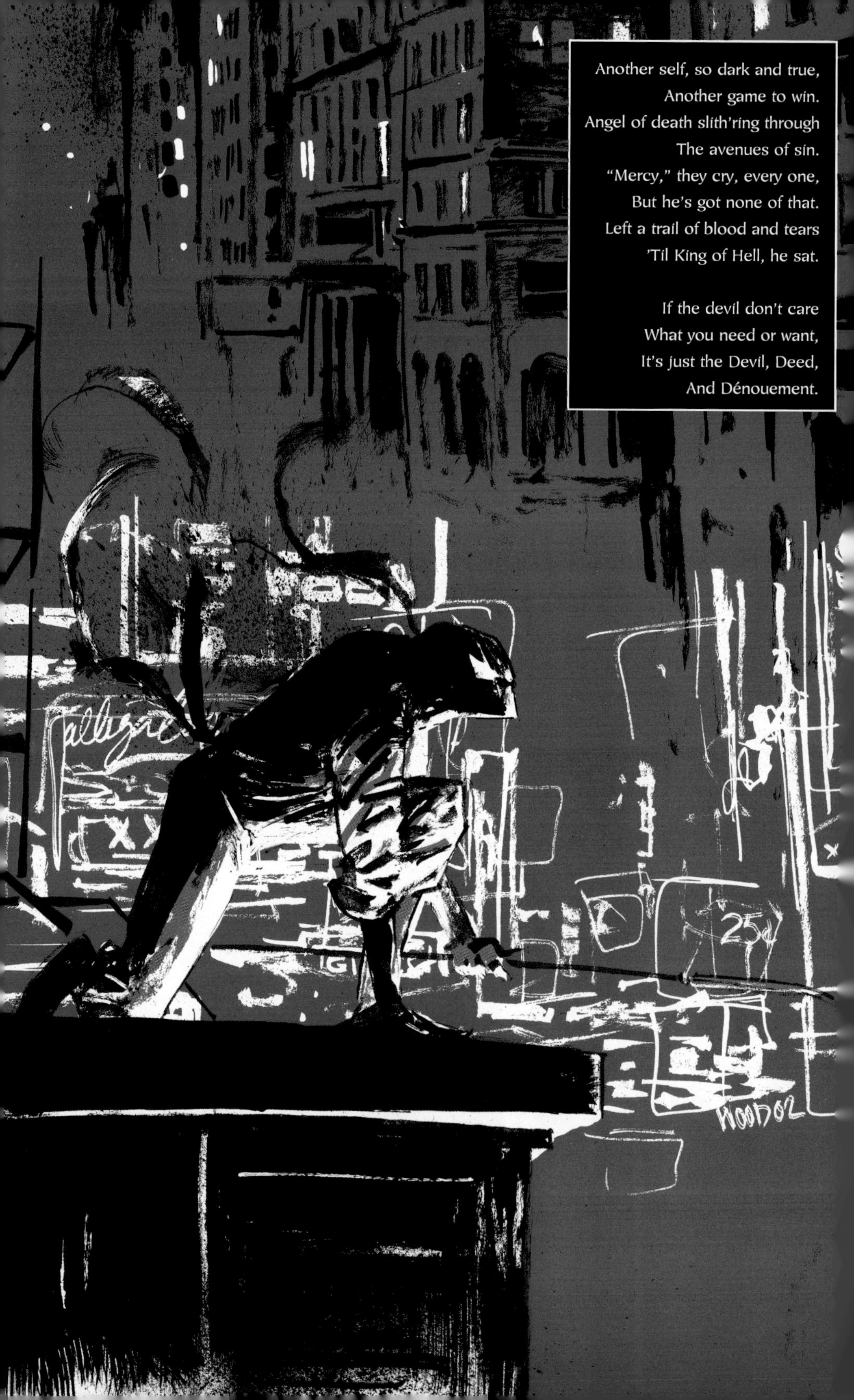
Another self, so dark and true,
Another game to win.
Angel of death slith'ring through
The avenues of sin.
"Mercy," they cry, every one,
But he's got none of that.
Left a trail of blood and tears
'Til King of Hell, he sat.

If the devil don't care
What you need or want,
It's just the Devil, Deed,
And Dénouement.

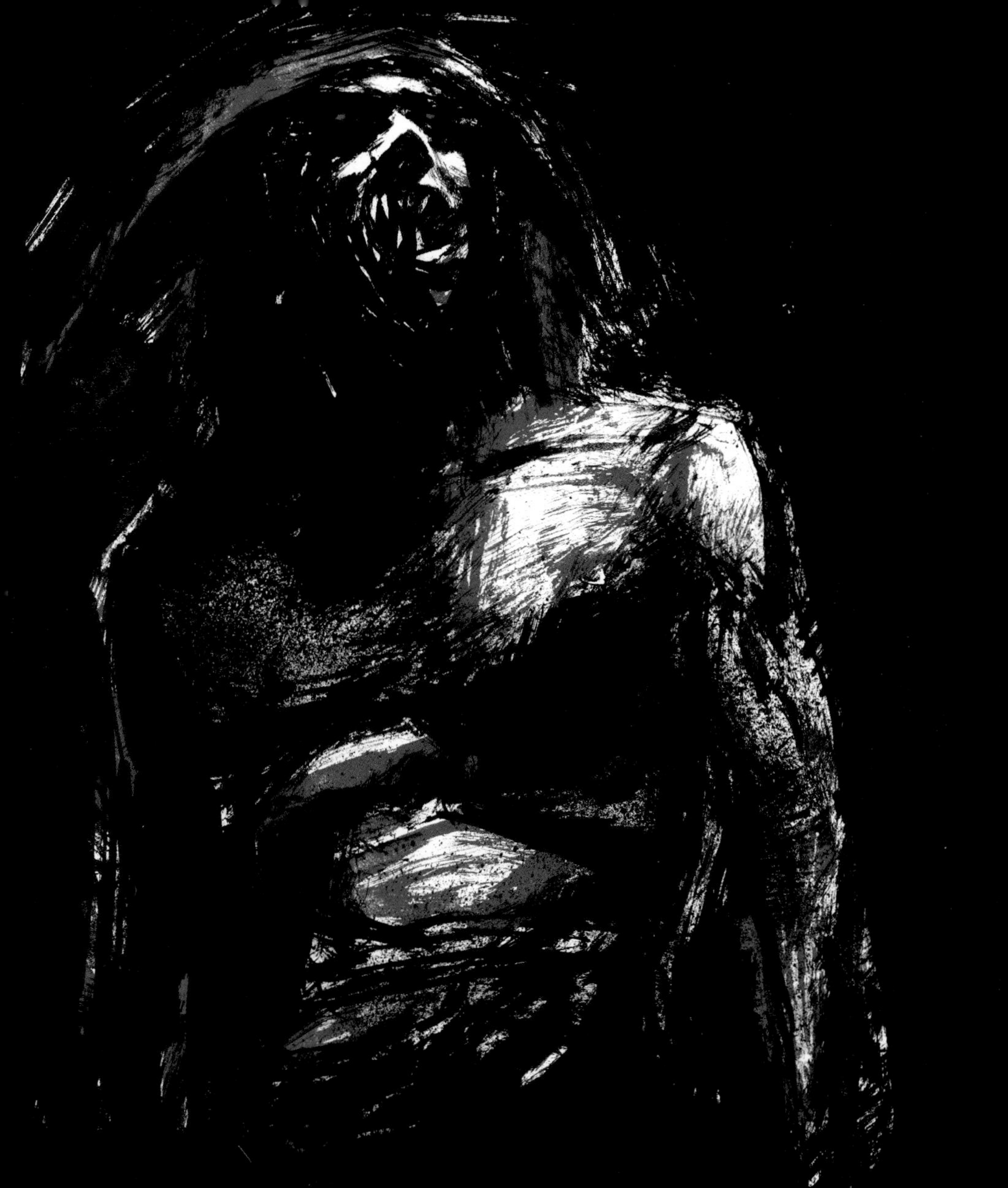

Let's not forget the Howlin' Wolf,
His plaything and his bane.
The only ugly challenge
To his vast and brutal reign.
The beast could tear and tatter,
Growl and grapple, rip and rend.
But its fearsome reputation
Was just fodder in the end.

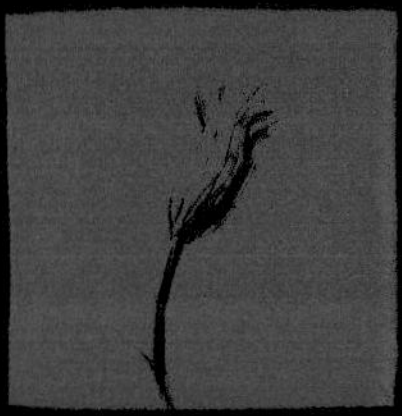

Well, the devil don't care
What you need or want.
He's only Devil, Deed,
And Dénouement.

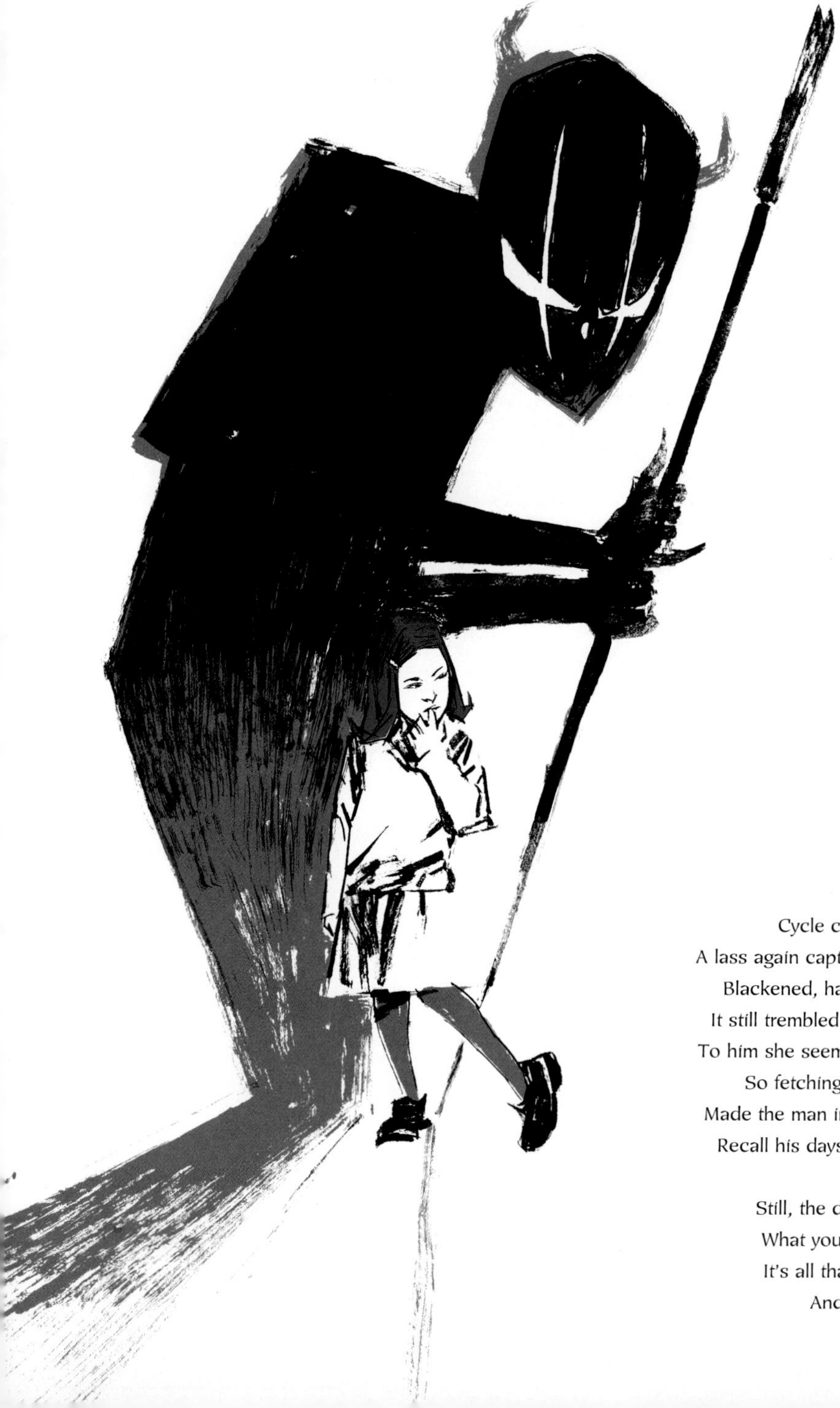

Cycle came full circle.
A lass again captured his heart.
Blackened, hard, and brittle,
It still trembled from the start.
To him she seemed a li'l angel,
So fetching, fair, and coy.
Made the man inside the fiend
Recall his days as just a boy.

Still, the devil don't care
What you need or want.
It's all that Devil, Deed,
And Dénouement.

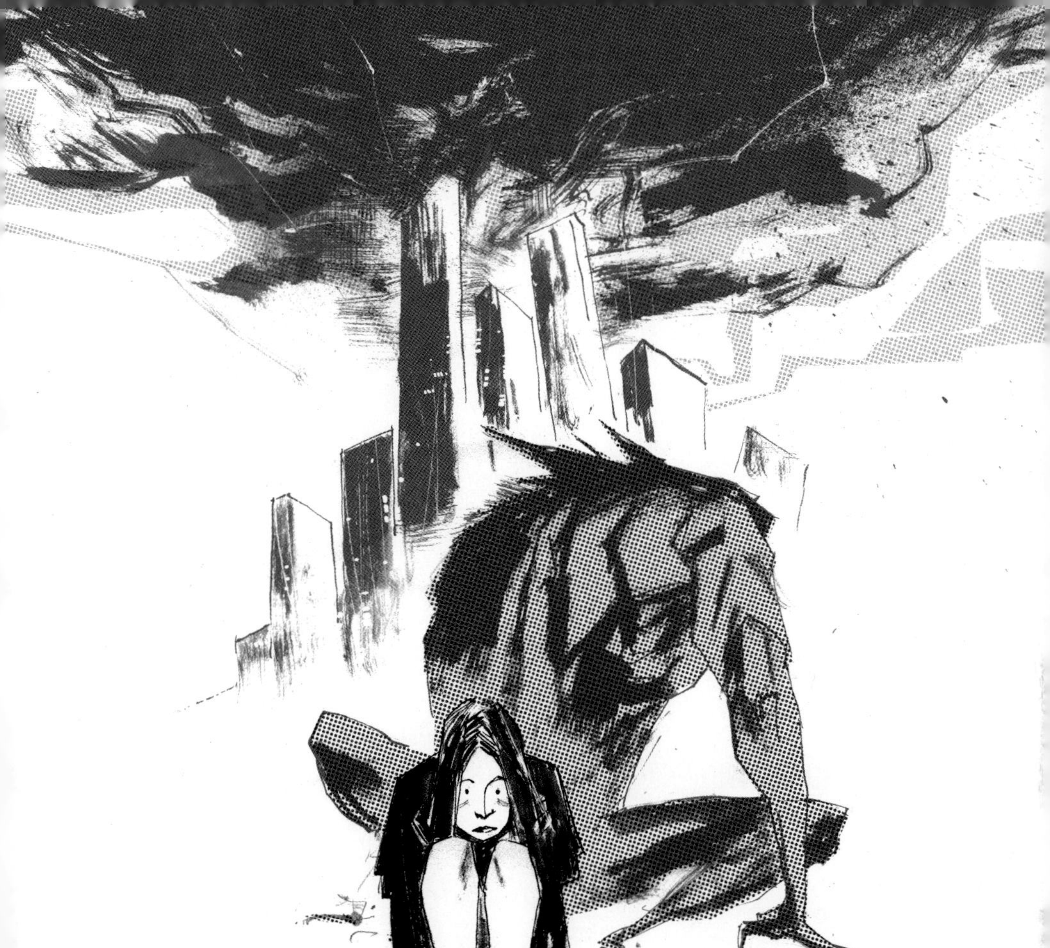

Ahead loomed only tragedy,
Bloodshed, treason, and pain.
The child devised a cunning trap
To end this horrid game.
He never once suspected
Such a ruse could douse his flame.
By fear and force he'd always ruled
And died so, just the same.

When the devil don't care
What you need or want,
There's only Devil, Deed,
And Dénouement.

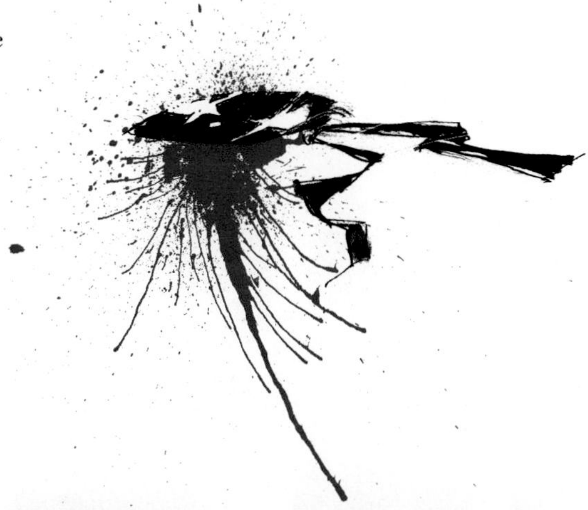

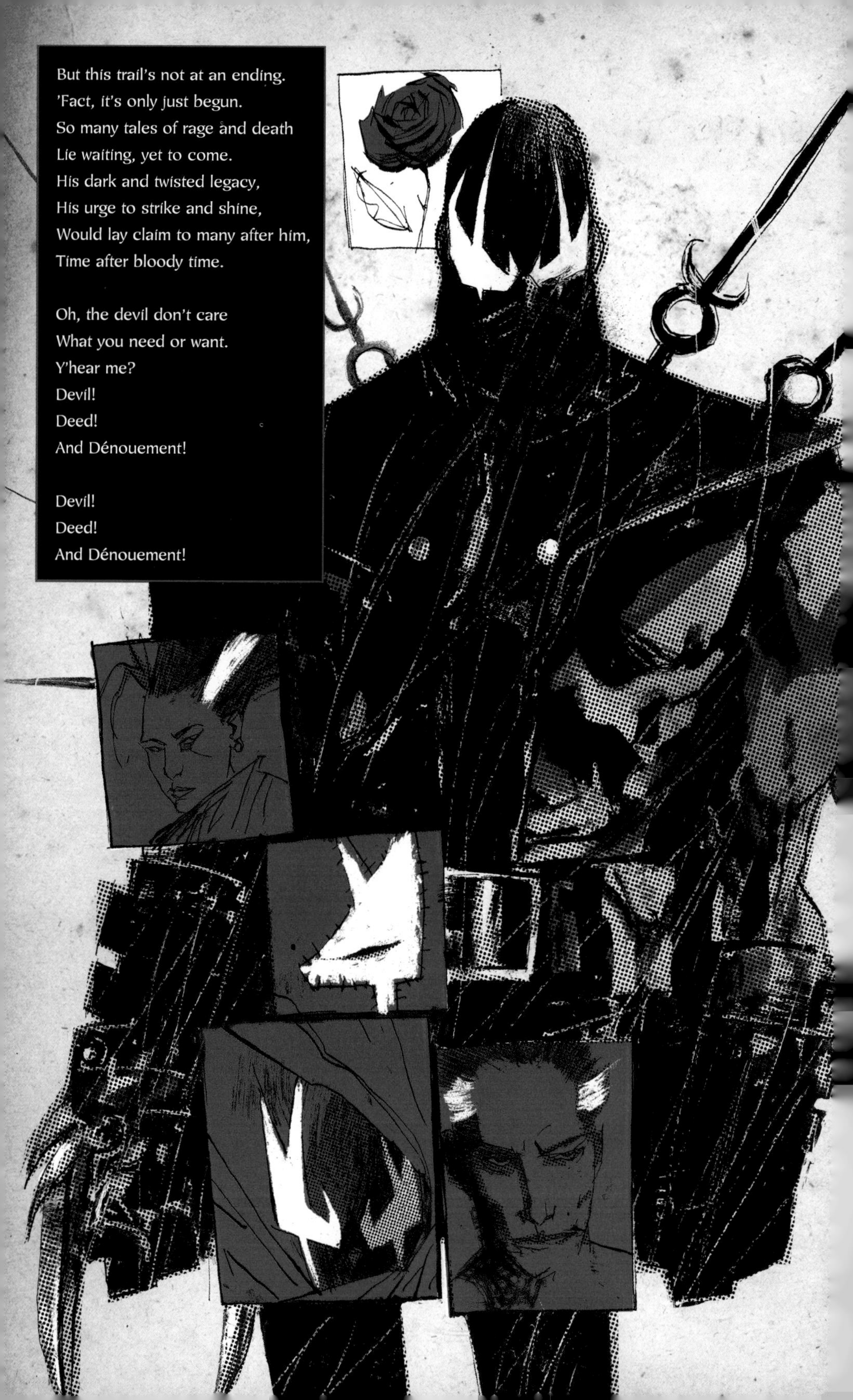
But this trail's not at an ending.
'Fact, it's only just begun.
So many tales of rage and death
Lie waiting, yet to come.
His dark and twisted legacy,
His urge to strike and shine,
Would lay claim to many after him,
Time after bloody time.

Oh, the devil don't care
What you need or want.
Y'hear me?
Devil!
Deed!
And Dénouement!

Devil!
Deed!
And Dénouement!

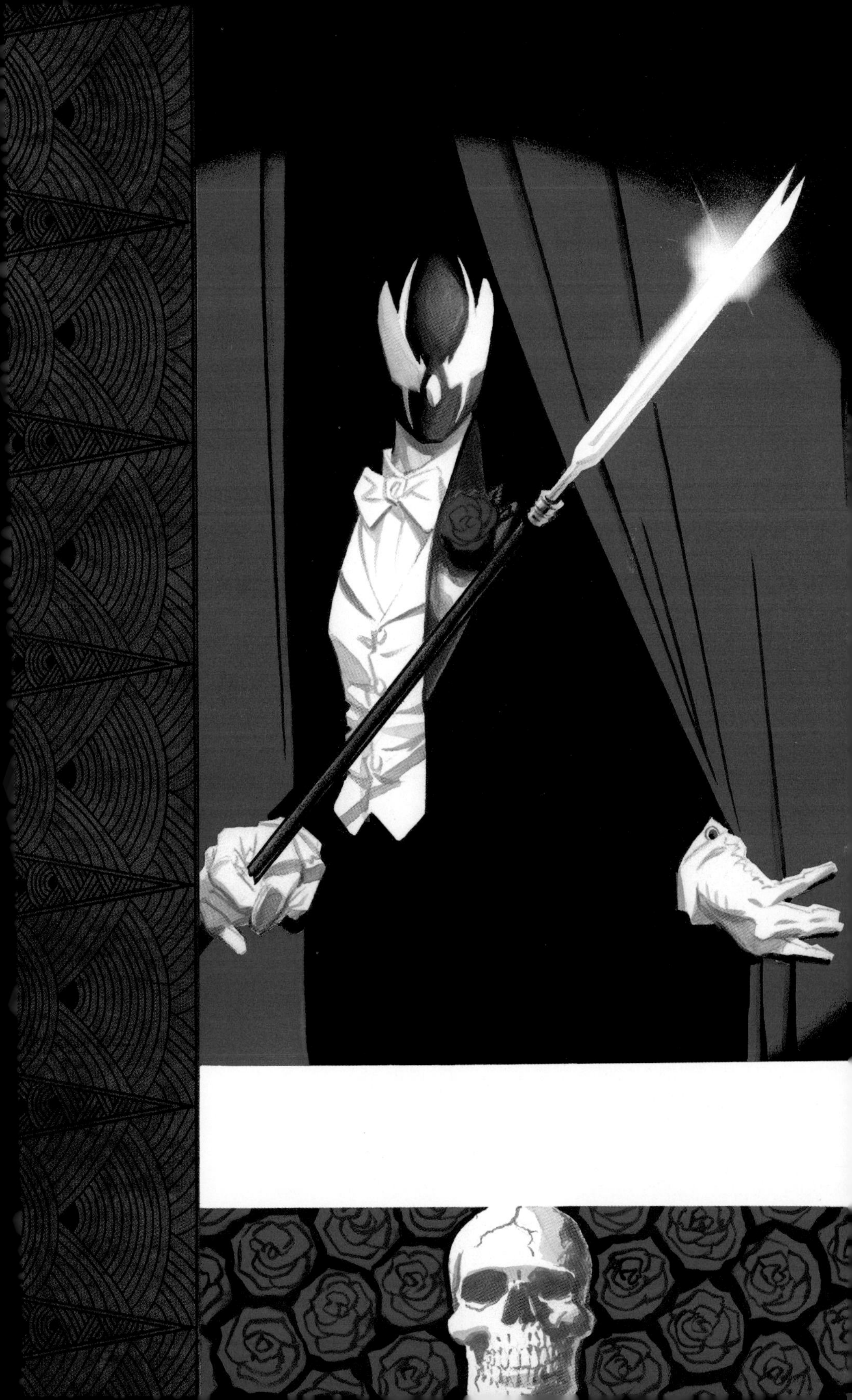

BEHOLD THE DEVIL
Created, written & illustrated by **MATT WAGNER**

Lettering by **TOM ORZECHOWSKI**

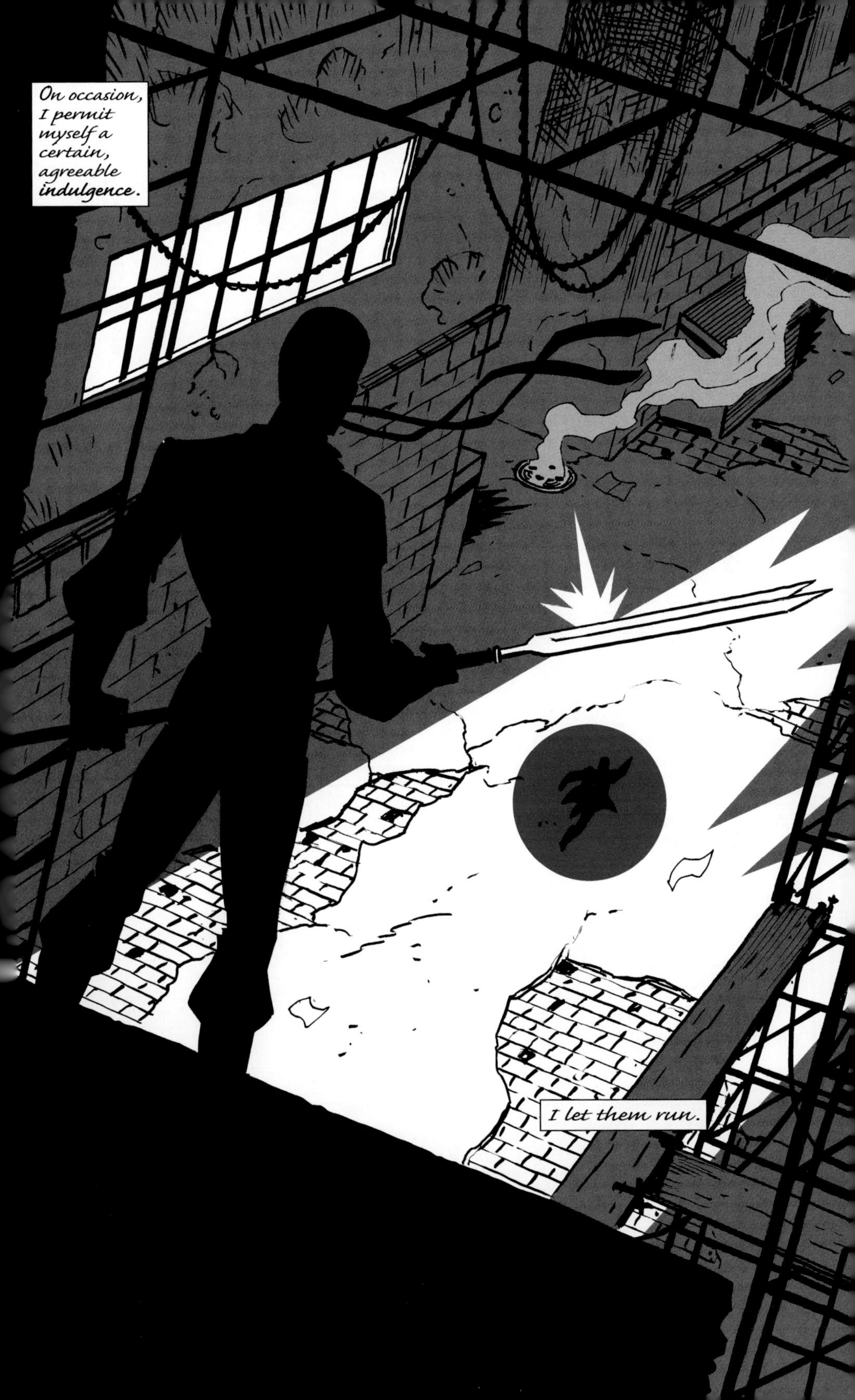
On occasion, I permit myself a certain, agreeable indulgence.
I let them run.

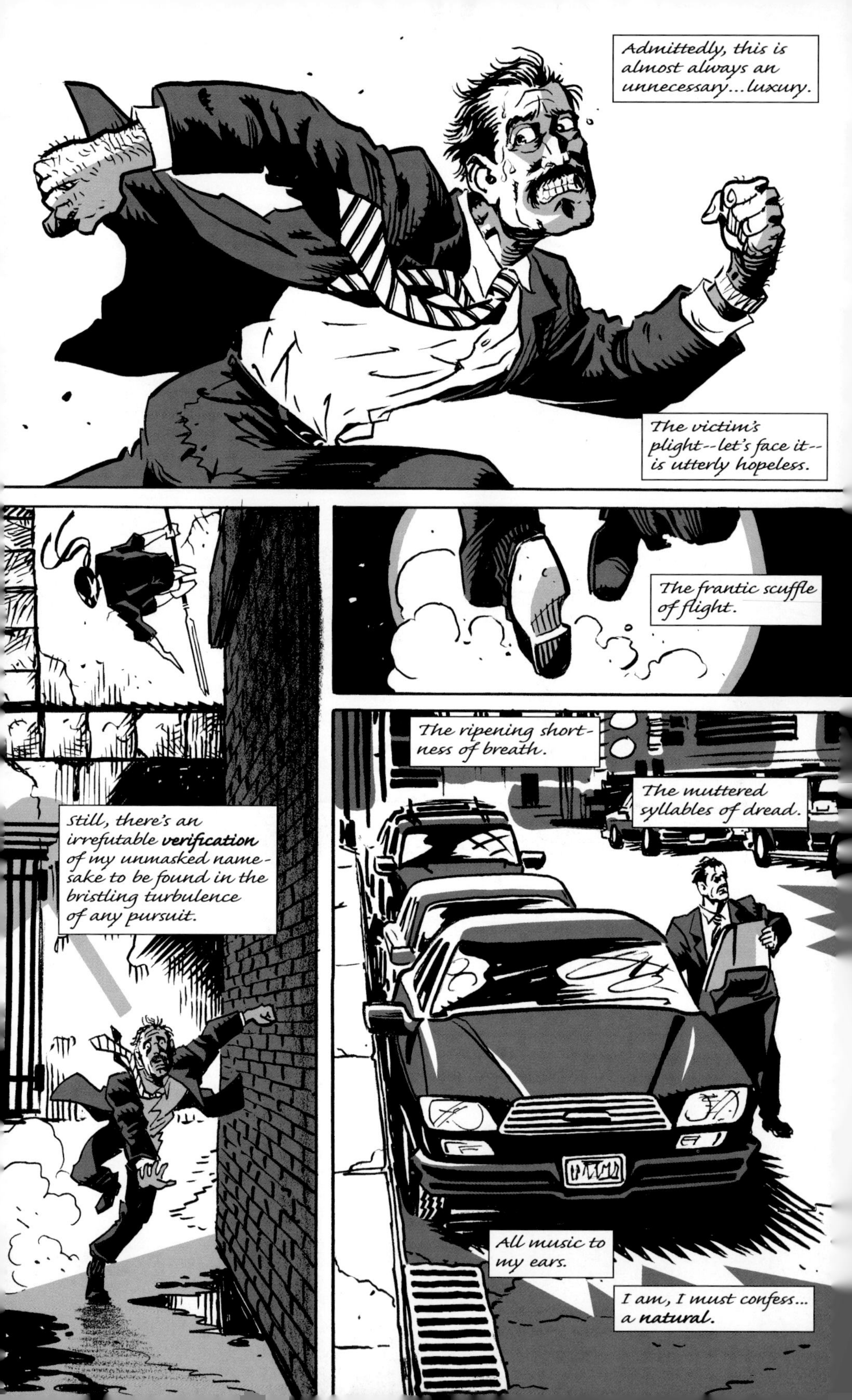
Admittedly, this is almost always an unnecessary...luxury.
The victim's plight--let's face it--is utterly hopeless.
Still, there's an irrefutable **verification** of my unmasked name-sake to be found in the bristling turbulence of any pursuit.
The frantic scuffle of flight.
The ripening short-ness of breath.
The muttered syllables of dread.
All music to my ears.
I am, I must confess... a **natural**.

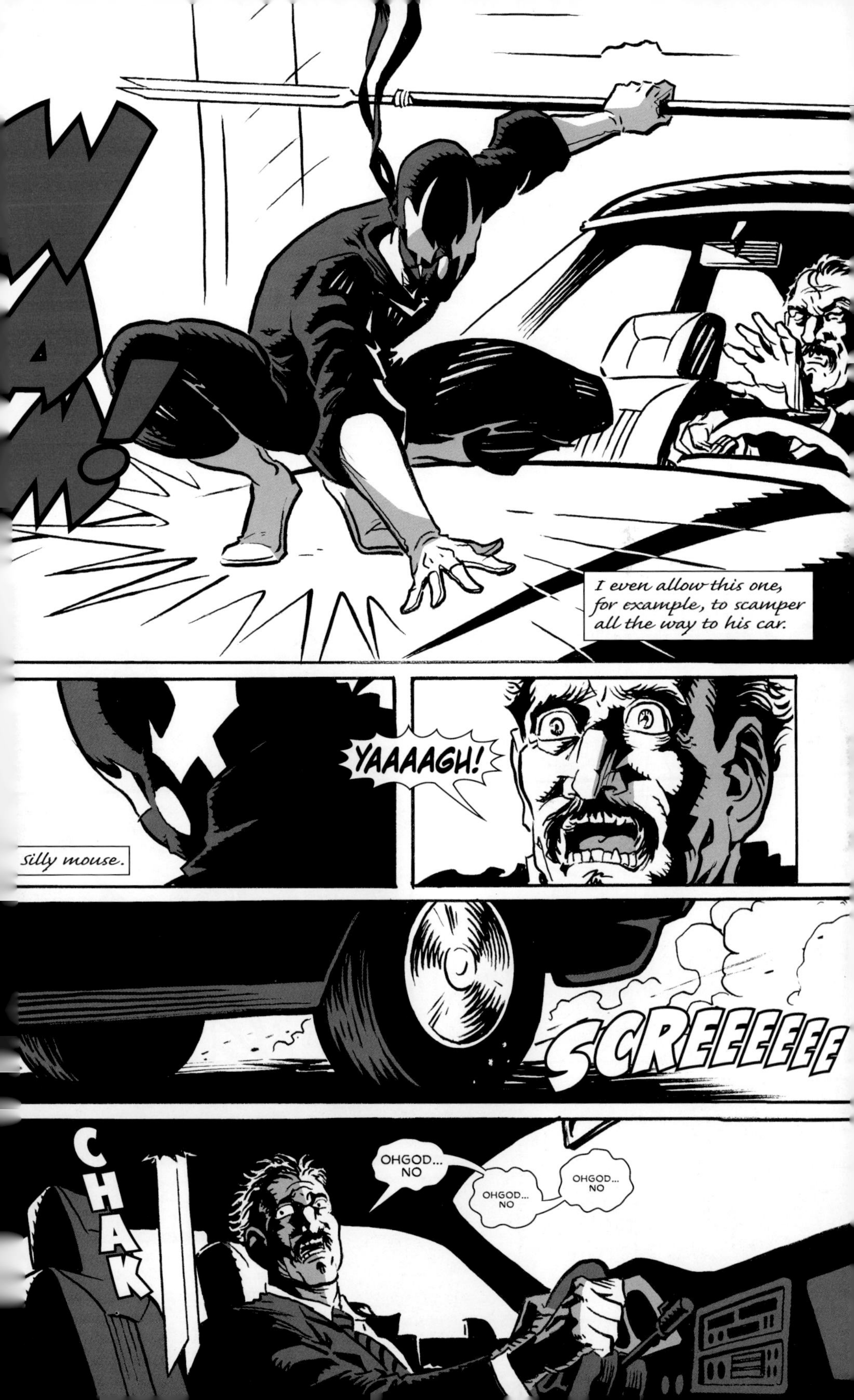

WAM!
I even allow this one, for example, to scamper all the way to his car.
silly mouse.
YAAAAGH!
SCREEEEEE
CHAK
OHGOD... NO
OHGOD... NO
OHGOD... NO

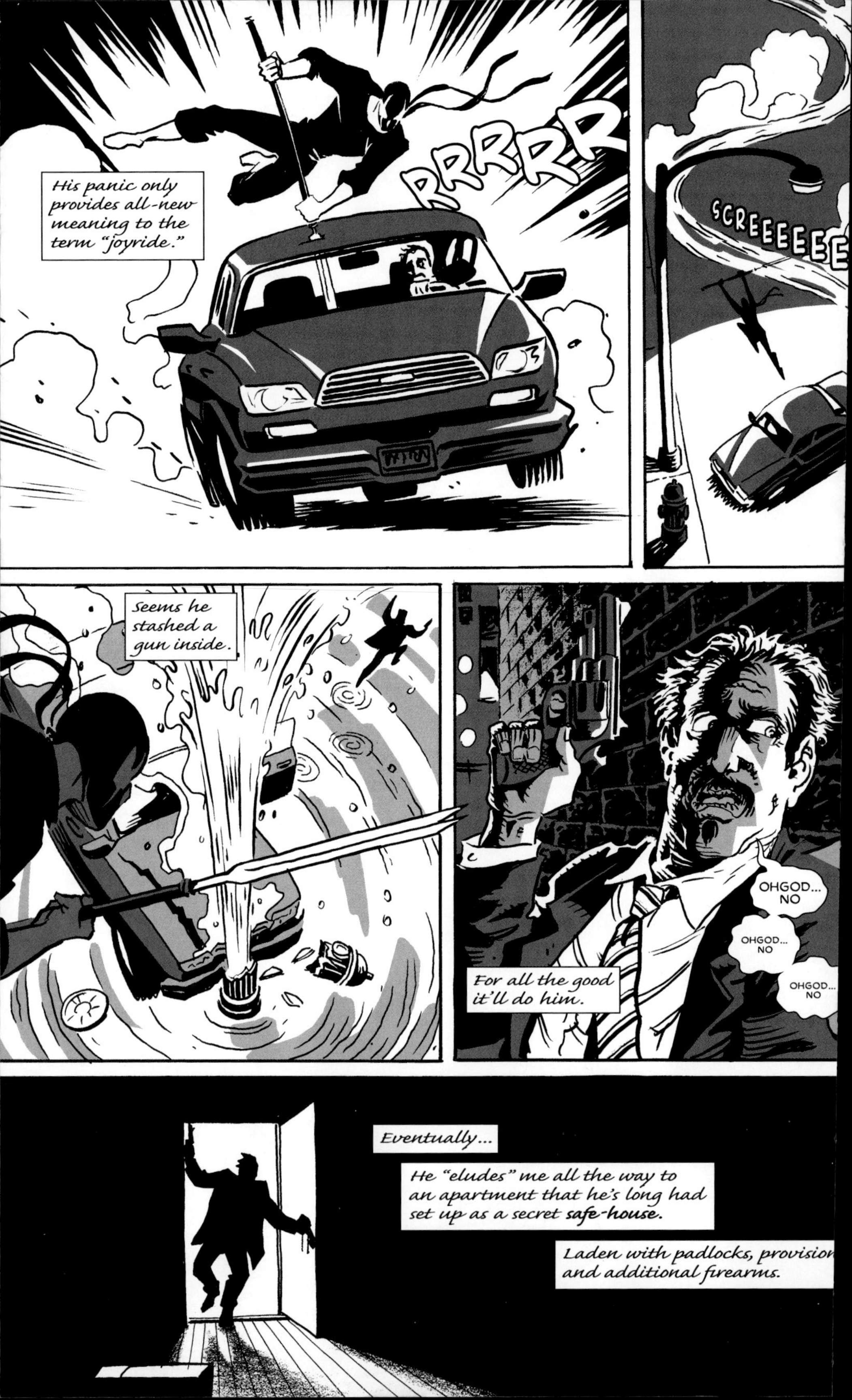
His panic only provides all-new meaning to the term "joyride."
RRRRR
SCREEEEEEE
Seems he stashed a gun inside.
OHGOD... NO
OHGOD... NO
OHGOD... NO
For all the good it'll do him.
Eventually...
He "eludes" me all the way to an apartment that he's long had set up as a secret safe-house.
Laden with padlocks, provision and additional firearms.

silly mouse.

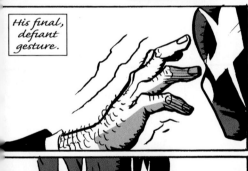

His final, defiant gesture.

Unmasking his undoer.

I let him sneak a peek.

Just before his eyes go slack and dim.

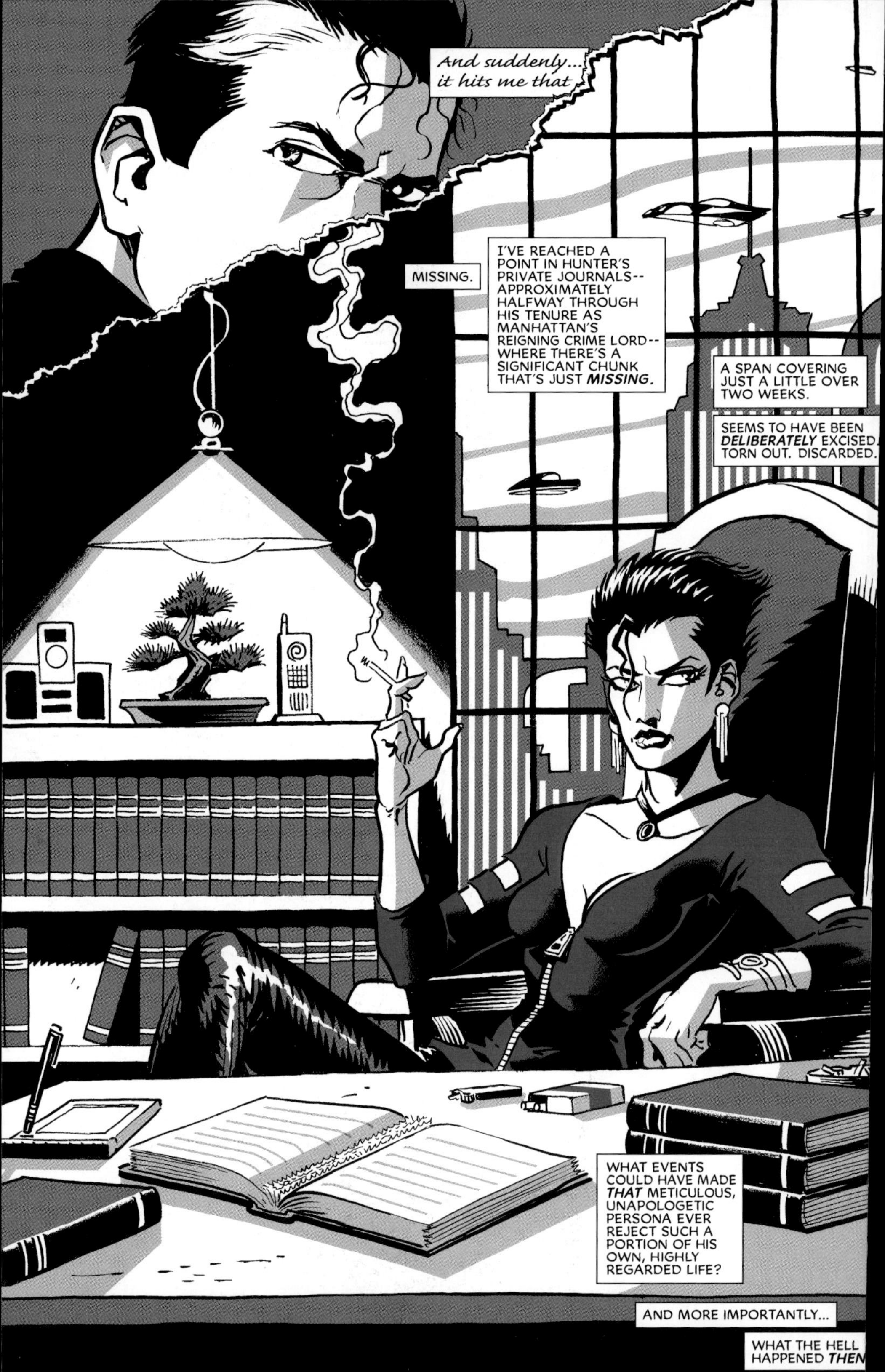
And suddenly... it hits me that
MISSING.
I'VE REACHED A POINT IN HUNTER'S PRIVATE JOURNALS--APPROXIMATELY HALFWAY THROUGH HIS TENURE AS MANHATTAN'S REIGNING CRIME LORD--WHERE THERE'S A SIGNIFICANT CHUNK THAT'S JUST MISSING.
A SPAN COVERING JUST A LITTLE OVER TWO WEEKS.
SEEMS TO HAVE BEEN DELIBERATELY EXCISED. TORN OUT. DISCARDED.
WHAT EVENTS COULD HAVE MADE THAT METICULOUS, UNAPOLOGETIC PERSONA EVER REJECT SUCH A PORTION OF HIS OWN, HIGHLY REGARDED LIFE?
AND MORE IMPORTANTLY...
WHAT THE HELL HAPPENED THEN

In the persona of Hunter Rose, his poignant and eloquent words captivated the attention of millions. His empathetic novels spoke of a common humanity and evoked wisdom well beyond his years. In the guise of Grendel, his nefarious deeds terrorized a city and eventually invoked dread in over half the nation. No less wordy in this other hidden identity, he reveals, in his extensive private journals, an inhuman thirst for domination and a sociopathic brilliance that can only be called—for lack of a better word—genius. How surprising then to find that a section of these meticulous, self-celebrating records had been excised from the final documents, seemingly by his own hand—a missing adventure from a life that was all but unsullied by any recognizable form of regret.

What events could have driven such a tsunamic psyche to such an act of self-censure? What realizations could've disrupted that steely resolve?

Perhaps we will never know.

—excerpt from *Devil by the Deed*
by Christine Spar

The first one never even sees it coming.

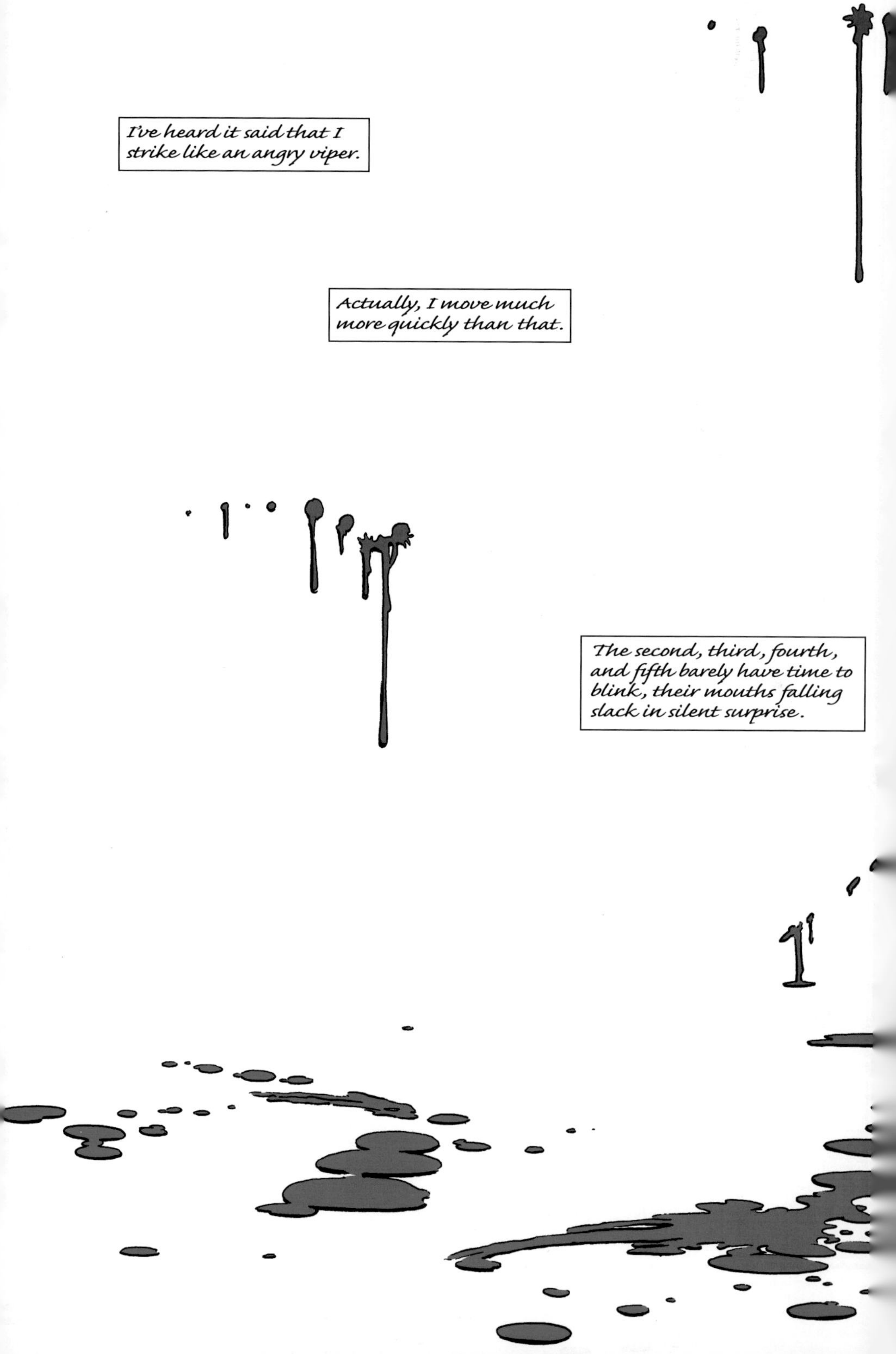
I've heard it said that I strike like an angry viper.
Actually, I move much more quickly than that.
The second, third, fourth, and fifth barely have time to blink, their mouths falling slack in silent surprise.

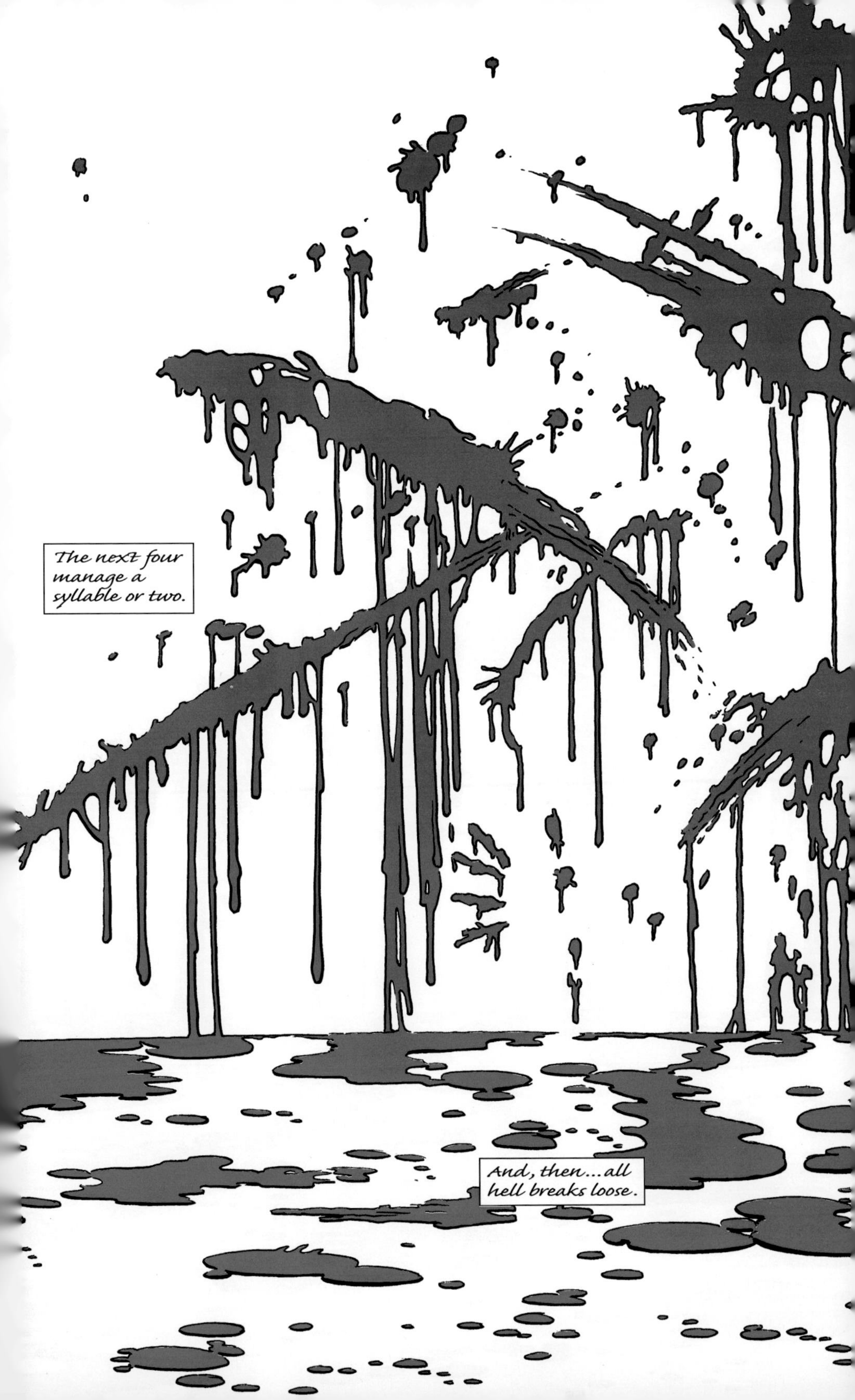
The next four manage a syllable or two.
And, then...all hell breaks loose.

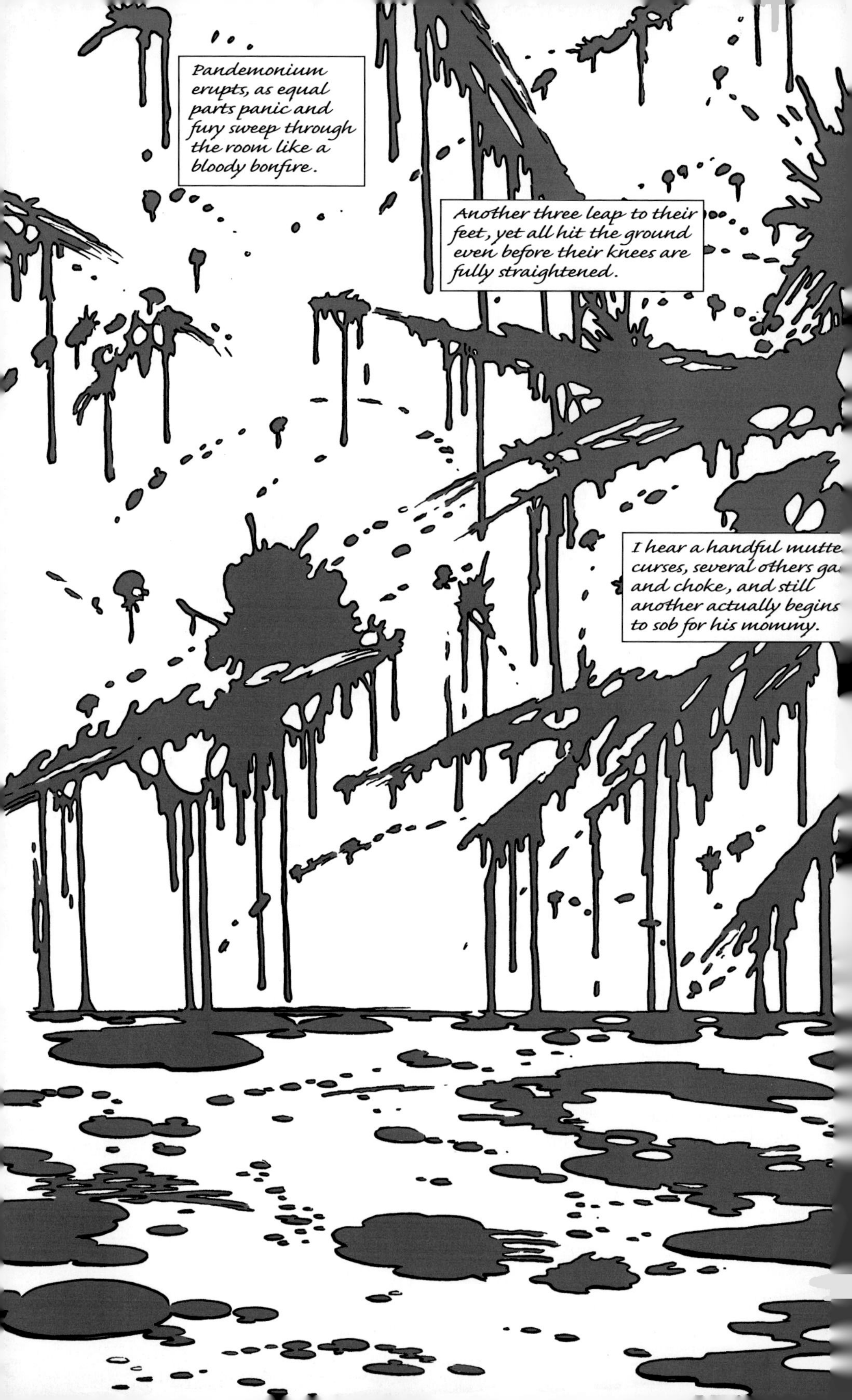
Pandemonium erupts, as equal parts panic and fury sweep through the room like a bloody bonfire.
Another three leap to their feet, yet all hit the ground even before their knees are fully straightened.
I hear a handful mutte curses, several others ga and choke, and still another actually begins to sob for his mommy.

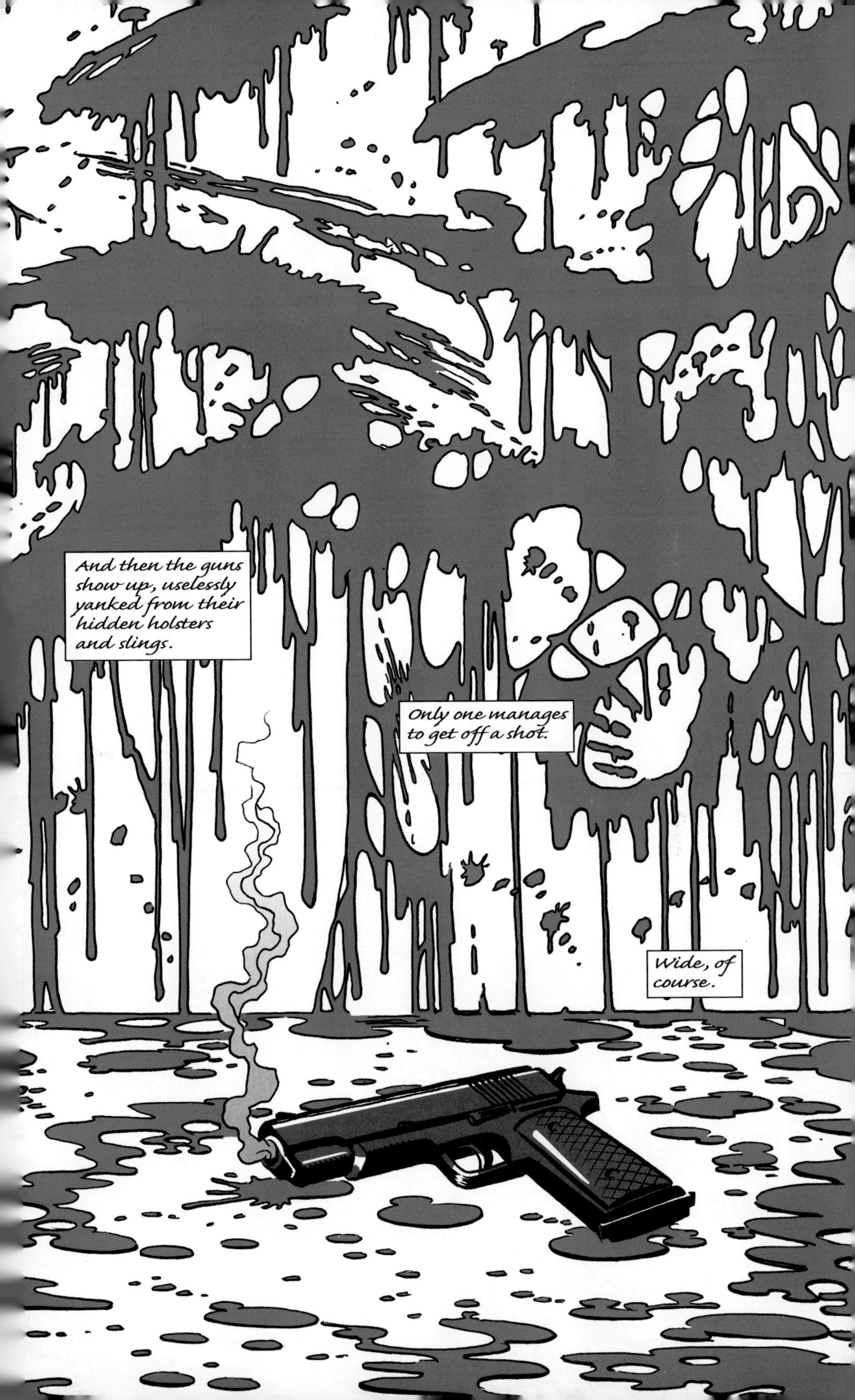
And then the guns show up, uselessly yanked from their hidden holsters and slings.
Only one manages to get off a shot.
Wide, of course.

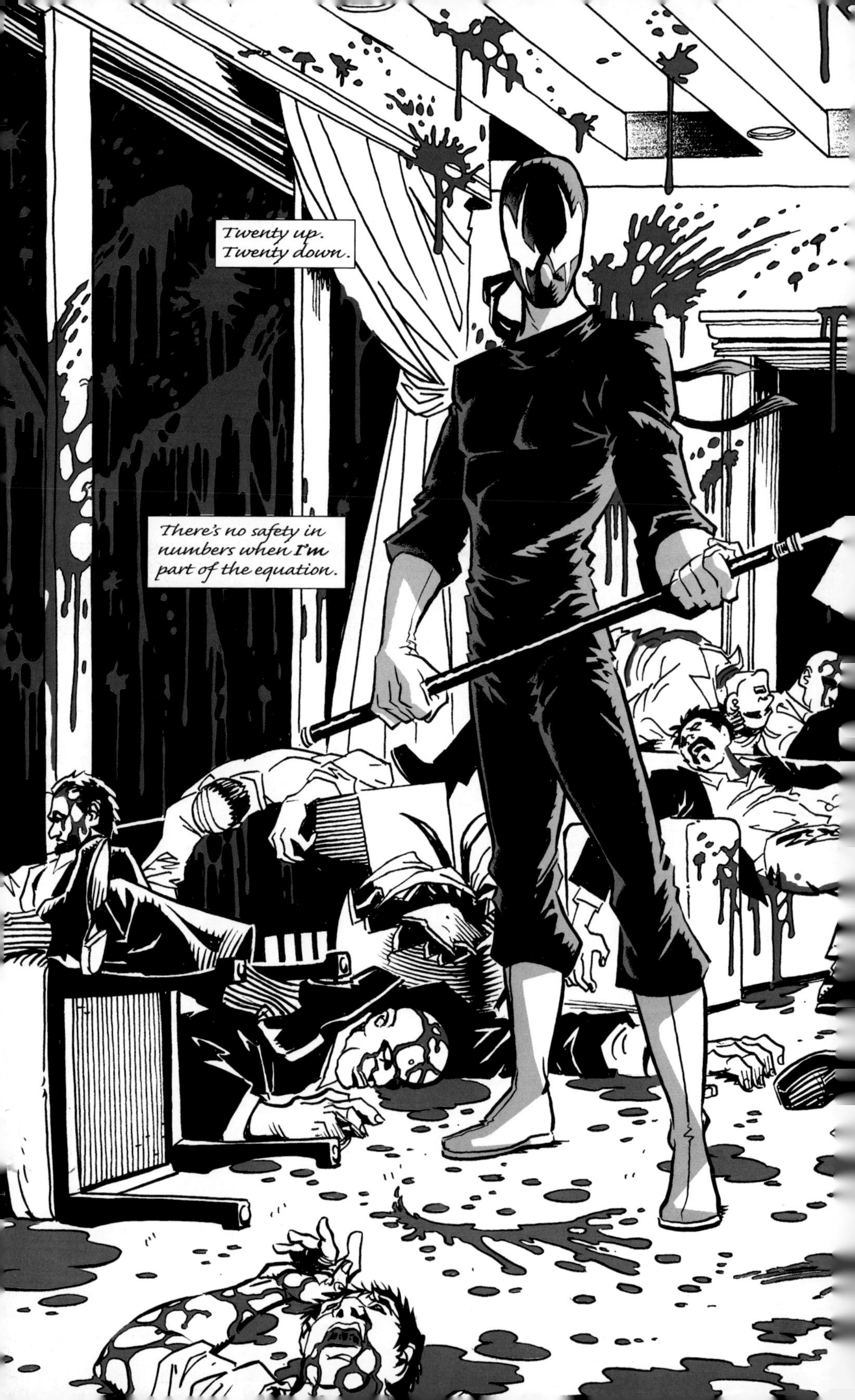
Twenty up. Twenty down.
There's no safety in numbers when I'm part of the equation.

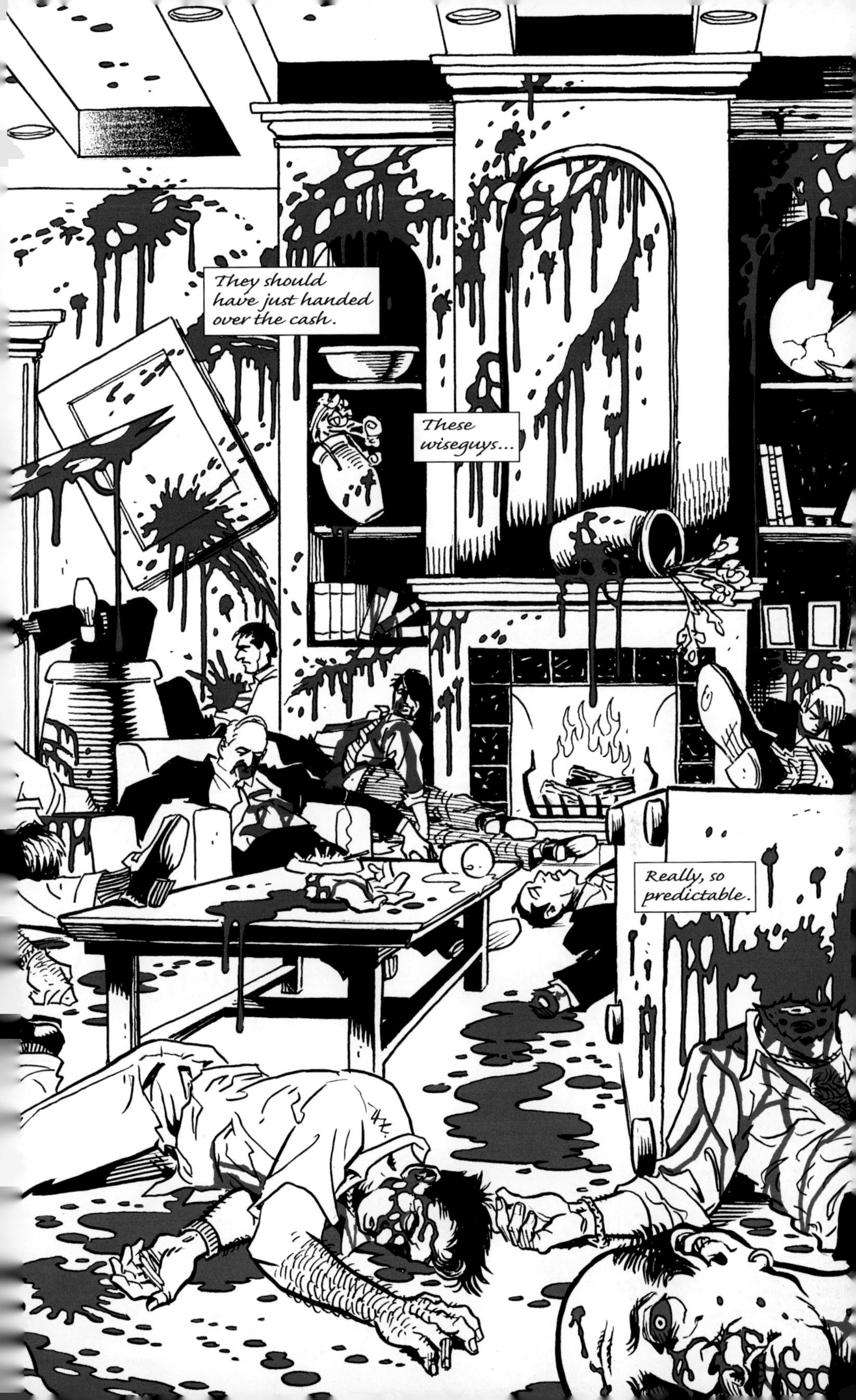
They should have just handed over the cash.
These wiseguys...
Really, so predictable.

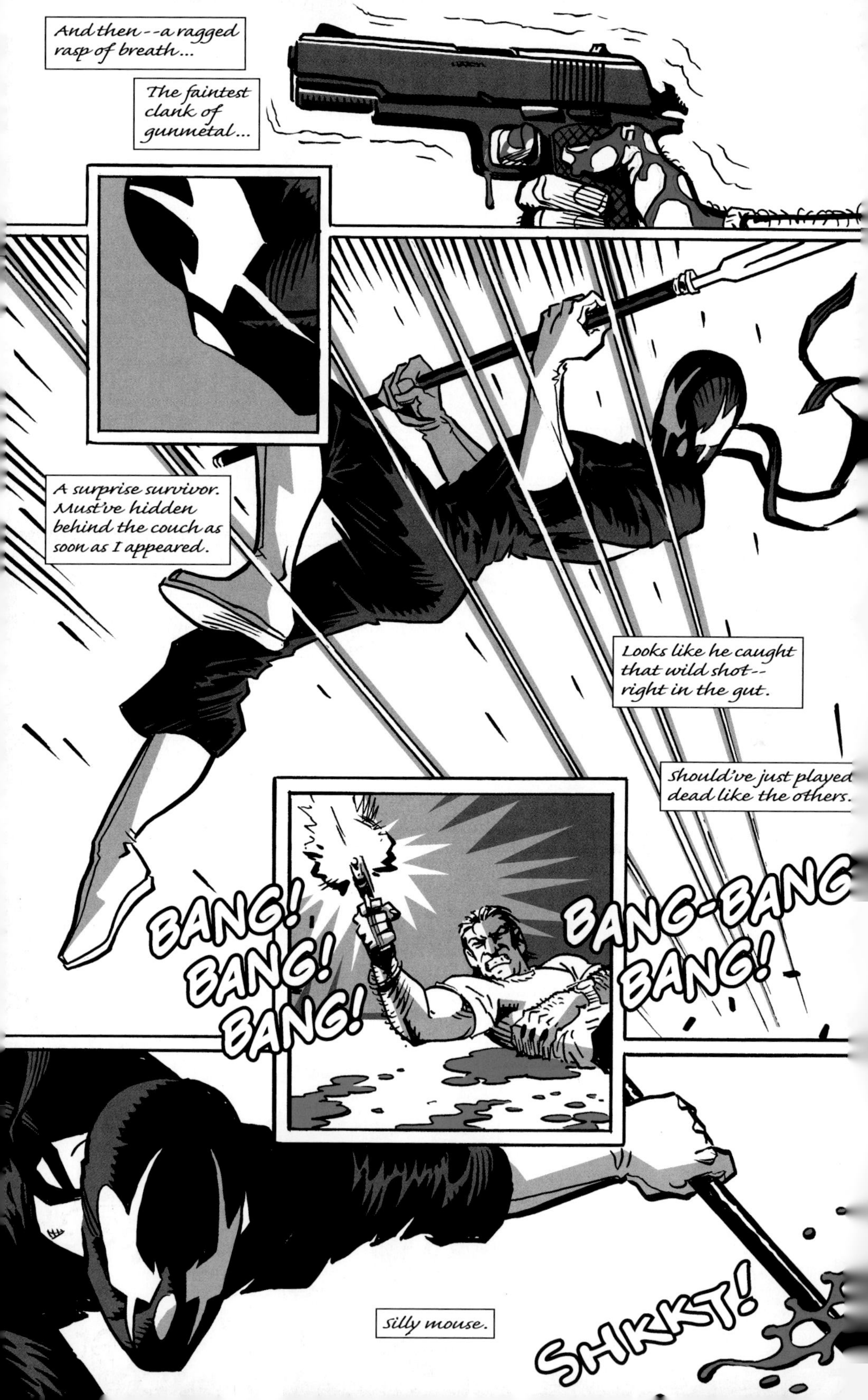
And then--a ragged rasp of breath...
The faintest clank of gunmetal...
A surprise survivor. Must've hidden behind the couch as soon as I appeared.
Looks like he caught that wild shot--right in the gut.
Should've just played dead like the others.
BANG! BANG! BANG!
BANG-BANG BANG!
Silly mouse.
SHKKT!

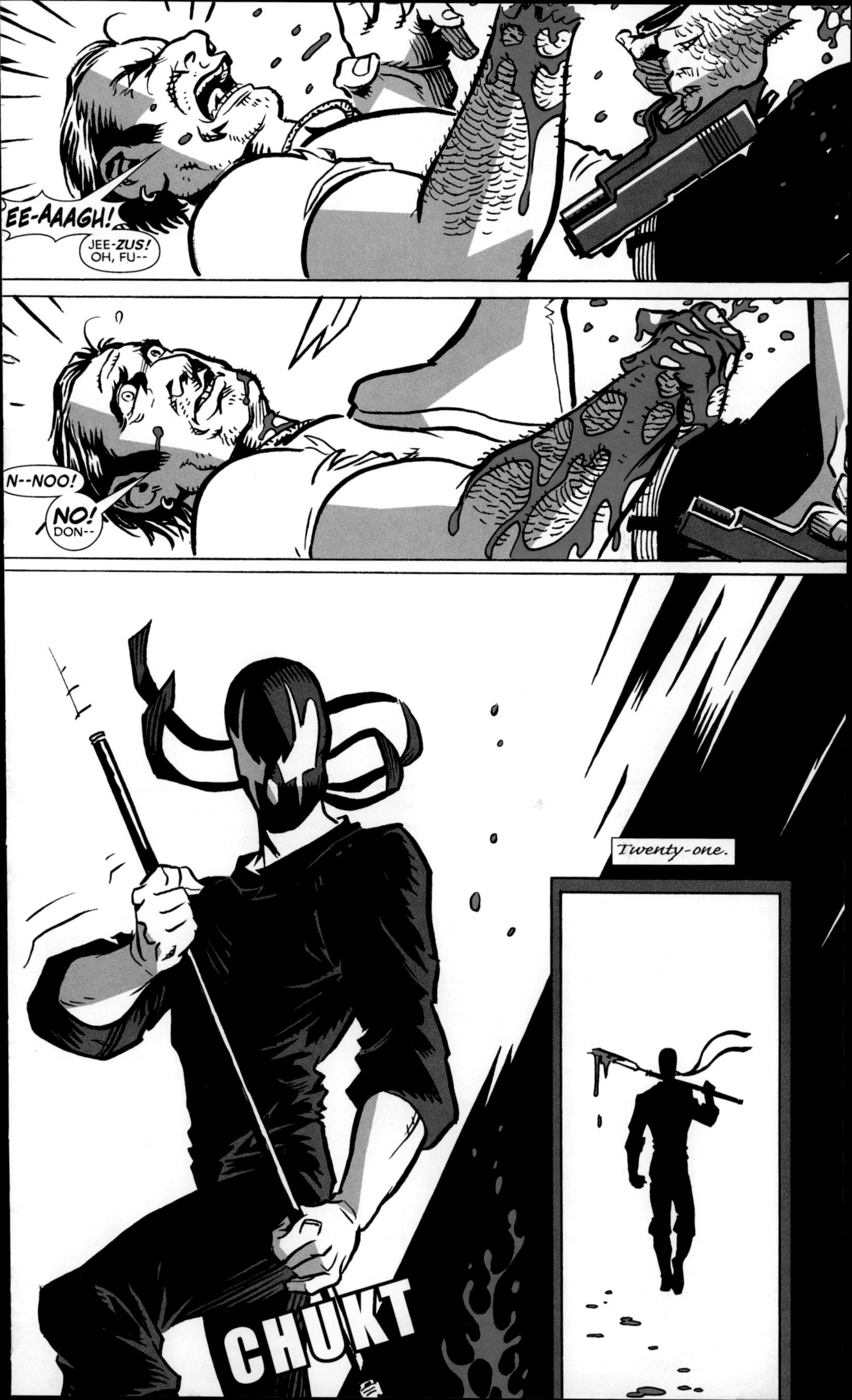
EE-AAAGH!
JEE-ZUS! OH, FU--
N--NOO!
NO! DON--
Twenty-one.
CHUKT

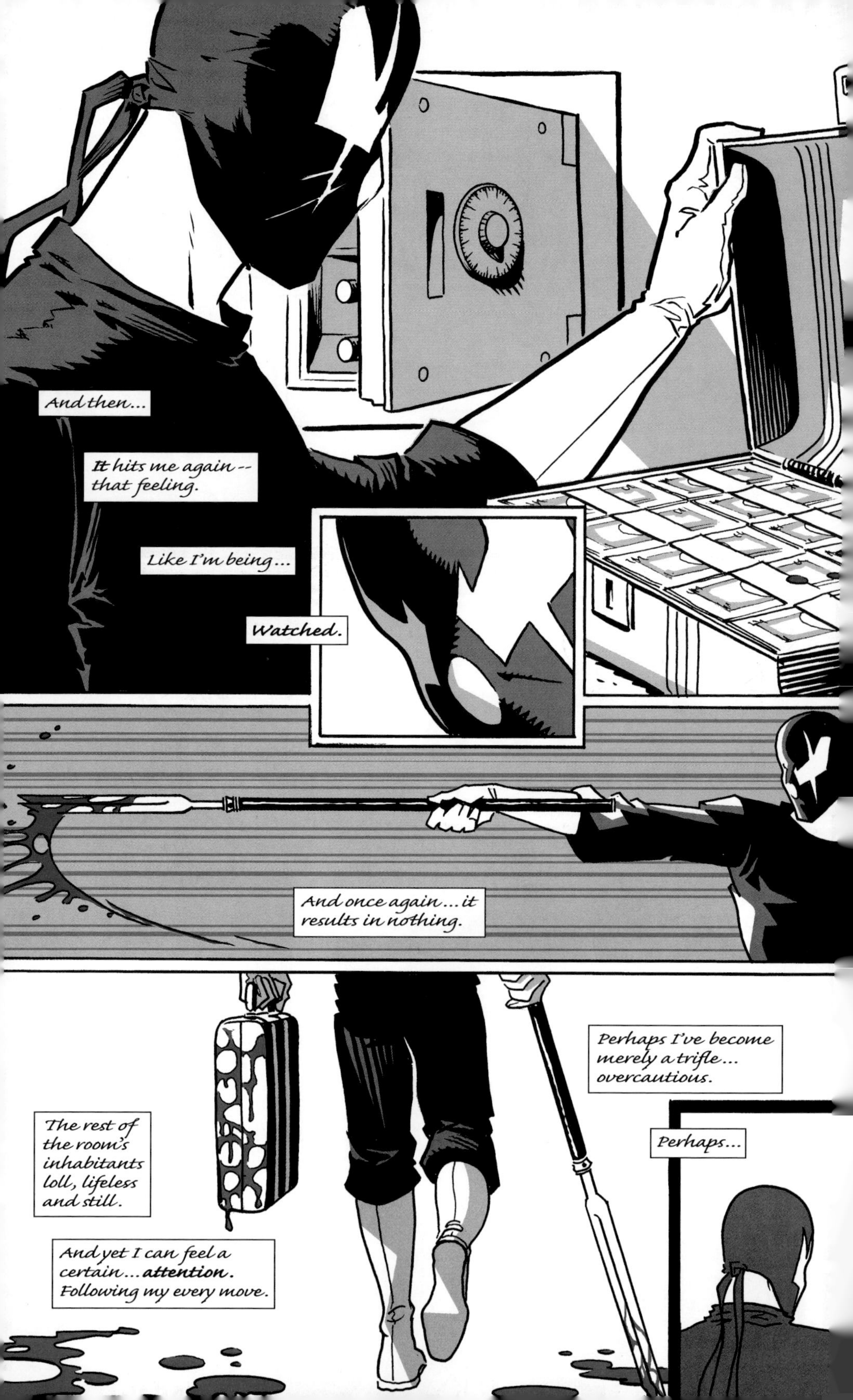
And then...
It hits me again -- that feeling.
Like I'm being...
Watched.
And once again... it results in nothing.
The rest of the room's inhabitants loll, lifeless and still.
And yet I can feel a certain... attention. Following my every move.
Perhaps I've become merely a trifle... overcautious.
Perhaps...

HANTOM
KES OVER MOB

NDEL STRIKES

RIME LORD ESC

DEAT

Udieresis aacute agrave acircumflex adieresis atilde aring. Ccedilla eacute egrave ecircumflex edieresis iacute igrave. Gant ba rry Icircumflex idieresis ntilde oacute. Ograve ocircumflex qw

All right, you…
— Degree Cent

ucircumflex.

ndy-boy Ciccone

Notdef AE oslash. Notdef plus inus notdef notdef yen mu notdef tdef notdef notdef notdef ordfemi-ne ord masculine.

Notdef ae oslash questiondown clamdow orin not ille mo grave at dash quo Udieres erling se rmandbls demark a

GRENDEL UN

STILL ON THE LOOS

ered. flex adieresis atilde aring. Ccedilla
mark eacute egrave ecircumflex edieresis
iacute igrave. Icircumflex idieresis
slash. ntilde oacute. Ogra
otdef odieresis otilde uac
otdef cumflex. Udieresis dagger degree
e ord cent sterling section bullet para

Mystery Man.

Ghost in the Machine.

Death Dealer.

NDEL

STERY ASSASS

ARTIST'S RENDERING

ntilde oacute. Ograve ocircumfl
odieresis otilde uacute ugrave uc

NDEL

SLAUGHT

te agrave acircumflex adieresis atilde
eacuteegrave ecircumflex edieresis
cumflex idieresis ntildeoacute. Ograve
esis otilde uacute ugrave ucircumflex

Who the hell **are** you?

URF WA

een Dead, No Witr

Udieresis aacute agrave acircum-
ex adieresis atilde aring. Ccedilla
cute egrave ecirc
cute igrave. Icirc
ilde oacute. Ograv
esis otilde uacute
ex idieresis ntilde.
Udieresis dagg
erling section bul
rmandbls register
ademark acute dier
ushmus notdef
tdef notdef notdef
dfeminine ord mas

sterling se
paragraph

GANGLAND SLA

POLICE BAFFLED BY BLACK-CLAD KI

Notdef ae oslash que
ondown exclamdownlog
lnot notdef. Florin not
dnotdef guillemotleft gu
motright ellipsis space.
rave atilde otilde oe
dash emdash quoted bl
ft quotedblright.

Quoteleft quoteright
ide notdef ydieresis. Yd
esis fraction currency
lsingleft guilsinglright

ANOTH

GRENDEL SIGHT

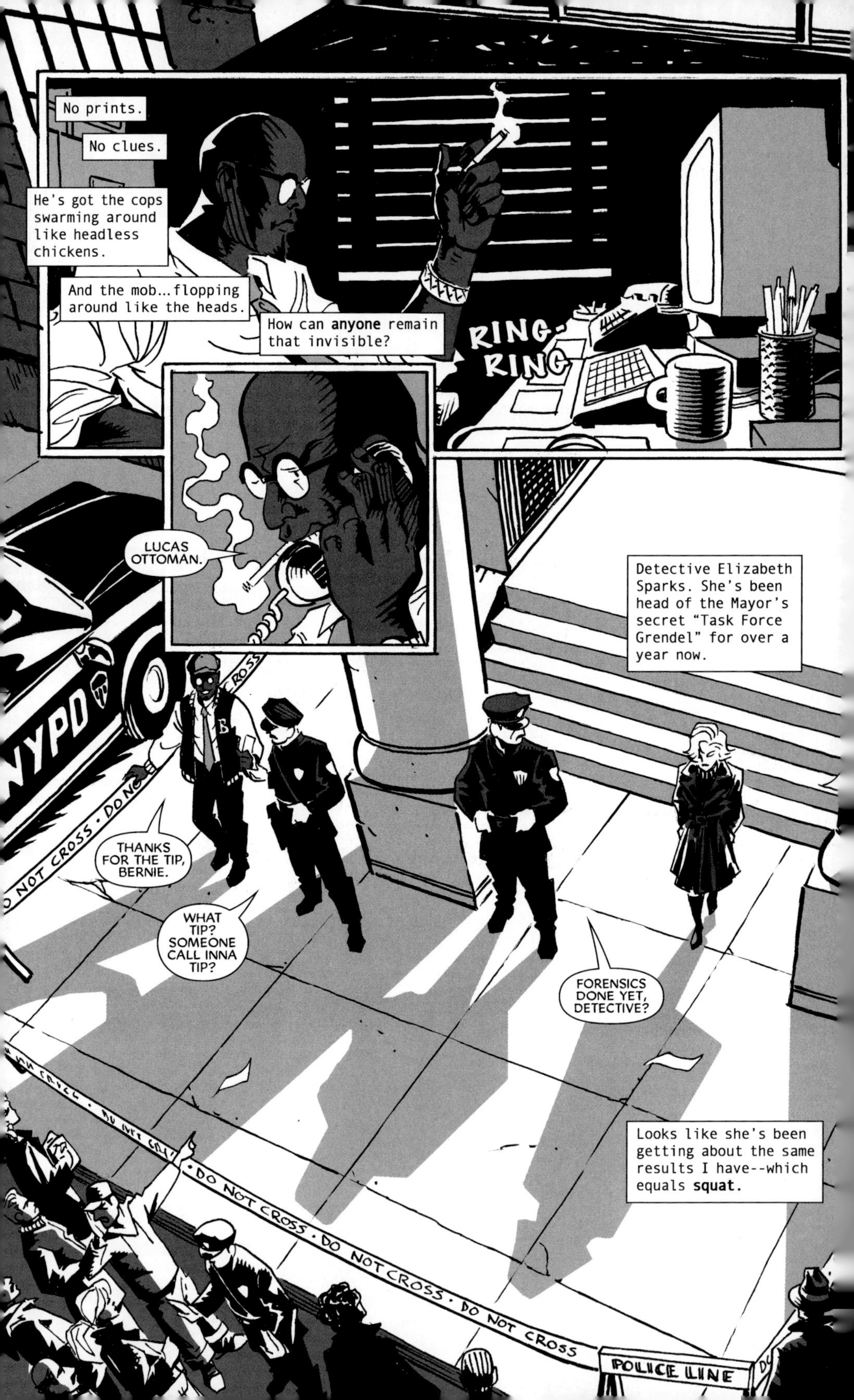
No prints.
No clues.
He's got the cops swarming around like headless chickens.
And the mob... flopping around like the heads.
How can **anyone** remain that invisible?
RING-RING
LUCAS OTTOMAN.
Detective Elizabeth Sparks. She's been head of the Mayor's secret "Task Force Grendel" for over a year now.
NYPD
THANKS FOR THE TIP, BERNIE.
WHAT TIP? SOMEONE CALL INNA TIP?
FORENSICS DONE YET, DETECTIVE?
Looks like she's been getting about the same results I have--which equals **squat.**
DO NOT CROSS · DO NOT CROSS · DO NOT CROSS
POLICE LINE

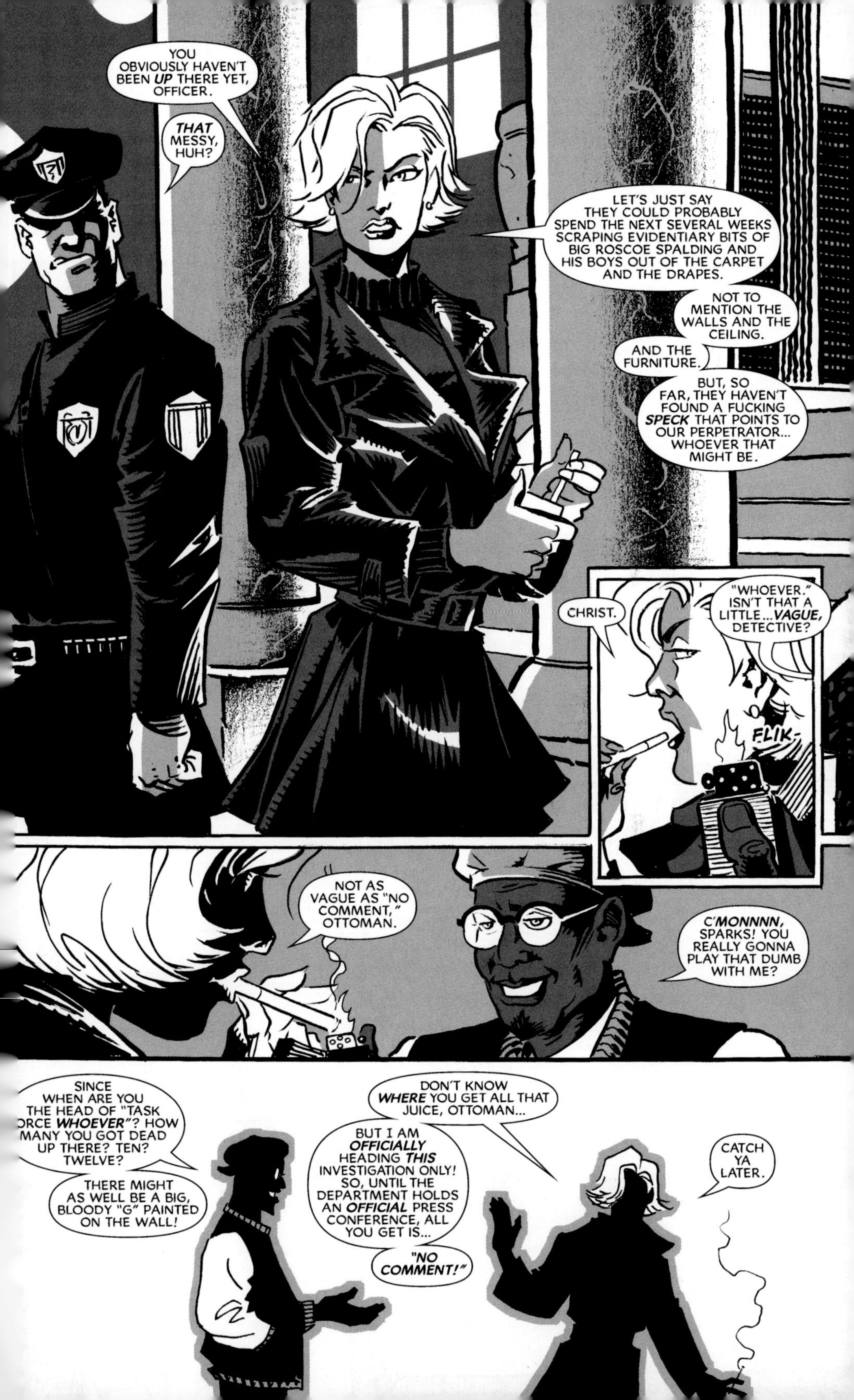

YOU OBVIOUSLY HAVEN'T BEEN UP THERE YET, OFFICER.
THAT MESSY, HUH?
LET'S JUST SAY THEY COULD PROBABLY SPEND THE NEXT SEVERAL WEEKS SCRAPING EVIDENTIARY BITS OF BIG ROSCOE SPALDING AND HIS BOYS OUT OF THE CARPET AND THE DRAPES.
NOT TO MENTION THE WALLS AND THE CEILING.
AND THE FURNITURE.
BUT, SO FAR, THEY HAVEN'T FOUND A FUCKING SPECK THAT POINTS TO OUR PERPETRATOR... WHOEVER THAT MIGHT BE.
"WHOEVER." ISN'T THAT A LITTLE...VAGUE, DETECTIVE?
CHRIST.
FLIK-
NOT AS VAGUE AS "NO COMMENT," OTTOMAN.
C'MONNNN, SPARKS! YOU REALLY GONNA PLAY THAT DUMB WITH ME?
SINCE WHEN ARE YOU THE HEAD OF "TASK ORCE WHOEVER"? HOW MANY YOU GOT DEAD UP THERE? TEN? TWELVE?
THERE MIGHT AS WELL BE A BIG, BLOODY "G" PAINTED ON THE WALL!
DON'T KNOW WHERE YOU GET ALL THAT JUICE, OTTOMAN...
BUT I AM OFFICIALLY HEADING THIS INVESTIGATION ONLY! SO, UNTIL THE DEPARTMENT HOLDS AN OFFICIAL PRESS CONFERENCE, ALL YOU GET IS...
"NO COMMENT!"
CATCH YA LATER.

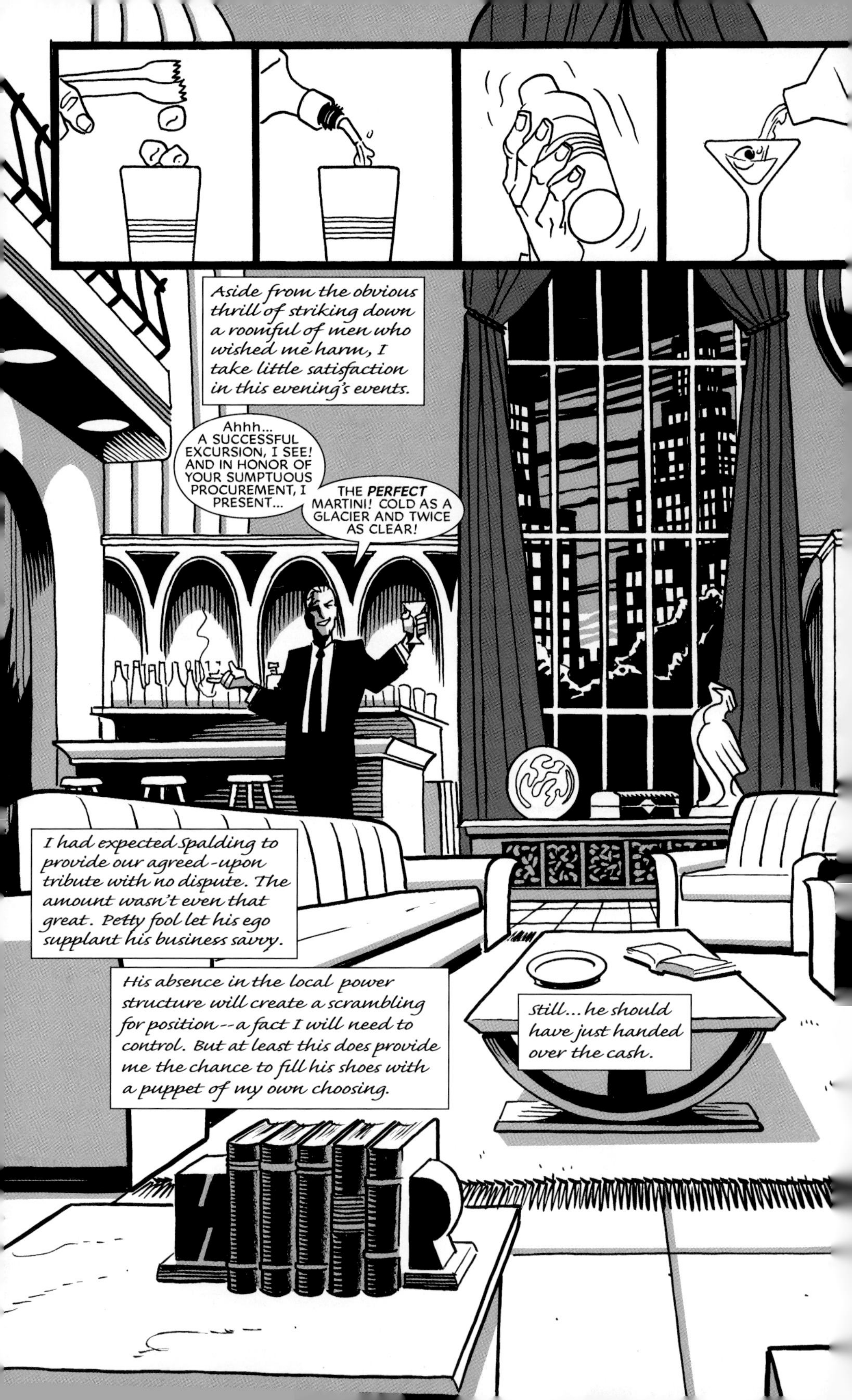

Aside from the obvious thrill of striking down a roomful of men who wished me harm, I take little satisfaction in this evening's events.
Ahhh... A SUCCESSFUL EXCURSION, I SEE! AND IN HONOR OF YOUR SUMPTUOUS PROCUREMENT, I PRESENT...
THE *PERFECT* MARTINI! COLD AS A GLACIER AND TWICE AS CLEAR!
I had expected Spalding to provide our agreed-upon tribute with no dispute. The amount wasn't even that great. Petty fool let his ego supplant his business savvy.
His absence in the local power structure will create a scrambling for position--a fact I will need to control. But at least this does provide me the chance to fill his shoes with a puppet of my own choosing.
Still... he should have just handed over the cash.

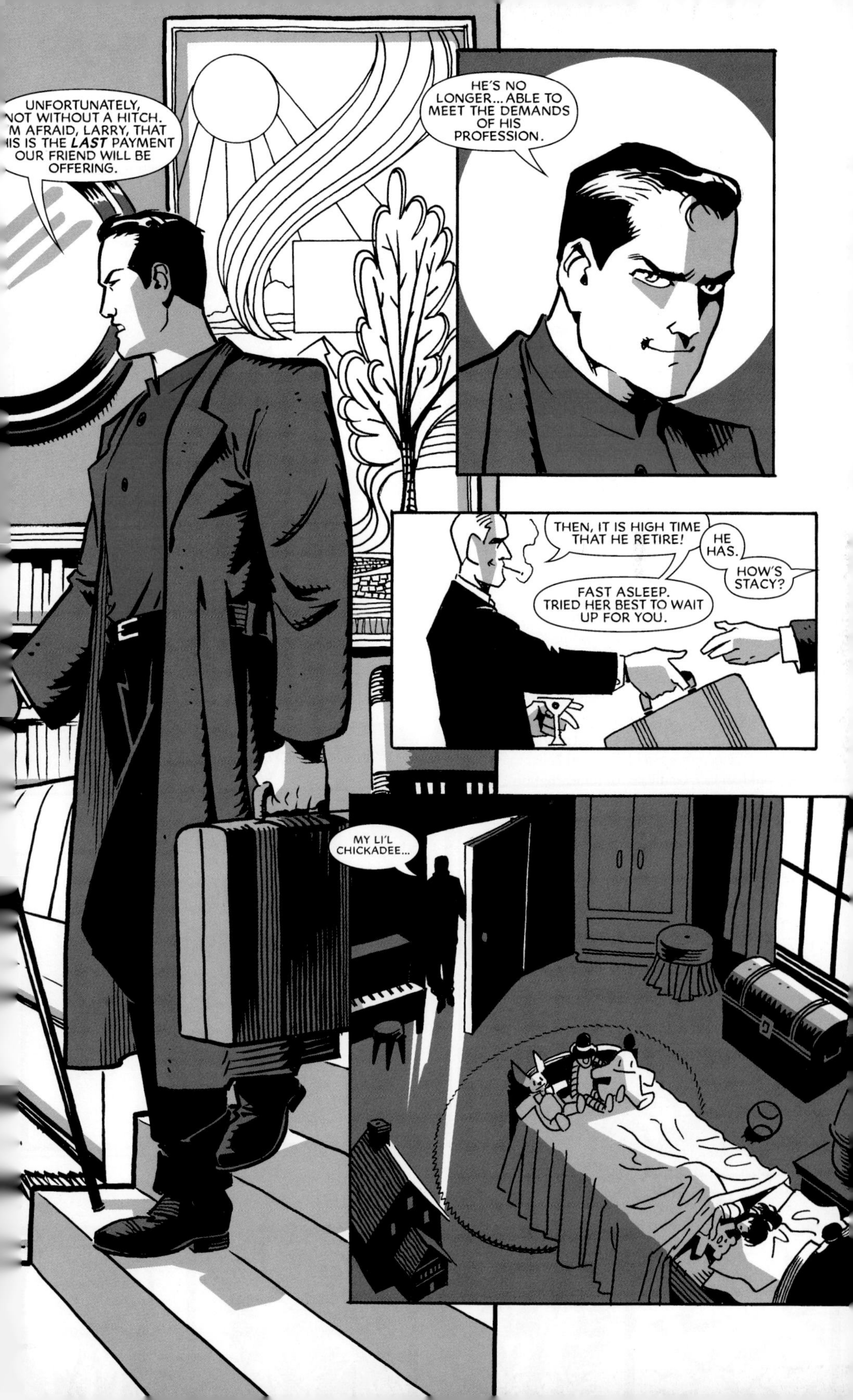
UNFORTUNATELY, NOT WITHOUT A HITCH. I'M AFRAID, LARRY, THAT THIS IS THE *LAST* PAYMENT OUR FRIEND WILL BE OFFERING.
HE'S NO LONGER... ABLE TO MEET THE DEMANDS OF HIS PROFESSION.
THEN, IT IS HIGH TIME THAT HE RETIRE!
HE HAS.
HOW'S STACY?
FAST ASLEEP. TRIED HER BEST TO WAIT UP FOR YOU.
MY LI'L CHICKADEE...

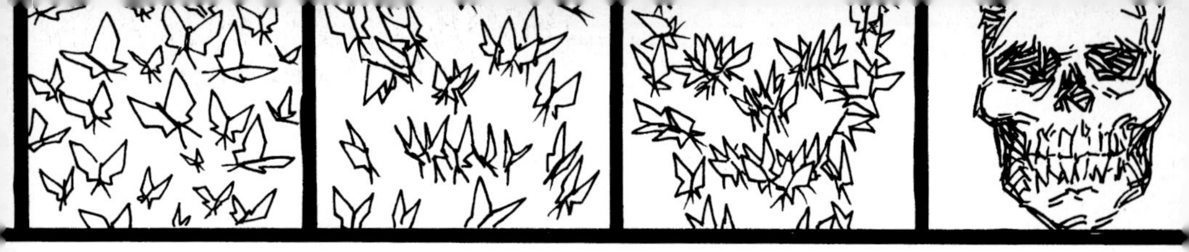

Much effort has been expended trying to explain and understand Hunter Rose's altruistic interest in my mother, the young and wayward Stacy Palumbo. By all examination of his own accounts, it was a relationship based upon genuine and supportive affection—the seemingly lone spark of humanity remaining kindled in a soul that had long ago left such considerations as love and charity behind. I maintain that his adoption and compassion towards his youthful ward weren't born from any pangs of guilt associated with his role in the death of Barry Palumbo, her uncle, former guardian, and only surviving family. As I have mentioned elsewhere, "guilt" is a human sentiment that found no exercise in the psyche of Grendel. Rather, I would posit that this atypical act of kindness was an emotional echo, a memory of the transformative blossoming he found in the patronage of his own mentor. Hunter saw in Stacy many of the same qualities that he adored about Jocasta Rose and, in turn, that Jackie had seen in him. There are several journal entries wherein he even refers to a halfhearted belief that Stacy could, in fact, be the actual reincarnation of his long-lost love. Of course it is *more* than ironic to consider that this isolated empathy would eventually lead to his ultimate downfall and, in turn, result in the utter tragedy that her life would inevitably become.

—excerpt from *Devil by the Deed*
by Christine Spar

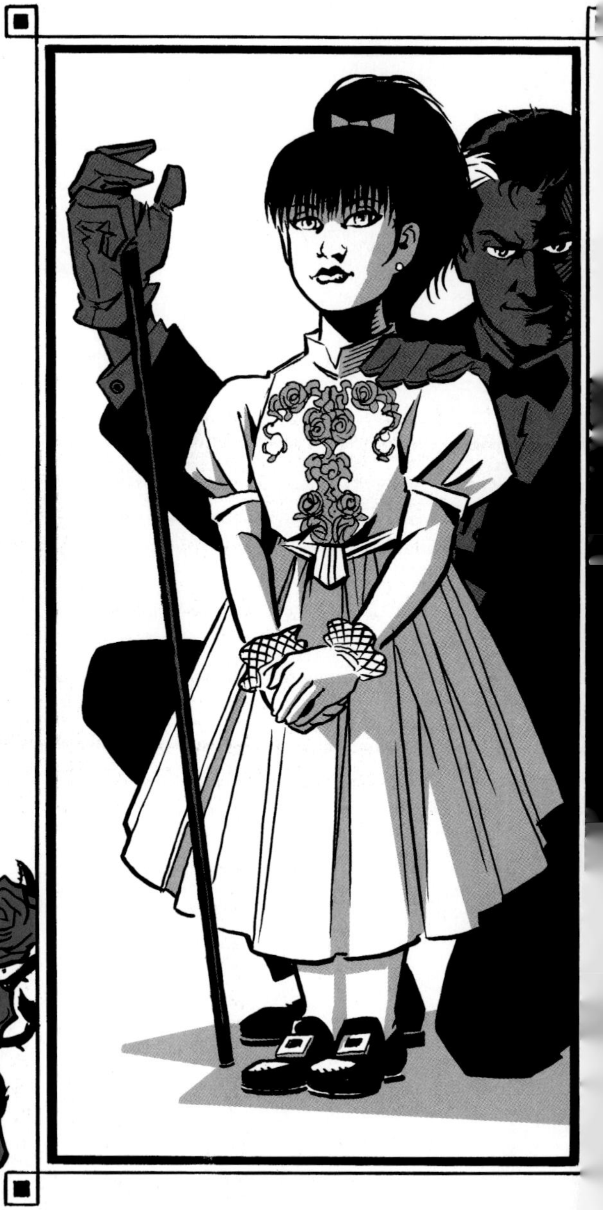

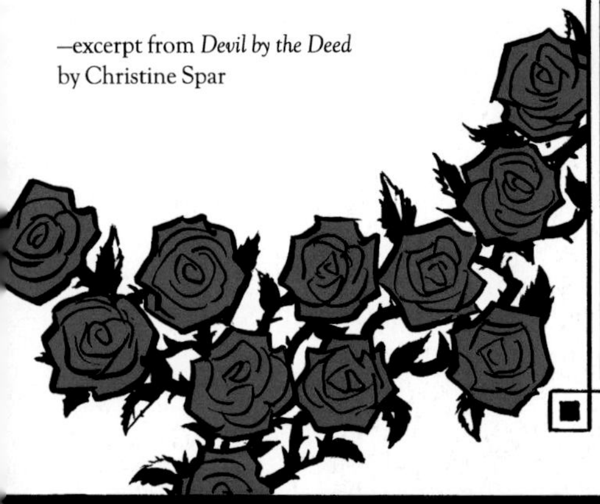

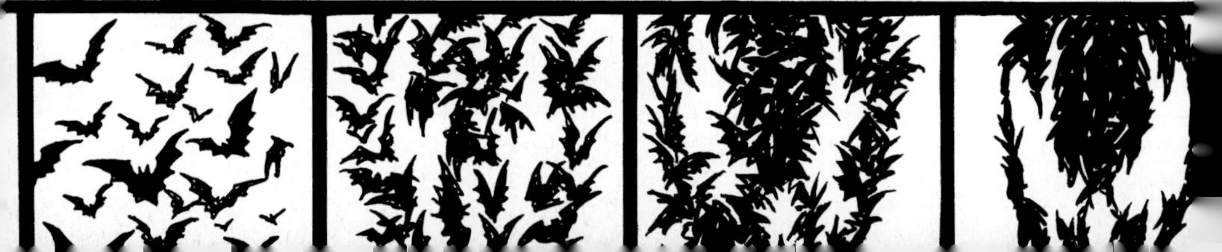

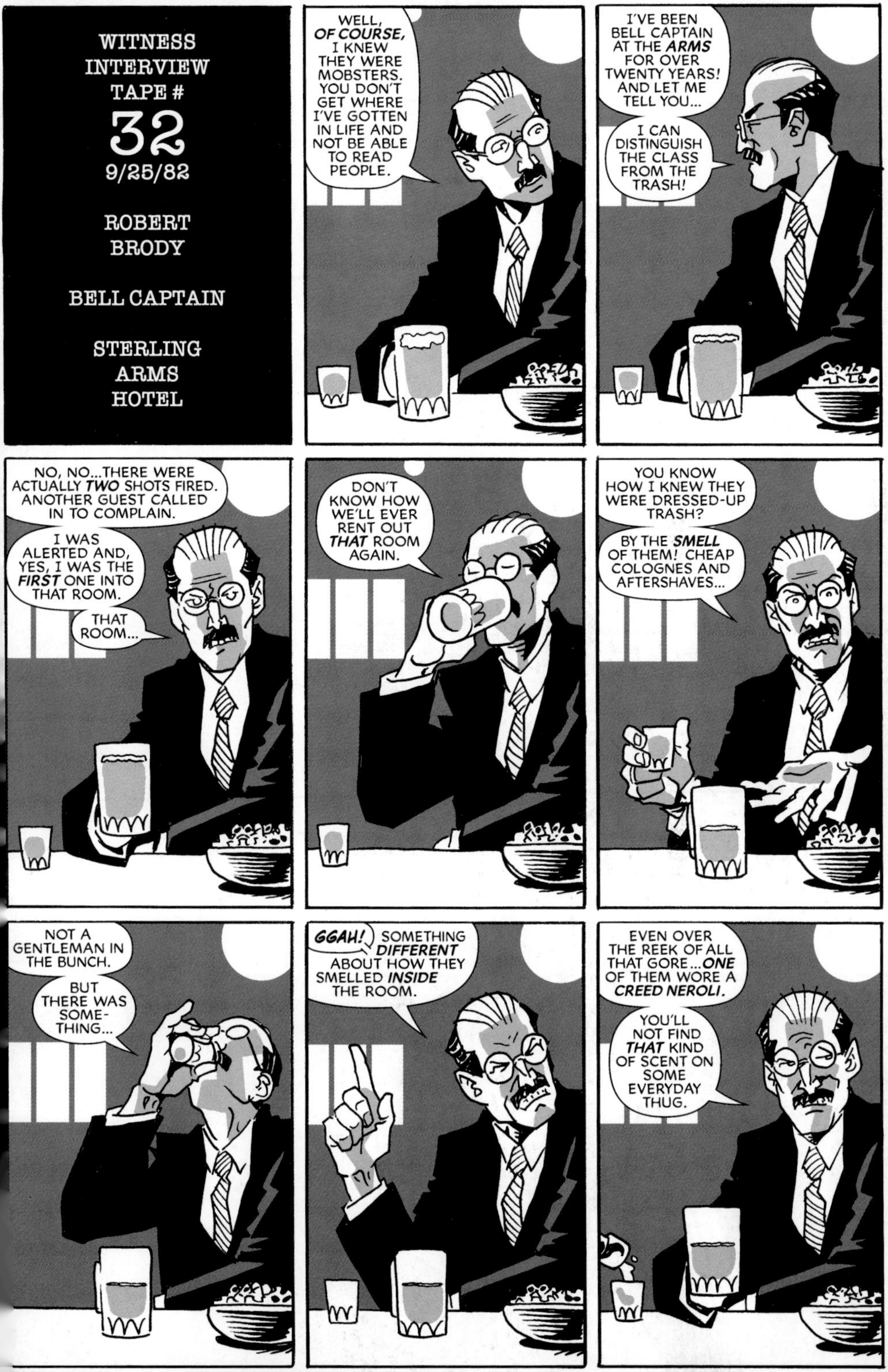
WITNESS INTERVIEW TAPE # 32
9/25/82
ROBERT BRODY
BELL CAPTAIN
STERLING ARMS HOTEL
WELL, OF COURSE, I KNEW THEY WERE MOBSTERS. YOU DON'T GET WHERE I'VE GOTTEN IN LIFE AND NOT BE ABLE TO READ PEOPLE.
I'VE BEEN BELL CAPTAIN AT THE ARMS FOR OVER TWENTY YEARS! AND LET ME TELL YOU...
I CAN DISTINGUISH THE CLASS FROM THE TRASH!
NO, NO...THERE WERE ACTUALLY TWO SHOTS FIRED. ANOTHER GUEST CALLED IN TO COMPLAIN.
I WAS ALERTED AND, YES, I WAS THE FIRST ONE INTO THAT ROOM.
THAT ROOM...
DON'T KNOW HOW WE'LL EVER RENT OUT THAT ROOM AGAIN.
YOU KNOW HOW I KNEW THEY WERE DRESSED-UP TRASH?
BY THE SMELL OF THEM! CHEAP COLOGNES AND AFTERSHAVES...
NOT A GENTLEMAN IN THE BUNCH.
BUT THERE WAS SOME-THING...
GGAH!
SOMETHING DIFFERENT ABOUT HOW THEY SMELLED INSIDE THE ROOM.
EVEN OVER THE REEK OF ALL THAT GORE...ONE OF THEM WORE A CREED NEROLI.
YOU'LL NOT FIND THAT KIND OF SCENT ON SOME EVERYDAY THUG.

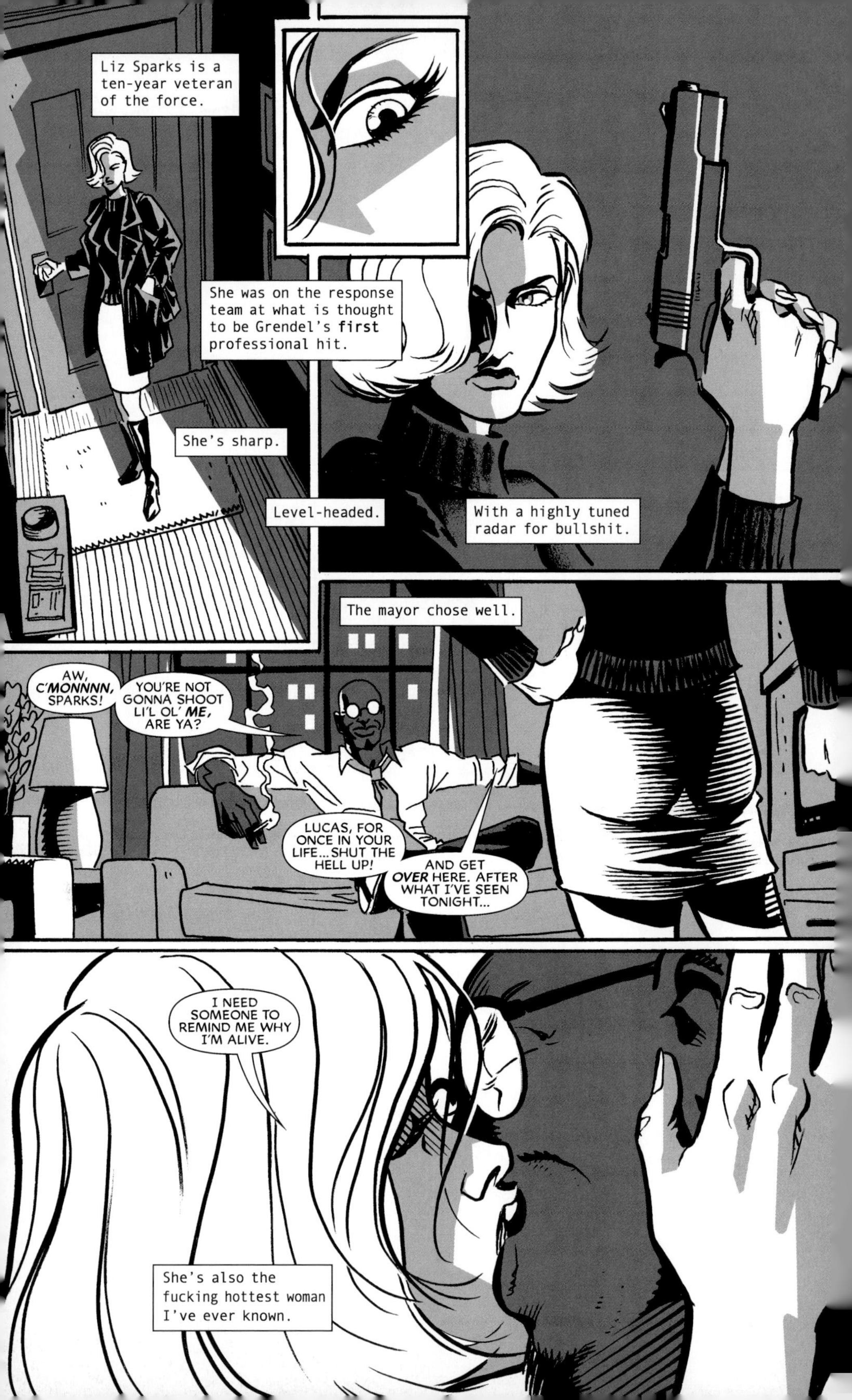
Liz Sparks is a ten-year veteran of the force.
She was on the response team at what is thought to be Grendel's **first** professional hit.
She's sharp.
Level-headed.
With a highly tuned radar for bullshit.
The mayor chose well.
AW, C'MONNNN, SPARKS!
YOU'RE NOT GONNA SHOOT LI'L OL' ME, ARE YA?
LUCAS, FOR ONCE IN YOUR LIFE... SHUT THE HELL UP!
AND GET OVER HERE. AFTER WHAT I'VE SEEN TONIGHT...
I NEED SOMEONE TO REMIND ME WHY I'M ALIVE.
She's also the fucking hottest woman I've ever known.

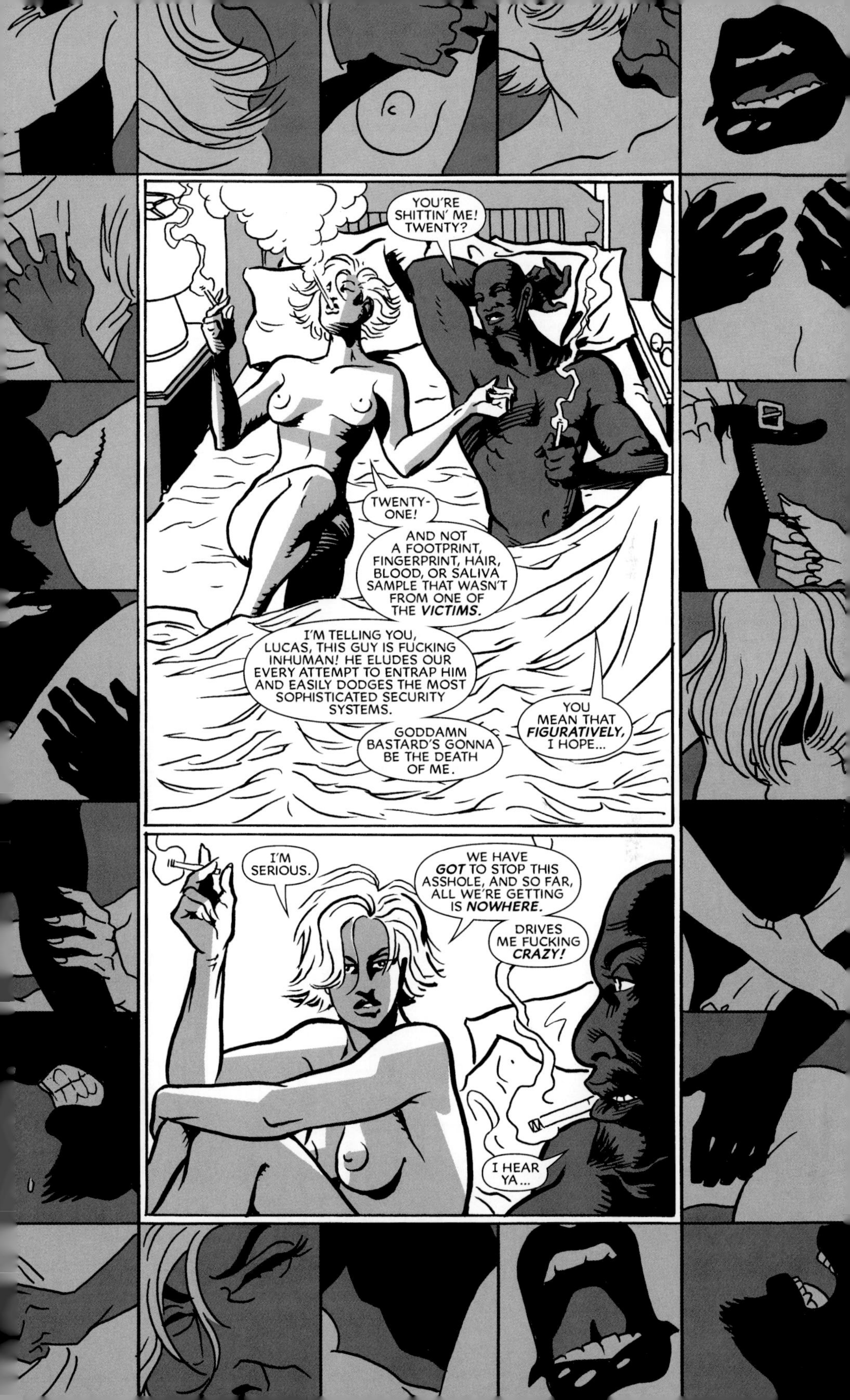
YOU'RE SHITTIN' ME! TWENTY?
TWENTY-ONE!
AND NOT A FOOTPRINT, FINGERPRINT, HAIR, BLOOD, OR SALIVA SAMPLE THAT WASN'T FROM ONE OF THE *VICTIMS.*
I'M TELLING YOU, LUCAS, THIS GUY IS FUCKING INHUMAN! HE ELUDES OUR EVERY ATTEMPT TO ENTRAP HIM AND EASILY DODGES THE MOST SOPHISTICATED SECURITY SYSTEMS.
GODDAMN BASTARD'S GONNA BE THE DEATH OF ME.
YOU MEAN THAT *FIGURATIVELY,* I HOPE...
I'M SERIOUS.
WE HAVE *GOT* TO STOP THIS ASSHOLE, AND SO FAR, ALL WE'RE GETTING IS *NOWHERE.*
DRIVES ME FUCKING *CRAZY!*
I HEAR YA...

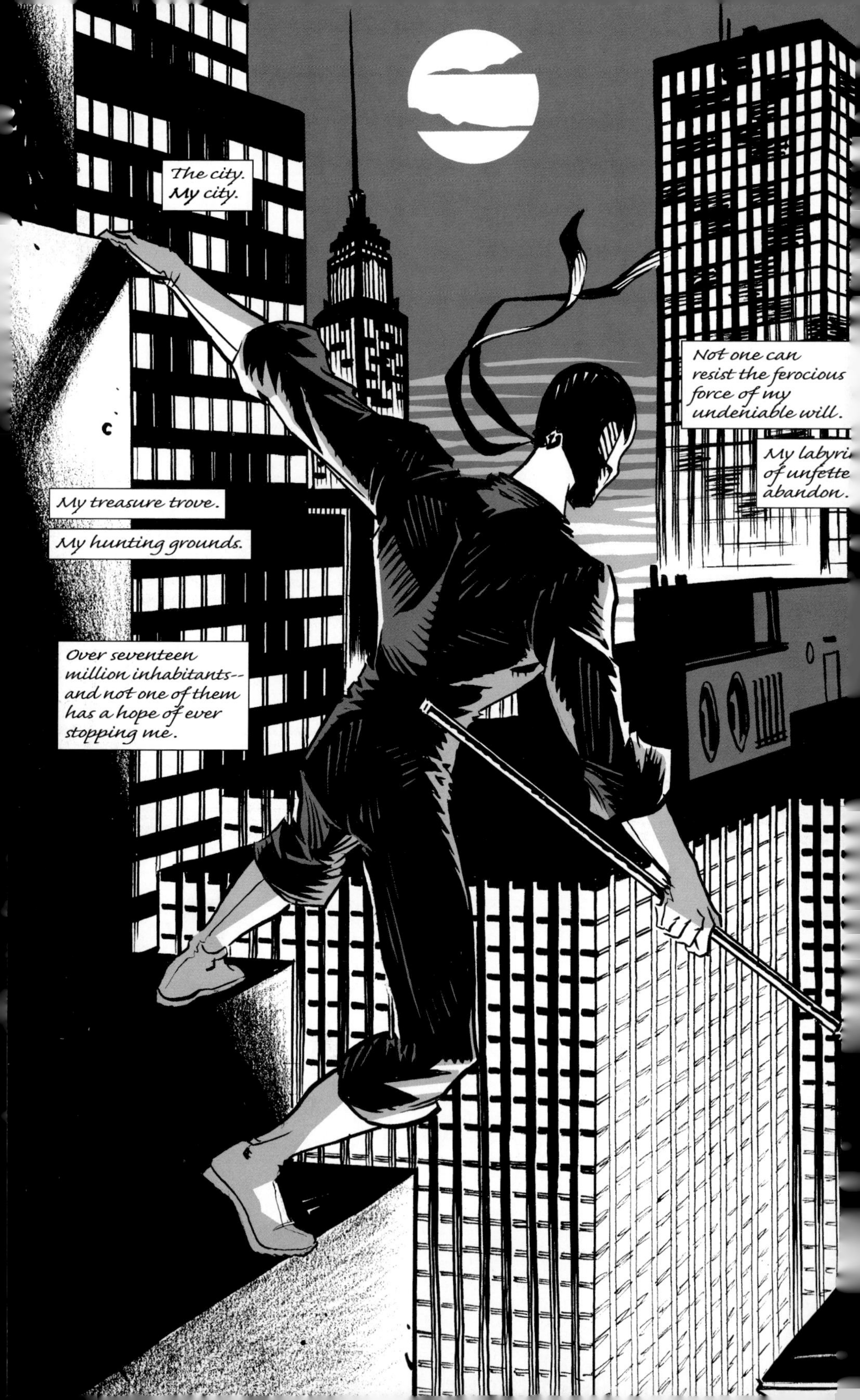
The city. My city.
My treasure trove.
My hunting grounds.
Over seventeen million inhabitants--and not one of them has a hope of ever stopping me.
Not one can resist the ferocious force of my undeniable will.
My labyri of unfette abandon.

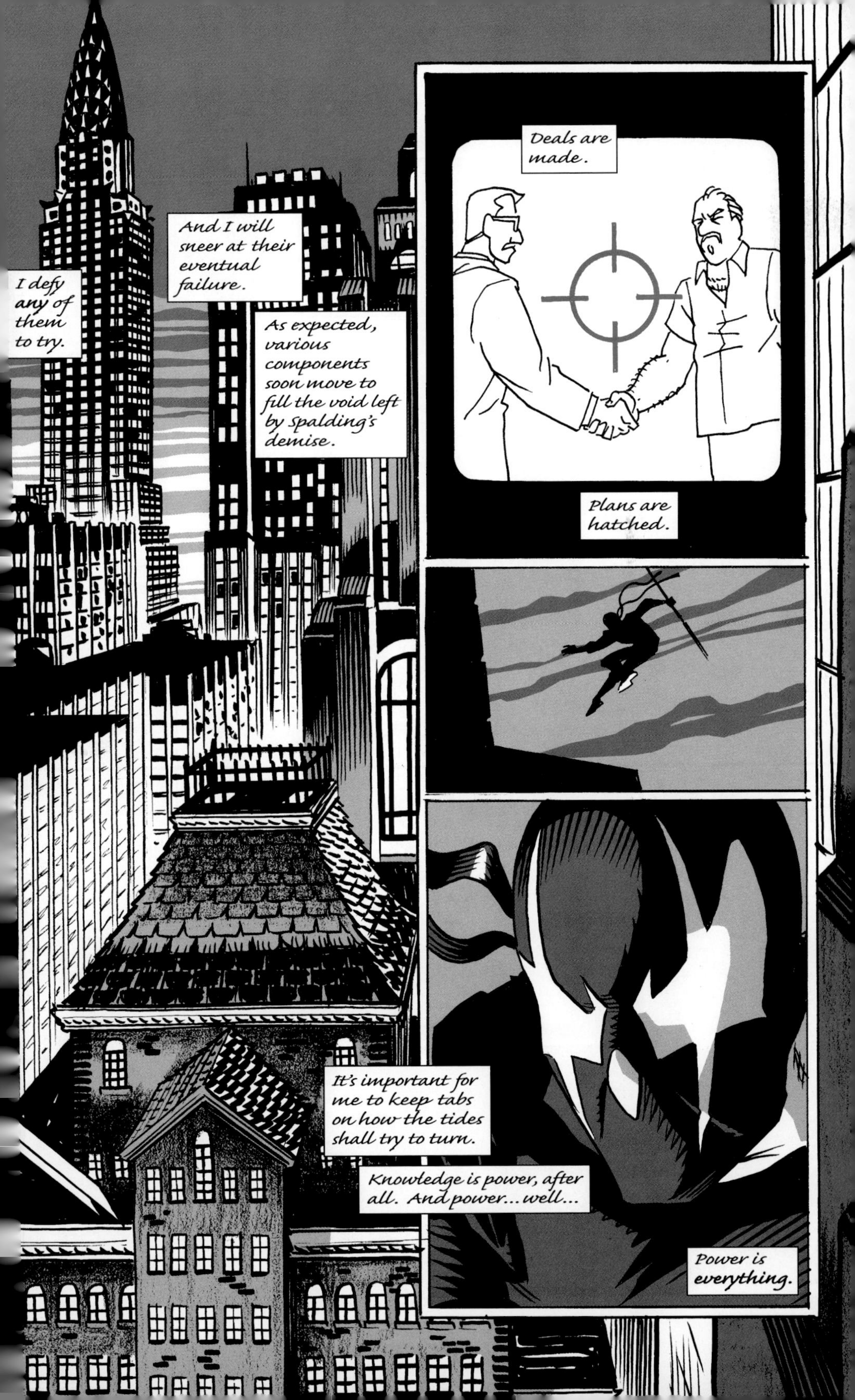
I defy any of them to try.
And I will sneer at their eventual failure.
As expected, various components soon move to fill the void left by Spalding's demise.
Deals are made.
Plans are hatched.
It's important for me to keep tabs on how the tides shall try to turn.
Knowledge is power, after all. And power... well...
Power is everything.

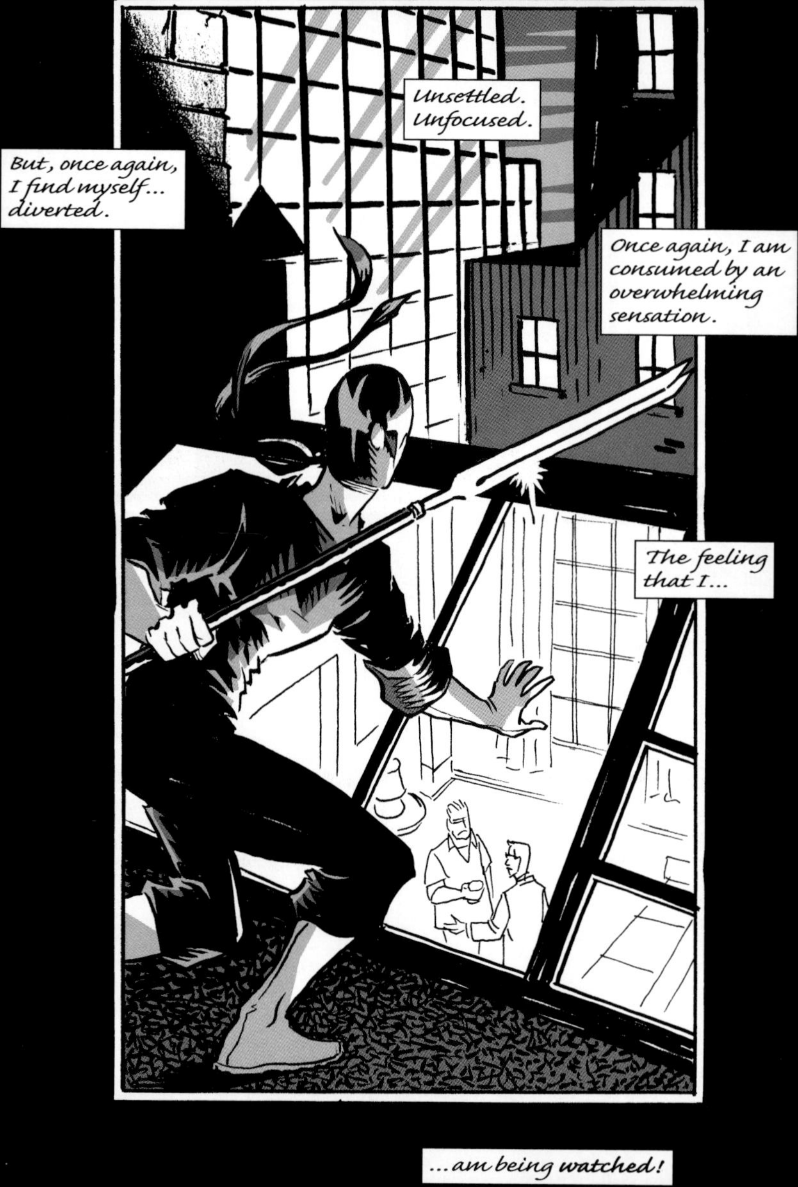
But, once again,
I find myself...
diverted.
Unsettled.
Unfocused.
Once again, I am
consumed by an
overwhelming
sensation.
The feeling
that I...
...am being watched!

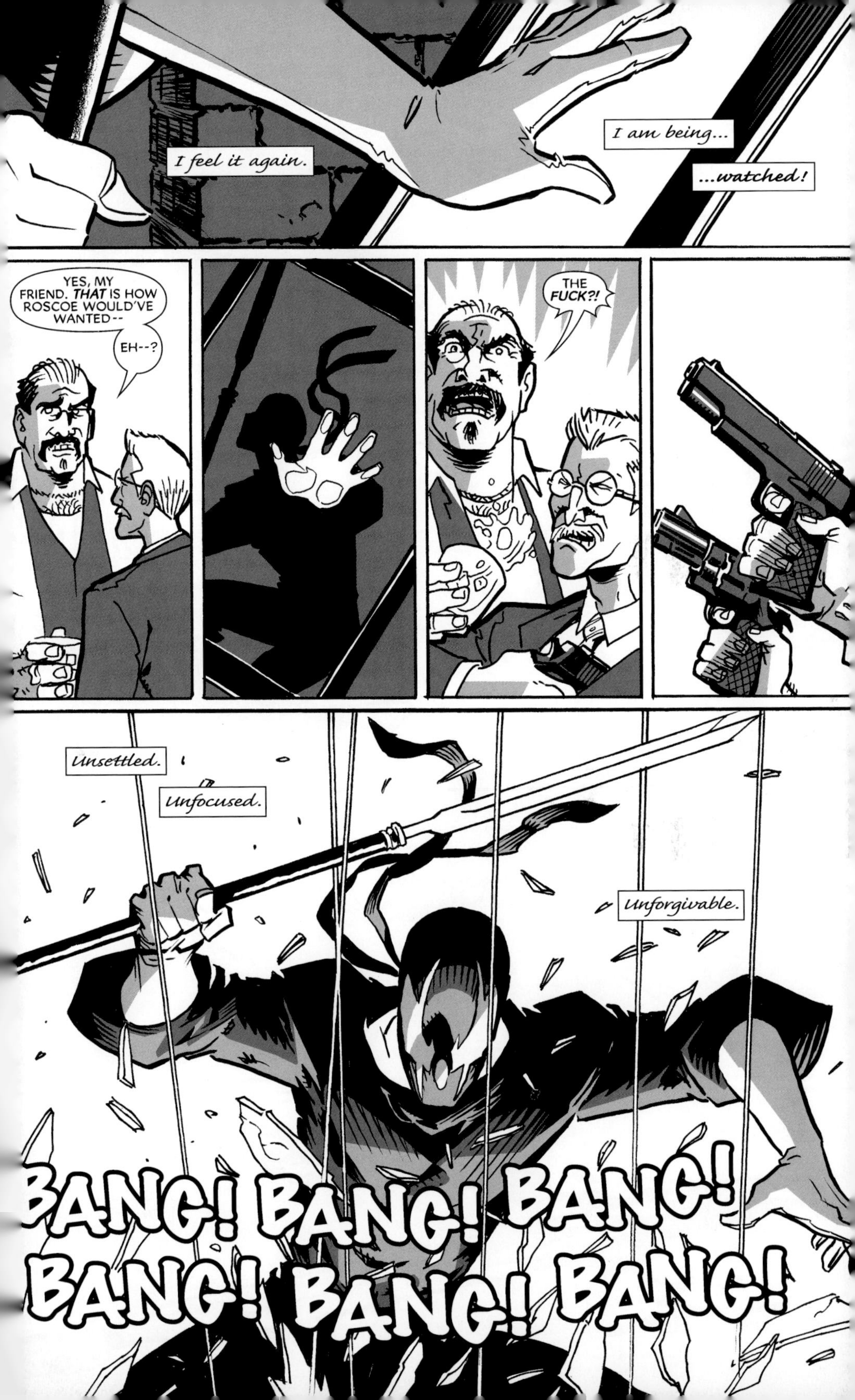
I feel it again.
I am being...
...watched!
YES, MY FRIEND. THAT IS HOW ROSCOE WOULD'VE WANTED--
EH--?
THE FUCK?!
Unsettled.
Unfocused.
Unforgivable.
BANG! BANG! BANG!
BANG! BANG! BANG!

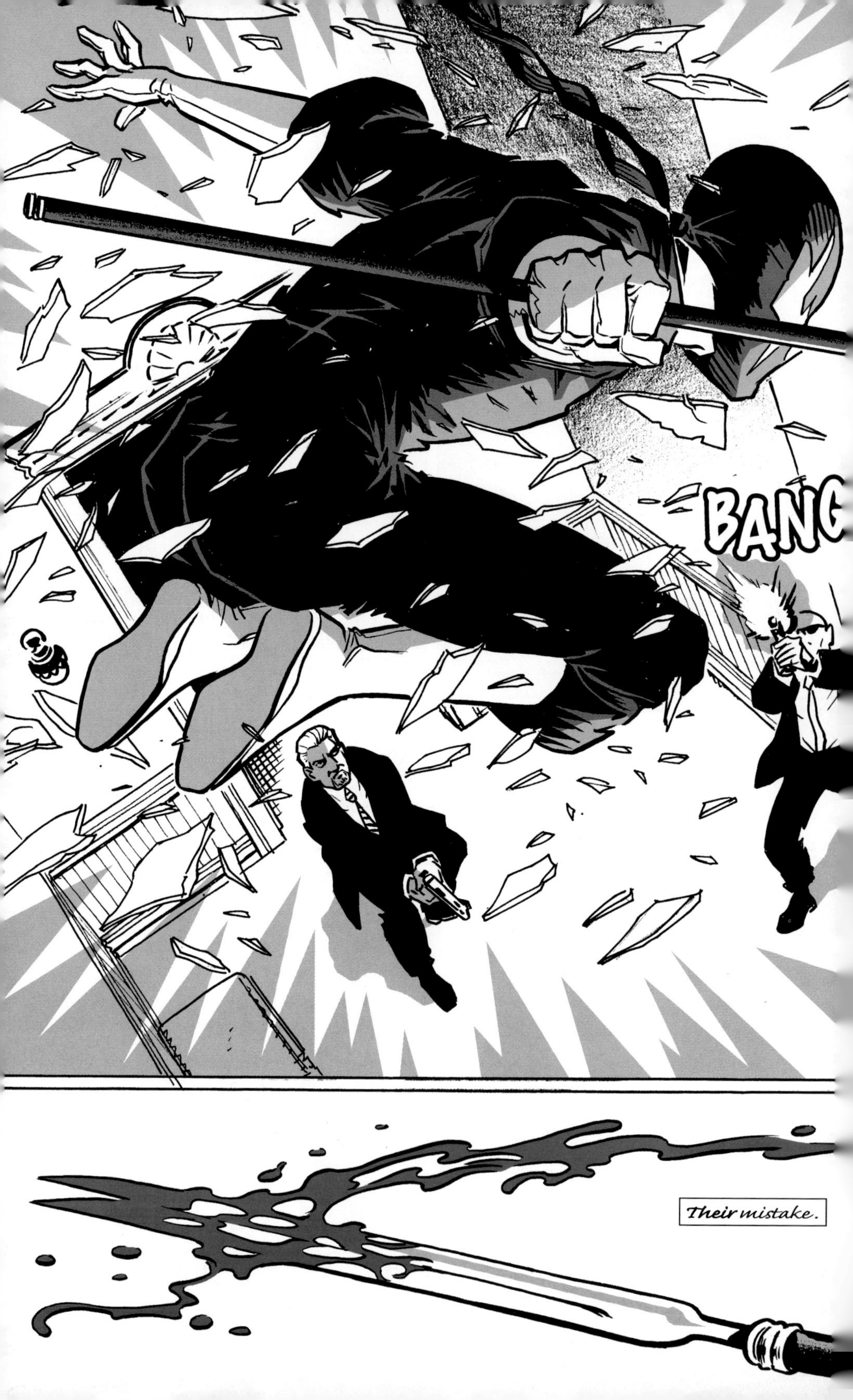
BANG
Their mistake.

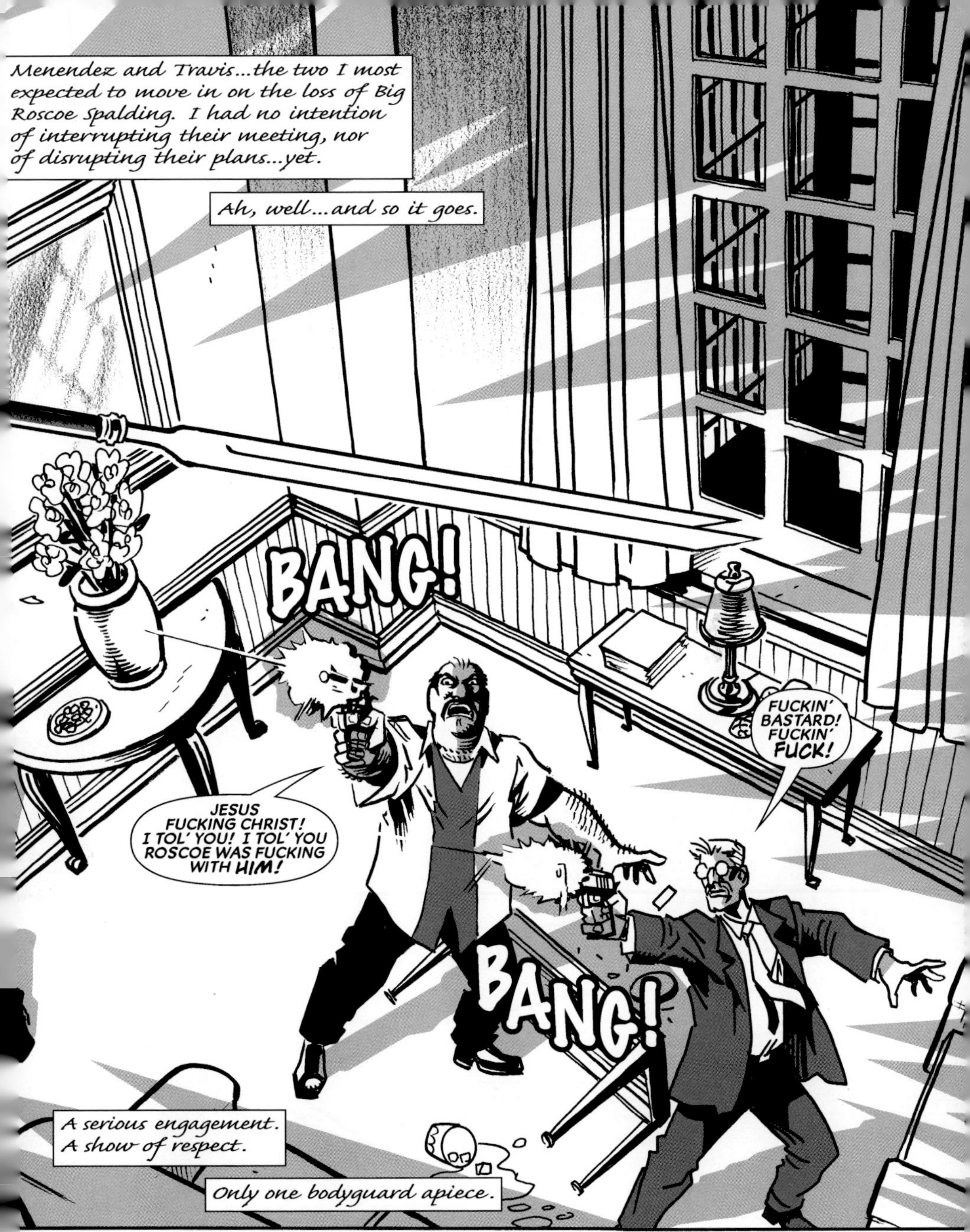
Menendez and Travis...the two I most expected to move in on the loss of Big Roscoe Spalding. I had no intention of interrupting their meeting, nor of disrupting their plans...yet.
Ah, well...and so it goes.
BANG!
FUCKIN' BASTARD! FUCKIN' FUCK!
JESUS FUCKING CHRIST! I TOL' YOU! I TOL' YOU ROSCOE WAS FUCKING WITH HIM!
BANG!
A serious engagement. A show of respect.
Only one bodyguard apiece.

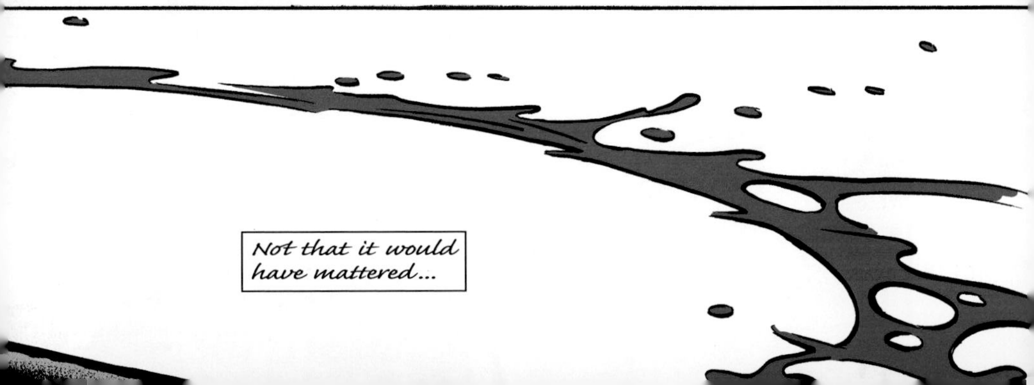
Not that it would have mattered...

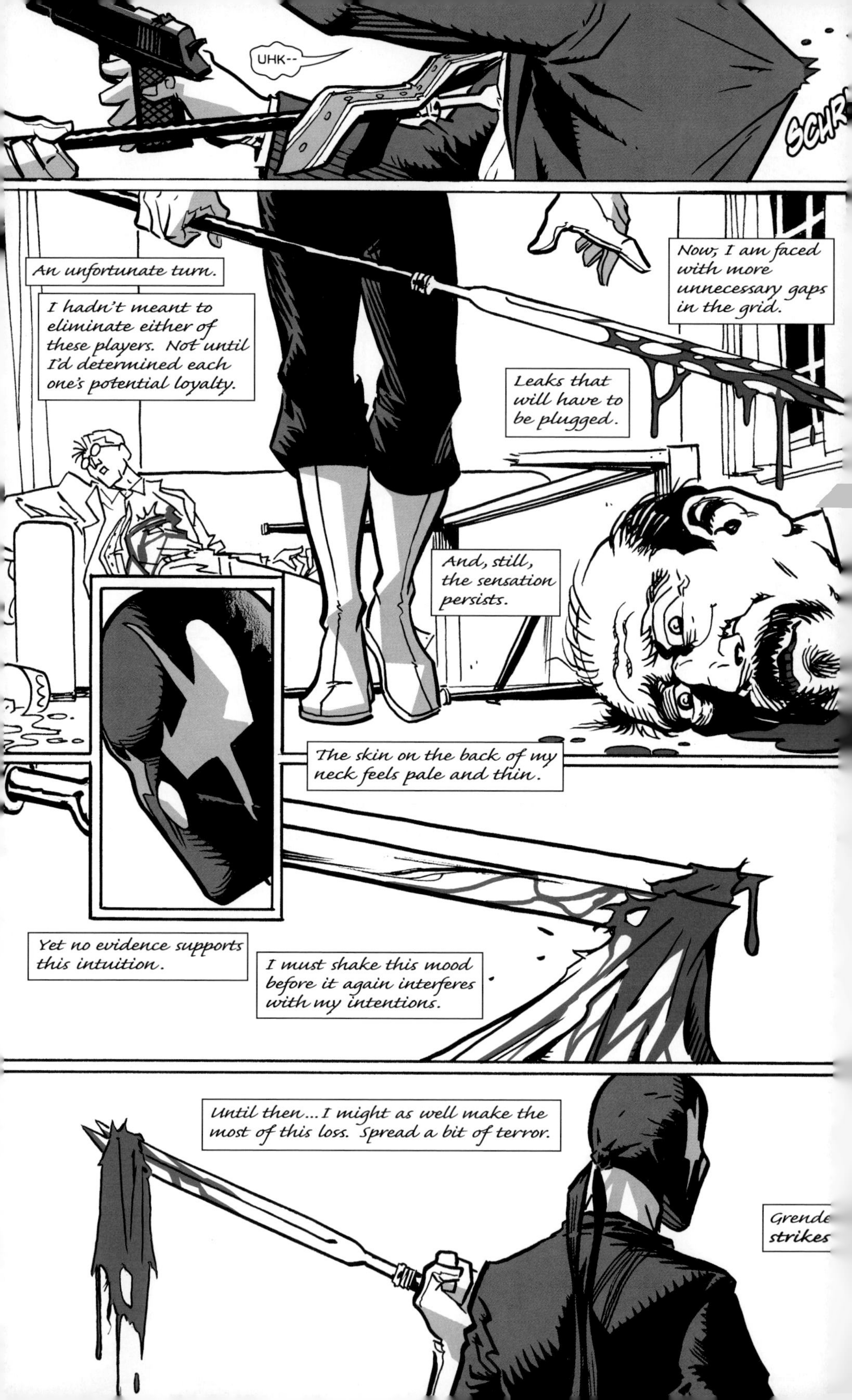
UHK--
SCHR
An unfortunate turn.
I hadn't meant to eliminate either of these players. Not until I'd determined each one's potential loyalty.
Now, I am faced with more unnecessary gaps in the grid.
Leaks that will have to be plugged.
And, still, the sensation persists.
The skin on the back of my neck feels pale and thin.
Yet no evidence supports this intuition.
I must shake this mood before it again interferes with my intentions.
Until then... I might as well make the most of this loss. Spread a bit of terror.
Grende
strikes

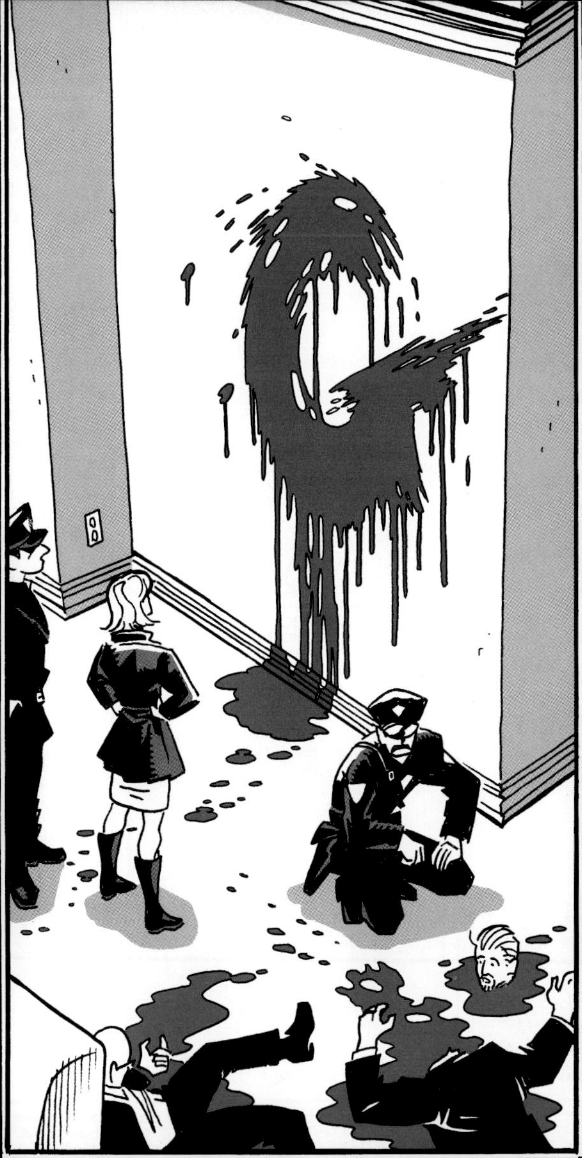

NEW YORK POLICE DEPARTMENT
OFFICIAL REPORT
MANHATTAN BUREAU

OFFENSE/INCIDENT: Homicide (multiple)
LOCATION: 1335 E. 25th St.
PRECINCT: 7th

CASE #: 5571932
DATE: 9/26/82
TIME: 11:30 P.M. (Approx.)

REPORTING OFFICER: Det. Elizabeth Sparks

EYES ONLY: Head of "Task Force G" alerted just after midnight by officers Anthony Dykstra and James McCall, who responded to a call of "Shots Fired" at the Eastview Apartments building. Officers discovered the aftermath of a gun battle that resulted in the deaths of four victims: Jorge Menendez (HM), William "Billy-Bone" Travis (WM), Pablo Lopez (HM), and Thomas McKinnon (WM). All four fatalities apparently resulted from deep stab wounds, including one complete decapitation. Officers referred case to Det. Sparks due to the presence of a large "G" insignia painted on the wall in the victims' own blood. Said graffiti has long been associated with the criminal boss and sometime-assassin code-named "Grendel." Assailant apparently entered the penthouse apartment through a shattered skylight and proceeded to engage the room's occupants in a seemingly short and decisive battle (motive unknown at this time). Assailant was apparently unharmed during the encounter, as all blood samples found on the scene match only the victims' types. No further physical evidence found to be associated with the assailant. Ballistics reports indicate a total of eleven shots fired from three of the victims' weapons. Thomas McKinnon's weapon had been drawn but was unfired. All bullets recovered from the room's walls and furniture.

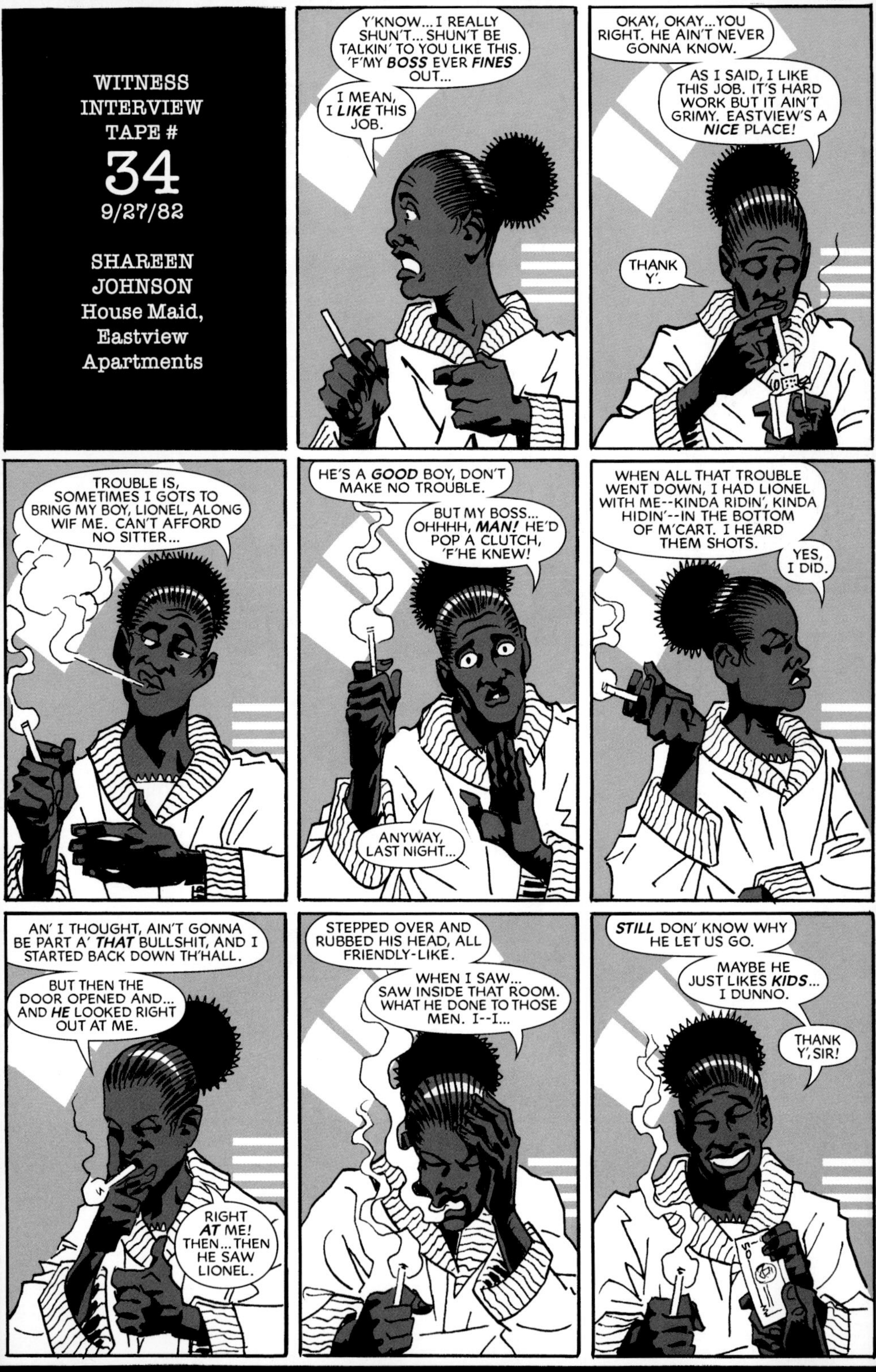
WITNESS INTERVIEW TAPE # 34 9/27/82
SHAREEN JOHNSON House Maid, Eastview Apartments
Y'KNOW... I REALLY SHUN'T... SHUN'T BE TALKIN' TO YOU LIKE THIS. 'F'MY BOSS EVER FINES OUT...
I MEAN, I LIKE THIS JOB.
OKAY, OKAY... YOU RIGHT. HE AIN'T NEVER GONNA KNOW.
AS I SAID, I LIKE THIS JOB. IT'S HARD WORK BUT IT AIN'T GRIMY. EASTVIEW'S A NICE PLACE!
THANK Y'.
TROUBLE IS, SOMETIMES I GOTS TO BRING MY BOY, LIONEL, ALONG WIF ME. CAN'T AFFORD NO SITTER...
HE'S A GOOD BOY, DON'T MAKE NO TROUBLE.
BUT MY BOSS... OHHHH, MAN! HE'D POP A CLUTCH, 'F'HE KNEW!
ANYWAY, LAST NIGHT...
WHEN ALL THAT TROUBLE WENT DOWN, I HAD LIONEL WITH ME--KINDA RIDIN', KINDA HIDIN'--IN THE BOTTOM OF M'CART. I HEARD THEM SHOTS.
YES, I DID.
AN' I THOUGHT, AIN'T GONNA BE PART A' THAT BULLSHIT, AND I STARTED BACK DOWN TH'HALL.
BUT THEN THE DOOR OPENED AND... AND HE LOOKED RIGHT OUT AT ME.
RIGHT AT ME! THEN... THEN HE SAW LIONEL.
STEPPED OVER AND RUBBED HIS HEAD, ALL FRIENDLY-LIKE.
WHEN I SAW... SAW INSIDE THAT ROOM. WHAT HE DONE TO THOSE MEN. I--I...
STILL DON' KNOW WHY HE LET US GO.
MAYBE HE JUST LIKES KIDS... I DUNNO.
THANK Y', SIR!

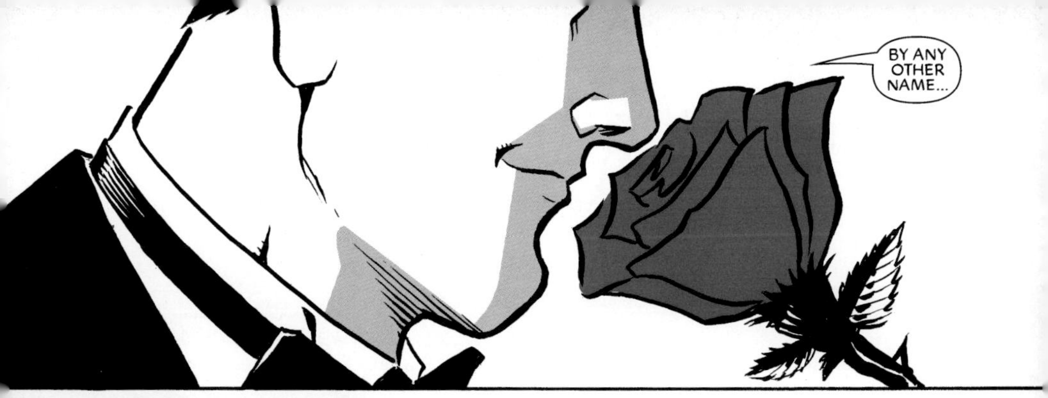

BY ANY OTHER NAME...

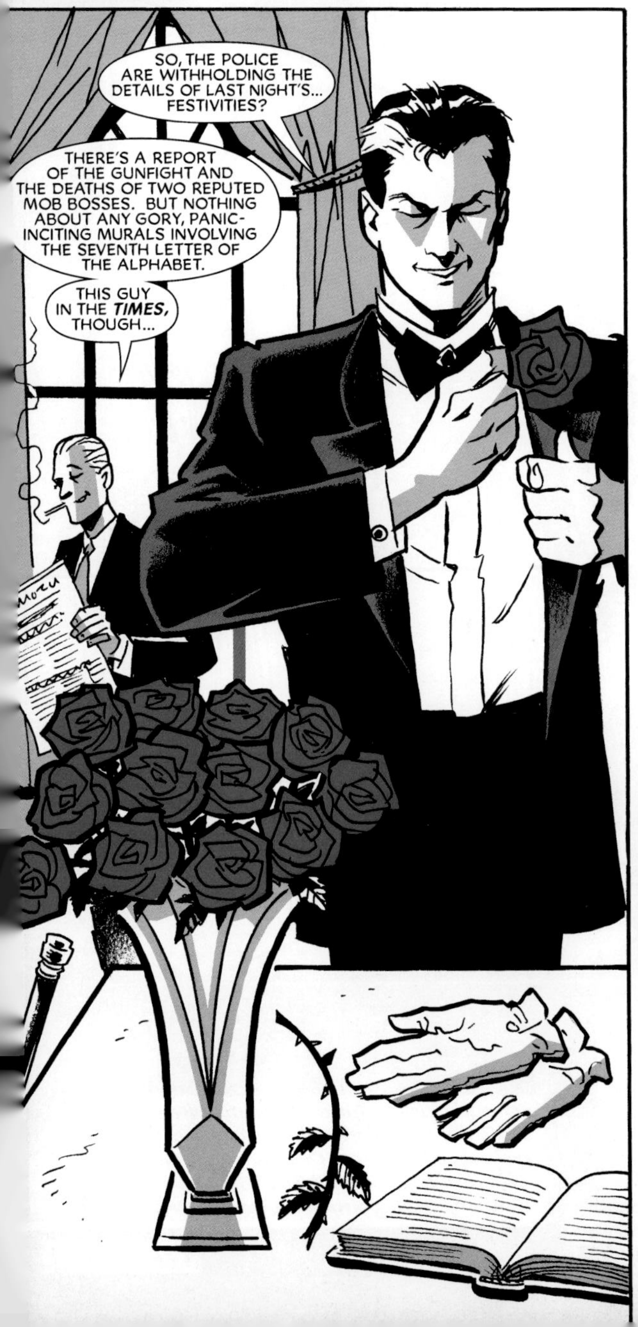

SO, THE POLICE ARE WITHHOLDING THE DETAILS OF LAST NIGHT'S... FESTIVITIES?
THERE'S A REPORT OF THE GUNFIGHT AND THE DEATHS OF TWO REPUTED MOB BOSSES. BUT NOTHING ABOUT ANY GORY, PANIC-INCITING MURALS INVOLVING THE SEVENTH LETTER OF THE ALPHABET.
THIS GUY IN THE ***TIMES,*** THOUGH...

It is doubtful that Grendel could have, in fact, risen to the top—or even maintained his dominance—of the criminal underworld without the presence and assistance of Larry Stohler. Like a sly jackal to Hunter's proud and ferocious lion, Larry stalked around the edges of his master's activities. His highly attuned ear for both news and gossip provided Grendel's network with an invaluable source of information, which was consistently quick and rarely in dispute.

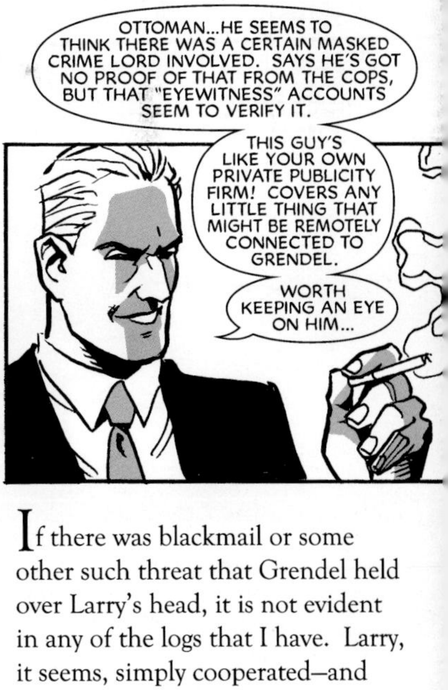

OTTOMAN...HE SEEMS TO THINK THERE WAS A CERTAIN MASKED CRIME LORD INVOLVED. SAYS HE'S GOT NO PROOF OF THAT FROM THE COPS, BUT THAT "EYEWITNESS" ACCOUNTS SEEM TO VERIFY IT.
THIS GUY'S LIKE YOUR OWN PRIVATE PUBLICITY FIRM! COVERS ANY LITTLE THING THAT MIGHT BE REMOTELY CONNECTED TO GRENDEL.
WORTH KEEPING AN EYE ON HIM...

If there was blackmail or some other such threat that Grendel held over Larry's head, it is not evident in any of the logs that I have. Larry, it seems, simply cooperated—and Grendel let him do so.

—excerpt from *Devil by the Deed* by Christine Spar

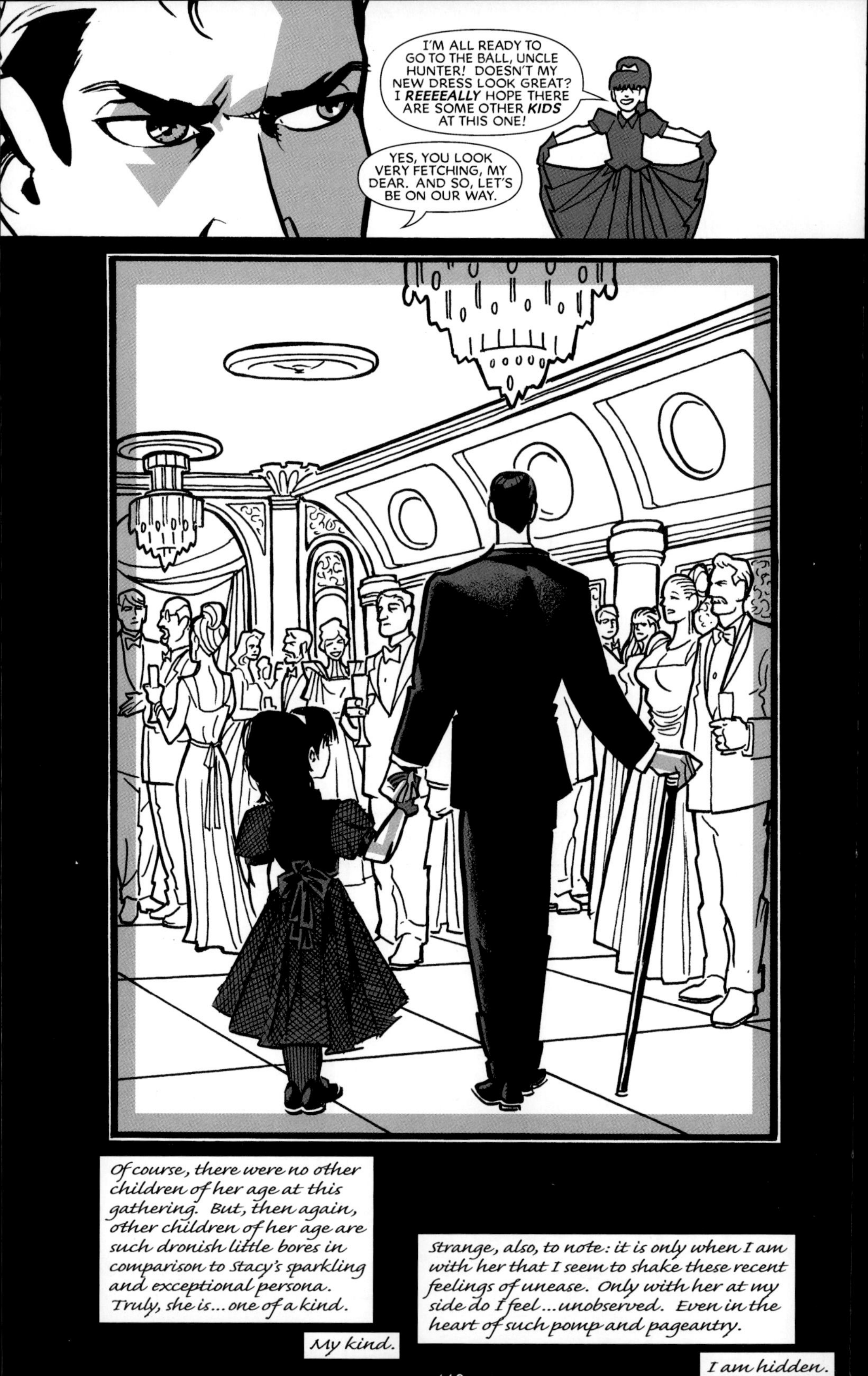
I'M ALL READY TO GO TO THE BALL, UNCLE HUNTER! DOESN'T MY NEW DRESS LOOK GREAT? I REEEEALLY HOPE THERE ARE SOME OTHER KIDS AT THIS ONE!
YES, YOU LOOK VERY FETCHING, MY DEAR. AND SO, LET'S BE ON OUR WAY.
Of course, there were no other children of her age at this gathering. But, then again, other children of her age are such dronish little bores in comparison to Stacy's sparkling and exceptional persona. Truly, she is... one of a kind.
My kind.
Strange, also, to note: it is only when I am with her that I seem to shake these recent feelings of unease. Only with her at my side do I feel... unobserved. Even in the heart of such pomp and pageantry.
I am hidden.

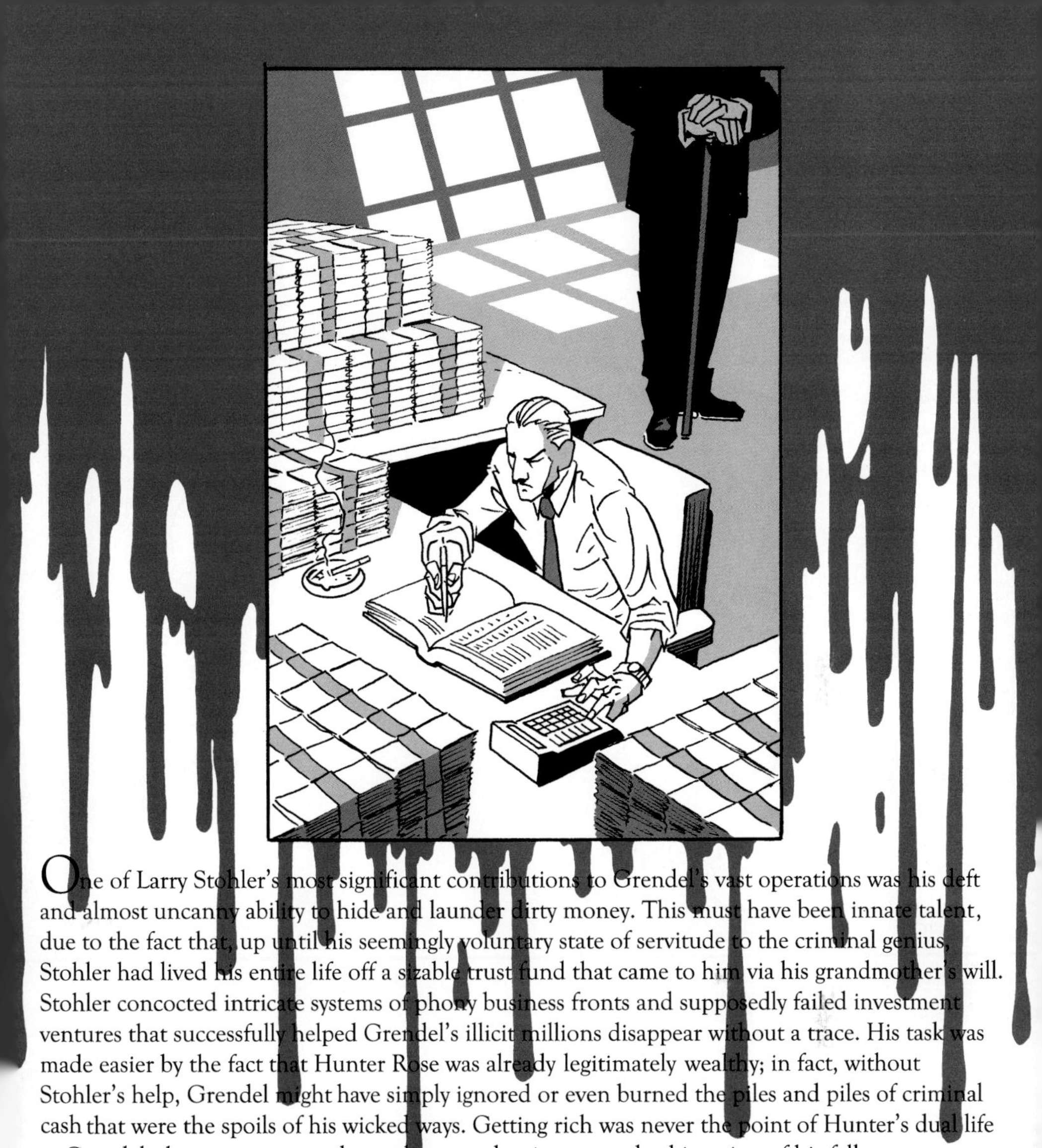

One of Larry Stohler's most significant contributions to Grendel's vast operations was his deft and almost uncanny ability to hide and launder dirty money. This must have been innate talent, due to the fact that, up until his seemingly voluntary state of servitude to the criminal genius, Stohler had lived his entire life off a sizable trust fund that came to him via his grandmother's will. Stohler concocted intricate systems of phony business fronts and supposedly failed investment ventures that successfully helped Grendel's illicit millions disappear without a trace. His task was made easier by the fact that Hunter Rose was already legitimately wealthy; in fact, without Stohler's help, Grendel might have simply ignored or even burned the piles and piles of criminal cash that were the spoils of his wicked ways. Getting rich was never the point of Hunter's dual life as Grendel; that purpose was always the utter dominance and subjugation of his fellow man.

—excerpt from *Devil by the Deed*
by Christine Spar

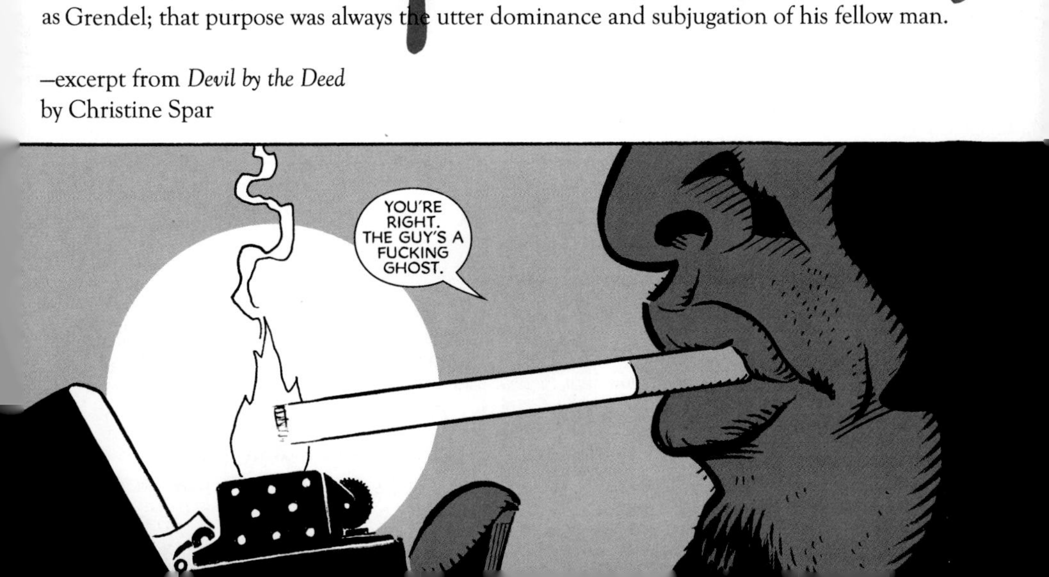
YOU'RE RIGHT. THE GUY'S A FUCKING GHOST.

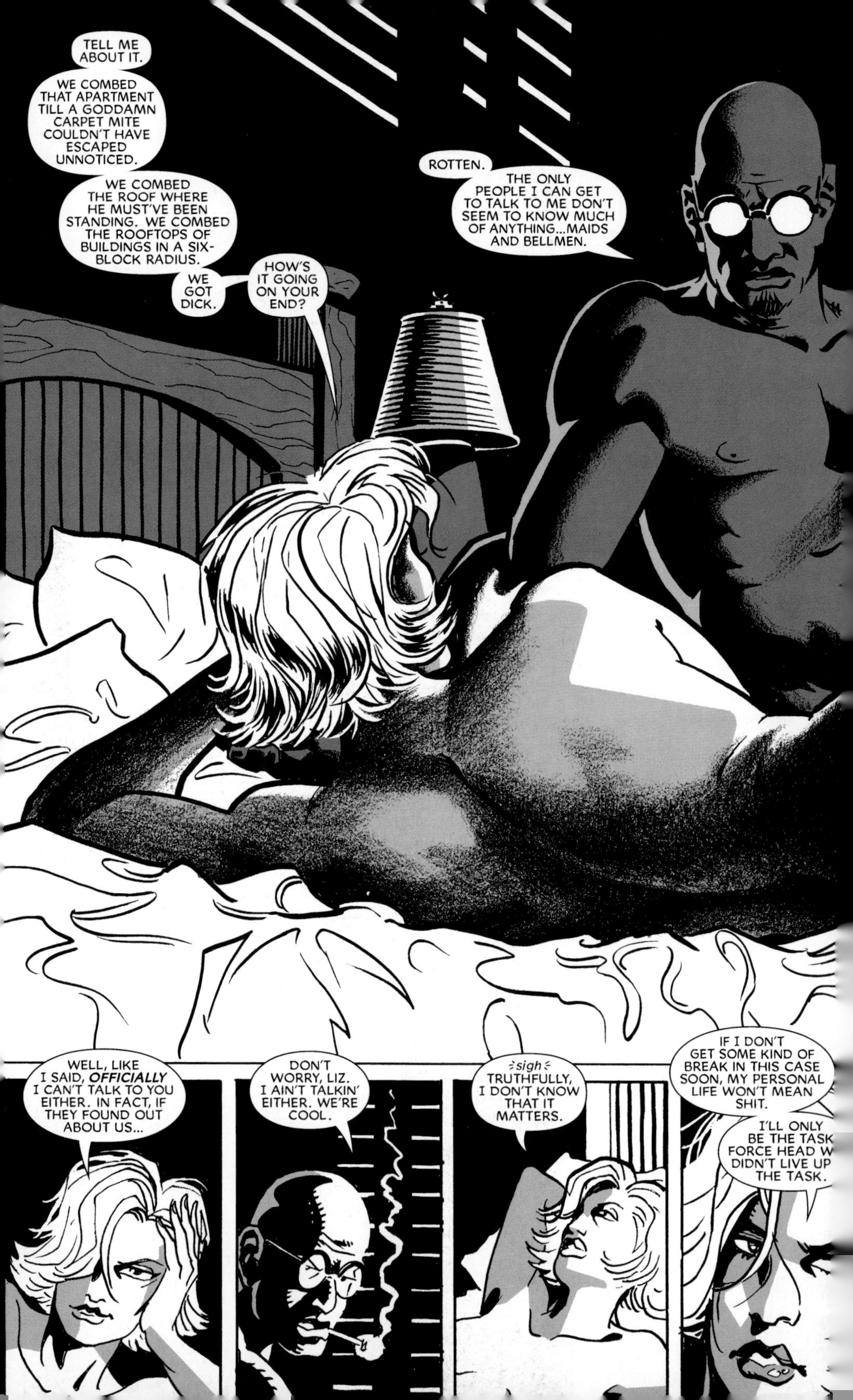
TELL ME ABOUT IT.
WE COMBED THAT APARTMENT TILL A GODDAMN CARPET MITE COULDN'T HAVE ESCAPED UNNOTICED.
WE COMBED THE ROOF WHERE HE MUST'VE BEEN STANDING. WE COMBED THE ROOFTOPS OF BUILDINGS IN A SIX-BLOCK RADIUS.
WE GOT DICK.
HOW'S IT GOING ON YOUR END?
ROTTEN.
THE ONLY PEOPLE I CAN GET TO TALK TO ME DON'T SEEM TO KNOW MUCH OF ANYTHING...MAIDS AND BELLMEN.
WELL, LIKE I SAID, *OFFICIALLY* I CAN'T TALK TO YOU EITHER. IN FACT, IF THEY FOUND OUT ABOUT US...
DON'T WORRY, LIZ. I AIN'T TALKIN' EITHER. WE'RE COOL.
sigh
TRUTHFULLY, I DON'T KNOW THAT IT MATTERS.
IF I DON'T GET SOME KIND OF BREAK IN THIS CASE SOON, MY PERSONAL LIFE WON'T MEAN SHIT.

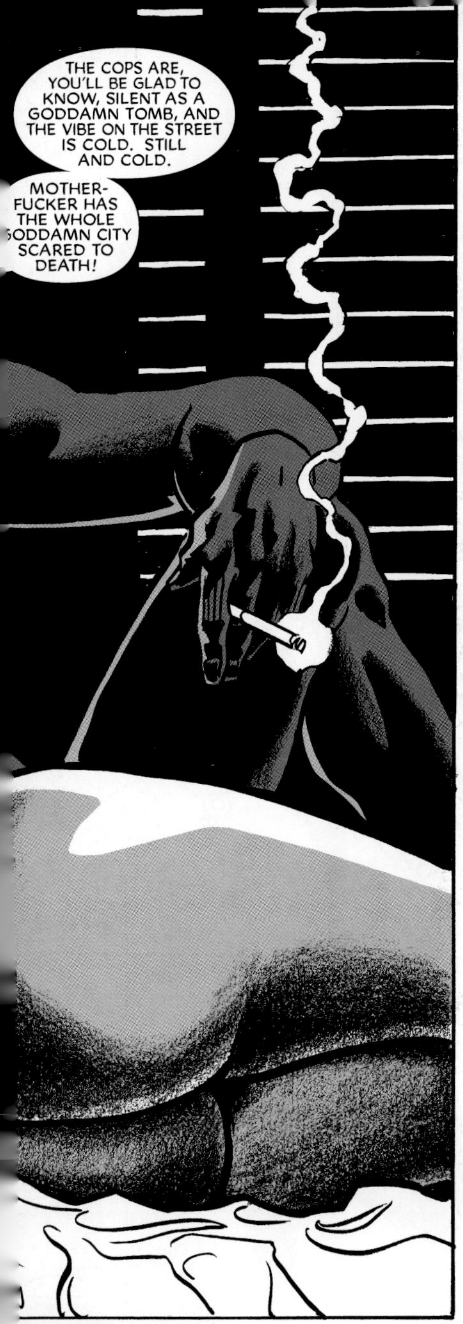
THE COPS ARE, YOU'LL BE GLAD TO KNOW, SILENT AS A GODDAMN TOMB, AND THE VIBE ON THE STREET IS COLD. STILL AND COLD.
MOTHER-FUCKER HAS THE WHOLE GODDAMN CITY SCARED TO DEATH!

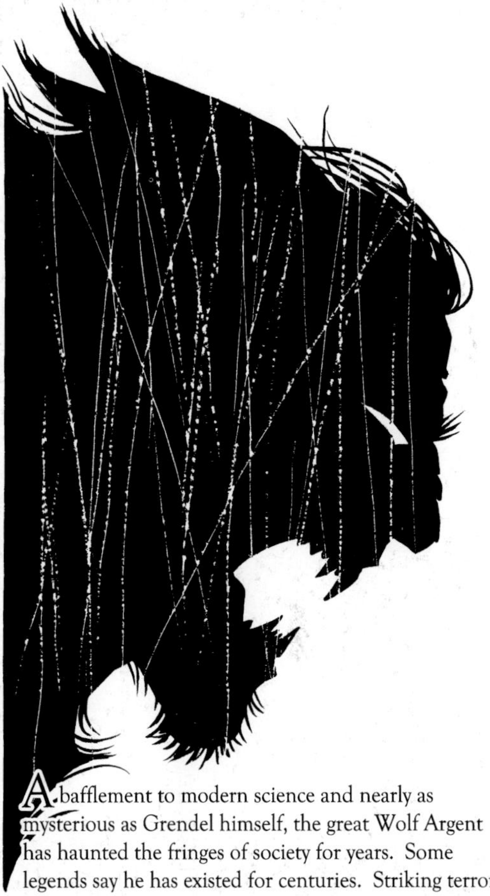

A bafflement to modern science and nearly as mysterious as Grendel himself, the great Wolf Argent has haunted the fringes of society for years. Some legends say he has existed for centuries. Striking terror into the hearts of evildoers everywhere (save, apparently, for one), the Wolf's violent attacks on the criminal underclass have lately been the subject of extreme controversy, with law-enforcement officials defending his actions as both necessary and justified. Some claim the Wolf is no better than the very villains he pursues, while still others claim that he is nothing more than an urban legend, concocted and maintained by authorities in order to act as a scapegoat for their own procedural infractions.

—excerpt from *Devil by the Deed*
by Christine Spar

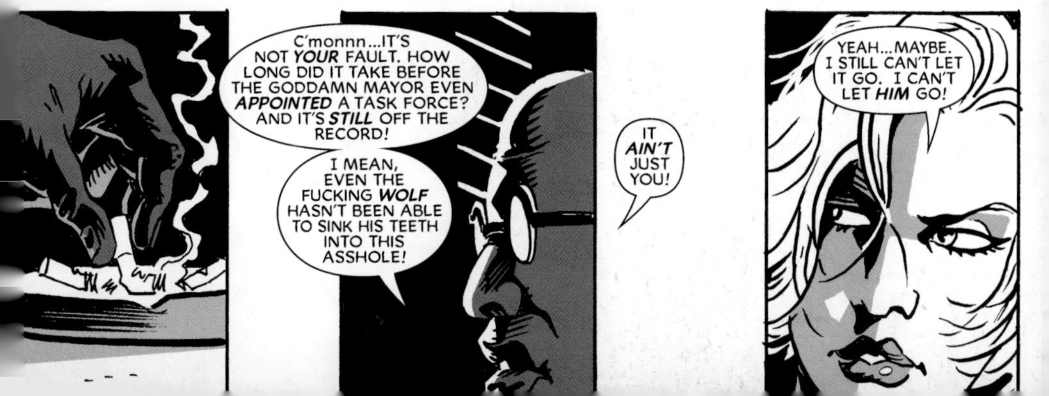
C'monnn...IT'S NOT *YOUR* FAULT. HOW LONG DID IT TAKE BEFORE THE GODDAMN MAYOR EVEN *APPOINTED* A TASK FORCE? AND IT'S *STILL* OFF THE RECORD!
I MEAN, EVEN THE FUCKING *WOLF* HASN'T BEEN ABLE TO SINK HIS TEETH INTO THIS ASSHOLE!
IT *AIN'T* JUST YOU!
YEAH...MAYBE. I STILL CAN'T LET IT GO. I CAN'T LET *HIM* GO!

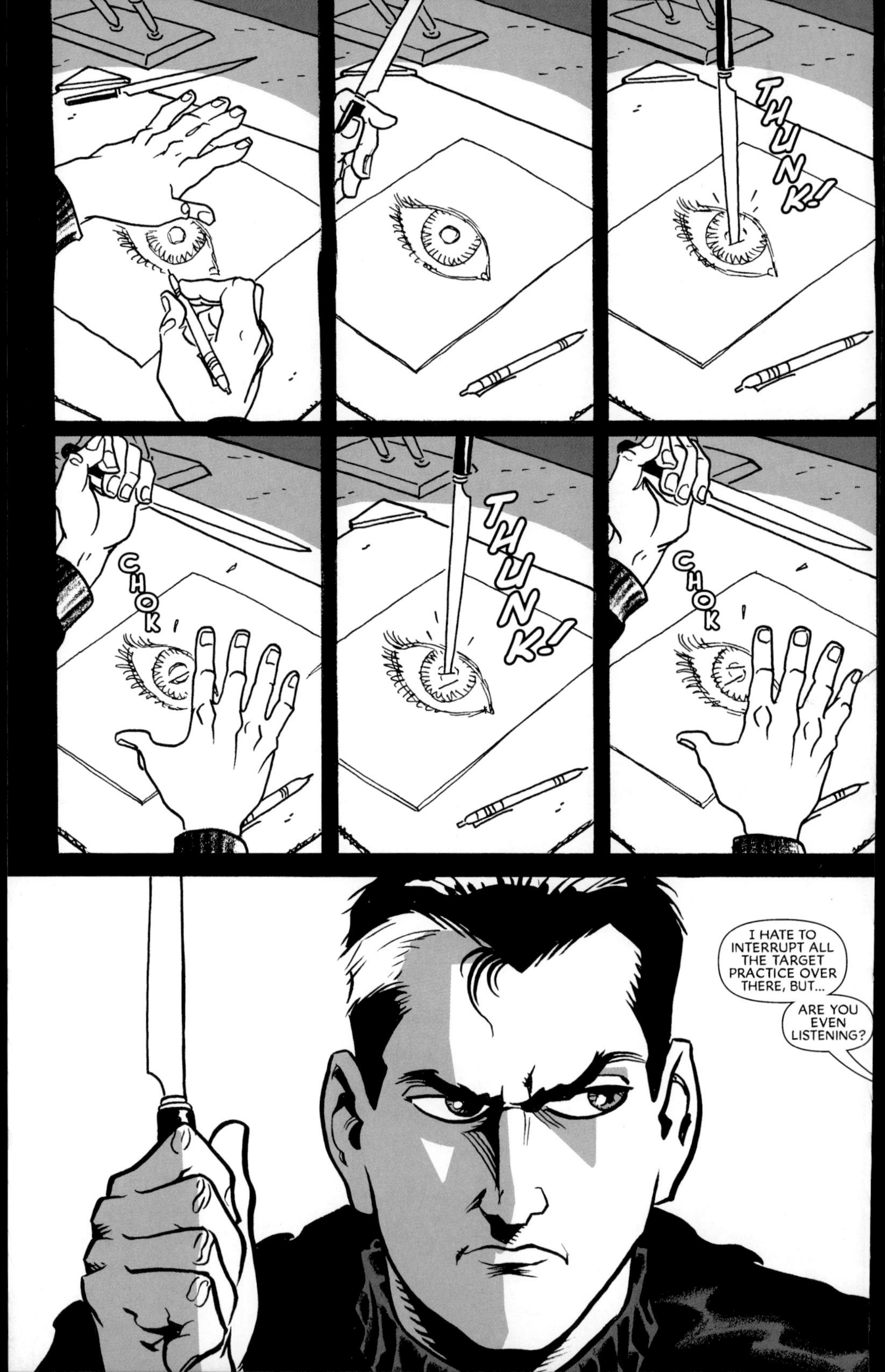
THUNK!
CHOK
THUNK!
CHOK
I HATE TO INTERRUPT ALL THE TARGET PRACTICE OVER THERE, BUT...
ARE YOU EVEN LISTENING?

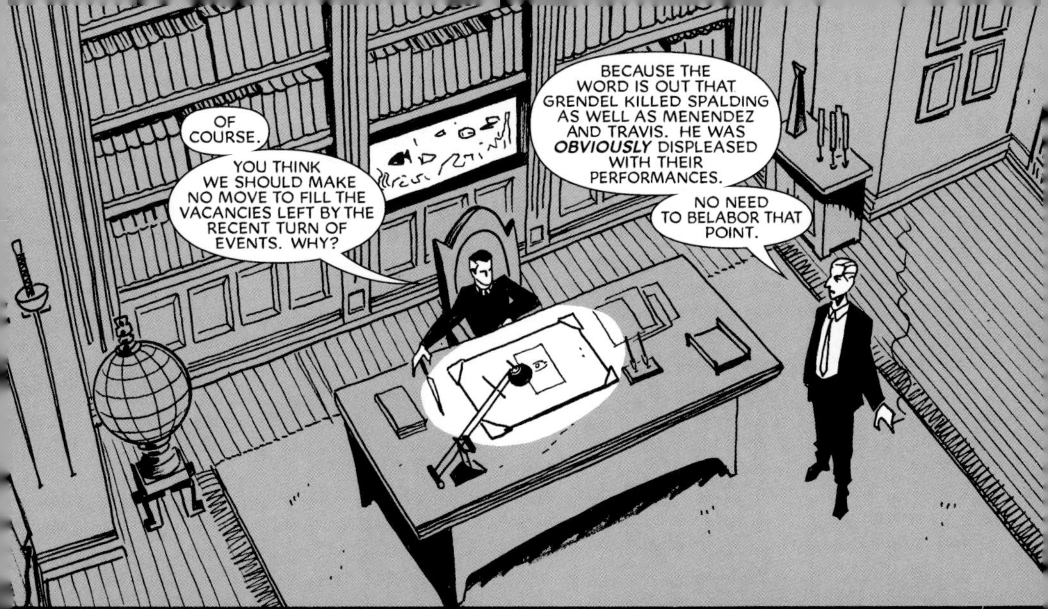
OF COURSE.
YOU THINK WE SHOULD MAKE NO MOVE TO FILL THE VACANCIES LEFT BY THE RECENT TURN OF EVENTS. WHY?
BECAUSE THE WORD IS OUT THAT GRENDEL KILLED SPALDING AS WELL AS MENENDEZ AND TRAVIS. HE WAS *OBVIOUSLY* DISPLEASED WITH THEIR PERFORMANCES.
NO NEED TO BELABOR THAT POINT.

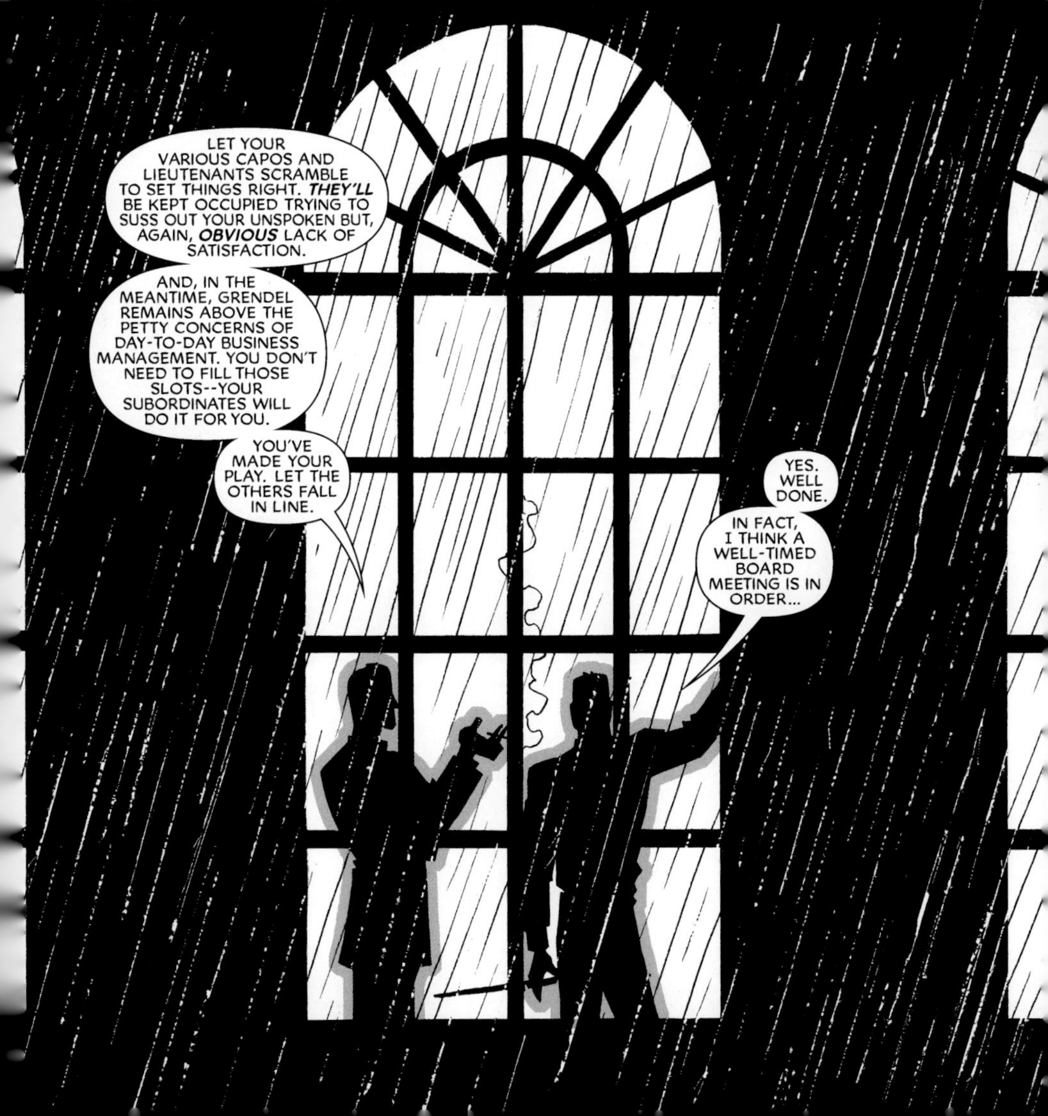
LET YOUR VARIOUS CAPOS AND LIEUTENANTS SCRAMBLE TO SET THINGS RIGHT. *THEY'LL* BE KEPT OCCUPIED TRYING TO SUSS OUT YOUR UNSPOKEN BUT, AGAIN, *OBVIOUS* LACK OF SATISFACTION.
AND, IN THE MEANTIME, GRENDEL REMAINS ABOVE THE PETTY CONCERNS OF DAY-TO-DAY BUSINESS MANAGEMENT. YOU DON'T NEED TO FILL THOSE SLOTS--YOUR SUBORDINATES WILL DO IT FOR YOU.
YOU'VE MADE YOUR PLAY. LET THE OTHERS FALL IN LINE.
YES. WELL DONE.
IN FACT, I THINK A WELL-TIMED BOARD MEETING IS IN ORDER...

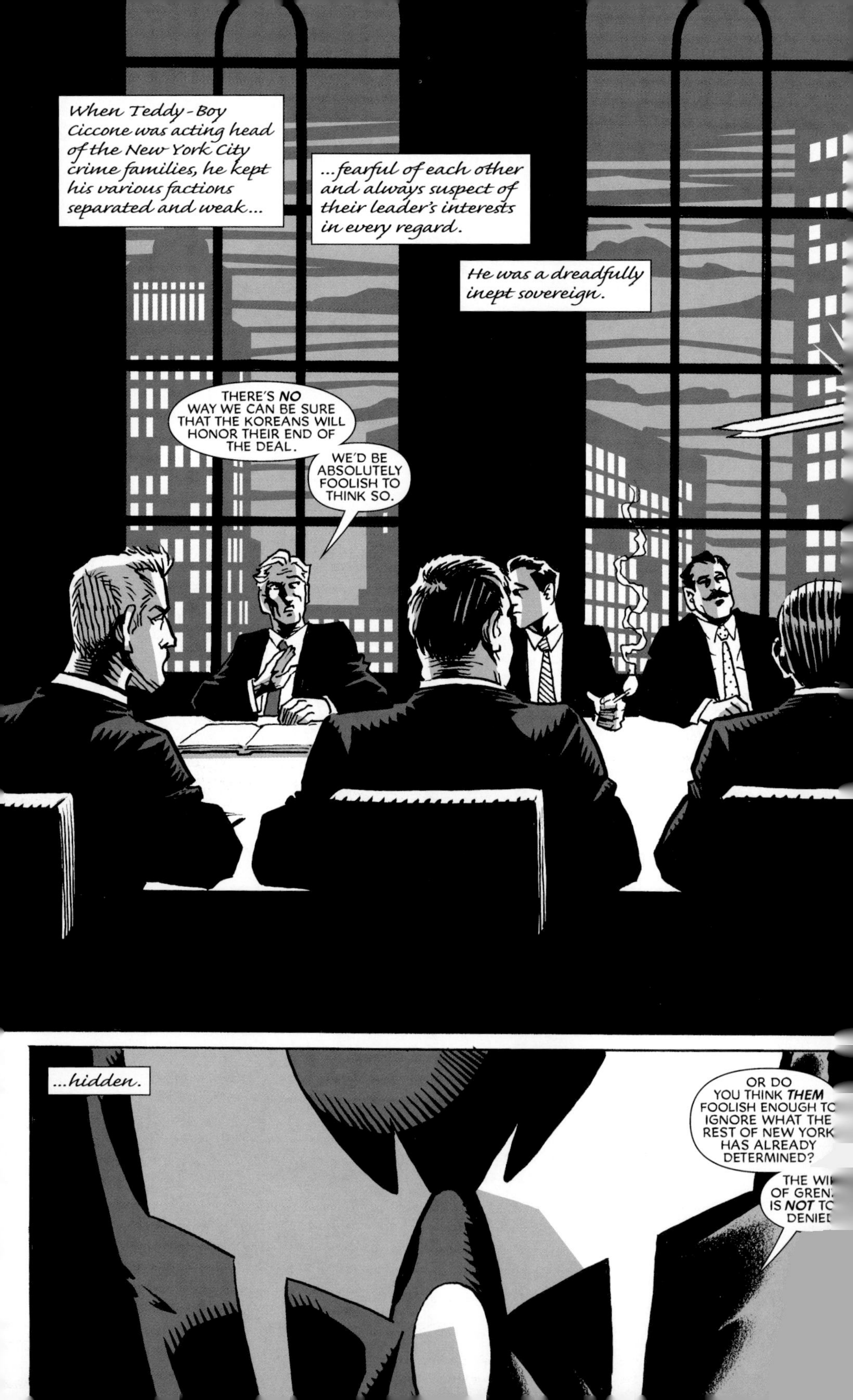
When Teddy-Boy Ciccone was acting head of the New York City crime families, he kept his various factions separated and weak...
...fearful of each other and always suspect of their leader's interests in every regard.
He was a dreadfully inept sovereign.
THERE'S *NO* WAY WE CAN BE SURE THAT THE KOREANS WILL HONOR THEIR END OF THE DEAL.
WE'D BE ABSOLUTELY FOOLISH TO THINK SO.
...hidden.
OR DO YOU THINK *THEM* FOOLISH ENOUGH TO IGNORE WHAT THE REST OF NEW YORK HAS ALREADY DETERMINED?
THE WI OF GREN IS *NOT* TO DENIED

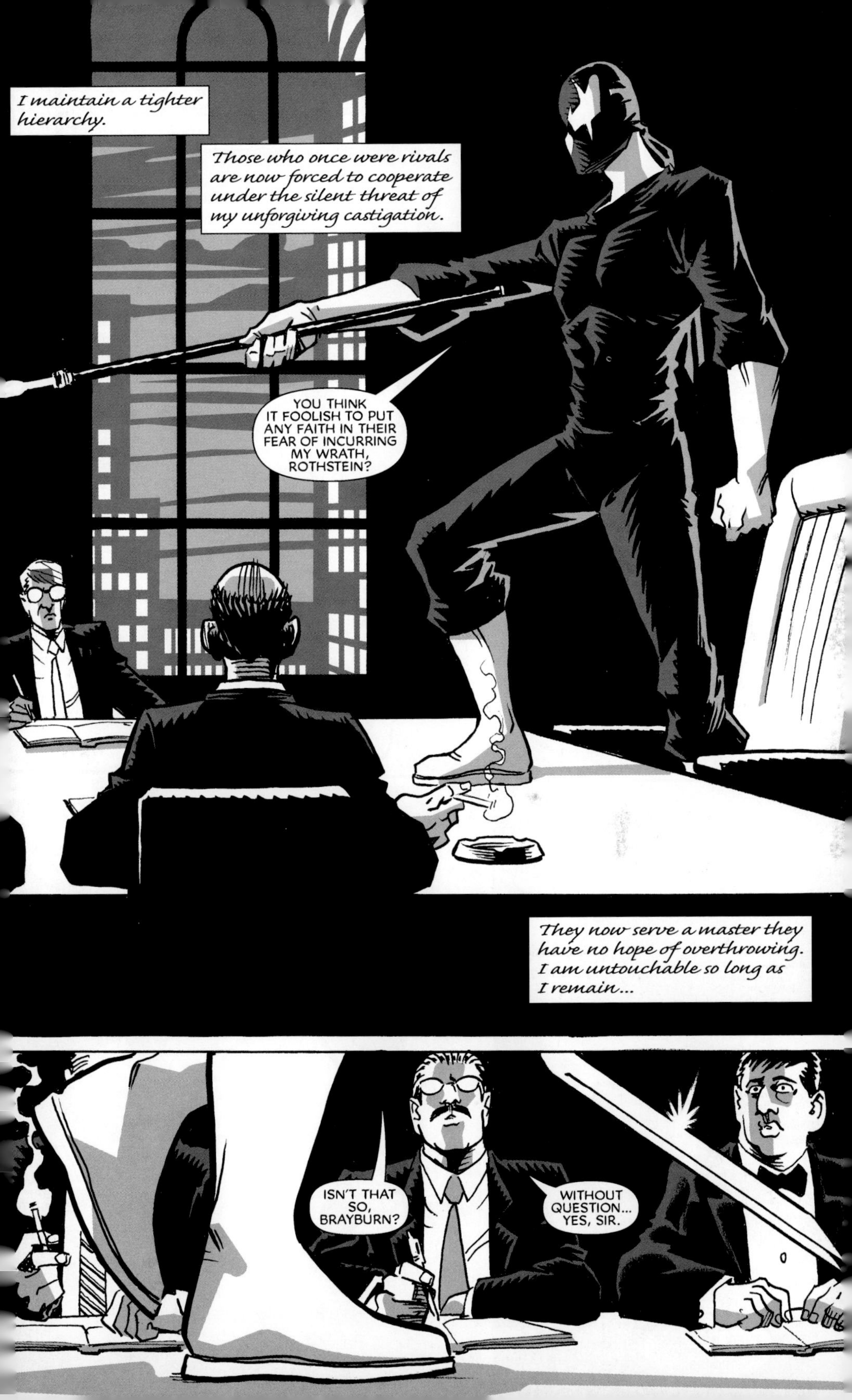
I maintain a tighter hierarchy.
Those who once were rivals are now forced to cooperate under the silent threat of my unforgiving castigation.
YOU THINK IT FOOLISH TO PUT ANY FAITH IN THEIR FEAR OF INCURRING MY WRATH, ROTHSTEIN?
They now serve a master they have no hope of overthrowing. I am untouchable so long as I remain...
ISN'T THAT SO, BRAYBURN?
WITHOUT QUESTION... YES, SIR.

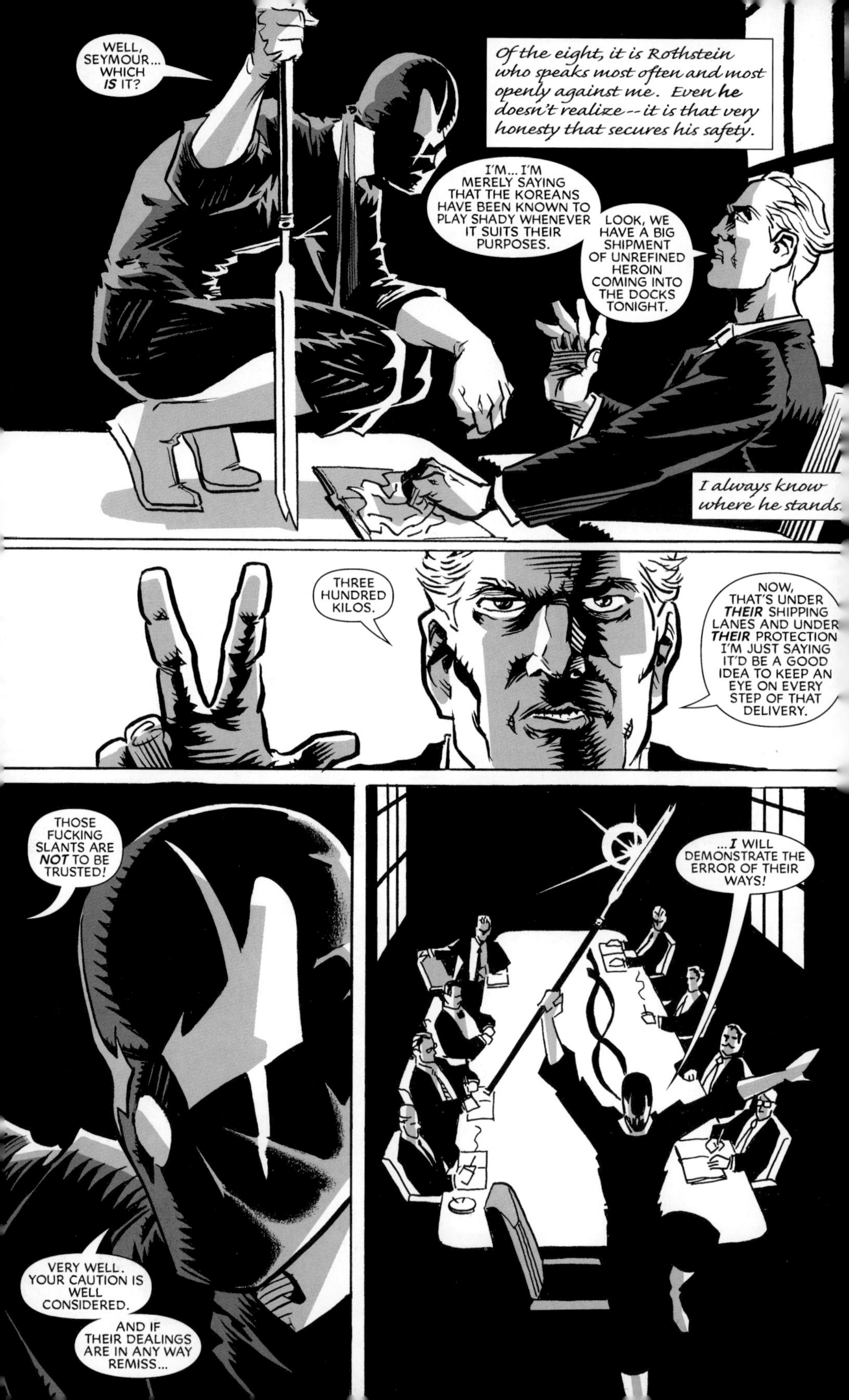

WELL, SEYMOUR... WHICH IS IT?
Of the eight, it is Rothstein who speaks most often and most openly against me. Even he doesn't realize--it is that very honesty that secures his safety.
I'M... I'M MERELY SAYING THAT THE KOREANS HAVE BEEN KNOWN TO PLAY SHADY WHENEVER IT SUITS THEIR PURPOSES.
LOOK, WE HAVE A BIG SHIPMENT OF UNREFINED HEROIN COMING INTO THE DOCKS TONIGHT.
I always know where he stands.
THREE HUNDRED KILOS.
NOW, THAT'S UNDER THEIR SHIPPING LANES AND UNDER THEIR PROTECTION. I'M JUST SAYING IT'D BE A GOOD IDEA TO KEEP AN EYE ON EVERY STEP OF THAT DELIVERY.
THOSE FUCKING SLANTS ARE NOT TO BE TRUSTED!
VERY WELL. YOUR CAUTION IS WELL CONSIDERED.
AND IF THEIR DEALINGS ARE IN ANY WAY REMISS...
...I WILL DEMONSTRATE THE ERROR OF THEIR WAYS!

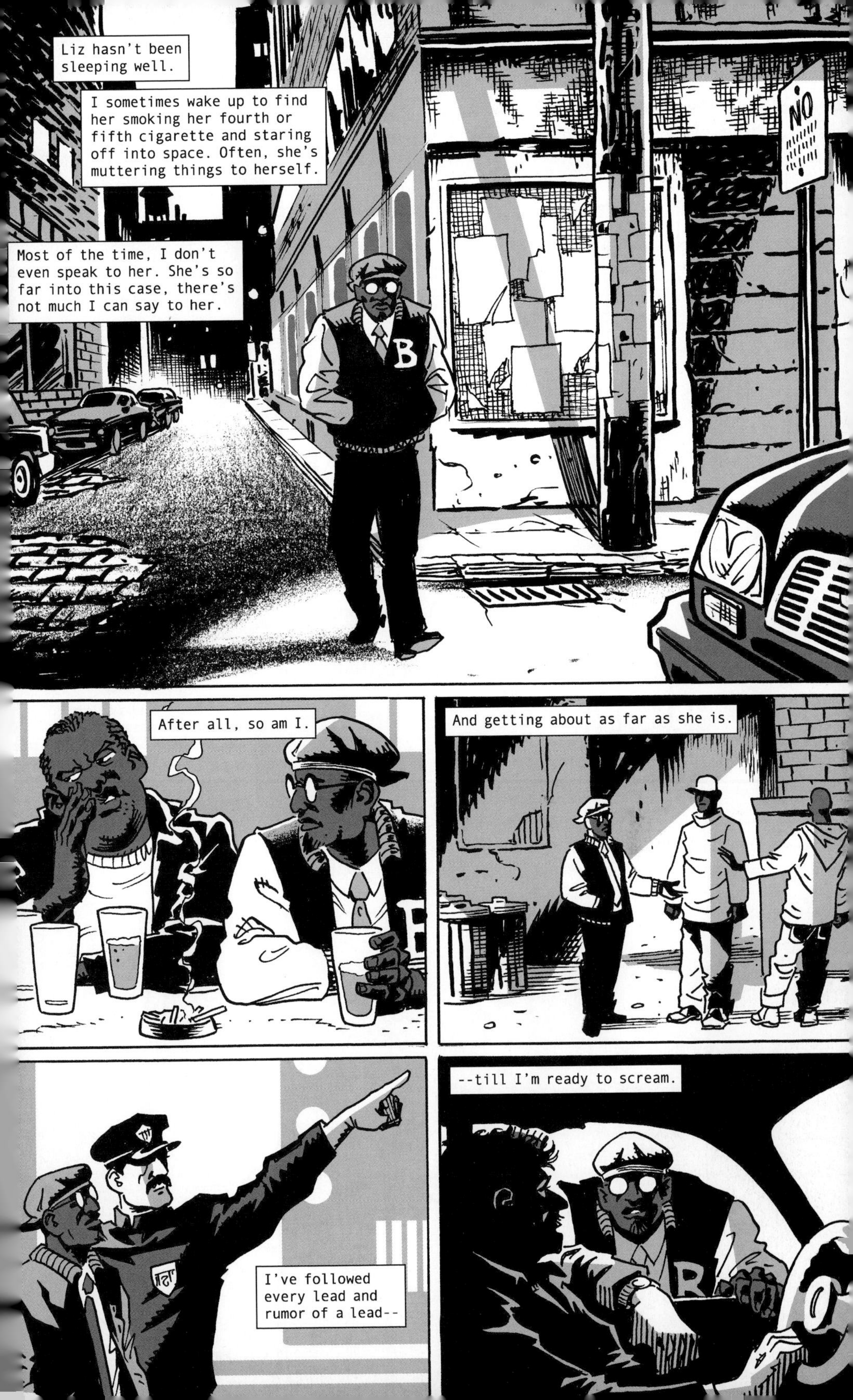
Liz hasn't been sleeping well.
I sometimes wake up to find her smoking her fourth or fifth cigarette and staring off into space. Often, she's muttering things to herself.
Most of the time, I don't even speak to her. She's so far into this case, there's not much I can say to her.
NO
After all, so am I.
And getting about as far as she is.
I've followed every lead and rumor of a lead--
--till I'm ready to scream.

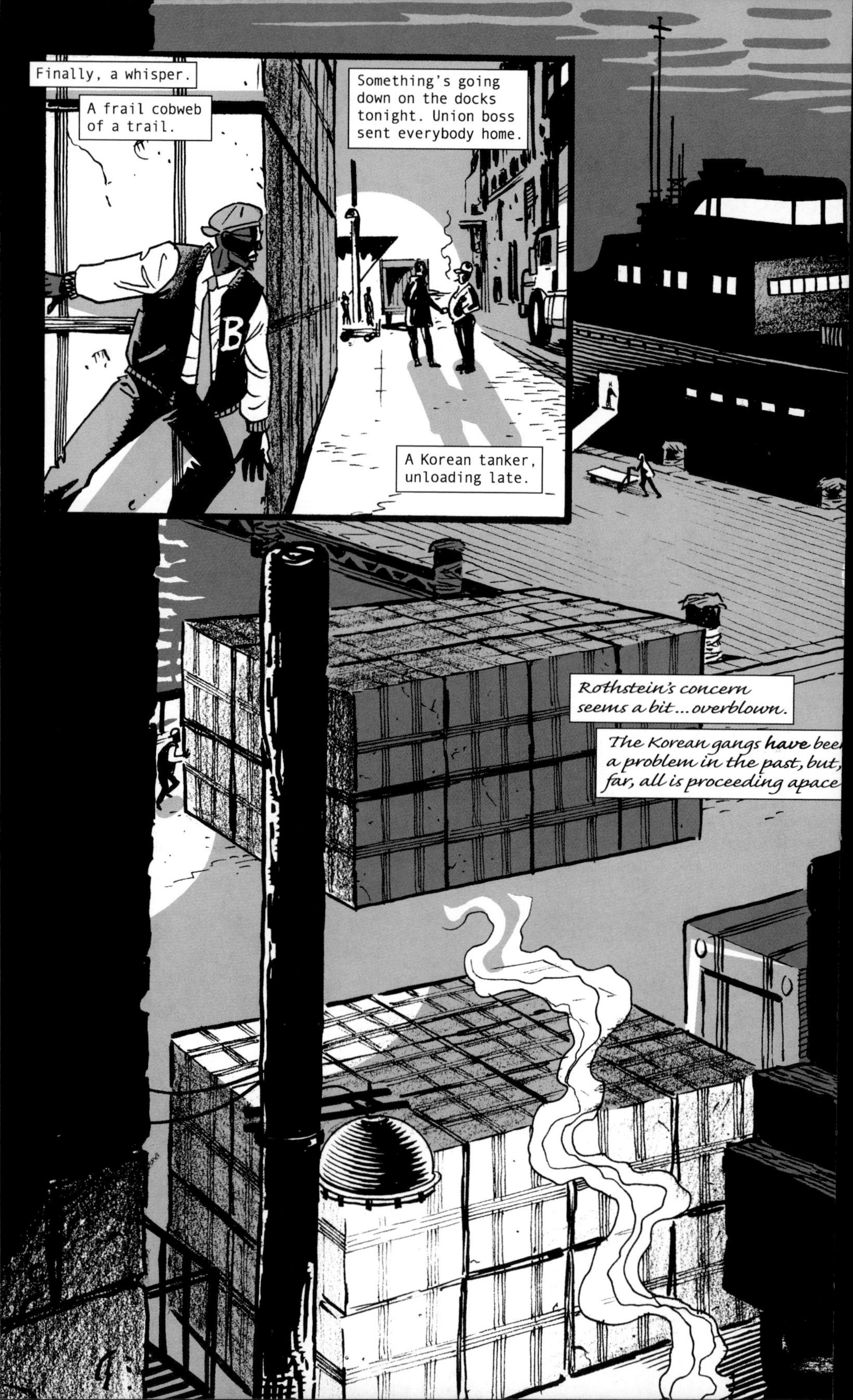
Finally, a whisper.
A frail cobweb of a trail.
Something's going down on the docks tonight. Union boss sent everybody home.
A Korean tanker, unloading late.
Rothstein's concern seems a bit...overblown.
The Korean gangs **have** bee a problem in the past, but, far, all is proceeding apace

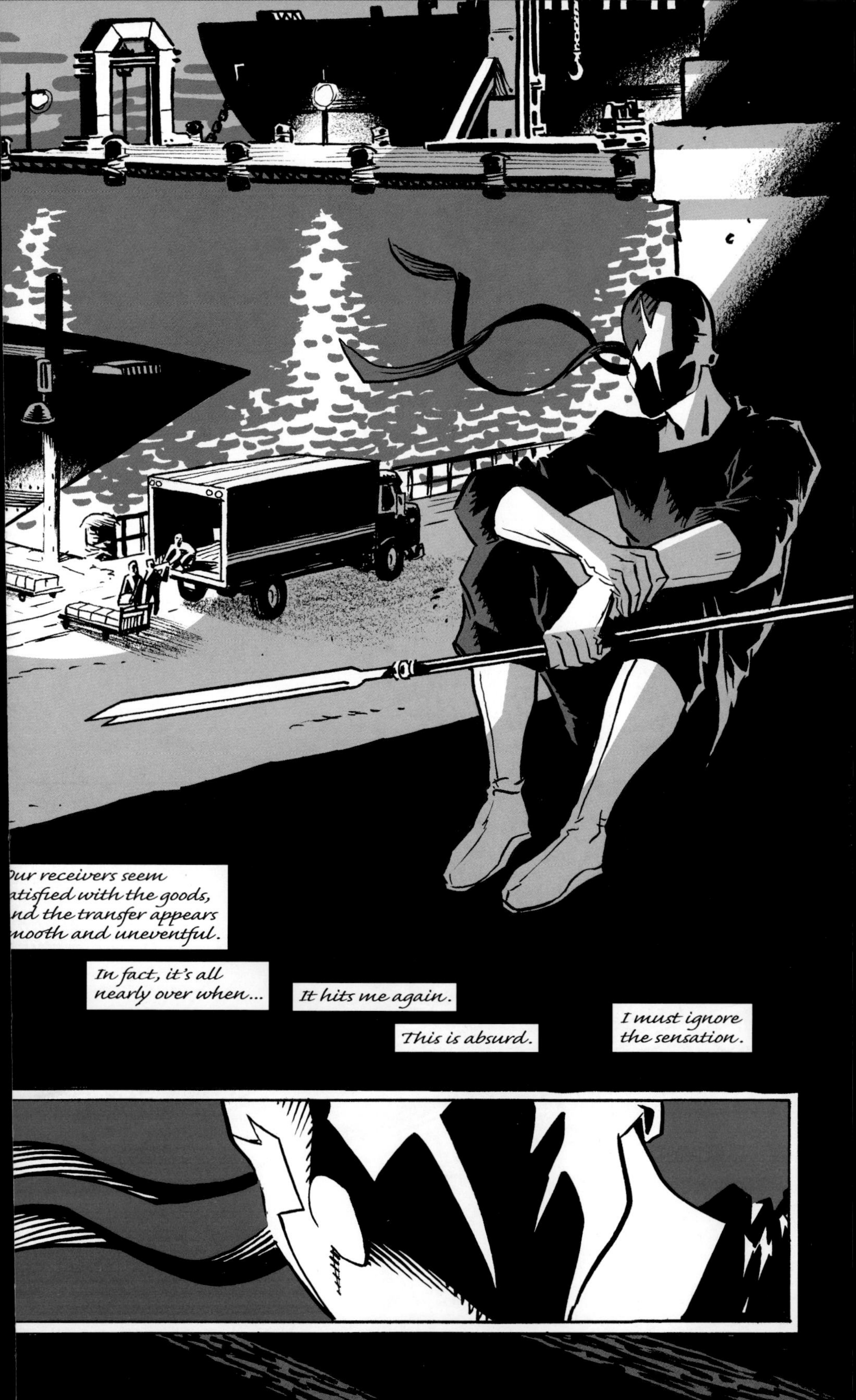
Our receivers seem satisfied with the goods, and the transfer appears smooth and uneventful.
In fact, it's all nearly over when...
It hits me again.
This is absurd.
I must ignore the sensation.

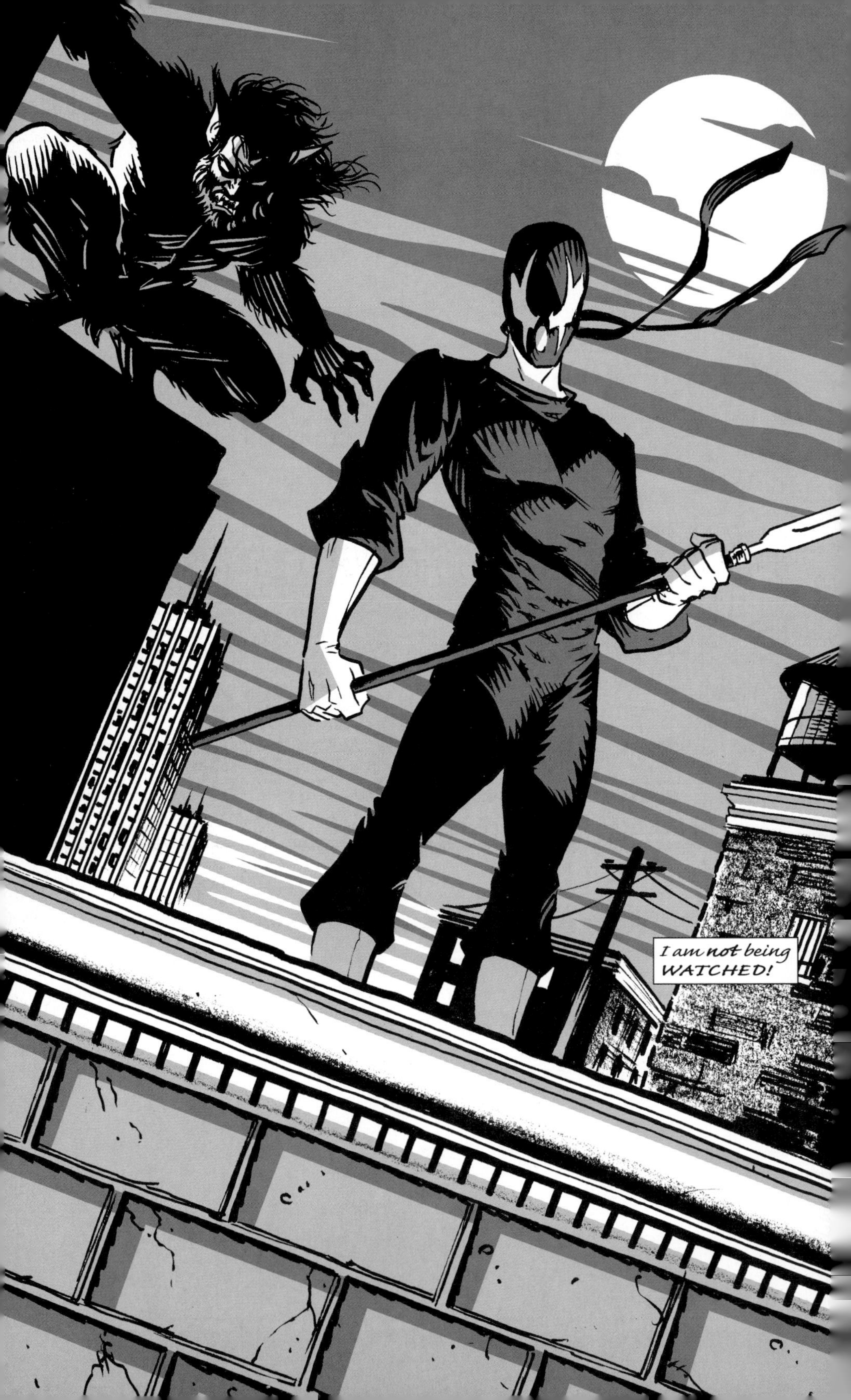
I am not being WATCHED!

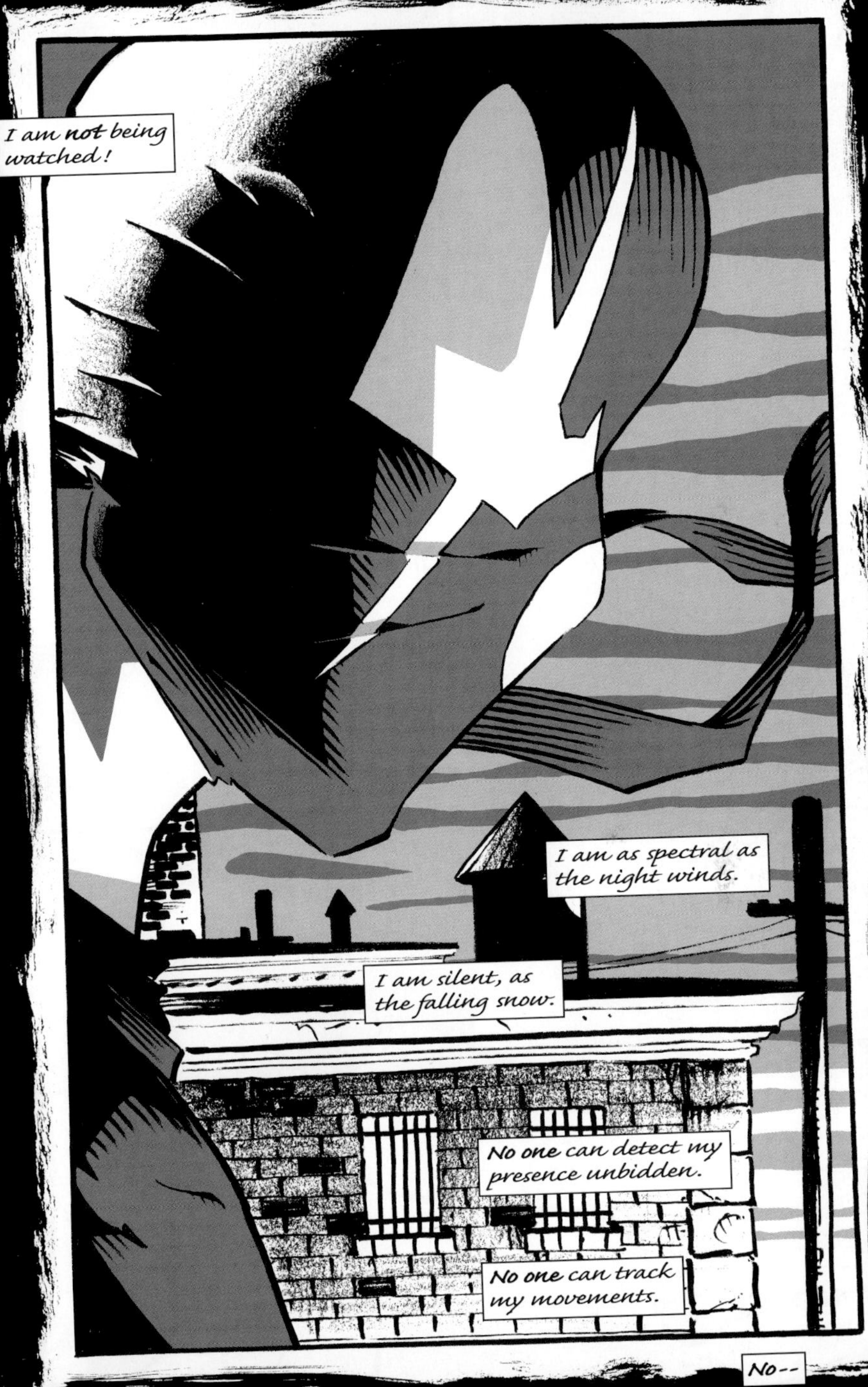
I am **not** being watched!
I am as spectral as the night winds.
I am silent, as the falling snow.
No one can detect my presence unbidden.
No one can track my movements.
No--

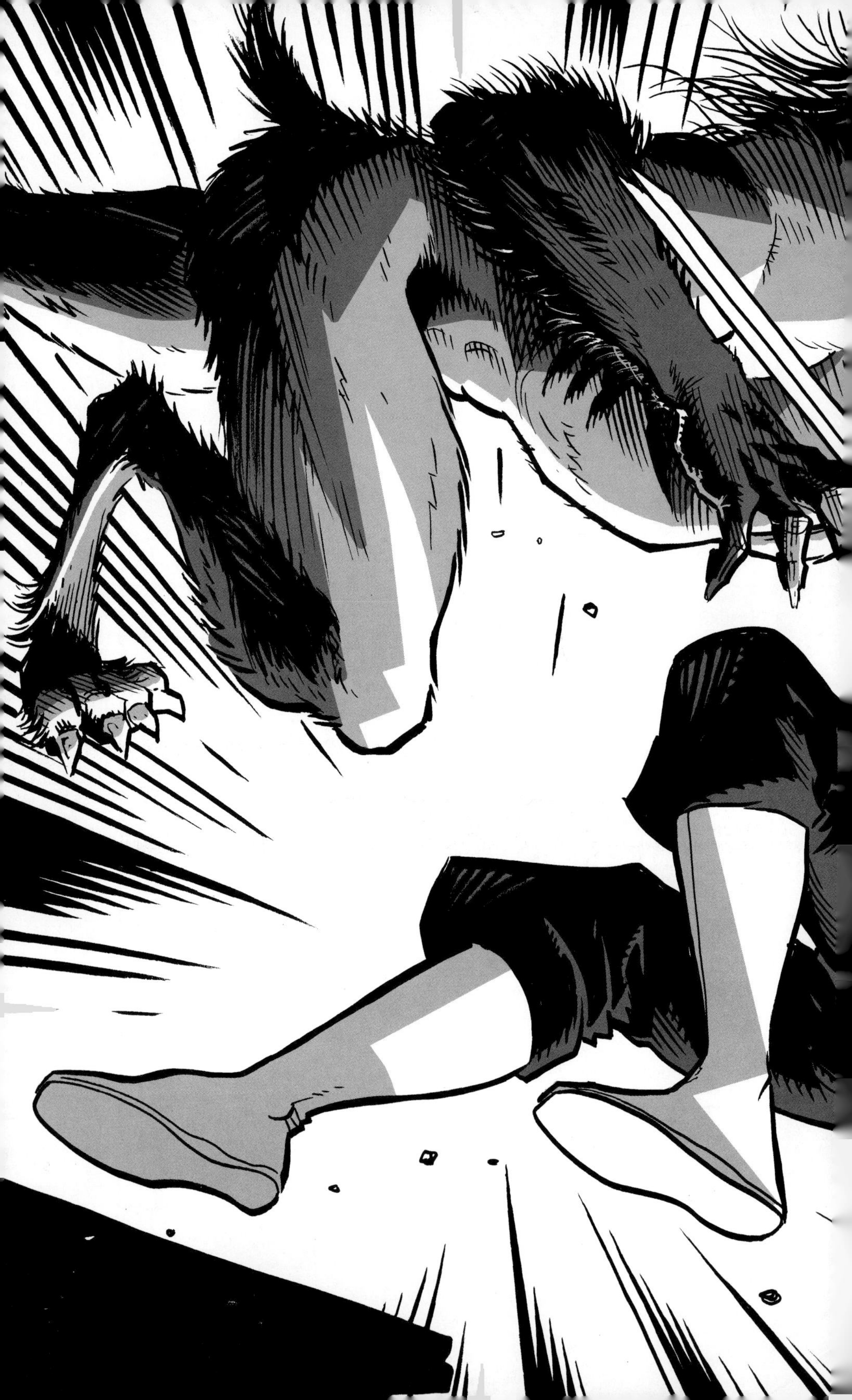

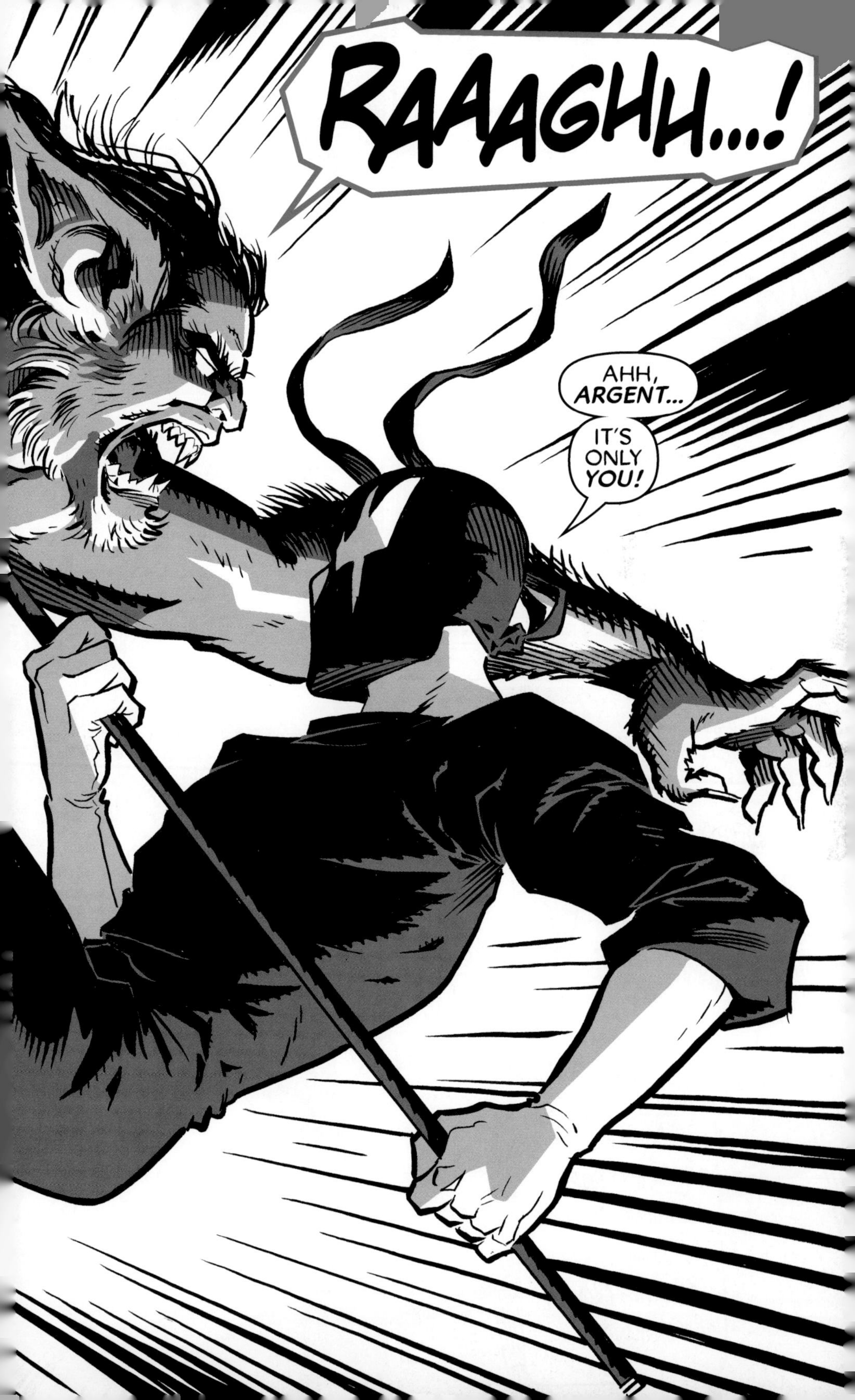
RAAAGHH...!
AHH, ARGENT...
IT'S ONLY YOU!

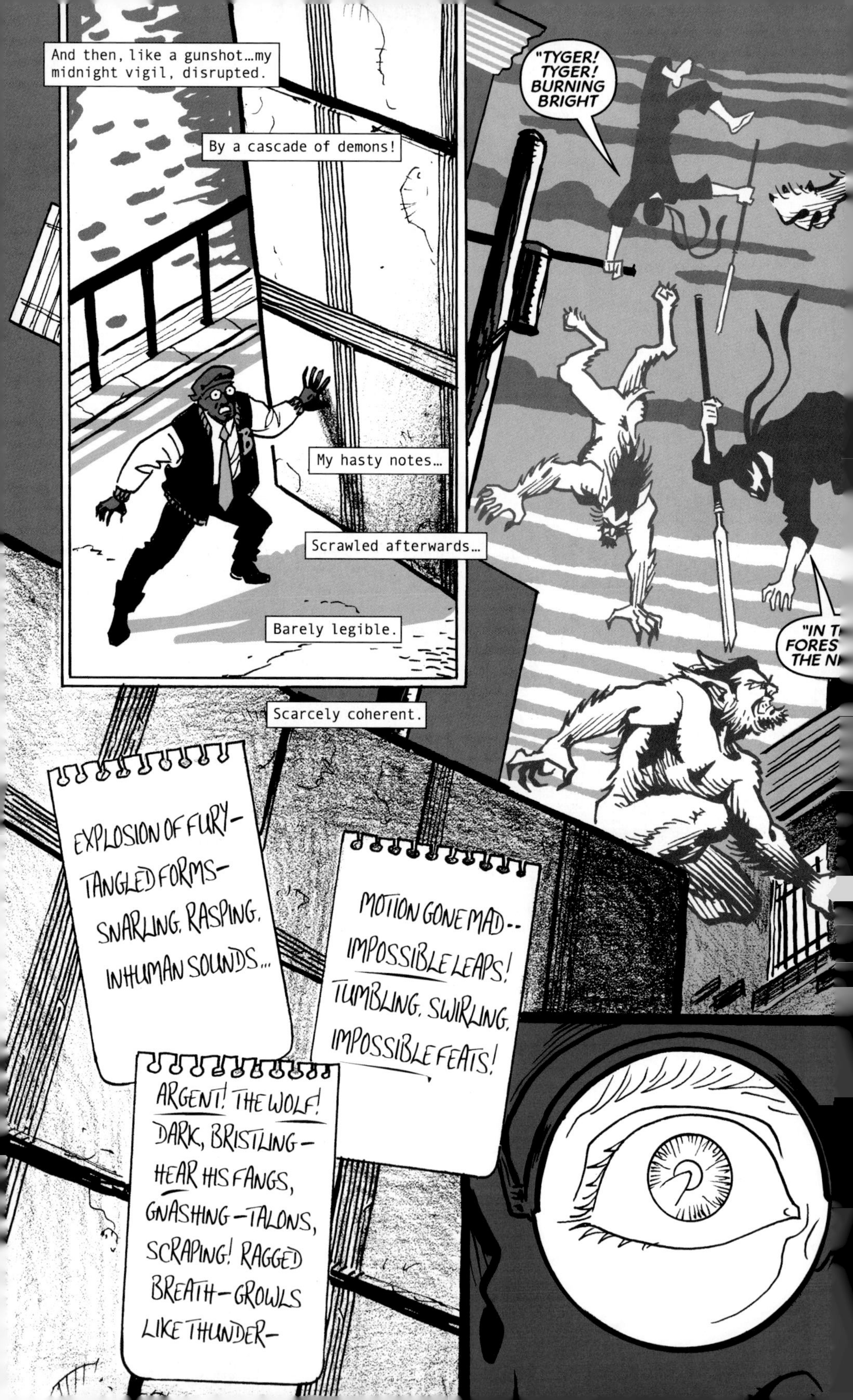

And then, like a gunshot…my midnight vigil, disrupted.
By a cascade of demons!
"TYGER! TYGER! BURNING BRIGHT
My hasty notes…
Scrawled afterwards…
Barely legible.
Scarcely coherent.
EXPLOSION OF FURY-
TANGLED FORMS-
SNARLING. RASPING.
INHUMAN SOUNDS…
MOTION GONE MAD--
IMPOSSIBLE LEAPS!
TUMBLING. SWIRLING.
IMPOSSIBLE FEATS!
ARGENT! THE WOLF!
DARK, BRISTLING-
HEAR HIS FANGS,
GNASHING-TALONS,
SCRAPING! RAGGED
BREATH-GROWLS
LIKE THUNDER-

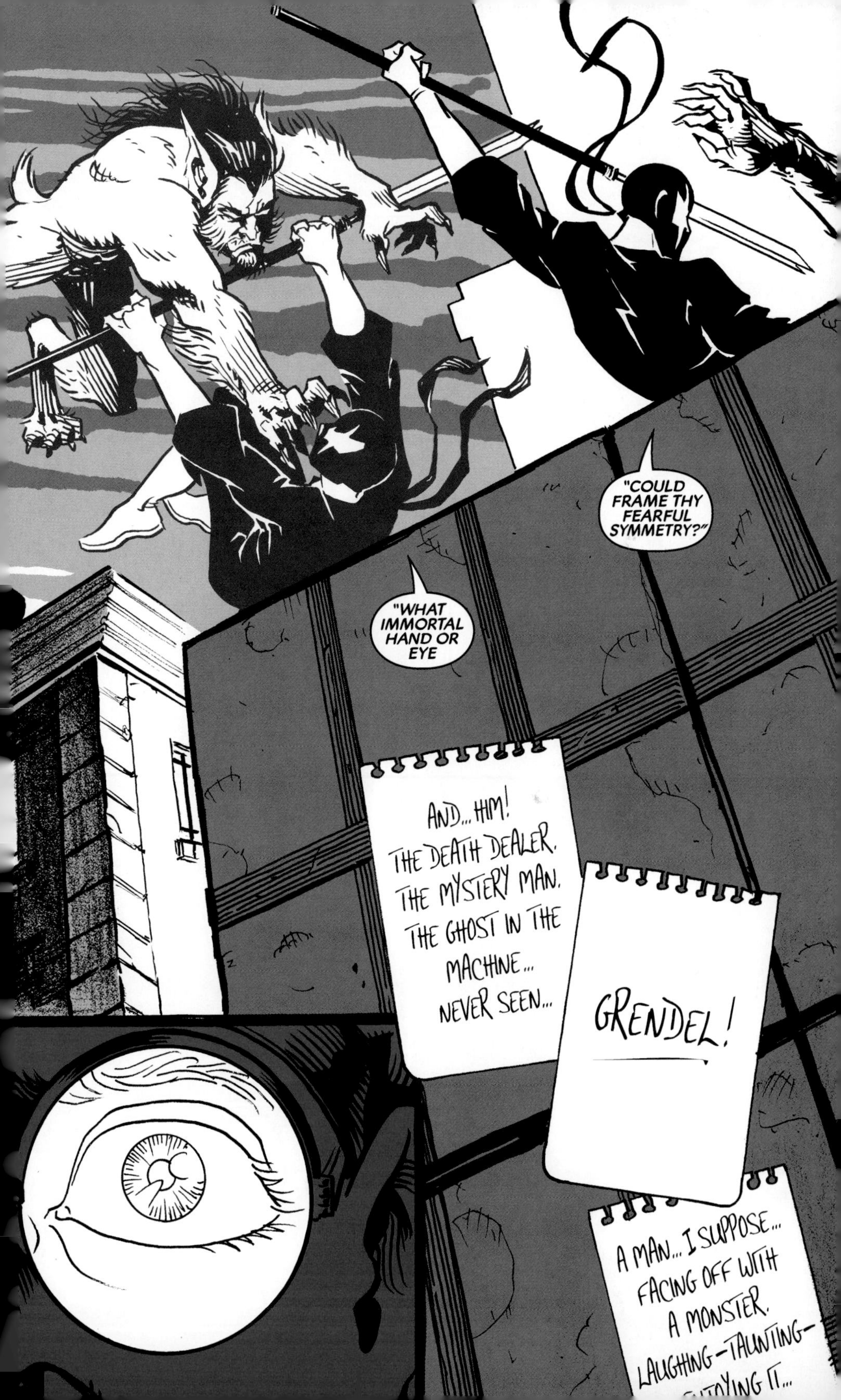

"COULD FRAME THY FEARFUL SYMMETRY?"
"WHAT IMMORTAL HAND OR EYE
AND... HIM! THE DEATH DEALER. THE MYSTERY MAN. THE GHOST IN THE MACHINE... NEVER SEEN...
GRENDEL!
A MAN... I SUPPOSE... FACING OFF WITH A MONSTER. LAUGHING-TAUNTING-

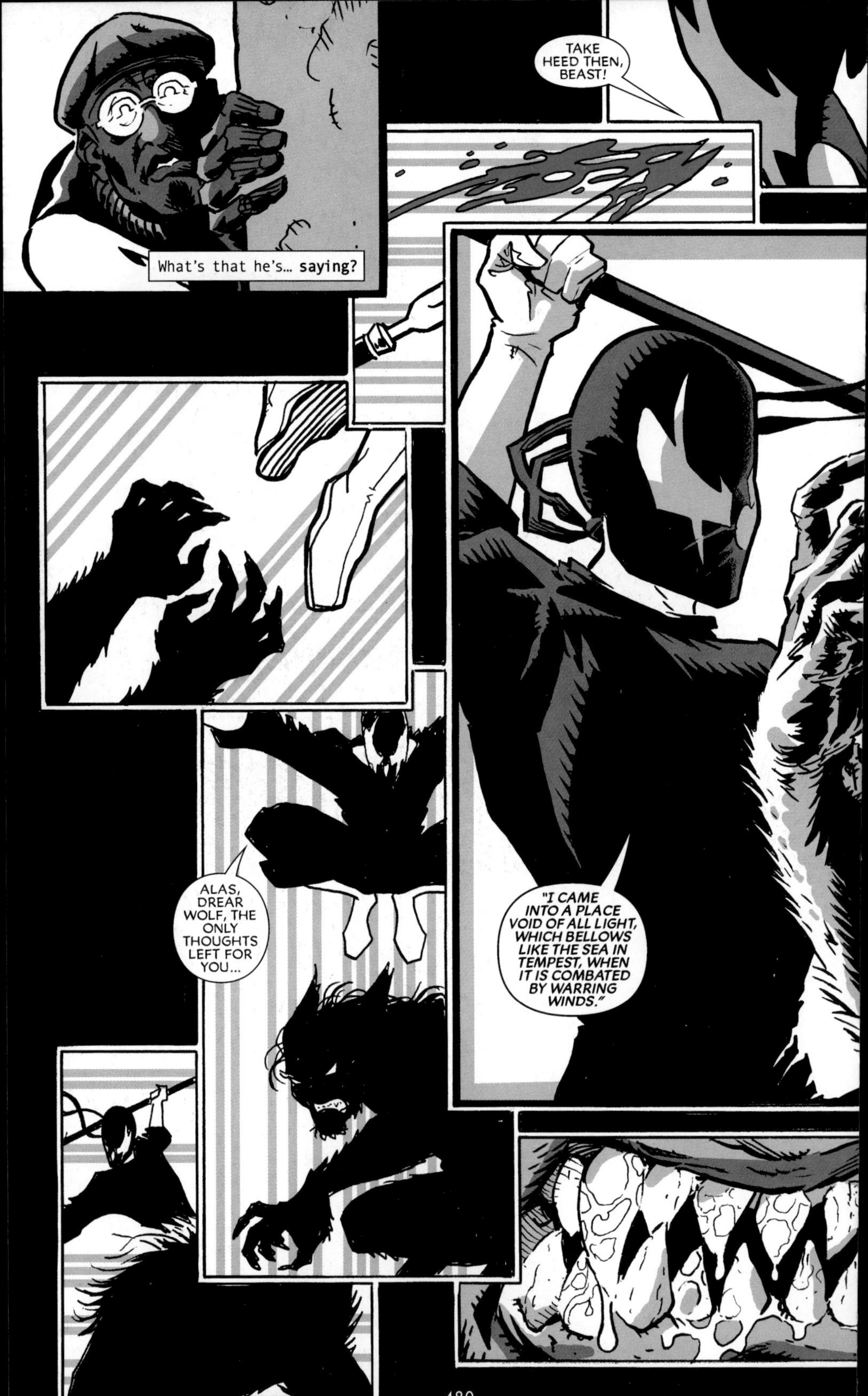

What's that he's... **saying?**
TAKE HEED THEN, BEAST!
ALAS, DREAR WOLF, THE ONLY THOUGHTS LEFT FOR YOU...
"I CAME INTO A PLACE VOID OF ALL LIGHT, WHICH BELLOWS LIKE THE SEA IN TEMPEST, WHEN IT IS COMBATED BY WARRING WINDS."

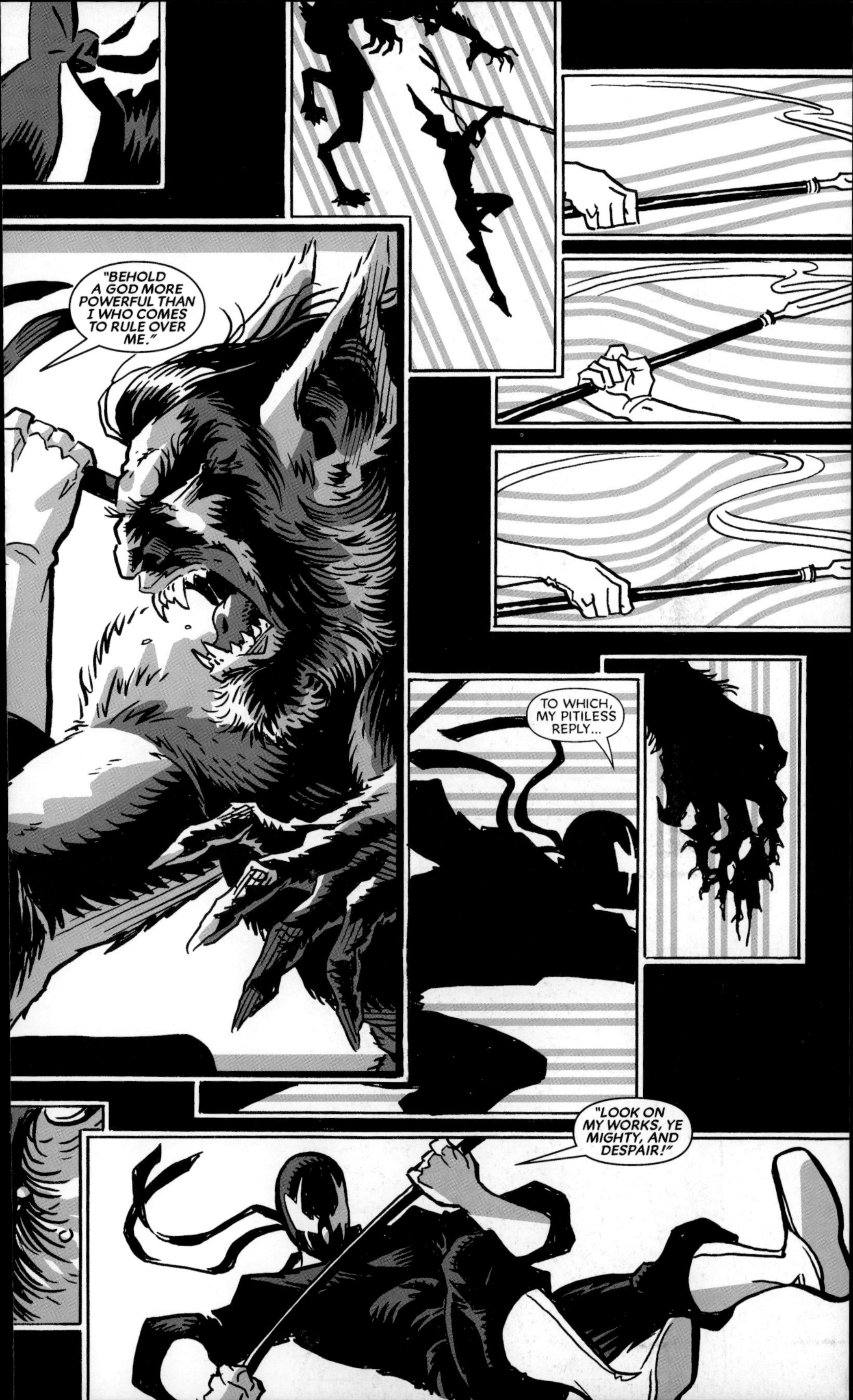
"BEHOLD A GOD MORE POWERFUL THAN I WHO COMES TO RULE OVER ME."
TO WHICH, MY PITILESS REPLY...
"LOOK ON MY WORKS, YE MIGHTY, AND DESPAIR!"

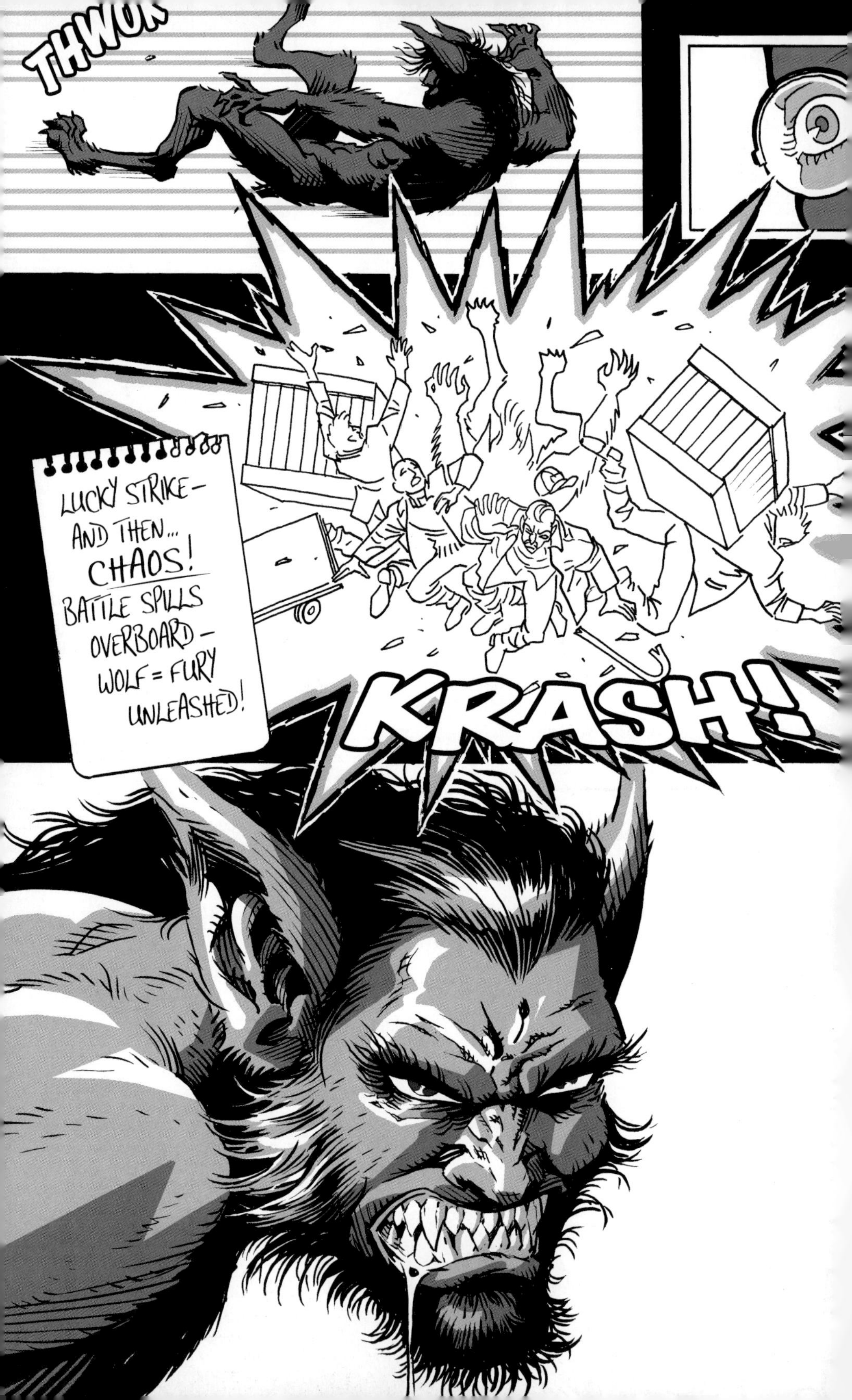
THWOK
LUCKY STRIKE—
AND THEN...
CHAOS!
BATTLE SPILLS
OVERBOARD—
WOLF = FURY
UNLEASHED!
KRASH!

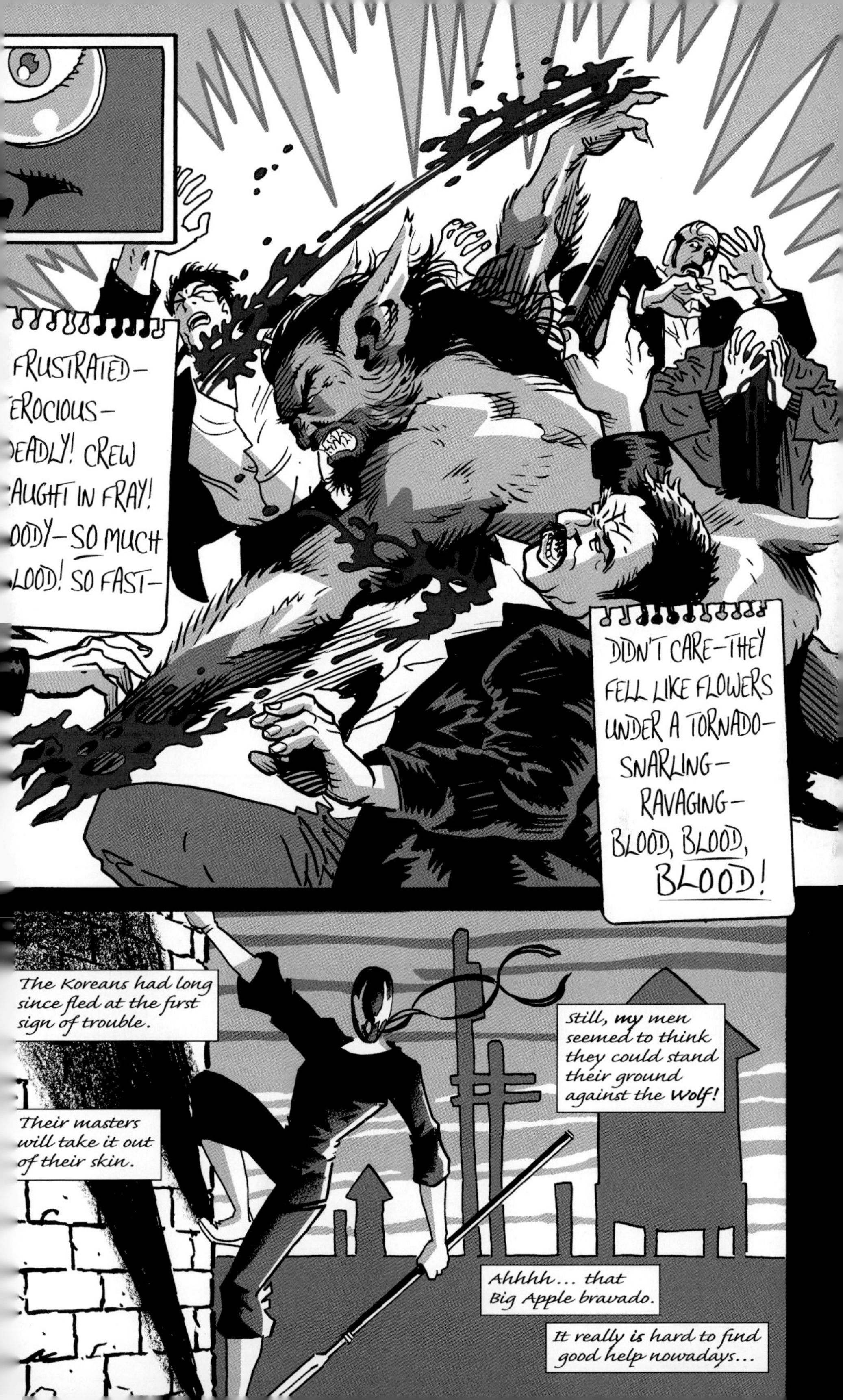
FRUSTRATED—
EROCIOUS—
EADLY! CREW
AUGHT IN FRAY!
OODY—SO MUCH
LOOD! SO FAST—
DIDN'T CARE—THEY FELL LIKE FLOWERS UNDER A TORNADO—
SNARLING—
RAVAGING—
BLOOD, BLOOD, BLOOD!
The Koreans had long since fled at the first sign of trouble.
Their masters will take it out of their skin.
Still, my men seemed to think they could stand their ground against the Wolf!
Ahhhh... that Big Apple bravado.
It really is hard to find good help nowadays...

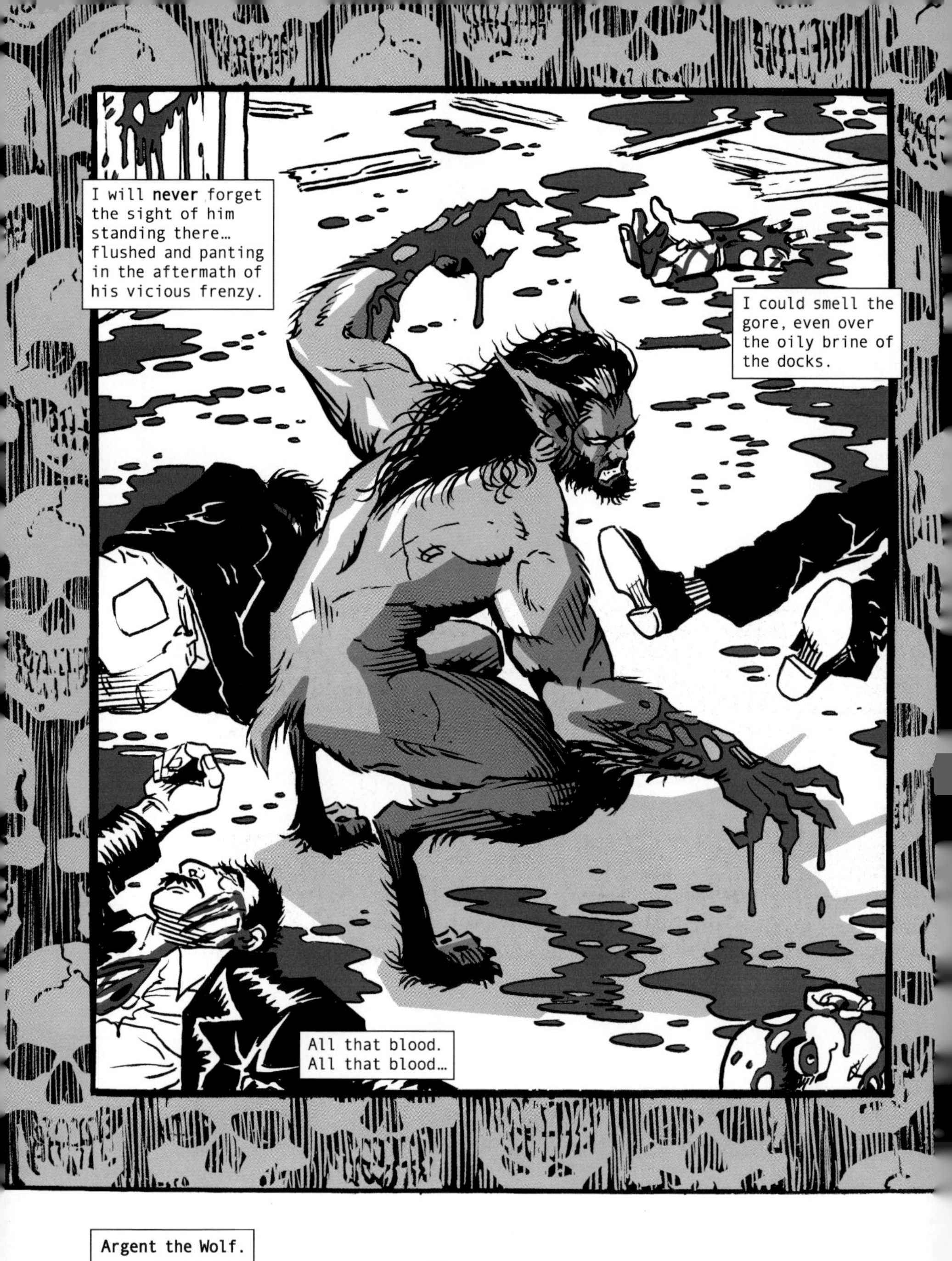
I will **never** forget the sight of him standing there… flushed and panting in the aftermath of his vicious frenzy.
I could smell the gore, even over the oily brine of the docks.
All that blood. All that blood…

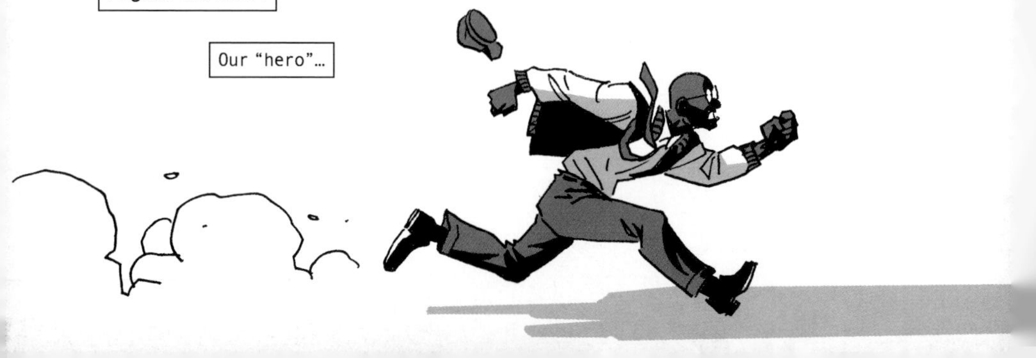
Argent the Wolf.
Our "hero"…

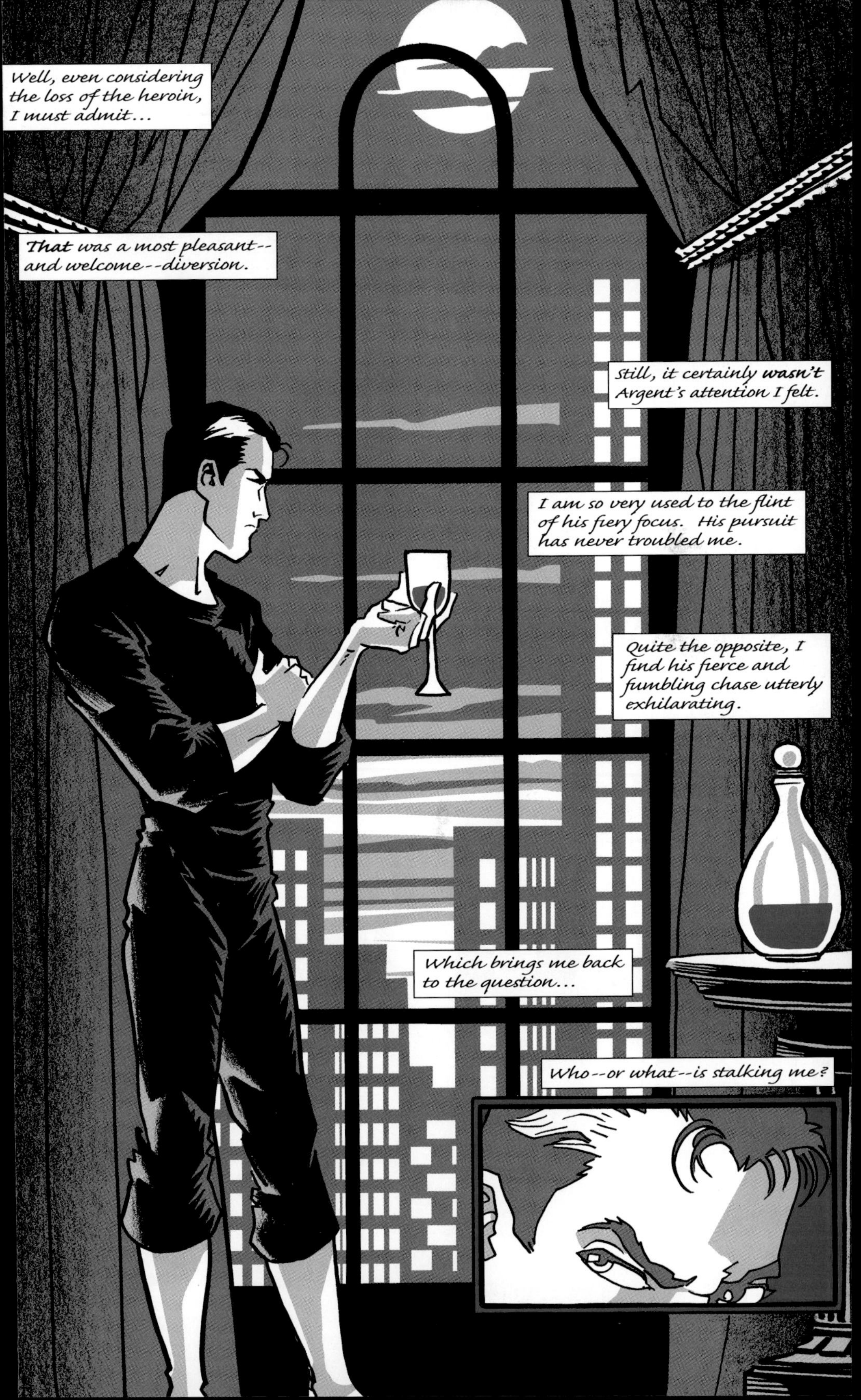
Well, even considering the loss of the heroin, I must admit...
That was a most pleasant--and welcome--diversion.
Still, it certainly wasn't Argent's attention I felt.
I am so very used to the flint of his fiery focus. His pursuit has never troubled me.
Quite the opposite, I find his fierce and fumbling chase utterly exhilarating.
Which brings me back to the question...
Who--or what--is stalking me?

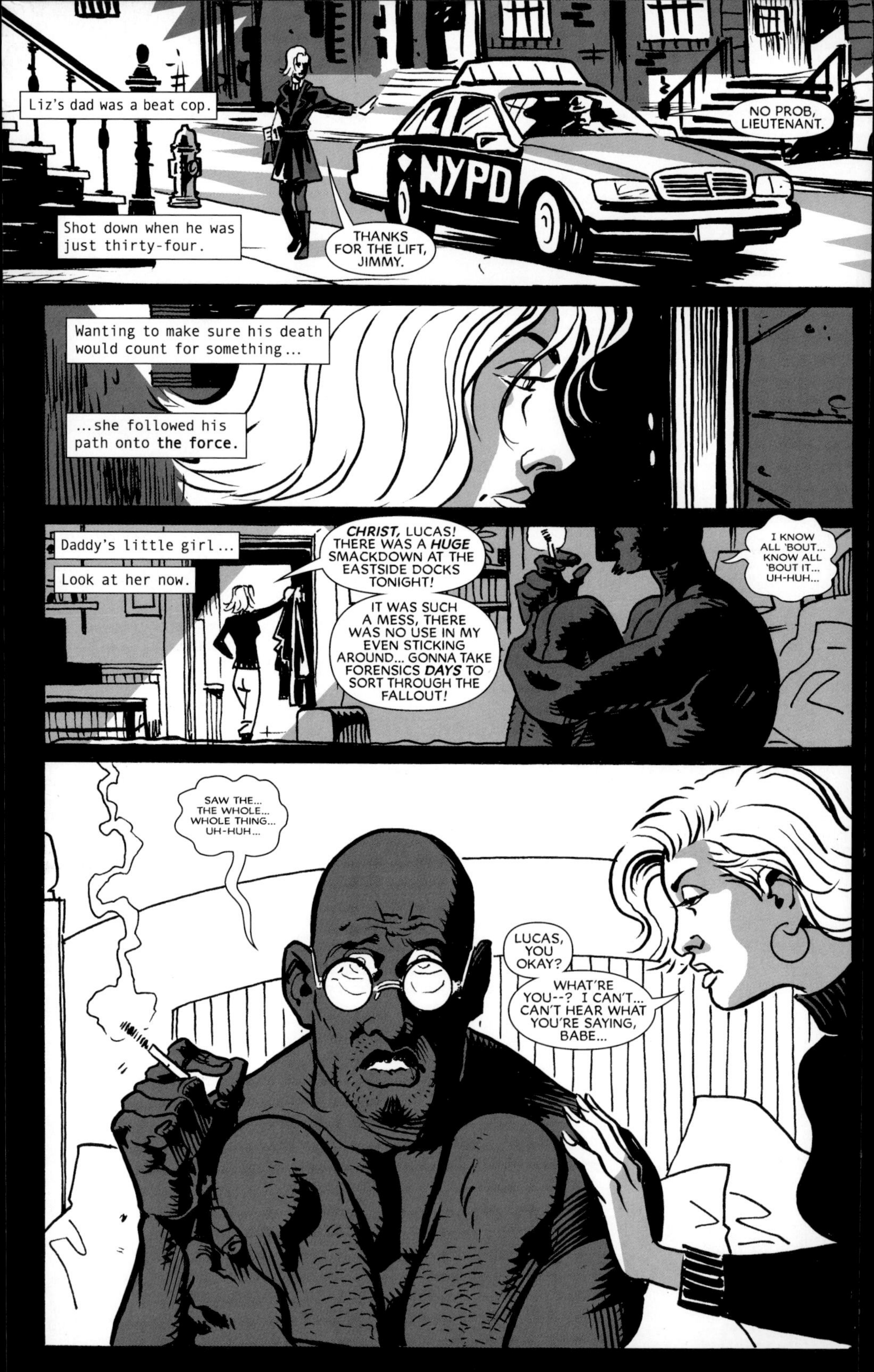
Liz's dad was a beat cop.
NO PROB, LIEUTENANT.
Shot down when he was just thirty-four.
THANKS FOR THE LIFT, JIMMY.
NYPD
Wanting to make sure his death would count for something...
...she followed his path onto **the force.**
Daddy's little girl...
Look at her now.
CHRIST, LUCAS! THERE WAS A *HUGE* SMACKDOWN AT THE EASTSIDE DOCKS TONIGHT!
IT WAS SUCH A MESS, THERE WAS NO USE IN MY EVEN STICKING AROUND... GONNA TAKE FORENSICS *DAYS* TO SORT THROUGH THE FALLOUT!
I KNOW ALL 'BOUT... KNOW ALL 'BOUT IT... UH-HUH...
SAW THE... THE WHOLE... WHOLE THING... UH-HUH...
LUCAS, YOU OKAY?
WHAT'RE YOU--? I CAN'T... CAN'T HEAR WHAT YOU'RE SAYING, BABE...

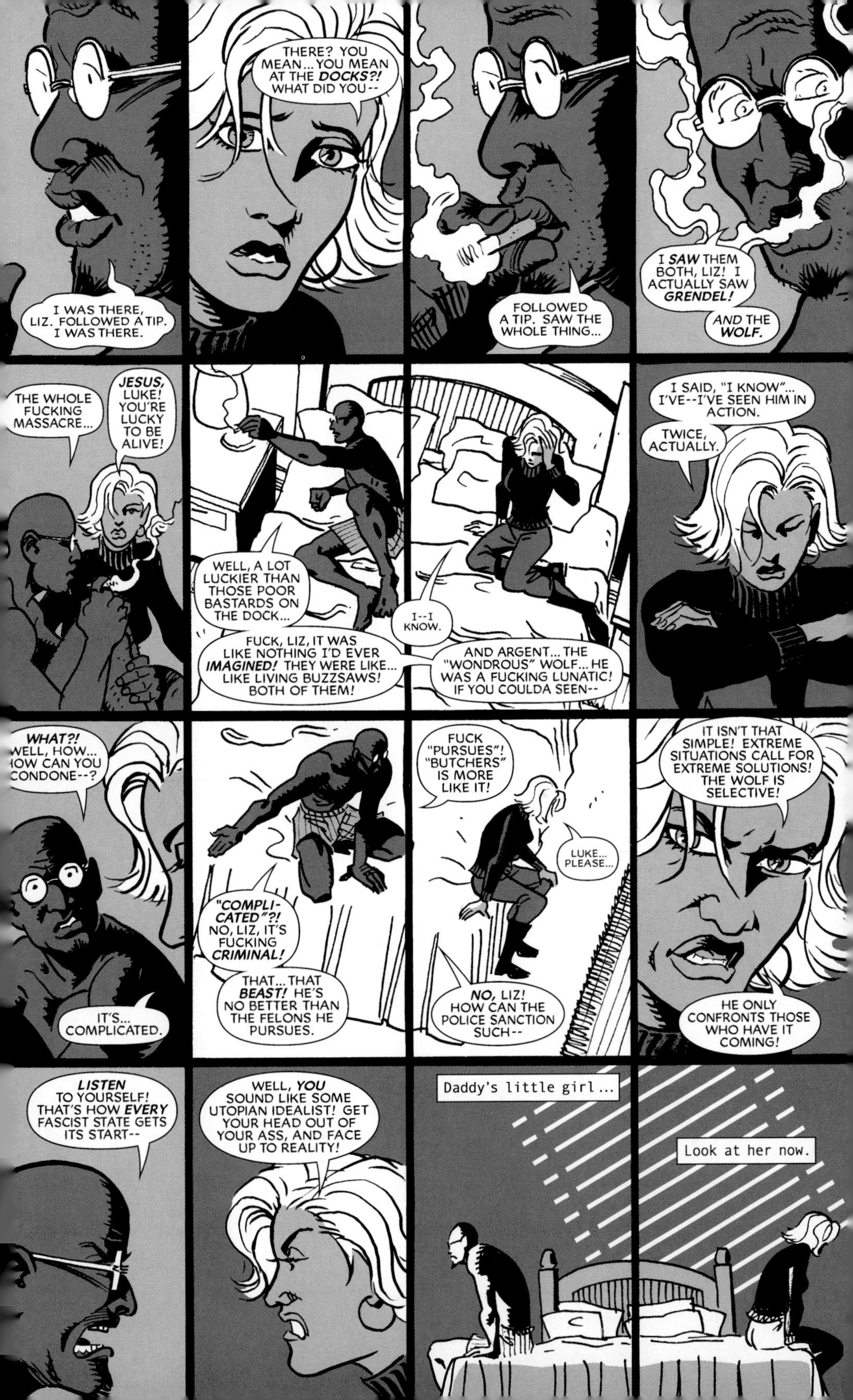
I WAS THERE, LIZ. FOLLOWED A TIP. I WAS THERE.
THERE? YOU MEAN... YOU MEAN AT THE *DOCKS?!* WHAT DID YOU--
FOLLOWED A TIP. SAW THE WHOLE THING...
I *SAW* THEM BOTH, LIZ! I ACTUALLY SAW *GRENDEL!*
AND THE *WOLF.*
THE WHOLE FUCKING MASSACRE...
JESUS, LUKE! YOU'RE LUCKY TO BE ALIVE!
WELL, A LOT LUCKIER THAN THOSE POOR BASTARDS ON THE DOCK...
FUCK, LIZ, IT WAS LIKE NOTHING I'D EVER *IMAGINED!* THEY WERE LIKE... LIKE LIVING BUZZSAWS! BOTH OF THEM!
I--I KNOW.
AND ARGENT... THE "WONDROUS" WOLF... HE WAS A FUCKING LUNATIC! IF YOU COULDA SEEN--
I SAID, "I KNOW"... I'VE--I'VE SEEN HIM IN ACTION.
TWICE, ACTUALLY.
WHAT?! WELL, HOW... HOW CAN YOU CONDONE--?
IT'S... COMPLICATED.
"COMPLICATED"?! NO, LIZ, IT'S FUCKING *CRIMINAL!*
THAT... THAT *BEAST!* HE'S NO BETTER THAN THE FELONS HE PURSUES.
FUCK "PURSUES"! "BUTCHERS" IS MORE LIKE IT!
LUKE... PLEASE...
NO, LIZ! HOW CAN THE POLICE SANCTION SUCH--
IT ISN'T THAT SIMPLE! EXTREME SITUATIONS CALL FOR EXTREME SOLUTIONS! THE WOLF IS SELECTIVE!
HE ONLY CONFRONTS THOSE WHO HAVE IT COMING!
LISTEN TO YOURSELF! THAT'S HOW *EVERY* FASCIST STATE GETS ITS START--
WELL, *YOU* SOUND LIKE SOME UTOPIAN IDEALIST! GET YOUR HEAD OUT OF YOUR ASS, AND FACE UP TO REALITY!
Daddy's little girl...
Look at her now.

Some of my mother's fondest memories of her tragically disrupted youth are those times she spent in idyllic wanderings through the historic and scenic pathways of Central Park. It was during those times, she later recalled, that she felt most serene and secure. Her life up until that point had been blurred by one calamity after another, and her current role as Uncle Hunter's social pet, while at first exciting to her inexperienced young mind, soon left her feeling lonely and numb.

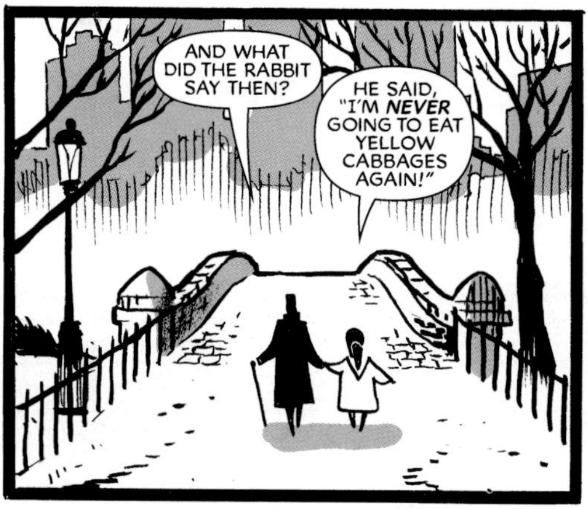
AND WHAT DID THE RABBIT SAY THEN?
HE SAID, "I'M *NEVER* GOING TO EAT YELLOW CABBAGES AGAIN!"

But in the park, she felt the full focus of Hunter's affections. She felt free to be herself—a child—and free to revel in this most "normal" aspect of an otherwise odd and troubled life. Little did she realize how very much worse it would eventually become.

—excerpt from *Devil by the Deed*
by Christine Spar

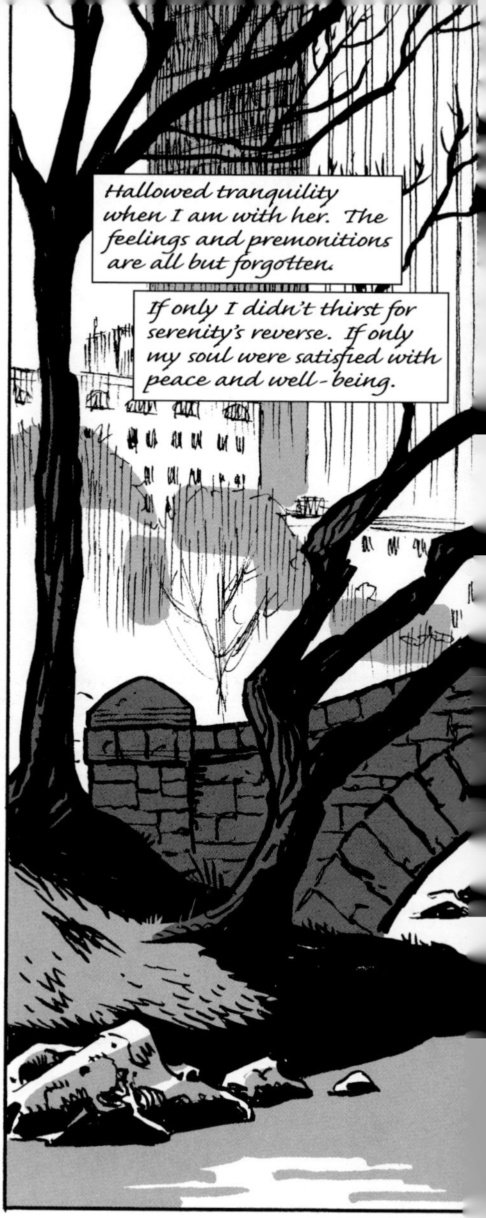
Hallowed tranquility when I am with her. The feelings and premonitions are all but forgotten.
If only I didn't thirst for serenity's reverse. If only my soul were satisfied with peace and well-being.

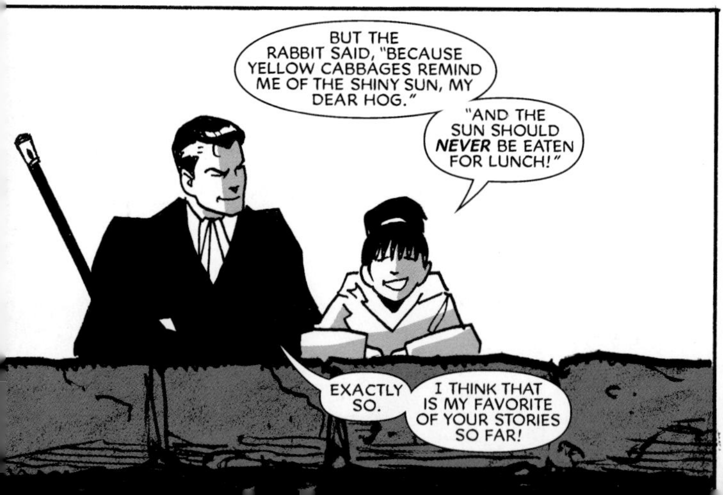
BUT THE RABBIT SAID, "BECAUSE YELLOW CABBAGES REMIND ME OF THE SHINY SUN, MY DEAR HOG."
"AND THE SUN SHOULD *NEVER* BE EATEN FOR LUNCH!"
EXACTLY SO.
I THINK THAT IS MY FAVORITE OF YOUR STORIES SO FAR!

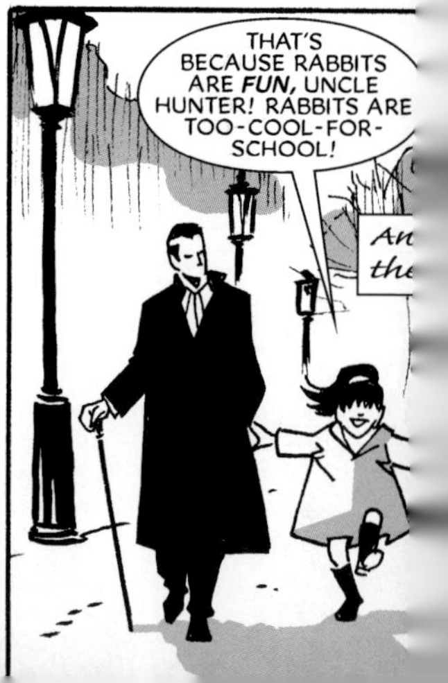
THAT'S BECAUSE RABBITS ARE *FUN*, UNCLE HUNTER! RABBITS ARE TOO-COOL-FOR-SCHOOL!

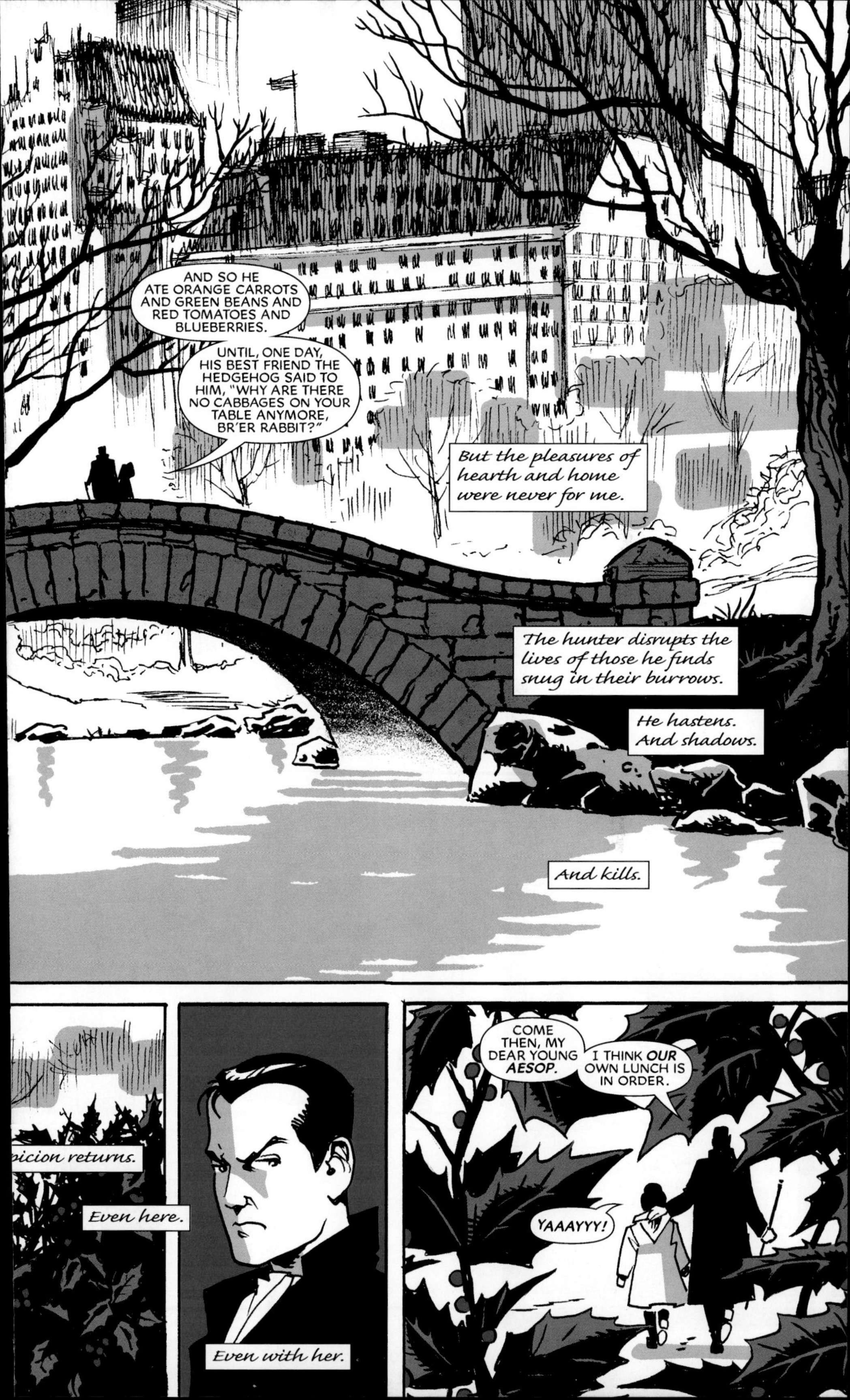
AND SO HE ATE ORANGE CARROTS AND GREEN BEANS AND RED TOMATOES AND BLUEBERRIES.
UNTIL, ONE DAY, HIS BEST FRIEND THE HEDGEHOG SAID TO HIM, "WHY ARE THERE NO CABBAGES ON YOUR TABLE ANYMORE, BR'ER RABBIT?"
But the pleasures of hearth and home were never for me.
The hunter disrupts the lives of those he finds snug in their burrows.
He hastens. And shadows.
And kills.
picion returns.
Even here.
Even with her.
COME THEN, MY DEAR YOUNG AESOP.
I THINK OUR OWN LUNCH IS IN ORDER.
YAAAYYY!

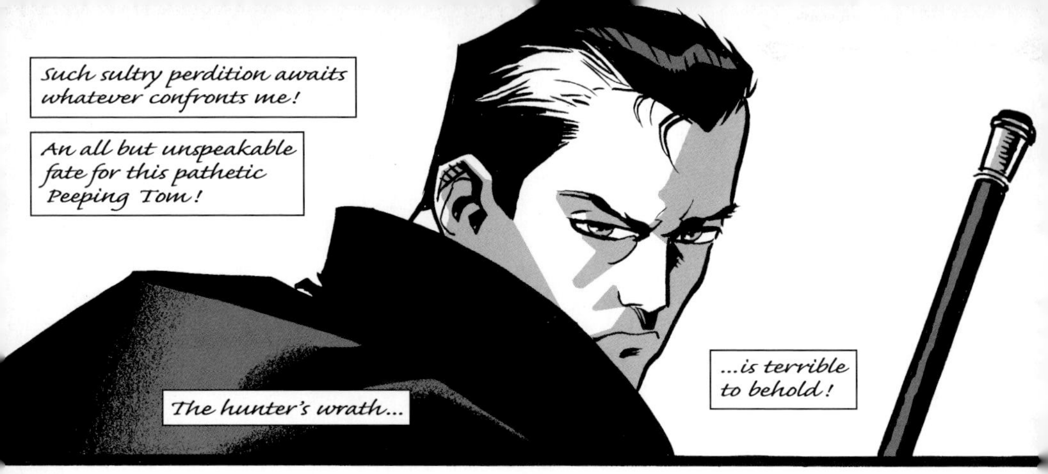
Such sultry perdition awaits whatever confronts me!
An all but unspeakable fate for this pathetic Peeping Tom!
The hunter's wrath...
...is terrible to behold!

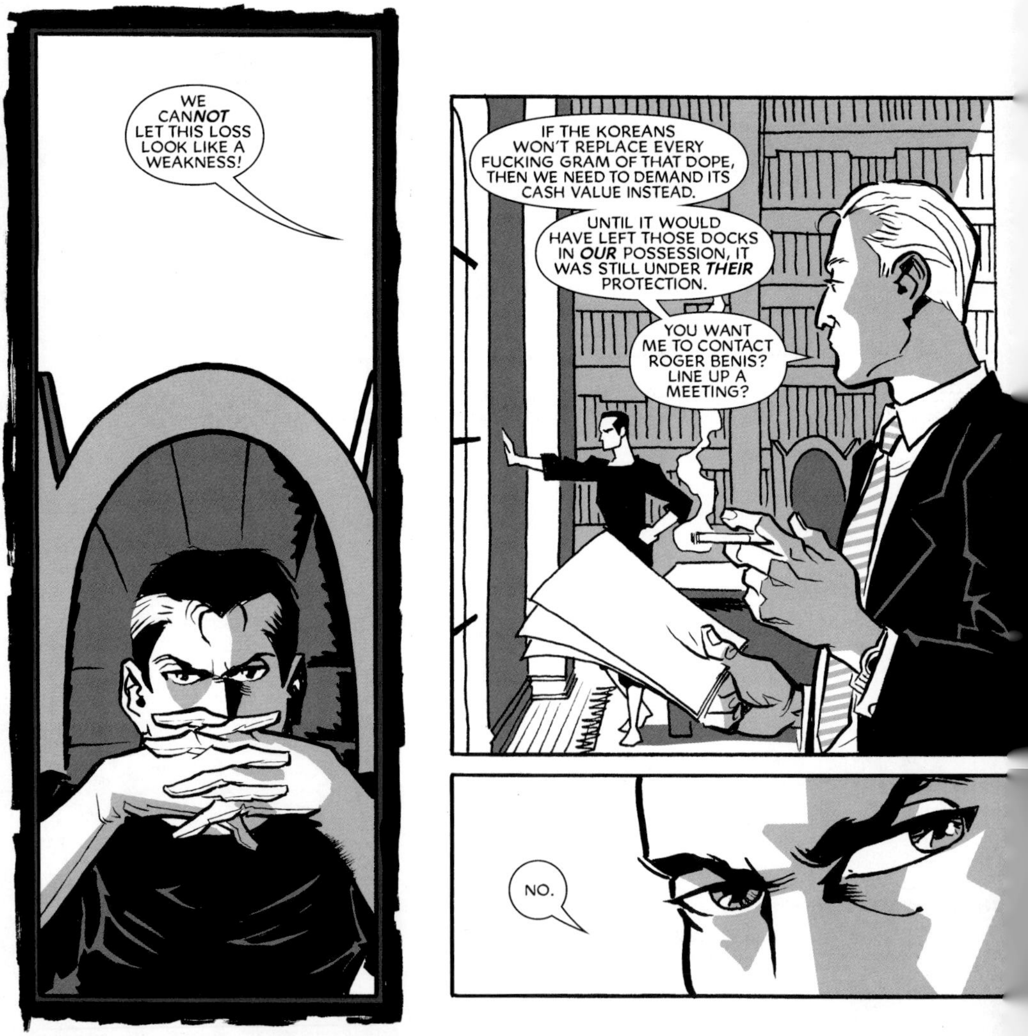
WE CANNOT LET THIS LOSS LOOK LIKE A WEAKNESS!
IF THE KOREANS WON'T REPLACE EVERY FUCKING GRAM OF THAT DOPE, THEN WE NEED TO DEMAND ITS CASH VALUE INSTEAD.
UNTIL IT WOULD HAVE LEFT THOSE DOCKS IN OUR POSSESSION, IT WAS STILL UNDER THEIR PROTECTION.
YOU WANT ME TO CONTACT ROGER BENIS? LINE UP A MEETING?
NO.

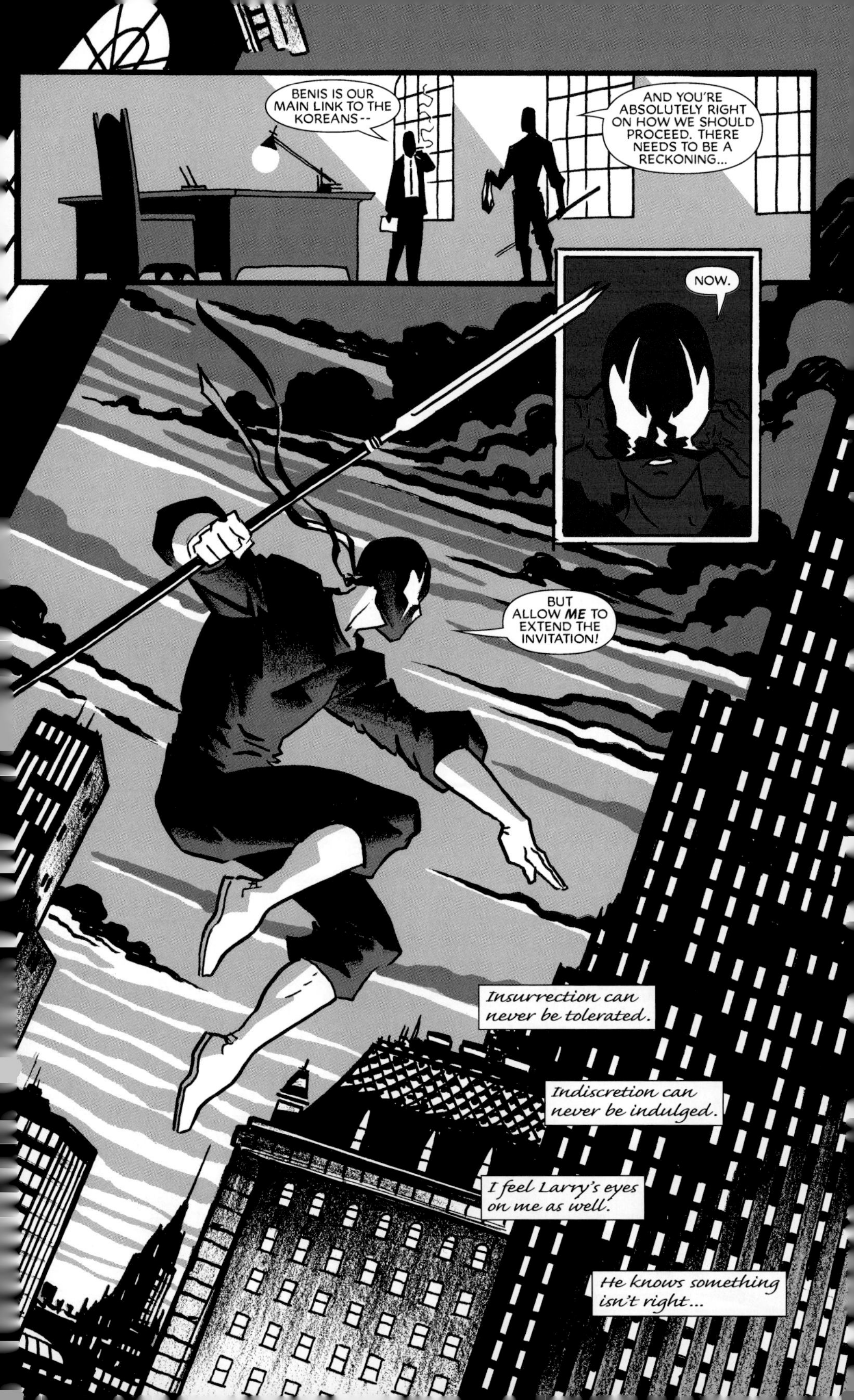
BENIS IS OUR MAIN LINK TO THE KOREANS--
AND YOU'RE ABSOLUTELY RIGHT ON HOW WE SHOULD PROCEED. THERE NEEDS TO BE A RECKONING...
NOW.
BUT ALLOW *ME* TO EXTEND THE INVITATION!
Insurrection can never be tolerated.
Indiscretion can never be indulged.
I feel Larry's eyes on me as well.
He knows something isn't right...

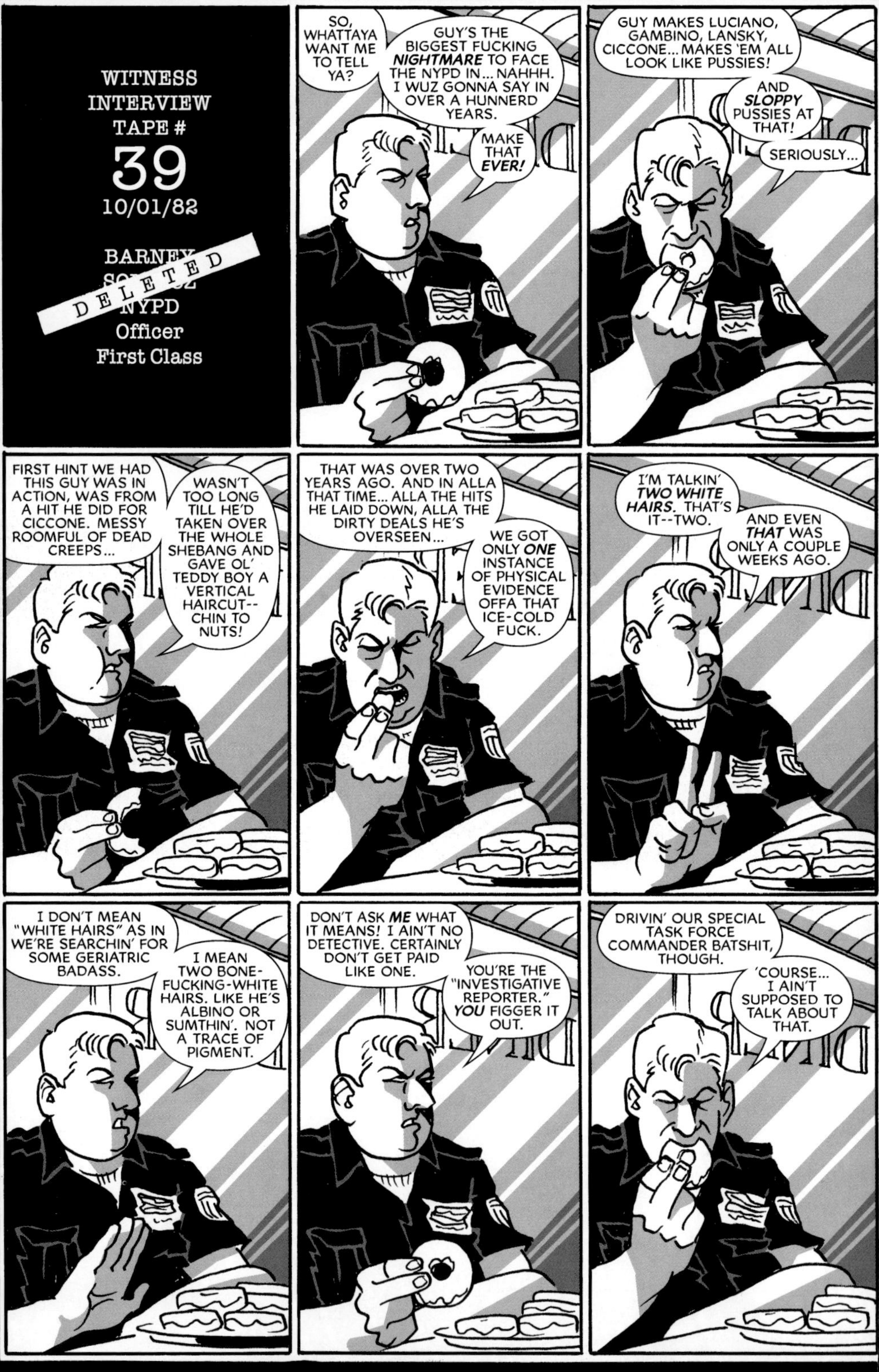
WITNESS
INTERVIEW
TAPE #
39
10/01/82
BARNEY
DELETED
NYPD
Officer
First Class
SO, WHATTAYA WANT ME TO TELL YA?
GUY'S THE BIGGEST FUCKING NIGHTMARE TO FACE THE NYPD IN... NAHHH. I WUZ GONNA SAY IN OVER A HUNNERD YEARS.
MAKE THAT EVER!
GUY MAKES LUCIANO, GAMBINO, LANSKY, CICCONE... MAKES 'EM ALL LOOK LIKE PUSSIES!
AND SLOPPY PUSSIES AT THAT!
SERIOUSLY...
FIRST HINT WE HAD THIS GUY WAS IN ACTION, WAS FROM A HIT HE DID FOR CICCONE. MESSY ROOMFUL OF DEAD CREEPS...
WASN'T TOO LONG TILL HE'D TAKEN OVER THE WHOLE SHEBANG AND GAVE OL' TEDDY BOY A VERTICAL HAIRCUT--CHIN TO NUTS!
THAT WAS OVER TWO YEARS AGO. AND IN ALLA THAT TIME... ALLA THE HITS HE LAID DOWN, ALLA THE DIRTY DEALS HE'S OVERSEEN...
WE GOT ONLY ONE INSTANCE OF PHYSICAL EVIDENCE OFFA THAT ICE-COLD FUCK.
I'M TALKIN' TWO WHITE HAIRS. THAT'S IT--TWO.
AND EVEN THAT WAS ONLY A COUPLE WEEKS AGO.
I DON'T MEAN "WHITE HAIRS" AS IN WE'RE SEARCHIN' FOR SOME GERIATRIC BADASS.
I MEAN TWO BONE-FUCKING-WHITE HAIRS. LIKE HE'S ALBINO OR SUMTHIN'. NOT A TRACE OF PIGMENT.
DON'T ASK ME WHAT IT MEANS! I AIN'T NO DETECTIVE. CERTAINLY DON'T GET PAID LIKE ONE.
YOU'RE THE "INVESTIGATIVE REPORTER." YOU FIGGER IT OUT.
DRIVIN' OUR SPECIAL TASK FORCE COMMANDER BATSHIT, THOUGH.
'COURSE... I AIN'T SUPPOSED TO TALK ABOUT THAT.

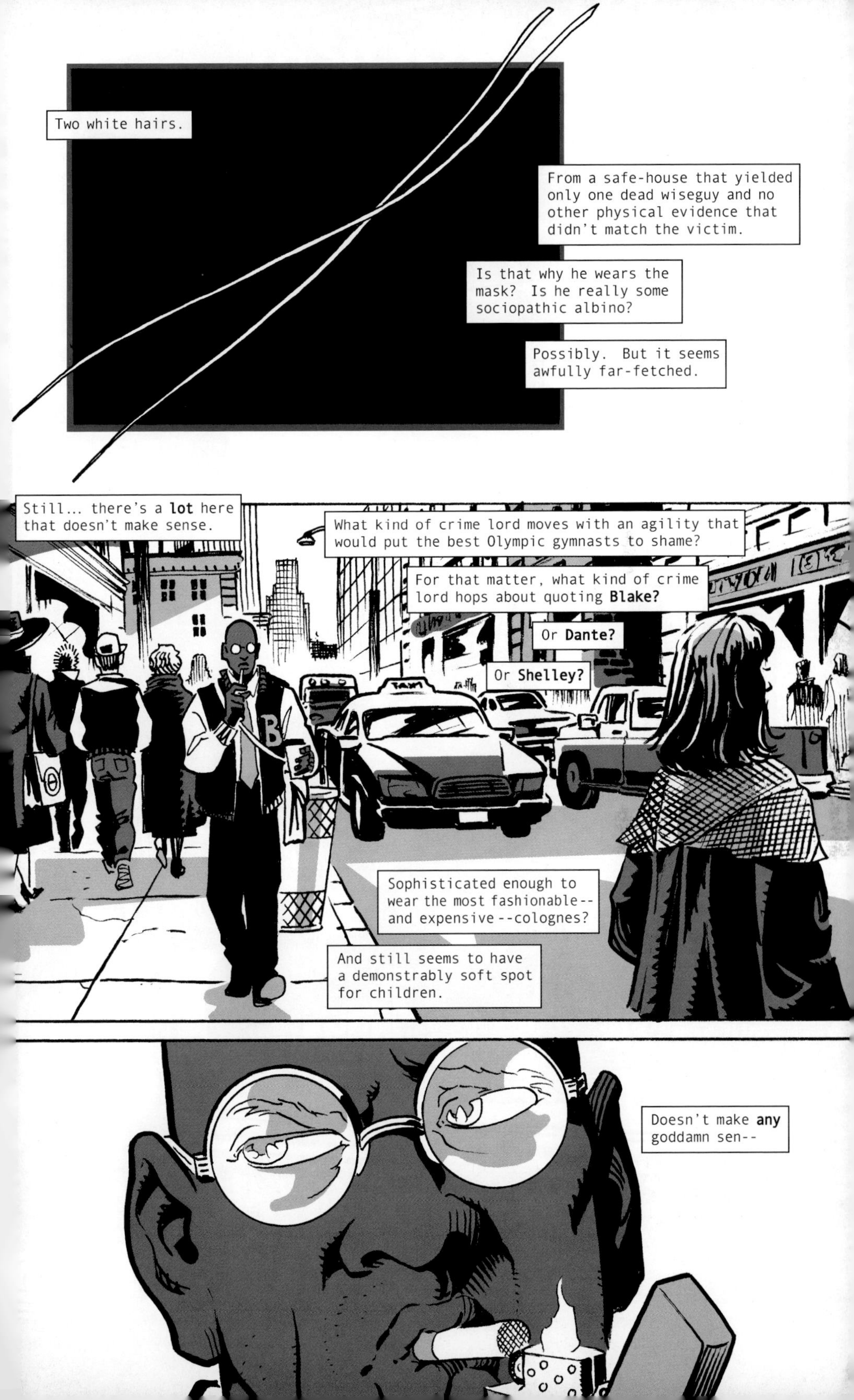
Two white hairs.
From a safe-house that yielded only one dead wiseguy and no other physical evidence that didn't match the victim.
Is that why he wears the mask? Is he really some sociopathic albino?
Possibly. But it seems awfully far-fetched.
Still... there's a **lot** here that doesn't make sense.
What kind of crime lord moves with an agility that would put the best Olympic gymnasts to shame?
For that matter, what kind of crime lord hops about quoting **Blake?**
Or **Dante?**
Or **Shelley?**
TAXI
Sophisticated enough to wear the most fashionable-- and expensive --colognes?
And still seems to have a demonstrably soft spot for children.
Doesn't make **any** goddamn sen--

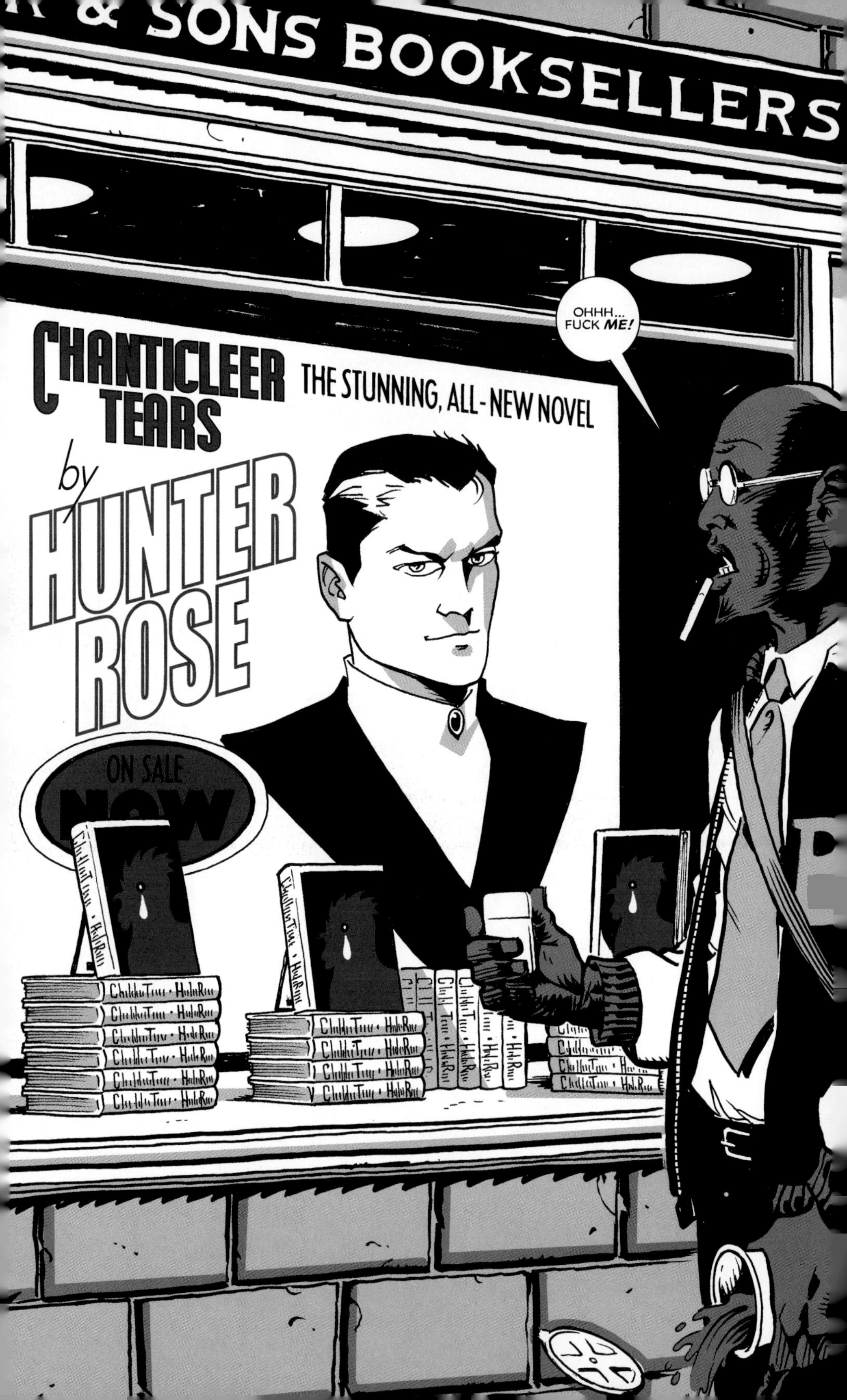
& SONS BOOKSELLERS
CHANTICLEER TEARS
THE STUNNING, ALL-NEW NOVEL
by HUNTER ROSE
ON SALE NOW
OHHH... FUCK *ME!*

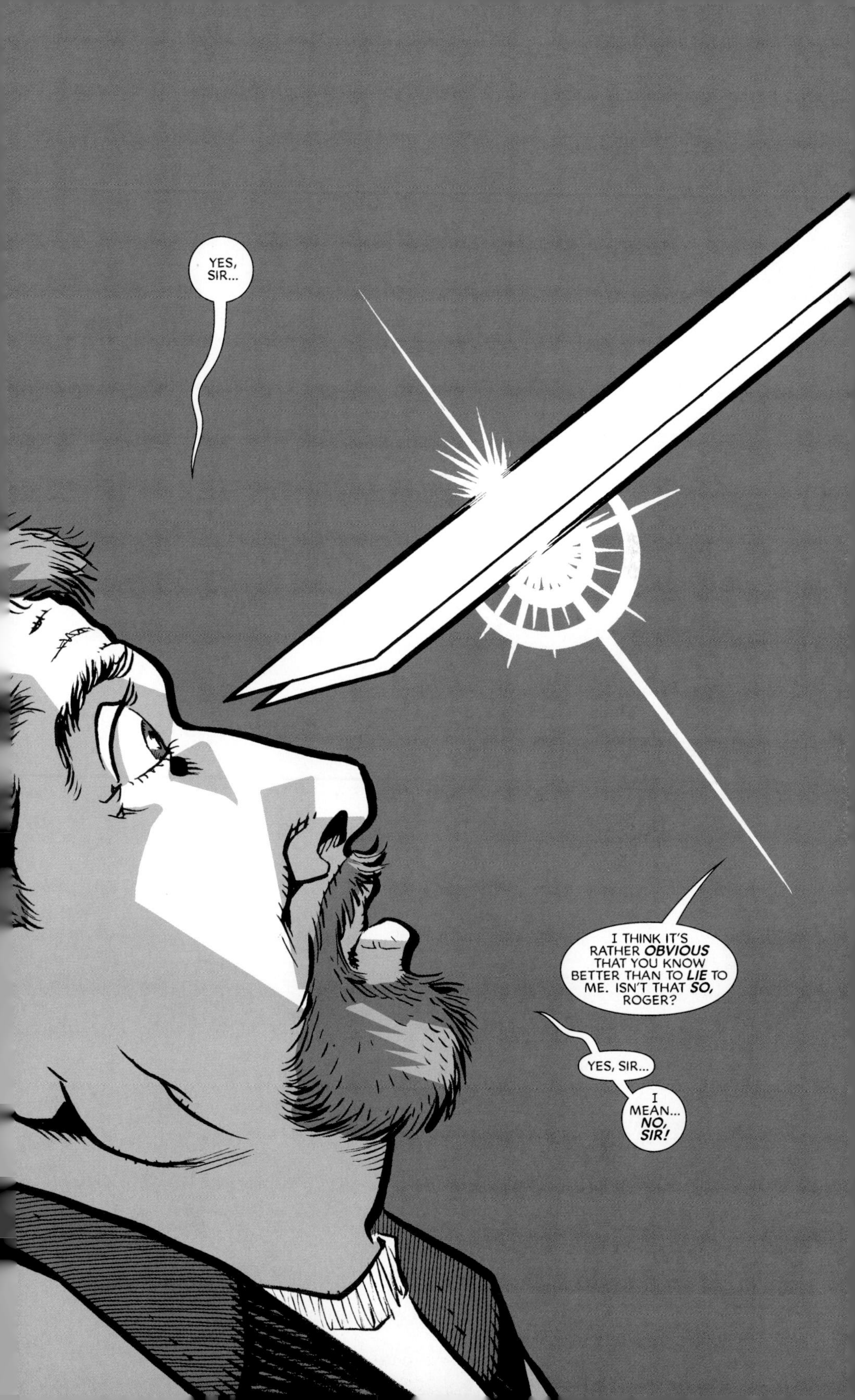
YES, SIR...
I THINK IT'S RATHER *OBVIOUS* THAT YOU KNOW BETTER THAN TO *LIE* TO ME. ISN'T THAT *SO,* ROGER?
YES, SIR...
I MEAN... *NO, SIR!*

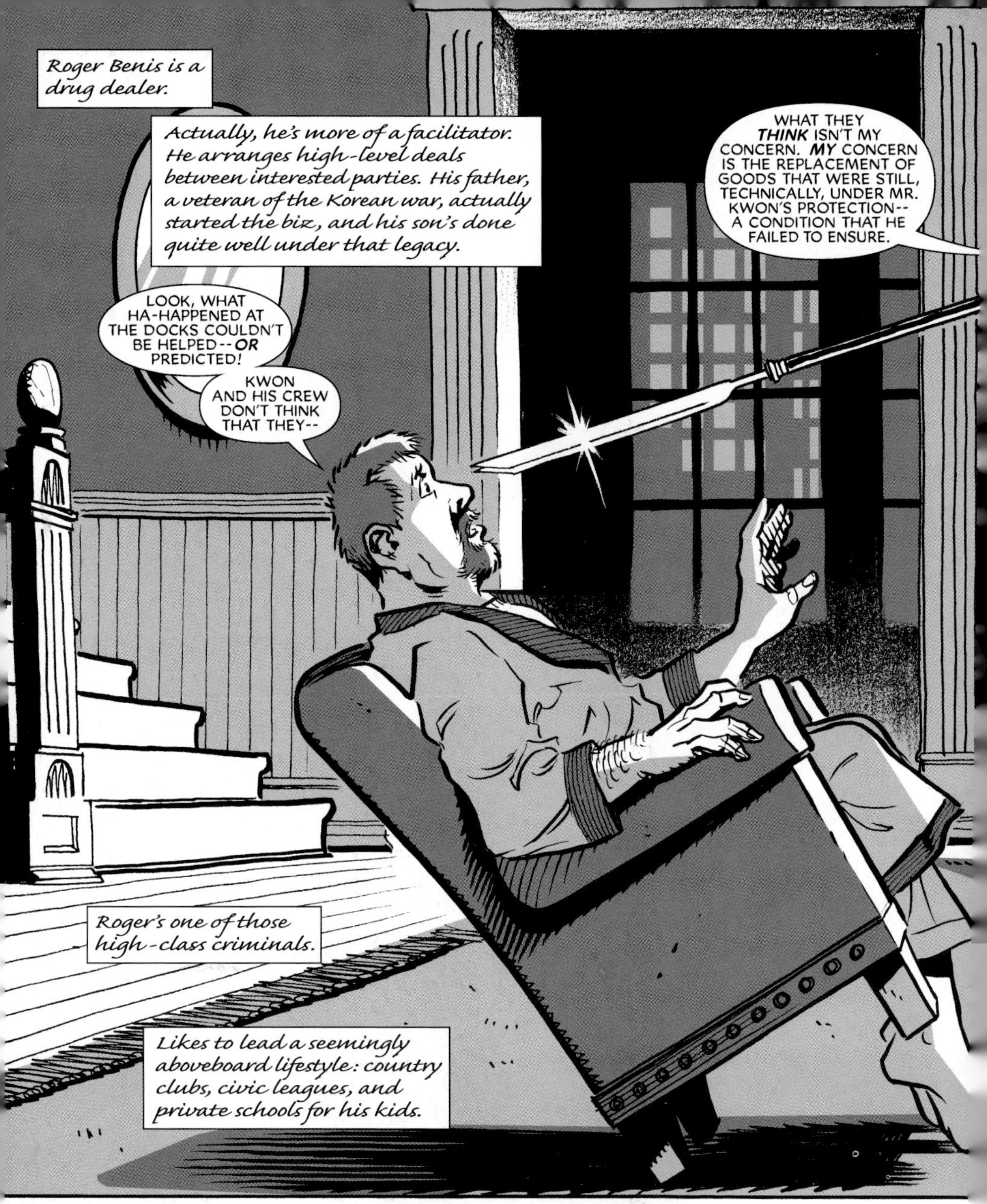
Roger Benis is a drug dealer.
Actually, he's more of a facilitator. He arranges high-level deals between interested parties. His father, a veteran of the Korean war, actually started the biz, and his son's done quite well under that legacy.
LOOK, WHAT HA-HAPPENED AT THE DOCKS COULDN'T BE HELPED--OR PREDICTED!
KWON AND HIS CREW DON'T THINK THAT THEY--
WHAT THEY THINK ISN'T MY CONCERN. MY CONCERN IS THE REPLACEMENT OF GOODS THAT WERE STILL, TECHNICALLY, UNDER MR. KWON'S PROTECTION--A CONDITION THAT HE FAILED TO ENSURE.
Roger's one of those high-class criminals.
Likes to lead a seemingly aboveboard lifestyle: country clubs, civic leagues, and private schools for his kids.

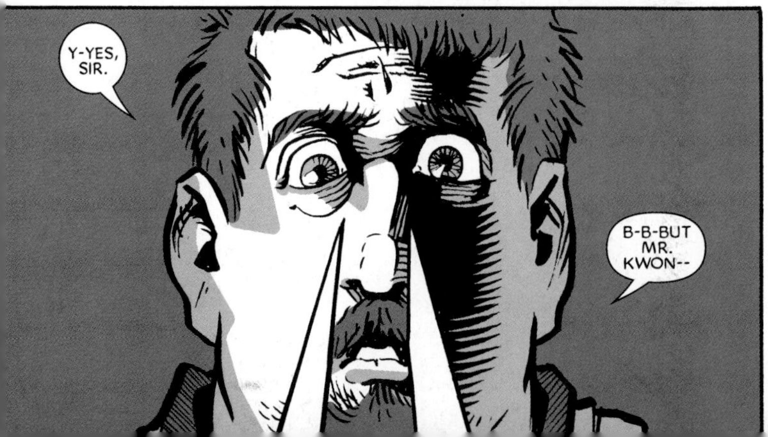
Y-YES, SIR.
B-B-BUT MR. KWON--

Due to the mysteriou
absence of this period i
Grendel's private journ
we can only speculate a
what led to this eventu
quite bloody conflict.

—excerpt from
Devil by the Deed
by Christine Spar

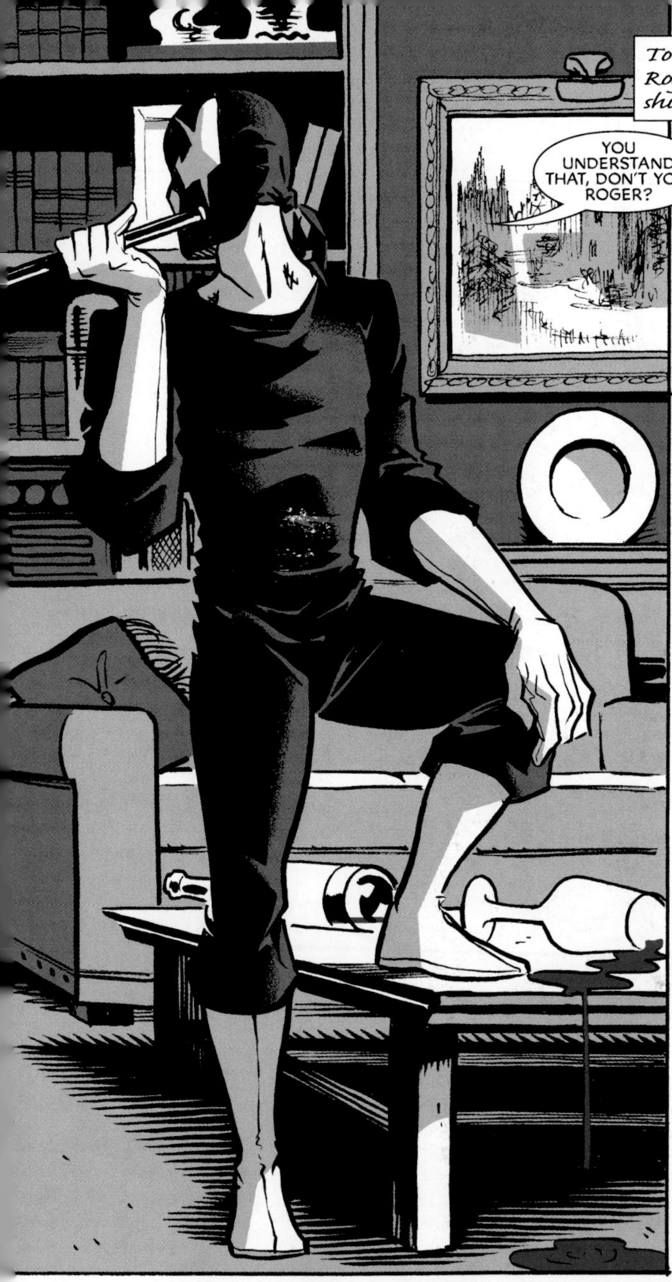
To quote the popular idiom, Roger likes to "pretend his shit doesn't stink."
YOU UNDERSTAND THAT, DON'T YOU, ROGER?

It was around this time—what I have now come to think of as the "lost days"—that Grendel apparently encountered some form of major contention with a renegade gang operating outside the confines of New York's "Five Families" criminal syndicate. Since the late 1950s, the Korean mob *Beomseobangpa* had managed to maintain their basic independence due to their ready control of various international shipping lines. This fact led to an uneasy alliance with the more traditional European-based mobs, a balance of power that had endured for decades but which was shaken to its very foundations by the ascent of a masked mastermind who had no seeming connection to any previous faction and little loyalty to any treaty that was not of his own making.

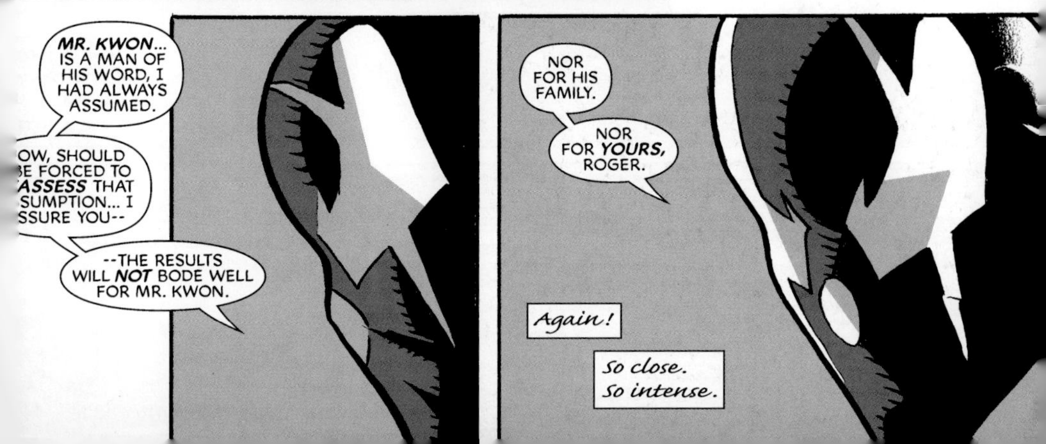
MR. KWON... IS A MAN OF HIS WORD, I HAD ALWAYS ASSUMED.
OW, SHOULD BE FORCED TO ASSESS THAT SUMPTION... I SSURE YOU--
--THE RESULTS WILL NOT BODE WELL FOR MR. KWON.
NOR FOR HIS FAMILY.
NOR FOR YOURS, ROGER.
Again!
So close. So intense.

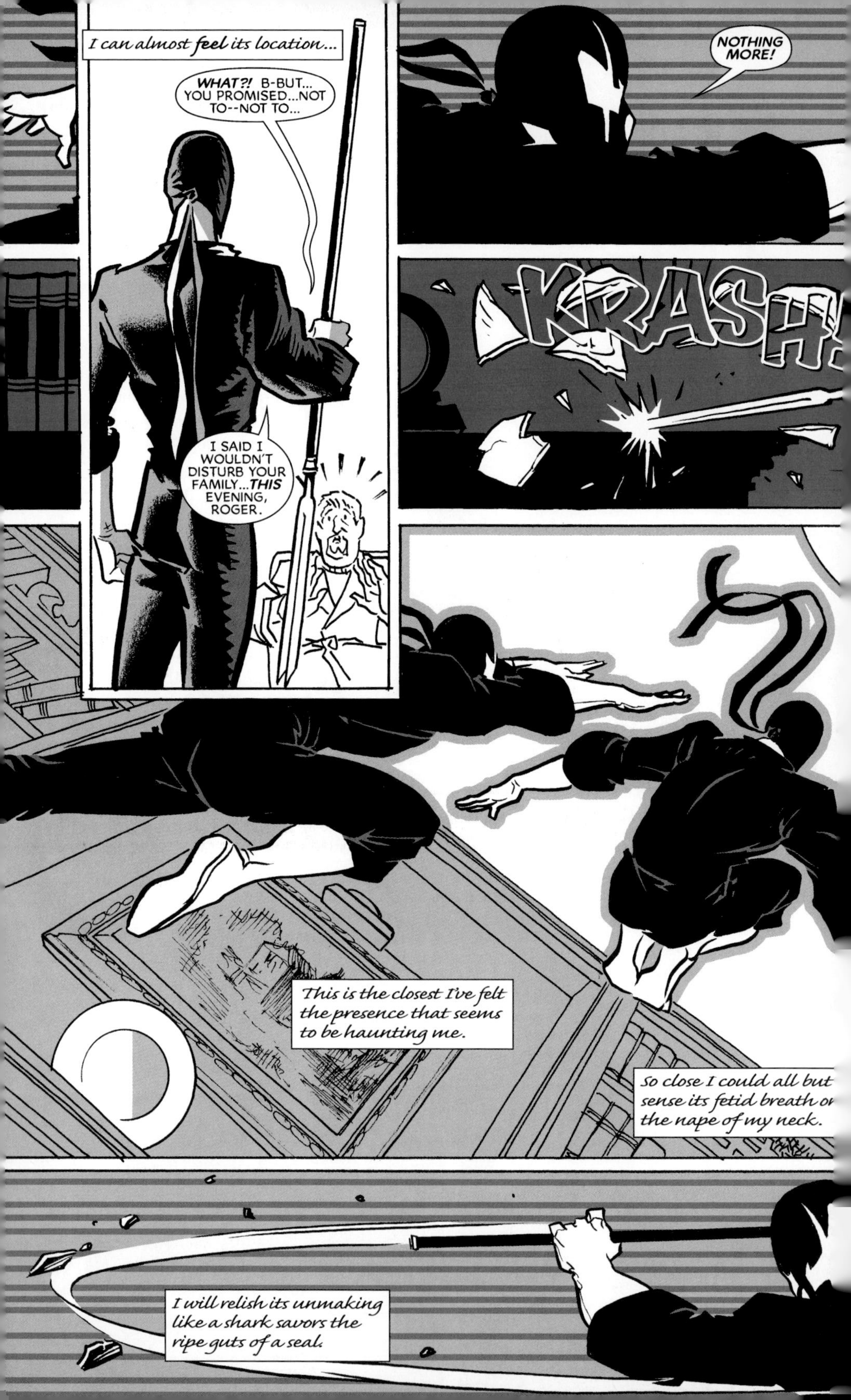

I can almost feel its location...
WHAT?! B-BUT... YOU PROMISED...NOT TO--NOT TO...
I SAID I WOULDN'T DISTURB YOUR FAMILY...THIS EVENING, ROGER.
NOTHING MORE!
KRASH!
This is the closest I've felt the presence that seems to be haunting me.
So close I could all but sense its fetid breath on the nape of my neck.
I will relish its unmaking like a shark savors the ripe guts of a seal.

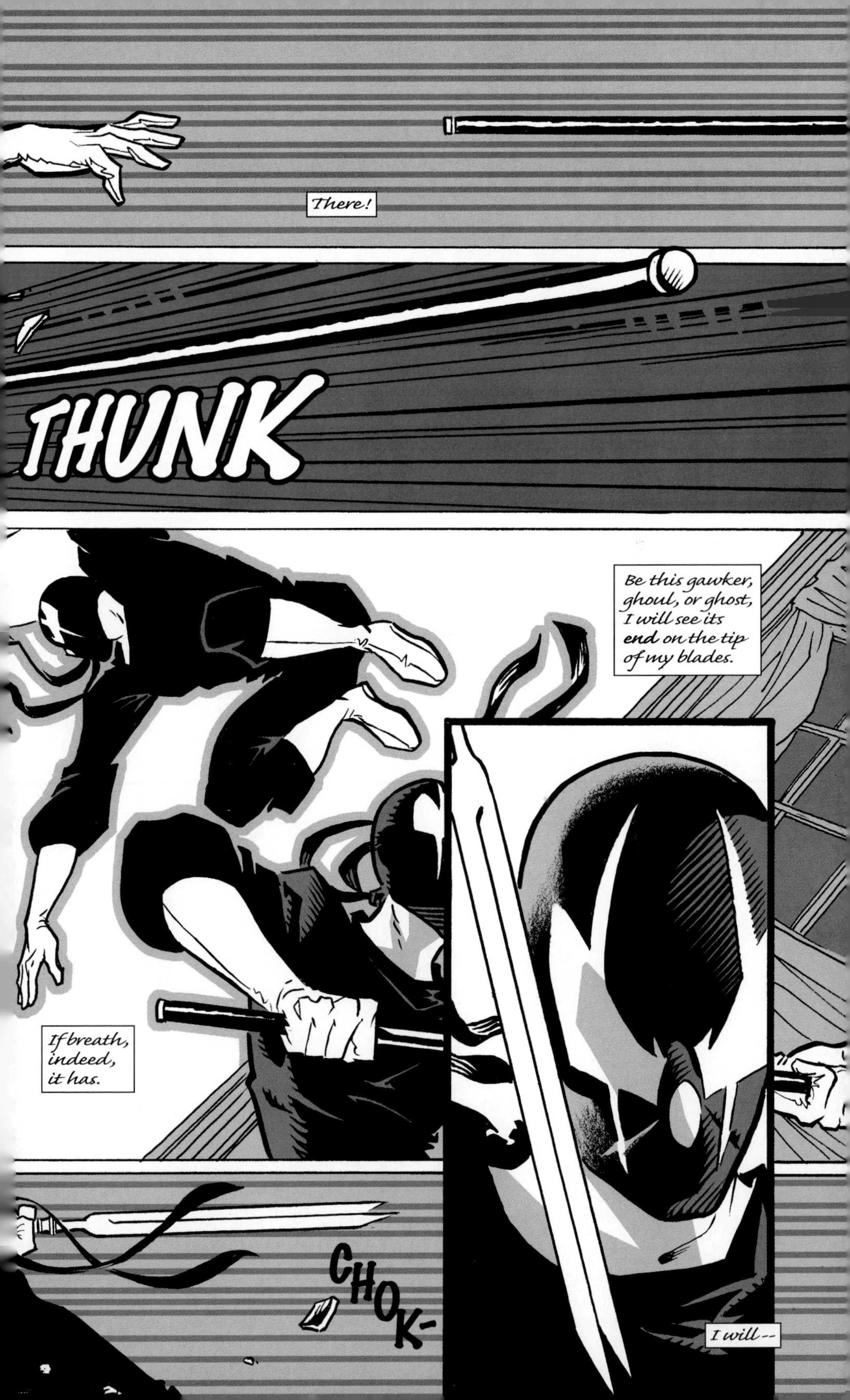
There!
THUNK
Be this gawker, ghoul, or ghost, I will see its **end** on the tip of my blades.
If breath, indeed, it has.
CHOK-
I will--

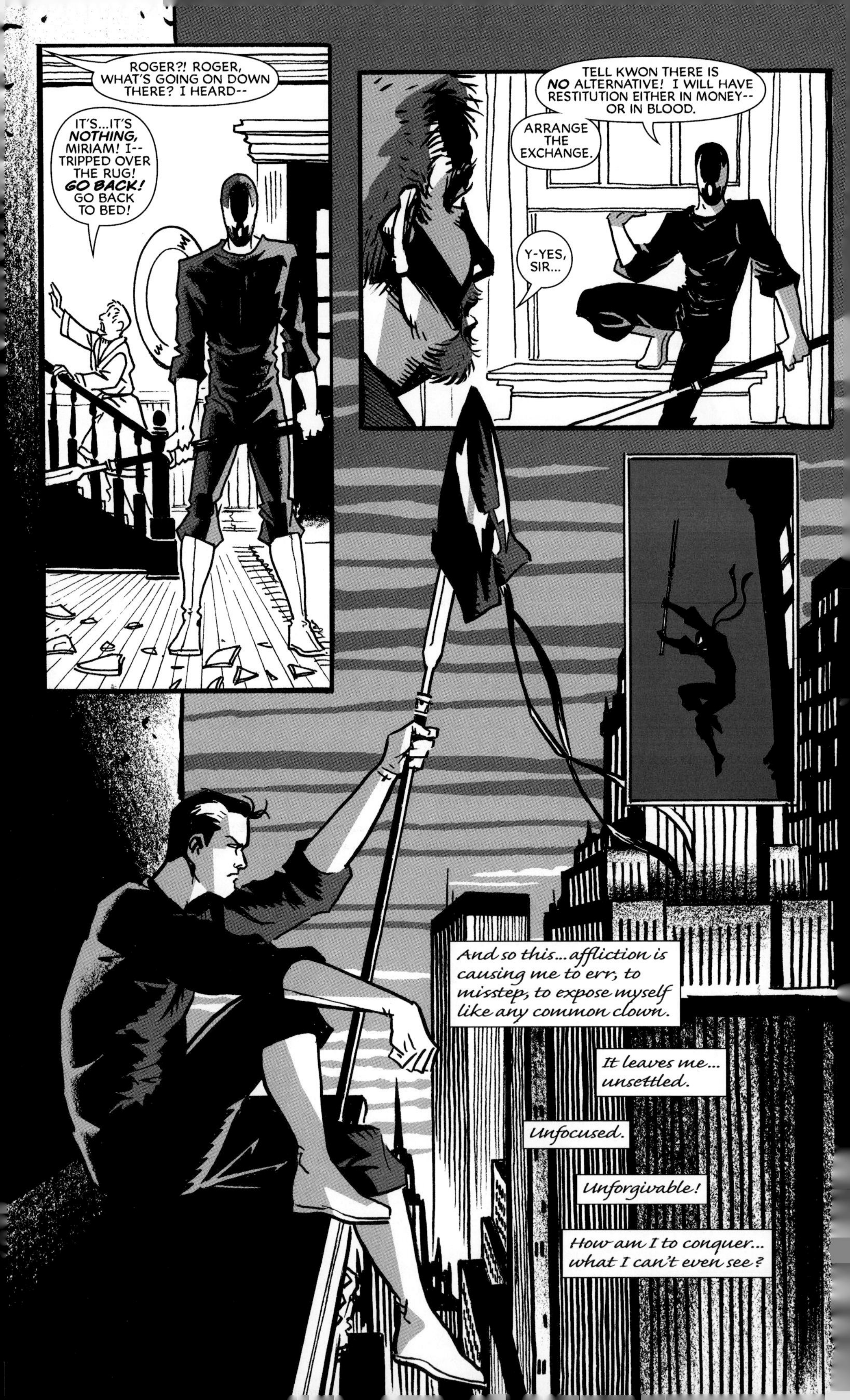

ROGER?! ROGER, WHAT'S GOING ON DOWN THERE? I HEARD--
IT'S...IT'S **NOTHING,** MIRIAM! I-- TRIPPED OVER THE RUG! **GO BACK!** GO BACK TO BED!
TELL KWON THERE IS **NO** ALTERNATIVE! I WILL HAVE RESTITUTION EITHER IN MONEY-- OR IN BLOOD.
ARRANGE THE EXCHANGE.
Y-YES, SIR...
And so this...affliction is causing me to err, to misstep, to expose myself like any common clown.
It leaves me... unsettled.
Unfocused.
Unforgivable!
How am I to conquer... what I can't even see?

...ARING YOUNG SENSATION

by QwvrduWBdW
M.../NrU+k08S+PlZNvxB1qQgsGOLV
3DORgQZ7EY... J/Kvl fEP7afrwi8G+LNW8E+Kf2mNT9e
0S7fT7+1g0m9
mxPG/ElWVDF
pVqVubs2afwt/
gIoTKIlfzJYDCGMhCBS28o8Sktbudfij4kg
K2tw4KywttYROQwVoSTggHAB7EL2rjznQeMuH8weAz

> Unthinkable.

> Surely...my mind is making connections and conclusions out of sheer desperation.

A WRITE SPEAKS

INDIGO: A LITERARY CURE FOR THE BLUE

Hunter Rose Delivers a Hit

PdJPpMtgIoTKIlfzJYDCGMhCBS28OR
HhHK9le6r8SktbudfiJ4kgK2tw4KywttYR
OQwVoSTggHAB7EL2rjznOeMuH8weA
zPEWnCzdpU3o0pa8jSybzlvbS1iTBYfK

PdJPpMtgIoTKIlfzJYDCGMhCBS28
HhHK9le6r8SktbudfiJ4kgK2tw4Kyw
ROQwVoSTggHAB7EL2rjznOeMuH
eAzPEWnCzdpU3o0pa8jSvbzlvbS1j
QdalRuvO9rrtovnojymy8aft
418QRW8zW66bLpA01riLzz
e3mnuY5ZCoX7LCZISsslqh
difiJ4kgK2tw4KywttYROQw

KsqlaC5nFW+Fvl2b
320d9lrqe7mNHJct
pVqVubs2afwt/aX8
NfG+/1PSfhb8bfFu
XmmQLPdJPpMtg
oTKIlfzJYDCGMh

PUBLISHER'S BULLETIN

NEW HUNTER ROSE NOVEL DUE THIS SUMMER

KsqlaC5nFW+Fvl2ba320d9lr
qe7mNHJctipVqVubs2afwt/a
X
GMhCBS28ORHhHK9le6r8S
ktbudfiJ4kgK2tw4KywttYR
OQwVoSTggHAB7EL2rjznO
eMuH8weAzPEWnCzdpU3o
0pa8jSvbzlvbS1jTBYfKMX
QdalRuvO9rrtovnojymy8aft
U6lZ3M99418QRW8zW66b
LpA01riLzZ4UskuWnle3mn
uY5ZCoX7LCZISsslqHCLz

> This just can**not** be so.

R ROSE
GENIUS

W+Fvl2ba320
-JctipVqVubs
fG+/1PSfhb8
QLPdJPpMtgI
GMhCBS28
6r8SktbudfiJ
wttYROQwV

> Hunter Rose is **not** Grendel...

El
vbS1jTBYfKM
9rrtovnojymy
99418QRW8
01riLzZ4Usku
5ZCoX7LCZI
KFX9oA2gmt

LoXlC7VRpJWYNKkERMqt
uVerUovdpvTo97rR+TvK/kl
RgQYpVk8qRJk2yRvGrIyuq
kf9wVoSTggHAB7EL2rjznO
eMuH8weAzPEWnCzdpU3

> Grendel is **not** Hunter Rose.

HUNTER ROSE

About Town

...nter Rose Takes ...eattle by Storm

KsqlaC5nFW+Fvl2ba320d
9lrqe7mNHJctipVqVubs2a
wt/aX8NfG+/1PSfhb8bfFu
qXmm
JYDC
9le6r8SktbudfiJ4kgK2tw
KywttYROQwVoSTggHA
7EL2rjznOeMuH8weAzP

PdJPpMtgIoTKIlfzJY
MhCBS28ORHhHK9
SktbudfiJ4kgK2tw4f
nOeMuH8weAzPEW
pU3o0pa8jSvbzlvbS
fKMXQdalRuvO9rrt
my8aftU6lZ3M99418

> Still...

...TERATI TURN
...CK-TIE AFFAIR

Hunter Rose

37EL2rjznOeMuH8weAzP... my8a

WEEKEND TIM...

CREON
...allenging ...ovel by ...nter Rose

KsqlaC5nFW+Fvl2ba
320d9lrqe7mNHJctip
VqVubs2afwt/aX8Nf
G+/1PSfhb8bfFuqXm
nQLPdJPpMtgIoTKI

-Fvl2ba320d   PdJPpMtgIoTKIlfzJYDCG
ipVqVubs2a   MhCBS28ORHhHK9le6r8

NEW STAR: ...UNTER ...ROSE
...Author ...akes On ...g Apple

New York Times - STYLE

MY LITTLE CHICKADEE SETS WEEK-END SALES RECORD

PdJPpMtgIoTKIlfzJYDCGMhCBS28ORHhHK9le
6r8SktbudfiJ4kgK2tw4KywttYROQwVoSTggHA
B7EL2rjznOeMuH8weAzPEWnCzdpU3o0pa8jSv
bzlvbS1jTBYfKMXQdalRuvO9rrtovnojymy8aftU

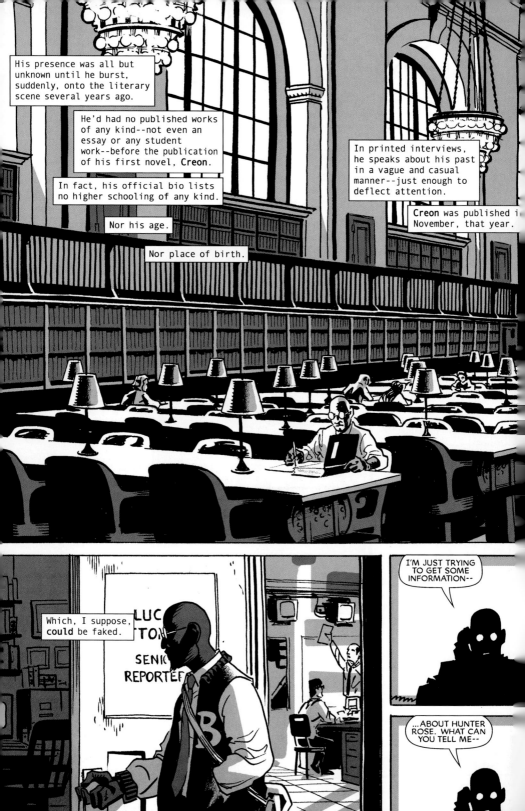

His presence was all but unknown until he burst, suddenly, onto the literary scene several years ago.

He'd had no published works of any kind--not even an essay or any student work--before the publication of his first novel, **Creon.**

In fact, his official bio lists no higher schooling of any kind.

Nor his age.

Nor place of birth.

In printed interviews, he speaks about his past in a vague and casual manner--just enough to deflect attention.

Creon was published i November, that year.

Which, I suppose, **could** be faked.

LUC
TO
SENI
REPORTE

I'M JUST TRYING TO GET SOME INFORMATION--

...ABOUT HUNTER ROSE. WHAT CAN YOU TELL ME--

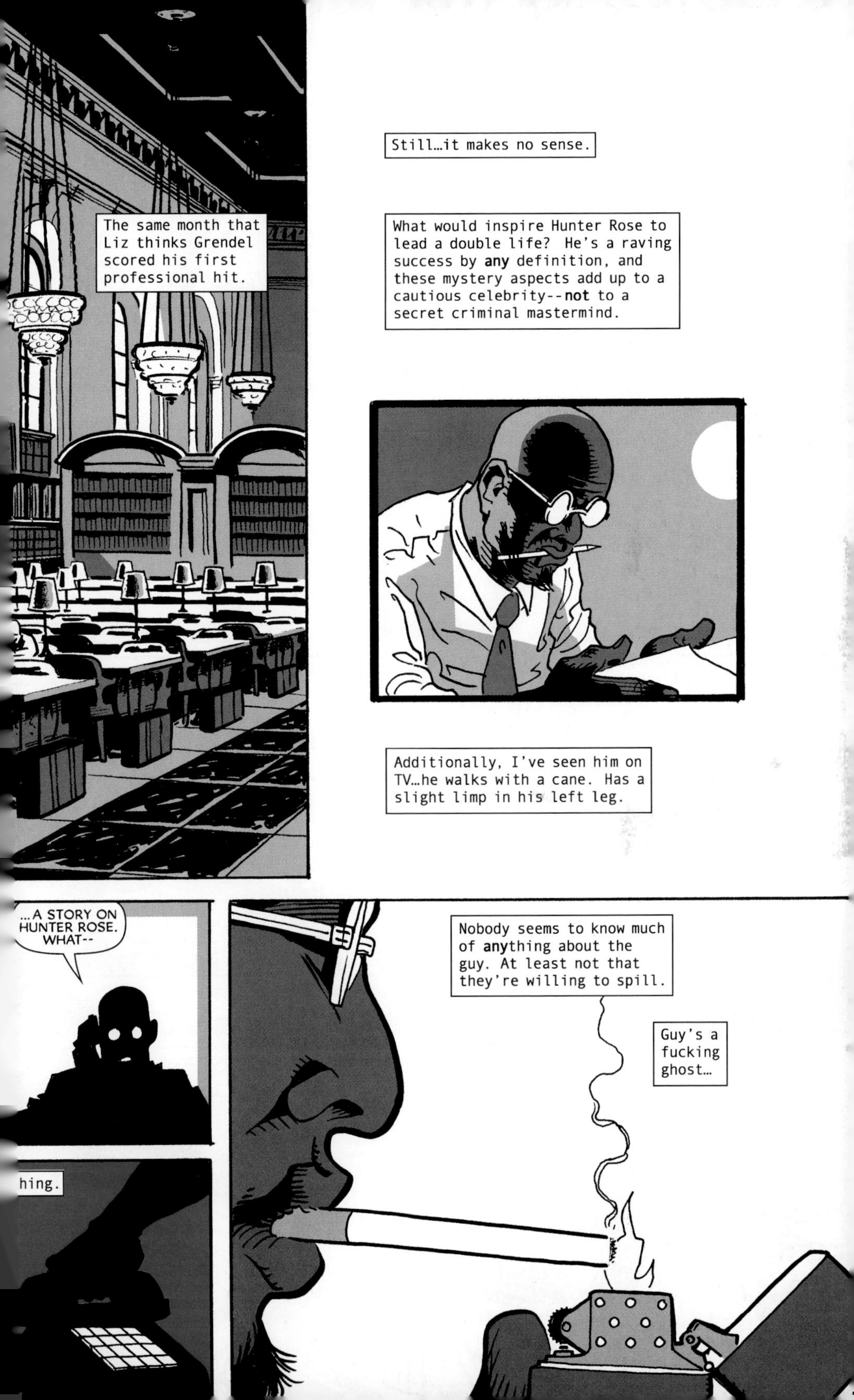
The same month that Liz thinks Grendel scored his first professional hit.
Still…it makes no sense.
What would inspire Hunter Rose to lead a double life? He's a raving success by **any** definition, and these mystery aspects add up to a cautious celebrity--**not** to a secret criminal mastermind.
Additionally, I've seen him on TV…he walks with a cane. Has a slight limp in his left leg.
...A STORY ON HUNTER ROSE. WHAT--
hing.
Nobody seems to know much of **any**thing about the guy. At least not that they're willing to spill.
Guy's a fucking ghost…

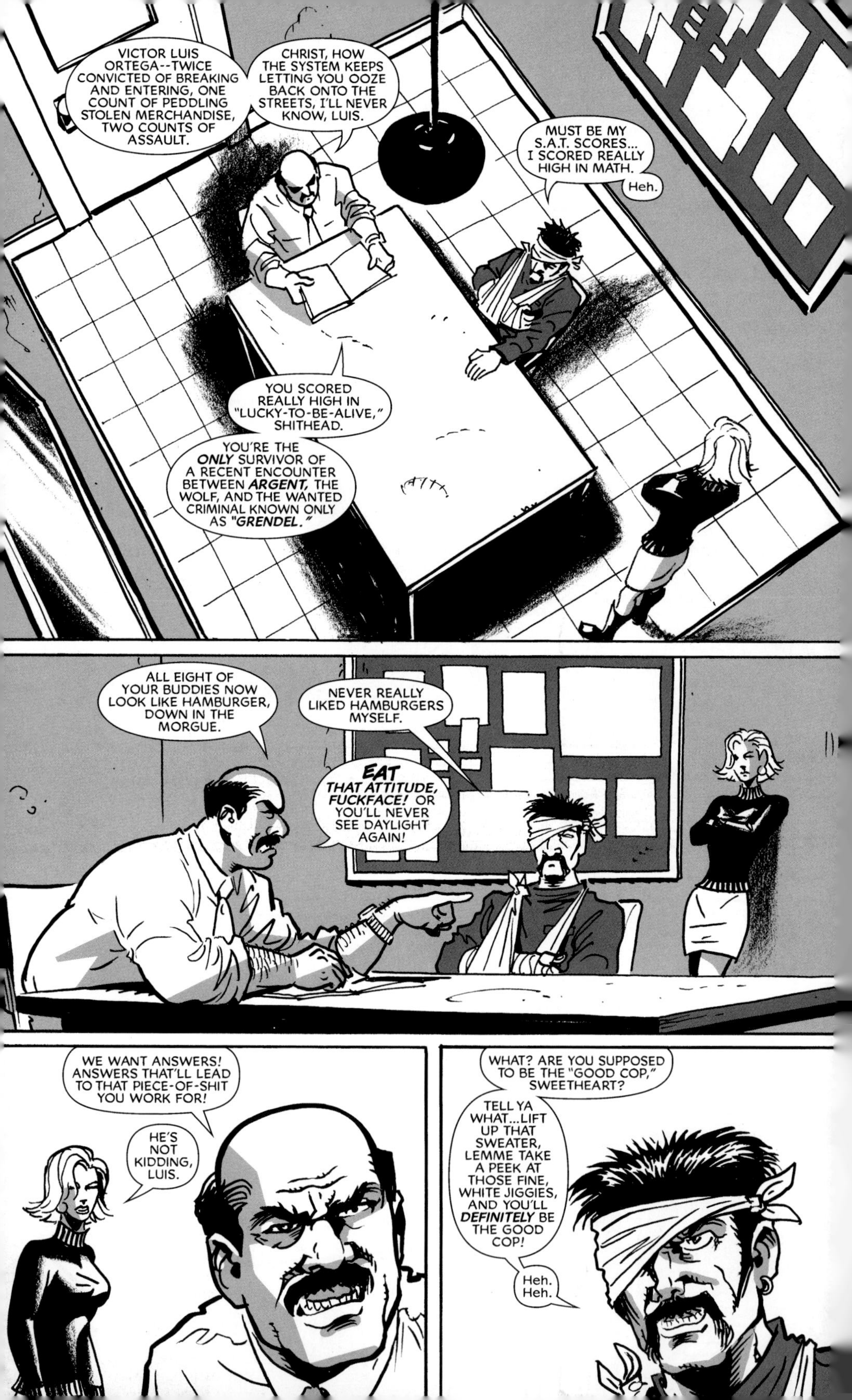
VICTOR LUIS ORTEGA--TWICE CONVICTED OF BREAKING AND ENTERING, ONE COUNT OF PEDDLING STOLEN MERCHANDISE, TWO COUNTS OF ASSAULT.
CHRIST, HOW THE SYSTEM KEEPS LETTING YOU OOZE BACK ONTO THE STREETS, I'LL NEVER KNOW, LUIS.
MUST BE MY S.A.T. SCORES... I SCORED REALLY HIGH IN MATH.
Heh.
YOU SCORED REALLY HIGH IN "LUCKY-TO-BE-ALIVE," SHITHEAD.
YOU'RE THE ONLY SURVIVOR OF A RECENT ENCOUNTER BETWEEN ARGENT, THE WOLF, AND THE WANTED CRIMINAL KNOWN ONLY AS "GRENDEL."
ALL EIGHT OF YOUR BUDDIES NOW LOOK LIKE HAMBURGER, DOWN IN THE MORGUE.
NEVER REALLY LIKED HAMBURGERS MYSELF.
EAT THAT ATTITUDE, FUCKFACE! OR YOU'LL NEVER SEE DAYLIGHT AGAIN!
WE WANT ANSWERS! ANSWERS THAT'LL LEAD TO THAT PIECE-OF-SHIT YOU WORK FOR!
HE'S NOT KIDDING, LUIS.
WHAT? ARE YOU SUPPOSED TO BE THE "GOOD COP," SWEETHEART?
TELL YA WHAT...LIFT UP THAT SWEATER, LEMME TAKE A PEEK AT THOSE FINE, WHITE JIGGIES, AND YOU'LL DEFINITELY BE THE GOOD COP!
Heh. Heh.

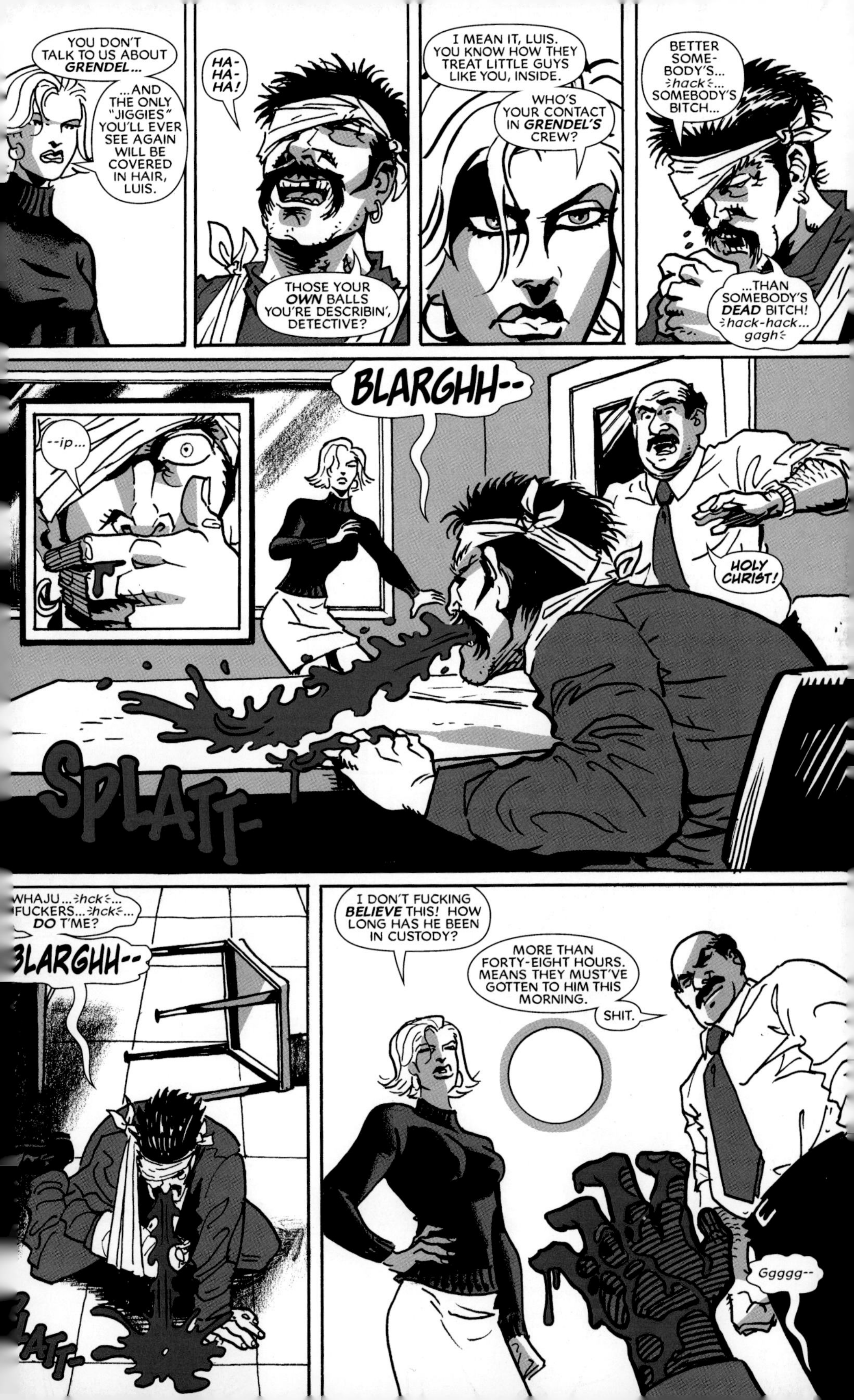
YOU DON'T TALK TO US ABOUT GRENDEL...
...AND THE ONLY "JIGGIES" YOU'LL EVER SEE AGAIN WILL BE COVERED IN HAIR, LUIS.
HA-HA-HA!
THOSE YOUR OWN BALLS YOU'RE DESCRIBIN', DETECTIVE?
I MEAN IT, LUIS. YOU KNOW HOW THEY TREAT LITTLE GUYS LIKE YOU, INSIDE.
WHO'S YOUR CONTACT IN GRENDEL'S CREW?
BETTER SOME-BODY'S... hack... SOMEBODY'S BITCH...
...THAN SOMEBODY'S DEAD BITCH! hack-hack... gagh
--ip...
BLARGHH--
HOLY CHRIST!
SPLATT-
WHAJU...hck... FUCKERS...hck... DO T'ME?
BLARGHH--
SPLATT-
I DON'T FUCKING BELIEVE THIS! HOW LONG HAS HE BEEN IN CUSTODY?
MORE THAN FORTY-EIGHT HOURS. MEANS THEY MUST'VE GOTTEN TO HIM THIS MORNING.
SHIT.
Ggggg--

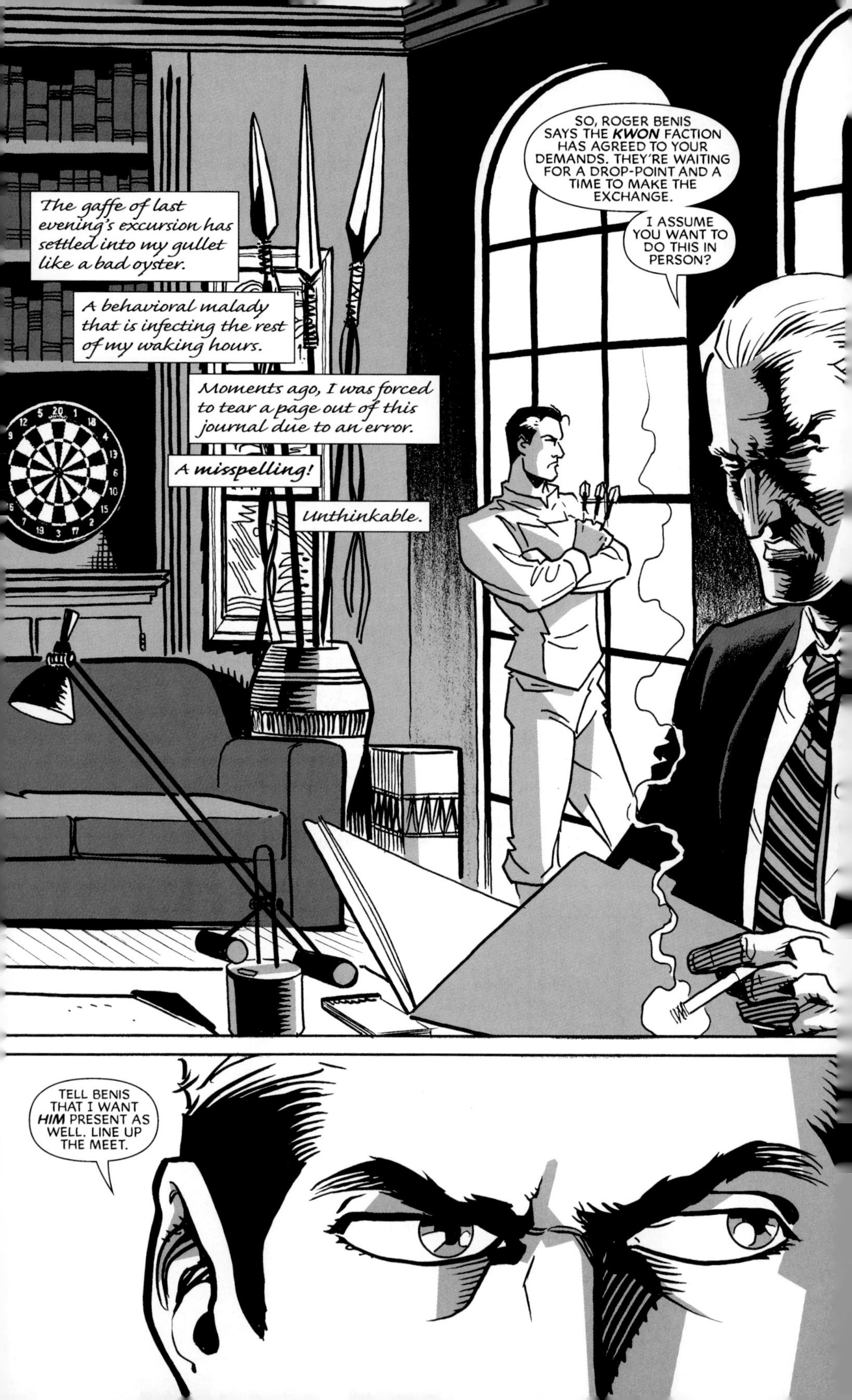

The gaffe of last evening's excursion has settled into my gullet like a bad oyster.
A behavioral malady that is infecting the rest of my waking hours.
Moments ago, I was forced to tear a page out of this journal due to an error.
A misspelling!
Unthinkable.
SO, ROGER BENIS SAYS THE KWON FACTION HAS AGREED TO YOUR DEMANDS. THEY'RE WAITING FOR A DROP-POINT AND A TIME TO MAKE THE EXCHANGE.
I ASSUME YOU WANT TO DO THIS IN PERSON?
TELL BENIS THAT I WANT HIM PRESENT AS WELL. LINE UP THE MEET.

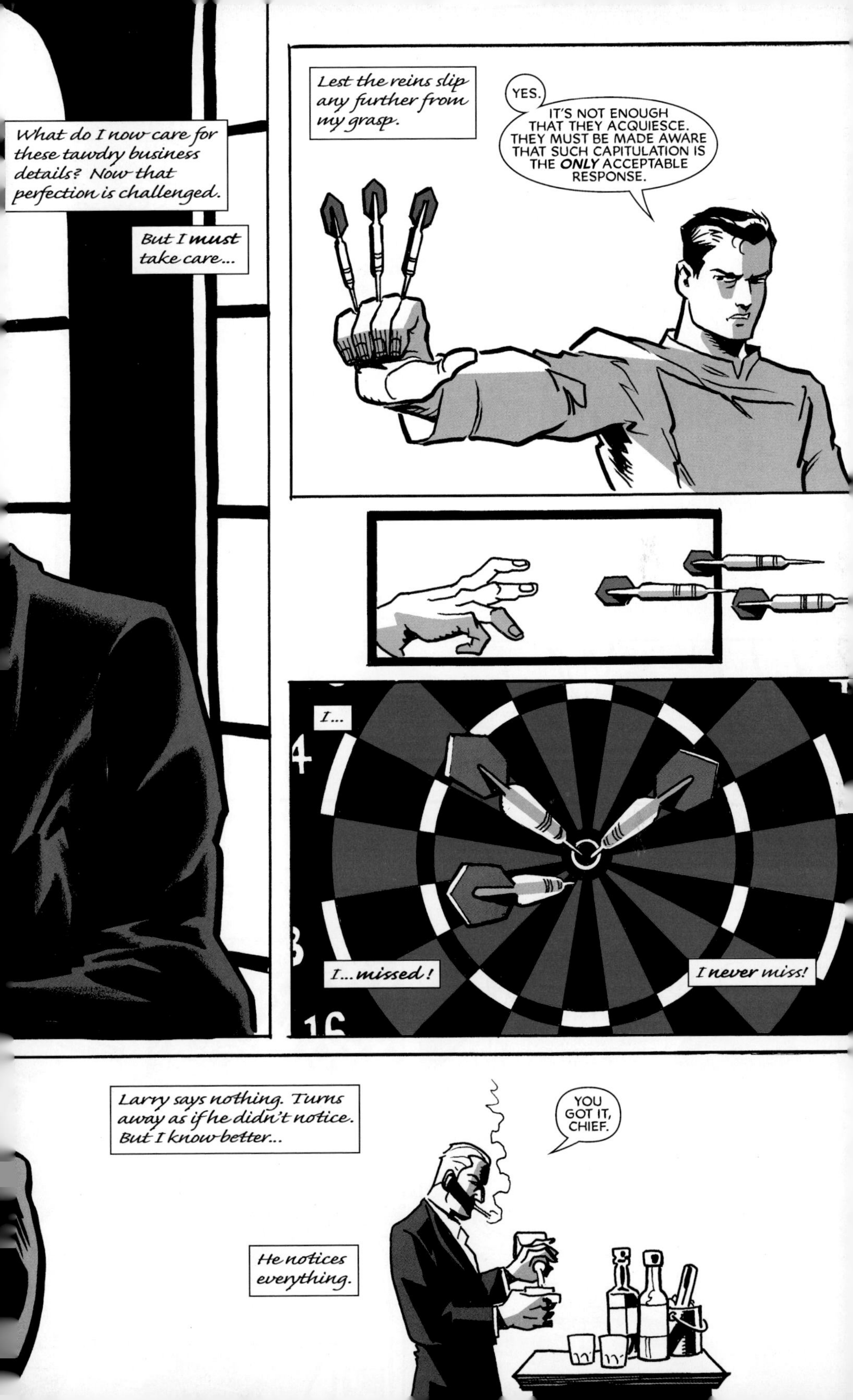

What do I now care for these tawdry business details? Now that perfection is challenged.
But I must take care...
Lest the reins slip any further from my grasp.
YES.
IT'S NOT ENOUGH THAT THEY ACQUIESCE. THEY MUST BE MADE AWARE THAT SUCH CAPITULATION IS THE ONLY ACCEPTABLE RESPONSE.
I...
I...missed!
I never miss!
Larry says nothing. Turns away as if he didn't notice. But I know better...
YOU GOT IT, CHIEF.
He notices everything.

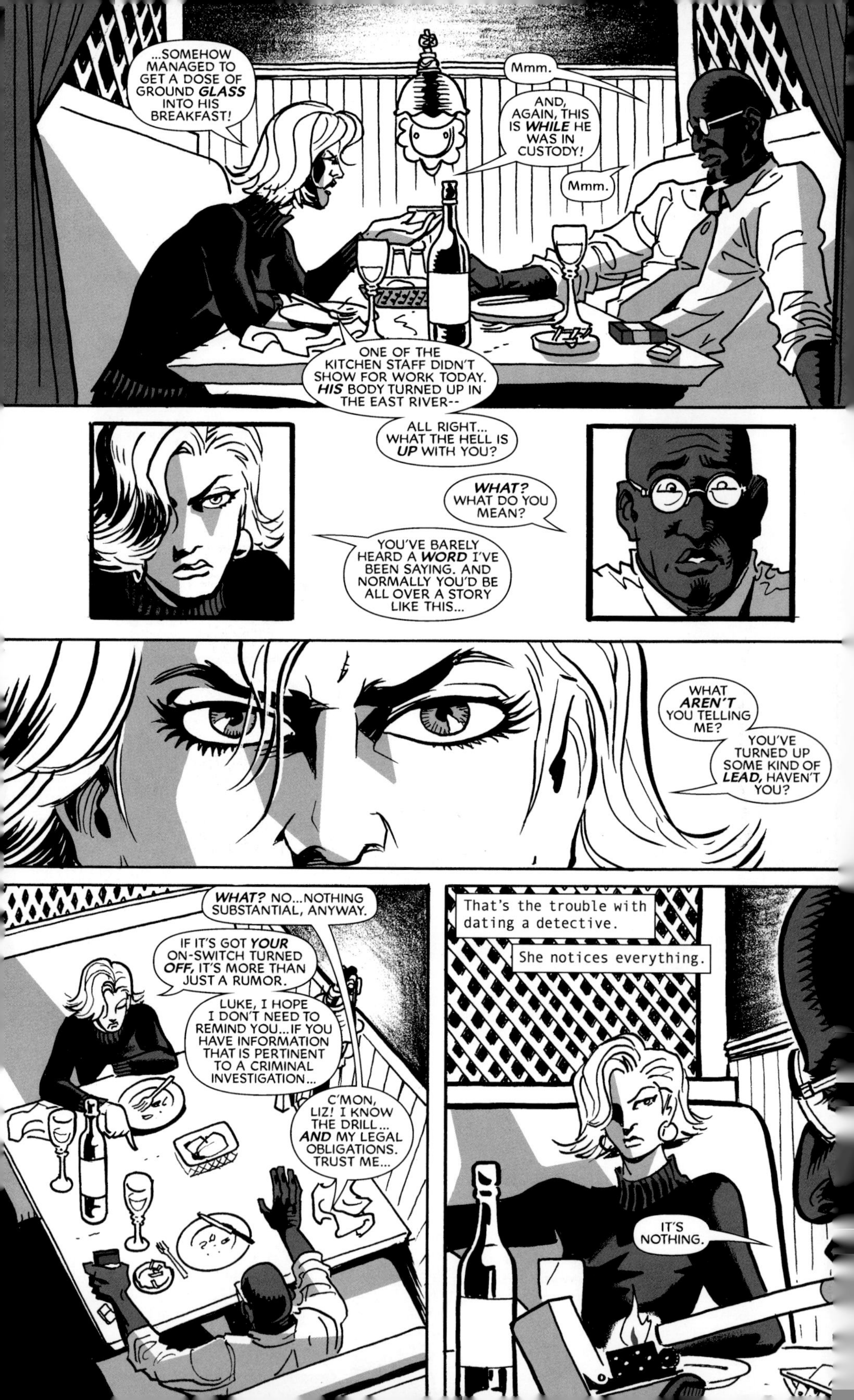
...SOMEHOW MANAGED TO GET A DOSE OF GROUND GLASS INTO HIS BREAKFAST!
Mmm.
AND, AGAIN, THIS IS WHILE HE WAS IN CUSTODY!
Mmm.
ONE OF THE KITCHEN STAFF DIDN'T SHOW FOR WORK TODAY. HIS BODY TURNED UP IN THE EAST RIVER--
ALL RIGHT... WHAT THE HELL IS UP WITH YOU?
WHAT? WHAT DO YOU MEAN?
YOU'VE BARELY HEARD A WORD I'VE BEEN SAYING. AND NORMALLY YOU'D BE ALL OVER A STORY LIKE THIS...
WHAT AREN'T YOU TELLING ME?
YOU'VE TURNED UP SOME KIND OF LEAD, HAVEN'T YOU?
WHAT? NO...NOTHING SUBSTANTIAL, ANYWAY.
IF IT'S GOT YOUR ON-SWITCH TURNED OFF, IT'S MORE THAN JUST A RUMOR.
LUKE, I HOPE I DON'T NEED TO REMIND YOU...IF YOU HAVE INFORMATION THAT IS PERTINENT TO A CRIMINAL INVESTIGATION...
C'MON, LIZ! I KNOW THE DRILL... AND MY LEGAL OBLIGATIONS. TRUST ME...
That's the trouble with dating a detective.
She notices everything.
IT'S NOTHING.

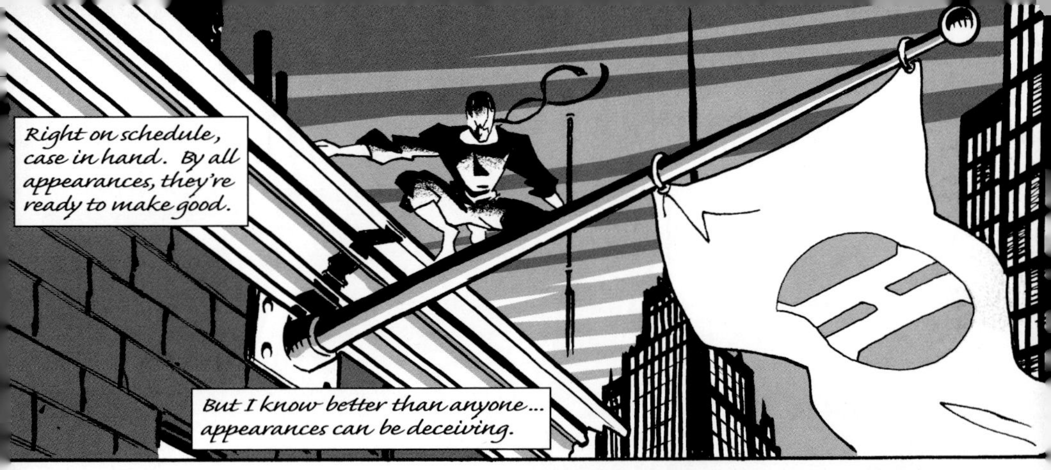
Right on schedule, case in hand. By all appearances, they're ready to make good.
But I know better than anyone... appearances can be deceiving.

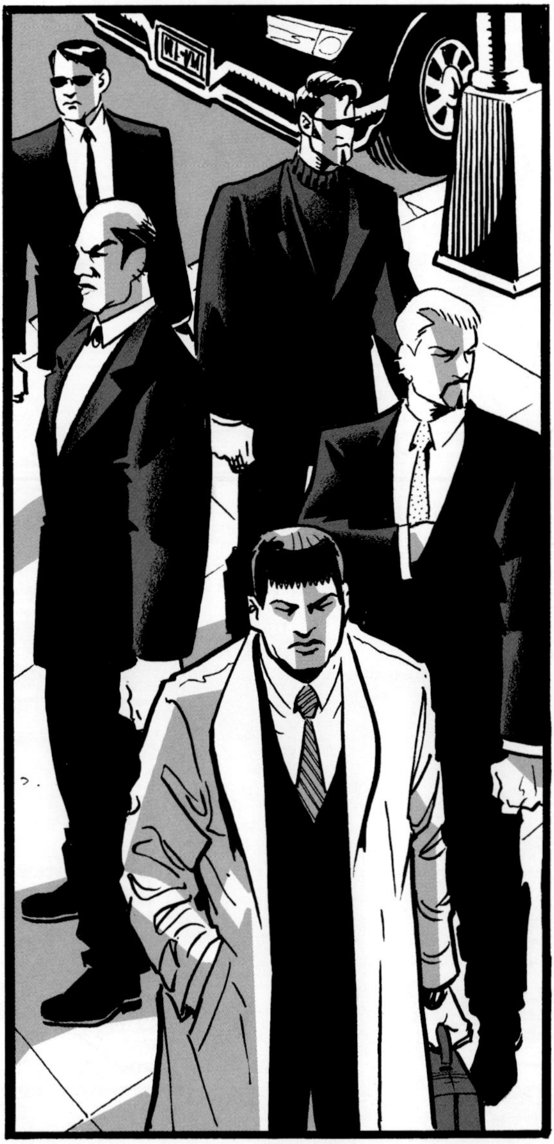

Kwon Hyun-Ki held his sovereignty over the Korean mob by a combination of ruthless business tactics and a canny sense of self-preservation. In his younger days, he had clawed his way to power by climbing over or even just outright killing whoever stood in his way. Legend has it that Kwon even murdered his own brother and uncle in order to secure his place at the top of the *Beomseobangpa* hierarchy. In addition to his fearsome reputation, Boss Kwon consolidated his authority with the help of his inner circle, "The Four Winds." Half bodyguards, half coordinators of his various criminal functions, this quartet of deadly martial-arts experts were almost always at Kwon's side and were rumored to have left a thresher's path of broken and bloody bodies in their wake. This formidable team must've granted their leader the added confidence necessary for attempting to take on the city's enigmatic new crime lord—a mistake they would eventually regret.

–excerpt from *Devil by the Deed*
by Christine Spar

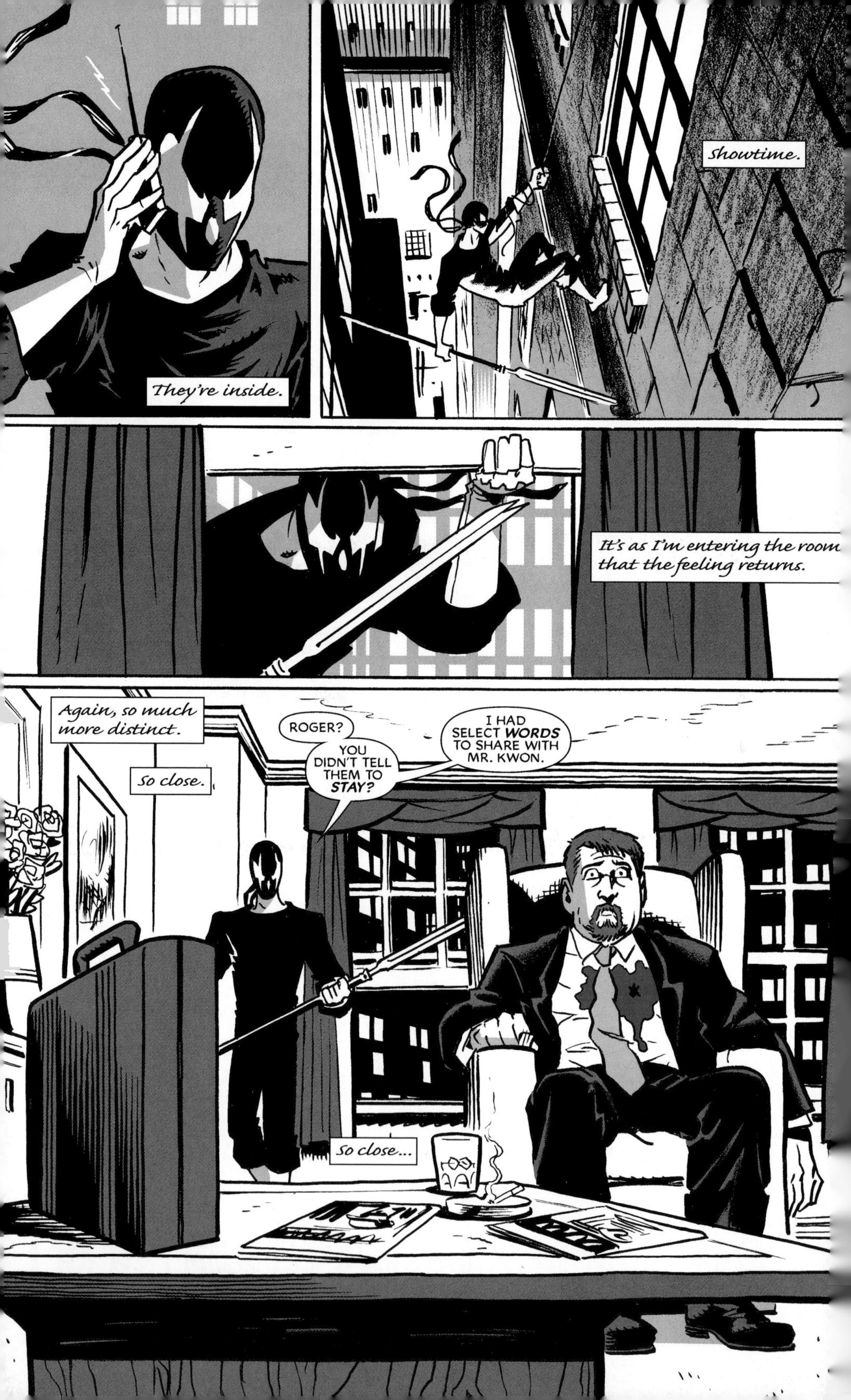
They're inside.
Showtime.
It's as I'm entering the room that the feeling returns.
Again, so much more distinct.
So close.
ROGER?
YOU DIDN'T TELL THEM TO STAY?
I HAD SELECT WORDS TO SHARE WITH MR. KWON.
So close...

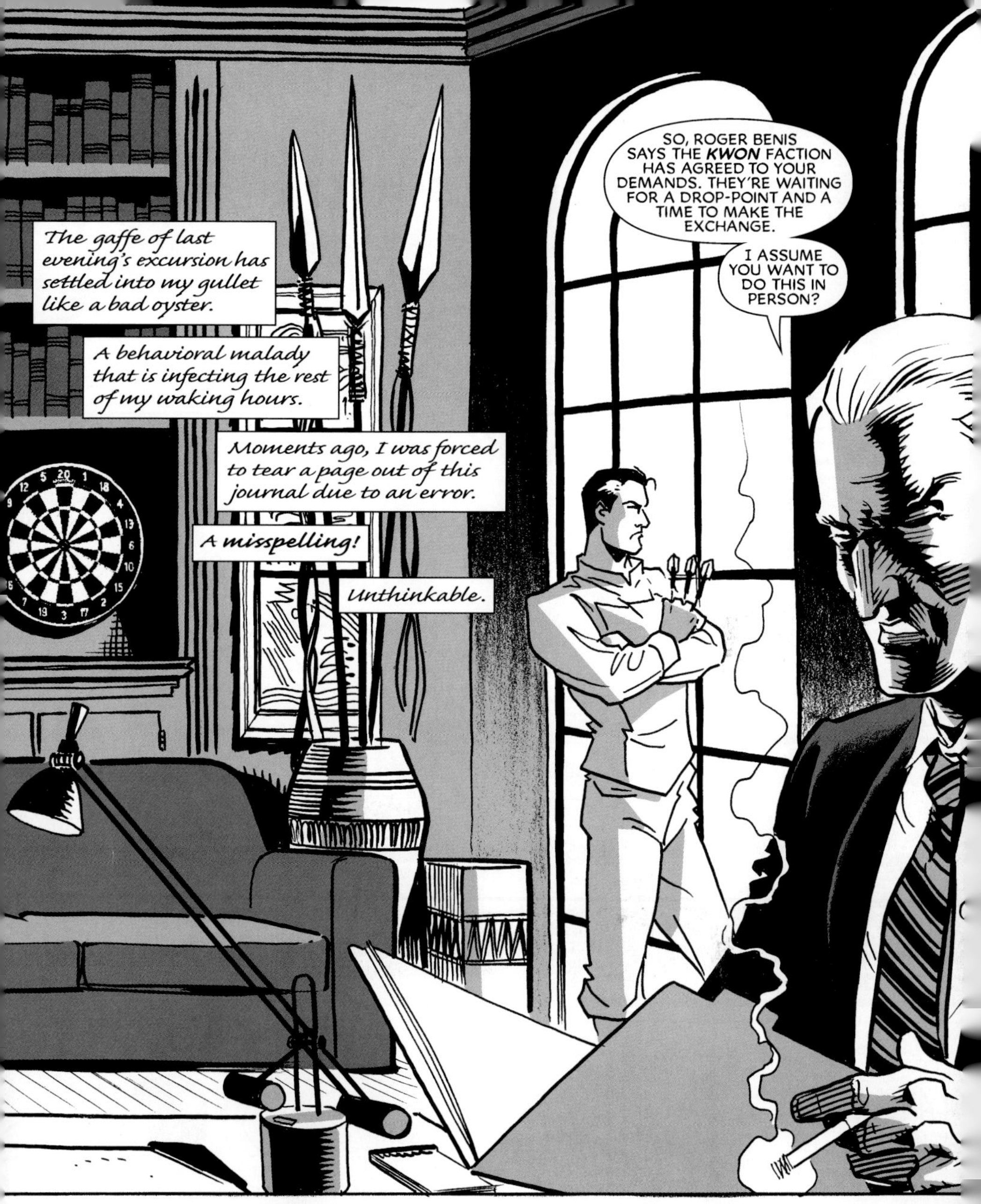
The gaffe of last evening's excursion has settled into my gullet like a bad oyster.
A behavioral malady that is infecting the rest of my waking hours.
Moments ago, I was forced to tear a page out of this journal due to an error.
A misspelling!
Unthinkable.
SO, ROGER BENIS SAYS THE KWON FACTION HAS AGREED TO YOUR DEMANDS. THEY'RE WAITING FOR A DROP-POINT AND A TIME TO MAKE THE EXCHANGE.
I ASSUME YOU WANT TO DO THIS IN PERSON?

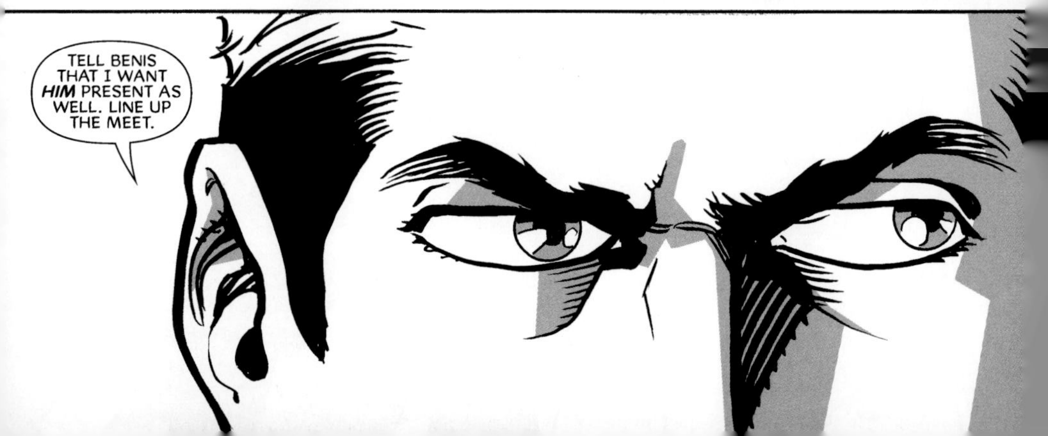
TELL BENIS THAT I WANT HIM PRESENT AS WELL. LINE UP THE MEET.

YOU DON'T TALK TO US ABOUT *GRENDEL*...

...AND THE ONLY "JIGGIES" YOU'LL EVER SEE AGAIN WILL BE COVERED IN HAIR, LUIS.

HA-HA-HA!

THOSE YOUR *OWN* BALLS YOU'RE DESCRIBIN', DETECTIVE?

I MEAN IT, LUIS. YOU KNOW HOW THEY TREAT LITTLE GUYS LIKE YOU, INSIDE.

WHO'S YOUR CONTACT IN *GRENDEL'S* CREW?

BETTER SOME-BODY'S... ⸗*hack*⸗... SOMEBODY'S BITCH...

...THAN SOMEBODY'S *DEAD* BITCH! ⸗*hack-hack... gagh*⸗

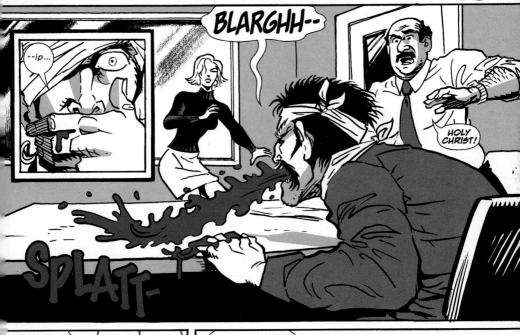

BLARGHH--

--ip...

HOLY CHRIST!

SPLATT-

WHAJU...⸗hck⸗... FUCKERS...⸗hck⸗... *DO* T'ME?

BLARGHH--

ATT-

I DON'T FUCKING *BELIEVE* THIS! HOW LONG HAS HE BEEN IN CUSTODY?

MORE THAN FORTY-EIGHT HOURS. MEANS THEY MUST'VE GOTTEN TO HIM THIS MORNING.

SHIT.

Gggggg--

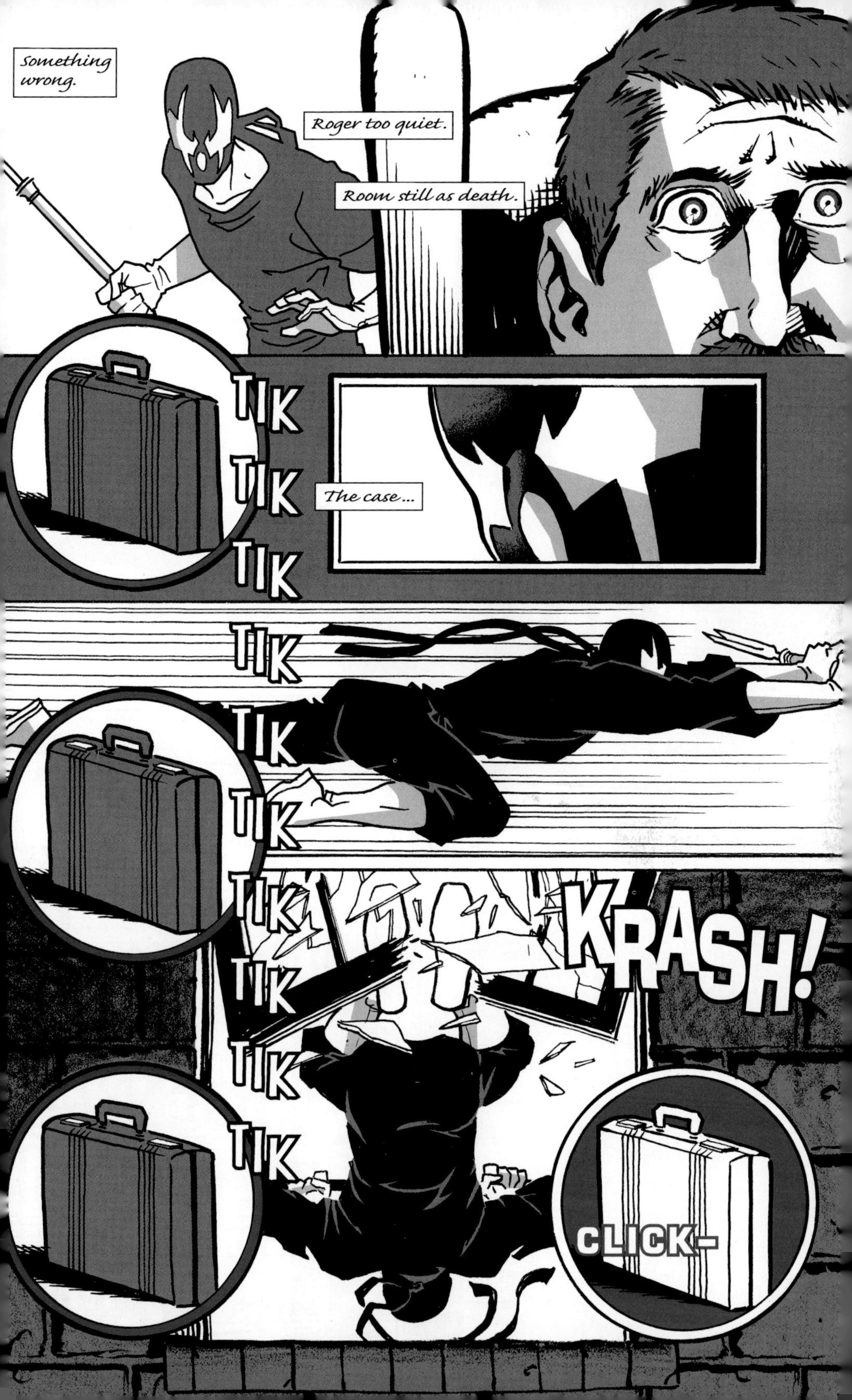
Something wrong.
Roger too quiet.
Room still as death.
TIK
TIK
The case...
TIK
TIK
TIK
TIK
TIK
KRASH!
TIK
TIK
TIK
CLICK-

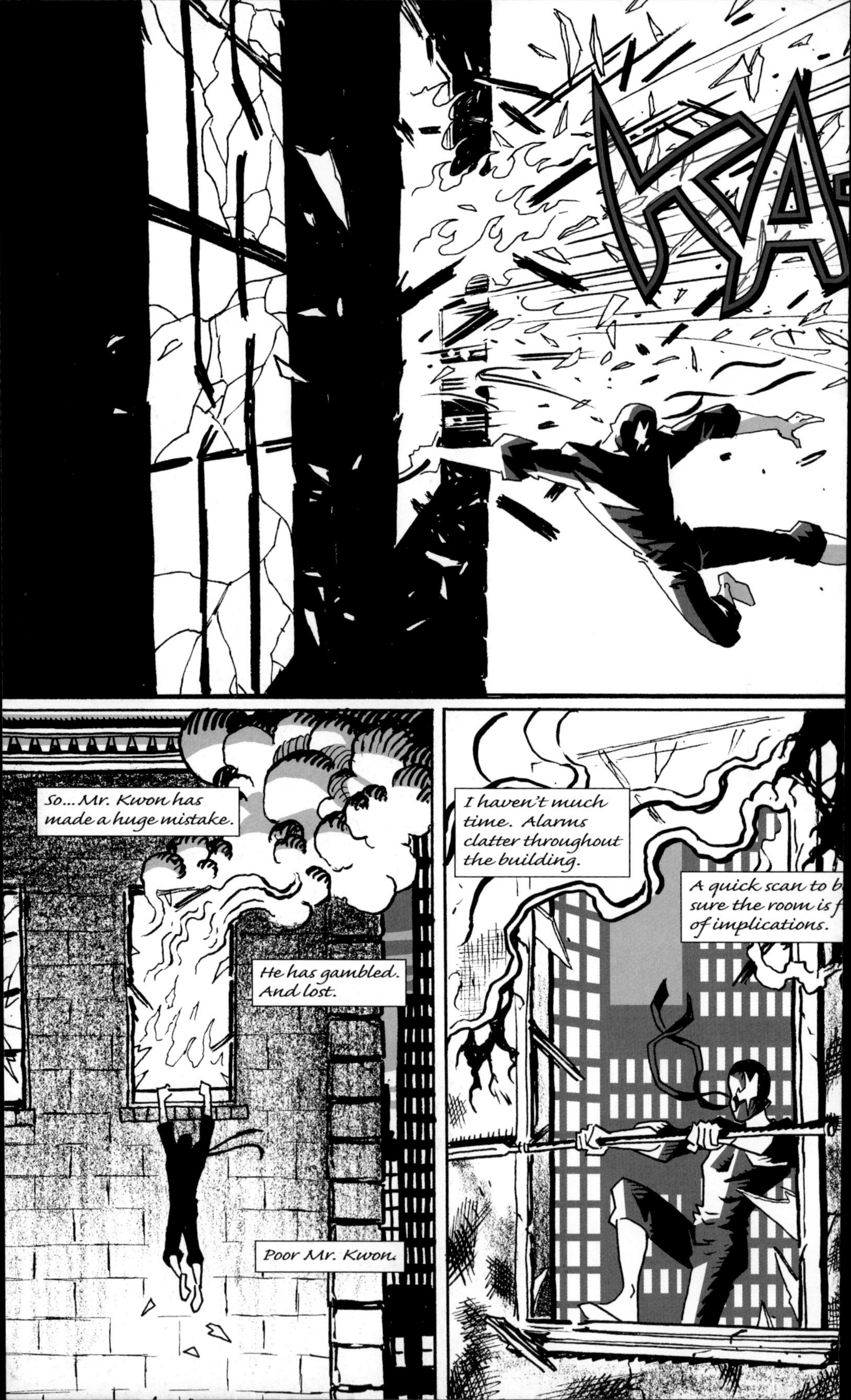
So... Mr. Kwon has made a huge mistake.
He has gambled. And lost.
Poor Mr. Kwon.
I haven't much time. Alarms clatter throughout the building.
A quick scan to b
sure the room is f
of implications.

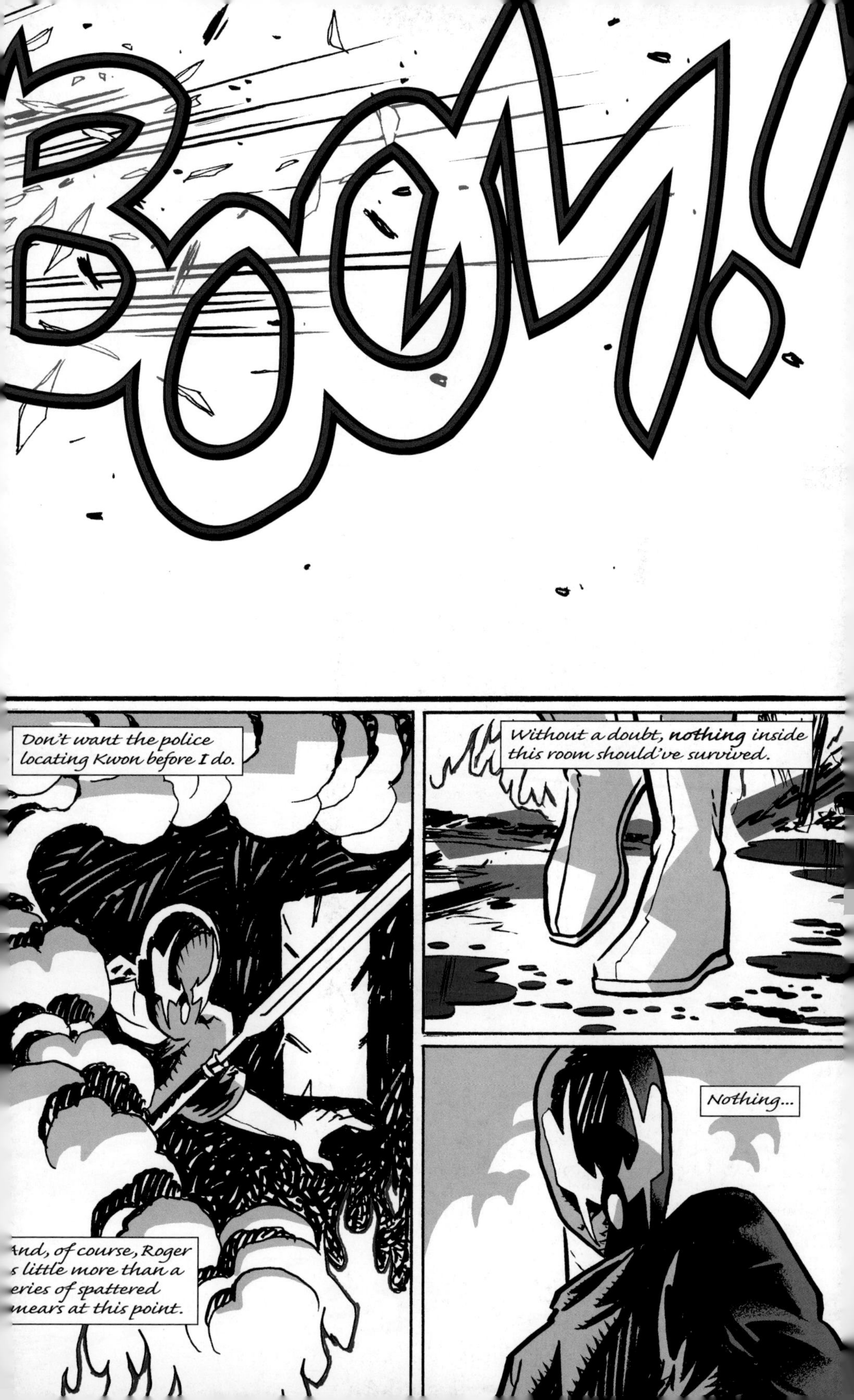
BOOM!
Don't want the police locating Kwon before I do.
Without a doubt, nothing inside this room should've survived.
And, of course, Roger
s little more than a
eries of spattered
mears at this point.
Nothing...

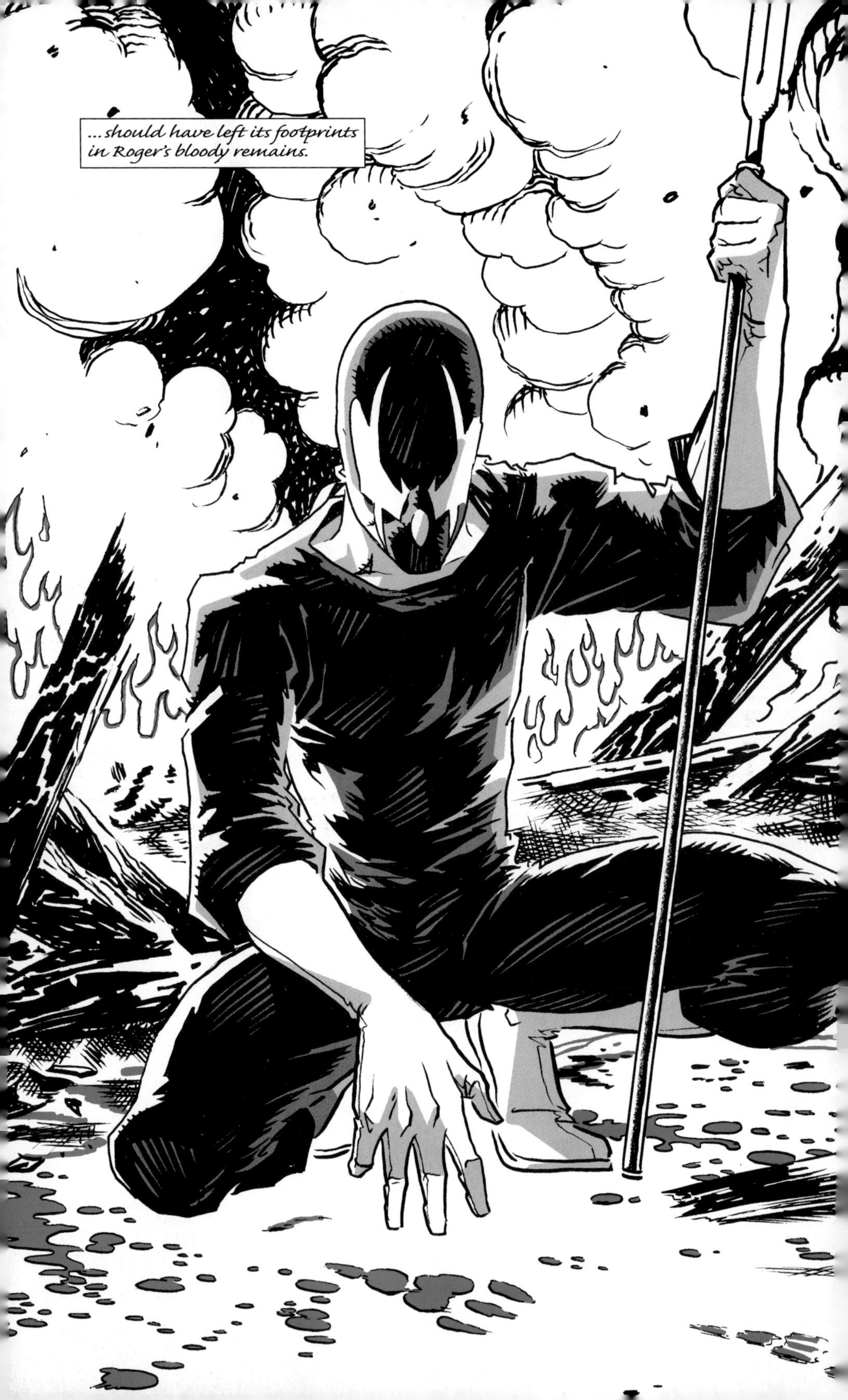
...should have left its footprints
in Roger's bloody remains.

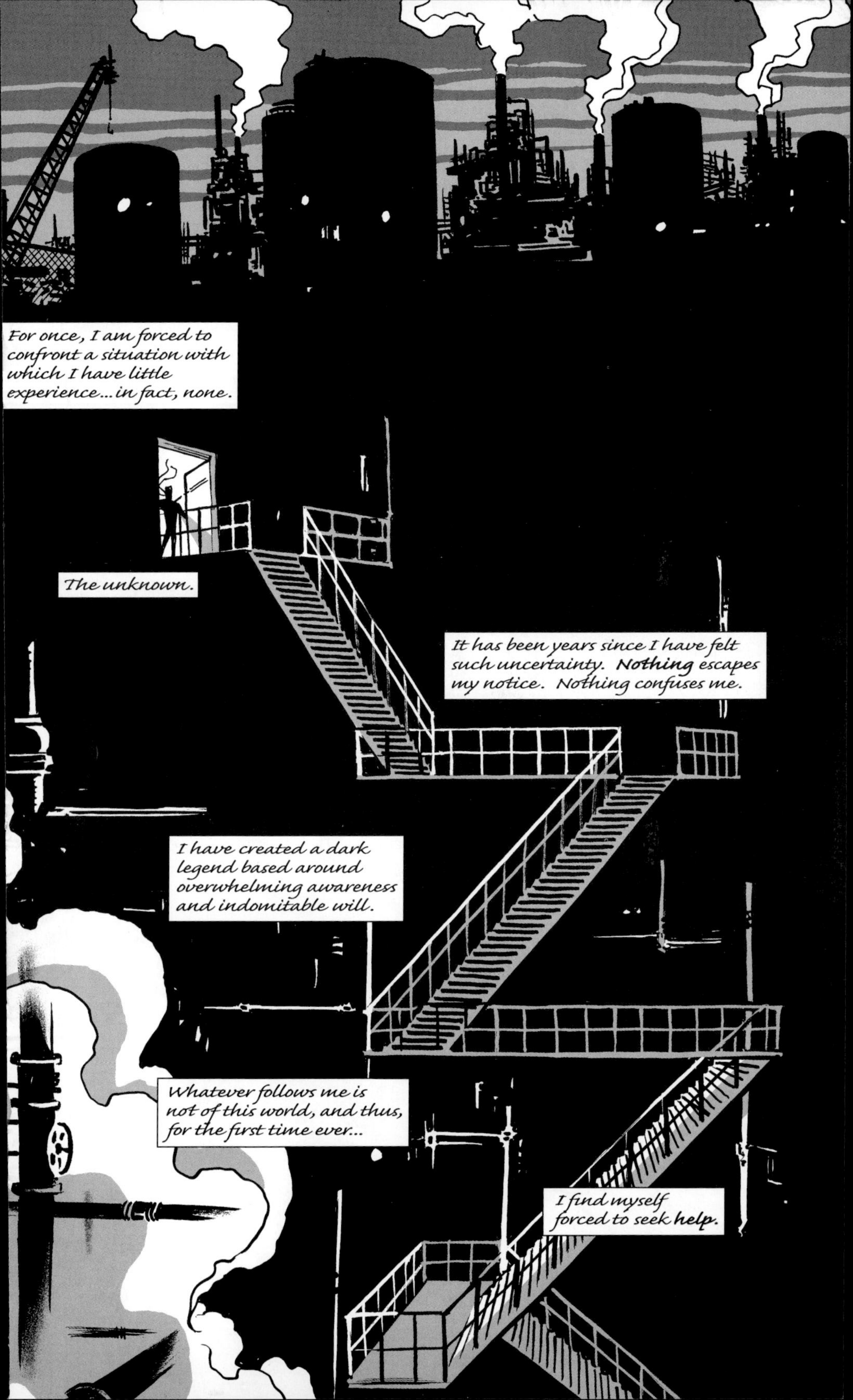
For once, I am forced to confront a situation with which I have little experience... in fact, none.
The unknown.
It has been years since I have felt such uncertainty. **Nothing** escapes my notice. Nothing confuses me.
I have created a dark legend based around overwhelming awareness and indomitable will.
Whatever follows me is not of this world, and thus, for the first time ever...
I find myself forced to seek **help**.

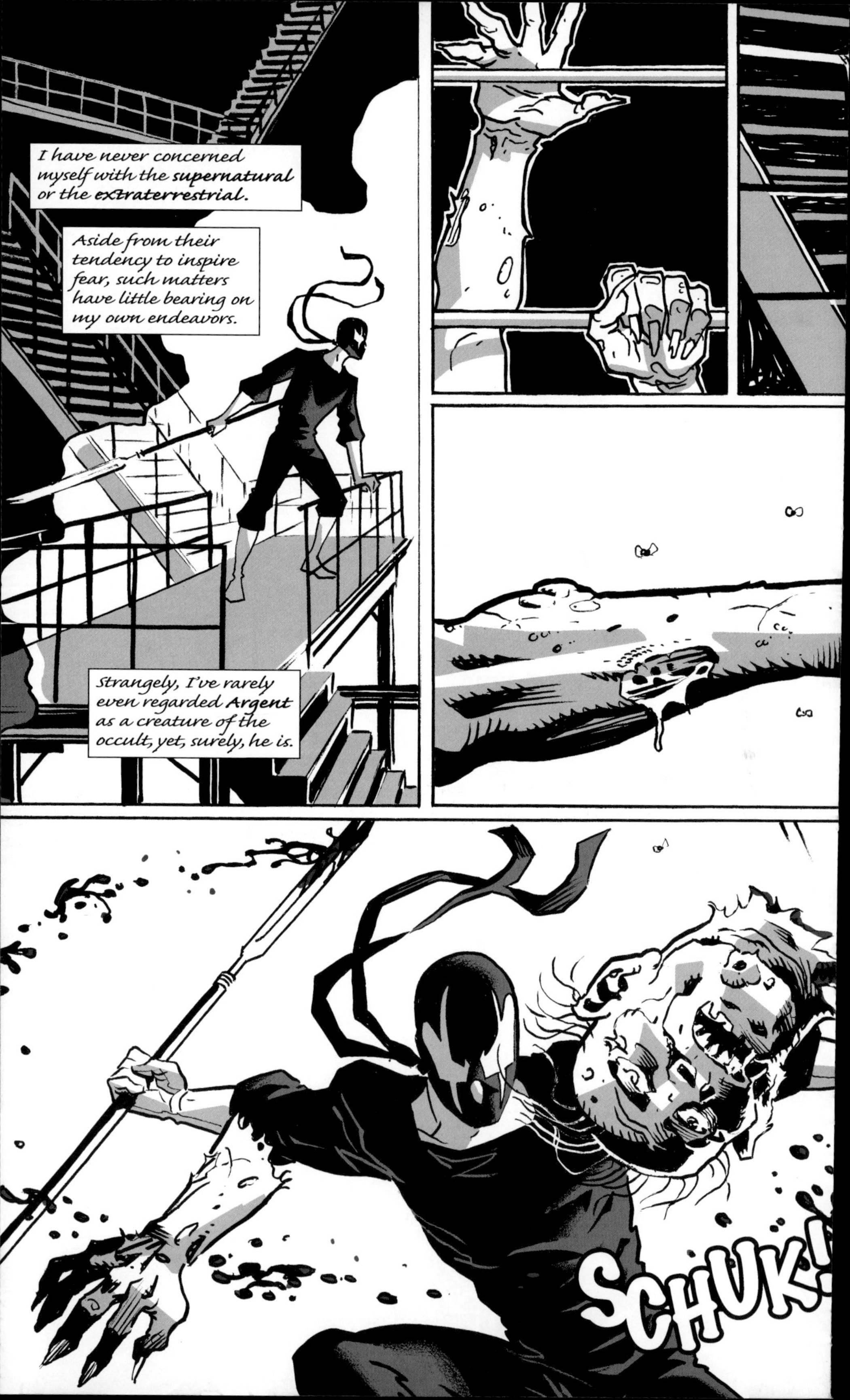
I have never concerned myself with the supernatural or the extraterrestrial.
Aside from their tendency to inspire fear, such matters have little bearing on my own endeavors.
Strangely, I've rarely even regarded Argent as a creature of the occult, yet, surely, he is.
SCHUK!

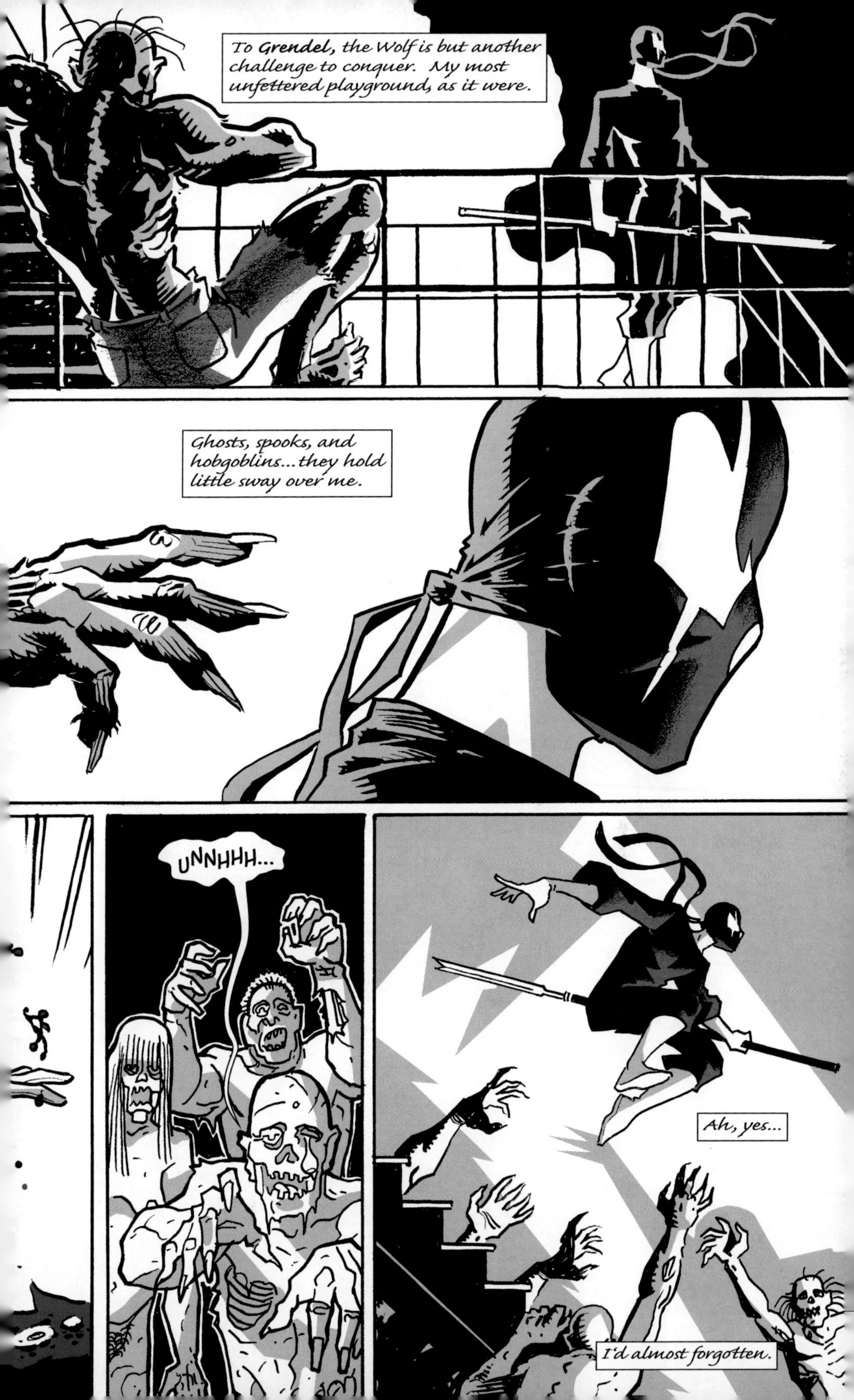
To Grendel, the Wolf is but another challenge to conquer. My most unfettered playground, as it were.
Ghosts, spooks, and hobgoblins... they hold little sway over me.
UNNHHH...
Ah, yes...
I'd almost forgotten.

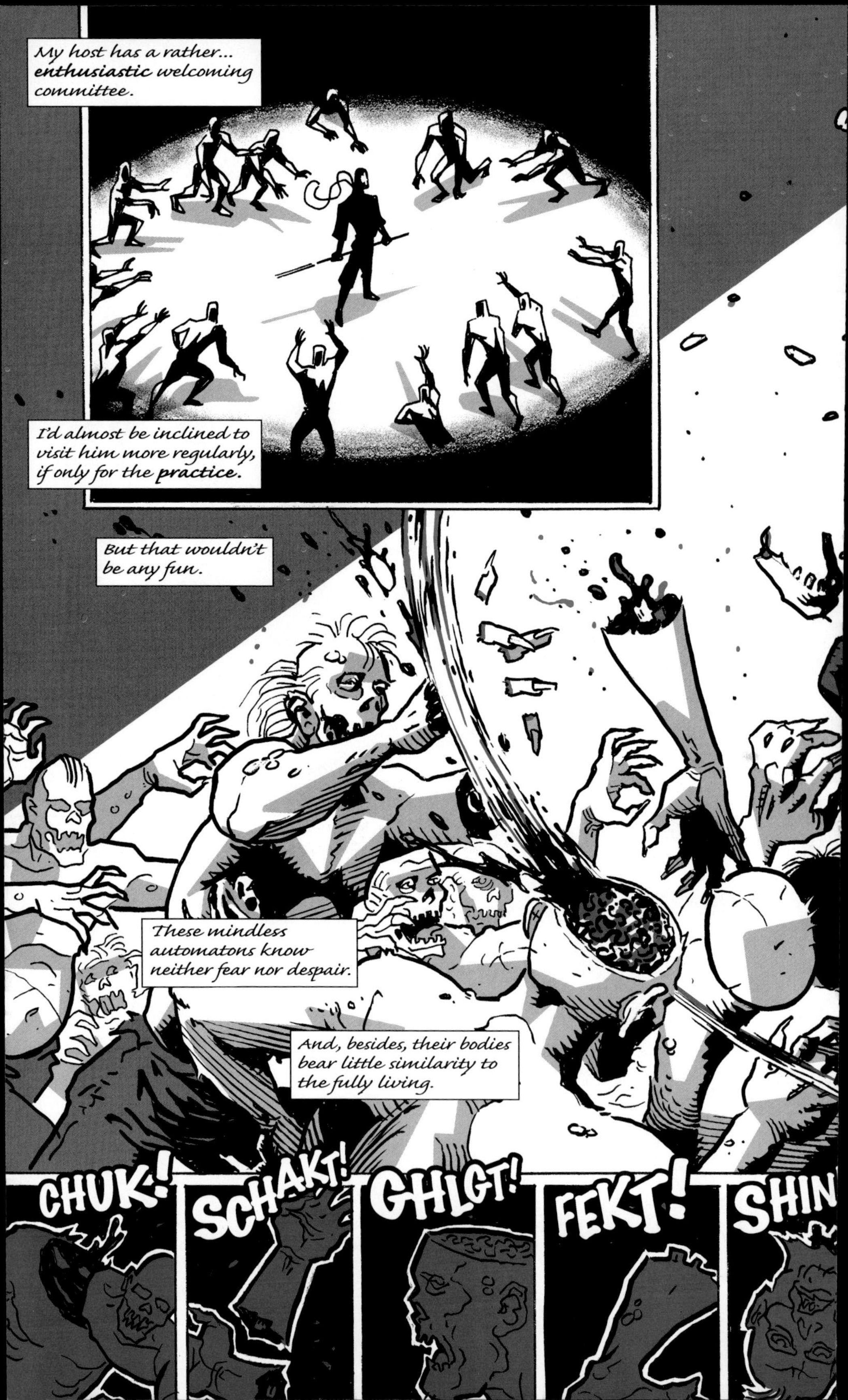

My host has a rather... **enthusiastic** welcoming committee.
I'd almost be inclined to visit him more regularly, if only for the **practice**.
But that wouldn't be any fun.
These mindless automatons know neither fear nor despair.
And, besides, their bodies bear little similarity to the fully living.
CHUK!
SCHAKT!
GHLGT!
FEKT!
SHIN

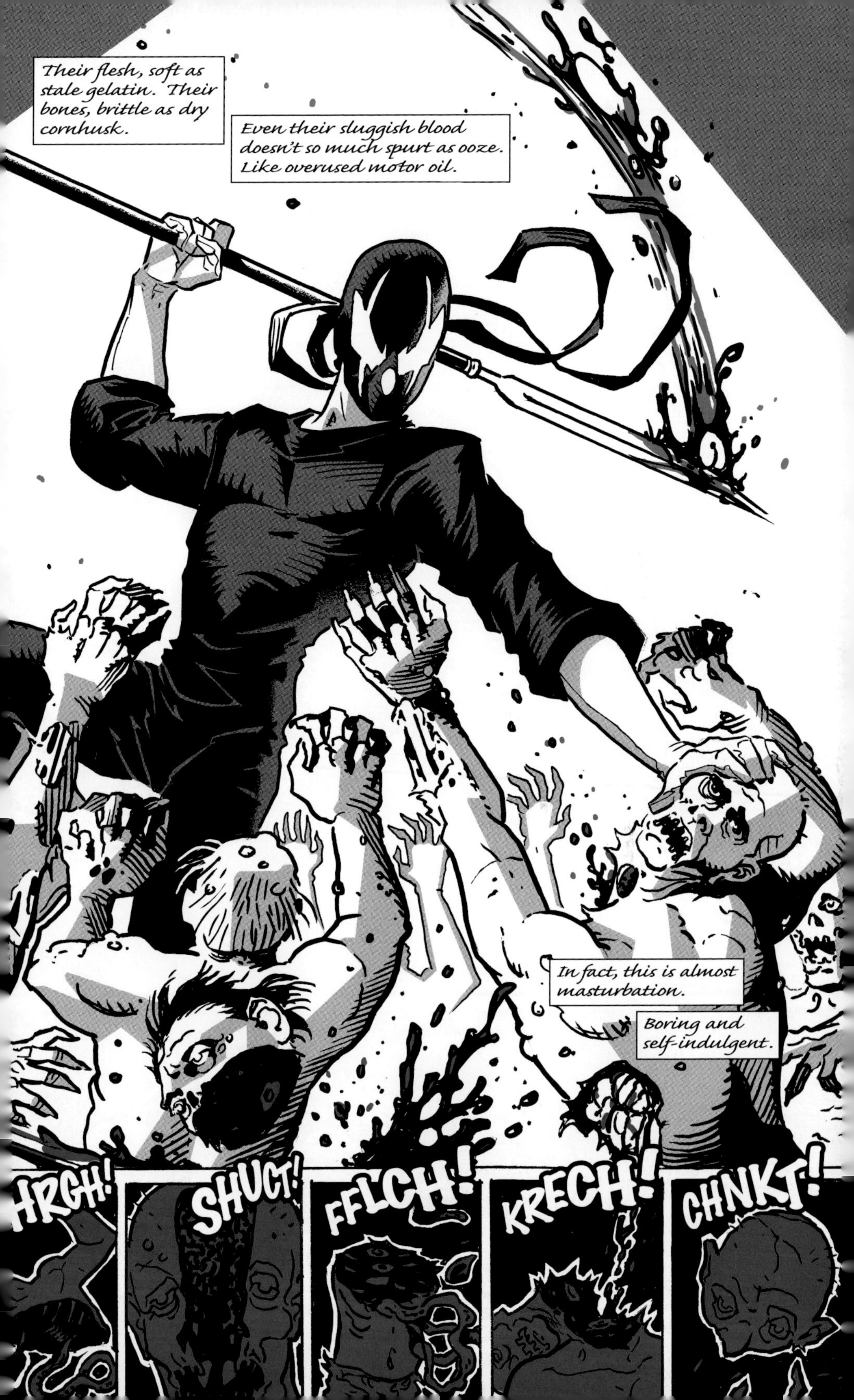
Their flesh, soft as stale gelatin. Their bones, brittle as dry cornhusk.
Even their sluggish blood doesn't so much spurt as ooze. Like overused motor oil.
In fact, this is almost masturbation.
Boring and self-indulgent.
HRGH!
SHUCT!
FFLCH!
KRECH!
CHNKT!

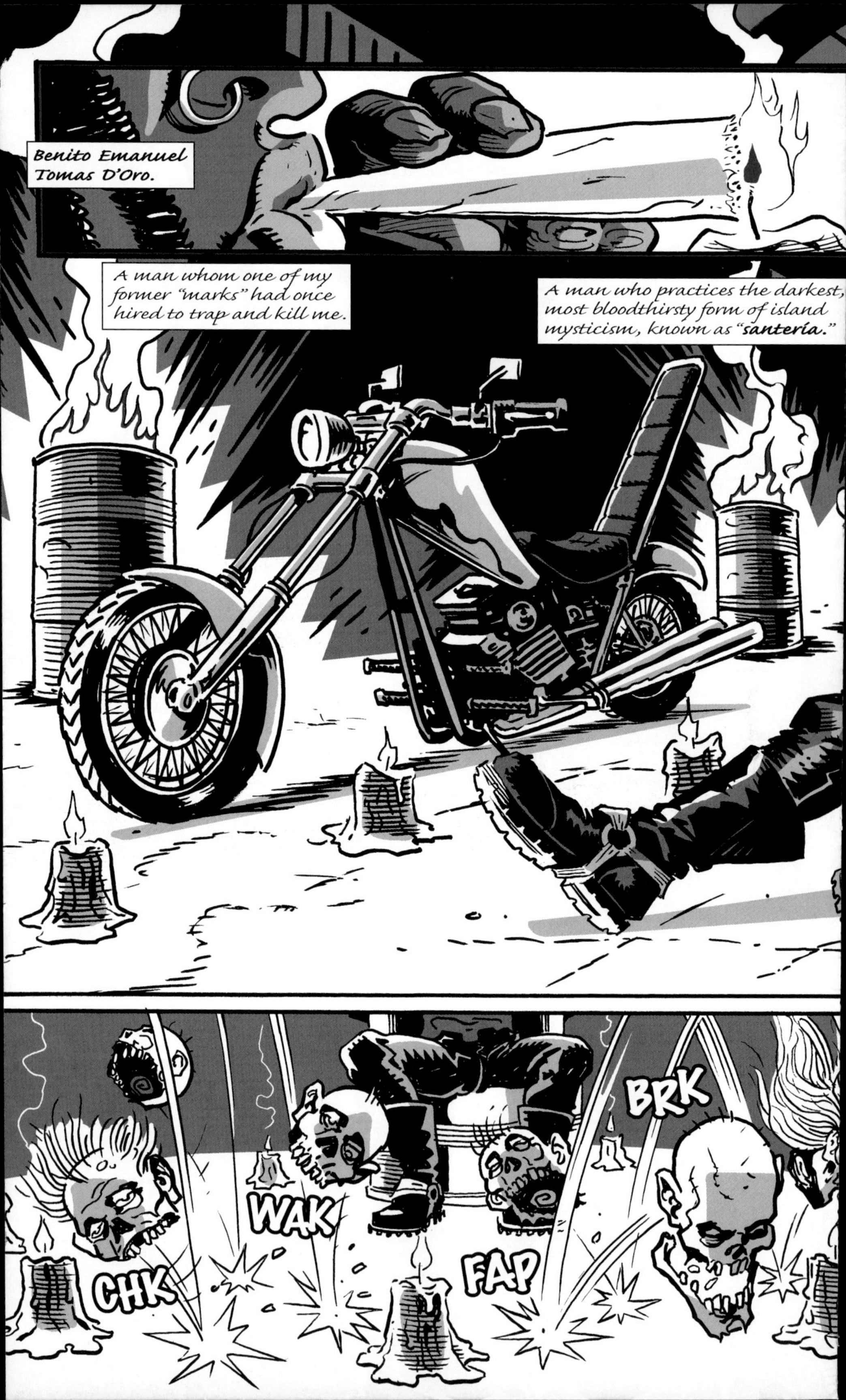
Benito Emanuel Tomas D'Oro.
A man whom one of my former "marks" had once hired to trap and kill me.
A man who practices the darkest, most bloodthirsty form of island mysticism, known as "santería."
BRK
WAK
CHK
FAP

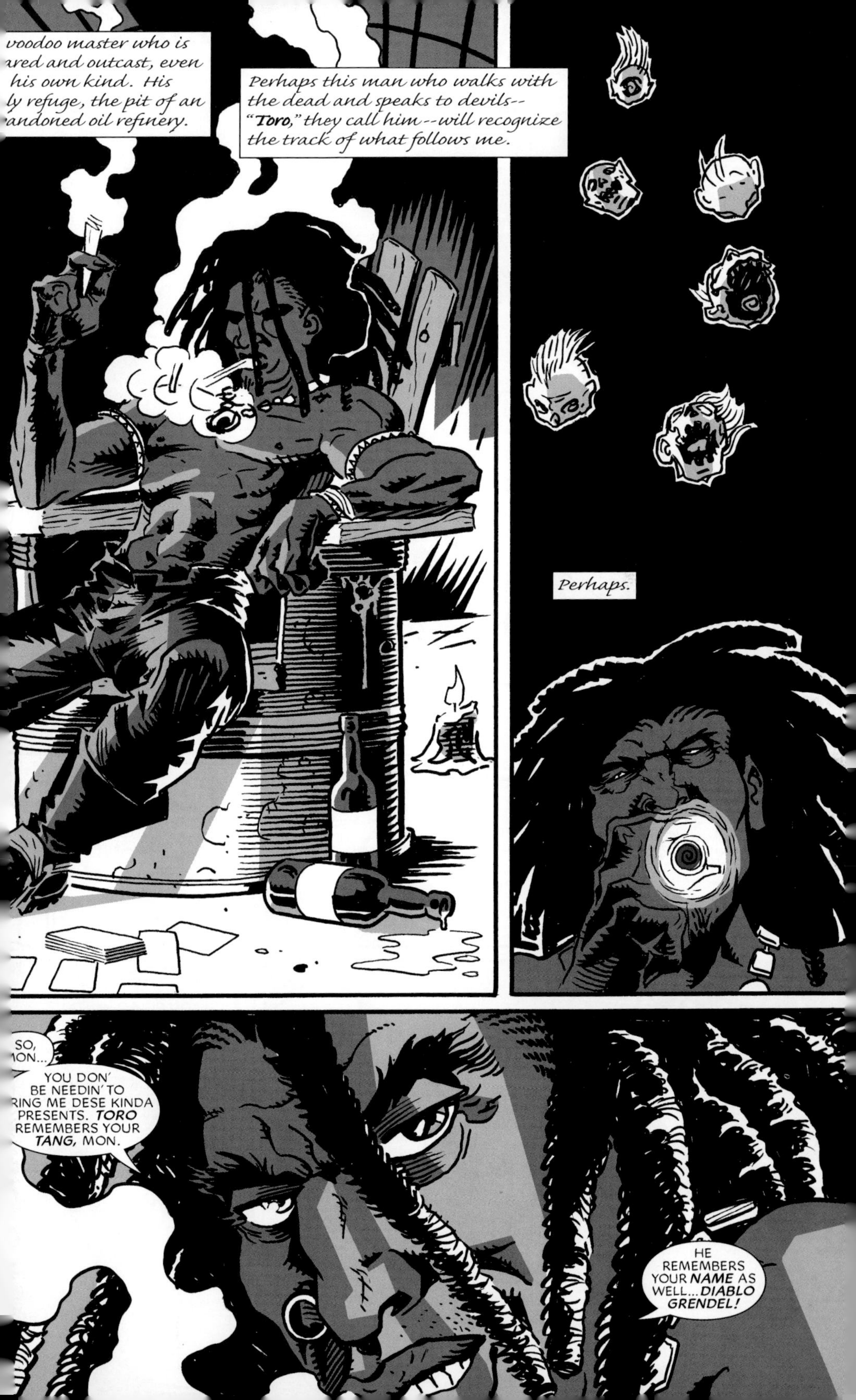
voodoo master who is
ared and outcast, even
his own kind. His
ly refuge, the pit of an
andoned oil refinery.
Perhaps this man who walks with the dead and speaks to devils-- "Toro," they call him--will recognize the track of what follows me.
Perhaps.
SO,
MON...
YOU DON' BE NEEDIN' TO
RING ME DESE KINDA PRESENTS. TORO REMEMBERS YOUR TANG, MON.
HE REMEMBERS YOUR NAME AS WELL... DIABLO GRENDEL!

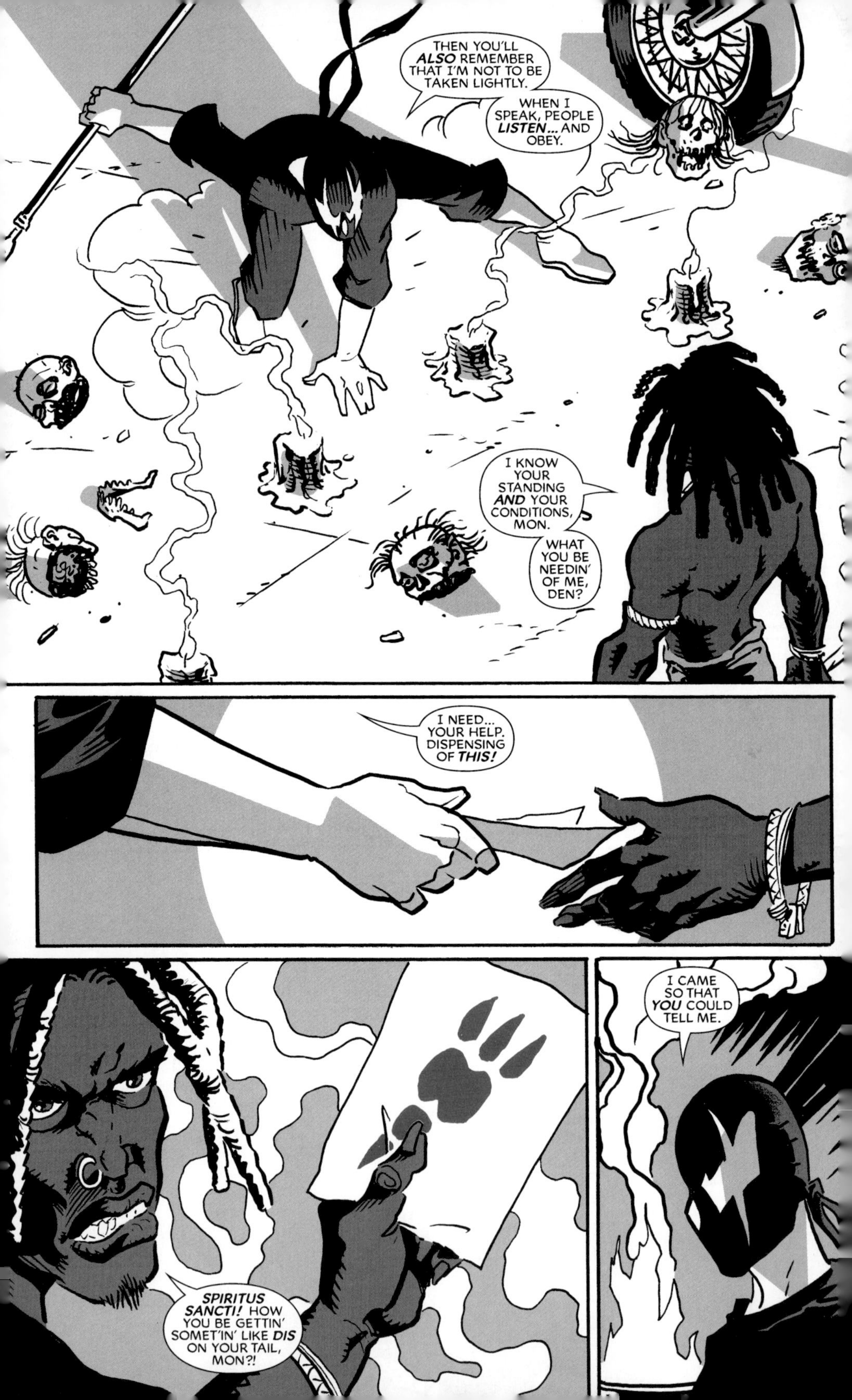
THEN YOU'LL ALSO REMEMBER THAT I'M NOT TO BE TAKEN LIGHTLY.
WHEN I SPEAK, PEOPLE LISTEN... AND OBEY.
I KNOW YOUR STANDING AND YOUR CONDITIONS, MON.
WHAT YOU BE NEEDIN' OF ME, DEN?
I NEED... YOUR HELP. DISPENSING OF THIS!
SPIRITUS SANCTI! HOW YOU BE GETTIN' SOMET'IN' LIKE DIS ON YOUR TAIL, MON?!
I CAME SO THAT YOU COULD TELL ME.

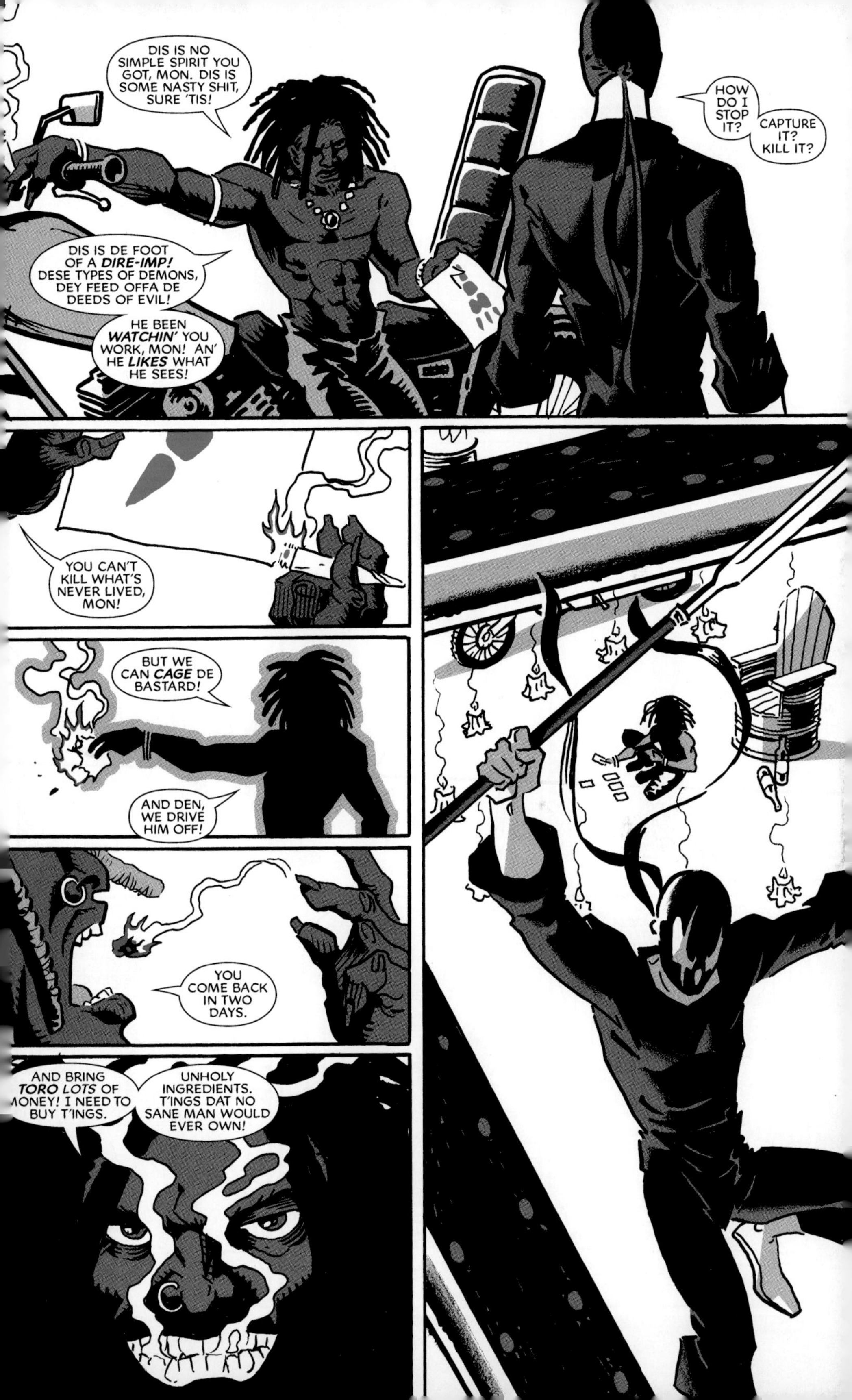
DIS IS NO SIMPLE SPIRIT YOU GOT, MON. DIS IS SOME NASTY SHIT, SURE 'TIS!
HOW DO I STOP IT?
CAPTURE IT? KILL IT?
DIS IS DE FOOT OF A DIRE-IMP! DESE TYPES OF DEMONS, DEY FEED OFFA DE DEEDS OF EVIL!
HE BEEN WATCHIN' YOU WORK, MON! AN' HE LIKES WHAT HE SEES!
YOU CAN'T KILL WHAT'S NEVER LIVED, MON!
BUT WE CAN CAGE DE BASTARD!
AND DEN, WE DRIVE HIM OFF!
YOU COME BACK IN TWO DAYS.
AND BRING TORO LOTS OF MONEY! I NEED TO BUY T'INGS.
UNHOLY INGREDIENTS. T'INGS DAT NO SANE MAN WOULD EVER OWN!

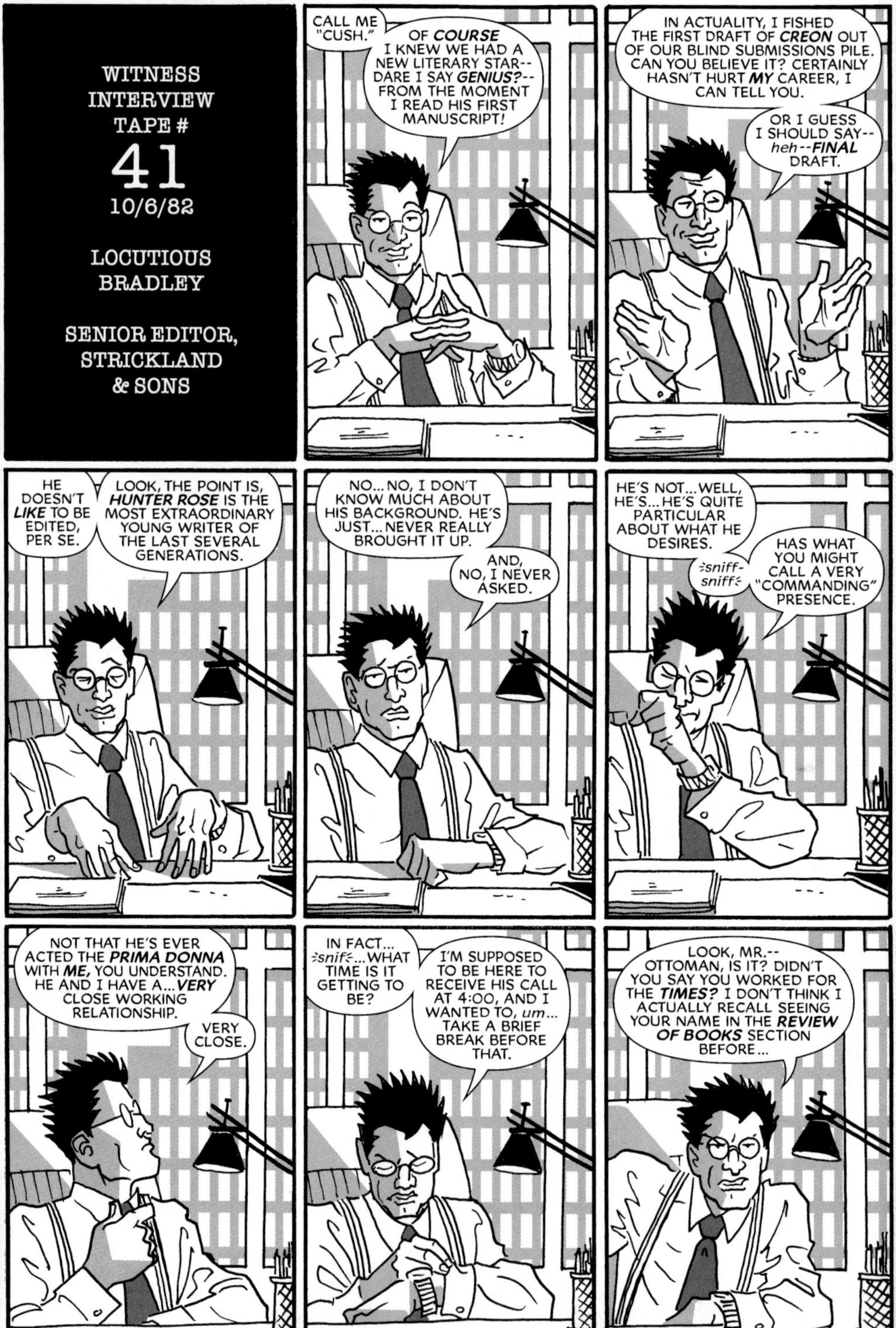
WITNESS INTERVIEW TAPE # 41
10/6/82
LOCUTIOUS BRADLEY
SENIOR EDITOR, STRICKLAND & SONS
CALL ME "CUSH."
OF COURSE I KNEW WE HAD A NEW LITERARY STAR-- DARE I SAY GENIUS?-- FROM THE MOMENT I READ HIS FIRST MANUSCRIPT!
IN ACTUALITY, I FISHED THE FIRST DRAFT OF CREON OUT OF OUR BLIND SUBMISSIONS PILE. CAN YOU BELIEVE IT? CERTAINLY HASN'T HURT MY CAREER, I CAN TELL YOU.
OR I GUESS I SHOULD SAY-- heh --FINAL DRAFT.
HE DOESN'T LIKE TO BE EDITED, PER SE.
LOOK, THE POINT IS, HUNTER ROSE IS THE MOST EXTRAORDINARY YOUNG WRITER OF THE LAST SEVERAL GENERATIONS.
NO... NO, I DON'T KNOW MUCH ABOUT HIS BACKGROUND. HE'S JUST... NEVER REALLY BROUGHT IT UP.
AND, NO, I NEVER ASKED.
HE'S NOT... WELL, HE'S... HE'S QUITE PARTICULAR ABOUT WHAT HE DESIRES.
sniff- sniff
HAS WHAT YOU MIGHT CALL A VERY "COMMANDING" PRESENCE.
NOT THAT HE'S EVER ACTED THE PRIMA DONNA WITH ME, YOU UNDERSTAND. HE AND I HAVE A... VERY CLOSE WORKING RELATIONSHIP.
VERY CLOSE.
IN FACT... snif... WHAT TIME IS IT GETTING TO BE?
I'M SUPPOSED TO BE HERE TO RECEIVE HIS CALL AT 4:00, AND I WANTED TO, um... TAKE A BRIEF BREAK BEFORE THAT.
LOOK, MR.-- OTTOMAN, IS IT? DIDN'T YOU SAY YOU WORKED FOR THE TIMES? I DON'T THINK I ACTUALLY RECALL SEEING YOUR NAME IN THE REVIEW OF BOOKS SECTION BEFORE...

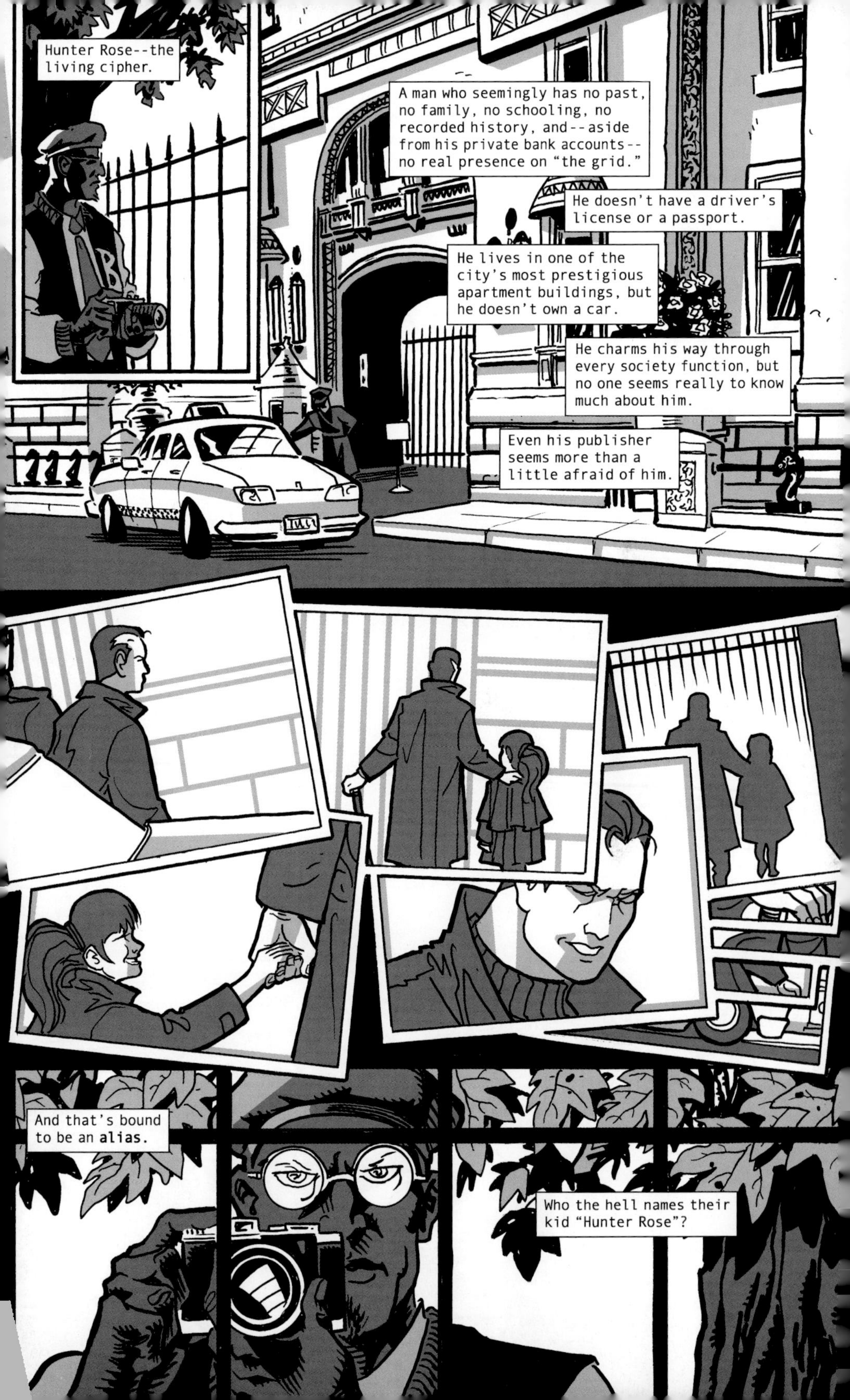
Hunter Rose--the living cipher.
A man who seemingly has no past, no family, no schooling, no recorded history, and--aside from his private bank accounts--no real presence on "the grid."
He doesn't have a driver's license or a passport.
He lives in one of the city's most prestigious apartment buildings, but he doesn't own a car.
He charms his way through every society function, but no one seems really to know much about him.
Even his publisher seems more than a little afraid of him.
And that's bound to be an **alias**.
Who the hell names their kid "Hunter Rose"?

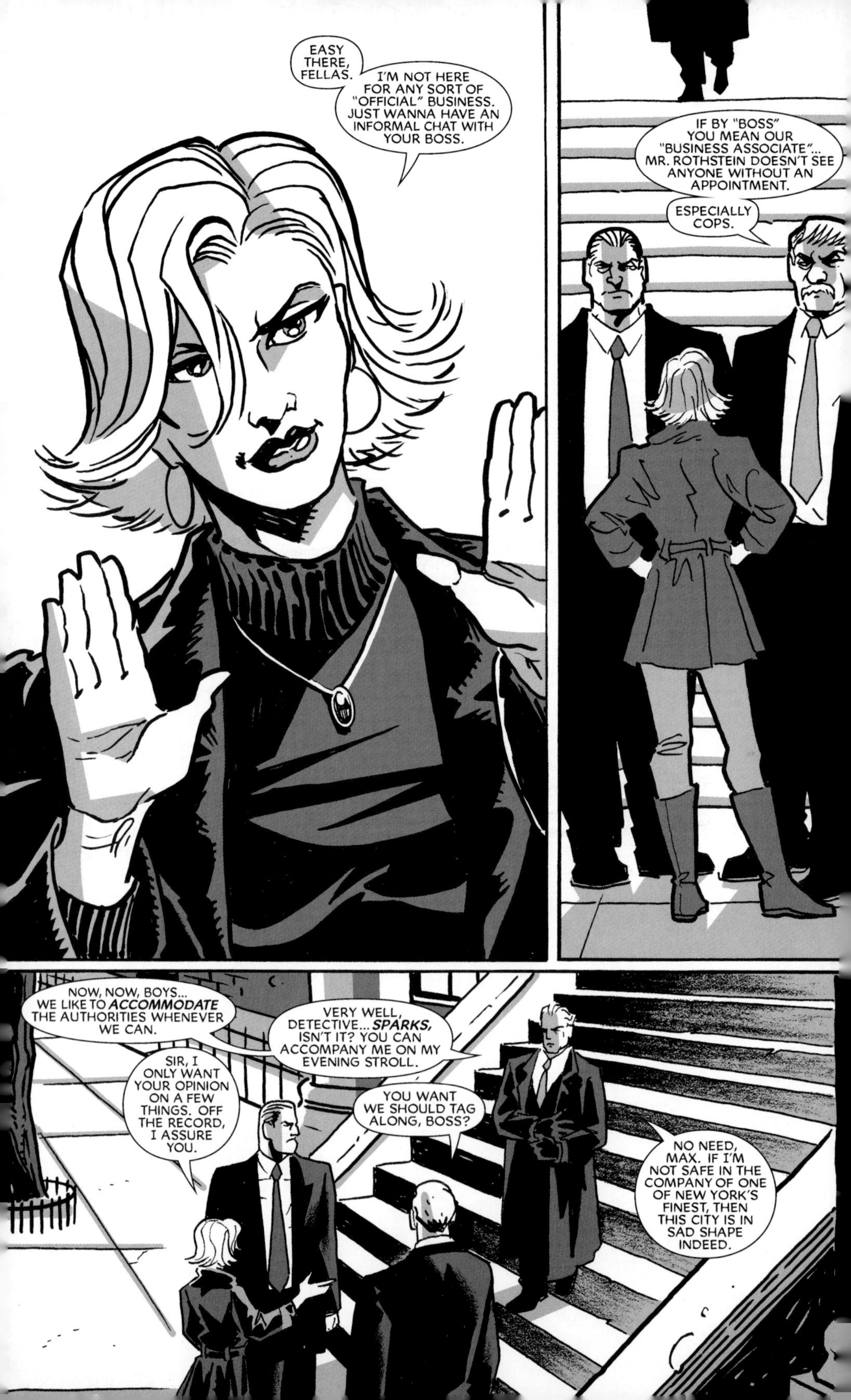
EASY THERE, FELLAS.
I'M NOT HERE FOR ANY SORT OF "OFFICIAL" BUSINESS. JUST WANNA HAVE AN INFORMAL CHAT WITH YOUR BOSS.
IF BY "BOSS" YOU MEAN OUR "BUSINESS ASSOCIATE"... MR. ROTHSTEIN DOESN'T SEE ANYONE WITHOUT AN APPOINTMENT.
ESPECIALLY COPS.
NOW, NOW, BOYS... WE LIKE TO ACCOMMODATE THE AUTHORITIES WHENEVER WE CAN.
VERY WELL, DETECTIVE... SPARKS, ISN'T IT? YOU CAN ACCOMPANY ME ON MY EVENING STROLL.
SIR, I ONLY WANT YOUR OPINION ON A FEW THINGS. OFF THE RECORD, I ASSURE YOU.
YOU WANT WE SHOULD TAG ALONG, BOSS?
NO NEED, MAX. IF I'M NOT SAFE IN THE COMPANY OF ONE OF NEW YORK'S FINEST, THEN THIS CITY IS IN SAD SHAPE INDEED.

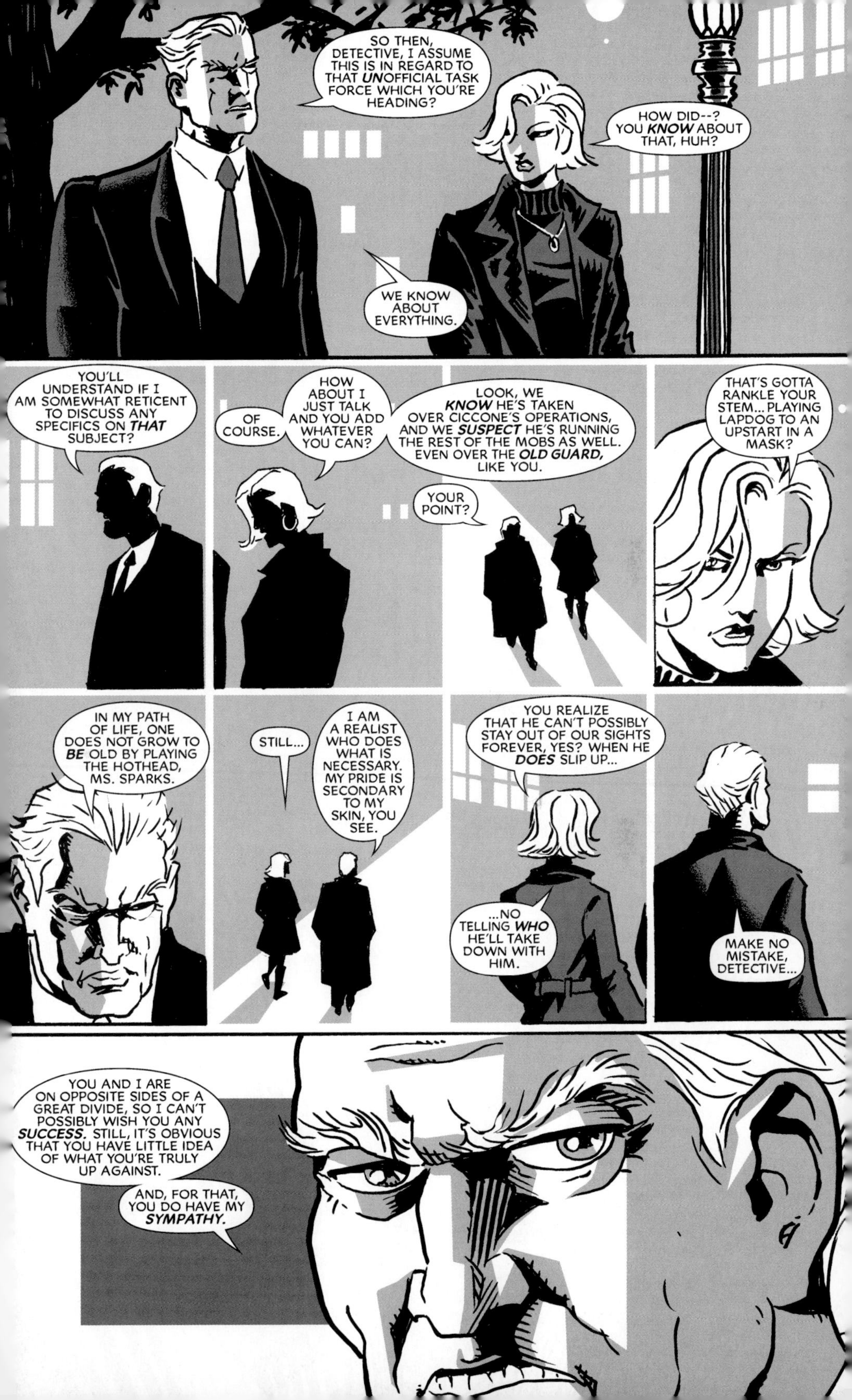
SO THEN, DETECTIVE, I ASSUME THIS IS IN REGARD TO THAT UNOFFICIAL TASK FORCE WHICH YOU'RE HEADING?
HOW DID--? YOU KNOW ABOUT THAT, HUH?
WE KNOW ABOUT EVERYTHING.
YOU'LL UNDERSTAND IF I AM SOMEWHAT RETICENT TO DISCUSS ANY SPECIFICS ON THAT SUBJECT?
OF COURSE.
HOW ABOUT I JUST TALK AND YOU ADD WHATEVER YOU CAN?
LOOK, WE KNOW HE'S TAKEN OVER CICCONE'S OPERATIONS, AND WE SUSPECT HE'S RUNNING THE REST OF THE MOBS AS WELL. EVEN OVER THE OLD GUARD, LIKE YOU.
YOUR POINT?
THAT'S GOTTA RANKLE YOUR STEM... PLAYING LAPDOG TO AN UPSTART IN A MASK?
IN MY PATH OF LIFE, ONE DOES NOT GROW TO BE OLD BY PLAYING THE HOTHEAD, MS. SPARKS.
STILL...
I AM A REALIST WHO DOES WHAT IS NECESSARY. MY PRIDE IS SECONDARY TO MY SKIN, YOU SEE.
YOU REALIZE THAT HE CAN'T POSSIBLY STAY OUT OF OUR SIGHTS FOREVER, YES? WHEN HE DOES SLIP UP...
...NO TELLING WHO HE'LL TAKE DOWN WITH HIM.
MAKE NO MISTAKE, DETECTIVE...
YOU AND I ARE ON OPPOSITE SIDES OF A GREAT DIVIDE, SO I CAN'T POSSIBLY WISH YOU ANY SUCCESS. STILL, IT'S OBVIOUS THAT YOU HAVE LITTLE IDEA OF WHAT YOU'RE TRULY UP AGAINST.
AND, FOR THAT, YOU DO HAVE MY SYMPATHY.

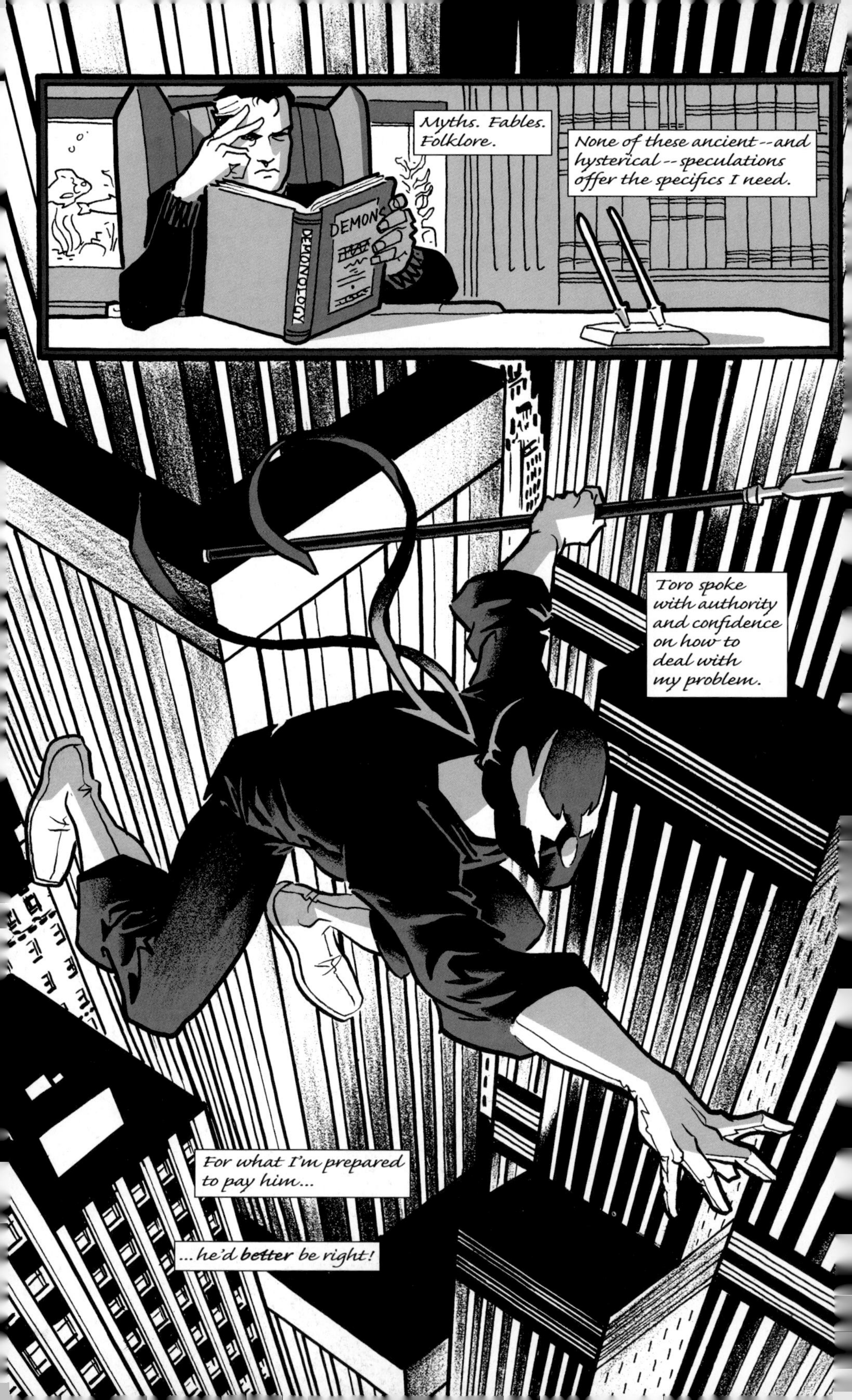
Myths. Fables. Folklore.
None of these ancient--and hysterical--speculations offer the specifics I need.
DEMONS
DEMONOLOGY
Toro spoke with authority and confidence on how to deal with my problem.
For what I'm prepared to pay him...
...he'd **better** be right!

During these "Lost Days" we do have some record, from alternative sources, of Grendel's various activities. His criminal endeavors still produced bloodshed and tragedy that left numerous evidentiary accounts with which we can, at least halfheartedly, attempt to fill in the course of events over those missing weeks. Almost out of character for him at the time was a somewhat "old-fashioned" armored-car heist that netted him nearly half a million dollars in one fell swoop. This sort of "highway robbery" wasn't in keeping with Grendel's normal style of doing business. We can only speculate as to what sort of sudden personal expense demanded that he secure such a vast sum of "mad money" on such an obviously short notice.

—excerpt from *Devil by the Deed*
by Christine Spar

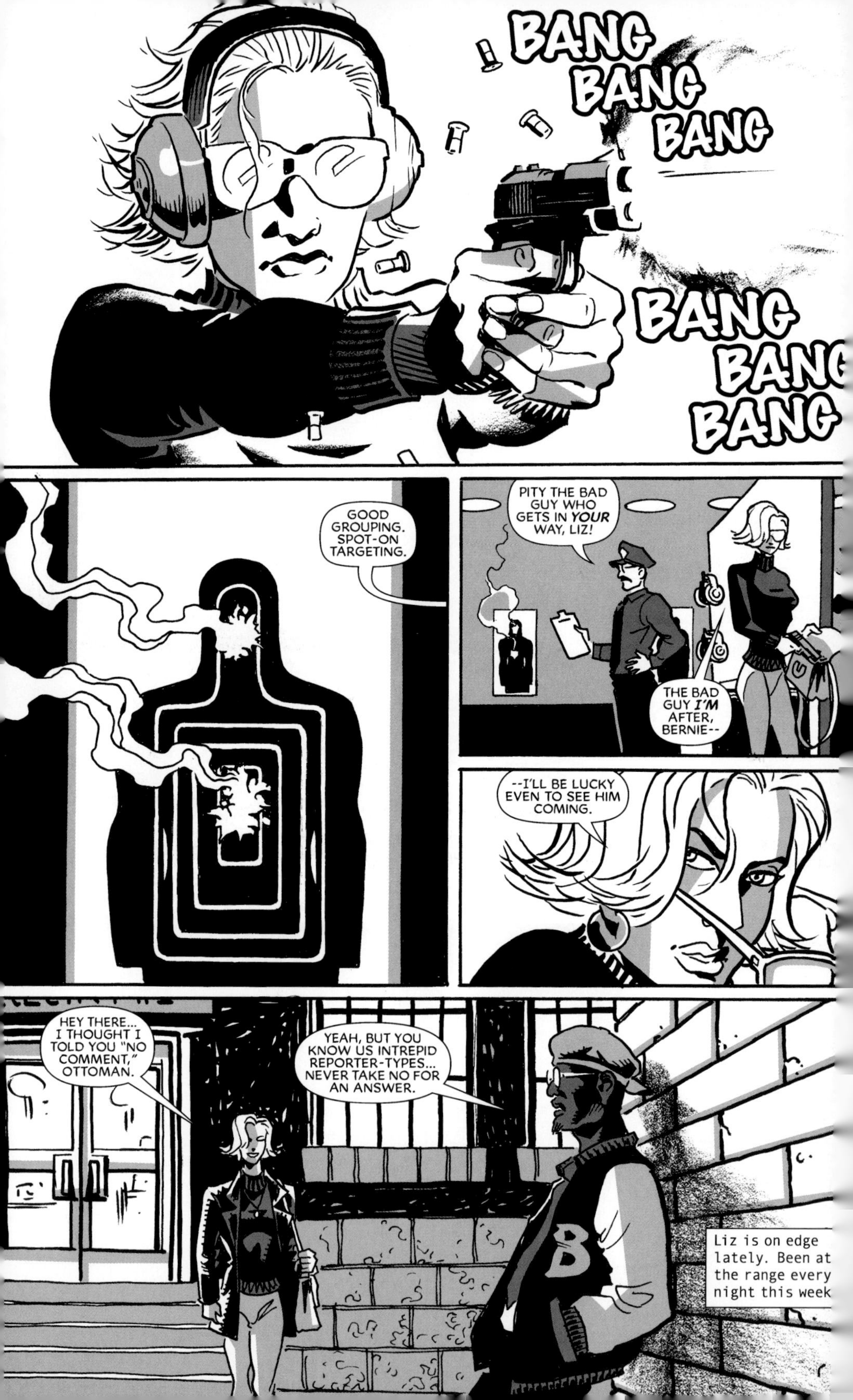
BANG
BANG
BANG
BANG
BANG
BANG
GOOD GROUPING. SPOT-ON TARGETING.
PITY THE BAD GUY WHO GETS IN YOUR WAY, LIZ!
THE BAD GUY I'M AFTER, BERNIE--
--I'LL BE LUCKY EVEN TO SEE HIM COMING.
HEY THERE... I THOUGHT I TOLD YOU "NO COMMENT," OTTOMAN.
YEAH, BUT YOU KNOW US INTREPID REPORTER-TYPES... NEVER TAKE NO FOR AN ANSWER.
Liz is on edge lately. Been at the range every night this week

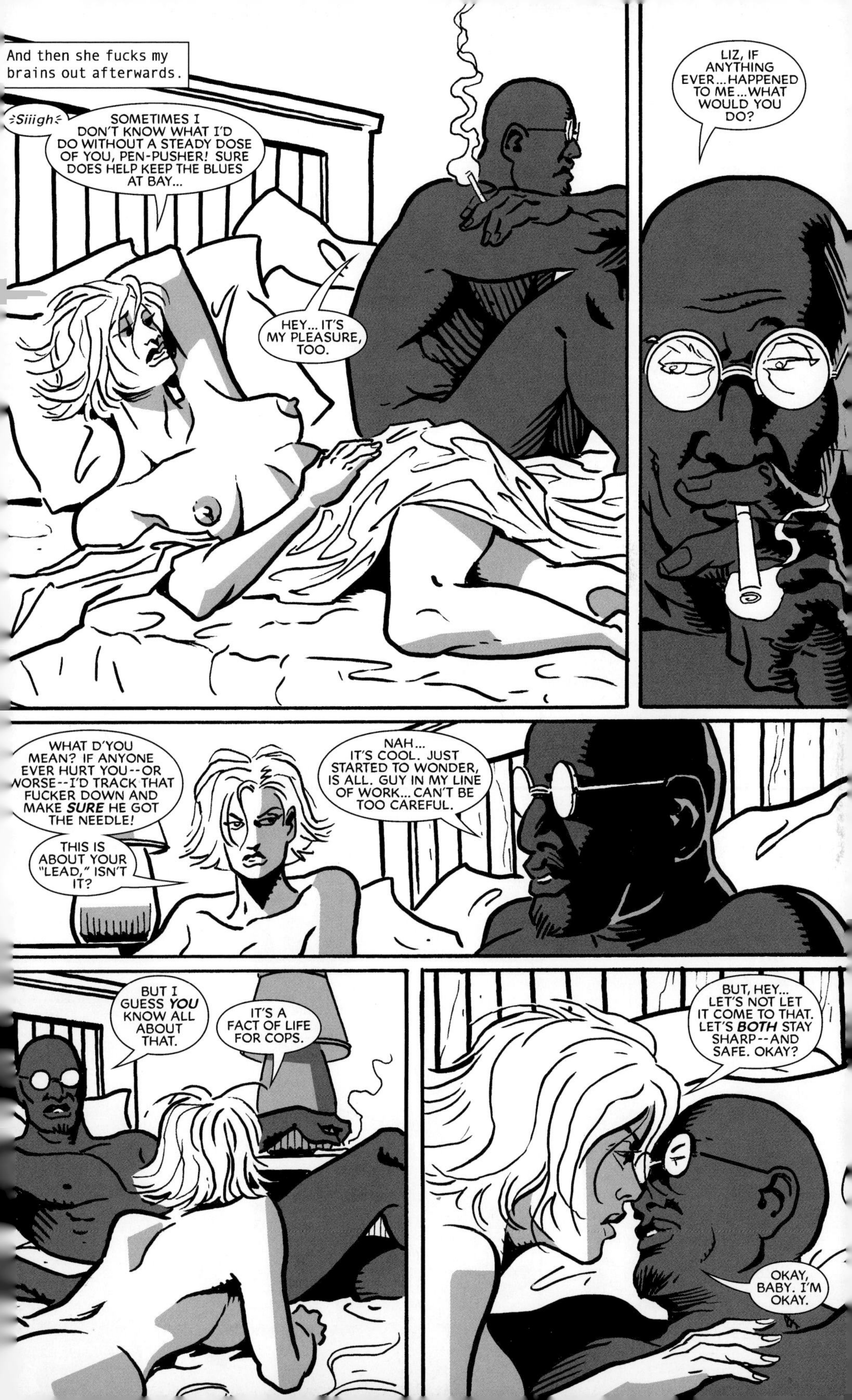

And then she fucks my brains out afterwards.
Siiigh
SOMETIMES I DON'T KNOW WHAT I'D DO WITHOUT A STEADY DOSE OF YOU, PEN-PUSHER! SURE DOES HELP KEEP THE BLUES AT BAY...
HEY... IT'S MY PLEASURE, TOO.
LIZ, IF ANYTHING EVER... HAPPENED TO ME... WHAT WOULD YOU DO?
WHAT D'YOU MEAN? IF ANYONE EVER HURT YOU--OR WORSE--I'D TRACK THAT FUCKER DOWN AND MAKE SURE HE GOT THE NEEDLE!
THIS IS ABOUT YOUR "LEAD," ISN'T IT?
NAH... IT'S COOL. JUST STARTED TO WONDER, IS ALL. GUY IN MY LINE OF WORK... CAN'T BE TOO CAREFUL.
BUT I GUESS YOU KNOW ALL ABOUT THAT.
IT'S A FACT OF LIFE FOR COPS.
BUT, HEY... LET'S NOT LET IT COME TO THAT. LET'S BOTH STAY SHARP--AND SAFE. OKAY?
OKAY, BABY. I'M OKAY.

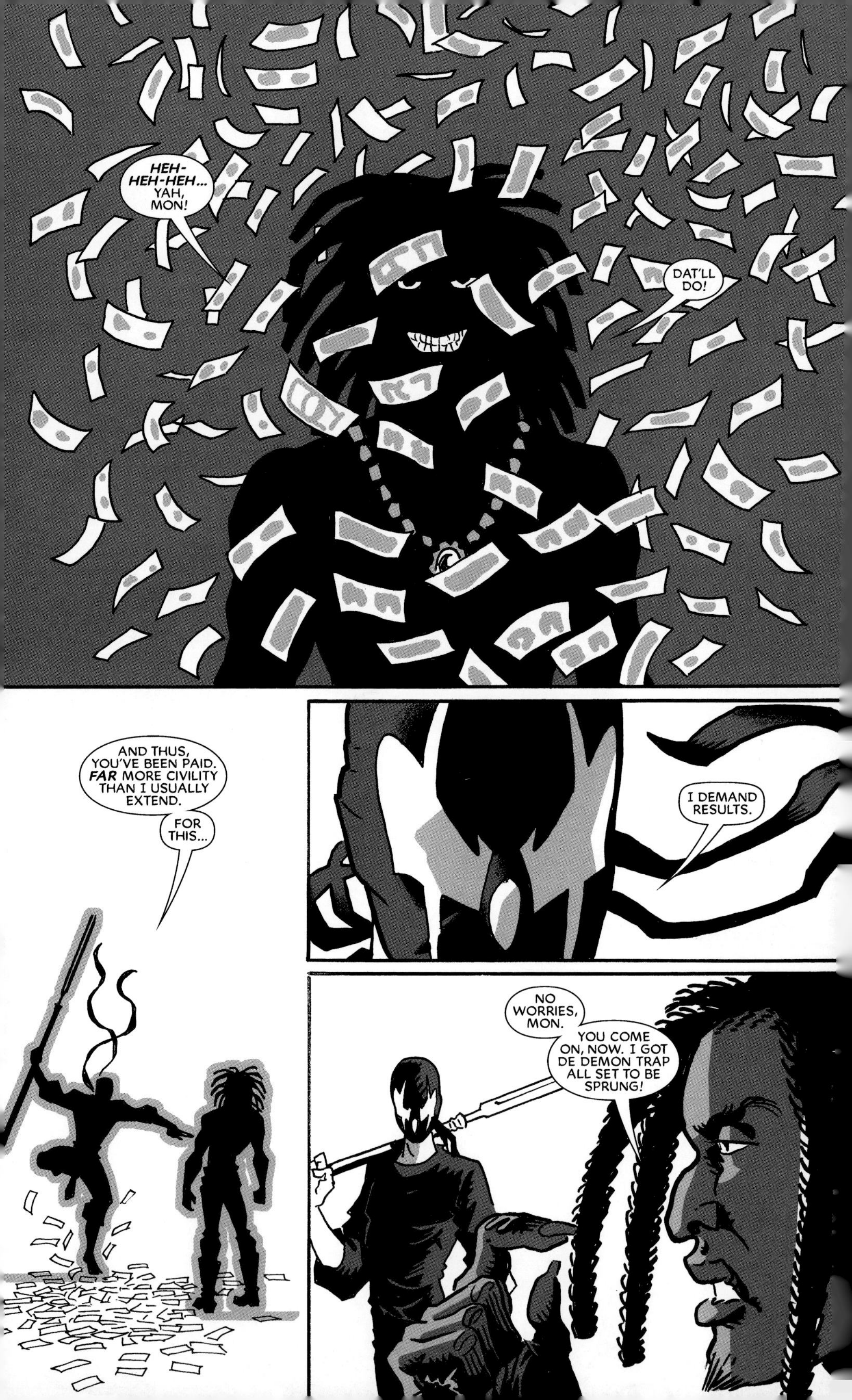

HEH-HEH-HEH... YAH, MON!
DAT'LL DO!
AND THUS, YOU'VE BEEN PAID. FAR MORE CIVILITY THAN I USUALLY EXTEND.
FOR THIS...
I DEMAND RESULTS.
NO WORRIES, MON.
YOU COME ON, NOW. I GOT DE DEMON TRAP ALL SET TO BE SPRUNG!

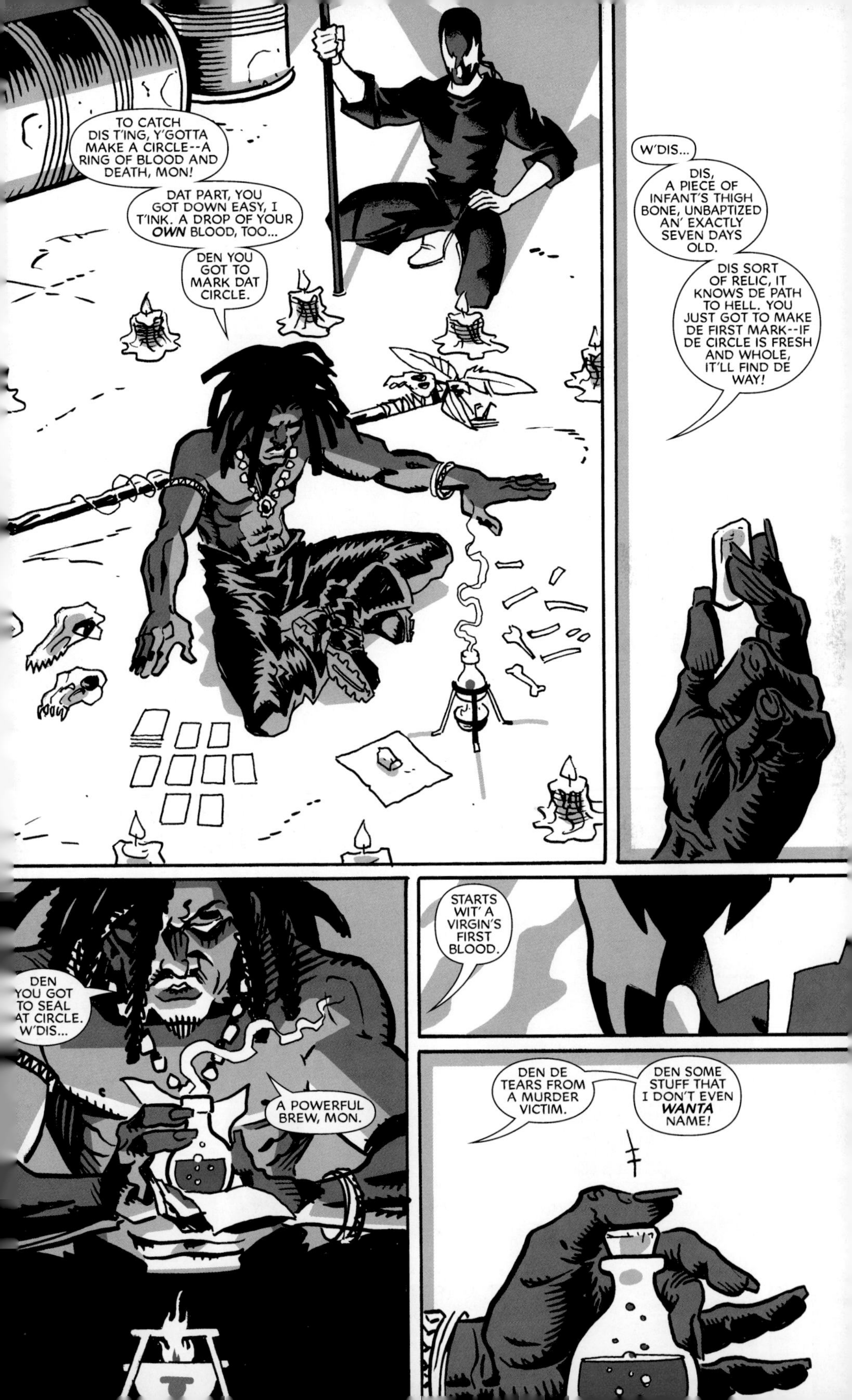
TO CATCH DIS T'ING, Y'GOTTA MAKE A CIRCLE--A RING OF BLOOD AND DEATH, MON!
DAT PART, YOU GOT DOWN EASY, I T'INK. A DROP OF YOUR *OWN* BLOOD, TOO...
DEN YOU GOT TO MARK DAT CIRCLE.
W'DIS...
DIS, A PIECE OF INFANT'S THIGH BONE, UNBAPTIZED AN' EXACTLY SEVEN DAYS OLD.
DIS SORT OF RELIC, IT KNOWS DE PATH TO HELL. YOU JUST GOT TO MAKE DE FIRST MARK--IF DE CIRCLE IS FRESH AND WHOLE, IT'LL FIND DE WAY!
DEN YOU GOT TO SEAL AT CIRCLE. W'DIS...
A POWERFUL BREW, MON.
STARTS WIT' A VIRGIN'S FIRST BLOOD.
DEN DE TEARS FROM A MURDER VICTIM.
DEN SOME STUFF THAT I DON'T EVEN *WANTA* NAME!

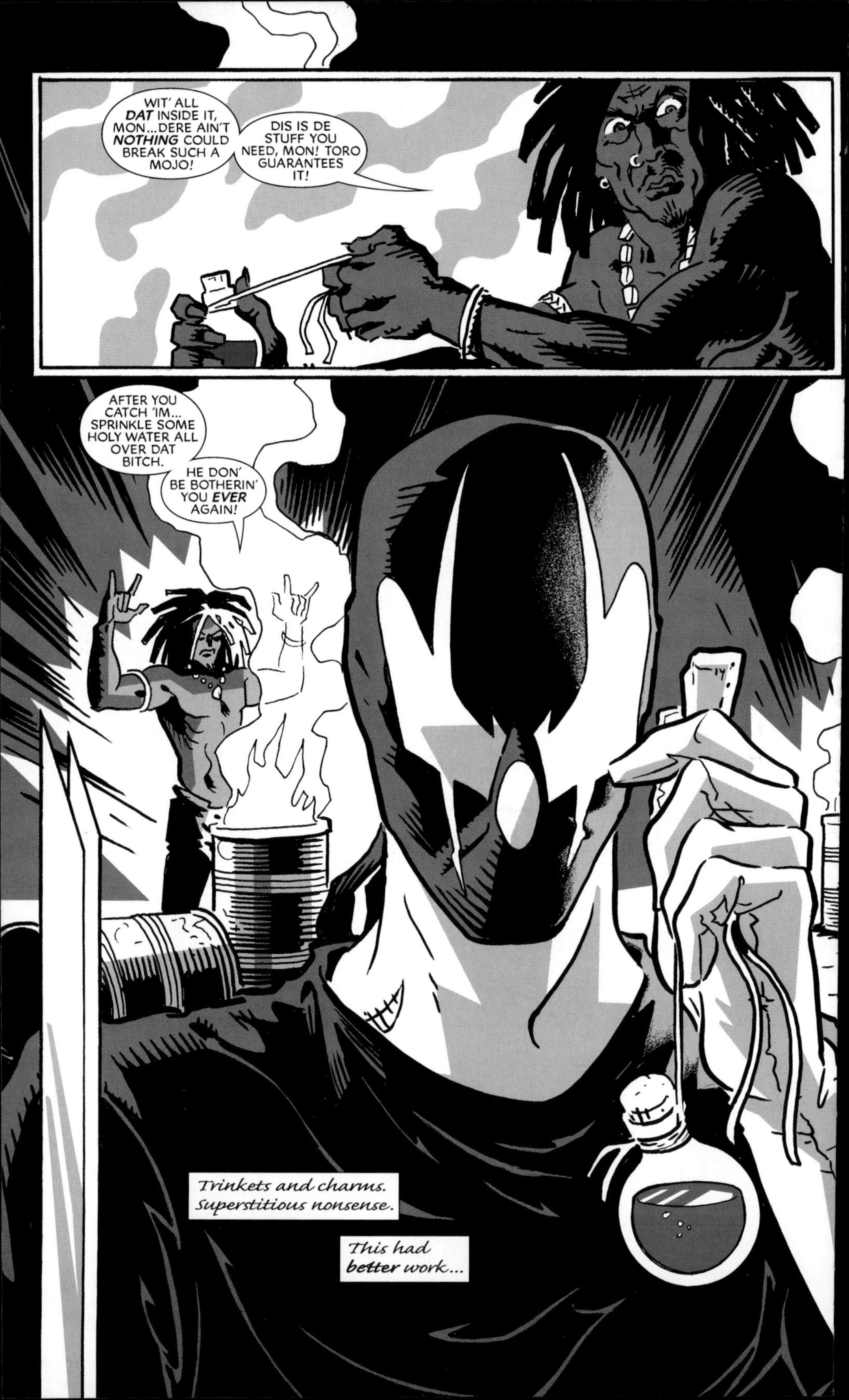
WIT' ALL DAT INSIDE IT, MON...DERE AIN'T NOTHING COULD BREAK SUCH A MOJO!
DIS IS DE STUFF YOU NEED, MON! TORO GUARANTEES IT!
AFTER YOU CATCH 'IM... SPRINKLE SOME HOLY WATER ALL OVER DAT BITCH.
HE DON' BE BOTHERIN' YOU EVER AGAIN!
Trinkets and charms. Superstitious nonsense.
This had better work...

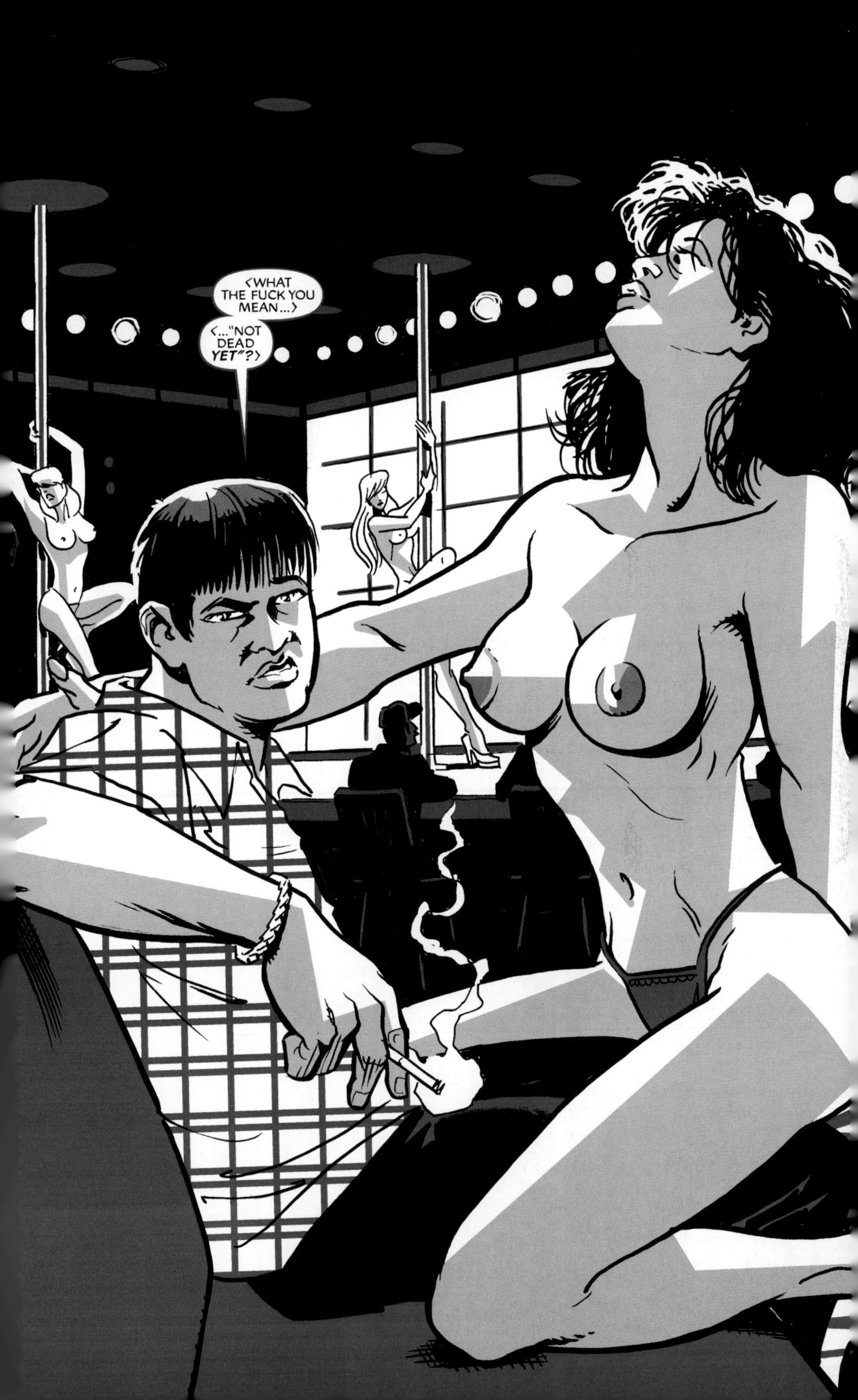

<WHAT THE FUCK YOU MEAN...>
<..."NOT DEAD YET"?>

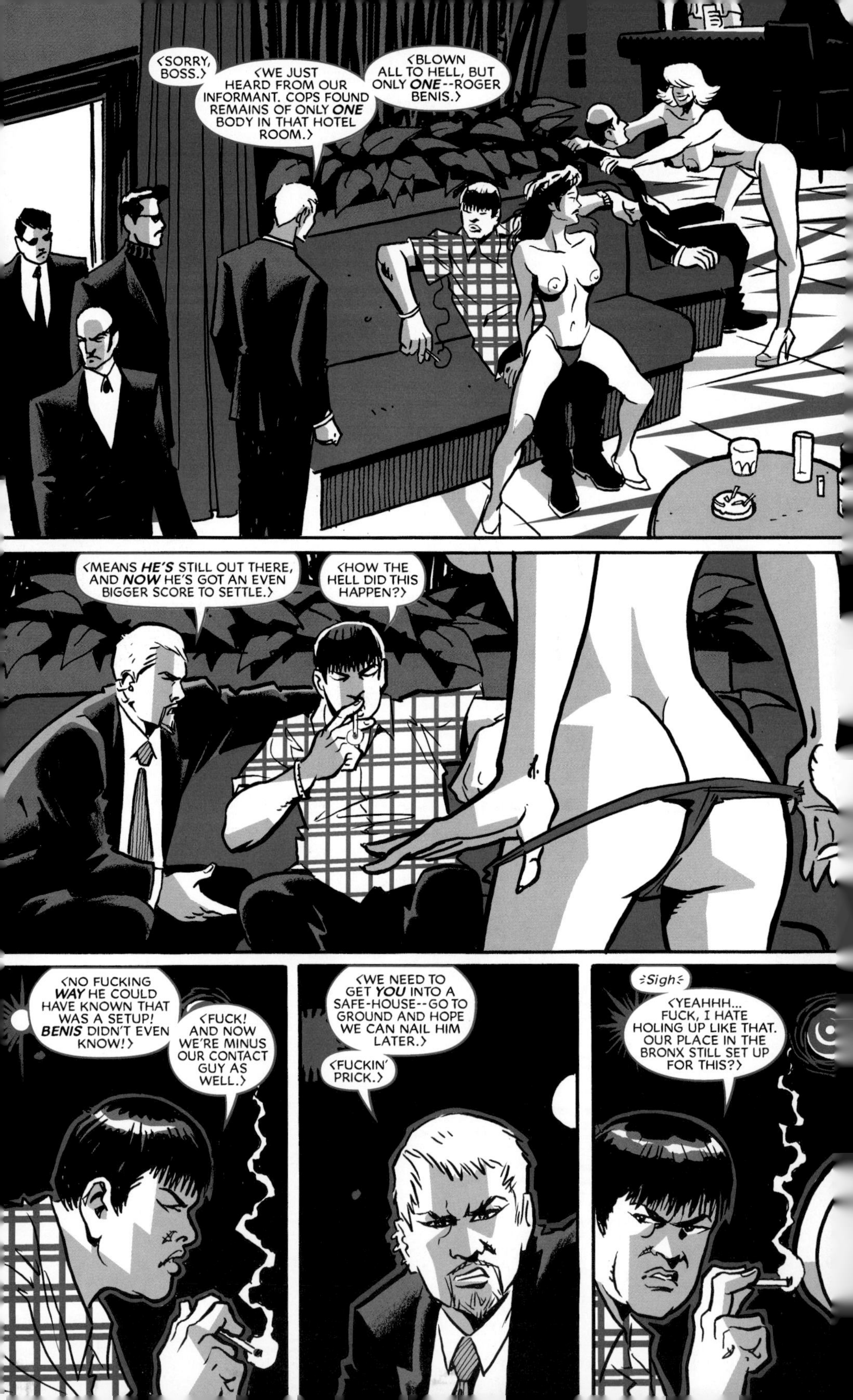
<SORRY, BOSS.>
<WE JUST HEARD FROM OUR INFORMANT. COPS FOUND REMAINS OF ONLY ONE BODY IN THAT HOTEL ROOM.>
<BLOWN ALL TO HELL, BUT ONLY ONE--ROGER BENIS.>
<MEANS HE'S STILL OUT THERE, AND NOW HE'S GOT AN EVEN BIGGER SCORE TO SETTLE.>
<HOW THE HELL DID THIS HAPPEN?>
<NO FUCKING WAY HE COULD HAVE KNOWN THAT WAS A SETUP! BENIS DIDN'T EVEN KNOW!>
<FUCK! AND NOW WE'RE MINUS OUR CONTACT GUY AS WELL.>
<WE NEED TO GET YOU INTO A SAFE-HOUSE--GO TO GROUND AND HOPE WE CAN NAIL HIM LATER.>
<FUCKIN' PRICK.>
Sigh
<YEAHHH... FUCK, I HATE HOLING UP LIKE THAT. OUR PLACE IN THE BRONX STILL SET UP FOR THIS?>

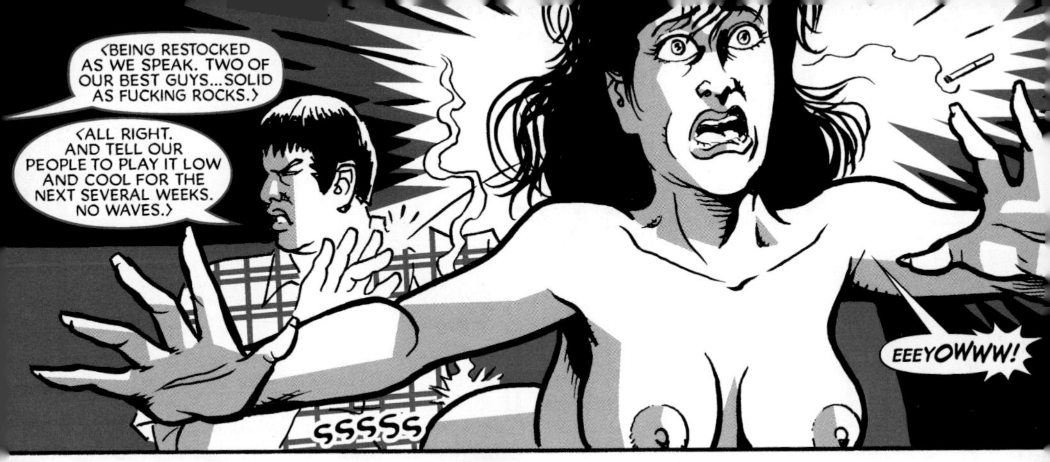
<BEING RESTOCKED AS WE SPEAK. TWO OF OUR BEST GUYS...SOLID AS FUCKING ROCKS.>
<ALL RIGHT. AND TELL OUR PEOPLE TO PLAY IT LOW AND COOL FOR THE NEXT SEVERAL WEEKS. NO WAVES.>
EEEYOWWW!
SSSSS

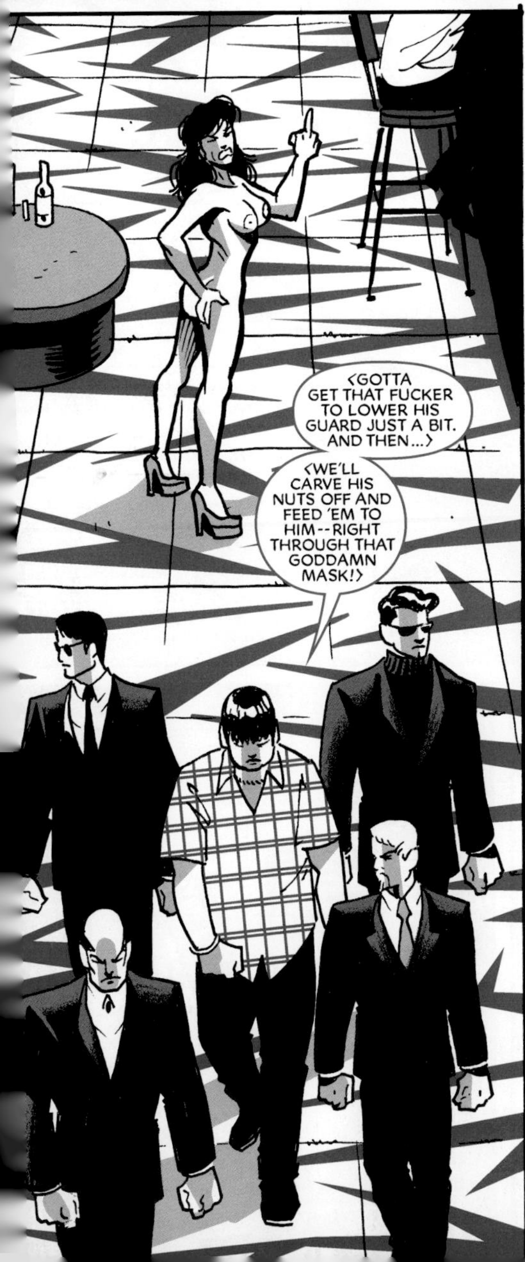
<GOTTA GET THAT FUCKER TO LOWER HIS GUARD JUST A BIT. AND THEN...>
<WE'LL CARVE HIS NUTS OFF AND FEED 'EM TO HIM--RIGHT THROUGH THAT GODDAMN MASK!>

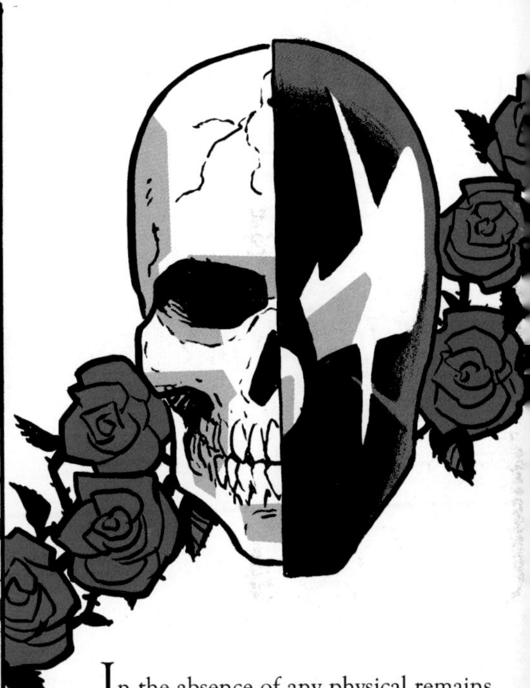

In the absence of any physical remains for Kwon Hyun-Ki and his deadly "Four Winds," we can only speculate as to their ultimate fate. Reports of an explosion later drew authorities to eventually discover the existence of an empty mob "safe-house," provisioned for what was obviously expected to be an extended state of siege. Still, other than some powdery ash of dubious origin, no evidence of the Korean hierarchy was ever seen again. In lieu of Grendel's firsthand account of this obviously deadly confrontation, their fate remains a mystery.

– excerpt from *Devil by the Deed*
by Christine Spar

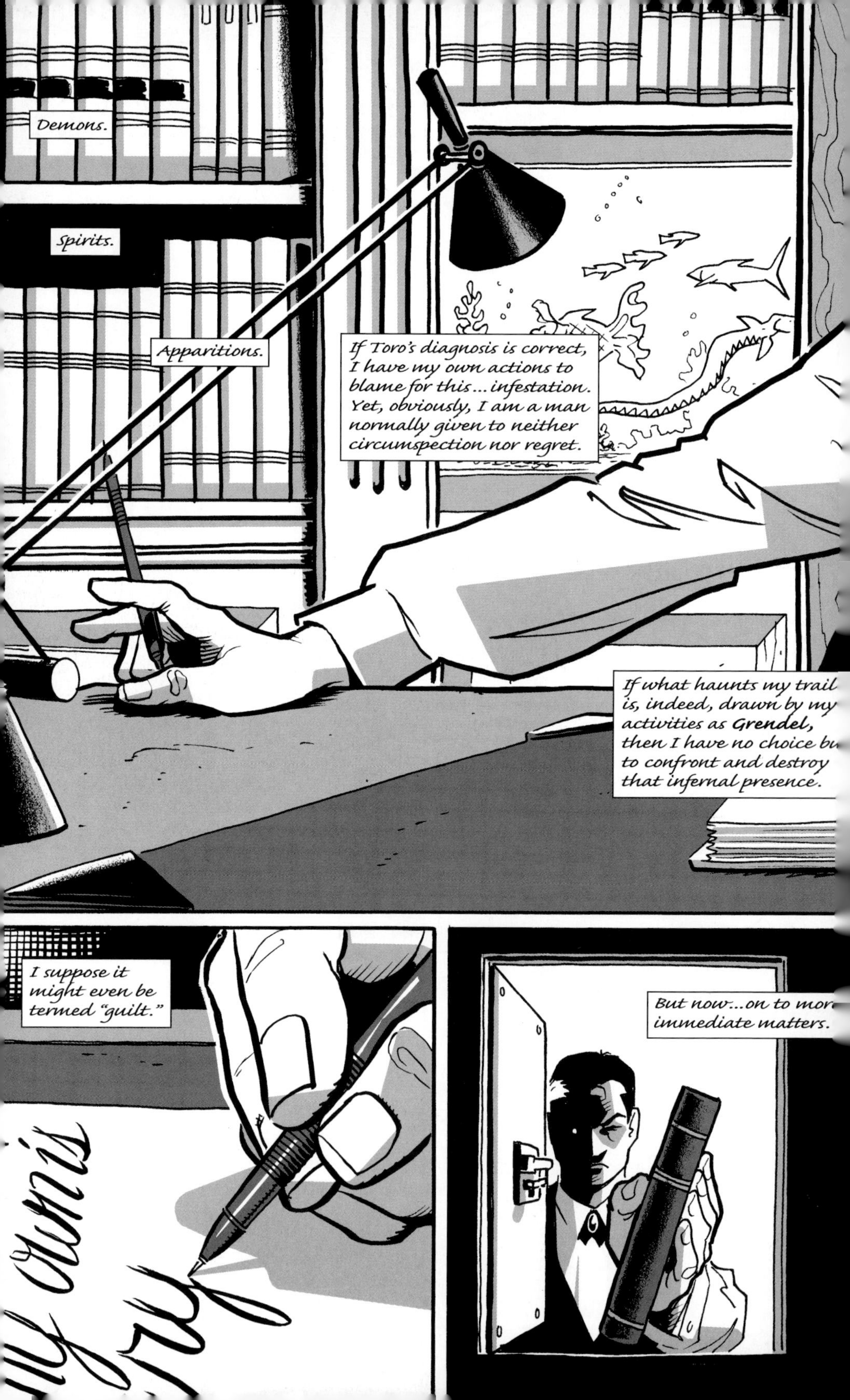
Demons.
Spirits.
Apparitions.
If Toro's diagnosis is correct, I have my own actions to blame for this...infestation. Yet, obviously, I am a man normally given to neither circumspection nor regret.
If what haunts my trail is, indeed, drawn by my activities as Grendel, then I have no choice bu to confront and destroy that infernal presence.
I suppose it might even be termed "guilt."
But now...on to mor immediate matters.

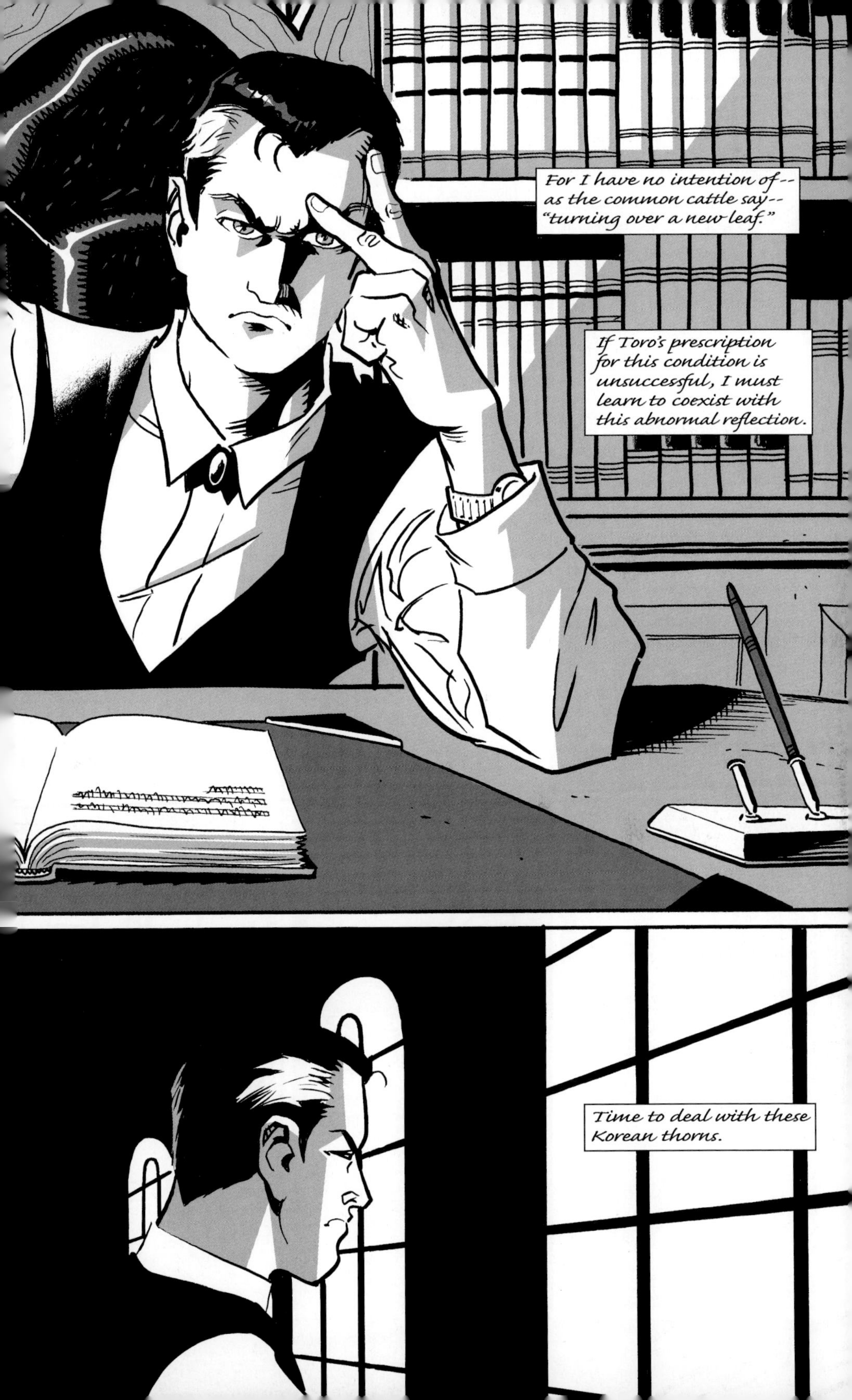
For I have no intention of--
as the common cattle say--
"turning over a new leaf."
If Toro's prescription
for this condition is
unsuccessful, I must
learn to coexist with
this abnormal reflection.
Time to deal with these
Korean thorns.

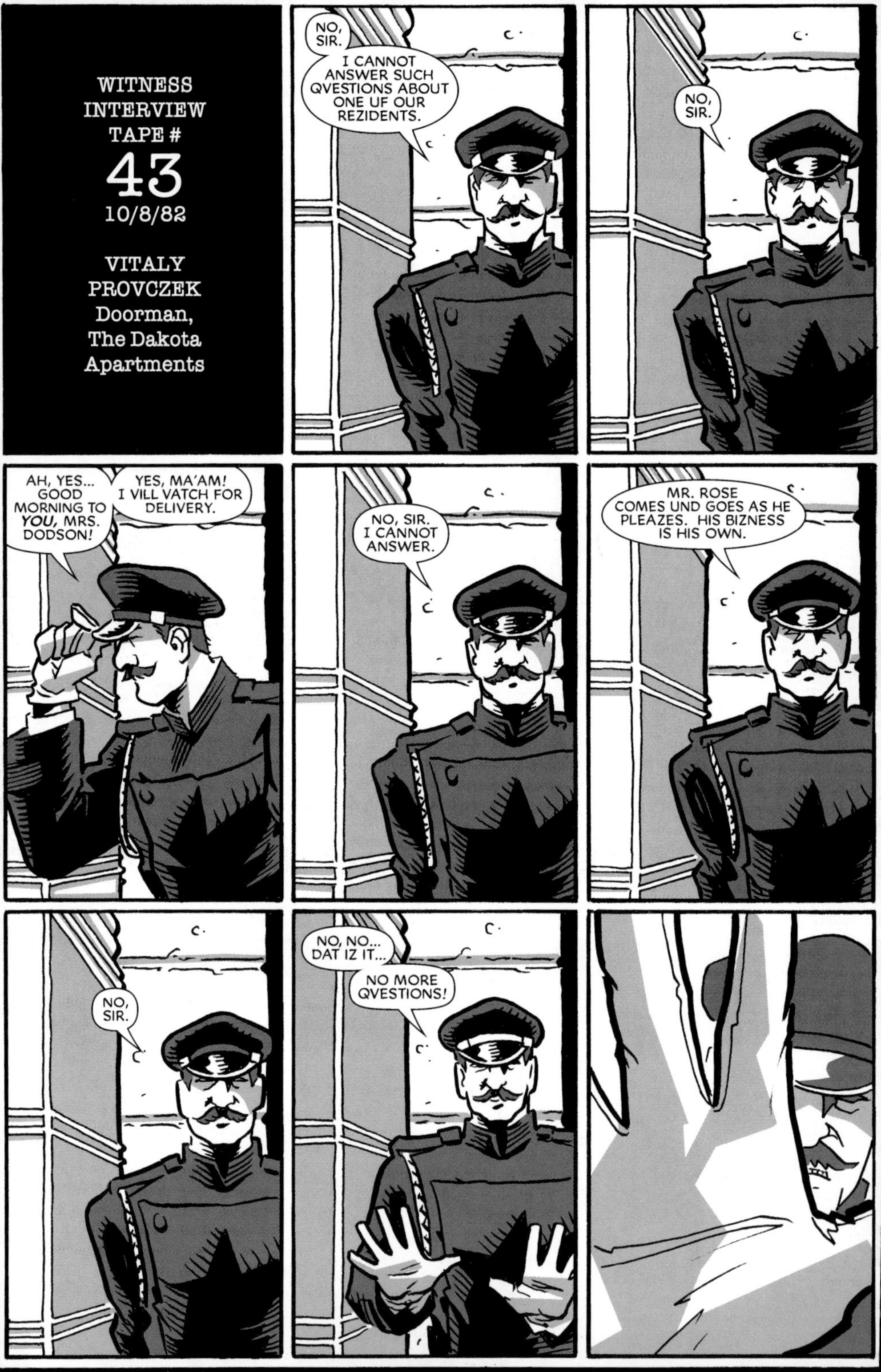
WITNESS INTERVIEW TAPE # 43
10/8/82
VITALY PROVCZEK
Doorman, The Dakota Apartments
NO, SIR.
I CANNOT ANSWER SUCH QVESTIONS ABOUT ONE UF OUR REZIDENTS.
NO, SIR.
AH, YES... GOOD MORNING TO *YOU,* MRS. DODSON!
YES, MA'AM! I VILL VATCH FOR DELIVERY.
NO, SIR. I CANNOT ANSWER.
MR. ROSE COMES UND GOES AS HE PLEAZES. HIS BIZNESS IS HIS OWN.
NO, SIR.
NO, NO... DAT IZ IT...
NO MORE QVESTIONS!

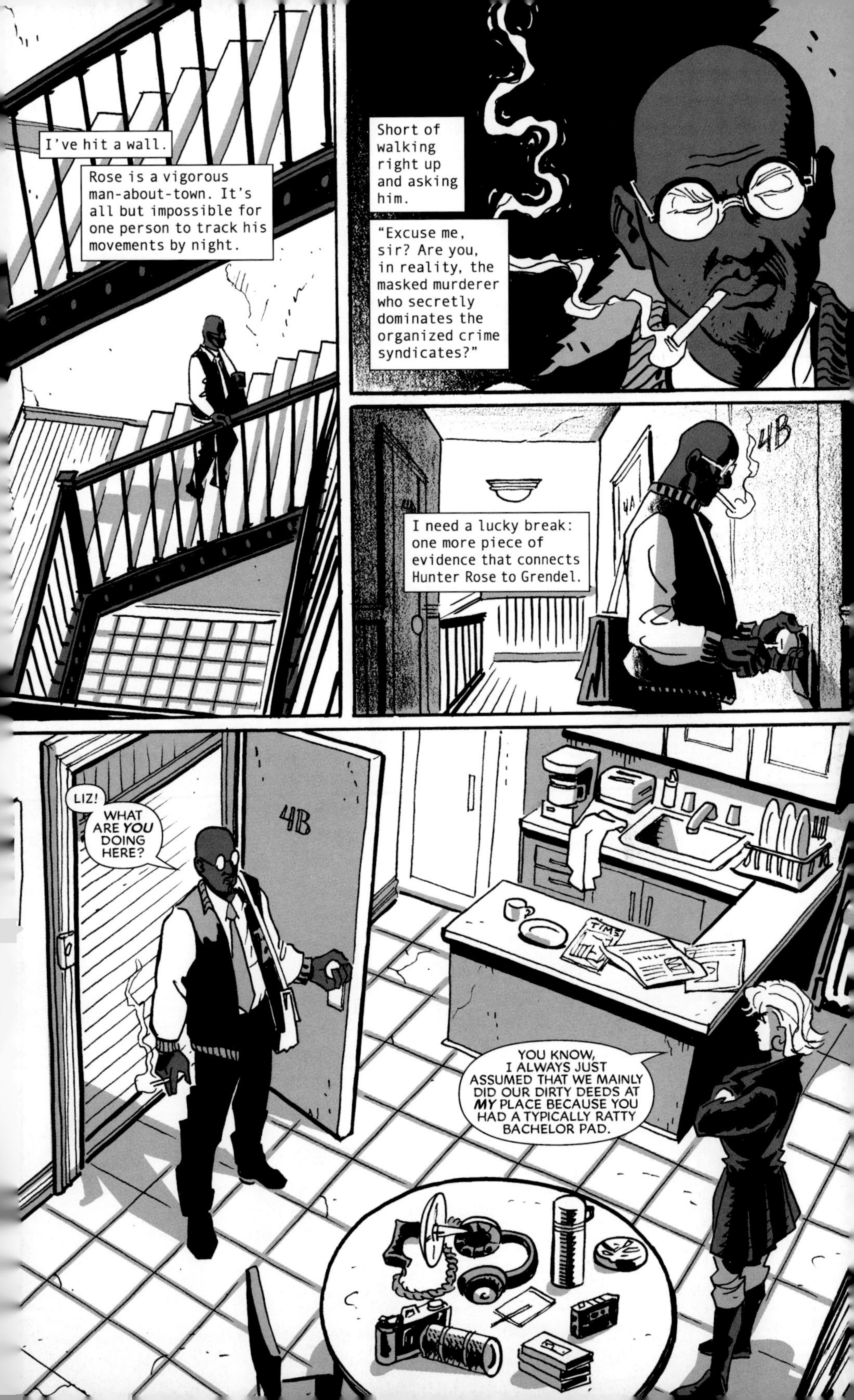

I've hit a wall.
Rose is a vigorous man-about-town. It's all but impossible for one person to track his movements by night.
Short of walking right up and asking him.
"Excuse me, sir? Are you, in reality, the masked murderer who secretly dominates the organized crime syndicates?"
4B
I need a lucky break: one more piece of evidence that connects Hunter Rose to Grendel.
4A
LIZ!
WHAT ARE *YOU* DOING HERE?
4B
YOU KNOW, I ALWAYS JUST ASSUMED THAT WE MAINLY DID OUR DIRTY DEEDS AT *MY* PLACE BECAUSE YOU HAD A TYPICALLY RATTY BACHELOR PAD.

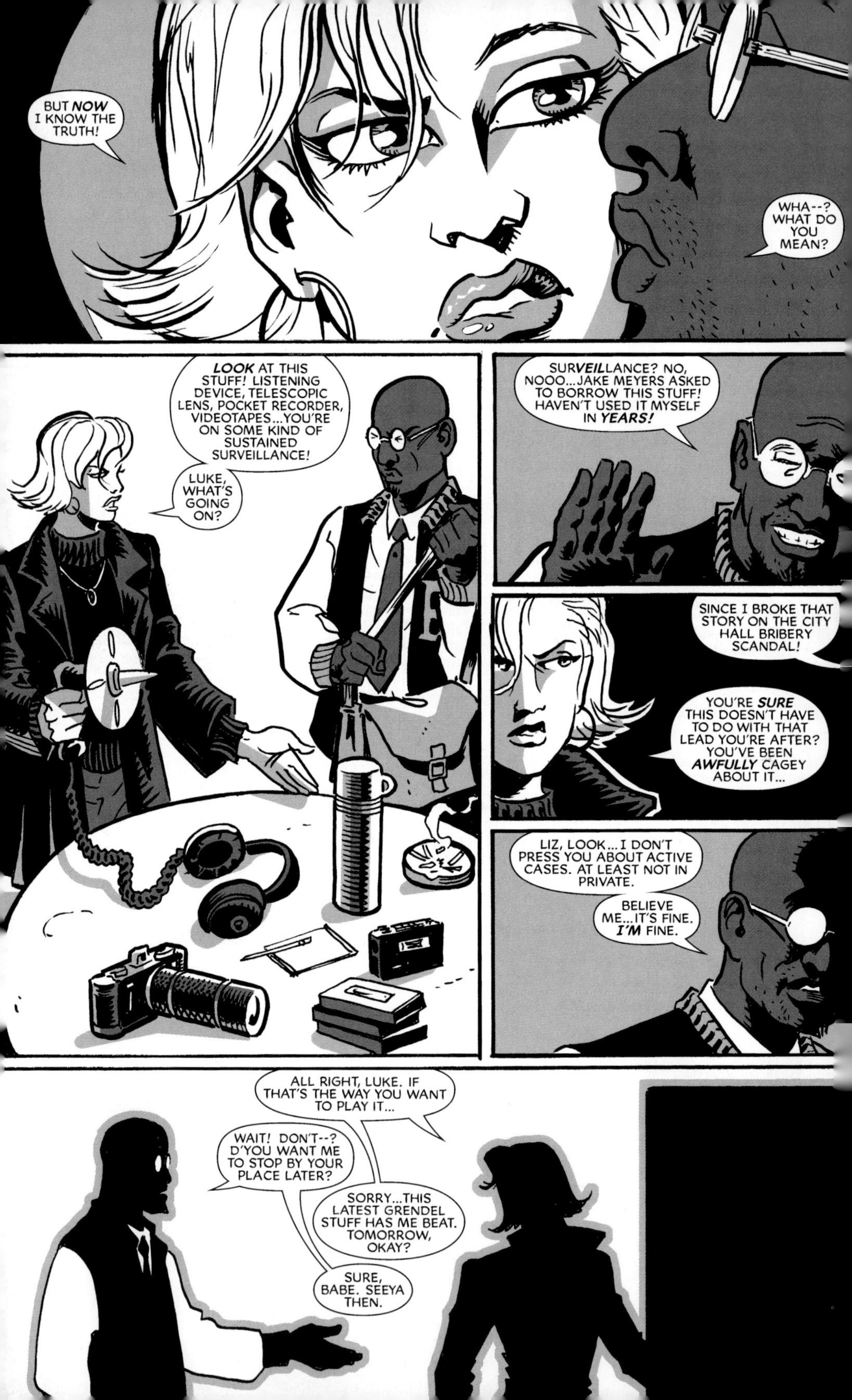
BUT NOW I KNOW THE TRUTH!
WHA--? WHAT DO YOU MEAN?
LOOK AT THIS STUFF! LISTENING DEVICE, TELESCOPIC LENS, POCKET RECORDER, VIDEOTAPES...YOU'RE ON SOME KIND OF SUSTAINED SURVEILLANCE!
LUKE, WHAT'S GOING ON?
SURVEILLANCE? NO, NOOO...JAKE MEYERS ASKED TO BORROW THIS STUFF! HAVEN'T USED IT MYSELF IN YEARS!
SINCE I BROKE THAT STORY ON THE CITY HALL BRIBERY SCANDAL!
YOU'RE SURE THIS DOESN'T HAVE TO DO WITH THAT LEAD YOU'RE AFTER? YOU'VE BEEN AWFULLY CAGEY ABOUT IT...
LIZ, LOOK...I DON'T PRESS YOU ABOUT ACTIVE CASES. AT LEAST NOT IN PRIVATE.
BELIEVE ME...IT'S FINE. I'M FINE.
ALL RIGHT, LUKE. IF THAT'S THE WAY YOU WANT TO PLAY IT...
WAIT! DON'T--? D'YOU WANT ME TO STOP BY YOUR PLACE LATER?
SORRY...THIS LATEST GRENDEL STUFF HAS ME BEAT. TOMORROW, OKAY?
SURE, BABE. SEEYA THEN.

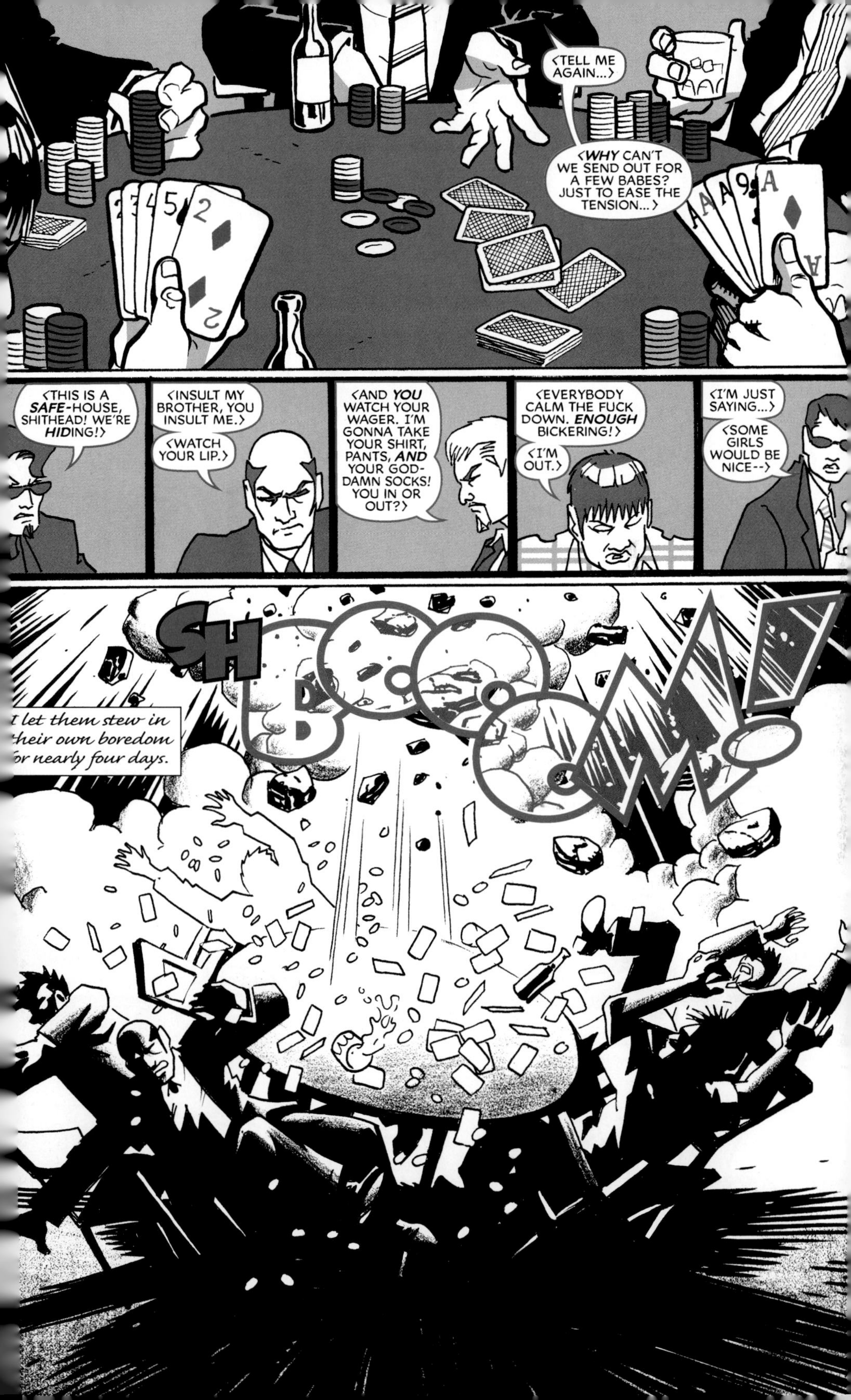

<TELL ME AGAIN...>
<WHY CAN'T WE SEND OUT FOR A FEW BABES? JUST TO EASE THE TENSION...>
<THIS IS A SAFE-HOUSE, SHITHEAD! WE'RE HIDING!>
<INSULT MY BROTHER, YOU INSULT ME.>
<WATCH YOUR LIP.>
<AND YOU WATCH YOUR WAGER. I'M GONNA TAKE YOUR SHIRT, PANTS, AND YOUR GOD-DAMN SOCKS! YOU IN OR OUT?>
<EVERYBODY CALM THE FUCK DOWN. ENOUGH BICKERING!>
<I'M OUT.>
<I'M JUST SAYING...>
<SOME GIRLS WOULD BE NICE-->
SHBOOOM!
I let them stew in their own boredom for nearly four days.

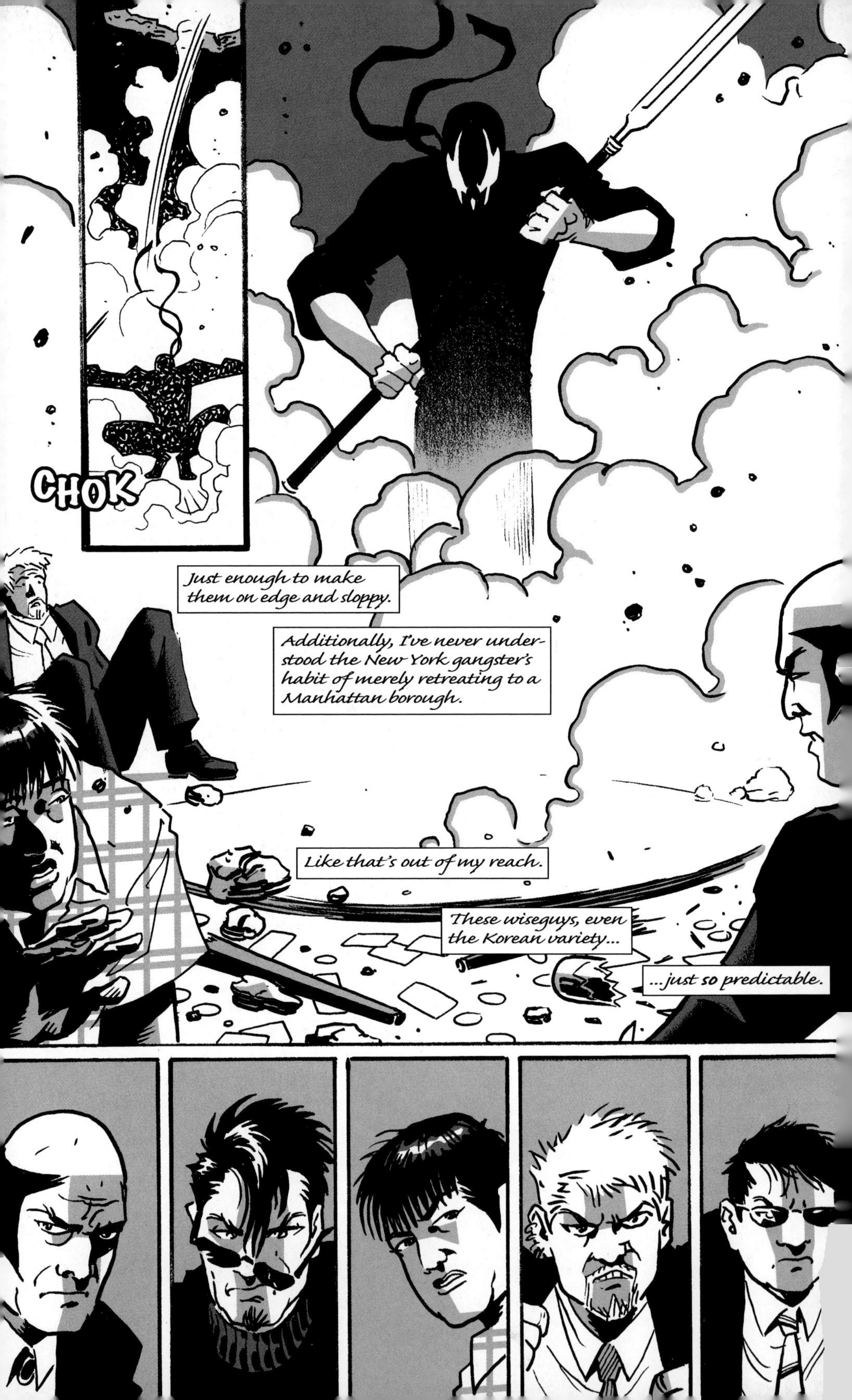
CHOK
Just enough to make them on edge and sloppy.
Additionally, I've never understood the New York gangster's habit of merely retreating to a Manhattan borough.
Like that's out of my reach.
These wiseguys, even the Korean variety...
...just so predictable.

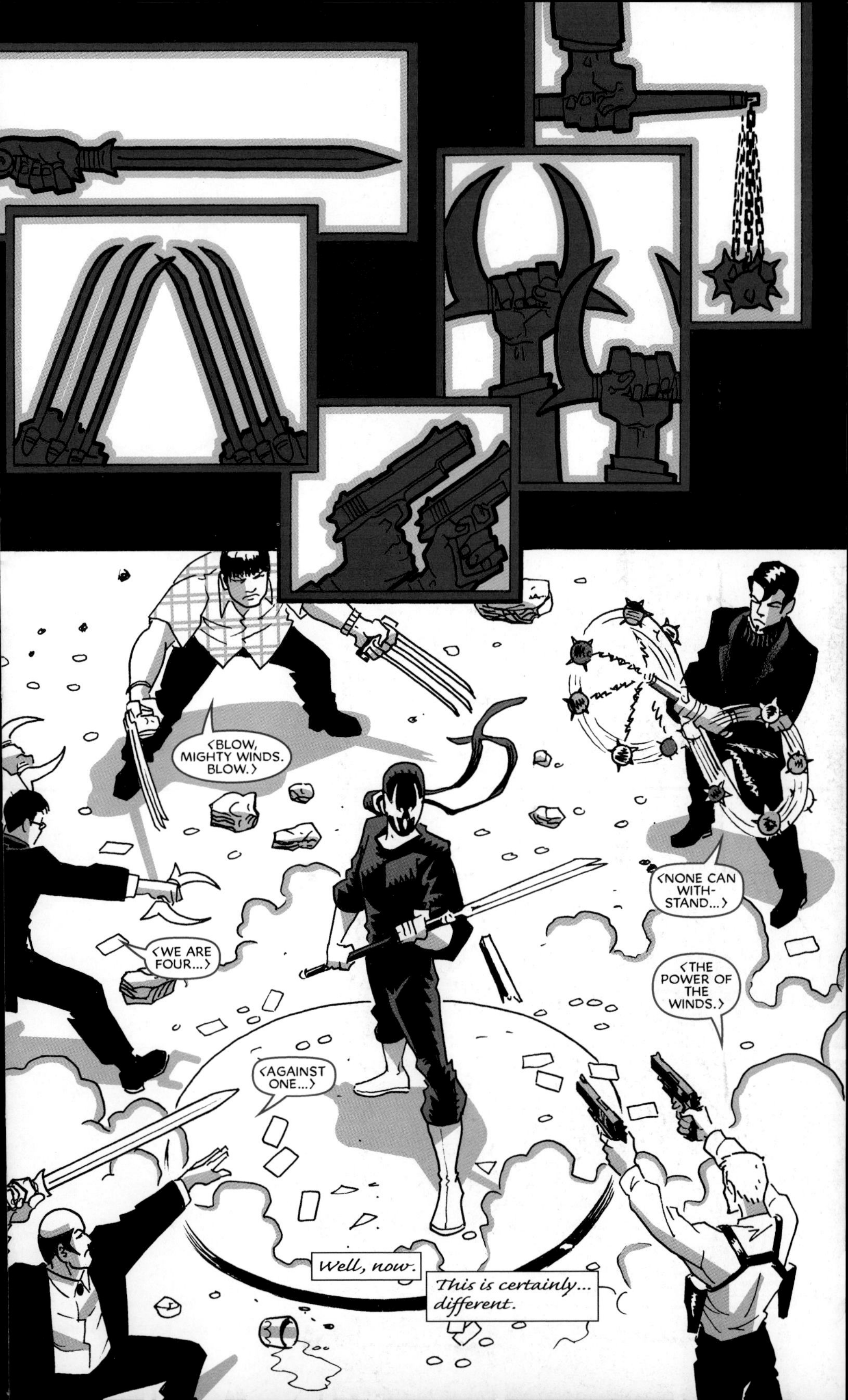

<BLOW, MIGHTY WINDS. BLOW.>
<NONE CAN WITH-STAND...>
<WE ARE FOUR...>
<THE POWER OF THE WINDS.>
<AGAINST ONE...>
Well, now.
This is certainly... different.

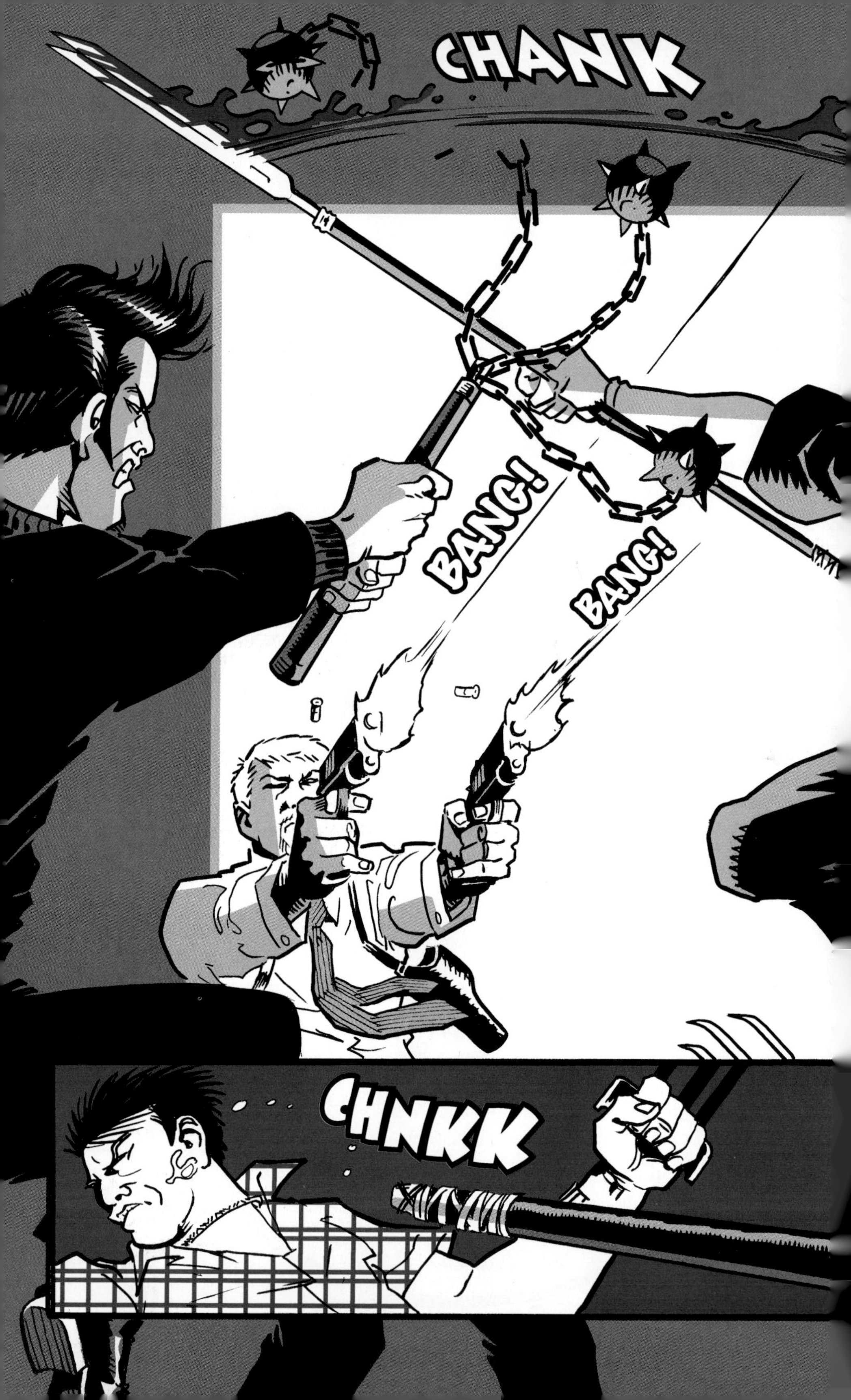
CHANK
BANG!
BANG!
CHNKK

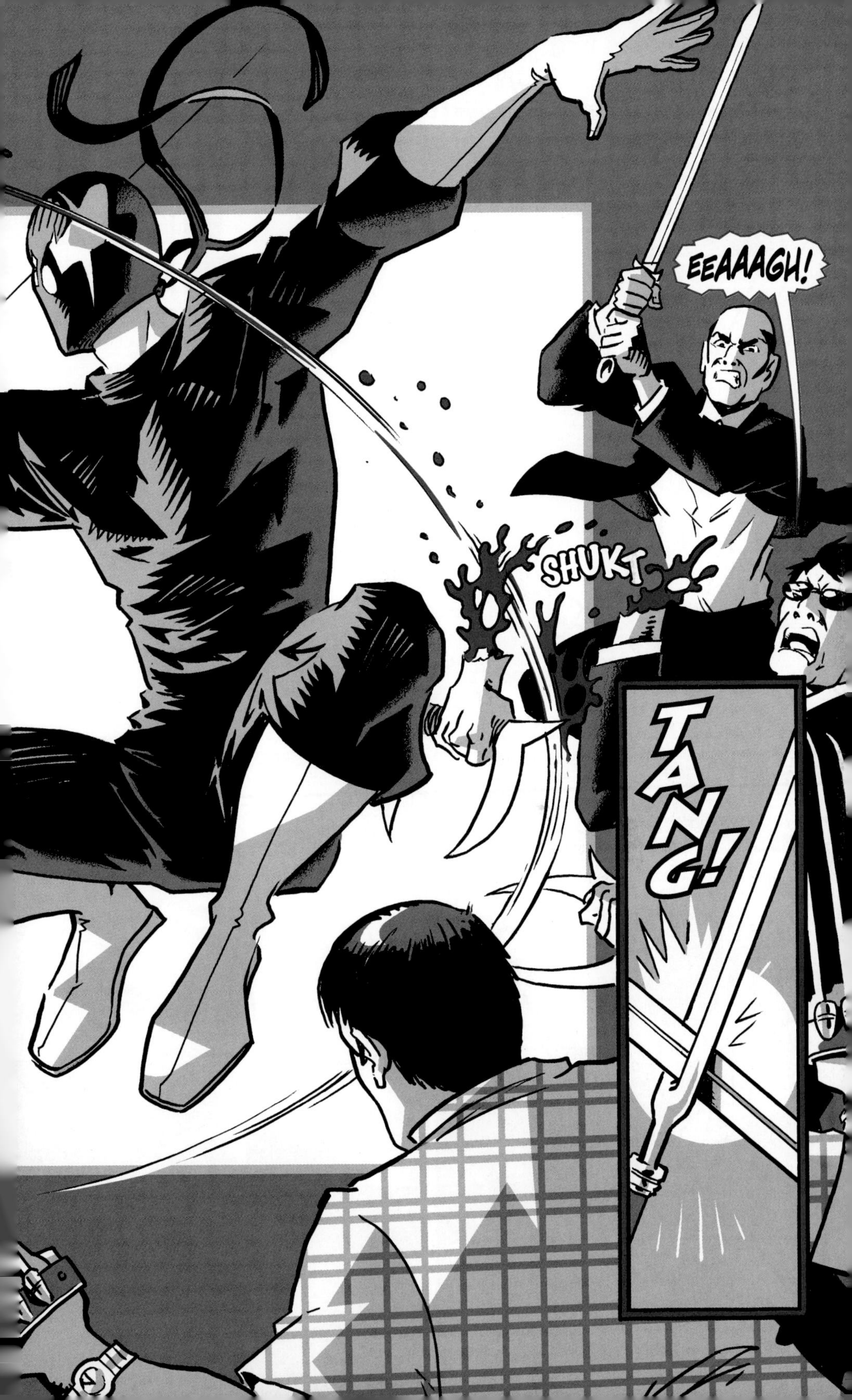
EEAAAGH!
SHUKT
TANG!

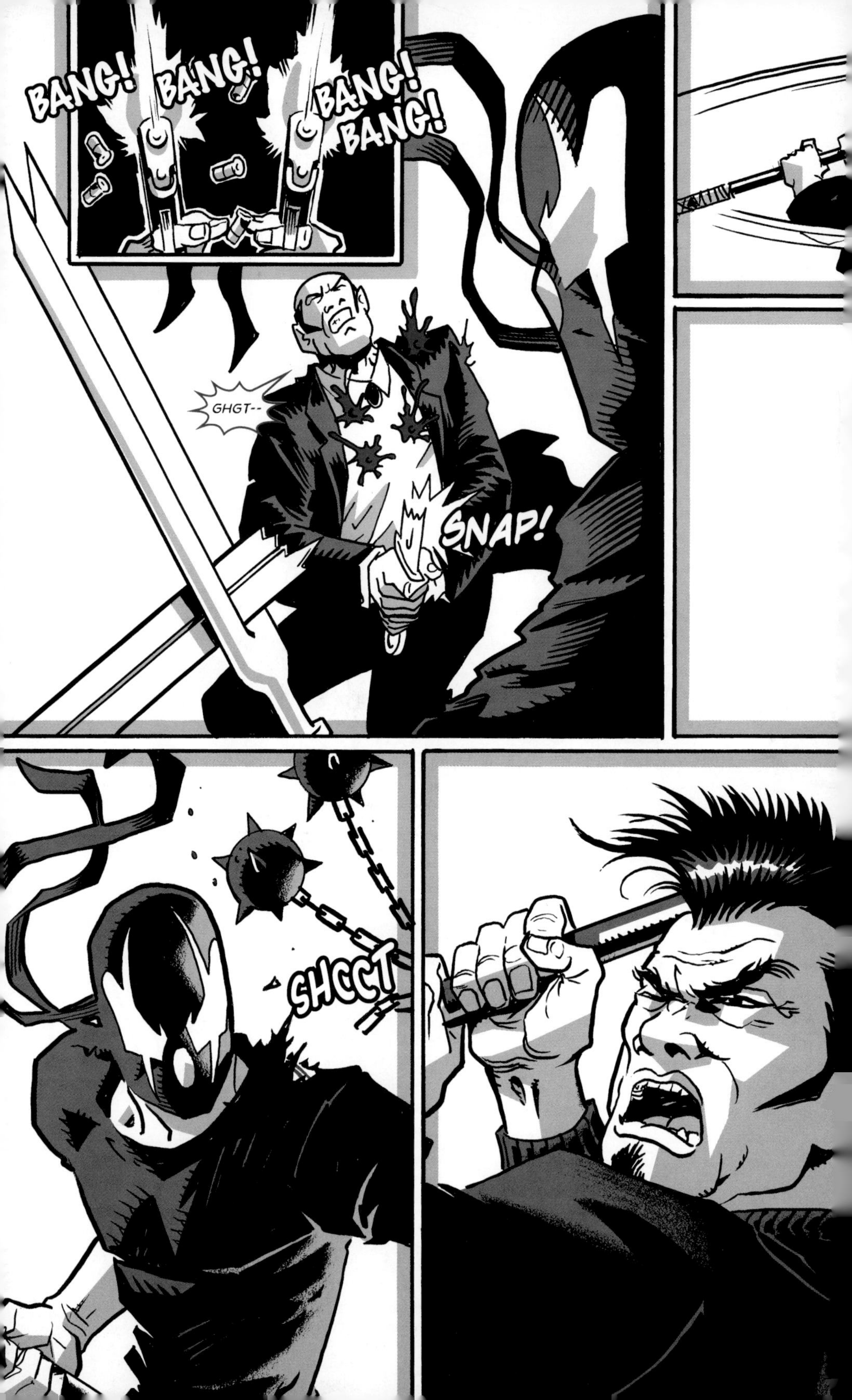
BANG! BANG!
BANG! BANG!
GHGT--
SNAP!
SHCCT

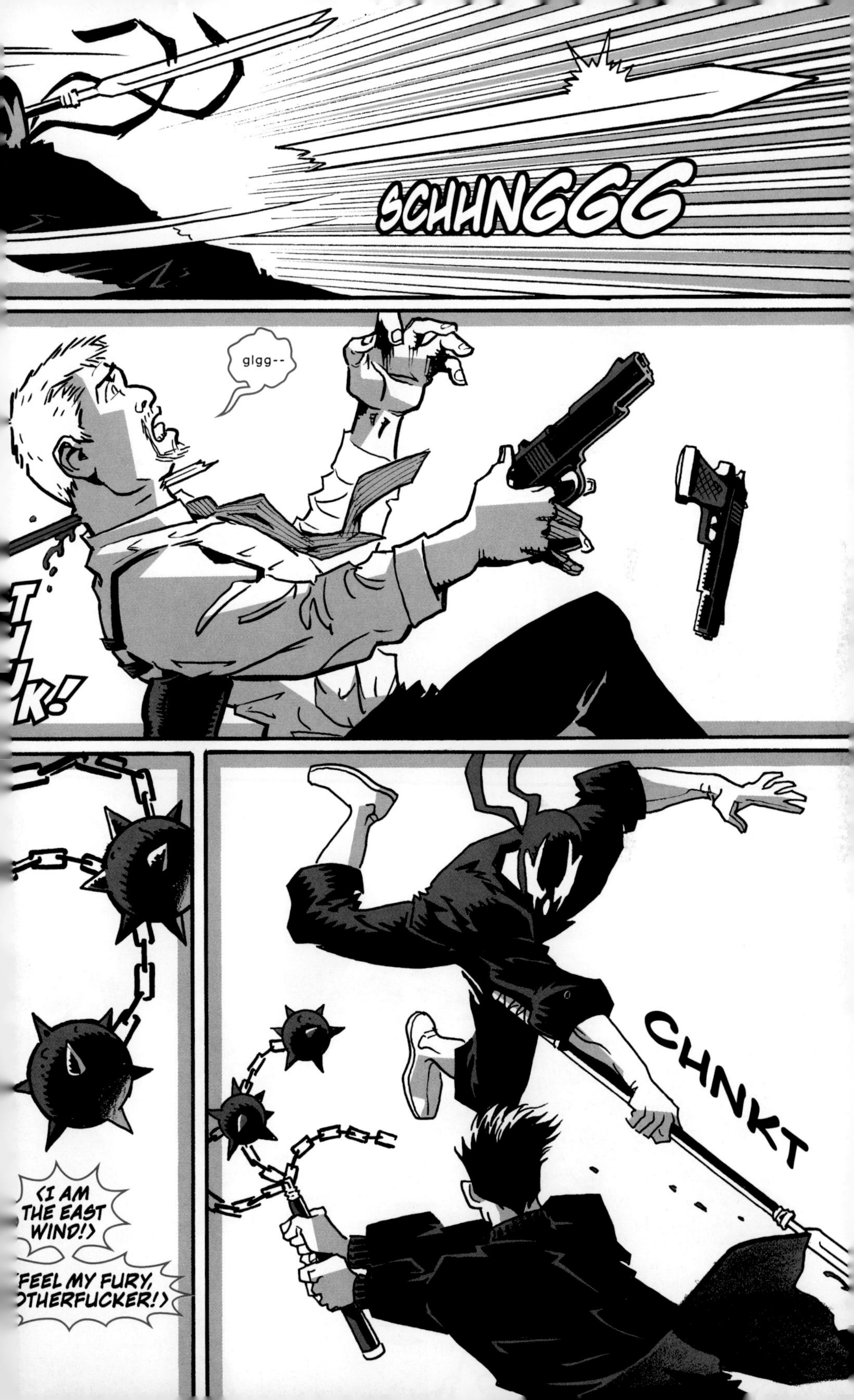
SCHUNGGG
glgg--
K!
CHNKT
<I AM THE EAST WIND!>
FEEL MY FURY, OTHERFUCKER!>

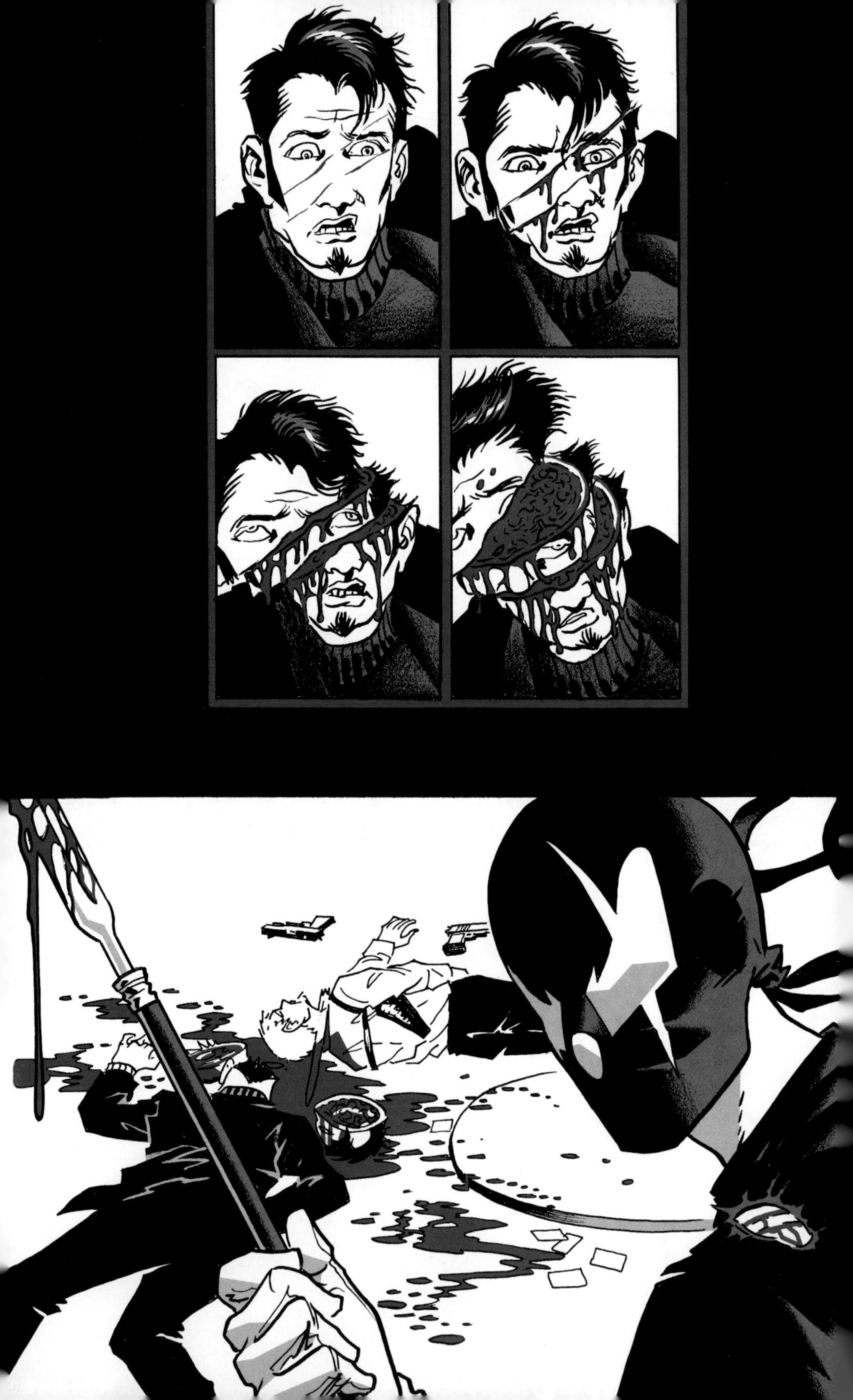

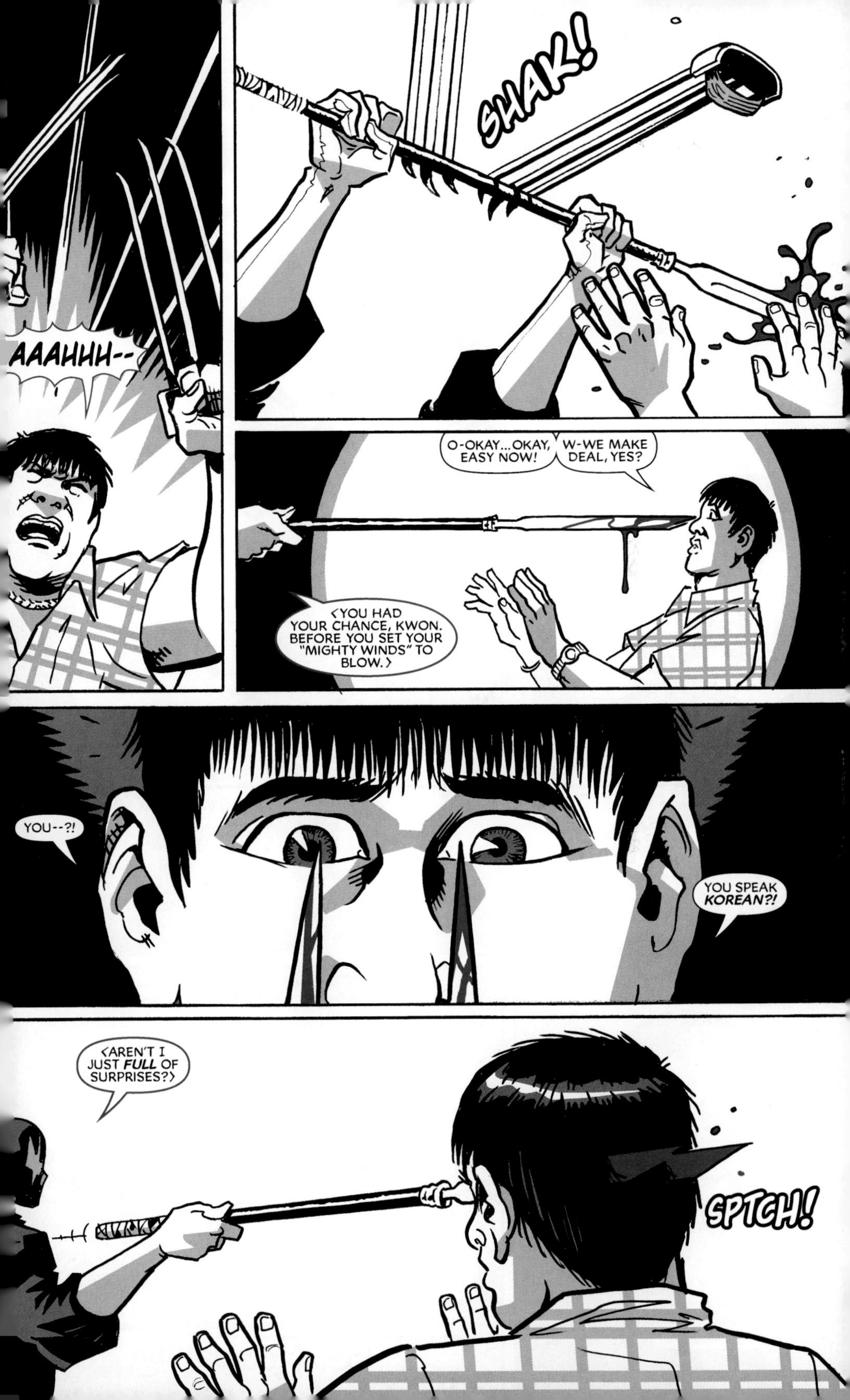
AAAHHH--
SHAK!
O-OKAY...OKAY, EASY NOW!
W-WE MAKE DEAL, YES?
<YOU HAD YOUR CHANCE, KWON. BEFORE YOU SET YOUR "MIGHTY WINDS" TO BLOW.>
YOU--?!
YOU SPEAK KOREAN?!
<AREN'T I JUST FULL OF SURPRISES?>
SPTCH!

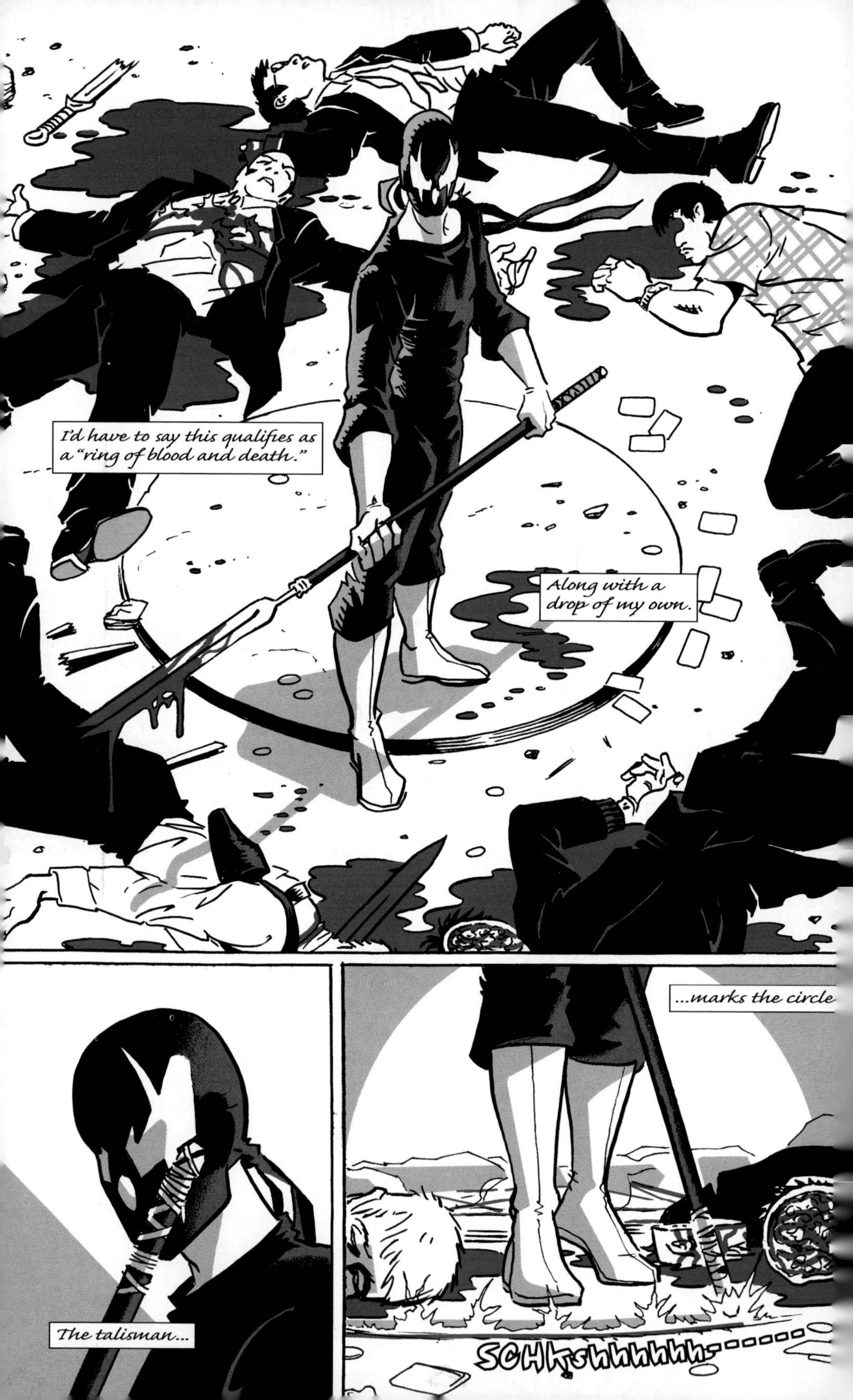
I'd have to say this qualifies as a "ring of blood and death."
Along with a drop of my own.
The talisman...
...marks the circle
SCHKshhhhhhh-oooooo

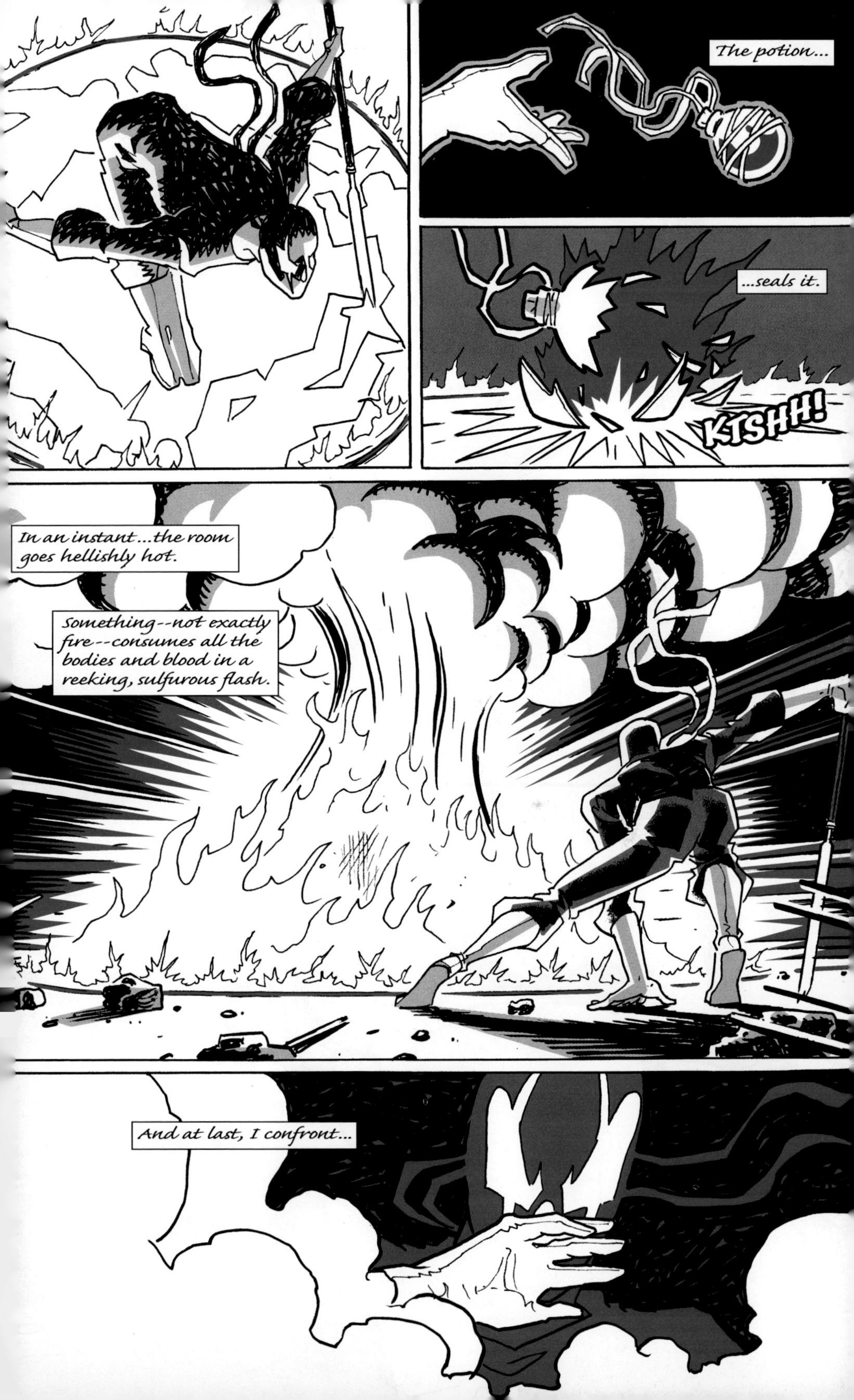
The potion...
...seals it.
KTSHH!
In an instant...the room goes hellishly hot.
Something--not exactly fire--consumes all the bodies and blood in a reeking, sulfurous flash.
And at last, I confront...

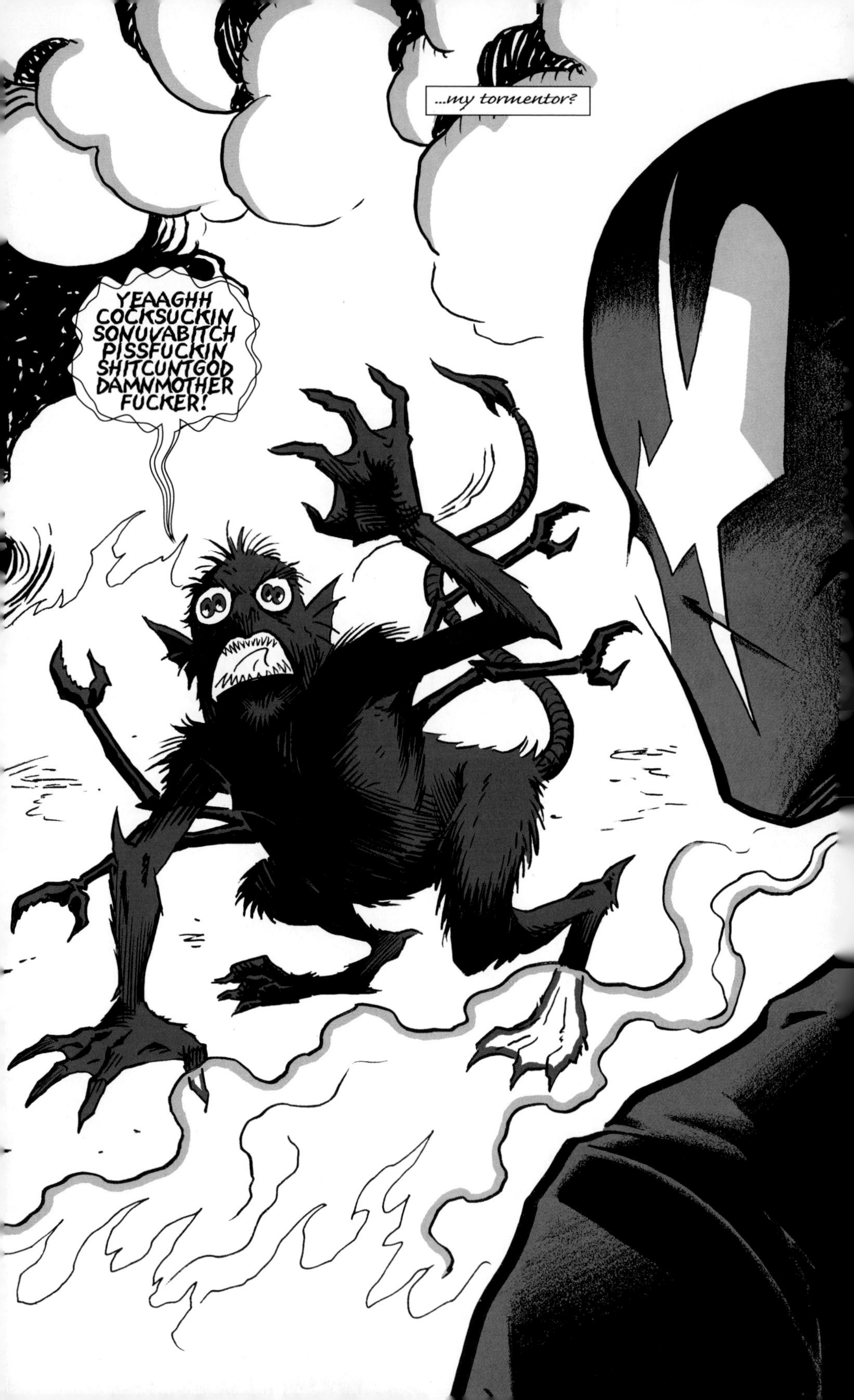
...my tormentor?
YEAAGHH COCKSUCKIN SONUVABITCH PISSFUCKIN SHITCUNTGOD DAMNMOTHER FUCKER!

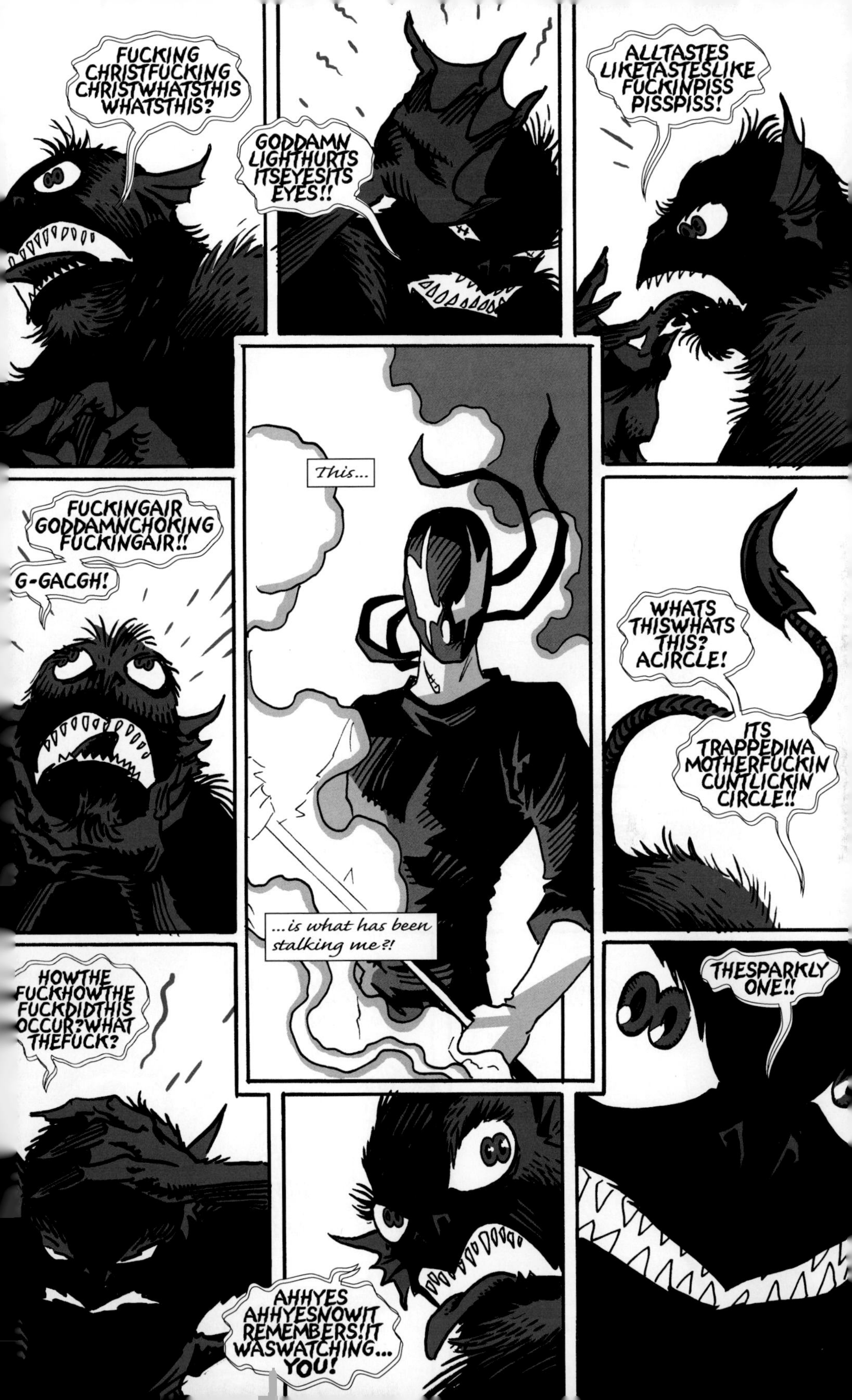
FUCKING CHRISTFUCKING CHRISTWHATSTHIS WHATSTHIS?
GODDAMN LIGHTHURTS ITSEYESITS EYES!!
ALLTASTES LIKETASTESLIKE FUCKINPISS PISSPISS!
This...
FUCKINGAIR GODDAMNCHOKING FUCKINGAIR!!
G-GACGH!
WHATS THISWHATS THIS? ACIRCLE!
ITS TRAPPEDINA MOTHERFUCKIN CUNTLICKIN CIRCLE!!
...is what has been stalking me?!
HOWTHE FUCKHOWTHE FUCKDIDTHIS OCCUR?WHAT THEFUCK?
THESPARKLY ONE!!
AHHYES AHHYESNOWIT REMEMBERS!IT WASWATCHING... YOU!

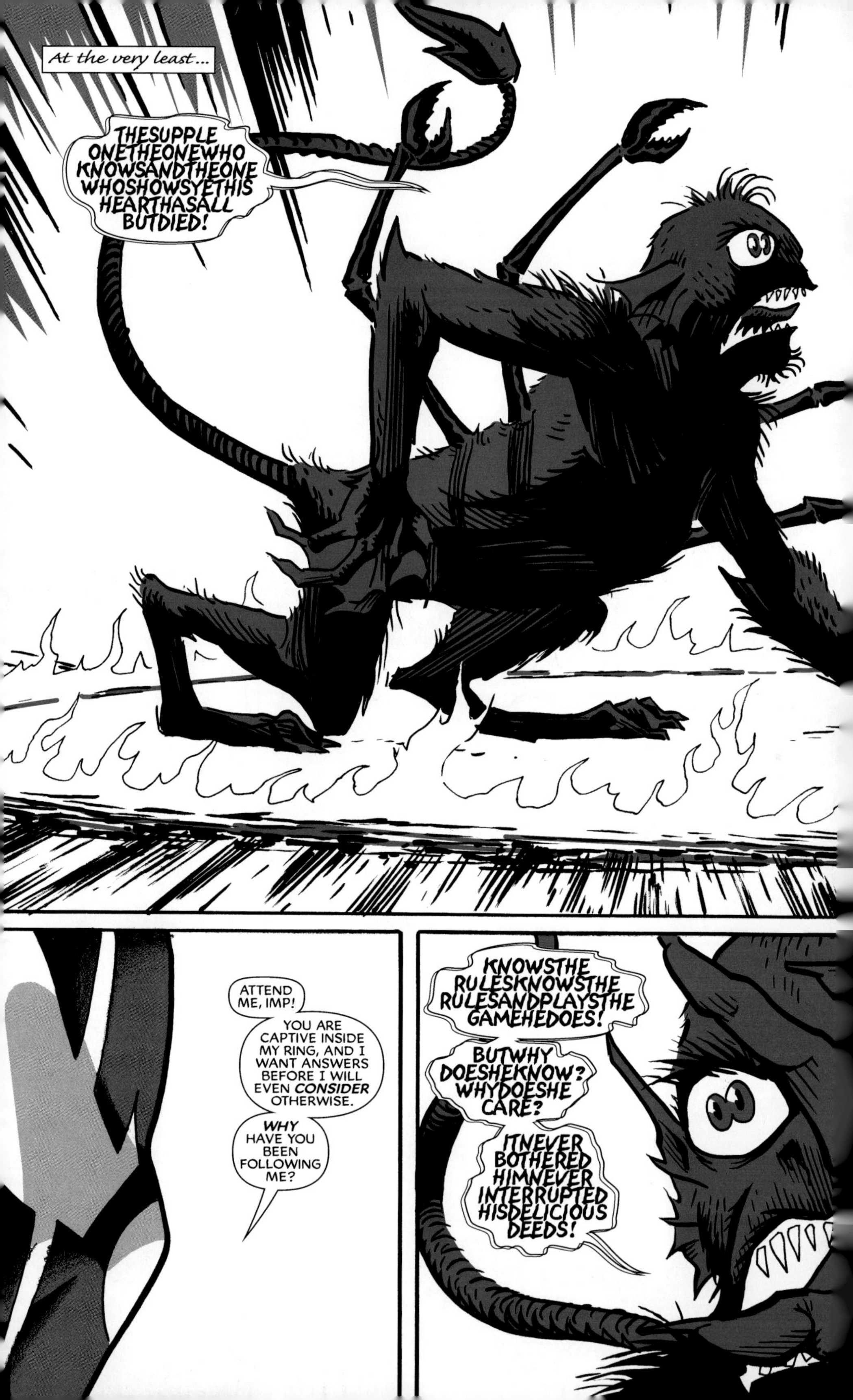
At the very least...
THESUPPLE ONETHEONEWHO KNOWSANDTHEONE WHOSHOWSYETHIS HEARTHASALL BUTDIED!
ATTEND ME, IMP!
YOU ARE CAPTIVE INSIDE MY RING, AND I WANT ANSWERS BEFORE I WILL EVEN CONSIDER OTHERWISE.
WHY HAVE YOU BEEN FOLLOWING ME?
KNOWSTHE RULESKNOWSTHE RULESANDPLAYSTHE GAMEHEDOES!
BUTWHY DOESHEKNOW? WHYDOESHE CARE?
ITNEVER BOTHERED HIMNEVER INTERRUPTED HISDELICIOUS DEEDS!

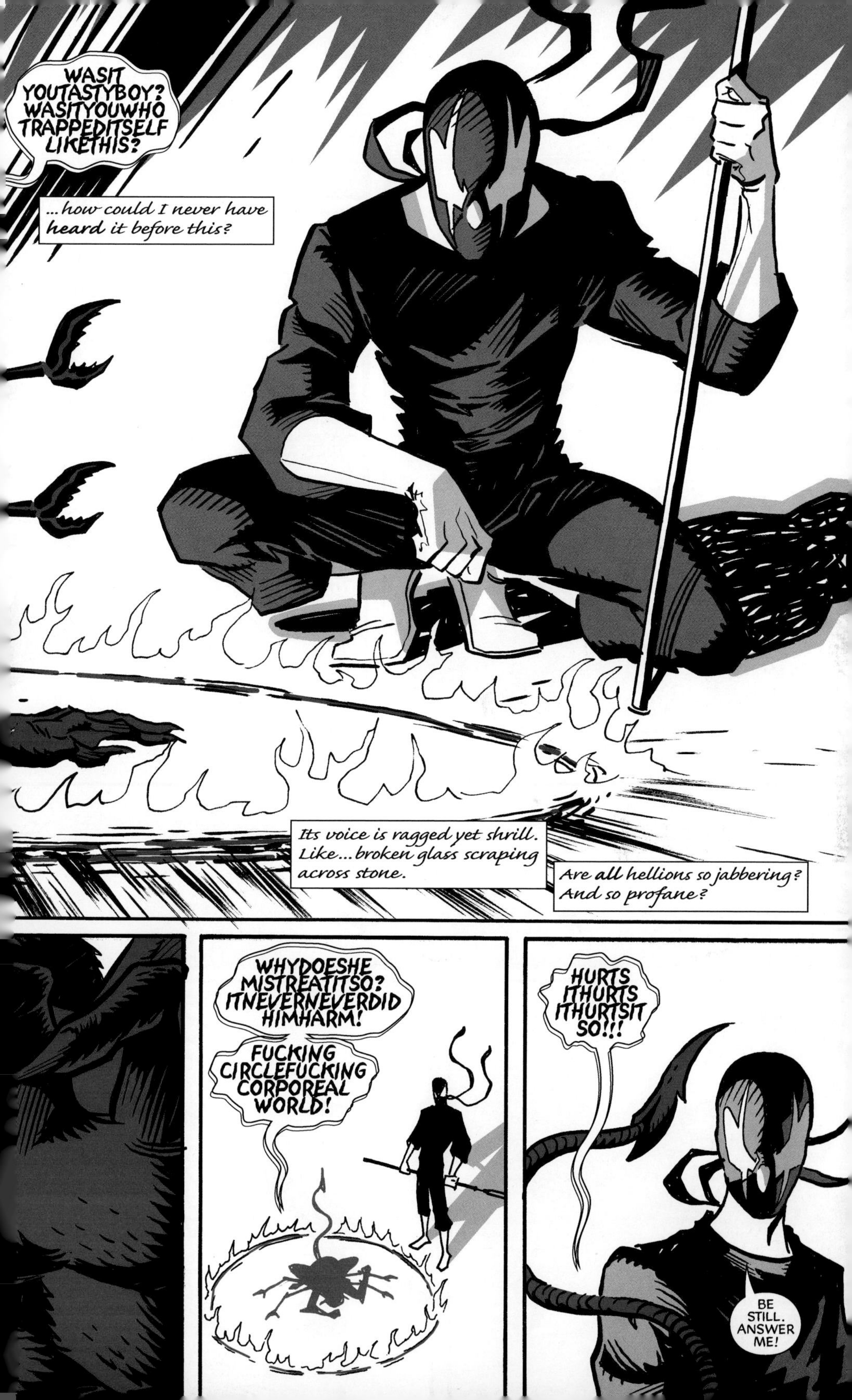
WASIT YOUTASTYBOY? WASITYOUWHO TRAPPEDITSELF LIKETHIS?
...how could I never have heard it before this?
Its voice is ragged yet shrill. Like...broken glass scraping across stone.
Are all hellions so jabbering? And so profane?
WHYDOESHE MISTREATITSO? ITNEVERNEVERDID HIMHARM!
FUCKING CIRCLEFUCKING CORPOREAL WORLD!
HURTS ITHURTS ITHURTSIT SO!!!
BE STILL. ANSWER ME!

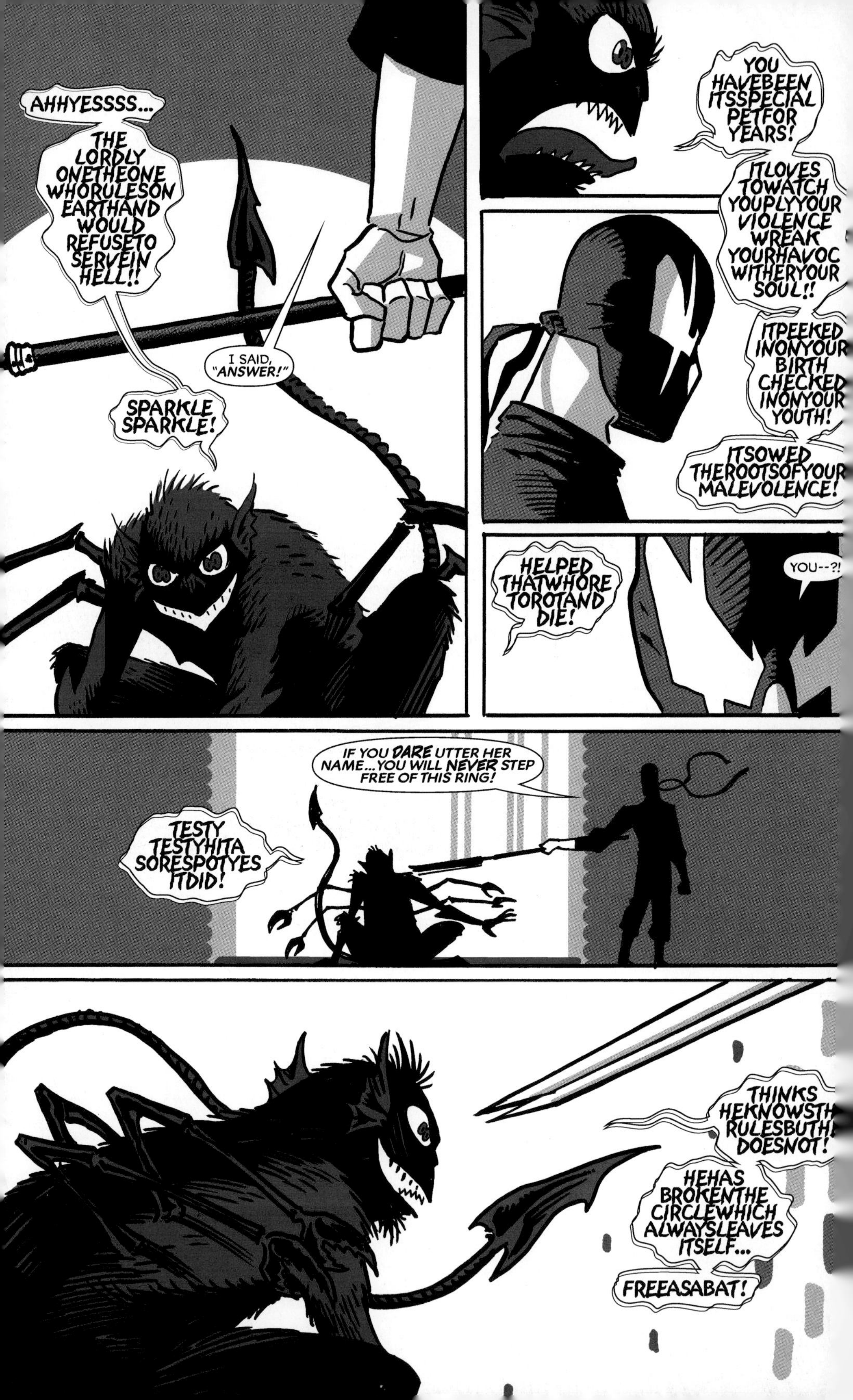
AHHYESSSS...
THE LORDLY ONETHEONE WHORULESON EARTHAND WOULD REFUSETO SERVEIN HELL!!
I SAID, "ANSWER!"
SPARKLE SPARKLE!
YOU HAVEBEEN ITSSPECIAL PETFOR YEARS!
ITLOVES TOWATCH YOUPLYYOUR VIOLENCE WREAK YOURHAVOC WITHERYOUR SOUL!!
ITPEEKED INONYOUR BIRTH CHECKED INONYOUR YOUTH!
ITSOWED THEROOTSOFYOUR MALEVOLENCE!
HELPED THATWHORE TOROTAND DIE!
YOU--?!
IF YOU DARE UTTER HER NAME... YOU WILL NEVER STEP FREE OF THIS RING!
TESTY TESTYHITA SORESPOTYES ITDID!
HEHAS BROKENTHE CIRCLEWHICH ALWAYSLEAVES ITSELF...
FREEASABAT!

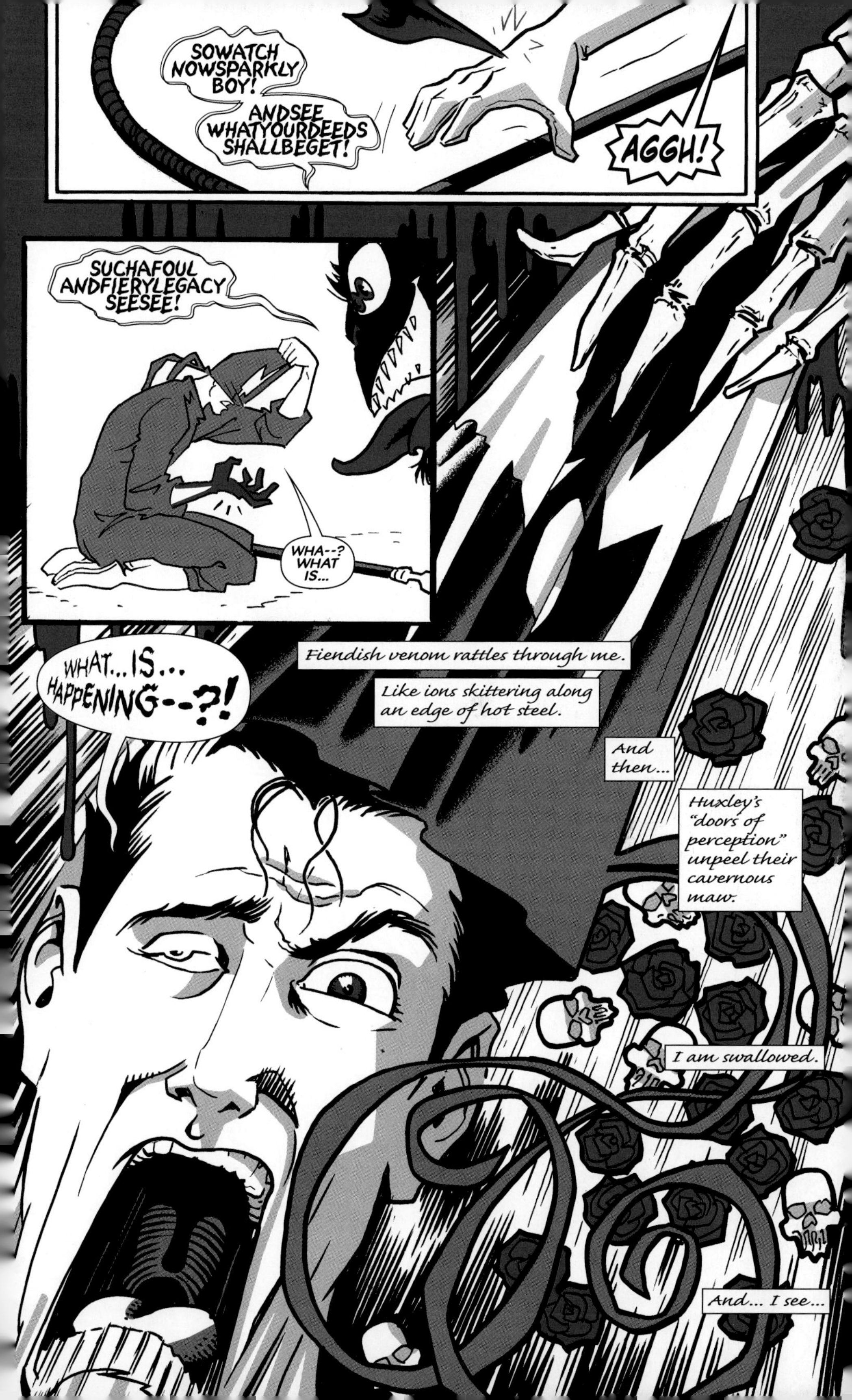
SOWATCH NOWSPARKLY BOY!
ANDSEE WHATYOURDEEDS SHALLBEGET!
AGGH!
SUCHAFOUL ANDFIERYLEGACY SEESEE!
WHA--? WHAT IS...
WHAT...IS... HAPPENING--?!
Fiendish venom rattles through me.
Like ions skittering along an edge of hot steel.
And then...
Huxley's "doors of perception" unpeel their cavernous maw.
I am swallowed.
And... I see...

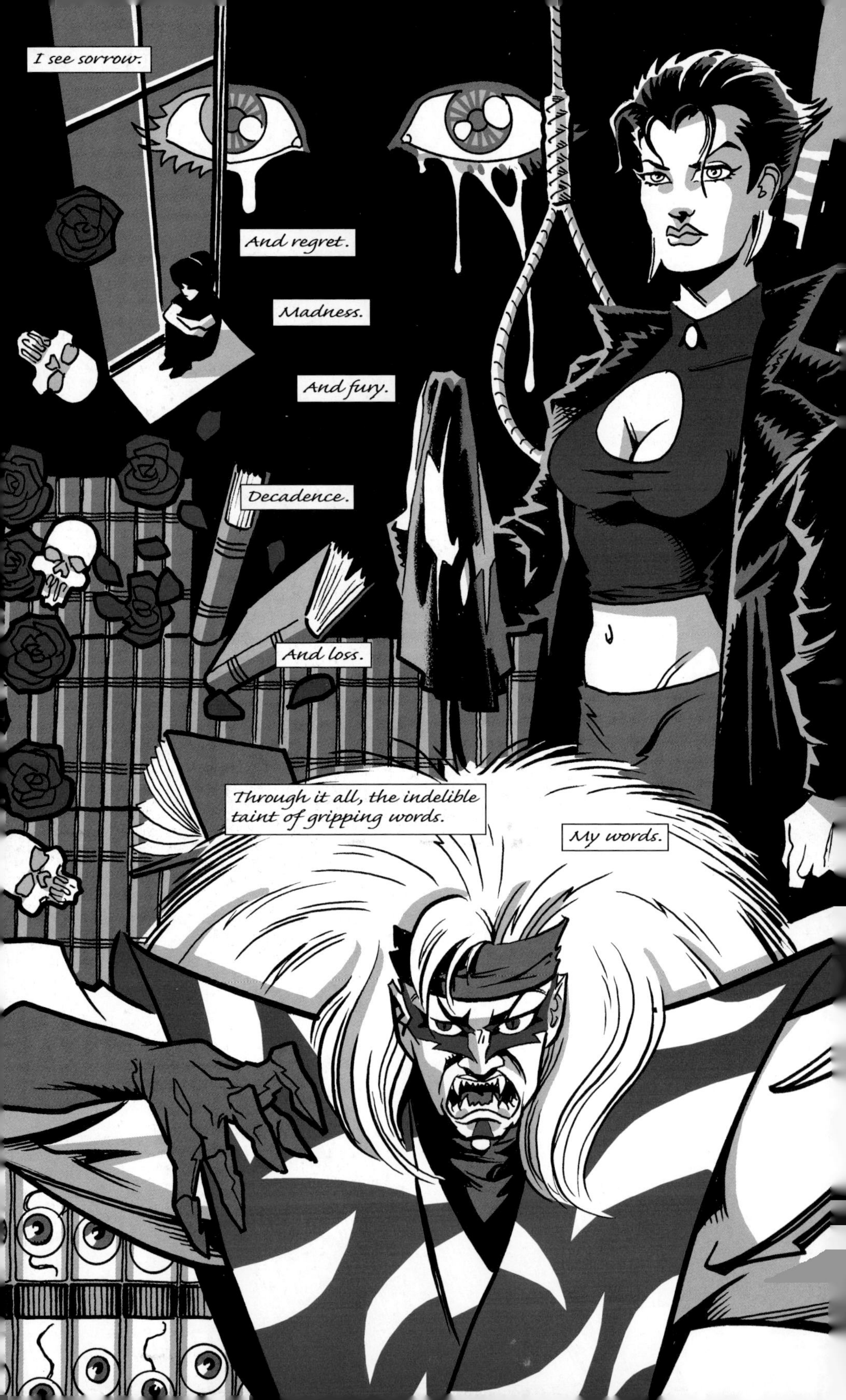
I see sorrow.
And regret.
Madness.
And fury.
Decadence.
And loss.
Through it all, the indelible taint of gripping words.
My words.

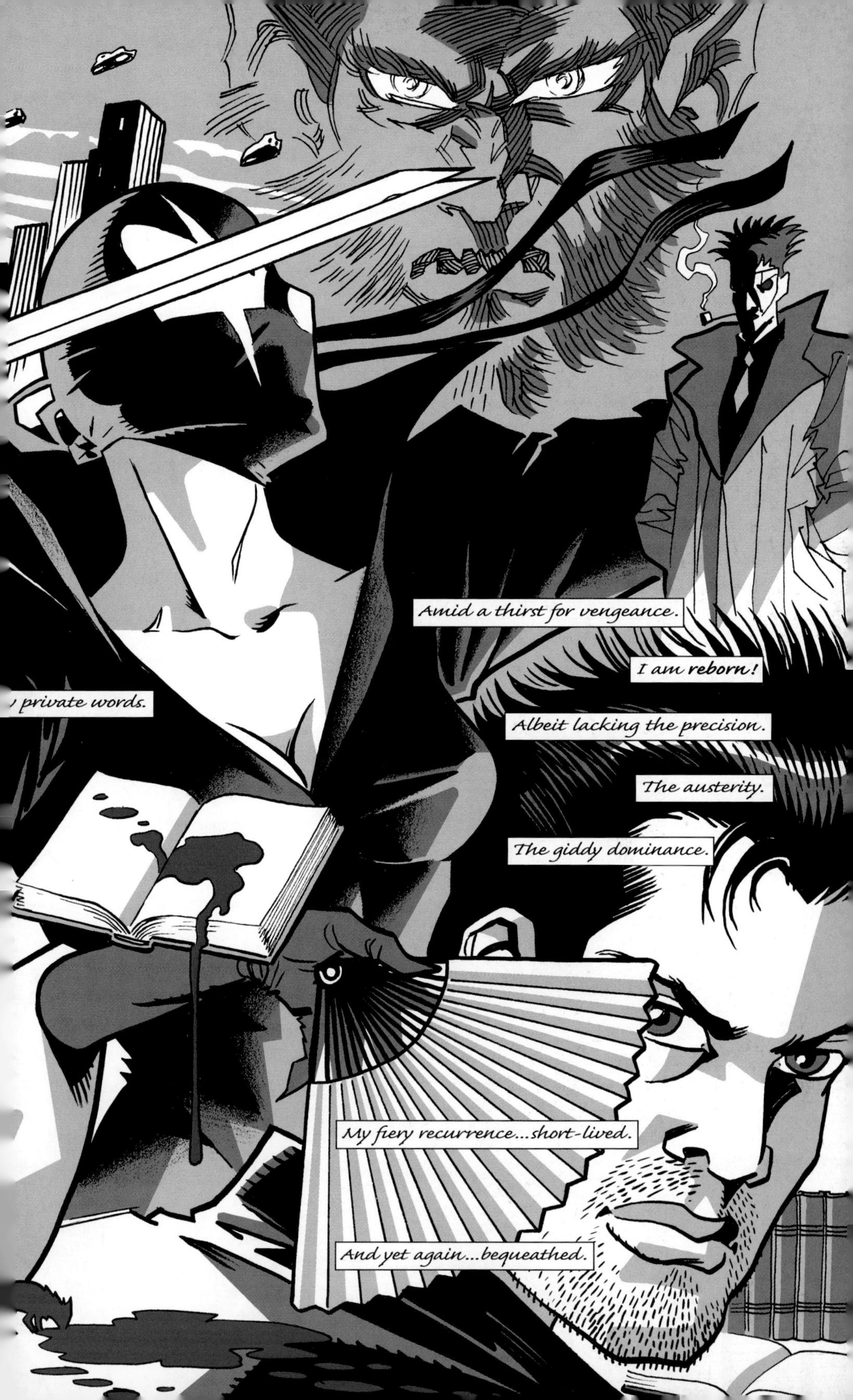
Amid a thirst for vengeance.
I am reborn!
private words.
Albeit lacking the precision.
The austerity.
The giddy dominance.
My fiery recurrence...short-lived.
And yet again...bequeathed.

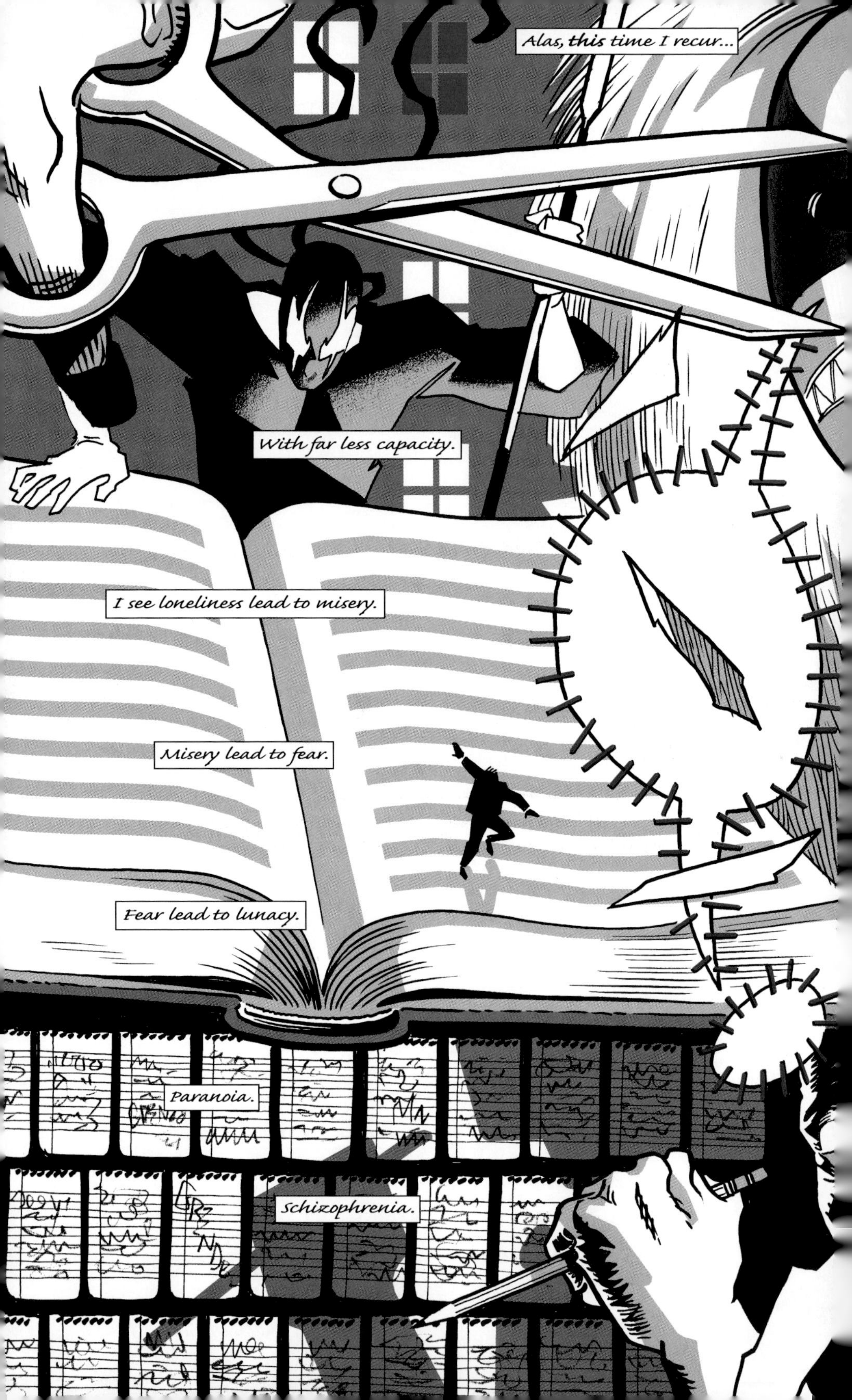
Alas, this time I recur...
With far less capacity.
I see loneliness lead to misery.
Misery lead to fear.
Fear lead to lunacy.
Paranoia.
Schizophrenia.

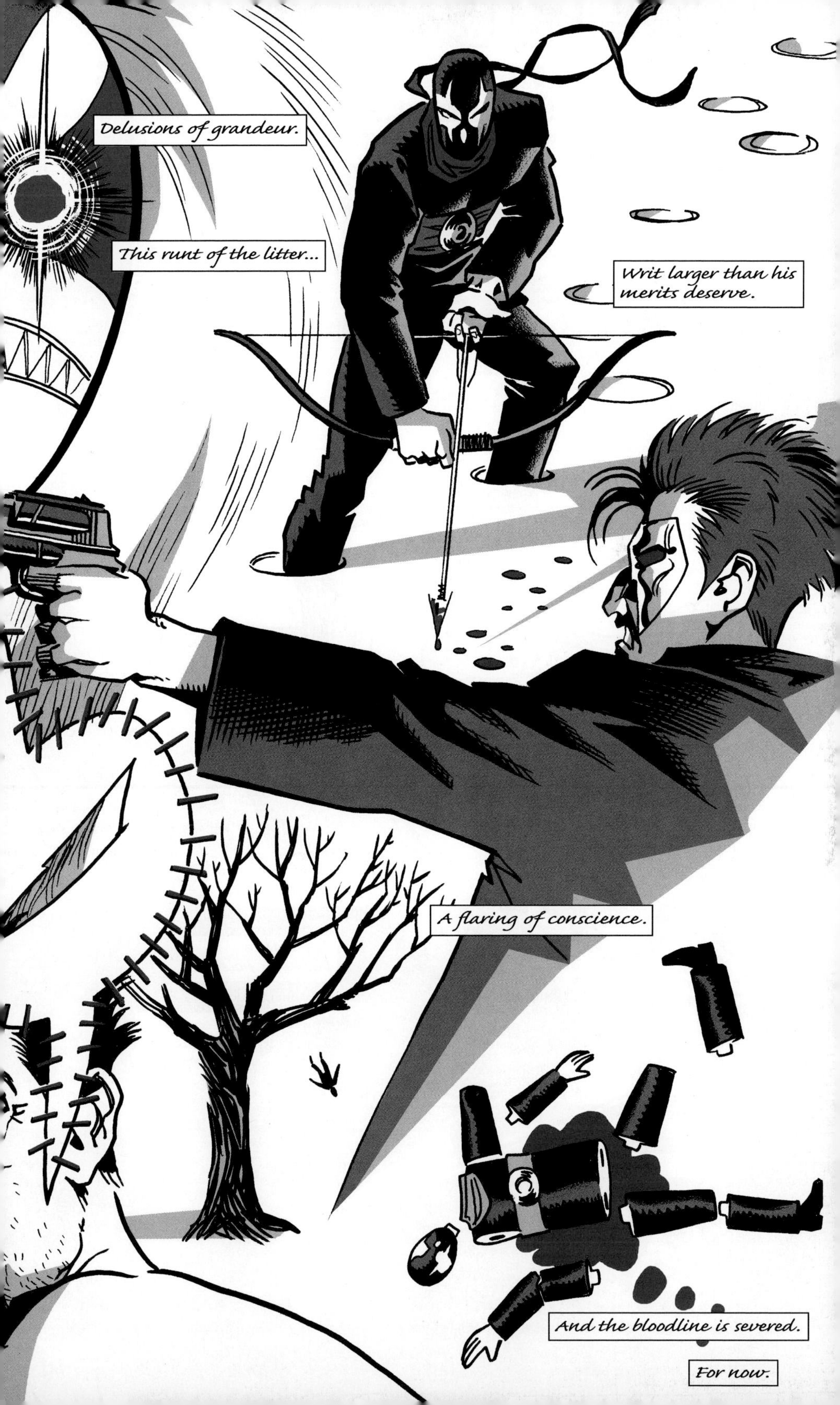
Delusions of grandeur.
This runt of the litter...
Writ larger than his merits deserve.
A flaring of conscience.
And the bloodline is severed.
For now.

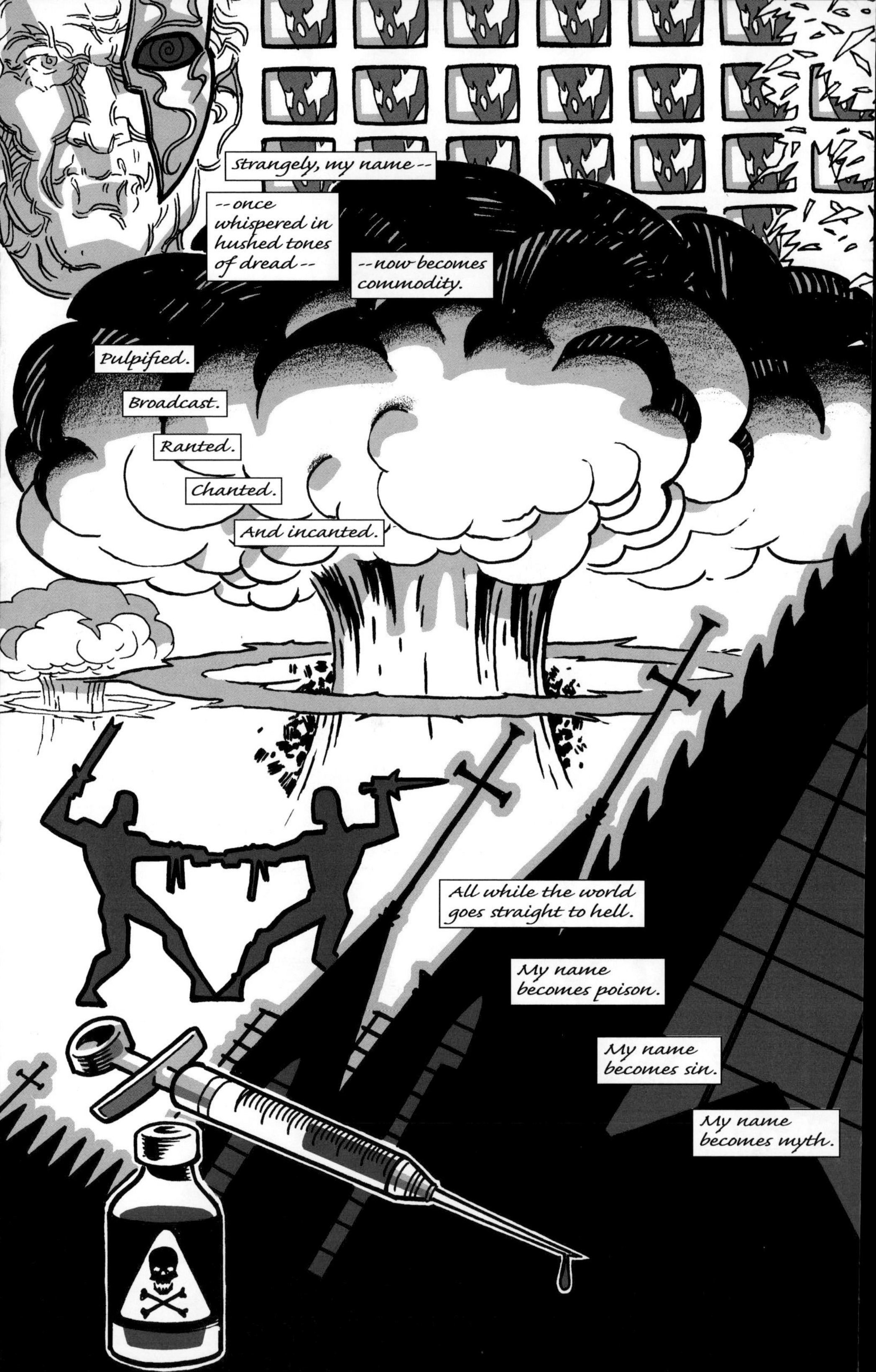
Strangely, my name--
--once whispered in hushed tones of dread--
--now becomes commodity.
Pulpified.
Broadcast.
Ranted.
Chanted.
And incanted.
All while the world goes straight to hell.
My name becomes poison.
My name becomes sin.
My name becomes myth.

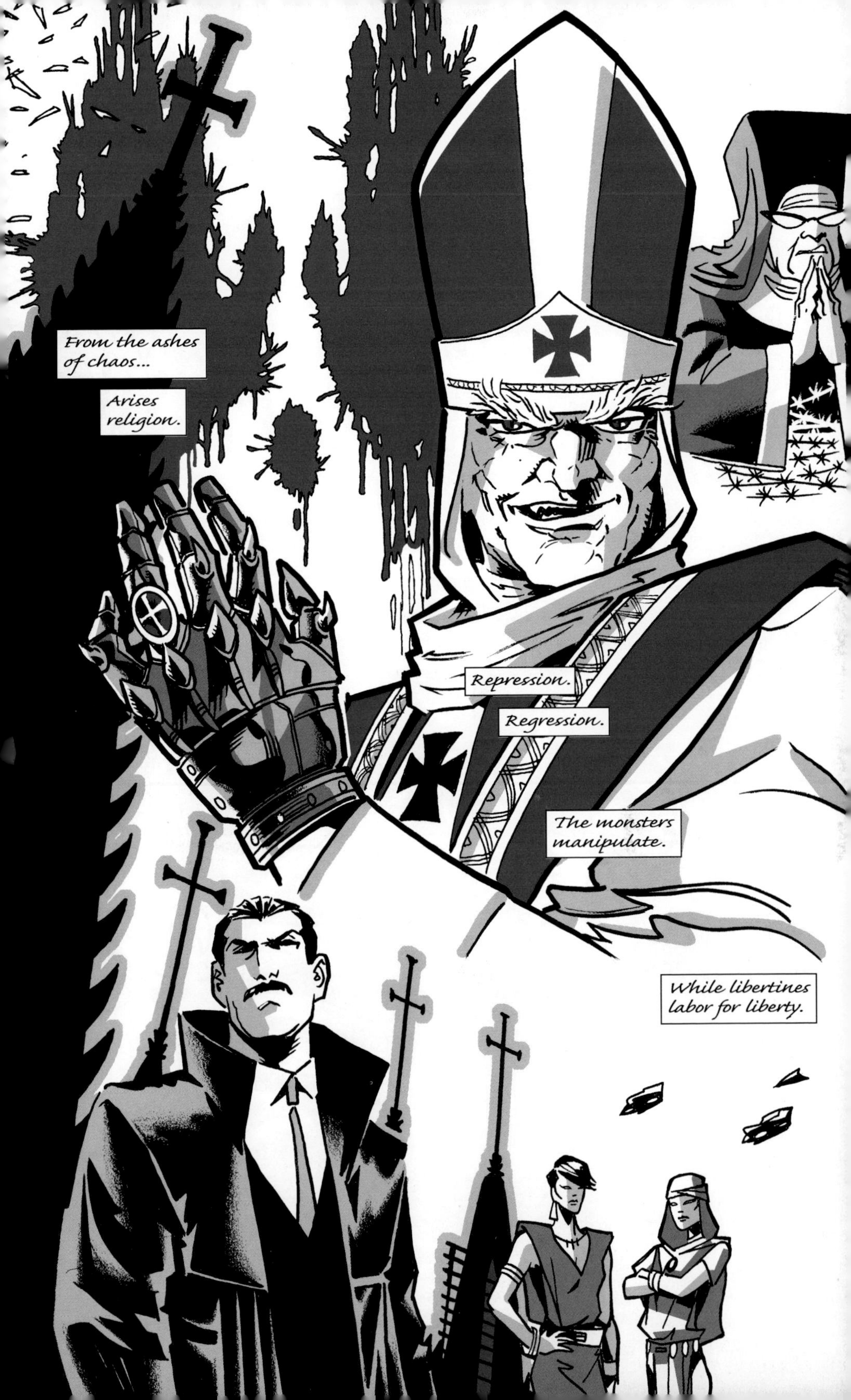
From the ashes of chaos...
Arises religion.
Repression.
Regression.
The monsters manipulate.
While libertines labor for liberty.

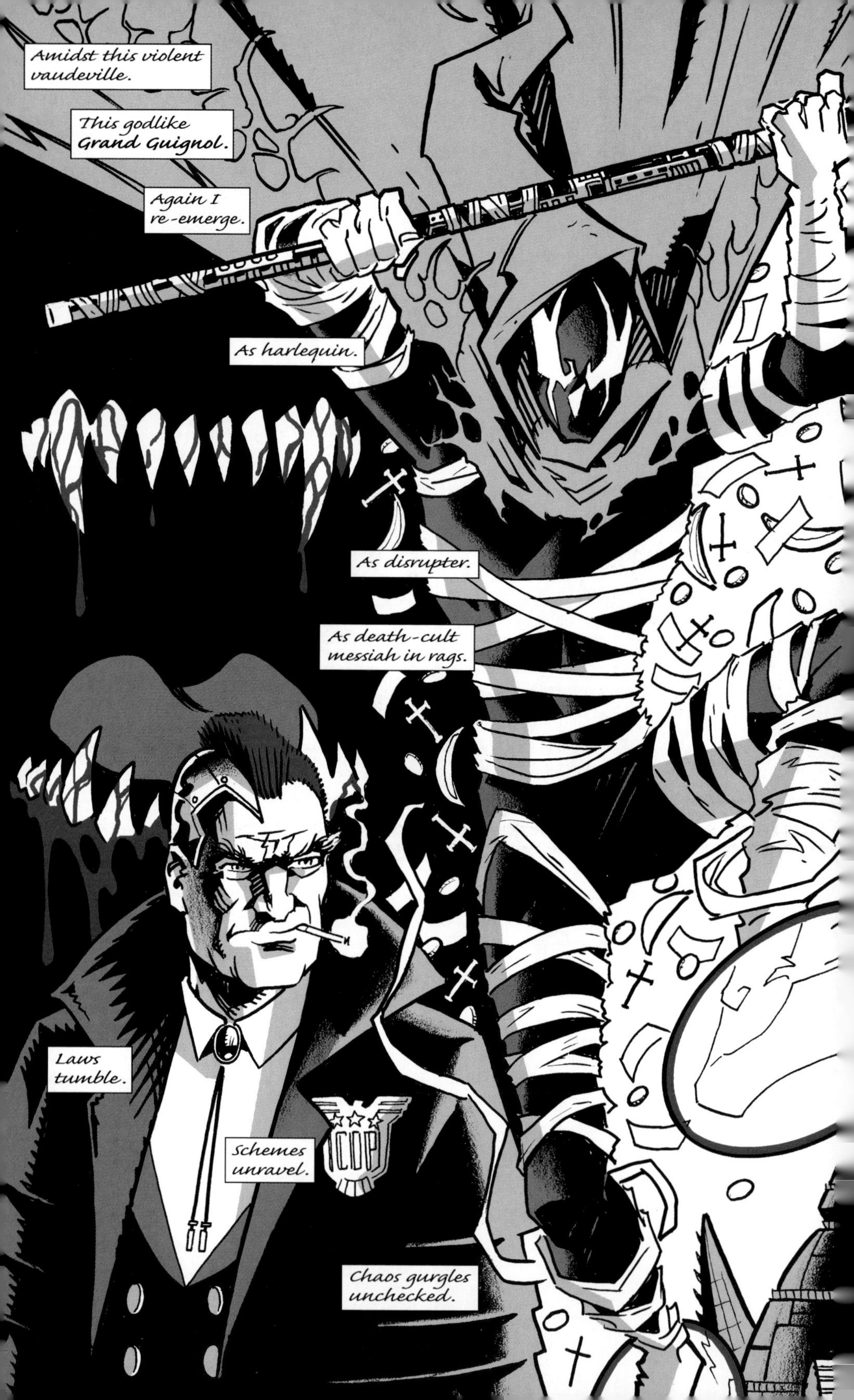
Amidst this violent vaudeville.
This godlike Grand Guignol.
Again I re-emerge.
As harlequin.
As disrupter.
As death-cult messiah in rags.
Laws tumble.
Schemes unravel.
Chaos gurgles unchecked.

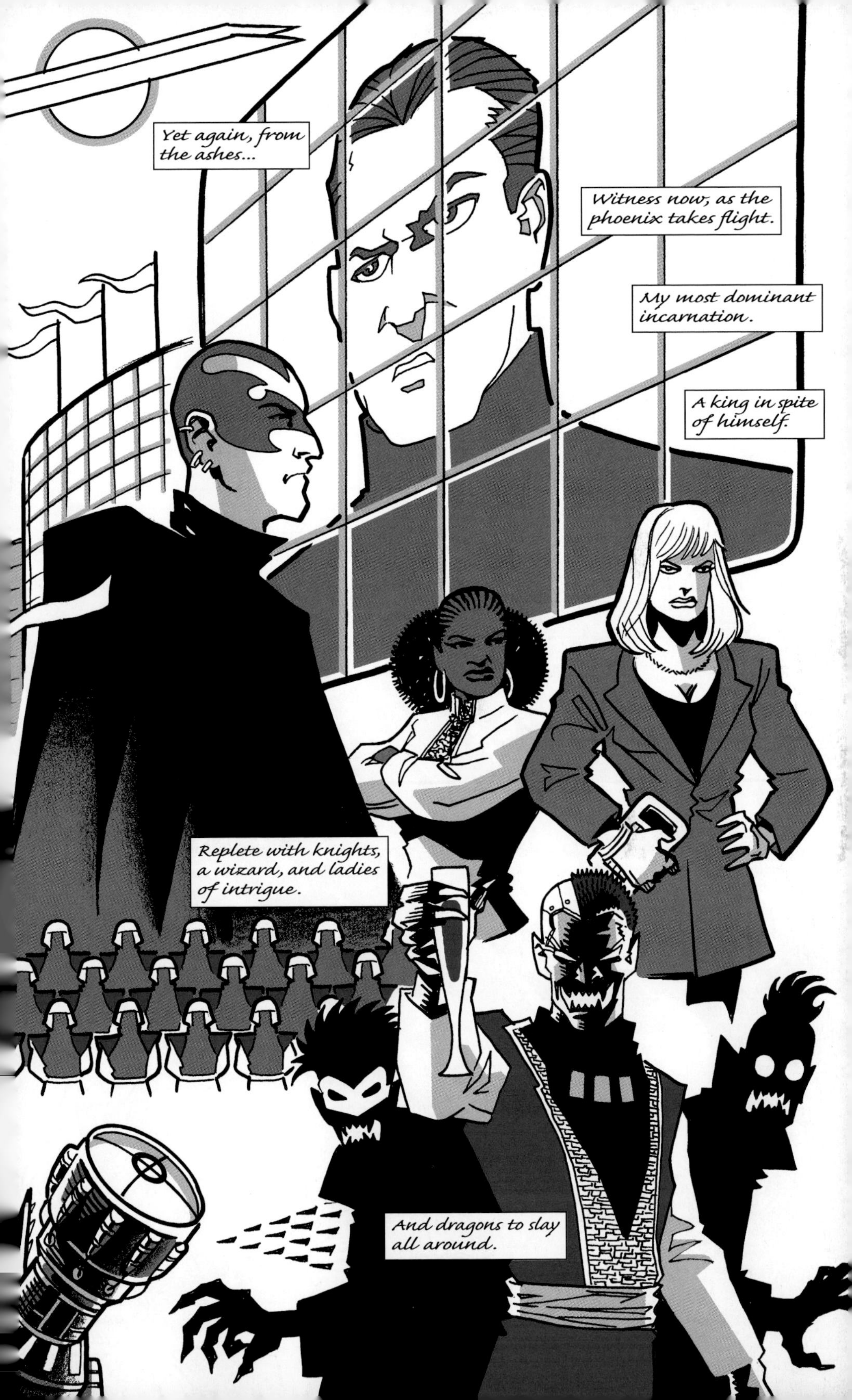
Yet again, from the ashes...
Witness now, as the phoenix takes flight.
My most dominant incarnation.
A king in spite of himself.
Replete with knights, a wizard, and ladies of intrigue.
And dragons to slay all around.

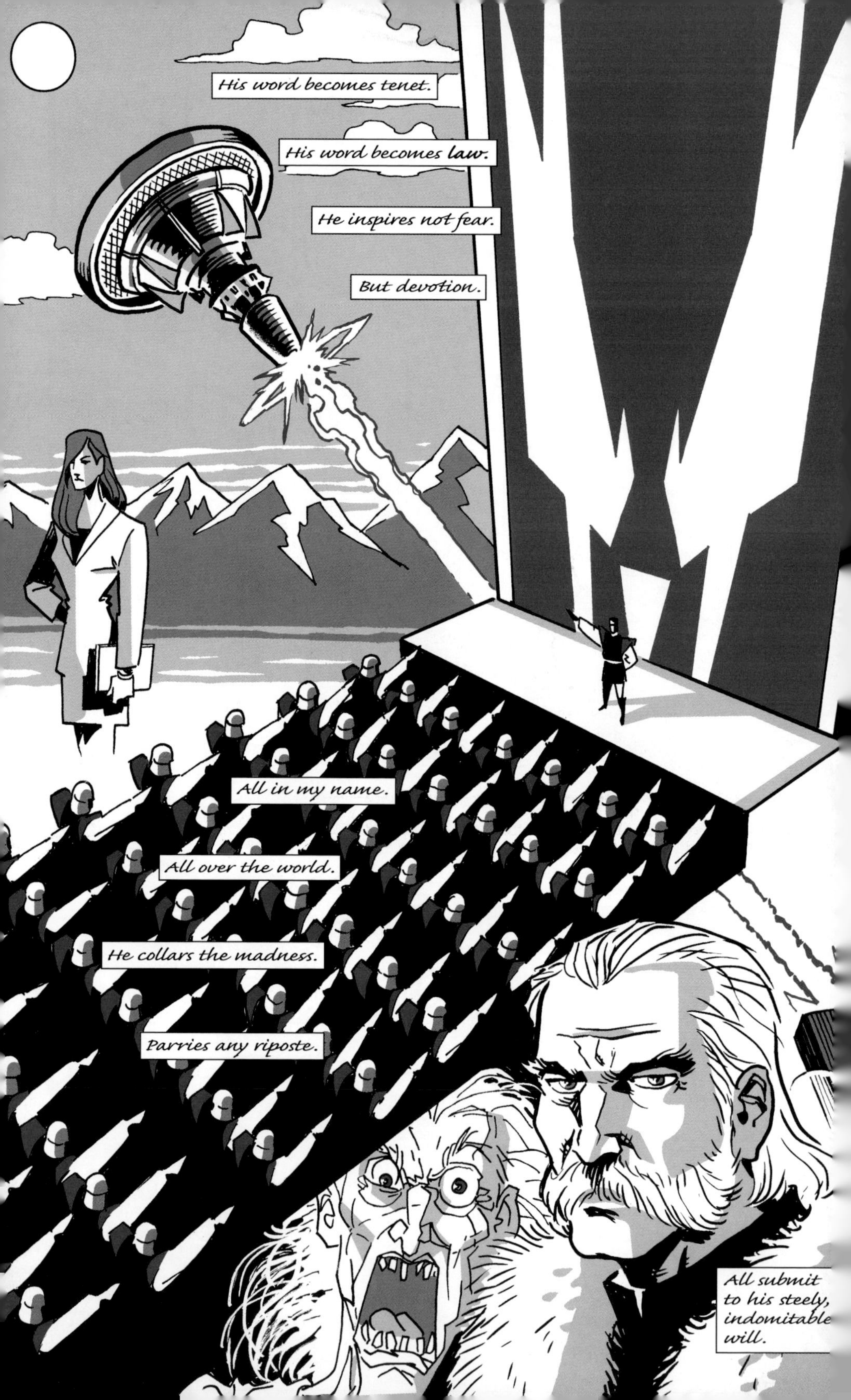
His word becomes tenet.
His word becomes **law.**
He inspires not fear.
But devotion.
All in my name.
All over the world.
He collars the madness.
Parries any riposte.
All submit to his steely, indomitable will.

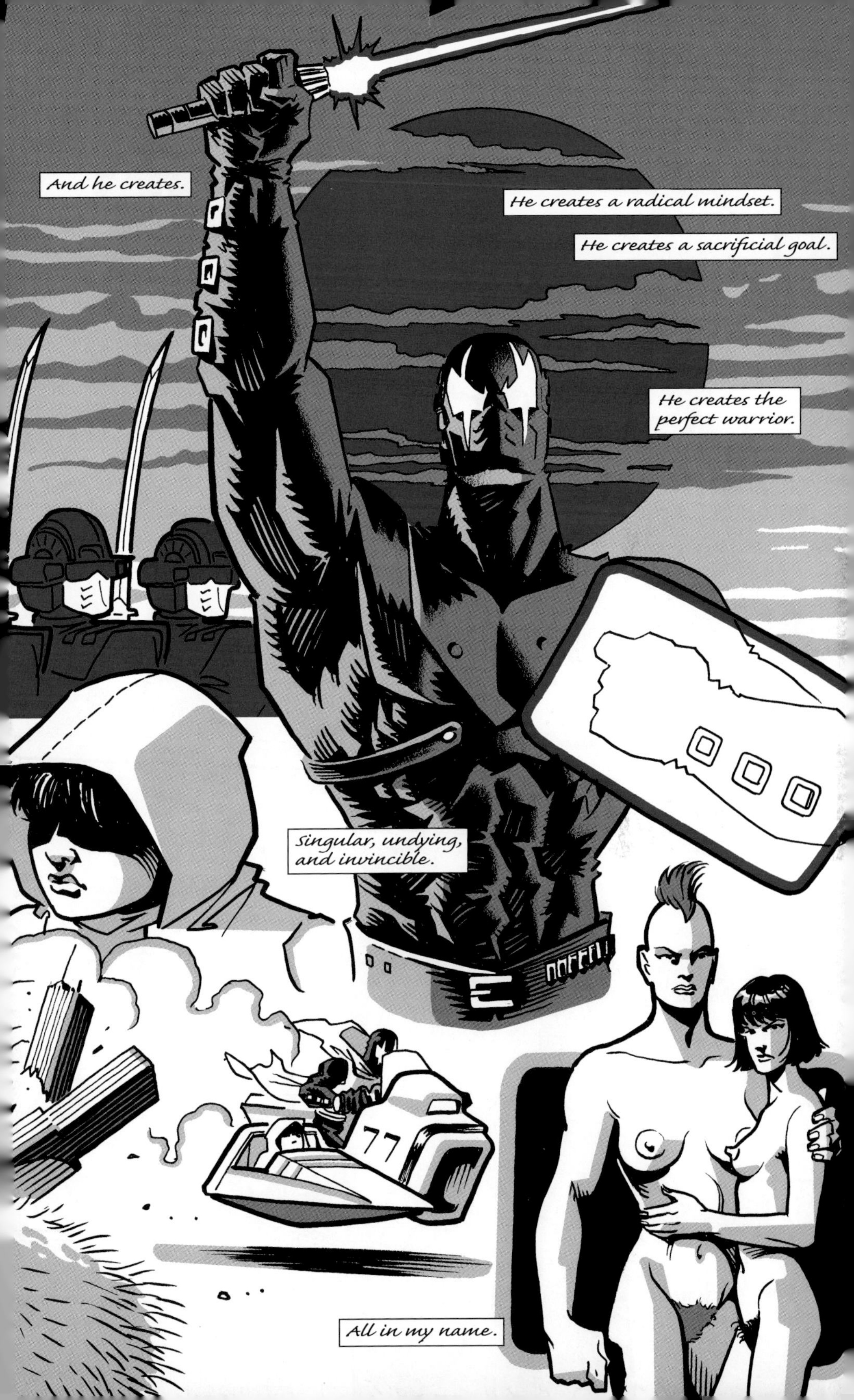
And he creates.
He creates a radical mindset.
He creates a sacrificial goal.
He creates the perfect warrior.
Singular, undying, and invincible.
All in my name.

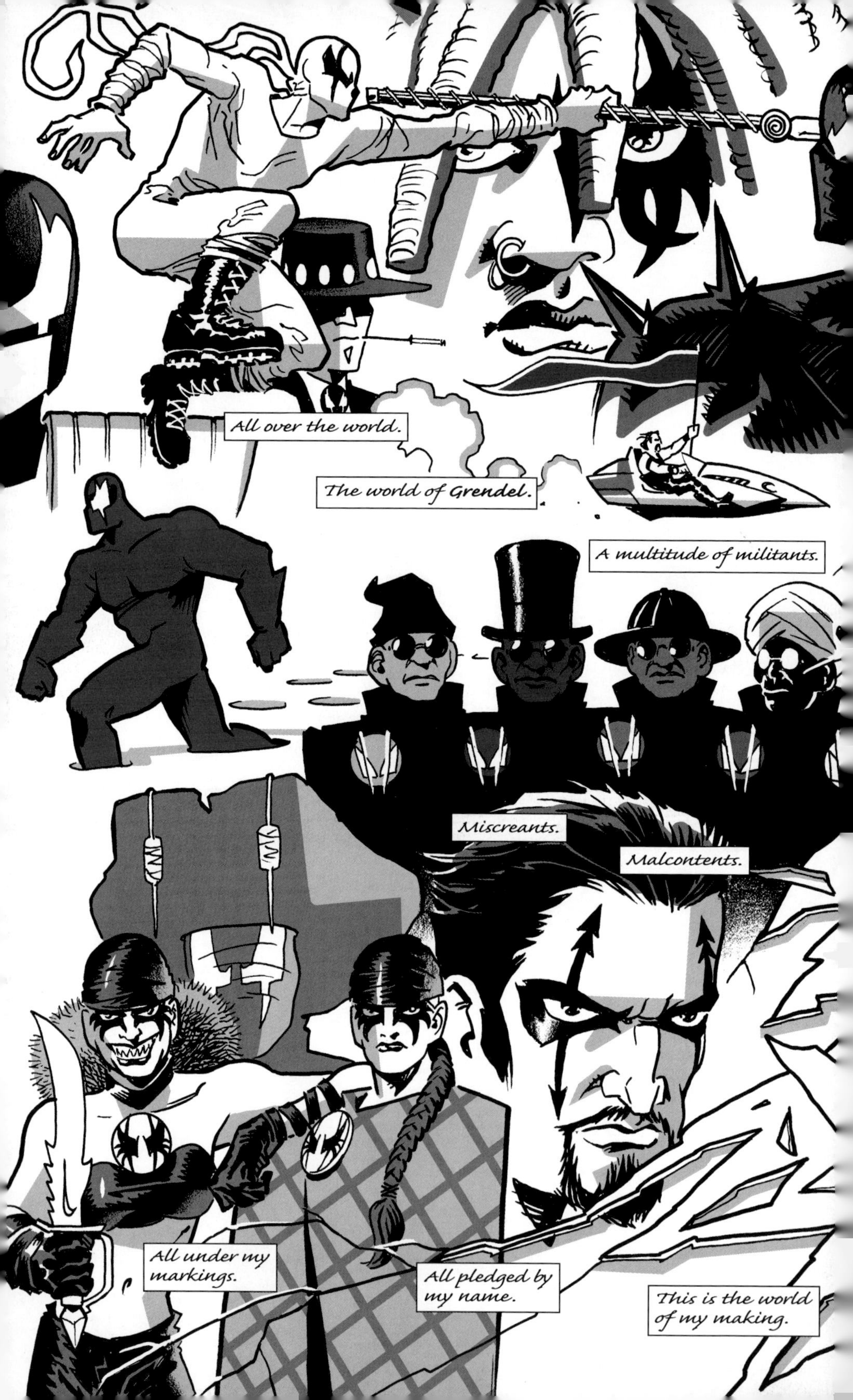
All over the world.
The world of Grendel.
A multitude of militants.
Miscreants.
Malcontents.
All under my markings.
All pledged by my name.
This is the world of my making.

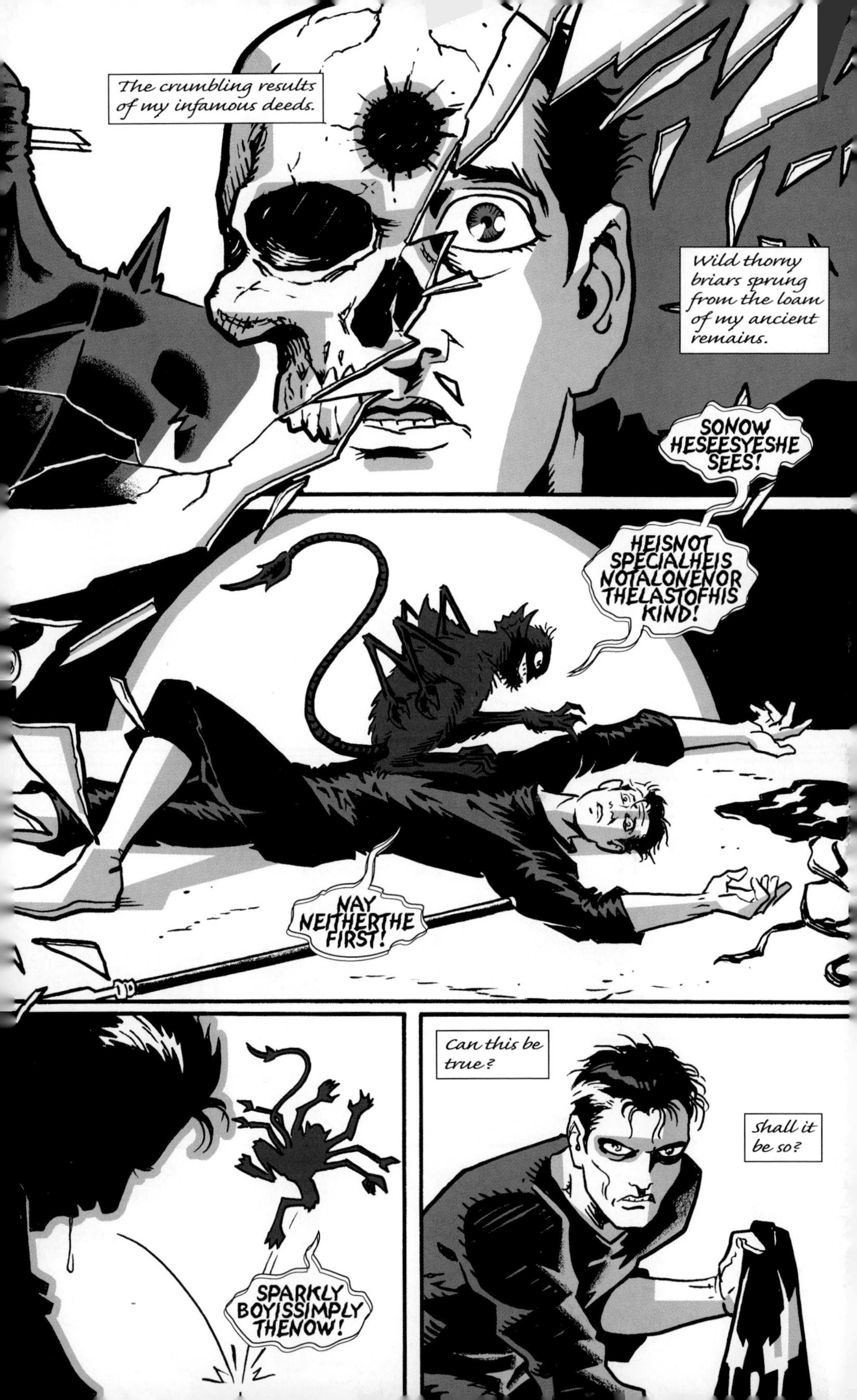
The crumbling results of my infamous deeds.
Wild thorny briars sprung from the loam of my ancient remains.
SONOW HESEESYESHE SEES!
HEISNOT SPECIALHEIS NOTALONENOR THELASTOFHIS KIND!
NAY NEITHERTHE FIRST!
SPARKLY BOYISSIMPLY THENOW!
Can this be true?
Shall it be so?

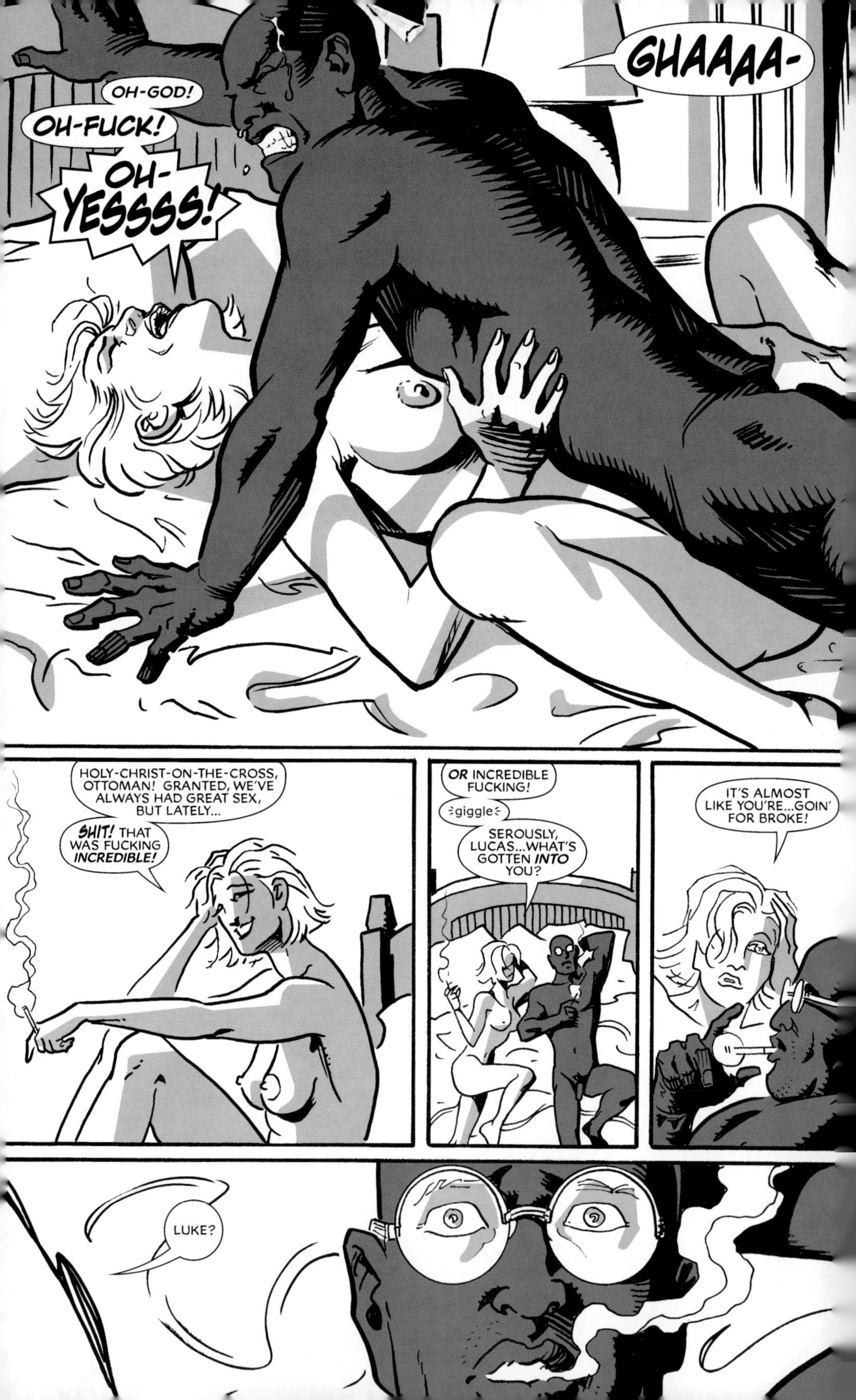
OH-GOD!
OH-FUCK!
OH-YESSSS!
GHAAAA-
HOLY-CHRIST-ON-THE-CROSS, OTTOMAN! GRANTED, WE'VE ALWAYS HAD GREAT SEX, BUT LATELY...
SHIT! THAT WAS FUCKING ***INCREDIBLE!***
OR INCREDIBLE FUCKING!
giggle
SEROUSLY, LUCAS...WHAT'S GOTTEN ***INTO*** YOU?
IT'S ALMOST LIKE YOU'RE...GOIN' FOR BROKE!
LUKE?

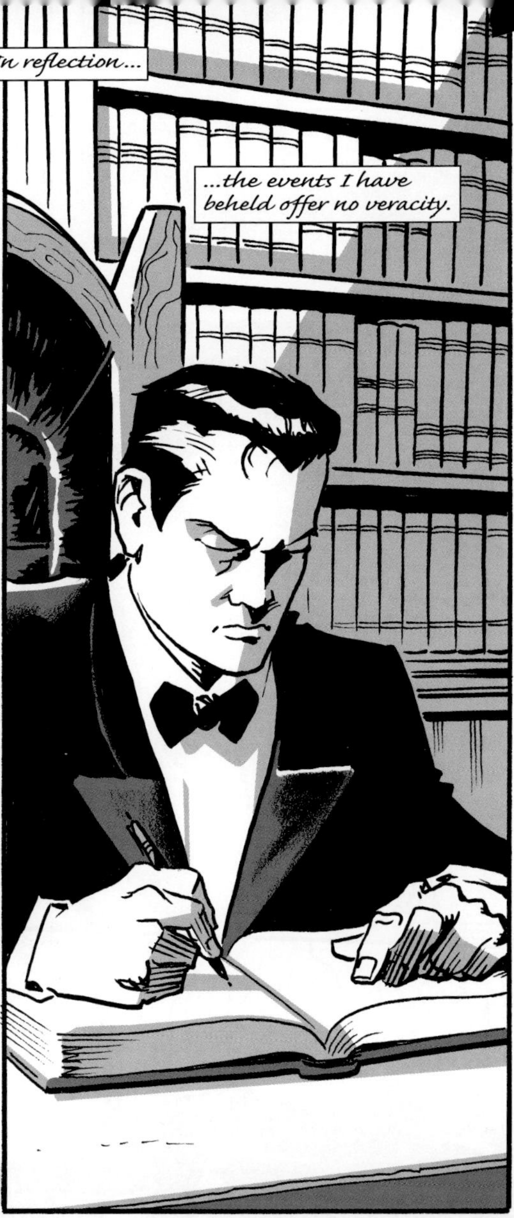
In reflection...
...the events I have beheld offer no veracity.

The demon's prophecy bears no more stamp of authentic revelation than any drug-induced hallucination. Aiding this suspicion is the fact that, since the encounter, I have felt no further evidence of the imp's pestering presence. I no longer feel pursued or observed in any fashion. Once again, I am a living phantom--master of the night.

The notion that I will spawn a history of **Grendels** *yet to come, a phenomenon that will someday encompass the globe, is absurd.*

I will be remembered, but only with awestruck alarm. I will be regarded, but only as a mysterious marvel.

Further, the thought that I am not utterly self-created stands contrary to every fiber of my being. I am **only** *the sum of my own decisions and my own inimitable deeds.*

I am not a resultant. I am extraordinary.

Again, these events I have beheld...

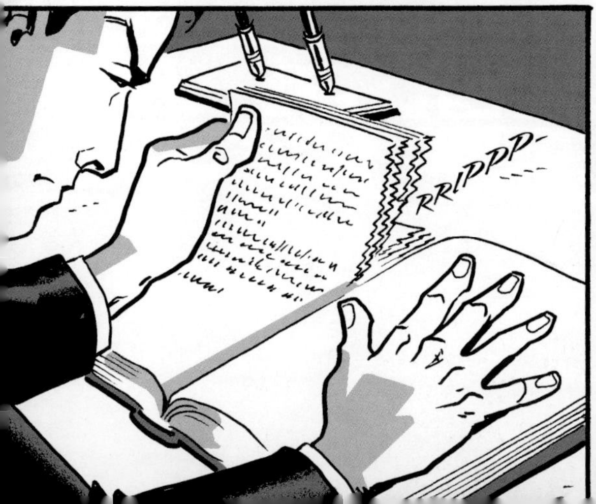
RRIPPP

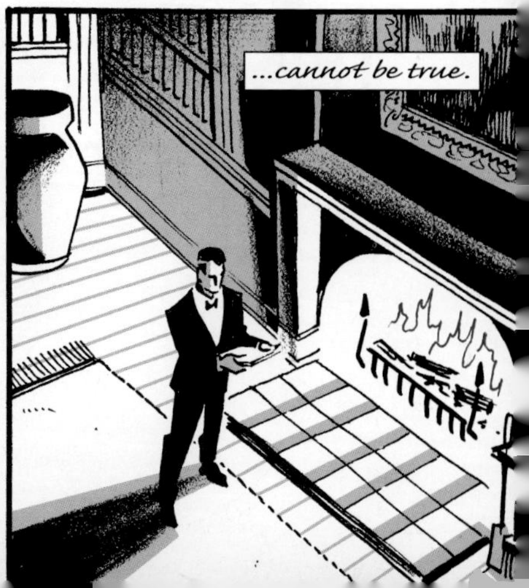
...cannot be true.

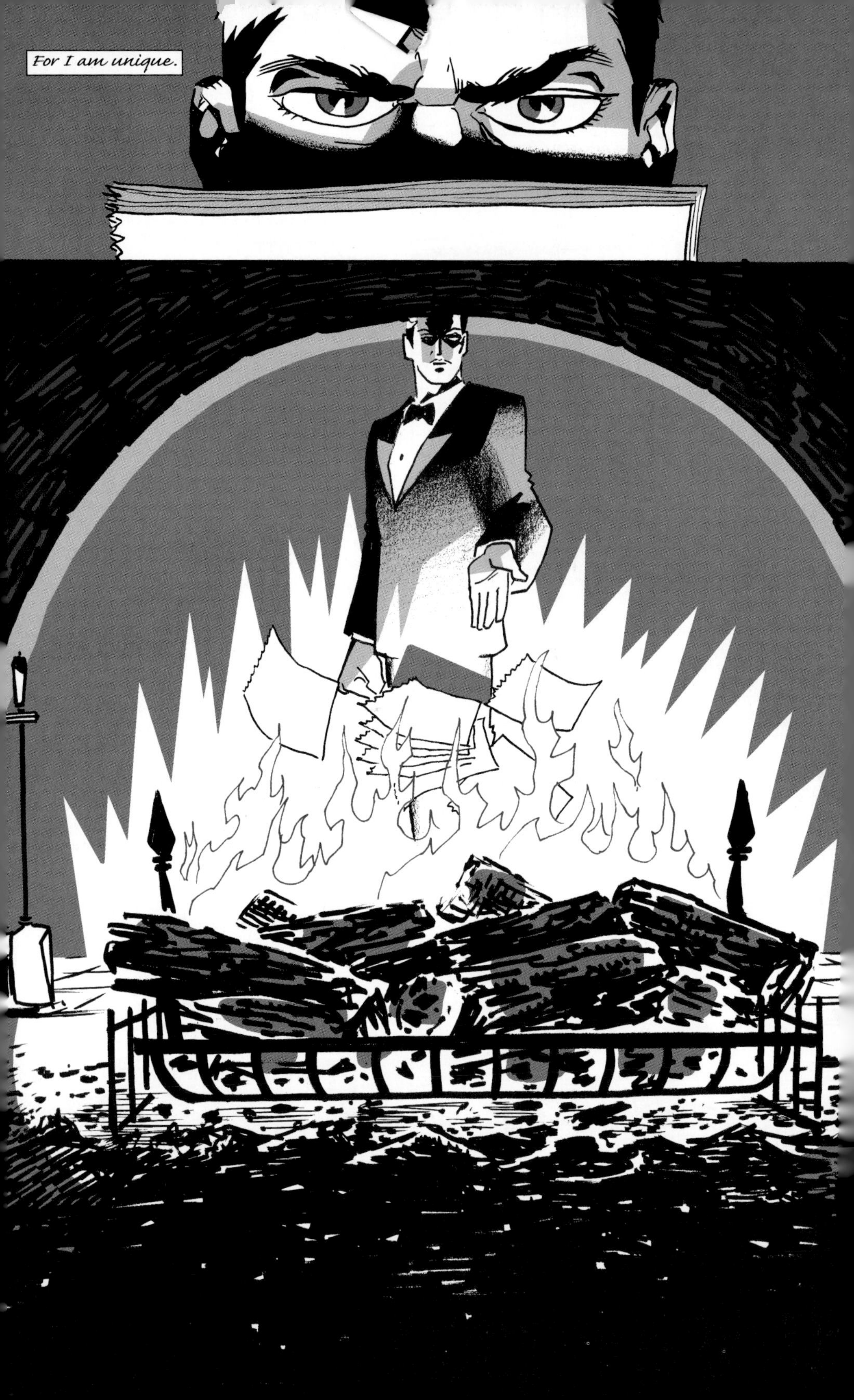
For I am unique.

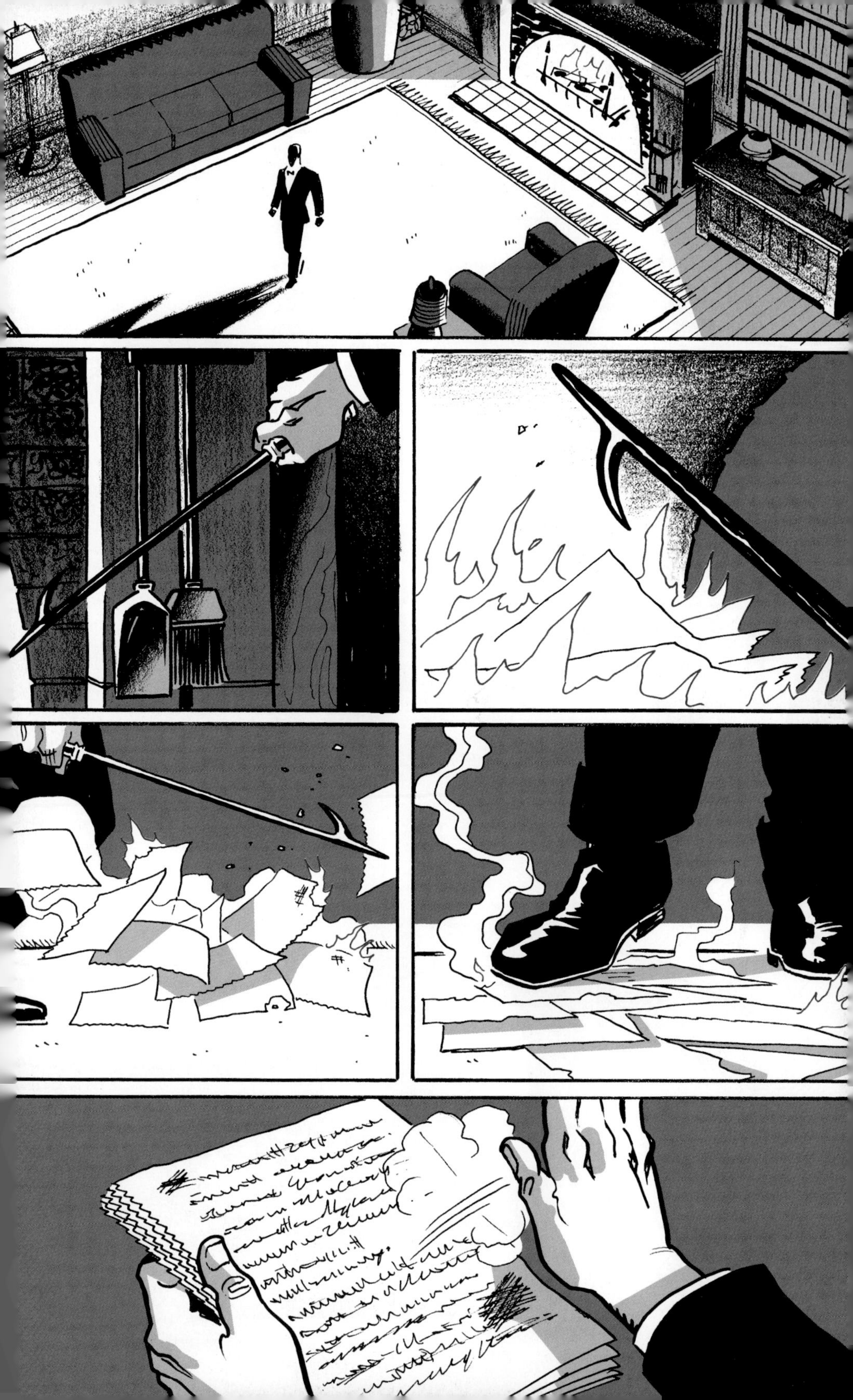

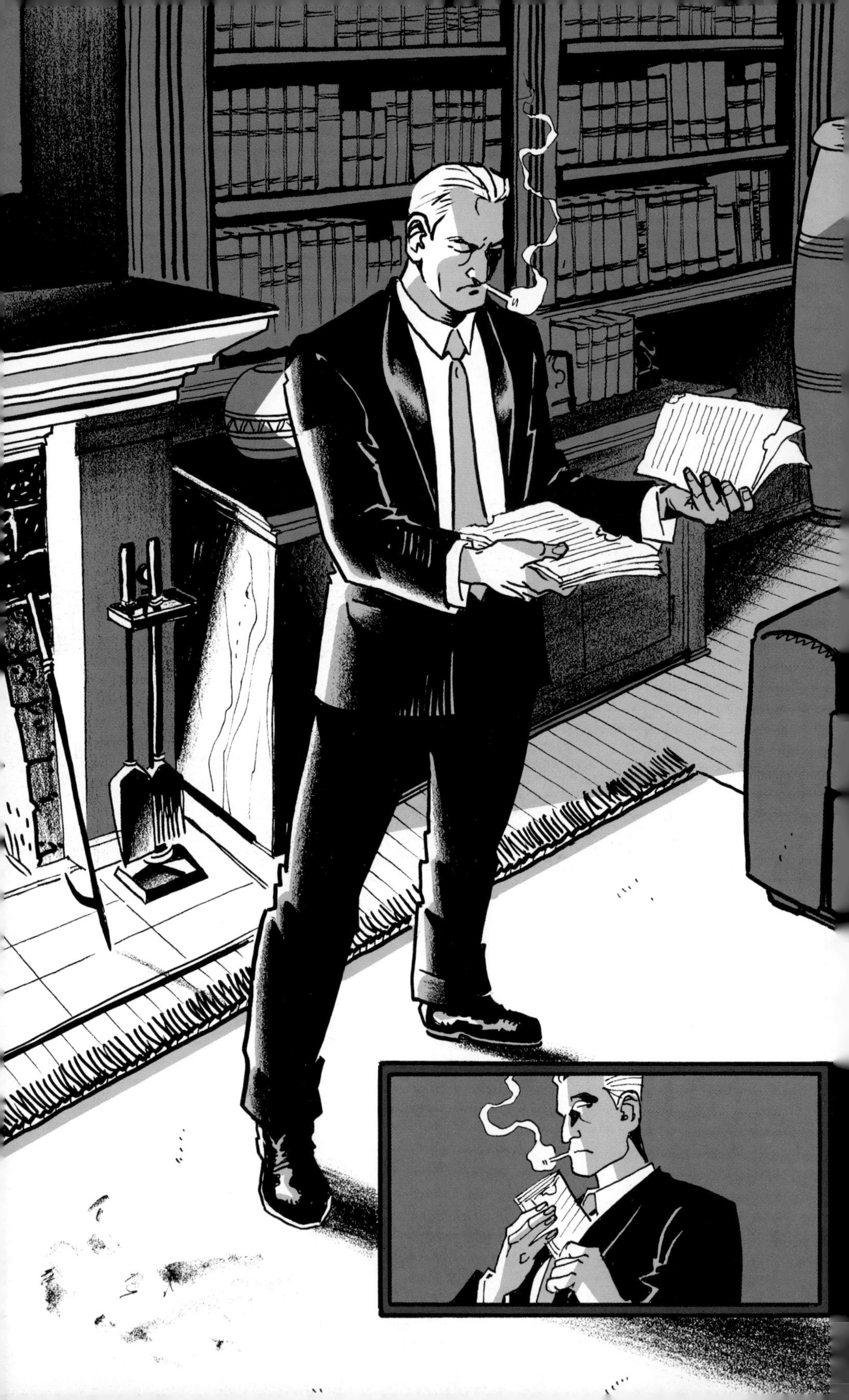

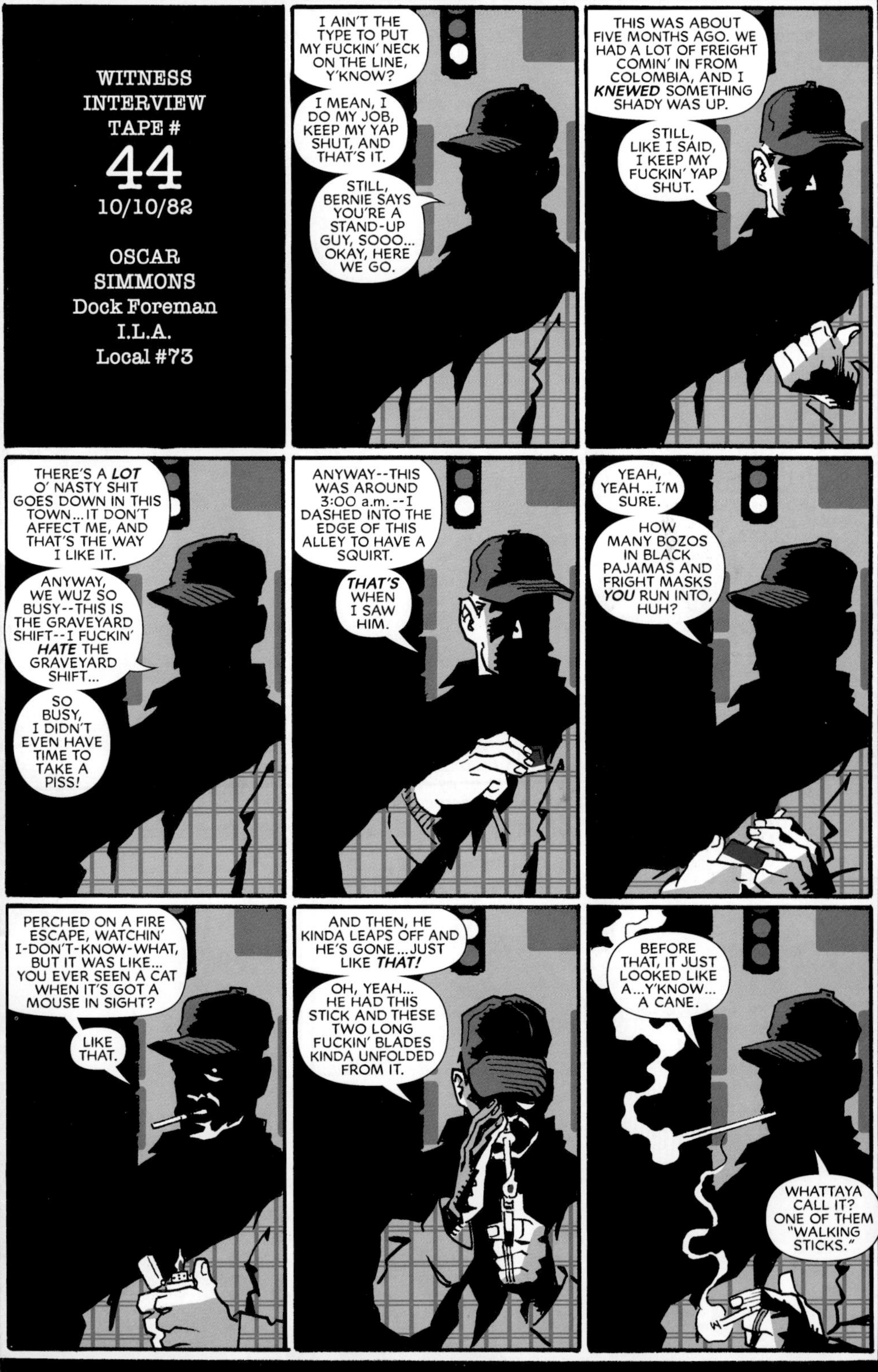
WITNESS INTERVIEW TAPE # 44 10/10/82
OSCAR SIMMONS Dock Foreman I.L.A. Local #73
I AIN'T THE TYPE TO PUT MY FUCKIN' NECK ON THE LINE, Y'KNOW?
I MEAN, I DO MY JOB, KEEP MY YAP SHUT, AND THAT'S IT.
STILL, BERNIE SAYS YOU'RE A STAND-UP GUY, SOOO... OKAY, HERE WE GO.
THIS WAS ABOUT FIVE MONTHS AGO. WE HAD A LOT OF FREIGHT COMIN' IN FROM COLOMBIA, AND I KNEWED SOMETHING SHADY WAS UP.
STILL, LIKE I SAID, I KEEP MY FUCKIN' YAP SHUT.
THERE'S A LOT O' NASTY SHIT GOES DOWN IN THIS TOWN... IT DON'T AFFECT ME, AND THAT'S THE WAY I LIKE IT.
ANYWAY, WE WUZ SO BUSY--THIS IS THE GRAVEYARD SHIFT--I FUCKIN' HATE THE GRAVEYARD SHIFT...
SO BUSY, I DIDN'T EVEN HAVE TIME TO TAKE A PISS!
ANYWAY--THIS WAS AROUND 3:00 a.m.--I DASHED INTO THE EDGE OF THIS ALLEY TO HAVE A SQUIRT.
THAT'S WHEN I SAW HIM.
YEAH, YEAH... I'M SURE.
HOW MANY BOZOS IN BLACK PAJAMAS AND FRIGHT MASKS YOU RUN INTO, HUH?
PERCHED ON A FIRE ESCAPE, WATCHIN' I-DON'T-KNOW-WHAT, BUT IT WAS LIKE... YOU EVER SEEN A CAT WHEN IT'S GOT A MOUSE IN SIGHT?
LIKE THAT.
AND THEN, HE KINDA LEAPS OFF AND HE'S GONE... JUST LIKE THAT!
OH, YEAH... HE HAD THIS STICK AND THESE TWO LONG FUCKIN' BLADES KINDA UNFOLDED FROM IT.
BEFORE THAT, IT JUST LOOKED LIKE A... Y'KNOW... A CANE.
WHATTAYA CALL IT? ONE OF THEM "WALKING STICKS."

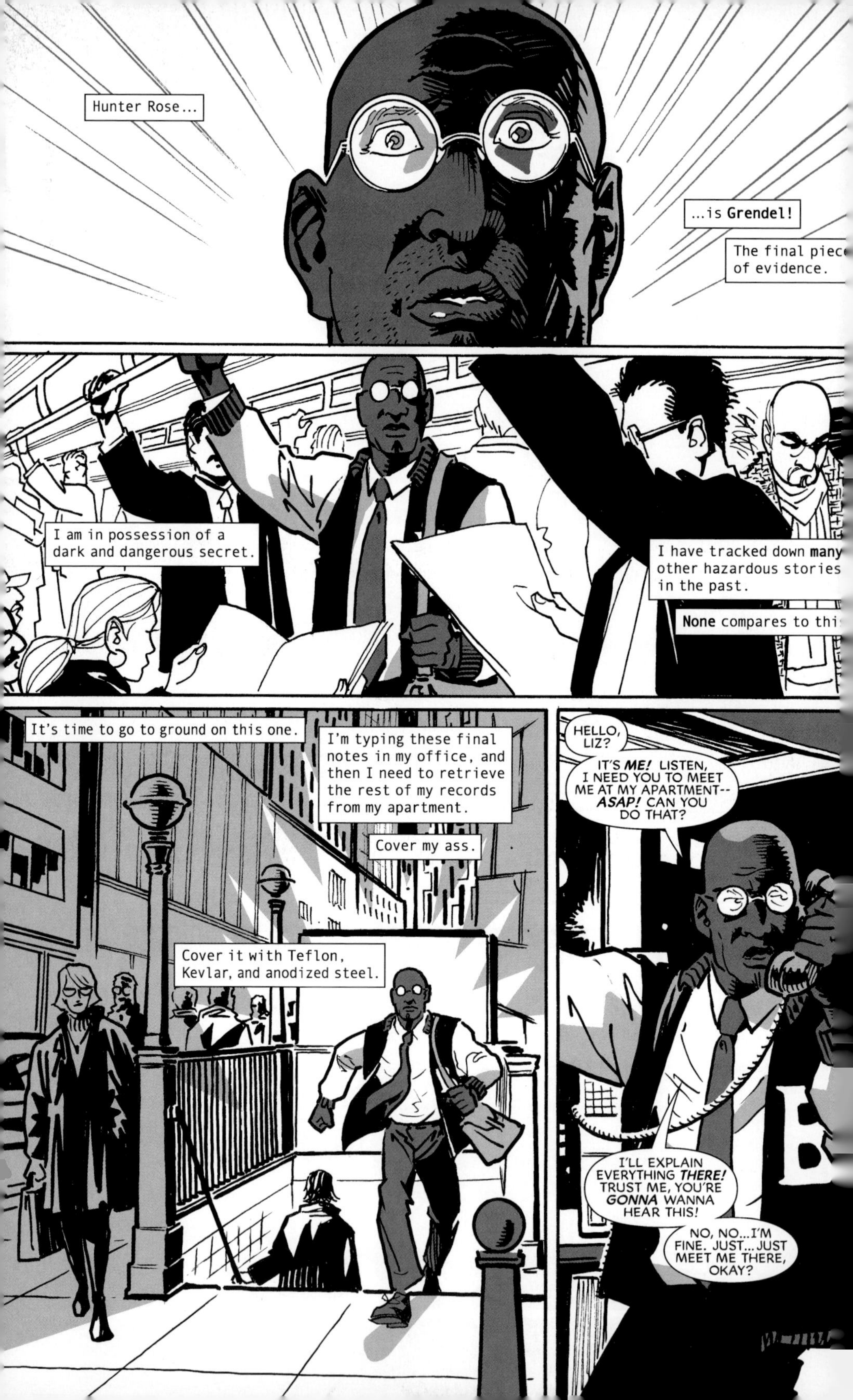

Hunter Rose...
...is **Grendel!**
The final piec
of evidence.
I am in possession of a dark and dangerous secret.
I have tracked down **many** other hazardous stories in the past.
None compares to thi
It's time to go to ground on this one.
I'm typing these final notes in my office, and then I need to retrieve the rest of my records from my apartment.
Cover my ass.
Cover it with Teflon, Kevlar, and anodized steel.
HELLO, LIZ?
IT'S ***ME!*** LISTEN, I NEED YOU TO MEET ME AT MY APARTMENT-- ***ASAP!*** CAN YOU DO THAT?
I'LL EXPLAIN EVERYTHING ***THERE!*** TRUST ME, YOU'RE ***GONNA*** WANNA HEAR THIS!
NO, NO...I'M FINE. JUST...JUST MEET ME THERE, OKAY?

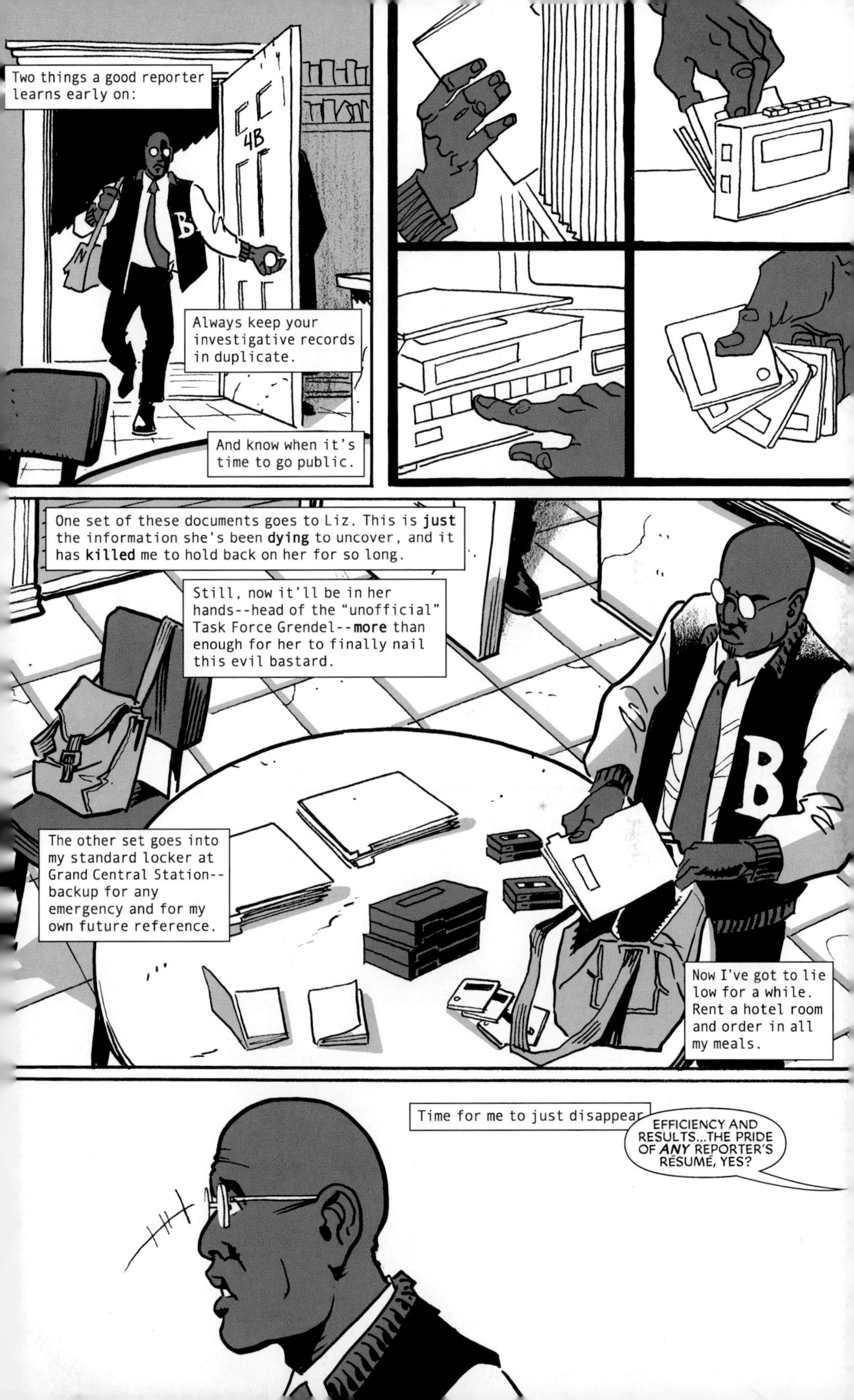

Two things a good reporter learns early on:
Always keep your investigative records in duplicate.
And know when it's time to go public.
One set of these documents goes to Liz. This is **just** the information she's been **dying** to uncover, and it has **killed** me to hold back on her for so long.
Still, now it'll be in her hands--head of the "unofficial" Task Force Grendel--**more** than enough for her to finally nail this evil bastard.
The other set goes into my standard locker at Grand Central Station--backup for any emergency and for my own future reference.
Now I've got to lie low for a while. Rent a hotel room and order in all my meals.
Time for me to just disappear.
EFFICIENCY AND RESULTS...THE PRIDE OF *ANY* REPORTER'S RÉSUMÉ, YES?

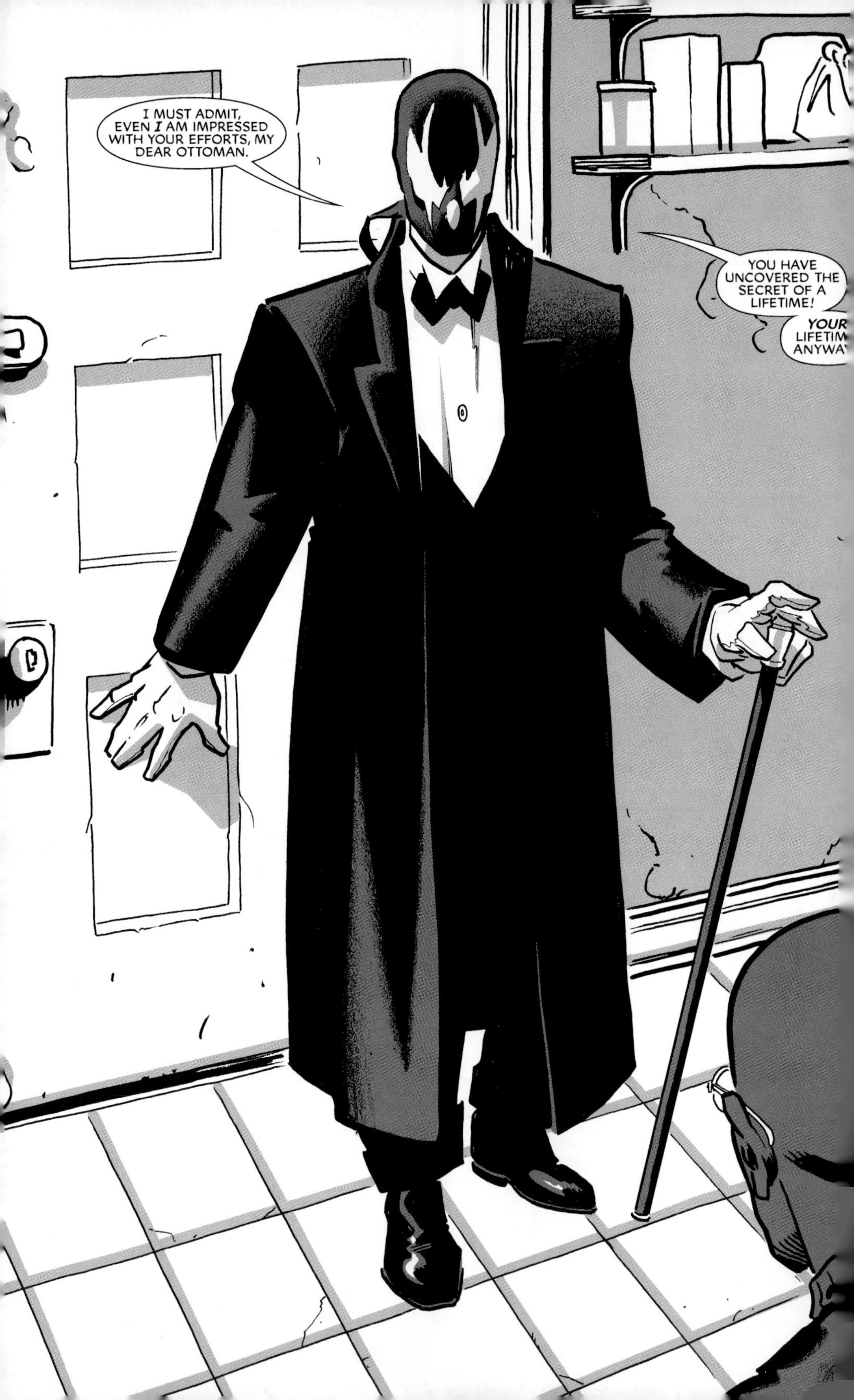
I MUST ADMIT, EVEN *I* AM IMPRESSED WITH YOUR EFFORTS, MY DEAR OTTOMAN.
YOU HAVE UNCOVERED THE SECRET OF A LIFETIME!
YOUR LIFETIM ANYWA

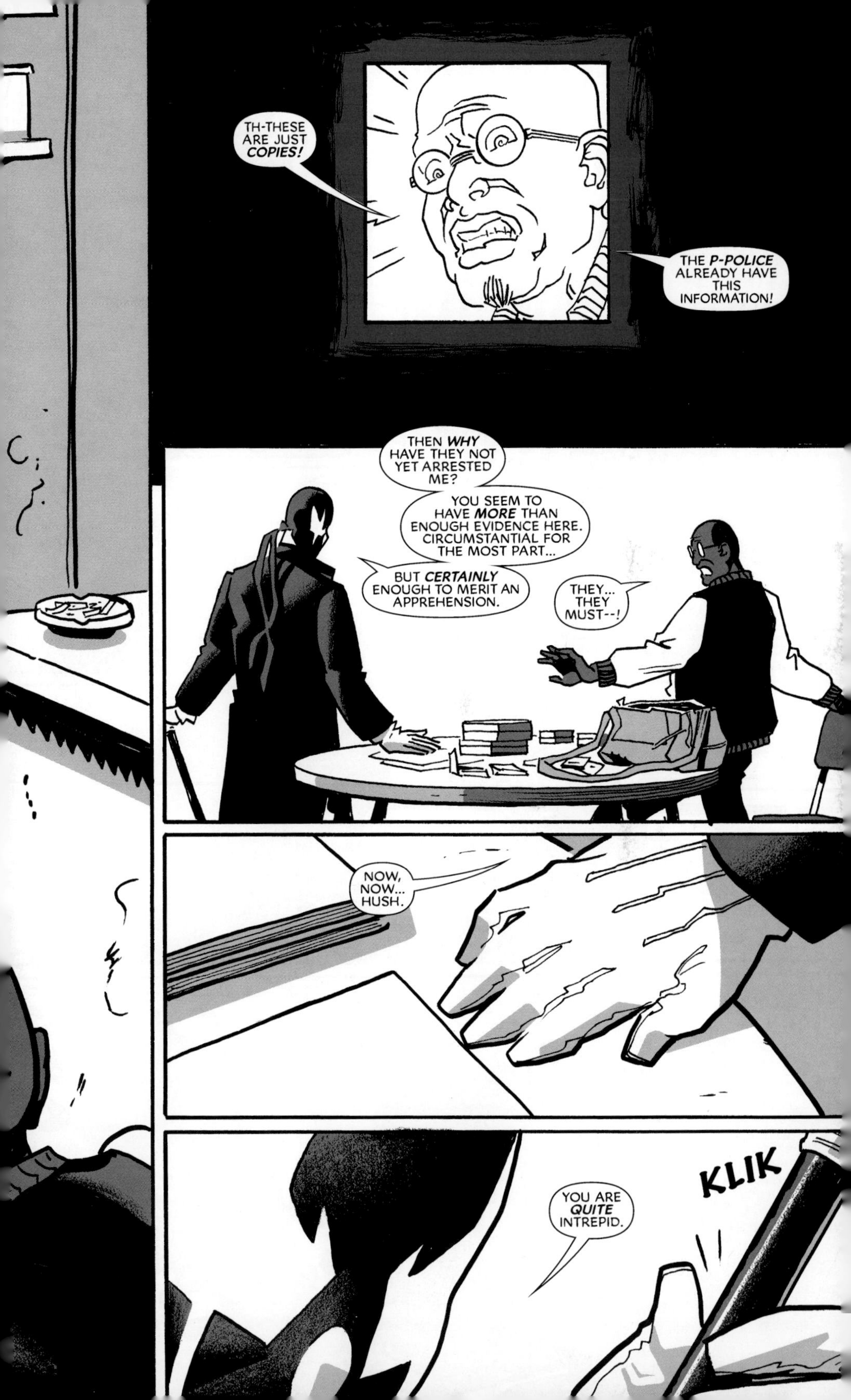
TH-THESE ARE JUST COPIES!
THE P-POLICE ALREADY HAVE THIS INFORMATION!
THEN WHY HAVE THEY NOT YET ARRESTED ME?
YOU SEEM TO HAVE MORE THAN ENOUGH EVIDENCE HERE. CIRCUMSTANTIAL FOR THE MOST PART...
BUT CERTAINLY ENOUGH TO MERIT AN APPREHENSION.
THEY... THEY MUST--!
NOW, NOW... HUSH.
KLIK
YOU ARE QUITE INTREPID.

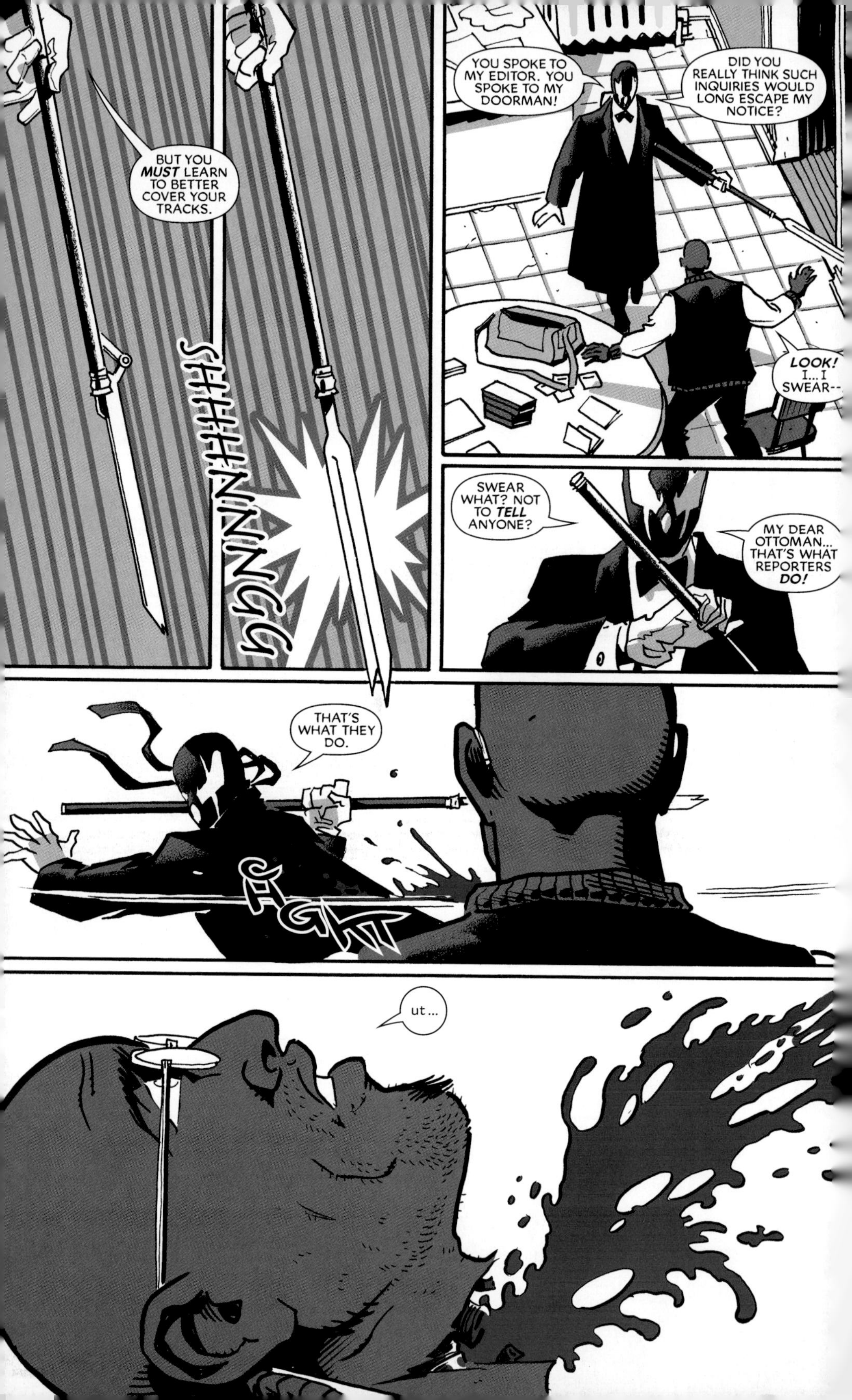
BUT YOU MUST LEARN TO BETTER COVER YOUR TRACKS.
SHHHHNNNGG
YOU SPOKE TO MY EDITOR. YOU SPOKE TO MY DOORMAN!
DID YOU REALLY THINK SUCH INQUIRIES WOULD LONG ESCAPE MY NOTICE?
LOOK! I... I SWEAR--
SWEAR WHAT? NOT TO TELL ANYONE?
MY DEAR OTTOMAN... THAT'S WHAT REPORTERS DO!
THAT'S WHAT THEY DO.
CHGHT
ut...

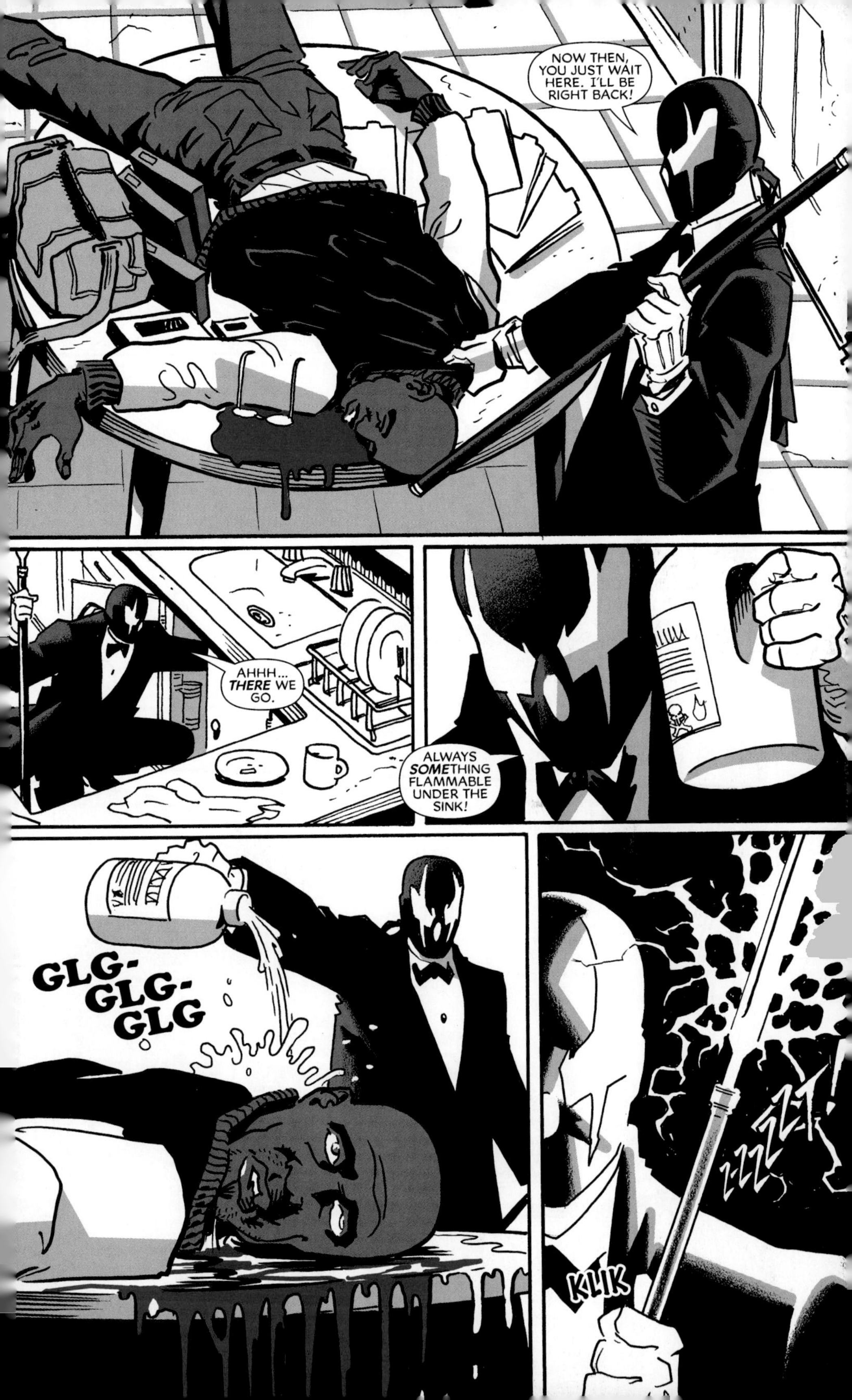
NOW THEN, YOU JUST WAIT HERE. I'LL BE RIGHT BACK!
AHHH... THERE WE GO.
ALWAYS SOMETHING FLAMMABLE UNDER THE SINK!
GLG-GLG-GLG
KLIK

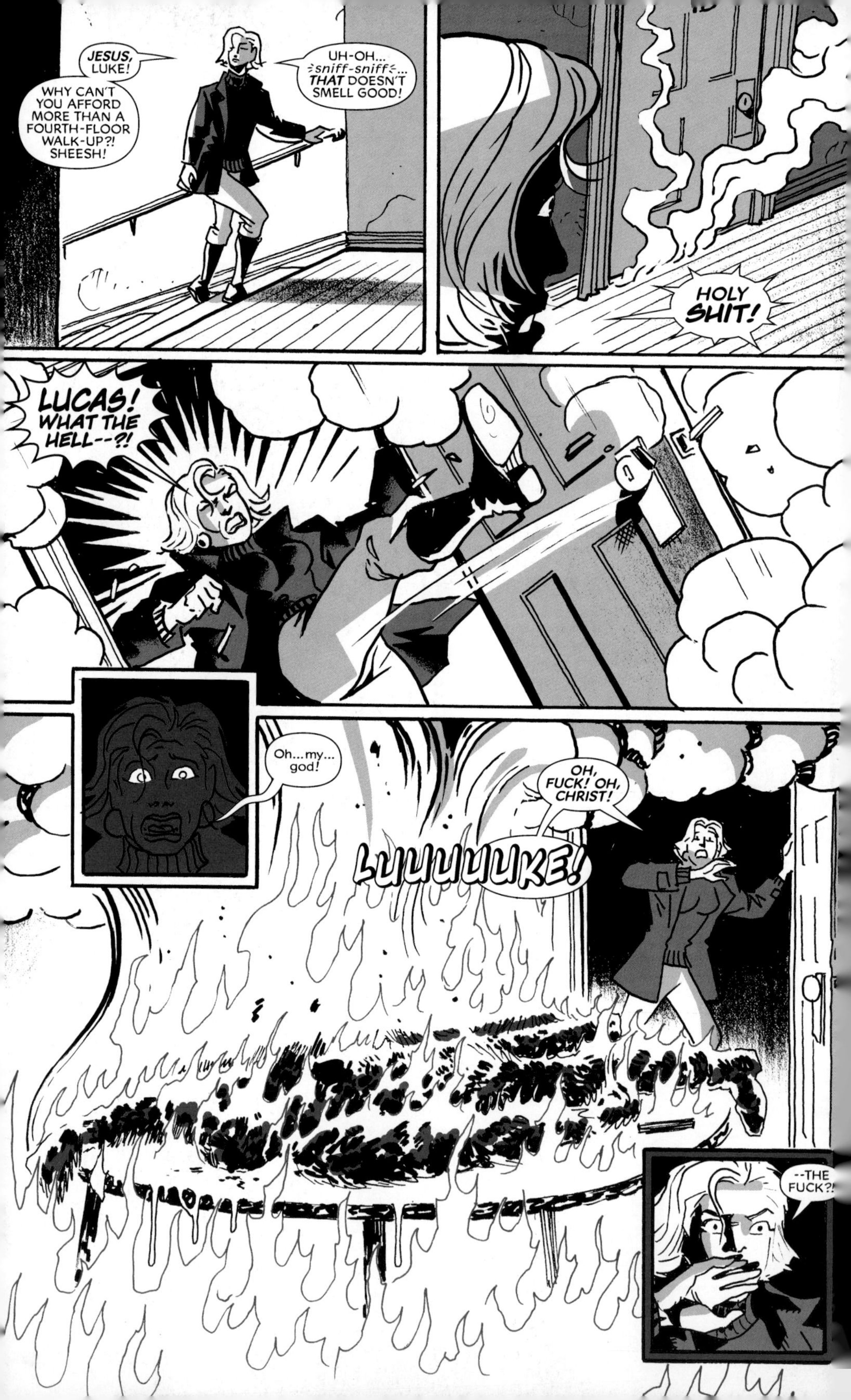
JESUS, LUKE!
WHY CAN'T YOU AFFORD MORE THAN A FOURTH-FLOOR WALK-UP?! SHEESH!
UH-OH... sniff-sniff... THAT DOESN'T SMELL GOOD!
HOLY SHIT!
LUCAS! WHAT THE HELL--?!
Oh...my... god!
OH, FUCK! OH, CHRIST!
LUUUUUKE!
--THE FUCK?!

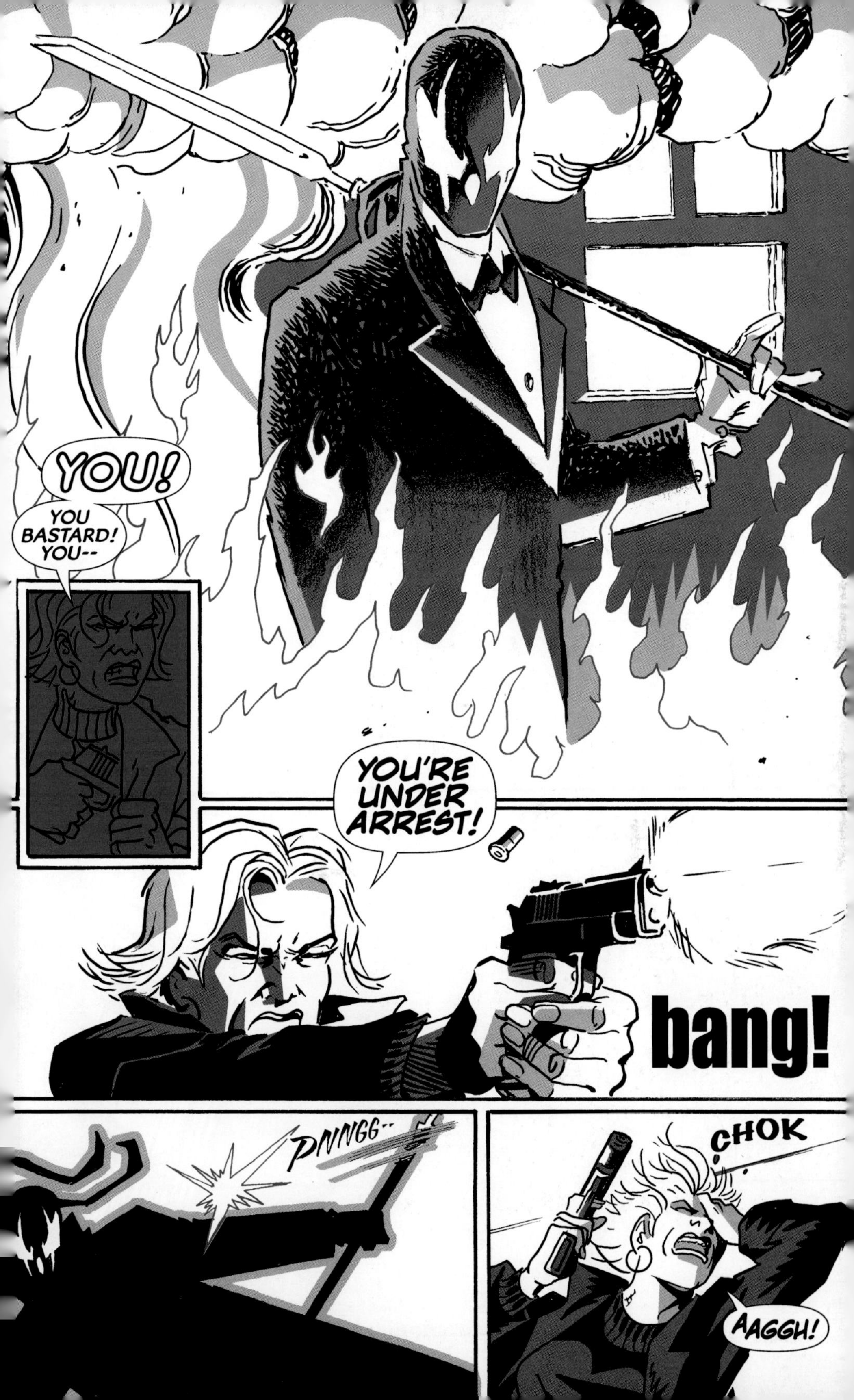

YOU!
YOU BASTARD! YOU--
YOU'RE UNDER ARREST!
bang!
PNNGG--
CHOK
AAGGH!

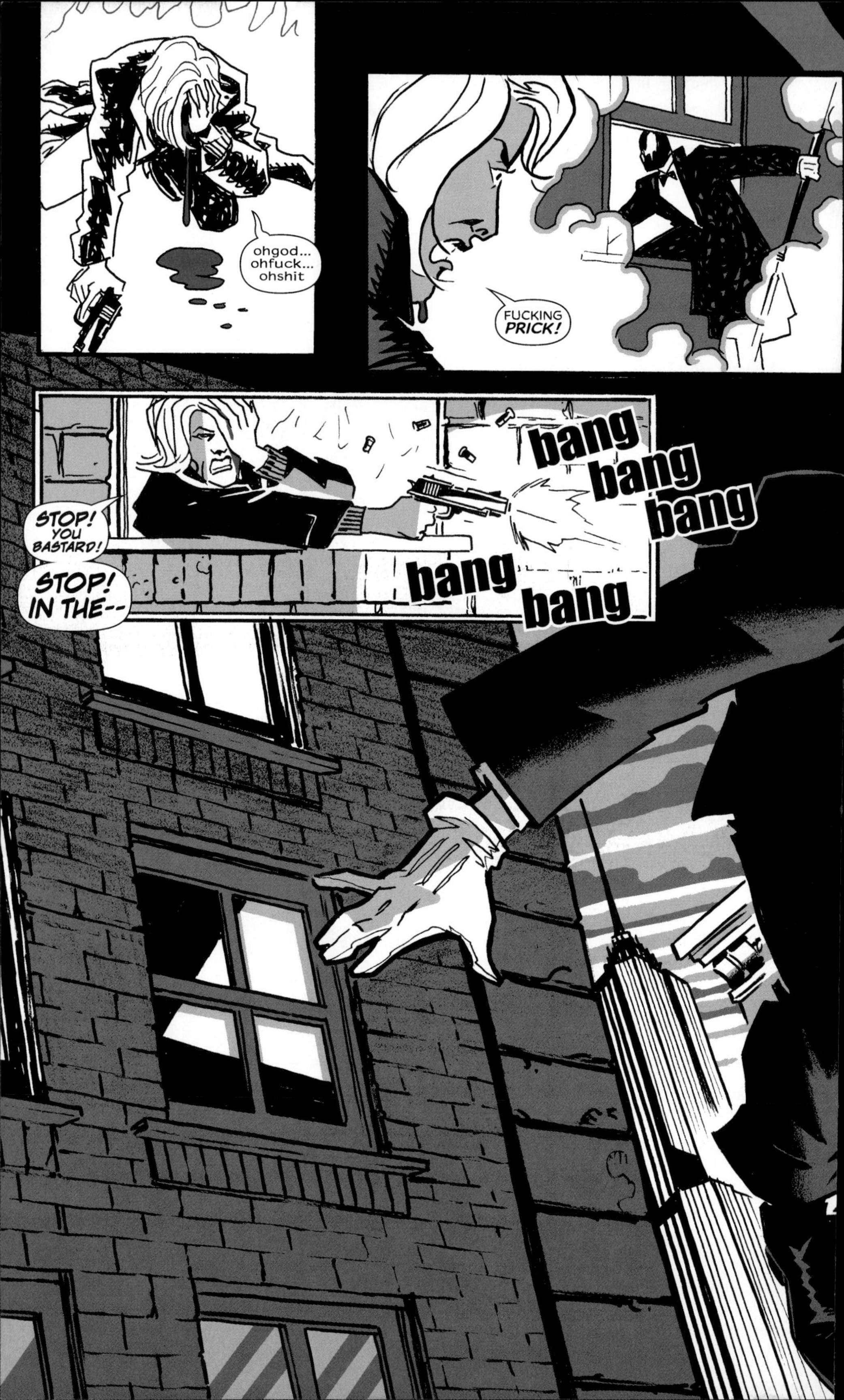
ohgod...
ohfuck...
ohshit
FUCKING PRICK!
STOP! YOU BASTARD!
STOP! IN THE--
bang
bang
bang
bang
bang

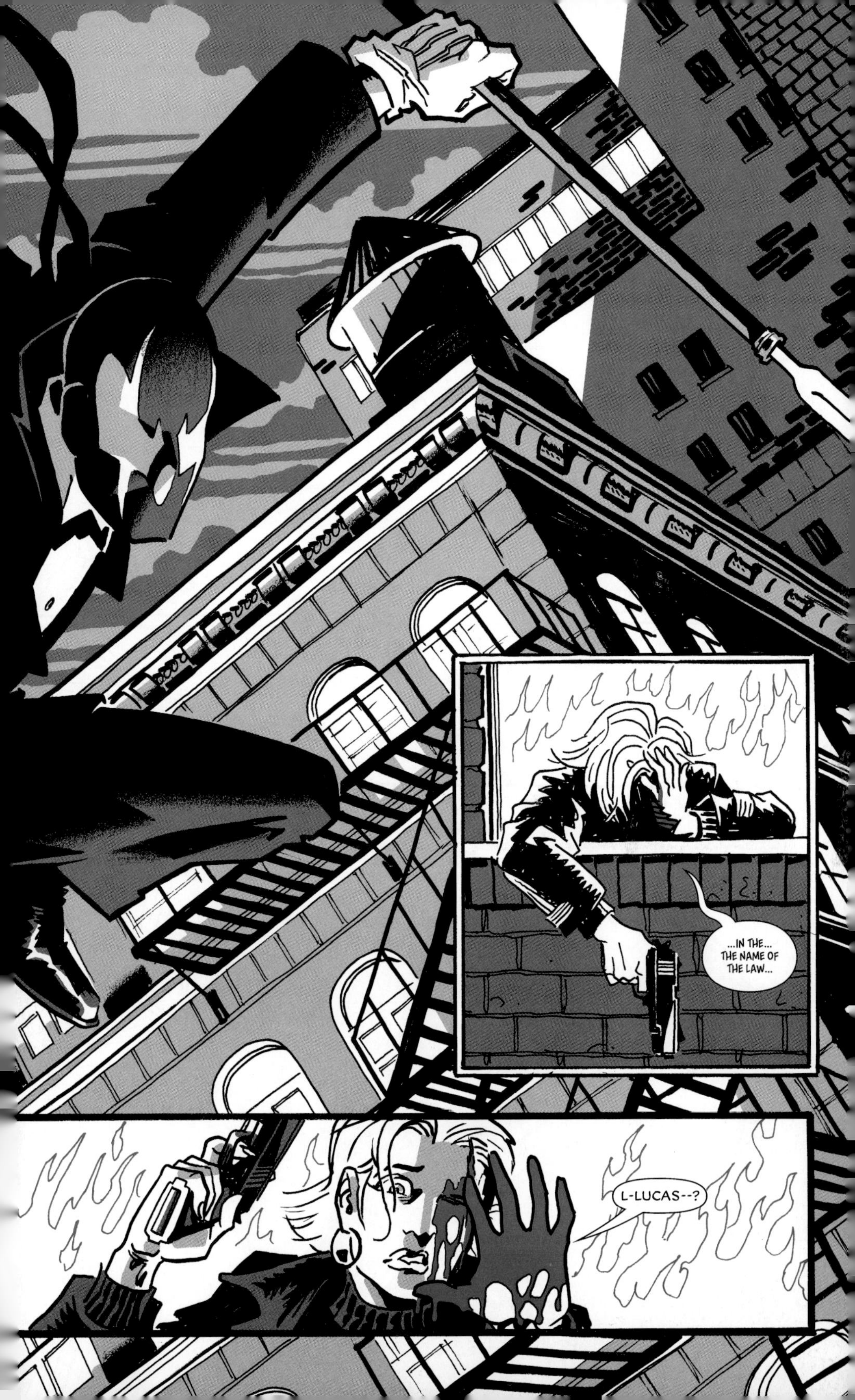
...IN THE...
THE NAME OF
THE LAW...
L-LUCAS--?

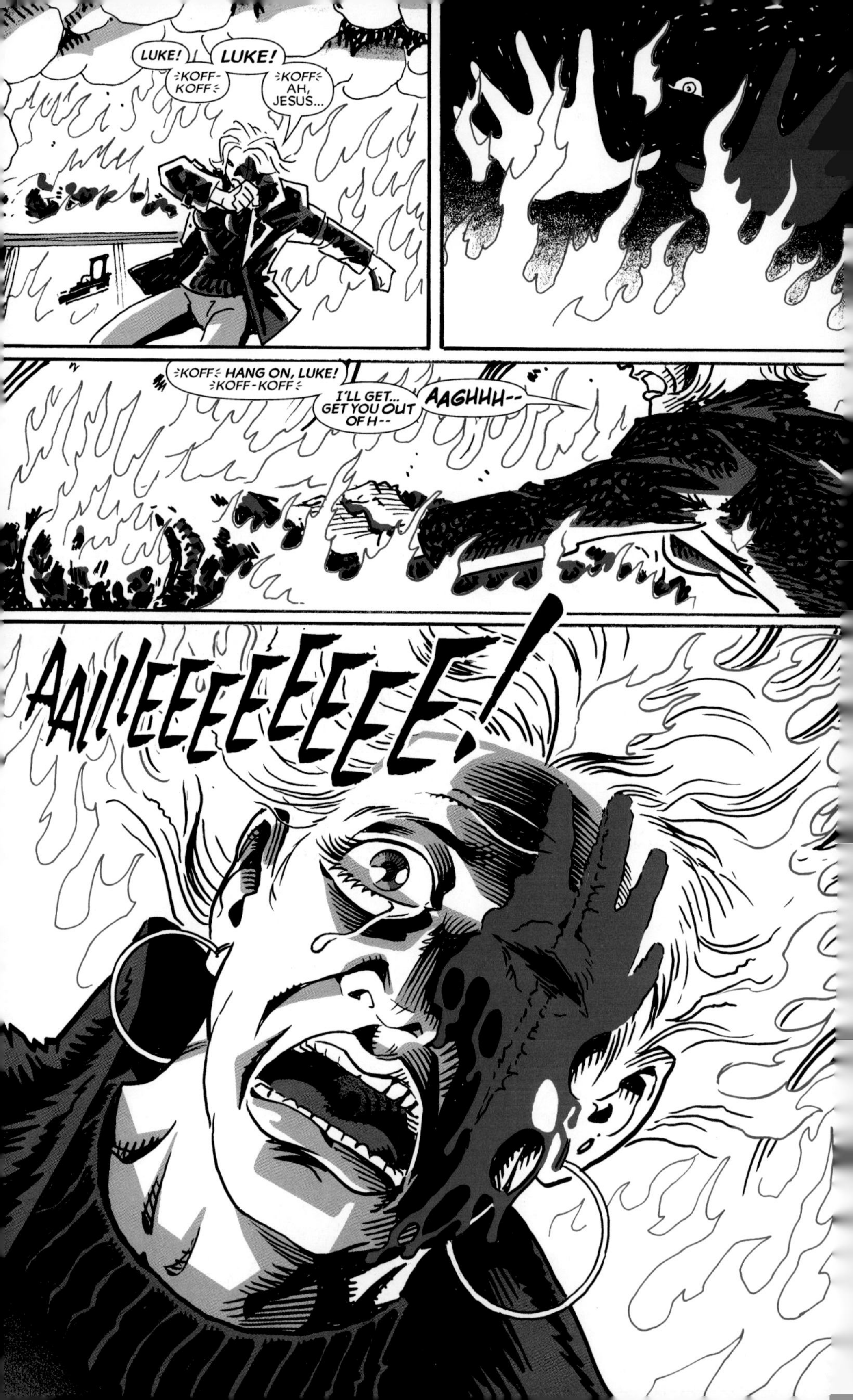
LUKE!
LUKE!
=KOFF- KOFF=
=KOFF= AH, JESUS...
=KOFF= HANG ON, LUKE! =KOFF-KOFF=
I'LL GET... GET YOU OUT OF H--
AAGHHH--
AAIIEEEEEEEEEE!

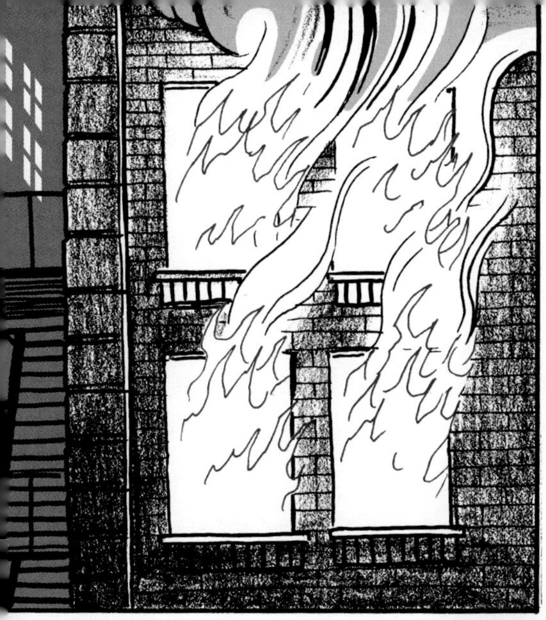

Grendel's activities soon returned to what can best be described as "normal"—the swift, efficient, and merciless maintenance of his criminal empire. His first entry following those "lost days" details the extermination of a newspaper reporter who had seemingly stumbled a bit too close to the alter ego of Hunter Rose. A bare blip on his danger radar, Grendel snuffed out this nuisance and started a blaze that successfully destroyed any existing evidence, while gutting over half the apartment building and killing fifteen others as well.

Of particular note was a victim who barely managed to survive the inferno. Records show that NYPD Detective Elizabeth Sparks had, for some time, been head of a secret Grendel Task Force. This incident brought to light her clandestine affair with the ill-fated reporter, Lucas Ottoman. Sparks later claimed to have encountered Grendel at the scene but was, obviously, unable to apprehend him. Her vain, desperate attempts to rescue her slain lover's corpse resulted in the loss of her left eye and six of her fingers, as well as third-degree burns over forty percent of her body. Her lungs ruined by the smoke and the heat, she ultimately retired from the force and spent the rest of her days in bitter seclusion.

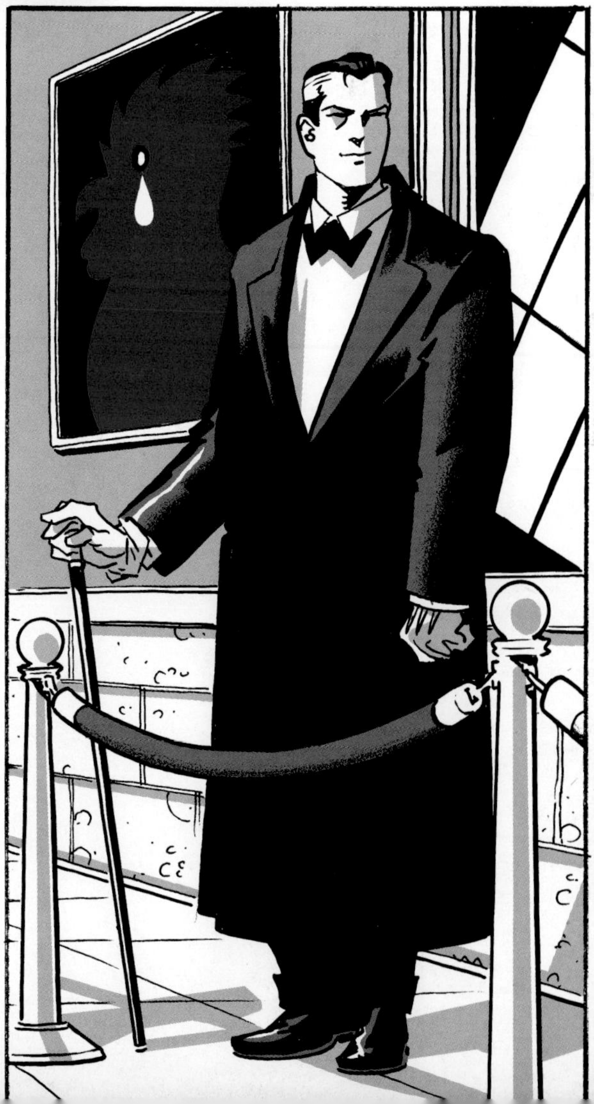

Later that same evening, Hunter Rose staged a live reading from his most recent bestseller, drawing a crowd of over seven hundred admirers.

The fate of his missing journal entries remains a mystery to this very day.

—excerpt from *Devil by the Deed* by Christine Spar

NINE
MONTHS
LATER...

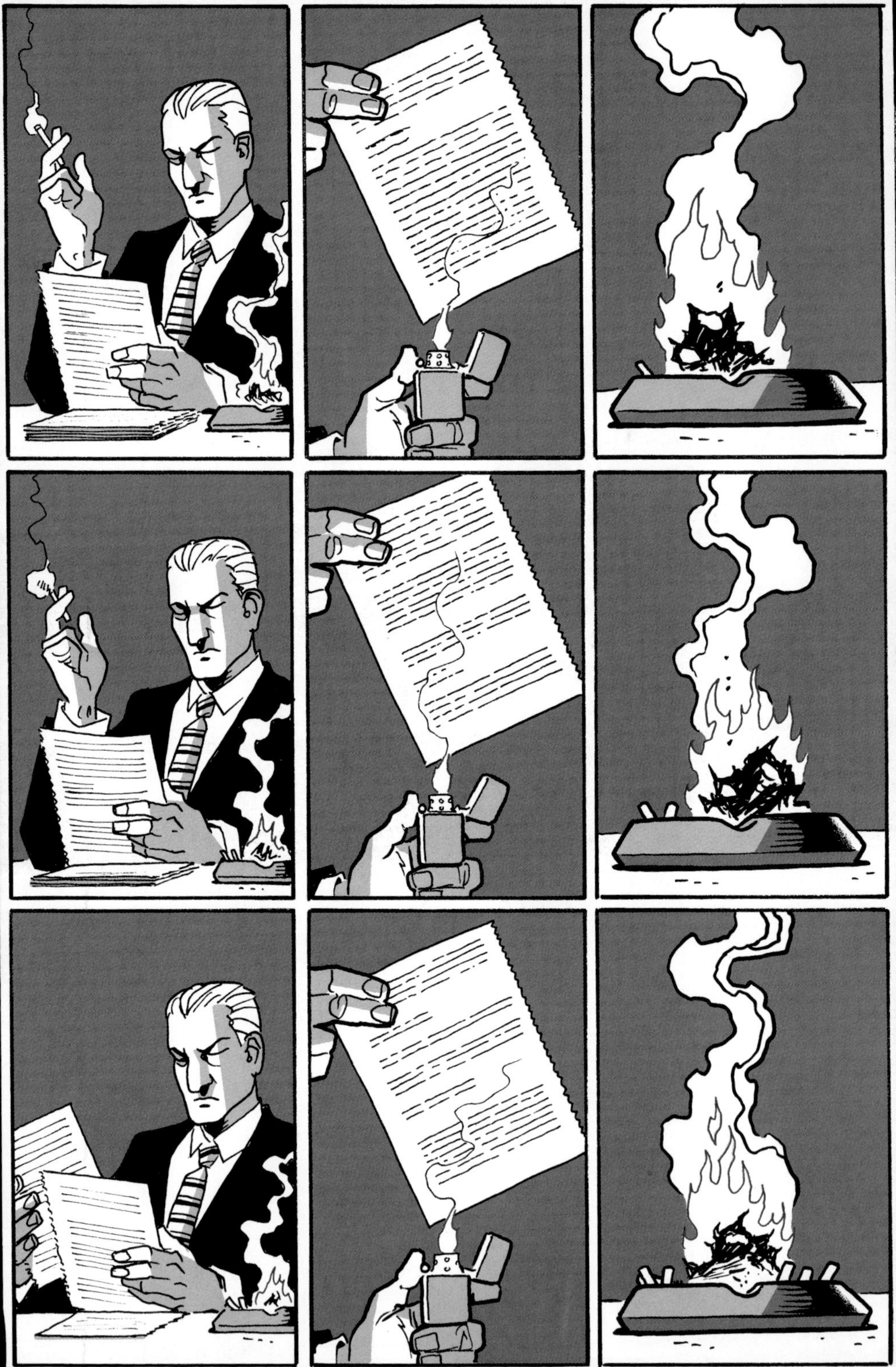

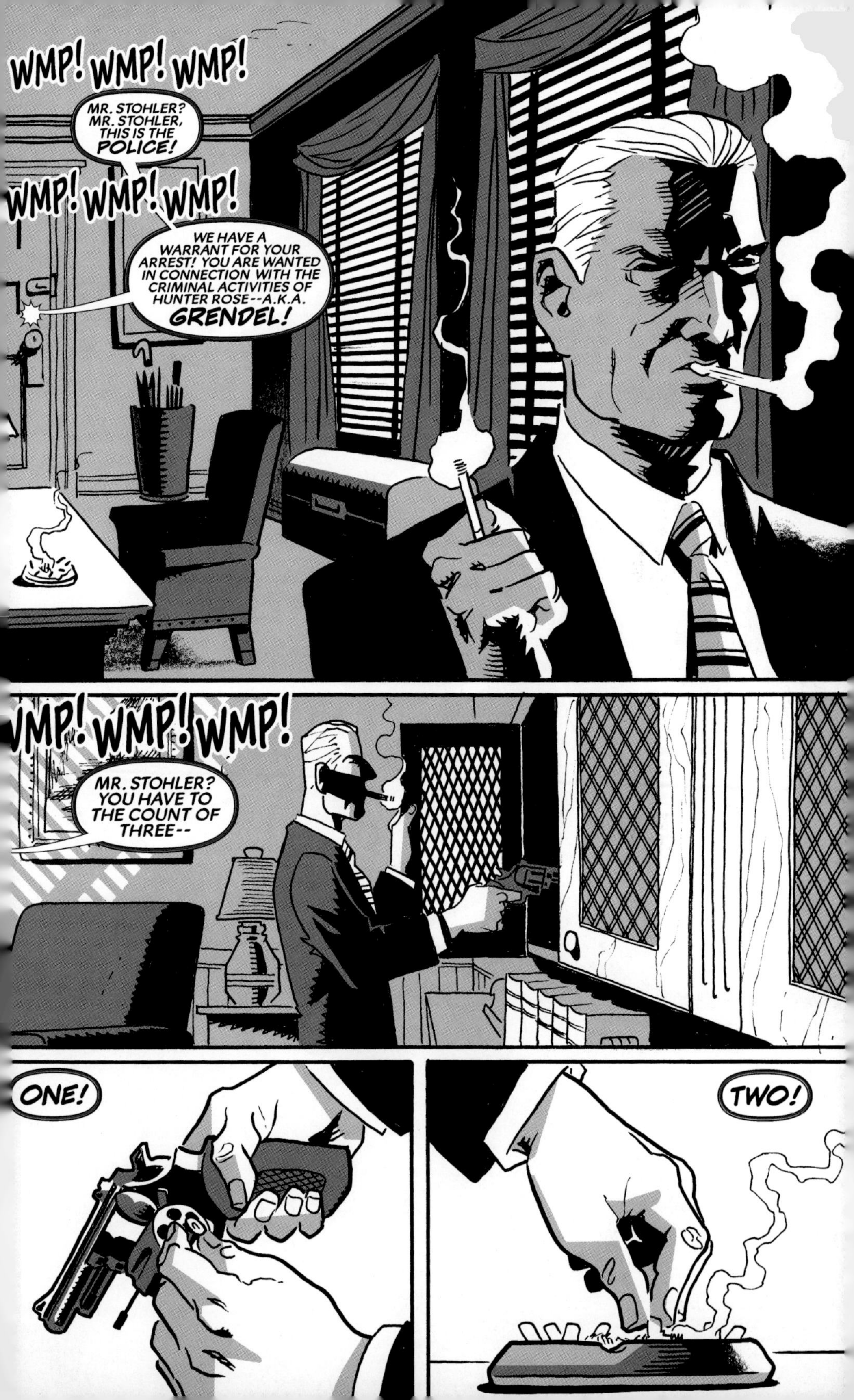
WMP! WMP! WMP!
MR. STOHLER? MR. STOHLER, THIS IS THE POLICE!
WMP! WMP! WMP!
WE HAVE A WARRANT FOR YOUR ARREST! YOU ARE WANTED IN CONNECTION WITH THE CRIMINAL ACTIVITIES OF HUNTER ROSE--A.K.A. GRENDEL!
WMP! WMP! WMP!
MR. STOHLER? YOU HAVE TO THE COUNT OF THREE--
ONE!
TWO!

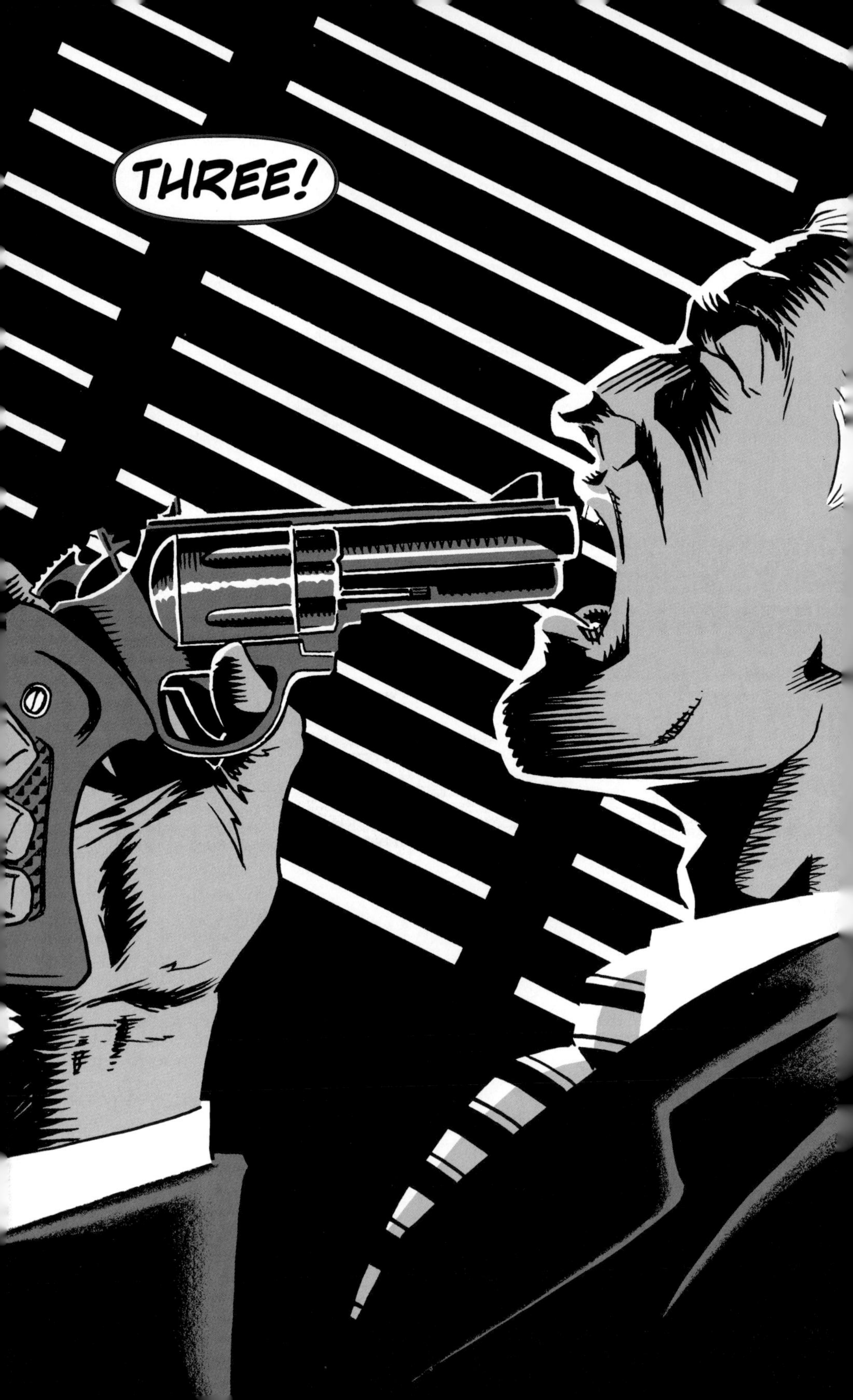
THREE!

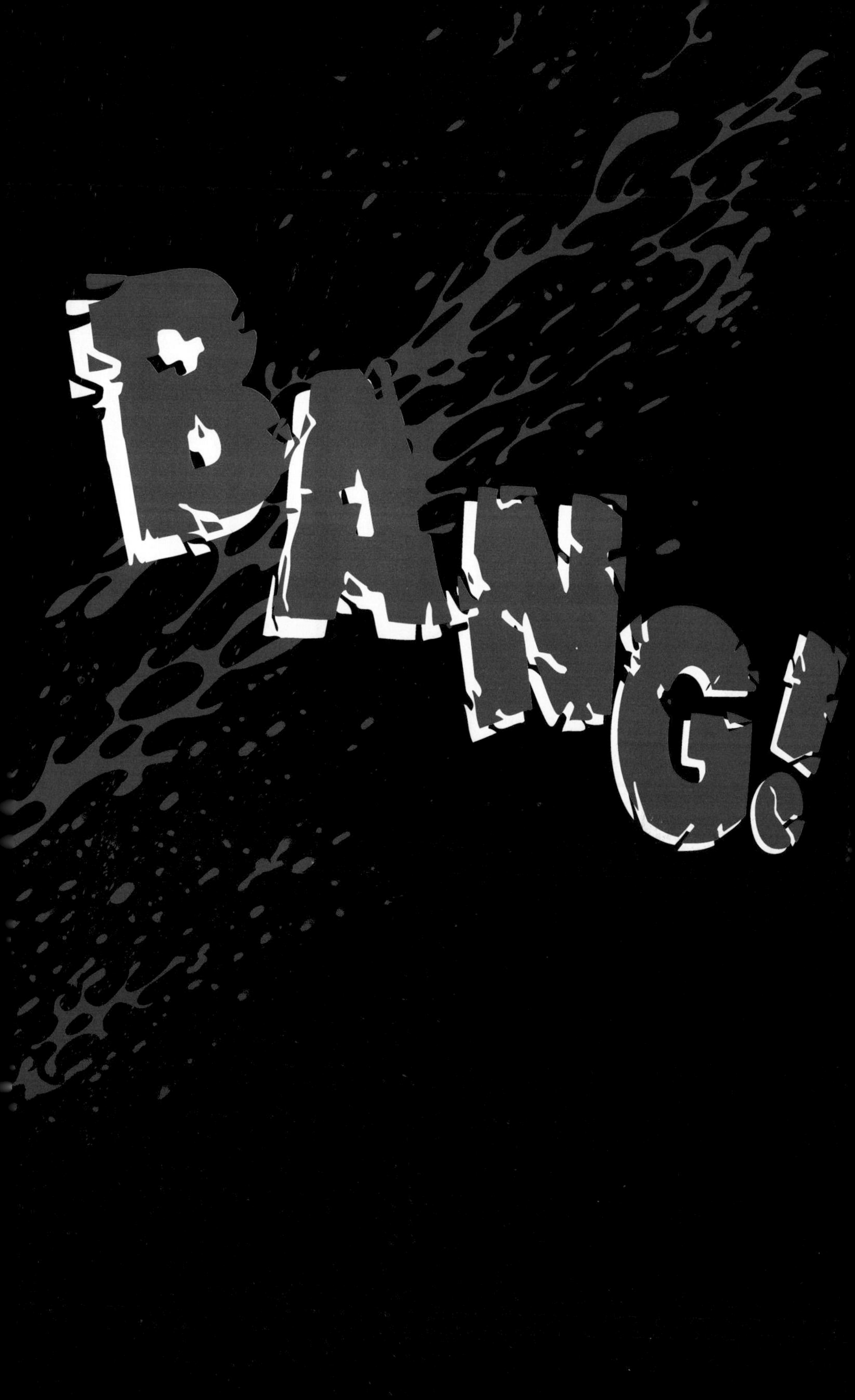
BANG!

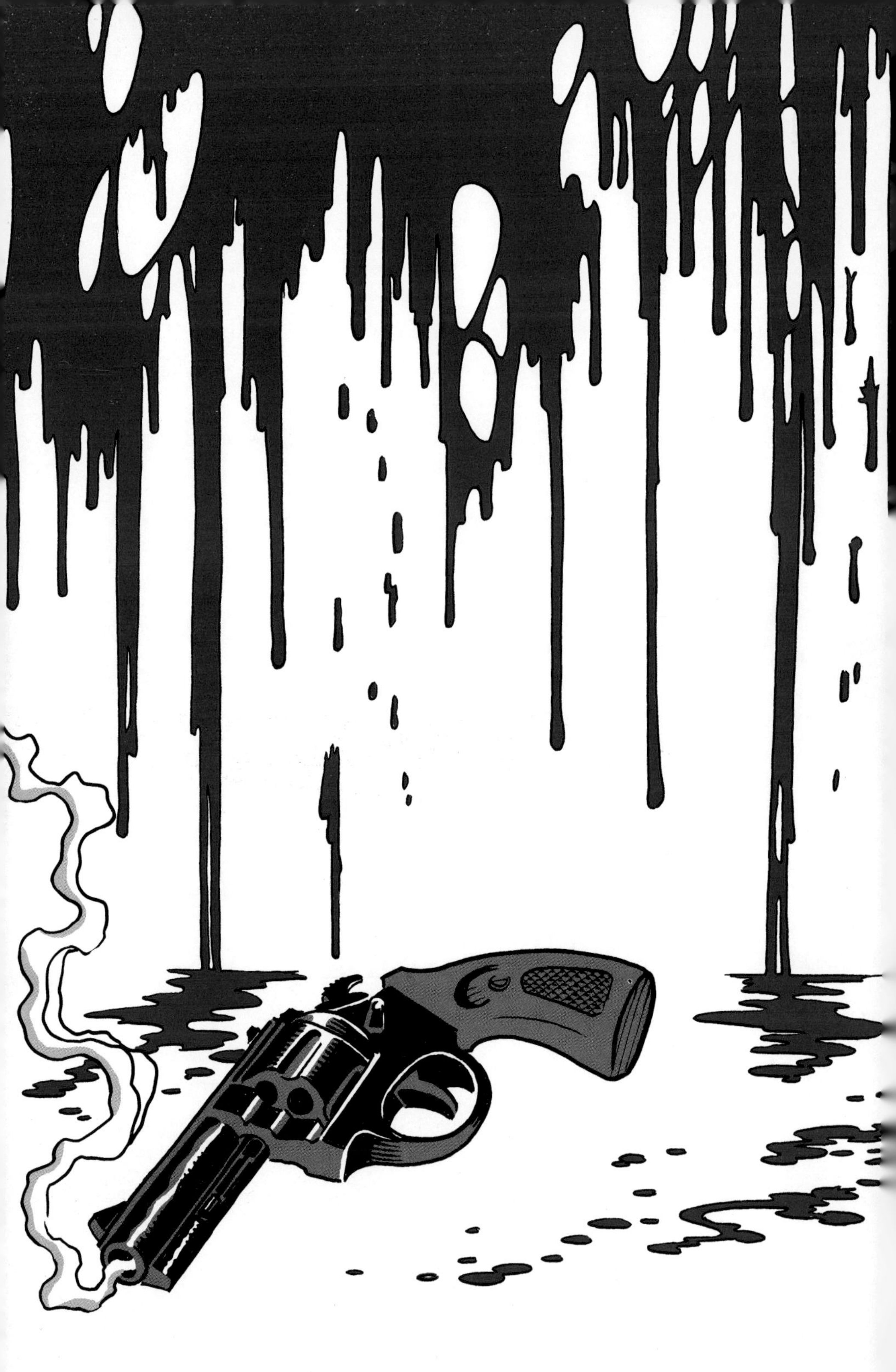

T H E   E N D